The Peoples of Africa

General Editor: Parker Shipton

This series is about the African peoples from their origins to the present day. Drawing on archaeological, historical and anthropological evidence, each volume looks at a particular group's culture, society and history.

Approaches will vary according to the subject and the nature of evidence. Volumes concerned mainly with culturally discrete peoples will be complemented by accounts which focus primarily on the historical period, on African nations and contemporary peoples. The overall aim of the series is to offer a comprehensive and up-to-date picture of the African peoples, in books which are at once scholarly and accessible.

Already published

The Shona and their Neighbours*
David Beach

The Berbers*
Michael Brett and Elizabeth Fentress

The Peoples of the Middle Niger*
Rod McIntosh

The Ethiopians*
Richard Pankhurst

The Egyptians*
Barbara Watterson

The Swahili
Mark Horton and John Middleton

In preparation

The Peoples of Kenya
John Middleton

* Indicates title commissioned under the general editorship of Dr David Phillipson of Gonville and Caius College, Cambridge

A Maasai herder stands next to a satellite communications tower in the Rift valley, Kenya.
Photo: Adrian Arbib.

PERSPECTIVES ON AFRICA

A READER IN CULTURE, HISTORY, AND REPRESENTATION

edited and introduced by

Roy Richard Grinker
George Washington University

and

Christopher B. Steiner
Connecticut College

Blackwell
Publishing

© 1997 by Roy Richard Grinker and Christopher B. Steiner

BLACKWELL PUBLISHING
350 Main Street, Malden, MA 02148-5020, USA
9600 Garsington Road, Oxford OX4 2DQ, UK
550 Swanston Street, Carlton, Victoria 3053, Australia

First published 1997

11   2008

Library of Congress Cataloging-in-Publication Data

Perspectives on Africa: a reader in culture, history, and representation / edited and introduced by Roy Richard Grinker and Christopher B. Steiner.
    p.   cm.
  Includes bibliographical references.
  ISBN: 978-1-55786-685-1 (hbk. : alk. paper); ISBN: 978-1-55786-686-8 (pbk. : alk. paper)
  1. Ethnology—Africa, Sub-Saharan. 2. Africa, Sub-Saharan—Politics and government.
3. Africa, Sub-Saharan—Economic conditions. 4. Africa, Sub-Saharan—Social life and customs.
I. Grinker, Roy R. (Roy Richard, 1961– . II. Steiner, Christopher Burghard, 1961– .
  GN645.P47   1996
  306'.096—dc20   96–21537
                                        CIP

A catalogue record for this title is available from the British Library.

Printed and bound in Singapore
by C.O.S. Printers Pte Ltd

The publisher's policy is to use permanent paper from mills that operate a sustainable forestry policy, and which has been manufactured from pulp processed using acid-free and elementary chlorine-free practices. Furthermore, the publisher ensures that the text paper and cover board used have met acceptable environmental accreditation standards.

For further information on
Blackwell Publishing, visit our website:
www.blackwellpublishing.com

To Colin Turnbull
and for
our children

CONTENTS

PREFACE

The idea for this volume emerged in 1992 when both of us were teaching courses in African studies but were unable to locate a suitable collection of readings for our students. Since that time, we have sought to construct for students enrolled in courses on African cultures a basic but representative guide to the vast literature in the study of sub-Saharan Africa.

Over the years, many of those who have taught courses on African cultures and societies have found it difficult, if not impossible, to assign their students the best and most influential works in African anthropology and cultural studies. Sometimes these works are articles in obscure and hard-to-find journals, small portions of larger books, or chapters in costly edited volumes that they would rather not assign. Furthermore, given copyright restrictions, it is often tedious and expensive to reproduce and distribute readings to our students. We intend *Perspectives on Africa: A Reader in Culture, History, and Representation* to make key articles in African studies accessible to a wide range of readers.

Since the 1960s, only a handful of edited volumes on African cultures have been published, and they differ sharply from this book in several ways. First, the majority are collections of descriptive articles on particular societies or ethnic groups, edited volumes consisting of summary chapters that offer general overviews of particular topics, or single author introductory texts. *Perspectives on Africa,* in contrast, consists of two kinds of readings: previously published articles that have proven to be classic and influential not only in anthropology but also in other related disciplines (such as history, cultural studies, and philosophy), and outstanding articles published within the last several years that we believe are significant to the development and intellectual vitality of African studies. Indeed, the two standard readers of previously published works in African anthropology – Elliot Skinner's *Peoples and Cultures of Africa* (American Museum of Natural History Press, 1973) and Simon Ottenberg's *Cultures and Societies of Africa* (Random House, 1960) – were published quite some time ago and, therefore, cannot reflect the issues and debates that have become central to African studies during the last few decades.

Second, in past collections little guidance has been offered to the reader to help locate the place or significance of the various essays within the historical contexts of anthropology and African studies. The articles contained in each section of this volume are arranged in more or less chronological order to show the continuities and transformations in both subject matter and theoretical perspective. Our introductory essays aim, at least in part, to situate the texts within the discipline of anthropology and, more generally, within the field of African studies. This book, therefore, is intended as both an introduction to the cultures of Africa and an intellectual history of the study of African cultures.

Third, whereas the majority of existing published readers are composed entirely of descriptive ethnographic overviews or vignettes, *Perspectives on Africa* contains both ethnography and theory. Our hope is that this book will help students to link theory with data, perspective with practice. We consider theory to be of special importance to the reader because the ethnography of Africa has so profoundly influenced the direction and development of anthropological theory in general – advances in social theory that have helped us interpret and understand cultures throughout the world. The great value of so many of the essays included here is that they teach us not only about particular societies – their social lives, belief systems, economies, and political structures – but also about how models and theories are generated and, sometimes, contested in the intellectual formation of an academic discipline.

Fourth, the sections of this book are, to some extent, organized around major debates. The debates illustrate the dynamic processes through which scholars have tried to describe and understand African cultures. Readers can explore the ways in which authors critically examine one another's work, and they can evaluate contrasting perspectives on the same sociocultural phenomena. In addition, because a number of the authors we have selected are historians, philosophers, and literary critics, the book highlights diversity of opinion, multiplicities of voice, and draws attention to the importance of interdisciplinary scholarship in African studies. Indeed, we have paid special attention to intertextuality, that is, we have sought to construct a text that highlights the interpenetration of ideas and concepts among the various readings, within and across

chapters, disciplines, regions, and historical periods.

The process of selecting topics and specific readings for this book was a daunting task. Commenting on the intellectual challenges of editing a volume such as this one, William Arens recently wrote in the pages of *American Ethnologist*:

> Compiling an overview of the social anthropology of a vast culture area such as sub-Saharan Africa . . . is a difficult and probably thankless undertaking, especially as the reviews begin to accumulate. Many are sure to quibble about what has been included and, even more important, who and what have been excluded from the discussion as representative topics and figures. (1995: 1081)*

African studies *is* encyclopaedic, and it is always difficult to know where to begin and where to end. For example, although we have decided to focus exclusively on scholarly works about Africa, how does one really define what is "scholarly"? Only those articles written by university professors for refereed journals and books? Do not the poems, novels, songs, and popular cultural products of Africa constitute a significant corpus of expressions and explanations about African cultures? Furthermore, given the size and complexity of the African continent, hard choices had to be made about which geographic areas should be represented. Is it possible to represent all of Africa in a single volume? Should North Africa be included in a reader on African studies, when historically the discipline has concentrated largely on regions south of the Sahara? Weighing up the volume of materials available to us, we ultimately decided that for the sake of our readers we needed to collect a fairly coherent body of works that would address one another with the same literary

---

* Arens, W. 1995. Review of *Anthropology and Africa: Changing Perspectives on a Changing Scene* by Sally Falk Moore. *American Ethnologist* 22(4): 1081–82.

genre and through the discourse of a similar academic paradigm. For that reason, we have not included many distinguished works outside of the disciplines of social science and cultural studies nor, for the most part, have we included works that go beyond the regional focus of sub-Saharan Africa.

After making a set of preliminary choices, we sent an abstract and table of contents to more than a hundred teachers and scholars of Africa in the United States, Canada, Great Britain, The Netherlands, Australia, New Zealand, Japan, Kenya, Zambia, Côte d'Ivoire, and South Africa. We are extremely grateful for the large number of responses we received, which included numerous suggestions for adding or deleting a number of works, assessments of the value of the topics we had chosen, and constructive criticisms of the book project as a whole. Several scholars suggested that we include sections devoted to development, medicine, and agrarian reforms. Some suggested that we were giving short shrift to early scholars, and others argued that we had included too many of the older works. Given the scope of this project, we were not able to give special attention to a number of important topics and had to present them under larger rubrics: these include, in no special order, Islam and Christianity, agriculture and food, matriliny, pastoralism and nomads, law, health and healing, migration and resettlement, and economic development, among others.

As one might expect, some scholars advised that we bring into sharper focus certain important issues addressed in the essays we had selected: the ruinous legacies of colonialism, racial and sexual discrimination, malnutrition, poverty, war, underdevelopment, and the plight of refugees. They were rightly concerned that, in the broad vision of Africa which we seek to present, these aspects of contemporary African life might elude some readers. This is, indeed, a problem of representation: how to evoke a coherent and balanced picture of critical research in African studies without losing sight of the predicaments of misfortune and human tragedy.

Few people who have lived in Africa can escape firsthand experience of the human suffering of those afflicted with AIDS and other diseases, those caught up in the wretched circumstances of destitution and famine, and those exiled or displaced by the political crossfire of military dictatorships. It is indeed urgent that scholars document and analyze such critical issues. Twenty-eight million Africans face famine today, and in countries like Ethiopia, Mozambique, the Sudan, Liberia, and Zaire the economies have virtually collapsed. Yet Africa is not only about the tragedies of human experience. It is also about joy, perseverance, the richness of life, and the endless creativity and diversity of human cultures. We would argue that in order to comprehend the inhumanity of violence and destitution it is also necessary to understand the humanity of the moral universe and the worlds of meaning within which these tragedies occur.

*   *   *

We would like to extend our sincere gratitude to the following individuals who have contributed their time and knowledge to advising us in the many difficult decisions and selections that were made in the course of editing this book: Monni Adams, Misty Bastian, David Beach, Maurice Bloch, Alison S. Brooks, Angela Cheater, Jean Comaroff, John Comaroff, Jeremy Coote, Irven Devore, Nancy Devore, Gillian Feeley-Harnik, Marianne Ferme, Gautam Ghosh, Andre Gingrich, Alma Gottlieb, Jane Guyer, W. D. Hammond-Tooke, Karen Tranberg Hansen, Kris Hardin, Grace Harris, Allan Hoben, J. Iliffe, Michael Jackson, A. A. H. M. Kirk-Green, Igor Kopytoff, Joel Kuipers, Murray Last, Richard B. Lee, Robert A. Levine, I. M. Lewis, Sally Falk Moore, Simon Ottenberg, Maxwell Owusu, David Parkin, Pauline Peters, David W. Phillipson, Allen F. Roberts,

Judy Rosenthal, Enid Schildkrout, Leslie Sharp, Anna Simons, Jacqueline Solway, Leroy Vail, M. G. Whisson, Jennifer Widener, Roy Willis, John Yellen, and Carolyn Yezer. Of course, we take full responsibility for the final editorial decisions that were made, and for any errors of fact or sins of omissions.

Many of the authors included in this volume were extraordinarily generous in the time and effort they took to help us produce this book. Those whose works were not reproduced in whole but excerpted deserve special recognition for their willingness to part with some of their words, tables, figures, and footnotes which could not be accommodated due to limitations of space. In these cases, footnotes have been renumbered and so may not be consistent with the numerical sequence found in the original publication.

John Davey, our editor at Blackwell, and Anna Harrison, his capable assistant, deserve great thanks. Their professionalism, competence, and attention to detail were all that any author could hope for. Parker Shipton, editor of the series in which this book appears, was always there for assistance and advice, and is, therefore, very much a part of this volume. The George Washington University and The Getty Center for the History of Art and the Humanities have also assisted us in numerous ways. We are grateful to Elisabeth Cameron for her help with bibliographic searches and locating obscure sources; to Kimberly Santini for preparing the maps of Africa; and to Jobe Benjamin and John Kiffe who reproduced with great care and speed the photographs that illustrate this volume.

Finally, we would like to extend our gratitude to our students and colleagues at the various institutions with which we have been affiliated over the past few years – The George Washington University, The Atlantic Council of the United States, Carleton College, Harvard University, The American Museum of Natural History, The Natural History Museum of Los Angeles County, The University of California–Los Angeles, the University of Southern California, The School of American Research, and The Getty Center for the History of Art and the Humanities. Special recognition goes to our families – Joyce Chung, Isabel and Olivia Grinker, and Rebecca and Kyra Steiner – for their love and tolerance. Joyce deserves special recognition for her initial suggestion of how to resolve the problem of finding a suitable teaching text – edit our own volume.

This book is dedicated to Colin Turnbull, who died in 1994 after an illustrious career as a teacher and scholar of Africa. We can think of few anthropologists who stimulated so many students to learn about Africa, to travel to all regions of the continent, and to respect the diversity and vitality of African cultures. Turnbull wrote mostly for the public at large, rather than for a small professional readership. Through his teaching, and through the publication of such works as *The Forest People* (Simon and Schuster, 1961) *The Lonely African* (Simon and Schuster, 1962) and *The Human Cycle* (Simon and Schuster, 1983), he has reached out to millions of people, telling the stories of African lives, and the many lessons Africa and Africans have to offer humanity. It is our hope that this volume will contribute in some way to moving us further along the exemplary path he forged.

Roy Richard Grinker
Washington, DC

Christopher B. Steiner
New London, CT

ACKNOWLEDGMENTS

The editors and publishers wish to thank the following for permission to use copyright material:

American Anthropological Association for material from Paul Bohannan, 'Some Principles of Exchange and Investment among the Tiv', *American Anthropologist*, 57:1, pt. 1, February (1955) pp. 67–70; Meyer Fortes, 'The Structure of Unilineal Descent Groups', *American Anthropologist*, 55:1, Jan.–March (1953) pp. 17–41; Sharon Hutchinson, 'The Cattle of Money and the Cattle of Girls among the Nuer', *American Ethnologist*, 19:2, May (1992) pp. 294–316; Maxwell Owusu, 'The Ethnography of Africa: The Usefulness of the Useless', *American Anthropologist*, 80:2, June (1978) pp. 310–34; and Parker Shipton, *Bitter Money*, American Ethnological Society Monograph Series, Number 1 (1989) pp. 1–2, 16–17, 19, 20, 21–36, 40–7, 56–7, 64–7, 81;

American Philosophical Quarterly for material from Peter Winch, 'Understanding a Primitive Society', *American Philosophical Quarterly*, I (1964) pp. 307–24;

The American Society for Aesthetics for James W. Fernandez, 'Principles of Opposition and Vitality in Fang Aesthetics', *The Journal of Aesthetics and Art Criticism*, XXV, no. 1 (1966) pp. 53–64;

E. J. Brill, Leiden, for material from Aidan W. Southall, 'The Illusion of Tribe' in *The Passing of Tribal Man in Africa*, ed. P. C. W. Gutkind, pp. 28–31, 32–5, 39–43, 44, 46–50;

Cambridge University Press for material from Keith Hart, 'Informal Income Opportunities and Urban Employment in Ghana', *Journal of Modern African Studies*, 11:1 (1973) pp. 61–89; and Terence Ranger, 'The Invention of Tradition in Colonial Africa; in *The Invention of Tradition*, ed. Eric Hobsbawm and Terence Ranger (1983), by permission of the author and Past and Present Society;

Elisabeth W. Case, Agent, on behalf of the author for material from Ester Boserup, 'The Economics of Polygamy' in *Women's Role in Economic Development* (1970), Allen & Unwin, pp. 37–50;

Frank Cass & Co Ltd for Catherine Coquery-Vidrovitch, 'Research on an African Mode of Production' in *Relations of Production*, ed. David Seddon (1978);

Edinburgh University Press for material from Peter Geschiere, 'Kinship, Witchcraft and the Market' in *Contesting Markets*, ed. Roy Dilley (1992) pp. 159–76;

Greenwood Publishing Group, Inc. for material from Mona Etienne, 'Women and Men, Cloth and Colonization: the Transformation of Production–Distribution Relations Among the Baule (Ivory Coast)' in *Women and Colonization*, ed. M. Etienne and E. Leacock (1980), Praeger, pp. 214–38;

HarperCollins Publishers Ltd and Grove/Atlantic, Inc. for material from Frantz Fanon,

The Wretched of the Earth, trans. Constance Farrington (1968, 1982) pp. 206–19, 226–7, 236–47. Copyright © 1963 by Presence Africaine;

Heinemann Publishers (Oxford) Ltd for material from Ngugi Wa Thiong'o from *Detained: A Writer's Prison Diary* (1981) pp. 29–38, 56–62;

Lawrence Hill Books for material from Cheikh Anta Diop, 'The Meaning of Our Work' in *The African Origins of Civilisation: Myth or Reality* (1974);

Howard University Press for material from Walter Rodney, *How Europe Underdeveloped Africa* (1972);

International African Institute for Karin Barber, 'How Man Makes God in West Africa: Yoruba Attitudes towards the Orisa', *Africa*, 51:3 (1981) pp. 724–45; Igor Kopytoff, 'Ancestors as Elders in Africa', *Africa*, 41:2 (1971) pp. 129–42; Robin Horton, 'African Traditional Thought and Western Science', *Africa*, Part I, 37:1 (1967) pp. 50–71; and material from M. Griaule, *Conversations with Ogotemmêli* (1948), Oxford University Press, pp. 11–32;

Longman Group UK Ltd for material from David Coplan, *In Township Tonight! South Africa's Black City Music and Theatre* (1985) pp. 143–82;

Northwestern University Press for Mary Douglas, 'The Lele: Resistance to Change' in *Markets in Africa*, ed. Paul Bohannan and George Dalton (1962);

Oxford University Press for material from E. E. Evans-Pritchard, *The Nuer* (1940) pp. 95–110, 113–17, 135–8; and E. E. Evans-Pritchard, *Witchcraft, Oracles and Magic Among the Azande* (1937; abridged edition 1976);

Peabody Museum of Archaeology and Ethnology for Uri Almagor, 'The Cycle and Stagnation of Smells: Pastoralists-Fishermen Relationships in an East African

Society', *RES: Anthropology and Aesthetics*, 13 (Spring 1987) pp. 107–121. Copyright © 1987 by the President and Fellows of Harvard College;

Scientific American, Inc. for Colin Turnbull, 'The Lessons of the Pygmies', *Scientific American*, 208:22 (1963) pp. 28–37. Copyright © 1963 by Scientific American, Inc.;

University of California Press for material from Roy Richard Grinker, *Houses in the Rainforest: Ethnicity and Inequality Among Farmers and Foragers in Central Africa* (1994). Copyright © 1994 The Regents of the University of California; and Leroy Vail, 'Introduction' to *The Invention of Tribalism in Southern Africa* (1988). Copyright © 1988 Leroy Vail;

The University of Chicago Press for material from Edwin Wilmsen, *Land Filled With Flies* (1989); Jean and John Comaroff, *Of Revelation and Revolution, Vol. I* (1991); and Jacqueline S. Soloway and Richard B. Lee, 'Foragers, Genuine or Spurious?: Situating the Kalahari San in History', *Current Anthropology*, 31:2 (1990) pp. 109–47;

University of Minnesota Press for Kwame Anthony Appiah, 'Racisms' in *Anatomy of Racism*, ed. David Theo Goldberg (1990) pp. 3–17 included as 'Europe Upside Down: Fallacies of the New Afrocentrism', *Times Literary Supplement*, 12 February 1993;

The University of Wisconsin Press for Simon Ottenberg, 'Humorous Masks and Serious Politics among the Afikpo Ibo' in *African Art and Leadership*, ed. Douglas Fraser and Herbert M. Cole (1972) pp. 99–121. Copyright © 1972 The University of Wisconsin Press.

Every effort has been made to trace the copyright holders but if any have been inadvertently overlooked the publishers will be pleased to make the necessary arrangement at the first opportunity.

INTRODUCTION

AFRICA IN PERSPECTIVE

Woman in window. Abidjan, Côte d'Ivoire, 1991.
Photo: Christopher B. Steiner.

INTRODUCTION:
AFRICA IN PERSPECTIVE

Even a rapid glance at the language we commonly use will demonstrate the ubiquity of visual metaphors. If we actively focus our attention on them, vigilantly keeping an eye out for those deeply embedded as well as those on the surface, we can gain an illuminating insight into the complex mirroring of perception and language. Depending, of course, on one's outlook or point of view, the prevalence of such metaphors will be accounted an obstacle or an aid to our knowledge of reality. It is, however, no idle speculation or figment of imagination to claim that if blinded to their importance, we will damage our ability to inspect the world outside and introspect the world within. And our prospects for escaping their thrall, if indeed that is even a foreseeable goal, will be greatly dimmed. . . . This opening paragraph should suggest how ineluctable the modality of the visual actually is, at least in our linguistic practice.

Martin Jay (1993). *On the ease with which twenty-one
visual metaphors can be used in only six sentences.*

French scholar Marcel Griaule, one of the first anthropologists to carry out extensive field research in West Africa, was acutely aware that anthropological observation depends upon perspective. He was known to have his field assistants hold his ankles so that he could safely peer out over the edge of high cliffs to observe from above the Dogon people, whom he studied. This practice tells us much about Griaule's anthropology, to say nothing of how much he trusted his assistants. Whether as an anthropologist, or as an avid pilot, he wanted the grand view – to see everything all at once and from above. He wrote: "Man is silly: he suspects his neighbor, never the sky . . . all his great and small intentions, his sanctuaries, his garbage, his careless repairs, his ambitions for growth appear on an aerial photograph." From above, Griaule wrote, he could discern "the underlying structure both of topography and of minds" (quoted in Clifford, 1988: 68).

Now imagine that you are atop the tallest structure in your community – it could be a mountain, a rooftop, the observation deck of a skyscraper or monument, or perhaps even the "Ivory Tower" of an academic institution.

The perspective appears to offer endless possibilities for sight, encumbered by little more than the biological limitations of human vision. The power of observation can be both liberating and daunting for we may sense not only how much we can see from certain places, but how little we see when we are elsewhere. From atop the imagined tower, you may cast your gaze over a wide expanse, and in so doing assume that your view is somehow "real" or "true" and that your perception is "total" and "collective."

Yet, if we can learn anything from Griaule's efforts, it is that our views are largely determined by the structures of observation. Each view frames an object or image that negates our liberation, for when we look *at* something we always, necessarily, look *from* somewhere else: whether it be from a particular place, a cardinal direction, an above or a below. Pure vision is an illusion. "There is no vision without purpose," writes literary critic W. J. T. Mitchell, for the "world is already clothed in our systems of representation" (1986: 38).

The structures that frame our perception may be as obvious as the windows of the Sears

Tower, the observation deck of the Washington Monument, or the placards reading "scenic view" that dot the highways of America indicating to tourists where to take a photograph and capture their visual memory. Sometimes these structures are much less obvious, however, as when we see things through the looking glass of our own values, assumptions, or beliefs – for example, when European explorers looked at Africa through the distorting lens of colonialism, when missionaries judged African religions in terms of Christian tenets and thought, or when anthropologists evaluated beliefs in witchcraft according to the laws and methods of Western science.

Some points of view also have masters or authors – a fact that once again negates the apparent liberation of what appears to be a privileged sight (or site): Sears, Eiffel, Hancock, and Washington, among others. Like these architects of national landscapes, the master authors of anthropology have constructed the sites (or sights) from which students of Africa have viewed the histories, societies, and cultures of the continent. Their own views, in turn, were of course heavily influenced by the values of their time – values which authorized certain perspectives and limited or prohibited others. When we critically assess these perspectives, the observers become the observed, surveyors are put under surveillance and are transformed at once into subject and object.

In an essay on the development of public exhibitions in Europe, cultural critic Tony Bennett (1994: 133) reminds us that observation can also be a form of domination or surveillance; that when we engage in survey and inspection we simultaneously become the seer and the seen. There is power with the knowledge of observation, writes Bennett, "the power to order objects and persons into a world to be known and to lay it out before a vision capable of encompassing it as a totality" (1994: 149).

Just as observation is a form of control, so too is the process of writing and representing what has been observed. In a study of language and colonialism in the former Belgian Congo, anthropologist Johannes Fabian argues that

> Colonial expeditions were not just a form of invasion; nor was their purpose inspection. They were determined efforts at *in-scription*. By putting regions on a map and native words on a list, explorers laid the first and deepest, foundations for colonial power. By giving proof of the 'scientific' nature of their enterprise they exercised power in a pure subtle form – as the power to name, to describe, to classify. (1986: 24)

To return for a moment to Griaule's station atop a cliff in the rocky escarpments of Mali, we might argue also that his position makes him something of a spy – able to look at others without being looked at by them. Griaule inspects his field site with the "imperial eyes" of the colonizer that sought to describe and, in so doing, possess "their" (dominated) others in Africa and elsewhere (Pratt, 1992). The anthropologist, in this case, is invisible while what he sees from his site of observation is rendered completely visible. This is what philosopher Michel Foucault calls "disciplinary power" – a form of authority and control which is "exercised through its invisibility" (1979: 89). In most cases, of course, the structural distance between the observer and the observed is less obvious than in the case of Griaule's panoptic vision of Africa, but the underlying principle of how power and control might be gained through observation and description is almost always present in transcultural encounters and in any system of representation. "It is the fact of being constantly seen," Foucault concludes, "that maintains the disciplined individual in his subjection" (1979: 87).

If ideas about ourselves and others derive from the ways in which we see and write, and if seeing and writing are implicated in power relations, then it would be reasonable to question critically some of the products of vision and writing. These include not only books and encyclopaedias, but the concepts and ideas that have emerged from them: family, kingship, clanship, tribe, culture, ethnicity, feudality, bureaucracy, state, nation, and Africa, among others. To question these terms is not to dismiss them but rather to determine how, why, and when they appeared, and assess to what degree they are "real" concepts, with reference to an objective reality, or whether they are cultural and heuristic constructs created for particular scientific, political, economic, or other purposes. The last term mentioned – Africa – is especially curious because, at one level, Africa refers to an actual geological unity (the second largest continent after Asia), but at another level it refers to much more. The naming of a continent may seem benign or innocuous, yet in past centuries, the term "continent" implied something that holds or retains. Indeed, the delineation and naming of a particular land mass by European explorers and geographers has often led to the implication that Africa has, until recently, remained relatively isolated from the currents of world history. Africa appears in European literature and art as a static, timeless, and separated land.

From this perspective, slaves may have left Africa for the New World, but little entered Africa or crossed its paths until the era of European colonialism. Such a view is absolutely wrong, since Africans have been a powerful and fundamental force in world history long before the rise of European civilizations. Africa has also been elaborated and articulated negatively in Europe and North America in broad cultural and racial terms, as "dark," "savage," "barbarous," "heathen," "uncivilized," and "underdeveloped" – expressions that have had profound ramifications on the idea of Africa in Western thought. Again, these terms mask more about Africa than they reveal, and tell us much more about Europeans than about Africans. But recognition of these views highlights the extent to which our visions or illusions of Africa are created out of particular assumptions – biases, prejudices, fantasies, or ideologies – and how these visions take shape in the various representational forms of art, literature, and scholarship.

This book is about scholarly perspectives. It is about how some writers have looked at Africa, and how we today look back at them and see scholarship in a new light. This book, then, is not only about perspectives on Africa as attitudes or points of view, but also about perspectives in a more technical and artistic sense, as the process through which scholars render complex and multidimensional experiences and phenomena as texts. Perspective – from the Latin *perspectiva,* meaning optic and clear to the sight (Jay, 1993: 53) – refers in art to the technique of rendering spatial extension into depth on a flat surface, such as drawing a three-dimensional scene on a shallow plane. The development of perspectivist technique as artistic convention during the European Renaissance privileged the viewer as the center of vision, and with the power to order conceptions of reality through his gaze (see Jay, 1993; Berger, 1972). We are concerned here with this aspect of perspective, because we believe that, as a metaphor rooted in the visual arts, it can help us understand intellectual history. Are there parallels, for example, between the illusionist painter's visual sleight-of-hand and the representation of Africa? How are the processes of seeing and looking transformed into writing, reading, and the production of knowledge?

One of the central goals of this volume is to highlight the relationship between "perspective" as technique, position, and metaphor, and "Africa" as an objective reality. We hope to uncover Africa as a concept; and to consider Africa as a subject that has been constructed, invented, and interpreted in writing. Is there such a "thing" as Africa? How can we group hundreds of different cultures and languages into a single category called Africa? How do we learn about its peoples and cultures? How can we study Africa and still comprehend it as a process of invention, and as a constructed entity that masks its own heterogeneity?

To some extent the history of learning about culture has involved a shifting of perspectives, from the privileged position of the observer looking at (or down at) objects of scientific scrutiny, to the position of a participant engaged in a dialogue, who looks with (rather than simply at) the people with whom he or she creates and shares a fieldwork experience. Many African authors, in fact, analyze their own cultures, or study the cultures of Europe that once studied them. Africanist scholars of the past largely looked from above, while many of those in the present look from a level position or from below. Looking from below implies being sensitive to the power of observation about which Bennett spoke, recognizing the biases inherent in any one perspective, and considering how anthropologists and their assistants (usually called "informants") come to understand culture together; sometimes it also means paying special attention to the beliefs, experiences, and interests of people whose voices may be relatively absent from the historical and ethnographic record: the poor, the marginalized, the oppressed. A critical reading of many texts in this volume may elicit questions about an author's perspective. Is his or her interpretation of culture a view from afar? Is it a view from close and within? Whose voices are heard? Whose voices are silent or muted?

One of the central paradoxes of intensive anthropological fieldwork is that it necessitates multiple positions: to be close for a time, during the period of field research, and then to step back and consider from afar the world in which one participated and lived. Like a pointillist painting by Seurat, which appears as a chaotic collection of dots from up close but reveals itself as a clear and detailed image from a distance, scholarly work requires movement and dynamics. The haggling one may have observed in a local cattle market in Kenya, or the witchcraft accusation one may have listened to in Zaire, may appear differently

from the remove of an academic vantage point. The one is now framed in terms of "the circulation of commodities," "the construction of value" or "spheres of exchange;" the other, in terms of "social control," "belief systems," or "modes of thought." Taking the language of psychoanalyst Heinz Kohut, some anthropologists have noted the value of distinguishing between "experience near" concepts – such as the Azande's conceptions of witchcraft or a Lese boy's affinity and affection for his mother's brother – and "experience distant" concepts – such as "cosmological belief" and "matrilateral alliance" (Geertz, 1983: 57). Or, to use an American example, "best friend" and "significant other" are near, while "social relations" and "love object" are distant. Sometimes the principles of culture (experience distant concepts) emerge out of the minutiae of everyday life, as a linguist might generalize from a collection of particular sentences to a set of abstract grammatical rules that stand apart from, and yet constitute, the act of speaking any one of those sentences. Stepping back is important because it is sometimes difficult to see things that are too close to us. We take them for granted and, as the saying goes, cannot see the forest for the trees.

Another paradox of movement, from far to close and from close to far, involves the dynamic relation between the exotic and the familiar. Often what piques our interest is something that seems peculiar and unfamiliar – a ritual practice, a marriage system, a religious belief. Seen from a distance, the values and practices of different cultures may even seem irrational or bizarre. How odd it must appear to some people that the Azande of central Africa, as Evans-Pritchard represented them, (see Part IV) explain all misfortunes, including the death of the eldest people in their communities, as caused by witchcraft. Yet, as we begin to understand a belief or practice in the context in which it exists, and from the perspective of those to whom it belongs, the irrational or the strange begins to make sense, and is thus translated into our own logic of understanding. The authors included in Part IV comprehend the logic of Azande witchcraft beliefs without judging them from their own scientific or philosophical perspectives. The central debate of Part IV, however, is precisely about the relation between the exotic and the familiar. Evans-Pritchard sees the Azande as not too different from Western scientists (although he considers that they are wrong to believe in witches), while Peter Winch and Robin Horton view the Azande as quite distinct. Winch, especially, resists strongly the impulse to view the Azande in *terms* of Western science, as merely "bad scientists," and illustrates for us the risk of making the unfamiliar familiar in the wrong terms, or to erase all difference and see everyone as essentially alike. And, therein lies the difficult paradox of simultaneously making the familiar strange and the strange familiar (Spiro 1990).

Much of the work of addressing these challenging problems is carried out by scholars at the typewriter or, today, on the word processor. The reason why we focus our attention in this volume on the act of writing is that we learn about Africa by reading texts, and we become scholars of Africa by writing them. Most anthropologists spend months, if not years, conducting research abroad, but when they return home they are confronted with translating experience into text. Ethnography, the general term for anthropological description, literally means "writing" (-graphy) "culture" (ethno-). The writing necessarily involves not only the translation of experience, but the actual construction of an ensemble of words that must fit the conventions of scholarly discourse: the words must form grammatical sentences, then paragraphs, chapters, and books. An ethnography might involve the division of a society into distinct parts, such as kinship, economy, religion, and politics, when in everyday life these aspects of culture are inextricably bound together. Certain voices may be made more salient than others simply because they were the voices the ethnographer heard. And the writer's own interests will determine how certain topics or ideas are selected for writing. Although authors seek to represent many dimensions, writing (like filmmaking) leaves a lot of social experience on the cutting room floor. Because writing is a process of selection, making and representing, scholarship and fiction, have more in common than meets the eye. They constitute forms of verbal painting (Pratt 1992).

Our concern with these problems, and what they mean for the future of African studies, led us to focus this volume on how African history and culture have been *represented* in writing. On what authority do authors represent a whole society and its identities? This is a particularly troublesome question, when we consider that many anthropologists have worked among people who cannot represent themselves in writing because they do not have a written language or because they are otherwise unable (or unauthorized) to write and publish. The academic degrees and the requirements of publishers and reading audiences may serve to authorize only certain people to speak – hence the relation between the word author and author*ize*. How do we identify, define, and characterize someone else's culture? How can we evaluate whether some characterizations are "better" or more "accurate" than others? Critical readers of scholarly work must give special care to analyzing the concepts, and the narrative strategies and structures which authors use to give themselves the authority to represent and to be believed (Clifford, 1983).

Culture

Few concepts in contemporary social science are as abstract and imprecise, and at the same time such a central object of study, as "culture." Anthropologist Clyde Kluckhohn (1952) once compiled several hundred different definitions of the term culture. Of course, the more abstract the term the more multiple are its possible meanings, and the more useful it can be as an analytic construct. It is thus not necessarily fruitful for us to offer a unified or precise definition of culture, especially since the more than fifty authors represented in this book employ the concept in different ways. For some, culture is a public system of symbols and classifications that gives meaning to an otherwise meaningless and disordered world; for others, culture is a form of integration, through which social, economic, religious, and political institutions are linked together into a coherent whole; for others yet, culture refers to the ways in which human beings create belief systems and social practices so that they are better able to benefit from the material world in which they subsist.

We would like to stress that it is extraordinarily difficult not only to define culture, but to determine if there is a place where one culture begins and another ends. Anthropologists have long been committed to identifying the boundaries of distinct cultures (in past times called "tribes," a subject addressed in Part I), and to salvaging cultures putatively on the brink of extinction in the rapid and sometimes destructive forces of modernization and globalization.

In recent years, however, anthropologists and other scholars from a variety of different disciplines have begun to question the conventional view that the non-Western world consists of "endangered authenticities" (Clifford, 1988: 5). They have begun to believe, instead, that different cultures have been in contact with one another for as long as humanity has existed, and that, in the late twentieth century, the boundaries of culture are even more permeable and fluid. Most readers of this book will be familiar with the concept of authenticity, and have at some time seen advertisements for restaurants or shops offering "authentic" goods from some "exotic" corner of the globe. At what point does something become "inauthentic"? Or are we all living within a complex matrix of inauthenticities that we try to represent as homogeneous or unique cultures?

The continent of Africa can be characterized as a collection of cultures, but it is also a place for the blending of many cultures, a process sometimes called "syncretism" (Stewart and Shaw, 1994). The term refers to the merging of different forms into one, as when the Nuer of the Sudan incorporate into their social organization rituals borrowed from the neighbouring Dinka and, in the process, may no longer view them as being of Dinka origin. Or when religious leaders in Africa combine elements of Christianity or Islam with indigenous ideas and rituals into a unified system of belief and practice.

The cover of this book highlights the blending of cultures in Africa. The image appears to depict the construction of Saint Peter's Basilica in Vatican City, Rome. But the photograph, as the figures in the foreground might indicate, was taken in Africa not Italy. During the 1980s, Félix Houphouët-Boigny, the first president of independent Côte d'Ivoire, and a devout Roman Catholic, built this variation of Saint Peter's in his natal village of Yamoussoukro. His rendition of the basilica was constructed to specifications that made it larger than the original. This post-Renaissance-style European church erected in the heart of Africa's savannah, engineered by a Lebanese architect, and built by Israeli and French workers, is the largest Christian edifice ever constructed, with a dome rising nearly forty feet higher than Saint Peter's. The Basilica of Our Lady of Peace, as it is called, incorporates 272 Greek columns, resplendent doors made of thirteenth-century stained glass from France, and a 7.4-acre esplanade of Italian marble tiles designed to hold 300,000 worshippers. Pope John Paul II consecrated the basilica in September, 1990, amid a ceremony of Baule dancers (Massaquoi, 1990: 116).

When Houphouët-Boigny was buried in Yamoussoukro in 1994, a spectacular event was held at the basilica. *The New York Times* reported at length on the dazzling assemblage of visual expressions that were present that day, while also commenting on the fascinating mix of cultural traditions:

> Two months after his death, President Félix Houphouët-Boigny of the Ivory Coast [Côte d'Ivoire], one of the last of a generation of African leaders to guide his people from colonialism, finally received a somber state funeral today in the world's largest church, which he had built in his ancestral village. . . . All the panoply of Western religious liturgy mixed with traditional African customs were on display here: the stirring music of Handel and Gounod; the undulating music and dance of ancient African rituals; a huge chorus dressed in bright batik dress singing "*laagoh budji gnia,*" the Baoule-language words for "Lord, it is you who has made all things"; a military honor guard dressed in bright red coats and brandishing glittering swords, and hundreds of village elders, resplendent in huge multi-colored strips of kente and korhogo cloth. (1994: A1)

This is a particularly spectacular example of cultural blending and the creative assembly of diverse traditions, but what it illustrates for us is the general condition in which so-called "distinct cultures" are actually composed of many threads, each of which emerge out of the complexities of history, and which sometimes come together to form a cultural fabric of new and seamless wholes. Other notable examples of blending include Zionism, perhaps the most popular form of Christianity in southern Africa (Sundkler, 1948; Comaroff, 1985) and the Kimbanguist church of Zaire (Martin, 1975). In Zionism, the prophet Isaiah Shembe not only brought together aspects of Christianity with Zulu culture, but also the cosmological beliefs and practices of several different southern African or "Bantu" cultures. Thus, the Zulu king becomes transformed in Zionism as the Bantu Church Father. In Kimbanguism, the prophet Simon Kimbangu articulated Christian ideas of salvation, but joined them with healing and anti-witchcraft rituals.

In addition to syncretism one also finds cultural pluralism, that is, the co-existence of alternative beliefs and practices without necessarily being merged together into new syncretic entities. For instance, in many parts of Africa there are different kinds of therapeutic alternatives, and they do not always conflict with one another; different illnesses may call for different kinds of therapies. For instance, John Janzen (1978) has shown how the Kongo of Zaire choose among a variety of techniques for healing: Western medical therapies, the art of the *banganga* or "traditional healers," kinship therapy, in which kin members become integrally involved in diagnosis and treatment, and a set of ritual healing choices that can be roughly grouped under the categories of initiation and purification. There are no clear or impermeable boundaries between these therapeutic systems – for example, kinship therapy usually involves some form of purification, and *banganga* usually try to involve kin members in therapy management – yet neither do they form a syncretic system that combines, or reconciles, all of them together.

History

The process of narrating and interpreting the African past has long been an intellectual struggle against European assumptions and prejudices about the nature of time and history in Africa. As historian David William Cohen states, "The major issue in the reconstruction of the African past is . . . the question of how far voices exterior to Africa shape the presentation of Africa's past and present" (1985: 198). Many historians, especially those without any background or training in African historiography, have assumed incorrectly that prior to European contact with Africa indigenous "traditions" were ancient, permanent, and reproduced from generation to generation without change. In a now famous statement made in the early 1960s, Hugh Trevor-Roper, an eminent professor of Modern History at Oxford University, declared that "Perhaps, in the future, there will be some African history to teach. But at present there is none: there is only the history of the Europeans in Africa. The rest is darkness . . . and darkness is not the subject of history" (quoted in Fage 1981: 31).

This false image of cultural isolation and temporal stagnation has been attributed not only to African history but prehistory as well. Graham C. Clark, for example, could write with "scientific" authority and confidence as recently as the 1970s that much of Africa during the Late Pleistocene "remained a kind of cultural museum in which Archaic traditions continued . . . without contributing to the main course of human progress" (1971: 181). Contrary to this view, however, research in paleontology and archaeology has shown that the first microlithic technology emerged in Africa, and that cattle domestication and pottery may have been indigenous African developments. We also often forget that the earliest complex states emerged on the continent of Africa, in what is today Egypt (McIntosh and McIntosh, 1983). If we cast our sights back to the evolution of humanity, we find that human-made tools appear in Africa at least 2.6 million years ago, long before they appear in Eurasia.

Africa was indeed the birthplace of human kind. The earliest available evidence of our hominid ancestors has been unearthed in the Afar region of Ethiopia, and in the Rift Valley of northern Kenya and Ethiopia, where the remains are dated at about 4.5 million years before present (see White, Suwa, and Asfaw, 1994; Leakey, Feibel, McDougall, and Walker, 1995). The first appearance in the world of modern human behavior – people acting like contemporary humans – is at least 200,000 y.b.p. in highland Ethiopia, and the first modern human beings – people who look like contemporary humans – appear at least 100,000 y.b.p. throughout east and southern Africa in what are today Ethiopia, Kenya, Tanzania, and South Africa. From prehistory

onward, Africa has remained a vital and central force in building the world we live in. Until the late 1950s, however, Africanist historical scholarship consisted almost entirely of the history of Europeans in Africa, and was taught in university courses under the rubric of "colonial history." Little or no attention was paid to indigenous African views of the past or to the role Africans played in shaping global developments, processes, and structures. Explanation in this type of historiography – exogenous rather than endogenous history – consisted of locating the external (rather that internal) causes for African events, and thus denied Africans their own historical agency.

Beginning sometime in the last several decades, a period which coincides with the dismantling of European colonialism and the rise of independent African nation-states, the study of African history has unfolded in two new, radically different, and more promising directions – both of which have shifted the gaze of the historian away from Europe, and its colonial preoccupations, and toward the continent of Africa itself. The first of these new histories of Africa has been written on a global scale, and "traces connections among discernible communities, regions, peoples, and nations that anthropologists have often separated and reified as discrete entities" (Roseberry, 1989: 125). Rather than view Africa as a set of cultural enclaves, this new historical approach looks at the place of Africa in shaping the world (Wolf, 1982). This kind of transnational focus demonstrates that precolonial, colonial, and postcolonial Africa has not simply been subjected to the progression of other peoples' histories but has produced, directed, and contributed to the course of world events.

The second type of history that is being written in Africa today is a type of "social history" that attempts to reconstruct the past from the records of ordinary lives. Rather than recount "official" histories from above – whether it be from European colonial archives or from African chronicles of conquest or kinglists of royal successions – this new history of Africa looks instead from below to discover the place and meaning of the past in the individual and collective thought of Africans. Because many African societies chronicled the past in oral rather than written form, the challenge of this type of history is to bring together a multitude of small fragments of local knowledge, myths, epic narratives, and oral texts (Vansina 1985). From a Western point of view, there is a tendency to perceive oral traditions as being less "accurate" or "reliable" than written histories (see Henige, 1972; Clifford, 1988: 277–346). If we take the position, however, that *all* history is in fact a highly biased and often haphazard and radical selection of only a few moments salvaged from a much denser swirl of past human activities and events, then the authority of the written word is no more credible than verbal accounts. Both are representations of reality that must be understood within the cultural context of their production and reproduction. The notion of perspective, of course, underlies all historical accounts, since "different people carry in their heads different modes and systems of arranging and simplifying the complex and massive information that the past remits to the living" (Cohen, 1977: 15).

Anthropology has always had a peculiar and rather uneasy relationship to history. In trying to define the field of anthropology as a distinct and unified discipline, many anthropologists in the early to mid twentieth century dismissed the study of history as something which was irrelevant to the anthropological inquiry (Schapera, 1962). (Evans-Pritchard, for example, in the days before he began to stress the importance of history to social anthropology, declared in 1950 that "a society can be understood satisfactorily without reference to its past" (1950: 120).) Today it is clear that anthropology cannot ignore history. The past conditions the present, and so the present must be understood as an isolated moment or a "slice of time" in what is a much broader and more complex process of change.

There have been two central shifts in historical perspective: one concerns the unit of analysis, the other social dynamics. First, whereas most anthropologists once treated African societies as discrete cultural isolates, contemporary anthropologists now view them as historically contingent, with permeable and changing boundaries. Second (as we note in Part I), although anthropologists once viewed societies synchronically as systems that maintained and reproduced themselves in harmonious balance, or oscillated between a small number of organizational principles (Leach, 1954), they now tend to emphasize that societies are constantly changing and in flux. Rather than looking at societies as closed "systems" from which one must attempt to distill pervasive patterns and structural principles, many anthropologists now look for "process" – shifting trajectories and the patterns of change that emerge through time. The problem with history for anthropology is that most ethnographic fieldwork is conducted in a limited geographic region and in the course of a relatively short span of time, where change may not be apparent or observable (Moore, 1986: 7). The challenge, then, is to fit the "ethnographic present" of field research into a larger framework of historical development, process, and change.

Representation

One of the key problems in contemporary anthropology is what George Marcus and Michael Fischer (1986) have called the "crisis of representation." By this they refer to the fact that anthropology, and the humanities and social sciences in general, can no longer make claims of representing objective truths and mimetic reality. If postmodern theory has taught us anything, it is that knowledge and its images are constructed from individual perspectives, and therefore, by definition, can only be biased, partial, and greatly simplified reductions of more complex and nuanced wholes. All descriptions of the social world are filtered through the subjective lenses of multiple frameworks of interpretation – whether it be the perception of the observer, the language of the narrator, or the assumptions of the reader. Representations, in short, can neither posit unmediated authenticity nor make claim to universal validity (Duncan and Ley, 1993: 3–5).

Those who teach and study Africa today must learn to problematize the issue of representation in order to locate and unpack the economic, political, personal, or other motivations that might underlie any particular image of Africa. In his seminal books, entitled *The Invention of Africa* (1988) and *The Idea of Africa* (1994), Zairian scholar and philosopher V. Y. Mudimbe has argued that since Greek times Africa has "been represented in Western scholarship by 'fantasies' and 'constructs' made up by scholars and writers" (1994: xv). What Mudimbe is arguing here is not that the continent called "Africa" is somehow detached from the globe or that it is a "geographic fiction," but rather he is saying that our knowledge of Africa has been constructed and disseminated through (mostly negative) images and theories by Europeans about Africa and Africans (Gyekye, 1995: xxiv). Such images of Africa have often been used by Western writers to "establish opposites and 'others' whose actuality is always subject to the continuous interpretation and reinterpretation of their differences from 'us'" (Said, 1995: 3). For this reason, representations of Africa generally tell us far less about those who are being represented than they do about the preoccupations and prejudices of those engaged in the act of representing.

At different moments in history, negative images of Africa have been used to endorse various Western activities on the African continent – such as the slave trade, military occupation, colonial expansionism, Christian evangelical conversion, or even the terms and conditions of international World Bank loans. The following is a clear and poignant example of how a particular representation of Africa could be used for self-interested goals and, in this case, for personal economic gain. In the late eighteenth century, Archibald Dalzel, a British adventurer and political envoy in Africa, published an historical account of the West African kingdom of Dahomey (1793). In this folio volume, illustrated (and, as it were, authenticated) by numerous copper-plate engravings, Dalzel painted an especially negative image of the peoples of Dahomey, describing them variously as a "savage," "warlike," and "ferocious" nation whose rulers legitimated their authority through the frenetic exercise of large-scale human sacrifices. He argued that the practice of raiding Dahomean villages to capture men and women for export as slave labor to the Americas could be justified on the grounds that it rescued potential victims of human sacrifice who would otherwise be killed by their own people. "Whatever evils the slave-trade may be attended with," wrote Dalzel, "this we are sure of, it is mercy to the unfortunate brave, and not less to poor wretches who, for a small degree of guilt, would otherwise suffer from the butcher's knife" (1793: xxv). Research into the life and career of Dalzel reveals, however, that he was heavily invested in the slave trade and, at the time that he published his account, his business was under direct attack by the anti-slave-trade movement, whose supporters were arguing in British parliament for the abolishment of slavery (Waldman, 1965). Thus, far from an objective representation of Dahomey and its inhabitants, Dalzel's account, like so many others before and after him, was but a veiled attempt to further the author's own interests and goals.

The problem with books such as Dalzel's is that their negative imagery lingers on long after the publication of the original account. Subsequent travellers to Dahomey, for example, relied heavily on Dalzel's report, and often copied verbatim his descriptions of Dahomean rites and customs, especially the human sacrifices which they themselves often admit not having seen. "When new generations of explorers or administrators went to Africa," notes Philip Curtin, "they went with prior impressions of what they would find" (1964: xii).

The process of transcultural representation goes both ways. Since earliest contact with foreign cultures, Africans have also represented "others" in their arts, rituals, myths, and oral narratives. Some of these representations offered satirical commentary on colonial and missionary activities, others sought to incorporate the symbolic power of the "distant" and the "foreign" into indigenous belief systems and religious practices, while yet others were intended as cultural expressions of protest and resistance.

In the 1940s, a Yoruba carver named Thomas Ona Odulate created miniature sculptures of Europeans dressed in their characteristic colonial attire. These sculptures were made for sale to travelers and colonial agents who brought them back to Europe as exotic keepsakes and souvenirs of Africa. Most of these carvings captured the elements of European demeanor that most amused the Yoruba: "the pith-helmet of the district officer (often likened to a calabash); the long moustache of the colonial governor (often compared to a cat's); the white wig of the lawyer (often likened to the head of a senile person), and the spectacles on the nose of the court-clerk (often likened to the eyes of an owl)" (Lawal, 1993: 9). While the artist is known to have told his clients that these carvings were not intended to ridicule Europeans, but were meant instead to project hierarchy and rank, Nigerian art historian Babatunde Lawal cannot help but wonder whether these carvings were not also intended as subversive images against colonial authority. Were they not satirical commentary on idiosyncratic British character? Were they not objects of ridicule which functioned to "savage" the European in an African visual art?

Representation is an issue which lies at the heart of a current debate in African studies regarding the cultural composition of Africa itself. On one side of the debate are those who argue that there is indeed such a thing as an "African" identity whose deep essence transcends the surface differences which distinguish one African culture from another. On the other side, are those who argue that the peoples of Africa have far less culturally in common than is usually assumed.

Anglo-Ghanaian philosopher Kwame Anthony Appiah is among those who have argued that there is no cultural unity in Africa, and that Africanist discourse has inaccurately grouped together vastly divergent cultures which have little or nothing in common. "Whatever Africans share," he writes, "we do not have a common traditional culture, common languages, a common religious or conceptual vocabulary . . . we do not even belong to a common race" (1992: 26). "The central cultural fact of African life," Appiah concludes elsewhere, "remains not the sameness of Africa's cultures, but their enormous diversity" (1995: 40).

Among those who maintain that there is in fact an underlying uniformity to the cultures of Africa is anthropologist Igor Kopytoff, who has argued that in the historical diffusion of cultures across the continent, "the frontiersmen were bringing with them a basically similar kit of cultural and ideological resources" (1987: 10). Thus, according to this perspective, cultures in Africa spread through time from place to place carrying with them comparable cultural baggage and deeply rooted worldviews, which today enable us to look at the continent of Africa as a coherent cultural system and an epistemological whole. As Kopytoff concludes: "it is not surprising that Sub-Saharan Africa should exhibit to such a striking degree a fundamental cultural unity" (1987: 10).

While Kopytoff's argument is largely historical and anthropological in nature, the debate over Africa's cultural unity has also been linked at times to political arguments about the place of modern Africa in a postcolonial world. Cheikh Anta Diop, for example, a Senegalese historian and outspoken proponent of Pan-African solidarity, argued beginning in the 1950s that African cultures needed to find a common historical root which could unify the inhabitants of the continent (1978). Diop asserted that just as Europe drew much of its strength from the unity it established by tracing its ancestry to a single Greco–Latin culture, so too Africa had to locate and exploit a similar unified cultural background in order to develop its own strength through a coalescing regime of self-awareness. Thus, the present diversity of Africa was, according to this argument, "more illusion than reality" (July 1987: 138).

Other arguments for the cultural unity of Africa, which were also largely political in character, were made, for instance, by some of the other proponents of the *négritude* movement, such as the Martiniquan poet Aimé Césaire and Senegalese intellectual Léopold Senghor; by the leader of independent Ghana, Kwame Nkrumah, in his discourse on "African Personality" (1963); and, more recently, by many African philosophers, including W. E. Abraham (1962), Kwesi Wiredu (1980), and Paulin Hountondji (1983), among others. What joins all of these perspectives is a common desire to go beyond the mere political or economic freedom which was offered by African independence in the 1960s. True "independence" depended upon liberating Africa from the ethical and aesthetic standards of the West, and on a process of "intellectual decolonization" which involved a search for a common African ancestry in order to reunite a divided continent (July, 1987: 18).

The question of Africa's cultural unity remains an important and controversial topic today. In a recent "blockbuster" exhibition of African art held at the Royal Academy of Arts in London, for example, the issue of cultural unity emerged as a central point of contention and debate. Unlike prior exhibitions of African art, which generally have concentrated on the arts of a more delimited or particular region – one defined as broadly, for example, as West

or Central Africa as a whole, or as narrowly as a single ethnic group, such as Yoruba, Dan, or Dogon – this exhibition, entitled *Africa: The Art of a Continent,* included works from the entire continent, embracing Ancient Egypt and Islamic North Africa as well.

The problem, however, is what do all these diverse cultures, separated by space and time, have in common with each other? Appiah, who commented critically on the exhibition, argued that what they have in common is merely their shared classificatory history in the Western taxonomy and representation of world art. "What unites these objects as African," he writes, "is not a shared nature, not the shared character of the cultures from which they came, but *our* ideas of Africa; ideas which . . . have now come to be important for many Africans, and thus are now African ideas too" (1995: 41). In our collective imagination we have come to accept a category of objects we call African art. But can geographic contiguity alone suffice as a criterion for cultural classification? How do we define the category European art? Surely, there are more nuances to such a category than merely including all art forms that emanate from the continent of Europe. Imagine, for example, an exhibition of European art which lumped together Greek statuary, illuminated Medieval manuscripts, paintings of the Italian Renaissance, and German Expressionist prints. Does an exhibition of "African art" amount to the same degree of cultural clustering of diverse artistic expressions and distinct historical moments? Or, conversely, is there a "deep" and "unconscious" African identity which unites all artistic expressions from the continent?

Museum exhibitions reveal to the viewer things that might otherwise remain unnoticed or unseen. They spotlight certain aspects of art and culture, while simultaneously masking others in the shadow of their own illuminations. To some extent, this book is itself a kind of exhibition – a collection of pieces that comes to stand for a version of what is commonly called African studies. Like an exhibition, this book offers what art historian Svetlana Alpers (1991: 27) calls "a way of seeing" – the structuring of vision which results from isolating an object of study in order to encourage the viewer to look at the familiar in an unfamiliar way or, conversely, to see the unfamiliar in a familiar way. Like a collection of objects displayed side-by-side in a museum case, this volume assembles and binds works of scholarship that might not otherwise have come together. Their juxtaposition is meant to encourage contrast and comparison, to spin the initial threads of intertextual dialogue and debate, and to engage with each other in a contest of methodology and interpretation. But the totality of this collection is inevitably artificial or, as it were, inauthentic since the field of study is constantly changing, growing, and redefining itself. Yet like the most timeless of exhibitions, which must eventually be dismantled and packed away to make room for something new, this book offers a timely collection of perspectives on Africa – a series of essays which represent our vision of African studies past and present, and a set of perspectives which will direct and condition the future of this discipline.

References

Abraham, W. E. 1962. *The Mind of Africa*. London: Weidenfeld and Nicolson.

Alpers, Svetlana. 1991. "The Museum as a Way of Seeing," pp. 25–41. In *Exhibiting Cultures: The Poetics and Politics of Museum Display*, edited by Ivan Karp and Steven D. Lavine. Washington, D. C.: Smithsonian Institution Press.

Appiah, Kwame Anthony. 1992. *In my Father's House: Africa in the Philosophy Culture*. New York and Oxford: Oxford University Press.

Appiah, Kwame Anthony. 1995. "Why Africa? Why Art?," *The Royal Academy Magazine* 48 (Autumn): 40–41.

Bennet, Tony. 1994. "The Exhibitionary Complex." In Nicholas B. Dirks, Geoff Eley, and Sherry B. Ortner, eds. *Culture/Power/History: A Reader in Contemporary Social Theory*. Princeton, NJ: Princeton University Press. Reprinted from *New Formations* 4: 73–102, 1988.

Berger, John. 1972. *Ways of Seeing*. New York: Viking.

Clark, Graham C. 1971. *World Prehistory: A New Outline*. Cambridge: Cambridge University Press.

Clifford, James. 1983. "On Ethnographic Authority," *Representations* 1(2): 118–46.

Clifford, James. 1988. *The Predicament of Culture: Twentieth-Century Ethnography, Literature, and Art*. Cambridge, MA: Harvard University Press.

Cohen, David William. 1977. *Womunafu's Banafu:* *A Study of Authority in a Nineteenth-Century African Community*. Princeton, NJ: Princeton University Press.

Cohen, David William. 1985. "Doing Social History from *Pim*'s Doorway," pp. 191–235. In *Reliving the Past: The Worlds of Social History* edited by Olivier Zunz. Chapel Hill: The University of North Carolina Press.

Comaroff, Jean. 1985. *Body of Power, Spirit of Resistance: The Culture and History of a South African People*. Chicago: University of Chicago Press.

Curtin, Philip D. 1964. *The Image of Africa: British Ideas and Action, 1780–1850*. 2 vols. Madison: University of Wisconsin Press.

Dalzel, Archibald. 1793. *The History of Dahomy, an Inland Kingdom of Africa, compiled from authentic memoirs; with an introduction and notes*. London: Spilsbury & Sons.

Diop, Cheikh Anta. 1978. *The Cultural Unity of Black Africa*. Chicago: Third World Press.

Duncan, James, and David Ley. 1993. "Introduction: Representing the Place of Culture," pp. 1–24. In *Place/Culture/Representation*, edited by James Duncan and David Ley. London and New York: Routledge.

Evans-Pritchard, E. E. [1950] 1960. "Social Anthropology: Past and Present," pp. 139–54 In Evans-Pritchard, *Social Anthropology and other essays*. New York: The Free Press.

Fabian, Johannes. 1986. *Language and Colonial Power: The Appropriation of Swahili in the*

Former Belgian Congo, 1880–1938. Cambridge: Cambridge University Press.

Fage, J. D. 1981. "The Development of African Historiography," pp. 25–42. In *General History of Africa, vol. 1: Methodology and African Prehistory*, edited by J. Ki-Zerbo. Paris: UNESCO and London: Heinemann.

Foucault, Michel. 1979. *Discipline and Punish: The Birth of the Prison.* Harmondsworth: Penguin.

Geertz, Clifford. 1983. "From the Native's Point of View: On the Nature of Anthropological Understanding." In Geertz, Clifford. *Local Knowledge: Further Essays in Interpretive Anthropolgy*, pp. 55–72. New York: Basic Books.

Gyekye, Kwame. 1995. *An Essay on African Philosophical Thought: The Akan Conceptual Scheme.* Philadelphia: Temple University Press. First published 1987.

Henige, David. 1972. *The Chronology of Oral Tradition.* Oxford: Clarendon Press.

Hountondji, Paulin J. 1983. *African Philosophy: Myth and Reality.* Bloomington: Indiana University Press.

Janzen, John. 1978. *The Quest for Therapy: Medical Pluralism in Lower Zaire.* Berkeley and Los Angeles: University of California Press.

Jay, Martin. 1993. *Downcast Eyes: The Denigration of Vision in Twentieth-Century French Thought.* Berkeley and Los Angeles: University of California Press.

July, Robert W. 1987. *An African Voice: The Role of the Humanities in African Independence.* Durham, NC: Duke University Press.

Kluckhohn, Clyde. 1978. *Culture: A Critical Review of Concepts and Definitions.* Milwood, New Jersey: Kraus. First published in 1952.

Kopytoff, Igor. 1987. "The Internal African Frontier: The Making of African Political Culture," pp. 3–84. In *The African Frontier: The Reproduction of Traditional African Societies*, edited by Igor Kopytoff. Bloomington: Indiana University Press.

Lawal, Babatunde. 1993. *Oyibo: Representations of the Colonialist Other in Yoruba Art, 1826–1960.* Discussion Papers in the African Humanities 24. Boston: African Studies Center, Boston University.

Leach, Edmund R. 1954. *Political Systems of Highland Burma.* Boston: Beacon Press.

Leakey, M. G., C. S. Feibel, I. McDougall, and A. Walker. 1995. "New Four-Million-Year-Old Hominid Species from Kanapoi and Allia Bay, Kenya," *Nature* 376(6541): 565–71.

Marcus, George E., and Michael M. J. Fischer. 1986. *Anthropology as Cultural Critique: An Experimental Moment in the Human Sciences.* Chicago: University of Chicago Press.

Martin, Marie-Louise. 1975. *Kimbangu: An African Prophet and his Church,* translated by D. M. Moore. Oxford: Basil Blackwell.

Massaquoi, Hans J. 1990. "The World's Largest Church." *Ebony* 46(2): 116–22.

McIntosh, S. K., and R. J. McIntosh. 1983. "Current Directions in West African Prehistory," *Annual Review of Anthropology* 12: 215–58.

Mitchell, W. J. T. 1986. *Iconology: Image, Text, Ideology.* Chicago: University of Chicago Press.

Moore, Sally Falk. 1986. *Social Facts and Fabrications: "Customary" Law on Kilimanjaro, 1880–1980.* Cambridge: Cambridge University Press.

Mudimbe, V. Y. 1988. *The Invention of Africa: Gnosis, Philiosophy, and the Order of Knowledge.* Bloomington: Indiana University Press.

Mudimbe, V. Y. 1994. *The Idea of Africa.* Bloomington: Indiana University Press.

Nkrumah, Kwame. 1963. *Africa Must Unite.* New York: Praeger.

Noble, Kenneth B. 1994. "For Ivory Coast's Founder, Lavish Funeral." *The New York Times,* 8 February, A1.

Pratt, Mary Louse. 1992. *Imperial Eyes: Travel Writing and Transculturation.* London and New York: Routledge.

Roseberry, William. 1989. "European History and the Construction of Anthropological Subjects," pp. 125–44. In *Anthropologies and Histories: Essays in Culture, History, and Political Economy.* New Brunswick, NJ: Rutgers University Press.

Said, Edward W. 1995. "East Isn't East: The Impending End of the Age of Orientalism," *Times Literary Supplement,* 3 February, pp. 3–6.

Schapera, I. 1962. "Should Anthropologists be Historians?" *Journal of the Royal Anthropological Institute* 92: 143–56.

Spiro, Melford. E. 1990. "On the Strange and Familiar in Recent Anthropological Thought." In *Cultural Psychology,* edited by J. Stigler, R. A. Shweder, and G. Herdt. Cambridge: Cambridge University Press.

Stewart, Charles, and Rosalind Shaw, eds. 1994.

Sycretism/Anti-syncretism: the Politics of Religious Synthesis. London and New York: Routledge.

Sundkler, Bengt G. M. 1948. *Bantu Prophets in South Africa.* London: Lutterworth Press.

Vansina, Jan, 1985. *Oral Tradition as History.* Madison: University of Wisconsin Press.

Waldman, Loren K. 1965. "An Unnoticed Aspect of Archibald Dalzel's *The History of Dahomy*," *Journal of African History* 6(2): pp. 185–92.

White, T. D., G. Suwa, and B. Asfaw. 1994. "*Australopithecus ramidus*, a New Species of Early Hominid from Aramis, Ethiopia," *Nature* 371(6495): 306–12.

Wiredu, Kwesi. 1980. *Philosophy and an African Culture.* Cambridge: Cambridge University Press.

Wolf, Eric. 1982. *Europe and the People Without History.* Berkeley: University of California Press.

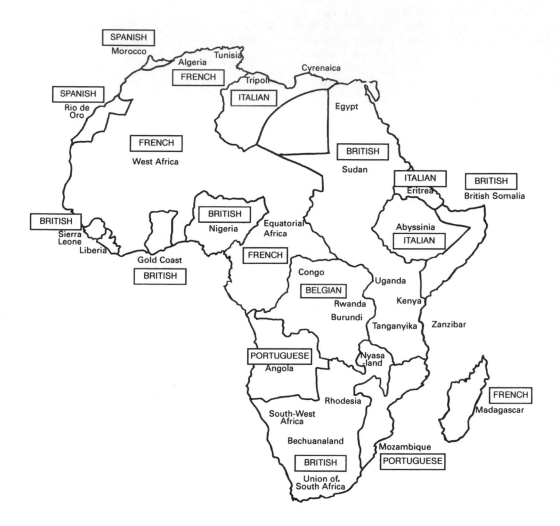

Map I   Africa in colonial era, c.1925

Map II   Africa today, showing ethnic groups discussed in book

PART I

FROM TRIBE TO ETHNICITY:
KINSHIP AND SOCIAL ORGANIZATION

Children in Swaziland.
Photo: Roy Richard Grinker.

FROM TRIBE TO ETHNICITY: KINSHIP AND SOCIAL ORGANIZATION

1.   Meyer Fortes. 1953. "The Structure of Unilineal Descent Groups". *American Anthropologist* 55: 17–41.

2.   Edward E. Evans-Pritchard. 1940. "Time and Space" From *The Nuer*. Oxford: Clarendon.

3.   Aidan W. Southall. 1970. From "The Illusion of Tribe." In P.C.W. Gutkind, ed. *The Passing of Tribal Man in Africa*, pp. 28–50. Leiden: E.J. Brill.

4.   Leroy Vail. 1988. "Introduction: Ethnicity in Southern African History," pp. 1–19. In Leroy Vail, ed. *The Invention of Tribalism in Southern Africa*. Berkeley: University of California Press.

5.   John L. Comaroff. 1984. "Of Totemism and Ethnicity: Consciousness, Practice and the Signs of Inequality." *Ethnos*, 52, no. 3–4: 301–323.

Introduction

Much of the history of anthropology, and of social theory in general, has been devoted to answering a central sociological question: Given that societies are made up of a multiplicity of individuals, with different interests and motivations, how do societies stay together? This is a question phrased and addressed most explicitly at the turn of the century by the French sociologist Emile Durkheim, and later, in the colonial period of the 1930s and 1940s, by anthropologists of Africa, and elsewhere, such as A.R. Radcliffe-Brown and E. E. Evans-Pritchard. They began to focus on how customs and social organizations contributed to social solidarity. The solidifying role played by a particular custom was said to be its function, and the kinship,

political, and legal systems that benefited from the functions were said to constitute the social structure. These anthropologists were often referred to as "structural-functionalists." The readings in this section include Meyer Fortes and Evans-Pritchard (so-called structural-functionalists) as well as other authors who both build upon, elaborate, and reject some of the early concepts, assumptions, and arguments.

The focus on function was the result of a movement in the discipline of anthropology away from speculative historical reconstructions and broad comparative work (such as evolutionism and diffusionism), and toward the study of how particular cultures functioned at particular historical moments. Continuing into the 1940s, many anthropologists continued to study the cultures of the world not "in their own right" (Lienhardt, 1976: 180) but to demonstrate the origins, evolution, or diffusion of cultures and culture traits in history. The new approach – sometimes called "synchronic" because of its focus on a single point in time – made anthropology more empirical and therefore more scientific. Instead of speculating about history, anthropologists wrote about what they actually observed. And instead of studying and comparing the parts of many different cultures, functionalists studied the systems of relations of particular cultures, that is, the ways in which the parts of a culture operated together to form and maintain the whole. Meyer Fortes (1953: 22–3) wrote: "A culture is a unity in so far as it is tied to a bounded social structure. In this sense I would agree that the social structure is the foundation of the whole social life of any *continuing* society" (original emphasis). Emphasizing the whole over the parts gave new life to the science of society, for anthropology now not only conformed more to the scientific method, but had in the concept "society" its own central object of study, its own raison d'etre, as well as a unique theoretical perspective to orient the collection and interpretation of ethnographic data. This movement is articulated clearly in the article by Meyer Fortes, included in this part.

Functionalism offered several new directions to anthropological fieldworkers. First, the focus on society diminished the importance of individual behaviour and, of course, individual variation. A major theoretical premise was that behind all individuals' actions, there had to be a social system. For example, individuals could be free to act only to the extent that there was a structure – economic, legal, political or otherwise – which permitted their acts. Second, since all societies constituted total working systems, all societies, including so-called "primitive" societies, had an understandable, rational, and valid reason for being. Thus, for example, societies without centralized states, such as the Nuer, or

societies where witchcraft was the primary explanation for harm-doing, such as the Tiv or Azande, were no longer seen as backward, abberant, or deficient, but rather as communities that operated according to a certain logic. The anthropologist's task was to identify and characterize that logic, usually analysing one specific system at a time, such as religion, kinship, or economics, and publishing each analysis as one of a sequence of monographs (Lienhardt, 1976: 181). Third, while functionalism did not help explain historical change, it did help explain historical continuity and social reproduction. Various institutions, whether belief systems, economic or political systems, were analyzed to determine how they contributed to the maintenance and perpetuation of the society as a whole. Indeed, even where anthropologists wrote a good deal of history, it was synchronic history: histories that focused on reproduction rather than change.

Kinship was one of the primary mechanisms for social reproduction, especially in stateless societies. In three extraordinarily important books, all published in 1940, the contours of British social anthropology and kinship studies were established, and a productive period of fieldwork in Africa was set into motion: *African Political Systems*, edited by Meyer Fortes and Edward E. Evans-Pritchard, with a foreward by A.R. Radcliffe-Brown; *The Nuer* by Evans-Pritchard; and *The Political System of the Anuak*, by Evans-Pritchard (Kuper, 1973: 107). In the first book, Fortes and Evans-Pritchard distinguished two fundamental types of African political systems: the state society, with a centralized authority (such as the Zulu and Tswana of southern Africa), and the stateless society, a category which encompassed every society without centralized authority, from the cattle-herding Nuer of Sudan to the hunter-gatherers, the !Kung San of southern Africa and the Efe and Mbuti of central Africa. This distinction had a profound influence on the development of the anthropology of Africa (see, for example, Tait and Middleton, 1958). Evans-Pritchard's landmark book, *The Nuer*, addressed the problem of how the Nuer could live together without any apparent political structure. But there was a political structure. Indeed, the answer to the problem was that the political structure and the kinship structure were one and the same.

Before addressing the details of the relation between kinship and politics, it is necessary to put these Africanists in more historical context. It is important to note that prior to the 1940s, few anthropologists had done intensive fieldwork, learned the languages of the people they studied, or lived with them for extended periods of time. Up until the four-year field-work of Bronislaw Malinowski in the Pacific Trobriand Islands during World War I, anthropology had consisted, by and large, of the study of customs and myths collected by travelers, missionaries and explorers, and the analysis of cultural patterns rather than the detailed workings of any one particular society. Intensive fieldwork during the late colonial period among the Nuer (Evans-Pritchard), Zulu (Max Gluckman), Tswana (Schapera), and Tallensi (Fortes), among others, demonstrated how fruitful a firsthand knowledge of language and social life could be. Other notable works based on fieldwork include Audrey Richards' *Land, Labour and Diet in Northern Rhodesia* (1939), Melville Herskovits' *Dahomey, an African Kingdom* (1967 [1938]), Hilda Kuper's *An African Aristocracy* (1947), and countless articles published in journals such as *Africa* (the journal of the International African Institute) and by the Rhodes-Livingstone Institute.

There were also more problematic uses of fieldwork, especially when colonial administrators funded anthropologists. Indeed, anthropology has often been called the "handmaiden of colonialism." At an abstract level, the relationship is not difficult to see. Recent post-modernist scholarship emphasizes how intellectuals in general are complicitous in

forms of domination, and anthropologists are no exception. First, administration could never be totally separated from the content and categories of *knowledge*. However much anthropologists might like to distinguish themselves, the colonists, administrators and anthropologists emerged out of the same intellectual climate using the same intellectual apparatuses, whether we are speaking generally about the idea of encountering and mastering an "other," or more specifically of how European categories of race, gender, or class, became incorporated into both scholarly analysis and colonial perspectives. And, in as much as anthropologists studied religion, they shared much with and learned much from the missionaries whose first task was often to learn the rituals and belief systems of the people with whom they would work. Second, however different they might have been, colonialism and anthropology had some similar results. For example, both introduced the concept of "tribe" to Africa, divided the world into a "West" and "others," reified "tribes" and "traditions," and ended up, often unwittingly, altering the modes of thought of many Africans so that people began to think of themselves in terms not of their own making.

However, according to two historians of African anthropology, the colonial administrator's uses of anthropologists were quite limited. In their accounts of the anthropology of Africa, both Adam Kuper (1973) and Sally Falk Moore (1994) look rather concretely at the relationship between the two professions, and point out that, despite the fact that much funding for anthropological work came from colonial administrators, and that many colonial administrators were themselves engaged in ethnographic work, seldom did the administrators listen to the anthropologists. According to Moore (1994: 19), they found, more often than not, that information on rituals, proverbs, and marriage systems were unimportant to their ability to govern, and that anthropologists often looked out for the well-being of the people with whom they lived and studied, and thus could act counter to colonial interests. Yet, there certainly were important connections to be made. Among other things, administrators were interested in anthropological work on African political systems because the methods by which Africans governed themselves impinged directly on the ability of the colony to govern. For example, the British could invest chiefs with political responsibilities in those societies with a pre-existing system of chiefs, while for other societies without chiefs, such as the hunter-gatherers and farmers of central Africa, the Belgians had to create chiefdoms and chiefs.

It is here, in the conjuncture of colonial and indigenous political systems, that we begin to see the linkage betwen politics and kinship. The Nuer of southern Sudan, the topic of Evans-Pritchard's chapter reprinted in this section, were scattered over an immense area of land, and without any discernible system of relationships linking them together (more than 200,000 persons over an area of more than 30,000 square miles – that is fewer than seven people per square mile). Moreover, according to seasonal changes, including availability of water during the dry season, and dangerous flooding during the rainy season, the Nuer would move often and far, in and out of villages, from inland to riverside camps. Such movement was troubling not only for ethnographers trying to understand social organization, but for the administrators who wanted to pacify, settle, and tax these communities. How could the British pacify and administer people whose order appeared only as disorder? Although there is no evidence that the British administration ever consulted Evans-Pritchard's works, or even asked for his advice, Evans-Pritchard concluded that one could make sense of the Nuer world, and that the Nuer had a well-organized political system. But it was one uniquely suited to their ecological and social needs, and one which operated according to genealogy and kinship relations.

Evans-Pritchard argued that the Nuer conceived their political relationships in terms of descent and lineage. According to this view, African societies, like the Nuer, consist of "descent groups," and these societies are organized and act according to the descent group's corporate organization. The descent group served as a legal system – a system that defined the norms and limits of behavior, and established lines of authority – as well as an economic system that governed the exchange of cattle between individuals and families. (In Part II Sharon Hutchinson highlights the tremendous importance of cattle to the Nuer). Anthropologists used the term "lineage" to describe descent groups in which the genealogical lines were clearly drawn, and the term "clan" to describe groups in which the individuals believed, but could not fully demonstrate, that they descended from a common ancestor. The Nuer had a segmentary lineage system that consisted of a number of groups descending from the most inclusive (the tribe) to the least (say, two brothers). Each descending level consisted of groups defined by their opposition to other like segments. The segmentary lineage was thus a balance of power with no center. At any point in time, however, opposed segments could unite into a more inclusive segment to take action against another set of united segments. Brothers could be naturally opposed to one another, but if a more distantly related third party fought with one of the brothers, the two brothers would unite to form a single segment. To quote a Nuer man, "We fight against the Rengyan, but when either of us is fighting a third party, we combine with them" (Evans-Pritchard, 1940: 143).

The system of oppositions and alliances may thus change according to social context. Evans-Pritchard (1940: 142) says, "Each segment is itself segmented and there is opposition between its parts. The members of any segment unite for war against adjacent segments of the same order and unite with these adjacent segments against larger sections." Analogies to this system can be found in international law, where there is no official ultimate authority, and where alliances and oppositions shift according to context; for example, though Syria was diplomatically opposed to the United States, and allied with its Arab neighbour Iraq before the Gulf War, during the war Syria and the United States became allies.

One of the theoretical outcomes of Evans-Pritchard's analysis is that it helped move anthropology away from a strict empiricism and toward the study of more structural, theoretical, organizing principles. The segmentary lineage is an abstract principle, a way of conceptualizing the world. For this reason, Evans-Pritchard also focused on concepts of time and space and the degree to which these abstractions were implicated in the organization of society. The selection from *The Nuer* included in this section focuses specifically on time and space and the manner in which these ostensibly common sense concepts are social concepts, socially constructed and socially enacted. Thus, Evans-Pritchard tells us that the Nuer words for ecological time (*tot*, village life, rainy season; *mai*, dry season) are not words for time reckoning but rather denote the cluster of social activities characteristic of the seasons. To quote Adam Kuper, "the Nuer do not say, it is *tot*, therefore we must move to the upland villages; rather they say we are in the villages, therefore it is *tot* (1973: 89)." In other words, concepts of time are determined by society and social life. In turn, social relationships could be construed in terms of time. People and cattle were more or less related in terms of the genealogical distance, that is their distance in time or generations from a common ancestor. Everyone had a measurable social or structural distance from everyone else.

The Nuer was thus not simply a book about a group of eastern Africans. It was about the future directions of anthropology. The genealogies of many major theoretical movements in structuralism, Marxism and

economic anthropology, among others, can be traced back to the Nuer and its theoretical insights and innovations. More specifically, the work established as a central problematic the complex relations between behaviour and structure, actual social interactions and the models for patterning them. All of this is not to say that the work is without criticism (see, for instance, Karp and Maynard, 1983; Gough, 1971; Kelly, 1985; Grinker, 1994). These criticisms suggest, in general, that Evans-Pritchard neglected social and historical complexities of the Nuer in the service of his one abstract model, that he focused on lineages when the household was also a major form of social and political organization, and that he wrongly emphasized the Nuer as a homogeneous and internally undifferentiated society, when, in fact, as subsequent work has shown, the Nuer of his time were differentiated according to rank as well as ethnicity (including aristocrats, Dinka, and other captives). Indeed, anthropologists soon began questioning some of the most basic assumptions of Evans-Pritchard, and other anthropologists of his era, including the concepts of descent, lineage, and tribe. Readings by Southall and Vail speak directly to the ubiquitous concept "tribe," and illuminate its complexities and limitations.

"Tribe" generally referred to a group of people bound by common language, territory, and custom, and more specifically to small scale agricultural societies considered more complex than "bands" – that is, small autonomous groups, usually hunter-gatherers and nomads, with what were sometimes called "simple" political organizations – but less complex than chiefdoms – that is, ranked societies with centralized political organizations. The segmentary lineage was, for Evans-Pritchard, a type of *tribal* organization well suited for societies that, for whatever reason, cannot sustain a fixed and centralized political system. The tribe consisted of descent groups, the basic units of collective identity and action.

The anthropologists Aidan Southall, Adam Kuper, Philip Gulliver, Morton Fried, Igor Kopytoff, June Helm, Peter Ekeh, and historian Jan Vansina, are among those who have leveled the harshest criticisms against the use of the term "tribe." These anthropologists challenged the typology that distinguished societies on the basis of authority structures, questioned the criteria used to hierarchically rank societies in terms of complexity, and pointed out the problems and limitations of the terms themselves. "Tribe" was a useful term for anthropologists, such as Evans-Pritchard, who tried to delineate the boundaries of groups with few distinct boundaries, and where ethnic identities and loyalites could shift rapidly. For the same reason, "tribe" turned out to be a useful term for administrators and local politicians because it drew the lines necessary for census taking, taxation and work recruitment. Yet, as Southall and others point out, boundaries between tribes were often drawn by anthropologists or administrators quite arbitrarily, sometimes according to language similarities and differences, and at other times according to differences in territory, religion, or dress – all, of course, as perceived by the Europeans. (Similarly, the boundaries between colonies and nations in Africa were often constructed more out of convenience than respect for local ethnic divisions, and so many societies found themselves virtually cut in half. The Azande, for instance today live in both Sudan, a former British colony and Zaire, a former Belgian colony).

There was another serious problem with tribe: it implied a distinction between Africa and Europe. Few Europeans of the twentieth century refer to themselves with the term tribe, yet the word continues to be used today in academic work, and especially in the mass media, to refer to Africa. When there is conflict between, say, the Flemish and the French speakers in Belgium, or between the Serbs and Bosnians of the former Yugoslavia, the international media refer to the conflict as "ethnic", yet, when the Hutu and Tutsi of Rwanda and Burundi, or the Xhosa and Zulu of South Africa, fight with one another, the media refer to the conflict as "tribal." "Tribe" is also linked to the concept "tribalism," and for this reason has a rather pejorative usage in Africa today, meaning those affiliations that pit identities against one another at the expense of unified national, political and economic development.

In sum, "tribe" hurts more than it helps, and obscures more than it reveals. What it obscures is identities that are both malleable and dependent upon their relations with other identities. It masks our ability to see the internal diversity of African communities and to look for models other than descent and lineage to account for social and political organization. If we characterize a society in tribal terms, including the focus on descent as the key organizing principle of society, we might easily view it as a homogeneous entity. To represent the same society in ethnic terms, however, might lead us to see transformation and diversity as well as continuity and similarity. Ethnicity helps us to see how individual societies integrate individuals and groups who are not members of descent groups, who may not speak the same language, or live in the same territory.

The focus on ethnicity was a particular advantage for the study of diverse and rapidly changing communities in African cities, and urban anthropologists such as Clyde Mitchell, Max Gluckman, A.L. Epstein and Abner Cohen, made some of the most important strides in the transition from tribal to ethnic studies. Unfortunately, rural areas continued to be seen as unchanging. Moore (1994: 69) writes:

> The fact is, of course, that conditions in the countryside changed at the same time that cities grew, often in related ways. But the "tribal" *model* was not changing, since its goal was a reconstruction of a precolonial African "type," not the recording of a full,

unexpurgated account of changing events and practices in the countryside at the time of fieldwork. To be sure, collective cultural differences were important then, and they have continued significance in Africa to this day. In many parts of the continent, tribal or ethnic identities have ongoing social and political salience. But this should not be mistaken for an unchanging traditionalism.

At a time, in the late twentieth century, when African cultures are no longer bound by location, but by migration, displacement, diaspora, travel, telephone and the internet, common territory cannot define identity. And the number of interactions between African societies, as demonstrated in ancient and modern African history, compels us to employ theoretical concepts that draw our attention to shifting identities, and to relations between groups rather than solely to relations within groups. This is, indeed, the direction in which Leroy Vail points us. We want to stress, however, that these problems in no way make the previous studies wrong or irrelevant. Critical approaches, and the development of new theoretical concepts, do not necessarily disprove; rather, they show us the limits of older approaches and concepts, open up new lines of inquiry, and lead us to see phenomena that we did not see before.

Leroy Vail and John L. Comaroff's works offer perspectives on the category ethnicity that help make it a more precise, helpful and analytical tool for African studies. To understand their essays, it is necessary to outline two contrasting views of ethnicity: primordialism and instrumentalism. The former holds that ethnicity arises from similarities between individuals of a group in physical characteristics, language, and cultural features thought to be "natural" or "inherited," as distinct from particular social or historical conditions. These features have the power to impart a sense of group and individual identity, a sense of belonging to a community.

In contrast, "instrumentalist" models hold that groups create ethnic identities for political and economic interests. Ethnicity, according to this view, is rationally oriented toward the fulfillment of specific goals like nationalism, access to economic power, or freedom from colonial rule. Primordialism was well suited to the synchronic tribal studies of the structural-functionalists, and instrumentalism more consonant with diachronic, historical analyses.

Most scholars today reject these simplistic alternatives and hold the position that neither is sufficient to explain ethnic group structure and sentiment. As Vail and Comaroff both note, primordialism overlooks the fact that ethnic identity is not a natural feeling that simply emerges mysteriously in all human communities, but a complex and dynamic set of symbolic meanings embedded in and patterned by history. Instrumentalists are so concerned with political and economic motivations that they sometimes ignore the question of how the particular elements or symbols of an ethnic identity are chosen. Vail, in particular, stresses that some ethnic features and ties are of long standing but a great many others are of recent origin – even though people may believe they are ancient. Moreover, the meaning and definition of ethnicities change over time and differ according to historical circumstance. In other words, as Comaroff tells us, all ethnicities have a history. If there is anything primordial, he writes, it is not any particular ethnicity but rather the process of symbolic classification, the mechanism by which people divide the world into a we and a they, and thereby give meaning to their lives. If we understand that process, we will better understand not only the people we study, but also the ways in which anthropologists and historians, past and present, have tried to make sense of Africa.

References

Evans-Pritchard, E.E. 1940. *The Nuer*. Oxford: Clarendon.

Evans-Pritchard, E.E. 1940. *The Political system of the Anuak of the Anglo-Egyptian Sudan*. London: P. Lund Humphries and Co., Ltd., for the LSE.

Fortes, Meyer. 1953. "The Structure of Unilineal Descent Groups." *American Anthropologist*, 55: 17–41.

Fortes, Meyer and E.E. Evans-Pritchard, eds. 1940. *African Political Systems*. London: Oxford University Press, for the IAI.

Gough, Kathleen. 1971. "Nuer Kinship: A Re-examination." In *The Translation of Culture*, ed. T. O. Beidelman, pp. 79–122. London: Tavistock.

Grinker, Roy Richard. 1994. *Houses in the Rainforest: Ethnicity and Inequality among Farmers and Foragers in Central Africa*. Berkeley: University of California Press.

Herskovits, Melville. 1967 [1938]. *Dahomey: An Ancient African Kingdom*. Evanston: Northwestern University Press.

Karp, Ivan and Kent Maynard. 1983. "Reading the Nuer." *Current Anthropology*, 24 (4): 481–502.

Kelly, R.C. 1985. *The Nuer Conquest: The Structure and Development of an Expansionist System*. Ann Arbor: Univeristy of Michigan Press.

Kuper, Adam. 1973. *Anthropology and Anthropologists: The Modern British School*. London: RKP.

Kuper, Hilda. 1961 [1947]. *An African Aristocracy: Rank Among the Swazi*. London: Oxford University Press, for IAI.

Lienhardt, Godfrey. 1976. "Social Anthropology of Africa." In Fyfe, Christoper, ed. *African Studies Since 1945*. pp. 179–185.

Middleton, John and D. Tait, eds. 1958. *Tribes without Rulers*. London: Routledge and Kegan Paul.

Moore, Sally Falk. 1994. *Anthropology and Africa; Changing Perspectives on a Changing Scene*. Charlottesville: University of Virginia Press.

Richards, Audrey. 1939. *Land, Labour and Diet in Northern Rhodesia: An Economic Study of the Beinba Tribe*. London: International Institute of African Language and Culture.

Suggested Readings

Bates, R., V.Y. Mudimbe, and J. O'Barr, eds. 1993. *African and the Disciplines: The Contribution of Research in Africa to the Social Sciences and Humanities*. Chicago: University of Chicago Press.

Cohen, Abner, 1965. *Custom and Politics in Urban Africa: A Study of Hausa Migrants in Yoruba Towns*. Berkeley: University of California Press.

Cohen, R. 1978. "Ethnicity: Problem and Focus." *Annual Review of Anthropology* 7: 379–403.

Colson, E. 1962. *The Plateau Tonga of Northern Rhodesia: Social and Religious Studies*. Manchester: Manchester University Press.

Comaroff, John L., ed. 1980. *The Meanings of Marriage Payments*. London: Academic Press.

Ekeh, Peter. 1990. "Social Anthropology and Two Contrasting Uses of Tribalism in Africa." *Comparative Studies in Society and History* 32(4): 660–700.

Fortes, Meyer. 1949. "Time and Social Structure: An Ashanti Case Study." In Fortes, Meyer, ed. *Social Structure*. Oxford: Clarendon Press. pp. 54–84.

Gluckman, Max. 1958. "Analysis of a Social Situation in Modern Zululand," Rhodes–Livingstone Paper no. 28. *Bantu Studies* 14: 1–30; 147–74.

Grayburn, Nelson. 1971. *Readings in Kinship and Social Structure*. New York: Harper and Row.

Gulliver, Philip. 1971 *Neighbours and Networks*. Berkeley and Los Angeles: University of California Press.

Gutkind, Peter. 1970. *The Passing of Tribal Man in Africa*. Netherlands: Brill.

Helm, June. ed. 1968. *Essays on the Problem of Tribe*. Proceedings of the 1967 Annual Spring Meeting of the American Ethnological Society. Seattle: University of Washington Press.

Hutchinson, Sharon. 1996. *Nuer Dilemmas: Coping with Money, War and the State*. Berkeley: University of California Press.

Kuper, Adam. 1982. "Lineage Theory: A Critical

Retrospect." *Annual Review of Anthropology* 11: 71–95.

Mair, Lucy. 1934. *An African People in the Twentieth Century*. London: Routeledge.

Radcliffe-Brown, A.R. 1952. *Structure and Function in Primitive Society*. New York: The Free Press.

Radcliffe-Brown, A.R. and Daryll Forde, eds. 1975 [1950]. *African Systems of Kinship and Marriage*. London: Oxford University Press for the IAI.

Schapera, Isaac. ed. 1937. *The Bantu-speaking Tribes of South Africa*. London: Routledge.

Sharp, J. 1980. "Can we Study Ethnicity? A Critique of Fields of Study in South African Anthropology. *Social Dynamics* 6 (1): 1–16.

Stocking, George. 1995. *After Tylor: British Social Anthropology: 1885–1951*. Madison: University of Wisconsin Press.

Turner, Victor. 1957. *Schism and Continuity in an African Society: A Study of Ndembu Village Life*. Manchester: Manchester University Press.

1

THE STRUCTURE OF UNILINEAL
DESCENT GROUPS[1]

MEYER FORTES

The most important feature of unilineal descent groups in Africa brought into focus by recent field research is their corporate organization. When we speak of these groups as corporate units we do so in the sense given to the term "corporation" long ago by Maine in his classical analysis of testamentary succession in early law (Maine, 1866). We are reminded also of Max Weber's sociological analysis of the corporate group as a general type of social formation (Weber, 1947), for in many important particulars these African descent groups conform to Weber's definition. British anthropologists now regularly use the term *lineage* for these descent groups. This helps both to stress the significance of descent in their structure and to distinguish them from wider often dispersed divisions of society ordered to the notion of common – but not demonstrable and often mythological – ancestry for which we find it useful to reserve the label *clan*.

The guiding ideas in the analysis of African lineage organization have come mainly from Radcliffe-Brown's formulation of the structural principles found in all kinship systems (cf. Radcliffe-Brown, 1950). I am sure I am not alone in regarding these as among the most important generalizations as yet reached in the study of social structure. Lineage organization shows very clearly how these principles work together in mutual dependence, so that varying weight of one or the other in relation to variations in the wider context of social structure gives rise to variant arrangements on the basis of the same broad ground-plan.

A lineage is a corporate group from the outside, that is in relation to other defined groups and associations. It might be described as a single legal personality – "one person" as the Ashanti put it (Fortes, 1950). Thus the way a lineage system works depends on the kind of legal institutions found in the society; and this, we know, is a function of its political organization. Much fruitful work has resulted from following up this line of thought. As far as Africa is concerned there is increasing evidence to suggest that lineage organization is

[1] *Editorial note:* This paper was presented by Professor Fortes at the Symposium on the "Positive Contributions of Social Anthropology," held at the 50th annual meetings of the American Anthropological Association in Chicago, November 15–17, 1951. Professor Fortes' participation in the symposium was made possible by the generosity of the Wenner-Gren Foundation for Anthropological Research, Inc.

most developed in what Evans-Pritchard and I (1940), taking a hint from Durkheim, called segmentary societies. This has been found to hold for the Tiv of Nigeria (P. J. Bohannan, 1951), for the Gusii (Mayer, 1949) and other East and South African peoples, and for the Cyrenaican Beduin (Peters, 1951), in addition to the peoples discussed in *African Political Systems*. In societies of this type the lineage is not only a corporate unit in the legal or jural sense but is also the primary political association. Thus the individual has no legal or political status except as a member of a lineage; or to put it in another way, all legal and political relations in the society take place in the context of the lineage system.

But lineage grouping is not restricted to segmentary societies. It is the basis of local organization and of political institutions also in societies like the Ashanti (Fortes, 1950; Busia, 1951) and the Yoruba (Forde, 1951) which have national government centered in kingship, administrative machinery and courts of law. But the primary emphasis, in these societies, is on the legal aspect of the lineage. The political structure of these societies was always unstable and this was due in considerable degree to internal rivalries arising out of the divisions between lineages; that is perhaps why they remained federal in constitution. In Ashanti, for instance, this is epitomized in the fact that citizenship is, in the first place, local not national, is determined by lineage membership by birth and is mediated through the lineage organization. The more centralized the political system the greater the tendency seems to be for the corporate strength of descent groups to be reduced or for such corporate groups to be nonexistent. Legal and political status are conferred by allegiance to the State, not by descent, though rank and property may still be vested in descent lines. The Nupe (Nadel, 1942), the Zulu (Gluckman in Fortes and Evans-Pritchard, 1940) the Hausa (Dry, 1950), and other state organizations exemplify this in different ways. There is, in these societies, a clearer structural differ-entiation between the field of domestic relations based on kinship and descent and the field of political relations, than in segmentary societies.

However, where the lineage is found as a corporate group all the members of a lineage are to outsiders jurally equal and represent the lineage when they exercise legal and political rights and duties in relation to society at large. This is what underlies so-called collective responsibility in blood vengeance and self-help as among the Nuer (Evans-Pritchard, 1940) and the Beduin (Peters, 1951).

Maine's aphorism that corporations never die draws attention to an important characteristic of the lineage, its continuity, or rather its presumed perpetuity in time. Where the lineage concept is highly developed, the lineage is thought to exist as a perpetual corporation as long as any of its members survive. This means, of course, not merely perpetual physical existence ensured by the replacement of departed members. It means perpetual structural existence, in a stable and homogeneous society; that is, the perpetual exercise of defined rights, duties, office and social tasks vested in the lineage as a corporate unit. The point is obvious but needs recalling as it throws light on a widespread custom. We often find, in Africa and elsewhere, that a person or descent group is attached to a patrilineal lineage through a female member of the lineage. Then if there is a danger that rights and offices vested in the lineage may lapse through the extinction of the true line of descent, the attached line may by some jural fiction be permitted to assume them. Or again, rather than let property or office go to another lineage by default of proper succession within the owning lineage, a slave may be allowed to succeed. In short, the aim is to preserve the existing scheme of social relations as far as possible. As I shall mention presently, this idea is developed most explicitly among some Central African peoples.

But what marks a lineage out and maintains its identity in the face of the continuous replacement by death and birth of its members is the fact that it emerges most precisely in a complementary relationship with or in opposition to like units. This was first precisely shown for the Nuer by Evans-Pritchard and I was able to confirm the analysis among the Tallensi (Fortes, 1949). It is characteristic of all segmentary socieites in Africa so far described, almost by definition. A recent and most interesting case is that of the Tiv of Northern Nigeria (P. J. Bohannan, 1951). This people were, until the arrival of the British, extending their territory rapidly by moving forward *en masse* as their land became exhausted. Among them the maximal lineages are identified by their relative *positions* in the total deployment of all the lineages and they maintain these positions by pushing against one another as they all move slowly forward.

The presumed perpetuity of the lineage is what lineage genealogies conceptualize. If there is one thing all recent investigations are agreed upon it is that lineage genealogies are not historically accurate. But they can be understood if they are seen to be the conceptualization of the existing lineage structure viewed as continuing through time and therefore projected backward as pseudo-history. The most striking proof of this comes from Cyrenaica. The Beduin there have tribal genealogies going back no more than the fourteen generations or thereabouts which we so commonly find among African Negro peoples; but as Peters points out, historical records show that they have lived in Cyrenaica apparently in much the same way as now for a much longer time than the four to five hundred years implied in their genealogies. Dr. P. J. and Dr. L. Bohannan have actually observed the Tiv at public moots rearranging their lineage genealogies to bring them into line with changes in the existing pattern of legal and political relations within and between lineages. A genealogy is, in fact, what Malinowski called a legal charter and not an historical record.

A society made up of corporate lineages is in danger of splitting into rival lineage factions. How is this counteracted in the interests of wider political unity? One way is to extend the lineage framework to the widest range within which sanctions exist for preventing conflicts and disputes from ending in feud or warfare. The political unit is thought of then as the most inclusive, or maximal, lineage to which a person can belong, and it may be conceptualized as embracing the whole tribal unit. This happens among the Gusii (Mayer, 1949) as well as among the Nuer, the Tiv and the Beduin; but with the last three the tribe is not the widest field within which sanctions against feud and war prevail. A major lineage segment of the tribe is the *de facto* political unit by this definition.

Another way, widespread in West Africa but often associated with the previously mentioned structural arrangement, is for the common interest of the political community to be asserted periodically, as against the private interests of the component lineages, through religious institutions and sanctions. I found this to be the case among the Tallensi (Fortes, 1940) and the same principle applies to the Yakö (Forde, 1950 (b)) and the Ibo (Forde and Jones, 1950). I believe it will be shown to hold for many peoples of the Western Sudan among whom ancestor worship and the veneration of the earth are the basis or religious custom. The politically integrative functions of ritual institutions have been described for many parts of the world. What recent African ethnography adds is detailed descriptive data from which further insight into the symbolism used and into the reasons why political authority tends to be invested with ritual meaning and expression can be gained. A notable instance is Dr. Kuper's (1947) account of the Swazi kingship.

As the Swazi data indicate, ritual institutions are also used to support political authority and to affirm the highest common interests in African societies with more complex political structures than those of segmentary societies. This has long been known, ever since the Divine Kingship of the

Shilluk (cf. Evans-Pritchard, 1948) brought inspiration to Sir James Frazer. But these ritual institutions do not free the individual to have friendly and co-operative relations with other individuals irrespective of allegiance to corporate groups. If such relations were impossible in a society it could hardly avoid splitting into antagonistic fractions in spite of public ritual sanctions, or else it would be in a chronic state of factional conflict under the surface. It is not surprising therefore to find that great value is attached to widely spreading bonds of personal kinship, as among the Tallensi (Fortes, 1949). The recent field studies I have quoted all confirm the tremendous importance of the web of kinship as a counterweight to the tendency of unilineal descent grouping to harden social barriers. Or to put it slightly differently, it seems that where the unilineal descent group is rigorously structured within the total social system there we are likely to find kinship used to define and sanction a personal field of social relations for each individual. I will come back to this point in a moment. A further point to which I will refer again is this. We are learning from considerations such as those I have just mentioned, to think of social structure in terms of levels of organization in the manner first explicitly followed in the presentation of field data by Warner (1937). We can investigate the total social structure of a given community at the level of local organization, at that of kinship, at the level of corporate group structure and government, and at that of ritual institutions. We see these levels are related to different collective interests, which are perhaps connected in some sort of hierarchy. And one of the problems of analysis and exposition is to perceive and state the fact that all levels of structure are simultaneously involved in every social relationship and activity. This restatement of what is commonly meant by the concept of integration has the advantage of suggesting how the different modes of social relationship distinguished in any society are interlocked with one another. It helps to make clear also how certain basic principles of social organization can be generalized throughout the whole structure of a primitive society, as for instance the segmentary principle among the Nuer and the Tallensi.

This way of thinking about the problem of social integration has been useful in recent studies of African political organization. Study of the unilineal descent group as a part of a total social system means in fact studying its functions in the widest framework of social structure, that of the political organization. A common and perhaps general feature of political organization in Africa is that it is built up in a series of layers, so to speak, so arranged that the principle of checks and balances is necessarily mobilized in political activities. The idea is used in a variety of ways but what it comes to in general is that the members of the society are distributed in different, nonidentical schemes of allegiance and mutual dependence in relation to administrative, juridical and ritual institutions. It would take too long to enumerate all the peoples for whom we now have sufficient data to show this in detail. But the Lozi of Northern Rhodesia (Gluckman, 1951) are of such particular theoretical interest in this connection that a word must be said about them. The corporate descent group is not found among them. Instead their political organization is based on what Maine called the corporation sole. This is a title carrying political office backed by ritual sanctions and symbols to which subjects, lands, jurisdiction, and representative status, belong. But every adult is bound to a number of titles for different legal and social purposes in such a way that what is one allegiance group with respect to one title is split up with reference to other titles. Thus the only all-inclusive allegiance is that of all the nation to the kinship, which is identified with the State and the country as a whole. A social stucture of such a kind, knit together moreover by a widely ramifying network of bilateral kinship ties between persons, is well fortified against internal disruption. It should be added that the notion of the "corporation sole" is found among many Central African peoples. It appears, in fact, to be a jural institution of the same generality in any of these societies as corporate groups are in others, since it is significant at all levels of social structure. A good example is the Bemba (cf. Richards, 1936, 1940b) among whom it is seen in the custom of "positional inheritance" of status, rank, political office and ritual duty, as I will explain later.

What is the main methodological contribution of these studies? In my view it is the approach from the angle of political organization to what are traditionally thought of as kinship groups and institutions that has been specially fruitful. By regarding lineages and statuses from the point of view of the total social system and not from that of an hypothetical EGO we realize that consanguinity and affinity, real or putative, are not sufficient in themselves to bring about these structural arrangements. We see that descent is fundamentally a jural concept as Radcliffe-Brown argued in one of his most important papers (1935); we see its significance, as the connecting link between the external, that is political and legal, aspect of what we have called unilineal descent groups, and the internal or domestic aspect. It is in the latter context that kinship carries maximum weight, first, as the source of title to membership of the groups or to specific jural status, with all that this means in rights over and toward persons and property, and second as the basis of the social relations among the persons who are identified with one another in the corporate group. In theory, membership of a corporate legal or political group need not stem from kinship, as Weber has made clear. In primitive society, however, if it is not based on kinship it seems generally to presume some formal procedure of incorporation with ritual initiation. So-called secret societies in West Africa seem to be corporate organizations of this nature. Why descent rather than locality or some other principle forms the basis of these corporate groups is a question that needs more study. It will be remembered that Radcliffe-Brown (1935) related succession rules to the need for unequivocal discrimination of rights *in rem* and *in personam*. Perhaps it is most closely connected with the fact that rights over the reproductive powers of women are easily regulated by a descent group system. But I believe that something deeper than this is involved; for in a homogeneous society there is nothing which could so precisely and incontrovertibly fix one's place in society as one's parentage.

Looking at it from without, we ignore the internal structure of the unilineal group. But African lineages are not monolithic units; and knowledge of their internal differentiation has been much advanced by the researches I have mentioned. The dynamic character of lineage structure can be seen most easily in the balance that is reached between its external relations and its internal structure. Ideally, in most lineage-based societies the lineage tends to be thought of as a perpetual unit, expanding like a balloon but never growing new parts. In fact, of course, as Forde (1938) and Evans-Pritchard (1940) have so clearly shown, fission and accretion are processes inherent in lineage structure. However, it is a common experience to find an informant who refuses to admit that his lineage or even his branch of a greater lineage did not at one time exist. Myth and legend, believed, naturally, to be true history, are quickly cited to prove the contrary. But investigation shows that the stretch of time, or rather of duration, with which perpetuity is equated varies according to the count of generations needed to conceptualize the internal structure of the lineage and link it on to an absolute, usually mythological origin for the whole social system in a first founder.

This is connected with the fact that an African lineage is never, according to our present knowledge, internally undifferentiated. It is always segmented and is in process of continuous further segmentation at any given time. Among some of the peoples I have mentioned (e.g. the Tallensi and probably the Ibo) the internal segmentation of a lineage is quite rigorous and the process of further segmentation has an almost mechanical precision. The general rule is that every segment is, in form, a replica of every other segment and of the whole lineage. But the segments are, as a rule, hierarchically organized by fixed steps of greater and greater inclusiveness, each step being defined by genealogical reference. It is perhaps hardly necessary to mention again that when we talk of lineage structure we are really concerned, from a particular analytical angle, with the organization of jural, economic, and ritual activities. The point here is that lineage segmentation corresponds to gradation in the institutional norms and activities in which the total lineage organization is actualized. So we find that the greater the time depth that is attributed to the lineage system as a whole, the more elaborate is its internal segmentation. As I have already mentioned, lineage systems in Africa, when most elaborate, seem to have a maximal time depth of around fourteen putative generations. More common though is a count of five or six generations of named ancestors between living adults and a quasi-mythological founder. We can as yet only guess at the conditions that lie behind these limits of genealogical depth in lineage structure. The facts themselves are nevertheless of great comparative interest. As I have previously remarked, these genealogies obviously do not represent a true record of all the ancestors of a group. To explain this by the limitations and fallibility of oral tradition is merely to evade the problem. In structural terms the answer seems to lie in the spread or span (Fortes, 1945) of internal segmentation of the lineage, and this apparently has inherent limits. As I interpret the evidence we have, these limits are set by the condition of stability in the social structure which it is one of the chief functions of lineage systems to maintain. The segmentary spread found in a given lineage system is that which makes for

maximum stability; and in a stable social system it is kept at a particular spread by continual internal adjustments which are conceptualized by clipping, patching and telescoping genealogies to fit. Just what the optimum spread of lineage segmentation in a particular society tends to be depends presumably on extra-lineage factors of political and economic organization of the kind referred to by Forde (1947).

It is when we consider the lineage from within that kinship becomes decisive. For lineage segmentation follows a model laid down in the parental family. It is indeed generally thought of as the perpetuation, through the rule of the jural unity of the descent line and of the sibling group (cf. Radcliffe-Brown, 1951), of the social relations that constitute the parental family. So we find a lineage segment conceptualized as a sibling group in symmetrical relationship with segments of a like order. It will be a paternal sibling group where descent is patrilineal and a maternal one where it is matrilineal. Progressive orders of inclusiveness are formulated as a succession of generations; and the actual process of segmentation is seen as the equivalent of the division between siblings in the parental family. With this goes the use of kinship terminology and the application of kinship norms in the regulation of intra-lineage affairs.

As a corporate group, a lineage exhibits a structure of authority, and it is obvious from what I have said why this is aligned with the generations ladder. We find, as a general rule, that not only the lineage but also every segment of it has a head, by succession or election, who manages its affairs with the advice of his co-members. He may not have legal sanctions by means of which to enforce his authority in internal affairs; but he holds his position by consent of all his fellow members, and he is backed by moral sanctions commonly couched in religious concepts. He is the trustee for the whole group of the property and other productive resources vested in it. He has a decisive jural role also in the disposal of rights over the fertility of the women in the group. He is likely to be the representative of the whole group in political and legal relations with other groups, with political authorities, and in communal ritual. The effect may be to make him put the interests of his lineage above those of the community if there is conflict with the latter. This is quite clearly recognized by some peoples. Among the Ashanti for instance, every chiefship is vested in a matrilineal lineage. But once a chief has been installed his constitutional position is defined as holding an office that belongs to the whole community not to any one lineage. The man is, ideally, so merged in the office that he virtually ceases to be a member of his lineage, which always has an independent head for its corporate affairs (cf. Busia, 1950).

Thus lineage segmentation as a process in time links the lineage with the parental family; for it is through the family that the lineage (and therefore the society) is replenished by successive generations; and it is on the basis of the ties and cleavages between husband and wife, between polygynous wives, between siblings, and between generations that growth and segmentation take place in the lineage. Study of this process has added much to our understanding of well known aspects of family and kinship structure.

I suppose that we all now take it for granted that filiation – by contrast with descent – is universally bilateral. But we have also been taught, perhaps most graphically by Malinowski, that this does not imply equality of social weighting for the two sides of kin connection. Correctly stated, the rule should read that filiation is always complementary, unless the husband in a matrilineal society (like the Nayar) or the wife in a patrilineal society, as perhaps in ancient Rome, is given no parental status or is legally severed from his or her kin. The latter is the usual situation of a slave spouse in Africa.

Complementary filiation appears to be the principal mechanism by which segmentation in the lineage is brought about. This is very clear in patrilineal descent groups, and has been found to hold for societies as far apart as the Tallensi in West Africa and the Gusii in East Africa. What is a single lineage in relation to a male founder is divided into segments of a lower order by reference to their respective female founders on the model of the division of a polygynous family into separate matricentral "houses." In matrilineal lineage systems, however, the position is different. Segmentation does not follow the lines of different paternal origin, for obvious reasons; it follows the lines of differentiation between sisters. There is a connection between this and the weakness in law and in sentiment of the marriage tie in matrilineal societies, though it is usual for political and legal power to be vested in men as Kroeber (1938) and others have remarked. More study of this problem is needed.

Since the bilateral family is the focal element in the web of kinship, complementary filiation provides the essential link between a sibling group and the kin of the parent who does not determine descent. So a sibling group is not merely differentiated within a lineage but is further distinguished by reference to its kin ties outside the corporate unit. This structural device allows of degrees of individuation depending on the extent to which filiation on the non-corporate side is elaborated. The Tiv, for example, recognize five degrees of matrilateral filiation by which a sibling group is linked with lineages other than its own. These and other ties of a similar nature arising out of marriage exchanges result in a complex scheme of individuation for distinguishing both sibling groups and persons within a single lineage (L. Bohannan, 1951). This, of course, is not unique and has long been recognized, as everyone familiar with Australian kinship systems knows. Its more general significance can be brought out however by an example. A Tiv may claim to be living with a particular group of relatives for purely personal reasons of convenience or affection. Investigation shows that he has in fact made a choice of where to live within a strictly limited range of nonlineage kin. What purports to be a voluntary act freely motivated in fact presupposes a structural scheme of individuation. This is one of the instances which show how it is possible and feasible to move from the structural-frame of reference to another, here that of the social psychologist, without confusing data and aims.

Most far-reaching in its effects on lineage structure is the use of the rule of complementary filiation to build double unilineal systems and some striking instances of this are found in Africa. One of the most developed systems of this type is that of the Yakö; and Forde's excellent analysis of how this works (Forde, 1950) shows that it is much more than a device for classifying kin. It is a principle of social organization that enters into all social relations and is expressed in all important institutions. There is the division of property, for instance, into the kind that is tied to the patrilineal lineage and the kind that passes to matrilineal kin. The division is between fixed and, in theory, perpetual productive resources, in this case farm land, with which goes residence rights, on the one hand, and on the other, movable and consumable property like livestock and cash. There is a similar polarity in religious cult and in the political office and authority linked with cult, the legally somewhat weaker matrilineal line being ritually somewhat stronger than the patrilineal line. This balance betwen ritual and secular control is extended to the fertility of the women. An analogous double descent system has been described for some Nuba Hill tribes by Nadel (1950) and its occurrence among the Herero is now classical in ethnology. The arrangement works the other way round, too, in Africa, as among the Ashanti, though in their case the balance is far more heavily weighted on the side of the matrilineal lineage than on that of the jurally inferior and noncorporate paternal line.

These and other instances lead to the generalization that complementary filiation is not merely a constant element in the pattern of family relationships but comes into action at all levels of social structure in African societies. It appears that there is a tendency for interests, rights and loyalties to be divided on broadly complementary lines, into those that have the sanction of law or other public institutions for the enforcement of good conduct, and those that rely on religion, morality, conscience and sentiment for due observance. Where corporate descent groups exist the former seem to be generally tied to the descent group, the latter to the complementary line of filiation.

If we ask where this principle of social structure springs from we must look to the tensions inherent in the structure of the parental family. These tensions are the result of the direction given to individual lives by the total social structure but they also provide the models for the working of that structure. We now have plenty of evidence to show how the tensions that seem normally to arise between spouses, between successive generations and between siblings find expression in custom and belief. In a homogeneous society they are apt to be generalized over wide areas of the social structure. They then evoke controls like the Nyakyusa separation of successive generations of males in age villages that are built into the total structure by the device of handing over political power to each successive generation as it reaches maturity (Wilson, 1951). Or this problem may be dealt with on the level of ritual and moral symbolism by separating parent and first born child of the same sex by taboos that eliminate open rivalry, as among the Tallensi, the Nuer, the Hausa and other peoples.

Thus by viewing the descent group as a continuing process through time we see how it binds the parental family, its growing point, by a series of steps into the widest framework of social structure. This enables us to visualize a social system as an integrated unity at a given time and over a stretch of time in relation to the process of social reproduction and in a more rigorous way than does a global concept of culture.

I do want to make clear, though, that we do not think of a lineage as being just a collection of people held together by the accident of birth. A descent group is an arrangement of persons that serves the attainment of legitimate social and personal ends. These include the gaining of a livelihood, the setting up of a family and the preservation of health and well-being as among the most important. I have several times remarked on the connection generally found between lineage structure and the ownership of the most valued productive property of the society, whether it be land or cattle or even the monopoly of a craft like blacksmithing. It is of great interest, for instance, to find Dr. Richards attributing the absence of a lineage organization among the Bemba to their lack of heritable right in land or livestock (Richards, 1950). A similar connection is found between lineage organization and the control over reproductive resources and relations as is evident from the common occurrence of exogamy as a criterion of lineage differentiation. And since citizenship is derived from lineage membership and legal status depends on it, political and religious office of necessity vests in lineages. We must expect to find and we do find that the most important religious and magical concepts and institutions of a lineage based society are tied into the lineage structures serving both as the necessary symbolical representation of the social system and as its regulating values. This is a complicated subject about which much more needs to be known. Cults of gods and of ancestors, beliefs of a totemic nature, and purely magical customs and practices, some or all are associated with lineage organization among the peoples previously quoted. What appears to happen is that every significant structural differentiation has its specific ritual symbolism, so that one can, as it were, read off from the scheme of ritual differentiation the pattern of structural differentiation and the configuration of norms of conduct that goes with it. There is, to put it simply, a segmentation of ritual allegiance corresponding to the segmentation of genealogical grouping. Locality, filiation, descent, individuation, are thus symbolized.

Reference to locality reminds us of Kroeber's careful argument of 1938 in favor of the priority of the local relationships of residence over those of descent in determining the line that is legally superior. A lineage cannot easily act as a corporate group if its members can never get together for the conduct of their affairs. It is not surprising therefore to find that the lineage in African societies is generally locally anchored; but it is not necessarily territorially compact or exclusive. A compact nucleus may be enough to act as the local center for a group that is widely dispersed. I think it would be agreed that lineage and locality are independently variable and how they interact depends on other factors in the social structure. As I interpret the evidence, local ties are of secondary significance, *pace* Kroeber, for local ties do not appear to give rise to structural bonds in and of themselves. There must be common political or kinship or economic or ritual interests for structural bonds to emerge. Again spatial dispersion does not immediately put an end to lineage ties or to the ramifying kin ties found in cognatic systems like that of the Lozi. For legal status, property, office and cult act centripetally to hold dispersed lineages together and to bind scattered kindred. This is important in the dynamic pattern of lineage organization for it contains within itself the springs of disintegration, at the corporate level in the rule of segmentation, at the individual level in the rule of complementary filiation.

As I have suggested before, it seems that corporate descent groups can exist only in more or less homogeneous societies. Just what we mean by a homogeneous society is still rather vague though we all use the term lavishly. The working definition I make use of is that a homogeneous society is ideally one in which any person in the sense given to this term by Radcliffe-Brown in his recent (1950) essay, can be substituted for any other person of the same category without bringing about changes in the social structure. This implies that any two persons of the same category have the same body of customary usages and beliefs. I relate this tentative definition to the rule of sibling equivalence, so that I would say that, considered with respect of their achievable life histories, in a homogeneous society all men are brothers and all women sisters.

Societies based on unilineal descent groups are not the best in which to see what the notion of social substitutability means. For that it is better to consider societies in which descent still takes primacy over all other criteria of association and classification of persons in the regulation of social life but does not serve as the constitutive principle of corporate group organization. Central Africa provides some admirable instances (cf. Richards, 1950; Colson and Gluckman, 1951). Among the Bemba, the Tonga, the Lozi and many of their neighbors, as I have already remarked, the social structure must be thought of as a system of interconnected politico–legal statuses symbolized and sanctioned by ritual and not as a collection of people organized in self-perpetuating descent units. The stability of the society over time is preserved by perpetuating the status system. Thus when a person dies his status is kept alive by being taken up by an heir; and this heir is selected on the basis of descent rules. At any given time an individual may be the holder of a cluster of statuses; but these many be distributed among several persons on his death in a manner analogous to the widespread African custom by which a man's inherited estate goes to his lineage heir and his self-acquired property to his personal heir. Ideally, therefore, the network of statuses remains stable and perpetual though their holders come and go. Ritual symbols define and sanction the key positions in the system. What it represents, in fact, is the generalization throughout a whole society of the notion of the corporation sole as tied to descent but not to a corporate group. Descent and filiation have the function of

selecting individuals for social postitions and roles – in other words, for the exercise of particular rights and obligations – just as in cross cousin marriage they serve to select ego's spouse.

The concept of the "person" as an assemblage of statuses has been the starting point in some interesting enquiries. A generalization of long standing is that a married person always has two mutually antagonistic kinship statuses, that of spouse and parent in one family context and that of child and sibling in another (cf. Warner, 1937). This is very conspicuous in an exogamous lineage system; and the tensions resulting from this condition, connected as they are with the rule of complementary filiation, have wide consequences. A common rule of social structure reflected in avoidance customs is that these two statuses must not be confounded. Furthermore, each status can be regarded as a compound of separable rights and obligations. Thus a problem that has to be solved in every matrilineal society is how to reconcile the rights over a woman's procreative powers (rights *in genetricem* as Laura Bohannan has called them in her paper of 1949) which remain vested in her brother or her lineage, with those over her domestic and sexual services (rights *in uxorem*, cf. L. Bohannan, *loc. cit.*) which pass to her husband. Among the Yao of Nyassaland, as Dr. Clyde Mitchell has shown (1950), this problem underlies the process of lineage segmentation. Brothers struggle against one another (or sisters' sons against mothers' brothers) for the control of their sisters' procreative powers and this leads to fission in the minimal lineage. It is of great significance that such a split is commonly precipitated by accusations of witchcraft against the brother from whose control the sisters are withdrawn. By contrast, where rights over a woman's child-bearing powers are held by her husband's patrilineal lineage the conflicts related to this critical interest occur between the wives of a lineage segment; and among the Zulu and Xhosa speaking tribes of South Africa these lead to witchcraft accusations between co-wives (cf. Hunter, 1936). As Laura Bohannan's paper shows, many widespread customs and institutions connected with marriage and parenthood, such as the levirate and the sororate, wife-taking by women, exchange marriage as practiced by the Tiv, and ghost marriage as found among the Nuer (Evans-Pritchard, 1951) have structural significance not hitherto appreciated if they are regarded from the point of view I have indicated.

But one thing must be emphasized. This method of analysis does not explain why in one society certain kinds of interpersonal conflict are socially projected in witchcraft beliefs whereas in another they may be projected in terms of a belief in punitive spirits. It makes clear why a funeral ceremony is necessary and why it is organized in a particular way in the interest of maintaining a stable and coherent social system. It does not explain why the ritual performed in the funeral ceremonies of one people uses materials, ideas and dramatizations of a different kind from those used by another people. In short, it brings us nearer than we were thirty years ago to understanding the machinery by which norms are made effective, not only in a particular primitive society but in a type of primitive society. It does not explain how the norms come to be what they in fact are in a particular society.

In this connection, however, it is worth drawing attention to certain norms that have long been recognized to have a critical value in social organization. Marriage regulations, incest prohibitions and the laws of homicide and warfare are the most important. Analysis of lineage structure has revealed an aspect of these norms which is of great theoretical interest. It is now fairly evident that these are not absolute rules of conduct which men are apt to break through an outburst of unruly instinct or rebellious self-assertion, as has commonly been thought. They are *relatively* obligatory in accordance with the structural relations of the parties. The Beduin of Cyrenaica regard homicide within the minimal

agnatic lineage, even under extreme provocation, as a grave sin, whereas slaying a member of a different tribal segment is an admirable deed of valor. The Tallensi consider sex relations with a near sister of the same lineage as incest but tacitly ignore the act if the parties are very distant lineage kin. Among the Tiv, the Nuer, the Gusii and other tribes the lineage range within which the rule of exogamy holds is variable and can be changed by a ceremony that makes formally prohibited marriages legitimate and so brings marriage prohibitions into line with changes in the segmentary structure of the lineage. In this way previously exogamous units are split into intermarrying units. In all the societies mentioned, and others as well, an act of self-help that leads to negotiations if the parties belong to closely related lineages might lead to war if they are members of independent – though not necessarily geographically far apart – lineages. Such observations are indications of the flexibility of primitive social structures. They give a clue to the way in which internal adjustments are made from time to time in those structures, either in response to changing pressures from without or through the momentum of their own development. They suggest how such societies can remain stable in the long run without being rigid. But this verges on speculation.

The contributions to African ethnography mentioned in this paper are only a small and arbitrary selection from a truly vast amoung of new work that is now going on in several countries. My aim has been to suggest how this work links up with a theoretical approach that is much in evidence among British social anthropologists. It is perhaps needless to add that this approach is also being actively applied by American, French, Belgian and Dutch anthropologists concerned with the problems of social organization. What I wish to convey by the example of current studies of unilineal descent group structure is that we have, in my belief, got to a point where a number of connected generalizations of wide validity can be made about this type of social group. This is an advance I associate with the structural frame of reference. I wish to suggest that this frame of reference gives us procedures of investigation and analysis by which a social system can be apprehended as a unity made of parts and processes that are linked to one another by a limited number of principles of wide validity in homogeneous and relatively stable societies. It has enabled us to set up hypotheses about the nature of these princi-

ples that have the merit of being related directly to the ethnographic material now so abundantly at hand and of being susceptible of testing by further field observation. It cannot be denied, I think, that we have here a number of positive contributions of real importance to social science.

UNIVERSITY OF CAMBRIDGE
CAMBRIDGE, ENGLAND

References

BATESON, G., 1937, *Naven*.

BOHANNAN, LAURA, 1949, Dahomean Marriage: a revaluation. *Africa*, 19. 4.

——, 1951, *A Comparative Study of Social Differentiation in Primitive Society*. (D.Phil. thesis, University of Oxford.

BOHANNAN, P. J., 1951, *Political and Economic Aspects of Land Tenure and Settlement Patterns among the Tiv of Central Nigeria*. (D. Phil. thesis, University of Oxford.

BUSIA, K. A., 1951, *The Position of the Chief in the Modern Political System of Ashanti*.

DRY, P. D. L., 1950, *The Social Structure of a Hausa Village*. (B.Sc. thesis, University of Oxford.

EGGAN, F., 1937, Cheyenne and Arapaho Kinship Systems, in *Social Organizations of North American Tribes*.

——, 1950, *Social Organization of the Western Pueblos*.

EVANS-PRITCHARD, E. E., 1933–35, The Nuer: tribe and clan. *Sudan Notes and Records*, Volume XVI, Part 1, Volume XVII, Part 1, Volume XVIII, Part 1.

——, 1937, *Witchcraft, Oracles and Magic among the Azande*.

——, 1940, (a), *The Nuer*.

——, 1940, (b), The Political System of the Nuer, in *African Political Systems*.

——, 1948, *The Divine Kingship of the Shilluck of the Nilotic Sudan*. Frazer Lecture.

——, 1951, *Kinship and Marriage among the Nuer*.

FIRTH, R., 1936, *We, the Tikopia*.

FORDE, C. DARYLL, 1938, Fission and Accretion in the Patrilineal Clans of a Semi-Bantu

Community. *Journal of the Royal Anthropological Institute*, Volume 68.

——, 1939, Kinship in Umor: Double Unilateral Organization in a Semi-Bantu Society, *American Anthropol*. Volume 41.

——, 1947, The Anthropological Approach in Social Science, in *The Advancement of Science*, Volume IV.

——, 1950 (a), Double Descent among the Yakö, in Radcliffe-Brown and Forde, 1950.

——, 1950 (b), "Ward Organization among the Yakö" *Africa*, 20. 4.

——, 1951, The Yoruba Speaking Peoples of South-Western Nigeria. *Ethnographic Survey of Africa*. Pt. IV.

FORDE, C. DARYLL and G. I. JONES, 1950, the Ibo and Ibibio-Speaking Peoples of South Eastern Nigeria, *Ethnographic Survey of Africa, Western Africa, Part III*.

FORTES, M., 1945, *The Dynamics of Clanship among the Tallensi*.

——, 1949, *The Web of Kinship among the Tallensi*.

——, 1949, Time and Social Structure: an Ashanti Case Study, in *Social Structure: studies presented to A. R. Radcliffe-Brown*, Ed. by M. Fortes.

——, 1951, Kinship and Marriage among the Ashanti, in Radcliffe-Brown and Forde, 1950.

FORTES, M., and E. E. EVANS-PRITCHARD 1940, (edit.) *African Political Systems*.

GLUCKMAN, M., 1950, Kinship and Marriage among the Lozi of Northern Rhodesia and the Zulu of Natal, in Radcliffe-Brown and Forde, 1950.

——, 1951, The Lozi of Barotseland in North

Western Rhodesia, in *Seven Tribes of British Central Africa*, edited by E. Colson and M. Gluckman.

HERSKOVITS, M. J., 1938, *Dahomey*.

——, 1948, *Man and His Works*.

HUNTER, MONICA, 1936, *Reaction to Conquest*.

GOUGH, E. K., 1950, *Kinship among the Nayar of the Malabar Coast of India*. (D.Phil. thesis, University of Cambridge.)

KUPER, HILDA, 1947, *An African Aristocracy*.

——, 1950, Kinship among the Swazi, in Radcliffe-Brown and Forde, 1950.

KROEBER, A. L., 1938, Basic and Secondary Patterns of Social Structure. *Journal of the Royal Anthropological Institute*, Volume 68.

LOWIE, R., 1921, *Primitive Society*.

MALINOWSKI, B., 1929, *The Sexual Life of Savages*.

MAINE, SIR HENRY, 1866, *Ancient Law*.

MAYER, P., 1949, The Lineage Principle in Gusii Society. *International African Institute, Memorandum XXIV*.

MITCHELL, J. CLYDE, 1950, *Social Organisation of the Yao of Southern Nyasaland*. (D.Phil. thesis, University of Oxford.)

——, 1951, The Yao of Southern Nyasaland, in *Seven Tribes of British Central Africa*, edited by E. Colson and M. Gluckman.

MURDOCK, G. P., 1949, *Social Structure*.

NADEL, S. F., 1942, *A Black Byzantium*.

——, 1950, Dual Descent in the Nuba Hills, in Radcliffe-Brown and Forde, 1950.

PETERS, E. L., 1951, *The Sociology of the Beduin of Cyrenaica*. (D.Phil. thesis, University of Oxford.)

RADCLIFFE-BROWN, A. R., 1930–31, "Social Organization of Australian Tribes," *Oceania*, 1.

——, 1935, Patrilineal and Matrilineal Succession. *Iowa Law Review*, Vol. XX. 2.

——, 1950, Introduction to *African Systems of Kinship and Marriage*.

RADCLIFFE-BROWN, A. R., and C. DARYLL FORDE (edit.), 1950, *African Systems of Kinship and Marriage*.

RATTRAY, R. S., 1929, *Ashanti Law and Constitution*.

RICHARDS, A. I., 1936, Mother Right in Central Africa, in *Essays presented to C. G. Seligman*.

——, 1939, *Land, Labour and Diet in Northern Rhodesia*.

——, 1940 (a), Bemba Marriage and Modern Economic Conditions, *Rhodes-Livingstone Institute Papers No. 3*.

——, 1940 (b), The Political System of the Bemba, in *African Political Systems*.

——, 1950, Some Types of Family Structure among the Central Bantu, in Radcliffe-Brown and Forde, 1950.

RIVERS, W. H. T., 1911, Presidential address, *British Association for the Advancement of Science*, Section H.

——, 1914, *Kinship and Social Organization*.

SCHAPERA, I., 1940, *Married Life in an African Tribe*.

——, 1950, Kinship and Marriage among the Tswana, in Radcliffe-Brown and Forde, 1950.

SELIGMAN, C. G. and B. Z. SELIGMAN, 1932, *Pagan Tribes of the Nilotic Sudan*.

SMITH, E. W., 1935, Africa: what do we know of it? *Journal of the Royal Anthropological Institute*, Volume 65.

SPOEHR, A., 1947, Changing Kinship Systems. *Anthropological Series, Chicago Natural History Museum*, Vol. 33, No. 4.

——, 1950, Observations on the Study of Kinship. *American Anthropologist*, Vol. 52.

WARNER, W. L., 1937, *A Black Civilization*.

WEBER, MAX, 1947, *The Theory of Social and Economic Organization*, translated by A. R. Hudson and Talcott Parsons.

WILSON, MONICA, 1950, Nyakyusa Kinship, in Radcliffe-Brown and Forde, 1950.

——, 1951 (a), Nyakyusa Age Villages, *Journal of the Royal Anthropological Institute*, Vol. 79.

——, 1951 (b), *Good Company: A Study of Nyakyusa Age Villages*.

2

THE NUER: TIME AND SPACE

E.E. EVANS-PRITCHARD

I

In describing Nuer concepts of time we may distinguish between those that are mainly reflections of their relations to environment, which we call oecological time, and those that are reflections of their relations to one another in the social structure, which we call structural time. Both refer to successions of events which are of sufficient interest to the community for them to be noted and related to each other conceptually. The larger periods of time are almost certainly structural, because the events they relate are changes in the relationship of social groups. Moreover, time-reckoning based on changes in nature and man's response to them is limited to an annual cycle and therefore cannot be used to differentiate longer periods than seasons. Both, also, have limited and fixed notations. Seasonal and lunar changes repeat themselves year after year, so that a Nuer standing at any point of time has conceptual knowledge of what lies before him and can predict and organize his life accordingly. A man's structural future is likewise already fixed and ordered into different periods, so that the total changes in status a boy will undergo in his ordained passage through the social system, if he lives long enough, can be foreseen. Stuctural time appears to an individual passing through the social system to be

entirely progressive, but, as we shall see, in a sense this is an illusion. Oecological time appears to be, and is, cyclical.

The oecological cycle is a year. Its distinctive rhythm is the backwards and forwards movement from villages to camps, which is the Nuer's response to the climatic dichotomy of rains and drought. The year (*ruon*) has two main seasons, *tot* and *mai*. *Tot*, from about the middle of March to the middle of September, roughly corresponds to the rise in the curve of rainfall, though it does not cover the whole period of the rains. Rain may fall heavily at the end of September and in early October, and the country is still flooded in these months which belong, nevertheless, to the *mai* half of the year, for it commences at the decline of the rains – not at their cessation – and roughly covers the trough of the curve, from about the middle of September to the middle of March. The two seasons therefore only approximate to our division into rains and drought, and the Nuer classification aptly summarizes their way of looking at the movement of time, the direction of attention in marginal months being as significant as the actual climatic conditions. In the middle of September Nuer turn, as it were, towards the life of fishing and cattle camps and feel that village residence and horticulture lie behind them. They begin to speak of camps as though they were already in being, and long to

Figure 2.1

be on the move. This restlessness is even more marked towards the end of the drought when, noting cloudy skies, people turn towards the life of villages and make preparations for striking camp. Marginal months may therefore be classed as *tot* or *mai*, since they belong to one set of activities but presage the other set, for the concept of seasons is derived from social activities rather than from the climate changes which determine them, and a year is to Nuer a period of village residence (*clieng*) and a period of camp residence (*wec*).

Seasonal variations in social activities, on which Nuer concepts of time are primarily based, have been indicated and, on the economic side, recorded at some length. The main features of these three planes of rhythm, physical, oecological, and social, are charted in Figure 2.1.

The movements of the heavenly bodies other than the sun and the moon, the direction and variation of winds, and the migration of some species of birds are observed by the Nuer, but they do not regulate their activities in relation to them nor use them as points of reference in seasonal time-reckoning. The characters by which seasons are most clearly defined are those which control the movements of the people: water, vegetation, movement of fish, &c.; it being the needs of cattle and variations in food-supply which chiefly translate oecological rhythm into the social rhythm of the year, and the contrast between modes of life at the height of the rains and at the height of the drought which provides the conceptual poles in time-reckoning.

Besides these two main seasons of *tot* and *mai* Nuer recognize two subsidiary seasons included in them, being transitional periods between them. The four seasons are not sharp divisions but overlap. Just as we reckon summer and winter as the halves of our year and speak also of spring and autumn, so Nuer reckon *tot* and *mai* as halves of their year and speak also of the seasons of *rwil* and *jiom*. *Rwil* is the time of moving from camp to village and of clearing and planting, from about the middle of March to the middle of June, before the rains have reached their peak. It counts as part of the *tot* half of the year, though it is contrasted with *tot* proper, the period of full village life and horticulture, from about the middle of June to the middle of September. *Jiom* meaning 'wind', is the period in which the persistent north wind begins to blow and people harvest, fish from dams, fire the bush, and form early camps, from about the middle of September to the middle of December. It counts as part of the *mai* half of the year, though it is contrasted with *mai* proper, from about the middle of December to the middle of March, when the main camps are formed. Roughly speaking, therefore, there are two major seasons of six months and four minor seasons of three months, but these divisions must not be regarded too rigidly since they are not so much exact units of time as rather vague conceptualizations of changes in oecological relations and social activities which pass imperceptibly from one state to another.

are the focal points. Nuer, especially the younger people, are still in camp for part of *tot* (the greater part of *rwil*) and are still in villages, especially the older people, for part of *mai* (the greater part of *jiom*), but every one is in villages during *tot* proper and in camps during *mai* proper. Since the words *tot* and *mai* are not pure units of time-reckoning but stand for the cluster of social activities characteristic of the height of the drought and of the height of the rains, one may hear a Nuer saying that he is going to "*tot*" or "*mai*" in a certain place.

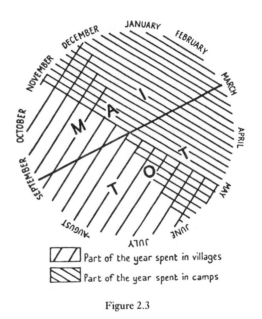

Part of the year spent in villages
Part of the year spent in camps

Figure 2.3

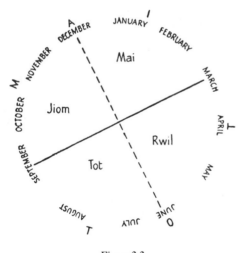

Figure 2.2

In the diagram above a line drawn from mid March to mid September is the axis of the year, being an approximation to a cleavage between two opposed sets of oecological relations and social activities, though not entirely corresponding to it, as may be seen in the diagram below, where village life and camp life are shown in relation to the seasons of which they

The year has twelve months, six to each of the major seasons, and most adult Nuer can state them in order. In the list of months given below it has not been possible to equate each Nuer name with an English name, because our Roman months have nothing to do with the moon. It will be found, however, that a Nuer month is usually covered by the two English months equated to it in the list and generally tends to coincide with the first rather than the second.

teer	Sept. – Oct.
lath (boor)	Oct. – Nov.
kur	Nov. – Dec.
tiop (in) dit	Dec. – Jan.
tiop (in) tot	Jan. – Feb.
pet	Feb. – Mar.
duong	Mar. – Apr.
gwaak	Apr. – May
dwat	May – June
kornyuot	June – July
paiyatni (paiyene)	July – Aug.
thoor	Aug. – Sept.

Nuer would soon be in difficulties over their lunar calendar if they consistently counted the succession of moons,[1] but there are certain activities associated with each month, the association sometimes being indicated by the name of the month. The calendar is a relation between a cycle of activities and a conceptual cycle and the two cannot fall apart, since the conceptual cycle is dependent on the cycle of activities from which it derives its meaning and function. Thus a twelve-month system does not incommode Nuer, for the calender is anchored to the cycle of oecological changes. In the month of *kur* one makes the first fishing dams and forms the first cattle camps, and since one is doing these things it must be *kur* or thereabouts. Likewise in *dwat* one breaks camp and returns to the villages, and since people are on the move it must be *dwat* or thereabouts. Consequently the calendar remains fairly stable and in any section of Nuerland there is general agreement about the name of the current month.

In my experience Nuer do not to any great extent use the name of the months to indicate the time of an event, but generally refer instead to some outstanding activity in process at the time of its occurrence, e.g. at the time of early camps, at the time of weeding, at the time of harvesting &c., and it is easily understandable that they do so, since time is to them a relation between activities. During the rains the stages in the growth of millet and the steps taken in its culture are often used as points of reference. Pastoral activities, being largely undifferentiated throughout the months and seasons, do not provide suitable points.

There are not units of time between the month and day and night. People indicate the occurrence of an event more than a day or two ago by reference to some other event which took place at the same time or by counting the number of intervening 'sleeps' or, less commonly, 'suns'. There are terms for to-day, to-morrow, yesterday, &c., but there is no precision about them. When Nuer wish to define the occurrence of an event several days in advance, such as a dance or wedding, they do so by reference to the phases of the moon: new moon, its waxing, full moon, its waning, and the brightness of its second quarter. When they wish to be precise they state on which night of the waxing or waning an event will take place, reckoning fifteen nights to each and thirty to the moon. They say that only cattle and the Anuak can see the moon in its invisible period. The only terms applied to the nightly succession of lunar phases are those that describe its appearance just before, and in, fullness.

The course of the sun determines many points of reference, and a common way of indicating the time of events is by pointing to that part of the heavens the sun will then have reached in its course. There are also a number of expressions, varying in the degree of their precision, which describe positions of the sun in the heavens, though, in my experience, the only ones commonly employed are those that refer to its more conspicuously differentiated movements: the first stroke of dawn, sunrise, noon, and sunset. It is, perhaps, significant that there are almost as many points of reference between 4 and 6 a.m. as there are for the rest of the day. This may be chiefly due to

---

[1] There is some evidence of an intercalary month among the Eastern Jikany, but I cannot be definite on this point, and I have not heard it mentioned in other parts of Nuerland.

striking contrasts caused by changes in relations of earth to sun during these two hours, but it may be noted, also, that the points of reference between them are more used in directing activities, such as starting on journeys, rising from sleep, tethering cattle in kraals, gazelle hunting, &c., than points of reference during most of the rest of the day, especially in the slack time between 1 and 3 p.m. There are also a number of terms to describe the time of night. They are to a very limited extent determined by the course of the stars. Here again, there is a richer terminology for the transition period between day and night than during the rest of the night and the same reasons may be suggested to explain this fact. There are also expressions for distinguishing night from day, forenoon from afternoon, and that part of the day which is spent from that part which lies ahead.

Except for the commonest of the terms for divisions of the day they are little used in comparison with expressions which describe routine diurnal activities. The daily timepiece is the cattle clock, the round of pastoral tasks, and the time of day and the passage of time through a day are to a Nuer primarily the succession of these tasks and their relations to one another. The better demarcated points are taking of the cattle from byre to kraal, milking, driving of the adult herd to pasture, milking of the goats and sheep, driving of the flocks and calves to pasture, cleaning of byre and kraal, bringing home of the flocks and calves, the return of the adult herd, the evening milking, and the enclosure of the beasts in byres. Nuer generally use such points of activity, rather than concrete points in the movement of the sun across the heavens, to co-ordinate events. Thus a man says, 'I shall return at milking', 'I shall start off when the calves come home', and so forth.

Oecological time-reckoning is ultimately, of course, entirely determined by the movement of the heavenly bodies, but only some of its units and notations are directly based on these movements, e.g. month, day, night, and some

parts of the day and night, and such points of reference are paid attention to and selected as points only because they are significant for social activities. It is the activities themselves, chiefly of an economic kind, which are basic to the system and furnish most of its units and notations, and the passage of time is perceived in the relation of activities to one another. Since activities are dependent on the movement of the heavenly bodies and since the movement of the heavenly bodies is significant only in relation to the activities one may often refer to either in indication of the time of an event. Thus one may say, 'In the *jiom* season' or 'At early camps', 'The month of *Dwat*' or 'The return to villages', 'When the sun is warming up' or 'At milking'. The movements of the heavenly bodies permit Nuer to select natural points that are significant in relation to activities. Hence in linguistic usage nights, or rather 'sleeps', are more clearly defined units of time than days, or 'suns', because they are undifferentiated units of social activity, and months, or rather 'moons', though they are clearly differentiated units of natural time, are little employed as points of reference because they are not clearly differentiated units of activity, whereas the day, the year, and its main seasons are complete occupational units.

Certain conclusions may be drawn from this quality of time among the Nuer. Time has not the same value throughout the year. Thus in dry season camps, although daily pastoral tasks follow one another in the same order as in the rains, they do not take place at the same time. They are more a precise routine owing to the severity of seasonal conditions, especially with regard to water and pasturage, and require greater co-ordination and co-operative action. On the other hand, life in the dry season is generally uneventful, outside routine tasks, and oecological and social relations are more monotonous from month to month than in the rains when there are frequent feasts, dances, and ceremonies. When time is considered as relations between activities it will be understood that it has a different connotation in rains and drought. In the drought the daily time-reckoning is more uniform and precise while lunar reckoning receives less attention, as appears from the lesser use of names of months, less confidence in stating their order, and the common East African trait of two dry-season months with the same name (*tiop in dit* and *tiop in tot*), the order of which is often interchanged. The pace of time may vary accordingly, since perception of time is a function of systems of time-reckoning, but we can make no definite statement on this question.

Though I have spoken of time and units of time the Nuer have no expression equivalent to 'time' in our language, and they cannot, therefore, as we can, speak of time as though it were something actual, which passes, can be wasted, can be saved, and so forth. I do not think that they ever experience the same feeling of fighting against time or of having to co-ordinate activities with an abstract passage of time, because their points of reference are mainly the activities themselves, which are generally of a leisurely character. Events follow a logical order, but they are not controlled by an abstract system, there being no autonomous points of reference to which activities have to conform with precision. Nuer are fortunate.

Also they have very limited means of reckoning the relative duration of periods of time intervening between events, since they have few, and not well-defined or systematized, units of time. Having no hours or other small units of time they cannot measure the periods which intervene between positions of the sun or daily activities. It is true that the year is divided into twelve lunar units, but Nuer do not reckon in them as fractions of a unit. They may be able to state in what month an event occurred, but it is with great difficulty that they reckon the relation between events in abstract numerical symbols. They think much more easily in terms of activities and of successions of activities and in terms of social

structure and of structural differences than in pure units of time.

We may conclude that the Nuer system of time-reckoning within the annual cycle and parts of the cycle is a series of conceptualizations of natural changes, and that the selection of points of reference is determined by the significance which these natural changes have for human activities.

II

In a sense all time is structural since it is a conceptualization of collateral, co-ordinated, or co-operative activities: the movements of a group. Otherwise time concepts of this kind could not exist, for they must have a like meaning for every one within a group. Milking-time and meal-times are approximately the same for all people who normally come into contact with one another, and the movement from villages to camps has approximately the same connotation everywhere in Nuerland, though it may have a special connotation for a particular group of persons. There is, however, a point at which we can say that time concepts cease to be determined by oecological factors and become more determined by structural interrelations, being no longer a reflection of man's dependence on nature, but a reflection of the interaction of social groups.

The year is the largest unit of oecological time. Nuer have words for the year before last, last year, this year, next year, and the year after next. Events which took place in the last few years are then the points of reference in time-reckoning, and these are different according to the group of persons who make use of them: joint family, village, tribal section, tribe, &c. One of the commonest ways of stating the year of an event is to mention where the people of the village made their dry season camps, or to refer to some evil that befell their cattle. A joint family may reckon time in the birth of calves of their herds. Weddings and other ceremonies, fights, and raids, may likewise give points of time, though in the absence of numerical dating no one can say without lengthy calculations how many years ago an event took place. Moreover, since time is to Nuer an order of events of outstanding significance to a group, each group has its own points of reference and time is consequently relative to structural space, locally considered. This is obvious when we examine the names given to years by different tribes, or sometimes by adjacent tribes, for these are floods, pestilences, famines, wars, &c., experienced by the tribe. In course of time the names of years are forgotten and all events beyond the limits of this crude historical reckoning fade into the dim vista of long long ago. Historical time, in this sense of a sequence of outstanding events of significance to a tribe, goes back much farther than the historical time of smaller groups, but fifty years is probably its limit, and the farther back from the present day the sparser and vaguer become its points of reference.

However, Nuer have another way of stating roughly when events took place; not in numbers of years, but by reference to the age-set system. Distance between events ceases to be reckoned in time concepts as we understand them and is reckoned in terms of structural distance, being the relation between groups of persons. It is therefore entirely relative to the social structure. Thus a Nuer may say that an event took place after the *Thut* age-set was born or in the initiation period of the *Boiloc* age-set, but no one can say how many years ago it happened. Time is here reckoned in sets. If a man of the *Dangunga* set tells one that an event occurred in the initiation period of the *Thut* set he is saying that it happened three sets before his set, or six sets ago. Here it need only be said that we cannot accurately translate a reckoning in sets into a reckoning in years, but that we can roughly estimate a ten-year interval between the commencement of successive sets. There are six sets in existence, the names of the sets are not cyclic, and the

order of extinct sets, all but the last, are soon forgotten, so that an age-set reckoning has seven units covering a period of rather under a century.

The structural system of time-reckoning is partly the selection of points of reference of significance to local groups which give these groups a common and distinctive history; partly the distance between specific sets in the age-set system; and partly distances of a kinship and lineage order. Four generation-steps (*kath*) in the kinship system are linguistically differentiated relations, grandfather, father, son, and grandson, and within a small kinship group these relationships give a time-depth to members of the group and points of reference in a line of ascent by which their relationships are determined and explained. Any kinship relationship must have a point of reference on a line of ascent, namely a common ancestor, so that such a relationship always has a time connotation couched in structural terms. Beyond the range of the kinship system in this narrow sense the connotation is expressed in terms of the lineage system. The base line of the triangle in Figure 2.4 represents a given group of agnates and the dotted lines represent their ghostly agnatic forebears, running from this base to a point in lineage structure, the common ancestor of every member of the group. The farther we extend the range of the group (the longer becomes the base line) the farther back in lineage structure is the common ancestor (the farther from the base line is the apex of the triangle). The four triangles are thus the time depths of four extensions of agnatic relationship on an existential plane and represent minimal, minor, major, and maximal lineages of a clan. Lineage time is thus the structural distance between groups of persons on the line *AB*. Structural time therefore cannot be understood until structural distance in known, since it is a reflection of it, and we must, therefore, ask the reader to forgive a certain obscurity at this point and to reserve criticism till we have had an opportunity of explaining more clearly what is meant by structural distance.

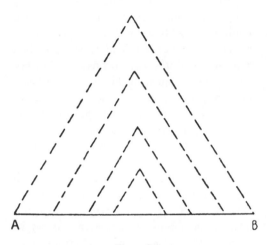

Figure 2.4

We have restricted our discussion to Nuer systems of time-reckoning and have not considered the way in which an individual perceives time. The subject bristles with difficulties. Thus an individual may reckon the passage of time by reference to the physical appearance and status of other individuals and to changes in his own life-history, but such a method of reckoning time has no wide collective validity. We confess, however, that our observations on the matter have been slight and that a fuller analysis is beyond our powers. We have merely indicated those aspects of the problem which are directly related to the description of modes of livelihood which has gone before and to the description of political institutions which follows.

We have remarked that the movement of structural time is, in a sense, an illusion, for the structure remains fairly constant and the perception of time is no more than the movement of persons, often as groups, through the structure. Thus age-sets succeed one another forever, but there are never more than six in existence and the relative positions occupied by these six sets at any time are fixed structural points through which actual sets of persons

pass in endless succession. Similarly, for reasons which we explain later, the Nuer system of lineages may be considered a fixed system, there being a constant number of steps between living persons and the founder of their clan and the lineages having a constant position relative to one another. However when many generations succeed one another the depth and range of lineages does not increase unless there has been structural change.

Beyond the limits of historical time we enter a plane of tradition in which a certain element of historical fact may be supposed to be incorporated in a complex of myth. Here the points of reference are the structural ones we have indicated. At one end this plane merges into history; at the other end into myth. Time perspective is here not a true impression of actual distances like that created by our dating technique, but a reflection of relations between lineages, so that the traditional events recorded have to be placed at the points where the lineages concerned in them converge in their lines of ascent. The events have therefore a position in structure, but no exact position in historical time as we understand it. Beyond tradition lies the horizon of pure myth which is always seen in the same time perspective. One mythological event did not precede another, for myths explain customs of general social significance rather than the interrelations of particular segments and are, therefore, not structurally stratified. Explanations of any qualities of nature or of culture are drawn from this intellectual ambient which imposes limits on the Nuer world and makes it self-contained and entirely intelligible to Nuer in the relation of its parts. The world, peoples, and cultures all existed together from the same remote past.

It will have been noted that the Nuer time dimension is shallow. Valid history ends a century ago, and tradition, generously measured, takes us back only ten to twelve generations in lineage structure, and if we are right in supposing that lineage structure never grows, it follows that the distance between the beginning of the world and the present day remains unalterable. Time is thus not a continuum, but is a constant structural relationship between two points, the first and last persons in a line of agnatic descent. How shallow is Nuer time may be judged from the fact that the tree under which mankind came into being was still standing in Western Nuerland a few years ago!

Beyond the annual cycle, time-reckoning is a conceptualization of the social structure, and the points of reference are a projection into the past of actual relations between groups of persons. It is less a means of co-ordinating events than of co-ordinating relationships, and is therefore mainly a looking-backwards, since relationships must be explained in terms of the past.

III

We have concluded that structural time is a reflection of structural distance. In the following sections we define further what we mean by structural distance, and make a formal, preliminary, classification of Nuer territorial groups of a political kind. We have classified Nuer socio-temporal categories. We now classify their socio-spatial categories.

Were a man to fly over Nuerland he would see white patches with what look like tiny fungoid growths on them. These are village sites with huts and byres. He would see that between such patches are stretches of brown and black, the brown being open grassland and the black being depressions which are swampy in the rains; and that the white patches are wider and more frequent in some parts than in others. We find Nuer give to these distributions certain values which compose their political structure.

It would be possible to measure the exact distance between hut and hut, village and village, tribal area and tribal area, and so forth, and the space covered by each. This would give us a statement of spatial measurements in bare physical terms. By itself it would have

very limited significance. Oecological space is more than mere physical distance, though it is affected by it, for it is reckoned also by the character of the country intervening between local groups and its relation to the biological requirements of their members. A broad river divides two Nuer tribes more sharply than many miles of unoccupied bush. A distance which appears small in the dry season has a different appearance when the area it covers is flooded in the rains. A village community which has permanent water near at hand is in a very different position to one which has to travel in the dry season to obtain water, pasturage, and fishing. A tsetse belt creates an impassable barrier, giving wide oecological distance between the peoples it separates, and presence or absence of cattle among neighbours of the Nuer likewise determines the oecological distance between them and the Nuer. Oecological distance, in this sense, is a relation between communities defined in terms of density and distribution, and with reference to water, vegetation, animal and insect life, and so on.

Structural distance is of a very different order, though it is always influenced and, in its political dimension, to a large extent determined by oecological conditions. By structural distance is meant, as we have already indicated in the preceding section, the distance between groups of persons in a social system, expressed in terms of values. The nature of the country determines the distribution of villages and, therefore, the distance between them, but values limit and define the distribution in structural terms and give a different set of distances. A Nuer village may be equidistant from two other villages, but if one of these belongs to a different tribe and the other to the same tribe it may be said to be structurally more distant from the first than from the second. A Nuer tribe which is separated by forty miles from another Nuer tribe is structurally nearer to it than to a Dinka tribe from which it is separated by only twenty miles. When we leave territorial values and speak of lineages and age-sets, structural space is less determined by environmental conditions. One lineage is closer to another than to a third. One age-set is closer to another than to a third. The values attached to residence, kinship, lineage, sex, and age, differentiate groups of persons by segmentation, and the relative positions of the segments to one another gives a perspective that enables us to speak of the divisions between them as divisions of structural space. Having defined what is meant by structural space we may now proceed with a description of its political divisions.

IV

We have noted that structural distance is the distance between groups of persons in social structure and may be of different kinds. Those which concern us in our present account are political distance, lineage distance, and age-set distance. The political distance between villages of a tertiary tribal section is less than the distance between tertiary segments of a secondary tribal section, and that is less than the distance between secondary segments of a primary tribal section, and so forth.

The lineage distance between segments of a minor lineage is less than the distance between minor segments of a major lineage, and that is less than the distance between major segments of a maximal lineage, and so forth. The age-set distance between segments of an age-set is less than the distance between successive age-sets and that is less than the distance between age-sets which are not successive. As we wish to develop our argument and therefore to avoid analysis which does not allow the reader to refer back to statements already made, we will give immediate consideration only to political distance and only to some characteristics of it.

Nuer give values to local distributions. It might be thought a simple matter to discover what these values are, but since they are embodied in words, one cannot understand their range of reference without considerable knowledge of the people's language and of the way they use it, for meanings vary according to the social situation and a word may refer to a variety of local groups. It is, nevertheless, possible to differentiate them and to make a crude formal classification of them, as we have done in Figure 2.5.

A single living hut (*dwil* or *ut*) is occupied by

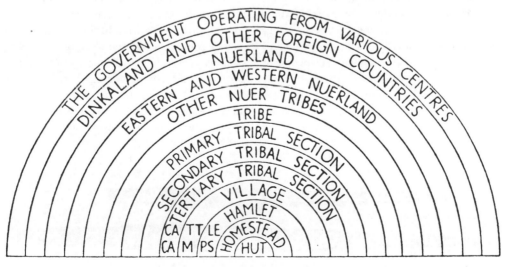

Figure 2.5   Nuer Socio-Spatial Categories

a wife and her children and, at times, by her husband. They constitute a simple residential family group. The homestead, consisting of a byre and huts, may contain a simple family group or a polygamous family and there are often one or two kinsmen living there as well. This group, which we call a household, is often referred to as the *gol*, a word which means 'hearth'. A hamlet with gardens and waste land around it is called *dhor* and each has its special name, often derived from some landmark or from the name of the senior kinsman living there. A hamlet is generally occupied by close agnatic kinsmen, often brothers, and their households, and we call this group of persons a joint family. As these groups are not treated in our account we say no more about them. It must be remembered, however, that a village is not an unsegmented unit but is a relation between a number of smaller units.

The village is a very distinct unit. It is sometimes referred to as *thur*, a ridge of high ground, but generally as *cieng*, a word which may be translated 'home', but which has such a variety of meanings that we shall devote a special section to it. A village comprises a community, linked by common residence and by a network of kinship and affinal ties, the members of which, as we have seen, form a common camp, co-operate in many activities, and eat in one another's byres and windscreens. A village is the smallest Nuer group which is not specifically of a kinship order and is the political unit of Nuerland. The people of the village have a feeling of strong solidarity against other villages and great affection for their site, and in spite of the wandering habits of Nuer, persons born and bred in a village have a nostalgia for it and are likely to return to it and make their home there, even if they have resided elsewhere for many years. Members of a village fight side by side and support each other in feuds. When the youths of a village go to dances they enter the dance in a war line (*dep*) singing their special war chant.

A cattle camp, which people of a village form in the drought and in which members of neighbouring villages participate, is known as *wec*. While this word has the meaning of "camp" in contrast with *cieng*, "village," both words are used in the same general sense of local community. Thus when it is said of a certain clan that they have no *wec* we are to understand that they nowhere in a tribal section or village form a dominant nucleus of the community and that, therefore, no local community takes its name from them. A large camp is called after the dominant lineage in it or after the village community who occupy it, and small camps are sometimes named after an old person of importance who has erected his windscreen there. We have seen that the social composition of a camp varies at different times of the drought from the people of a hamlet to the people of a village, or of neighbouring villages, and that men sometimes camp with kinsmen living in camps other than those of their own villages. Consequently, while local communities of the rains tend to be also local communities in the drought their composition may be somewhat different. We again emphasize that not only are the people of a camp living in a more compact group than the people of a village, but also that in camp life there is more frequent contact between its members and greater co-ordination of their activities.

Figure 2.6 Horn and ebony spears.

The cattle are herded together, milked at the same time, and so on. In a village each household herds its own cattle, if they are herded at all, and performs its domestic and kraal tasks independently and at different times. In the drought there is increasing concentration and greater uniformity in response to the greater severity of the season.

We sometimes speak of a district to describe an aggregate of villages or camps which have easy and frequent intercommunication. The people of these villages take part in the same dances, intermarry, conduct feuds, go on joint raiding parties, share dry season camps or make camps in the same locality, and so on. This indefinite aggregate of contacts does not constitute a Nuer category or a political group, because the people do not see themselves, nor are seen by others, as a unique community, but 'district' is a term we employ to denote the sphere of a man's social contacts or of the social contacts of the people of a village and is, therefore, relative to the person or community spoken about. A district in this sense tends to correspond to a tertiary or a secondary tribal segment, according to the size of the tribe. In the smallest tribes a whole tribe is a man's district, and a district may even cut across tribal boundaries in that in a large tribe a border village may have more contacts with neighbouring villages of another tribe than with distant villages of its own tribe. The sphere of a man's social contacts may thus not entirely coincide with any structural division.

A number of adjacent villages, varying in number and total extension according to the size of the tribe, are grouped into small tribal sections and these into larger ones. In the larger tribes it is convenient to distinguish between primary, secondary, and tertiary tribal sections. These sections, of whatever size, are, like a village, spoken of as "*cieng*". Since the next chapter is devoted to these tribal segments no more is said about them here.

V

In our account of Nuer time-reckoning we noted that in one department of time their system of reckoning is, in a broad sense, a conceptualization, in terms of activities, or of physical changes that provide convenient points of reference for activities, of those phases of the oecological rhythm which have peculiar significance for them. We further noted that in another department of time it is a conceptualization of structural relations, time units being co-ordinate with units of structural space. We have given a brief description of these units of structural space in its political or territorial dimension and have drawn attention to the influence of oecology on distribution and hence on the values given to the distribution, the interrelation between which is the political system. This system is not, however, as simple as we have presented it, for values are not simple, and we now attempt to face some of the difficulties we have so far neglected. We start this attempt by asking what it is the Nuer mean when they speak of their *cieng*.

Values are embodied in words through which they influence behaviour. When a Nuer speaks of his *cieng*, his *dhor*, his *gol*, &c., he is conceptualizing his feelings of structural distance, identifying himself with a local community, and, by so doing, cutting himself off from other communities of the same kind. An examination of the word *cieng* will teach us one of the most fundamental characteristics of Nuer local groups and, indeed, of all social groups: their structural relativity.

What does a Nuer mean when he says, "I am a man of such-and-such a *cieng*"? *Cieng* means "home," but its precise significance varies with the situation in which it is spoken. If one meets an Englishman in Germany and asks him where his home is, he may reply that it is England. If one meets the same man in London and asks him the same question he will tell one that his home is in Oxfordshire, whereas if one meets him in that county he will tell one the name of the town or village in which he lives. If questioned in his town or village he will mention his particular street, and if questioned in his street he will indicate his house. So it is with the Nuer. A Nuer met outside Nuerland says that his home is *cieng Nath*, Nuerland. He may also refer to his tribal country as his *cieng*, though the more usual expression for this is *rol*. If one asks him in his tribe what is his *cieng*, he will name his village or tribal section according to the context. Generally he will name either his tertiary tribal section or his village, but he may give his primary or secondary section. If asked in his village he will mention the name of his hamlet or indicate his homestead or the end of the village in which his homestead is situated. Hence if a man says "*Wa ciengda*," "I am going home," outside his village he means that he is returning to it; if in his village he means that he is going to his hamlet; if in his hamlet he means that he is going to his homestead. *Cieng* thus means homestead, hamlet, village, and tribal sections of various dimensions.

The variations in the meaning of the word *cieng* are not due to the inconsistencies of language, but to the relativity of the group-values to which it refers. I emphasize this character of structural distance at an early stage because an understanding of it is necessary to follow the account of various social groups which we are about to describe. Once it is understood, the apparent contradictions in our account will be seen to be contradictions in the structure itself, being, in fact, a quality of it.

A man is a member of a political group of any kind in virtue of his non-membership of other groups of the same kind. He sees them as groups and their members see him as a member of a group, and his relations with them are controlled by the structural distance between the groups concerned. But a man does not see himself as a member of that same group in so far as his is a member of a segment of it which stands outside of and is opposed to other segments of it. Hence a man can be a member of a group and yet not a member of it. Thus a

man is a member of his tribe in its relation to other tribes, but he is not a member of his tribe in the relation of his segment of it to other segments of the same kind. Likewise a man is a member of his tribal segment in its relation to other segments, but he is not a member of it in the relation of his village to other villages of the same segment. A characteristic of any political group is hence its invariable tendency towards fission and the opposition of its segments, and another characteristic is its tendency towards fusion with other groups of its own order in opposition to political segments larger than itself. Political values are thus always, structurally speaking, in conflict. One value attaches a man to his group and another to a segment of it in opposition to other segments of it, and the value which controls his action is a function of the social situation in which he finds himself. For a man sees himself as a member of a group only in opposition to other groups and he sees a member of another group as a member of a social unity however much it may be split into opposed segments.

Therefore Figure 2.5 illustrates political structure in a very crude and formal way. It cannot very easily be pictured diagrammatically, for political relations are relative and dynamic. They are best stated as tendencies to conform to certain values in certain situations, and the value is determined by the structural relationships of the persons who compose the situation. Thus whether and on which side a man fights in a dispute depends on the structural relationship of the persons engaged in it and of his own relationship to each party.

We need to refer to another important principle of Nuer political structure: the smaller the local group the stronger the sentiment uniting its members. Tribal sentiment is weaker than the sentiment of one of its segments and the sentiment of a segment is weaker than the sentiment of a village which is part of it. Logically this might be supposed to be the case, for if unity within a group is a function of its opposition to groups of the same kind it might be surmised that the sentiment of unity within a group must be stronger than the sentiment of unity within a larger group that contains it. But it is also evident that the smaller the group the more the contacts between its members, the more varied are these contacts, and the more they are co-operative. In a big group like the tribe contacts between its members are infrequent and corporate action is limited to occasional military excursions. In a small group like the village not only are there daily residential contacts, often of a co-operative nature, but the members are united by close agnatic, cognatic, and affinal ties which can be expressed in reciprocal action. These become fewer and more distant the wider the group, and the cohesion of a political group is undoubtedly dependent on the number and strength of ties of a non-political kind.

It must also be stated that political actualities are confused and conflicting. They are confused because they are not always, even in a political context, in accord with political values, though they tend to conform to them, and because social ties of a different kind operate in the same field, sometimes strengthening them and sometimes running counter to them. They are conflicting because the values that determine them are, owing to the relativity of political structure, themselves in conflict. Consistency of political actualities can only be seen when the dynamism and relativity of political structure are understood and the relation of political structure to other social systems is taken into consideration.

3

THE ILLUSION OF TRIBE[*]

AIDAN W. SOUTHALL

Introduction

Controversial though the matter is, the most generally acceptable characteristics of a tribal society are perhaps that it is a whole society, with a high degree of self-sufficency at a near subsistence level, based on a relatively simple technology without writing or literature, politically autonomous and with its own distinctive language, culture and sense of identity, tribal religion being also co-terminous with tribal society. Some would insist on further differentiation of the tribal level of social and cultural organization, on the one hand, from the very small scale band level characteristic of hunting and gathering peoples without agriculture, and on the other, from state or state-like organizations found at the upper limit of scale and complexity within the range of non-literate societies. Thus, Sahlins (1961: 323) speaks of the "tribal level, as distinguished from less-developed *bands* and more advanced *chiefdoms*". This point of

view has not found much favour and can be criticised on a number of counts. At the empirical level, tribes and bands do not appear as distinct as is implied, and the concept of "chief" and "chiefdom", while clear to some writers, is highly variable and inconsistent in the ethnographic literature as a whole. The empirical difficulties of distinguishing the tribal level in the broad sense have been considerable, and the addition of two further levels seems to make them insurmountable. It is not by multiplying global distinctions of this sort that we shall progress, but by dealing with more specialized categories of phenomena while retaining the general concept of tribe as a convenient initial descriptive label. Dozens of definitions could, of course, be quoted from authoritative anthropological writings, but for the most part, they add nothing to understanding and vary only in emphasis, one stressing language, another politics, another self-identity, and so forth.

[*] It was only after completing this paper that "Essays on the Problem of Tribe" (Helm, ed., 1968) became available to me. Many of the same problems are raised, as indeed they have been raised explicitly or implicitly, many times before by the whole body of ethnographic material.

However, Fried's original paper (1966) which provided the stimulus for these essays, was obviously intended as introductory and exploratory rather than conclusive, while the essays themselves are necessarily as diverse as their authors. Moreover, the predominating concern of many of them with evolutionary perspectives and with more purely taxonomic and allied statistical problems are matters which I have deliberately omitted.

There may therefore be a case for a further attempt – and doubtless many others – at a more synoptic statement with some new illustrative materials.

For present purposes, to simplify the argument, we shall use tribal society in the more inclusive sense of all those societies which exhibit the first mentioned set of characteristics. On this basis, to what extent do such societies still exist? In the strict sense they cannot exist, since there are no areas of the inhabited earth unclaimed by one sovereign state or another. They can only exist in dwindling pockets so remote that such sovereign claims have not yet been made effective and can be ignored. No tribal society which has lost its political autonomy can continue to be a tribal society in the full sense of this meaning, although many of its members may retain vivid and even nostalgic memories of its former full existence and may continue to be strongly influenced by the values belonging to this former state and still endeavour to act according to them in those fields where new controls and changed needs allow them to do so. It is the melancholy paradox of anthropology that effective study of such social systems dates only from a period so late that they had already ceased to exist in this full sense, so that an element of reconstruction has always entered into the study of them in these terms. But it would be foolish to deny that the end of their existence in the full sense was the beginning of a long transitional period in which their members were in varying degrees becoming incorporated into wider systems, yet continued to retain strong elements of their former state. Neglect of this has vitiated much of the work carried out supposedly in their interests by the development disciplines.

It is not only political autonomy which has been lost, though that was fundamental, and it is well to specify the changes which have generally occurred in respect of the other stated characteristics. They are no longer self sufficient, because various pressures from without and then from within have brought them to depend extensively on goods and services which they cannot produce for themselves. Even where their material well being is still little better than their former subsistence,

they have none the less become involved with the wider market economy in countless seemingly irrevocable ways. By the same token, their technology is no longer simple. Even where it is little improved in efficiency, it has come to reflect in its array of tools and weapons, clothes and even foodstuffs, the vast, unseen and distant complex of the industrial world. Almost invariably some of its members have become literate, and even if they have often at the same time tended to become absentees, they none the less remain vital members of it and the very symbols of its passing. Furthermore, they have often, and necessarily, become literate in a foreign language. They have also adopted, of course under strong external persuasion if not pressure, new religious beliefs, practices, and memberships, or at least new sets of ideas, which are incompatible with tribal society. In all these ways, the close identity of language, culture and society (if ever existed) is now blurred and has become a series of alternatives. To say "I am a Kikuyu, a Kenyan, an African," means three very different things. The latter two identities did not exist three quarters of a century ago. What has been said here is obviously only a minimal statement of the changes that have occurred. It goes without saying that in many cases the transformation is much greater.

So far we have given a definition of what a tribal society is, conceptually, and presumably was, empirically, but have argued that it can no longer exist in this full sense, however potent many of its features may remain. The carrying over of such features into a different system is tribalism. Tribalism is usually regarded in pejorative light and the rational basis for this is that to carry over elements specific to one system into another is inappropriate. It is in the political context that tribalism is regarded with particular disfavor, and in a number of social and economic contexts also. But those who rightly stigmatise the carryover which is tribalism in these contexts would in others often favor it, especially with respect to certain family values and to aesthetic modes of expression, as for example in music, dancing and plastic arts. Thus President Julius Nyerere of Tanzania: "It has been said – and this is quite right – that Tanganyika is tribal, and we realise that we need to break up this tribal consciousness among the people and to build up a national consciousness" (Nyerere, 1966: 38–9). Yet on the other hand, "I have set up this new Ministry to help us regain our pride in our own culture. I want it to seek out the best of the traditions and customs of all our tribes and make them a part of our national culture" (op. cit. 187). "The traditional order is dying; the question which has yet to be answered is what will be built on our past, and, in consequence, what kind of society will eventually replace the traditional one" (op. cit. 6).

This is the oft discussed problem of trying to retain the good which was in the old and grafting it on to the new. But the characteristics of tribal society which we gave constitute a set of highly dependent variables. Dependent variables, whether we like it or not, constitute a functional system. We say "highly dependent" because we reject the extreme claims of total functional integration which are widely recognised as false. Tribal societies were not totally integrated. There were areas of partial integration and partial dependence in the system, allowing for the possibility of moderate change from within or without. But they were certainly quite highly integrated systems and to pick and choose among supposedly desirable and undesirable elements in them is a fatal misunderstanding of their intrinsic nature. Of course there is continuity as well as change. There are harder and softer elements in the system. But the interdependence, although partial and not total, is none the less real. There is therefore some possibility of preserving some desirable elements, but it can only be done in submission to the limitations imposed by the degree of interdependence of variables. Unfortunately, this requirement is far from being taken seriously into account by the policy makers concerned.

This is particularly relevant to those formerly tribal populations which have not lost their demographic vitality, or will to live, but rather are in many cases on the brink of, or already involved in, a dangerous population explosion, rapidly entering the modern world and usually forming the major population component of new nations, or of colonial territories in their last stages, as in most of Africa and New Guinea. The other side of the coin is the more tragic situation reported by Levi-Strauss in "A World on the Wane" of those pathetic remnants which "had learnt from the ferocious persecutions of the previous hundred years to keep themselves entirely hidden from the outer world", – people who "were neither 'true Indians', nor, for that matter, 'true savages', but former 'savages' on whom civilization had been abruptly forced; and, as soon as they were no longer 'a danger to Society', civilization took no further interest in them" (1961: 134–5). This is the characteristic situation of aboriginal peoples throughout the Americas, except for those who have successfully made the transition into peasantries, or as individuals, become lost in industrial society. Such tragic situations are also reported sporadically from Africa where, according to Diamond (1964a: 45) the Anaguta of the Nigerian Plateau "*decided* not to join the modern world" but "move like ghosts on the outskirts of civilization . . . Their culture crumbles, their population declines, their lands shrink and as an ethnic entity they change only disintegratively. They accept, they pursue their decline; for them the world ends." Or, again, the fragmentary Ik of north-eastern Uganda, where, according to Turnbull (1967: 70) "social disintegration has gone to the limit" and "at the present rate the Ik are not likely to survive much longer." . . .

According to Steward (1958: 44–5) "the concept of primitive or 'tribal' is based on three fundamental aspects of the behavior of members of tribal societies". These are, in brief, that it is a construct representing the ideal, normative aspect of the behaviour of "all members of a fairly small, simple, independent, self-contained and homogeneous society" . . . "Tribal society is not divisible into genuine subcultural groups." Secondly, tribal culture has pattern, or configuration, some underlying unity and overall integration, and thirdly, that it is "essentially relativistic" and unique in relation to other cultures with which it contrasted. While it has been "a useful tool for analysis and comparison, especially when contrasts are sought, . . . as a tool for dealing with culture change it has found little utility." To the present writer its deficiencies are more fundamental than this, for as we shall see, the cultures which lie at the lower end of the range in terms of social scale are not in fact unique and independent entities which can properly be seen as unequivocally distinct from one another. Indeed, to do so is frequently to misunderstand their essential nature. On the other hand, cultures which lie at the higher end of the scale are not as homogeneous and lacking in subcultural divisions as is implied. These divergences are much too general and glaring to be regarded as permissible deviations from a consistent core.

The ideal type or analytical model of the tribe varies a good deal in the versions of different writers, as we have seen, but it is fair to say that these variations do play round recurring common themes. However, we shall give examples to document the fact that, whichever particular choice of definition is made, empirical divergences are so gross, widespread and frequent as to render the concept of tribe as it exists in the general literature untenable. In many cases the definitions generally current actually hinder understanding of the entities to which they are supposed to refer. The named tribes which appear in the literature frequently represent crystallizations at the wrong level, usually a level which is too large in scale because foreign observers did not initially understand the lower levels of structure or failed to correct the misrepresentations of their predecessors, or because some arbitrary and even artificial entity was chosen for the sake of easy reference, despite a realisation that it was fallacious and misleading. Furthermore, such fabrications of the foreign observer have often themselves acquired validity in the course of externally induced change and amalgamation, while the indigenous peoples concerned have also become aware of the need for larger scale as the modern world closed in upon them.

The Concept of Tribe in Africa

Since the birth of African nationalism, tribalism has always been a sore subject and for very good reasons. Some nationalists have even gone so far as to claim that tribal divisions were the deliberate creation of a Machiavellian colonial policy of divide and rule. While it is doubtful whether most colonial administrators most of the time had sufficient knowledge of the internal structure of the traditional societies they ruled and sufficient expertise in social engineering to achieve what is credited to them by this view, there is a certain element of truth in it to the extent that many of the named entities which appear as tribes in the literature appeared for the first time during the colonial period and must in this sense necessarily be considered a product of it. One of the most striking and well documented cases is that of the Luhia in Kenya.

When the German anthropologist Günter Wagner went to Kenya in 1934, Kavirondo was simply a geographical area, so named from the time of the earliest Arab, Swahili and European traders and explorers, but not so known by any of its indigenous inhabitants. Wagner notes that "owing to its constant use by Europeans, the term 'Kavirondo' has nowadays been to some extent adopted by the natives, but they use it with reference to the district rather than to themselves. When talking to other natives – even outside the district – they always style themselves by the name of their respective sub-tribe, such as Wanga, Vugusu, Logoli, Nyole, etc. Among politically minded natives who for a number of years have been pleading for a political unification of all Bantu Kavirondo tribes under a paramount chief according to the Buganda pattern, the word *avaluhia*, meaning 'those of the same tribe', is propagated as a common designation for all Bantu Kavirondo. The term 'Kavirondo', on the other hand, is generally rejected in these quarters as being of European origin" (Wagner 1949: 20). Many other writers have pointed out that the term Kavirondo was regarded as opprobrious for various reasons, though agreement has never been reached as to its meaning or derivation.

Wagner himself, like many another ethnographer, vacillates over his use of the term tribe, applying it sometimes to one level, sometimes to another. "In pre-European days the various sub-tribes of Bantu Kavirondo were, for their greater part, very loosely organized politically, each sub-tribe consisting of a number of more or less sovereign clans. Since British rule was established in the middle of the nineties, they have been organized into chieftaincies." However, since traditional groupings varied in size and the colonial administration aimed at uniformity and convenience in the size of administrative units, there was the usual discrepancy between the definition of groupings on the one hand and administrative chieftaincies on the other. Next Wagner distinguishes the following tribes, corresponding to what he referred to as subtribes in the previous passage: Vagusu, Tadjoni, Wanga, Marama, Tsotso, Tiriki, Nyala, Kabras, Hayo, Marach, Holo and Logoli, to which must also be added the Idaxo, Isuxa, Kisa, Nyole and Samia. Among such acephalous peoples the exact number of groups properly to be distinguished may be genuinely ambiguous and debatable in some instances, but the above list would generally be accepted. Bethwell Ogot (1967: 138) speaks of "the seventeen Luyia tribes." Ogot further states (1967: 139) that "the name 'Baluyia' was first adopted by the North Kavirondo Central Association in June 1935. *The elders rejected the*

name, (italics mine) and it was only after the Second World War that it gained general currency." This entirely accords with the experience of the present writer, who, arriving to teach at Makerere College in 1945, found that the whole group of Bantu speaking students from North Kavirondo called themselves Abaluyia and were never known as anything else.

It may be said that the Luyia people came into existence between approximately 1935 and 1945. Before that time no such group existed either in its own or anyone else's estimation. It was clearly due to the reaction of younger and more educated men to the exigencies of the colonial situation. It arose out of previous attempts at intertribal or supratribal organization and unity such as the North Kavirondo Central Association and Bantu Kavirondo Tax-payers' Association and led to further important organizations such as the Abaluyia Union, which came to represent the Luyia away from home, especially in the big towns such as Nairobi in Kenya and Kampala in Uganda. This new supertribe was closely linked to the colonial administrative framework, being in effect based upon and in part suggested by the administrative and territorial framework of the North Kavirondo District (subsequently renamed North Nyanza District because of the already noted pejorative aura of the word Kavirondo). In language and culture the Samia were just as much Luyia as the Hayo or Marach, but the unfortunate Samia were not only cut in two by the frontier between Kenya and Uganda, but even their Kenya half was situated administratively in Central and not North Nyanza District. Consequently Samia were never considered Luyia, and Samia away from home their own separate ethnic association.

In the original conglomeration of the Luyia in the 1930s and 40s the Vugusu were the largest numerical component. This in itself favored secessionist tendencies on their part, since they occupied a compact territory on the north side of the Luyia area. During the 1950s they began to agitate for, and eventually succeeded in winning, their own administrative district, which became known as Elgon Nyanza. With this the integrity of the Luyia supertribe began to crumble and it is now arguable whether the Vugusu are Luyia or not. . . .

The fact is that many tribes have come into existence in a similar way to the Luyia, through a combination of reasonable cultural similarity with colonial administrative convenience, which in more recent times has often coincided with peoples' own sense of need for wider levels of organization to enable them to exert more effective pressure on events. The Luyia never did conform to the criteria of a tribe with which we started. Indeed, by the time they first came into existence they already diverged somewhat from every criterion mentioned.

The meaning of the name Luyia is instructive. Wagner explains (1949: 55) that "the stem -*hia* means 'to be hot', 'to burn'" and in a concrete sense the word *olu-hia* means "fire place on a meadow", hence "the fire-place as the centre of public life of the clan." "It is at this *oluhia* that the old men of the clan community meet every morning to warm themselves and to discuss the events and news of the day as well as to settle all important matters of the clan." Despite linguistic variation between the different Luyia groups they nearly all have this term and concept. The case of the Luyia is instructive because it is comparatively rare that an adequate documentation is available to demonstrate the process of appearance of new "tribes" with reasonable completeness. But the Luyia are far from being an isolated case and the process has close counterparts in many regions of the world.

To take an example from the other side of the continent of Africa, Labouret (1931), Fortes (1945), Goody (1957) and Tait (1961) have all extensively documented the fact that in a large and populous region, including adjacent parts of Ghana, Ivory Coast and Upper Volta, any single definitive boundary drawn between one 'tribe' and another was bound to be relative, arbitrary and a misrepresentation of the facts. Colson (1951: 95) has demonstrated the same point for the Plateau Tonga of Central Africa (Zambia). It was not that these peoples were an undifferentiated mass, but that they were differentiated in many subtle and complex ways for different purposes. Any idea of the Lobi, Tallensi, LoDagaba or Konkomba as clearcut, isolated, enclosed tribes is a complete travesty of the facts. Legitimate authority did not inhere to or flow from any one unequivocal level of organization, but was contingent upon the situation. . . .

Much the same process of the picking up, fixing and generalizing by colonial authorities of names applied to vaguely defined peoples by their neighbors or other foreigners, seems to have occurred in the case of the Yoruba. "The term Yoruba is sometimes said to have been derived from a foreign nickname, meaning cunning, given to the subjects of the Alafin of Oyo by the Fulani and Hausa. The Hausa word for the Yoruba language is *Yarbanci*. Yoruba has been commonly applied to a large group, united more by language than by culture, *whose members speak of themselves* (italics mine) as Oyo, Egba, Ijebu, Ife, Ilesha and the other names of the various tribes" (Forde, 1951: 1). However, it is debatable whether the latter named entities are any more justly designated as tribes than the Yoruba as a whole. They might just as well be called city states. Johnson seems to agree with the Hausa or Fulani derivation of the name Yoruba, suggesting that the country was first known to Europeans from the north "for in old records the Hausa and Fulani names are used for the country and its capital; thus we see in Webster's Gazetteer 'Yarriba'," (1921: xix). This he equates with Yoruba but attempts no other derivation. But he continues "this country comprises many tribes governed by their own chiefs and having their own laws. At one time they were all tributaries to one sovereign, the King of Yoruba, including Benin on the East, and Dahomey on the West, but are now independent." There appears to be no historical foundation for this title of "the King of Yoruba," except for the supposedly wider influence of the kingdom of Old Oyo before the eighteenth century, and the ritual focus of all Yoruba upon Ife. It is like the legenday crediting of former suzerainty over Buganda, Ankole and other· Interlacustrine states to a supposed Bunyoro-Kitara "Empire." Here too there has been a persistent confusion between political and ritual relations.

Group names with an ecological referent are common all over the world and often show a very poor correlation with valid divisions between one tribe and another on the basis of political, social, cultural and linguistic facts. Madagascar is a striking case. There we have the following generally accepted names and meanings, which may none the less be apocryphal in some cases: *Antanala* (the forest people), *Antandroy* (the people of the thorny cactus forest,) *Antankarana* (the people of the rocks and caves), *Antanosy* (the people of the islands), *Antefasy* (the people of the sands) *Antemoro* (the people of the coast), *Antesaka* (the people who catch small fish with the hands),* *Antsihanaka* (the people of the lake), *Betanimena* (the people of the red land), *Bezanozano* (the bush people), and *Sakalava* (the people of the long valleys, or of the broad and long plain). A few other Malagasy peoples have acquired non-ecological designations: *Betsileo* (the many who are not conquered), *Betsimisaraka* (the many who do not separate), *Mahafaly* (those who cause joy) and *Tsimihety* (those who do not cut their hair). – It is said that growing their hair long made Tsimihety men look like women and facilitated their escape from slave raiders.

Even where these ecological terms are accurate, as in the case of Antanala, they refer to people in a particular habitat rather than to people with distinct socio-cultural characteristics. Ecology can be very important, but no

one now would hold it responsible for all social and cultural differences. Other terms are vague and overlapping. Many Malagasy live on the sand besides the Antefasy, very many on the coast besides the Antemoro, and very many on red earth besides the Betanimena. The Antanosy do not in fact live on islands. *Antandroy* is a fair description, but these people were neither a cultural, historical nor political unity . . . Another common basis of tribal naming which is in a sense more structurally genuine than many of those so far discussed is derived from the names of primal ancestors which appear in genealogies, myths and legends as founders of the people. It is obvious that this kind of eponymy is particularly to be expected in the case of segmentary lineage systems with their strong emphasis on genealogical reckoning. In such society's conception of itself and its past there is usually a series of levels which phase into one another as they proceed further back in time. The nearest level largely consists of the ancestors of specific contemporary groups, whose genealogical relationships tend to express the contemporary relations of such groups and from one or other of whom every full member of the society can trace himself directly. Beyond this there is a vaguer level of tribal heroes about whose exploits, genealogical connections and even names there are differences of opinion between different members and sections of the modern community, though these are usually recognisably common variations upon central themes. Beyond this is the yet more shadowy realm of figures who represent the origins of man and society, the differentiation of human and divine, the expression of ultimate cultural meanings in symbolic form.

In these reaches all is relative, that which is "first" is so only in relation to that which followed. "For the deeper we sound, the further down into the lower world of the past we probe and press, the more do we find that

---

*   But see Deschamps & Vianès (1959) p. 92 for another interpretation.

the earliest foundations of humanity, its history and culture, reveal themselves unfathomable . . . Thus there may exist provisional origins, which practically and in fact form the first beginnings of the particular tradition held by a given community, folk or communion of faith; and memory, though sufficiently instructed that the depths have not actually been plumbed, yet nationally may find reassurance in some primitive point of time and, personally and historically speaking, come to rest there" (Mann, 1963: 3). Not only is the beginning thus always relative, but almost invariably there is asymmetry and contradiction associated with it.

In the case of the great Somali people, who may justifiably be called a nation as forming the basis of a new nation state, among the usual rival derivations one of the most plausible is that which traces Somali to the eponymous ancestor of most of the northern pastoral Somali. The asymmetry and contradiction lies in the fact that "the Somali nation is composed of two parts, the Somali and the Sab. Strictly, the word 'Somali' does not apply to the Sab, who say themselves that they are 'Sab' and are so described and distinguished by the 'Somali'; nor is the Sab group subsumed under the name 'Somali' in the total genealogy of the Somali nation." (Somali and Sab appear in the genealogy in the structural position of brothers, both of common descent from the Qurayshitic lineage of the Prophet Mohammed). "The Sab stand opposed to the Somali, and are grouped with them only at a higher genealogical level, when the two ancestors Sab and Somali, are traced back to Arabian origins, in the total genealogy of the inhabitants of Somaliland" (Lewis, 1955: 15 and 1961: 12). Instances of eponymous tribal naming are very numerous among peoples with segmentary lineage organization, such as the Tiv, Gusii and others already mentioned earlier.

The difficulty of identifying one "tribe" clearly and distinctly from another is often represented as a troublesome test which the anthropologist must pass. Thus, of the Australian Tiwi, because they lived on two islands, "fuzziness on the edges of tribal territory – a chronic headache to anthropologists working with mainland tribes – did not exist" (Hart and Pilling, 1964: 11). Or again of the Tiv, "the Tiv do not present that difficulty so common in Africa: identifying the tribe" (Bohannan, 1958: 35). The difficulty is undeniable, particularly in the case of stateless societies, and meticulous exploration of the distribution, interconnections and meaning of the various elements in culture and social structure is of vital importance in such situations, but insistence on defining some global discrete entity as a tribe may simply be a refusal to recognise the fundamental characteristics of this kind of society. I have argued elsewhere (Southall, 1968) that stateless societies have the combined characteristics of: multi-polities, ritual superintegration, complementary opposition, intersecting kinship and distributive legitimacy. The contingent nature of their structure, subdivisions and boundaries is of their essence, not something to be swept away by penetrating analysis. The representation of adjacent stateless societies as a neatly discrete series of named units is to misunderstand and misrepresent them.

Despite Bohannan's categorical statement on Tiv identity, Tiv is in fact a set of contradictions, as any stateless society must be when mistakenly regarded as a discrete tribe. "A Tiv is a Tiv and can prove it" because "every Tiv can trace his descent from Tiv himself." Yet this genealogy is "not in itself a record of ancestry," nor "a portrait of political structure, for its field of relevance is greater than that of the political while, on the other hand, not all political relationships are capable of expression in its idiom." For Tiv is actually the ancestor of non-Tiv peoples also, such as the Uge and Utange, and "the name of a linguistic and cultural entity which never (prior to British Administration) acted as a political unit." As with the Nguru-Luguru-Kaguru cluster of Tanzania, the named entity is, quite characteristically, at once too large and too small.

The Tiwi also, despite the apparent clarity with which they are defined by the accident of island isolation, turn out on closer inspection to have just that fuzziness which Hart and Pilling deny. For the Tiwi "did little as a member of a tribe. Only when an outsider turned up did he need to think of himself as a Tiwi, and outsiders were very rare. For the rest of the time he thought of himself as a member of his band, thought of his band as his people, and of his band territory as his country . . . The nine bands thus acted, psychologically, as small tribelets or semi-sovereign groups" (op. cit. 12–13). Thus Tiwi too turns out to be something of an illusion. Even the band was "a flexible and constantly shifting collection of individuals" (op. cit. 1. 12). "The casual way in which people left one band and joined another shows that the band was in no sense a tight political or legal group" (op. cit. p. 31).

The further illusion seems to be cherished that at least with language we are on safer ground with an unequivocal factor defining clearcut groups. "All Tiwi, *of course*, spoke the same language" (op. cit. p. 11, italics mine). Yet among the Murngin, who are not so distant from the Tiwi, either culturally or geographically, "the members of each moiety are supposed to speak different languages . . . Even each clan is said to have a 'language'; and some have a different dialect, but most within a given area speak the same one. The clans claim 'languages' of their own by giving themselves linguistic names in addition to group names" (Warner, 1937: 30). Rather than assume that language always defines a cultural entity, even when most other factors fail, we should assume that language is also one of the elements which groups in an acephalous, stateless society may purposefully and almost "artificially" use as a basis of distinction and identification, even when observed empirical differences are slight. "Of course," we may add, "the tribe is almost a non-existent unit

among the Murngin" (Warner, 1937: 9). "The tribes of northeastern Arnhem Land, of which Murngin is one, are very weak social units, and when measured by the ordinary definitions of what constitutes a tribe fail almost completely. The tribe is not the war-making group. On the contrary, it is usually within it that the most intensive feuds are found. Tribal membership of the clans on the borders of two tribes is uncertain and changing, or the people may sometimes insist that they belong to both tribes. Even clans well toward the center of a tribe's territory will, under certain circumstances, range themselves with another group" (Warner, op. cit., 35). The name Murngin is little used and the moiety names are used much more commonly.

Warner's account makes it very clear that the conventional concept of tribe was quite inappropriate to what he nonetheless called his "Social Study of an Australian Tribe." He uses the name Murngin purely for convenience. "The word Murngin (fire sparks) was found as a designation only after much effort. The people do not think of themselves under this name or classification. The word has been used by me as a general term for all of the eight tribes in the area and for the groups of people located in the central part of the territory of the eight tribes. I have seized upon this name as a convenient and concise way of talking about this whole group of people; had any of the other tribes who possess the particular type of social organization found in this area been located in the center of the group, I should have used the name of that tribe rather than Murngin" (Warner, op. cit. 15). Thus, Warner constantly uses the term tribe having said that "the tribe can hardly be said to exist in this area" (ibid). Nor, of course, was the area of Warner's eight "tribes" clearly distinguished from neighbouring areas. It was simply the area within which he was able to accomplish field work. The relativities of the Murngin and Tiwi situations are duplicated in other instances too numerous to mention, such as the Yir Yoront (Sharp, 1958), which chiefly show that the situation long ago revealed by Radcliffe-Brown and others is no peculiar anomaly, but far more prevalent than they can have realized.

It is not so unlike the case of the Amba in Western Uganda, who include two main groups, the Bulibuli and the Bwezi, who speak two entirely different languages. By an asymmetry which is also a further characteristic of stateless societies, while both Bulibuli and Bwezi are Amba, the Bulibuli are also known as the Amba proper. Each village is either Bulibuli or Bwezi, but Bulibuli and Bwezi villages are interspersed. Each village was an independent political unit and "warfare between various villages was a constant feature" (Winter, 1958: 138). But the village was not a "self-sufficient system of action" chiefly because "the men of the village must obtain wives from the outside" therefore "even the internal organization of the village can only be understood . . . in terms of its interrelationship with the larger structure of which it is a part" (Winter, op. cit., 139). Each village had a maximal lineage as its core and villages based on maximal lineages belonging to the same named clan and exogamous group were linked together in important ways. Thus we have again no one categorical level of organization which can properly be picked out from the rest, but rather a number of levels, all equally important for different purposes, a number of criteria defining essentially overlapping groups and categories, so that "friends on one basis are enemies on another" and conflicts become cohesion (Gluckman, 1955: 4, 19).

Needless to say, language is even less necessarily or obviously a criterion of tribe where higher levels of political specialization have been reached and diverse groups incorporated by conquest or assimilation. Thus, Alur society contained Nilotic, Sudanic and Bantu speakers, of half a dozen different languages, (Southall, 1956, passim) and such situations were common in more elaborate state systems. The Azande, Lozi and many other conquering groups incorporated numerous diverse elements, which retained considerable cultural diversity . . .

An attractively precise definition of tribe was developed by Evans-Pritchard (1940: 122). Although he defines Nuer tribes by nine very concrete and culture bound criteria (loc. cit) the essence of the definition, which was adopted and long retained by many British social anthropologists is contained in the simple sentence: "local communities have been classed as tribes or tribal segments by whether they acknowledge the obligation to pay blood-wealth or not" (ibid). Evans-Pritchard applied the same criterion to the Kenya Luo and other Nilotic peoples, Lienhardt applied it to the Dinka, Middleton to the Lugbara, Tait to the Konkomba and so on. For a while it became an article of faith in the context of a particular approach. It was most effective in relation to the immediate matter at hand: – the exposition and clarification of segmentary lineage systems. Its chief disadvantages were that there were many other varieties of socio-political structure which it did not fit and that it further confused and outraged the commonsense of the general reader by suddenly transforming what had always been known as single "tribes," "peoples," "societies," or "cultures," into tens, dozens and even hundreds of different distinct "tribes." For example, the Dinka were divided by Lienhardt (1958: 102) into some twenty five "tribal groups," and the three of these which he happened to know well contained 27, 10 and 6 "tribes" respectively, suggesting that the total number of Dinka "tribes" would amount to many hundreds.

As the enthusiasm for segmentary lineage systems passed its peak, this precise but severely limited usage of the term tribe lost ground and eventually fell into disuse. In practice, the term sub-tribe is now substituted for it in the same context. Thus Middleton (1960: 7) refers to the Lugbara as consisting of about sixty tribes, but subsequently (1963: 82) changed this to sixty sub-tribes.

Conclusion

The problem of ethnic classification as such is a special problem which we do not attempt to cover. We can only reiterate that no uni-dimensional classification of socio-cultural groups can provide an adequate basis for the comparative study of specific problems, let alone for frequency distributions, because the proper units of classification and analysis will vary according to the phenomenon and the problem studied. We must expect that comparative and generalizing studies of kinship systems or specific components of them, religious, symbolic or identity systems or specific components of them, political and economic systems or their components, and so forth, will always involve a plurality of units of analysis and fields of distribution. All attempts at establishing unequivocal, all-purpose, unidemensional classifications of socio-cultural groups involve grave danger of misrepresenting the nature of societies as anthropology knows them. To hammer home the importance of interlocking, overlapping, multiple and alternative collective identities is one of the most important messages of social and cultural anthropology . . . There are three sets of problems associated with the tribal concept as we have examined it: problems of definition (ambiguous, imprecise or conflicting definitions and also the failure to stick to them consistently); problems of illusion (false application of the concept to artificial or misconceived entities) and problems of transition and transformation (use of the concept of tribe unjustifiably with reference to phenomena which are a direct product of modern influences). There is a considerable overlap between the last two sets of problems. As we have seen, there are many stateless societies where inaccurate definition has simply been the product of ignorance, illusion, or inattention; but very often the "definition by illusion" has been a definition of larger scale which became permanently adopted for administrative convenience and ultimately accepted by the people themselves. We may thus say that the problems of illusion have frequently been perpetuated by those of transition and transformation . . .

Problems of nomenclature may seem trivial, except insofar as they breed confusion and misunderstanding among anthropologists themselves, while at the same time rendering nugatory any influence which anthropology might have upon the world of scholarship as a whole. Where unresolved problems remain, agreement upon nomenclature is unlikely. What may legitimately be demanded is that nomenclature should be clear and consistent in each discourse, so that the problems of greater moment which lie behind it can be tackled. It is simply with this in mind that we would suggest calling "tribal" that traditional form of society which we described at the beginning. Once the empirical facts are recognized there should be enough consensus for adequate communication despite many minor differences of opinion. Tribal society may be largely a phenomenon of the past, but it is still of enormous intellectual and human importance.

The distinguishing of individual tribal units is a different and perhaps misconceived problem as we have seen. The solution should be very simple. Where discrete tribal units can be empirically demonstrated – well and good, where not, the temptation to speak or write as though some unique and all embracing discrete level of organization exists when the facts belie it should be resisted. The analysis and comparative study of tribal society should proceed on the basis of more specialized categories in the fields of kinship, ritual, politics, economics, language and so forth. Stateless societies cannot be expected to present discrete boundaries except where special geographical or historical circumstances favour it. But chiefdoms and tribal states are more likely to do so the greater the degree of their political specialization. Yet by the same token they are less homogeneous and un-differentiated than has commonly been supposed. All out social and cultural constructs are bound to encounter intermediate cases when applied to empirical data, but it must be remembered that the intermediacy is as likely as not a product of the constructs rather than of the data. Nonetheless, the distinction of tribal societies in their lack of writing and records, their simple technology and direct subsistence economy, the absence of highly differentiated consumption patterns, the importance of the domain of kinship and multiplex relationships with all the institutional implications of these characteristics holds fairly well empirically.

When we move on from tribal societies in the full sense, which must increasingly be regarded as phenomena of the past, to the transitional situations which are prevalent today, there are again two main empirical types to be distinguished. There are the tribal societies which have been transitional sometimes for long periods, in relation to the dominant influence of ancient pre-industrial states and there are those which are transitional in relation to the post-industrial states which are almost exclusively those of the western world. This distinction has been important but is now itself becoming transitory. On another dimension there is the distinction between the transitional situation of communities, necessarily usually rural, and the transitional situation of individuals derived from such communities, which may also be urban, and indeed industrial. For the reasons already stated, it seems required by consistency and also by the human situation itself that the condition of individuals and groups in all the transitional situations of the contemporary world should now be described in ethnic and not in tribal terms. While all formerly tribal peoples are becoming increasingly subject to the ubiquitous pressures of the modern industrial world, there is the paradox that the former tribal peoples are mainly to be found within the confines of the less developed nations, whose economic condition, radically transformed though it is, is being left relatively further and further behind by the developed nations, so that in this

sense one dichotomy is being substituted for another at a higher level.

For anthropologists this involves a poignant dilemma. Their whole discipline has been reared upon the discovery and study of forms of culture and society which held up a contrasting mirror to their own. More recently they have been adjusting, albeit slowly, to the prospective resolution of this contrast and to joining in the further exploration of man and society with colleagues who have actually emerged from the other side of it. But although these colleagues from the other world, the *tiers monde*, can truly enter an international world of anthropological scholarship, their hands are still tied by the fact that their new world has a meaning for them and us which is in unexpected ways as contrasted to ours as was the old tribal world which has passed away. This imposes a heavy strain and responsibility of understanding and sympathy.

Anthropology claims to be a universal discipline. Committed above all things to cross-cultural perspectives and to the transcendence of the ethnocentric myopia, it is naturally embarrassed by the colonialist taint which besmirches it in so much of the *tiers monde*. If western, and especially American, anthropologists are to avoid the charge that they are prostituting the discipline to assuage their personality problems, they will have to take much more seriously the complementarity of the contribution required from the new breed of anthropologists whose fathers or grandfathers were members of non-literate societies. If this contribution is to be made, and anthropology to avoid drifting into a blind alley as a bourgeois, essentially Western culture bound pastime, western anthropologists will have to stop calling primitive and tribal the contemporary communities from which their colleagues of the new breed come. This may be a case in which human feelings have to prevail over strict logic. It is also essential if anthropologists, preeminently equipped and destined for the task as they should be, are to contribute to bridging and healing the widening economic and credibility gap between the *tiers monde* and the West.

If asked what terms then can we use, since even the most neutral and logical can so easily become contaminated (as the disheartening sequence of: undeveloped, underdeveloped, less developed, developing, has shown), I should have to answer simply for the strategic moment, for the present critical and vital generation, that for the present the word prim-

itive should be dropped from the vocabulary of social anthropology, however much it wounds our romantic souls, that the term "tribe" should usually be applied only to the small scale societies of the past which retained their political autonomy, and that the new associations derived from them in the contemporary context should be referred to as ethnic groups as other members of the category are.

References

Bohannan, Laura (1958) Political Aspects of Tiv Social Organization, in Middleton and Tait (1958).

Colson, E. (1951). "The Plateau Tonga of Northern Rhodesia", in E. Colson and M. Gluckman (eds.). *Seven Tribes of British Central Africa*, Oxford University Press.

Colson, E. (1953). *The Makah Indians*, Manchester University Press.

Deschamps, Hubert and Suzanne Vianès (1950). *Les Malgaches du Sud-Est*, Presses University taires de France.

Diamond, Stanley (1964). "What History Is", in Robert A. Manners (ed.). *Process and Pattern in Culture, Essays in Honor of Julian H. Steward*, Aldine, Chicago.

Evans-Pritchard, E. E. (1940). *The Nuer*, London, Oxford University Press.

Forde, C. Daryll (1951). *The Yoruba-Speaking Peoples of South-Western Nigeria*, International African Institute, London.

Fortes, M. (1954). *The Dynamics of Clanship among the Tallensi*. Oxford University Press, London.

Fried, Morton H. (1966). On the Concepts of "Tribe" and "Tribal Society", *Transactions of the New York Academy of Sciences*, Vol. 28, No. 4, 527–40.

Gluckman, Max (1955). *Custom and Conflict in Africa*, Blackwell, Oxford.

Goody, J. (1957). Fields of Social Control Among the LoDagaba, *Journal of the Royal Anthropological Institute*, vol. 87, pt. 1, p.75.

Hart, C. W. M., and Pilling, A. R. (1964). *The Tiwi of North Australia*, Holt, Rinehart and Winston, New York.

Labouret, Henri (1931). *Les tribus du rameau Lobi.*

Paris, Institut d'ethnologie.

Lévi-Strauss, C. (1961). *A World on the Wane*, Criterion Books, New York.

Lewis, I. M. (1955). Peoples of the Horn of Africa, Ethnographic Survey of Africa, International African Institute, London.

Lewis, I.M. (1961). *A Pastoral Democracy*, Oxford University Press (for International African Institute), London.

Mann, Thomas (1963). *Joseph and his Brothers*, trans. H. T. Lowe-Porter, Secker and Warburg, London.

Middleton, John (1960). *Lugbara Religion*, Oxford University Press (for International African Institute), London.

Middleton, John (1963). The Yakan or Allah Water Cult among the Lugbara, *Journal of the Royal Anthropological Institute*, Vol. 93, pt. 1.

Nyerere, Julius K. (1966). *Freedom and Unity: Uhuru na Umoja*, London, Oxford University Press.

Sahlins, Marshall D. (1961). The Segmentary Lineage: An Organization of Predatory Expansion, *American Anthropologist*, Vol. 63, No. 2, Part 1, pp. 322–345.

Sharp, Lauriston (1958). "People without Politics", in Verne F. Ray (ed.). *Systems of Political Control and Bureaucracy*, American Ethnological Society, University of Washington Press, Seattle.

Southall, A. W. (1956). *Alur Society: A Study in Processes and Types of Domination*, Heffer, Cambridge.

Southall, A. W. (1968). Stateless Society, *Internation Encyclopaedia of the Social Sciences*, Vol. 15, *Macmillan, New York*, pp. 157–168.

Steward, Julian H. (1958). *Theory of Culture Change*, University of Illinois Press, Urbana.

Tait, David (Jack Goody, ed., 1961). The Konkomba of Northern Ghana, Oxford University Press (for International African Institute), London.

Turnbull, C. (1967). "The Ik: alias the Teuso", *Uganda Journal*, Vol. 31, No. 1, March, pp. 63–71.

Wagner, G. (1949). *The Bantu of North Kavirondo*, Vol. I, Oxford University Press.

Warner, W. L. (1937). *A Black Civilization: A Social Study of an Australian Tribe*, Harper, New York.

4

ETHNICITY IN SOUTHERN AFRICAN HISTORY

LEROY VAIL

Out of the crooked timber of humanity
no straight thing can ever be made.
Immanuel Kant

Interpretations

African political leaders, experiencing it as destructive to their ideals of national unity, denounce it passionately. Commentators on the Left, recognizing it as a block to the growth of appropriate class awareness, inveigh against it as a case of "false consciousness." Apologists for South African apartheid, welcoming it as an ally of continued white dominance, encourage it. Development theorists, perceiving it as a check to economic growth, deplore it. Journalists, judging it an adequate explanation for a myriad of otherwise puzzling events, deploy it mercilessly. Political scientists, intrigued by its continuing power, probe at it endlessly. If one disapproves of the phenomenon, "it" is "tribalism"; if one is less judgmental "it" is "ethnicity."

Ethnicity's emergence as a central concern for a wide range of students of African affairs is relatively recent, and its forceful intrusion upon the dominant nationalist paradigm of the 1950s and early 1960s was both unexpected and unwelcome.[1] At that time, it was accepted that Africans were organized naturally into "tribes," but, as nationalist movements in Africa were then apparently enjoying great success, most observers believed that parochial ethnic loyalties were merely cultural ghosts lingering on into the present, weakened anomalies from a fast receding past. As such, they were destined to disappear in the face of the social, economic and political changes that were everywhere at work. People from all sectors of the political spectrum believed in this vision. For those on the Right and in the Centre, "modernization" would do the job.

---

[1] As I was preparing to write this Introduction, I was fortunate to have made available to me a preliminary version of Crawford Young's magisterial summing up of the literature on "Class, ethnicity and nationalism," which has influenced my approach considerably. Young's stimulating and valuable essay was written for the Social Science Research Council, and it will be published in a future issue of *Cahier d'études africaines."* Two other studies which influenced my writing markedly are Anthony Giddens, *A Contemporary Critique of Historical Marxism* (Berkeley and Los Angeles, 1981), and Donald L. Horowitz, *Ethnic Groups in Conflict* (Berkeley and Los Angeles, 1985). The literature on ethnicity is immense and I have decided to eschew any attempt to produce a bibliographical essay. I shall attempt to write an interpretative overview.

Greater access to education, improved communications, and the shifting of people from the slumbering "traditional" rural sector of the economy to the vibrant "modern" industrial sector by the beneficent forces of economic growth guaranteed that ethnic loyalties would fade away. In their place would grow a new, nation-oriented consciousness which would underpin progressive "nation-building," especially if the new nation states could make good their promises of a better life for all their citizens. Africa would be a continent of new Switzerlands in which cultural divisions would be of little political importance.

For those on the Left, too, "modernization" was the key, although it was viewed from a somewhat different perspective. The breakdown of "traditional" societies by the forces of new, state-sponsored welfare socialism, with its expanded facilities in public education, medicine and agricultural programmes, would allow newly independent African states to "skip a stage" in the evolution of their societies towards socialism and to enter directly into that blessed condition. In effect, socialism would then provide the material base for a pan-ethnic class consciousness that would transcend, if not negate, cultural differences. Africa would be a continent of new Yugoslavias.

The general paradigm of "modernization," then, appealed to almost every political viewpoint. For almost every observer nationalism seemed progressive and laudable, while ethnicity – or, as it was usually termed, "tribalism" – was retrogressive and divisive.

Ethnicity, however, failed to cooperate with its many would-be pall-bearers. It soon became clear that African nationalist movements, ideologically shaped by the basically negative sentiments of anti-colonialism and with little substantive philosophical content

relevant to the day-to-day life or ordinary Africans living in post-colonial states, were simply unable to provide them with compelling intellectual, social, and political visions. Once the attainment of independence had made most of its anti-colonial message irrelevant, nationalist "thought" was transformed into a gloss for the manipulation of the institutions of the new nation-states on behalf of the interests of the ruling political parties in a succession of one party states.[2] Much state activity was devoted to the pursuit of variously defined forms of "economic development," but such development proved elusive and the much-desired economic Fruits of Independence generally failed to ripen. That growth which did occur, moreover, was usually to the benefit of the dominant political classes and possessed little popular appeal.

As a result of this quick reining in of nationalism's popular thrust within the bureaucratic structures of essentially artificial post-colonial states, ethnic or regional movements rooted in the colonial era had fresh life breathed into them and came to be seen as attractive alternatives to the dominant political parties with their demands for uncomplaining obedience from the governed. In effect, the revitalization of "tribalism" was structured into the one-party system by the very fact of that system's existence. Ethnicity became the home of the opposition in states where class consciousness was largely undeveloped. Ethnic particularism has consequently continued to bedevil efforts to "build nations" to the specifications of the ruling party for the past two decades or more. This hard political fact has called forth ever more systematic repression of dissent by those in control of the state, thus, in effect, strengthening the appeal of the ethnic alternative. Ethnicity's future, even in countries such as South Africa, where

---

[2] The situation is reflected in the fact that many political leaders felt the need to fabricate a "philosophy" of government in an attempt to compensate for the intellectual banality of the nationalist movements after independence. These "philosophies" generally had far greater appeal for well-intentioned non-nationals than for those dwelling within the particular countries for which they were composed.

industrialization has proceeded further than anywhere else on the continent, seems secure because it is likely to provide an important focal point for whatever opposition to the dominant political classes that might exist.

With its power to divide people politically, then, and with its sturdy resistance to erosion by the ideological forces of national or class consciousness, ethnicity came to demand close – albeit often very grudging – attention after decades of neglect. Its source and appeal needed reasonable explanations, and interpretations of it have ranged widely, reflecting its multidimensional nature.

The most prominent explanation – if only because of its widespread use – is the one that, despite the great frequency with which one encounters it in media coverage of Africa, is plainly the least satisfactory. In effect, this interpretation is a restatement of the old assumption that Africans are by nature "tribal" people and that "tribalism" is little more than an irrelevant anachronism, an atavistic residue deriving from the distant past of rural Africa. It should have evaporated with the passage of time, but, inexplicably, something went wrong, and it continues to refuse to obey the laws of social and political change. It thus remains able to motivate Africans to frequent actions of conflict and violence. Ethnic consciousness is, in this view, a form of collective irrationality.

The problems with this interpretation are clear. First, it is always dangerous to assume that people consistently act out of mass irrationality. People tend to act rationally, and there is no reason on the face of it to accept that Africans are exceptions. Second, this argument is, in effect, also a tautology with no analytical power, arguing as it does that Africans act "tribalistically" because they are naturally "tribal." Third, and most tellingly, empirical evidence shows clearly that ethnic consciousness is very much a new phenomenon, an ideological construct, usually of the twentieth century, and not an anachronistic cultural artifact from the past. As an offspring

of the changes associated with so-called "modernization", therefore, it is unlikely to be destroyed by the continuation of these same processes. For all these reasons, then, this interpretation must be discarded.

Other, more scholarly interpretations have been suggested to explain the origin and persistence of ethnicity in Africa. All these interpretations have two things in common. First, they derive mainly from the work of anthropologists, sociologists and, especially, political scientists, observers who have been primarily concerned with the situation in Africa at the time they actually studied it. This has meant that their interpretations have usually been concerned with ethnicity's role at the moment of observation and its potential for the future. As such, they usually give only brief attention to its history, presenting whatever history that might be uncovered as mere "background" to ethnicity's contemporary role.

Second, all these interpretations are also marked by the fact that they have evolved out of the nationalist paradigm dominant from the 1950s into the 1970s. They implicitly accept a basically evolutionary view of human history. In this view, the future ought to be better than the past, and "better" has been identified with improvements assumed to flow from an increase in political scale and the growth of national unity – in short, from "nation-building." As a consequence, most such analyses of ethnicity are concerned with the way it has traduced the promise of modernizing nationalism and are thus predisposed to negative judgments. Their emphasis, therefore, has been on ethnicity's role as a disrupter of the promising trends of secular nationalism that seemed to characterize African politics in the late 1950s and early 1960s and to promise a rosy future.

The intellectual range of these interpretations of ethnicity has been wide. One viewpoint encountered frequently – especially within Africa itself – is that ethnicity is primarily the result of a history of "divide-and-rule" tactics which colonial governments cannily employed. European anthropologists connived at such policies by specifying "tribes" culturally within the context of a uniquely colonial sociology, thereby giving the "tribe" a real, but specious, identity. The element of truth in this explanation has made it superficially attractive, especially as the South African government today actively uses both approaches in its Bantustan policies and in its stress on the uniqueness of "tribal" culture, patent efforts to promote political divisions among the country's African population.

Yet whatever its merits, it is an explanation clearly insufficient to explain the persistence of ethnic consciousness. This is so for several reasons. First, it fails to explain why, in a particular territory throughout which the colonial state employed roughly the same divide-and-rule policies, ethnic consciousness developed unevenly, strong among certain peoples but not among others, a situation common throughout Africa. Second, it tends to depict Africans as little more than either collaborating dupes or naive and gullible people, beguiled by clever colonial administrators and untrustworthy anthropologists, a situation which empirical evidence fails to corroborate. Finally, it does not explain how, three decades after the departure of the colonialists, "tribalism," or its close kin, "regionalism," lives on as strongly as ever in independent African states, the governments of which have been actively trying to suppress it, and why in some places it is growing up for the first time. The clever blandishments of subtle European administrators are clearly insufficient to explain either the origins of ethnic consciousness or its continuing appeal today.

A second interpretation, especially prominent in the 1950s and early 1960s, arose from the study of urban sociology, especially in the mining areas of Central Africa.[3] Intellectually, it was linked to the Dual Economy model of "modernization" theory, and it located its interpretation of the development of new ethnic consciousness in the experiences of rural people in industrial workplaces. As members of various cultural groups left their isolated rural areas and interacted with each other in industrial or urban locales, they formed stereotypes of themselves and others, and these stereotypes effectively highlighted and strengthened culturally defined distinctions amongst peoples. The tendency of employers to prefer certain ethnic groups for certain types of work and their conscious manipulation of ethnic differences to keep the workforce disunited resulted in competition between ethnic groups being built into the hierarchically structured workforce. In this view, ethnicity was a recent phenomenon of the modern urban workplace in which boundaries and distinctions between people had been built up. It was not a phenomenon of the rural areas, where people were assumed to live in accordance with prescriptive patterns derived from a "traditional" past and where they were largely isolated from peoples of differing cultures. As such, some scholars, as well as most African politicians of the time, assumed that the but recently formed ethnic identities were still malleable and that they would prove susceptible to an easy transformation into a national identity through processes of political mobilization associated with "nation-building," especially if the labour unions representing such workers could be coopted into the national political establishment.[4]

This interpretation is certainly valuable for its underscoring of the important point that ethnic stereotypes were indeed largely produced in work situations and in urban settings. Yet it too is unable to serve as a general explanation of ethnicity's origin or, especially, its

---

[3] Most notably, A.L. Epstein, *Politics in an Urban African Community* (Manchester, 1958), and J.C. Mitchell, *The Kalela Dance* (Manchester, 1958).

[4] For example, I. Wallerstein, "Ethnicity and national integration," *Cahiers d'études africaines*, 1 (1960), pp. 129–39.

persistence. First, by emphasizing the boundaries that the creation of ethnic stereotypes
among urban Africans produced, which, in
turn, created opposing notions of "them" and
"us", it overlooks the more substantive intellectual content contributed by African
intellectuals to the specification of concepts of
ethnic self-identity within those boundaries.
Positive views about one's history, the heroes
of one's ethnic past, and the manifestations of
one's culture, especially language, quite simply did not spring automatically from the work
situation or the urban centre, yet they have all
been central in defining ethnic identities and
ethnic ideologies.

Second, by stressing the essentially non-
rural nature of the growth of ethnic
stereotypes, this interpretation implicitly
accepts the notion that rural Africa was
preserved in some sort of "traditional" pickle,
antithetically opposed to "modern" industrial
Africa and largely untouched by the forces of
change associated with capitalist expansion
and urbanization. Such a view of the existence
of "two Africas" with but insubstantial linkages between them has by now been
convincingly discredited.[5] Quite simply, the
rural areas of southern and central Africa did
not remain unchanged in a brine of
"tradition", with meaningful change restricted
to areas of obvious economic growth.
Historical change affected the rural areas as
much as it did the industrial and urban areas.
More to the point, empirical evidence abundantly demonstrates that it is to the rural areas
that one must look for most of the intellectual
content of ethnic ideologies as they developed

during the twentieth century in response to
such change.

A third interpretation of the growth of
ethnicity is that it resulted from uneven development within African colonial territories.[6]
Certain people were able to do comparatively
well from the educational and employment
opportunities that colonial capitalism
presented unevenly, with aspirant petty bourgeois groups able to establish themselves in
some areas but not in others. When it became
clear that the colonial era was nearing its end,
these petty bourgeois groups mobilized
support along ethnic lines so that they would
be in a position to maximize their opportunities for access to resources and power after
independence. This situation led in turn to the
continuation of specifically ethnic politics in
many countries of Africa, resulting in a rash of
coups d'état and civil wars as ethnic fragments
of the national petty bourgeoisie competed for
their own advantage. From this perspective,
ethnicity tends to be seen instrumentally, as
little more than an ideological mask employed
by ambitious members of upwardly-aspiring
groups as a way of papering over growing class
divisions within their ethnic group so as to
secure their own narrow interests through
demagoguery and mystification. Ethnicity,
then, when ordinary people embrace it, is the
very epitome of "false consciousness." . . .

Finally, deriving from a Durkheimian
notion of the importance of the role of the
"community," or Gemeinschaft, there is the
"primordialist" interpretation of ethnicity, an
interpretation which now appears to be in the
ascendancy amongst many scholars.[7] Its

---

[5] As in R. Palmer and N. Parsons, eds., *The Roots of Rural Poverty in South and Central Africa* (Berkeley and Los
Angeles, 1977), *passim*.
[6] This point was developed at an early point of study in J.S. Coleman, *Nigeria: Background to Nationalism* (Berkeley
and Los Angeles, 1958) and in R. Lemarchand, *Political Awakening in the Congo* (Berkeley and Los Angeles, 1964).
Interest in it has been stimulated more recently by the publication of such influential books as M. Hechter, *Internal
Colonialism* (Berkeley and Los Angeles, 1975) and T. Nairn, *The Break-up of Britain: Crisis and Neo-Nationalism*
(London, 1977).
[7] As, for example, in Horowitz, *Ethnic Groups in Conflict, passim* and A. Giddens, *The Nation-State and Violence*
(Berkeley and Los Angeles, 1985), *passim*, but especially pp. 212–221. See also J.F. Stack, Jr., ed., *The Primordial
Challenge: Ethnicity in the Contemporary World* (Westport, CT, 1986).

attraction lies in its serious attempt to answer the crucial question as to why the ethnic message possesses such strong appeal. This interpretation seeks the explanation in the realm of psychology. Africans, it is argued, were badly affected by the disruptive socio-economic and political changes of the late nineteenth and twentieth centuries. Pre-capitalist and pre-colonial hierarchies and elements of order in social life were undermined by the growth of capitalist relations and the impact of colonialism, thereby depriving people of social and psychological security. As a result, in a hostile world they have instead sought security through the invocation of a lost past of firm values as a way of recreating a life in which they can achieve emotional and, even, perhaps, physical safety. Ethnic identity provides a comforting sense of brotherhood in a world tending towards social atomization and rootlessness. Ethnic leaders represent and embody the unity of the cultural group. In this view, ethnicity is a kind of romantic rejection of the present. Enduring rather as religious fundamentalism or faith healing do in western societies, it is a reaction to the sterility of modern positivism and has become something akin to a civil religion with great emotional appeal.

Once again, this argument is attractive, particularly as the ethnic message, once established amongst people, does appear to be a part of the natural order of the universe. It categorizes people in accordance with inevitable, largely unselfconscious ascription: people belong to tribe X because they were born in tribe X and are, regardless of personal choice, characterized by the cultural traits of tribe X. Thus one is a member of a "tribe" not by choice, but by destiny, and one thus partakes of a set of "proper" customs.

Yet there are three serious problems with this interpretation. First, the mere appeal of, or belief in, a generalized idyllic past and the presumed unity of the ethnic group seem insufficiently definite to explain the relevance to people in specific historical situations of the statements that comprise constructed ethnic ideologies. Why have vague cultural statements about language or a common history or a hero from the past succeeded in "comforting" people or mobilizing them? Does ethnicity appeal because it is intrinsically "primordial," or is it constructed as "primordial" in its discourse to render it more generally appealing? What specific messages within the ethnic ideology actually appeal the most and to whom? And why? In short, the stress upon the "primordial" aspect of ethnicity tends to overlook both the actual intellectual content of the message, which can vary from group to group, and its varying appeal among different members of the same ethnic group.

Second, by stressing the backward-looking, "primordial" aspect of ethnicity, this interpretation fails to answer the central empirical question of how the most backward-looking ethnic ideologies, with their glorification of long-dead heroes and their delight in "traditional values," have been able at the same time to contain within them a powerful acceptance of western education and skills and a willingness to "change with the times." The emphasis on the primordial past does not take into account ethnicity's forward-looking aspect which, as commentators have frequently observed, gives it a Janus-like appearance. This is so, I suggest, largely because the role of class actors in creating and shaping ethnic ideologies has been largely overlooked. It is the direct appeal of fresh ideas and institutions to certain new classes that appeared in twentieth century Africa that has been translated into the progressive face of ethnic identity. The psychological appeal of primordialism and the concern for specific present-day interests of specific classes perhaps seem unlikely bed-fellows, but they are real ones nonetheless and must be explained.

Third, and directly related to the first two problems, the emphasis upon a comforting past projects upon African people's ideas an unconvincing stasis. It is simply impossible to accept that Africans, living through some of the most rapid changes that any people have lived through in all human history, have attached themselves blindly, like so many limpets, to a vision of the past that has little relevance to the present and the future just because it is "comfortable." As an interpretation, the "primordialist" explanation of ethnicity, on its own, is simply too ahistorical and non-specific to convince. In analyzing ethnicity's real appeal one must instead try to relate its actual assumptions about the past to the current historical reality of those accepting them.

A History

Thus far historians have not devoted much attention to the history of ethnicity and ethnic ideologies in southern Africa. This is somewhat puzzling, especially as many have been aware for some time that ethnicity is not a natural cultural residue but a consciously crafted ideological creation.[8] It is likely that the explanation for this relative neglect lies in the fact that historians were, like other scholars, caught up in the nationalist paradigm that dominated the entire range of African studies in the 1950s and 1960s. They thus saw studies of the growth of ethnic consciousness as parochial, misconceived, and largely irrelevant to their main concerns at that time: the recovery of Africa's pre-colonial past and the exploration of the growth of anti-colonial resistance and its flowering into progressive nationalism. In the optimistic nation-building

mood of the time, studies of ethnicity were also extremely unpopular with African opinion-makers, embarrassing even to mention, and they exerted pressure against studies that might further divisiveness in the new nation states they thought they were "building." Thus, the history of ethnic identities largely remained to be written. . . .

The event which served as the catalyst for the melding of diverse peoples into such a unit as southern Africa, a region extending from Namibia to Mozambique, was the discovery of gold on the Witwatersrand in 1886. This initiated the building of Africa's single most potent economic force and attracted capital investment to other, less important focuses of investment, such as the copper mines of Zaire and Zambia, the farms and ranches of Zimbabwe, and the plantations of central Mozambique and southern Malawi. The links that were rapidly constructed to weld together the various territories of the region – and their societies – included ties of finance, trade, political influence, and, especially, migrant labour.

Yet the creation of such ties was necessarily differential, and great variation is to be found from one area to another within the region. In some places, such as Lesotho, the Transkei, southern Mozambique, northern Malawi, and western Zambia, links with the Rand's mines were direct and obvious: large-scale and persistent male labour migrancy organized through the Witwatersrand Native Labour Association demonstrated clearly the dependence of these regions. In other places, such as the Zambian and Zairian Copperbelts, central Mozambique, and southern Malawi,

---

[8] Iliffe's *A Modern History of Tanganyika* (Cambridge, 1979) contains much relevant material regarding the history of ethnicity in Tanganyika. For the Afrikaners of South Africa, one should see D. Moodie, *The Rise of Afrikanerdom: Power, Apartheid and the Afrikaner Civil Religion* (Berkeley and Los Angeles, 1975); H. Adam and H. Giliomee, *Ethnic Power Mobilized* (New Haven 1979); and D. O'Meara, *Volkskapitalisme: Class, Capital and Ideology in the Development of Afrikaner Nationalism*, 1934–1938 (Cambridge, 1983). This point has been made often for European nationalism, in such important studies as Barrington Moore's *Social Origins of Dictatorship and Democracy: Lord and Peasant in the Making of the Modern World* (Harmondsworth, 1967).

local capitalist interests were able to dominate and the influence of the Rand was less obvious and less direct. In still other locales, such as parts of central Malawi, southern Zambia, and parts of Zaire and Swaziland, successful peasant production permitted local Africans to avoid both long-distance labour migrancy and working for local entrepreneurs. Nonetheless, the Rand's influence was everywhere present, if only as a model of labour relations and a distant, but powerful, economic presence. Although certainly uneven, the Rand's influence knitted the region's territories together.

As a consequence of the growth of capitalist relations of production both on the Rand itself in the 1890s and in other centres of capitalist endeavour that were established throughout the region shortly afterwards, the people of virtually all its societies experienced pervasive social, economic, and political change. The range of such change was broad, and many of the changes were clearly disadvantageous to the people affected. The capitalist enterprises of the region were all highly labour-intensive, requiring large and constant supplies of cheap African labour. To push Africans into the service of these enterprises, colonial governments imposed taxes, which in many areas could be paid only through men leaving their homes to participate in labour migrancy. These taxes were imposed during, or immediately after, a series of ecological disasters during the 1890s and the early 1900s that greatly weakened the fabric of local African societies. These disasters included drought, locusts and famine, but perhaps the key one was the great rinderpest epidemic of the mid-1890s, which killed livestock through the whole of southern Africa. Because livestock was widely reckoned as the embodiment of wealth, rinderpest's impact effectively constituted a gigantic mass bankruptcy for many societies. Moreover, as the exchange of cattle for women through the system of bridewealth (*lobola*) payments was the principal way in which many of the region's societies regulated

marriage and the establishment of new families, it became socially necessary to work for money, using it either to restock the herds or as a substitute for cattle in the making of bridewealth payments.

Later, widespread alienation of African land, the establishment of overcrowded "native reserves," and the entrenchment of patterns of labour migrancy resulted in both impoverished villages and strained relationships within divided families. The labour demands of mines, plantations, and industries, coupled with governmental tax and land policies and the rising needs of people to purchase discretionary goods, pressed men out of the rural areas as workers, especially after the outbreak of World War I in 1914. It should be stressed that this process of rural transformation was not restricted to black Africans. The commercialization of agriculture in large areas of South Africa also undermined an Afrikaner society that had hitherto been characterized by paternalistic relations of clientage between Afrikaner grandees and poor Afrikaner tenants. This commercialization forced from the land white Afrikaners who had long had direct access to it. They moved into the growing cities of South Africa, where, because of their lack of education or marketable skills, they came to constitute a "poor white" problem of startling dimensions.

What was common for all the region's peoples – blacks and whites alike – was that many of them were gradually losing control over their lives as control over that most basic factor of production, the land, slipped from their grasp. No longer were rural communities – whether black or white – able to exist autonomously, beyond the reach of capitalism and colonial administration. At the same time that this rural transformation was occurring, the region's mixed-race groups, such as the "Cape Coloureds" of South Africa and the Luso-Africans of Mozambique, were suffering an erosion of their positions. Earlier, through possession of language and other skills, they had enjoyed relatively secure social and economic positions as intermediaries between whites and blacks. After the 1890s, however, these positions were successfully challenged by poor Afrikaners in South Africa and immigrant Portuguese whites in Mozambique, both of which groups increasingly benefited from the support of racist state institutions. Thus they, like blacks and some white Afrikaners, were also caught in a process of declining control over their lives and destinies.

People of all these groups fought against the erosion of their positions. For many involved in this struggle land, and access to land, came to stand at the very centre of their consciousness, being fixed there not only at the beginning of the process of the undermining of rural autonomy, but also in succeeding decades. For white Afrikaners, land ownership was also important, kept alive as the ideal Afrikaner way of life even among the poor whites of the cities and towns.

For Africans, however, access to land remained a central issue for a more pressing reason. This was because, from the very start of the industrialization process, employers and government officials alike were determined to create a system in which unskilled workers would oscillate from the rural villages to work sites and then back to the villages and in which skilled positions would be held by whites. In this way, their wives and children would remain permanently behind in the rural areas, while the men would dwell in bachelor dormitories at the work sites for the duration of their contracts. Such a system had many advantages for both capitalist entrepreneurs and European administrators. For the employers it helped keep the working class fragmented and unorganized, and it allowed them to pay wages that were less than what would have had to be paid if the whole of a worker's family migrated and settled permanently as fully proletarianized people. For the officials it assured that there would be at least some money brought into the rural areas to help sustain village life there. In some cases, moreover, the migrant

labour system also enabled governments to collect capitation fees for each worker recruited.

Migrant labour had less appeal for the workers themselves, but they had little choice in the matter. The need for money and the official pressures upon the men to work as migrants on contract, coupled with the establishment of effective recruiting agencies, resulted in the rapid institutionalization of the system of oscillating migrant labour as the standard mode of labour mobilization. But because the system was one in which workers were to move back and forth, even rural areas that were little more than unproductive rural slums necessarily remained of central concern for the migrants. On the one hand, they could not remain at home to supervise life in the village and oversee their wives and children. On the other hand, they could not abandon their rural homes. Laws prevented the relocation of families to work sites and strictly regulated the length of contracts a worker could assume. Thus, it was in the rural areas that the workers' long-term interests necessarily lay, for they would eventually return there when their working life was over. Even while absent for decades from the rural areas, then, the workers' concerns typically remained sharply focused on what was occurring at home. This situation could not but produce profound apprehensions in the migrants, and the capitalist era for them was – and still is – truly an age of anxiety.

While the majority of people were affected adversely by the changes produced by industrialization and capital investment, not everyone suffered. Indeed, the establishment of capitalist enterprises and colonial administrations provided a range of opportunities that many whites and some Africans could seize. Certain people were able to respond to the growing markets for produce, becoming peasant producers or even small-scale farmers, while in South Africa, Afrikaner agriculturalists on medium-sized and large farms prospered. Others, especially those able to gain an education or useful skills, were able to take up places in the social interstices that the changing economy opened up, becoming relatively well-rewarded teachers, ministers of religion, artisans, government clerks, or even small businessmen. In effect, then, the economic changes that followed on the establishment of the Rand's gold industry and the binding together of the far-flung areas of southern and central Africa into a regional economic unit were accompanied by a rapid and increasingly sharp differentiation of the region's peoples into more favoured and less favoured societies and of the societies themselves into more favoured and less favoured classes-in-the-making.

Such rapid social and economic change eroded earlier political relationships based on clientage both within and outside of lineages, social patterns, and religious beliefs, all of which had characterized societies during the nineteenth century. This erosion in turn opened the way for new forms of consciousness throughout the region. Worker consciousness amongst both whites and blacks appeared spasmodically in situations of localized stress on the work site. Evidence of such class solidarity was shown at times of rapid socio-economic change, appearing in such events as the Rand Rebellion of 1922, the strike of copper miners on the Zambian Copperbelt in 1935, and the African mineworkers' strike of 1946 on the Witwatersrand gold mines. But class consciousness remained exceptional for as long as the working class was weak and fragmented and difficult to infuse with a sense of community.

New types of popular religious consciousness also appeared in the form of mainline Christian churches as well as separatist churches such as Watch Tower and a myriad of Zionist sects, and these shaped their adherents' evolving new self-identities. And among the educated clerks, teachers, clerics, and businessmen who emerged in the black, "coloured" and mixed race communities a petty bourgeois consciousness, with an accept-

ance of Victorian notions of respectability, progress and individual uplift through hard work, gained prominence.

One of the most far-reaching and important of these new forms of consciousness was a new ethnic – or tribal – consciousness that could and did encapsulate other forms of consciousness. Ethnicity could coexist with other types of consciousness without apparent unease because it was cultural and hence based on involuntary ascription, not on personal choice. People were members of a particular ethnic group whether they liked it or not. It was simply a fact of existence. As such, ethnic identity could inhere in both petty bourgeois and worker, in both peasant farmer and striving politician.

A Model

. . . The creation of ethnicity as an ideological statement of popular appeal in the context of profound social, economic and political change in southern Africa was the result of the differential conjunction of various historical forces and phenomena. It is the very unevenness of their co-appearance and dynamic interaction that accounts for the unevenness of ethnic consciousness in the region. One may discern three such variables in the creation and implanting of the ethnic message. First, as was the case in the creation of such ideologies elsewhere, for example in nineteenth century European nationalism, it was essential to have a group of intellectuals involved in formulating it – a group of culture brokers. Second, there was the widespread use of African intermediaries to administer the subordinate peoples, a system usually summed up in the phrase "indirect rule," and this served to define the boundaries and texture of the new ideologies. Third, ordinary people had a real need for so-called "traditional values" at a time of rapid social change, thus opening the way for the wide acceptance of the new ideologies. What emerges perhaps most clearly from these studies is the fact that intellectuals carefully crafted their ethnic ideologies in order to define the cultural characteristics of members of various ethnic groups. . . .

The role of missionaries was especially crucial in at least one – and sometimes all – of three ways, and it is evident that their influence upon the development of African history in the twentieth century has been far greater than they have been given credit for over the past two decades. First, missionaries themselves were often instrumental in providing the cultural symbols that could be organized into a cultural identity, especially a written language and a researched written history. Samuel Johnson long ago recognized that "languages are the pedigree of nations," and missionaries accepted this dictum wholeheartedly. They had the skills to reduce hitherto unwritten languages to written forms, thereby delivering the pedigrees that the new "tribes" required for acceptance. It was the missionaries who chose what the "proper" form of the language would be, thus serving both to further unity and to produce divisions by establishing firm boundaries.[9]

In addition to creating written languages, missionaries were instrumental in creating cultural identities through their specification of "custom" and "tradition" and by writing "tribal" histories. Once these elements of culture were in place and available to be used as the cultural base of a distinct new, ascriptive ethnic identity, it could replace older organizing principles that depended upon voluntary clientage and loyalty and which, as such, showed great plasticity. Thus firm, non-porous and relatively inelastic ethnic boundaries, many of which were highly arbitrary, came to be constructed and were then strengthened by the growth of stereotypes of "the other".

Second, and of considerable practical importance, European missionaries, assuming that Africans properly belonged to "tribes," incorporated into the curricula of their mission schools the lesson that the pupils had clear ethnic identities, backing up this lesson with studies of language and "tribal custom" in the vernacular. Thus, mission education socialized the young into accepting a tribal membership, and to be a member of a "tribe" became "modern" and fashionable through its close association with education.

Third, and finally, missionaries educated local Africans who then themselves served as the most important force in shaping the new ethnic ideologies. These people – usually men – were keenly aware of the forces that were pulling apart their societies and, with the examples of nationalism in Europe derived from their own mission education before them, they sought to craft similar local movements as a means of countering these problems. Despite their own western-style education, they realized that such a construct would best be understood and accepted if it were put in a cultural idiom easily accessible to the people. Thus, in formulating their new ideologies, they looked to the local area's past for possible raw material for their new intellectual bricolage.[10] Like their European predecessors during the initial stages of nineteenth century nationalism, they "rediscovered" the "true values" of their people and so defined the "ethnic soul." Their cultural strongbox was the "customs" and "traditions" of the people, identification with which they saw as giving an automatic, ascriptive cultural unity to "their" people as they

---

[9]   For an interesting, although not wholly convincing, assessment of the central role of language in the building of nationalism, see B. Anderson, *Imagined Communities: Reflections on the Origin and Spread of Nationalism* (London, 1983).
[10]   It should be noted that intellectuals discussed in the chapters of this volume are all literate intellectuals. The nature of the evidence makes it difficult to ascertain the nature of the thought and work of non-literate intellectuals, yet it should be kept in mind that such non-literate intellectuals have indeed worked to further ethnic ideologies through oral genres. This whole topic is the subject of a forthcoming study by L. Vail and L. White.

confronted the challenge of colonialism and the impact of industrialization. Several studies have been made which demonstrate the role of educated people as key actors in the creation of such ideology.

In those societies where missionaries did not work, or where they did work but did not introduce education along western lines, or where African intellectuals emerged only at a late period or not at all, the development of ethnic ideologies was either stalled or never occurred. The unevenness of education in southern Africa largely determined the unevenness of the development of ethnic consciousness. In many locales it is only today, after the post-independence expansion of education and the emergence of local intellectuals, that the process of creating such ethnic ideologies and "forging traditions" has emulated what happened earlier in other societies.

It was not sufficient, however, that there should be local intellectuals – white or black – interested in the recovery of the ethnic past. A second, more instrumental factor was also required. All of southern Africa was under direct European administration of various types, and by the period after World War I, virtually all administrations were engaged in implementing systems of indirect rule, using African "traditional" authorities as intermediaries between the white administration and the ruled. Thus, if language in the form of written discourse was central in specifying the forms of culture, indirect rule provided the institutional framework for articulating these forms. Communications between the European administrators and subordinate Africans was distinctly tribal in its tone and content. Africans were talked to in terms deemed suitable, and these terms were ethnic. In the cases of the "Cape Coloureds" and the Luso-Africans of Mozambique, and, to some extent, the Afrikaners, for whom the conven-

tions of indirect rule were not suitable, they were simply denied representation.

There were several reasons for the European policy of indirect rule. First, there was the realization that the use of so-called "traditional" African leaders could be markedly less expensive than the employment of expensive European officials. Second, administrators assumed that Africans were naturally "tribal" people. If the natural ethnic units could be strengthened, it would help ensure their continuation as discrete "tribal" groups and prevent the emergence of "de-tribalized" Africans of whom whites were deeply suspicious. This, in turn, would slow the emergence of any potentially dangerous territory-wide political consciousness that might develop. The remarks of a British War Office official in 1917 reflect these divide-and-rule tactics:

> [The] spirit of nationality, or perhaps it would be more correct to say, of tribe, should be cultivated and nowhere can this be done with better chance of success than in British East Africa and Uganda, where there are numerous tribes ethnographically quite distinct from one another. It is suggested that in each ethnographically distinct district the schools should, as far as possible, form integral parts of the tribe and centres of folk-lore and tradition. . . .
>
> . . . a method may also be found whereby the efforts of missionaries may also assist in the cultivation of national spirit. This it seems might be done by allowing only one denomination to work in each demographic area and by not allowing the same denomination to work in two adjacent areas.[11]

Third, by the end of World War I it was becoming increasingly evident that the chronic absence of men from rural societies was producing great social stresses. The administrators became convinced that the

---

[11] Malawi National Archives, GOA 2/4/12, "Mohammadanism and Ethiopianism", Circular letter, Lt. Col. French to Gov. Smith, 7 Aug. 1917.

rural disintegration occurring before their eyes could be slowed, if not stopped, by the encouragement of "traditional authorities" to use "traditional sanctions" in exercising control over the rural areas to counter the forces of social decay.

This acceptance of indirect rule by European administrations obviously gave opportunities to African political authorities to augment their personal power. More importantly, I suggest, it gave opportunities to the intellectuals of the areas concerned – both European missionaries and African members of the educated petty bourgeoisie – to implement their ideological programmes through alliances with the newly recognized chiefs. In this way the cultural ideals contained in their new ideologies could be at least partially actualized in the day-to-day workings of African administrations under indirect rule. Ethnic identity, thus, came to be specified not only by the written histories, grammars, and accounts of "traditional customs" produced by local culture brokers, but also – and in many respects, far more importantly – by the actual operation of the administrative mechanisms of indirect rule. This aspect of the development of ethnic identity was the consequence of the dynamic interaction of African initiative with the expectations of European administrators and forward-looking missionaries. It should be remembered, however, that the subordinate peoples did not have a free hand in their work as they had to operate within the severe constraints imposed by racist administrators who were ever alert to check initiatives deemed either unseemly or dangerous.

The presence of intellectuals, the socialization of ethnic ideas through mission schools and through the actual operation of administrative systems under indirect rule to strengthen "tribal" rule were, however, by themselves inadequate to produce a broad acceptance of an ethnic ideology. The ideology itself needed a raison d'être and an appeal, and it was this appeal that constitutes the third factor in our model of the growth of ethnicity in southern Africa.

The ideologies of nationalism have often been described as "Janus-like." They are in one aspect profoundly reactionary, looking backwards to a Golden Past: they concentrate upon its heroes, its historical successes, and its unsullied cultural purity, and are decked out with the mythic "rediscovered" social values of that past. In Africa, the explicit association of such ethnic ideologies with chiefs and headmen whose position was often firmly rooted in the past was an additional factor in accentuating the backward-looking face of ethnicity. Yet these ideologies were also clearly products of the present, concerned with current conditions, and they typically exhibited a forward-looking concern for the future. Nationalism – and tribalism – have thus appeared uncertain and ambiguous to many observers.

Yet when one looks closely at the situation in southern Africa, one comes to realize that the ethnic message's backward-looking aspects and its forward-looking concerns have been in no way contradictory. The emphases on past values, "rediscovered" traditions, and chiefly authority were truly conservative – that is, they were calculated to conserve a way of life that was in the process of being rapidly undermined by the forces of capitalism and colonialism. Forward-looking members of the petty bourgeoisie and migrant workers alike attempted to shore up their societies and their own positions in them by embracing ethnicity and accepting tribal identities.

Ethnicity appealed to the petty bourgeoisie because its forward-looking aspects ensured them a leadership role in the newly defined "tribe" as the well-informed interpreters of "tribal tradition." Their position as allies of chiefs further legitimized their role, blunting consciousness of the class divisions that were then appearing in local societies. In this situation, it was generally accepted that they also had a duty to improve their own social and economic positions "for the good of the tribe."

Far more importantly, ethnicity appealed strongly to ordinary African men, not primarily because it gave them a sense of psychological comfort, as the primordialist interpretation argues, but because it aided them in bringing a measure of control to the difficult situations in which they found themselves in their day-to-day life. The word "control" is crucial. It was the element of control embedded in tribal ideologies that especially appealed to migrant workers, removed from their land and families and working in far distant places. The new ideologies stressed the historical integrity of the tribe and its land and, especially, the sanctity of the family and its right to land.[12] Land stood at the very centre of ethnic ideologies.

The place of women was also a central issue dealt with in ethnic ideologies. In the early decades of the century bridewealth steadily inflated in value, and women thus represented a greater "investment" by men in cattle or money. With most men absent as migrant labourers, women were also becoming more important to the day-to-day survival of the family through their work on the land. Yet such valuable women naturally often sought to act independently, even to the extent of seeking divorces or leaving the rural areas illegally to move to industrial and urban areas. This produced acute conflict between the genders. Therefore an emphasis on the need to control women and a stress on the protection of the integrity of the family came to be intrinsic to both ethnic ideologies and the actual institutional practices of indirect rule. Ethnicity's appeal was strongest for men, then, and the Tswana proverb to the effect that "women have no tribe" had a real – if unintended – element of truth in it.

Ethnic ideologies helped to provide the control necessary to minimize migrants' natural anxieties about what occurred at home. In the system of indirect rule, the chiefs were of central importance. It was they, with their new official histories, their new censuses and lists, their new courts and records, all of which employed for the first time that most fundamentally powerful invention, writing, who were now able to exercise a greatly increased degree of surveillance over both women and land in the absence of the men. It was they who brought into daily practice those "rediscovered traditions" which emphasized control in the name of "custom." The old dictum that "all politics is local" was especially valid throughout southern Africa. African men and their lineages accepted that it was in their essential interest to support the new structures of chiefs, their courts, and their educated petty bourgeois spokesmen and agents. It was also for this reason that men, when returning at the end of their contracts from the mines or farms or plantations, gave chiefs the gifts that constituted one of their most important sources of income. The good chief was a proxy who protected the interests of the migrant workers and, for that, they were ready – if not eager – to reward him materially. In effect, the bureaucratized chief of the newly constituted "tribe" had replaced the lineage head or independent patron of earlier times, and the old language of kinship came to be employed as metaphor to sustain and legitimize this new, obviously non-kinship relationship.[13]

It was for very real reasons of exercising at least a measure of control over land and women, thereby bringing at least a measure of peace to their minds, that African men welcomed the new ethnic ideologies which involved augmenting powers of chiefs in a

---

[12] M. Chanock, *Law, Custom and Social Order: The Colonial Experience in Malawi and Zambia* (Cambridge, 1985), is an important study that goes far in exploring the role of the perceived need to control women in the development of concepts of law during the colonial period.

[13] The relevance of the language of kinship ties to the development of ethnic identity is explored, within a basically primordialist interpretation, in Horowtiz, *Ethnic Groups in Conflict*, pp. 55–92.

situation of rapid social decay. Ethnicity, insofar as it was a mechanism of such control, may be interpreted, then, as a form of popular male resistance to the forces that were reshaping African lives throughout southern Africa. It was for this reason also that the appeal of ethnic ideologies was strongest amongst those who were migrant labourers. The ethnic identity that was rooted in the realities of the countryside was, rather incidentally, strengthened in the workplace, where migrants found themselves in the company of, and often in competition with, workers from other cultural groups, a situation which generated sets of largely negative ethnic stereotypes.

Men came to think of themselves as belonging to particular ethnic groups, then, not because they especially disliked their fellow workers, nor because being a member of the group made them feel good, but rather because the ethnic apparatus of the rural area – the chiefs, "traditional" courts, petty bourgeois intellectuals, and the systematized "traditional" values of the "tribe" as embodied in the ethnic ideology – all worked to preserve the very substantial interests which these men had in their home areas. Without ethnicity – or tribalism – the migrants would have been less able to exercise the control that was necessary for them to assure the continuation of their positions in rural societies and their ultimate retirement in their home areas.

In those situations in which labour migrancy was not a pressing reality (the Afrikaners, the "Cape Coloureds," the Luso-Africans of Mozambique and, to a lesser extent, contemporary Swaziland and Ciskei) . . . or in areas from which men did not emigrate in large numbers, such as southern Zambia and central Malawi, the ethnic message has clearly had less popular appeal, reaching no further than the petty bourgeoisie

in most cases. In the case of the Afrikaners, effective class alliances between the bourgeois elements of society and the "poor whites" were brought into being only in the 1940s and afterwards. In the case of the "Cape Coloureds" and the Mozambican Luso-Africans – and possibly Swaziland and the Ciskei – the gaps between well-off and poor were too great to be easily overcome by appeals to ethnicity. In these situations, class identity – or at least class tension – has tended to overshadow ethnicity.

The Situation Today

For large areas of southern Africa, independence came in the 1960s and 1970s. But the condition which stretches basic economic, familial and welfare concerns between rural residence and work site endures down to the present. Migrant labour is still a dominant form of labour mobilization throughout the region, and the mental attitudes intrinsic to it continue. Even in situations where men have been permanently resident in the urban areas with their families for decades, these attitudes are widely found. This is so not because Africans are inherently rural people or are in close harmony with Nature, but because housing and living expenses are far lower in the rural areas than they are in urban areas. This lower cost of living serves as a constant reason for those dwelling in urban locales to keep the rural areas always in mind and to view their urban sojourn as only temporary.[14] Thus, because at the end of one's period of employment retirement benefits are usually given in the form of a single lump sum of money rather than in monthly payments, if they are given at all, a person – whether unskilled migrant or educated white collar worker – has little choice but to return

---

[14]   In a recent survey the author conducted among women dwelling in the squatter locations around Lusaka, Zambia, not a single woman interviewed admitted a preference for the urban environment, and all said they looked forward to returning "home" in the future because of the lower cost of living and greater tranquillity there.

"home" to live out the rest of his days, spending as little money as possible.

The preoccupation with one's connection to the land has been overwhelming, with virtually everyone either possessing a piece of land in actuality or desiring it in his or her fantasies. This continuing fixation on land, I suggest, has resulted from decades of the existence of an oscillating workforce that has only partially proletarianized workers and from the failure to establish the sort of welfare measures that would support a fully urbanized population after retirement. The concern for land as an ultimate fall-back means of survival is clearly an economic concern, then, and, in the circumstances, it is quite understandable. Even in South Africa, the most industrialized of all the countries of the region and one in which complete proletarianization on a substantial scale in secondary and tertiary industry has existed at least since the 1940s, lack of adequate welfare and retirement measures keeps alive deep concerns about access to land. Thus the African National Congress still finds that to contend publicly that one of the fundamental roots of the political conflict between black and white in South Africa is the Native Land Act of 1913, and to talk about a land reform that would give dispossessed blacks renewed access to land, have great appeal to their constituency.

Added to this economic concern is the fact that the nation states that have appeared since the 1960s have suffered profoundly from economic weakness, a weakness which has grown more serious with each passing year. Quite naturally, this has had a negative effect on the possibility of the creation of broad loyalty to the nation state itself. The nationalist message before and immediately after the end of colonialism was that the new dispensation would result in economic improvements and much increased welfare benefits. Unfortunately, this progress has not occurred, and instead the nation state's administrative structures have faltered and shrivelled.

There are thus further economic reasons

why sentiments which would be described as "nationalist" do not converge with citizenship in a new nation state, as it has come to be identified as at least the occasion, and sometimes as the cause, of a declining standard of living for the majority of people. People perhaps accept that they are citizens of the country in which they live, but this acceptance of civil status does not produce the same loyalty as does their ethnic identity. There has therefore been an increased concern with ethnic identities over the past two decades, and with it has come a great acceleration in the "rediscovery" of culture for more and more ethnic groups.

For economic reasons, therefore, as well as for reasons of psychological satisfaction, it seems clear that ethnic loyalties will continue in southern Africa for the foreseeable future. The exact forms of future ethnic identities are still cloudy, largely because conditions related to certain variables have changed since the development of ethnic consciousness in the colonial period, a process which has for the most part provided the model used in this volume. Education, for example, is now almost wholly under the control of the nation state, and, hence, will not be as easily employed to bring about acceptance of specific ethnic identities among children. In some countries – such as Malawi and Swaziland – the chiefs remain as influential figures in the rural areas. In others, such as Zambia, the chiefs remain, but most of their power has been taken from them. In yet others, such as Mozambique, chiefs have been abolished totally. Therefore it is likely that the symbols of ethnicity will vary from place to place and from country to country depending on the nature of local government and the way the state communicates with ordinary people.

Furthermore, the potential culture brokers are far more numerous now than sixty years ago, and they have been exposed to a far wider variety of thought, usually not associated with missions. This means that while the backward-looking aspects of future ethnic phenomena – concern for the glories of past history, culture heroes, the central importance of language, and the like – will remain pretty much the same as for examples in the past, the forward-looking aspect of the Janus of ethnicity has the potential of wide variation across the political spectrum. In contemporary Zambia, for example, a main focus of ethnic identity for the Bemba-speaking people who see themselves cut off from state power is the predominantly Bemba miners' union.

The unevenness of development that has marked southern Africa since 1886 shows no sign of ceasing now. Therefore it is likely that the content of the ethnic message itself will continue to vary from people to people, as the culture brokers craft messages that will resonate with their own clienteles. For the serious student of political history in the region, then, it will not be adequate to approach ethnicity, or "tribalism," as if all examples were essentially the same. Concern with the content of the message will be of ever greater importance if we are to understand it.

Finally, as ethnicity and parochial loyalties within the borders of nation states are likely to continue, it is important to cease approaching them from the perspective of the nation state itself. Ignoring them as embarrassing epiphe-nomena that should have long ago disappeared will do no good. Condemning them as "reactionary" or "divisive" will accomplish very little. Instead, granted that it is virtually certain that the nation states of southern Africa are going to continue as institutionalized governing states in tension with those whom they govern, it will be necessary for the region's politicians and scholars alike to work towards accommodating ethnicity within these nation states.[15] States like Lesotho and Botswana, where the nation state and ethnicity are largely coterminous, are exceptional. Multi-ethnic states like Mozambique and Zaire, Zambia and, most crucial of all, South Africa are typical. The western model of the nation state which sees it as identical with the cultural nation itself simply does not obtain in such situations and to insist upon its superior claims to legitimacy and loyalty is simply myopic. Instead, accepting that ethnicity does exist as a potent force, Africans will have to produce political solutions derived from African experience to solve African problems, and this is clearly of great importance in the evolving situation in South Africa, the political and economic centre of the region.

---

[15]   This point is developed in Horowitz, *Ethnic Groups in Conflict*, pp. 563–580, in a rather interesting and realistic fashion.

5

OF TOTEMISM AND ETHNICITY: CONSCIOUSNESS, PRACTICE AND THE SIGNS OF INEQUALITY*

JOHN L. COMAROFF

Is ethnicity an object of analysis, something to be explained? Or is it an explanatory principle capable of accounting for significant aspects of human existence? Because it has been treated in both ways, sometimes simultaneously, there is disagreement over even the most fundamental issues: What is ethnicity, one thing or many? Does it have the capacity to determine social and material life? Or is it determined by other forces and structures? And how does it relate to race, class and nationalism? Drawing examples primarily from Africa, this essay posits five propositions about the nature of ethnicity in an effort to illuminate its historical character and diverse experiential forms.

There is a Socratic parable, well-known in some quarters, about a teacher who gives his students two magnifying glasses and invites them to look at the one through the other. When each has told of all he has learned, the sage delivers his lesson in the form of a question, a *coup de grace*:

"Of what have you told me," he asks, "the thing you have seen or the thing through which you have seen it?"

The same conundrum lurks, usually unremarked, behind the study of ethnicity. Is the latter an object of analysis, something to be explained? Or is it an explanatory principle capable of illuminating significant aspects of human existence? Does it really refer to "idols of the tribe" (Isaacs 1975), or is it in fact an idol of the scribe (Mafeje 1971)? It certainly has been treated in both ways, sometimes simultaneously. As a result, there is still a notable lack of agreement on even the most fundamental of issues: What is ethnicity? Is it a monothetic or a polythetic class of phenomena, one thing or many? Has it the capacity to determine social activity, or is it a product of other forces and structures? Do its roots lie in so-called primordial consciousness or in a reaction to particular historical circumstance? And how is it related to race, class, and nationalism? In addressing these questions, I shall use a wide-angle lens

* I should like to thank William Julius Wilson, Jean Comaroff, Carole Nagengast, Kathleen Hall and Jean Lave for their insightful criticism of earlier drafts of this essay.

rather than a magnifying glass, and shall focus it, somewhat eclectically, on various African contexts. In so doing, moreover, I seek deliberately to turn the sage's moral on its head. For I am concerned to examine, at once, *both* an analytic object and its conceptual subject: on one hand, those processes involved in the rise of ethnic consciousness in Africa and elsewhere, and, on the other, the theoretical terms by means of which ethnicity may itself be comprehended.

Contrary to the usual canons of scholarly enquiry, I proceed not by situating my discussion within the relevant literature, but by stating five propositions about the nature of ethnicity. These propositions, though, are not presented in axiomatic form; rather, they are developed and exemplified as cumulative, if yet tentative, steps in pursuit of an analytic position capable of accounting for the genesis, persistence, and transformation of ethnicity and ethnic consciousness. This is not to pretend that any of them, regarded in isolation, is necessarily new – although each does fly in the face of some, and sometimes most, received wisdom. Whatever their individual provenance, however, their theoretical significance lies more in the systematic relations among them than in the substance of each in its own right.

I

The first proposition is intended primarily as a point of departure, a very general statement of orientation toward the conception of ethnicity: *Contrary to the tendency, in the Weberian tradition, to view it as a function of primordial ties,*[1] *ethnicity always has its genesis in specific historical forces, forces which are simul-taneously structural and cultural.* The corollary of this proposition ought also to be underscored. If it is true that ethnicity is a product of particular historical conditions (cf. Wallerstein 1979, Chapters 10–11), and not an ontological feature of human organization, it follows that it cannot be treated as a truly "independent" explanatory principle, a "first cause" in and of itself (Moerman 1967:167).[2] This is not to deny either its reality or the fact that action is regularly conducted in its name. Nor is it to ignore that such action has concrete implications for everyday relations. It is, rather, to recognize that, in order to understand ethnicity at all, we have not merely to reveal the conditions of its genesis, but also to establish its place in the sociological chain of being. It is to these two problems that much of this essay is addressed; for it is only by resolving them that the first proposition – and the overall position to which it speaks – may finally be sustained.

It is instructive to begin with the long-standing contention that the roots of ethnicity lie in the original "fact" of human cultural difference and ascribed status group affiliations; after all, the tenacity of the "primordial" thesis is itself significant. Now that thesis rests, in large part, on the compound notion (i) that culturally defined communities – or, in Weberian terms, "status groups" (*stande*) – everywhere share an intrinsic awareness of their own identity; (ii) that the traditional loyalties vested in this identity are the source of ethnic consciousness and affiliation; and (iii) that the latter provide the basis for collective action and intergroup relations. The counter thesis, of course, suggests that expressions of ethnicity do not arise in any community save as a *reaction* to threats against its integrity and

---

[1] For discussion of this tendency and its Weberian origins, see, among others, Hechter (1975:313f); Greenberg (1980:13f).

[2] The treatment of ethnicity as a "first cause" capable of producing autonomous effects remains the same throughout the human sciences; see, for example, Bronfenbrenner (1978:258) in respect of psychology, Cohen (1978) of anthropology, and Wilson (1980) of sociology.

self-determination. As long as that integrity remains unchallenged, goes the argument, ethnic sensibilities either do not exist or remain dormant.[3]

Both these theses, I believe, are simultaneously correct and incomplete. On the one hand, the precapitalist world, where primordial affiliations and loyalties are tacitly presumed to have had their origins, was never so atomistic that communities did not have relations with others. And, in so far as this is true, it would be plainly absurd to pretend that their members could have lacked common identities or a concern for sociocultural differences; consider, for example, the acute awareness that the diverse peoples of the Luapula valley are known to have had for each others' "customs" (Cunnison 1959:53–61). On the other hand, this form of awareness is distinctly different from ethnic consciousness *sui generis* (Skinner 1978:193).

Let me elaborate. In as much as collective social identity always entails some form of communal self-definition, it is invariably founded on a marked opposition between "we" and "others"; identity, that is, is a *relation* inscribed in culture. Patently, the social and material boundaries involved in any such relations – not to mention their content – are historically wrought; they change in the course of economic and political processes (see below). Still, whatever the substance of particular relations between groupings, the irreducible fact of identity implies the cultural structuring of the social universe. All this merely echoes the anthropological truism, after Durkheim and Mauss (1963), that classification, the meaningful construction of the world, is a necessary condition of social existence. But, I stress, it is the *marking* of relations – of identities in opposition to one another –

that is "primordial," not the substance of those identities.

This, it will be recalled, was the point that Bergson (1935:172–5) made about the essence of totemism, the point upon which Lévi-Strauss (1963) was to build his famed thesis. The genius of Bergson's insight lay in the observation that it was not the intrinsic nature of totemic objects ("their animality") that gave them their significance. It was, rather, "their duality"; the fact that relations between these objects stood for relations between social groups (p. 175). Totemism, then, is just one form – and, it is to be added, an historically specific form – of the universal process of classification. It is one in which groupings define themselves as independent or interdependent units within a common humanity; formulate collective identities in contrast to one another; and portray themselves and others, in symbolic terms, as similar yet different. Whether such relations are signified in animate or inanimate objects makes little difference. These are the media of *totemic consciousness*, a particular species of *conscience collective*.

Ethnic consciousness also entails the formulation of collective identities and their symbolic embodiment in markers of contrast between social groupings. For ethnicity, like totemism, exists above all else as a set of relations. In this respect, they are formally similar. But they differ clearly in their substance. However the former is defined – and, to be sure, it has been defined in very many ways (see, for example, R. Cohen 1978) – it appears to have two generally recognized and closely related properties. One refers to the subjective classification, by the members of a society, of the world into social entities according to cultural differences. The other involves the

---

[3] See, for instance, du Toit (178:10f); Fried (1967:15, 170); Skinner (1978:192f); and Cohen & Middleton (1970). As Wallerstein (1979:184) puts it, "Ethnic consciousness is eternally latent everywhere. But it is only realized when groups feel either threatened with a loss of previously acquired privilege or conversely feel that it is an opportune moment politically to overcome longstanding denial of privilege."

stereotypic assignment of these groupings – often hierarchically – to niches within the social division of labor.[4] Neither property, of course, is unique to ethnic consciousness; the first applies equally to totemism, the second to class. But it is in their fusion that the particular character of ethnicity resides. Moreover, it is not coincidental that these features among all those associated with ethnic consciousness, are the most commonly observed: for reasons which will become evident, they reflect the manner in which the forces that yield an ethnically ordered universe impress themselves upon human experience.

II

There is a good deal more to ethnicity than this, however. Not only may its character change over time – which is one reason why it is so resistant to easy definition (Hechter 1975:311) – but the way in which it is experienced and expressed may vary among social groupings according to their positions in a prevailing structure of power relations. For dominant groupings – be they Afrikaners, self-styled chosen people of South Africa (Adams & Giliomee 1979; Coetzee 1978:249), or precolonial Alur, spreading their particular concepts of chiefship over the hinterland of Uganda (Southall 1953:181) – it takes on the assertive stamp of a protectionist ideology; a legitimation of control over economy and society. Concomitantly, it involves the negation of similar entitlements to others, often on putative cultural or "civilizational" grounds, and may call into doubt their shared humanity. Thus R. Gordon (1978:215f) notes that Kavango and Ovambo mineworkers in Namibia believe, correctly, that their white supervisors "think we are animals." And nine-

teenth century Tswana saw Sarwa (bushmen), who peopled their underclass, as *phologolo*, beasts of the wild. Although these Sarwa allegedly controlled wondrous knowledge of herbal substances, they were thought properly to live in the undomesticated bush, and were only allowed into the towns of their masters by night (Mackenzie 1871:368). Ironically, the Tswana, themselves being subjected increasingly to the domination of Boer (Afrikaner) settlers, had become known to the whites as *skepsels*, "creatures" (cf. Marais 1939, quoted in Crapanzano 1985:31; also Livingstone 1858:37). According to Crapanzano (1985:40), who recently did fieldwork among Afrikaners, this perception persists into the present. Indeed, he tells an anecdote that makes the point with frightening clarity. It concerns an elderly informant who, though deeply religious, had developed a quixotic theory as to why the bible should not be taken literally:

> [If you read it literally . . .] "you wouldn't be able to explain how the Black man got here," he said. "They come from baboons. That's what evolution has taught us, and the Bible doesn't say anything about evolution. God created the White man in a day. *That*, the Bible tells us. It took evolution to create the Black man."

For the subordinate, ethnic affiliation may originate in an *attribution* of collective identity to them on the part of others. On occasion, as we shall see, the creation of such identities has little foundation in pre-existing sociological reality, in which circumstances it usually involves what has been termed "the invention of tradition" (Hobsbawm & Ranger 1983). But even where they have had a social identity contrived for them, subordinate groupings typically come to define their "ethnicity" as an

---

[4]   These properties appear with equal regularity in Weberian and Marxist discourses on ethnicity – albeit with different analytic weight. Rex (1970:48), in fact, sees them as the defining conditions for what sociologists treat under the rubric of "race relations."

emblem of common predicament and interest; through it, too, they may begin to assert a shared commitment to an order of symbols and meanings and, sometimes, a moral code (Moerman 1967). This, moreover, is often expressed in the reciprocal negation of the humanity of those who dominate them. Those same Kavango and Ovambo mineworkers, for instance, repay their degradation by referring to the Europeans as "barbarians" (R. Gordon 1978:216). Similarly, the Tswana vernacular for "whites" *makgoa*, belongs to a class of nouns (sing. prefix: *le-*; pl. prefix: *ma-*) reserved for non-human animate objects and human pests; it includes such terms as *legodu* (thief) and *letagwa* (drunkard). The word *makgoa* itself originally denoted the "white bush lice" associated with the hindquarters of large animals (J. Comaroff 1985:137). In sum, then, ethnic identity, which always assumes *both* an experiential and a practical salience for those who bear it, entails the complementary assertion of the collective self and the negation of the collective other; it may call into question shared humanity; and its substance is likely to reflect the tensions embodied in relations of inequality.

I shall explore these substantive features below. For now, it is enough to reiterate that, while ethnicity is quite different in its *content* from totemism, there is, beneath this difference, a common denominator: both are, ultimately, modes of social classification and consciousness, markers of identity and collective relations. Herein, in fact, lies the point of interrogating them together. For it calls into question the roots of the contrast and, by extension, the particularity of ethnicity: why should the primordial fact of social classification, of the consciousness of identity and distinction, take on such diverse forms? The easy answer, of course, would be an evolutionary one: that totemism is the precursor of ethnicity, the latter being a product of the movement from "simple" to more "complex" social systems. But this explanation will not do. Just as it is demonstrable that ethnic consciousness existed in precapitalist Africa so, as Linton's classic ethnographic vignette proves (1924; see Lévi-Strauss 1963:7–8), totemic consciousness occurs in industrial societies. The solution, I suggest, is to be sought elsewhere; namely, in the historically specific social structures in which totemism and ethnicity, respectively, arise and persist. For the signs and practices involved in each have their source in the very construction of economy and society.

Drawing all this together, then, the second proposition may be stated thus: *ethnicity, far from being a unitary "thing," describes both a set of relations and a mode of consciousness; moreover, its meaning and practical salience varies for different social groupings according to their positions in the social order. But, as a form of consciousness, it is one among many – totemism being another – each of which is produced as particular historical structures impinge themselves on human experience and condition social action.*

This proposition also has important corollaries, among them, the final repudiation of the "primordial" thesis. For, as the comparison of totemism and ethnicity has revealed, this thesis flows from a confounding not merely of two modes of consciousness, but also of quite separate levels of analysis. I reiterate that the marking of contrasting identities – of the opposition of self and other, we and they – is "primordial" in the same sense that classification is a necessary condition of social existence. But the way in which social classification is realized in specific forms of collective identity, ethnicity no less than any other, is always a matter to be decided by the material and cultural exigencies of history.[5]

---

[5]   Another variant of the "primordial" argument is the "human nature" thesis. For example, Milton Gordon (1978:73) holds that, since ethnicity cannot be shed by mobility, it "becomes incorporated into the self." Man acting in the name of his ethnic group, then, is man defending himself; and, given that "human nature" is aggressively narcissistic, ethnic

III

This leads directly to the third proposition, which addresses these forces that produce totemism and ethnicity, and their associated modes of consciousness. In its most general form, it may be put as follows: *while totemism emerges with the establishment of symmetrical relations between structurally similar social groupings – groupings which may or may not come to be integrated into one political community – ethnicity has its origins in the asymmetric incorporation of structurally dissimilar groupings into a single political economy.*

More specifically, totemic consciousness arises with the interaction of social units that retain – or appear from within to retain – control over the means of their own production and reproduction. It is, in short, a function of processes in which autonomous groupings enter into relations of equivalence or complementary interdependence and, in so doing, fashion their collective identities by contrast to one another. At times, such relations are enshrined in cycles of exchange of varying kinds; at others, they may entail raiding, hostility and warfare; often they embrace both. Moreover, it is possible, in fact usual, that such encounters yield short-term inequalities among the parties to them. But, if each retains its integrity and is not subordinated as a group in and of itself – which is most likely where the units bear formal structural similarity – the overall symmetry of relations is perpetuated. And, as long as it is, totemic

identities and affiliations, in the general terms in which I have defined them, will be sustained – with the added qualification that the particular content of these identities will depend both on the sociocultural orders of those who bear them and on the exact nature of their engagement with others.

Totemic consciousness, and the processes that give rise to it, occurred widely in precapitalist Africa. It was realized, for instance, in relations among Sotho-Tswana chiefdoms, and between so-called acephalous societies such as the Nuer and Dinka in the Sudan (Evans-Pritchard 1956: 82–4); to be sure, the ethnographic literature abounds with examples. It is true that, historically, totemic relations have also arisen in circumstances where a political community has incorporated either immigrant or conquered populations. Significantly, though, this seems to happen only when such populations are assimilated into an existing social order, not as a subordinate class, but as units of structure like those already there. In such situations, a form of totemic pluralism tends to emerge. The most striking case of this is provided by the Tswana *merafe* ("nations"), which regularly absorbed groupings from outside. These incoming groupings, whose totems differed from those of the host chiefdoms, were generally established as integral and independent wards and sections, the major politico-residential divisions within Tswana politics; their internal organization, distributions of authority and productive arrangements became an

---

consciousness and conflict is endemic. Wilson (1981:113) has countered by pointing out that this "human" predisposition is always mediated by social and cultural factors – the implication being that it may be a necessary, but can never be a sufficient condition for ethnic antagonism. I would go still further, however. It seems that Gordon has confused precisely the two levels of which I have spoken. Certainly, "I" is fused into "we" in the construction of collective identity; that is an irreducible *social* fact, whether or not "human nature," if it exists at all, is as Gordon asserts. But why *ethnic* identity? For Gordon, the answer finally comes down to the assertion that it cannot be willingly shed. Yet the anthropological evidence is unequivocal. Ethnic identity often *can* be set aside, and may be a highly situational attribute (see below). Of course, the relative ease with which it is sloughed off varies dramatically: for, say, Jews in Nazi Germany – who shared language, skin color, and (to a large extent) culture with their oppressors – it was well-nigh undeniable; for Central Africans on the copperbelt, although divided by language, culture, and diverse skin pigmentation, it seems always to have been negotiable. Quite clearly, ethnic mobility – like all social identity – is historically determined. But then, for many anthropologists and comparative sociologists, so too is "human nature."

indistinguishable element of the structure in place (Schapera 1938; J. L. Comaroff 1973). Consequently, Tswana chiefdoms usually contained a large number of totemic groupings whose identities in contrast to each other were marked in ritual contexts (Schapera 1952).[6] As this implies, totemic consciousness might also surface in the wake of conquest and in complex states, depending on the manner in which social units are ordered within the polity. Where they are incorporated into symmetrical relations with other like units – as they were, say, in the "snowball state" of nineteenth century Ngoni (Barnes 1954) – the historical conditions for the production of totemic consciousness may be expected to take their due course.[7]

The emergence of ethnic groups and the awakening of ethnic consciousness are, by contrast, the product of historical processes which structure relations of inequality between discrete social entities. They are, in other words, the social and cultural correlates of a specific mode of articulation between groupings, in which one extends its dominance over another by some form of coercion, violent or otherwise;[8] situates the latter as a bounded unit in a dependent and unique position within an inclusive division of labor; and, by removing from it final control over the means of production and/or reproduction, regulates the terms upon which value may be extracted from it. By virtue of so doing, the dominant grouping constitutes both itself and the subordinate population as classes; whatever the prior sociological character of these aggregations, they are, in the process, actualized as groups *an sich*.

The creation of structured inequality of this kind, as I have already noted, demands meaningful signification; there can, after all, be no social division of labor without its representation in culture. And, in a stratified, segmentary social environment, this entails marking out the social world into identifiable classes.[9] Now these representations are not arbitrary: since they apprehend and rationalize the unequal distribution of material, political and social power by virtue of *group* membership, they must, by definition, ascribe such inequalities to the *intrinsic* nature of the groups concerned. It is thus that the "ascriptive" character of each becomes its "ethnic" identity – even though the groups themselves might only have been established, at least in their contemporary mould, in the very process of articulation which contrived that identity in the first place.

It follows that the identity imputed to a social group from the outside may be quite different from that same identity as subjectively experienced. For the construction of the collective self – and, by extension, any accounting of its entitlements (for the dominant) or predicament (for the subordinate) – depends on its *differentiation* from the collective other. "Otherness," then becomes a contrivance in the counter image of social selfhood, not an empirical description of any

---

[6] Schapera (1952) refers to these groupings as "ethnic." By any definition of ethnicity, however, this usage is inappropriate; clearly, it reflects the ambiguities surrounding the term in the 1950s (du Toit 1978:1 ff).

[7] A comparable argument could be made for the rise of the Zulu state in the early nineteenth century. Here, it seems, most vanquished populations had social orders which did not differ greatly from that of their conquerors. When absorbed into the Zulu polity, they became integral units in its social and productive structure rather than a subordinate class (cf. Suret-Canale 1969; Walter 1969; Guy 1980). For a complementary discussion on ethnic identities in precapitalist Africa, see Wallerstein (1979).

[8] McGuire (1982:168), following Spicer (1971:797), offers the parallel observation that ethnic groups, the bearers of "persistent cultural systems," are born out of "opposition"; that is, out of the "efforts by those in control of the surrounding state apparatus to incorporate or assimilate" minority populations.

[9] Warren's (1978) revealing study of collective identity among Guatemalan Indians – among whom subordination within a class society is vividly portrayed in ethnic terms – is built on this very premise; it analyses, in considerable detail, the elaboration of the signs of inequality into a coherent set of cultural representations.

particular population. Indeed, the Janus-faced nature of ethnic consciousness – the fact that it involves both the assertion of a collective self and the negation of collective others – is a cultural expression of the structuring of inequality; it emerges as groupings come to signify and symbolize their experience of a world of *asymmetrical* "we–them" relations.

The extent to which ethnic identities are rooted in previous cultural realities, moreover, is highly variable (Young 1976:34). Apart from all else, cultures tend to be transformed as the groups who bear them interact with one another (Sahlins 1982). But even if they were not, it is rarely the case, for reasons just given, that they are accurately represented in the identity assigned to others – this being true even where emergent ethnic affiliations are created out of previously bounded, homogeneous populations. Thus, just as the agencies of British colonialism had little appreciation of African social orders and acted upon distorted impressions of them – witness the common view that the natives had no religion (e.g. Moffat 1842:244; Burchell 1822–4 [2]:383) – so Tswana held an equally skewed image of the culture of their nineteenth century Sarwa serfs. This is yet more likely to occur when underclasses are composed of people of diverse origins: in such circumstances, the substance of their identities, as contrived from both within and outside, is inevitably a *bricolage* fashioned in the very historical processes which underwrite their subordination.

Ethnic consciousness, as I stated earlier, existed in precapitalist Africa. It is not purely the product of colonialism or urbanization, as has sometimes been suggested, although both do contain the requisite conditions and are generally accompanied by manifestations of ethnicity. Perhaps the most celebrated instance in the precolonial context lies in Tutsi–Hutu relations in Rwanda and Burundi (Maquet 1961), the history of which conformed closely to the above characterization. But there are many other examples (see Wallerstein 1979), the conquest and subordi-

nation of the Bairu by the Bahima in Ankole providing another immediately familiar one (Oberg 1940). Less well-known is the case of the Betsileo of Malagasy, of whom Kottak (1980:4–5) writes:

> Betsileo have not always shared . . . consciousness of themselves as a distinct ethnic unit. Prior to their conquest by the Merina, there appear to have been no Betsileo. Rather, there were several statelets and chiefdoms located in different parts of what is now the Betsileo homeland. Their conquerors . . . created the Betsileo province of the Merina state . . . and, in so doing, provided a basis for Betsileo ethnic consciousness to develop through the present.

Kottak goes on to note (1980:303, n.1) that Bara ethnicity also originated in the nineteenth century under very similar conditions (see Huntington 1974). Ethnic consciousness, it seems, has increased throughout Malagasy as a function of political consolidation.

With colonial penetration into Africa, indigenous populations were integrated – to differing degrees and with varying rapidity – into the political economies of Europe, thereby becoming part of an increasingly global division of labor. And, as we might expect, their asymmetric incorporation into a wider order or productive and exchange relations yielded novel ethnic affiliations and groupings (Wolf 1982:380 f). As Greenberg (1980:14) observes:

> The Kikuyu, for example, whose coherence is now so important to understanding Kenyatta and nationalism in Kenya, had no certain identity before the imposition of British rule and the alienation of land to the settlers; distinctive groups like the Sikhs in India, Ibo in Nigeria, and Malays in Malaysia were barely conscious of their "sameness" one hundred years ago.

But there were differences between the forms of ethnicity which had prevailed in the pre-colonial epoch and those bred in the wake of the expanding world system. As has been argued elsewhere (Long 1984; J. L. Comaroff 1982), the leitmotif of modern Third World history lies in a mutually determining interaction, a "dialectic of articulation," between global forces and the diverse social orders of Africa and elsewhere. This encounter established new, multilevelled structures of inequality both within Africa itself and between Africa and Europe. And, in so doing, it laid the basis for what might be termed "segmentary ethnicity" (cf. R. Cohen 1978:387); that is, a nesting hierarchy of ethnic identities.

At the lowest levels, local groups, which often became bounded political units by bureaucratic fiat, sought and gained dominance over others within colonial – and, later, postcolonial – states, thereby constructing internal ethnic relations. At the highest levels, the conjuncture of "Europeans" and "Africans" expressed itself in an encompassing ethnicity. This was reflected, on the one hand, in the growth of post-Africanism and the concept of an "African culture"; on the other, it saw the crystallization of a settler–colonial social order wrought largely out of a caricature of (aristocratic) Victorian English society (Ranger 1983, see Chapter 35, this volume). And, between these polarities, there developed a variety of middle-order allegiances, attachments that crossed parochial boundaries but justified common political cause with reference to shared cultural affinities; these have been described by terms such as "supertribalism." Of the three levels, significantly, the lowest has conventionally come to be portrayed as "tribalism"; the middle, as "nationalism," sometimes with the qualifier "ethnic"; and the highest, as "race." But all had their genesis alike in the processes that gave rise to ethnic consciousness in its more complex segmentary guise. They are *interrelated* products of an historically specific confrontation between the populations of Africa and the various agencies of colonial domination.

It is not difficult to point to cases of segmentary ethnicity, since the emergence of a hierarchy of identities, all culturally marked and politically salient, has been a recurrent theme throughout modern Africa. For example, the colonial history of Zimbabwe called into being an intricate ethnological map of "tribes" whose administration under indirect rule *demanded* that their "traditional" political constitution be recognized – even, in places, where they had none. It also fostered the pre-eminence of two such entities, the Shona and Ndebele, each of which spawned the core of a (supratribal) nationalist movement. The alliance of these movements within a "patriotic front," in turn, fought the war of liberation that led to Zimbabwean independence; a war between adversaries – each with allies beyond the national borders – riven along the *racial* line of fault that divides southern Africa into inclusive (transnational) pigmentary groupings. Similar processes, if not always with the same climax, have occurred in East Africa, most notably in Uganda (Mazrui 1978) and Kenya (Parkin 1978), and in West Africa. The exact hierarchy of groupings yielded by such processes varies, of course. But the overall *structure* of nesting, opposed identities – of "tribe," "nation" and "race," each a particular refraction of ethnicity – manifests itself with remarkable frequency.

IV

The fourth proposition, which takes all this a step further, concerns the distinction between historical forces and structures, and the manner in which they are experienced in everyday life. I have argued that the forces which produce consciousness – totemic, ethnic or any other – lie in the construction and transformation of economy and society. But the terms in which they are understood by social actors have to do with the way in which the world is signified: human beings perceive and act upon their contexts not as they are formally constituted, but as they are construed in shared signs and symbols. With the emergence of class formations in which positions in the division of labor are signified by ascribed status and cultural distinction, ethnicity becomes a dominant medium through which the social order is to be interpreted and navigated.

In other words, where it becomes the basis of social classification and status relations, ethnicity, rather than the forces that generate it, takes on the ineffable appearance of determining the predicament of individuals and groups. After all, viewed from *within* any such social context, ethnic affiliation cannot but be represented as the "independent variable" that shapes careers and biographies. For, at the experiential level, it *does* seem to be ethnicity which orders social status, class membership, and so on – and not class or status that decides ethnic identities. In fact, Marx's image of the *camera obscura* (1970:36), whatever its other limitations (Lichtman 1975:49), is apposite here: the origins of ethnic groups and consciousness may lie in the structuring of inequality. But, once objectified as a "principle" by which the division of labor is organized, ethnicity assumes the autonomous character of a prime mover in the unequal destinies of persons and populations. To wit, just as working class black Americans do not view their blackness as a function of their class positions, but their class position as a function of their blackness,[10] so underclass Hutu in Rwanda or Kgalagadi in Botswana see their status as being ascribed by virtue of their ethnic affiliation and not vice versa.

Under these conditions, then, ethnicity becomes an essential feature of the "natural" order of things, the given character of the world with regard to which people must conduct their lives. Nor is this confined to any particular sociological category. It applies as much to those for whom ethnic ideologies legitimize dominance as it does to those for whom ethnic labels are signs of subordination. As this suggests, such labels are not merely terms in a system of classification, although they are certainly that too. They also become a pragmatic basis for the formation of interest groups and networks, social resources for pursuing individual and communal utilities. Consequently, ethnic consciousness enters a dialectical relationship with the structures that underlie it: once ethnicity impinges upon experience as an (apparently) independent principle of social classification and organization, it provides a powerful motivation for collective activity. And this, by turn, must perforce realize an everyday world dominated by ethnic groups and relations, thereby reproducing the very social order that gave rise to ethnic consciousness in the first place. However, as we shall see, the matter is yet more complex. For social action conducted in the name of ethnicity also reveals contradictions inherent in systems of structured inequality and may transform those systems from within.

All this may sound much the same as saying that ethnicity is merely a form of false consciousness, a "phantasmic" mystification of class. But that would miss the point. For the way in which relations in any system are signified is an irreducible part of its reality. As Genovese (1968:32; see Greenberg 1980:390) puts it,

> . . . once an ideology arises it alters profoundly the material reality and in fact

[10] It is precisely this point that lies behind much of the debate over Wilson's claim (1980) of the declining significance of race in America. Wilson's critics have argued that skin color remains the main factor shaping the lives of blacks; its salience, therefore, cannot have decreased. At the *experiential* level, this may be true. But, whatever other arguments may be brought to bear on his case, Wilson, to his credit, does *not* deny the experiential importance of race. His thesis, rather, is that the life chances of blacks are determined primarily by other structural factors; namely, class differences. The controversy, in sum, flows from the confusion of social experience with the forces that give rise to it.

becomes a partially autonomous feature of that reality.

Indeed, structures of inequality and the terms of their cultural representation, whether they be subsumed in "ethnicity" or anything else, are mutually constitutive. For reasons already given, the one cannot exist without the other: both alike are elements of the dialectic of structure and practice which shapes concrete social relations – and, therefore, the very essence of economy and society.

The fourth proposition, in sum, argues that, *while ethnicity is the product of specific historical processes, it tends to take on the "natural" appearance of an autonomous force, a "principle" capable of determining the course of social life.* That is, by (i) configuring the particular manner in which a social system is experienced from within, it (ii) motivates social practice and rationalizes the pursuit of individual and collective utilities. This, in turn, (iii) shapes manifest relations, groups and identities; and, so (iv) a dialectic is established between structure and practice that, in time, reproduces and/or transforms the character of the social order itself.

V

This brings me to the fifth and final proposition, which echoes a very general analytic injunction: not only are the conditions that produce an historical phenomenon to be distinguished from those that sustain it, but any such phenomenon, once created, may acquire the capacity to affect the structures that gave rise to it. So it is with ethnic identity. *Where it becomes an objectified "principle" in the collective consciousness of a society, ethnicity may be perpetuated by factors quite different from those that caused its emergence, and may have a direct and independent impact on the context in which it arose.*

I have already stressed that, in systems where "ascribed" cultural differences ratio-nalize structures of inequality, ethnicity takes on a cogent existential reality. It is this process of reification, as we have seen, that gives it the appearance of being an autonomous factor in the ordering of the social world. As a result, ethnic identities regularly assume, for those who share them, a pervasive functionality in everyday social, economic, and political life (cf. Patterson 1977:102f). What is more, this functionality may *itself* seem to sustain the practical relevance of ethnic affiliation for both persons and groups. Behind it, however, there lies a subtle relationship between social experience and the forms of collective and individual practice.

Since it is cultural indices that are perceived to underlie inequalities in these systems, it follows, in the very nature of social experience, that such asymmetries would be eliminated (for groups) and upward mobility be possible (for persons) if the relevant cultural markers could be reversed or relinquished. After all, in order to have meaning, any sign must imply its complementary opposite. Thus, if the signs and principles which apparently mandate relations of inequality were no longer to apply, the inequality itself would be removed – or so it seems from the actors' perspective. In other words, such systems represent themselves as potentially navigable, their internal lines of division more or less porous, to the extent that sociocultural differences may be negotiated. This, in turn, establishes the appropriate terms in which social action is to be joined, and interests to be pursued, at the levels of both collective and individual enterprise. Let us examine each, for not only do they have contrasting dynamics, but a complex connection obtains between them.

At the level of collective action, the logic of common interest is, for the dominant, plain enough (see above). It lies in the authoritative protection of their exclusive cultural identity and, with it, their material position. In ideological terms, such protectionism entails a stress upon the contrasts between themselves and others; although the creation of alliances with particular groupings, the internal segmentation of the underclass, and the admission of individuals into their ranks may become strategic considerations in the defense of privilege. For the subordinate, the issue is not so clear cut. If and when any cohesive response to the common predicament is perceived as possible, two options present themselves. Either they can engage in some form of concerted direct effort – usually, but not always, political – to remove entirely the structures of inequality. Or they can seek to negate cultural differences by "proving" that these have ceased to be relevant: *vide* the attempts of South African and American blacks, earlier this century, to claim their civil rights by establishing that they had "become" sufficiently like those who oppressed them (i.e. "civilized"). It is not surprising, in light of the manner in which such systems engrave themselves upon human consciousness, that the second option tends to be the one of first resort (cf. Greenberg 1980:7–8); nor is it difficult to understand why it regularly fails, and gives way sooner or later to overt political action. In the colonial context, with the emergence of segmentary ethnicity, parochial groups (i.e. "tribes") find that such exertions, while not removing higher order inequalities, bring relative success as they "rise" within the lower reaches of the (colonial) division of labor at the expense of similar groupings.

However these historical movements work themselves out in particular contexts, a fundamental contradiction inheres in them. For any activity aimed at the reversal of "ascribed" inequalities may reinforce the primacy of ethnicity as a principle of social differentiation: the very fact that such activity is conducted by and for groupings marked by their cultural identities confirms the perception that these identities *do* provide the only available basis of collective self-definition and action. This is more dramatically the case where common action is seen to have been successful, but failure also tends to affirm shared affiliations, and the attribution to them

of social predicament. The affirmation is clearly tautological; in analytic terms, though, it will be evident that the reproduction of ethnicity, and the reinforcement of its pragmatic salience, is as much a function of efforts directed at its erosion as it is of activities that assert its positive value. And as long as social practice continues to be pursued *as if* ethnicity did hold the key to the structures of inequality, the protectionism of the dominant and the responses of the dominated alike serve to perpetuate an ethnically ordered world.

For the same reasons that collective melioration is held by the subordinate to lie in the negation of ethnic differences, individual mobility is often perceived as a matter of relinquishing those cultural attributes which appear to ascribe social status. For individuals, the adoption of new identities is relatively easier than it is for groups; again, there is abundant documentation from Africa of the renegotiation of such identities, perhaps the most poignant case being the practice of "trying for white" by those classified as "colored" in South Africa (Watson 1970). At this level, then, the lines of ethnic division may indeed be breached if and when particular persons accumulate the social and material wherewithall to do so. As noted before, too, there may be little resistance, on the part of the dominant, to the rise of a limited proportion of the underclass. If anything, as indicated by the entire history of capitalism, the promise of upward mobility, as just reward for industrious achievement, is ordinarily seen to enjoy both practical and ideological virtue.

Once upward mobility is seen as a possibility and energies are expended to achieve it, ethnic groups must inevitably become *internally* stratified. For, in order to garner the assets with which to renegotiate their class position, individuals require first to consolidate their situations within the underclass itself. Thus Wallerstein (1979), among others, has shown that intra-ethnic relations provide the arena in which such persons might acquire the resources for upward movement; indeed, there are few other contexts within which they might do so.[11] In addition, under colonialism, where segmentary ethnicity developed, lower order ethnic groups often assumed the character of fractions of the underclass; fractions more or less exclusively associated – much as in the segmented labor markets of the industrialized world – with relatively stratified niches within the division of labor.[12] This, in turn, opens the way for individuals to manipulate ethnic identities so as to ascend within the nether echelons of the hierarchy: it charts a series of steps that may finally lead out of the underclass itself. The regular effort to navigate this route, of course, is the very stuff of the ethnography of urban Africa. It gives rise to what is usually glossed as "situational ethnicity" (R. Cohen 1978; A. Cohen 1974), the strategic management of personal identity for social and material gain. Those who traverse the route, and ascend far enough within the class structure, become an identifiable fragment of the dominant class, an emergent local bourgeoisie. Both as individuals and as a group, however, they face an unavoidable choice. For, on leaving the underclass, they must either seek to discard their ethnic identities – which, after all, marked the predicament from which they contrived to escape – or sustain the contradiction of being a member of a group whose primary class position is different from their own. In either case, their situation is paradoxical, since the two dimensions of their identity are at odds with each other – a contradiction most vividly embodied in the classical "black white men" of Africa (cf. Fanon 1968).

Drawing together the collective and individual perspectives, a significant pattern emerges. On one hand, as long as ethnic affiliations and identities provide the terms of communal action, such action – whatever its immediate goals, and regardless of the successes or failures of any given grouping – reinforces the experiential salience of ethnicity as a social principle. In consequence, the seemingly ascribed character of ethnic identities is repeatedly confirmed; so, also, is the conception of ethnic groups as bounded units (cf. Barth 1969), despite the reality that membership in them is frequently the subject of social management. On the other hand, at the individual level, the achievement of upward mobility transforms the relationship of ethnicity and class. For it leads both to the internal differentiation of ethnic groups and, with the emergence of bourgeois fractions, to the loss of a one-to-one correspondence between ethnic affiliation and class membership. (Were that correspondence to be sustained, self-evidently, the paradoxes involved in both collective and individual action would either not surface, or would take a different form.) This does not obliterate the fact that, as a *statistical* frequency – and as an indigenous perception – ethnic groups continue to be predominantly associated with particular class positions. Nonetheless, class and sociocultural differences cease to be coterminous in any absolute or prescriptive sense.[13]

All this is nicely exemplified in ethnic political movements which arise among populations that were once subordinated *in toto* but, over time, have become diversified to the extent that some of their numbers have left the underclass. These movements are often

---

[11]   Greeley and McCready (1974:300) make much the same point about ethnic relations in the United States – a point classically illustrated, as William Wilson has reminded me, by E. Franklin Frazier's *Black Bourgeoisie* (1957).

[12]   For an especially clear example, see Mazrui's account (1978) of colonial Uganda, where the cleavage between Nilotes and Bantu was unambiguously reflected in the contemporary division of labor. Mazrui might easily have extended his analysis to take in the Indian and white settler communities, which had equally well-defined niches in that division of labor.

[13]   See Wilson (1984), whose penetrating analysis of race and social policy in America illuminates and gives comparative support to this aspect of my discussion.

joined, and led, by such upwardly mobile members – sometimes, I suggest, in the effort to resolve the contradiction in their own lives – and are usually framed in the rhetoric of protest and resistance; of rebellion rather than revolution, to invoke Gluckman's well-worn distinction. In some instances they have a single sociocultural grouping at their core, as did Mau Mau in Kenya; in others, like the African National Congress in South Africa and many nationalist political parties throughout the continent, they cut across local "tribal" divisions. In the latter case, too, they may reinforce a shared symbolic order where it existed only tenuously before, and weld a relatively heterogeneous social entity into a bounded status group that acts *für sich*. In so doing, ethnic political movements underscore, at once, the continuities and discontinuities in the articulation of ethnicity and class. In one respect, they express the strong (statistical) association between the two; such action *is*, patently, directed against a prevailing distribution of social, economic, and political power, and its mass support comes from those who most palpably suffer inequality. Yet they also breach the lines of class division and, as such, give the appearance of being manifestations of status group solidarities. Moreover, the dualistic character of these movements – as statements of underclass resistance, and as assertions of status group unity – may have implications that are not envisaged by those who engage in them.

Thus, under colonialism in Africa, ethnic struggles certainly had an impact on the surface contours of the social world, and they did occasionally lead to significant liberal reforms. But, insofar as they refracted class antagonisms in the cause of status group interests, they did not finally remove the *structures* of subordination. If anything, they masked those structures in an ideology of individual achievement, and, by leaving intact the correlation between ethnicity and class, served ultimately to consolidate relations of collective inequality. Nor was this restricted to Africa.

As Post (1978) reveals, much the same applied to black nationalist organizations in Jamaica in the 1930s, Marcus Garvey's Universal Negro Improvement Association (UNIA) among them. These organizations tended to acquire a solidly middle class leadership (for whom political action often involved demands made in their collective *class* interest; 1978:208), and a large following among the poor, who had come to experience their suffering, "in the natural order of things" (1978:145), as the heritage of color. Post goes on to argue that such "generalized Black nationalism" (1978:161) ultimately "refracted and atomized potential collective class consciousness" (1978:187), especially when it either receded into Ras Tafarian millennialism, or sufficed itself with the crumbs of economic palliation. In other words, by virtue of its dualistic quality, ethnicity itself became a factor in the maturation of a colonial and post-colonial capitalist order characterized by marked asymmetries. On the one hand, it continued to provide a cultural and organizational basis for a highly stratified division of labor; on the other, it rationalized the possibility of upward mobility and an ethos of achievement.

More generally, then, as ethnic groups become internally differentiated and lose their uniform correspondence to class – as they must inevitably do in the long run – they *mature* into status groups in the classical Weberian sense of the term. Now there is a double theoretical irony in this. First, in as much as ethnic affiliations are realized and solidify into status groups by virtue of such *historical* processes, they have precisely the opposite trajectory to that theorized by Weber. In the Weberian tradition, affinities based on status, being primordial, ought to come before those based on class; and they should only give way to the latter with the growth of an increasingly rationalized industrial economy (Hechter 1975:313; Greenberg 1980:6). They certainly should not emerge *with* the genesis of class structures, let alone enter a complex dialectical relationship with them. But, second, it is not only Weber who is turned on his head by the rise and persistence of ethnic groupings. In classical Marxian terms too, ethnicity should not appear with the emergence of class differences. Quite the converse: the processes that produce class societies ought to submerge "traditional" ideologies and, eventually, cause them to wither away as class consciousness is brought to the fore. However, far from disappearing, or remaining a mere epiphenomenon of "real" antinomies, ethnic identity assumes an important role in the dynamics of many historical systems – sustaining yet masking, reinforcing yet refracting, their dominant lines of cleavage. For the contradictions inherent in structures and signs of inequality not only give ethnicity the appearance of an objectified "force"; they also motivate and rationalize the very social practices which assert, with baroque circularity, that ethnicity truly is a pervasive force in the social world.

Conclusion

If the five propositions bear scrutiny, it is no wonder, *pace* both Weberian and Marxian orthodoxies, that ethnicity is as ubiquitous and tenacious as it is; and that, in spite of undergoing changes in its content, experiential character and historical relevance, it refuses to vanish – notwithstanding the once commonplace sociological tendency to predict its imminent demise. The major problem, in both theoretical and empirical terms, it seems to me, is not to account for the genesis and persistence – or even the transformation – of ethnic consciousness and affiliation. Once ethnicity is understood to exist as a set of relations, a product of specifiable historical forces and processes rather than a primordial "given," those issues become readily understandable. Much more vexing, in light of everything I have argued, is the question of when and why ethnic ideologies break down and class consciousness rises to replace it – if, indeed, this ever happens in such straightforward terms. But that is a problem which demands separate treatment. The purpose of the present exercise has been more modest. It has been to explore just some of the fundamental analytic issues surrounding the signs and practices of inequality. And, if the propositions formulated along the way remain tentative for now, they are offered in the belief, to parody Lévi-Strauss, that ethnicity is good to rethink.

References

ADAMS, H. and H. GILIOMEE. 1979. *Ethnic Power Mobilized*. New Haven: Yale University Press.

BARNES J. A. 1954. *Politics in a Changing Society*. London: Oxford University Press for the Rhodes–Livingstone Institute.

BARTH, F. (ed.). 1969. *Ethnic Groups and Boundaries: The Social Organization of Cultural Difference*. Boston: Little, Brown and Co.

BERGSON, H. L. 1935. *The Two Sources of Morality and Religion*. Translated by Audra, A. and C. Brereton. New York: Henry Holt and Co.

BRONFENBRENNER, U. 1979. *The Ecology of Human Development: Experiments by Nature and Design*. Cambridge: Harvard University Press.

BURCHELL, W. J. 1822–4. *Travels in the Interior of South Africa* (two volumes). London: Longmans.

COETZEE, J. H. 1978. Formative Factors in the Origins and Growth of Afrikaner Ethnicity. In *Ethnicity in Modern Africa*, edited by B. M. du Toit. Boulder: Westview Press.

COHEN, A. (ed.). 1974. *Urban Ethnicity*. London: Tavistock.

COHEN, R. 1978. "Ethnicity: Problem and Focus in Anthropology." *Annual Review of Anthropology*, 7:349:403.

COHEN, R. and J. MIDDLETON (eds). 1970. *From Tribe to Nation: Studies in Incorporation Processes*. Scranton: Chandler.

COMAROFF, J. 1985. *Body of Power, Spirit of*

Resistance: The Culture and History of a South African People. Chicago: University of Chicago Press.

COMAROFF, J. L. 1973. *Competition for Office and Political Processes among the Barolong boo Ratshidi.* University of London: Ph.D. Thesis.

– 1982. Dialectical Systems, History and Anthropology. *Journal of Southern African Studies,* 8(2):143–72.

CRAPANZANO, V. 1985. *Waiting: The Whites of South Africa.* New York: Random House.

CUNNISON, I. 1959. *The Luapula Peoples of Northern Rhodesia.* Manchester: Manchester University Press.

DURKHEIM, E. and M. MAUSS. 1963. *Primitive Classification.* Translated and edited by R. Needham. Chicago: University of Chicago Press.

DU TOIT, B. M. 1978. Introduction. In *Ethnicity in Modern Africa,* edited by B. M. du Toit. Boulder: Westview Press.

EVANS-PRITCHARD, E. E. 1956. *Nuer Religion.* Oxford: Oxford University Press.

FANON, F. 1968. *Black Skin White Masks.* London: MacGibbon and Kee.

FRAZIER, E. F. 1957. *Black Bourgeoisie.* New York: The Free Press.

FRIED, M. H. 1967. *The Evolution of Political Society: An Essay in Political Anthropology.* New York: Random House.

GENOVESE, E. D. 1968. *In Red and Black: Marxian Explorations in Southern and Afro-American History.* New York: Pantheon Books.

GORDON, M. 1978. *Human Nature, Class, and Ethnicity.* New York: Oxford University Press.

GORDON, R. 1978. The Celebration of Ethnicity: A "Tribal Fight" in a Namibian Mine Compound. In *Ethnicity in Modern Africa, edited by B. M. du Toit. Boulder: Westview Press.*

GREENBERG, S. B. 1980. *Race and State in Capitalist Development.* New Haven: Yale University Press.

GREELEY, A. M. and W. C. McCREADY. 1974. *Ethnicity in the United States.* New York: Wiley.

GUY, J. 1980. Ecological Factors in the Rise of Shaka and the Zulu Kingdom. In *Economy and Society in Pre-Industrial South Africa,* edited by S. Marks and A. Atmore. London: Longman.

HECHTER, M. 1975. *Internal Colonialism: The Celtic Fringe in British National Development,* *1536–1966.* Berkeley and Los Angeles: University of California Press.

HOBSBAWM, E. J. and T. O. RANGER (eds). 1983. *The Invention of Tradition.* Cambridge and New York: Cambridge University Press.

HUNTINGTON, W. R. 1974. *Religion and Social Organization of the Bara People of Madagascar.* Ann Arbor: University Microfilms International.

ISAACS, H. R. 1975. *Idols of the Tribe: Group Identity and Political Change.* New York and London: Harper and Row.

KOTTAK, C. P. 1980. *The Past in the Present: History, Ecology, and Cultural Variation in Highland Madagascar.* Ann Arbor: University of Michigan Press.

LÉVI-STRAUSS, C. 1963. *Totemism.* Translated by R. Needham. Boston: Beacon Press.

LICHTMAN, R. 1975. Marx's Theory of Ideology. *Socialist Revolution,* No. 23, 5(1):45–77.

LINTON, R. 1924. Totemism and the A.E.F. *American Anthropologist,* 26:296–300.

LIVINGSTONE, D. 1858. *Missionary Travels and Researches in South Africa.* New York: Harper and Brothers.

LONG, N. 1984. Creating Space for Change: A Perspective on the Sociology of Development. Inaugural Lectureship for Professorship of Empirical Sociology. Wageningen: The Agricultural University.

MACKENZIE, J. 1871. *Ten Years North of the Orange River.* Edinburgh: Edmonston and Douglas.

MAFEJE, A. 1971. The Ideology of Tribalism. *Journal of Modern African Studies,* 9(2):253–62.

MAQUET, J. J. 1961. *The Premise of Inequality in Ruanda.* London: Oxford University Press for the International African Institute.

MARAIS, J. S. 1939. *The Cape Coloured People, 1652–1937.* London: Longmans, Green.

MARX, K. and F. ENGELS. 1970. *The German Ideology.* New York: International Publishers.

MAZRUI, A. A. 1978. Ethnic Tensions and Political Stratification in Uganda. In *Ethnicity in Modern Africa,* edited by B. M. du Toit. Boulder: Westview Press.

McGUIRE, R. H. 1982. The Study of Ethnicity in Historical Archeology. *Journal of Anthropological Archeology,* 1:159–78.

MOERMAN, M. 1967. Being Lue: Uses and Abuses of Ethnic Identification. In *Essays on the Problem of Tribe,* edited by J. Helm. American

Ethnological Society: Proceedings of the Annual Meeting (1967).

MOFFAT, R. 1842. *Missionary Labours and Scenes in Southern Africa*. London: Snow.

OBERG, K. 1940. The Kingdom of Ankole in Uganda. In *African Political Systems*, edited by M. Fortes and E. E. Evans-Pritchard. London: Oxford University Press for the International African Institute.

PARKIN, D. 1978. *The Cultural Definition of Political Response*. London and New York: Academic Press.

PATTERSON, O. 1977. *Ethnic Chauvinism: The Reactionary Impulse*. New York: Stein and Day.

POST, K. 1978. *Arise Ye Starvelings: The Jamaican Labour Rebellion of 1938 and its Aftermath*. The Hague and London: Martinus Nijhoff.

RANGER, T. O. 1983. The Invention of Tradition in Colonial Africa. In *The Invention of Tradition*, edited by E. J. Hobsbawm and T. O. Ranger. Cambridge and New York: Cambridge University Press.

REX, J. 1970. The Concept of Race in Sociological Theory. In *Race and Racialism*, edited by S. Zubaida. London: Tavistock.

SAHLINS, M. 1982. *Historical Metaphors and Mythical Realities*. Ann Arbor: University of Michigan Press.

SCHAPERA, I. 1938. *A Handbook of Tswana Law and Custom*. London: Oxford University Press for the International African Institute.

– 1952. *The Ethnic Composition of Tswana Tribes*. London: London School of Economics.

SKINNER, E. P. 1978. Voluntary Associations and Ethnic Competition in Ouagadougou. In *Ethnicity in Modern Africa*, edited by B. M. du Toit. Boulder: Westview Press.

SOUTHALL, A. 1953. *Alur Society*. Cambridge: W. Heffer and Sons.

SPICER, E. H. 1971. Persistent Cultural Systems. *Science*, 174:795–800.

SURET-CANALE, J. 1969. Tribes, Classes, Nations. *La Nouvelle Revue Internationale*, 130 (June):110–124.

WALLERSTEIN, I. 1979. *The Capitalist World-Economy*. Cambridge: Cambridge University Press.

WALTER, E. V. 1969. *Terror and Resistance: A Study of Political Violence*. Oxford and New York: Oxford University Press.

WARREN, K. B. 1978. *The Symbolism of Subordination: Indian Identity in a Guatemalan Town*. Austin and London: University of Texas Press.

WATSON, G. 1970. *Passing for White: A Study of Racial Assimilation in a South African School*. London and New York: Tavistock.

WEBER, M. 1968. *Economy and Society*. New York: Bedminister Press.

WILSON, W. J. 1980. *The Declining Significance of Race: Blacks and Changing American Institutions*. Chicago: University of Chicago Press.

– 1981. Shifts in the Analysis of Race and Ethnic Relations. In *The State of Sociology: Problems and Prospects*, edited by J. F. Short, Jr. Beverley Hills: Sage Publications.

– 1984. Race-Specific Policies and the Truly Disadvantaged. *Yale Law and Policy Review*, 2(2):272–90.

WOLF, E. R. 1982. *Europe and the People Without History*. Berkeley and London: University of California Press.

YOUNG, C. 1976. *The Politics of Cultural Pluralism*. Madison: University of Wisconsin Press.

PART II

ECONOMICS AS A CULTURAL SYSTEM

Vegetable market in Treichville Quarter, Abidjan, Côte d'Ivoire, 1987.
Photo: Christopher B. Steiner.

Economics as a Cultural System

6   Mary Douglas. 1962. "Lele Economy Compared with the Bushong: A Study of Economic Backwardness." In Paul Bohannan and George Dalton (eds.), *Markets in Africa*. Evanston, Il: Northwestern University Press.

7   Paul Bohannan. 1955. "Some Principles of Exchange and Investment among the Tiv." *American Anthropologist*, 57:60–70.

8   Catherine Coquery-Vidrovitch. 1978. "Research on an African Mode of Production." In David Seddon (ed.) *Relations of Production*. London: Cass.

9   Keith Hart. 1973. "Informal Income Opportunities and Urban Employment in Ghana." *Journal of Modern African Studies* 11 (1):61–89.

10   Parker Shipton. 1989. *Bitter Money: Cultural Economy and Some African Meanings of Forbidden Commodities*. Washington, D.C. American Anthropological Association.

11   Sharon Hutchinson. 1992. "The Cattle of Money and the Cattle of Girls Among the Nuer 1930–83." *American Ethnologist*, 19 (2):294–316.

Introduction

The extraordinary variety and number of studies on African economics make it virtually impossible for us to summarize them in the scope of this introduction and this volume. These studies include ethnographic analyses of households (Guyer, 1981), local and regional economic histories, including histories of the slave trade and state formation (Harms, 1981; Kopytoff and Miers, 1977; Southall, 1974), the impact of migrant labor on local community life (Murray, 1981), Marxism (Meillassoux, 1981; Coquery-Vidrovitch, 1978; Donham, 1990), migration and urbanization (Southall, 1973; Cohen, 1969; Mayer, 1962; Epstein, 1958; Watson, 1958; Mitchell, 1956), political economy (Hart, 1982; Berry, 1978; 1984), economic development and trans-formations in agrarian and pastoral systems (Ferguson, 1990; Robertson, 1987; Little and Watts, 1994; Fratkin et al., 1994; Werbner, 1982), and the economics of gender (Apepoju and Oppong, 1994; H. Moore and Vaughan, 1994; Moodie and Ndatshe, 1994; Boserup, 1970). Given the vast number of different kinds of economic studies conducted in Africa, the reader may well question whether it is possible, or fruitful, to treat economics as a distinct domain of analysis. We have therefore limited ourselves in this section to a few key texts that illustrate some central perspectives on the study of African economies, and which quite directly inform, or speak to, the readings in other parts. For example, Hutchinson (Chapter 11) and Evans-Pritchard (Chapter 2) worked in the same part of Africa, with the same population, and on similar issues, and so each of these articles contributes to a fuller understanding of the other.

In this volume, the texts that make up the chapters on social organization (Part I), hunter-gatherers (Part III), gender (Part VII), and colonialism (Part VIII) are very much concerned with economics; although the putative focus is on issues such as sex roles, ethnicity as a social boundary, or the impact of European domination upon local values, the essays are more broadly concerned with how these issues are integrated with production and material and social exchanges. Other works, such as Geschiere's essay on witchcraft and the market in Cameroon (Chapter 20), and Rodney's selection on underdevelopment (Chapter 34), are explicit about how economics relate to other domains. Such attention to integration is, for many scholars, the hallmark of an anthropological economics, if not of the study of social organization in general, and distinguishes anthropology from the economic sciences. LeClair and Schneider thus write about the anthropologist's emphasis on social and cultural factors in economics (1968: 7):

> Economists traditionally could and did take the economic system as something of an isolate in the total social system. It could be studied in its own terms, and it was simpler to do so. By the same token, economists did not delve too much into ends in themselves; operating within a single cultural context, they could take ends as they were and felt no need for explaining them. Operating within a single social framework, they could afford to concentrate their attention on the economic system. Thus, the social and cultural systems were "given" parameters which did not need to be taken into account in the analysis.

From an anthropological viewpoint, economics must always be situated in its total sociocultural context. To illustrate how anthropologists developed such a perspective, we shall briefly outline some of the most important works and debates in the history of economic anthropology.

In a seminal work on inter-island exchange in a place far from Africa – the Trobriand Islands near Papua/New Guinea – the early anthropologist Bronislaw Malinowski (1922) described a fascinating exchange system called the Kula ring. His data suggested that Western models of economic behavior were not applicable to all societies, and more specifically, that the model of the economizing individual, motivated to employ scarce means for the maximum benefit, might not be fruitfully applied to non-capitalist, non-industrial societies. Malinowski's description of the Kula ring, in which the Trobrianders move among a ring of islands to give and receive valuable armshells and necklaces supported such a conclusion because the Trobriands expend more time and energy on the collection of the valuables than would seem economically "rational" to many western observers. The armshells and necklaces were not, at the time of his study, convertible to cash or many other goods, nor did owning these goods translate directly into greater wealth. The meaning of the trade was symbolic and aesthetic, defined by cultural values and not by the standard sorts of maximization models one finds in American economics textbooks: that, "all other things being equal," individuals will maximize their gains with an insufficiency of means. Anthropological economics thus developed as a perspective that emphasized social values and conformity over and above individual choice, utilitarianism, and "rationality."

Of course, all other things are never equal, and so such models may also not be applicable to all social and economic behavior in western societies. We know, for example, that in the United States businesses succeed and fail on the basis of religious holidays, such as Christmas, Hannukah, Kwanzaa, and Easter, that we often spend far more on our vacations, automobiles, and children's weddings than is truly "economical," and that, indeed, the whole set of practices we call gift giving constitutes a system in which we pay for symbols and meanings, prestige, love, favor, and for the future, rather than for immediate gratifications of material goods. Economists would, no doubt, be among the first to argue that they are always concerned with the non-material questions of economics, such as how much people will pay for, or fail to maximize for, leisure, vacations, or prestige and luxury goods. Yet, conventional economic perspectives frame these questions *in terms* of maximization and choice, rather than in terms of cultural value.

For many economic anthropologists, however, there can be considerable value in applying economic theories across cultures if we search for the fit and non-fit between scientific and local models. Assessing the degree of fit can quickly bring to light how people define their economic needs differently, and we may even learn that certain economic needs are characteristic of particular kinds of societies. Marshall Sahlins (1968; 1973), for instance, has suggested that hunter-gatherer societies in general, and the !Kung San of Botswana in particular (see Part III), do not try to maximize their economic benefits. Responding to some conventional assumptions that the subsistence economies of all hunter-gatherers, past and present, have been dismal and "poor," Sahlins calls hunter-gatherers the "original affluent society":

> . . . This was, when you come to think of it, the original affluent society. By common understanding an affluent society is one in which all the people's wants are easily satisfied; and though we are pleased to consider this happy condition the unique achievement of industrial civilization, a better case can be made for hunters and gatherers . . . For wants are "easily satisfied," either by producing much or desiring little, and there are, accordingly, two possible roads to affluence. The Galbraithean course makes assumptions peculiarly appropriate to market economies, that man's wants are

great, not to say infinite, whereas his means are limited, although improvable . . . But there is also a Zen solution to scarcity and affluence, beginning from premises opposite from our own, that human material ends are few and finite and technical means unchanging but on the whole adequate (1968:85).

Sahlins' argument is framed very much in terms of maximization models, but it is, at the same time, a powerful critique of the assumptions surrounding the concept of scarcity in the economic sciences (see Bird-David, 1992). The readings in Part III on hunter-gatherers address this issue again in the context of a debate about the !Kung San, and presents the more general problem of how and why we sometimes group culturally variable societies under single economic categories, such as "hunter-gatherer," "pastoralist" or "peasant."

We want to stress that practices which do not fit the Western model of "Economic Man" (*Homo Economicus*) are therefore not irrelevant to more conventional economic analyses, and while the kinds of economic activities anthropologists sometimes describe, such as the Kula ring, or gift-giving, may seem abstract or symbolic rather than material and productive, these activities often have significant effects on material life. For example, recent research in the Trobriand Islands has shown that when Trobrianders go on trading trips, made ostensibly to obtain Kula valuables, they actually engage in a wide range of other trading activities, including trade for foodstuffs and other important materials for house and canoe building. The trade for Kula valuables functioned to reduce the variable scarcity of certain foods and other products over a wide geographical area in the Trobriand archipelago, and the trading activities themselves helped to solidify partnerships and alliances that could be exploited in the event of future crises such as natural disasters, food depletions, or war (Singh, 1962). Establishing a single determining role is, of course, a chicken and egg problem – whether the adaptive advantages of trading Kula objects determined the values attributed to them, the adaptive advantages were an unintended byproduct of the Kula system, or the consequent adaptive advantages led Trobrianders to reinforce a pre-existing Kula trade. The point to be stressed here is that economics must be seen in their total social context, not only because economic behavior is always, already, socially meaningful, but because it ramifies to all areas of social life, including those we might not assume to fall under the rubric "economy."

One of the scholars most impressed by Malinowski's Kula data was the French anthropologist Marcel Mauss, a student and nephew of Emile Durkheim. Like his uncle, Mauss focused on the society rather than the individual, and was thus interested in answering the questions we raised in the first chapter. How do societies cohere? In his book, *Essai sur le don* (translated as *The Gift*), Mauss (1954 [1925]) concluded that social solidarity is generally achieved by means of gift exchange, and therefore that gift giving and receiving are fundamental to social life. He argued that reciprocity, while seemingly a voluntary behavior, involves complex moral and social obligations because the objects that people give are never totally separated from them: gifts bind people together in social relationships, and so we are socially and morally obliged to reciprocate. If you are an anthropologist and you need to understand a society, looking at gifts is a good way to go about it. Gifts, he said, betray "all the threads of which the social fabric is composed" – religious, legal, moral, economic, aesthetic, and morphological (Mauss, 1954:1).

Gifts may not exactly fit economists' models of "economic rationality," but they are perhaps "socially rational," to the extent that gift giving is an economic activity that is fundamental to ongoing social life. Mauss had a profound impact on anthropology, and economic anthropology in particular, because his focus on gifts led cross-cultural economics away from the study of individual rationalities

and toward the study of social, collective values; moreover, he showed that exchanges can also involve persons and symbols.

Marriage, for example, is a common form of social and economic exchange, or gift exchange, in which two families join together through the "giving" of the bride and groom, the transfer of gift objects, or the establishment of bridewealth or other debt, between families. There is an old saying in many parts of the world: "marry your enemies." Thus, in Shakespeare's *Henry V*, when England and France seek to end their war, young Prince Hal of England marries Princess Catherine of France, and the result is peace and social solidarity between in-laws and also between countries (see Geschiere, chapter 20, p. 355). In the United States, we often think of marriage as defined by a single event – a wedding – but in many parts of the world, especially in sub-Saharan Africa, marriage is a complex political and economic process of gift giving and payment that can take many years, if not generations, to complete. Some African men and their families give marriage their highest priority, working for years to save enough money or goods for bridewealth, and subsequent payments. Among the Lese of Zaire, for example, a man must pay an initial amount of money to the bride's father or brother to set a marriage in process, another amount for rights of sexual access, and, over the years, later payments for rights in his offspring (what we might call "childwealth," and which the Lese call an "umbilical cord payment"); if the childwealth is not paid, the father cannot claim the child as his own, and the child must take his mother's clan identity. The first editor, who worked in a Lese community, could not find a single case in which all the payments had been made in full. When someone approached completion of payment, the in-laws would raise the price, justifying it on the basis of inflation, or the wife's fertility and good work. In fact, in-laws want their daughter's husband to remain in debt, fearing that if all the payments were made, the husband (and wife) might sever connections with them. Money may be spent, goats and chickens may be eaten; but debts remain. Even after all of these payments have been made, a man's in-laws may demand gifts to compensate the wife and her family for all the hard work entailed in raising small children (the Lese call this a "feces and urine payment" because the payment refers to the time of childrearing prior to toilet-training), or may require a death payment when she dies. On one occasion, a man was denied access to land and wealth he thought he had the rights to when it was determined that his grandfather (father's father) had failed to make the umbilical cord payments for genetricial rights. He and his deceased father were thus denied full membership in the clan, and rights in the clan's land.

That gift giving is a powerful institution with important social and symbolic ramifications is illustrated by an interesting variation in the sound /gift/ across some different European languages. In English, /gift/ means "present", in German, /gift/ means "poison"; and in Danish and Swedish, /gift/ means both "married" and "poison." The definitions of "married" and "present" are by now clear, but what of "poison"? The poison in the gift lies in its ability to obligate; it coerces reciprocation and constitutes a relationship into which the receiver may not have wished to enter. Whether we like it or not, when someone gives us a gift, we are powerfully affected; depending on our culture's values associated with gifts, we may feel compelled to accept it, to reciprocate in some way, to define or re-define the social relationship created by the gift, to feel unworthy of the gift, to seek an escape from the relationship, interpret why the gift was given, or why a particular kind or quantity of gift was given. Gifts, like words, communicate, and they can communicate good things or bad. We may feel burdened and uncomfortable if we are given a gift larger than what we deem to be socially appropriate, or if we are given a gift from an inappropriate sphere of exchange.

For example, it is generally appropriate in the United States for parents to give their children gifts of money, but money is not an appropriate gift between friends or peers. Or, as another example, when an American couple receives silverware or a toaster as a wedding gift, it is because the gift is intended to symbolize the formation of a new household; were they to receive a crate of lemons, the meaning might be entirely different. When a Lese man in Zaire receives cultivated foods from an Efe hunter-gatherer, it is a form of denigration meant to highlight the Lese man's inability to grow his own food, yet when he receives *meat* from the same man, it is a positive and welcome sign for the Lese man that he and his people are of higher social status than the Efe. The semantics and spheres of economic exchange are highlighted in several of the articles presented in Part II, especially those by Bohannan, Hutchinson and Shipton.

The sort of culturally embedded economics we are describing here, however, does not comprise the entire field of economic anthropology, for there are many economic anthropologists who apply formal western-derived models to other cultures, and who seek to discern economic laws, or develop economic hypotheses and theories, that help us understand, and even predict, the economic behavior of a large number of different kinds of societies (Burling, 1962; Firth, 1967; Cook, 1968). Such scholars have often been crudely labeled "formalists," while those who believe that the application of economic theory to non-industrial societies is limited, if not wrong-headed, have been called "substantivists." The concept of substantivism comes from the economic historian Karl Polanyi, who argued that organized markets in Europe are only a very recent invention, and that they have detached economics from the rest of social life. Although classical economic theories are useful for analyzing these markets, he argued, they are not useful for analyzing the economies of other societies; for Polanyi, "market" is narrowly defined as the impersonal, modern market of Europe and North America, whereas other societies engage in what he called "marketless trade," reciprocity or redistribution. He thus excludes from his definition the many complex marketplaces throughout Africa, with their various forms of production and exchange systems, indigenous currency, and artisan guilds (Bohannan and Dalton, 1962). Polanyi defined his substantivist position in opposition to formalism (1958:243–44).

> The substantive meaning of economic derives from man's dependence for his living upon nature and his fellows. It refers to the interchange with his natural and social environment, in so far as this results in supplying him with the means of material want satisfaction.
> The formal meaning of economic derives from the logical character of the means–ends relationship, as apparent in such words as "economical" or "economizing." It refers to a definite situation of choice, namely, that between different uses of means induced by an insufficiency of means.
> . . . It is our proposition that only the substantive meaning of "economic" is capable of yielding the concepts that are required by the social sciences for an investigation of all the empirical economics of the past and present.

As a named division, the debate between substantivists and formalists is now largely relegated to the history of anthropology, and most scholars today employ some mixture of the two, taking the cultural embeddedness of economy for granted, but appreciating the roles individual choice and risk play in economic practices. Still, the tension between these two perspectives continues to influence anthropological research on economics. Major questions persist about how much substantive perspectives overemphasize conformity to social values and patterns (or give too little emphasis to the choices individuals must make in selecting their economic transactions and

social relationships), and how much formalist perspectives detach the individual from social context. In denying the applicability of economic theories designed for industrial societies to the analysis of non-industrial societies, do scholars with a substantivist perspective risk endorsing the existence of two separate types of societies, the industrial and non-industrial, market and nonmarket, "primitive" and peasant? What is the value of employing a particular definition of "market" to distinguish among different economies? There are other important questions that emerge from this debate:

How can we use our own categories of understanding to comprehend the economies of other cultures, economies that may be constructed with categories, concepts, and symbolic schemes very different from our own?

Is it possible that a focus on cultural values might impede some analyses of human economic behavior?

In its emphasis on social patterns, are there aspects of economic anthropology that resemble functionalism?

What is the relationship between individual and social economic patterns? What is the value of making a distinction between the individual and the social?

In light of the readings included in this volume, have Africanist scholars represented the economies of Africans as distinct from industrial, market economies?

Does European domination, colonialism, and the emergence of capitalist, class societies in Africa mean that formal western-derived models are now applicable to African economies?

In Chapter 6, Mary Douglas addresses the problem of poverty among the Lele of the Kasai region of Zaire. In a comparative analysis of the Lele and Bushong economies, she argues that economies are deeply embedded in social ideas and practices. She takes as her case two neighboring groups with starkly different levels of economic productivity: the Lele are poor, while the Bushong are rich. To some extent, their differences can be explained by the fact that the Lele have less fertile soil and less efficient technology, but they also work less at the production of goods. However, working less cannot be explained by environment, but by the social and cultural values and organization of work. She pays special attention to the interesting fact that Lele men begin working at age thirty, while the Bushong begin work at age eighteen; and whereas the Lele retire in middle-age, the Bushong retire only when they are in their sixties, or are unable to work. Douglas carefully and systematically compares the two societies' authority structures, age of marriage, incidence of polygyny, and importance of seniority, to show why and how they produce different work schedules, and therefore very different levels of production, scarcity and wealth.

Chapter 7, "Some Principles of Exchange and Investment among the Tiv," considers the cultural constitution of the economy from another perspective: the organization and semantics of exchange. In this influential essay, Paul Bohannan elaborates a concept he calls "spheres of exchange." As with many anthropological developments, this concept brings us back to Malinowski. In the Trobriands, Kula exchanges constitute a realm of transaction distinct from barter or trade, which is called *gimwali*. *Kula* valuables, then, could not be bought, sold, or exchanged in everyday markets, but rather only in the series of exchanges of *Kula* goods that linked the various islands. *Kula* valuables, in turn, were made up of several spheres; the most important one included the armshells and necklaces, while another comprised axe-blades and lime spoons, and another involved certain foods, such as yams, bananas and taro, that could be presented or offered as gifts (Gudeman, 1986:123). As Bohannan tell us,

among the Tiv of Nigeria goods are placed in particular categories or spheres of exchange; goods within the same sphere are interchangeable, or exchangeable, but goods from different spheres are not. Chickens, goats, and everyday *subsistence goods* constitute one sphere; *prestige goods* such as cattle, rituals offices, and medicines constitute a second sphere; and *rights in people*, such as wives and children, make up the third. Although an item in any single sphere was usually exchangeable only for another item in the same sphere, some movement was possible, even desirable, because each sphere was differently valued in terms of prestige, status, and morality: the first sphere was less highly valued than the second, and the second less highly valued than the third. Many Tiv looked for opportunities to convert a first sphere good to a second sphere good, while converting a good the other way was considered quite undesirable, even shameful. Indeed, Bohannan suggests that when the Tiv invest their wealth, they invest only if it can convert to a higher category: converting subsistence wealth into prestige wealth, prestige wealth into rights in people.

In Chapter 8, Coquery-Vidrovitch's Marxist essay offers a contrasting example of economic anthropology. Marxism has had an important place in economic anthropology's move toward studying regional and local economic histories. Coquery-Vidrovitch moves beyond the study of any single community to articulate a pervasive pattern of production throughout Sub-Saharan Africa: an African mode of production. Coquery-Vidrovitch argues that most Africanist scholars have not taken economic inequality or class relations as central topics of study, and have instead looked primarily at egalitarianism and kinship organization in subsistence and stateless societies. This is where Marxism becomes relevant. One of the central features of Marxist economics is a focus on how power and wealth are unequally distributed in society. In one of the most famous works on inequality and production, for example,

Claude Meillassoux (1981) describes how, among the Guro of Côte d'Ivoire, elders exploit young men by controlling the *means of reproduction* (wives), either through polygynous marriages that deplete the supply of available women, or by demanding bridewealth payments so high that young men are coerced into working for the elders. Most Marxist scholars emphasize production as the building block of other aspects of society, which then in turn support or reinforce production. While the concept of mode of production is complex, and has been subject to a wide range of interpretations and uses, Marx wrote quite clearly the following definition in the preface to *Contributions to a Critique of Political Economy*:

> The sum total of these relations of production constitutes the economic structure of society – the real foundation on which rise legal and political superstructures and to which correspond definite forms of social consciousness. The mode of production in material life determines the general character of the social, political, and spiritual processes of life (1859 [1983]: 49).

Coquery-Vidrovitch argues that the social organization of production is not defined by political organization, such as the commonly used dichotomy of state and stateless societies (see Part I), but rather by the control over long distance trade by kinship or other groupings. Although the particular form of power that obtains in any given society is largely dependent upon the kind of groups that rise to power, the kinship system, and the general organization of labor and value, the social system is epiphenomenal, or secondary, to production. The African mode of production constitutes the basic organization of African societies.

One of Marx's most important contributions was to shed light on the social relations of production, especially through his concept "commodity fetishism." For Marx, commodity fetishism illustrates the tendency in a capitalist mode of production to attribute value to things (the products of labor) rather than to labor (social relations). In other words, the relationships between people appear as relationships between things. Commodity fetishism refers to the reification of capital, as in the Luo case described by Parker Shipton, in which people attribute moral power and agency to money, or more generally speaking when we conceive of money as having an intrinsic value apart from the actions and beliefs of human beings. This is not to say that this conception is false, since "things" are indeed meaningfully related to one another; Marx's point is that commodity fetishism conceals the social relationships that constitute value, and masks the relations of oppression or exploitation between laborers and those who control the means of production. Precisely because it hides these relations from view, workers remain unaware of the nature of their exploitation, and commodity fetishism thus becomes an instrument of oppression.

Shipton and Hutchinson elaborate upon Bohannan's work by situating the concept of spheres of exchange in the histories of the Luo and Nuer (a group historically related to the Luo) respectively, but they also bring into relief some fascinating aspects of fetishism, and the social meanings of money. Both Shipton and Hutchinson reveal the ways in which the members of these African societies classify money in cultural, moral terms. Just as religions are sometimes shaped in the image of society (see Part V), the economy is a metaphor and model of, and for, the moral and social order. The Luo distinction between good and evil money reflects relationships between men and women, youths and elders, and is framed in terms of ancestors, lineage, and marriage payments. For Luo, an ostensibly simple good, such as a homestead rooster, should not be sold because it symbolizes masculinity, sexual potency, and the continuity of the lineage, among many other things; thus to sell a rooster for money is tantamount to selling one's masculinity and violating the integrity of the lineage, and money earned from such a sale is tainted and brings "bitter" blessings.

The Nuer distinction between good and bad uses of cattle and money turns about a distinction between blood and non-blood spheres of exchange: because the Nuer equate cattle and people, cattle represent the blood of both the animal and the lineage, and should therefore be used in exchanges that create enduring bonds between people (such as marriage), or that relate people and the supernatural (in religious ritual); money, in contrast, should be used for impersonal transactions such as paying taxes. The Nuer, like the Luo, further classify money into good and bad types. Some Nuer beer sellers, for example, separate the monies collected from Nuer and non-Nuer clients. They use money from selling beer to non-Nuer to pay taxes, and use money collected from Nuer to buy cattle. The Nuer also differentiate cattle into the "cattle of girls" (usually acquired as bridewealth) and the "cattle of money" (usually acquired through purchase), and draw a parallel between these two kinds of cattle and the blood and non-blood spheres of exchange. The former cattle ideally circulate only among kinsmen, and the latter is more freely circulated. However, Hutchinson details the complicated ways in which these distinctions are muted, or in which one kind of cattle is converted into another – from a blood sphere of exchange to a non-blood sphere exchange. The symbolic and political import of girls and women becomes central to these distinctions, as does the fact that the equation between people and cattle quite differently affected men and women. These are subjects Hutchinson takes up in great detail in a larger and more comprehensive study (Hutchinson, 1996).

For our purposes here, the larger significance of these studies is that the European introduction of certain kinds of money and modes of exchange into Africa resulted in their transformation rather than replication. Economists and evangelists have often puzzled over their inability to introduce western concepts and practices into Africa, as if they expected them to be reproduced perfectly in all times and places. Such a perfect reproduction could occur only if economics were *isolable* from other aspects of society and history. When Islam, Christianity, European styled nationalism and democracy, and other ideas entered into Africa, they entered into a dialogic relation with African ideas. These studies including Geschiere's study of economics and witchcraft (Chapter 20) show how global phenomena, such as capital, money, taxes, and war are given culturally specific meanings across time and space. Indeed, their historical treatments of these pastoralists contrasts with Evans-Pritchard's ahistorical treatment of the Nuer in Chapter 2, and represent one of the important changes in intellectual perspective we outlined in the Introduction.

Hutchinson, especially, details the ways in which moral distinctions between good and bad sorts of commodities or spheres of exchange are embedded in a particular history of civil war, and other turbulence. Such distinctions serve not only as responses to history, but as history itself, shaping strategies of resistance to money and capitalism. Indeed, as Hutchinson shows, the Nuer have good reason to fear the encroachment of external political and economic forces. The attribution of life and morality to money is one way to symbolically (and unconsciously) articulate displeasure with social and cultural change. Both Shipton and Hutchinson illustrate that the process by which people simultaneously resist and comply with economic change is marked by extraordinary ambivalence and uncertainty. It is a process in which people creatively seek ways of having a dynamic economy that still resonates with local meanings, and, in the case of the Nuer, preserves the important equation between humans and cattle.

Keith Hart complements all of these studies by illustrating the failure of western categories of the economy to account for the economic and social behaviour of urban Africans. In his essay on the informal economy in Accra, Ghana, Hart explores the linkages among economic development, unemployment, wage income, and rural–urban migration. He shows how little economists actually discern of the economy when they consider unemployment rates, and the conventional indicators of economic growth, in the absence of data on informal productive activities. Rural–urban migration often appears to result in a burgeoning number of unemployed, passive and exploited poor, yet he discovers that a significant portion of the urban economy is made up by people who, though unemployed in the formal sector for formal wages, actually accumulate a great deal of income, and have a powerful effect on the total economy, through "legitimate" informal activities, such as farming and gardening, transport, street hawking, laundering, vehicle repair, or begging, and "illegitimate" informal activities such as theft, prostitution, gambling, smuggling, bribery, and embezzlement. In fact, these opportunities may be alluring enough

that some people choose to participate in the informal sector instead of, or in addition to, the formal sector of the economy. Although economists had long argued that the central conflict (or obstacle) in African economic development was between capitalist/precapitalist, modern/traditional economic activities, Hart tells us that such a distinction is seldom fruitful in the analysis of African economies. Many African nations have dual economies (MacGaffey, 1987; 1991) – wage earners and the self-employed – and the economies complement rather than conflict with one another (Smith, 1989: 301; Gerry, 1987; Hill, 1970). The co-existence of these two sectors, and its profound economic consequences, are not revealed in the sorts of data or statistics that form the basis of most economic work, but rather in the ethnographic studies that describe actual social and individual practices, and that illuminate the many ways in which formal and informal sectors articulate with one another. Hart thus points the way to an especially promising area of research for anthropologists: where econometric techniques fail, the anthropologist often succeeds.

References

Adepoju, Aderanti and Christine Oppong. eds. 1994. *Gender, Work and Population in Sub-Saharan Africa*. Portsmouth, NH: Heinemann.

Berry, Sara S. 1978. *Cocoa, Custom and Socio-economic Change in Rural West Nigeria*. Oxford: Clarendon.

Berry, Sara. 1984. *Fathers Work for their Sons: Accumulation, Mobility, and Class formation in an Extended Yoruba Community*. Berkeley and Los Angeles: University of California Press.

Bird-David, Nurit. 1992. "Beyond the 'Original Affluent Society:' A Culturalist Reformulation." *Current Anthropology* 33 (1): 25–47.

Bohannan, Paul and George Dalton, eds. 1962. *Markets in Africa*. Evanston: Northwestern University Press.

Boserup, Ester. 1970. *Women's Role in Economic Development*. London: George Allen and Unwin.

Burling, Robbins. 1962. "Maximization Theories and the Study of Economic Anthropology." *American Anthropologist* 64: 802–21.

Cohen, Abner. 1969. *Custom and Politics in Urban Africa: A Study of Hausa Migrants in Yoruba Towns*. Berkeley: University of California Press.

Cook, Scott. 1973. "Economic Anthropology: Problems in Theory, Method, and Analysis." In John J. Honigmann, ed. *Handbook of Social and Cultural Anthropology*. Chicago: Rand McNally and Company, pp. 795–860.

Coquery, Catherine. 1978. "Research on an African Mode of Production." In David Seddon (ed.) *Relations of Production*. London: Cass.

Donham, Donald. 1990. *History, Power, Ideology*. Cambridge: Cambridge University Press.

Epstein, A. L. 1958. *Politics in an Urban African Community.* Manchester: Manchester University Press.

Ferguson, James. 1990. *The Anti-Politics Machine.* Cambridge: Cambridge University Press.

Firth, Raymond, ed. 1967. *Themes in Economic Anthropology.* London: Tavistock.

Fratkin, Elliot, Kathleen A. Galvin and Eric Abella Roth, eds. 1994. *African Pastoralist Systems: An Integrated Approach.* Boulder: Lynne Rienner.

Gerry, Chris. 1987. "Developing Economies and the Informal Sector in Historical Perspective." In Louis A. Ferman, Stuart Henry, and Michele Hoyman, eds. *The Informal Economy.* Special Issue of The Annals of the American Academy of Political and Social Science. Newbury Park, CA.: Sage Publications.

Gudeman, Stephen. 1986. *Economics as Culture: Models and Metaphors of Livelihood.* London, Boston and Henley: Routledge and Kegan Paul.

Guyer, Jane. 1981. "Household and Community in African Studies." *African Studies Review,* 24: 37–137.

Harms, Robert. 1981. *River of Wealth, River of Sorrow: The Central Zaire Basin in the Era of the Slave and Ivory Trade. 1500–1891.* New Haven: Yale University Press.

Hart, J. K. 1982. *The Political Economy of West African Agriculture.* Cambridge: Cambridge University Press.

Hill, Polly. 1970. *Studies in Rural Capitalism in West Africa.* Cambridge: Cambridge University Press.

Hutchinson, Sharon. 1996. *Nuer Dilemmas: Coping with Money, War and the State.* Berkeley and Los Angeles: University of California Press.

Kopytoff, Igor and Suzanne Miers, eds. 1977. *Slavery in Africa: Historical and Anthropological Perspectives.* Madison: University of Wisconsin Press.

LeClair, Edward E. Jr., and Harold K. Schneider, eds. 1968. *Economic Anthropology: Readings in Theory and Analysis.* New York: Holt, Rinehart and Winston.

Little, Peter D. and Michael J. Watts, eds. 1994. *Living under Contract: Contract Farming and Agrarian Transformation in Sub-Saharan Africa.* Madison: University of Wisconsin Press.

MacGaffey, Janet. 1987. *Entrepreneurs and Parasites: The Struggle for Indigenous Capitalism in Zaire.* Cambridge: Cambridge University Press.

MacGaffey, Janet. 1991. *The Real Economy of Zaire: The Contribution of Smuggling and other Unofficial Activities to National Wealth.* London: James Currey.

Malinowski, Bronislaw. 1922. *Argonauts of the Western Pacific.* New York: Dutton.

Marx, Karl. 1859 [1983]. "Mode of Production, Civil Society, and Ideology." From Karl Marx, *A Contribution to the Critique of Political Economy,* reprinted in Tom Bottomore and Patrick Goode, eds. *Readings in Marxist Sociology,* pp. 49–50. Oxford: Oxford University Press.

Matory, J. Lorand. 1994. *Sex and the Empire That Is No More: Gender and the Politics of Metaphor in Oyo Yoruba Religion.* Minneapolis: University of Minnesota Press.

Mauss, Marcel. [1925] 1954. *The Gift: Forms and Functions of Exchange in Archaic Society,* trans. Ian Cunnison. London: Cohen & West.

Mayer, Phillip. 1962. Migrancy and the Study of Africans in Town. *American Anthropologist,* 64: 576–92.

Meillassoux, Claude. 1981. *Maidens, Meal and Money.* Cambridge: Cambridge University Press.

Mitchell, Clyde. 1956. "The Kalela Dance." *Rhodes-Livingstone* Paper, no. 27.

Moodie, T. Dunbar with Vivienne Ndatshe. 1994. *Going for God: Men, Mines and Migration.* Berkeley and Los Angeles: University of California Press.

Moore, Henrietta and Megan Vaughan. 1994. *Cutting Down Trees: Gender, Nutrition, and Agricultural Change in the Northern Province of Zambia. 1890–1990.* Portsmouth, NH: Heinemann.

Morgan, Lewis Henry. [1877] 1963. *Ancient Society.* Cleveland: Meridian Books, World Publishing Co.

Murray, Colin. 1981. *Families Divided: The Impact of Migrant Labor in Lesotho.* Johannesburg: Ravan.

Polanyi, Karl. 1958. "The Economy as Instituted Process." In Karl Polanyi, Conrad Arensberg and Harry W. Pearson, eds. *Trade and Markets in the Early Empires,* pp. 243–270. Glencoe: The Free Press.

Robertson, A. F. 1987. *The Dynamics of Productive*

Relationships: African Share Contracts in Comparative Perspective. Cambridge: Cambridge University Press.

Sahlins, Marshall. 1968. "Notes on the Original Affluent Society." In Richard B. Lee and Irven DeVore, eds. Man the Hunter, pp. 84–89. Chicago: Aldine Publishing Company.

Sahlins, Marshall. 1972. Stone Age Economics. Chicago: Aldine Publishing Company.

Singh, Uberoi J. P. 1962. Politics of the Kula Ring: An Analysis of the Findings of Bronislaw Malinowski. Manchester: Manchester University Press.

Smith, M. Estellie. 1989. "The Informal Economy." In Stuart Plattner, ed. Economic

Anthropology, p. 292–317. Stanford, CA.: Stanford University Press.

Southall, Aidan, ed. 1973. Urban Anthropology: Cross-Cultural Studies of Urbanization. Oxford: Oxford University Press.

Southall, Aidan. 1974. "State Formation in Africa." Annual Review of Anthropology, vol. 3: 153–165.

Watson, W. 1958. Tribal Cohesion in a Money Economy: A Study of the Mambwe People of Northern Rhodesia. Manchester: Manchester University, for the Rhodes–Livingstone Institute.

Werbner, Richard, ed. 1982. Land Reforms in the Making: Tradition, Public Policy, and Ideology in Botswana. London: Rex Collings.

Suggested Readings

Berry, Sara. 1984. "The Food Crisis and Agrarian Change in Africa: A Review Essay." African Studies Review, 27 (2): 59–112.

Bohannan, Paul and Laura Bohannan. 1968. Tiv Economy. London: Longman.

Chayanov, A. V. [1925] 1966. The Theory of Peasant Economy. Homewood, Ill.:Irwin.

Comaroff, John L. ed. 1980. The Meaning of Marriage Payments. London: Academic Press.

Creevey, Lucy, ed. 1986. Women Farmers in Africa: Rural Development in Mali and the Sahel. Syracuse, N.Y.: Syracuse University Press.

Curtin, Philip D. 1984. Cross-Cultural Trade in World History. Cambridge: Cambridge University Press.

Evans-Pritchard, E. E. 1940. The Nuer. Oxford: Clarendon Press.

Firth, Raymond. 1957. "The Place of Malinowski in the History of Economic Anthropology." In Raymond Firth, ed. Man and Culture: An Evaluation of the Work of Bronislaw Malinowski. pp. 209–228. London, Boston and Henley: Routledge and Kegan Paul.

Forde, Daryll. [1934] 1963. Habitat, Economy, and Society. New York: Dutton.

Freund, Bill, 1984. "Labor and Labor History in Africa: A Review of the Literature." African Studies Review, 27 (2): 1–58.

Geertz, Clifford. 1963. Agricultural Involution. Berkeley: University of California Press.

Godelier, Maurice. 1977. Perspectives in Marxist

Anthropology. Cambridge: Cambridge University Press.

Goody, Jack and Stanley Tambiah. 1973. Bridewealth and Dowry. Cambridge: Cambridge University Press.

Gras, N. S. B. 1927. "Anthropology and Economics." In W. F. Ogburn and A. A. Goldenweiser, eds. The Social Sciences and their Inter-relations, pp. 10–23. Boston: Houghton Mifflin.

Greenfield, Sidney and Arnold Strickon, eds. 1986. Entrepreneurship and Social Change. Monographs in Economic Anthropology, no. 2, Lanham, Md.: University Press of America, for the Society of Economic Anthropology.

Guyer, Jane I. 1984. "Naturalism in Models of African Production." Man 19: 371–88.

Guyer, Jane I. 1991. "Female Farming in Anthropology and African History." In Michaela di Leonardo, ed. Gender at the Crossroads of Knowledge: Feminist Anthropology in the Postmodern Era. Berkeley and Los Angeles: University of California Press.

Herskovits, Meville J. and M. Harwitz, eds. Economic Transition in Africa. Evanston, Ill.: Northwestern University Press.

Hill, Polly. 1969. "Hidden Trade in Hausaland." Man 4: 393–409.

Homans, George. 1958. "Social Behavior as Exchange." American Journal of Sociology 63: 597–606.

Iyam, David Uru. 1995. *The Broken Hoe: Cultural Reconfiguration in Biase Southeast Nigeria.* Chicago: University of Chicago Press.

Leach, Jerry Wayne and Edmund Ronald Leach, eds. 1983. *The Kula: New Perspectives on Massim Exchange.* Cambridge: Cambridge University Press.

Lee, Richard B. 1979. *The !Kung San: Men, Women and Work in a Foraging Society.* Cambridge: Cambridge University Press.

Lee, Richard B., and Irven De Vore, eds. 1962. *Man the Hunter.* Chicago: Aldine Publishing Company.

Ortiz, Sutti. 1983. *Economic Anthropology: Topics and Theories.* Monographs in Economic Anthropology, no. 2. Lanham, Md.: University Press of America, for the Society for Economic Anthropology.

Rappaport, Roy A. 1968. *Pigs for the Ancestors.* New Haven: Yale University Press.

Rigby, Peter. 1969. *Cattle and Kinship among the Gogo.* Ithaca, NY.: Cornell University Press.

Robbins, Lionel. 1935. *An Essay on the Nature and Significance of Economic Science.* New York: St Martins Press.

Salisbury, Richard F. 1962. *From Stone to Steel.* Melbourne: University of Australia Press.

Schneider, Harold K. 1964. "A Model of African Indigenous Economy and Society." *Comparative Studies in Society and History,* 7: 37–55.

Tambiah, Stanley Jeyaraja. 1968. "The Magical Power of Words." *Man* 3: 175–206. Also reprinted in Stanley Jeyaraja Tambiah. 1985. *Culture, Thought and Social Action: An Anthropological Perspective.* Cambridge: Harvard University Press.

Wolf, Eric. 1966. *Peasants.* Engelwood Cliffs, N.J.: Prentice-Hall.

6

LELE ECONOMY COMPARED WITH THE BUSHONG

MARY DOUGLAS

The Lele[1] and the Bushong[2] are separated only by the Kasai River. The two tribes recognize a common origin, their houses, clothes and crafts are similar in style, their languages are closely related.[3] Yet the Lele are poor, while the Bushong are rich. The Lele produce only for subsistence, sharing their goods, or distributing them among themselves as gifts and fees. The Bushong have long been used to producing for exchange, and their native economy was noted for its use of money and its specialists and markets. Everything that the Lele have or can do, the Bushong have more and can do better. They produce more, live better, and populate their region more densely.

The first question is whether there are significant differences in the physical environment of the two peoples. Both live in the lat. 5 Degrees, in the area of forest park merging into savannah, which borders the south of the Congo rain forest. They both have a heavy annual rainfall of 1400 to 1600 mm. (40 to 60 inches) per annum. The mean annual temperature is about 78°F. (25°C.). As we should expect from their proximity, the climatic conditions are much the same for both tribes.

Nonetheless, a curious discrepancy appears in their respective assessments of their climate. The Bushong, like the local Europeans, welcome the dry season of mid-May to mid-August as a cold season, whereas the Lele

---

[1]   The Lele are a tribe, inhabiting the west border of the Bakuba Empire. They are divided into three chiefdoms, of which only the most westerly has been studied. The Chief of the eastern Lele, at Perominenge, apes Kuba fashions in his little capital; the men wear basketry hats held on with metal pins, the chief has some of the dress and paraphernalia of the Nyimi. How much deeper this resemblance goes, it is impossible to say, since conditions at the time of field work were not favorable for study of this chiefdom. Everything that is said here concerning the Lele refers to the western Lele, whose chief, when visits were made in 1949–50 and 1953, was Norbert Pero Mihondo. The field work was carried out under the generous auspices of the International African Institute, and of the *Institut de Recherche Scientifique en Afrique Centrale*.
[2]   The Bushong are the ruling tribe of the Kuba Kindom. They were studied in 1953–56 by Dr. Vansina, to whom I am deeply indebted for his collaboration and for supplying unpublished information for this paper.
[3]   According to the Lexico-statistical survey conducted by Dr. Vansina, there is an 80 per cent similarity between the two languages.

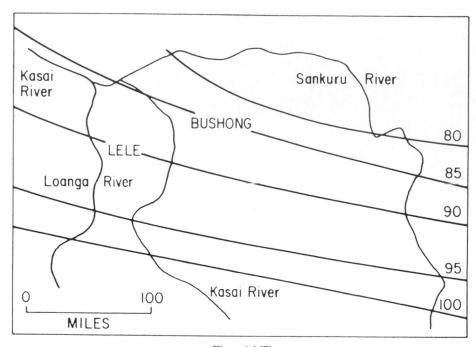

Figure 6.1 [7]
Average Length of Dry Season Expressed in Days
(From: F. Buitot – "Saisons et Périodes Sèches et Pluvieuses au Congo Belge." Bruxelles, 1954)

regard it as dangerously hot. The Bushong in the north tend to have a dry season ten days shorter (Bultot 1954) than most of the Lele, (see figure 6.1), and the Lele soils retain less moisture, and the vegetation is thinner, so that the impression of drought is more severe, but otherwise there seems no objectively measurable difference in the climate to account for their attitudes.

There are certainly important differences in the soil, drainage and vegetation. The Lele are distinctly less fortunate. Their soils belong to the most easterly extension of the Kwango plateau system, and to some extent share in the sterility characteristic of that region. On that plateau, the soils are too poor to support anything but a steppe-like vegetation in spite of the ample rainfall. The soils consist of sands,

poor in assimilable minerals of any kind, lacking altogether in ferro-magnates or heavy minerals, and so permeable that they are incapable of benefiting from the heavy rainfall[4] (see Figure 6.2). On the Bushong side of the Kasai River the soil is altogether richer, and mineral deposits, particularly of iron ore, occur. Whereas Lele country is characterized by rolling grasslands with forest galleries along the river banks, Bushong country is relatively well-forested, although the sketch map tends to exaggerate the forested area on their side of the Kasai.

With such important differences in their basic natural resources, we are not surprised that Lele country is poorer and more sparsely populated. But how much poverty and how low a density can be attributed to

[4]   We are very grateful to M. L. Cahen, Director of the *Musée du Congo Belge*, Tervuren, for guidance on the physical environment of the two tribes.

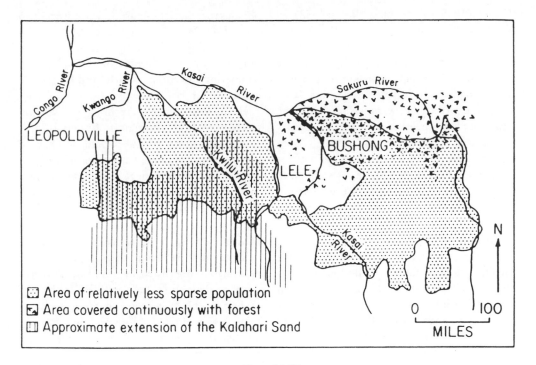

Figure 6.2 [8]
(From: N. Nicolai & J. Jacques – "La transformation du paysage Congolais par Chemin de Fer" 1954 p. 112)
Population Density and Forest Cover (Lele and Bushong)

the environmental factor? Can we leave the matter here?

There is no certain method of estimating the extent to which environment itself limits the development of an area. The Pende of Gungu, immediate neighbors of the Lele, inhabit an area even poorer in soils than the Lele area, and as poor as those worked by the notoriously wretched Suku of Kahemba and Feshi. The Lele are poor, but the Suku are known as a miserable, dispirited people, incapable of exploiting to the full such resources as their poor environment offers. The Pende are famous as energetic cultivators, well-nourished and industrious. All three peoples grow different staple crops; the Pende, millet; the Suku, manioc; the Lele, maize. There is obviously no end to the speculation one could indulge as to what the potentialities of the environment might be.

Congo geographers have been much occu-

pied by the question of the relation between soil and population density. The whole Belgian Congo is an area of very low density. Fifty per cent of its surface has a population of less than 2.4 to the square kilometer (roughly 6 to square mile) (Gourou 1955 : 4). It is generally agreed (Gourou 1955 cites Cohen; Nicolai 1952 : 247) that there is a rough correlation of poor sandy soils with low densities, insofar as the small stretch of relatively more populous country occurs in a favored gap between the Kwango "kalahari" plateau and sands to the north. However, it is also agreed that soil poverty in itself is not an adequate explanation of the pockets of extra low density which occur, especially on the second and fifth parallels of South latitude. Professor Gourou says emphatically and repeatedly that the sterility of the soils cannot be held to account for all the densities of less than 2 to the square kilometer (5 to the square mile) in the Belgian Congo

(Gourou 1955 : 52, 57, 109; Nicolai 1952). In Northern Rhodesia we have an illuminating case. The Ndembu live at an average density of 6 to the square mile, in many areas at a density of only 3, but according to a careful calculation of the capacity of their land, worked according to their own methods, the area should be capable of supporting a population of from 17 to 38 to the square mile, (6.8 to 15 per square kilometer) (Turner 1957).

In short, we cannot assume, as some have done, that there is any universal tendency to maximize food production (Harris 1959), or that the food resources of a region are the only factor limiting its population.

For the Lele and the Bushong the relative densities are as follows. The territory of Mweka, where the Bushong live, has an average density of 4–5 to the square kilometer (11 to the square mile). The BCK railway running through the area has attracted an immigrant population of Luba. If we abstract the railway zone from our figures, we find that the Bushong proper live at a density of (Gourou 1955 : 109) only 3 or 4 to the square kilometer, (7–10 to the square mile). The Lele[5] inhabit Basongo territory, where the average density is from 2 to 4 to the square kilometer (5–7 to the square mile), but since the Lele account for only half the population (among recent immigrants of foreign tribesmen to work in the Brabanta oil concession, refinery and port, and among Cokwe hunters), we can suppose that until recently Lele themselves used to live at a mere 1.7 to the square kilometer (4 to the square mile).

When the geographers agree that poverty of soil is not a sufficient explanation for the degree of poverty prevailing in similar areas, we are justified in looking for a sociological explanation to supplement the effect of environmental factors. For one thing, it is obvious that the demographic factor works two ways. Low density is partly the result of inferior technology, applied to inferior resources, but it may also inhibit development by hampering enterprises which need large-scale collaboration.

If we now consider technology, we find many suggestive differences. In certain processes marked superiority would be likely to increase output. Others are proof of a higher standard of living. Surveying these, we find that in hunting, fishing and housebuilding, the Bushong worker uses more specialized materials and equipment than the Lele, and in cultivation he spends more energy and time.

Take hunting first, since the Lele are passionately interested in it and pride themselves on their skill (Douglas 1954). In the eyes of their neighbors, it seems that they are notorious as inefficient hunters, particularly because they do not use nets, and only rarely make pit traps.

Hunting is the only occupation in which large numbers of Lele men regularly combine. They reckon that fifteen to twenty men and ten dogs are necessary for a good hunt. Using nets, the Bushong need a team of only ten men, and can hope to do well with five. In short, the Bushong hunter uses better capital equipment, and his hours of hunting are more productive.

Why should the Lele not have nets? The materials are present in the forest on both sides of the river, and the Lele know what nets are. Making a net is presumably a long task. In view of the local deforestation and the resulting paucity of game, it may be a case in which costly capital equipment is simply not worthwhile. Bushong nets are made by their women. Perhaps the rest of the answer lies in the different division of labor between men and women in each tribe, and the larger proportion

---

[5]   According to P. Gourou, 1951, the average density of the population of all tribes for the Basongo–Port Francqui region, in which the Lele now account for only half, is 3 to 4 to the square kilometer. This agrees with calculations based on the total number of Lele in that area, about 26,000, and the extent of their territory, about 63 by 110 miles, which give a Lele density of roughly 4 to the square mile, or 1.7 to the sq. km.

of the total agricultural work which Lele leave to their women. Whatever the reason, we note that the absence of nets is consistent with a general Lele tendency not to invest time and labor in long-term equipment.

The same applies to pit-traps. Lele know how to make these, and frequently talk about them. The task requires a stay in the forest of several days and nights, or regular early dawn journeys and late returns. The traps are hard work to dig with only a blunt matchet for spade, and once set, they need to be watched. In practice few men ever trouble to make them. I suspect that the reason in this case is again that the amount of game caught by pit-traps tends to be disappointing in relation to the effort of making them, and that the Lele have felt discouraged when using a technique which is more productive in the thicker forests on the other side of the river.

Lest it be thought that the Lele neglect capital-intensive aids because hunting is a sport, a pleasure, and a religious activity, let me deny any parallel with English fox-hunting. The Lele would have applauded the French Brigadier of fiction who used his sabre to slay the fox. Their eager purchase of firearms whenever they can get the money and the license shows that their culture does not restrict them to inferior techniques when these do not require long-term collaboration and effort.

In fishing the Lele are also inferior. Their country is well watered by streams and rivers, and bounded on two sides by the great Kasai, and on the west by the swift-flowing Loange. Along the banks of the Kasai are fishing villages, whose men dot the river with elaborate traps and fishing platforms. These fishermen are mostly Dinga, or Bushong, and not often Lele. In one northern village, near the Kasai, Lele women used to go every two days to the nearest Dinga village where, lacking claims of kinship, they obtained fish by bartering manioc. Compared with the Bushong the Lele as a whole are not good at fishing, nor at canoe making. There is no need

to describe in detail the diversity and elaborate character of Bushong fishing equipment, but it is worth noting that in some types of fishing, using several canoes trailing nets, the team may consist of twenty men or more. These skills may be a legacy from their distant past, since the Bushong claim to have entered the territory in canoes along the Kasai river, while the Lele claim to have travelled overland (Vansina 1956) and to have found the river banks already occupied by Dinga fishing villages.

If the Lele were originally landsmen, and the Bushong originally fishermen, this might account for more than the latter's present technical superiority in fishing. For primitive fishermen are necessarily more heavily equipped than are primitive hunters and cultivators. The need for fishing tackle, nets, lines, hooks, traps, curing platforms, and for watercraft as well as for weirs and dams makes quite a different balance in the allocation of time between the consumer's and producers' goods. If they started in this area with the typical balance of a fishing economy, this may have meant an initial advantage for the Bushong in the form of a habit of working for postponed consumption.

Be that as it may, Lele mostly leave fishing to their women. Their simple method is to block a slow-moving stream, so as to turn the nearest valley into a marsh. In this they make mud banks and ponds, where they set traps for fish scarcely bigger than minnows. A morning's work draining out such a pond and catching the fish floundering in the mud yields a bare pint or so of fish. In the dry season they make a two-day expedition to the Lumbundji, where they spread a saponaceous vegetable poison over the low waters, and pull out the suffocated fish by hand, or in baskets.

As to housing, Lele and Bushong huts look much alike. They are low rectangular huts, roofed with palm thatch. The walls are covered with rows of split bamboos or palm ribs, lashed onto layers of palmleaf, on a frame of strong saplings. Deceptive in appearance,

Lele huts when new look much sturdier than those of the Bushong, but in practice they last less well: the Lele hut is more roughly and quickly made. A well-built one will last about six years without repair, and, as they are capable of being renewed piecemeal, by the substitution of new walls or roof thatch, they are not replaced until the whole village is moved to a new site, and the owner decides that he has neglected his hut so long that it will not stand removal. A hut in good condition is transported to a new site, with from six to eight men carrying the roof, and four at a time carrying the walls.

Bushong huts are also transportable. They are made with slightly different materials. For the roof thatch, they use the leaves of the raffia palm, as do the Lele. For the walls, they use the reputedly more waterproof leaves of a dwarf palm growing in the marshes. Over this, instead of palm ribs split in half, they sew narrow strips of bamboo, where available. Lele consider bamboo to be a tougher wood than palm, but it is rare in their region. The narrow strips are held in place by stitching in pleasing geometric patterns (Nicolai & Jacques 1954 : 272ff). A rich Bushong man, who can command labor, can build a hut that will last much longer than the ordinary man's hut, up to fifteen years without major repairs. The palace of the Nyimi at Mushenge, which was still in good condition in 1956, had been originally built in 1920.

The Bushong use an ingenious technique of ventilation, a movable flap between the roof and the walls, which lets out smoke. It is impossible to say whether they do this because their building is too solid to let the smoke filter through the walls, or whether they are more fastidious and painstaking about their comfort than the Lele, whose huts do certainly retain some of the smoke of their fires.

Within the hut, the furnishings illustrate the difference in material wealth, for the Bushong have a much greater refinement of domestic goods. They sit on stools, lay their heads on carved neck rests (often necessary to accommodate an elaborate hair style). They eat from basketry plates, with iron or wooden spoons. They have a bigger range of specialized basketry or wooden containers for food, clothing, cosmetics. A man who has more than one hat needs a hat box and a place for his metal hat pins. Lele do not make fibre hats, and only a few men in the village may possess a skin hat. The beautiful Bushong caskets for cosmetics are prized objects in many European museums. When a Lele woman has prepared some cosmetic from camwood, she uses it at once, and there is rarely enough left over for it to be worth storing in a special container. Only a young mother who, being cared for by her own mother after her delivery, has nothing else to do but grind camwood for herself and the baby, stores the prepared ointment in a little hanging basket hooked into the wall, enough for a few days.

Dr. Vansina was impressed with the high protein content of the Bushong diet, with the large quantities of fish and meat they ate, and the variety in their food. The Lele gave an impression of always being hungry, always dreaming of meat, often going to bed fasting because their stomach revolts at the idea of a vegetable supper. They talk a lot about hunger, and *ihiobe*, an untranslatable word for meatlessness and fishlessness. The Bushong cultivate a wider range of crops and also grow citrus fruits, pineapples, pawpaws, mangoes, sugar cane and bananas, which are either rare or completely absent in the Lele economy.

In short, the Bushong seem to be better sheltered, better fed, better supplied with goods, and with containers for storing what they do not immediately need. This is what we mean by saying that the Bushong are richer than the Lele. As to village-crafts, such as carving and smithing, the best of the Lele products can compete in quality with Bushong manufacture, but they are much scarcer. The Lele are more used to eating and drinking out of folded green leaves than from the basket plates and carved beakers common among the Bushong. Their medical instruments, too, are simpler. If, instead of cutting down a gourd top, they carve a wooden enema funnel for a baby, they make it as fine and thin as they can, but do not adorn it with the elaborate pattern found on some Bushong examples.

Before considering agriculture, we should mention the method of storing grain, for this is a rough index of output. Both Lele and Bushong houses are built with an internal grain store, suspended from the roof or supported on posts over the hearth. Here grain and even fish and meat can be preserved from the ravages of damp and of insects by the smoke of the fire. Most Lele women have no other grain store. Bushong women find this too small and use external granaries, built like little huts, raised a few feet above ground. These granaries, of which there may be one or two in a Lele village, are particularly characteristic of the southern Bushong villages, while in the north the huts which are built in the fields for a man to sleep in during the period of heaviest agricultural work are used as temporary granaries. The Lele are not in the habit of sleeping in their fields, except to shoot wild pig while the grain is ripening. This may be another indication that they do less agricultural work than the Bushong.

When we examine the techniques of cultivation, we find many contrasts. The Bushong plant five crops in succession in a system of rotation that covers two years. They grow yams, sweet potatoes, manioc, beans, and gather two and sometimes three maize harvests a year. The Lele practice no rotation and reap only one annual maize harvest. If we examine the two agricultural cycles, we see that the Bushong work continuously all the year, and that the Lele have one burst of activity, lasting about six weeks, in the height of the dry season.

Here is the probable explanation of their dread of the dry season. There is, in fact, surprisingly little range in the average monthly temperatures throughout the year. For the coldest month, July, it is only 2°C. less than the hottest month, January (Vandenplas 1947 :

33–38). Nonetheless, the Europeans and the Bushong welcome the period from mid-May to mid-August as the "cold season", probably because they enjoy the cooler nights and the freedom from humidity. But the Lele, enduring the sun beating on them from a cloudless sky while they are trying to do enough agricultural work for the whole year, suffer more from the dust and impurities in the atmosphere and from the greatly increased insolation. The relatively cooler nights may make them feel the day's heat even more intensely.

Apart from the differences in crops cultivated, we may note some differences in emphasis. Lele give hunting and weaving a high priority throughout the year, while the Bushong think of them as primarily dry-season activities. Traditionally, the Lele used to burn the grassland for big hunts (in which five or six villages combined for the day) at the end of the dry season, when the bulk of their agricultural work was done. If the first rains had already broken, so much the better for the prospects of the hunt, they said, as the animals would leave their forest watering places to eat the new shoots. At the end of the dry season is the time in which the firing could do the maximum damage to the vegetation, it has been forbidden by the administration, and if permission is given at all, the firing must be over by the beginning of July. The Bushong used to burn the grassland in mid-May or early June, at the beginning of the dry season, when the sap had not altogether died down in the grass.

The cycle of work described for the Lele is largely what the old men describe as their traditional practice. It was modified by the agricultural officers of the Belgian Congo. Lele are encouraged to sow maize twice, for harvesting in November, and in April. Manioc is now mainly grown in the grassland, instead of in the forest clearings. There are some changes in the plants cultivated. Voandzeia has been replaced by groundnuts, some hill rice is sown, and beans in some parts. These are largely treated as cash crops by the Lele, who sell them to the Europeans to earn money for tax. The other occupation which competes for their time is cutting oil-palm fruits to sell to the *Huileries du Congo Belge*, whose lorries collect weekly from the villages. Lele complain that they are now made to work harder than before, to clear more land, keep it hoed, grow more crops. They never complain that cutting oil-palm fruits interferes with their agricultural program, only that the total of extra work interferes with their hunting.

This is not the place for a detailed study of Bushong agriculture. It is enough to have shown that it is more energetically pursued and is more productive. One or two details of women's work are useful indications of a different attitude to time, work and food. Lele like to eat twice a day: in the morning at about 11 o'clock or midday, and in the evening. They complain that their wives are lazy, and only too often the morning meal consists of cold scraps from the previous night; they compare themselves unfavorably with Cokwe, who are reputed to have more industrious wives. In practice the Lele women seem to be very hard-working, but it is possible that the absence of labor-saving devices may make their timetable more arduous.

Table 6.1 [28] Annual Cycle of Work

	Bushong		Lele
Dry Season			
Mid-May	Harvest beans, maize II, yams. Clear forest	Hunt, weave draw wine	Clear forest for maize
	Burn grassland for hunt		
June	Hunt, fish, weave, repair huts	" "	
Mid-July to Aug. 15	Burn forest clearings, gather bananas and pineapple. Plant hemp	" "	Women fish in low waters
	Hunt, fish, plant sugar cane and bananas		Burn forest clearings
	Send tribute to capital period of plenty		Sow maize
Wet Season			
Mid-August	Lift ground nuts	" "	Fire grassland for hunting
Sept.	Sow ground nut. Sow maize I	" "	Sow voandzeia, plant manioc, bananas
	Collect termites		
Oct.		" "	peppers; sugar cane, pineapples
Nov.		" "	(occasional) and raffia palms in
Mid-Dec.		" "	forest clearings with maize
Little Dry Season			
Mid-Dec.	Sow maize II; sow voandzeia	" "	Green maize can be plucked
Jan.	Sow tobacco, sow maize II	" "	Maize harvest
Wet Season			
Feb.	Lift ground nuts, sow beans, collect termites and grubs	" "	Lift voandzeia
	Reap maize I (Main crop)		
March	Reap maize I. Sow tobacco, beans, yams, manioc	" "	
April to Mid-May	Gather beans, sow voandzeia and tobacco	" "	

For example, one of their daily chores is to fetch water from the stream. At the same time, they carry down a heavy pile of manioc roots to soak for a few days before carrying them back to the village. Bushong women, on the other hand, are equipped with wooden troughs, filled with rain water from the roofs, so that they can soak their manioc in the village, without the labor of transporting it back and forth. Bushong women also cultivate mushrooms indoors for occasional relish, while Lele women rely on chance gathering.

Bushong women find time to do the famous raffia embroidery, perhaps because their menfolk help them more in the fields. Lele men admiring the Bushong *Velours*, were amazed to learn that women could ever be clever enough to use needle and thread, still less make this elaborate stitching. The Bushong culinary tradition is more varied than that of the Lele. This rough comparison suggests that Lele women are less skilled and industrious than Bushong women, but it is probable that a time-and-motion study of women's and men's work in the two economies would show that Lele men leave a relatively heavier burden of agricultural work to their women, for reasons which we will show later.

Another difference between Bushong and Lele techniques is in the exploitation of palms for wine. Lele use only the raffia palm for wine. Their method of drawing it kills the tree; in the process of tapping, they cut out the whole of the crown of the palm just at the time of its first flowering. During the few years before the palm has matured to this point, they take the young yellow fronds for weaving, and after drawing the sap for wine, the stump is stripped and left to rot down. Lele have no use for a tree which has once been allowed to flower, except for fuel and building purposes. The life of a palm, used in this way, is rarely more than five years, although there seems to be some range in the different times at which individual palms mature.

The Bushong also use this method on raffia palms, but they have learnt to tap oil palms by making an incision at the base of the large inflorescene, a technique which does not kill the tree. Presumably this technique could be adapted to raffia palms, since the Yakö of Cross River, Nigeria use it (Forde 1937). But neither Lele nor Bushong attempt to preserve the raffia palm in this way, and Lele do not draw any wine from oil palms, although these grow plentifully in the north of their territory. According to Lele traditions oil palms were very scarce in their country until relatively recently, and this may account for their not exploiting it for wine. But here again, consistently with other tendencies in their economy, their techniques are directed to short-term results, and do not fully use their resources.

To balance this picture of Lele inefficiency, we should mention the weaving of raffia, for here, at least, they are recognized as the better craftsmen. Their raffia cloth is of closer texture than Bushong cloth, because they use finer strands of raffia, produced by combing in three stages, whereas the Bushong only comb once. Incidentally, the fine Lele cloth is not suitable for velours embroidery.

Lele take pride in producing a cloth of a regular and fine weave, and they refuse inferior cloth if it is preferred for payment. A length of woven raffia is their normal standard of value for counting debts and dues of all kinds. How little it has even now become a medium of exchange has been described elsewhere (Douglas 1958). Raffia cloth is not the medium of exchange for the Bushong, who freely used cowries, copper units, and beads before they adopted Congolese francs as an additional currency. Raffia cloth is the principal export for the Lele, whereby they obtain knives, arrowheads and camwood. This may explain why unadorned raffia cloth holds a more important place in the admittedly simpler economy of the Lele than its equivalent in the diversified economy of the Bushong.

If we ask now why one tribe is rich and the other poor, the review of technology would seem to suggest that the Lele are poorer not only because their soil is less fertile, but because they work less at the production of goods. They do not build up producer's capital, such as nets, canoes, traps and granaries. Nor do they work so long at cultivation, and their houses wear out quicker. Their reduced effort is itself partly a consequence of their poorer environment. It is probable that their soil could not be worked by the intensive methods of Bushong agriculture without starting a degenerative cycle. Hunting nets and pit-traps are less worthwhile in an area poor in forest and game. But certain other features of their economy cannot be fully explained as adaptations to the environment.

When Lele timetables of work are compared with those of the Bushong, we see no heavy schedules which suggest that there would be any shortage of labor. Yet, their economy is characterized paradoxically by an apparent shortage of hands, which confronts anyone who seeks collaborators. When a sick man wants to send a message, or needs help to clear his fields, or to repair his hut, or to draw palm wine for him, he will often be hard put to find anyone whose services he can command. *"Kwa itangu bo – No time,"* is a common reply to requests for help. His fields may lie uncleared, or his palm trees run to seed for lack of hands. This reflects the weakness of the authority structure in Lele society, and does not imply that every able-bodied man is fully employed from dawn to dusk.

Some anthropologists write as if the poorer the environment and the less efficient the techniques for exploiting it, the more the population is forced to work hard to maintain itself in existence; more productive techniques produce a surplus which enables a part of the population to be supported as a "leisure class."[6] It is not necessary to expose the fallacies of this approach, but it is worth pointing out that, poor as they are, the Lele are

less fully employed than the Bushong. They do less work.

"Work," of course, is here used in a narrow sense, relevant to a comparison of material wealth. Warfare, raiding, ambushing, all planning of offensive and defensive actions, as also abductions, seductions, and reclaiming of women, making and rebutting of sorcery charges, negotiations for fines and compensations and for credit – all these absorbingly interesting and doubtless satisfying activities of Lele social life must, for this purpose of measuring comparative prosperity, be counted as alternatives to productive work. Whether we call them forms of preferred idleness, or leisure activities, or "non-productive work," no hidden judgment of value is implied. The distinction between productive work and other activities is merely used here as rough index of material output.

If we wish to understand why the Lele work less, we need to consider whether any social factors inhibit them from exploiting their resources to the utmost. We should be prepared to find in a backward economy (no less than in our own economy) instances of decisions influenced by short-term desires which, once taken, may block the realization of long-term interests.

First, we must assess in a very general way, the attitudes shown by the Lele towards the inconveniences and rewards of work.

For the Bushong, work is the means to wealth, and wealth the means to status. They strongly emphasize the value of individual effort and achievement, and they are also prepared to collaborate in numbers over a sustained period when this is necessary to raise output. Nothing in Lele culture corresponds to the Bushong striving for riches. The Bushong talk constantly and dream about wealth, while proverbs about it being the steppingstone to high status are often on their lips. Riches, prestige, and influence at court

---

[6] For the most widely read statement of this view, see Herskovits 1952 (Part V, The Economic Surplus) and for a list of reputed subscribers to this view, see Harris 1959.

are explicitly associated together (Vansina 1954).

On the other hand, Lele behave as if they expect the most satisfying roles of middle and old age to fall into the individual's lap in the ripeness of time, only provided that he is a real man – that is, normally virile. He will eventually marry several wives, beget children, and so enter the Begetter's cult. His infant daughters will be asked in marriage by suitors bearing gifts and ready to work for him. Later, when his cult membership is bringing in a revenue of raffia cloth from fees of new initiates, his newborn daughter's daughters can be promised in marriage to junior clansmen, who will strengthen his following in the village. His wives will look after him in his declining years. He will have stores of raffia cloths to lend or give, but he will possess this wealth because, in the natural course of events, he reached the proper status for his age. He would not be able to achieve this status through wealth.

The emphasis on seniority means that, among the Lele, work and competitiveness are not geared to their longings for prestige. Among the Bushong, largely through the mechanism of markets, through money, and through elective political office, the reverse is true. It also means that Lele society holds out its best rewards in middle life and after. Those who have reached this period of privilege have an interest in maintaining the *status quo*.

All over the world it is common for the privileged sections of a community to adopt protective policies, even against their own more long-term interests. We find traces of this attitude among old Lele men. They tend to speak and behave as if they held, collectively, a position to be defended against the encroachments of the young men. Examples of this attitude have been published everywhere (Douglas 1959). Briefly, secrets of ritual and healing are jealously guarded, and even knowledge of the debts and marriage negotiations of their own clans are deliberately withheld from the young men, as a technique for retarding

their adulthood. The old are realistic enough to know that they are dependent ultimately on the brawn and muscle of the young men, and this thought is regularly brought up in disputes, when they are pressing defense of their privileges too far: "What would happen to us, if we chased away the young men? Who would hunt with us, and carry home the game? Who would carry the European's luggage?" The young men play on this, and threaten to leave the village until eventually the dispute is settled. Although it does not directly affect the levels of production that we have been discussing, this atmosphere of jealousy between men's age-groups certainly inhibits collaboration and should probably not be underestimated in its long-term effects.

Lele also believe in restricting competition. At the beginning of the century, the Lele chief NgomaNvula tried to protect the native textile industry by threatening death for anyone who wore European cloth (Simpson 1911 : 310). If a Lele man is asked why women do not weave or sew, he instantly replies: "If a woman could sew her own clothes, she might refuse to cook for the men. What could we give them instead of clothes to keep them happy?" This gives a false picture of the male contribution to the domestic economy, but it is reminiscent of some modern arguments against "equal pay" for both sexes.

Within the local section of a clan, restrictions on entry into the skilled professions are deliberately enforced. A young boy is not allowed to take up a craft practiced by a senior clansman, unless the latter agrees to retire. In the same clan, in the same village, two men rarely specialize in the same skill. If a man is a good drummer, or carver, or smith, and he sees an aptitude for the same craft in his son or nephew, he may teach the boy all he knows and work with him until he thinks the apprenticeship complete. Then, ceremonially, he hands over his own position, with his tools, and retires in favour of the younger man. This ideal is frequently practiced. The accompanying convention, that a boy must not compete with his elder kinsman, is also strong enough to stop many a would-be specialist from developing his skill. Lele openly prefer reduced output. Their specialist craftsmen are few and far between because they are expected to make matters unpleasant for rivals competing for their business. Consequently the Lele as a whole are poorer in metal or wooden objects for their own use, or for export.

Lastly, it seems that Lele old men have never been able to rely on their junior clansmen for regular assistance in the fields. As a junior work-mate, a son-in-law is more reliable than a fellow-clansman. This is so for reasons connected with the pattern of residence and the weak definition of authority within the clan (Douglas 1957). An unmarried youth has no granary of his own to fill. Work which he does to help his maternal uncles, father, or father's brothers, is counted in his favor, but he can easily use the claims of one to refuse those of another, and escape with a minimum of toil. Boys would be boys, until their middle thirties. They led the good life, of weaving, drinking, and following the manly sports of hunting and warfare, without continuous agricultural responsibilities.

The key institution in which the old men see their interests as divorced from those of the young men is polygyny. Under the old system, since the young girls were pre-empted by the older men, the age of marriage was early for girls (eleven or twelve), and late for men (in their thirties). It would be superficial to suppose that these arrangements were solely for the sexual gratification of the old men. One should see them as part of the whole economic system, and particularly as one of the parts which provide social security of the old.

The division of labor between the sexes leaves the very old men with little they can do. An old woman, by contrast, can earn her keep with many useful services. But old men use their rights over women to secure necessary services, both from women and from men. Through polygyny, the principles of male dominance and of seniority are maintained to

the end. To borrow an analogy from another sphere, we could almost say that the Lele have opted for an ambitious old-age pensions scheme at the price of their general standards of living. We shall see that the whole community pays for the security in old age which polygyny represents.

In the kingdom of ends peculiar to the Lele, various institutions seem to receive their justification because they are consistent with polygyny of the old men and delayed marriage of the young. The latter were reconciled to their bachelorhood, partly by the life of sport and ease, and partly by the institution of wife-sharing by age-sets. They were encouraged to turn their attention away from the young wives in their own villages by the related custom of abducting girls from rival villages (Douglas 1951). Intervillage feuding therefore appears to be an essential part of the total scheme, which furthermore commits the Lele to small-scale political life. The diversion of young men's energies to raiding and abducting from rival villages was a major cause of the low levels of production, for its effects were cumulative. The raiding gave rise to such insecurity that at some times half the able-bodied males were engaged in giving armed escort to the others. Men said that in the old days a man did not go to the forest to draw palm wine alone, but his age-mate escorted him and stood with his back to the tree, bowstring taut, watching for ambush.

Coming from Bushong country in 1907, Torday was amazed at the fortified condition of Lele villages:

> Here, too, we found enclosures, but instead of the leaf walls which are considered sufficient among the Bushongo, the separations were palisades formed by solid stakes driven into the ground. Such a wall surrounded the whole village, and the single entrance was so arranged that no more than one person was able to enter at one time. (Torday 1925 : 231)

Simpson also remarked that Lele men, asked to carry his baggage from their own village to the next, armed as if going into strange country. Such insecurity is obviously inimical to trade.

We have started with polygyny as the primary value to which other habits have been adjusted, because the Lele themselves talk as if all relations between men are defined by rights to women.

The point is the more effective since the Bushong are monogamous. We know well that polygyny elsewhere does not give rise to this particular accumulation of effects. Are there any features peculiar to Lele polygyny? One is the proportion of polygynous old men, indicated by the high rate of bachelorhood. Another is in the solutions they have adopted for the problems of late marriage. In some societies with extensive polygyny, the institutions which exist for the sexual satisfaction of the young men[7] are either wholly peaceful, or directed to warfare with other tribes and not to hostilities between villages. Thirdly, where the chain of command is more sharply defined (as in patrilineal systems, or in matrilineal societies in which offices are elective or carry recognizable political responsibilities, as among the Bushong), then polygyny of older men is less likely to be accompanied by attitudes of suspicion and hostility between men's age-groups.

Having started our analysis with polygyny and the high rate of bachelorhood, tracing the various interactions, we find the Lele economy constantly pegged down to the same level of production. Something like a negative feedback appears in the relations of old to young men: the more the old reserve the girls for themselves, the more the young men are resentful and evasive; the more the young men are refractory, the more the old men insist on their prerogatives. They pick on the most unsatisfactory of the young men, refuse to allot him a wife, refuse him cult membership; the others note his punishment, and either come to heel or move off to another village. There cannot be an indefinite worsening in their relations because, inevitably, the old men will die. Then the young men inherit their widows, and, now not so young, see themselves in sight of polygynous status, to be defended by solidarity of the old.

So we find the Lele, as a result of innumerable personal choices about matters of immediate concern, committed to all the insecurity of feuding villages, and to the frustration of small-scale political life and ineffective economy.

If we prefer to start our analysis at the other end, not with polygyny but with scale of political organization, we come to the same results. For whatever reason, the Bushong developed a well organized political system (Vansina 1957), embracing 70,000 people. Authority is decentralized from the Nyimi, or paramount chief, to minor chiefs, and from these to canton heads, and from these to village heads. Judicial, legislative, and administrative powers are delegated down these channels, with decisions concerning war and peace held at the center by the Nyimi. Political office is elective or by appointment. Appropriate policing powers are attached to leaders at each point in the hierarchy. Leaders are checked by variously constituted councils, whom they must consult. The Nyimi maintains his own army to quell rebellions. Tribute of grain, salt, dried foods, and money is brought into the capitals, and redistributed to loyal subjects and officials. The chiefly courts provide well-rewarded markets for craftsmen's wares so that regional specialities are salable far from their sources. Even before the advent of Europeans there was a food-market at Musenge, the Nyimi's capital. No doubt the Kasai River, protecting them from the long arm of the Bushong Empire, is partly responsible for the Lele's never having been drawn, willy-nilly, into its orbit, and accepting its values.

---

[7] For example, Tiv "sister-marriage" of the "manyatta" of the Masai.

The Lele village, which is their largest autonomous unit, is not so big as the smallest political unit in the Bushong system. (The Lele villages average a population of 190, and the Bushong villages 210.) True, there are Lele chiefs, who claim relationship with Bushong chiefs. Each village is, indeed, found within a chiefdom – that is, an area over which a member of the chiefly clan claims suzerainty. But in practice his rights are found to be ritual and social. Each village is completely independent. The chief has no judicial or military authority. He claims tribute, but here we have no busy palace scene in which tribute payers flock in and are lavishly fed by the special catering system which chiefly polygyny so often represents.

When a chief visited a village, he was given raffia cloths, as many as could be spared. Then the villagers asked what woman he would give them in return. He named one of his daughters, and they settled a day to fetch her. The girl became the communal wife of one of the age-sets, the whole village regarding itself as her legal husband and as son-in-law to the chief. Son-in-lawship expressed their relation to him until the day that he claimed the girl's first daughter in marriage. Then the relation became reversed, the chief being son-in-law to the village. The raffia gifts and women which went back and forth between the chief and village were not essentially different from those which linked independent villages to one another in peaceful exchange. None of this interfered with the autonomy of the village.

The simple factor of scale alone has various repercussions. There is no ladder of status up which a man may honorably climb to satisfy his competitive ambitions. There is no series of offices for which age and experience qualify a man, so that in his physical decline he can enjoy respect and influence and material rewards. The Bushong lay great emphasis on individual effort and achievement, but the Lele try to damp it down. They avoid overt roles of leadership and fear the jealousy which individual success arouses. Their truncated status system turns the Lele village in on itself, to brood on quarrels and sorcery accusations, or turns it, in hostility, against other villages, so promoting the general feeling of insecurity. The latter makes markets impossible, and renders pointless ambition to produce above home needs. The old, in such an economy, unable to save, or to acquire dignity in their declining years by occupying high political office, bolster their position by claiming the marriageable women, and building up a system of rewards reserved for those who begat in wedlock. And so we are back again to polygyny and prolonged bachelorhood.

This picture has been partly based on deductions about what Lele society must have been like twenty years before fieldwork was begun. Before 1930 they could still resort to ordeals, enslave, raid and counterraid, abduct women, and pursue blood-vengeance with barbed arrows. They still needed to fortify their villages against attacks. By 1949 the scene had changed. The young men had broken out of their restraining social environment – by becoming Christians. They enjoyed protection, from mission and government, from reprisals by pagans. They could marry young Christian girls who, similarly, were able to escape their expected lot as junior wives of elderly polygynists. Raiding was ended, age-sets were nearly finished. Old men had less authority even than before. The young Christian tended to seek employment with Europeans to escape the reproaches and suspicions which their abstention from pagan rituals engendered.[8]

It would be interesting to compare their performance as workers in the new and freer context. One might expect that, away from the influence of their old culture, Lele performance might equal or surpass that of Bushong.

[8]   This process has been described in Douglas 1959 b.

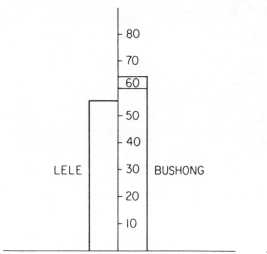

Figure 6.3 [9]
Age of Retirement from Work

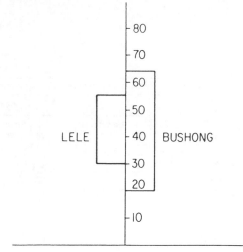

Figure 6.4 [10]
*Period of Full Work, Showing Age of Entry into Full
Agricultural Responsibility*

Unfortunately the framework for such a comparison is lacking. Neither tribe has a high reputation for industry with its respective employers, compared with immigrant Cokwe, Luba and Pende workers. This may simply be because the best reputations are earned by tribes which have longest been accustomed to wage-labor.

One is tempted to predict that, in so far as it is due to social factors, Lele are likely to change their name for idleness and lack of stamina before long. In 1949–50 they were not forthcoming in numbers for plantation labor or for cutting oil-palm nuts. By 1954, when a scattering of small shops through the territory had put trade goods within their reach, they had become eager to earn money. The restrictive influence of the old social system was already weaker.

We may now look again at the demographic factor, and distinguish some effects on it of the economy and the political system. It is obvious that in different types of economy, the active male contribution may have different time spans according to the nature of the work. If there were a modern community whose breadwinners were international skating champions, footballers, or miners at the coal-face, their period of active work would be briefer than in economies based on less physically exacting tasks. A primitive economy is, by definition, one based on rudimentary technology, and the more rudimentary, the more the work consists of purely individual physical effort. Moreover, the simpler the economy, the smaller the scope for managerial roles and ancillary sedentary work. The result, then, is that the period of full, active contribution to the economy is shorter.[9]

If we compare Lele and Bushong economies on these lines, we see that the "age of retirement" is likely to be earlier for the Lele. The typical Bushong man is able, long after he has passed his physical prime, to make a useful contribution to production, either by using his experience to direct the collaboration of others or in various administrative roles which are important in maintaining the security and

---

[9] This approach was suggested by Linton 1940.

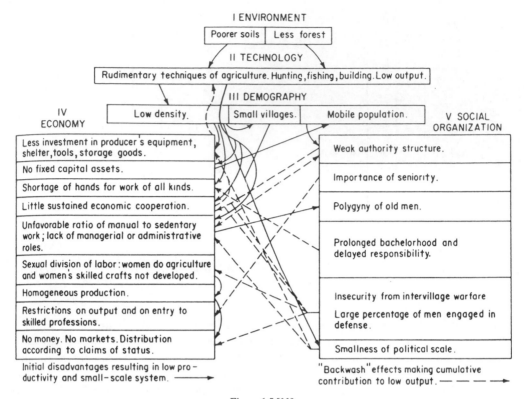

I ENVIRONMENT

| Poorer soils | Less forest |

II TECHNOLOGY

Rudimentary techniques of agriculture. Hunting, fishing, building. Low output.

III DEMOGRAPHY

IV
ECONOMY

| Low density. | Small villages. | Mobile population. |

V SOCIAL
ORGANIZATION

Less investment in producer's equipment, shelter, tools, storage goods.

No fixed capital assets.

Shortage of hands for work of all kinds.

Little sustained economic cooperation.

Unfavorable ratio of manual to sedentary work; lack of managerial or administrative roles.

Sexual division of labor: women do agriculture and women's skilled crafts not developed.

Homogeneous production.

Restrictions on output and on entry to skilled professions.

No money. No markets. Distribution according to claims of status.

Weak authority structure.

Importance of seniority.

Polygyny of old men.

Prolonged bachelorhood and delayed responsibility.

Insecurity from intervillage warfare

Large percentage of men engaged in defense.

Smallness of political scale.

Initial disadvantages resulting in low productivity and small-scale system. ⟶

"Backwash" effects making cumulative contribution to low output. — — — ⟶

Figure 6.5 [11]
Lele Economy and Social Organization

order necessary for prosperity. The Lele economy, on the other hand, with its emphasis on individual work, gives less weight to experience and finds less productive work for the older man to do. We can only guess at the differences, but it is worth presenting the idea visually, as in Figure 6.3.

Furthermore, at the other end of the life span, the same trend is increased because of the late entry into agricultural work of Lele men. The young Lele is not fully employed in agriculture until he is at least thirty and married, the Bushong man when he is twenty. Figure 6.4 illustrates the idea that the active labor force in the Lele economy, as a proportion of the total population, is on both scores smaller than it is with the Bushong. The total output of the economy has to be shared among a larger population of dependants.

The comparison of the two economies has shown up something like the effects of "backwash" described by Professor Myrdal (1957). First we see that in the environment there are initial disadvantages which limit development. Secondly, we find that in the social organization itself there are further inhibiting effects which are cumulative, and which work one on another and back again on the economy, technology and population, to intensify the initial disadvantages. We have tried to present the interaction of these tendencies in a simplified form in Figure 6.5.

"Nothing succeeds like success." Somehow, sometime, the Bushong took decisions which produced a favorable turn in their fortunes and set off interactions which resulted in their political hegemony and their wealth. The Lele missed the benefits of this civilization because of their location on the other side of the Kasai River, their poorer soils, their history. The decisions they took amounted to an accommodation of their life to a lower political and economic level. Their technology was inferior, so their efforts were backed with less efficient equipment, and their economy was less productive. Their old social system barred many of the chances which might have favored economic growth.

Anthropologists sometimes tend to discuss the adoption or rejection of new techniques in terms of a cultural mystique, as if dealing with irreducible principles, of which no analysis is feasible.[10] The Lele may be taken as a case in point. Their preference for their own inferior techniques, in spite of awareness of better methods used across the river, depend on certain institutions, and these again on their history and environment. Through economic analysis we can break down the effect of choices, each made reasonably enough in its own restricted context. By following up the interactions of these choices, one upon another, we can see how the highly idiosyncratic mold of Lele culture is related to a certain low level of production.

References

BENEDICT, RUTH
  1956 "The Growth of Culture," in *Man, Culture and Society* (H. Shapiro, ed.). New York: Oxford University Press.
DOUGLAS, MARY
  1951 "A Form of Polyandry among the Lele," *Africa*, Vol. 21, pp. 1–12.
  1954 "The Lele of the Kasai," in *African Worlds* (D. Forde, ed.). London: Oxford University Press.
  1957 "The Pattern of Residence among the Lele," *Zaïre*, Vol. 11, pp. 818–43.
  1958 "Raffia Distribution in the Lele Economy," *Africa*, Vol. 28, pp. 2 ff.
  1959a "Age-Status among the Lele," *Zaïre*, Vol. 13, pp. 386–413.
  1959b "The Lele of the Kasai," in *The Church and the Nations* (A. Hastings, ed.). London: Sheed & Ward.
  —— "Blood-debts among the Lele," *Journal of the Royal Anthropological Institute*, forthcoming.
FORDE, D.
  1937 "Land and Labour in a Cross River Village," *Geographical Journal*, Vol. 40, No. 1.
GOUROU, P.
  1955 *La Densité de la population rurale au Congo Belge, etc*. Brussels: Acad. Roy. Sci. Col. Mem. 8,1,2.
HARRIS, M.
  1959 "The Economy Has No Surplus?" *American Anthropologist*, Vol. 61, No. 2, pp. 185–200.
MYRDAL, GUNNAR
  1957 *Economic Theory and Underdeveloped Regions*. London: G. Duckworth.
NICOLAI, H.
  1952 "Problèmes du Kwango," *Bulletin de la Société Belge d'Études Géographiques*, Vol. 25, No. 2.
NICOLAI, H. AND JACQUES, J.
  1954 *La Transformation du paysage Congolais par le Chemin de Fer, L'Exemple du B.C.K.* Acad. Roy. Sci. Col. Brussels, Sect. des Sci. Natu. et Med. Mem. in 8, XXIV, L.
TORDAY, E.
  1925 *On the Trail of the Bushongo*. London: Seeley, Service & Co., Ltd.
TURNER, V. W.
  1957 *Schism and Continuity in an African Society*. Manchester: Manchester University Press.

[10] See Benedict (1956 : 187): "Among primitive peoples, this lack of interest in 'progress' has been proverbial . . . Every primitive tribe has its own cultural arrangements which ensure its survival . . . They may be culturally uninterested in labor-saving devices. Often the value they put on time is extremely low, and 'wisdom' is far more valued than efficiency. Our cultural system and theirs are oriented around different ideals."

VAN DEN PLAS, A.
  1947 *La Température au Congo Belge.* Pub.
  Minis. Colon., pp. 33–38.
VANSINA, JAN
  1954 "Les Valeurs Culturelles des Bushong,"
  Zaïre, No. 9, pp. 900–910, November.
  1955 "Initiation Rituals of the Bushong,"
  Africa, Vol. 25, pp. 138–52.
  1956 "Migration dans la Province du Kasai,"
  Zaïre, pp. 69–85.
  1957 "L'État Kuba dans le cadre des institutions politiques Africaines," *Zaïre*, Vol. 11, pt.
  1, pp. 485–92.

7

SOME PRINCIPLES OF EXCHANGE AND INVESTMENT AMONG THE TIV[1]

PAUL BOHANNAN

Tiv are a pagan people numbering over 800,000 who live in the middle Benue Valley of northern Nigeria. The basis of their economy is subsistence agriculture, supplemented by an effective network of markets particularly in the southern and central portions of their country. Tiv pride themselves on their farming abilities and their subsistence wealth.

Today, however, their ideas of economic exchange and their traditional methods of investment and economic aggrandizement are being undermined by a new economic system which demands different actions, motives and ideas. This article deals with: (I) Tiv ideas of exchange as expressed in their language, (II) some traditional modes of investment and exchange, based on a ranked hierarchy of spheres or categories of exchangeable commodities, and (III) the impact of Western economy on such aspects of subsistence, exchange and investment which Tiv consider in terms of these spheres or categories.

I

Distribution of goods among Tiv falls into two spheres: a "market," on the one hand, and gifts, on the other.

The several words best translated "gift" apply – besides the cases which we in the West would recognize as "gift" – to exchange over a long period of time between persons or groups in a more or less permanent relationship. The gift may be a factor designed to strengthen the relationship, or even to create it. There are several Tiv words for "gift," the examination of which would require another article the length of this one. For our purposes, it is primary that any of these "gift" words implies a relationship between the two parties concerned which is of a permanence and warmth not known in a "market," and hence – though "gifts" should be reciprocal over a long period of time – it is bad form overtly to count and compute and haggle over gifts.

A "market" is a transaction which in itself calls up no long-term personal relationship, and which is therefore to be exploited to as

---

[1] Twenty-six months' research was carried out between July 1949 and January 1953 among the Tiv, under the auspices of the Social Science Research Council and the Wenner-Gren Foundation for Anthropological Research, with supplementary grants from the Colonial Social Science Research Council and the Government of Nigeria, to all of which bodies grateful acknowledgment is made.

great a degree as possible. In fact, the presence of a previous relationship makes a "good market" impossible: people do not like to sell to kinsmen since it is bad form to demand as high a price from a kinsman as one might from a stranger. Market behavior and kinship behavior are incompatible in a single relationship, and the individual must give way to one or the other.

The word "market" (*kasoa*) has several meanings in Tiv. It refers primarily to any transaction which is differentiated from gift exchange (and, as we shall see, from exchange marriage). It is also a meeting of people at a regular place and time for the primary purpose of exchanging food and other items. One's "market" is also an aspect of one's luck (*ikôl*) – some people have "good market [luck]" and some have "bad market [luck]." Therefore, one's market can be affected by one's ritual condition, for fetishes (*akombo*) – not to mention witches (*mbatsav*) – can spoil a man's market (*vihi* or *kasoa*); indeed, curses and broken promises can also affect a person's market.

Everything, including women, which is exchanged has an exchange value or equivalent (*ishe*), whereas no gift has an exchange value. In a market situation *ishe* means vaguely "exchange equivalent" – one might even sometimes translate it "price" – though Tiv seldom ask or quote equivalents in their own trading. Rather, they effect bargains, usually without recourse to this word. An expensive item is a "thing of great value" or "thing of high equivalent" (*kwagh u kehe ishe*), and to haggle is to dispute the value or equivalent (*kperen ishe*). The general term both for economic trading and for exchange marriage can be translated roughly as "trading value" (*yamen ishe*).

In every market transaction, there is a man who sells (*te*) and a man who buys (*yam*). These words must be carefully examined for they do not exactly parallel their English equivalents. *Te* means to spread something out on the ground to the public view, as in a market place. By extension, it means "to sell" – there is no other way to say "to sell," and no other verb to designate that half of an exchange in which one releases or gets rid of an article. *Yam*, on the other hand, means "trade" in the widest sense, but refers primarily to that half of the exchange in which one takes or gains an article. It can, therefore, often be translated by the English word "buy." Its difference, however, can be seen in sentences such as "I bought money with it" (*m yam inyaregh a mi* – more accurately translated "I realized money on it," and still more accurately but less literally, "In this exchange what I received was money"). Activities of traders are called *yamen a yam*; exchange marriage is often called "woman trading" (*kwase yamen*) or, more politely, "value trading" (*ishe yamen*).

Although Tiv have a word which means approximately the same as the English word "exchange" (*musan*), which can sometimes be used to differentiate barter from money transactions, this word is not ordinarily used of trade or commerce.

II

Within the bounds of these words and basic concepts, Tiv image and communicate their ideas of economic transactions and investments. It is important to realize, however, that the ideas themselves may never be articulated as principles or as logical systems. The systematization may be, as in this case, the work of the ethnographer. Yet, this systematization is – or at least is consistent with – the Tiv covert ideology in the matter; its empirical validity is demonstrated when, in terms of it, the ethnographer can both sensibly discuss the ideas and images with Tiv in their language, and communicate them in another language to his colinguals and colleagues.

It is in these terms that we can say that in Tiv ideology it is neither usual nor desirable to exchange a commodity for just any other commodity. Rather, there are several different categories of interchangeable commodities and items, each of which is felt to be more or less exclusive. It seems to be necessary to distinguish three such categories.

The most apparent category of exchangeable items among Tiv consists primarily of foodstuffs (*yiagh*). All locally produced foodstuffs (imported, particularly European, food is not *yiagh*) are said by Tiv to be of a single economic kind, and immediately interchangeable. To trade pepper for locust-bean sauce or yams for guinea corn is a common transaction or "market" among Tiv. The quantities to be exchanged are never prescribed,[2] as they are in some societies – the bargain which any individual may drive within the sphere of foodstuffs is a reflection of the market aspect of his luck. If I, selling pepper, can get locust beans of a quality and quantity whose value I myself consider to be greater than the value of the pepper I gave for them, my market is good; if I get less, my market is bad – or, more commonly, the market of the other person is better than mine. The obvious advantage of such a line of reasoning is that, in really successful transactions, everybody's market is good.

Included within this same category are chickens and goats, as well as household utensils (mortars, grindstones, calabashes, baskets and pots) and some tools (particularly those used in agricultural pursuits), and also raw materials for producing any items in the category. For a woman to sell yams to buy a pot, for her to make a pot and sell it to buy yams – these are considered to be normal buying and selling (*yamen a yam*).

The second important category is that which includes slaves, cattle, that type of large white cloth known as *tugudu*, and metal bars. One is still entitled to use the present tense in this case, for ideologically the category still exists in spite of the fact that brass rods are today very rare, and that slavery has been legally abolished. Tiv still quote prices of slaves in cows and brass rods, and of cattle in brass rods and *tugudu* cloths. Akiga, in a hitherto untranslated part of his book, tells us that,

> You could buy one iron bar (*sokpo*) for a *tugudu* cloth. In those days five *tugudu* cloths were equivalent to a bull! A cow was worth ten *tugudu*. One brass rod (*bashi*) was worth about the same as one *tugudu* cloth; thus five brass rods were worth a bull.

Other Tiv would disagree about the actual values of these various commodities.[3] The value of the brass rod is said by all to have declined considerably just before the arrival of the Europeans in Tivland. None, however, would disagree with Akiga's grouping of commodities.

This second category is associated with prestige (*shagba*) in the same way that the first category is associated with subsistence. Although slaves and brass rods, at least, had some economic value beyond their value as prestige-conferring property, this latter was their main use.

The supreme and unique category of exchange values contains only one item: rights in human beings other than slaves, and particularly rights in women. Even twenty-five years after official abolition of exchange marriage, it is this category of exchange in which Tiv are emotionally most entangled (L. and P. Bohannan 1953: 69–71). All exchanges within this category are exchanges of rights in human beings, usually dependent women and children, so that the category may be called the category of dependent persons, and many of its values are expressed in terms of kinship and marriage.

---

[2] This fact may be a function of the time observations were made, which was a time of inflation in Tivland as elsewhere.

[3] I believe Akiga to be giving examples of a category rather than quoting prices here. But the price stability may have been generally recognized in the pre-money days of stable exchange to which Akiga refers.

This plan or scheme leaves out several important items of Tiv material culture: particularly weapons, specialists' tools like diving apparatus, etc., which do not, generally speaking, enter into exchange situations. Since I have no record of hearing these items discussed in a situation of exchange, I have no basis for assigning them to one category or another – indeed, I doubt that Tiv would do so. My purpose in reporting these categories is not the pedantic one of putting every commodity into one or the other; rather, the categories represent the fundamentals of Tiv notions of exchange and investment.

Further, several items which we consider as exchangeable wealth, and as bases for investment, are not included by Tiv in this system of thought. Services and labor, for example, are by and large reciprocal and form part of the age-set, kinship and domestic group structures and moralities. Tiv consider it rude and improper to discuss services in terms of "exchange" but insist rather that such matters be viewed as individual acts of generosity or as kinship or age-set obligations. They recognize the reciprocity, of course, but do not themselves cast it into terms which we would consider "economic." Land, which many peoples – including, perhaps, ourselves – consider to be the ultimate wealth, is not exchangeable among Tiv, not even for other land. Land is, to Tiv, the spatial aspect of social organization; land rights are conditions of agnation. It is impossible for a Tiv to invest in land, since his basic right in land is a right to sufficient land, and only secondarily a right to specific lands. No Tiv can control more land than he can use. (Both land rights and labor are discussed at some length in Bohannan 1954.) Therefore, it should be noted, we are dealing with Tiv exchange and investment, but the notions cover only a part of the range to which the English words "exchange" and "investment" refer.

It is instructive of Tiv modes of thought about these three main categories of exchangeable items to note the manner in which individual items can be "removed" from the categories, or made incapable of further exchange. Individual items are removed from the category of subsistence by expenditure, including sacrifice to fetishes. Although yams have an exchange value as well as a utilitarian value, once eaten they no longer have either. Household equipment breaks or is worn out. All items which are removed from this sphere of exchangeable goods are removed either by being used up or by being sacrificed (and subsequently used up).

Removing individual items from the second category – that centering around prestige – is more complex, and its very complexity makes possible some of the characteristics of Tiv economy. Some individual items – cloth – can be removed by expenditure; other individual items – slaves – can be removed by death of human beings. Most of the items, however, are removed by an act which increases the prestige of the owner of the item by diminishing its utility or exchangeability. Thus, brass rods can be converted into jewelry, thereby increasing the prestige of ownership but diminishing the range of utility; cows can be butchered on festive occasions (cattle are never sacrificed for religious purposes among Tiv), thereby increasing the prestige of the owner but diminishing the utility of the commodity and nullifying its exchangeability.

Individual items are removed from the third category – that of rights in dependent persons – by death of the human beings, and by death alone.

The three chief categories of exchangeable items among Tiv, while considered of equal practical importance, are nevertheless arranged in a hierarchy on the basis of moral values. The category of prestige is superior to (but no more important than) the category of subsistence; great prestige assumes adequate or ample subsistence means. The category of dependent persons is superior to (but no more important than) the categories both of prestige and of subsistence. A large number of dependent persons, demonstrating success in attracting, getting, and keeping dependents, assumes adequate or ample prestige and subsistence goods. But, conversely, many dependents give one prestige and enable one to produce ample and generous amounts of subsistence wealth.

The moral basis of the hierarchy is evident in the fact that the ethics of kinship are more compelling than the ethics of mere prestige (and always take precedence – ideally one must always sacrifice prestige or hope of gain to aid a kinsman); the ethics of prestige are more compelling than the mores of markets and exchange of subsistence wealth – a man forgoes gain in subsistence wealth for the sake of prestige or to fulfill kinship obligations.

The hierarchical nature of the values involved in the three main categories of exchangeable goods provides a basis for investment and economic endeavor in Tiv society. The drive toward success leads most Tiv, to the greatest possible extent, to convert food into prestige items; to convert prestige items into dependents – wives and children. Tiv say that it is good (*do kwagh*) to trade food for brass rods, but that it is bad (*vihi kwagh*) to trade brass rods for food; that it is good to trade your cows or brass rods for a wife, but very bad to trade your marriage ward for cows or brass rods. Seen from the individual's point of view, it is profitable and possible to invest one's wealth only if one converts it into a higher category: to convert subsistence wealth into prestige wealth and both into women is the aim of the economic endeavor of individual Tiv.

That Tiv do conceptualize exchange articles as belonging to different categories, and that they rank the categories on a moral basis, gives rise to the fact that two different kinds of exchange may be recognized: exchanges of items contained within a single category, and exchanges of items belonging to different categories. For Tiv, these two different types of exchange are marked by separate and distinct moral attitudes.

Exchanges within a category – particularly that of subsistence, the only one intact today –

excite no moral judgments beyond comments regarding the "market" luck of one or both of the parties to the exchange. Exchanges between categories, however, excite a completely different sort of moral reaction: the man who exchanges lower category goods for higher category goods does not brag about his market luck but about his skill in investment, his personal magnetism, and his "strong heart." The man who exchanges high category goods for lower rationalizes his action in terms of high-valued motivation (most often the needs of his kinsmen).

To maintain this distinction between the two types of exchanges which Tiv mark by different behavior and different values, I shall use separate words. I shall call those exchanges of items within a single category "conveyances" and those exchanges of items from one category to another "conversions." (Steiner [1954] uses "translations" for what I have called conversions.) For purposes of analysis, I shall maintain the dichotomy between the two words representing types of exchanges more rigidly than would any Tiv between the two types of moral behavior in the normal course of living. Roughly, conveyances are – to Tiv – morally neutral; conversions have a strong moral quality in their rationalization.

The two institutions most intimately connected with conveyance are markets and marriage, particularly exchange marriage. Both these are special subjects and must be dealt with separately. The remainder of this section is concerned with conversion.

Conversion, unlike conveyance, is not mere exchange of equivalent goods. Because there is a definite moral dimension to conversion, it forms a strong source of motivation to individual action. It is in the light of such motivation that we must evaluate the fact that a very high percentage of autobiographies collected from Tiv contain variants of this story: "When I was a very small child, my kinsman gave me a baby chicken. I tended it carefully and when it grew up it laid eggs and hatched out more chickens; I exchanged these chickens for a young nanny goat, who bore kids, which I put out with various kinsmen until I could exchange them for a cow. The cow bore calves, and eventually I was able to sell the calves and procure a wife." Every successful man considers such a story one of the most important sequences of his biography; it proves that he has been successful.

Tiv say that it was often possible in the old days to buy brass rods for food, but usually only if the owner of the brass rods were short of food or required an unusually large amount to give a feast, making too heavy a drain on his wives' food supplies. They also say that no honorable man would exchange slaves for food – there were other means of getting food, especially along the extended web of kinship. Although all Tiv with whom I discussed the matter denied emphatically that Tiv would ever sell a kinsman, wife or ward to get food (there are other reasons for which such sales were made), Akiga – in an untranslated section of his book – mentions a famine which was so severe that, as a last resort, men sold their daughters to foreigners in exchange for food so that they could keep their sons alive.

Another conversion found among Tiv is marriage by bride wealth (which may be of several types, usually all lumped together and called *kem kwase*). Although some forms of marriage by bride wealth were in the past actually delayed exchanges (and today can be seen as substitutes for exchanges [L. and P. Bohannan 1953:71–73]), to "receive a woman" (*ngoho kwase*) – to get wife or marriage ward without giving one in exchange – is every man's goal. A wife is traditionally acquired by being granted a sister or cousin (any woman in one's marriage-ward sharing group – the *ingôl* group of Akiga 1939 and Abraham 1940) to exchange for a wife, either directly or by means of bride wealth. A wife whom one acquires in any other way is not the concern of one's marriage-ward sharing group because the woman or other property exchanged for her

did not belong to the marriage-ward group. The daughters of such a wife are not divided among the members of a man's marriage-ward group, but only among his sons. Such a wife is not only indicative of a man's ability and success financially and personally, but rights in her are the only form of property which is not ethically subject to the demands of his agnates.

Wives may sometimes be acquired by means of much more elaborate conversions. We discovered one case (in the course of a witchcraft moot) in which a man two generations ago had traded a slave for a cow, which he in turn traded for a marriage-ward to exchange for a wife; the distribution, as marriage-wards, of the daughters of this marriage (among his sons rather than his marriage-ward group) was called into question. Sometimes Tiv acquire foreign wives for cattle, from tribes whose custom it is to marry with cattle; the daughters of such women are considered to be Tiv, and can be exchanged in regular Tiv fashion – they do not go into the "pool" of wards in the marriage-ward group unless a man's agnates force him by threats of witchcraft to share his "property" with them.

There are many social sanctions for conversion of one's wealth to higher categories: Tiv are very scornful of a man who is merely rich in subsistence goods (or, today, in money); they say that if he has not converted his goods the reasons must be personal inadequacy. Tiv also say that jealous kinsmen of a rich man will bewitch him and his people by means of certain fetishes in order to make him expend his wealth in sacrifices to "repair" the fetishes. Once the conversion is made, demands of kinsmen are no longer effective – at least they must take a new form.

A man who persists in a policy of converting his wealth into higher categories instead of letting it be dispersed by his dependents and kinsmen is said to have a "strong heart" (*taver shima*). He is both feared and respected: because he is strong enough to resist the excessive demands of his kinsmen, but still fulfills his kinship obligations generously, he is feared as a man of special, potentially evil, talents (*tsav*).

III

Tiv notions of exchange and investment are among the hardest hit of all their ideas by impact of Western ideology and by colonial economy and social organization because these ideas are immediately and obviously in conflict with Western ideas and practice. Today, Tiv are concerned because their categories of exchangeable items cannot be maintained. There are three main reasons for this fact: (1) two of the categories today have no overt validity, (2) many new commodities have been introduced which do not belong to any category, and (3) money has provided a common denominator among the categories which was previously lacking.

A moment's consideration makes it obvious that the category of prestige goods, centering mainly about cattle, slaves and brass rods, has ceased to exist in material terms, although the category is maintained ideally. Slave dealing was prohibited from the first effective European control (about 1910); brass rods are no longer generally available because the Administration regarded them primarily as currency and "replaced" them with pounds, shillings and pence. Perhaps of even greater moment was the fact that in 1927 the highest exchange category, that of rights in women, was dealt a crippling blow by Administrative abolition of exchange marriage and substitution of marriage by bride wealth (payable in money) as the legal form. The category of subsistence items is the only one that today can still be found in anything like its original form.

European and African traders have introduced many new commodities to Tivland, both of Nigerian and European manufacture, and have increased many fold the quantity of some other commodities which were formerly present in small amounts or small numbers.

These goods, particularly European goods, were introduced concurrently with money, and they are considered part of the money complex. They do not enter into any formerly existing category, but form their own category only very imperfectly. Thus, there are today many more commodities than ever before which do not fit precisely into traditionally structured exchange situations.

Finally, and perhaps more important, is the introduction of currency, the very nature of which is to standardize the exchangeability value of every item to a common scale. The introduction of currency was not only to be expected with the extension of Western economic ventures, it was hurried by the Administration in its desire to collect tax in a convenient and readily transportable form. A money tax, payable by all adult males, was imposed throughout Tivland by the end of the first World War. Imposition of this tax coincided with the initiation of large-scale growing of beniseed (*sesamum indicum*) as a cash crop. Beniseed, although long known to Tiv, is today often called by the word for "tax" or "tribute" (*kpandegh*).

Even though it is possible to consider brass rods as "currency" in the old system, because they were a commodity whose exchange value was more far-reaching than that of any other commodity and because they belonged to the intermediary category, the introduction of coinage was not a simple "substitution" of one form of currency for another as was thought at the time to be the case. Brass rods were, it is true, the main medium of conversion in the old days: brass rods could be and sometimes were used to buy food, they could be and often were used to get a wife. But the penetrability of brass rods into the other categories of exchange, while more pronounced than that of any other commodity, did have limitations. Brass rods never provided a standard gauge against which the exchangeability value of all commodities was reckoned, as is the case with the coinage issued by the West African Currency Board.

Today all conversions and most conveyances are made in terms of money. Yet Tiv constantly express their distrust of money. They compare the monetary system to the subsistence system at great length, always to the disfavor of the former. Money does not (they say) reproduce itself or bear seed. You spend (*vihi*, literally "spoil") money and it's gone – a man can't spend a field, and though he sacrifices a goat, it has already borne kids. Money, they feel, is the root of much of their trouble.

Tiv, both desiring and distrusting money as they do, have attempted at least in some contexts to relegate it to a fourth and lowest category of exchangeable goods. The logical end of such a classification, however, would be either that money is exchanged only for money, or that it is exchanged only for those European goods which were introduced more or less concurrently with it. That is precisely the view that many Tiv elders expound. It is a view, however, which cannot be maintained in the present situation in Tivland.

Concurrently with the introduction of money, pacification of the countryside and introduction of cash crops, a further factor arose: men's trading developed very rapidly. Men's trade, like women's, tends to be based on subsistence goods, but unlike women's, on goods which must be procured and traded over long distances: smoked fish from the Benue and Katsina Ala Rivers, camwood and kolas from Ogoja Province, and items such as cotton which are grown in some parts of Tivland and not in others. Today men up to the age of forty may carry their goods as much as 150 miles to market where it commands the highest price. This trade is usually carried out in terms of money, by semiprofessional traders. These men start with money and end with money; their purpose is to increase their money. Tiv consider this legitimate enterprise.

Tiv also say that women's trade is legitimate and sensible: a woman may sell one type of food to buy another, or sell food to buy a waist cloth for herself or small gifts and latter-day necessities for her children. All Tiv say that the fact that these transactions are carried out in money is beside the point: the woman has not made a conversion, for she has sold expendable subsistence goods and bought expendable subsistence goods.

The difficulty arises when the semiprofessional traders begin trading in the foodstuffs which were formerly the province solely of women. These men may invest sums of their capital in food for resale; in fact, these young semiprofessional traders are the most active buyers and sellers of grain at Tiv markets today, although women also speculate in grain and in yams to a smaller extent. A young trader buys grain in small quantities – often in two- and three-penny lots – from women who are selling it in the market. He collects this grain, may hold it for a while and almost certainly will transport it to another market for sale either to another middleman or to the Hausa or Ibo lorry drivers who visit the larger markets to buy food for export to the over-populated areas of the Eastern Provinces or the new urban areas in Tivland.

Both the trade carried on by women and that carried on by these ambitious young professional traders are considered admirable by Tiv. The trader is not granted so favorable a position in Tiv society as he is in some other West African societies, and mere monetary or subsistence wealth is not sufficient in itself to afford great prestige. Trade of women stays within the category of subsistence (if one considers the end in view and discounts the presence of money, as Tiv do in the situation), while the trade of professionals stays within the monetary category.

Yet Tiv see truckload after truckload of foodstuffs driven away from their large markets every fifth day. They say that food is less plentiful today than it was in the past, though more land is being farmed. Tiv elders deplore this situation and know what is happening, but they do not know just where to fix the blame. In attempts to do something about it, they sometimes announce that no women are to sell any food at all. But when their wives disobey them, men do not really feel that they were wrong to have done so. Tiv sometimes discriminate against non-Tiv traders in attempts to stop export of food, but their actions are seldom upheld by the courts to which the outsiders scurry, and in any case Tiv themselves are occupied in the export of food. In their condemnation of the situation which is depriving them of their food faster than they are able to increase production, Tiv elders always curse money itself. It is money which, as the instrument for selling one's life subsistence, is responsible for the worsened situation – money and the Europeans who brought it.

Yet they cannot fix the blame or stop the situation. When women sell to middlemen, Tiv class this exchange in the category of subsistence exchange. When middlemen sell to other middlemen or exporters, it falls within the ethics of money trade. That the two spheres have overlapped they find mysterious and frustrating, and in the nature of money. Yet, so long as a woman does not sell too much food, there is no feeling that she has done wrong; so long as a man buys a commodity with money and sells it for money, he has done nothing blameworthy.

Of even greater concern to Tiv is the influence money has had on marriage institutions, by affecting the interchange of rights in women. In response to what appeared superficially to be popular demand, the Administration (encouraged by the Missions and with the apparent concurrence of the tribal councils) abolished exchange marriage and substituted for it a form of marriage by bride wealth. It is the writer's opinion that both Tiv and Administration today believe this action to have been precipitate and ill-advised. Today every woman's guardian, in accepting money as bride wealth, feels that he is converting down. Although attempts are made to spend money which is received in bride wealth to acquire brides for one's self and one's sons, it is in the nature of money, Tiv insist, that this is most difficult to accomplish. The good man still spends his bride wealth receipts for brides – but good men are not so numerous as would be desirable. Tiv deplore the fact that they are required to "sell" (*te*) their daughters and "buy" (*yam*, but more euphemistically *kem*, to accumulate) wives. It smacks, they tell the investigator in low tones, of slavery. There is no dignity in it since the possibility of converting a bride wealth marriage into an exchange marriage has been removed.

The fact that Tiv, in the face of the introduction of a money economy, have retained the motivations commensurate with their old ideology of investment based on a scheme of the discreteness of several categories of exchangeable items, hierarchically arranged, has created several difficulties and inconsistencies. It is considered admirable to invest one's wealth in wives and children – the least expendable form of wealth traditionally known to Tiv, and that form most productive of further wealth.

But Tiv have come upon a simple paradox: today it is easy to sell subsistence goods for money to buy prestige articles and women, thereby aggrandizing oneself at a rapid rate. The food so sold is exported, decreasing the amount of subsistence goods available for consumption. On the other hand, the number of women is limited. The result is that bride wealth gets higher – the price of women becomes inflated. Under these conditions, as Tiv attempt to become more and more wealthy in people, they are merely selling more and more of their foodstuffs and subsistence goods, leaving less and less for their own consumption.

Indigenous Tiv ideas of the sort we would call economic not only formed a basis for their intellectual ordering of their economic exchanges, but also supply motivation for their personal economic striving. These ideas are inconsistent with a monetary economy on the fringe of industrial society. Tiv, to whom these are not "economic ideas" but a "natural" ordering of phenomena and behavior, tend to see the difficulty as being with the monetary economy. The ethnographer can only look on and attempt to understand the ideas and motivations, knowing that the discrepancy between ideas and the actual situation will become greater until one is smashed and then adapted to suit the other – and he knows also that the conclusion is foregone.

References

ABRAHAM, R. C.
    1940   The Tiv people. 2nd ed. London, Crown Agents.
AKIGA
    1939   Akiga's story. Translated by Rupert East. London, Oxford University Press. For International African Institute.
BOHANNAN, PAUL
    1954   Tiv farm and settlement. London, Her Majesty's Stationery Office.

BOHANNAN, LAURA and PAUL
    1953   The Tiv of central Nigeria. London, International African Institute.
STEINER, FRANZ
    1954   Notes on comparative economics. British Journal of Sociology.

8

RESEARCH ON AN AFRICAN MODE OF PRODUCTION*

CATHERINE COQUERY-VIDROVITCH

Until recently, African traditional societies have generally been studied in isolation and with emphasis on the particular. Economic anthropologists are only just beginning to understand the kinship structures of subsistence societies.[1] But by concentrating on the fact of subsistence, they have underestimated the importance of the organization of production and of the social hierarchy. Subsistence, which is not autarchy, does not imply the absence of a division of labour or of elementary methods of exchange, in particular, local food markets. These are not "class societies" as Marxists understand the term nowadays, and they differ from pre-capitalist Western societies in the absence of any private appropriation of the land. However, throughout Africa, they have gone beyond the stage of "primitive community". Even the economic organization of the Pygmies in the forest is based on an exchange of goods from hunting and gathering for the agricultural produce of sedentary tribes.

Thus the problem of a mode of production arises, which even Soviet historians[2] hesitate to compare to one of the stages defined for Western Europe: slavery, feudalism, and capitalism. Since Marx and Engels had outlined another mode of production, the Asiatic, Marxists naturally thought of extending to Africa this concept hitherto used for societies of the Near East (Egypt and Mesopotamia) and Far East (China).[3]

The Asiatic mode of production presupposes villages based on collective production and bound to a "higher unity" in the form of a state capable of compelling people to work. Behind this "generalized slavery", a despot

---

* Originally published as "Recherches sur une mode de production africain," *La Pensée*, 144, Editions Sociales, Paris, 1969. Translated in M.A. Klein and G.W. Johnson (eds), *Perspectives on the African past*. Little, Brown and Company, New York, 1972.

[1] Especially Claude Meillassoux "Essai d'interprétation du phénomène économique dans les sociétés traditionnelles d'autosubsistence." *Cahiers d'Études Africaines*, 4, pp. 3–67, 1960, and *Anthropologie économique des Gouro de Côte-d'Ivoire* (Paris 1964).

[2] On the opening of the debate on the Asiatic mode of production in the Soviet Union, see J. Chesneaux "Où en est la discussion sur le mode de production asiatique. II," *La Pensée*, 129 (1966).

[3] On this, see the synthesis of J. Chesneaux: "Le mode de production asiatique. Quelques perspectives de recherche." *La Pensée*, 114 (1964). "Où en est la discussion sur le mode de production asiatique?," *La Pensée*, 122 (1965). "Où en est . . . II." 129 (1966). "Où en est . . . III." 138 (April 1968), pp. 21–42.

"exploits these communities economically while he rules them".[4] The State becomes an entrepreneur capable of massive public works despite a limited technical capacity: irrigation systems (the river states of the Near East), military defence (the Great Wall of China), or prestige (the pyramids).[5] In this extreme form, the Asiatic mode of production is clearly not found in Black Africa. Even if we could compare certain forms of African despotism with it, we would find ourselves without the dynamic element, the "generalized slavery," which is found only perhaps in the massive constructions of the "Builders of Stone" in Southern Africa (Zimbabwe, 11th to 18th centuries).

Conscious that some of the Asian characteristics mentioned by Marx are not found in Black Africa, researchers have been generally reluctant to push their analysis to its limits. Although they would be reluctant to admit it, their problem is an excess of respect for the master, who could not have analysed societies which were unknown in his time.

The most striking effort was Jean Suret-Canale's attempt to describe an Asiatic mode of production in pre-colonial Black Africa in terms of an evolution in three stages: the *primitive community* (which has, in fact, disappeared); the tribal or *tribo-patriarchal* structure of segmentary societies called "anarchic" or "stateless", where the basic social unit is the extended family, and which is the transition to clearly differentiated *class societies*, or *states* in which privileged aristocracies seem to have created the State above the patriarchal village.[6]

By elimination – since African societies were neither slave-based (as the term is used in ancient history) nor feudal – Suret-Canale compares their system to that of Asian societies. He has to recognize the absence of *despotism*, but is anxious to relate the African mode of production to his general plan, and hence gives a broad definition of an Asiatic mode of production: "The coexistence of an instrument of production based on the rural community . . . and the exploitation of man by man in diverse forms . . . which consistently use the intermediary of the community."

Suret-Canale assigns to the difference between "a stateless society" and a State an importance which is now debated for Black Africa.[7] In addition, his definition of a surplus exclusively based upon the privileged class's appropriation of the products of village labour appears to be erroneous (we shall return to this later) and his definition of an Asiatic mode of production, if not false, is too general since it omits the essential point: the motivating factor of the exploitation of man by man, that is to say the kind of these "diverse forms."

A similar problem prompted Godelier, in a study of the Asiatic mode of production,[8] to distinguish between "an Asiatic mode of production with public works" and "an Asiatic mode of production without public works." The latter seems more debatable. Once again this limited definition omits the dynamic element from a mode of production, by leaving out its economic foundation at the level of production. In fact, public works, which surpass the means of particular communities, create the conditions of productive activity for these communities: "The State and the ruling class directly intervene in the conditions of

[4] J. Chesneaux: "Le M.P.A. quelques perspectives . . ." *La Pensée*, 114 (1964).

[5] Ch. Parain: "Protohistoire méditerranéenne et mode de production asiatique." *La Pensée*, 127, pp. 26–27 (1966).

[6] Jean Suret-Canale. "Les societétés traditionnelles en Afrique noire et le concept du mode de production asiatique," *La Pensée*, 177, pp. 19–42 (1964).

[7] Whatever type of society is considered, political institutions are based upon principles of descent and two categories of relationships – lineage and political – always appear both complementary and antagonistic. G. Balandier: *Anthropologie politique*, Paris 1967, p. 61.

[8] M. Godelier: *La notion de mode de production asiatique et les schémas marxistes d'évolution des sociétés*. C.E.R.M., Paris, 1963.

production, and the connection between productive capacity and production lies directly with the organization of public works.[9] These public works give rise to a bureaucracy and an absolute power, which is centralized and 'despotic'."

Suret-Canale had already noted that the states of West Africa were set up differently: "they were clearly based on the union of a tribal confederation (headed by a 'king', the chief of the land), and a *market* to which the king gives security and from which he takes an important part of his revenue."[10] Godelier is also aware that the rise of empires in tropical Africa (such as mediaeval Ghana, Mali, and Songhai) was not related to the organization of public works but "to the control by tribal aristocracies of inter-tribal or inter-regional trade involving an exchange of precious products – gold, ivory, skins, etc. . . . between black and white Africa."[11]

In completing his presentation, Suret-Canale unconvincingly eliminates the dynamic element in African history which stemmed from foreign contacts. He resorts to a local example rather than to scientific reasoning: his proof is the existence of the Mossi States in whose formation "trade apparently played no role whatever,"[12] – which remains to be verified. Godelier, on the other hand, accepts the consequences of his analysis. He proposes "to add a second hypothesis to that of Marx . . . that there can be another path and another form for the mode of production, by which a minority dominates and exploits the community without directly interfering with their conditions of production, but by profitably taking a surplus in labour and in products."[13]

We are in complete agreement with this, and the object of this article is to show why. We take exception to the comparison between the "Asiatic mode of production" and the mode of production found in some African societies, and therefore will use the term "African mode of production." The only thing the two systems have in common is the existence of subsistence village communities. In Asia, however, it is a question of despotism and direct exploitation through generalized slavery, whereas in Africa, as we shall see, there is a superimposed bureaucracy which interferes only indirectly with the community. We do not see the necessity of examining these two types of production, which differ in so many respects, together. By considering the original features of both, and analysing the productive relationships in Africa, it will be possible to discern an "African mode of production."

Long-Distance Trading

One characteristic of African societies is that they were never truly isolated. The African continent has known two major phenomena: the mobility of its people and the volume of long-distance trade. Migrations – collective movements or progressive infiltrations – came to an end only in the colonial era when colonial régimes fixed populations for more effective police control or for such administrative goals as tax collection or the allocation of lots for private property. Previously, the history of Africa was indistinguishable from the movements of its peoples. These were partly attributable to the existence of low population densities and large, relatively open areas. Nearly everywhere, except along the coasts,

---

[9] Godelier, *op. cit.*, p. 29.
[10] Suret-Canale: "Les sociétés traditionnelles . . .," *op. cit.*, p. 37.
[11] Godelier, *op. cit.*, p. 30.
[12] "This hypothesis is invalidated by the existence of the Mossi States . . . ," Suret-Canale, *op. cit.*, p. 37.
[13] Godelier, *op. cit.*, p. 37.

the land is open to movement and even the dense forest is cut by large navigable rivers such as the Congo.

Examples of movement are numerous. The most spectacular was the Bantu expansion which overflowed most earlier populations in the central and southern part of the continent.[14] The Fulbe, who took refuge in the Senegalese Tekrur after prehistoric migrations from the Sahara, moved in the opposite direction from the 17th century. Today they are scattered from Senegal to Lake Chad. The history of the Fang since the early 19th century is that of movement from Cameroon toward the Atlantic.[15] Finally, there were Nilotic movements which spread south from the Sudan throughout eastern Africa between the 15th and 19th centuries and perhaps their superior techniques reached the Lake Region, Katanga, and Rhodesia.[16] In brief, there is no ethnographic monograph which cannot present for the people studied a map of their origins marked with criss-crossing arrows, symbols of the complexity of its successive and often recent migrations.

Following these continual upheavals, African societies were at all times under foreign influence, which came from Egypt, from the Arab world, from Europe, indeed, even from Asia. The heritage of ancient Egypt spread into Nubia, to Napata and then to Meroe (the Kingdom of Kush, 600 B.C. to A.D. 300), and from there to Axum in Ethiopia. Southwest Asia looked to East Africa, which offered a reserve of manpower, a place for immigration, and numerous early ties. From the 9th century on, members of persecuted sects took refuge on the Coast. Kilwa, in Swahili country, is said to have been founded in the 10th century by a group of Iranians. Other places along the coast – Mogadiscio, Mombasa, Malindi, Pemba and, further south, Sofala (opposite Madagascar), which were great centres of Arab mercantile activity, at least until the Portuguese discovery, had a comparable origin. Indian merchants, between the 11th and 13th centuries, had enough influence to introduce their system of weights and measures, and their money practices to the region, and in Kilwa, enough to even bring an adventurer of their choice (Al Hasan ibn Talut) to power in the thirteenth century. In the South, even before Islam, Malayan canoes opened the way to the Comaro Islands and Madagascar, and Malacca had regular relations with the western coasts of the Indian Ocean from the ninth and tenth centuries. Finally, the Chinese at least twice made contact with East Africa, in 1417–19 and in 1431–33, and the archaeological discoveries of Chinese and Persian pottery are numerous enough for this to have been written: "From the 10th century onwards, the buried history of Tanganyika is written in Chinese porcelain."[17]

In West Africa, contacts with the Maghreb were even earlier: in 734 an expedition from the Sous reached Sudan. Contacts were established which were never broken: in 757–58 the founding of Sijilmassa in southern Morocco

---

[14]   J. H. Greenberg: *Languages of Africa* (Bloomington, 1962).

[15]   P. Alexandre: "Proto-histoire du groupe beto-bulu-fang: essai de synthèse provisoire." *Cahiers d'Études Africaines,* V, pp. 503–60 (1965).

[16]   Oliver and Mathew: *History of East Africa,* chap. VI. "Discernible developments in the interior. c. 1500–1840" (London, 1962), pp. 169–211. R. Oliver and J. D. Fage, *A short history of Africa* (London, 1962), p. 52.

[17]   Sir Mortimer Wheeler, "Archaeology in East Africa." *Tanganyika notes and records,* 40 p. 46 (1955). G.S.P. Freeman-Grenville has done important studies of money found on the coast, which confirms commercial contacts with Yemen, Arabia and Asia. Cf. "East African coin finds and their historical significance," *Journal of African History, I,* pp. 31–44 (1960). On the history of the contacts between East Africa and the Indian Ocean see Auguste Toussaint: *History of the Indian Ocean.* Tr. by Jane Guicharnaud (London, 1966). A. Villers, *The Indian Ocean* (London, 1952); J. M. Gray, *History of Zanzibar from the Middle Ages* (London, 1962); G.S.P. Freeman-Grenville, *The mediaeval history of the Tanganyika coast* (London, 1962); J-L Duyvendak, *China's discovery of Africa* (London, 1949).

opened the Sudan road for the gold caravans. As for the Europeans, they moved along the coasts from 1434 (the date when Cape Bojador, opposite the Canary Islands, was crossed) to 1487 (when they doubled the Cape of Tempests, later the Cape of Good Hope).

These contacts led to long-distance commerce across the Sahara and the Indian Ocean. This cannot be reduced to external factors: the Arab conquest, the Portuguese Exploration, or the colonial impact. They profoundly affected the interior too by encouraging the collaboration of coastal kingdoms (slave-traders, for example), and of inland tribes who acted as intermediaries. In the Congolese basin, merchandise got through long before white men did, preceding the half-breed Portuguese traders, the "pombeiros" who had been trickling toward the Pool along the caravan trails since the end of the fifteenth century. In the Gabonese back country, the people of the Ogooué had European-made textiles, pearls, and "neptunes"[18] in their possession. The Fang of Woleu-Ntem, an area barely penetrated before the twentieth century (within the borders of southern Cameroon), had guns from trading before anyone there had ever seen a white man.[19] Likewise, during his mediaeval Sudanese empires, the people of the forest regions, including the Gold Coast, whose mines were opened in the mid-14th century by Mandé initiative, had received merchandise of Maghreb origin (glass beads, salt) in exchange for iron ore, ivory, or kola nuts which had been sent up North.

It was not necessary for trading to achieve a large volume in order to exercise great influence. History shows, however, that it often reached considerable proportions: gold and salt in medieval West Africa, or the gold and copper exported via the Monomotapa, rulers of an empire centred in the bend of the Zambesi river and Sofala on the Indian Ocean. In addition, there were slave traders. At least 10 to 20 million were sent to the Atlantic trade between the sixteenth and nineteenth centuries.[20] The trans-Sahara trade to the Ottoman empire was at about 10,000 a year in the nineteenth century (compared to 70,000 sent to America)[21] and in the same period, large numbers were being shipped from the Congo basin to Zanzibar and the Indian Ocean trade.

A critique of the traditional contrast in Black Africa: states *vs* stateless societies

The economic life of pre-colonial African societies was characterized by the juxtaposition of two apparently contradictory levels: the local subsistence village and international, even transcontinental commerce. This economic phenomenon is paralleled by and inseparable from a political one pointed out by Balandier, the conflict between a kinship-based tribal structure and a territorial organization with centralizing tendencies.[22] Does that mean we must link (as Suret-Canale implicitly does) first subsistence to "tribo-patriarchal" or stateless society and, second, long-distance trade and the more or less despotic state? The analogy is questionable. In order to show this, we shall limit ourselves to a few examples. Let historians and anthropologists make the case which will permit us to verify what in our

---

[18] Great plates of embossed copper which were used for money, especially for the payment of dowries (originally produced by the Portuguese, they were in use until the 20th century).

[19] Catherine Coquery-Vidrovitch (ed.), *Brazza et la prise de possession du Congo* (Paris: Mouton, 1970).

[20] For a long time it was estimated at 20–50 million. Philip Curtin estimates that 10 million would be the maximum. See *The Atlantic slave trade* (Madison, 1970).

[21] A. Adu Boahen: *Britain, the Sahara and the Western Sudan* (London, 1965).

[22] G. Balandier: *Anthropologie politique, op. cit.*

present state of knowledge must be considered a research hypothesis.

Anthropologists have certainly proved to what degree kinship structures are associated with the economic structures of subsistence. Segmentary societies, until recently placed in the poorly defined and poorly studied category of primitive "classless societies," show themselves on closer analysis to be rather diversified. Once again, it is Balandier who reminds us that in Black Africa "all societies are heterogeneous to varying degrees."[23] This primitive community is made up of "social strata" which are involved in "antagonism, competition and conflict."[24] In its simplest form, it is the domination of the elder over the younger, the elder controlling the means of production because they can demand that the younger "remit the product of their labour."[25] They can exclusively hoard or exchange "prestige goods," which reinforce their position – and, thus, we have a process of accumulation in the villages, capable of developing and accentuating inequalities. This is not a full outline. It is sufficient to underline the danger of denying that subsistence is "an economic, scientific, and Marxist category" because "it is only a void, the absence of a market economy and market goods."[26] Such a negative definition risks the rejection of "all pre-capitalist societies . . . in the vague concept of traditional society,"[27] which would explain in part the lack of interest shown in this problem by Europocentric historians, including Marxists. We find no such strong

refusal in Marx himself. On the contrary, he states that

> the specific economic form in which unpaid surplus labour is exacted from the direct producers . . . is the basis of *any form of economic* community . . . and, at the same time, the basis of its *specific political form*. It is always necessary to seek the hidden foundation of any *social edifice*, and consequently, of any political form which draws its relationship from sovereignty and dependence in the immediate relationship between the manager of the means of production and the direct manager (a connection whose different aspects naturally correspond . . . to a *certain degree* of productive social force."[28]

Is it necessary, on the contrary, to associate long-distance trading and centralized power? This seems much more dubious. To be sure, the most striking examples have been studied within states: Ghana and Mali were tied to trade with Maghreb; Benin and Dahomey experienced a similar development with the slave-trade; Zanzibar flourished in the 19th century with slave and ivory trading in East Africa. But recent studies prove that long-distance trade influenced the most diverse societies. Along the Congo River and its main tributaries (the Oubangui, Sangha, Likouala, Alima, to mention only the north bank), trade was the only means of existence for certain segmentary peoples. In the 16th century trading took place between the Portuguese and the Kongo Kingdom situated on the south of

---

[23]   Ibid. p. 93.

[24]   Ibid. p. 93

[25]   Cf. Meillassoux: *Anthropologie économique des Gouro, op. cit.*, p. 217.

[26]   Suret-Canale, "Structure et anthropologie économique," *La Pensée*, 135, p. 99 (1967). In saying this, Suret-Canale evidently goes beyond his own line of thought, since he has devoted himself to an analysis of the "tribe-patriarchal" society and has defined the *productive forces* based on communal agriculture: "Les societés traditionnelles . . .," *La Pensée*, 117, pp. 19–42 (1964).

[27]   Hence Godelier's contradiction: he reproaches Meillassoux while accusing him at the same time of over-emphasizing "the fact of inequality . . . in most classless societies." "A propos de deux textes d'anthropologie économique," *L'homme* (1967), p. 86.

[28]   Marx: *Le capital*, III, Ed. Soc., pp. 171–172. On this subject see, Parrain: "Proto-histoire méditerranéenne . . . ," *La Pensée*, 127, p. 26 (1966).

the Congo. But, by 1850, the latter no longer existed. Beyond the Bakongo of the coastal zone, trade had reached the Bateke of Stanley Pool, and, further up-river, the Bubangi who lived where the Sangha and Oubangui rivers met the Congo.[29] There, the power of the chief rarely extended beyond the village or fraction of a village. Nonetheless, these river people, isolated on knolls along a complex system of lagoons, constituted a dynamic whole; unable to earn a living from the marshy soil, they turned to trade in local food products and in slaves. On the upper Alima, the Bubangi (locally called Lakuba) set up temporary encampments for the dry season and traded about 20 tons a day of manioc from the Batekes of the plateau and the Mbochi of the river. In return they offered the fruits of their activity: mats, pottery, paddles, nets, harpoons, and dried fish which they produced in large amounts.

With these activities, which were indispensable to the maintenance of their position in this strategic, though barren area, they combined their role as agents for long-distance Congolese trading: in exchange for European merchandise, they received ivory from Likouala. Further upstream came slaves, wood, ivory and, before long, rubber from the Sangha and the Oubangui. Important markets developed around Pool and along the rivers. These products were provided by similar segmentary groups operating further upstream. The inhabitants of the forest knew that the river came from "the land of white men" armed with guns, who were certainly Arabs. This fact, amongst others, confirms the extent of Congolese trade which handled products and men over great distances.

No matter what society is examined, the permanence of trade transcends the traditional contrast between states and stateless societies.

Balandier has already shown the coexistence of apparently contradictory elements at the heart of *all* African politics, state or stateless. In both, all forms of transition can be discovered. To be sure, there is a progress toward centralized organization, but the difference is qualitative rather than essential; even in the most "despotic" societies (mediaeval Sudanese kingdoms, the Kongo in the sixteenth century, and Dahomey in the nineteenth century), the authority of the sovereign never replaced the tribe-patriarchal organization. At most, it involved a superimposed bureaucracy, which respected the structures of rural life. To recognize this trait common to all African societies is, at the same time, to seek its economic basis. One of the motives of African history is to be found in the dialectical interplay, or the absence of interplay, between apparently heterogeneous socio-economic levels within the same unit (the coexistence of communal clan structures and territorial entities, the superimposition of subsistence and long-distance trade). At any given moment, their history reveals a certain stage of development in these relationships, whose contradictions were perpetually generating disequilibrium and conflict.

Toward an "African mode of production?"

By taking into account these specific traits it becomes possible to discern an *African mode of production* distinct from the classic model of the *Asiatic mode of production*.

Black Africa, as we have stated, never had an Asiatic type of despotism. That does not mean that there were no aristocracies or privileged classes. But the rulers who had power in various places were hastily identified as

[29] G. Sautter: *De l'Atlantique au fleuve Congo* (Paris, 1965), pp. 215–325. Also see: C. Coquery-Vidrovitch (Ed.), *Brazza et la prise de possession du Congo, op. cit.* and J. Vansina: "Long-distance trade routes in Central Africa." *Journal of African History*, III, 3, 375–90 (1960).

"absolute monarchs" by European observers. The demands which they made with the aid of the ruling class were neither, nor exclusively, wrought on "the hard-working peasantry, made up both of free men and captives," which was, in Africa, as elsewhere, "the fundamental exploited class."[30] To be sure, there were exceptions. In pre-colonial Senegal the families which had power also possessed rights to land and to work from the peasants (as a collectivity, however, with neither the exploiters nor the exploited considered as individuals).[31] In Burundi, property (livestock and pastures) was controlled by the *Tutsi* at the expense of the *Hutu*. This suggests a relationship of a feudal nature.[32]

However, it seems excessive to seek the only motive for this development of African societies in the productive forces of a subsistence economy. Such a statement, which seeks within African society the opposition of exploiters and the exploited reveals a lack of observation of the actual data. Black Africa is the one place in the world where agriculture was least liable to produce a surplus. Agricultural and craft techniques were particularly rudimentary (no wheel nor plow: the only tool was the hoe). The necessity of improving production with the aid of new tools or large public works was never felt. A rather sparse population was able to meet its needs without too much effort from land which was abundant, though not fertile. No ruler, in order to live, ever needed to take food from village production *in quantity*. At most,

he was content to organize for his own benefit the labour of his wives (the case of Dahomey, for example), and "domestic" slaves, but this was not comparable to what has been called the "slavery mode of production." The tribute levied by the best-organized despots (the kings of the Kongo and Dahomey) does not seem to have been used as payment for services or to provide labor needed on tasks of public utility. It is not certain that tribute was regularly used to feed the people of the court, and nothing indicates that it was even used as a public aid fund to which those in need could appeal.[33] In the Kongo, the King and the nobles redistributed what they had received among vassals who requested it.[34] In Dahomey, the "customs festival," an annual ceremony celebrated since the eighteenth century in honour of the royal ancestors, fulfilled the same function. It was an occasion for the sovereign to collect the tribute but, above all, to dazzle his assembled subjects for several weeks with the dynasty's wealth and bounty, either by the public sacrifice of hundreds of slaves,[35] or by the distribution of spirits, poured out in great quantities, or of cowries (local money) and cloth cast out from public platforms.[36] In brief, the fees demanded were, above all, of symbolic value, a guarantee of the social structure. Not that the relationship of exploiters to exploited did not exist; rather the African despot exploited his subjects less than the neighbouring tribes. In fact, it was long-distance trading which provided the major part of his surplus. From

---

[30]   J. Suret-Canale: "Les sociétés traditionnelles . . ." *op. cit.*, *La Pensée*, 117, p. 30 (1964). Godelier expresses the same thing in an analogous, although less categorical, form: the aristocracy, "assures the *bases* of its class exploitation by the deduction of a part of the communities' product (in work and goods)," *La notion de M.P.A.* . . . , *op. cit.*, p. 30.

[31]   Kalidou Deme: "Les classes sociales dans le Sénégal pré-colonial," *La Pensée*, 130, p. 17 (1966).

[32]   J.-J. Maquet: *The premise of inequality in Ruanda*, London, 1961.

[33]   Peter C. Lloyd: "The political structure of African kingdoms," *Political systems and the distribution of power* (London, 1965), p. 78.

[34]   W. G. L. Randles: *L'ancien royaume du Congo des origines à la fin du XIXᵉ siècle*, Chap. 5, "La fiscalité," Paris, 1969.

[35]   About a hundred each year, and more than five hundred for the grand Customs Festival celebrated the year of the King's funeral.

[36]   Coquery-Vidrovitch: "La fête des coutumes au Dahomey, historique et essai d'interprétation," *Annales*, 4, pp. 696–716 (1964).

this point of view, the customs festival was not a retrograde institution which limited or paralysed European contacts – on the contrary, it stimulated the economic life of the country and encouraged the intense trading activity necessary to supply this "fair" with all sorts of products (slaves in exchange for European merchandise). Let us not be reproached here for excessively favoring the *mode of circulation of goods* at the expense of the *mode of production*; the fundamental problem was not to transport merchandise but to procure it – in a certain sense to "produce" it. It was evidently a bastardized form of production, both immediate and apparent, which was in fact ruinous, since, in the long run, it sterilized the country instead of enriching it. There were two ways of procuring goods: war (in the case of slave raids),[37] or peaceful exchanges with neighbouring peoples (the case of salt and gold in the Sudan), a type of externally oriented exchange comparable to a form of production and opposed to circulation within a given society.

Suret-Canale noted the basic role of trade in Black Africa, "the decisive element in the consolidation of the first states in tropical Africa."[38] He has not sufficiently explored its significance, however, because of his concern to establish *direct* domination of the aristocracy over the peasantry. The control of long-distance trading demanded the subordination of the bulk of the population to those who benefited from it. Yet the control exercised by the ruling class was manifested *indirectly*, by the exclusive possession of goods which were accumulated in a process analogous to the way "prestige goods" are often amassed by the

elders in a subsistence society: for example, red cotton fabric from Europe which the Bateke chiefs kept for their funerals[39] and weapons accumulated in the arsenals of the Sultans of Haut-Oubangui. Furthermore, indirect domination did not exclude its corollary, direct domination, especially in the case of the gun trade, which conditioned them both. In acquiring arms, the sovereign assured himself of control of military enlistment, the payment of tributes and the work of the plantations which in turn promoted the accumulation of an exportable surplus (for example, palm oil cultivated by the king's plantations in Dahomey since the mid-19th century). But, let us repeat, the major revenues came not from village communities, but from outside the territory, from the annual raids or from peaceful commercial transactions which secured products at rates much lower than their actual value. Thus, life in the kingdom of Dahomey was marked by military expeditions launched each dry season towards the Ashanti in the West or the Yoruba cities in the East, in order to bring back the slaves required by the economy. This was also true in the Kongo and probably in Benin. In central Africa, the Likouba (Bubangi) obtained manioc from the Bateke and the Mbochi "at ridiculously low prices."[40] At Stanley Pool they resold the red wood, the ivory and the slaves brought upstream at five or six times, indeed, perhaps ten times the price.[41] Even in the case of the empires founded on mineral wealth (gold from the Sudan or from southern Africa), the ruler's problem was not to impose on his subjects a collective effort to extract the ores. It was to obtain, at a low price, a metal sometimes

---

[37] "War, *which is one of the forms of production*, in a characteristic fashion generates what is called 'parasitic-military States' found in Ancient times as well as in the Middle Ages." G-A Melekechvili: "Esclavage, féodalisme et mode de production asiatique dans l'Orient ancien," *La Pensée*, No. 132 (1967), p. 41.

[38] Suret-Canale: "Les sociétés traditionnelles . . . ," *La Pensée*, No. 117 (1964), p. 36.

[39] G. Sautter: "Le plateau congolais de Mbé," *Cahiers d'Études Africaines*, No. 2, 1960, p. 37.

[40] From the testimony of European observers. C. Coquery-Vidrovitch (ed), *Brazza et la prise de possession du Congo*.

[41] A knife bought for 3 bars of copper in Ikelemba was resold for 60 bars in Bonga; a slave bought for 20 bars was resold for 400–500 bars. *Ibid.*

located far from his territory. Neither the King of Ghana, nor the Emperor of Mali controlled the producers who probably operated within a hunting and gathering economy. They knew even less about them because of silent barter. This oft-described process forbade the two parties to enter into direct contact. The merchants who came from the North displayed their merchandise (salt) in a specific place and then they withdrew. The next morning, opposite each object they wanted to sell, they found an amount of gold-dust. If they thought the offer sufficient, they took the gold; if not, they touched nothing, until a supplementary amount was added or, if their demand was too high, it was all taken away. When the Emperor of Mali had one of the traders carried off in order to discover "what kind of men did not allow themselves to be seen or to be spoken to," the only result was the suspension of trade for three years.[42] In addition, Arab writers reported absurd stories about cannibals or deformed savages who worked the veins of gold after the rains. . . .[43] In southern Africa, the ore-bearing sites spread from Katanga to the Limpopo are more extensive than the ruins of the "stone builders," which testify to a political organization around Zimbabwe and Mapungubwe (South Rhodesia) and seem to corroborate an analogous hypothesis of "production" by trade rather than by direct exploitation.[44]

The African mode of production is based then upon the combination of a patriarchal–communal economy and the exclusive ascendancy of one group over long-distance trade. The form of power at any given moment depends upon the nature of this group. If political authority was in the hands of the heads of kinship groups at the village level, their preeminence was then uncontested. In the case of the Fang or the Bubangi, it was only

threatened by the rivalry of small groups involved in the same trade. In the middle Congo, the system collapsed only under the pressure of external factors: the intrusion of Europeans who seized control of trade for their own profit and eliminated the traditional middlemen.

If, on the other hand, in a more differentiated political system, a privileged class succeeded in controlling long-distance trade by means of a hereditary caste or because of an accumulation of capital, the régime combined the tribo-patriarchal system and a new kind of territorial ambition. The mediaeval Sudanese empires, for example, were characterized by the utilization of traditional animist structures by an Arabized aristocracy which controlled trade. It would be an error to imagine these to be Islamic states (especially since Ghana was already declining when Islam took root). The function of these empires was to control and exploit trade between the western Sudan and North Africa. Their goal was domination for profit and this economic objective allowed them to realize their political form. The ruling class was interested in presenting a Moslem facade, through the organization of its Courts and the pilgrimages, which would favour good relations with the Maghreb, a client and supplier. However, Islamic proselytizing would have threatened internal stability. We have no evidence that Islam had a solid base outside of the large cities; on the contrary, even within monarchical institutions the descriptions left by Arab geographers show that the leaders felt the need to graft their power onto a typically pagan structure, probably of Mandé origin. Hence the pomp which surrounded the King, the rites he had to follow (not to drink in public, not to converse directly with his subjects . . .), and the submissive demonstrations of his dignitaries (who prostrated

[42] A. Ca' da Mosto: *The Voyages of Cadamosto*. Tr. and ed. G. R. Crone (London, 1937).

[43] See the evidence in: Al-Bakri, 1068: *Description de L'Afrique*, trans. (Algiers, 1913), p. 381; Al-Omari, 1338: *L'Afrique moins l'Egypte*, trans. (Paris, 1927), pp. 70–1; A. Ca' da Mosto, *The Voyages* . . .

[44] See R. Summers: *Ancient Mining in Rhodesia* (Salisbury, 1969).

themselves in the dust or performed sacramental dances in honour of the sovereign). To abandon these traditions would have provoked hostility, since the masses were attached to patriarchal forms. The evolution of the empires resulted from the equilibrium between these two antagonistic currents: in Songhai, for example, Sonni Ali (1464–92), a champion of militant paganism, aroused a Moslem reaction against himself. To be sure, he subdued the whole loop of the Niger river, but the history of the Empire became a constant competition between pagans and Moslems, which weakened the state and encouraged the Moroccan conquest in 1591. This resolved the conflict by uniting all in resistance in the name of the animist cause – but at the price of economic supremacy.[45] . . .

When a privileged group or a despot lost control of long-distance trade this eventually led to the decline of his political power: this was the case in the Kingdom of the Kongo. At first it owed its cohesion to the King's monopoly of long-distance trade which probably existed within central Africa from the twelfth century: lumps of sea salt were carried inland, as well as the "zimbu" shellfish from the isle of Luanda which was used as money. On the other hand, raffia mats and ivory were received at the Pool from forest areas. When the ruler lost control of trade with Europe, he also lost control of outlying provinces. Chiefs on the coast from Loango and Soyo north of the river's mouth to Angola in the south profited by the distance from the capital to seize control of markets, with the aid of Portuguese merchants from Saô Tomé. From the sixteenth century on, these peripheral coastal peoples gradually freed themselves. The vassals became brokers, and from this trade they took a power which permitted them to compete with the authority they henceforth rejected.[46]

The examples presented do not in themselves claim to establish a general law. In the present state of our knowledge, they are simply an effort to explain the coexistence of contradictory political and economic elements. This coexistence was undoubtedly explained by the preference of the minorities in power to exploit their neighbours rather than their subjects. No African political régime, no matter how despotic, felt the need to eliminate communal village structures within their borders which did not interfere with their exploitation. As long as the village transmitted its tribute to the chief of the district or of the province, it ran the life of the collectivity as it pleased. The elders assured the worship of the clan's ancestors; the chief of the land allotted arable land to each family and to each generation; groups of women dominated the local food markets. There was no need to supply the ruler with a contingent of plantation labourers or porters, tasks generally performed by royal slaves seized in foreign countries. The most frequent obligations were limited to military service, or, as in Dahomey, the selection of some girls for the harem of the "Amazon" corps, the élite female warriors of the King.

To be sure, in many African societies trade played a lesser role; this was the case of the Gouro of the Ivory Coast, even though kola markets existed and played a dynamic role. Trade was a way for the younger Gouro, who controlled it, to challenge the supremacy of their elders.[47] In any case, wherever trade was limited, it seems that nothing endangered the "tribe-patriarchal" structures because nothing was capable of assuring enough of a surplus. As to the "military hegemonies" which prevailed elsewhere, were they as extraneous to a long-distance trade economy as is said? For example, it would be necessary to study further the role played by the little known

[45] J. D. Fage, "Some thoughts on state formation in the Western Sudan before the 17th century," *Boston Univ. Papers in African History*, I, pp. 17–34, 1964.
[46] W. G. L. Randles, Chap. IV, "L'Économie"; XI, "Les conséquences de l'ouverture de la nouvelle frontière," *op. cit.*
[47] Meillassoux: *Anthropologie économique . . . , op. cit.*

merchant class in the Mossi kingdoms. Elsewhere, pastoral occupations encouraged the development of the Fulbe, by favouring the accumulation of wealth in the form of livestock. Whatever might be said of them, their prosperity first manifested itself in active cattle markets. The Fulbe States, heirs to Ousman don Fodio, especially, controlled in the nineteenth century, and no doubt before that, the slave trade which supplied all of Sudan with slaves.[48] It is not necessary, however, to require identification of everything. We admit that in Africa there were several types of ascendency by a ruling class over the rest of the population: control of long-distance trade often implied military power (for example, the slave-trade kingdoms). No doubt the latter prevailed, sometimes by itself in certain "parasitic military States" (Buganda, for example, where the State appeared to be a war machine designed to plunder slaves, cattle, and prestige objects destined for the chiefs, the military officers, and the bravest warriors, thereby making possible the mobilization of a large part of the population for two annual campaigns).[49] It would also be necessary to distinguish between West Africa and the inter-lacustrine zone. In the former, land was controlled collectively by the village community (only the King of Dahomey in the nineteenth century asserted his right of eminent domain, when he took over land for the palm plantations sought by Europeans). In the latter, phenomena akin to the appropriation of land by the ruling class are discerned quite early (the case of Ruanda, for example).

These examples prove the need for more case studies. It would be equally desirable to begin a comparison with other so-called subsistence societies, beginning with the Maghreb. There we also find this juxtaposition of two economic systems impervious to each other on the village and on the State level. Perhaps we could then also clarify the reasons for a dichotomy which has struck all African historians: the *invariability* of the communal bases of subsistence as opposed to the *instability* of the socio-political level. The second term, although inseparable from the first, could be explained by other factors. It might arise from the complex interplay of diverse elements. Among these, long-distance trade was among the most dynamic, but also the most vulnerable, since it was subject to external as well as internal factors.

We can see how much the African mode of production, which cannot be reduced to the pre-capitalist modes of production in the West, is also radically different from those of Asia, because there is no true despotism directly exploiting a peasant class. A final problem remains: the possible evolution of this mode of production. It has often been suggested that the Asiatic mode of production was doomed to stagnation. Godelier, on the contrary, insists that the movement of a society toward an Asiatic mode of production, revealing the emergence of a fluid class structure "is the greatest advance of productive forces possible on the basis of early communal forms of production". Evolution beyond this stage (providing that it is not petrified at this stage), could only come from the working out of its internal contradictions. Class structures would progressively take precedence over communal ones, through the development of private property.[50]

Can a comparable evolution of the African mode of production be conceived? Stagnation

---

[48] C. Coquery-Vidrovitch: "La politique française en Haute-Sangha," *Revue française d'histoire d'outre-mer*, 186, pp. 29–31 (1965).
[49] D. Sperber: *Les paysans-clients au Buganda*, Communication au Colloque du Groupe de Recherche en Anthropologie et Sociologie Politique (CRASP) (Paris, 29 March 1968). However, this thesis assumes that Buganda was more independent of commercial relationships with the coast than Dahomey or Ashanti, which can be debated.
[50] M. Godelier, *op. cit.*, pp. 31–33.

is more frequent than elsewhere, for the productive forces are not real forces. Founded upon war or trade, production is sterile. To be sure, a surplus is guaranteed for the privileged class, but it is an apparent surplus, whose long-term price is the impoverishment of the country. The Sudanese Empires disappeared without leaving a trace, as soon as commerce was reversed, the trade to the North of gold for salt, being redirected to the Guinea area discovered by the Portuguese, where gold and then slaves were traded for European merchandise. The States founded upon the slave trade were finally overcome by that which created their prosperity: the Kongo, starting in the seventeenth century, Benin, even before the eighteenth century, and the Ashanti Confederation (Gold Coast) in the nineteenth century. Is that to say that the Africa mode of production was condemned to be engulfed, or to be disintegrated? In one case at least, that of Dahomey, it was capable of evolution: King Ghézo agreed to renounce the increasingly uncertain slave trade in the middle of the nineteenth century in favour of a "legitimate commerce," encouraged by Europeans and based upon actual production: palm oil and palm kernels.

Sufficient accumulation of capital allowed him to develop huge plantations under his direct control. It was the beginning of the passage to a mode of production having some characteristics of the *ancien régime* (most labour was servile, supplied by annual slave raids), and certain forms akin to feudalism, but with monarchy increasingly claiming the right of eminent domain over property. By the carefully maintained confusion between "lands of the kingdom" and "lands of the king," he proceeded to the private appropriation of land. The peasants were compelled to maintain trees and collect oil; the *topo* took care of applying strict regulations. Those who possessed palm groves were obligated to take care of the soil and harvest the fruit, under penalty of a fine or loss of land. They could not cut a palm tree without royal authorization. Palm oil made the king wealthy through taxes levied on trade. His subjects owed him a tax in kind on the oil sold, estimated at one-eighteenth of the harvest. Special officials, stationed in the various cities, collected the taxes which multiplied in Dahomey. In Allada, the former capital, every vessel which passed through "the large and the small," was taxed.[51]

Would this development have been possible elsewhere? It seems to be outlined, at least, in the interlacustrine area – a system with feudal tendencies in Ruanda, based on the capitalization of cattle. All this was shattered by the conquest, which altered relationships between the colonizers and the colonized and caused African societies to move toward a capitalist system which was "adulterated in that capitalist relationships were closely linked to more archaic forms to the greater profit of the privileged."[52] However, these examples indicate that one African society was no less capable than any other of assimilating elements from the West, and of overcoming its contradictions, provided that she could control herself the transformation of her economy. By substituting the exploitation of the palm groves for the destructive slave trade, Dahomey was integrated into a new economic system without a shattering of its equilibrium. It began by altering the mode of production.

[51]   C. Coquery-Vidrovitch: "Le blocus de Whydah (1876–1877) et la rivalité franc–anglaise au Dahomey," *Cahiers d'Études Africaines*, II, p. 384 (1965).
[52]   Y. Lacoste. *Géographie du sous-développement*, pp. 230–31. Paris, 1965.

9

Informal Income Opportunities and Urban Employment in Ghana

KEITH HART*

This article originated in the study of one Northern Ghanaian group, the Frafras, as migrants to the urban areas of Southern Ghana. It describes the economic activities of the low-income section of the labour force in Accra, the urban sub-proletariat into which the unskilled and illiterate majority of the Frafra migrants are drawn.

Price inflation, inadequate wages, and an increasing surplus to the requirements of the urban labour market have led to a high degree of informality in the income-generating activities of the sub-proletariat. Consequently, income and expenditure patterns are more complex than is normally allowed for in the economic analysis of poor countries. Government planning and the effective application of economic theory in this sphere have been impeded by the unthinking transfer of western categories to the economic and social structures of African cities. The question to be answered is this: Does the "reserve army of urban unemployed and underemployed" really constitute a passive, exploited majority in cities like Accra, or do their informal economic activities possess some autonomous capacity for generating growth in the incomes of the urban (and rural) poor?

The Economic Situation of the Urban Sub-Proletariat in Accra

International and long-distance migrants comprised 29 per cent of Ghana's labour force in 1960, while intra-regional migrants accounted for a further 24 per cent. As far as Accra was concerned, many of these mobile workers were housed in the slum on the northern outskirts, of which the centre is Nima. Over a third of the Accra labour force came to live in such areas – which included New Town and Sabon Zongo but the Nima district alone in 1960 constituted some 8 per cent (31,000) of the city's population of just under 400,000. Nima's workforce (those aged 15 years or more) was then enumerated as 20,800 (males 63 per cent, females 37 per cent); but, of these, only 16,000 (77 per cent) were listed as "economically active".

Table 9.1 shows that, while the public and

*   An earlier version of this article was presented to the Conference on Urban Unemployment in Africa held at the Institute of Development Studies, University of Sussex, in September 1971. The anthropological fieldwork was undertaken during 1965–8, and the ethnographic present, whenever used, refers to this period.

Table 9.1 – Economic Situation of working age population in Accra and Nima, 1960

Percentage

Economic situation	Males		Females		Total	
	Accra	Nima	Accra	Nima	Accra	Nima
Public-sector employee	30.3	29.3	6.9	2.6	22.4	22.9
Private-sector employee	31.6	31.2	6.3	2.7	23.0	24.6
Employer/self-employed	21.5	18.2	67.5	81.6	37.1	32.9
Other non-wage earning	4.2	2.7	3.9	2.4	4.1	2.7
Unemployed	12.4	18.7	15.5	10.8	13.5	16.9
Total economically active	100.0	100.1	100.1	100.1	100.1	100.0
Not economically active (as % of working age population)	15.1	6.3	42.0	52.0	26.6	23.3

Source: *Census of Population, 1960*

private sectors have a roughly equal share of wage employment among the economically active population, over half the total is listed as self-employed, non-wage earning, and un-employed. In addition, a quarter of the working-age population is described as not economically active (mostly female home-makers, plus some students, disabled persons, and others). Leaving aside problems of def-inition and of accuracy of enumeration, it is clear that a very large part of the urban labour force is not touched by wage employment: 40 per cent of active males and 95 per cent of active females in Nima. The question is, How many are truly unemployed? Census statistics cannot help us here.

The great differences between males and females of various ages are well illustrated by Table 9.2. Taking the active labour force alone, unemployment seems to fall heaviest on teenage boys (38 per cent) and girls (31 per cent), young men (22 per cent), and men in their prime (15 per cent). But this tripartite classification into employed (including

Table 9.2 – Nima: sex, age and economic situation, 1960

Age group	Total		Employed		Unemployed		Non-active	
	Number	%	Number	%	Number	%	Number	%
Males	13,110		10,040		2,240		830	
15–19		11.1		46.6		28.6		24.8
20–24		20.4		73.6		20.4		6.0
25–44		57.9		83.0		14.9		2.1
45+		10.6		79.1		10.8		10.1
Females	7,720		3,280		420		4,020	
15–19		18.1		32.3		14.3		53.4
20–24		26.2		37.7		3.1		59.2
25–44		46.8		47.2		3.6		49.2
45+		8.9		52.00		4.7		43.3
Total	20,830		13,320		2,660		4,850	

Source: *Census of Population, 1960*

self-employed), unemployed, and non-active may well be unreliable. Let it suffice to indicate the sheer size of the population which does not earn wages in Accra.

The range of occupations filled by Nima inhabitants is restricted. In 1960, 80 per cent of employed women were sales workers, the remainder being scattered through various manual occupations, of which tailoring provided the only significant percentage; but 90 per cent were self-employed. Male workers were concentrated in manual occupations also, mostly as artisans (32 per cent) and labourers (31 per cent); white collar occupations accounted for less than 8 per cent.

The Frafras exhibited an even narrower and more poorly paid range of occupations within the organized labour force, being located mainly in domestic, labouring, and similar jobs which lacked high skill requirements. Even long-term southern residents from this group were to be found at or near the government minimum wage of £8. 10s. per month (6/6d. per day) in 1966.[1] Cooks and stewards could earn from £10 to £15 per month according to experience, and nightwatchmen received £14. These figures represent a ceiling wage for all but a small majority of Frafras. The only opportunity to earn sums in excess of this from wage employment lay in joining the armed forces, where private soldiers were paid £16 and non-commissioned officers much more.

The pattern of economic life

Evidence for Ghana in the 1960s shows declining real incomes for urban wage-earners. Thus, three separate indices of real earnings revealed decreases over the 5-year period 1960–1 to 1965–6 of 55 per cent, 46 per cent, and 36 per cent respectively.[2]

Index A refers to the minimum real wage based on the year 1939 = 100, and shows a drop from July 1960 to December 1965 of 119 to 52.[3]

Index B has a base year of 1952 = 100, and drops similarly from 132 to 72 in the period 1960–6.[4]

Index C refers to average real earnings of male African employees in private establishments, and reveals a decrease from the base year 1961 = 100 to 64 in 1965.[5]

These findings are borne out by an *ad hoc* comparison between my own 1966 figures and those given by Jean Rouch for immigrants from the French territories to Accra in 1953–4.[6] At that time the basic wage for an urban labourer was 4s. 6d. per day, and increases in the money earnings of unskilled workers over the intervening 12 years were in most cases less than 40 per cent. Many commodity prices, on the other hand, doubled or trebled in the period.

Rouch presents an average monthly budget for migrant wage-earners in 1953–4 as follows: £3. 10s. on food (about 2s. 6d. per day for three meals), and £2. 10s., for sundries – i.e. rent

[1] Prices are given in Ghanaian pounds (£G), which, before the introduction of the Cedi and later the new Cedi, were officially at parity with the £ sterling.

[2] See Douglas Rimmer, "Wage Politics in West Africa", University of Birmingham, 1970. All three indices showed a slight upturn in real earnings for 1967–8, following an 8 per cent increase in the minimum wage.

[3] W. Birmingham, I. Neustadt, and E. N. Omaboe (eds), *A Study of Contemporary Ghana*, vol. 1, *The Economy of Ghana* (London, 1966), p. 141.

[4] Mills Odoi, *Report of the Commission on the Structure and Remuneration of the Public Service in Ghana* (Accra–Tema, 1967), p. 26.

[5] F. Stoces, "Agricultural Production in Ghana, 1955–65", in *The Economic Bulletin of Ghana* (Legon), x, 3, 1966, p. 27.

[6] See Jean Rouch, *Notes on Migrations into the Gold Coast* (Paris, 1954) – English translation by P. E. O. and J. B. Heigham (Accra, 1956), pp. 46–8.

(share of a room, costing £1. 10s. for up to ten occupants), clothing, cigarettes, and entertainments – which is reducible to £1. 10s., or less, if stringent economy is observed. He goes on to claim that, out of average monthly earnings of £6, a migrant can save £1, an annual total of £12. These budget figures give the impression that individual expenditure patterns may meaningfully be expressed as regular daily or monthly rates. In my experience, expenditures were highly irregular, as the discussion below attests.

Nevertheless, it is possible to state that, at 1966 Accra food prices, it would be difficult for a man with a wife and child to eat regularly for less than 5s. per day – almost 80 per cent of the minimum daily wage. Room rents were mostly in the range of £2 to £4 per month, and the average number of adult males per room was only 1.5, in contrast with Rouch's sample. Transport to place of work could cost 1s. per day; even water for bathing, cooking, and drinking cost a penny a bucketful in Nima. A few other prices in the "sundries" category – gin 6s. a bottle, beer 5s. a bottle, cigarettes 2s. 6d. to 5s. for 20, clothes on the whole more expensive than in the U.K., a girl for a few shillings – should suffice to indicate the nature of the budgetary battle fought by workers earning around £10 per month. The claims of visitors, relatives, and similar costs only added to this burden.

Not surprisingly, faced with the impossibility of making ends meet, the urban worker of 1966 often ran up considerable debit accounts, used some of his pay to settle a few bills, went on a short-run binge until penniless, and spent the majority of the month in penury and increasing debt, relying on extended credit facilities and a wide range of putative kin and friends to provide occasional meals, and even lodging, if necessary. The pattern of everyday economic life for these workers was thus a hand-to-mouth existence characterized by unevenness of expenditures over a pay period, flexibility of consumption units, and the proliferation of credit in all commodities. *Haushalten* (budgeting), one of Max Weber's two types of rational economic activity, is not widespread in places like Nima. Moreover, prices at the local retail level take into account the default rate which results when so large a proportion of turnover is inevitably taken up by credit sales. The number of dependants laying claim on a single wage is rendered highly variable through the continuous exchange of personnel, goods, and services within an extended kin-group resident in both urban and rural areas. Migrant remittances to their rural families are likewise irregular, being paid often by means of loans incurred in response to pressures brought to bear by visitors from home in the dry season.

The chronic imbalance between income from wage employment and expenditure needs is only partly mitigated by the generosity of kinsmen and neighbours, and only temporarily deferred by manipulation of the credit system. A more lasting solution may be sought from supplementary income sources; and it is with the analysis of these opportunities, rather than the consumption patterns and the structure of dependency relationships, that this article is mainly concerned.

One solution to the inadequacy of urban wages, however, lies in duplication of wage employment within the organized labour force. The practice of holding down more than one job at a time, doubling up of shifts worked, "moonlighting", and similar examples of industry, were extremely common in Nima. The incidence of this phenomenon is of some significance for urban labour statistics; for widespread job duplication would raise the already substantial residue calculated by subtracting the number of enumerated jobs from the total economically active population. "One man, one job" is a risky assumption, especially when low-paid, low hours employment is involved.

Frequently, even when jobs were relatively scarce during the 1960s, a labourer would make a financial arrangement with the timekeeper to turn a blind eye to his disappearance after mid-day in order to work on an afternoon job. Nightwatchmen, by sleeping on the job, are often able to be employed in the daytime as well. The willingness of workers to put in long hours on a multiplicity of occupations, both in and out of the organized labour force, is testified by many cases of which the following is one example.

Mr A. D. in 1966 worked as a street-cleaner at 6*s.* 6*d.* per day (which brought in between £6 and £7 per month, after deductions for social benefits and the timekeeper), as an afternoon gardener at £6 per month, and as a nightwatchman at £14. In addition to this annual income of approximately £320, he grew vegetables on his own plot of land which brought in another £100 or so. An average monthly income of £35 is not overmuch for incessant productive activity, but it is four times the minimum wage. He was 45 years old, unmarried, and used his 15–day annual leave for weeding and planting his "farm"; he had never been home to the Frafra area during his stay of almost 20 years in Accra. Accumulated profits went into a savings account towards his "big plan" for a gracious retirement in his home village.

As this case shows, it is erroneous to assume that such behaviour is typical only of short-term "target" migrants. Seasonal or yearly migration has become a much less common contributor to the urban labour supply in recent years. This is largely attributable to the difficulty of obtaining employment under present-day conditions in cities like Accra. While a few may retain relatively fixed, immediate goals, for most workers long-term residence (sometimes of an intermittent nature) in the urban areas of Southern Ghana is the norm. The system of rewarding lengthy service, particularly in the public sector, by gratuities and pensions is an important stabilizing element. The desire of migrants to improve their living standards, and to accumulate against retirement in the country, is not easily satisfied; as a result, most stay for a number of years, perhaps for all their working lives, in pursuit of a goal which for many is simply unrealizable.[7]

The "way out" of this persistent dilemma for urban workers is seen by many to lie in emulating the role of the small-scale entrepreneur, as exemplified by the success of some of their fellows who started off with similar life-chances. Rouch made this point in relation to the immigrants of 1953–4:

> A comparison between the wages paid unskilled workers and the earnings of traders shows that the same migrants can attain to more profitable situations . . . In a month or two a *kayakaya* (market porter) can hope to become a truck boy and make 10*s.* a day . . . Finally the migrant has all around him the encouraging example of the great success of his comrades (cattle, timber and transport operators). One can understand why the emigrants try as quickly as possible to amass a small nest-egg in wage-earning employment so that they can also enter into trading careers.[8]

Petty capitalism, often as a supplement to wage-employment, offers itself as a means of salvation. If only the right chance came, the urban workers could break out of the nexus of high living costs and low wages which is their lot. This hope is comparable with the promise of wealth which a large win on the football pools holds out for the British worker over-burdened by hire-purchase payments. As it is, the monthly equation of income and expenditure is usually negative, and few manage to escape from the spiral of ever-increasing debt.

---

[7]   The empirical basis for these statements concerning the length of stay in urban areas is contained in my unpublished Ph.D. thesis: J. K. Hart, 'Entrepreneurs and Migrants – a study of modernization among the Frafras of Ghana', University of Cambridge, 1969.

[8]   Rouch, op. cit. p. 45.

But the lives of the majority are sustained by hopes of this kind and, as a result, most are ready to involve themselves, both on a casual and regular basis, in petty enterprises of all types ranging in scale from the most trivial activities to major businesses.

Another way of putting this is to say that, denied success by the formal opportunity structure, these members of the urban sub-proletariat seek informal means of increasing their incomes. This is not unique: of many prominent examples, we may compare the dilemma of slum-dwellers in the United States,[9] and of those who live in the "culture of poverty" in Central America[10] – and, perhaps above all, the high degree of informality in the economic lives of the nineteenth-century London poor.[11] It is this world of economic activities outside the organized labour force which is the subject of detailed examination here.

The Informal Sector

The distinction between formal and informal income opportunities is based essentially on that between wage-earning and self-employment. The key variable is the degree of rationalization of work – that is to say, whether or not labour is recruited on a permanent and regular basis for fixed rewards. Most enterprises run with some measure of bureaucracy are amenable to enumeration by surveys, and – as such – constitute the "modern sector" of the urban economy. The remainder – that is, those who escape enumeration – are variously classified as "the *low-productivity* urban sector," "the reserve army of *underemployed and unemployed*," "the urban *traditional* sector," and so on. These terms beggar analysis by assuming what has to be demonstrated.

A typology of urban income opportunities

It has been shown for Accra that the number of those outside the organized labour force is very large. The significance of the activities of this residue is subject to some dispute however. The semi-automatic classification of unorganized workers as "underemployed shoeshine boys and sellers of matches" contrasts with a view which stresses the important part played by these workers in supplying many of the essential services on which life in the city is dependent. I have discussed elsewhere the role of small operators in distribution, transport, and other tertiary activities in Ghana.[12] In practice, informal activities encompass a wide-ranging scale, from marginal operations to large enterprises; whether their productivity is relatively high or low remains a question for empirical verification.

Moreover, a consideration of income opportunities outside formal employment must include certain kinds of crime. The incidence of illegitimate activity in Nima was, to my knowledge, all-pervasive. It was difficult indeed to find anyone who had not at some time transgressed the law, usually with some profitable result, if undetected. The following typology, therefore, distinguishes between legitimate and illegitimate activities in the informal sector. It should be emphasized that the typology refers to activities or roles, *not* persons: actual individuals are often to be found on both sides of the analytical divide and in more than one capacity.

[9]   W.F. Whyte, *Street-Corner Society* (Chicago, 1943).
[10]   O. Lewis, *La Vida* (New York, 1966).
[11]   H. Mayhew, *London Labour and the London Poor* (London, 1851), vols. 1–4.
[12]   See J. K. Hart, "Small-Scale Entrepreneurs in Ghana and Development Planning," in *The Journal of Development Studies* (London), July 1970, pp. 103–20.

Formal income opportunities
  (a) *Public sector wages.*
  (b) *Private sector wages.*
  (c) *Transfer payments* – pensions, unemployment benefits.

Informal income opportunities: legitimate
  (a) *Primary and secondary activities* – farming, market gardening, building contractors and associated activities, self-employed artisans, shoemakers, tailors, manufacturers of beers and spirits.
  (b) *Tertiary enterprises with relatively large capital inputs* – housing, transport, utilities, commodity speculation, rentier activities.
  (c) *Small-scale distribution* – market operatives, petty traders, street hawkers, caterers in food and drink, bar attendants, carriers (*kayakaya*), commission agents, and dealers.
  (d) *Other services* – musicians, launderers, shoeshiners, barbers, night-soil removers, photographers, vehicle repair and other maintenance workers; brokerage and middlemanship (the *maigida* system in markets, law courts, etc.),[13] ritual services, magic and medicine.
  (e) *Private transfer payments* – gifts and similar flows of money and goods between persons; borrowing; begging.

Informal income opportunities: illegitimate
  (a) *Services* – hustlers and spivs in general; receivers of stolen goods; usery, and pawn-broking (at illegal interest rates); drug-pushing, prostitution, poncing ("pilot boy"), smuggling, bribery, political corruption Tammany Hall-style, protection rackets.
  (b) *Transfer* – petty theft (e.g. pickpockets), larceny (e.g. burglary and armed robbery), peculation and embezzlement, confidence tricksters (e.g. money doublers), gambling.

This list is by no means exhaustive, but it serves to illustrate the range of income opportunities widely available to the urban sub-proletariat living in areas such as Nima. There are two ways of looking at these activities: first, from the perspective of individuals,

as potential sources of incomes; and, secondly, from the aggregate perspective of total income and expenditure flows in the urban economy. An important consideration is the degree of regularity (one might say of professionalism) with which the individual is engaged in informal activities. Only in the case of regular involvement can we talk of "informal employment" as distinct from casual income flows of an occasional nature. But clearly this is a question of degree, which is in turn dependent on whether one is concerned with time inputs, or the relative size of cash returns for different activities. Thus, while there is a world of difference between the full-time street hawker and the casual dealer, the latter may make a coup in one afternoon equivalent to the former's earnings for several weeks. Most informal roles, therefore, contain considerable variations in these respects.

Another variable, referred to briefly already, is the relationship of individuals to informal undertakings. Although most are self-employed, some may be hired by small enterprises which escape enumeration as "establishments." Into this category fall many apprentices, assistants of traders with and without fixed premises, and a variety of casual employees including – to take an exotic example – the paid stooge in a confidence trick. On the whole, however, the ensuing analysis is restricted to those who, whether working alone or in partnership, are self-employed.

My first concern is with the availability of these informal means, particularly to those who lack wage employment of the formal kind ("the residual underemployed and unemployed.") The next six sub-sections deal, in a highly disaggregated manner, with what is often referred to as "ease of entry into petty trading and similar occupations," using the opportunity at the same time to introduce additional information on certain activities.

---

[13] See Polly Hill. "Landlords and Brokers," in *Markets and Marketing in Africa* (Edinburgh, 1966), pp. 1–14.

Primary and secondary activities

Many urban dwellers purchase, rent, or occupy plots of land to farm on as a sideline. One migrant even once remarked that "the trouble with Accra is that there is not enough land to farm on"! Despite this, a good number manage to find a small place on the outskirts of the city to grow corn and vegetables. The high cost of food makes gardening, whether for one's own consumption or for sale, a profitable business. Cannabis is also grown openly in city gardens. Similarly many raise fowls and small livestock even in the heart of a slum like Nima. Access to these income sources is limited primarily by the availability of space.

Artisans need not only small capital sums in order to set up their own sewing machine, bench and tools, or other equipment, but also a considerable amount of learned expertise. For those who have such training, practice of their craft is not necessarily burdened with heavy overheads in rents and the like – the weather is predictable enough to permit work in the open under a shady tree, while others may establish themselves on a verandah, or even partition off working-space in their own living quarters. The same applies to female gin-distillers and beer-brewers operating from their small compounds. These occupations are, by definition, not available to unskilled workers, but a young man or woman may acquire the necessary skills by informal apprenticeship (with scanty pay) to one of these operators over a lengthy period of time.

Tertiary enterprises

Entrepreneurial activities in the services sector – transport operators, landlords, corn-mill owners, commodity speculators, and so on – represent the apex of informal economic opportunities to the sub-proletariat. Their essential characteristic is that they are frequently part-time roles, entered by individuals who have accumulated savings by some other means and, in the absence of an advanced capital market, re-invest income under their own management in taxis and lorries, accommodation, bulk purchases of maize, and the like. Successful performance is not, however, solely dependent on capital supplies or bureaucratic knowledge (many are illiterate); these constraints are overshadowed by the need for specialized "know-how" and the ability, through diversification of investments and delegation of tasks, to accommodate the considerable risks attendant on these one-man enterprises. Though income from such activities may be very high, they are often combined with a formal job.

Small-scale distribution

Traders fall into a number of groups. Among Frafra migrants who were engaged more or less full-time in trade were those who bring goods for sale in the South and return immediately, those who retail in the South and make periodic visits home to replenish stock, those who are sedentary retailers and wholesalers in the city, and those who form a partnership with others to combine all these operations. An individual may at any time exchange one of these roles for another – an itinerant trader, for example, may settle temporarily in the South. There are other axes of differentiation, such as the nature of the trading medium (market stalls, roadside booths, hawking) and, more importantly, the commodity being traded. Frafras specialize in fowls, Northern artifacts of straw and leather, and also as bread-sellers. It is common to find a small niche in the distribution system dominated by one ethnic group in this way. Possibly by access to supply sources, and certainly through information control, trust and co-operation, these social segments in the city acquire competitive advantage over others in relation to specific commodities. A further differentiating factor is the trader's position in the chain of distribution of his chosen commodity: some are carriers, some are middlemen; some buy and sell in bulk, others buy on credit and retail in small quantities; bread-sellers retail on a commission basis for bakeries, while some cattle dealers act merely as brokers. All maintain a flexible attitude to their trading role and are apt to switch from one to another, or to combine several at once. Finally, they differ in the time-input and scale of their activities. Petty traders, brokers, wholesale merchants, commission agents, and occasional dealers – all these roles are played in varying degrees by large numbers of the urban sub-proletariat.

Occasional buying and selling of consumer goods is a common means of increasing one's income. Most urban workers are "out for a quick buck" and, given the chance, an individual with some cash to spare will buy an object for which he thinks he can find a buyer at a higher price, preferably after he himself has had some use of it. The objects most commonly traded are consumer items ranging from wrist-watches to refrigerators, and running the gamut of clothing, furniture, and household effects. Some have refined this trading into a lucrative art, the main aim of which is to place oneself between the owner and a would-be purchaser. Naturally, in a place like Nima, these activities often shade into the receiving of stolen goods. The main assets for this occupation are a well-tried sense of value and a wide range of contacts: an individual with both may, by maintaining a fast flow of single items through his hands, achieve considerable profits without needing much capital or storage space.

Trade is not the only place for the middleman – any deal in which one is instrumental is a source of "commission" from all parties involved; thus some men of experience and influence make a substantial living from acting as a broker in business deals, and as a witness and go-between in court actions. There are thus fruitful areas in brokerage and middlemanship for the enterprising worker, whether employed or not.

Distribution has been discussed at length owing to its significance in urban economic life. One frequently reads that ease of entry into trade in cities like Accra is so total that, with the consequent proliferation of small operatives, returns to the individual are less than for an equivalent time spent in formal wage-employment at the minimum rate. The low opportunity cost of labour thus justifies the classification of most traders as "underemployed" and, incidentally, argues for the efficiency of the system through the effects of competition on prices. For example, in a study of peasant marketing in Java, the author remarks that profits are kept down, since, if people thought profits were high, they would go in for trading themselves.[14] This assumption discounts constraints on entry such as social networks, informal skill, and knowledge, as well as the availability of time, capital, or credit.

The pervasiveness of credit at all levels, and the difficulties of trading without literate aids, make this an activity which must be learnt just as any other skilled or, at least, semi-skilled occupation. Ethnic group concentrations of this kind already mentioned also act as informal rings inhibiting entry into certain commodity trades. The whole of meat distribution, from cattle trading to butchering, is dominated by the Islamic Hausa community, and non-Muslims have great difficulty breaking in, even at the lowest level. It must be acknowledged, however, that opportunities for trading on a regular or casual basis are extremely widespread in Accra, if not completely unrestricted in their modes of entry. Moreover, the trading role (part-time as well as full-time) offers potentially much higher returns than wage-employment of the kind available to the urban proletariat.

---

14   See A. Dewey, *Peasant Marketing in Java* (Glencoe, Ill., 1962). p. 85.

Other services

Secondary occupations are a marked feature of rural society in Ghana. The Frafra homeland is no exception – the farming season there is so short and the fruits so meagre that most men derive some earnings from the practice of a learned skill. It is not surprising, therefore, that many migrants to the towns of Southern Ghana continue to derive supplementary income from these skills. An expert musician or praise-singer is rewarded handsomely at parties and drinking houses. There is also a good market for diviners and other ritual specialists: the urban employment potential for religious and related workers is at least as great as in rural areas. Islamic teachers (*mallams*) would also fall into this category of the full-time informally employed. Payment for such services is irregular, but frequently lucrative. For skilled, semi-skilled, and un-skilled service occupations – fitters, barbers, and washerwomen, etcetera – learned exper-tise and small capital/overhead requirements restrict entry to a varying degree. Unskilled service occupations, such as night-soil remover, are available freely within the limits of market demand and personal distaste.

Private transfer payments

The ability of an individual to draw on the resources of others, either consistently (as a client to a patron, or as a dependent to a highly paid worker) or in emergencies, involves the entire structure of rural-urban and urban community relationships. Economists are increasingly likely to draw on such sociological information in reaching estimates of urban real incomes.[15] We should remember that income flows between kin outside the elementary family tend to be essentially irregular. The meaning of "dependency" is thus highly vari-able. Last of all, of course, there is begging on the streets: there are no limits, save personal pride, to the availability of this expedient. But in Accra, begging is largely restricted to disabled persons and children.

Illegitimate activities

Although under-represented in the literature of developing countries, the question of differ-entials in the availability of illegitimate means to disadvantaged groups has received much attention in western (particularly American) criminology.[16] There is a distinction to be drawn between "illegitimacy" and "illegality." The system of bourgeois values enshrined in a nation's code of laws may not coincide with concepts of legitimacy prevalent in certain subcultures of that society. The notion of legitimacy used in this article is derived essen-tially from Ghana's laws, and presumably coincides with the morality of "respectable" Ghanaians.

Nima is notorious for its *lack* of respect-ability, for the dominance of a criminal element, and for the provision of those goods and services usually associated with any major city's "red-light district." In this environment, the availability of certain illegitimate means (particularly of a casual, rather than a pro-fessional kind) is scarcely less than infinite; moreover these activities, while recognized as illegal, and therefore, somewhat risky, meet with little of the opprobrium found elsewhere in the city. These illegitimate activities may be classified into "services" and "transfers" for the reason that, while the former constitute

---

[15] A recent survey of Dakar workers produced an average dependency rate of 9.6 persons per worker; G. Pfefferman, *Industrial Labor in the Republic of Senegal* (New York, 1968), pp. 166–70. It is unlikely that up to 20 people (as reported) were *supported* in any permanent sense at one time by an individual wage-earner; see the reference made by Rimmer, op. cit. pp. 56–7.

[16] For a general review of the problem see R.A. Cloward, "Illegitimate Means, Anomie and Deviant Behaviour," in *American Sociological Review* (Washington), xxiv, April 1959.

deviant forms of services which may be said to be purchased, the victims of the latter cannot be said to have voluntarily initiated the income flows concerned.

The most common category, which straddles the borders of legality, is the "hustler" or "spiv" – a jack of all trades, mostly shady. He can be found pushing Indian hemp, selling smuggled or stolen goods, touting for a prostitute, operating a street roulette wheel, getting involved in a rigged horse race, money-lending at a gamblers' party, and generally behaving in a Runyonesque way. The nearest vernacular equivalent is "pilot boy," which, however, has certain overtones of street violence and gangs of delinquent youths. Although it is easy to depict the character as a person, the phenomenon is better classed as a diverse range of activities, or perhaps as a rôle played by many urban sub-proletarians occasionally or with regularity. In Nima, for this mildest of activities there is virtually no public disapproval, and access to such opportunities is unlimited.

Hoarding of scarce commodities and other trading malpractices, on the other hand, generate considerable odium; but this did not prevent traders from continuing in these practices.[17] Money-lending and pawn-broking at usurious rates (15–50 per cent per month, as against the legal maximum of 30 per cent per annum) are not popular, but the scarcity of liquid capital and frequent defaults are a part justification, as I have suggested elsewhere.[18] Only those with a capital surplus can enter this profitable occupation.

The confidence trickster is a folk hero in Ghana – traditional tales celebrating the exploits of Ananse, the Ashanti spider, or of the northern "bush rabbit," betray this admiration for cunning deceit. The modern equivalent is the money-doubler, a type which appears frequently in present-day Ghanaian literature.[19] Under this rubric we range from the great men of the profession with their teams of supporting actors (one of whom built four houses on his takings), to the amateur who tries to con a tourist in a bar. Migrants and lower-paid workers in general gamble prolifically, and there are always a few who, by sharp practice and skill, or by putting themselves in the position of the bank, make a consistent profit. For all occupations of this kind, native wit is the sole prerequisite for entry.

Many jobs are a source of additional perquisites, but some wage-earners also have access to a marketable commodity in the form of supplies, cash, or bribes. Discreet peculation of valuable goods (such as gold, building materials, food, and liquor) by mine workers, construction-site labourers, storeboys, cooks, and the like, can be an important source of regular income. And anyone who is perceived by his fellows to be influential is the recipient of bribes: some are in positions of real power (notably police and foremen), but others foster an illusion among their illiterate brethren that they exert an influence which they do not in fact possess – hospital orderlies, high-court caretakers, mortuary assistants, messengers, and the domestic servants of important men are among the unlikely occupations which may be fruitful in this way. The main areas for bribes are in helping to secure employment and in making available concessions from the bureaucracy. The Ghanaian preference for particularistic approaches to authority is a ready source of income to those near, and not so near, to the centres of decision-making.

For women, informal opportunities outside trading lie mainly in "the oldest profession." But prostitutes, like other traders, in Nima, need regular credit customers in order to sell their wares in a situation characterized by the

---

[17]   See W. E. Abraham, *Report of the Commission of Enquiry into Trade Malpractices in Ghana* (Accra-Tema, 1966).

[18]   Hart, loc. cit. p. 114.

[19]   See Gustav Jahoda, 'Money Doubling in the Gold Coast: with some cross-cultural comparisons', in *The British Journal of Delinquency* (London), VIII, 1957, pp. 266–76, and countless short stories and local newspaper articles.

general scarcity of cash. Given that promiscuity and direct or delayed money payments are quite normal in Ghanaian sexual relationships, it is difficult to point to a clear-cut distinction between any "good-time girl" and the prostitute proper. Only when a girl is protected by a pimp and receives cash on delivery may we speak of prostitution *per se*. This is largely a western practice, and most such transactions are with white men or bourgeois black men. Within Nima itself, the scarce minority of single women are not averse to being the kept concubine of a number of men (both simultaneously and serially), but organized prostitution is not widespread. Similarly, some young men receive payment in cash or kind as the sexual partners to older, prosperous women.

Finally, there is theft – over the whole gamut from pickpocketing to armed robbery. The degree of organization varies but never reaches the level found in developed countries. "Fences" and their gangs are common but, to the extent that admission into cliques like this is necessary for practising some forms of larceny, entry to this profession is limited. Thieves practise openly, but usually outside their home neighbourhood. This explains the paradox (paralleled in traditional justice) that, while respected and even admired by his immediate social milieu as long as his victims are outsiders, the thief is hounded by crowds, beaten up and vilified wherever he is caught. The permissiveness of the slum, and ease of association with criminals (owing to their numbers and proximity), remove most obstacles facing the would-be thief or receiver and, in Nima at least, the dictum that "an inclination to steal is not a sufficient explanation of the genesis of the professional thief" does not hold.[20]

Some Choices Facing the Urban Poor

Recruitment to formal and informal employment is, of course, determined on a far from random basis, even allowing for differences in the qualifications of would-be aspirants to the various jobs. The uneven distribution of economic opportunities between the regional/ethnic groups of Ghana is striking. Thus while 21 per cent of Gas (the dominant tribe of Accra) had a white-collar job in 1960, only 1 per cent of the northern Mole-Dagbani group of tribes fell into this category. The extremes are well illustrated by comparing the 200 Frafra white-collar workers with the 5,000 from the smaller number of Akwapims in Southern Ghana; the latter rate is 75 times the former. These differences, which add an explosive regional/tribal element to Ghana's emergent class structure, are largely attributable to differing lengths of exposure to colonial rule and the spread of western education.[21]

Job-seeking

Frafras, and other groups like them, when seeking employment in the South are very conservative; few will apply for a job where they have no particularistic relationship – such as a previously employed kinsman – and perhaps their view of the recruitment process is justified. Information about vacancies tends to travel along informal social networks rather than through employment exchanges, and nepotism is not unknown in Ghana. The result is that migrants from one village or area tend to be clustered occupationally – out of 22 Accra residents from one village section, 20 were employed as cooks; from another section, half were employed as construction workers, and so on. This is perhaps why virtually none of the 5,000 adult male Frafras in Accra-Tema

[20] See E. H. Sutherland, *The Professional Thief* (Chicago, 1937), p. 19.
[21] See J. K. Hart and A. F. Robertson, "Länderstudien zum Problem des Tribalismus in Afrika: Ghana," in *Internationales Afrika Forum* (Munich), July–August 1970, pp. 432–5.

were employed in factories during the mid–1960s.[22] We have already seen the same phenomenon in specialized commodity trading. Thus, a significant constraint limiting access to urban employment of all kinds is the actor's perception of the competitive advantage or disadvantage to himself of ethnic or kin-group membership.

All types of work in the city are therefore viewed differently according to the standpoint of the job-seeker. Apart from ethnic affiliation, the status-ranking of occupations varies between other social categories; thus, while the Islamic community, for example, may accord high prestige to commercial success, others look down on all informal occupations. The education variable is, of course, extremely significant in this respect. The high rates of "unemployment" recorded among the young in the 1960 Census – see Table 9.2 – undoubtedly reflect the influence of exposure to western education. If, to the illiterate Frafra migrant, informal opportunities offer a ladder out of poverty, to the educated youth, with his eyes on a conventional bureaucratic career, such employment may seem both socially inferior and undesirable. However, an increasing number of middle-school leavers in the urban labour market find their qualifications inadequate for scarce white-collar jobs, so that they must compete with illiterates for manual work. Under these circumstances, informal occupational roles take on a more favourable aspect as a substitute for, or complimentary to, forms of employment with a low wages ceiling. One may speculate on the result, when literacy comes to be widely added to existing aptitudes in the pursuit of informal means of advancement.

Combinations of income sources

If job duplication in the formal sector is common, multiple informal employment – both with and without simultaneous wage employment – is almost universal in the economic behaviour of Accra's sub-proletariat. Only rarely is an individual or family dependent on one source of income. This preference for diversity of income streams has its roots in the traditional risk-aversion of peasants under conditions of extreme uncertainty, and is justified by the insecurity of urban workers today.[23] The most salient characteristic of wage-employment in the eyes of the sub-proletariat is not the absolute amount of income receipts but its reliability. For informal employment, even of the legitimate variety, is risky and expected rewards highly variable. Thus, for subsistence purposes alone, regular wage-employment, however badly paid, has some solid advantages; and hence men who derive substantial incomes from informal activities may still retain or desire formal employment. An acquaintance in Nima earned on an average over £100 a month from rents, receiving stolen goods, and a host of trading operations (though the dispersion of his earnings from month to month was very wide); yet he referred to himself as an "unemployed cook/steward," the occupation which he had left some five years before. Time is an important constraint for successful operators and, in the absence of scope for delegation, the opportunity cost of time foregone for the sake of keeping on a job may be too high. But what about the situation of the "unemployed" in relation to the informal opportunity structure?

---

[22] Margaret Peil discovered one or two Frafras working in an unskilled capacity in factories covered by her survey in 1966; see *The Ghanaian Factory Worker: industrial man in Africa* (Cambridge, 1972).

[23] For diversification in the activities of small entrepreneurs, see Hart, loc. cit. pp. 107–9.

The following case-history serves to illustrate the place of informal activities in the economic lives of Nima's labour force. Atinga was given a medical discharge from the army at Christmas 1965. He was 28 years old, had been in the South for nine years, and now lived in Nima with his wife and a brother's teenage son. He was without work and had not yet been paid any gratuity or pension; but he had £10 from his last pay packet. At first he thought of going home to farm, but the prospect of getting another job in Accra was more attractive. However, he had to finance the period of his unemployment and decided to set up as a retailer of *akpeteshi* or crude gin.

First he converted his room (rent £3 per month) into a bar-cum-living quarters by the simple expedient of hanging a cloth down the centre and piling his accumulated possessions on both sides – chairs and a table (bought for 15*s*.) occupied the "bar" section. For next to nothing he got some small plastic glasses, an assortment of used bottles, and an old, rusting funnel, which were placed on the table. He then went to a nearby distiller and bought a 4–gallon drum of *akpeteshi* for £5. 10*s*. He handed over what was left (just under £4) to his wife for food, borrowed £4 elsewhere out of which to pay the month's rent, and opened his new business on 30 December.

The retail price of gin was fixed throughout Nima at 6*s*. a bottle, and smaller quantities *pro rata*; allowing for wastage, gross receipts from a drum came to £8 to £7. 10*s*. Profit margins could be varied by buying gin wholesale at prices ranging from £4 to £5. 10*s*. a drum, according to quality and method of payment (cash or credit). Atinga bought the best gin in order to attract a clientele, and because he knew that increased turnover compensated for reduced item profit.

His main problem related to the extension of credit; adequate turnover, given the improvidence of his customers, could only be maintained by generous credit facilities. But Atinga needed a high proportion of cash sales to replenish stock and to feed his family, as well as to pay other costs. His average daily expenditure was 7*s*. 6*d*. or £14–£15 per month, including rent. So he had to sell a lot of gin. He also tried to diversify; but his wife's sugar-lump sales business foundered under a saturation of competition in the neighbourhood, and his own attempts to sell Coca Cola were doomed without a refrigerator.

In the first three weeks Atinga ran into a crisis: he over-extended credit to the tune of £14 (a third of total sales) in order to keep up a turnover rate of one gallon a day and attract a clientele, some of whom were clearly out to take him for a ride. His stocks ran out before pay-day, leaving him with inadequate funds to replenish them. However, he weathered the crisis, borrowing in order to maintain supplies (otherwise his clients would take their custom, and their debts, away), and gaining repayment of enough credit to go on with. He now cracked down on credit facilities and, though this naturally slowed turnover, he built up a small regular clientele whom he trusted and who came to him whatever the quality of his gin; he was thus able to economise by buying gin at £4 a drum. The core of his regular customers consisted of young men from his home village.

By now Atinga saw that his bar was only viable as a sideline, supplementary to regular employment; moreover his wife was pregnant. For some time he tried persistently to get back into the army, while his wife looked after the bar. When things were bad, his landlord's wives helped out with meals and food supplies. Attempts to diversify in trade failed for lack of capital and expertise. Meanwhile his personal loans and debts were extended to roughly equal effect, a backlog of rent being the most significant item. After his narrow escape, turnover steadied out to around four or five drums a month, giving rise to a monthly income of between £10 and £12; moreover this was being realized (eventually) in cash, for his total outstanding credit in April 1966 was only £12 – a much smaller percentage of turnover – of which £5. 10s. had been written off as bad debts.

The remainder of 1966 saw a gradual decline in the fortunes of Atinga's bar, if not in his total income. For in September he got a job as a watchman at 8s. per day, leaving his wife to look after the customers. Turnover, however, slowed to a trickle and his wife consumed most of the gin. Occasionally he supplemented their income with a once-and-for all enterprise, like the purchase of a stray dog for sale as meat and soup. At times like this, his bar did a roaring trade for a brief spell; but more often it was empty at night because he had no gin to sell, or his customers no money, or, more likely, both.

In December his wife gave birth to a son. In February 1967 the military bureaucracy got round to paying him £40 as an advance on his gratuity. The bar took on a new lease of life – £20 was spent on wood for a counter, partition, door, and shelves. Atinga even bought a gin-seller's licence; he did not, however, pay off any of his accumulated debts. For a few weeks he used the remainder of his capital to keep up an artificial rate of business, but he was soon back in the vicious circle of credit and turnover. In May he lost his job as a watchman, but was lucky to be accepted almost immediately for training as an escort policeman. In June he went off to Winneba and visited his wife and child at weekends. On one of these visits, in August 1967, he was thrown out of the house by his landlord, who accused him of being the informer behind a police raid on the premises. The room and all its wooden fittings were seized as part compensation for a debt of £32. 10s. owed to the landlord.

Atinga left the neighbourhood with his family, and the gin bar enterprise was at an end – his landlord's wife took it over, but was unsuccessful as she offered no credit whatsoever. Some 20 months of unemployment and intermittent formal employment had been negotiated satisfactorily by means of an informal operation which was always rickety, but which had been the main basis of his family's survival in the city. Atinga's story provides a case study of how informal employment may act as a buffer, for those who are "out of work," against destitution or dependence on others.

How easy is it for someone who lacks alternative means of supporting himself to find work of this kind? The answer, of course, will vary according to the type of work. Nevertheless, despite the constraints on entry to informal occupations, the range of opportunities available outside the organized labour market is so wide that few of the "unemployed" are totally without some form of income, however irregular. By any standards many of them are poor, but then so are large numbers of wage-earners.

The Structure of Urban Employment

It is generally understood that growing residual underemployment and unemployment in the cities of developing countries is "a bad thing." But why should this be so? In what way precisely does this phenomenon constitute a *problem*? Is it from the viewpoint of poverty (inadequate personal or family incomes), social disorganization and public morality (the crime rate or prostitution), overcrowding (pressure on social infrastructure in towns), political unrest (the danger to politicians of a concentration of frustrated slum-dwellers), rural depopulation (reductions in agricultural capacity)? Or, expressed in terms of the productivity of labour, is it an economist's problem (inefficient utilization of manpower or reduced contribution to growth in national income)?

Rethinking employment policy

Employment policy frequently confronts all of these questions and some objectives may be seen to be in conflict. But by focusing on "unemployment," with its attendant western folk images of Tyneside or New York in the 1930s, of dole queues and Keynesian solutions, the goals of employment policy are confused, when they should be made explicit. What happens if the problem is restated in terms of formal and informal employment structures? The question becomes not "How can we create work for the jobless," but rather "Do we want to shift the emphasis of income opportunities in the direction of formal employment for its own sake, or only to reduce participation in socially disapproved informal activities and in those informal occupations whose marginal productivity is too low"? Perhaps it will be argued that some movement should be encouraged away from tertiary activities (both formal and informal) towards primary and secondary production in town and country-side. These are matters of political economy and empirical verification which demand a more sophisticated approach to *all* forms of employment, both inside and out of the formal or wages sector.[24]

Several examples from Ghana's recent history illustrate these points. In the early 1960s the Workers' Brigade was seen as a partial solution to the employment problem – a public-sector, para-military organization which provided opportunities for work in primary and secondary production. Recruitment in urban areas heavily favoured women, as an explicit measure to diminish prostitution by providing alternative sources of incomes for city girls. The success of this may be judged by the observation, which was commonplace in Nima, that Workers' Brigade girls were "easier game" than most, and more ready to extend credit to their lovers when they already had a steady income from their job. Which may be fine from the viewpoint of parties to these liaisons, but does nothing to diminish sexual licence in Nima.

Another failure was the Lonrho *pito* brewery, a capital-intensive concern set up in Tamale to compete with petty manufacturers of a beer made from northern millet. Other examples of a more general kind may be multiplied – food supermarkets, automatic car-washers, and so on – most of which diminish the dependence of the urban middle classes on goods and services supplied by the informal sector. In view of the factory endowments of cities like Accra, is the justification for such developments (that the "productivity" of labour so employed is high) sufficient to offset the cost of reduced demand for informal goods and services?

In the midst of this haphazard modernization, one strand of employment policy emerges as the cornerstone of government planning in many African states: that is, the goal of maximizing employment opportunities through keeping down the wages of those who are already employed – job creation with wage restraint. As long as urban wage-earners could be described as an "aristocracy of labour" – the lucky few who had won a passport from unemployment (or, at best, underemployment) to the automatic affluence of a job – any policy aimed at reducing the queue of those playing the "urban lottery" would be demonstrably rational. The only problem is then to stem the tide of farmworkers rushing to town in pursuit of these lucrative jobs, an objective to which modern sector wage restraint is admirably suited. Unfortunately this view of the situation, in Ghana's case at least, has for long been so far removed from reality as to invite political catastrophe.

Who are the unemployed and underemployed?

This article has attempted to show that for many urban wage-earners poverty is ever

---

[24] See U.N.D.P./I.B.R.D., *Report on Development Strategies for Papua New Guinea*, 1973–8 (Port Moresby, 1972), for an implementation of the approach recommended here.

present, and that the informal sector provides opportunities of improving real incomes for this category as well as for the "jobless." The difficulty of placing many individuals unequivocally in either the formal or informal sectors (owing to the widespread incidence of multiple income sources), when combined with the low ceiling to wage employment relative to informal maximum incomes, makes it empirically and theoretically absurd to maintain the notion of a significant status transition from unemployment or under-employment to full-time employment through the mere acquisition of a job in the organized labour force.

We must re-examine and refine our terms. Most urban workers lacking formal employ-ment and therefore "out of work" may be said to be, in the most basic sense, unemployed. For they would usually take a wage job, as long as it did not seriously limit the scope for continuing informal activities, on the grounds that the income provided is *secure*, i.e. fixed, regular, and relatively permanent. But the urgency of their plight varies, and this may be measured by the amount of time which is spent, while out of work, actively canvassing for formal employment. The truly "un-employed" are those who will not accept income opportunities open to them for which they are qualified, and this often means rejecting informal means of making a living. It may be that in Accra only the educated youth contains a high proportion of persons who would fall into this category.

All the residue of the unorganized urban work-force is commonly subsumed in the term "underemployed," which is grounded in an assumption about their level of productivity. But these are vague, value-laden concepts – what criteria are being used? Is it to be taken for granted that income returns to a given time input, at a certain level of skill, are usually lower in the informal than in the formal sector?

Few are as "underemployed" by this criterion as full-time workers employed at the govern-ment minimum wage. And, when a wage job alone cannot provide for a family's subsistence needs, the question of poverty and income levels in general becomes more relevant than the definition of underemployment.

Some questions about the informal sector

Informal activities are recognized as typical of economic life in the cities of developing and developed countries, but their overall signifi-cance could be dismissed as negligible – except, of course, for the unfortunate indi-viduals forced to live in this way. The Jamaican urban unemployed are thus said to make a living from "scuffling . . . a hand-to-mouth existence which includes begging, borrowing, stealing, finding, receiving as gifts, with a little casual work and selling thrown in."[25] All of this counts as income from the individual view-point, but it is mostly transfers combined with productive activities of little aggregative consequence. The informal sector has there-fore been assumed to depend on demand created by current levels of activity in the formal sector, as measured by movements in gross national product or total formal wage expenditure. Such a picture leaves many ques-tions unresolved, although it allows economists to equate significant economic activity with what is measured.

Just what is the relationship between the formal and informal sectors of the urban economy? Do they move in parallel – or does the level of some informal activities vary inversely with formal trends? In particular, what are the effects of transfers through urban crime? In looking at the determinants of growth in informal output we need to distinguish between demand and supply constraints. Is the demand curve perfectly elastic or downwards sloping? If the latter,

---

[25]   See K. Norris, *Jamaica: the search for identity* (London, 1962), p. 40.

by how much is average income decreased by the addition of labour seeking work in the informal sector? Is the urban economy relatively stable or dynamic in this respect? Might not the removal of some supply constraints push the demand curve outwards? What is the state of trade between formal and informal sectors? Does the informal economy resemble *in scale* the U.S. or U.K. economies in its dependence on outside factors? How much income is generated by internal transactions, and how much by export activity? Finally, is there a net transfer of resources either way between the formal and informal sectors? What about relationships with the rural sector? Inasmuch as the informal sector is identifiable with a socio-economic category (the sub-proletariat living in Accra's slums and earning a maximum from wage-employment of £15 to £20 per month), what are the income distribution effects of informal activities?

So many of the goods and services purchased in the city are informally produced that their exclusion from economic analysis is unwarrantable. This article cannot provide empirically determined answers, but it is possible to suggest ways of conceptualizing these problems in a fairly rigorous way.

An input-output approach to income flows

One way to chart income flows within the urban economy would be to set up an input-output matrix of formal and informal activities (using a typology such as that drawn up on p. 150) based on surveys of income and expenditure patterns. Additional rows and columns would account for trade and transfers with the rural sector and the "rest of the world". Ignoring measurement problems and the question of short- and long-term changes (which could be resolved only by time-series data), this mode of analysis ·arguably refines

the questions and generates testable hypotheses.

Thus, all informal purchases paid for from wages earned in the formal sector would be classified as "exports"; set against this would be the volume of "imports," i.e. purchases in the formal sector financed by informal incomes. The "balance of payments" between the sectors would be completed by net transfers, particularly those occasioned by theft. Assuming that the formal sector monopolizes trade with the "rest of the world," the only other relevant balance of payments for the informal sector would then be that with the rural sector. A current account surplus in favour of the informal sector *vis-à-vis* the formal might be offset by capital flows in the opposite direction, or by a deficit with the rural sector – there are several possibilities here.

Apart from import–export activities, a most significant question relates to the amount of income generated by transactions *within* the informal sector; the "spread effects" of informal purchases or transfers could be quantified by an analysis of expenditure patterns. Demand creation thus depends on the internal income multiplier, as well as on sales to the formal sector. Informal occupations might therefore by classified according to their "export coefficients." Whatever its drawbacks, at least this approach has the merit of directing attention to all income flows in the urban economy.[26]

The structure of the urban economy

The informal sector may be identified for heuristic purposes with the sub-proletariat of the slum – a reasonable assumption despite the participation of many in the wage economy, and of a few members of higher income groups in certain lucrative informal activities. On

---

[26] I am grateful to John Bryden of the University of East Anglia, Norwich, for suggesting this approach, as well as for his numerous valuable comments on this article.

inspection, the informal sector seems to support a high level of export activity: much primary and secondary production, as well as many service activities (distribution, transport, and so on), are for the general market and therefore paid for in large measure by those living outside the slum. The biggest export coefficients (combining services and transfers in this context) are to be found in such illegitimate occupations as prostitute, burglar, embezzler, and con-man, in contrast with the hustler, money-lender, drug-pusher, and gambler, whose customers are generally sub-proletarians also.

Most current expenditures are internal transactions – rents, profits from food and similar sales, personal services, and entertainments are paid for mainly within the informal economy. Public transfers are of negligible significance in Accra, and private transfers circulate within the sub-proletariat, with some leakage to the rural sector; but illegitimate transfers are borne predominantly by the urban middle classes. We may hypothesize, therefore, that the current-account balance of payments between the informal and formal economies favours the former, and that informal activities constitute a net addition to the income resources of the sub-proletariat.

Urban crime may then be seen as a redistribution of wealth with income effects throughout the informal economy. "Loot" – or static wealth lying idle in the homes of the bourgeoisie – is a stock, independent of current income flows, which is mobilized through theft into direct and indirect income for sub-proletarians. In this sense, increases in crime may act as a buffer against falls in G.N.P., since national income accounting does not normally include transfers by theft. The tie-up between urban unemployment and crime rates in Africa is receiving much press publicity at present. It is interesting that Ghana's repatriation of many foreign nationals in 1969, which has been interpreted by at least one commentator as a response to growing unemployment, should have been conducted with references by the Government to the "lawlessness" of the immigrant community.[27] This area of analysis clearly deserves a more comprehensive approach than it has hitherto been accorded.

When we turn to the question of internal income distribution in the slum, the informal economy emerges as a source of differentiation within the sub-proletariat which far surpasses the homogeneous impression given by the ranges of wages in formal employment. These differences in life-style, wealth, and social status are, however, mitigated by the system of patronage and familial/ethnic obligation which ensures a more equitable distribution. It is the "big men" of each ethnic division of the sub-proletariat who provide the newcomer and the newly out of work with a certain refuge, where food and a place to sleep may always be found in emergencies. On a smaller scale and more intermittently, any ephemeral increases in disposable income, which more insignificant persons may derive from informal activities, are quickly dissipated through entertainment of kin and friends, as well as by loans given with dubious prospects of gaining repayment. The egalitarian philosophy of peoples, inured by generations of peasant insecurity to the disbursement of surpluses as a form of social insurance, makes private accumulation a difficult, though not impossible, task, and allows those who do not benefit from the informal economy to consume the earnings of those who do.[28]

Finally, what can be said about the relationship between wage-employment levels and the informal sector? It is clear that an increasing

[27] Rimmer, op. cit. p. 69.
[28] Cf. G. Foster, 'Peasant Society and the Image of the Limited Good', in *The American Anthropologist* (Washington), II, 1965, pp. 293–315; and K. Hart, 'Migration and Tribal Identity among the Frafras of Ghana', in *The Journal of Asian and African Studies* (Leiden), VI, 1 January 1971, pp. 26–35.

surplus to the labour requirements of the formal sector (whether occasioned by rural–urban migration, or by redundancies in a period of deflation), must increase the supply of labour to the informal economy. Not only that – if wage incomes are inadequate, the needs of the "employed" create added pressures on the supply side. The question is, Does the informal sector have any autonomous capacity for growth?

The dynamics of informal growth depend on a number of factors: changes in the pattern of final demand in favour or goods and services produced informally, changes in the rates of savings and capital formation in the informal sector, and on the volume of transfers via theft which is independent of demand. The possibility that the informal economy, with its emphasis on tertiary activities, may be developing at a rate faster than other sectors of the national economy, and thus taking up some of the slack created by inadequate rates of growth in the well-documented modern sector, cannot be dismissed on *a priori* grounds. When half of the urban labour force falls outside the organized labour market, how can we continue to be satisfied with indicators of economic performance which ignore their productive activities?

Understanding urban drift

The implied criticisms of the previous section apply to no field more strongly than to the analysis of urban drift in developing countries. One theory which incorporates wage-employment levels in comparing the expected real incomes of rural–urban migrants is M. P. Todaro's often-quoted East African model.[29] Stated in terms of the subjective probability of improving real incomes, this model may account for much of the variation in rural–urban movements, *provided that* the measurements chosen for the income and probability factors approximate to reality.

This article has argued that wage incomes are only part of the urban opportunity structure, and we need not think all of those who enter informal occupations do so as a result of failure to obtain a wage-job. The magnetic force of the town may be derived from the multiplicity of income opportunities rather than merely from wage levels. A decision to come to the city would then have some objectively rational motive if, despite the paucity of formal employment opportunities and the low ceiling to wage renumerations, the migrant could look to the prospect of accumulation, with or without a job, in the informal economy of the urban slums.

The implications for the study of rural–urban migration are thus considerable. Before basing policy on causal inferences drawn from observable trends in conventional indicators, we must be sure that they measure what they are supposed to. For an overview of productivity in the economy, we must ascertain whether labour drawn off from agriculture into the informal urban sector is more or less productively engaged there, and with what consequences. The "reserve army of underemployed and unemployed" in towns may or may not be the economic disaster it is often thought to be.

Conclusions

This article lacks an overview of informal urban activities in relation to underdevelopment of the Ghanaian type. Socialists may argue that foreign capitalist dominance of these economies determines the scope for informal (and formal) development, and condemns the majority of the urban population to deprivation and exploitation. More

---

[29]   See M. P. Todaro, 'A Model of Labour Migration and Urban Unemployment in Less-Developed Countries', in *The American Economic Review* (Providence, R.I.), 69, 1, March 1969.

optimistic liberals may see in informal activities, as described here, the possibility of a dramatic "bootstrap" operation, lifting the underdeveloped economies through their own indigenous enterprise. Before either view – or a middle course stressing both external constraint and autonomous effort – may be espoused, much more empirical research is required.

It may be that an important source of variance is the level of industrial activity as a proportion of total urban employment and consequent differences in the structure of wages. Old cities like Accra, lacking significant industrial development, may be contrasted with newer urban complexes such as the Zambian Copperbelt in the scope and relative attractiveness of informal opportunities – a contrast which is sustainable for western cities in the industrial revolution, for example between London and Manchester in the nineteenth century. One thing is certain: Accra is not unique, and a historical, cross-cultural comparison or urban economies in the development process must grant a place to the analysis of informal as well as formal structures. It is time that the language and approach of development economics took this into account.

10

BITTER MONEY: FORBIDDEN EXCHANGE IN EAST AFRICA

PARKER SHIPTON

No society uses money in all economic exchanges. The most urban, literate, and industrial peoples offer some gifts in kind, as in rites of passage (birthdays, retirements) or gestures of diplomacy (statues, pandas). They also use specialized currencies, like food stamps, coupons, or poker chips. Barter, the direct exchange of goods without money, now accounts for a sizable part of international trade. It also occurs, and is perpetually reborn, in war-torn countries or countries with high inflation rates. These nonmonetary forms of exchange can come and go, expand and contract, as social, economic, and political circumstances change. But some rural people who have limited, tenuous contact with states, markets, and international religious and cultural traditions – those some call "peasants" – seem to hold particularly ambivalent feelings about money, and to seek ways to channel it out of special social relations.

This chapter is about some East African farmers, in a partly monetized economy and a partly Christianized religious environment, who have decided that there are two kinds of money, one good and one evil. Among the Kenya Luo, the classification of cash reflects important conceptual and social tensions, stemming partly from disjunctions between new kinds of private accumulation and other,

indigenous forms of economic activity. Luo associate some new forms of exchange with spiritual forces, lately with the devil of Christian dogma. Money from forbidden transactions is conceived of as barren, and ultimately useless to its owner. But money is ritually transformable between good and evil states.

This much the Luo have in common with some other peoples in roughly comparable circumstances elsewhere, including some well-known cases in Latin America (Nash 1979; Taussig 1980). On both continents, distinctions between good and evil money, or its sacred and profane states, relate to recent histories of contact with foreign forms of enterprize. These beliefs and practices can be interpreted as ideological responses of poor and powerless peoples to rapid involvement in market economies, and to discomforts in adjustment as inequalities widen. Some of the parallels are striking.

The Luo beliefs, however, also reflect particularly African family tensions, and they call for other special interpretations. Luo ideas about good and evil money highlight tensions arising between the sexes, and between elders and juniors, as new ways of handling family property emerge and fortunes become more volatile. The Luo beliefs about evil money are expressed in an idiom of ancestors, unilineal kin groups, and bridewealth, reflecting views of social order that few Latin American peoples share. . . .

Anthropology today is without a commonly accepted paradigm for understanding the meaning of money in African economic life. Instead the scene is something like the stage floor at the end of a Shakespearean tragedy, strewn about with the bleeding cadavers of actors who have slain each other one by one, lingering and overlapping in their throes. Evolutionists in the nineteenth century, diffusionists from the 1890s to the 1920s, functionalists from the 1920s to the 1960s, structuralists from the 1950s to the 1970s, dependency theorists and neo-Marxists from the 1960s to the early 1980s, less radical but still critical political economists and moral economists from the 1970s, and postmodernists more recently have all had their turns on center stage. Each school has criticized its predecessors, particularly its immediate ones.

All serious analysts of economic life in Africa – mainstream or radical, formalist of substantivist, relativist or absolutist – can agree that real people in Africa do not sort neatly into market and nonmarket types. Asking why market and nonmarket behavior appear in the same societies at once, anthropologists have tried to slice the economy in several ways. Countless studies divide populations in half: capitalist urbanites versus traditionalist country folk; ambitious, entrepreneurial juniors versus social conscious elders; market-integrated, individualistic men versus close-knit, subsistence-oriented women; the self-aggrandizing rich versus the redistributive poor. Another angle is a public–private dichotomy: generosity and sharing in public, accumulation in private. Or society is divided up in time and space. There are times and places for "structure," individual profit, and social distance (like weekly marketplaces), and others for "communitas" and sharing (like special groves at initiation

time, or churches on sabbath days). Ethnic and religious divisions too provide convenient demarcation lines: the "minority middleman" or "pariah capitalist" phenomenon has been studied most everywhere. Deconstructionists have sought to tease out the selfish within the ostensibly redistributive customs and ceremonies, attempting to probe deeper levels of awareness and to demystify exploitation. Feminist scholars and others have scrutinized the smallest units of social aggregation, finding competing interests within families or households that were once assumed to be solidary decisionmaking units. Each of these approaches has been challenged, suggesting perhaps that each is realistic enough to deserve the scrutiny in the first place.

Money, exchangeable for almost anything, and variously symbolizing almost anything, provides special fascination. Since well before Mauss (1967) attempted to distinguish gift from commodity economies, anthropologists have presumed money to be a sign of market and commodity relations. Substantivists like Bohannan (1955, 1959) and transactionalists like Barth (1967), following examples from the Pacific, tried in the 1950s and early 1960s to sort out local cognitive categories for exchanges that they called "spheres of exchange" – subsistence goods exchangeable only for other subsistence goods, prestige goods exchangeable only for other prestige goods, and so on. "Special purpose currencies" like cloth or brass rods, exchangeable only for particular other objects, were standard elements of these analyses. Much attention was paid to proscriptions (or "taboos") about exchange, and to the opprobrium for those who broke them. Such research phased away in the 1960s as the powerful wave of Levi-Straussian structuralism channeled cognitive inquiry away from economic subjects into more overtly "symbolic" ones like myth and ritual.

But symbolics and economics need not, and should not, be discrete topics. Anthropologists are now reawakening their interest in the symbolic and cognitive aspects of material life, and vice versa. Values, beliefs, and ideals are very much a part of production, exchange, and consumption; and these economic concerns have their own affects in turn on cognitive categories that structure the values' and so on. Bohannan has conceived of money, among Tiv, as something that scrambles previously distinct spheres of exchange, being easily exchangeable for anything. The findings to be discussed here on Kenya Luo suggest a somewhat different picture. To the extent that spheres of exchange exist among the Luo, money does not necessarily scramble the spheres. But it is usually classed as belonging to one sphere or another. How money is obtained determines how it is classed, and how it is classed determines how people think it should be used. Here money is not just money.

In all societies, it seems, some goods are not deemed properly salable, including, in Europe and North America, gifts or heirlooms, things we say have "sentimental value," whether this be an accurate reason or not (and often it is not). The origin of a thing determines how it may be used or disposed of. As Arjun Appaddurai (1986) and some other contributors to his volume have recently observed, goods in any society may slide in and out of commodityhood in their "lifetimes" of ownership and circulation. We must ask not only why some things are sold and others not, but how and why a thing

may *become* salable or unsalable.[1] And what relations might there be between sales taboos and purchase taboos?

Following an object through its "social life," in Appadurai's terms, may tell more about people than about the thing itself. The Luo of Kenya, as we shall see, follow a person's money and other wealth from acquisition to disposal. How one obtained money affects how one may dispose of it. The attachment between particular persons or groups, and particular property of special kinds, is expected not to be broken. These things may be considered special property, or perhaps *anticommodities*. When they are sold, money obtained in exchange for them becomes tainted, unusable for some other kinds of exchanges. While "special-purpose currencies" are now commonplace in the anthropological literature – special shells, brass rods, or barkcloths supposed to be exchanged for specific other kinds of goods, but not others – the Luo case presents a kind of *special-purpose cash*. Luo beliefs about tainted money link both sales taboos and purchase taboos, and not all money is freely interchangeable with other money, though of equivalent amount and appearance. . . .

After 70 years under British rule and 25 more within the margins of a pro-Western, pro-enterprise state, the two million Luo (or Joluo) of the Nyanza Province of Kenya are well familiar with, though not wholly absorbed in, market economy.[2] They are also partially

---

[1] This idea explored in Appadurai's book is not entirely new. Over a century ago, an informant of James G. Swan on Prince of Wales Island, off the northwest coast of Canada, illustrated nicely how the social history of a thing, rather than its inherent nature, determines its salability. Silver-laden and on a buying spree for the Smithsonian Institution in 1875, Swan found he could buy almost anything, including the largest canoe in the region. All the Northwest Coast inhabitants refused to sell was the beautifully carved columns in their villages. The local explained, "These posts are monuments for the dead and we will not sell them any more than white people will sell the grave stones or monuments in cemeteries but you can have one made for you" (Swan's diary, quoted in Doig 1980:157). A century before that, in a wholly different setting, Samuel Johnson gave this advice to a friend: "An ancient estate should always go to males. It is mighty foolish to let a stranger have it . . . As for an estate newly acquired by trade, you may give it, if you will, to the dog *Towser*" (quoted in Boswell 1917 [1792]).
[2] Kenya is divided administratively into provinces, districts, divisions, locations, and sublocations. The Luo comprise the great majority of the populations of three districts in Nyanza Province: Siaya, Kisumu, and South Nyanza. In the Luo language (dhoLuo), prefixes can denote person. *Jaluo* thus refers to one Luo, *Joluo* to more than one.

integrated into an international religious tradition.

Having moved over the past 450 to 500 years (Crazzolara 1950:31–32; Ogot 1967: 28–41) from the Bahr el Ghazal region of the Sudan, where their cousins the Nuer and Dinka now live, Kenya Luo live in a densely settled land of separated farmsteads in three districts around the eastern shore of Lake Victoria, an area now rather loosely webbed with roads. The landscape changes from flat and dry by the lake, to green and hilly in eastern uplands. Occupying a unified territory, from close to the Ugandan border in the northwest into Tanzania in the south, the Luo are fairly homogeneous in language, and their communities are interlinked throughout by marriage and other kin ties. Luo have market contacts with members of several neighboring groups, though some of the boundaries are considered sharp. Clockwise from the north on a map, their neighbors are the Luhya, Nandi, Gusii, Maasai, and Kuria.[3] They also have dealings with immigrant Indian, Middle Eastern, and Somali traders in the towns of the region. These groups are endogamous, and while rural Luo depend on them for provisions, the relations between the majority and minorities are generally cool. The provincial capital, Kisumu, connects by rail and air to Nairobi. . . .

Rural Luo cobble together their livelihood from many activities, on and off the farm, and many have several "occupations" simultaneously. With ox-plows and hand hoes they grow maize, sorghum, millet, and many other vegetable foods, and several cash crops including coffee, sugarcane, tobacco, cotton, and groundnuts, depending on altitude and rainfall, soils, and access to markets. They also herd cattle – cherished animals still used for bridewealth payments among other things – and sheep and goats, and raise chickens; some also fish in the lake and streams. For about fifty years, about a third of the middle-aged men have lived outside the Luo homeland at any given time in their search for wage labor either in Kenya's plantations, towns, and cities, or in other countries of East Africa (see Parkin 1978; Stichter 1982; Whisson 1964). Within Nyanza Province, several large sugar plantations established under Asian management early in the century, and one from the late 1970s, provide some manual jobs, mostly "casual." Rural families depend on members' labor migrations for remittances in cash and kind, but migrants also depend on rural farms as safety nets, sources of occasional food, and eventual retirement homes.

Luo speak of themselves as an egalitarian people. While inequalities in wealth show up clearly in Luo neighborhoods – tin roofs among thatched roofs, motor vehicles among pedestrians, pressed shirts among tattered rayon ones and bare chests – Luo are known for, and proud, of their leveling ideology.[4] Fears of witchcraft accusations, gossip, and general ostracism check fast grabbing and ostentation: getting rich too quickly subjects a Luo to rumors about cattle thievery or worse sins like father-beating. Beliefs about "bitter money" will be seen to reflect similar concerns. . . .

Luo political organization ties directly into relations of kinship, gender, and age. The Luo are a classic case, and one of the best available, of a segmentary lineage society (Evans-Pritchard 1965; Goldenberg 1982; Parkin 1978; Shipton 1984a, 1984b; Southall 1952). This means that kin groups based on real or putative descent through one sex, in this case male, divide and subdivide like

---

[3] Some groups of Luo-speakers of Bantu origins, called Suba, live in parts of South Nyanza District, including its islands. Culturally they are almost fully assimilated. South of the Luo in Tanzania live Kuria and Jita groups.

[4] For more on Luo egalitarian ideals, see Goldenberg (1982:137–140), P. Mboya (1938), Ocholla-Ayayo (1976:242, 236–239), Odinga (1967:1–14), Parkin (1978:92–98), Shipton (1985), Waligorski (1970:20), and Whisson (1962b:7, 1964:44–45). In age hierarchy and in a few other ways, however, Luo are decidedly inegalitarian, in fact.

branches of a tree. Patronymic in naming, virilocal in postmarital residence, and, in a third of the family homesteads, polygynous, the Luo give a high public profile to males. Patriliny, bridewealth, and polygyny all reinforce each other.[5]

Reproduction is a key underlying concern. It is a basis of the value system by which men judged exchanges in the past, in a pattern, locally called *rundo* (or turning ground), familiar elsewhere in Africa. As a Luo informant characteristically told Judith Butterman, "That was the big trade in the past: cultivation to chickens, chickens to goats, goats to cows; cows to women" (1979:61).[6] With women, children: hands to cultivate. As discussed later, Luo say that misusing money can cause human and animal infertility – for them about the worst fate imaginable. . . .

Religion: Mixtures of Old and New

In religion, education, and some other aspects of culture, Christian mission influences in Luo country and environs have been heavy, making for a rich and complex mixture of old and new.[7] The scant available evidence on the Luo in precolonial Kenya suggests their religious tradition included a high god (or at least creator and life force) Nyasaye or Were, manifested in the sun and extraordinary earthly things. Ancestral and other spirits were, and still remain, active forces in local conceptions of the world. Luo refer to spirits by the terms *tipo* (pl. *tipo*), or shadow; *kwaro* (pl. *kwere*), grandfather or earlier agnatic forebear; and various other terms, depending on the locality and context, the type of behavior of the spirit, and the use of euphemism.[8] They identify spirits with male or female ancestors, and pay most attention to those of people who were somehow important when alive, or who are related in particularly important ways to the living concerned. Ancestors in the male line usually are the most respected and feared. People perceive spirits as agents of good, evil, or both. They may see, hear, feel, or smell them, or see them in their dreams. They also sense their presence in their own turns of fortune, including those involving money. Spirits watch some money more than other money, as we shall see, and beliefs in spirits may cause humans to worry, to sacrifice, to debate, and sometimes to change their minds about how to spend.

Sudden gains and losses in life also call into play Luo beliefs in witchcraft and magic of benevolent and malevolent sorts, practiced by men or women. These beliefs persist, some in changing forms, despite strong challenges from churches and schools. Concepts corresponding to witchcraft or magic are denoted by *juok* (pl. *juogi*), *bilo*, (pl. *bilo*), *nawi* (pl. *nepe*), and numerous other terms, again, depending

---

[5] A central argument of Parkin (1978). For other examinations of Luo bridewealth, see also Ocholla-Ayayo (1979), Parkin (1980), and Wilson (1961).

[6] *Rundo* (v.t.) also means to rotate, to sell crops for money, or to confuse or mislead. This combination of meanings hints that crops and money – and perhaps the other commodities – may belong to ideally separate spheres, but the evidence is not conclusive.

[7] Whisson (1964) broadly describes changes in Luo religion up to then; Hauge (1974) and Ocholla-Ayayo (1976), Luo ethics and indigenous spiritual life generally, and Evans-Pritchard (1950) and Abe (1978), some Luo beliefs and practices concerning ancestral spirits.

[8] Terms for spirits include *tipo* (pl. *tipo*), shade or shadow, a term often used for the spirits of the newly dead, as in funerals; *juok* or *juogi*, (pl. *juogi*), also used in the singular for the supreme being, or in other contexts meaning witchcraft – *juogi* also means possession by a spirit; *jakwath* (pl. *jokwath*), guardian spirit or herdsman; *jachien* (pl. *jochiende*), an unhappy spirit or demon that haunts or troubles; or *jagunda* (pl. *jogunda*), one that inhabits an abandoned homestead site. *Chuny* (pl. *chuny*) means liver or sometimes heart, but also the spirit or soul, often used of the living. In the past, particular animals or inanimate objects were also associated with spirits.

on the locality, the intention, the agency, and the kinds of objects or substances manipulated, if any.[9] . . .

Since before the turn of the 20th century, British, American, and other Catholic and Protestant missions have competed for converts in the Luo country, the strongest churches carving up the region sharply into hegemonic territories smaller than districts.[10] The Seventh-Day Adventist mission was set up in 1906, and by 1913, the Gospel According to St. Matthew was translated into Luo. . . . Some churches have profoundly influenced local education in establishing mission schools, which, among other things, have served and molded local elites; and Luo have taken advantage of the chances more generally in forming a kind of ethnic intellectual elite in Kenya.[11]

In addition to foreign-based missions, countless and diverse independent African Christian churches have appeared since the first, the Nomiya Luo Church, began in 1914.[12] Most of the independent African churches in western Kenya have begun as direct or indirect offshoots of particular foreign churches, and many of the larger ones have sprouted separatist churches themselves. . . .

Taken together, Christianity as foreign missionaries conceive of it has only partly eradicated indigenous Luo religion. The traditions of thought and practice found today in the region weave together local and exogenous strands, in a variegated fabric not devoid of stresses and strains. Indigenous and exogenous marriage systems, methods of praise and prayer, food and drink taboos, and dress codes all interthread, but not in a static or homogeneous way. Individuals who find that the strictures of their churches do not fit their habits or ambitions – for example, monogamists who become interested in plural marriage, or drinkers who wish to quit drinking – commonly switch to sects that fit

[9] Some concepts corresponding to "witchcraft" or "magic" are *juok* (pl. *juogi*), witchcraft, also an inherited name; *nawi* (pl. *nepe*), poison, magic, or spell; *bilo* (pl. bilo), medicine, often powder and usually protective, and *yath* (pl. *yien, yiedhe*), medicine or poison; *manyasi*, a solution of medicinal herbs and water; and *ndagla*, evil magic using an offensive object. The standard prefix *ja* (pl. *jo*) is used to refer to one who manipulates spiritual forces. Thus *ajuogo* (pl. *ajuoge, ajuoke*), from *juok*, is a broadly used term meaning diviner, witch, or medicine man or woman; a *jadil* (pl. *jodil* – from *dilo*, cleansing ritual) is a specialist in spirits or ghosts. *Japuok* (pl. *jopuok*) refers to a night runner or a woman with the power of the evil eye which causes internal illness; this power is called *sihoho* and is thought to belong only to some women.

[10] In the parts of South Nyanza District where most of the fieldwork for this study was done, the strongest foreign-based church is the Seventh-Day Adventist Church, which started work in what is now Nyanza Province in 1906. The Kenya SDA church is part of the East African union of SDAs; the mother SDA church is headquartered in Washington, D.C. Anglicans of the Church of the Province of Kenya (CPK), Diocese of Maseno South, carry on the tradition imported to the Lake Victoria Basin in the late decades of the 19th century by missionaries of the London-based Church Missionary Society. Also strong is the (Roman) Catholic Church in Kenya, founded upon the local establishment of the London-based Mill Hill Fathers, who also first began proselytizing in the region in the late 19th century. Other foreign-based churches active in the area include those of Pentecostal Evangelists and the Salvation Army.

[11] Some consider the Luo dominance in Kenya's intellectual scene a response to a lack or loss of economic and political power, or a kind of holding pattern.

[12] The oldest independent African church sect in Nyanza is Nomiya Luo Church, formed as the Nomiya Luo Mission in 1914 as the first independent African church in Kenya, and headquartered now in Kisumu. Other especially important independent churches in the Luo country are the following: the Maria Legio of Africa, a female-founded church dating from the early 1960s, headquartered in South Nyanza, and mixing elements of Catholicism and indigenous Luo practice; the African Israel Church Nineveh, founded in 1942 from Canadian Pentecostalist roots, and based north of Kisumu; and several churches using the name Roho (spirit) or Roho Maler (Holy Spirit), including the Roho Church of God in Israel, founded in 1963 by a former Pentecostalist as the African Spiritual Israel Church and renamed twice later in the decade; and the Roho mar Nyasaye Mission (Spirit of God Mission). For basic information on these and other Kenyan independent churches, see D. Barrett et al. (1973), an annotated directory; Whisson (1964); and Wipper (1977).

their needs or ambitions more closely. In the choices among beliefs there is some syncretism. Though missionaries have tried hard to stamp out ancestral spirits, these remain active in the minds of many Luo who consider themselves Christian.

Money

Money as coinage or printed notes has been in general use in the Luo country only since the turn of the 20th century: it came at about the same time as the Bible. Most of Luo country lay well away from the major long-distance trade routes of the 19th century. Although Luo knew specialized or "intermediate" currencies like iron wire (*nalo*) for arm or leg bands, and doubtless some knew money too, before the establishment of the British East Africa Protectorate in 1895, it was the colonial impetus, particularly taxation from 1900 on, that first caused money's spread, and Luo have always associated it with alien authority while finding it convenient for their own purposes.[13] . . . An ethnographer studying the Luo northwest of Kisumu town in the late 1940s noted that metal ornaments as trade currency were then a thing of the past (Waligorski 1970:19). Barter was still seen, though cash seemed to be increasingly supplanting it too.[14]

As "intermediate currency," as minted tender, or as credit, money tends to free an African farmer from depending on the elements or the goodwill of his or her neigh-

bors, for food and other provisions each year. Saved in padlocked boxes, mattresses, and by a few men, in banks, money can buy a Luo what might otherwise require cooperation.[15]

But money has not taken over all transactions and is unlikely to do so soon. Farmers continue to engage in permanent or temporary local contracts exchanging land, labor, and livestock directly – to name only three factors of production (Johnson 1980; Shipton 1985; cf. Robertson 1987). Rural Luo now pay bridewealth in livestock, though they supplement this with cash (cf. Parkin 1980). Kin appearing at funerals present the immediate family of the dead with grain or other edibles; only those living too far to come are likely to send money instead. Household guests bring gifts like tea, sugar, or clothes, but not money. As everywhere, exchanges in kind are warmer and more personal than those with cash. Money creeps into most kinds of transactions, but in some, Luo discernibly try to keep it out.

Luo remain acutely conscious of what they see as their past, jealously guarding what remains of their cultural, political, and economic independence. To the accelerating pace of change their responses remain deeply ambivalent. It is this ambivalence, and the attempts to reconcile ideals with actions, that their current beliefs about bitter money may serve to illustrate. . . .

---

[13]   Money is defined here as serving at least several of the following purposes: a medium of exchange, a standard of value, a store of value or wealth, a standard of deferred payment, or a unit of account. For discussions of these and other definitions see Neale (1976), Simmel (1978), and Weber (1947:172–181, 280–309).

[14]   Northcote (1907:58), Waligorski (1970:19), and Whisson (1962a:13) discuss early 20th-century "intermediary" currencies like iron wire, brass rings, and hoes, and standards of measurement and value like grain baskets of graduated sizes. For information on barter in the mid-century, see these sources and Wagner (1956, vol. II: 161–162). Substitutions of cash for other exchange media are not necessarily irreversible.

[15]   Margaret Field (1940:217) wrote of the Ga of Ghana, "The first step in the loss of the sense of togetherness was the coming of money. Money could buy you food and make you independent of the yearly gifts of the earth and the help of relatives. Its possession did not depend on goodness – rather it was the contrary." The functionalist cast of her words was distinctly 20th century, but the basic idea can be found in John Locke's second treatise of government (1960 [1689], sect. 50; see also MacPherson 1962:208–209).

Bitter Money

Pesa makech is a term Luo use to describe ill-gotten money.[16] *Pesa* is money; anglophone Luo commonly translate *makech* in this context as "bitter," but the word can mean other things at the same time: biting, nasty, cruel, evil, dangerous.[17] A near English equivalent is "dirty money," but this idea does not capture the spiritual dimensions of the Luo concept, or the restrictions Luo place on the money's uses.[18]

Bitter money is a special instance of what Luo sometimes call *gueth makech*, best translated as "bitter blessings" or "bitter rewards." These are benefits deriving from unfair or unjust activities, and therefore unable to help one in the long run. The "bitterness" is figurative. How one has gained a reward determines whether or how one should use it. Luo pay special attention to money.

To Luo, bitter money is dangerous to its holder and the holder's family, because of its associations with spirits, and, in the minds of some Luo, with divinity. It must be kept strictly apart from transactions involving permanent lineage wealth and welfare, notably from livestock or bridewealth transactions.

Money obtained in several ways is thought bitter. One way is by "windfall," unearned gain: finding someone's lost money, or winning a lottery. Another is by a reward for killing or hurting others, as with a hired criminal or (according to some) a mercenary soldier. Theft is another source of bitter money, dangerous to its spender. This money is rather like stolen food, which Luo, like some other East Africans warn themselves not to eat for fear it will harm them.[19] The danger or "bitterness" in bitter money does not follow it as it circulates, but sticks with the one who procured it by misdeed. The "spirit of the gift" is here inverted. Bitter money contains instead something one might call the "spirit of the theft."[20]

Most commonly, though, bitter money comes from sales. In southern Luoland there are several commodities normally thought to

---

[16]   The findings about bitter money sketched here were made toward the end of (and incidentally to) a field research project on rural land rights, credit, and debt, between 1980 and 1983. Since only a short time could be devoted in the field to bitter money beliefs, their variations over time and space are not yet known. Most of the information on bitter money here comes from Kanyamkago Location, South Nyanza District, but bitter money from forbidden transactions is a familiar idea throughout Luoland at least, and widely associated with the commodities discussed here.

[17]   The root in DhoLuo is *kech; ma* is an adjectival prefix. The term conflates various meanings of evil or harm; in noun form *kech* also means hunger or famine. Though many Lui speak of money's "bitterness" with the explicit simile of taste in the mouth, there seems to be no opposite like "sweet" money; instead, money that is not *makech* is simply *pesa maber*, "good money." The evil state is thus marked, while the opposite is unmarked.

[18]   Once "dirty money" is in our possession, we may feel little compunction about the uses to which we can put it. To North American academics, the origin of grant money does not normally restrict its usability. Fulbright awards come from American arms sales abroad, Rhodes scholarships from gruesome racial exploitation in southern African mines, Nobel prizes from high explosives. Academic scholarships are a favorite way for weapon mongers to launder "dirty money" back into respectability, a kind of atonement. Scholars seems to use these funds with more pride than shame, reasoning sometimes that the real dirty work was done by someone else, and that taking is different from contributing. But where the initial earner of "dirty" money also spends it on other ethnically dubious purposes, public opprobrium can be great. The American press deemed the "Iran-Contra" scandal of the Reagan administration in the United States worse than the sum of two separate scandals in different parts of the world, because the funds earned in one covert illegal military activity were used in another, allegedly by some of the same people.

[19]   Ocholla-Ayayo (1976:241) lists the Luo proverb, *Kik icham gima Jamichiere onego, kata chiemo mokwal*, "Do not eat stolen food, especially meat of stolen livestock." It can make one ill at least: in a way more literal than in the proverb, one man's meat *is* another man's poison. Compare the Kikuyu proverbs, *Indo ciene irir mutino*, "Stolen things bring in misfortune," and *Mũguĩ utarĩ wa awa nĩ ũkũndembũrĩra thiaka* "The arrow which is not my father's pierces my quiver," meaning roughly the same (Barra 1987:26, 55).

[20]   The "spirit of the gift," reported by Robert Hertz among the Maori and made famous by Marcel Mauss, is what

yield the seller bitter money. These include land, gold, tobacco, and cannabis. Many also say that selling a homestead rooster will produce money that is bitter. These material things are not necessarily considered evil or dangerous in themselves. What makes the rewards of land (for instance) dangerous is the selling, and the implicit disrespect or denial of someone else's right or claims to it. The commodities listed seem to be the ones whose sale is most likely to involve some perceived unfairness or injustice. Nor, probably, is the list complete, but these were the only transactions yielding bitter money of which I have been able, in a brief time, to learn; and as discussed later, there are many other transactions that are forbidden in various ways but do not produce bitter money.

We deal now first with land, tobacco, cannabis, and gold in turn. As it happens, each of these commodities has been associated with major social, economic, or political changes in the South Nyanza district of Luoland, where most of my interviews were conducted.[21] Roosters, considered last, are special in that their individual economic value is small but their symbolic associations strong.

Land

A profound and wide-ranging change in 20th-century Luo country has been the growth of a market in land, a process lately stimulated by the Kenya government's nationwide program of registering all farmland as private, individual property.

Like agrarian people all over eastern Africa, the Luo had no strictly private ownership (or, for that matter, communal ownership) in land as Europeans understand it before the arrival of Europeans in the late 19th century. Rather, Luo land rights depended on a complex interaction of principles that can only be sketched in roughest outline here.[22] Individuals and families acquired land use rights by the act of clearing new land, by real or putative membership in patrilineages or patriclans, by long residence in the territory of these groups or their larger federations (*ogendni*), or by territorial encroachments or conquest. Over the long term one could maintain cultivation rights to a particular piece of land by investing labor: in this respect, the Luo case was characteristic of land right systems all over the continent.[23] The system oscillated seasonally between individualistic and collectivistic principles, never reaching extremes: land to which an individual or family held fairly exclusive rights during the growing season became open grazing ground for neighbors after harvest. At any time, many different people and groups could have rights of different orders in a particular piece of land; and the rights of use, administration, and disposal were often held by different people.

---

compels a gift recipient to reciprocate or pass the gift along, and thus to be a member of society. Mauss writes of the Maori *hau*,

> Even when abandoned by the giver, it still forms a part of him . . . To keep this thing is dangerous, not only because it is illicit to do so, but also because it comes morally, physically, and spiritually from a person. Whatever it is, food, possessions, women, children or ritual, it retains a magical and religious hold over the recipient. The thing given is not inert. It is alive and often personified, and strives to bring to its original clan and homeland some equivalent to take its place. [Mauss 1967 [1925]:8–10]

Much of this comes close to the Luo conception of bitter money, except that the giving and taking may be reversed.

[21] In fieldwork I learned that sales of several commodities produced bitter money, and saw only after learning this that the commodities tended to be associated with major changes I had been observing in Luo society.

[22] See Shipton (1984a, 1984b), and sources cited there specifically on the preregistration systems of tenure in Luoland; Okoth-Ogendo (1976, 1978) discusses Kenyan tenure systems more generally from a sociolegal perspective.

[23] The best general survey of African systems of land tenure with reference to the principle that "work creates rights" remains Meek (1946). (It also contains useful chapters on other parts of the then British empire.) The idea that the investment of labor is what creates property relations between people and things (or between people in respect of things) is an old idea, however; it was the central point of John Locke's "labor theory of value" in the *Second Treatise of Government*.

Land was not normally salable until well into the colonial period, though relatives could swap holdings or, where lineage elders agreed, invite outsiders onto lineage lands. Though women did not normally inherit land, when married they held well-recognized rights in the lands of their conjugal families, holding these in trust for their own unmarried sons.[24]

Territorial confinement of ethnic groups under colonial authority, the advent of the ox-plow, and the falling death rate due to medicine and consequent rises in population growth all contributed to competition for land and to local imbalances in the ratio of population to land in the first three decades of the 20th century. In Luoland the competition led to some strengthening of individual claims in places. But there were already strong sanctions against land sales. Toward the end of the 19th century, for instance, the last *jabilo* (diviner for the *oganda*) of Kanyamkago is said to have placed a curse on the selling of land there – a sign that at least someone was trying to sell. Kanyamkago residents now hold that his curse has killed neighbors who have sold their land – nearly everyone can think of examples – and that even the cattle of those guilty have died off. (Such curses are known elsewhere in East Africa.)[25] In the early 20th century, overt or covert land sales became a more familiar idea if not a common practice.[26]

Now they are becoming common practice. This was a part of the original design behind the registration of all farmland as private property. Set in motion by the British colonial government in 1954 as the continent's first nationwide attempt to "individualize" land, the processes of land consolidation, adjudication, and registration have continued under the national government since independence in 1963. Those who have studied the tenure reform in Luoland agree on several things. The registration has been a hard process for the government and for rural people, has endangered or diminished the legal land rights of women and other categories of persons, has failed to achieve its planned goals (except for a probable concentration of holdings, an explicit aim of the original plan), and is producing a land register that is quickly becoming obsolete.[27]

Luo stiffly resisted the process until after Kenya's independence in 1963. They resisted for many reasons, some concerning preservation of their social structure and process. It is well known to East Africanists that the Luo conceive of land as a permanent lineage asset, closely linked with genealogical position, and as something not to let go lightly. Luo assess and defend claims to land by reference to ancestral graves: the dead are buried in the homestead, and the spirits remain around there when the homestead is eventually abandoned.

All in Luo country agree that the ancestors disapproved of land sales, and many Luo still

---

[24]   The listed works of Pala (1977, 1980) and Hay (1972, 1982) discuss the preregistration land rights of Luo women in some detail.

[25]   Compare this findings of Moore's (1986:267) on the Chagga of Mt. Kilimanjaro, Tanzania:

It is said even today that cursed land, lands wrongfully appropriated and then cursed by the rightful owner cannot be sold by the appropriator or his descendants at any price if the story of the curse is known and believed. Thus there are supernatural reasons to have clear "title," that is, in this system, a clear right to sell land.

Farther afield, Bourdieu (1977:175) describes how the land of Kabylia "settles its scores" with farmers who have abused it.

[26]   See DeWilde 1967:130–131; Dundas 1913:55; Fearn 1961:34; and the notes of the Kenya Land Commission (1934:2294, 2299).

[27]   See Coldham (1978, 1979), Okoth-Ogendo (1976, 1978), Pala (1977, 1983), and Shipton (1988) on the registration process and its effects there. These sources also cite other reports based on first-hand observations in Luoland. See also Glazier (1985) and Haugerud (1983) on Embu District.

do today. In explaining why, an elderly Kanyamkago woman told me cryptically that the land is (like) a magician (*lowo jajuok*), adding that

> When we are born, we find it there; all that we eat comes from it; what we excrete goes back to it, and when we die we return to it. It feeds us and it swallows us.[28]

In a sense, selling land is selling the ancestors, and thus one's patrilineal kin; for these are so closely identified as to be in some respects the same.[29] The rewards that come from one come from the others too.

Luo say that ancestral spirits follow money obtained in land sales and ensure that it comes to no good for the seller. This money is *makech*, bitter. If a man sells land and buys livestock with it, either directly or indirectly, the animals of their offspring will die off by disease or other misfortune. If he first uses the animals in a bridewealth payment, the bride will die before long. According to one informant, this is because the bride, coming into the patrilineage, will eat the food from the land that has been cast out of the lineage. Seemingly everyone in Kanyamkago knows someone whose patriline has been ruined by the use of bitter money in bridewealth. A middle-aged man told his own story. In 1954, he said, he had harvested some tobacco, sold it, and bought a goat with the money. His goats multiplied, and he exchanged these for cattle, which he used in bridewealth payments for his sons' marriages. Now the sons wanted to have families of their own, but because of the bitter

money, he doubted whether they and their wives would be able to produce healthy offspring.

Whether land sales will lead to ruin even today is a subject of much debate in Luo country. Many say they are waiting to see. It may be that selling land that one inherited is more likely to produce bitter money, in Luo eyes, than selling land that one recently purchased, for the latter is less likely to involve the overlapping claims of one's kin. One of my eldest women informants sighed that since the blacks had taken over from the whites in Kenya, everything had turned upside down, and perhaps now it was possible to get rich by selling land.[30]

Tobacco

Money from tobacco resembles money from land, in that it involves the spirits of ancestors, and it is partly these associations with ancestors that appear it make it "bitter." Tobacco also resembles land in that it has been the subject of an ambitious recent campaign from outside Luo country to push Luo agriculture into a market economy.

The Luo have known tobacco (*Nicotinia tabacum*; in Luo, *ndawa*) for generations, possibly since shortly after its introduction on the continent in the 16th century.[31]

Smoked mainly by elders until recent years, tobacco was grown in small quantities in the abandoned homes of dead relatives, where manure from the old cattle enclosures had made the soil especially fertile.[32] In Luo country the abandoned homestead enclosures

---

[28] The phrase *chamo lowo*, to eat (from) land, can also mean to inherit it.

[29] See Gudeman (1986:40–41) for a discussion of the continuum from "as if" to "as being" models. The ontological problems implied in "as being" models are old, however, and much debated since Evans-Pritchard's famous reports (1956) that to the Nuer, "twins are birds" and sacrificed cucumbers "are" bulls.

[30] Of course, not all shared her political views!

[31] The crop has spread quickly through the continent upon its introduction (Akehurst 1981; Brooks 1937, vol. I:41–42). Luo call local strains of tobacco *ndap nyaluo*, "Luo tobacco," suggesting how well the crop had become incorporated into Luo life before the start of the BAT project. Until colonial times, Luo elders smoked tobacco in fairly short-stemmed pipes made of clay, Kisii soapstone, or goatskin; but over the past few decades home-rolled and mass-produced cigarettes have almost completely taken over.

[32] Some elders say that in precolonial times the Luo harvested tobacco where elephants had defecated.

are also the sites of ancestral graves. It was perhaps for this reason, combined with the fascination of fire and smoke, and the sometimes narcotic and even hallucinogenic effects of nicotine (see Schweinfurth 1878, vol. I:254) that Luo thought of tobacco as a crop of the spirits of the dead.

Luo have believed, and many still do today, that spirits watched over the growing tobacco plants and followed the crop after harvest. Elders of both sexes smoked as a way of contacting spirits in times of trouble. They found smoking gave them extraordinary powers of memory: ancestors from the distant past with whom the smoker was not acquainted would appear to him or her, just as they could during a sleeping dream. Informants say the ancestors often appeared smoking pipes themselves. Evoking spirits by smoking was something of a gamble: the smoker had no choice of what spirit might appear, and the appearance of an unwelcome one could drive him or her insane. It was the spirits, too, who caused tobacco addiction and urged an elder to plant more of the crop.

Smoke appears to constitute its own conceptual category for the Luo. It is as much like a liquid as it is like air. The usual term for "to smoke" is *madho ndawa*, literally, to drink tobacco. Smoke is thought to wash away problems as water washes away dirt; and it could do so for a smoker just as for participants in special ritual sacrifices where meat was cooked. Elders will also say *ndawa mach*, tobacco is fire. So it is a product of the earth that may be associated with air, water, and fire at the same time. Tobacco connects elements of the ordinary world, and it connects the ordinary world with the spirit world. This last is a theme common to other Nilotic peoples too.[33]

Luo say that the spirits follow transactions where tobacco is involved and render unproductive wealth acquired through it. Like money from land sales, money from tobacco is *makech*, and it has to be kept strictly separate from lineage stock or bridewealth. If a man exchanges tobacco for livestock, either directly or indirectly, and uses the animals in bridewealth payment, the bride will perish in fire and smoke, since she will have been procured through fire and smoke. Not even the animals' calves will do.[34] Selling tobacco involves the spirits in profane commerce, and this action taints wealth. It affects not only money, but also animal and human wealth.

There are other trepidations, too, surrounding tobacco. Of the countless Catholic and Protestant churches that together claim as members most of the Luo today, nearly all have objections, strong or mild, to tobacco production or use.[35] Among these are sects opposed to tobacco in their European

[33] Johnson (1980:216) mentions the elder Suba (Luo speakers of Bantu descent living near Kanyamkago in South Nyanza) use tobacco in purification ceremonies for accidental killers, though its significance there is unclear. R. G. Abrahams (personal communication) has observed that among the Labwor, a Lwoo-speaking Ugandan group related to the Kenya Luo, tobacco is an especially potent article used in interpersonal blessings (pressed against the forehead, inserted between toes and into armpits, and held in hand). His unpublished field notes read, "It seems its [the blessing's] strength is connected with kec-ness [like Luo *kech*-ness] of tobacco. Other aspects of this are that a person who steals tobacco will die very quickly if its owner curses him and there is also some belief that a person who has very, very much tobacco in his house will be killed by it." Evans-Pritchard (1956:221) has noted that "In violent storms Nuer, fearful of the lightning, throw small pieces of tobacco into the air, asking God to take them, and saying that they have paid him ransom with this offering." Lienhardt observed on the Nuer and Dinka shrines of their deity Deng Dit, "No man can safely approach it without making some small offering, usually by throwing tobacco in the direction of the shrine" (1961:101; see also pp. 153–154, 259 on tobacco offerings to divinity, clan divinities, and ancestral ghosts).

[34] Tobacco taboos also apply to women's out-marriages as well as to in-marriages. A bridegroom must not take tobacco to the home of his bride – as one elderly widow put it, she would then have to make up some excuse not to marry him, like "he's not beautiful enough," or "he's not wealthy enough." Nor must her family give any to him, or sell any for food or livestock to be given to him, or the marriage will be spoiled.

[35] But packaged cigarettes and home-rolled tobacco are now ubiquitous commodities in Luoland, and despite the disapproval of many of the Euro-American and independent churches, many men and women of all ages smoke.

mother churches (e.g., the popular Seventh-Day Adventist Church), others whose African missions have imposed new strictures not found in the European mother churches (notably Anglican and Catholic churches), and a vast number of independent African Christian churches. Though smoking is nowhere explicitly condemned in the Judeo-Christian Bible, many Luo find passages there to support its condemnation, such as Mark 7:21: "That which proceedeth from the man, that defileth the man" – in this case, smoke from the smoker's mouth. During the colonial period many converted Luo decided tobacco was not just an ancestral spirit's crop, but Satan's crop; others decided it was both. The new beliefs overlaid the old but by no means expunged them. Tobacco was cursed, and most still seem to think it is today.

But none of this has prevented the recent spread of tobacco as a cash crop. In the late 1960s the British-American Tobacco Company (BAT), the largest tobacco company in the Western world, had established its buying centers at Oyani and Taranganya, in South Nyanza.[36] By 1982, BAT had contracted over 4000 farmers in Luo locations of South Nyanza to build tobacco drying barns and to grow Virginia flue-cured and other types of tobacco on parts of their own landholdings.

Tobacco has proved an extremely lucrative crop for smallholders.[37] They have made more money per hectare with tobacco than with any other seasonal crop they grow.[38] But the inequalities in the distribution of the profits among local growers are enormous.[39] Men are contracted and paid in cash as individuals, though they use mainly family labor. The burden of the longer and duller tasks, especially weeding, has been shifting to women. The scheme appears to be concentrating family wealth into male hands.[40] It is also undermining the authority of elders, since BAT prefers younger men because of their supposed energy, and since now, for the first time, junior men can become richer than their fathers while staying at home. Tobacco has called for adjustments in patterns of labor recruitment. Some men are hiring help on a cash basis for the first time, for the day-and-night chore of feeding wood into the curing barns in drying time. Others are adapting old Luo forms of exchange labor, notably the *rika* (a small circle of neighbors who work for each other in rotation). Though tobacco has brought about visible improvements in housing in Kanyamkago, many of the farmers are spending a large part of their tobacco earnings on town drinking, prostitution, and other entertainments of which their relatives disapprove. The spread of the tobacco crop in an area where fundamentalist Christian churches predominate has necessitated adjustments in religious belief and practice.[41] While a few of the churches have remained dead set against

---

[36]   The occasion was the nationalization of its Tanzanian tobacco operations, which until then had supplied tobacco to Kenya.

[37]   This paragraph is a cursory summary of findings presented in more detail in Shipton (1985:288–309); see also Acland (1980).

[38]   Except perhaps cannabis; records on this are lacking.

[39]   In 1982, for instance, the highest-earning quartile of 128 registered BAT tobacco growers in a sublocation of Kanyamkago earned 68% of the total tobacco earnings, while the lowest-earning quartile earned only 1% (compiled from BAT records). One reason for the poor distribution of the rewards is that tobacco is graded on a wide scale according to quality, and therefore quality can be multiplied by quantity for the best growers.

[40]   As of 1982, 96% of the 128 registered tobacco growers in the Kanyamkago sublocation studies were male.

[41]   Long's study of the Lala of Zambia (1968:242) found that Jehovah's Witnesses were often the first to adopt a new commercial Turkish tobacco crop. His explanation, inspired by Weber (1930), focuses on what he perceives as their individualistic ethic.

tobacco growing, most have found rather
clever ways to reconcile themselves with it.[42]
In several, members who grow tobacco protect
themselves by giving their local clergy a
portion of their tobacco profits – call it a tithe
or otherwise, the pattern is familiar from other
walks of life – and the clergy arrange the rest
with the spiritual or ecclesiastical powers, as
need be.

Is tobacco money still bitter? Do the ancestral spirits and Christian demons still follow
tobacco and the wealth that comes from it, now
that the crop is big business? Some think not,
and I have heard the reason given that the new
tobacco is not grown just at abandoned homestead sites and therefore lacks some of the
spiritual charges. But many Luo think old and
new tobacco are bitter alike. Some will point to
the frequent barn fires, others to floods and
hailstorms. "*Piny okethore*," some elders will
say, "the country is being spoiled."[43] Older
women warn that tobacco wealth will not last,
and will not help anyone's lineage, and many
will tell of marriages and families that
collapsed when tobacco money worked its way
into bridewealth. It is widely claimed that
money earned by growing tobacco gets spent
faster than other money. Many farmers believe
this is because the money is bitter and followed
by spirits.[44] But others say they are unsure
whether the new BAT tobacco yields bitter
money, like the old local tobacco. As in the case
of newly registered land, many say they have
not had time to watch the effects on families
and lineages: they are waiting to see.

To be on the safe side, farmers say, it is good
to use tobacco money on food and clothes, or
iron roofs – things not expected to last forever
anyway. They say, do not use it to buy cattle
or pay bridewealth; use maize money for that.
But there seems to be a disjunction here
between the real and the ideal. For when
tobacco growers were questioned on how they
had used their tobacco earnings in the previous
year, livestock purchases were the most
common response. A likely reason is that men,
being the first to receive the tobacco earnings,
are seeking to preserve part of the wealth as
unchallengeable male property by converting
it to livestock. But by converting bitter money
into lineage property, they are risking the
wrath of the spirits and of God. Some who
have obtained livestock through tobacco earnings, and want to use it for bridewealth, are
trying to "launder" the wealth by selling the
stock, buying other animals with the proceeds,
and using them instead. Conservatives say this
will never work.

Cannabis

Cannabis sativa (marijuana, called *njaga* in Luo
and *bhang* in many East African languages) is
another crop that Luo elders grew and smoked
in the past. They planted it where tobacco
grew, in the abandoned homestead sites, and
Luo men smoked it to communicate with the
ancestors, among other purposes. The ancestral spirits were thought to protect cannabis
gardens, as they protected tobacco gardens. At

---

[42]   In the early 1980s, the Gospels Church warned members who grow tobacco but did not expel them. The Roho
Msanda Holy Ghost Church and the Pentecostal Holiness Church had decided that their lay members may grow tobacco,
but not their clergy. The Seventh-Day Adventist Church and the Legio Maria, two of the churches that most adamantly
resisted tobacco growing in the early BAT years in South Nyanza, had later, after much debate, allowed their members
to grow tobacco. But they stipulated that none who did so could take communion.

[43]   Compare the Bemba attribution of 1930s copper price collapses to the displeasure of the ancestors (Richards
1939:235; also discussed in Gudeman 1986:94). Findings like these are fairly common patterns in rural African studies.

[44]   In part of a survey I conducted, men and women of 107 households in Kanyamkago Location were asked whether
farmers found this a problem and if so, why it happened. (Possible answers were not prompted.) Thirty-eight percent
responded that it was a problem because of the spirits of the dead; this was by far the most common answer. This is not,
of course, the kind of question best answered by survey, and I believe the proportion of farmers who think the spirits
cause the money to disappear quickly may be rather higher.

the same time, however, a small amount of cannabis kept inside a house was believed to ward away malevolent spirits and to protect a family from cholera, believed to be a spirit-borne disease. Cannabis was a medicine, then, associated with ancestors in both positive and negative ways.

Cannabis smoking, like tobacco smoking, has now spread to juniors and cannabis has become a common commodity in the informal economy of both city and countryside in Kenya. Cannabis is forbidden both by national law and by Kenyan Christian churches – frequent condemnations appear in Kenyan newspapers – but the commerce, particularly among young men with buyers in the towns, is lively. Once planted, cannabis can grow and reproduce quickly and with little labor input. "It's like stealing," stated a Luo man. This seems to be another reason why money or other goods obtained through cannabis are bitter.

Gold

Another economic and social change of the 20th century has been the use of Luo land and labor from the 1930s onward for foreign-owned gold mines, including Macalder's Mine, a small British-owned gold mine in the western part of the location, 15 kilometers from Lake Victoria and the same distance from the Tanzanian border.[45] Though the "Native Reserves" had been protected by the Native Trust Lands Ordinance of 1930, mineral rights still belonged to the British Crown and a new Mining Ordinance was passed in 1931 that effectively allowed the Provincial Commissioner to issue prospecting permits to settlers on payment of a 20 shilling fee and a £25 deposit (Fearn 1961:128–129; Hay 1972:221). Small prospectors flowed into the province, followed by agents of larger,

London-registered companies. These companies acquired land rights on leasehold. Their invasions of local farm and homestead lands were compensated by commuted rent, in cash. This was unacceptable to the Nyanza Africans, whose land transactions had customarily been redeemable at will by the original owner. It was particularly unacceptable to those who had learned of the supposed "protection" under the 1930 ordinance (Fearn 1961:143–146; cf. Hay 1972:221). Five thousand and eighty-one Luo and as many Luhya, mostly men, were at work in the Nyanza mines by 1935. In that year, the peak year of the industry, the Africans worked for an average of £6 a year (Fearn 1961:130). This was not a bad wage by the standards of other opportunities Africans had (Hay 1972:222–223). But the European staff members earned 39 times as much per capita (calculated from Fearn 1961:130). Cash wages paid to Africans attracted new Indian and other Asian traders, with new commodities. Most of the gold was exported from Kenya as bullion. So while the gold rush brought some welcome new jobs and commerce to the region, it also meant land dispossessions, a gender differential in earning power, discriminatory licensing, locally unprecedented wage inequalities, and ultimate extraction of the precious metal for parts unknown.

The Second World War and its equipment shortages brought problems to the European mining firms from which they never recovered, and they abandoned the Nyanza mines by the early 1950s. Although Macalder's is still officially defunct, some local farmers still mine the shafts and surrounding fields, illegally, on a small scale.[46] A few also pan for gold in local streams. Local traders serve as middlemen in a covert trade linking these small prospectors to Nairobi gold buyers.

[45]   For historical reconstructions of the mining era, see Fearn (1961:123–150) and Hay (1972:218–224).
[46]   The Trading in Unwrought Precious Metals Act of 1933, revised 1984, states that "No person shall buy, sell, deal in, receive, or dispose of by way of barter, pledge or otherwise, either as principle or agent, any unwrought precious metal" without a license from the Commissioner of Mines and Geology or an agent (*Laws of Kenya*, Ch. 309, sect. 3).

As with the other commodities, Kan-yamkago informants will tell of neighbors whose families have suffered grave misfortunes after selling gold to buy livestock. (This is not, of course, the kind of story that anyone is likely to tell about him or herself.) An elderly woman in Kanyamkago told of her husband's brother, Dalmas Nyayal, who, when young in the 1930s, had found gold on a visit to Kihancha, part of the Kuria country.[47] He used the gold to buy cows and distributed these to the eldest three of his four brothers. They used the cows for their bridewealth, but he did not. The brothers all died, and so did all their wives but one. But, at the time of field-work, Dalmas Nyayal was still alive and living with his three wives and their children – to the informant, the picture of a successful man.

In another rumored instance, Okello Okwach of Karachuonyo, South Nyanza, is said to have sold a substantial amount of gold, and used the proceeds to buy 80 head of cattle, which he used to marry two more wives. He also used some to educate his son to secondary level, enabling his son to find work later as a headmaster in several successive primary schools. But very gradually Okello Okwach's cattle all died off, forcing him away to seek work in some of the towns. The son went to search for him, found him, and persuaded him to return home. Okwach is said to have turned foul-tempered toward his wives and other members of the family. He began beating the wives and coercing them into sexual acts at strange times. The son and the son's mother conspired to murder him, and they cut his body to pieces. Nor was peace restored even then: the family continued to decline and was reported almost gone by the time of the telling.

Some informants say that money from gold sales is bitter because it is a product of the land that is obtained with very little work, in relation to its value. Unlike money from, say, sorghum or maize, bitter money has involved too little sweat (*luya*). Gold sales are illegal except with a license, virtually impossible for a Luo smallholder to obtain, but elders today say gold rewards were *makech* even before it became illegal. There are women working independently or grinding, panning, and washing what their male relatives dig up, but it seems the rewards have most often gone directly into men's hands.

Roosters

Beliefs about bitter money are full of metaphors. Just as the bride procured through tobacco sales can be expected to die in fire and smoke, Luo remember their elders' saying in the past that a bride obtained through the sale or barter of roosters for cattle would fly about like a hen, in adultery. Roosters remain among the objects of sales taboos; they still yield bitter blessings.

Why roosters are included, in Luo minds, must be explained in terms of their symbolism, since the individual economic value of the birds is small. Luo consider a home incomplete without a rooster. Like the sharpened pole sticking straight up from a thatch rooftop in a homestead with a living male head, the rooster stands for maleness. A Luo term for rooster, *thwon*, also means male or hero, rather as the English term "cock" has referred for centuries to the male organ as well as the animal. The rooster's polygamy is associated with human polygyny, a man's route to prestige and, in the past at least, often to wealth. It stands for sexual potency.

The rooster carries other related meanings. It is conceptually linked with the continuity of the lineage, and with the progress of civilization into the wilderness. In the Luo *buru* ceremony, which commemorates a man's death some time after the funeral, a rooster is taken from his homestead and cooked and eaten in the *thim* or bush. Among other things,

---

[47]   In reports about incidents concerning bitter money, I have changed the personal names.

this is thought to mark the end of his homestead as well as of the man's life. When a young married man and his wife found a new homestead, the man ritually receives a rooster and an axe from his father's. In the past, Luo say, it was variously customary to take fire, a spear, a shield, and a euphorbia plant (used for enclosing the homestead) too. Now these things are no longer taken along, but significantly, the rooster still is: it is considered absolutely essential. The homestead rooster is a special one. Its health is associated with the well-being of the family.[48] A bird with a floppy crest is a bad sign; this should stand up tall. When the rooster grows old and weak, a man cooks it and consumes it ritually with elders, to ensure the family does not decline with it, and thereafter he regards a young offspring rooster as the living symbol of his family.[49]

The rooster is not a peculiarly Luo symbol; it is important to other Kenyan ethnic groups and has been adopted as a national symbol as well. The rooster appears brandishing an axe (inside a shield, between lions rampant, with crossed spears – all associated with wilderness) in the center of the emblem of the Kenya African National Union, now the sole legitimate political party in the nation. The emblem is emblazoned on the reverse of all coins. The rooster was sometimes associated with the late President Jomo Kenyatta, and Jogoo House (*jogoo* is Swahili for rooster) in Nairobi remains the office of the Vice President.

To sell the homestead rooster, among the Luo at least, is to sell one's masculinity and authority, and to betray one's home and patriline. This powerful, polysemic symbol means too much to be converted freely to 20 shillings. . . .

Belief in bitter money is very much alive today. For many it is science – there is evidence all around to support it, and little to contradict it. It is most often elders who believe today in bitter money, as one might expect; juniors tend to be more skeptical or unsure on the subject, and usually turn to elders when wanting to know more. But the age division is far from clear: a few of all ages will profess to reject the entire notion, and perhaps some will grow to accept it later in life, even as formal schooling and Christianity lead others to reject it. The fluidity with which Luo mix elements of their local beliefs with elements of Christianity from various churches suggests that the idea may be adapted to new circumstances for some time to come.

The Ritual Purification of Money and Its Holders

Bitter money is convertible to good money, which will "stick" to its owner's homestead by a purification ceremony (*oso*) led by a ritual specialist (*ajuoga*, pl. *ajuoge*).[50] A purification ritual for bitter money can be a rather frightening thing because of the unknown forces invoked, and it is performed only where a large amount of money is concerned: in the early 1980s some considered 10,000 to 20,000 shillings as a minimum, but there was no clear cutoff.[51] Nor is a ceremony performed for just *any* bitter money. The ceremonies are more common for gold than for tobacco. This may

---

[48] Far afield, Clifford Geertz's well-known article (1972) on the Balinese cockfight describes some other ways men can identify with roosters. More broadly, Eugenia Shanklin (1985) reviews anthropological literature on domestic animals and their symbolism; see pp. 392–396 on "animals as metaphors" for humans.

[49] Compare some other eastern African peoples' historical customs of killing a leader weakening from age or illness to ensure that society does not weaken with him. Some variants have been found or indirectly reported among the Nilotic Dinka (Lienhardt 1961:298–319) and Shilluk (Evans-Pritchard 1963:76) of Sudan, distant cousins of the Luo; and the Bantu-speaking Nyoro of Uganda (Beattie 171:105n) and Bemba of what is now Zambia (Richards 1940:98n).

[50] *Dolo, misango,* and *liswa* (which can all mean sacrifice) are other terms I have heard denoting purification rituals, and *dilo* is also reported.

[51] In the early 1980s, the Kenya shilling was worth about 10 U.S. cents.

be because gold is considered in a sense to be money already when it reaches one's hands, whereas tobacco is not. Purification ceremonies appear to be most common during the rainy seasons, when anxieties about damages to forthcoming harvests are highest. Most think a purification rite should be conducted soon after the money is brought home: the day after, ideally, or as soon thereafter as a ritual specialist can be engaged and provisions procured. As it happens, however, unrelated *ajuoge* living far from one's home are often preferred. They are considered not only to have greater power than those who are neighbors or kin, but also to be more discreet, being less entangled in local social life, and less jealous of the new wealth.[52]

No great rewards in Luo life are obtained without spiritual intervention, and an ostensible aim of a purification ceremony is to thank the spirit or spirits that provided the bitter money. If this is not done, they will ensure the money comes to no good. Most often, the spirit is assumed to be one in the male line. A son might let his father arrange the ritual, and a male homestead head may have it performed on behalf of his homestead.

Descriptions of the ceremonies vary.[53] Informants asked about standard practice sometimes begin by describing an "ideal" ceremony, with a large crowd assembled and the sacrifice of a bull, and end up talking about something much more modest, apparently more in line with present convention at least. All members of the lineage (in this context, *anyuola*) must come, some informants claim – but in a segmentary system, this must of course depend on how ones defines the lineage, as well as on how seriously the ideal is taken. Recently, it seems to have been more common for the owner of the bitter money to hold a smaller meal with a few guests from the neighborhood who may or may not be kin.[54]

An ideal purification rite must involve blood sacrifice. The animal should be male: a bull (which must have horns), a ram, or other; but a female may be used on occasion.[55] The *ajuoga*, who may have come the night before the ceremony, may witness the slaughter in the morning, but it may be done by anyone. The sacrificer slices the animal's throat with a knife. Members of the homestead roast the meat, including the intestines, over fire, and all present eat of it. Beer is drunk (traditionally grain beer, with long straws from a single pot) and may contribute to singing; some also mention food including sesame gruel, cow's

---

[52]   The preference for shamans, diviners, etc. living far away from one's home is a pattern observed in many other societies, in Africa south of the Sahara and elsewhere. Some may be considered more powerful precisely *because* their ordinary social roles are less familiar.

[53]   I have not had the opportunity to witness an *oso* ritual. In Hubert's and Mauss's classic schema emphasizing the distinction between sacred and profane in ritual and the difference between "sacralization" and "desacralization" (1964), the sacrifices the Luo describe would be "desacralization" in that they are attempts to free someone of tainting impurity. De Heusch analyzes African animal sacrifices, modifying Hubert's and Mauss's distinction (de Heusch 1985: chapts. 5–6, p. 213; see also Shanklin 1985:396–398 and sources cited therein). De Heusch also analyzes some apparent meanings of chyme in sacrificial rites on the Thonga in southern Africa (pp. 72–82); human contact with chyme is also important in Luo rituals of peacemaking, and of separation as in the establishment of new land boundaries. See also Abe's description (1978:10–11) of purification rituals (which he calls *dilo*) among Luo of Kamagambo Location, South Nyanza.

[54]   This diminution of ceremony through time, or because of practical constraints, is reminiscent of the famous Nuer sacrifices of cucumbers in lieu of bulls (Evans-Pritchard 1956:128). Of course, ritual gestures may also be exaggerated in oral lore, or concealed from foreigners suspected to be opposed.

[55]   No special color has been mentioned for these animals, but in other Luo sacrifices, red, black, or white animals are variously preferred, as in many other African societies south of the Sahara. There are many surface parallels between Luo sacrifices and those studied in more detail by Evans-Pritchard (1956) among the Nuer and Linehardt (1961) among the Dinka: for instance, in the uses of chyme and medical solutions, and beliefs about blood and smoke.

butter, and fish. The meal should be eaten in the center of the homestead.

In most versions, in Kanyamkago at least, the *ajuoga* openly prepares a mixture of water and herbal medicines (together called *manyasi*) together with chyme from the animal's stomach, in a small calabash. The possessor of the bitter money sips it, and the *ajuoga* sprinkles it into the money (or the gold, in one report), and around the homestead, inside and outside the house or houses, and on animals of the homestead. He pours it on the adults of the homestead, but not on children, since they are assumed unable to make money. The possessor of the bitter wealth is expected to explain to the gathering how he obtained it.[56] The *ajuoga* may add herbal medicines to the food and conduct prayers. The blood of the sacrificed animal, the smoke of the fire, and the remnants of meat left around and outside the homestead are all thought to reach the ancestors; the blood and meat feed them. The flowing blood and the smoke are also thought to wash away evil. Some also say the departing guests take the spirits away with them.

Luo Christians commonly claim not to conduct such purification rites, at least not with animal sacrifices; but some are said to convene religious gatherings in their houses, with sermons, prayers, meals, and drink, in order to bless bitter money.[57] In these meetings they may drink tea, or as one informant told me rather to my surprise, even bottled soft drinks.

If the details of a purification rite are not attended to properly, it is said, it may do more harm than good. Some try to conduct the rites after spending the money, but this sequence is frowned upon. Informants told me of acquaintances who had died or gone insane because the wrong herbs had been used; one contrasted three of these with a man whose ritual had been well conducted and who had grown very rich: "ten wives or more."

Oso is more than a purification of money itself. It is a rite of passage for the transgressor of a norm – the one who has received the "bitter blessing" – and his family.[58] Selling land, tobacco, gold, cannabis, or the homestead rooster is rather like selling one's mother or father, and in a sense it *is* selling them; it is a gravely antisocial act.[59] Not just the money earned, but also the seller and those in close contact, become *makech*. If bitter money continues to circulate from one holder to another, the danger is not thought to circulate with it, but sticks with the one who committed the evil act and with his family. The purification ritual makes him or her fit to act as a member of society again. Bitterness is not just as attribute of money: it is an attribute of people.

Criteria Determining Bitterness: A Polythetic Class

There is no single element in common to all the kinds of transactions that yield bitter money, which cannot be found in some other kinds of transactions that do not. And no commodity yielding bitter money has all of the attributes associated with bitterness. Clearly no simple explanation of bitter money will do. Instead, there seems to be a set of recurring themes, no one of which needs to be present

---

[56] For this reason, it is said, thieves are not likely to have purification ceremonies, though their wealth is bitter. But I have heard of rituals conducted such that their reason remains secret to the convener and *ajuoga*.

[57] Nor, of course, should one overlook the similarities between "traditional" Lui blood sacrifices and Catholic communion rites.

[58] See van Gennep 1960; Ocholla-Ayayo 1976:240–241; Turner 1969. Purification rites are performed upon many other transgressions of norms in Luo culture, for instance where one has committed murder, where land has been cursed, where a woman has refused to sleep with her husband, or where two women with breast-feeding children have fought.

[59] Indeed, a Luo arguing against land alienations before the Kenya Land Commission in 1932 summed up his feelings by saying, "The land is our mother" (Kenya Land Commission 1934:2166).

Table 10.1 Some attributes of forbidden commodities

	Commodities Associated with bitter money				Commodities not associated with bitter money			
	Land	Tobacco	Cannabis	Gold	Sugarcane cotton	Smuggled goods	Local liquors	Sexual services (prostitution)
Produced from the land	•	•	•	•			•	
Associated with ancestors (and thus with descent groups)	•	•	•					
Associated with Europeans or Asian as an alienable commodity	•	•		•	•			?
Produced by men and women; sold by men	•	•	•		•			
Controlled by elders in the past; sold now by juniors	•	•	•					
Easy money, in relation to labor required		•	•	•		?		
Condemned by Christian churches		•	•				•	•
Illegal to produce or sell		•	•			•	•	•

for a transaction to be classified as bitter. A commodity with all the traits we have identified with bitterness would be a product of the land, associated with ancestors and family, extracted by or for foreigners with unfair compensation, involving female labor but yielding disproportionate profits for men and especially young men, easily obtained in relation to its value, condemned as sinful in Christian churches, and perhaps illegal in national law. But there seems to be no such commodity (see Table 10.1)

To understand the phenomenon like this we need to resort to a form of classification in which no single attribute defines a class. This is what biological taxonomists call a "polythetic" or "polytypic" class and the philosopher Ludwig Wittgenstein called a "family likeness" (1958:17). Wittgenstein's metaphor illustrates the general idea: "the rope consists of fibres, but it does not get its strength from any fibre that runs through it from one end to another, but from the fact that there is a vast number of fibres overlapping" (1958:87); see also Beckner (1959:22), Needham (1975). . . .

So if we have several objects, each of which has several attributes, allocated in this way:

Object	Attributes
1	a/b/c
2	b/c/d
3	c/d/e
4	d/e/f

we may come to recognize a "family resemblance" among them, and call them a kind of class, even though there is no single attribute that members all have in common, and no member that possesses all the attributes that define the class.[60] It is this kind of thought that

---

[60] Needham traces the roots of polythetic classification to the 18th-century French biologist Michel Adanson, but states

I think lies behind the Luo notion of bitter money. This is a "sliding" category.[61]

There may be a lesson in this for economic anthropology. Just as the defining quality of bitter money is not to be found in any single attribute of the commodities that produce it, but only in several combined, perhaps the deeper explanation of bitter money – the real cause – is not to be understood with any one theoretical approach. Perhaps the causes are multiple (as causes, alas, so often are); and perhaps, moreover, they cannot be grasped within a single paradigm, like "diffusion," "function," or "cognitive structure." To understand a phenomenon like bitter money may require thinking in several ways at once.

Why Bitter Money?

The task of explaining why a complex of beliefs and perceptions like the one described should exist at all can be undertaken in several ways. To begin with an approach that may seem outmoded, a diffusionist would ask first where else it all came from, and look to influences from outside the Luo country that might have been transmitted through travel, trade, and other contact. An obvious possibility is religious scripture. Certainly distinctions between good and evil wealth are widely found in Judeo-Christian sacred writings, and numerous passages of the Bible warn against ill-gotten gain. Old Testament's Book of Proverbs, in particular, contains admonitions like "Wealth gotten by vanity [in the New English version, "quickly"] shall be diminished: but he that gathereth buy labour shall increase" (10:16), or

"So are the ways of those that are greedy of gain, which taketh away the life of the owners thereof" (1:19). In the New Testament are found exhortations against being "greedy of filthy lucre" (1 Tim. 3:3). Judas Iscariot's betrayal or "sale" of Christ earns him thirty pieces of silver, which become, in some versions, an essential part of his violent end: "Now this man purchased a field with the reward of iniquity; and falling headlong, he burst asunder in the midst, and all his bowels gushed out" (Acts 1:18). The list could be extended. But just why Luo would have adopted beliefs about spiritual or divine retribution for unethical exchange, once exposed to these, would still need explaining, and another theoretical approach would be necessary.

A functionalist might offer several kinds of explanations at once. For psychological function, such a system of beliefs and perceptions may help explain or control otherwise inexplicable misfortune, and to reduce anxieties. For social function, the emphasis on ancestors would seem to bolster the power and legitimacy of elders – and the emphasis on divinity, the social control exercised by church leaders. For economic functions, beliefs in bitter money might may serve to regulate transactions, restricting land alienation and the concentration of wealth into fewer hands; and to help spread wealth too in purification rituals. The concept of shared fate, whereby not just infractors but their kin are expected to suffer as well, must encourage all to keep their kinmen's behavior in check. With functionalist approaches like these one cannot, however, readily take account of historical change, or show how society decides what it

---

that the "achievement" was not consummated until after 1950 (1975:353). "Polythetic" comes from the Greek *poly*, many; *thetos*, arrangement; the contrasting term is "monothetic." The use of the concepts in this work does not necessarily imply endorsement of Needham's broader views on the relation of anthropology to science, as they appear in sections IV and V of his article.

[61] Some other Luo conceptual categories "slide" in simpler ways. For instance, term *jokakwaro*, which literally means "descendents of one grandfather," can telescope to mean a patrilineage several or even many generations deep. (Early European land adjudication officers in the area had trouble understanding this one; they sought to identify groups of a single size as "the *jokakwaro*".) The elements comprising bitter money differ not in scale, but in kind.

really "wants" and makes sure its members conform to expectations. It is easy to mistake effects for causes, and one risks descending into tautology in trying too hard to portray these as circularly self-reinforcing.

A political–economic approach emphasizing domination and ideological resistance would add some advantages that neither classic diffusionist nor functionalist approaches offer. Kenya's history of land alienation to colonial settlers, and Luoland's own history with foreign mining firms and lately tobacco firms, have caused some deep and lasting public resentments. Popular ideological resistance to a land market that threatens ultimate expropriation, or to a big new multinational cash crop like tobacco, would not be hard to explain this way. A people who may once have thought themselves central have become involved in a world where the real centers of wealth, power, and influence seem to lie far away and out of reach.

But there are snags with this kind of explanation too, as a simple comparison between two crops, sugarcane and tobacco, can make clear. Through the internationally financed establishment of a sugar factory at Awendo in the 1970s, with a nucleus plantation and a wider catchment are of "outgrowing" or contract farming, both human lives and the land have been dramatically transformed, and not just for the better. Sugarcane has involved just as much risk for high gains, just as much callous corporate subjugation of farmers' labor and workers' lives, and just as reckless an alteration of the landscape as tobacco has. And yet sugarcane earnings have not, in my experience, been classed as bitter money, as tobacco money has. Moreover, where agrarian change is concerned, dominators and resistors are seldom discrete groups in the Luo country any more than elsewhere in contemporary rural Africa.

Anomaly, Liminality, and Spheres of Exchange

Certainly not all the explanations for bitter money will be found in social structures and political–economic processes. Other explanations might be found in cognitive structures, and in the symbolic meanings of the commodities themselves and the forms of exchange they have come to represent. One way of analyzing beliefs in bitter money is to conceive of the Luo economy as divided into "spheres of exchange" (cf. Barth 1967; Bohannan 1955, 1959), one for permanent lineage property and one for other property. Writing on Lesotho, Ferguson (1985) has suggested, like others before him elsewhere in Africa, that similar spheres are separated by a one-way barrier: cash is convertible to cattle, but not vice versa. In these terms, the Luo would appear to have a two-way barrier between their "spheres." Like Sotho men, Luo men try to prevent conversions of cattle or land into cash or other forms in which women gain better claims over them: this state is what Ferguson has called a "domain of contestation." At the same time, however, the beliefs about bitter money ostensibly prohibit Luo men from using just any money to buy cattle or land for their patrilineages. But today, at least, the barrier is semipermeable: land or livestock may be rented out for money, and money can be ritually purified for buying land or livestock.

Part of what separates money and other commodities would seem to be a distinction between what is subjectively appreciated and socially embedded, and what is counted and socially unattached. Like many other Africans south of the Sahara, Luo consider counting people or livestock an antisocial act, a breach of etiquette. It dries out flesh and blood to a talliable quantum. Like enumerating people, selling commodities associated with relatives and ancestors seems to Luo an unnatural reduction.

Bitter money is an unusual medium of exchange. It falls between ordinary categories, and it is perhaps this that makes it dangerous (Douglas 1966). A sale that converts the fixed and inalienable (the ancestral graves and the land) into the quintessentially movable commodity, money, has breached a fundamental distinction. So has a transaction that reduces quality to quantity, or a personal relationship to an impersonal one.

Commodities that yield bitterness are ones that breach or transcend ordinary categories themselves. Tobacco is grown on the spot where a homestead was, but is no longer. This is not the domestic sphere but not the wilderness either. Tobacco smoke to the Luo is neither air nor water, but something of both. The rooster crows between day and night, dividing sleep from waking time; to the Luo it also stands at the frontier of civilization and wilderness. Bitter money is held in the hands of the living, but watched over by spirits of the dead: it comes from involving the sacred in commerce that is profane. It mediates what Luo think of as their old, group-based redistributive modes of livelihood, and what they see as the new, individualistic mode of the market. Cash is a paradoxical joiner:

> Money . . . divides into two alternate ways — spiritual and worldly . . . in money are both the inherent tendency to split into spirit and matter and the possibility to hold them together. [Hillman 1982:34, 38]

More than just any money, bitter money seems to reinforce such divisions while bridging them.

Bitter money and the surrounding complex of beliefs suggest a fascination with the cyclical dimensions of life, and with contradictions they contain. The land is a "magician" because it both feeds us and devours us. Luo cite this as a reason why humans must not sell land; land is something with powers beyond human understanding or control. And there is a sense of respect and justice toward the land. The bride cannot be procured by exchanging away lineage land, because on coming into the lineage she would have to eat the products of the same land. Tobacco, like land, involves mystical cycles of its own: the bride procured in fire and smoke will perish in fire and smoke. The smoker who sees an ancestor is likely to see him or her smoking too. Bitter money of any kind, if ritually purified, will keep returning to its owner's homestead . . . not like a bad penny, for the Luo, but like a good one.

The Europeans whose religions have been spliced together with indigenous beliefs to produce today's bitter money beliefs may themselves be seen an anomalous, enigmatic creatures. While they appear as missionaries preaching brotherly love and sharing, many of them live in isolated fenced-off mission compounds. While they instruct about equality, they dress and eat unlike peasant farmers, keep fancy vehicles these local people cannot afford, and educate just a few privileged local sons for lucrative salaried futures. The disjunctions between white ideals and white behavior, and between the European and African cultures generally, are harsh realities that bitter money beliefs would seem both to express and to try to control.

But these interpretations can be pushed too far, and the problem is that we seldom know when we have done so. Spheres of exchange, liminality, and the cosmic paradoxes may sometimes exist only in discourse or interpretation. Every African society doubtless has some individuals who privately suppose they can transfer any commodity in any direction they want, who are quite happy to live with some ambiguity, and who are not particularly puzzled by positive or negative feedback loops. Some may suppose their *own* society's cultural emphasis on ancestors, lineage, and livestock controlled by elders to be something like "false consciousness" or mystification, continually maintained by local-born male elders, even while they play along with it in practice. Private ideology tempers and qualifies public ideology, and vice versa; and these can contradict each other. Cognitive categories may not be static: Luo or any other humans may modify them or formulate new ones as the commodities in their lives take on new meanings, and this very fluidity defies verification. Finally, spheres of exchange or liminal mediators sometimes appear as figments of the anthropological imagination, one inclined to build on received theory as well as on recorded fact, and to create order on paper where order is hard to find *in situ*. All cognitive interpretation is debatable; interpretation itself is a "domain of contestation." . . .

There are several ways, then, to begin to explain why Luo perceive bitter money, and they lead to different kinds of answers. Diffusionism asks from whom the idea or belief came. Functionalism asks what good it does for the people who hold it. Political economy asks whose interests it serves, how it gets manipulated for wealth or power, and to whose detriment. The structural analysis of symbols asks how the parts fit together, and why they were chosen in the first place. Each of these approaches yields a part of an understanding that will always be incomplete. And in the end, none of these schools of thought can truly debunk another, because no two ask "why" the same way.

A Recurring Theme

The motley assortment of commodities and forms of exchange yielding bitter money suggests that no simple explanation for the belief will suffice. But there is a recurring theme. Luo perceive a problem in the rise of possessive individualism. The theme emerges regularly, both in informants' discussions of their beliefs and their meanings (the "emic," or insiders' perspectives) and in the comparative analysis of the symbols and behavior involved (the "etic," or outsiders' perspectives). Bitter money is a fluid category. The commodities to which it refers probably vary from one time and place to another, and the concept may thus provide a window on what economic changes the members of the society

consider harmful or dangerous. Tracking the changes through time and space is a task for further research. The Luo country in the early 1980s was undergoing rapid social and economic change, and the bitter money concept pointed to specific perceived threats to family and community. There are no rules, often, until they are broken; and taboos on purchases and sales reflect real exchanges that the Luo consider in one sense or another as betrayals.

It is not all individualism that society reacts against with these cultural sanctions. Rather, it is self-indulgence in unaccustomed or newly politicized contexts: in forms of property in which group membership has entitled other individuals to overlapping claims in the past. It is the individual usurpation of benefits, and symbols, for which others have lived and worked. Whom transgressors are betraying depends on the circumstances, and on interpretation. It can be family or lineage, or perhaps even neighborhood or ethnic group. It can be ancestors, a debt to whom one can repay only by handing on an inheritance to the future. In the abstract, the principle of betrayal is the same; at this level, bitter money is a monothetic class. In the 20th century the Luo have tasted money and private property as never before, and refused to swallow these ideas whole. . . .

The Luo response to money, the market, and private property has been ambivalent and complex. The Luo have sold land and its most symbolically potent products for many decades, and they are doing so now on an unprecedented scale. But they are doing so with anxiety. The sales are sparking debate, challenging family unity, and further separating the real from the ideal in Luo behavior. For these rural Africans, in a sense, the real "black market" seems to be a white market. Regardless of one's theoretical or political persuasion, it is hard not to conclude that bitter money represents a reaction against new strains of possessive individualism in this rather egalitarian society, as devil's money represents in some Latin American contexts. The lineage-based conception of bitter money, however, is specifically African. The Luo emphasis on ancestors and bridewealth suggest that Luo have been trying to adjust to new experiences with older and more familiar local concepts. Bitter money contains a plea for personalized relations, and for the restitution of some family and community controls over vital resources. There is more to it than just an economic or political issue: there is also a motion for more autonomy in local culture. A sale of a bitter commodity is not a simple sale. It is a multifaceted transaction involving the autochthonous and the alien, the male and the female, the living and the dead.

Bitter money is a quintessentially anthropological phenomenon, in a traditional sense of the discipline: it is about economics, politics, law, kinship, the life cycle, and religion and ritual all at once. The anthropology to explain such a thing as this must be correspondingly multifaceted. It must not only consider symbolic polyvalence – the variety of things that the beliefs are consciously or unconsciously "about" – but it must also draw eclectically from diverse theoretical orientations in social science, accept multiple causes, and remain open to interpretations that seem on the surface to conflict.

References

Abe, Toshiharu
1978 *A Preliminary Report on Jachien among the Luo of South Nyanza*. Institute of African Studies, University of Nairobi, discussion paper no. 92.

Acland, J. D.
1980[1971] *East African Crops*. Hong Kong: Longman.

Appadurai, Arjun, ed.
1986 *The Social Life of Things: Commodities in Cultural Perspective*. Cambridge: Cambridge University Press.

Barrett, David B., George K. Mambo, Janice McLaughlin, and Malcolm J. McVeigh, eds.
1973 *Kenya Churches Handbook*. Kisumu, Kenya: Evangel Publishing House.

Barth, Fredrik
1967 Economic Spheres in Darfur. *In Themes in Economic Anthropology*. Raymond Firth, ed. Pp. 149–189. London: Tavistock.

Beattie, John H. M.
1966 Ritual and Social Change. *Man* (NS) 1:60–74.
1971 *The Nyoro State*. Oxford: Oxford University Press.

Beckner, Morton
1959 *The Biological Way of Thought*. New York: Columbia University Press.

Bohannan, Paul
1955 Some Principles of Exchange and Investment among the Tiv. *American Anthropologist* 57:60–70.

1959 The Impact of Money on an African Subsistence Economy. *Journal of Economic History* 19(4):491–503. [Reprinted in *Tribal and Peasant Economies*. George Dalton, ed. New York: Natural History Press]

Butterman, Judith
1979 Luo Social Formations in Change: Kanyamkago and Karachuonyo, c. 1800–1945. Ph.D. dissertation, Syracuse University.

Crazzolara, J. P.
1950 *The Lwoo, Part I*. Verona: Museum Combonianum.

Douglas, Mary
1966 *Purity and Danger*. New York: Praeger.

Evans-Pritchard, Edward E.
1956 *Nuer Religion*. London: Oxford University Press.
1963 The Divine Kinship of the Shilluk of the Nilotic Sudan. *In Essays in Social Anthropology*. Edward Evans-Pritchard ed. Pp 66–86. New York: Free Press.
1965[1949] Luo Tribes and Clans. *In The Position of Women in Society and Other Essays*. E. Evans–Pritchard, ed. Pp. 228–244. London: Faber and Faber.

Fearn, Hugh
1961 *An African Economy: A Study of the Economic Development of the Nyanza Province of Kenya, 1903–1953*. London: Oxford University Press.

Ferguson, James
1985 The Bovine Mystique. *Man* (NS) 20:647–674.
Field, M. J.
1940 *The Social Organization of the Ga People.* London: Crown Agents for the Colonies.
van Gennep, Arnold
1960[1909] *The Rites of Passage.* Monika B. Vizedom and Gabrielle A. Caffee, trans. Chicago: University of Chicago Press.
Goldenberg, David A.
1982 *We Are All Brothers: The Suppression of Consciousness of Socio Economic Differentiation in a Kenya Luo Lineage.* Ph.D. dissertation, Brown University. Ann Arbor: University Microfilms International.
Gudeman, Stephen
1986 *Economics as Culture: Models and Metaphors of Livelihood.* London: Routledge & Kegan Paul.
Hay, Margaret Jean
1972 *Economic Change in Luoland: Kowe, 1890–1945.* Ph.D. dissertation. University of Wisconsin. Ann Arbor: University Microfilms International.
1982 Women as Owners, Occupants, and Managers or Property in Colonial Western Kenya. *In African Women and the Law: Historical Perspectives.* Margaret Jean and Marcia Wright, eds. Pp. 110–123. Boston: African Studies Center, Boston University.
de Heusch, Luc
1985 *Sacrifice in Africa.* Bloomington: Indiana University Press.
Hillman, James
1982 A Contribution to *Soul and Money. In Soul and Money.* Russell A. Lockhart, James Hillman, Arwind Vasavada, John Weir Perry, Joel Covitz, and Adolf Guggenbuehl-Craig. Pp. 31–43. Dallas: Spring Publications.
Johnson, Steven Lee
1980 *Production, Exchange, and Economic Development among the Luo-Abasuba of Southwestern Kenya.* Ph.D. dissertation, Indiana University. Ann Arbor: University Microfilms International.
Lienhardt, Godfrey
1961 *Divinity and Experience: The Religion of the Dinka.* Oxford: Oxford University Press.
Locke, John
1960[1689] *Two Treatises of Government.* Peter

Laslett, ed. Cambridge: Cambridge University Press.
Long, Norman
1968 *Social Change and the Individual.* Manchester: Manchester University Press.
MacPherson, C. B.
1962 *The Political Theory of Possessive Individualism.* London: Oxford University Press.
Mauss, Marcel
1967[1925] *The Gift.* Ian Cunnison, trans. New York: Norton.
Meek, Charles Kingsley
1946 *Land Law and Custom in the Colonies.* London: Oxford University Press.
Nash, June
1979 *We Eat the Mines.* New York: Columbia University Press.
Neale, Walter C.
1976 *Monies in Societies.* New York: Chandler and Sharp.
Needham, Rodney
1975 Polythetic Classification. *Man* (NS) 10:349–367.
Northcote, G.A.S.
1907 The Nilotic Kavirondo. *Journal of the Royal Anthropological Institute* 38:58–66.
Ocholla-Ayayo, A. B. C.
1976 *Traditional Ideology and Ethics among the Southern Luo.* Uppsala: Scandinavian Institute of African Studies.
Ogot, Bethwell A.
1967 *People of East Africa: History of the Southern Luo. Vol. I: Migration and Settlement 1500–1900.* Nairobi: East African Publishing House.
Pala, Achola Okeyo
1977 Changes in Economy and Ideology: A Study of the Juluo of Kenya (with Special Reference to Women). Ph.D. dissertation, Harvard University.
1980 Daughters of the Lakes and Rivers: Colonization and the Land Rights of Luo Women in Kenya. *In Women and Colonization: Anthropological Perspectives.* Mona Etienne and Eleanor Leacock, eds. Pp. 186–213. New York: Praeger.
Parkin, David J.
1972 *Palms, Wine and Witnesses.* San Francisco: Chandler.
1978 *The Cultural Definition of Political Response:*

Lineal Destiny among the Luo. New York: Academic Press.

1980 Kind Bridewealth and Hard Cash. *In The Meaning of Marriage Payments.* John Comaroff, ed. Pp. 197–220. New York: Academic Press.

Richards, Audrey I.

1939 *Land, Labour and Diet in Northern Rhodesia.* London: Oxford University Press.

1940 The Bemba Tribe of North-Eastern Rhodesia. *In African Political Systems.* Meyer Fortes and Edward Evans-Pritchard, eds. Pp. 83–120. London: Oxford University Press, for International African Institute.

Robertson, A. F.

1984 *People and the State: An Anthropology of Planned Development.* Cambridge: Cambridge University Press.

1987 *The Dynamics of Productive Relationships: African Share Contracts in Comparative Perspective.* Cambridge: Cambridge University Press.

Schweinfurth, George

1878[1873] *The Heart of Africa.* Vol. I. London: Sampson, Low.

Shanklin, Eugenia

1985 Sustenance and Symbol: Anthropological Studies of Domesticated Animals. *Annual Review of Anthropology* 14:375–403.

Shipton, Parker

1984a Lineage and Locality as Antithetical Principles in East African Systems of Land Tenure. *Ethnology* 23(2):117–132.

1984b Strips and Patches: A Demographic Dimension in Some African Landholding and Political Systems. *Man* (NS) 19:613–634.

1985 *Land, Credit, and Crop Transitions in Kenya: The Luo Response to Directed Development in Nyanza Province.* Ph.D. dissertation, Cambridge University. Ann Arbor: University Microfilms International.

Simmel, Georg

1978[1907] *The Philosophy of Money.* Tom

Bottomore and David Frisby, trans. Boston: Routledge & Kegan Paul.

Southall, Aidan

1952 Lineage Formation among the Luo. *International African Institute Memorandum* 26. Pp 1–43. London: Oxford University Press.

Taussig, Michael

1980 *The Devil and Commodity Fetishism in South America.* Chapel Hill: University of North Carolina Press.

Turner, Victor

1969 *The Ritual Process: Structure and Anti-Structure.* Chicago: Aldine.

Waligorski, Andrzej

1970 Les Marchés des Luo vers 1946–1948. *Africana Bulletin* (Warsaw) 11:9–24.

Weber, Max

1947[1904] *The Theory of Social and Economic Organization.* A. M. Henderson and Talcott Parsons, trans. New York: Oxford University Press.

1958[1904] *The Protestant Ethic and the Spirit of Capitalism.* Talcott Parsons, trans. New York: Scribner's.

Whisson, Michael G.

1962a *The Will of God and the Wiles of Men: An Examination of the Beliefs Concerning the Supernatural Held by the Luo with Particular Reference to Their Functions in the Field of Social Control.* East African Institute of Social Research Conference Papers, Makerere University College, Kampala.

1962b *The Journeys of the JoRamogi.* East African Institute of Social Research Conference Papers. Makerere University College, Kampala.

1964 *Change and Challenge: A Study of the Social and Economic Changes among the Kenya Luo.* Nairobi: Christian Council of Kenya.

Wipper, Audrey

1977 *Rural Rebels: A Study of Two Protest Movements in Kenya.* London: Oxford University Press.

11

THE CATTLE OF MONEY AND THE CATTLE OF GIRLS AMONG THE NUER, 1930–83

SHARON HUTCHINSON

Money's uniqueness, Simmel suggests, lies in its ability to extend and diversify human interdependence while excluding everything personal and specific (1978[1900]:297–303). Money distances self from other and self from object, generating within the individual dissident feelings of self-sufficiency and alienation, powerlessness and personal freedom (Simmel 1978[1900]:307–311):

> In as much as interests are focused on money and to the extent that possessions consist of money, the individual will develop the tendency and feeling of independent importance in relation to the social whole. He will relate to the social whole as one power confronting another, since he is free to take up business relations and co-operation wherever he likes. [Simmel 1978[1900]:343]

The "close relationship . . . between a money economy, individualization, and enlargement of the circle of social relationships" enables the individual to buy himself not only out of bonds with specific others but also, Simmel notes, out of those bonds rooted in his possessions (1978[1900]:347, 403ff.). As "the embodiment of the relativity of existence," money drives a wedge between "possessing" and "being": "through money,

man is no longer enslaved in things" (Simmel 1978[1900]:409, 307, 404).

While Simmel welcomes elimination of the personal element of exchange as the gateway to "human freedom" (1978[1900]:297–303), he is acutely aware, nonetheless, of the potential instability, disorientation, and despair generated by money's perpetual wrenching of the personal values from things. The development of a money economy, he notes, encourages avarice and other socially detrimental forms of possessive individualism (Simmel 1978[1900]:247). Moreover, as money's empty and indifferent character wears away the "direction-giving significance of things," individuals strive, Simmel observes, to reinvest their possessions with "a new importance, a deeper meaning, a value of their own":

> If modern man is free – free because he can sell everything, and free because he can buy everything – then he now seeks (often in problematical vacillations) in the objects themselves that vigor, stability and inner unity which he has lost because of the changed money-conditioned relationship that he has with them. (Simmel 1978[1900]:404)

For Marx, in contrast, money is a "privileged commodity" to the extent that the congelations of human labor embodied in all other commodities come to express their values in it (1967[1867]:93). The development of "a 'money-form' of commodity exchange" is thus critical, he argues, for the recognition of human labor and productive powers as an abstract totality and, concomitantly, for the creation of a universal labor market (1967[1867]:35–84). Yet in making possible the sale of human labor as a general commodity, "a 'money-form' of commodity exchange" also facilitates relations of exploitation and alienation within the production process by effectively disassociating the value of concrete labor from the value of the products it can produce (Marx 1967[1867]:167ff., 195–198). The monetization of production relations, in other words, tends to intensify the "fetishism" inherent in simpler forms of commodity exchange by further obscuring the subjective relatization of the contribution that the producer makes to the product. For it is "just this ultimate money-form of the world of commodities," Marx states, "that actually conceals, instead of disclosing, the social character of private labor, and the social relations between individual producers" (1967[1867]:76). In brief, money plays privileged symbolic as well as material roles in the transformation of "direct social relations between individuals at work" into "material relations between persons and social relations between things," a transformation that lies at the heart of Marx's analysis of capitalism (Marx 1967[1867]:73).

In this article, I draw on the theoretical perspectives of Marx and Simmel in an effort to understand how a particular cattle-raising people in Africa, the Nuer of southern Sudan, have creatively incorporated "a 'money-form' of commodity exchange" into their culture and social life over the last half century. Following Marx, I highlight social and economic processes connected with the spread of colonialism and of capitalist relations of production underlying the gradual empowerment of money in Nuer eyes. Yet I also aspire to a more phenomenological understanding – à la Simmel – of money's enigmatic qualities as variously perceived, experienced, and evaluated by Nuer. How have these people been grappling with the allegedly "liberating" and "alienating" potentials of a rapidly expanding regional money economy?

In exploring these issues, I will concentrate on how Nuer have gradually interdefined cattle and money so as to create a unique system of wealth categories. Significantly, this system appears to exceed, both in complexity and in inner dynamism, anything previously reported in the burgeoning literature on the "commoditization" of human/cattle relations in other parts of Africa (see, for example, Comaroff and Comaroff 1990; Ferguson 1985; Murray 1981; Parkin 1980; Sansom 1976; Shipton 1989). Unlike the "one-" and "two-way barrier" systems recorded among the Basotho (Ferguson 1985) and the Luo (Shipton 1989) respectively, this system of wealth categories does not pivot on a simple opposition between "cattle" and "cash". Nor may it be characterized as an unambiguous attempt to dam the corrosive flow of cash, as appears to be the case among the southern Tswana (Comaroff and Comaroff 1990:212). Rather, Nuer attitudes toward money appear far more ambivalent and contextually differentiated. Although individuals may "resist" equating money with cattle in some contexts, they actively seek out and use money in others as a means of tempering instabilities and inequalities within the cattle economy itself. In developing these points here, I try to show how the various wealth categories collectively devised by Nuer facilitate movements of money and cattle between "market" and "nonmarket" spheres of exchange at the same time as they affirm the existence of an axiological boundary between these spheres. I also reflect more generally on how the increasing use of money by Nuer has contributed over the last half century to a profound reevaluation of the place of cattle in their lives. All in all, it is hoped that this article will enrich our appreciation of the myriad ways in which market and non-market forms of consciousness and sociality are empirically entwined in the world today.

On the Oneness of Cattle and People: 1930

According to Evans-Pritchard (1940, 1951, 1956), the Nuer of the early 1930s were almost totally absorbed in the care, exchange, and sacrifice of their beloved cattle. Few Nuer at that time understood the concept of currency; fewer still understood the impersonal principles of market exchange; and literally no one parted willingly with a cow for money. Wage-labor opportunities were universally spurned as being tantamount to slavery. Rather, people at that time were bound to their herds in an intimate symbiosis of survival (Evans-Pritchard 1940: 16–50). Mutual "parasites" is how Evans-Pritchard characterized them (1940:36). Whereas cattle depended on human beings for protection and care, people depended on cattle as insurance against ecological hazards and as vital sources of milk, meat, leather, and dung. Yet cattle were value far beyond their material contributions to human survival: cattle were the principal means by which Nuer created and affirmed enduring bonds among themselves as well as between themselves and divinity. In sacrificial and exchange contexts, cattle were considered direct extensions of the human persona. Their vitality and fertility were continuously being equated with, and opposed to, those of human beings. This human/cattle equation was perhaps most obvious in moments of bloodwealth and bridewealth exchange. However, it permeated myriad other contexts, saturating, as it were, the whole of Nuer social life at that time.

What is perhaps less evident from Evans-Pritchard's descriptions is that something was definitely gained by Nuer communities as a whole through the cultural assertion of a fundamental identity between cattle and people. Because cattle and people were in some sense "one," individuals were able to transcend some of the profoundest of human frailties and thereby achieve a greater sense of mastery over their world: death became surmountable, infertility reversible, and illness something that could be actively defined and cured. This equation gave "life," as it were, a second chance. Were a man to die without heirs, his relatives were able – indeed obliged – to collect cattle and marry a "ghost wife" to bear children for him. Likewise, were a woman to prove infertile, she was "free" to become a social man, gather cattle, and marry a wife to produce children for her. And were it not for rites of cattle sacrifice, people would have stood condemned at that time to a passive forebearance of severe illness, environmental crises, and countless other difficulties. But because human and bovine vitality were identified in such contexts, all these experiences of vulnerability and hardship could be lifted to a collective plane where they could be given form and meaning and actively coped with. Lastly, the ever-present possibility of translating human values into cattle values enhanced people's abilities to achieve lasting periods of peace among themselves. Although cattle were frequent subjects of dispute among kinsmen as well as non-kinsmen, there is a well-known saying that runs, "*Thilɛ duer mi baal yaŋ*" ("No [human] error exceeds the cow"). Cattle, in other words, were – and to a large extent continue to be – the conflict resolvers par excellence.

It was thus the ideological assertion of a fundamental "oneness" between cattle and people that enabled people to extend the potency of human action in tempering the perplexing vicissitudes and vulnerabilities of life. In a society where procreation, physical well-being, and communal peace were – and continue to be – among the highest cultural values, these "extensions" or "augmentations of life" should not be underestimated. To ignore them or to gloss over them by thinking of cattle exchange and sacrifice solely in terms of "reciprocity," "compensation," and "restitution" would be to reduce, I think, the creative potency of Nuer culture as a whole at that time.*

The Creation of Cattle and Labor Markets in Nuerland: 1930–83

The experience of British colonial conquest (1898–1930), swiftly followed in some regions by that of famine, made the early 1930s deeply disillusioning years for many Nuer. Effectively barred from replenishing their stock through raiding, men stood idle as successive waves of rinderpest decimated their herds (see Johnson 1980:469). For the conquering Anglo-Egyptian regime, in contrast, this was a period of optimism and of rapid political and economic advances. The radical administrative measures imposed as part of the "Nuer settlement" of 1929–30, which required among other things separation of the (Lou and Gawaar) Nuer from their Dinka neighbors, appeared to herald a new era of interethnic peace. Similarly, the successful elimination or capture of all major Nuer prophets seemed to clear the way for the birth of a new breed of tractable government chiefs (Johnson 1979, 1980:403–467). Such optimism, though shortlived in most instances, also sparked off scores of government work projects – carried out with conscripted Nuer labor – which included the construction of roads, steamer stations, administrative centers, and the like (END 66.A.2, 22 February 1934, "Assistant District Commissioner to Governor"). Conditions formerly hindering the expansion of northern trade into the region also ended abruptly (cf. Evans-Pritchard 1940:87–88). Improvements in public security and transport greatly facilitated the penetration of seasonal merchants, while cattle epidemics and food shortages ensured the rapid development of a hide export/grain import trade. . . .

Although seasonal markets and local British administrative officials were frequently at odds, these two groups nevertheless shared a common economic objective: the creation and maintenance of a profitable export trade in Nuer cattle. The greatest difficulty they faced in this regard was to advise adequate ways to tempt, force, cajole, or otherwise pressure Nuer into handing over their largest and fattest oxen for sale to meat markets in the north (WND 64 B.1., 25 March 1941, "J. Wilson, Assistant District Commissioner, to Governor").[1]

By 1933, seasonal Arab merchants had taken the lead by establishing two modes of cattle extraction, both of them circuitous. The first, a sort of cow/ox conversion racket, took advantage of interethnic cycles of trade then developing between the western Nuer and their Twic Dinka and Baggara Arab neighbors:

> The Nuer . . . have no desire to sell bulls [oxen] for money but they will exchange them for cow calves. [Baggara] Arabs [bordering the Leek and Bul Nuer in the west] and Twij Dinka are willing to sell cow calves. Thus . . . the merchants buy cow calves for money from the former and exchange them to the Nuer and [other] Dinka for big bulls. [WND 64 B.1., c. 1933, "Assistant District Commissioner to Governor"][2]

---

* Editor's Note.

On the ways in which the equation between people and cattle differentially affected men and women, see Sharon Hutchinson. 1996. *Nuer Dilemmas: Coping with Money, War and the State*. Berkeley and Los Angeles: University of California Press.

[1] Since steamer charges for the northern transport of oxen were calculated on a per capita rather than a per pound basis, export merchants sought to obtain the largest, fattest oxen possible.

[2] The willingness of the Twic Dinka to sell heifers at that time was due to the ease with which they could acquire them from the Baggara in exchange for female goats and sheep.

In eastern Nuerland, where neighboring ethnic groups were both more distant and more cattle-poor than in the west, merchants relied instead on seasonal fluctuations in local grain supplies to generate a cattle export trade:

> The agents go out to various trading posts in September and October [at harvest time] and buy grain and hides in exchange for trade goods [such as fishing hooks, beads, spears, and cloth] mostly though occasionally money is used. A second series of posts along the rivers catch the more distant tribes on their way to the dry weather camp. From February to April trade is practically at a standstill but then the reverse flow begins and grain is sold back to the improvident at enhanced prices for animals. Generally speaking, the grain bought from the Nuer is sold for Province requirements, i.e. police, Army, merkaz [town] requirements, and the grain resold to the natives is imported. This naturally depends largely upon prices but few merchants can afford to keep their capital locked up. The turnover is small but the profits are large as the grain and hides, etc., are bought cheap for trade goods acquired at trade prices and imported grain

is sold at a profit for animals valued cheaply. [SAD 212/13/3, 1930 "Eastern Nuerland, Province Handbook"]

Add to these extractive strategies the confiscation of cattle in annual tribute collections and in court fines and it's not surprising that the oxen export trade grew rapidly during the 1930s and 1940s.

But individual Nuer were still neither buying nor selling their cattle with money. The mutual convertibility of these two media had simply not been established for them. This situation continued, moreover, despite post-1935 administrative efforts to shift the basis of tribute collection in eastern Nuerland from cattle to cash (officials discovered early on that this "changeover . . . nearly always ends in more cash for Government" [UN 1/45/332, 1939, "E. G. Coryton, Handing Over Notes"][3] as well as to provide conscripted Nuer labor with "a small pecuniary reward."[4] Barter continued to dominate the private sector, and government wages remained far too low to permit a ready conversion of coins into cattle.[5] The situation changed dramatically, however,

---

[3] Unlike itinerant merchants, who stood to gain from a continued barter economy, the colonial administration sought the rapid "monetization" of the regional economy.

[4] "A note in the Luo Nuer District Annual Report of 1953–55 (WND 57 A. 3) reveals how long it took for cash to displace cattle in the collection of tribute among the Luo and other eastern Nuer groups: "For the first time [1954] cattle were spared being dragged off for sale by Government, a thing which they never escaped in previous years." Nuer west of the Bahr al-Jabal, in contrast, were never formally taxed in cattle. Hoping to avoid the bitterness generated by earlier tribute raiding campaigns among the eastern Nuer, the officer commissioned with opening up western Nuerland to British administration, Captain V. H. Ferguson, introduced instead compulsory cotton cultivation in 1925. Western Nuer adult males experienced their first annual tax of five piasters four years later (SAD 212/14/9, 1930, "Western Nuerland, Province Handbook"). The initial success of this cotton-for-tribute campaign was short-lived, however, owing to widespread corruption among the (primarily Dinka) cotton cultivation overseers appointed by the local administration. The overseers were in the habit of arbitrarily imposing "cattle fines" on individual Nuer who failed to produce the required cotton. Unable to curb these abuses, the administration revoked compulsory cotton cultivation in western Nuerland in 1934. However, many western Nuer continued to produce significant quantities of cotton until World War II.

[5] Throughout the famine era of the early 1930s, thousands of Nuer were conscripted to clear, bank, and bridge roads, to raise government "rest houses," and to cut and stack wood fuel for government steamers. In principle, these people were paid for their efforts at the rate of one or two piasters per day plus grain rations. In practice, however, few coins changed hands. As one British officer explained:

> Owing to the people's ignorance which renders them as easy prey for the average Northern accountant, I have been unable to devise any workable system whereby some 10,000 men are given a few pt. [piasters] each, for the purpose of paying it in as tribute after various pieces of different colored paper have been inscribed by a foreigner in an unknown language. So in practice no money changes hands, and each

following the introduction during the late 1940s of government-sponsored cattle auctions for the disposal of livestock acquired through court fines. By this time, government chiefs' courts were well established throughout Nuerland and were generating increasingly vital administrative revenues.[6] More important for our purposes, government fines' cattle, unlike tribute oxen, often included a large proportion of heifers.[7] Thus, for the first time Nuer men were able to purchase what they desired most: young, fertile heifers to increase their herds. And it was this opportunity that motivated them to enter the cattle market as buyers – and as money-paying ones at that. Because these auctions were carried out strictly on a cash basis, individuals wishing to participate were normally forced to sell an ox to a private merchant before the auction in order to have the requisite cash.[8] Hence from the government's perspective, these auctions had the added benefit of stimulating the export trade in Nuer oxen. Eventually, the administration established dry-season public auctions (to which anyone could bring cattle) in various district centers of Nuerland, first on a weekly and later on a daily basis. . . .

Nevertheless, the two basic extractive strategies established by itinerant merchants during the 1930s had really changed very little. Famine continued to fuel the grain import/cattle export trade, though coinage had replaced barter to some extent. The cow/ox conversion racket, in contrast, had been effectively captured by the government, with many local export merchants benefiting from this "takeover" as well. The net result was that individual Nuer were now replenishing their herds at one another's expense rather than at the expense of outlying neighbors. As far as Nuer were concerned, money remained in such contexts little more than a means of swapping cattle with the government. In other words, cattle only became money in order to become cattle again: C→M→C.

. . . By 1959, these schemes required an estimated 15,000 seasonal pickers in addition to permanent tenant labor (UNPAR, 1959–60). And thus each year the government would relay increasingly urgent appeals for additional "Nilotic" labor to migrate to these sites through local Dinka, Shilluk, Nuer, Atuot, and Anuak chiefs. Significantly, Nuer men were consistently singled out by scheme owners and by government administrators alike as the most desirable "backwater" recruits, for reasons made clear in the following quotation:

> Nuers proved the best of the lot. They usually arrived in high spirits and spent the hours proceeding to their station, dancing

sub-shen [*cien*] is required to do a definite piece of work every year under the supervision of its chiefs. [SAD 212/14/8, 1930, "Revenue, Zeraf Valley, Province Handbook"]

As the years passed and the famine subsided, "normal road maintenance," portage, and other government tasks were increasingly defined as the "normal duty of our tribesmen," and the pretense of a "small pecuniary reward" was dropped (UN 1/45/331, 1934, "Upper-Nile Province Roads"). Yet even when monetary payments were made, at the rate of one piaster a day – standard throughout much of the 1930s – a man would have needed the equivalent of 150 days of wages in order to purchase a small heifer in the marketplace. Consequently, the small amounts of money that entered Nuer hands were normally invested in grain or in cloth for mosquito netting.

[6] Government cattle fines were routinely imposed as "deterrents" in cases of fighting, homicide, theft, and slander as well as in certain types of adultery and fornication suits (cf. Howell 1954:63, 168).

[7] The ratio of cows to oxen among fines cattle collected by the government in homicide cases, for instance, was approximately seven to three (UNPMD, November 1940).

[8] In a letter to the governor dated 15 March 1947, J. Wilson, the Assistant District Commissioner of the western Nuer, reported: "Two items have a big influence on the cattle trade: 1. the government's sale of fines cattle, which causes people to sell bulls [oxen] to the merchants for money in order to have the ready cash to buy a government cow and 2. famine" (WND 64 b. 1.).

and singing in the field; they show enthusiasm and interest in their work. Unlike
comers from other localities who started
grumbling the moment they arrived and
when they are transported to the fields it
needs a miracle to make them refrain from
going on strike [*sic*]. [WND 57. A., 1959–60,
"Eastern Nuer District Annual Report"]

Before long, however, these unwitting strike-
breakers began venturing farther and farther
north, encouraged by the promise of higher
wages. By 1960, scores of young Nuer men had
reached Khartoum, where they commonly
obtained employment as day laborers in the
constructions industry. Because of these
increasingly lucrative wage-labor opportunities, it actually became possible for a man to
earn enough money during a dry season to
purchase a cow calf or two on his return to
Nuerland. Hence a new relationship between
cattle and money was forged: no longer was it
necessary for a man to give up a cow in order
to get one. Money could yield cattle directly:
$M{\rightarrow}C$ [9]

With the explosion of the civil war in Nuerland in 1963–64, all this economic activity
ground to a sudden halt. Regional cattle and
grain markets collapsed as their northern Arab
controllers retreated to heavily garrisoned
towns. Scores of villages were razed by rebel-
seeking army battalions while local herds were
plundered mercilessly by both parties to the
conflict. Families living within reach of
government roads and towns scattered deeper
and deeper into the bush. Hundreds of young
men working or studying in the north flocked
back to join southern secessionist forces while
others fled in the opposite direction. The
eastern Jikany and Lou Nuer suffered most

intensely. And thus, by the time a negotiated
peace settlement was signed in 1972, some
40,000 eastern Nuer had abandoned their
homes to seek refuge in Ethiopia.

As part of the Addis Ababa Agreement of
1972, thousands of southern rebels (including
an unknown number of Nuer) were integrated
into the national army and police forces.
Hundreds of others were offered civilian posts
in the newly established southern regional
government, only to be laid off a few months
later due to inadequate funds. These new
posts, though temporary in many cases,
injected large amounts of paper currency into
the regional economy, currency which Nuer
were increasingly willing to accept in exchange
for their cattle. Bachelors hoping to replenish
their war-ravaged herds and thereby achieve a
quicker road to marriage adopted short-term,
seasonal labor migration to northern cities on
a massive scale. Following employment
patterns set by their predecessors, most of
these youths became day laborers in the
Khartoum construction industry.[10] After
working some four to 18 months, many of
them returned laden with colorful clothes,
mosquito nets, plastic shoes, blankets,
mattresses, sunglasses, and other highly
valued goods and courting paraphernalia.
Indeed, failure to obtain imported display
items left young men in parts of eastern
Nuerland vulnerable to the coordinated
insults and rejection of marriageable girls. "If
he comes back from the north and his dog
recognizes him, don't converse with him!"
runs the famous dictum of Nyaboth Nguany
Thoan, an influential Lou girl leader. Among
Nuer communities west of the Bahr al-Jabal,
where during the early 1980s a fat stately ox
was still more likely to catch a girl's eye than

---

[9]   Marx, of course, would not have differentiated this economic stage in the commoditization of human/cattle relations
from the preceding one, since both are part of a money-mediated chain of commodity exchange. In one case, cattle are
the commodities exchanged; in the other, cattle and labor are. However, this second mode of commodity exchange was
a definite economic "breakthrough" in local terms. For the commoditization of labor/cattle relations suddenly empowered money in ways previously unperceived or, at least, undervalued by most Nuer.

[10]   For information on Nuer labor migrants in Khartoum, see Kameir (1980).

the flamboyant dance leggings so avidly adopted in the east, most migrants preferred to invest their earnings in bridewealth cattle.

During the post- (or, rather inter-) civil war era between 1972 and 1983, the economic vacuum created by the hasty departure of northern merchants during the war began to suck in Nuer adventurers desiring to try their luck at trading. Although some of these would-be merchants managed to start their businesses with funds gained through wage labor or the sale of fish, grain, crocodile skins, and other local resources, most relied on a sale of family livestock. Eventually, the more prosperous of these succeeded in penetrating the long-distance grain import/cattle export trade formerly monopolized by their northern Arab counterparts. And as more and more Nuer began to appreciate the enormous prof- its that could be reaped by driving cattle overland to Kosti or by founding a modest "bush shop," it became easier for a young man to persuade his elders to sell a few head of cattle in order that he might become a part- time trader. This is not to say that the local customers benefited from the changeover. On the contrary, many of the newly established Nuer merchants proved to be even more rapacious than their Arab predecessors. Markups of over 200 percent on trade goods were standard in many outlying "bush" shops throughout the early 1980s. Furthermore, it was not uncommon at that time to hear ordi- nary people complain that the newly emerging class of Nuer merchants had begun to adopt novel attitudes toward money. As David Kek Moinydet, as eastern Gajiok Nuer, explained:

> The trouble with these young [Nuer] merchants is that they treat their money like cattle. In the old days, you didn't give a cow to just anyone. An [unrelated] man might have to live and work in your homestead for years before receiving a cow. Well, now, these young merchants are taking this same attitude toward their money: if you're not close enough to be "counted" a cow [in

marriage], you're not close enough to be lent money!

However, these merchants were not the only ones who began to view money in a new light. During the same inter-civil war era, scores of Nuer communities initiated, under the auspices of local chiefs, "self-help" projects, including the construction of primary schools, veterinary facilities, and medical dispensaries as well as the repair and extension of local roads. These projects were invariably funded by local cattle contributions – some being more voluntary then others. Tragically, most of the buildings later remained idle owing to the central government's failure to provide promised staff and supplies. Yet even so, these developments would seem to reflect a definite attitudinal shift. Increasingly, cattle were being viewed, in some contexts at least, as potential sources of capital to be invested in specific projects, some private and others collective: C→M.

And thus, by the time I began investigating these issues firsthand in 1980, money had become a part of everyday social life. Or as one wry old eastern Gajaak man quipped: "Today everyone wants to die with a piaster in his hand!"

The three basic stages I have identified in the gradual forging of the cattle/money equation (namely C→M→C, M→C and C→M) are helpful, I think, in understanding the nature and limits of the mutual convert- ibility of cattle and money as these are revealed through a half century of archival records. They do little justice, however, to the intricacy of cattle/money ties as more recently defined by Nuer. For the various Ms and various Cs of which they consist are by no means inter- changeable. Rather contemporary Nuer, as we shall see, regard neither money nor cattle as "things in themselves."

The Circulation of Blood, Cattle, and Money: 1980–83

First formulation: "money has no blood" To what extent did the increased mutual convertibility of cattle and money stimulate Nuer to reassess critically the inherent logic and general significance of the cattle/human equation so central to their culture during the early 1930s? I begin with the observation that by 1983, money (*you*) had penetrated some fields of exchange more thoroughly than others. In exchange for grain, fishing hooks, cloth, guns, and medicines, as well as in the payment of taxes, court fines, school fees, and the like, people gladly substituted money for cattle whenever they could. Indeed, the giving up of a cow in such contexts was regarded as a truly lamentable loss: ideally, Nuer reserved cattle for more important occasions such as marriage, initiation, and sacrifice, or – as I would summarize Nuer statements in this regard – for the creation and affirmation of enduring bonds among themselves as well as between themselves and divinity. In contrast, the role of cattle as sacrificial victim and as the indispensable exchange object at times of initiation, feud settlement and, to a lesser degree, marriage had scarcely been affected by the massive introduction of currency. This is not to say that people's attitudes toward these rites remained constant between 1930 and 1983. On the contrary, the significance of cattle sacrifice, for instance, was steadily undermined by mounting waves of Christian conversion, by increased Nuer acceptance of Western medicines and concepts of illness, and by growing expectations that a host would provide meat for guests. Even so, money could not replace cattle in these contexts. Nor could it replace the gift of a "personality ox" at initiation, though the overall significance of this ox also declined in regions where increasing numbers of Nuer youths rejected scarification. Furthermore, most people actively resisted the idea that money was an adequate substitute for cattle in bridewealth

and bloodwealth exchange – although small amounts of money, as I noted, had begun to infiltrate some marriage payments by the early 1980s.

I hasten to add that this characterization of the unequal penetration of money into Nuer social life – based as it is upon a distinction between "blood" and "nonblood" associated spheres of exchange – is entirely my own construction: Nuer would not use such terms. This idea developed, rather, out of numerous comments made by individual Nuer (during general discussions about cattle sacrifice, feuding, marriage, incest, pollution, and other issues) to the effect that "cattle, like people, have blood" but "money has no blood." I interpreted these comments to mean that money was an "inappropriate" medium of exchange in certain contexts because it could not bind people together like *riem*, "blood" – whether that "blood" were conceived as human, bovine, or both in relation to particular types of enduring ties.

For instance, I was once asked by a highly intelligent and unusually well traveled eastern Gajaak youth, who had ventured at one point as far as Iraq in search of profitable employment, whether I knew the ultimate source of money (*you*). After remarking spontaneously to the effect that he realized different countries used different currencies, Peter Pal Jola went on to say:

> But there's something I still don't understand about money. Money's not like the cow because the cow has blood and breath and, like people, gives birth. But money does not. So, tell me, do you know whether God [*kuɔdh*] or Man [*raan*] creates money?

Widespread as these uncertainties may be have been among Nuer, they in no way prevented people from appreciating and using money as an everyday medium of exchange. Indeed, individual musings about money's ultimate origin were in many ways extraneous to the immediate feel of the various bits of metal and paper ever passing through their hands. It was not the mystery of money's generative powers that colored the give-and-take of daily life but rather, as we shall see, money's "sterility" as compared with the self-generating capacity of cattle. Similarly, it was the immediate, not the ultimate, source of money that defined what Nuer considered to be very different sorts of money. In order to understand why this was so, we must delve into the symbolism of "blood."

Although not equated with "life" (*tëk*) itself, blood or *riem* is the substance with which each and every human life begins. Conception is understood by Nuer as a mysterious merger of male and female "blood" flows, forged by the life-creating powers of *kuɔdh* (divinity). Without the direct participation and continual support of divinity, no child could be born or survive long enough to bring forth another generation. Moreover, since procreation is the paramount goal of life for everyone and the only form of immortality valued, "blood" may be understood as that which fuses the greatest of human desires with that profound humility with which Nuer contemplate the transcendent powers of divinity. A newborn child *is* "blood" and is referred to as such during the first month or two of life. Milk, semen, sweat – these too *are* "blood." It is as if *riem* were the mutable source of all human – and hence all social – energy.

As an element of life, blood converges with two other powerful forces of vitality: *yieɣ* (breath) and *tiiy/tiei* (awareness). Blood, however, is unique among these cardinal principles of life in that it is eminently social. Unlike either "breath" or "awareness," blood passes from person to person and from generation to generation, endowing interpersonal relations with a certain substance and fluidity. Both the coming of manhood and the coming of womanhood are marked by passages of blood. For a girl, the blood that flows during her first childbirth ushers her into adulthood; for a boy, it is the blood shed during the ordeal of scarification at initiation. The perpetual expansion, union, and contraction of kin groups are likewise spoken about in terms of the creation, transferral, and loss of *riem*. And thus, by emphasizing the fact that cattle, like people, have "blood," individuals were calling attention to the fact that cattle and people are capable of a parallel extension of vitality through time. Money, of course, is not augmentative in that sense. If anything, it appears condemned in Sudan to a continual loss of force, to a perpetual withering in the face of mounting inflation.

Now, insofar as individuals actually succeeded in restricting their use of cash to "nonblood" as opposed to "blood" associated fields of exchange, money was less a challenge than a support for the life-affirmed and life-affirming "truth" that "cattle and people are one." As Nyacuol Gaai, an elderly Leek woman, put it: "Money protects cattle" (*"Gangɛ ɣɔk piny"*; literally, "[Money] delays them on the ground"). People with money, in other words, could keep their cattle with them longer.

Yet why, one might ask, all this emphasis on "blood" when there were so many other differences between cattle and money that people could have stressed as well? Money is not only "bloodless" (and hence milkless) but also devoid of "breath," "awareness," and individualizing names, colors, temperaments, exchange histories, and so forth (cf. Comaroff and Comaroff 1990:211). Money is an utterly depersonalized medium in this sense. Moreover, unlike cattle, money can pass in relative secrecy from one locked metal footlocker to another. In my experience, nevertheless, Nuer men and women did not mention these elements of contrast when debating the nature and limits of convertibility between cattle and money. This is not to say that they did not appreciate or take advantage of them from time to time; it is to say, rather, that the symbolism of "blood" which so pervades their culture had been taken up and elaborated once again – this time, it would seem, so as to deny the possibility of a direct equation between money and people. It was as though people were attempting to reassure themselves that, though cattle and people were equated in some contexts and cattle and money in others, money and people were – and always would be – incommensurate. The gulf that divided them ran as deep and broad as Nuer images of "blood" in the generation of life and in the continuation of the social order. By stressing the unique "blood" linkage between cattle and people so as to exclude the intrusive medium of money, many Nuer, it would seem, were also rallying to the defense of those "augmentations of life" made possible by the ideological truth that "cattle and people are one."

Everything I have said thus far presumes that "cattle" and "money" are discrete units of comparison. But for Nuer, as I hinted, these were not "things in themselves." Rather, Nuer successfully crossbred the concepts of "money" and "cattle," bringing forth a generation of hybrid categories that proved exceptionally adaptable to an increasingly unstable social and economic environment. And nowhere did these hybrid categories thrive so well as in the vast field of bridewealth exchange. For it was here, in an open environment, where negotiations ranged freely and where there were no rigid rules to mar the horizon, that these categories first came into their own. It was here, too, that my initial observation regarding the differential penetration of money into "blood" and "nonblood" associated spheres of exchange could be exposed as excessively static. For in reality, money and cattle were flowing increasingly out, in, and between these opposed spheres of exchange.

Second formulation: the cattle of money and the cattle of girls   I should, perhaps, first check the assumption that "money" and "cattle" were wholly interchangeable: not all money was good, I was told, for buying cattle. There was something called *you ciɛth* – literally, the "money of shit" – that allegedly could not be invested fruitfully in cattle. Strikingly similar in some ways to the cattle-harming money of the Kenyan Luo (Shipton 1989), the "money of shit" was, nevertheless, defined differently.[11] Whereas the "bitter money" of the Luo originates in the sale of specific resources such as land, tobacco, cannabis, and gold, *you ciɛth* was quite literally money people earned in local towns by collecting and dumping the waste of household bucket latrines. Following the colonial administration's introduction of bucket latrines during the 1940s, it was difficult, of course, to find people willing to empty them each day – or rather under the cover of night. Eventually, the administration came to depend on prisoners for this service. In the interim, however, it seems Nuer women and men collectively rejected this type of work by convincing one another that "a cow bought with 'shit money' cannot live" (*"yaŋ mi ci kok ke you ciɛth, lcɛ bi tëɣ"*). What began, I suspect, as a prideful statement that "we, the people of the people, will not do such work" soon became an accepted fact of social life. . . . In this way, individuals sought to prevent the contaminating source of this money from polluting their cherished cattle, which were, after all, consumed as well as exchanged.

In addition to the "money of shit," there were five basic categories of monetary and cattle wealth prevalent during the 1980s – all of them important for understanding contem-

---

[11]   Shipton's (1989 – see extract, Chapter 10, this volume) stimulating analysis of "bitter money" among the Luo draws attention to the fact that people can and often do trace sums of money from source through release in the hope of protecting treasured possessions, like cattle, from potentially polluting influences. Shipton's development of this important theme might have been even stronger, however, had he more fully explored the interface between cattle and money among the Luo. It would be interesting to know, for instance, whether or not those cattle and sums of money that actually slip through the "two-way barrier system" he constructs blaze a trail, like "bitter money," through Luo social relations – as is the case among Nuer.

porary patterns of bridewealth circulation.[12] The first of these, *ɣɔk nyiët*, "the cattle of girls/daughters," referred to bridewealth cattle received by specific relatives of the bride on the basis of a system of "inheritable rights" *(cuɔŋ)* and "obligations" *(laad*; singular, *lat)* (cf. Evans-Pritchard 1951: 74–89; Howell 1954: 97–122; Hutchinson 1985)[13] Although nominally owned by the official recipient, these cows formed part of "the ancestral herd" from which close agnates ideally drew in order to marry, have sons, and thereby extend the patriline (see Evans-Pritchard 1951: 83, 1956:285).

In contrast, purchased cattle, *ɣɔk youni* or "the cattle of money," were less subject to the claims of extended kinsmen. They circulated between extended kinsmen, I was told, more as a "privilege" – that is, as a *muc* (a "free gift") or a *lony* (a "free" releasing) – than as a *cuɔŋ*, or inheritable right. Their purchaser, in other words, was somewhat freer to dispose of them as he wished – especially if he acquired them after having married and established a household of his own. In contrast, it was far more difficult – though by no means impossible during the early 1980s – for an unmarried youth residing in his father's household to differentiate effectively between cattle acquired through his own labor and those gained through his sister's marriages, for the father retained formal rights of disposal over all cattle entering his household throughout his lifetime. He could, if he desired, re-distribute cattle purchased by his sons among various wives' households as well as draw freely upon them in meeting cattle obligations toward extended kin. Indeed, during the 1980s

it was commonly expected in some parts of Nuerland – most notably in regions west of the Bahr al-Jabal – that bachelors engaged in seasonal labor migration would reaffirm their kinship solidarity upon their return home by freely giving one of the first bull calves purchased with their wages to a favorite maternal uncle, paternal uncle, paternal cousin, or other close relative. This gesture of solidarity was often complemented with a special sacrifice, carried out by a distant patrilineal kinsman (*guan böthni*), which was intended both to bless and to integrate other cattle purchased into the familial herd. The "cattle of money," in other words, could be ritually transformed in these regions into the "cattle of girls." Significantly, these expectations and concomitant rites were not, to the best of my knowledge, prevalent among the Nuer groups east of the Bahr al-Jabal before the eruption of the second civil war (1983 to the present).

Following the father's death, there was considerably more room for negotiation and dissent among brothers – particularly paternal half brothers – over shared rights in the familial herd. Hence, when I questioned various men and women on this score, I received a wide range of opinions – each expressed with an air of uncompromised certainty. A group of middle-aged eastern Gajiok men, for instance, assured me that following the father's death, "cattle of money" passed only as a "privilege" between paternal half brothers; full brothers, they argued, would normally be more supportive of one another and would thus willingly pool all cattle wealth. In contrast, several other Gajiok and

---

[12] Bridewealth rates for previously unmarried girls rose during the late 1970s and early 1980s from between 20 and 25 head of cattle to between 25 and 30. Bridewealth rates for divorcées, in contrast, ranged between 10 and 15 head of cattle during this period.

[13]Regional variations in the transgenerational scope of bridewealth claims are discussed in Hutchinson 1985. There I point out that, during the early 1980s, Nuer east of the Bahr al-Jabal were less likely to honor the bridewealth claims of distant kinsmen than their western cousins were. What is important to stress here, however, is simply that "cattle of girls" were associated with a system of collective rights and obligations – however those rights may have been negotiated and defined in specific instances.

western Leek men and women argued that half brothers retained full rights to one another's cattle, however acquired, until such time as all had married. A third opinion ran that a married man could own purchased cattle individually, regardless of the marital status of his half brothers. Finally, there were some Nuer (notably several western youths in the process of collecting sufficient cattle for their own marriages) who boldly declared: "A cow of your wages is a cow of your sweat and no one has rights in it other than you." In brotherly disputes over "rights" and "obligations" held in cattle, the ability to assert one or an other of these interpretations of "cattle of money" would thus seem crucial.[14] Indeed, from this perspective it would seem that the concept of *ɣɔk youni* had added a new twist to what was otherwise a longstanding "zone of contestation" among patrilineal kinsmen by giving hardworking younger brothers and sons a bit of turf from which to begin negotiating for a greater share of status and autonomy within the family fold.[15]

But not all money could be turned into the "cattle of money." Only money earned as wages or through the sale of grain, gum, fish, crocodile skins, or other goods obtained by self-exertion could become *ɣɔk youni*. Money acquired by these means was closely associated with *leth puany*, "human sweat," and was referred to as *you lad*, "the money of work."[16] This type of money stood opposed to that gained by the sale of collectively owned cattle:

you ɣɔɔk, or "the money of cattle." Whereas the former was individually owned, the latter carried with it all of the collective rights held in the cattle sold. Being an individual possession, the "money of work" could be "requested" (*thieiɛ*) or "begged" (*liimɛ*) from its owner by persistent relatives in need of school fees or simply desirious of a refreshing bowl of beer in the marketplace. The "money of cattle" was of a different order. Ideally, it was never squandered on small requests or projects but was instead reserved to purchase younger, fertile cattle to expand and upgrade the familial herd.

It is noteworthy that this distinction often worked to the disadvantage of Nuer whose immediate livelihood depended less on cattle than on wages. As a poorly paid, junior administrative official in Bentiu lamented:

> When a man goes to sell a cow [ox] at market, we, the relatives, usually don't bother him because we know that he is going to use that money to buy [female] cattle that will increase the herd. But then that same man can come and pester me here [in Bentiu] to give him money for beer. He may have a thousand pounds in his pocket from the cattle he has just sold. But that money is different; he wouldn't think of using it for beer. Nor could it be begged from him like the money of work. That's why it is so difficult for us who now live in town.

---

[14]   Admittedly, relations among the various strains of opinion about "cattle of money" outlined above were, sociologically and historically, far more complex than is suggested here. Failure to work out these relations in any detail (even though such is impossible within the scope of this article) remains one of the shortcomings of my argument.

[15]   "Zone of contestation" is a phrase adopted from Ferguson's intriguing analysis of the "category interests" upholding the "mystique" of bovine wealth among the Basotho (1985). Basotho men value cattle wealth, Ferguson argues, less for its self-reproducing capacities than for its relative immunity, as compared with money, to the claims of other household members – most notably, dependent wives. Significantly, in his analysis of the key power axes in Basotho society Ferguson does not mention the possibility of disputes over cattle wealth arising between men of the same household, extended family, or lineage. This, however, was the most important "zone of contestation" shaping contemporary Nuer attitudes toward both cattle and money wealth.

[16]   The fact that the potential link between human blood and sweat on the one hand and between human sweat and money on the other was never explicitly noted or developed by any of my informants would seem to lend support to my earlier observation that Nuer conceived of the "blood-bonds" between cattle and people primarily in procreative terms.

This fifth and final wealth category was also referred to as *ɣɔk youni* "the cattle of money." However, these were not real cows at all but rather sums of money substituted for a usually quite small portion of bridewealth cattle requested. There was no possibility during the early 1980s of linguistically eliding the distinction between money parading as cattle and real cattle purchased in the marketplace in such contexts, despite the fact that both could be referred to as *ɣɔk youni*, "the cattle of money." For real cattle, regardless of their exchange origins, were invariably identified during bridewealth negotiations on the basis of their sex, color, age, horn shape, and other distinguishing features. Hence any reference to "cattle of money" in such contexts was unambiguously understood to mean "money cattle" as opposed to "purchased cattle." (For clarity's sake, I will use the term "cattle of money" here to mean only purchased cattle and will use the inverse term "money cattle," when referring to cash passed in lieu of bridewealth cows.)

Now, whether or not a young man could pass money in lieu of a bridewealth cow or two depended entirely, I was told, on the will of his would-be father-in-law. The latter could always refuse, demanding that the young man take his money and buy a real cow instead. Hence only a "generous" father-in-law, I was told, would accept such a "cow." And for this reason, the number of "money cattle" transferred in Nuer marriages before the reeruption of civil war in 1983 was remarkably small.

The first thing to note about the various wealth categories outlined is that they facilitated movements of cattle and money between "blood" and "nonblood" spheres of exchange at the same time as they confirmed the presence of a conceptual boundary between these spheres. Social principles characteristic of "kinship" exchange were continuously being drawn, together with cattle and money, into the marketplace and vice versa. Consider the following hypothetical – though by no means atypical – series of cattle and money exchanges.

Imagine that an ox, originally obtained as bridewealth, is sold at market and the money so acquired is later invested in a young heifer: "cattle of girls" $\rightarrow$ "money of cattle" $\rightarrow$ "cattle of girls" (Cg$\rightarrow$Mc$\rightarrow$Cg). Now, in this sequence, the collective rights and privileges held in the original bridewealth ox are not lost as it is transformed into money and later back again into cattle. As a concept, then, the "money of cattle" both affirms and protects these collective cattle rights based as they are on shared "blood," as cattle pass in and out of the marketplace, a "nonblood" -associated sphere of social relations and exchange. Conversely, a successful migrant who invests his savings in cattle ("money of work" $\rightarrow$ "cattle of money" [Mw$\rightarrow$Cm]) is able to smuggle principles of personal autonomy and private ownership associated with market exchange into the realm of kinship relations via the concepts "money of work" and "cattle of money."[17] In this system, there are no absolutes: it is always a matter of specific cattle and specific sums of money, defined in terms of their immediate sources.

The relativity with which different sorts of cattle and money are classified is readily apparent in bridewealth exchange. For whether or not a particular cow is collectively defined as a "cow of money" or a "cow of girls" depends entirely on the negotiating position of the exchange partners. Whereas the groom and his party are normally quite conscious of which cows are "cattle of money" and which are "cattle of girls," from the perspective of the bride's family, all cattle

---

[17] The hybrid wealth system of the Nuer raises interesting questions with regard to Bohannan's (1955, 1959) famous hypothesis about money's scrambling effect on traditional exchange spheres among the Tiv. I have found Bohannan's thesis somewhat difficult to relate to the Nuer case, however, because it is premised on the idea that "things in themselves," rather than the social relations through which things flow, differentiate "spheres of exchange."

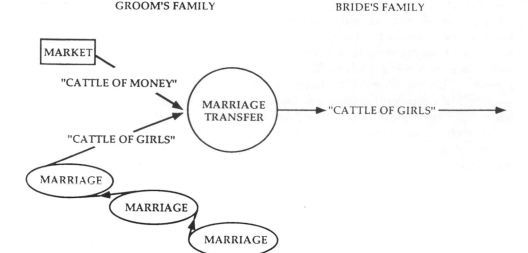

Figure 11.1 [1] The relativity of the "cattle of money"/"cattle of girls" distinction

received in marriage are "cattle of girls" (see figure 11.1). . . .

But what interests, one might ask, has this system of cattle/money distinctions really served? What has been its role, if any, in patterning relations of autonomy and dependence between men and women, young and old, kin and non-kin, wife-takers and wife-givers, and cattle-rich and cattle-poor, wage earners and nonwage earners, and so on?

With respect to familial and extended kin ties, this system of wealth distinctions certainly enhanced individual possibilities for autonomy by weakening feelings of mutual dependence among agnates and among cognates. With the expansion of the market economy, young men became far less dependent on the good will of their fathers, older brothers, and paternal and maternal uncles in the collection of bridewealth cattle than they were, say, during the 1930s and 1940s. The abilities of senior men to amass power in the form of cattle wealth declined accordingly – though, as I noted earlier, western Nuer elders developed ritual means of muting the "cattle of money"/"cattle of girls" distinction. Although one might suspect that these devel-

opments may contribute in the long run to the development of sharper inequalities of wealth among men, it would be difficult, I think, to convince many contemporary Nuer of this. In fact, several men and women argued that the introduction of money and the creation of local cattle, grain, and labor markets had significantly eased social inequalities inherent in the cattle economy itself – most notably, inequalities based on birth order and on relative family size. Whereas a sisterless man was often condemned to a bachelor's life during the 1930s and 1940s, he was "free" during the early 1980s to take up trading and wage labor in order to obtain marriage cattle. The money economy, in other words, was valued by many for having provided industrious individuals with additional opportunities to transcend poverty and misfortune. As one optimistic eastern Gajiok youth exclaimed, *Ci caan ŋɔɔk* ("Poverty [misfortune] has ended").

With regard to affinal ties, this system of wealth categories had an additional advantage, for it provided a farsighted individual with an opportunity to reduce the risk that his own marriage would someday be negatively affected by the divorce of a close female relative. When one considers the fact that divorce rates among Nuer nearly tripled between 1936 and 1983, this was not an insignificant advantage. Indeed, for reasons described in detail elsewhere (Hutchinson 1990), Nuer men and women of the 1980s were divorcing not only more frequently than earlier generations but also at later and later points in the marriage. Whereas Evans-Pritchard claims that during the 1930s divorce was "highly unusual" after the birth of a child to the union and "impossible" after the birth of a second (1951:94), during the 1980s it was not uncommon for government courts to sever unions involving, two, three, or even four children (Hutchinson 1990:402–404). Recovery of the original bridewealth cattle and their offspring was especially arduous in such cases since the cattle had usually long been dispersed through a multitude of other marriages. If they had not spread too far afield and the woman's husband knew of their whereabouts, he was likely to push in court for the return of those cows and their calves. If not, the courts maintained that substitutes be provided. Yet sometimes the family of the wife was unable to muster suitable substitutes without recalling cattle used in other marriages. Although the bride's people were not responsible for replacing cows that had died naturally in their own homestead, they were expected to replace all those that "had accomplished something" ("*mi ci duɔr laat*") for the bride's family – that is, those that had been used to solidify a second marriage, nullify a familial debt, or otherwise further the bride's family's objectives before dying in other people's homesteads. As a result of these rather stringent court-sanctioned interpretations of the cattle obligations of the wife's family vis-à-vis the divorcing husband,

the rupture of one marriage sometimes weakened others. If the marriage secondarily affected was a relatively recent one, it too could end in divorce.[18]

What must be realized, however, is that these potential difficulties could be avoided by far-sighted individuals through the skillful manipulation of the cattle/money categories outlined above. A young man could attempt to reduce the risk that his own marriage would someday be weakened by the divorce of a female relative by including as many "cattle of money" in his bridewealth settlement as possible. For, unlike the "cattle of girls," purchased cattle did not conduct shock waves created by other people's divorces. Since they came from the market, they could only be reclaimed, in principle, by the groom himself. During the 1980s this marriage strategy was especially favored by western Nuer men.[19] I often heard men advocate the advantages of marrying with "cattle of money" as opposed to "cattle of girls" with the expression "*Yaŋ mi ci kok ke you, thilɛ riɛk*" ("A cow bought with money is risk-free").

For all of these reasons, many men and women had come to regard "cattle of money" as a more secure form of wealth than "cattle of girls." Hence, contrary to what one might have expected, the growth of cattle and labor markets in Nuerland actually contributed in some ways to the stability of marital alliances: the more rapidly "cattle of girls" were transformed via market exchanges into "cattle of money," the less likely it was that the rupture of one marriage would adversely affect others. In other ways, of course, the expanding market economy had a profoundly negative impact on Nuer marriages. During the 1980s, marriages were often strained to breaking point by the

---

[18]   I documented three cases of "chain divorces" in the west and two in the east – all of them occurring relatively early in the second marriage.

[19]   As noted earlier, western Nuer migrants were more likely to invest their full earnings in bridewealth cattle than were their eastern counterparts. Moreover, as is explained in detail elsewhere (Hutchinson 1985), western Nuer marriages tended to be more extensively interwoven than eastern marriages since the bridewealth claims of distant kinsmen continued to be honored in that region.

extended absences of husbands striving to earn a bit of cash in Khartoum.[20] Age- and gender-based asymmetries within the community were also reduced to some extent by the continual transformation of "cattle of girls" into "cattle of money" via the marketplace. For in principle, anyone could earn money and purchase cattle – although, as I have explained, the rights of bachelors and married women were far more circumscribed in this regard than were those of married men and unmarried women.

At the same time, however, "cattle of money" were continually being transformed into "cattle of girls" via bridewealth transfers and special sacrificial offerings. As "cattle of girls," they could be used to justify and support the same age and gender asymmetries that they would tend to undermine as "cattle of money." In this way, Nuer were able to integrate and, in some sense, even synthesize practices and principles of monetary exchange with those characteristic of more enduring bonds of kinship and community. The synthesis achieved, however, was based on a perpetual alternation between, rather than a definitive fusion of, the conflicting social principles concerned.

From a slightly different perspective, one might argue that Nuer fused the concepts of cattle and money in such a way as to permit certain market values to bleed into bridewealth exchange without threatening the uniqueness of the cattle/people equation so fundamental to their social order. One did not actually need to use money in bridewealth transfers in order to take advantage of principles of private property and of limited liability associated with money: a few "cattle of money" would do. Thus, the self-generating aspect of bridewealth cattle, so central to Nuer images of perpetuation of alliances, was preserved – and all those "augmentations of life" rooted in the cultural assertion of an identity between cattle and people were protected.

Yet money, as I noted, had begun to make some inroads into the field of bridewealth exchange via the concept of "money cattle." Though these inroads were still limited during the early 1980s, there is every reason to believe that the tremendous hardships of war, famine, and disease Nuer are currently suffering will so decimate their herds that more and more people will be reduced to marrying with "money cattle" in the future.[21] A major shift from cattle to cash as the dominant medium of bridewealth exchange would require, however, a radical rethinking of the nature and logic of alliance. The notion that alliances are founded on an equation between human and bovine "blood" and perpetuated through a parallel extension of cattle and people through time would have to be totally reformulated in order to take account of money's "bloodless" nature. It remains to be seen whether or not the Nuer communities will transcend the overwhelming hardships they are currently experiencing to create more radical reformulations of their concepts of alliance, descent, and personhood in the future.

---

[20] Furthermore, due to transformations in Nuer customary law wrought by the British colonial regime, it was increasingly easy for husbands to divorce their wives on grounds of adultery. For an extended discussion of these legal complexities, see Hutchinson 1990.

[21] Although I reserve for future publications a discussion of the impact of the continuing Sudanese civil war on Nuer marriage practices, I should perhaps note here that the proportion of "money cattle" offered in bridewealth negotiations has grown rapidly among the communities of Nuer refugees currently camped on the outskirts of Khartoum. By 1990, most of these Nuer had responded to the inaccessibility of whatever cattle remained with their extended families in the south by nominally doubling bridewealth rates from some 25 to some 50 head of cattle. Up to half this amount could then be offered in the form of "money cattle" (at mutually agreed upon rate lower than the market value of real cattle). Although this money transfer enabled the initiation of the union, the groom was not thereby relieved of the obligation to provide his in-laws with a comparable payment of real cows at some admittedly vague point in the future: "when the world becomes good again." In contrast, those Nuer remaining in their southern homelands – the vast majority in 1990 – have continued to negotiate bridewealth settlements with real cattle, though at greatly reduced rates.

Conclusions

As of 1983, money had not developed into a generalized medium of exchange among Nuer. Nor had its introduction over the previous half century precipitated the emergence of a "unicentric economy" (Bohannan 1959:501). Rather, Nuer incorporated money into a weighted exchange system in which cattle remained the dominant metaphor of value. The elaborate system of cattle and money wealth categories they devised provided them with a sense of stability in the midst of change. Cattle and money were able to move freely between "market" and "kinship" spheres of exchange without threatening the cattle/human equation so fundamental to cultural concepts of personhood and transgenerational alliance. Money's powers of effacement were largely checked by an ideological elaboration of the unique "blood" links binding people and cattle. At the same time, the hybrid cattle/money categories developed greatly enhanced the abilities of young Nuer migrants, in particular, to understand and come to terms with the noncattle, "nonblood" forms of sociality increasingly binding them to the world at large.

Although the emergence of the cattle/money equation did not sunder the strong human bonds of identification with cattle, it contributed to a significant contraction of Nuer concepts of selfhood and sociality. Before the introduction of currency, the sense of self people cultivated in and through their relations with cattle invariably implied the support and participation of a collectivity of persons, including ancestors and divinities as well as numerous contemporaries. Cattle's role in creating and maintaining this socially enriched sense of self was subsequently weakened, as we have seen, by the emerging opportunities for individually acquiring and owning cattle made possible by "a 'money-form' of commodity exchange." Although cattle could now be converted into money and vice versa, the "cattle of money" and the "money of work" could not be used to augment self and society in the same way as the "cattle of girls" because, as Nuer put it, "money has no blood."

While the wealth system that Nuer developed would appear, from this perspective, to be an ingenious compromise between market and nonmarket forms of consciousness and sociality, it also reflected, as I have shown, major socioeconomic transformations in the relative autonomy and dependence of senior men versus junior men, cattle owners versus those without cattle, full brothers versus half brothers, wage earners versus nonwage earners, men versus women, husbands versus wives, married women versus unmarried women, wife-takers versus wife-givers, and merchants versus nonmerchants. I have pointed out, for instance, how this system of categories contributed to a marked decrease in the ability of senior men to amass power in the form of cattle wealth. "Cattle of money" and "money of work" played key roles in this power shift by giving wage-earning younger brothers and sons a potential basis from which to assert greater autonomy and status within the family. With respect to patrilineal connections, this system also aggravated conflicts of interest, inherent in the very structure of agnatic descent, between the collective and the individual procreative goals of lineage members. Nevertheless, older men and women continued to maintain strong moral pressure on the younger generation to reject formal division of the family's "energy" before marriage and the establishment of an independent household.[22]

---

[22] Significantly, I learned during my return visit to Sudan in 1990 that the ritual transformation of "cattle of money" into "cattle of girls" common among the western Nuer during the early 1980s had subsequently gained popularity among eastern Nuer as a means of affirming familial support in a period of extreme insecurity and hardship.

These issues, however, were far from resolved in 1983. Moreover, Nuer at that time were profoundly aware of the increasing precariousness of their social world in general and their cattle wealth in particular with respect to the widening vortex of violence then gaining momentum throughout the southern Sudan. More recently, the traumas of an increasingly brutal civil war have been exacerbated by encroaching rinderpest epidemics, slave raids, disease, and unprecedented famine. Thousands upon thousands of Nuer have been forced to seek refuge in northern cities or across the international frontier (see Hutchinson 1991). Their herds are being steadily decimated, their communities and families severed and destroyed. This continuing tragedy will undoubtedly provoke further reexaminations of their notions of selfhood and sociality in the years to come.

References

Archives and manuscript collections

DAK   Dakhlia (Interior) Files, National Records Office, Khartoum, Sudan
END   Eastern Nuer District Files, Nasir, Upper Nile Province, Sudan
SAD   Sudan Archive, Oriental Library, University of Durham, England
UN   Upper Nile Province Files, National Records Office, Khartoum, Sudan
UNPAR Upper Nile Province Annual Reports, Western Nuer District Files, Bentiu, Upper Nile Province, Sudan
UNPMD Upper Nile Province Monthly Diary, University of Khartoum Library, Khartoum, Sudan
WND   Western Nuer District Files, Bentiu, Upper Nile Province, Sudan

Bohannan, Paul
    1955 Some Principles of Exchange and Investment among the Tiv. *American Anthropologist* 57:60–70.
    1959 The Impact of Money on an African Subsistence Economy. *Journal of Economic History* 19:491–503.
Comaroff, Jean, and John L. Comaroff
    1990 Goodly Beasts, Beastly Goods: Cattle and Commodities in a South African Context. *American Ethnologist* 17:195–216.
Evans-Pritchard, Edward E.
    1940 *The Nuer*. Oxford: Clarendon Press.
    1951 *Kinship and Marriage among the Nuer*. Oxford: Clarendon Press.
    1956 *Nuer Religion*. Oxford: Oxford University Press.

Ferguson, James
    1985 The Bovine Mystique. *Man* (n.s.) 20:647–674.
Howell, Paul P.
    1954 *A Manual of Nuer Law*. London: Oxford University Press.
Hutchinson, Sharon
    1980 Relations between the Sexes among the Nuer: 1930. *Africa* 50:371–387.
    1985 Changing Concepts of Incest among the Nuer. *American Ethnologist* 12:625–641.
    1988 *The Nuer in Crisis: Coping with Money, War, and the State*. Ph.D. dissertation. Anthropology Department, University of Chicago.
    1990 Rising Divorce among the Nuer, 1936–83. *Man* (n.s.) 25:393–411.
    1991 War through the Eyes of the Dispossessed: Three Stories of Survival. *Disasters* 15:166–171.
Johnson, Douglas
    1979 Colonial Policy and Prophets: The "Nuer-Settlement," 1929–1930. *Journal of the Anthropological Society of Oxford* 10:1–20.
    1980 History and Prophecy among the Nuer of Southern Sudan. Ph.D dissertation. University of California, Los Angeles.
Kameir, Elwathig
    1980 Workers in an Urban Situation: A Comparative Study of Factory Workers and Building Site Labourers in Khartoum. Ph.D. dissertation. University of Hull.
Marx, Karl
    1967[1867] *Capital: A Critique of Political Economy*. Vol. 1. New York: International Publishers.
Murray, Colin
    1981 Families Divided: The Impact of Migrant

Labour in Lesotho. New York: Cambridge University Press.

Parkin, David

1980 Kind Bridewealth and Hard Cash: Eventing a Structure. *In The Meaning of Marriage Payments.* J. L. Comaroff, ed. pp. 197–200. New York: Academic Press.

Sansom, Basil

1976 A Signal Transaction and its Currency. *In Transaction and Meaning.* B. Kapferer, ed. pp.

143–161. Philadelphia: Institute for the Study of Human Issues.

Shipton, Parker

1989 *Bitter Money: Cultural Economy and Some African Meanings of Forbidden Commodities.* Washington, DC: American Anthropological Association.

Simmel, Georg

1978[1900] *Philosophy of Money.* London: Routledge and Kegan Paul.

PART III

Hunter-Gatherer Studies in Africa: The Mbuti, the !Kung San, and Current Debates

A Lese farmer (left) teases his Efe partner.
Photo: Roy Richard Grinker.

Hunter-Gatherer Studies in Africa: The Mbuti, the !Kung San, and Current Debates

12   Colin M. Turnbull. 1963. "The Lessons of the Pygmies." *Scientific American*, January: 303–311.

13   Roy Richard Grinker. 1994. "Houses in the Rainforest: Gender and Ethnicity among the Lese and the Efe in Zaire." From Roy Richard Grinker, *Houses in the Rainforest: Ethnicity and Inequality among Farmers and Foragers in Central Africa*. Berkeley and Los Angeles: University of California Press.

14   Edwin N. Wilmsen. 1989. *Land Filled with Flies*. Chicago: University of Chicago Press.

15   Jacqueline S. Solway, and Richard B. Lee. 1990. "Foragers, Genuine or Spurious?: Situating the Kalahari San in History." (*Current Anthropology*, 31, no. 2:109–147)

Introduction

Because cultural anthropology is defined, in large part, by the writing of ethnographies, we tend to associate major ethnographic topics with certain authors and societies – for example, "lineage theory" with Meyer Fortes and the Tallensi, witchcraft with Edward Evans-Pritchard and the Azande, and ritual with Victor Turner and the Ndembu. When we think about the study of hunter-gatherers, the first names that come to mind are Colin Turnbull and Richard B. Lee, the Mbuti Pygmies of central Africa and the !Kung San of southern Africa.

Turnbull's accounts of the Mbuti Pygmies of the Ituri Rainforest of Zaire, and Richard B. Lee's analyses of the !Kung San of the Kalahari Desert in Botswana and Namibia, have had a profound impact upon the teaching and study of cultural anthropology. Throughout the world, Turnbull's two major publications, *The Forest People* (1961) and *Wayward Servants* (1965), have been standard reading in courses on anthropology and African cultures, and have been the basis for a significant number of comparative studies on economic, political, and gender egalitarianism. His data have been cited, analyzed, and incorporated by hundreds of authors in anthropology books and articles on subjects as varied as cultural and biological evolution, sex roles, violence, and political economy.

One reason these ethnographies can be considered among the great works in the history of anthropology is that they have stimulated dialogue and debate between anthropologists of different sub-fields.

Cultural anthropologists have studied the San and the Mbuti to learn about key features of all hunter-gatherer societies: these features include egalitarianism, sharing, few exclusive rights to resources, and the absence of food surplus. Cultural anthropologists have also addressed the question of how and why these groups maintain a hunting and gathering lifestyle in the face of political, economic, and social change in Africa. Paleontologists and archaeologists have been especially interested in the San as a model for humanity's pre-agricultural past; many of these specialists argue that since 99 per cent of human existence has been spent hunting and gathering (agriculture is a mere 10,000 years old), contemporary hunter-gatherers provide us with a window, albeit an imperfect one, into our past. As Sherwood Washburn writes in his foreword to Richard Lee and Irven De Vore's *Kalahari Hunter-Gatherers*:

> The importance of the San comes from the fundamental role which hunting has played in human history. Large-brained humans (Homo Erectus and subsequent forms) supported themselves by hunting and gathering for at least a million years prior to the advent of agriculture . . . Before the onset of agriculture man had evolved into his present form, and all the basic patterns of human behavior had appeared: language, complex social life, arts, complex technology. It was during this span of about 99 per cent of the duration of the genus Homo that hunting was a major factor in the adaptation of man. If we are to understand the origin of man, we must understand man the hunter and woman the gatherer (1976: xv).

As we shall in the readings below, the use of hunter-gather societies as analogies for human life in the distant past is highly problematic.

Indeed, since the 1970s an enormous number of critical questions have been asked about the San and the Mbuti, and the extent to which contemporary peoples can teach us about human history:

Can these societies tell us something meaningful about human nature and evolution?

To what degree does the study of these societies separate hunter-gatherers from the total cultural and historical context in which they are embedded?

Is it useful to group culturally variable societies under the single category "hunter-gatherer" simply because of their subsistence strategy?

By defining societies in these terms, does the category itself favor certain theoretical approaches, such as Marxism, cultural evolutionism, or cultural materialism, that account for social and cultural differences in terms of technology and economy?

Since archaeological evidence now shows that ancestors of the San have engaged in regional trade as far back as 500 A.D., to what extent have the San, and other hunter-gatherer groups, been embedded in regional interactions or in world political and economic systems?

Is it possible that the people we assume to have been hunter-gatherers for hundreds or even thousands of years have long oscillated between a variety of subsistence strategies, including herding and agriculture?

If the archaeological evidence cited by recent authors is accepted, are hunter-gatherer societies therefore misrepresented in the literature as ahistorical primitive isolates?

So-called "revisionists," such as Edwin Wilmsen and James Denbow, find these to be compelling questions and want to challenge previous representations of hunter-gatherers in general, and Lee's characterizations of the San, in particular. They claim that Lee treats the San as pure, isolated and timeless hunter-gatherers.

The chapters by Turnbull, Solway and Lee, Wilmsen, and Grinker, reveal the complexity of this debate. Turnbull describes how the Mbuti Pygmies divide their universe into two spheres: a forest world, that is completely good, and a village world that is malevolent. He analyzes the many social and economic relationships between the Mbuti Pygmies and Bila farmers in the Ituri forest, Zaire, but argues that they can be viewed as autonomous societies. He also claims that, despite the many social arenas in which the two groups interact, and the ostensible dominance of the farmers over the hunter-gatherers, the Mbuti are independent actors who, in the village world, merely pretend to be subordinates so that they can exploit the farmer's foods. In Chapter 13, Grinker argues, in contrast to Turnbull, that the separation of forest and village worlds is an ethnic classification, and that the two groups are integral parts of the same but differentiated social system. Whereas Turnbull explores the hunter-gatherer/farm relationships primarily from the hunter-gatherer perspective, Grinker takes the farmer perspective. In his study of the Lese farmers and Efe (Pygmies), who live just to the north of the Mbuti with whom Turnbull worked, he finds that both groups depend upon one another for their own distinctive social and cultural identities. In addition, he argues that previous hunter-gatherer studies focus so much on economics that they often overlook the role that symbols, ideas, and social organization play in structuring relations of inequality between hunter-gatherers and farmers. Grinker elaborates the Lese house as one of the mechanisms the Lese and the Efe use to integrate themselves into an asymmetrical social system defined by both ethnicity and gender. The focus on the house stands in contrast not only to Turnbull's portrait of the Mbuti, but also to the work of other authors who have taken the clan and lineage as the central organizing principles of society and economy (see Part I, for example). The house helps us to comprehend certain kinds of relationships – ethnic and gendered relationships – that remain virtually invisible from the perspective of descent models. Elsewhere, Grinker (1994: 197–98) writes:

> It is in light of inequality that the house holds promise for a critical anthropology of Africa, a field that has relied so heavily on analyses

of clans, descent groups, and other units that are, sometimes by definition, egalitarian social organizations, and often have little to do with gender or ethnic relations . . . Clans tell us something very important about the ideologies framed by men about men, but they often tell us mainly about sameness and equality, egalitarianism and solidarity. It is in the context of egalitarianism, of course, that the clan, descent and lineage become so important to the Lese. The organization of descent lines into clans is especially important in times of conflict . . . for collective action in the case of dispute or illness. But while the clan is essential to Lese social life, it is simply one level, one location, from which to analyze social organization. One location is not more important than the other, but an accurate anthropological picture depicts society as the product of the relationship between these two co-existing models.

Richard Lee has addressed some of the critical questions we listed above in his 1979 book *The !Kung San: Men, Women, and Work in a Foraging Society*. Lee attempts to show that the !Kung data, especially those concerning demography, mobility, food acquisition, and the division of labor, are directly relevant to the study of human evolution. One of Lee's more profound and influential conclusions is that our human ancestors, like the !Kung and other hunter-gatherers, forged a relatively peaceful collective existence in which human beings shared their resources, and suppressed antisocial individualism. He suggests, "a truly communal life is often dismissed as a utopian ideal . . . but the evidence of foraging peoples tells us otherwise" (1979: 461).

The 1980s was a fertile time for hunter-gatherer studies, especially for Lee's critics. Numerous authors, such as Edwin Wilmsen and James Denbow (1992), provided their own data to challenge Lee's conclusions. Among other things, they argued aggressively that the !Kung were contemporary people who should not be compared with humans living in the

Stone Age. As Wilmsen states clearly, the !Kung that we observe today, are the product of a long history influenced by complex international and regional forces. Solway and Lee respond to these so-called "revisionists" by showing how problematic the concept of history can be. First, in many of the works that situate the San in regional and international systems, the history of the San has been defined as "contact," that is, as social change motivated by forces external to the group itself. Contrary to the revisionist's intentions, this view, Solway and Lee argue, perpetuates the idea of the hunter-gatherer as fragile, pristine, and unable to produce or adapt to innovation and change. Hunter-gatherers can make their own histories in a complex process that includes exogenously and endogenously produced forces. In arguing that contact between groups does not always lead to relations of domination and subordination, they also suggest that hunter-gatherers have the agency, resistance, and resilience to remain relatively autonomous even in the face of powerful outside influences.

Second, history is as variable as culture. The historical processes that affect just one area of the Kalahari desert (an area roughly the size of France) may not affect another. Following up on this point, the authors show, through oral history, archaeology, and ethnography, that the Dobe San (among whom Lee conducted most of his fieldwork) and the Western Kweneng San have had radically different historical experiences. Whereas the latter were intimately involved with Bantu pastoralists and fur traders for several hundred years, and were directly affected by both the Difaqane wars of the early 1800s, and British colonial rule, the Dobe San have remained isolated and independent of other ethnic groups even to this day. Anthropologists, they argue, cannot generalize from one San area to the other without taking into account the total historical contexts of each group.

These arguments are hotly contested by Wilmsen and by Schrire (1992), and by Wilmsen and Denbow (1992). In sharp contrast to Solway and Lee, Wilmsen and Denbow claim that the San of the Dobe region were subordinated to a dominant Early Iron Age society in the first millennium, A.D. The San, they claim, are Botswana's underclass. San identity is the result of a long and complicated past in which they were marginalized from the centers of economic and political power, and forced into poverty and occasional isolation. The category "San," they suggest, is an invented anthropological category that overlooks the realities of San life, and masks their true history.

The Kalahari debate draws our attention to several important methodological and theoretical issues in anthropology: as discussed above, these include the problems of (1) how to situate the local communities anthropologists often study in the larger social, economic, and historical contexts in which they exist, (2) how to conceptualize history and contact, and (3) how anthropologists interested in human and cultural evolution can find fruitful ethnographic analogies among contemporary peoples. These readings also force us to consider the problematic relationship between ethnographic cases and analytic categories. Argument over the San is in many respects an argument over the very nature of anthropological classification because the comparative categories we employ are often only as good as the individual ethnographies that constitute them. "Hunter-Gatherer," as a category, is equated so often with Lee's specific presentation of the San, that criticisms of Lee's ethnography may apply equally well to the general study of hunter-gatherers as a cross-cultural type. This debate thus illustrates the theoretical perils encountered when, as we noted in the opening paragraph of this introduction, certain societies become the quintessential examples of particular topics, theories, or classifications.

References

Grinker, Roy Richard. 1994. *Houses in the Rainforest: Ethnicity and Inequality among Farmers and Foragers in Central Africa*. Berkeley: University of California Press.

Lee, Richard B., 1979. *The !Kung San: Men, Women, and Work in a Foraging Society*. Cambridge: Cambridge University Press.

Washburn, S. 1976. "Foreward." In R. B. Lee and I. DeVore, eds. *Kalahari Hunter-Gatherers: Studies of the !Kung San and their Neighbors*.

Wilmsen, E. and Denbow, J. 1990. "Paradigmatic History of San-Speaking Peoples and Current Attempts at Revision." *Current Anthropology* 31:589–524.

Suggested Readings

Aunger, R. V. 1992. An Ethnography of Variation: Food Avoidances among Horticulturalists and Foragers in the Ituri Forest, Zaire. Ph.D. Dissertation, Department of Anthropology, UCLA. Los Angeles, California.

Bahuchet, S. and H. Giullaume. 1982. "Aka-Farmer Relations in the Northwest Congo Basin." In Richard Lee and Eleanor Leacock (eds.), *Politics and History in Band Societies.*, pp. 189–212. Cambridge: Cambridge University Press.

Bailey, R. C. 1985. The Socioecology of Efe Pygmie Men in the Ituri Forest, Zaire. Ph.D. Dissertation, Department of Anthropology, Harvard University.

Bailey, R.C., G. Head, M. Jenike, B. Owen, R. Rechtman, and E. Zechenter. 1989. "Hunting and Gathering in Tropical Rain Forest: Is it Possible?" *American Anthropologist*, 91 (1):59–83.

Bailey, R. C. and N. R. Peacock. 1989. "Efe Pygmies of Northeast Zaire: Subsistence Strategies in the Ituri Forest." In I. de Garine and G. A. Harrison (eds.), *Coping with Uncertainty in the Food Supply*, pp. 88–117. Oxford: Clarendon Press.

Barnard, Alan. 1992. *Hunters and Herders of Southern Africa: A Comparative Ethnography of the Khoisan Peoples*. Cambridge: Cambridge University Press.

Bird-David, Nurit. 1992. "Beyond 'The Original Affluent Society': A Culturalist Reformulation." *Current Anthropology* 33 (1):25–47.

Cavalli-Sforza, L. 1987. *African Pygmies*. Orlando: Academic Press.

Hart, J. A. and T. B. Hart. 1984. The "Mbuti of Zaire: Political Change and the Opening of the

Ituri Forest." *Cultural Survival Quarterly* 8 (3):18–20.

Hewlett, Barry. 1991. *Intimate Fathers: The Nature and Context of Aka Pygmy Paternal Care*. Ann Arbor: University of Michigan.

Ichikawa, M. 1978. "The Residential Groups of the Mbuti Pygmies." *Senri Ethological Studies* 1:131–188.

———. 1981. "Ecological and Sociological Importance of Honey to the Mbuti Net-Hunters, Eastern Zaire." *African Study Monographs* 1:55–68.

Ingold, T. D. Riches, and J. Woodburn, eds. *Hunters and Gatherers*, 2 vols. New York: Berg.

Johnson, M. 1931. *Congorilla: Adventures with Pygmies and Gorillas in Africa*. New York: Bewer, Warren, and Putnam.

Johnston, Sir H. H. 1903. The Pygmies of the Great Congo Forest. *Annual Report of the Board of Regents of the Smithsonian Institution, the Year ending 1902*. pp. 479–91.

Katz, Richard. 1982. *Boiling Energy: Community Healing among the Kalahari !Kung*. Cambridge, MA: Harvard University Press.

Kuper, Adam. 1993. "Post-Modernism, Cambridge, and the Great Kalahari Debate." *Social Anthropology* 1(1):57–71.

Lee, R. B. and I. DeVore, eds. 1968. *Man the Hunter*. Chicago: Aldine.

Lee, R. B. and E. Leacock, eds. 1982. *Politics and History in Band Societies*. Cambridge: Cambridge University Press.

Marshall, Lorna. 1976. *The !Kung of Nyae Nyae*. Cambridge: Cambridge University Press.

Mosko, M. S. 1987. "The Symbols of the 'Forest': A Structural Analysis of Mbuti Culture and Social Organization." *American Anthropologist* 89 (4):896–9 913.

Schebesta, P. 1933. *Among Congo Pygmies.* London: Hutchinson and Co.

——. 1936. *My Pygmy and Negro Hosts.* London: Hutchinson and Co.

——. 1952. "Les Pygmées du Congo Belge." *Mem. Inst. Roy. Colonial Belge,* ser. 8, vol. 26, fasc. 2.

Schrire, C. 1984. *Past and Present in Hunter-Gatherer Studies.* Orlando: Academic Press.

Shostak, Marjorie. 1981. *Nisa: The Life of a !Kung Woman.* London: Allen Lane.

Silberbauer, George. 1981. *Hunter and Habitat in the Central Kalahari Desert.* Cambridge: Cambridge University Press.

Tanno, T. 1976. "The Mbuti Net-Hunters in the Ituri Forest, Eastern Zaire: their Hunting Activities and Band Composition." In *Kyoto University African Studies.*

Terashima, H. 1983. "Mota and other Hunting Activities of the Mbuti Archers: a Scioecological Study of Subsistence Technology." *African Studies Monographs* 3:60–71.

——. 1984. "The Structure of the Band of Mbuti Archers." In J. Itani and T. Yoneyama (eds.), *Afurika Bunka no Kenkyu.* Kyoto: Academica Shuppan-kai, pp. 3–41.

——. 1985. "Variation and Composition Principles of the Residence Group (Band) of the Mbuti Pygmies – Beyond a Typical/Atypical Dichotomy." *African Study Monographs,* Supplementary Issue, 4:103–20.

——. 1987. "Why do Efe Girls Marry Farmers?: the Socio-ecological Backgrounds of Inter-Ethnic Marriage in the Ituri Forest of Central Africa." *African Study Monographs* 6:65–84.

Turnbull, Colin. 1961. The Forest People. New York: Simon and Schuster.

——. 1965a. *The Mbuti Pygmies: An Ethnographic Survey.* Anthropological Papers of the American Museum of Natural History 50 (3): 139–282.

——. 1965b. *Wayward Servants: The Two Worlds of the African Pygmies.* New York: Natural History Press.

——. 1983a. *The Mbuti Pygmies: Change and Adaptation.* New York: Holt, Rinehart and Winston.

——. 1983b. *The Human Cycle.* New York: Simon & Schuster.

Vansina, Jan. 1990. *Paths in the Rainforest.* Madison: University of Wisconsin Press.

Yellen, John E. "The Present and the future of Hunter-Gatherer Studies." In C. C. Lamberg-Karlovsky, ed. *Archaeological Thought in America.* Cambridge: Cambridge University Press.

12

The Lesson of The Pygmies

COLIN M. TURNBULL

It has long been assumed that these inhabitants of the African rain forest had adapted to a kind of serfdom in villages. The discovery that they have not has implications for the problems of Africa today.

In the welter of change and crisis confronting the lives of the peoples of Africa it would seem difficult to work up concern for the fate of the 40,000 Pygmies who inhabit the rain forests in the northeastern corner of the Congo. The very word "pygmy" is a term of derogation. According to early explorers and contemporary anthropologists, the Pygmies have no culture of their own – not even a language. They became submerged, it is said, in the village customs and beliefs of the Bantu and Sudanic herdsmen – cultivators who occupied the periphery of the forest and reduce them to a kind of serfdom some centuries ago. By the testimony of colonial administrators and tourists they are a scurvy lot: thievish, dirty and shrouded with an aura of impish deviltry. Such reports reflect in part the sentiments of the village tribes; in many villages the Pygmies are regarded as not quite people.

To argue that the Pygmies are people – even to show that they maintain to this day the integrity of an ancient culture – will not avert or temper the fate that is in prospect for them. The opening of the rain forests of Central Africa to exploitation threatens to extinguish them as a people. The Pygmies are, in truth, *bamiki nde ndura*: children of the forest. Away from the villages they are hunters and food gatherers. The forest provides them with everything they need, generally in abundance, and enables them to lead an egalitarian, cooperative and leisured existence to which evil, in the sense of interpersonal malevolence, is so foreign that they have no word for it. After centuries of contact with the "more advanced" cultures of the villages and in spite of all appearances, their acculturation to any other mode of life remains almost nil. They have fooled the anthropologists as they have fooled the villagers. For this reason if for no other, the Pygmies deserve the concerned attention of the world outside. Their success should make us pause to reconsider the depth of acculturation that we have taken for granted as existing elsewhere, as industrial civilization has made its inexorable conquest of the earth.

The reason for the prevailing erroneous picture of the Pygmies is now clear. It had hitherto been generally impossible to have access to them except through the offices of the village headman, who would call the local Pygmies in from the forest to be interviewed. To all appearances they lived in some sort of symbiosis, if not serfdom, with the village people, subject to both the secular and the religious authority of the village. The fact that Pygmy boys undergo the village ritual of initiation in a relation of subservience to village boys was cited as evidence of ritual dependence, and it has been held that the Pygmies are economically dependent on the villages for metal and for plantation foods, presumably needed to supplement the meat they hunt in the forest. The few investigators who got away from the villages did not manage to do so without an escort of villagers, acting as porters or guides. Even in the forest the presence of a single villager transforms the context as far as the Pygmies are concerned; therefore all such observations were still basically of Pygmies in the village, not in their natural habitat.

My own initial impression was just as erroneous. By good fortune my contact with the Pygmies circumvented the village and was established from the outset on a basis that identified me with the world of the forest. Seeing them almost exclusively in the context of the forest, I saw a picture diametrically opposed to the one generally drawn. Instead of dependence, I saw at first independence of the village, a complete lack of acculturation – in fact, little contact of any kind. It was only after two additional stays in the Ituri Forest, the home ground of the Congo Pygmies, that I was able to put the two contradictory pictures of their life together and to see the whole. It turned out that neither is wrong; each is right in its particular context. The relation of the Pygmies to the villagers is a stroke of adaptation that has served their survival and even their convenience without apparent compromise of the integrity of their forest-nurtured culture.

The BaMbuti, as the Pygmies of the Ituri Forest are known to themselves and to their neighbors, may be the original inhabitants of the great stretch of rain forest that reaches from the Atlantic coast right across Central Africa to the open grassland country on the far side of the chain of great lakes that divides the Congo from East Africa. Their origin, along with that of Negrito peoples elsewhere in the world, is lost in the prehistoric past. Most Pygmies have unmistakable features other than height (they average less than four and a half feet) that distinguish them from Negroes. They are well muscled, usually sway-backed and have legs that are short in proportion to their torsos. Their faces, with wide-set eyes and flat, broad noses, have a characteristically alert expression, direct and unafraid, as keen as the attitude of the body, which is always poised to move with speed and agility at a moment's notice. They do not envy their neighbors, who jeer at them for their puny stature; in the enclosure of the forest, where life may depend on the ability to move swiftly and silently, the taller Negroes are as clumsy as elephants. For his part the Pygmy hunter wins his spurs by killing an elephant, which he does by running underneath the animal and piercing its bladder with a succession of quick jabs from a short-shafted spear.

A BaMbuti hunting band may consist of as many as 30 families, more than 100 men, women and children in all. On the move from one encampment to another they fill the surrounding forest with the sound of shouted chatter, laughter and song. Along with the venting of high spirits, this ensures that lurking leopards and buffaloes will be flushed into the forest well ahead of the band and not be accidentally cornered on the trail. The women, carrying or herding the infants, dart from the trail to gather food, and the men scout the forests for game on the flanks and in the van of the ragged procession. Arriving at the campsite in no particular order, all join in the task of building huts. The men usually cut the saplings to make the frames and sometimes also the giant Phrynium leaves to cover them; the women take charge of the actual building. The saplings are driven securely into the ground around a 10-foot circle, then deftly bent and intertwined to form a lattice dome; on this structure the leaves are hung like shingles, in overlapping tiers. Before nightfall, with the first arrivals helping the stragglers to complete their tasks, the camp is built and the smoke of cooking fires rises into the canopy of the forest.

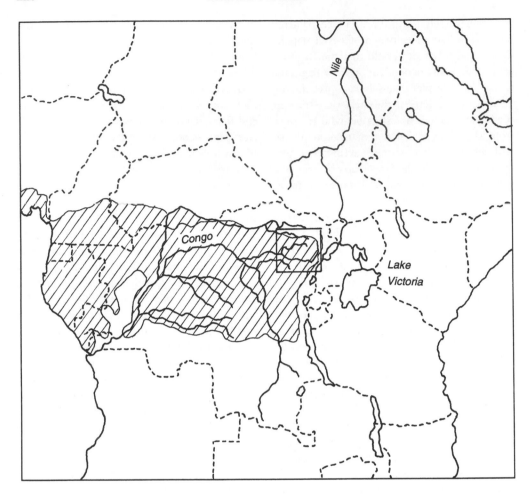

Figure 12.1 ITURI FOREST inhabited by the Pygmies occupies an area of roughly 50,000 square miles in the northeastern corner of the tropical rain forest of the Congo, in Central Africa.

The entire enterprise serves to demonstrate a salient feature of BaMbuti life: everything gets done with no direction and with no apparent organization.

A morning is usually all that is needed to secure the supply of food. The women know just where to look for the wild fruits that grow in abundance in the forests, although they are hidden to outsiders. The women recognize the undistinguished *itaba* vine, which leads to a cache of nutritious, sweet-tasting roots; the kind of weather that brings mushrooms springing to the surface; the exact moment when termites swarm and must be harvested to provide an important delicacy. The men hunt with bows and poison-tipped arrows, with spears for larger game and with nets. The last involves the Pygmy genius for co-operation. Each family makes and maintains its own net, four feet high and many yards long. Together they string the nets across a strategically chosen stretch of ground. The hunters, often joined by the women and older children, beat the forest, driving the game into the nets.

By afternoon they have brought enough food into camp and sometimes a surplus that

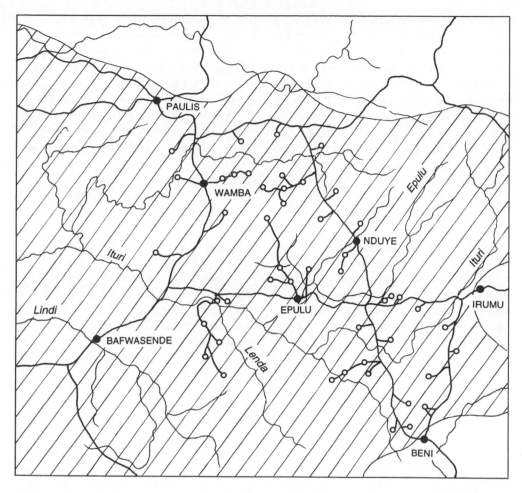

Figure 12.2   DETAIL MAP OF THE ITURI FOREST shows the Pygmy camps visited by the author *(small open circles)*, villages *(black dots)* and various rivers *(blue lines)*. The camps are connected by forest paths *(Thin black lines)*, the villages by roads *(heavy black lines)*.

will enable them to stay in camp the next day. Time is then spent repairing the nets, making new bows and arrows, baskets and other gear and performing various other chores. This still leaves a fair amount of free time, which is spent, apart from eating and sleeping, either in playing with the children and teaching them adult activities or in gathering in impromptu groups for song and dance.

The BaMbuti have developed little talent in the graphic arts beyond the occasional daubing of a bark cloth with red or blue dye, smeared on with a finger or a twig. They do, however, have an intricate musical culture. Their music is essentially vocal and noninstrumental. It displays a relatively complex harmonic sense and a high degree of rhythmic virtuosity. With the harmony anchored in the dominant and therefore all in one chord, the singing is often in canon form, with as many parts as there are singers and with improvisations and elaborations contributed freely by each. A song may have some general meaning, but it may also be totally devoid of words and consist simply of a succession of vowel sounds. The real meaning of the song, its importance and power, is in the sound. In the crisis festival of the *molimo*, the closest approximation to a ritual in the unformalized life of the BaMbuti, the men of the band will sing, night after night, through the night until dawn. The function of the sound now is to "awaken the forest" so that it will learn the plight of its children or hear of their joy in its bounty.

The spirit of co-operation, seen in every activity from hunting to singing, takes the place of formal social organization in the BaMbuti hunting band. There is no headman, and individual authority and individual responsibility are shunned by all. Each member of the band can expect and demand the co-operation of others and must also give it. In essence the bonds that make two brothers hunt together and share their food are not much greater than those that obtain between a member of a band and a visiting Pygmy, even if he is totally unrelated. Any adult male is a father to any child; any woman, a mother. They expect the same help and respect from all children and they owe the same responsibilities toward them.

When the Pygmies encamp for a while near a village, the character of the band and its activities undergo profound and complete transformation. This happens even when a lone villager pays a visit to a Pygmy camp. Not only do such activities as singing and dancing and even hunting change, but so also do the complex interpersonal relations. The Pygmies then behave toward each other as they would if they were in a village. They are no longer a single, united hunting band, co-operating closely, but an aggregate of individual families, within which there may even be disunity. On periodic visits to the village with which their hunting band is associated, the Pygmies occupy their own semipermanent campsite between the village and the forest. Each family usually has a particular village family with which it maintains a loose and generally

friendly exchange relation. At such times the Pygmies not only supply meat, they may also supply some labor. Their main function, as the villagers see it, is to provide such forest products as meat, honey and the leaves and saplings needed for the construction of village houses. The villagers do not like the forest and go into it as seldom as possible.

It is on these occasions that travelers have seen the Pygmies and decided that they are vassals to the villagers, with no cultural identity of their own. It is true that this is how the BaMbuti appear while they are in the villages, because in this foreign world their own code of behavior does not apply. In the village they behave with a shrewd sense of expediency. It in no way hurts them to foster the villagers' illusion of domination; it even helps to promote favorable economic relations. As far as the BaMbuti are concerned, people who are not of the forest are not people. The mixture of respect, friendship and cunning with which they treat their village neighbors corresponds to the way they treat the animals of the forest: they use them as a source of food and other goods, respecting them as such and treating them with tolerant affection when they are not needed. The Pygmies have a saying that echoes the proverb of the goose and the golden egg, to the effect that they never completely and absolutely eat the villagers, they just eat them.

In the mistaken interpretations of this peculiar relation the fact that the Pygmies seem to have lost their original language is often cited as evidence of their acculturation to the village. Linguists, on the other hand, see nothing surprising in this fact. Small, isolated hunting bands, caught up in the intertribal competition that must have attended the Bantu invasion that began half a millennium ago, could well have lost their own language in a couple of generations. It is by no means certain, however, that the Pygmy language is extinct. Certain words and usages appear to be unique to the Pygmies and do not occur in the languages and dialects of any of the numerous

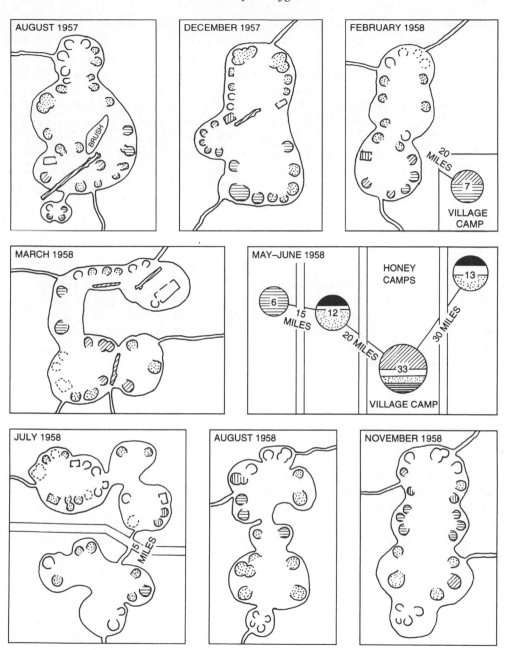

Figure 12.3 FOREST CAMPS change structure and constitution in cyclical fashion as Pygmies move from one campsite to another; they become increasingly fragmented at the approach of the honey season (May through June), break up during the season *(figures show number of families)* and re-form afterward. The disposition of huts, direction in which they face and their shapes are as shown; some were later abandoned *(broken lines)*. Of the clans constituting the group with which the author stayed during the period, the main one was the Bapuemi *(solid-coloured areas)*. A quarrel resulted in a split camp *(lower left)*, which gradually re-formed.

neighboring tribes. What is more, the Pygmies' intonation is so distinctive, no matter which of the languages they are speaking, as to render their speech almost unintelligible to the villager whose language it is supposed to be.

Some authorities maintain that the Pygmies rely on the villagers for food and metal. As for food, my own experience has shown that the BaMbuti hunting bands are perfectly capable of supporting themselves in the forest without any help from outside. The farther away from the villages they are, in fact, the better they find the hunting and gathering. If anything, it is the villagers who depend on the Pygmies, particularly for meat to supplement their protein-deficient diet.

It is more difficult to determine to what extent the BaMbuti are dependent on village metal. A few old men speak of hardening the points of their wooden spears in fire, and children's spears are still made in this way. Except for elephant hunting the spear is mostly a defensive weapon, and the loss of metal spear blades would not be serious. Knife and ax blades are more important; the word *machetti* – for the long, heavy-bladed brush-slashing knife – is well established in the Pygmy vocabulary. There are thorny vines, however, that can serve adequately as scrapers and others that when split give a sharp if temporary cutting edge, like that of split bamboo. When I have pressed the question, it has been stated to me that, in the absence of metal blades, "we would use stones." On the other hand, I have never succeeded in persuading a Pygmy to show me how. The answer to such a request was invariably: "Why should I go to all that trouble when it is so easy to get metal tools from the villagers?"

This is in fact the core of the Pygmies' economic relation with the villagers, and it renders the term "symbiosis" inapplicable. There is nothing they need badly enough to make them dependent on the villagers, although they use many artifacts acquired from them. Metal cooking utensils are a good example: the Pygmies can get along without

these comfortably. They use them only for the cooking of village foods that require boiling, such as rice; forest foods call for no such utensils. The BaMbuti will exchange goods with the villagers and even work for them, but only as long as it suits their convenience and no longer. No amount of persuasion will hold them. If a villager attempts coercion, the Pygmy simply packs up and goes back to the forest, secure in the knowledge that he will not be followed. On the next occasion he will offer his goods in another village. Tribal records are full of disputes in which one villager has accused another of stealing "his" Pygmies.

In the absence of effective economic control the villagers attempt to assert political and religious authority. The villagers themselves are the source of the myth that they "own" the Pygmies in a form of hereditary serfdom. They appoint Pygmy headmen, each responsible for his band to the appropriate village headman. Because the bands not only shift territorially but also change as to their inner composition, however, a village headman can no more be sure which Pygmy families comprise "his" band than he can tell at any time where the band has wandered. In his appointed Pygmy headman he has a scapegoat he can blame for failure of the band to fulfill its side of some exchange transaction. But the Pygmy has no wealth with which to pay fines and can rarely be caught for the purpose of enforcing any other restitution.

The villagers nonetheless believe themselves to be the masters. They admit it is a hard battle and point out that the Pygmies are in league with the powerful and tricky spirits of the forest. The fear the villagers have of the forest goes beyond a fear of the animals; it is also a respect based on the knowledge that they are newcomers, if of several hundred years' standing. This respect is even extended to the Pygmies. Some villages make offering to the Pygmies of the first fruit, acknowledging that the Pygmies were there before them and so have certain rights over the land. This offering is also expected to placate the forest spirits. Ultimately, however, the villagers hope to subject the Pygmies to the village spirits and thereby to assume total domination.

In carrying the contest into the realm of the supernatural, the villagers invoke the full armory of witchcraft and sorcery. To the villagers these methods of social control are just as scientific and real as, say, political control through armed force. Moreover, although witchcraft and sorcery generally get their results by psychological pressure, they can sometimes be implemented by physiological poisons. There are strange tales of illness and of death due to sorcery, and no Pygmy wants to be cursed by a villager. On receiving threats of this kind the hunting band takes to the forest, secure in the belief that village magic is no more capable of following them into the forest than are the villagers themselves.

More subtly, the villagers engage the Pygmies in the various important rituals of the village culture. A Pygmy birth, marriage or death, occurring when the hunting band is bivouacked near a village, sets in motion the full village ceremonial appropriate to the occasion. The "owner" of the Pygmy in each case assumes the obligation of providing the child-protecting amulet, of negotiating the exchange of bride wealth or of paying the cost of the obsequies. Such intervention in a Pygmy marriage not only ensures that the union is regularized according to village ritual; it also gives the owners in question indissoluble rights, natural and supernatural, over the new family. The Pygmies willingly submit to the ritual because it means a three-day festival during which they will be fed by the villagers and at end of which, with luck, they will be able to make off with a portion of the bride wealth. On returning to the forest the couple may decide that it was just a flirtation and separate, leaving the villagers to litigate the expense of the transaction and the wedding feast. Although they are economically the losers, the villagers nonetheless believe that by forcing or cajoling the Pygmies through the

ritual they have subjected them, at least to some extent, to the control of the village supernatural.

The same considerations on both sides apply to a funeral. The ritual places certain obligations on the family of the deceased and lays supernatural sanctions on them; death also involves, almost invariably, allegations of witchcraft or sorcery. Once again, therefore, the villagers are eager to do what is necessary to bring the Pygmies within the thrall of the local spirit world. And once again the Pygmies are willing to co-operate, knowing that the village funerary ritual prescribes a funerary feast. Even though their custom calls for quick and unceremonious disposal of the dead, they are glad to let the villagers do the disposing and even to submit to head-shaving and ritual baths in return for a banquet.

By far the most elaborate ritual by which the villagers hope to bring the Pygmies under control is the initiation of the Pygmy boys into manhood through the ordeal of circumcision, called *nkumbi*. All village boys between the ages of nine and 12 are subject to this practice, which takes place every three years. Pygmy boys of the appropriate age who happen to be in the vicinity are put through the same ceremony with the village boys. A Pygmy boy is sent first "to clean the knife," as the villagers put it, and then he is followed by a village boy. These two boys are thereafter joined by the blood they shed together in the unbreakable bond of *kare*, or blood brotherhood. Any default, particularly on the part of the Pygmy, will invoke the wrath of the ancestors and bring all manner of curses on the offender. So once more the Pygmies are placed under the control of the village spirits and the putative bonds between the serfs and their owners are reinforced. Some villagers also see this practice as a means of securing for themselves an assured complement of Pygmy serfs to serve them in the afterworld.

As in all the other ritual relations, the BaMbuti have their own independent motivation and rationalization for submitting their sons to the pain and humiliation of *nkumbi*. For one thing, the Pygmy boys acquire the same secular adult status in the village world as their village blood brothers. The Pygmies, moreover, have the advantage of knowing that the bonds they do not consider unbreakable nonetheless tie their newly acquired village brothers; they made use of this knowledge by imposing on their *kare*. Finally, for the adult male relatives of the Pygmy initiates the ceremony means three months or so of continuous feasting at the expense of the villagers.

Once the *nkumbi* is over and the Pygmies have returned to the forest, it becomes clear that the ritual has no relevance to the inner life of the family and the hunting band. The boys who have gone to such trouble to become adults in the village sit on the laps of their mothers, signifying that they know they are really still children. In Pygmy society they will not become adults until they have proved themselves as hunters.

Back in the forest the Pygmies once again become forest people. Their counter to the villagers' efforts to bring them under domination is to keep the two worlds apart. This strategy finds formal expression in the festival of the *molimo*. The *molimo* songs are never sung when a band is making a visitation to a village or is encamped near it. Out in the forest, during the course of each night's singing, the trail leading off from the camp in the direction of the village is ceremonially blocked with branches and leaves, shutting out the profane world beyond.

The relation between Pygmy and the village cultures thus resolves itself in a standoff. Motivated as it is by economics, the relation is inherently an adversary one. The villagers seek to win the contest by domination; the Pygmies seek to perpetuate it by a kind of indigenous apartheid. Because the relation is one of mutual convenience rather than necessity, it works with reasonable success in the economic realm. The villagers ascribe the success,

however, to their spiritual domination; any breakdown they cannot correct they are content to leave to rectification by the supernatural, a formula that works within their own society. The Pygmies hold, on the other hand, that the forest looks after its own, a belief that is borne out by their daily experience. In the nature of the situation, each group is able to think it has succeeded, as indeed in its own eyes it has. The very separateness of the two worlds makes this dual solution possible. But it is a solution that can work only in the present context.

A breakdown began when the Belgians insisted that the villagers plant cotton and produce a food surplus. The villagers then needed the Pygmies even more as a source of manpower. At the same time, with roads being cut through the forest, the movement of game became restricted. If the process had continued, the Pygmies would have found it increasingly difficult to follow their hunting and food-gathering way of life and would indeed have become the economic dependents of the villagers. The present political turmoil in the Congo has given the Pygmies a temporary reprieve.

In some areas, however, the Belgians had decided to pre-empt the untapped Pygmy labor force for themselves and had already set about "liberating" the Pygmies from the mythical yoke of the villagers, persuading them to set up plantations of their own. The result was disastrous. Used to the constant shade of the forest, to the purity of forest water and to the absence of germ-carrying flies and mosquitoes, the Pygmies quickly succumbed to sunstroke and to various illnesses against which the villagers have some immunity. Worse yet, with the abandoning of hunting and food gathering the entire Pygmy social structure collapsed. Forest values were necessarily left behind in the forest, and there was nothing to take their place but a pathetic and unsuccessful imitation of the new world around them, the world of villagers and of Europeans.

This whole problem was much discussed among the Pygmies just prior to the independence of the Congo. In almost every case they reached the determination that as long as the forest existed they would try to go on living as they had always lived. More than once I was told, with no little insight, that "when the forest dies, we die." So for the Pygmies, in a sense, there is no problem. They have seen enough of the outside world to feel able to make their choice, and their choice is to preserve the sanctity of their own world up to the very end. Being what they are, they will doubtless continue to play a masterful game of hide-and-seek, but they will not easily sacrifice their integrity.

It is for future administrations of the Congo that the problem will be a real one, both moral and practical. Can the vast forest area justifiably be set aside as a reservation for some 40,000 Pygmies? And if the forest is to be exploited, what can one do with its inhabitants, who are physically, temperamentally and socially so unfitted for any other form of life? If the former assessment of the Pygmy-villager relation had been correct and the Pygmies had really been as acculturated as it seemed, the problem would have resolved itself into physiological terms only, serious enough but not insuperable. As it is, seeing that the Pygmies have for several hundred years successfully rejected almost every basic element of the foreign cultures surrounding them, the prospects of adaptation are fraught with hazards.

Traditional values die hard, it would seem, and continue to thrive even when they are considered long since dead and buried. In dealing with any African peoples, I suspect, we are in grave danger if we assume too readily that they are the creatures we like to think we have made them. If the Pygmies are any indication, and if we realize it in time, it may be as well for us and for Africa that they are not.

13

Houses in the Rainforest: Gender and Ethnicity among the Lese and Efe in Zaire

ROY RICHARD GRINKER

We [the Lese] gained our independence from the Belgians in 1960, but the Efe [Pygmies] have not gained their independence from us.

A Lese man at the funeral of his Efe partner

At night in Lese villages, men sit outside their houses in their *pasa*, the roofed meeting places in the village plaza, and tell stories. At the center of the pasa is a fire. The nights are chilly in the rain forest and children may come to warm themselves by the fire while their mothers sit on makeshift chairs on the edge of the pasa. At these times, men and women will talk about the forest, of its dangers and darkness, and and of the tricksters and other spirits that harass and torment the farmers who try to enter. It seemed to me that the stories were directed toward the children and even intended to frighten them. One story tells of a man who goes to the forest and is seduced by a female forest spirit. She forces her way into his body and rips open his skin, disemboweling and killing him. Another story tells of a farmer who goes to the forest to set an animal trap. He meets a female forest spirit with leprosy who tells him that he can pass by only if he licks the blood and pus from her lesions. Even after he agrees, she transforms herself into a knife and impales him. A third story tells of an Efe spirit named Befe who comes from the forest into the village, exhumes and rapes the corpse of a Lese girl, and then rapes the village houses by penetrating the doors with his large phallus.

This chapter is about the village and the forest. But it is more generally about the opposition between the Lese and the Efe. It is difficult to imagine oppositions that are more sharp and fundamental than those which the Lese make between themselves and the Efe: village versus forest, culture versus nature, the civilized versus the savage, male versus female, white versus red, light versus dark. The Lese hold that they are civilized and cultural, because, among other things, they live in villages, cultivate food crops, and go to school and church, whereas the Efe are savages who live in the forest, hunt and gather, have only temporary settlements, and know nothing of God, mathematics, and the French language. Through metaphor, the Lese seek both to define themselves and to denigrate the Efe.

Gender is perhaps the most salient metaphor for characterizing the Efe; Lese men and women frequently characterize the Efe, and the forest in which the Efe live, as female.[1] The Lese, in contrast, characterize themselves, and the village in which they live, as male. In fact, the distinctions they make between themselves and the Efe, as groups, can be seen to parallel those between men and women in general, and between Lese men and their wives in particular. The Lese see the Lese–Efe relationship as part of a series of male–female oppositions, which, by implication, puts the Efe in the subordinate female position. The metaphor also implies a more specific relationship between the Efe and Lese men's wives and draws an analogic equivalence between them. In the Lese house, these two groups of people are subordinate to Lese men, and are thus culturally represented in similar ways. The central argument of this chapter is that the symbolic incorporation of the Efe into the Lese house is made possible by a particular Lese discourse about Lese–Efe differences . . .

The Forest and the Village

Although both the Lese and the Efe live in the Ituri forest, the Lese of Malembi with whom I lived deny that they themselves live in the forest. They say they live in the village and the Efe live in the forest. This dichotomy, repeated time and time again in Turnbull's work, is as fundamental to the Lese as was the opposition between Europe and the "dark continent," the white and the black. The forest for the Lese is analogous to the "jungle" for the European, conceived as impenetrable, dark, and dangerous. Stanley's description of the "green hell" (Vansina 1990a:39) he traveled through while crossing the Ituri forest is echoed in the experience of other explorers, missionaries, and administrators in the Congo.

And the Lese of Malembi, recalling the missionaries and other Europeans, are proud that they are "of the village," whereas the Efe are "of the forest." The forest is the place where the hostile ancestral spirits of the Lese dwell, spirits the Lese call *tore*, and translate into Swahili as *shaitani* (Satan), and the attributes associated with the forest – darkness, wetness, danger, and uncertainty, among other things – are therefore also associated with the Efe. The construction of ethnic boundaries goes hand in hand with the construction of inequality, in which the village is made to represent everything good, while the forest represents everything bad. This division of the world is echoed by Bahuchet and Guillaume (1982) in their account of Aka–Bantu relations, as well as by E. Waehle (1985:392), who writes: "The Efe are savages and sub-humans (likened to chimpanzees or forest hogs); they are thieves; the forest is the contradiction to the village (almost as nature to culture)."

The two worlds are diametrically opposed, and the difference between them represents one of the most significant and basic markers of ethnic distinction. For example, when an Efe woman marries a Lese man, and moves, as she must, to the village, the Efe and the Lese say that she has married the village (*anga-ni ubo-ke*); the groom is said to have "married [a girl] of the forest" (*anga-ni meli-ba*). Lese men insult other Lese men who engage in extensive hunting with the term "forest people," and any man who behaves in a manner believed by the Lese to be stereotypical of the Efe will be referred to by the Lese, disparagingly, as either a "forest person" or an "Efe."

For both the Lese and the Efe, the forest begins and ends with areas cleared for Lese houses and pasa. The forest is where the cleared land surrounding the village becomes

---

[1] Feminizing the subordinate or subordinating by feminizing is extremely common. Two of the most compelling examples are Jean and John Comaroff's discussion of the feminization of Africa and Africans by nineteenth-century Europeans (Comaroff and Comaroff 1991) and Jean Jackson's description of the Tukanoan denigration of the Maku in the central Northwest Amazon (1983:227–239).

wild and overgrown. Even a small patch of wild foliage creeping into the village area will be called forest, and the Lese may say that the forest "is coming closer." With the exception of forest paths, any area in which trees and shrubs have not been cut down and weeds and vines have not been removed will be considered forest. . . . Efe camps, even when they are situated only a few hundred meters from the village, sometimes within the garden of their Lese partners, are said to be in the forest.

Even with this close proximity, thcrc is a noticeable difference between Lese and Efe settlements. Though the Efe usually cut down some trees and vines, their camps are not cleared of all plant life, as are the Lese villages. The borders of Efe camps form a circle, or at least a highly curved and ambiguously defined domain. The huts are hemispherical, made of leaves and sticks, and the land of the camp area is black, brown, green, moist, and full of plant and insect life. Because the land is rarely weeded and so many trees are left standing, the sun cannot penetrate the canopy of the forest, and the land on which the Efe live remains damp and soft. The Lese villages, in addition to being well-defined and impeccably cleared areas of land, contain square or rectangular houses that are placed symmetrically in relation to the road and to other houses.

The Efe also find the opposition between the forest and the village to be significant. During my fieldwork, the Efe complained, in particular, about the insects in the village. Echoing Turnbull's reports of the Mbuti attitude toward the village (1965:18), Efe told me that the mosquitos are far more common in the villages, and that when Efe live in the villages for a long time they become ill. Indeed, outside the villages mosquitoes remain in the higher levels of the forest, where the trees have not been cut, and because the mosquitoes feed upon the monkeys and other arborial organisms, they are less irritating to human beings. In addition, when Efe camps become polluted with refuse and begin to attract fleas, the Efe can abandon the camp and quickly build

another one nearby. The Efe would surely agree with Turnbull's characterization:

> Where in the villages, and in the plantations that surround them, the midday temperatures soar well into the nineties, and the ground is covered with a dry, choking dust that quickly turns to mud, in the shade of the forest the world is cool and fresh, with only rare places, such as along river banks or at salt licks, where sunlight reaches the ground without first being filtered through a leafy roof. Also from the point of view of comfort, and of health, where village conditions lead to gatherings of flies and mosquitoes, these disease bearers are seldom if ever seen in the depths of the forest, except at such sites as are easily avoided. The Mbuti frequently compare their lot, in these respects, with that of the villagers, who in turn grudgingly admit to some advantages of forest life. (1965:18)

Yet Lese men, women, and children asserted that they could not live in the forest, that they would be cold, hungry, wet, and prone to disease; they might be bitten by snakes or insects, or, worse, they might encounter trouble from supernatural forces. The Lese often complained about the insects of the forest, namely, fleas and other creatures that are attracted by the garbage that collects in Efe camps.

Lese Representations: Hygiene and Sexuality

For the Lese, then, Efe camps represent a whole set of ideas about dirt, health, bodily odors, and secretions. Lese children were particularly illuminating about these ideas. Once when I accompanied a Lese family through an area of forest to check on a fish trap in a river, we found ourselves in an Efe camp that had been abandoned for about a year. One hut was still standing, and I held the hand of a six-year-old boy to whom I was especially close as I went to look inside it. He pulled away from me suddenly, and when I asked him why he was afraid, he said that he did not want to go inside the hut. I told him I only wanted to look inside, and he said that he did not even want to look, that he might get lice or fleas or become sick and die. The huts, his father explained, still contain body products, "things of their bodies," as he put it. The same little boy once shrieked with disgust after he smelled the scent of my shaving cream; he said that it smelled like the Efe, and that the odor "made [his] stomach unhappy." Lese adults, especially women, spoke to me about Efe hygiene, and cited Efe body odor as one of the main reasons why they would not engage in sexual intercourse with Efe men (indeed, I know of no cases, and only a few rumors, of this). Moreover, though under special circumstances some Lese may eat food out of the same cooking pot as an Efe, they will not eat food off the same plate, or banana leaf, as the Efe. This is more than a simple display of inequality. Serving food on the same plate is considered to be an unclean and unsafe act. . . .

When I asked one woman whether she "liked" Efe, her answer moved from comments about manners and habits to comments about cleanliness and dirt:

> I like Efe. No problem if they steal from me. I will not beat them. I get angry just to frighten them. They are not like *muto* (people). They have no *akiri* (intelligence, in KiSwahili). Our heart is the same, but their *akiri* is not the same. Their thoughts are different. They forget quickly, like conflicts with other people, they forget them quickly. But their eyes are the same as the eyes of people. They have the same sweat, but it smells different. It is pungent (*ikochi*). They sleep [live] for two months sometimes without bathing, or maybe they don't bathe for two weeks. Their underarms smell and they sleep on old banana leaves, and the old banana leaves smell too. They do not like to wash; they are used to old things – it is their custom (*desturi* in KiSwahili). And their chests get very dirty, and if you give them

soap, they do not wash their bodies, they will only wash their clothes.

Finally, the Lese of Malembi often spoke among themselves about how Efe defecate. Lese build outhouses, but the Efe do not, and, according to my informants, Efe will defecate anywhere in the forest. One Lese legend tells of an Efe girl who drowns in her own relative's diarrhea, and many other legends about the Efe incorporate excremental or anal themes. Two Lese men tried to help their Efe partners build outhouses, but said their attempts were in vain because the Efe are not "civilized" (*civilisé*), that they still live like "animals" (*ura*).

The excremental theme is used primarily to characterize the Efe, but it can be used by the Lese self-referentially in joking contexts. One joke concerning the physical differences between the Lese and the Efe asks: When someone defecates the feces falls and can be heard hitting the ground, but when someone urinates, the urine falls lightly onto the ground, and is silent – what am I talking about? The answer is: the Lese and the Efe. The Lese are fatter, taller, and heavier; the Efe are leaner, shorter, and lighter. But whereas height may be the most significant difference for American or European observers, the Lese pay closer attention to weight, skin color, the *shape* of the body, odor, the hair, and the eyebrows. The joke itself concerns the differences between the weight of Efe and Lese. One aspect of the joke that is not obvious is the analogy of color between the pairs, feces–urine, and Lese–Efe. Both the Efe and urine are considered to be red in color, since Efe skin color is lighter and more reddish than Lese skin color, and urine is also red (there is no word in either the Lese or Efe dialects for yellow). Likewise, both feces and Lese skin color are considered to be black. The Lese admire the Efe's lighter skin color, find it more beautiful, and value highly reddish skin color among themselves.

Lese also note the variation in muscle tone

and fatness. Whereas the Efe have little body fat and are very muscular, the Lese are fatter and appear less robust. The Efe are light-footed, an advantage for hunters, whereas the Lese are heavy-footed and make noise that frightens off the animals. In addition, the Efe are more hirsute. Their eyebrows are much fuller than those of the Lese, and the Lese say that when they travel in areas where there has been extensive intermarriage between Efe and Lese, where some of the physical distinctions are thus blurred, and where differences between the Lese and Efe dialects are not as clear, they can distinguish between Efe and Lese by looking first at the eyebrows. Moreover, Efe women have more chest hair than Lese women. Another joke told by Lese to refer to body hair as well as duplicity and shiftiness is the following: Efe have hairy chests – what am I talking about? The answer is: an *ene* animal trap, a large trap hole covered and hidden by leaves, sticks, vines, and other wild plants.

Lese men are extremely attracted to their stereotypical characterization of Efe women, specifically Efe women's body hair. Thirty-three out of forty men I interviewed (83%) on the subject of sexual attraction reported that during their lives they had engaged in sexual intercourse with an Efe woman; only five (12.5%), the youngest men in the sample, had never had sex with an Efe woman (two men did not wish to answer my question). In fact, the one physical attribute of the Efe women that the Lese men consistently reported as the most distinctive, attractive, and sexually arousing was body hair. Lese men speak among themselves of how exciting *torumbaka* (or pubic hair) is to them. *Torumbaka* literally means "hair from the crotch," but it is used specifically to refer to hair around the navel, or between the breasts; it is said to be unique to the Efe and is also said to have the power to produce instant erections in men.

Controlling Nature and Culture

Lese men project their own anxiety about control of their sexual desires for Efe women onto the Efe, whom they perceive to be sexually wild – like the forest in which they live. Indeed, the issue of control is central to Lese conceptions of the Efe and of themselves. From the Lese point of view, the Efe are uncontrolled, unrestrained; they act without planning or meditation, and their social organization is turbulent and disorderly and permits sexual relationships that the Lese consider incestuous. Efe men, according to Lese men, are addicted to sex and must engage in intercourse at least once a day. Lese men also say that the Efe's desire for marijuana predisposes the Efe toward violence and disorder. Lese men place a high value on their own self-control and for this reason very seldom smoke marijuana in adulthood. In addition, the Lese want to control the Efe. What Turnbull writes of the Bila and the Mbuti (1965:42, 83–84) applies somewhat to the Lese and the Efe, since the Lese do not use physical force and rarely go into the forest to control the Efe: "The villagers themselves admit their inability to exert physical force to bend the Mbuti to their will, for the Mbuti always have the ultimate escape of flight to the sanctuary of the forest. The villagers are completely unequipped to pursue the Mbuti into the forest and never attempt it" (1965:84). On one occasion when I was traveling to an Efe camp, an excited Lese villager named Filipe gave me a note he had written in Swahili ordering his Efe partner, Abdala, to come to the villages. The Efe who live near Malembi do not know how to read, so I read the note to them. Abdala then asked me to tell Filipe that he would come soon. When I returned to the village and reported Abdala's reply, Filipe became irate and asked, "But when? When will he come? I do not know where he is." In fact, Filipe knew very well where Abdala was, but he was perhaps expressing outrage at being unable to control his Efe's movements.

Indeed, the desire to control the Efe seems to be not a desire for political domination so much as an expression of anxiety about Efe mobility. Lese men and women often seemed disturbed when they heard, sometimes by word of mouth, that their Efe partner had moved from one camp to another or had gone to a plantation to sign up for wage labor. They also seemed worried when they learned that their Efe were traveling or living near the Lese gardens – partly because of the unpredictability of their Efe's whereabouts, partly, too, because they were afraid the Efe would steal their cultivated food. Like the forest growth that encroaches upon the swept earth of the village, the Lese say the Efe encroach upon the village gardens and threaten to ruin the carefully tended fields of cultivated food. . . .

In contrast to the Efe, the Lese consider themselves to be predictable and stable, controlled, restrained, organized, and thoughtful. They also believe that they have a greater *akiri* (intelligence) than the Efe. For the Lese, someone with akiri is educated, speaks several languages, can offer advice, can be trusted, is dependable, and is not self-destructive. At one Efe funeral, a Lese man simultaneously criticized and complimented the Efe in my presence by saying, "The Efe of before had no akiri, but now they do. Look at this white person [the author] who doesn't go to the forest everyday, but resides more often with the Lese. He has akiri. To go to the forest every day is bad and without akiri." In addition to being more sedentary, someone with akiri is also well-liked and diplomatic: "Someone with akiri doesn't say what he wants very quickly; he waits, and when he thinks that the person he is with likes him, and is calm, he will say what he wants." In contrast, the Efe are unwilling to "sooth" (*iruka*) their partners, and will let their desires be known at the start of a conversation with an exchange partner. . . .

One of the most common and explicit ways that the Lese disparage the Efe is to accuse them of stealing ("like baboons") foods out of their garden and destroying (*ima-ni*) the garden, even after they have been given food by the Lese partner. Lese make a connection between the Efe, a specific kind of insect, and rainbows, all three of which are believed to damage or destroy the Lese crops. Efe are frequently called *kongu*, the name for a species of large flies that can always be seen buzzing near the prized *njeru* variety of bananas, and that, in legend, inhabits the far end of rainbows (*raba* – for the Lese, an extremely dangerous phenomenon) and helps the rainbow to enter into the village from outside and destroy cultivated foods. The Lese also speak of the Efe as gluttonous in their appetite for food, tobacco and marijuana, and sex. The Efe, the Lese say, cannot farm for themselves because they have no *sibosibo* (patience), and because they lack the capacity to engage in a productive activity that does not offer immediate gratification. . . .

As noted earlier, the Efe and Lese speak differently. In addition to some differences in vocabulary, where the Lese use glottal consonants, the Efe instead place faucial gaps. But many Lese say that the difference is not so much in the words and grammar as in the organization of ideas. The Lese say that Efe speech is often incoherent and babbling, that when they speak they jump from one idea to the next, that their "ideas have no straight path" (*ide-ba todi a upu kikikiko embi-ani*). Paralleling what some Lese seem to think is an attention deficiency, Efe men are also said to have short and violent tempers and to murder without much provocation. These perceptions have their basis in the angry and sometimes violent fights that punctuate the daily life of many Efe camps, but actual murders are extremely rare. In addition, the Efe are the most fierce and frenzied actors at funerals. The fact that Efe always carry their bow and arrows and/or spear also contributes to the perception of the Efe as wild or savage. . . .

In terms of the classification of living things, in both the Efe and the Lese dialects, the Lese are called *muto* and the Efe are called *Efe*. *Muto* means "person," as I was called a *mutotufe* (white person), and Africans are in general called *mutokosa* (black person). In terms of classification of ethnicity, the Lese are called *Lese* or *Dese*, and the Efe are called *Efe*. Thus, while the Lese have three terms, one to distinguish themselves from the Efe and animals (*muto*), one to distinguish themselves from other groups (*Lese*), and another to distinguish themselves from other Lese (*Dese*), the Efe have only one term. The term *Efe* thus denotes nothing other than the archer Pygmies, and, unlike the word *muto*, has no other usage. The term *Efe* is not subsumed within the term *muto*. Linguistically, then, one might think that the *Efe* are not considered to be people. However, there is little uniformity regarding the location of the Efe in humanity; in the Lese language, Efe are under no circumstances called *muto*, nor do Efe refer to themselves as *muto*. In the KiNgwana form of Swahili, however, I was told, "yes the Efe are *watu* ['people,' in Swahili] but they are not muto ['people,' in Lese]." It is entirely possible that the Lese word for person, *muto*, also means "farmer." . . .

Nonetheless, the extent to which the Lese hope to surpass the Efe in terms of status cannot be overemphasized because this ideology of inequality bears directly on the argument that the two groups must be considered as one. It is easy enough to simply record denigrations. The Lese are quick to say that they believe the Efe should be *amu-ba-ni karu-ta* (under our feet) as the Efe have always been *amu kondu-ni karu-ta* (under our ancestor's feet). The more difficult task is to analyze the various denigrations of distinct contexts for symbolic patterns and associations. Indeed, analysis of the characterizations tells us something more general, something central to the very fabric of Lese identity. What all these characterizations of inequality suggest is that the Efe are not wholly "other" to the Lese because they are such a strong component and defining characteristic of Lese representations of themselves. For example, for the Lese, the dirtiness of the Efe is paired with their own

cleanliness, the wildness of the Efe is paired with their own wish for self-control. The Lese and the Efe are thus less in conflict than they are mutually constitutive. According to the Lese, Efe men and women act according to physical instincts involving food, sex, and aggression, and they are driven primarily by somatic influences. They are unable to harness their anger and are not capable of logical or rational thinking; they live with the forest rather than against it and, as represented in mythology, are closer to nature. The Lese believe themselves to be capable of mediating between their drives and the exigencies of proper and ordered social life. They represent rationality and reason, whereas the Efe stand for untamed passions. The Lese and the Efe are two interrelated organizations, and the Lese find meaning in their contrasts.

The contrast between the Lese as cultural and the Efe as natural is highlighted in a story that can serve as an introduction to the way in which the Lese establish unconscious symbolic oppositions about themselves and the Efe. This is one of many stories about the origin of Lese–Efe contact; every Lese phratry preserves a legend about the first meeting. Here, the narrator tells of how the Efe taught the Lese the difference between male and female genitals, and how to have sexual intercourse; the Lese in turn taught the Efe ingenuity and the value of tool use.

The Efe of long ago were Andisamba, my Efe. Andisamba's great grandfather was named Abeki. He was the Efe of Andali, of all the Lese-Dese. His wife's name was Matutobo. His grandmother's name was also Matutobo. Abeki went to the forest and returned. His grandmother came to wipe her anus on the top of his thigh. Abeki had many children, a boy here, a girl there. One day, Abeki took off to the forest, and arrived at a garden where there were ripe bananas. Efe ruin (deplete) our gardens, so the Efe went to take the bananas. He thought a lot about what his grandmother did to him, and so he thought a lot about the feces on his thigh. He had never seen bananas before, and he tried one, and he liked it. So he took bananas for his children. He now returned to the garden a third time. The villager left his village and saw footprints. The man saw the Efe sitting there, and then they saw each other. The man called out "ungbatue!" and the Efe said "ungbatue!" and the man asked the Efe to come to his village. "Do not be afraid! I will not hurt you" They went together.

The man was named Aupa. The Efe said again "ungbatue! See it is stupid, the feces on my thigh, it is by the hand of my grand-mother [*andu*]. Every day she does this." The man said, "Soon we will sharpen my knife [to kill the woman]." The man said he would rip open [*ataba*] the Efe's thigh and insert the knife inside it. Then her anus would rip, and the corpse would fall to the ground. The Efe returned until he reached his camp, and his grandmother said to Abeki's wife, "So your man returns?" The children said yes. Then she came to ask him to straighten out [*itesi*] his leg. She wiped herself, and the knife cut her. Corpse. They destroyed her house, and then the Efe moved with his wife to the villager's garden.[2]

From there, the Efe man came to the village woman, and her man was waiting there. "She is ill my woman." The Efe asked "Where is she?" "She is lying down in the pasa." The man went to get some alcohol, and with the Efe, the two of them drank together. The Efe asked, "Am I not able to see this illness?" The man told the Efe to go and look. He said, "My wife has no penis or testicles, only a wound in her crotch, and every month she bleeds from it, and I cannot stop the bleeding for several days."[3] The Efe said, "I will teach you." So he had sex with the village woman, and she became pregnant, and a child came, the first child. Later he gave her another pregnancy. The villager got mad at the Efe and said, "You will have sex with my woman? I will try myself." From there the Efe and Lese were together.[4]

By illustrating sex between a Lese woman and an Efe man, the characters reverse the condi-tions of the present day, in which intercourse between Lese women and Efe men is prohib-ited. But the origin story dramatizes the fact that it is the Efe who symbolically contribute knowledge of the natural world, while it is the

[2] The content of the story, in which the Efe and Lese partner collude to murder the Efe's grandmother, deserves some attention. The term *andu*, used for the grandmother, is a term of reference and address for any woman of a given Ego's grandparents' generation reckoned either matrilineally or patrilineally (including the biological grandmothers). Here, *andu* may refer simply to an elderly woman living in the same residence as the Efe man, Abeki. We can assume coresi-dence, since the man and woman have frequent and intimate contact. Most of the listeners to this story believed that the woman was unmarried, or widowed. Elderly women, especially widows, are not enjoyed by the Lese, and they are rarely encouraged to remain with their children. Widows whose children have died are encouraged even more strongly to leave the affinal village and return to their natal village. They are thought to be dangerous as witches and to be needy and unproductive drains on the economy. Infertile widows are psychologically abused, and sometimes physically abused, until they pack their belongings and return to their natal village. Thus, listeners to this story did not consider Abeki and his Lese partner's murder of the grandmother to be unmotivated. She offers the Lese and Efe partners a common task: for the Efe, the removal of a nuisance and an unproductive consumer; for the Lese, the removal of someone who would be unable to reciprocate his gifts of food. The story is essentially about the ideal relationship between Lese and Efe part-ners, a relationship that can be enjoyed when the partners are free of intragroup burdens and responsibilities, potential competition, and the envy of others.
[3] Blood is equated with being wounded, and young Lese children will often make the mistake of saying "I'm bleeded" (*be kutu*) or "the knife bleeded me" instead of using the proper verb for "to wound."
[4] Joset (1949) reports a similar story among the Lese-Obi. "The origin of this friendship between the Mambuti and the WaLese is given to us by a known legend: One day, a MoLese was in the forest. On the trail, he met a Mambuti who was walking with his daughter. In honor of this meeting the Mambuti gave his daughter as a gift. However, [the MoLese] did not know what to do. For him, the sexual parts of the woman were a wound, which he tried, in vain, to cure with medicines. Some years later the Mambuti returned and asked his son-in-law where were the children. The MoLese [sic] declared to his father-in-law that he didn't know what to do to have them. The Mambuti stopped the medication, and fornicated with the woman. Nine months later, the first child was born" (my translation from French).

Lese who contribute knowledge of the cultural world, to the Lese–Efe relationship. The forest, and the Efe who inhabit it, represent the wild and uncontrollable aspects of humanity, while the village, and the Lese who inhabit it, represent the civilized and controlled aspects of humanity. The Lese-Efe relationship binds the Efe to the Lese village. Conceptually, the villager's power lies in his exclusive knowledge of farming technique, and in the Efe's intractable and gluttonous desire for cultivated foods. The production of these foods attracts the Efe to the village and thereby controls them.

The nature/culture dichotomy so pronounced in this story appears to parallel the distinctions between men and women noted by S. B. Ortner (1974) in her well-known essay on the universal subordination of women. Through their social roles and reproductive functions, women are identified with the natural world, while men are identified with the cultural world. Correspondingly, sexual ideologies hold that women's creativity is expressed through childbirth while men's creativity is expressed through the development of technology. Ortner's dichotomy has been subject to criticism, primarily on the grounds that it is not universal, and that conceptions of nature and culture are Western categories whose relevance in ethnographic analysis is limited (H. Moore 1988, MacCormack and Strathern 1980; Mathieu 1978). More precise and meaningful criticisms emerge from the analysis of gender in detailed ethnographic studies (MacCormack and Strathern 1980). Do the Lese pair Efe and women together as representations of nature? If so, what is the nature of the relationship between these two categories of person? The Lese and Efe case appears to support the applicability of such a dichotomy to male–female relations in general, but it does not. For, as we shall see, the idiom of gender used to denigrate the Efe does not derive from women qua woman, but from wives. And wives are denigrated not because they are

women but because they are outsiders.

To answer the questions posed in the preceding paragraph, let us now look more deeply into the construction of Lese identity to examine the symbolic organization of the images of the Efe as women. We will find not only that Lese identity is formed through the conjunction of gender and ethnicity but also that the house is a basic locus of the gender and ethnic differentiation that encompasses many of the symbolic representations. . . .

Metaphor and the House

We can discern an analogy whereby Lese is to male as Efe is to Lese men's wives. But this does not mean that wives and Efe have sexual similarities. The analogy juxtaposes village insiders (Lese men) and village outsiders (wives and Efe); wives and Efe are structurally similar as village outsiders. More specifically, gender symbolism creates an analogic equivalence between the Lese men's wives and the Efe by stressing the parallels between the relationship the Efe have to the residences of their Lese partners, and the relationships wives have to their husband's residences. There is a paradoxical usage of the gender idiom by Lese women; Lese women denigrate Efe women in the same way as they denigrate Efe men – as "female." This usage highlights the point that the most cultural saline aspect of the idiom is not differentiation between male and female, but differentiation between "outsiders" and "insiders." The Lese feminization of the Efe arises not out of perceived similarities between women and Efe, but rather out of the structural similarities established by the use of gender as a metaphor of denigration.

The gender metaphor is an "external" or "analogic" metaphor which, as defined by Aristotle in the *Poetics*, is "when one thing is in the same relationship to another as a third is to a fourth" (Sapir 1977:22–23). Metaphor is ordinarily conceived as the juxtaposition of two terms from separate domains, such that they share certain features. To use Sapir's example, "George is a lion," conveys the sense that, although George is not really a lion, he and the lion are alike because they share courage or ferociousness (1977:23). Efe and women are not alike but are arranged in metonymic juxtaposition. As Sapir phrases it, "The similarity now derives from the relationship each term has to its proper domain" (1977:23). In the case of the Lese denigration of the Efe, the two terms "woman" (which we have already seen is more accurately defined as "wife") and "Efe" are linked not because they are similar but because they share a common link to a third domain: the Lese village and house.

What appears to be the characterization of the Efe as women is actually the characterization of the Efe as Lese men's wives. Both the Efe and wives are outsiders in relation to any Lese house or village. . . .

Conceptually, Efe partners and wives are brought together in the Lese house. Marriage and the Lese–Efe relationship are the basic constituents of the house, and ideally they are formed at the same time. A man sets up a house only after he is married, and all married Lese men should have Efe partners that they inherited following the marriage.[5] In a man's first marriage, the arrival of his wife should be within a year or two of the inheritance and establishment of a partnership with an Efe man.[6] In fact, on a few occasions, Lese men described their relationship to their Efe partners with the term *anga-ni*, which means

"marriage" but also refers to the joining together of two separate things. Marriages and houses, like husbands and wives, Lese and Efe, go hand in hand in social life. Houses are thus places for the coming together of things from the outside and things from the inside.

Marriage is considered to be in process from the earliest negotiations of bridewealth or classificatory sister exchange, but the union is not fully legitimized until the bride actually comes to the husband's village to stay in a house with him. Children born to a woman not living in the house of the father are thus frequently the subject of custody disputes between the families of the future bride and groom. The house is also the symbol of the dissolution of marriage. When a woman arrives at her husband's house she brings with her a *membo*, the collection of materials also called "things of the house" – such things as utensils for food gathering, processing, and cooking, and blankets, baskets, combs. The presence of the membo in the house represents the continuity of the union. A woman who wishes to leave her husband permanently will collect her membo and leave with it, thus "destroying" (*ima*) the house, and therefore the marriage. A woman who wishes to frighten her husband will take her membo and hide it in another place in the village, and a woman who simply wishes to separate from her husband for a short time will leave her membo intact, thus assuring her husband that the separation, even if carried out in the wake of a fight, is not permanent. Similarly, an Efe man identifies himself with a particular house by aligning himself

---

[5]   Maurice Bloch (1991) makes a similar point for the Zafimaniry of Madagascar: "Marriage without a house is a contradiction in terms, simply because the Zafimaniry notion which I choose to translate as "marriage" is distinguished from other forms of sexual union precisely by the existence of a house, and because the normal way of asking the question corresponding to our 'are you married?' is phrased, literally, to mean 'Have you obtain a house with a hearth?'" (p. 3).

[6]   All of these Lese of Malembi claimed to have Efe partners. Although most men inherit their Efe partners from their fathers, variations in demography prevent every man from inheriting in this way. A man's father's Efe may be childless, or he may have fathered girls only. Still more problematic, a Lese man may have more brothers than his father's Efe has sons. As a result, older sons inherit partners, and the other sons must try to establish partnerships elsewhere, usually by inheriting a partner from a patrilineally related man, such as a father's brother, or, as in a few cases, by reaching a partnership agreement with an Efe man who was not inherited, or whose *muto* died. These partnerships, far from the ideal, lack the trust and permanency of those that are inherited.

specifically with his partner, rather than with other men in the village. Before the actual inheritance of the partnership, Efe men and women will perform services and provide goods for a number of Lese within a village, but once the Efe man is "shown," he is expected to limit his village interactions to the house of his partner. One way that the alliance is expressed is by the giving of products designated as "forest goods" to his Lese partner. These include things such as arrows designed for monkey hunting, termites, and fruits. The Lese partner may in turn give his partner the dog from the house, to be used by him when hunting. The Lese partner will also give his Efe kitchen items, such as metal pots and pans for cooking. Just as a marriage dissolves with the removal of kitchen items from the Lese house, the Lese–Efe partnership is seen to dissolve when the Efe man returns kitchen items to the Lese house. While these two actions may seem to be the opposite of one another, the difference between taking and returning the goods reflects differences in residence. Efe men are members of the house, although they do not actually live in the house. They are incorporated, in part, by possessing "goods of the house." The return of these goods separates the Efe partner from the house, just as the removal of the goods by wives separates women from the house.

The terminology used to characterize marriage parallels the terminology used at the onset of the Lese–Efe relationship. A Lese man may establish a relation with an Efe partner by inheritance or by some other sort of arrangement. But even in the case of a direct inheritance passing from father to son, the recipient must have been "shown" the Efe either by his father or by another Lese in his own village. The term for "to show" is *itadu*, a word that is used to describe personal interactions in only two other contexts: that is, the "showing" of a wife to her future husband, and the "showing" of an unmarried woman to a man as a real or classificatory sister to exchange for a wife. The person who "shows" someone either a wife, or an Efe partner, is called *lakadu*, and the use of this term in Lese-Efe society is exclusive to these two contexts. This points to an equivalence, from the Lese men's perspective, between relationships with Efe men and relationships with wives. "Showing" establishes the dominance of the Lese men in both marriage and ethnic relations. I should also add that, just as some few Lese men marry polygynously, so too is it possible (although it is rare) for a Lese man to be shown and to maintain partnerships with more than one Efe. . . .

Aku-Dole: The Denigration of Lese Men

Lese men who are outsiders are also frequently denigrated in the form of "feminization." Lese men, women, and children who come to villages as visitors are not explicitly denigrated, but Lese men who have come from far away to live in a particular village to which they are distantly related are often treated badly. They are asked to help wives in some of their chores, a humiliating task for most men, because, they say, they are asked to behave like Efe men and like Lese men's wives, sitting and working with women in the kitchen. These men are then criticized for doing precisely what they are asked to do and are referred to pejoratively as *aku-dole*, literally "man-woman" – that is, a man who is like a woman (or like an Efe man). Village agnates also refer to such immigrants as *meremere*, a pejorative term meaning specifically someone who has come to the village but is not a direct patrilineal descendent. Thus, outsider Lese men are denigrated with the same idiom used to denigrate Efe men and Lese men's wives.

Red and White, Female and Male

Having demonstrated the saliency of gender as a metaphor for relationships between insiders and outsiders, we can now explore the metaphors of "red" and "white." Both "red" and "white" are open-ended in that they have a variety of different meanings. But the meanings together constitute a specific pattern of metaphoric relationships. The colors red and white are related to one another in the same way as female and male; wives (as a gender) and the Efe (as an ethnic group) are symbolized by redness, whereas men (as a gender) and the Lese (as an ethnic group) are symbolized by whiteness. Red, white, Efe, Lese, female, male are all of a piece, as we shall see in the symbolic constitution of human bodies, the Lese–Efe partnership, and house construction.

Lese relate lack of control, wildness, anger, and violence directly to the color red (*ikomba*), and more specifically to blood (*kutu*). Someone who is angry has hot blood (*kutukemu*); he is "with blood" or his blood is "traveling fast." Anger stimulates the circulation of blood within the internal organs and promotes a loss of control. When Lese describe the internal organs, they say that the heart should ideally be without blood, that blood should remain in the stomach; a heart that is filled with blood will cause death. Blood is also a life-giving substance. The patriline, as a life-giving force, passes to its members the same blood. Long ago, opposing clans fused and became "brothers" after the leaders of the two clans made incisions in their palms and then shook their hands, thus "mixing the blood." When an elderly man was on his deathbed in 1987, members of his clan reported to me that he confessed to murdering seven Lese witches during the 1950s after he administered *sambasa* poison to them at a witchcraft ordeal. He was reported as feeling remorseful and saying, "Their blood made our clan strong, but blocked my path to God."

The colors are also related to fertility. Menstrual blood is said to be the *tisi*, or semen, of the woman. Women are thought to be most fecund during, and just after, menstruation because the blood has begun to flow and can

mix with the *tisi*, or semen, of the men. The theory of conception is thus encompassed within the red (*ikomba*) – white (*itufe*) categories. When a child is born, its white aspects, the bones, bone marrow, and brain, are attributed to the contribution of the father's *tisi*, while its red aspects, the organs and blood, are attributed to the contribution of the mother's *tisi*. The bones are said to protect the organs, as a man protects a woman, as a Lese protects his Efe partner by feeding him and raising his children within the structure of the Lese partner's house.

J. W. Fernandez (1982:122–23) notes a nearly identical theory of conception for the Fang of central Africa and similarly describes how Fang women's symbolic role in house building parallels the Fang theory of conception: "The extension and replication of corporeal experience which was involved in the older procedure [of traditional house building] lay in the Fang belief that in the creation of the infant the red drop of female blood containing the homunculus was surrounded by the protective and fostering shell of white male semen. In the adult person the male element was the skeletal structure and tissues and tendons, all white, within which the sources of vitality – the blood and bloody organs – carried on their primary activity." Turner (1967) has also written of the red-white dichotomy, stating that, for the Ndembu, red is directly related to women's blood, the blood of murdering or stabbing, the blood of circumcision, and, in general, to power, anger, and danger. White, on the other hand, relates to semen, life, goodness, fertility, health, and good fortune. In addition, Turner notes that although the colors red and white are not always sex-linked, the incorporation of the two colors in ritual contexts often stands for the opposition of the sexes. The main contrast with the Ndembu is that, for the Lese, red and white together, *as opposed to white on its own*, represent fertility.

Blood flow signifies life, but the excessive flow of blood can lead to death and must be stopped with white bark powder. In the most common Lese origin myth, the story of Hara, the creator, the deceased are brought back to life when white bark powder is placed on their bleeding sores; in the Hara story, the main character Akireche starts life by first causing a man's tongue to bleed, and then stopping the flow of blood with white bark powder, thus separating him as a human being distinct from the trees and plants of the forest; finally, in the origin myth presented above, the Lese man fears that his wife will bleed to death, and the Efe man stops the woman from menstruating by inseminating her with semen [white *tisi*].

The symbolism extends to house building. When Lese build houses, men travel into the forest, or recruit their Efe to travel there, to find the appropriate small trees and vines for building material. Lese men take the trees and build the walls (*ai-ba*) and doors (*ai-ti*) of the house (*ai*). After the walls are complete, Lese men and women and Efe men begin digging up the reddish iron-rich earth at the edge of the village, arrange barrels or pots with which to collect water, and wait for a rainy day. The water or rain turns the earth into mud, and, on the day of mudding, women and children begin to mud the walls. Mudding is considered to be women's work. Men contribute the sticks – the skeleton – while the women contribute the mud. The mud is wet and red, as opposed to the dry, hard, light-colored trees, and must be supported by the structure of the walls. The notion that one element supports the other resembles the statements of the earliest observers of the Lese and the Efe (Schweinfurth in 1918 and Schebesta in 1938–1948) that their relations were characterized by dependency (Waehle 1985:391). Indeed, the dependency relations of both conception and the construction of the house parallel the relations between the two ethnic groups. The mud and the organs depend on (*ogbi*) the structure, as the Lese say that the Efe depend on (*ogbi*) them for their subsistence.[7] The house is thus a combination of the male and the female, in which the female depends upon and is encompassed by the male, just as the Efe depend upon and are encompassed by the Lese.

The Efe are indeed described as being red in color, and their habitat is described as being dark and wet and dirty. In contrast, the sunny village is bright, dry, and clean. The goods that the Efe are supposed to give to the Lese (meat and honey) are called red; these are, of course, also wet goods – bloody, sticky, moist. Thus meat and honey are red like the Efe who acquire those goods, and wet and dark, like the forest. The village, and the Lese, represent the production and accumulation of white, dry goods – cassava, potatoes, corn – which are cultivated, cultural products. Iron, also given by the Lese to the Efe, is referred to as white. I would even suggest that the red-white dichotomy also includes sexual relations and intermarriage between the Efe and the Lese: Lese men give white *tisi* to the Efe women, who contribute red *tisi* to the production of a child within the village context. . . .

The red-white dichotomy contains within it symbolic oppositions of social relations, sexual relations, house building, and exchange relations, and constitutes a specific pattern of meaning. The Efe, as (1) red, (2) hot-blooded partners contributing (3) red and bloody goods are integrated symbolically into a pattern of Lese beliefs. Moreover, each of the oppositions presented above (Efe–Lese, fertile–infertile, dark–light, red–white, meat–cultivated foods, wet–dry, wet goods–dry goods, dirty–clean, natural–cultural) are functions of the ideas about the differences between the inside and outside of the village,

---

[7] Curiously, the term *ogbi* is rarely used, and I have heard it used only with reference to contexts of dependence, including any situation in which someone cannot carry out a task without the help of someone else, on whom he/she therefore depends. It follows, then, that the symbolic meanings Lese attach to the Efe parallel those attached to the ideas of dependence inherent in conception and house building.

and between men and women. The oppositions also bring us back to the symbolic material out of which ethnic relations are constructed. We can imagine a series of nesting structures, each encompassing and encompassed by another. Blood is encompassed by semen, organs by the skeleton, the body by the house, female and Efe by Lese and male.

European Images

The consistent use of metaphors of gender to differentiate between the two ethnic groups is striking in its similarity to the use of metaphors of gender in European constructions of Africans and Africa. In an eloquent description of the place of Africa and Africans in the European scientific and religious discourse of the eighteenth and nineteenth centuries, Comaroff and Comaroff note that the "thrust into the African interior likened the continent to a female body" (1991:98). Gender was as salient a category as race, a lens through which domination at home could be projected onto domination abroad; as the Comaroffs put it, "In late eighteenth century images of Africa, the feminization of the black 'other' was a potent trope of devaluation. The non-European was to be made as peripheral to the global axes of reason and production as women had become at home" (Comaroff and Comaroff 1991:105). Africa was imagined as female in a number of ways: as a body to be penetrated by Europe, as mysterious and erotic, deprived of power, natural rather than cultural, and irrational and labile rather than rational and stable. These characterizations grew out of fundamental changes in gender ideology in Europe; whereas in the eighteenth century, maleness and femaleness were often thought of as fluid and imprecise categories, nineteenth-century scientific discourse held that a single sex could be discovered (Comaroff and Comaroff 1991:106). The scientist's challenge was to

discover the true nature of women, which, it was imagined, was embedded in the body in general, and the uterus in particular. The uterus became the center and cause of emotional and neurological disorders (Sulloway 1979:23–69), such as hysteria (from the Greek word for womb or uterus, *hystera*). Men, in contrast, were driven not by their organs or sexual nature but by reason, sensibility, and rationality. As we saw above, Lese distinctions between male and female are grounded upon distinctions in mental capacity, and between culture and nature.

I would not argue that the Lese appropriated the European metaphor; there are no data to support such an argument. But Europeans and the Lese may have formed similar characterizations because they use the same cultural material for their symbolic representations of the denigrated other. "Female," a meaningful category of domination in both local European and Lese contexts, becomes the basis for domination in other areas as well. The category served both colonists and the Lese as a way to define and maintain both difference and social boundaries (see Cooper and Stoler 1989:610).

Certainly there is some similarity between the Lese dehumanization of the Efe and the European dehumanization of all Africans and of foragers such as the Efe in particular. In an early example, the physician Edward Tyson presented the body of a chimpanzee as the body of a "Pygmy." Chimpanzees were not named until 1816, so Tyson believed that his chimp specimen was an ancient dwarf, not quite monkey and not quite human. Tyson's title placed the Pygmies squarely within the animal kingdom: *The Anatomy of a Pygmy Compared with that of a Monkey, an Ape, and a Man, with an Essay concerning the Pygmies of the Antients. Wherein it will appear that they are all either Apes or Monkies, and not Men, as formerly pretended, to which is added the Anatomy and Description of a Rattlesnake: also of the Musk-hog. With a Discourse upon the Jointed and Round-Worm* (Tyson 1751 [1699]). But if Africans were not human, then the missionaries had their work cut out for them; they were in the business of saving souls, and only human beings had souls. However, nineteenth-century scientists appreciated the idea of a chain of being, within which a variety of different kinds of human beings were organized hierarchically (Comaroff and Comaroff 1991:98). Biologists were mapping the mind of God, and every new discovery of different, and supposedly inferior, human beings led to further knowledge of the greatness of Western civilization, and the intricacies of God's creations (DeVore 1989). Thus, even when it was concluded that Africans, including Pygmies, were human, writers continued to describe these peoples using nonhuman images. Sir Harry H. Johnston, for example, reported to the Smithsonian Institution (1903) that the "Pygmies of the Great Congo Basin" were "ape-like negroes" (p. 481) with "baboon-like adroitness" (p. 482) reminiscent of the "gnomes and fairies of German and Celtic tradition" (p. 482).

The metaphor of the Efe as children also echoes the way that Europeans denigrated Africans. Alongside the popular European image of the noble savage ran the arrogant and patronizing image of Africans as children – children who were pure and unadulterated by an existence outside the Western world, and childlike in their naïveté. The Comaroffs note of the Tswana (1991:117),

> By the time our missionaries encountered the Tswana and began to write their own texts, the infantilization of Africans was firmly established. Adult black males were the "boys" whom the civilizing mission hoped one day to usher into "moral manhood." And "boys" they would remain well into the age of apartheid, whether or not they actually became Christian. Even at their most subtle and well meaning, the various discourses on the nature of the savage

pressed his immaturity upon European consciousness, adding to his race and symbolic gender yet a third trope of devaluation. This was no less true of the abolitionist movement, the most self-consciously compassionate voice of the age.

If adults were seen as children, one wonders what African children were likened to. In his report on the "dwarfs" of the Congo, Johnston described "a survival in the adult of that hair which appears in the fetus in all human races, a soft brownish down" (1903:488). Martin Johnson (1931), in his popular account of the Pygmies of the Ituri, *Congorilla: Adventures with Pygmies and Gorillas in Africa*, continued the image:

> The pygmies lead happy lives of carefree slavery in their Utopian forest homeland. They are mere children mentally as well as physically, always ready to sing, dance and make merry. They spend their days like youngsters at an endless picnic and there is nothing mean or malicious about them. They are truly unspoiled children of nature. (1931:62).[8]

Even today, the image of Africans as children runs through much of the literature on the Pygmies, such as K. Duffy's recent book, *Children of the Rainforest* (1984), and Turnbull's romantic depiction of the Mbuti as carefree, happy, and playful (1961).

Metaphors of Denigration in the Lese House

The Lese view of the Efe as children extends beyond the level of everyday discourse to the symbolic representation of Lese houses, into which the Efe are symbolically incorporated as children. This view is directly connected with

---

[8] To these images one might add that of Ota Benga, the African Pygmy man, from Kasai, Congo Free State, brought to the United States in 1904 by Dr. Samuel P. Verner. Ota Benga was displayed at the 1904 St. Louis World's Fair, and later, in the Monkey House at the Bronx Zoo (Bradford and Blume 1992).

Lese conceptions of the house as a reproductive domain.

Lese clans present a contradiction. One's membership in a clan depends on one's descent as reckoned patrilineally, and though every woman is a member of a clan, clans are idealized as groups of men. But social relationships reckoned through the mother are just as important to every Lese man or woman. Like clans, houses are constituted by both males and females, despite the fact that it is men who found and give identity to the house. Clans and houses are, in fact, conceived in a way that mediates the contradiction between their character and composition. They are both personified as mothers, and are said to be *ochi-ani*, to contain birth potential, or more literally, a uterus or womb (*ochi*). Clans and houses are reproductive organs. Marriage creates the uterus for the house and therefore also for the clan. Conflicts within the house, from dispute to divorce, disturb the uterus and produce infertility. To increase the fertility of the uterus, the Lese bury the placentas of the live births of Lese men's wives and sometimes Efe partner's wives inside the house into which the child was born. Stillbirths, the placentas of stillbirths, and the remains of miscarriages are all buried outside the house. The house is also said to contain a specifically Efe uterus, meaning that the house can produce Efe children and eventually Efe partners for one's family.

In addition to making children from adults, houses also make adults out of children. As one informant phrased the ideal, "most people in a village are either parents or children." People are "children" until they marry and have their own house, at which time they should become parents. The few Lese men who are thirty or forty years old but still unmarried and childless are in fact considered to be children. Although Lese men refer to their Efe partners and others of his generation as *imamungu*, literally, "my mother's child," or "sister/brother," Efe partners are considered to be the "children" of a particular house and, as in the Lese kitchen, are frequently denigrated by forms of teasing reserved for children. Many Efe partners at some time during their childhood lived in their father's Lese partner's houses, and are then said to be the children of the village, and to have been "raised" (*ire*) by the Lese. Even Lese children tease Efe men. One three-year-old boy was chasing a chicken around the periphery of the kitchen when he looked up and said to a member of his father's Efe's camp, "I won't let you take care of my chicken because it would get sick and die." It was a childishly innocent remark, perhaps, but an insult nonetheless. Children also denigrate Efe children as objects for manipulation and control. In children's play, Lese girls treat Efe girls as if they were dolls, braiding their hair and adorning them with beads, earrings, and other forms of ornamentation.

Are the Europeans who came to the Ituri forests ultimately to blame for the Lese treatment of the Efe as children? The Lese were likely introduced to some of the European images of denigration, and, I would suggest, the Lese were often the ones denigrated. But where the Lese were treated like children, they in turn treated the Efe like children. By using images provided by Europeans, the Lese may have been able to construct a more positive image of themselves. Frequently during my stay in Zaire, my Lese informants justified their denigration of the Efe by referring to their experiences with colonial administrators, and it seemed to me more than just an attempt to speak to me in a language they thought I might find meaningful; in several contexts in which I was a distant observer, I heard that the Lese had "colonized" (*colonisé*) the Efe, that the Efe were "savage" (*sauvage*) and needed to be tamed. One informant said, "We [Lese] gained our independence from the Belgians in 1960, but the Efe have not gained their independence from us." To some extent, these Lese are merely saying that the Efe cannot live without the Lese because they are culturally and materially deficient. Informants cited the fact that the Efe do not speak French and speak

Swahili poorly; in situations that demand communication with state authorities, such as the settlement of disputes, the paying of taxes, and participation in state-organized work groups Lese men represent their Efe before the authorities. The Lese also say that although the Efe work for them in their gardens, they know little or nothing about horticultural techniques and cannot even feed themselves; the Efe can become independent, according to these informants, but only after they learn to govern themselves.

The Efe's inability to govern themselves is shown, my informants say, in the absence of Efe houses. While the Lese stay put in village houses, the Efe do not have houses and may move their residence many times a year. Houses, my Lese informants said, could bring the Efe into civilization, but the Efe refuse to build them. Permanent settlements, they insisted, could also "civilize" the Efe, but again the Efe refuse. The Lese themselves were, of course, very mobile until they were relocated by the Belgians, who hoped the Lese would remain in their villages at least seven years, and did their best to restrict mobility by allotting strictly delimited areas of land to each clan with a chiefdom. Today, the Lese say that the Efe need to be settled, and one of the best ways to do that is to make sure they are integrated into Lese life. If the Efe ever separate from the Lese, my informants said, the Efe would be in a situation of chaos or disorder (*ovio*). The integration into the Lese social world gives the Efe a "place" (*fazi*).

The question of independence raises two other issues: the relation between the Efe and humanity, and the relation between the Lese as the saved, and the Efe as the heathen. It is commonplace in Africa for intergroup comparisons to involve mythical representations of one group as nonhuman, or else descended from the nonhuman. Lese origin stories tell of how the Lese came from a mountainous region ravaged by wars and famine, to find the Efe already living in the forest; other stories tell of the Efe's relation to nature. The story in which the Lese free the Efe from a life in trees is a story of liberation from savage ways. The missionaries under the colonial administration, like the Lese today, argued that membership in a civilized community like a mission was dependent not only on conversion to Christianity but also on the formation of permanent houses and gardens. Savages are accepted as mobile, but the civilized are always permanent. In the Lese language, a church is "God's House" (*mungu-ba ai*): heaven is called the "giant house" (*ai-tudu*), echoing another Lese notion that in ancient times all Lese lived in one house and the men gathered under one pasa. The Efe are thus the heathen (*paien*) who have not been admitted to the house of God and therefore have little hope of attaining salvation and humanity.

References

Bahuchet, S., and H. Guillaume. 1982. "Aka-Farmer Relations in the North-west Congo Basin." In *Politics and History in Band Societies*, ed. Richard Lee and Eleanor Leacock, pp. 189–212. Cambridge: Cambridge University Press.

Bloch, M. 1991. "The Resurrection of the House." Ms., Departmental Seminar; Dept. of Anthropology, University of California, Berkeley, Spring, 1991.

Bradford, P. V., and H. Blume. 1992. *Ota Benga: The Pygmy in the Zoo*. New York: St. Martin's Press.

Comaroff, Jean, and J. L. Comaroff. 1991. *Of Revelation and Revolution*, vol. I: *Christianity, Colonialism, And Consciousness in South Africa*. Chicago: University of Chicago Press.

Cooper, F., and A. L. Stoler. 1989. "Tensions of Empire: Colonial Control and Visions of Rule." *American Ethnologist* 16 (4):609–621.

DeVore, I. 1989. "The Human Place in Nature." *NAMTA Journal* 15 (1):35–46.

Duffy, K. 1984. *Children of the Rainforest*. New York: Dodd, Mead & Co.

Fernandez, J. W. 1976. *Fang Architectonics. Working Papers in the Traditional Arts*. Philadelphia: Institute for the Study of Human Issues.

——. 1982. *Bwiti*. Princeton, N.J.: Princeton University Press.

Jackson, J. 1983. *The Fish People: Linguistic Exogamy and Tukanoan Identity in Northwest Amazonia*. Cambridge: Cambridge University Press.

Johnson, M. 1931. *Congorilla: Adventures with Pygmies and Gorillas in Africa*. New York: Bewer, Warren & Putnam.

Johnston, H. H. 1903. "The Pygmies of the Great Congo Forest." Annual report of the Board of Regents of the Smithsonian Institution, for the year ending 1902, pp.479–91.

MacCormack, C., and M. Strathern, eds. 1980. *Nature, Culture, and Gender*. Cambridge: Cambridge University Press.

Mathieu, N. 1978. "Man-Culture and Woman-Nature?" *Women's Studies* 1:55–65.

Moore, H. 1988. *Feminism and Anthropology*. Minneapolis: University of Minnesota Press.

Ortner, S. B. 1974. "Is Female to Male as Nature Is to Culture?" In *Woman, Culture, and Society*, ed. M. Rosaldo and L. Lamphere, pp. 67–88. Stanford, Calif.: Stanford University Press.

Sapir, J. D. 1977. "The Anatomy of Metaphor." In *The Social Uses of Metaphor*, ed. J. D. Sapir and J. C. Crocker, pp. 3–33. Philadelphia: University of Pennsylvania Press.

Schebesta, P. 1933. *Among Congo Pygmies*. London: Hutchinson & Co.

——. 1936. *My Pygmy and Negro Hosts*. London: Hutchinson & Co.

——. 1952. "Les Pygmées du Congo Belge." Mémoire de l'institut Royal Colonial Belge, ser. 8, vol. 26, fasc. 2.

Schweinfurth, G. 1874. *The Heart of Africa*, Vol. II. New York: Harper & Brothers.

Turnbull, C. 1961. *The Forest People*. New York: Simon & Schuster.

——. 1965. *Wayward Servants: The Two Worlds of the African Pygmies*. New York: Natural History Press.

Turner, V. 1967. *The Forest of Symbols*. Ithaca, N.Y.: Cornell University Press.

Tyson, E. 1751 [1699]. *The Anatomy of a Pygmy Compared with That of a Money, an Ape, and a Man*. Second ed. London: T. Osborne in Gray's Inn.

Vansina, J. 1990. *Paths in the Rainforest*. Madison: University of Wisconsin Press.

Waehle, E. 1985. "Efe (Mbuti Pygmy) Relations to Lese-Dese Villagers in the Ituri Forest, Zaire: Historical Changes during the last 150 Years." Paper presented at the International Symposium: African Hunter-Gatherers, Cologne, January.

14

LAND FILLED WITH FLIES: THE EVOLUTION OF ILLUSION

EDWIN N. WILMSEN

The world of humankind constitutes a manifold, a totality of interconnected processes, and inquiries that disassemble this totality into bits and then fail to reassemble it falsify reality. Concepts like "nation," "society," and "culture" name bits and threaten to turn names into things. Only by understanding these names as bundles of relationships, and by placing them back into the field from which they were abstracted, can we hope to avoid misleading inferences and increase our share of understanding.

Eric Wolf, *Europe and the People without History*, 1982

Man the Hunter: A Nineteenth-Century Legacy

In company with many others called foragers in faraway corners of the earth, the San-speaking peoples of southern Africa have been relegated to an existential remoteness in time and space and being (fig. 14.1). This remoteness, as it is conceived to exist for the Kalahari, is represented as having been bridged only in recent decades, and that bridging itself is said to have been accomplished as often as not by social scientists seeking the wellspring of human existence. There is a basis for this perspective: unlike all other native peoples of southern Africa, among those called "Bushman" (most, but not all, of whom speak San languages) none have been able, in this century, to accumulate sufficient capital to maintain significant cattle herds of their own.[1] . . .

At the same time, in this century in Botswana and Namibia, an overwhelming majority of peoples so labeled have pursued a substantially pastoralist way of life in symbiosis with, employed by, or enserfed to Bantu-speaking cattle owners, primarily Batswana and Ovaherero. As we shall see, this is equally true of earlier centuries, with the modification that some proportion of San-speakers themselves then owned herds of respectable size. And all "Bushmen foragers," no matter how far out into the Kalahari they may have been found at any particular moment, were in those previous centuries – and remain now – enmeshed in the dominant pastoralist economies of the region through kinship and material production networks. Despite this, during this century few contemporary San-speaking herders have been able to establish livestock-based domestic economies independent of Bantu-speaking pastoralists

---

[1] Some San-speaking peoples, the Bateti, for example, are usually not included among "Bushmen" because of their known history of pastoralism and their present large herds.

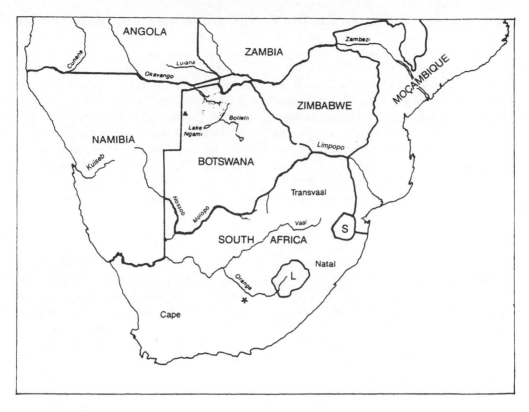

Figure 14.1 [1] Map of southern Africa showing the countries mentioned in the text; L is Lesotho, S is Swaziland. In colonial times Botswana was known as the Bechuanaland Protectorate or simply the Protectorate; Namibia was South-West Africa to the British and Südwestafrika to the Germans. Ngamiland is the part of northwestern Botswana west of the Okavango Delta and north of Lake Ngami, in which the location of CaeCae is marked by a triangle; the asterisk marks the location of Barrow's 1797 observations.

until this decade, when some are managing to do so. None have yet been able to enter into commodity production of cattle for readily available commercial markets now dominated by Tswana and Herero producers. What are the reasons for this state of affairs?

As we shall see, the current status of San-speaking peoples on the rural fringe of African economies can be accounted for only in terms of the social policies and economies of the colonial era and its aftermath. Their appearance as foragers is a function of their relegations to an underclass in the playing out of historical processes that began before the current millennium and culminated in the early decades of this century. The isolation in which

they are said to have been found is a creation of our view of them, not of their history as they lived it. This is as true of their indigenous material–social systems as it is of their incorporation in wider spheres of political economy in southern Africa.

A false dichotomy has crept in, a line drawn between those who produce their means of existence and those who supposedly do not, between those who live on nature and those who live in it, between those whose social life is motivated primarily by self-interest and those guided by respect for reciprocal consensus. Both ecologists and materialists locate foragers in an evolutionarily prior history; we still hear contemporary forager societies spoken of as living in nature, bound together in prepolitical community.[2] An endless, aboriginal continuity of social relations is envisioned, its alterations wrenched from resistance by external impositions in the form of drastic changes in a fickle environment or of imperative direction – usually technological or economic at base – from a hostile outside world. Foragers, in this scenario, are assigned the role of passive receptor and becoming the testing laboratory for our own ideological preoccupations regarding historical transformations of social forms.

In the prevailing paradigm of anthropology applied to the Kalahari, that of evolutionary ecology, the questions posed above have been nonquestions, never asked, without answers. This is because a distinction drawn by Lévi-Strauss (1967:47) has fundamentally informed all anthropological approaches to San-speaking "foragers"; that distinction is between "societies, which we might define as 'cold' in that their internal environment neighbours on the zero of historical temperature, [and] are, by their limited total manpower and their mechanical mode of functioning, distinguished from the 'hot' societies which appeared in different parts of the world following the Neolithic revolution." In fact, Lee (1979:6) goes so far as to believe that it is the very act of ethnographic fieldwork itself that "can begin to place this 'ahistorical' society into history." Ethnographers of San-speakers have assumed that these peoples were quintessential aboriginal hunters and gatherers whose way of life had changed little for millennia – those "cold" societies of Lévi-Strauss (1966:233–34), " 'peoples without history' . . . seeking, by the institutions they give themselves, to annul the possible effects of historical factors on their equilibrium and continuity."

Both geographic isolation and cultural conservatism were invoked to account for this static condition. It was asserted, without investigation, that neither African agropastoralists nor any other external influence had impinged significantly on their isolation until the middle third of this century. As a consequence, San-speakers were declared to be socially and culturally uninterested in and unprepared for participation in independent pastoral economies. Oddly, at the same time they were acknowledged to be seasoned herdsmen for others. We shall discover the reasons for this discordance.

These reasons lie in the epistemological discourse of Euroamerica's representation of its own past. Once established in scholarly and scientific – and of parallel importance, popular – lexicons, the events, peoples, and categories that become the objects of this discourse are transmuted into "indexical signs which perpetually point to their status as realities constituted independently of the process of representation itself" (Alonso 1988:36). The categories "Bushman," "San," "hunter-gatherer," "forager," and so forth are products of just such transmutation; they become objects and function to illuminate and legitimize a crucial area in Euroamerica's symbolic reconstruction of its own ontology.

It was just this discourse, Pratt (1985) tells us, that formed "what Mr. Barrow saw in the land of the Bushmen" in 1797 (fig. 14.1). In what follows, I shall trace the form that this discourse continues to dictate for modern ethnographies of "Bushmen." These ethnographies serve to authenticate our own subjective ontology by fitting an iconic "Bushman" into a prefigured category labeled "primitive." By displaying objectified peoples as examples of this category who exist "in a

---

[2]   For example, in their introduction to *Politics and History in Band Societies*, Leacock and Lee (1982:10) assert the anomaly that in societies free from fundamental conflicts of interest (as they say foragers are), techniques for decision making and conflict resolution are necessary; however, as with Steward's (1938) earlier *Basin-Plateau Aboriginal Sociopolitical Groups*, no clear analysis of these techniques is attempted, and few of the papers included in the book address political structure.

timeless present tense . . . not as a particular historical event but as an instance of a pregiven custom or trait" (Pratt 1985:120), ethnography validates the epistemological program. Consequently, the intrinsic realities of these objects are, as themselves, of little or no interest to this program. What is important is that its objects conform to a discursive narrative; while any of the parts may be questioned at any time, the ontological reconstruction itself becomes increasingly unchallengeable as a whole.

Since about 1960, most students of "forager" social formations have self-consciously espoused either some form of ecological or Marxian model or some combination of such models as the foundation of their work. This may be especially true of those whose attention is on African "foragers" and their relation to "food producers"; the general formulations of Meillassoux, Terray, Dupré and Rey, and Godelier in France, of Hindess and Hirst in England, and of Sahlins in the United States along with the particular field of studies of Lee, Silberbauer, and Tanaka in the Kalahari come readily to mind and will be examined in the course of our discussion. It is true that tenets of Marxian theory figure prominently in the presentations of the first five of these authors and infiltrate in decreasing degree those of the others. It is equally true that ecological parameters are recognized as important by all (at least to the extent that they are among the forces of production defined by Marx) and are invoked as primary explanatory factors by the last four of these writers. But the intellectual basis upon which they all construct their theoretical foundations has a far more ancient pedigree and is to be found in two corollary trajectories of nineteenth-century European thought. The first of these was an antiquarian and ethnological interest aroused by the realization that the biblical account of history could no longer accommodate accumulating empirical observations of geological, biological, and social processes made both at home and in exotic

parts of the hitherto unknown world. The second was an idealist sociology that in part arose to answer questions about human society thus exposed.

It has often been remarked that these trajectories have long histories in Western thought (see, for example, Worsaae 1849:138; Sorokin 1957:vii–viii; Leacock 1972:8; Stocking 1987:9–10, passim), and this is true, with the proviso that neither their referents nor the problematic engagement with those referents has remained constant. It is nevertheless worth quoting briefly from Hesiod (Athanassakis 1983: 70–71), whose words on the subject resonate in many rationalizations of the study of "primitive foragers" today:

> At first the immortals who dwell on Olympus
> created a golden race of mortal men.
> That was when Kronos was king of the sky,
> and they lived like gods, carefree in their hearts,
> ·
>   They knew no constraint
> and lived in peace and abundance as lords of
> their land.

Then, after recounting the second, silver, and third, bronze, races and the fourth, "divine races of heroes," Hesiod continues:

> I wish I were not counted among the fifth race
> of men,
> but rather had died before, or been born after it.
> This is the race of iron. Neither day nor night
> will give them rest as they waste away with toil
> and pain
> (*Works and Days*, lines 110–13, 119–20, 174–78)

These themes, of an early era of ease and equality contrasted with an ever more baneful present existence, recur regularly again in post-World War II ethnographies of African foragers, as they did in the eighteenth century. Leslie White, who helped inspire a renewed anthropological quest for human authenticity in the evolutionary "primitive" cultures, gave voice to a common feeling when he declared that these cultures – crude and limited as they may be – were infinitely superior in meeting human needs to any other ever realized, including our own (1959:23).

In the nineteenth century, especially after about 1860, the same bi-polar eras were identified, but their attributes were reversed by evolutionists of that time, for whom foragers lived as savage brutes (Guenther 1980 assembles many of the more lurid details), a condition from which the peak of Euroamerican civilization had long ago escaped. Those who pursued a sociological search for the nature of human nature were not so sure.

Even so, two fundamental constants run through both conceptions: first, an era of pure hunters (we now say hunter-gatherers, of course) did exist separately from other eras; second, that era – although its roots lay in the prehistoric past – is represented by "hunting" peoples who live at any time, prehistoric, historic, or present. Thus, peoples living today who may be classified as foragers bear witness not only to their own lives but to those of prehistoric foragers as well. That is, not only are living peoples conceived to be fit models for the remote past, but that remote past itself is said to establish the parameters of life of these living peoples.

Lee and DeVore are unequivocal on this point. Reporting the difficulties in defining "hunters" encountered at the 1966 Man the Hunter conference, they state (1968:4): "An evolutionary definition would have been ideal; this would confine hunters to those populations with strictly Pleistocene economies – no metal, firearms, dogs, or contact with non-hunting peoples. Unfortunately such a definition would effectively eliminate most, if not all, of the peoples reported at the symposium since, as Marshall Sahlins pointed out, nowhere today do we find hunters living in a world of hunters."

The Received Past

The present without a past

The history of the Kalahari, as written, reads like a kaleidoscope of unconnected slide shows thrown up on segregated screens. That southern African savanna called a desert still functions for many as an imaginary map – almost in the tradition of medieval geographers – on which names of various exotic peoples are entered or erased in accordance with some historiographic need of the moment to segregate those peoples conceptually – more urgent than spatially – from each other. . . .

Until recently, historians of the region were concerned primarily with tracing the emergence of first tribal, then modern, national states through the colonial nineteenth century and its aftermath. They did not find it necessary to elaborate the roles played by peoples considered marginal to this process. In Botswana, Tlou (1972:147)[3] began the move to broaden historical interest when he asserted that "the history of an area is more than just that of the ruling groups." He has taken his own admonition seriously and written extensively on all the Bantu-speaking peoples of Ngamiland, not just Batawana, but even he has relatively little to say about San-speakers (and Bakgalagadi) except that they were there first and live in the sandveld. Parsons (personal communication) has suggested that these peoples have been ignored because it has been too difficult to incorporate them into the narrative center of state political historiography, owing in large measure to a supposed lack of historical sources.

Recent interest in specific issues – the politics of traditional land tenure (Hitchcock 1978; Wilmsen 1982a, 1989) and a reevaluation of the nature of slavery and serfdom in the Kalahari (Tlou 1979; Miers 1983; Mautle

---

[3] Citations to Tlou (1972) are to his original Ph.D. dissertation; this dissertation has since been published (Tlou 1985) and is also listed in the References.

1986; Miers and Crowder 1988) – has stimulated research into the historical relations between San-speakers and the other peoples of the region. In Botswana, the establishment of the Bushman Development Programme in 1975 (later the Remote Area Dwellers Programme) at a ministerial level of government led to the first significant investigations into relations among San and Bantu peoples since the League of Nations – inspired investigations of the 1930s (Wily 1979). And for Namibia, Lau (1979, 1981, 1984) has begun to correct the historiographic imbalance in that country. Nonetheless, in general San-speakers are still set at the threshold of history and then effectively lost from sight. Even in as encyclopedic a work as *A New History of Southern Africa* (Parsons 1983), Khoisan peoples are discussed – uncommonly fully but nonetheless mainly in terms of Stone Age and Iron Age development – in an opening chapter and then rarely mentioned again. . . .

Such remoteness from the flow of history – a remoteness in the mind, as we shall see – was felt to be necessary in order to support the professed research goals of generating new insights into cultural evolution and reconstructing the properties of societies and economies of earlier human populations. Lee and DeVore tell us they chose to work in the northern Kalahari because "the research goals required a population as isolated and traditionally oriented as possible" (Lee 1965:2). For as they will say when we examine their motivation for joining Leslie White in a renewed search for lost authenticity in human relations, "The human condition was likely to be drawn more clearly here than among other kinds of societies" (Lee and DeVore 1968:ix). I (Wilmsen 1983) have noted that most students, including myself, of Bushmen, as they were then still called, were swept into this intellectual stream and the evolutionary paradigm from which it flows. . . .

It is, as a consequence, still too easy to follow Van Der Post (1958) into *The Lost World of the Kalahari* and to suppose that *The Harmless*

People of Thomas (1959) are not only enchanting but factual. These authors, to be sure, wrote partly fictionalized travelers' accounts for a popular audience, but they had a serious purpose: "A search for some pure remnant of the unique and almost vanished First People of my native land, the Bushmen" (Van Der Post 1958:3); and "studying the life and customs of the people of the Kalahari, who are called the Bushmen . . . the earliest human inhabitants still living in southern Africa" (Thomas 1959: 6–8). This purpose was in tune with the anthropology of their time: "To find and study Bushmen who were living in their own way . . . we observed a way of life that had not changed radically in ages," as Marshall (1957:1; reprinted unchanged in 1976: 14) thought, echoing Murdock's (1959:61) influential text, which concluded that Bushmen were Paleolithic people who represented "actual remnants of that ancient population and their cultures [who] have survived into the historical period." To which Herskovitz (1962:61), in his equally praised *The Human Factor in Changing Africa*, added of the Khoisan that they had a "negligible degree of participation in influencing the course of events in the territories they inhabit." One wonders, then, if they were indeed part of the human factor.

Anthropology was itself in tune with the history of the region: "There are also the original people of the land, the Bushmen . . . moving about their traditional hunting grounds from water hole to water hole. . . . sometimes one may be lucky enough to come across a family group" (Sillery 1952:xii). Later historians, even those sensitive to the colonial destruction of indigenous societies, also spare little concern for San-speakers. Bley (1971:xxii) could write, "Like the Bushmen and Berg-Damara, the Saan were displaced by the arrival of later, more powerful tribes, and by 1830 none of the original inhabitants occupied a position of any importance in the territory." And this from Clarence-Smith (1979:8): "In between [agricultural and pastoralist groups] live roving bands of Khoi or Twa hunter-gatherers, who have been of little or no historic importance." . . .

Ethnography and historiography, thus segregated from each other, are linked with fiction in perpetuating a conceptual isolation of San-speakers, a conceptualization that tautologically justifies its own fictitious state. Paradoxically, these peoples, who are universally considered to be the longest-term living residents of the Kalahari, are permitted antiquity while denied history.

Like the rest of southern Africa, the political and economic structures of the Kalahari in the nineteenth century were differentiated in recognizable terms. A number of diverse social groups were articulated with what appears to have been a degree of relative autonomy for each in the early years of the century. There were Tswana agropastoral incipient states on the southern and eastern margins of the Kalahari by the mid-eighteenth century, but what the economies of the peoples they encountered may have been has not yet been made so clear. It is usually assumed that these latter were strictly foragers, or at most kept small stock, but this is poorly founded speculation. The situation was not so simple.

It is clear, however, that as the nineteenth century progressed the various Tswana groups were able to consolidate their positions and gain hegemony over the other Kalahari peoples and to appropriate an extractable surplus from them in the form of tribute. In the process, they incorporated these weakened indigenous peoples into their own social formations as a servile class. In the last quarter of the nineteenth century and the first half of the twentieth, Batswana were actively abetted in this process by a British colonial administration acting, above all, in its own interest. Gadibolae (1985; see also Wiley 1985), on the basis of previously unexamined archival records and recently acquired oral histories, reaffirms that even the minimum efforts made to control the conditions of San serfdom were initiated by the Colonial Office primarily to

forestall adverse world opinion of their administration of the Protectorate.

The first question that begs to be asked, then, is to what extent these indigenous Kalahari social formations were altered, initially by African state expansion alone and later by colonial capital acting through those established states. It was, as it happened, at precisely the end of this period of hegemonic consolidation that the subjugated peoples of the Kalahari – especially those called Bushmen, San, or foragers – became the focus of anthropological attention. Consequently, a corollary question that must be asked is how this historic coincidence has led to a distortion of the ethnographic record of these peoples.

The uneven penetration of European merchant capital into the region is a second crucial factor. European traders were well established in eastern Botswana by the mid-1940s and only ten years later had saturated the farthest corners of Ngamiland in northwestern Botswana as well as adjacent Namibia (Parsons 1977: 117; Tlou 1972; Tabler 1973). These traders, however, only consolidated to themselves what had been in effect long before they arrived. Marks (1972), Clarence-Smith and Moorsom (1975), Elphick (1975, 1977), Kienetz (1977), Lau (1982), Nangati (1980), and practically all the authors in Gray and Birmingham (1970), Palmer and Parsons (1977), Marks and Atmore (1980), and Birmingham and Martin (1983) provide overwhelming evidence that European-inspired market factors were felt in every part of central and southern Africa before the actual appearance of white men in those parts. As we shall see, European trade items were received into Namibia–Ngamiland more than two hundred years before the first white man set foot there.

To be sure, the preponderance of the new wealth thus generated in the nineteenth century went directly to European traders, while the small, but still significant, remainder available to indigenous economies flowed mainly to, or at least through, chiefs and local headmen who retained the lion's share for themselves. An example encapsulates the process:

> Khama's income, now apparently freed from burdensome political reciprocities, came from his measure of monopolistic control over the market between internal and external trades at Shoshong. The income of the Ngwato king was estimated at £3,000 in 1874 and at £2,000 to £3,000 in 1877, though it is not clear whether this was in cash or cash value. The cash income was due in large measure to predominant royal ownership of the means of production – the king "owned" the land and the elephants and employed or hired out his serf hunters. He extracted a 50 per cent levy on ivory production – the "ground tusk" of every elephant shot in his domains, a common and venerable royal prerogative in Southern-Central Africa. (Parsons 1977:120)

There were exceptions, of course, but even where most rigidly true, the subjugated peoples – San-speakers and others – actually produced much of the surplus product channeled into commercial trade. This suggests that these peoples lived in societies already structured in such a way that they could organize themselves very quickly to produce an extractable surplus beyond what they had been providing as tribute to Batswana for decades and to earlier Iron Age chiefdoms for centuries.

Thus this case echoes others in southern Africa's colonial history. San traditionalism, so called, and the cultural conservatism uniformly attributed to these people by almost all anthropologists who have worked with them until recently, is a consequence – not a cause – of the way they have been integrated into the modern capitalist economies of Botswana and Namibia. The trajectory of this integration can be traced in the written and oral records.

Setting the Savage Stage

In 1819, Christian Jurgensen Thomsen, secretary of the then recently established Danish National Museum of Antiquities, synthesized the work of his predecessors and arranged the museum's collections by "classifying them into three ages of Stone, Bronze, and Iron on the basis of the material used in making weapons and implements, dividing the specimens into three groups representing what he claimed were three chronologically successive ages" (Daniel 1950:41).

Contemporary, living peoples entered as models into this scheme from the beginning; J. J. A. Worsaae, Thomsen's student, wrote in his *Primeval Antiquities of Denmark* (1849) that "having read how stone implements were at present used by Pacific islanders, and knowing that the Goths made no such use of stone implements, he concluded that there must have been a Stone Age" (Daniel 1950:44). Worsaae had been anticipated by Nilsson in 1834:

> As witnesses throwing light upon ancient times I count not only antiquities, monuments, their different shapes, and the figures engraved on them, but also *popular tales*, which most frequently originate from traditions, and are therefore remnants of olden times. . . . [We ought to be able, by collecting] the remains of human races long since passed away, and of the works which they have left behind, to draw a parallel between them and similar ones which still exist on earth, and thus cut out a way to the knowledge of circumstances which may have been, by comparing them with those which still exist. (Nilsson, quoted in Daniel 1950:49)

Following his own recommended procedure, Nilsson distinguished four stages in man's development. The first – naturally – was the savage stage, when man was still a hunter.

Lubbock's *Prehistoric Times* ([1865] 1913) not only gave a name to this time before history[4] but set the savage Stone Age on bedrock by separating a Paleolithic hunting stage in prehistory from its Neolithic fishing and ceramic-making successor. Lubbock devoted fully a third of his long book to "the consideration of modern savages [because] if we wish clearly to understand the antiquities of Europe, we must compare them with the rude implements and weapons still, or until lately, used by the savage races in other parts of the world" (Lubbock [1865] 1913:430–31). Lubbock not only made it clear, as in this passage, that Europe was the center of interest in all these staged scenarios, he also anticipated another modern concern that troubled Lee and DeVore in 1968 – that there were no longer any hunters living in a world peopled exclusively by hunters: "The present habits of savage races, while throwing, no doubt, much light on those of our earliest ancestors, are not to be regarded as representing them exactly, because they have been to some extent modified by external conditions, influenced by national character, which, however, is after all but the result of external conditions which have acted on previous generations" (Lubbock [1865] 1913:544).

In other words, if foragers were to be useful, it would be necessary to filter out from them what may have sifted down from the contamination of contact. Nevertheless, with suitable precautions in the employment of what we now call ethnographic analogy, "the archaeologist is free to follow the methods which have been so successfully employed in geology – the rude bone and stone implements of bygone ages being to the one what the remains of extinct animals [in relation to living species] are to the other" (Lubbock [1865] 1913:430).

The stage having been set, some action was called for. Morgan's *Ancient Society* ([1877] 1964:41–42) provided this:

Savagery was the formative period of the human race. Commencing at zero in knowledge and experience . . . our savage progenitors fought the great battle, first for existence, and then for progress, until they secured safety from ferocious animals, and permanent subsistence. . . . the inferiority of savage man . . . is, nevertheless, substantially demonstrated by the remains of ancient art in flint stone and bone implements, by his cave life in certain areas, and by his osteological remains. It is still further illustrated by the present condition of tribes of savages in a low state of development, left in isolated sections of the earth as monuments of the past.

Tylor ([1881] 1909:24) added a mobile element: "The lowest or *savage* state is that in which man subsists on wild plants and animals, neither tilling the soil nor domesticating creatures for his food. . . . [in some] regions they have to lead a wandering life in quest for the wild food which they soon exhaust in any place. In making their rude implements, the materials used by savages are what they find ready to hand, such as wood, stone, and bone, but they cannot extract metal from the ore, and therefore belong to the Stone Age."

There were confusions about just who fit where in these schemes. Worsaae's deduction from Polynesians using stone tools was one such, although this might be reconcilable with the fact that a distinction between a paleohunting and a neopotting Stone Age had not been made when he wrote. Lubbock ([1865] 1913:431) could say that "in some savage tribes we even find traces of improvement; the Bachapins, when visited by Burchell, had just introduced the art of working in iron."

These Tswana-speaking Batlhapa of southern Africa were possessors of vast herds

---

[4] Lubbock is generally credited by English-speaking scholars with introducing the term prehistoric, but it seems to have been in use in Germany at least by 1845, twenty years before Lubbock's book. For example, Marx and Engels ([1846] 1977:49) rebuke their German critics, who, they say, accuse them of speculating about "not history at all, but the 'prehistoric era.'"

of cattle and other domestic stock, long accustomed to ironsmithing. In the same breath, Lubbock asserts as proof of the eternal constancy of forager life that Bushmen, among others, 'lived when first observed almost exactly as they do now," although it is unlikely that he was acquainted with more than the latest thirty or forty of the then three hundred years of European reporting on these peoples. These confusions are hardly to be wondered at, given the embryonic state of ethnographic reporting at the time.

Yet by 1880 the basic defining characteristics of a savage, foraging stage of human existence were in place. These will seem familiar to any survivor of a standard contemporary introductory course in anthropology: (1) the foraging way of life has its roots in a Paleolithic past that occurred long before recorded history; (2) this way of life depends exclusively on hunting and gathering wild foods regardless of when in time (Paleolithic or later) and where it is found; (3) its technology is simple and based entirely on naturally occurring raw materials; (4) social groups, limited by these constraints, are necessarily small and are virtual relicates of each other; (5) these groups are usually compelled to be highly mobile in their search for food. There was also already the caution that the effects of contact with higher cultures had to be accounted for before inferences about the evolutionary significance of any particular group of foragers could be justified. Engels ([1884] 1972:97) added some now quaint speculations on stage variations in sexuality and marriage, noting, however, that some things are just too bizarre to exist any longer, even among savages: "The primitive social stage of promiscuity, if it ever existed, belongs to such a remote epoch that we can hardly expect to prove its existence *directly* by discovering its social fossils among backward savages."

But it was Pitt-Rivers in 1875 who sounded a note whose echoes we will hear a full century later (p. 159). Borrowing from Lubbock the analogy of ethnological to paleontological materials, he asserts the by now unremarkable dogma that "amongst the arts of existing savages we find forms which, being adapted to a low condition of culture, have survived from the earliest times, and also the representatives of many successive stages through which development has taken place in times past"; he adds, however, that "two nations in very different stages of civilization may be brought side by side, as is the case in many of our colonies, but there can be no amalgamation between them. Nothing but the vices and imperfections of the superior culture can coalesce with the inferior culture without break of sequence" (Pitt-Rivers [1875] 1906:18–19).

It is in fact precisely this latter argument that is invoked by both anthropologists and administrators in decrying the present condition and future prospects of southern African San-speaking peoples. In the next chapter we shall hear it said that these San peoples are on the "threshold of the Neolithic, stripped of the accretions and complications" of later evolutionary stages, and furthermore that this condition retards their social incorporation into and economic participation in modern national states. It is taken as axiomatic that peoples in a "lower stage of evolution" will eagerly grasp at the vices of their betters while remaining ignorant of those benefits that could raise them materially and morally to new heights. Implicit in this is the notion that forager social formations are incapable of change on their own. Furthermore, change, in the event that it is stimulated by external agencies, will be gradual. Contrarily, those on a "higher plane" never wish to fall beneath themselves, although they may sometimes be compelled to do so by a capricious nature.

All of this raises a fundamental question: Before there were peoples on a higher plane, how did anyone ever become anything other than a foraging savage? The answers offered pointed to that same capricious nature, which either elevated population numbers above the sustaining capacity of resources or depressed the

resources below the requirements of populations. Either condition forced innovation.
After "higher levels" were attained, the answer
was obvious: those in a lower condition would
naturally aspire to the higher once it was made
known to them. But they could reach this
apotheosis only through a "break in the
sequence" – that is, by escaping their intrinsic
primitiveness. Morgan ([1877] 1964:540) was
among the few who thought that savages might
sometimes rise, "for it was by this process [of
imitation] constantly repeated that the most
advanced tribes lifted up those below them, as
fast as the latter were able to appreciate and to
appropriate the means of progress."

Primitive critique of civilization

We must turn to the second intellectual trajectory of nineteenth-century Euroamerica to
unravel the reasoning behind these rather odd
propositions. The architects of the developing
Continental sociology of the latter half of the
nineteenth century shared many of the
precepts of their ethnological contemporaries,
although they had different agendas and were
generally not preoccupied with evolution in
itself. Loomis and McKinney (1957:1) point
out that Tönnies ([1887] 1957), in
Gemeinschaft und Gesellschaft (translated by
them as *Community and Society*), was concerned to address the questions "What are we?
Where are we? Whence did we come? Where
are we going?" These are, with perhaps the
exception of the last, the classic antiquarian
and evolutionary questions: posing them
presupposes a recognition of, if not an intent
to investigate, the proposition that there are
problematic historical antecedents to where it
is we are.

Tönnies was aware of this and wished to
merge formal and historical sociology in order
to better address his questions. He is quite
clear on this point ([1887] 1957:34, 42, 252),
although he does not dwell on historical, let
alone prehistoric, referents: "Gemeinschaft is
old. . . . the natural relationship is, by its very

essence, of earlier origin than its subject or
members. . . . Gemeinschaft by blood,
denoting unity of being, is developed and
differentiated into Gemeinschaft of locality . . .
a further differentiation leads to the
Gemeinschaft of mind, which implies only co-
operation and co-ordinated action for a
common goal." That is to say, original kinship
among individuals is natural and unanalyzable
– either by those in it or by those observing it
– but this kinship eventually becomes identified with territory and ultimately emerges as
an ideology of sociality through which individuals recognize their community of
interests. Or, "all three types of Gemeinschaft
are closely interrelated in space as well as in
time. . . . the earlier type involves the later one,
or the later one has developed to relative independence" (Tönnies [1887] 1957:42).

Gemeinschaft is the earlier, simpler stage of
sociality when all associations of persons were
replicate segments, the polar opposite of
modern Gesellschaft, characterized by atomization of social forms and alienation of
individuals. The crucial theme here is that
small-scale, earlier, "old" Gemeinschaft is the
authentic, "natural" state of human sociality,
whereas large-scale, current, derivative society
is artificial. The key attribute making
Gemeinschaft the center of focus is this
authenticity – the true state of human existence, one that may be regained by study and
effort. I argue that it is this quest for authenticity that fuels the fascination with foragers –
with true, untrammeled "primitives" – that
exists to this day in Euroamerican thought and
its authenticating agent, ethnography.

Later, in a convoluted passage – resonant of
German mystical painters and architects of the
time – concerning centers of development
radiating toward new nuclei spawning yet
others in the evolving chain, Tönnies ([1887]
1957:252) says that this "refers only to
different stages and types of collective life."
But the Gemeinschaft stage, at least, cannot
change without external stimuli, particularly
trade; it continues to exist in varying forms

today. There is a vague, unstated suggestion that it cannot change because it is pure.

I am unable to find that Tönnies specifically attributed Gemeinschaft to a savage – or any other kind of – Stone Age, but the passages quoted above, along with his occasional references to the primeval core of spouses, the tents of nomads, and other then-current ethnographic attributes of that primitive stage, plus the fact that we know Tönnies was conversant with the ethnology of his day, seems to suggest that he had in mind something of the kind. He says, for example ([1887] 1957:37), that Gemeinschaft is characterized by a "perfect unity of human wills as an original or natural condition," that is, by a collective conscience. Perhaps more tellingly, he quotes copiously from Maine's *Ancient Law* ([1887] 1957:182–183) wherein the condition of the modern family is traced through reverse evolution to its simple roots in prehistory.

Durkheim too eschewed evolutionary intentions, but he called upon historical transformation processes in aboriginal societies that in the words of mid-twentieth-century anthropologists sound very familiar today. He followed Tönnies in contrasting simple, original society to complex, derived society such as he saw his contemporary Europe to be. This original, simple society was based upon mechanical solidarity, an unproblematic cultural unity. Its attributes are (1) aggregation of replicate segments composed of relatively undifferentiated individuals; (2) common beliefs and sentiments; (3) communal, collective property; (4) uninhibited mobility within the group's domain; and (5) self-sufficiency of segments. . . .

Mechanically solidary societies continue to exist throughout time essentially unchanged from their initial state; indeed, they cannot change except through external stimuli. Such societies are incapable of generating any other social form from within themselves (Hirst 1975:132), for "we know that the segmental arrangement is an insurmountable obstacle to the division of labor, and must have disap-

peared at least partially for the division of labor to appear . . . [and this is contingent upon] an exchange of movements between parts of the social mass which, until then, had no effect on one another" (Durkheim [1893] 1964:256). For such change to occur, "relationships must have formed where none previously existed, bringing erstwhile separate groups into contact . . . [thus breaking down] the isolated homogeneity of each group" (Giddens 1971:78).

Before such contact went too far, one could still turn to "the simplest and most primitive" peoples to study the origins of human institutions. For Durkheim these were the Australian aborigines to whom he turned – apparently after reading English ethnologists (Giddens 1971:105) – to "discover the causes leading to the rise of the religious sentiment in humanity." Such a turn seems to contradict Durkheim's avowal that "man if a product of history. If one separates men from history, if one tries to conceive of man outside time, fixed and immobile, one takes away his nature" (quoted in Giddens 1971:106). It is a turn from which few have retraced their steps.

Earlier, with Engels in *The German Ideology* ([1846] 1977:68–69), Marx had specified the social conditions of the prior ages – conditions, moreover, that survived in the "antagonism between town and country [which] begins with the transition from barbarism to civilization, from tribe to State, from locality to nation, and runs through the whole of history to the present day." Those aboriginal conditions were (1) individuals united by bonds of family, tribe, and land; (2) human individuals as themselves instruments of production subservient to nature; (3) landed property relations those of direct natural domination and communality; (4) the premise of locality; (5) exchange chiefly that between men and nature.

In *Capital*, Marx ([1867] 1906:366–67) elaborates on this theme: "Co-operation, such as we find it at the dawn of human development, among races who live by the chase, . . .

is based, on the one hand, on ownership in common of the means of production, and on the other hand, on the fact that in those cases, each individual has no more torn himself off from the navel-string of his tribe or community, than each bee has freed itself from connexion with the hive." Such individuals and such "tribes living exclusively on hunting or fishing are beyond the boundary line from which real development begins" (Marx and Engels [1846] 1977:146).[5] . . .

The invention of "Bushmen"

It fell to the nineteenth century to invent its nativity in ancient hunting savagery, which is quite a different thing from simply gaining awareness of its ancient hunting ancestors. Hobsbawm (1983:3, 8) has remarked that in the profound and rapid social transformation of the later nineteenth century, with its attendant need to accommodate the aspiring political ambitions of an expanding bourgeoisie, invented traditions served a reassuring function. In this atmosphere, constructions of evolutionary stages and sociological forms molded in imaginable configurations played important roles. To paraphrase Hobsbawm (1983:2), these stages and forms established their own past that, in contrast to the constant change and innovation of the current world, offered an unchanging, invariant structure for at least some parts of social life; they provided "sanction of precedent, social continuity and natural law as expressed in history."

"Bushmen" were invented in this intellectual environment. They, or something like them, had to be made available to certify the ontological quest. The historical dimensions of this invention are the subject of "the past recaptured," but first we must grasp the ideological components, in extension of the foregoing discussion, that dictated the mod-

ern shape given the "Bushman" image. Gilman (1985) points out that it was physiognomy that first aroused scientific and popular interest – the black body as opposed to the white. But the mere noting of difference was not enough for "the radical empiricists of late eighteenth- and early nineteenth-century Europe. To meet their scientific standards, a paradigm was needed . . . rooted in some type of unique and observable physical difference" (Gilman 1985:212). The antithetical position to the white body was found in the black, especially the Bushman-Hottentot female, with her "primitive" steatopygous physique, her "primitive" genitalia, and her "primitive" sexual appetite. Gilman (1985:229) notes that Hegel and Schopenhauer believed that all blacks remained at this most primitive stage and that their contemporary presence served to indicate how far Europeans had extricated themselves from this swamp. Bushmen were placed at the nadir of this scale of humanity. Bachofen drew on these ideas to construct this primitive promiscuous horde as the initial stage of human sociality.

But "Bushmen" as social beings rather than natural history specimens did not yet figure prominently in those formulations. Although various of these peoples were mentioned in many travelers' accounts, official reports, and dispatches from 1761 onward (even much earlier at the Cape), the first full-scale ethnographic field investigation of any "Bushmen," that by the German Siegfried Passarge among the Zhu, was conducted in the 1890s. The resulting publications did not appear until 1905 and after; though of considerable merit considering their time, they appeared too late to have much influence on theoretical constructions, which in any case were by then moving in new directions. "Bushmen" did not yet carry the ethnographical authority accorded the often-cited American Indians,

---

[5] In a footnote to this passage, Marx ([1867] 1906:366–67) says, "Linguet is probably right, when in his 'Theorie des Lois Civiles,' he declares hunting to be the first form of cooperation."

Australian Aborigines, and Eskimos, among others.

That did not, however, shield "Bushmen" from being categorized along with these other colonized peoples, or from being isolated conceptually as an undifferentiated enclave among more "advanced" Africans (those at a "higher" evolutionary stage). This conceptual isolation was a prerequisite to their administrative isolation and was a major contributing factor in their deepening social and economic isolation in the emerging colonial social formation that has left its legacy in Botswana and Namibia today. This was the path to the divided present; it led from an indigenous past that was very different: "The colonial reification of rural custom produced a situation very much at variance with the pre-colonial situation" (Ranger 1983:254 and also Chapter 35 this volume) and had replaced prior relations among peoples with a created microcosmic society. Iliffe's (1979:324) observation that Tanganyikan natives created tribes in order to function within the colonial framework applies very much to the Kalahari. It was also in the interests of colonial administration to codify and reify custom as a means of consolidating its control. Ethnographers were recruited to provide this codification and to help ensure that this colonial world was manageable by certifying that it was divisible.

Their own words on the matter are revealing. Radcliffe-Brown (1923:142–43), newly appointed first head of the School of African Life and Languages at the University of Cape Town, wrote in the *South African Journal of Science*, "[The study of African culture] can afford great help to the missionary or public servant who is engaged in dealing with the practical problems of the adjustment of the native civilization to the new conditions that have resulted from our occupation of the country."

Seven years later, in their "introductory Note" to *The Khoisan Peoples of South Africa*, the first volume in a series on native peoples published by that very same school, Driberg and Schapera (1930:v) reiterated Radcliffe-Brown's thesis:

> To the administrator, the missionary, the economist, and the educationist, each in his own way now moulding the life of the Native into conformity with the standards of European civilization, a thorough knowledge and understanding of the people with whom he is concerned is an indispensable preliminary to the completion of his task. It is the hope of the editors that applied anthropology no less than the academic science will in this series the groundwork upon which it may build for the future.[6]

---

[6]   The ethnographic studies were carried out without any illusions about their primary beneficiaries, as the following *Circular Memorandum* (Botswana National Archives 1940b) makes clear:

27th.June 1940

To all District Commissioners, the Chief Veterinary Officer and the Chief Agricultural Officer

Subject: *Revision of Professor Schapera's Handbook on Tswana Law and Custom, Land Tenure, etc.*

I am directed by the Resident Commissioner to inform you that Professor Schapera is expected to arrive in Mafeking on the 30th.June and to leave Palapye on Monday the 8th.July. He will probably stay in Ngamiland for about six weeks, then go to Serowe for a month and then work southwards. More precise information as to his movements after leaving Maun will be communicated to each District Commissioner by Professor Schapera but it is requested now that the following arrangements be made for him at each centre in turn:

(a)   arrangements for his accommodation;

(b)   arrangements for the services of one, or preferably two, literate young natives who can be employed as full-time assistants while Professor Schapera is in the district concerned. These natives, if satisfactory, will be paid at the same rate as school teachers.

(c)   The Chief to be informed beforehand of the date of Professor Schapera's arrival so that there will be no delay in his commencing work as soon as he arrives.

Source: V. Ellenberger
for GOVERNMENT SECRETARY

This anthropological program was designed to serve the emerging segregationist solution to the harsher effects of domination; it was a "synthesis of liberalism and 'scientific racism,'" which would hold out the prospect of evolution for individual blacks while avoiding genetic degeneration [of whites]" (Marks and Trapido 1987:8). "An intellectual organizing principle was required to validate this synthesis or compromise. The development of an anthropological notion of 'culture' came to serve this purpose admirably" (Dubrow 1987:80).

Wright (1986:105–6) draws the inescapable conclusion that this ideological context in which anthropologists operated "served to orient their critical faculties in a way which made for the existence of an intellectual blindspot as far as questioning the notion of tribe was concerned." He goes on to observe that the thus reinforced continuance of a system of administration that emphasized "tribal" divisions was one of the major structural reasons why collective terms – such as "Bushmen" and later San (Wright, however, referred specifically to Nguni) – survived so long without being called into question. . . .

The need to name

In the invention of the requisite categories of tribal administration, considerable effort was devoted to investing names with meaning. The epistemological status of these names, as of all categorial names, is constituted in the ideological valuation of their predicates. For example, living in a "state of nature" was savagery to nineteenth-century evolutionists, so much so that savagery was considered to be the defining characteristic of the initial stage of human existence. In the later half of the twentieth century, however, living in this same state is again considered by some to be utopian (or at least quasi-utopian), so much so that it could be called the original affluent existence. In both cases the terms are applied attributively to anyone (or any group) who satisfies the predicate requirements of the concept "initial stage of human life"; these are the defining criteria mentioned several times in the preceding discussion of nineteenth-century evolutionary and sociological schemes. Everything else but such individuals or groups is contingent, both as empirical fact and as observational object; those things that in the next chapter we shall find Howell and Burchell avoiding are examples (cf. Schwartz 1977:13–41). In this investment process, language – not only the names that as labels encode the predicates of the categories of discourse but the specialized lexicon of the discourse itself – carries the burden of the work of reifying those categories and "helps to establish the authority which re-presentations require if they are to be seen as representative" (Alonso 1988:35).

By now it is well known that the term "Bushman" is anglicized from Dutch/Afrikaans "Bosjesmans/Bossiesmans" in its many spellings. The etymology of the Dutch term is in constant and sometimes contentious debate, revolving around the ideological investment of this term itself. It is important to emphasize that "Bushman" came into use during the 1680s in the Cape area only after thirty years of Dutch applications of other "terms obviously derived from native usage" (Parkington 1984:156). "Within a few years it had, along with 'Bosjesman Hottentot,' become the standard Dutch equivalent of the older [indigenous] Khoikhoi terms" (Elphick 1977:24). Those terms were Soaqua or Sonqua (Elphick (1977:24; Parkington 1984:151), which some authors derive from a root common to San of current usage; I shall take up this term in a moment.

Parkington (1984:156) sets "Bushman" in its original context of use. Within a few years of the founding of the Cape settlement in 1652, local pastoralist groups were called by their generic self-referents or by the names of their leaders; when explorations into the interior beyond the Cape boundaries became frequent, unknown peoples – many without domestic stock – were encountered. Europeans relied on their interpreters to supply names for these peoples, and "a new link in the chain of terminology was added. Before the end of the seventeenth century the term *Bushmen* or *Bushmen Hottentot* complemented and replaced *Sonqua Hottentot* to describe these peoples" (Parkington 1984:156–57). These changes occurred at a time "when increased Dutch interference was causing massive, and irreversible, changes in indigenous group relations. *Bushmen* relates more clearly to these changes" (Parkington 1984:164). Parkington suggests that Soaqua should be understood to refer to the aboriginal hunter-gatherer social formation of southern Africa, whereas Bushman refers to pastoralists and foragers whose social and material fabric had been disrupted by Dutch intervention. As these dispossessed groups – along with escaped slaves and deserters from the Cape Colony, some of whom were white Europeans – sought to establish a mode of existence away from Dutch control, "Bushmen," as applied to them, "became a wastepaper basket term for all those who lived by hunting, gathering, and stealing" (Goodwin and van Riet Lowe 1929:147). Or as Gordon (1984:196), citing Nienaber (1952), glosses it, " 'bandit.' " Elphick (1975:23–42), however, marks the much broader indigenous use of the term "San": "KhoiKhoi themselves made no such clear and systematic distinction between peoples, their term 'San' having wide reference to both hunter and small-scale pastoral groups" (Elphick 1975:41).

Gordon contributes to the many confusions to be found in the literature of the region that perpetuate distortions in the application of this term. He says (1984:216, citing Moritz 1980:21) that the missionary Carl Hugo Hahn, in 1851 one of the first Europeans to enter the northern part of what is now Namibia, recorded in his diary that "his Herero servants referred to the Bushmen as 'Ozumbushmana' [*sic*], a term clearly derived, as he recognized, from Dutch." But Hahn recognized a great deal more; his original published account (*Petermanns* 1859:299) reads: "Our people call the Bushmen Ozombusumana (Sing – Ombusumana), a corruption of the Dutch name. The true name, by which they have otherwise been known to the Ovaherero, is Ovaguma [Lau tells me this is written ova-guruha in Hahn's diary]. The new name will surely displace the older, and its etymology will perhaps later give philologists a headache."[7]

Gordon is eager to show that penetration by outsiders (in this case, Ovaherero) is recent; he therefore overlooks the obvious – Hahn's Herero servants were employing pidgin language forms in conversing with a European. This is an instance of the expediency with which, in the early years of their association, "Africans as a rule adopted the restricted jargon of their immediate European masters" (Fabian 1986:139).

Hahn's Herero servants no doubt did say to him that certain "Bushmen" were ozombusumana. But what were they telling him? The form of the term used provides a clue: the Otjiherero noun prefix (class 10) ozo- is applied to livestock as well as to most animals in general. The use of ozo- in this case thus carried the meaning "those Bushmen are our chattel," hardly an indication of unfamiliarity. Hahn was clearly aware of this; in his own dictionary (1857:151) he gives omu-kuna (pl. ova-kuna) as "Buschmann." The first full study of Otjiherero, that by Brincker ([1886] 1964:145), who worked among Ovaherero from 1863 to 1889, has omukuru as "einer, der verlängst gewesen ist . . . die Alten, Ahnen":

---

[7] "Unsere Leute nennen die Buschmänner Ozombusumana (Sing – Ombusumana), eine Verstümmelung des Holländischen Namens. Der eigentliche Name, unter welcem sie sonst bei den Ovaherero bekannt sind, ist Ovaguma. Der neue Name wird sicher den alten verdrangen und die Etymologie wird vielleicht später den Philologen Kopfbrechen machen" (*Petermanns* 1859:299, reprinted in Moritz 1980:2).

"one who formerly existed . . . the ancients, ancestors." More recently, Katjavivi (1988:1) writes Ovakuruvehi, "the ancient (or original) ones." Irle (1917:16), in his German–Otjiherero dictionary, translates Ahne (ancestor) as "omukuru." These glosses are in keeping with Guthrie (1970, 3:310), who attaches the notions of ancestor and grand-parent to his proto–Bantu root *-kúúkù. Modern ethnographers note the same term applied by Herero-speakers to specific peoples. Marshall (1976:17) says that Ovakuruha is the Herero term for Zhu. Vedder (1938:136) restricted Ovakuruha to those people he called Saan, the Heixum (Hai-‖'om) of current terminology, whom he distinguished from other Bushmen.

Otjiherero has another term, ovatua, derived from the proto–Bantu root *-túá (Guthrie 1970, 4:122): "The most likely original meaning was probably either 'pygmy' or 'Bushman,' and presumably referred to the indigenous inhabitants originally encountered by the speakers of the proto–Bantu." This root also has the apparently secondarily acquired connotation "member of neighboring despised tribe." Hahn (1857:150) has the form omukoatoa, which he glosses "Eingeborener": "native." Brincker ([1886] 1964:157) has omutua, "Volker vorzukommen": "people who came before" and notes that it appears as such in many Bantu languages; these glosses reflect Guthrie's first meanings. Brincker, however, captures the derogatory connotation as well: "Die Grundbedeutung scheint 'Buschmann' im verächtlichen Sinne zu sein": "The original meaning appears to be 'Bushman' with its contemptuous connotations." Local usage conforms to these

dictionary glosses. The Ovambandru people with whom I work in Botswana insist that Zhu – who are the archetypal "Bushmen" of ethnography – are not Ovatua (that is, not "Bushmen" or "member of despised tribe") but Ovakuruha (that is, "ancestral," "those who came before"). Ovatua do exist, they say, but in distant places.

Setswana elides the common Bantu root as rwa; with the plural prefix (class 1) ba-, desig-nating the noun class pertaining to humans, this becomes Barwa. Brown ([1875] 1979:16) renders this term "Bushmen." However, the root with the locative prefix (class 7) bo-becomes "borwa": "the country of the Bushmen, hence the south to people living farther north" (Brown [1875] 1979:34); and "kwa ntlha ea Borwa" refers to the south. Digging deeper, we find "batho ba ntlha": "the first people" (Brown [1875] 1979:231); hence, except for the reference to the south, this term is cognate with other Bantu forms meaning aborigines. In practice, as we shall shortly see, it was applied to all sorts of people in partic-ular circumstances, not only to those we today identify as San-speakers. The current form in use in Botswana is Basarwa, but this form does not occur in the nineteenth century and begins to appear only in the 1960s. A related form, Masarwa, was commonly used from the early nineteenth century or perhaps somewhat earlier to denote "Bushmen of the Bechuanaland Protectorate" (Brown [1875] 1979:183), that is, of the Kalahari;[8] this form employs the plural noun prefix (class 3) ma-, which is applied to non-Tswana and to persons of undesirable characteristics or social inferiority (Cole 1975:81). This term appears to derive from the secondary, acquired

---

[8] The source of the element sa in Basarwa (and Masarwa) is not known; it is not a noun prefix in Setswana. My own hypothesis is that it is the Nama noun Sa(n), incorporated into Baraw when Batswana first encountered peoples referred to by this term when they entered the western Kalahari in the mid-eighteenth century. The evolution may have been something like Masa → Masarwa, with the attachment of the root * -rwa possibly an accompaniment to reduction in status of peoples called Masa. Rainer Vossen has pointed out to me that Köhler (1975:305) proposed a similar hypoth-esis more than a decade ago: "Und es liegt nahe anzunehmen, dass diesem Namen der Wortstamm *Sa* zugrunde liegt, mit dem die Rinderhirten die nomadischen Jäger bezeichneten und der vielleicht in Ma-*Sa*-rwa wiederlebt, einem Namen, den die Tswana die hellhäutigen Jäger gaben."

meaning of the root *-túá, "despised neighboring tribe."

Thus we find three sets of contrasting pairs: Dutch, Sonqua/Bosjesmans; Otjiherero, Ovakuru/Ovatua; Setswana, Barwa/Masarwa. In each case the first term referred to known peoples of proximate location and carried neutral or positive connotations of aboriginality in some sense. The second term referred to newly encountered frontier peoples or rumored peoples of distant location and carried negative connotations of despised foreigner. In Dutch and English these transformations in usage occurred during the period – late eighteenth and early nineteenth centuries – when those groups were rapidly expanding geographically and consolidating their gains. These changes in nomenclatural referents were ideological impositions by newly hegemonic powers upon subordinated peoples who were thus interpellated as subjects in a new order of social relations. No longer a serious threat to European power, San-speakers acquired "characteristics that the powerful commonly find in those they have subjugated: meekness, innocence, passivity, indolence coupled with physical strength and stamina, cheerfulness, absence of greed or indeed desires of any kind, internal egalitarianism, a penchant for living in the present, inability to take initiatives on their own behalf" (Pratt 1986:46). This appears to be the first transition toward "bushmanness"; these same characteristics are attributed ethnographically to "Bushmen" today.

At the beginning of this transition the various Tswana groups were not yet dominant over other groups, but as their hegemony solidified during the course of the nineteenth century, the predicate attributes of San-speakers in Tswana ideology changed from original inhabitant to bloodthirsty marauder to childlike dependency. On the other hand, Ovaherero never established lasting hegemony in their sphere of influence; as a consequence, ovatua for them are situated somewhere over the horizon, and this term, when it is used at all, has only vague referents. Ovaherero usually refer to most local groups by their generic self-referents.

This brings us back to San. As noted already, Parkington derives this term from the same Khoikhoi root as Soaqua, which he says (1984:164) "should be referred to not as a title but as a description of a set of strategies that varied from almost complete independence [from livestock keeping] to clientship [of livestock keepers]." He says further (1984:158) that it seems certain that Soaqua was not originally meant to be capitalized "in the sense of referring to named communities" but referred to a particular and widespread life-style, which depended heavily – but apparently not exclusively – on foraging. Indeed, Vedder (1938:124) derives San from the Nama verb "sa": "to gather wild foods." Sixty-five years earlier, however, Theophilus Hahn ([1881] 1971:3) – although confessing that he was uncertain of the derivation – traced this term to the root "SA, to inhabit, to be located, to dwell, to be settled, to be quiet. Sã(n) consequently would mean Aborigines or Settlers proper. These Sã-n . . . as they are styled in the Cape Records, are often called Bushmen . . . a name given to indicate their abode and mode of living. . . . Sã(b) has also acquired a low meaning, and is not considered to be very complimentary."

This Khoikhoi/Nama term, now written San, thus seems to be fully parallel in meaning and history to Bantu rwa/tua-kuruha, moving from proteneutral/positive to acquired negative value. As we shall see, however, Nama-speakers in northern Namibia seldom used San but usually addressed and referred to peoples by their generic self-referents, by leader names, or by borrowed terms such as Bosjesmans.

Thus, before the emergence of ethnicity as a central logic, which began toward the end of the seventeenth century at the Cape but not in the Kalahari until the nineteenth century was well begun, Khoikhoi "sa" and Bantu "tau/rwa" forms were primarily epithets of origins with economic connotations. Group identification followed the self-usage of individual social units. As a consequence of struggles to control, first, commodity production for the European mercantile market and, later, units of labor for industrializing South Africa, all of these native terms acquired negative connotations and became categorical denominations that replaced group denotations in general reference. Their origins aside, all these forms are impositions upon peoples to whom they are foreign; they retain their acquired derogatory signification and are intensely disliked by those to whom they are applied. This dislike is gaining recognition in Botswana's popular press (Leepile 1988:9),

reflecting a growing awareness within the country of the pejorative connotations of Basarwa as well as of Bushman. These terms should all be relegated to archives, and the use of self-referents of self-defined social groups should be reinstated.[9] . . .

Primitive, savage, hunter-gatherer, forager, Bushman, Basarwa, San; the names have changed, their predicates and the premises from which these are drawn retain their negation of historically constructed objects. An analytical discourse that unquestioningly accepted these homogenizing categories, appropriate only to the needs of its own moment, has left us nothing but a stereotype of its subject.

---

[9] I employ self-referents in all appropriate cases. One of these needs special mention: those people of Botswana and Namibia known as !Kung in the literature refer to themselves as žu|'õasi (žu = person, |'õa = finished or complete, si = plural suffix; hence, completed people). !Xũ, which is the source of the term !Kung, is the self-referent name of a people who live in Angola and speak a dialect very similar to žu|'õasi; the name has been applied to both languages indiscriminately, since it was used this way by Bleek, who worked with a few prisoner !Kung or Zhu informants at the Cape in the 1880s. I have also adopted Setswana spelling of Khoisan words to reduce orthographic obstructions in the text; in this orthography, the dental and alveolar clicks (usually represented by | and ≠ are written as c, the lateral click (‖) as x, and the palatal click (!) as q. When necessary to give more precise phonological representation of words, I employ Snyman (1975 and to a lesser extent 1969) for Zhu, Traill (1974) for Kqoo, and Barnard (1985) for Nharo. I use Zhu instead of the longer form, a practice in keeping with these people's own usage. I use the term Bushman and rwa/tua forms only when their historical or connotational aspects are clear. I use San only to indicate that set of peoples who speak what used to be called the "Bush" languages of Khoisan. Although it is sometimes a bit awkward, this usage takes the form of San-speakers or San-speaking peoples except when used adjectivally.

A note is also in order regarding Bantu-language words. Until this century, there was no unified Tswana polity; rather, several independent polities of Tswana-speakers were known by their eponymous names; the Bakwena, Bangwato, and Batawana will concern us most. The geographical space of each such polity takes the locative prefix (Class 9) ga-; hence Gakwena, Gangwato, Gatawana. The locative (Class 7) bo- is applied to both the conceptual landed space and the actual geographical space of all the people conceived to be associated in language and culture (as in Botswana, the true place of all peoples who speak Setswana – that is, people with Tswana culture). All, or any plural fraction, of these peoples are Batswana; those identified with a specific smaller polity are Bakwena, Bangwato, Batawana, and so forth. A single individual takes the prefix (Class 1) mo-, thus Mokwena, Mongwato, Motawana. An individual Sarwa person is a Mosarwa; two or more are Basarwa. Otjiherero has a parallel structure: ova- is the equivalent of ba-, omu- of mo-; hence Ovaherero, Ovambanderu, Ovakuruha, and so on, and their singulars Omuherero, Omumbanderu, Omukuruha. Ovambanderu are the eastern branch of Herero in general; there are slight differences in speech, beliefs, and practices between the two groups. As adjectives, these roots take no prefix; thus Tswana agriculture, Mbanderu cattle, Sarwa hunters. For the spelling of geographical names in Botswana, I follow the *Third Report of the Place Names Commission* (GoB 1984).

References

Alonso, A.
1988 The effects of truth: Re-presentations of the past and the "imaging of community." *Journal of Historical Sociology* 1:33–57.

Athanassakis, A.
1983 *Hesiod: Theogony, Works and Days, Shield*. Baltimore: Johns Hopkins University Press.

Barnard, A.
1985 A Nharo word list. Department of African Studies, University of Natal, *Occasional Papers* 2.

Birmingham, D., and P. Martin, eds.
1983 *History of central Africa*. London: Longman.

Bley, H.
1971 *South-West Africa under German rule 1894–1914*. Evanston, Ill.: Northwestern University Press.

Brincker, H.
1964 *Wörterbuch und kurzgefasste Grammatik des Otji-Hérero*. Ridgewood, N.J.: Gregg Press. Fascimile reprint of 1886 original.

Brown, T.
1979 *Setswana-English dictionary*. 3d ed. Braamfontein: Pula Press. Originally published about 1875.

Clarence-Smith, W.
1979 *Slaves, peasants, and capitalists in southern Angola, 1840–1926*. Cambridge: Cambridge University Press.

Cole, D.
1975 *An introduction to Tswana grammer*. Cape Town: Longman.

Daniel, G.
1950 *A hundred years of archaeology*. London: Duckworth.

Driberg, J., and I. Schapera
1930 Introductory note. In *The Khoisan peoples of South Africa*, by I. Schapera, pp. v–vi. London: Routledge.

Dubrow, S.
1987 Race, civilization, and culture: The elaboration of segregationist discourse in the inter-war years. In *The politics of race, class, and nationalism in twentieth-century South Africa*, ed. S. Marks and S. Trapido, pp. 71–94. London: Longman.

Durkheim, E.
1964 *The division of labour in society*. New York: Free Press. Reprint of 1893 original.

Elphick, R.
1975 *Khoikhoi and the founding of white South Africa*. New Haven: Yale University Press.
1977 *Kraal and castle*. New Haven: Yale University Press.

Engels, F.
1972 *The origin of the family, private property, and the state*. New York: International. Ed. E. Leacock from 1884 original.

Fabian, J.
1986 *Language and colonial power: The appropriation of Swahili in the former Belgian Congo, 1880–1938*. Cambridge: Cambridge University Press.

Gadibolae, M.
1985 Serfdom (Bolata) in the Nata area. *Botswana Notes and Records* 17:25–32.

Giddens, A.
1971 *Capitalism and modern social theory*. Cambridge: Cambridge University Press.

Gilman, S.
1985 Black bodies, white bodies: Toward an iconography of a female sexuality in late nineteenth-century art, medicine, and literature. In Race, writing, and difference, ed. H. Gates, Jr., pp. 204–42. *Critical Inquiry* 12.

Goodwin, A., and C. van Riet Lowe
1929 The Stone Age cultures of South Africa. *Annals of the South Africa Museum* 27: 1–289.

Gordon, R.
1984 The !Kung in the Kalahari exchange: An ethnohistorical perspective. In *Past and present in hunter gatherer studies*, ed. C. Schrire, pp. 195–224. Orlando, Fla.: Academic Press.

Government of Botswana (GOB)
1984 *Third Report of the Place Names Commission*. Gaborone.

Gray, R., and D. Birmingham
1970 *Pre-colonial African trade*. Oxford: Oxford University Press.

Guenther, M.
1980 From "brutal savages" to "harmless people": Notes on the changing Western image of the Bushmen, *Paideuma* 26:123–40.

Guthrie, M.
1970 *Comparative Bantu: An introduction to the comparative linguistics and prehistory of the Bantu languages*. Ridgewood, N.J.: Gregg.

Hahn, T.
1971 *Tsuni-‖goam: The supreme being of the Khoi-Khoi.* Freeport: Books for Libraries. Reprint of 1881 original.

Herskovitz, M.
1962 *The human factor in changing Africa.* New York: Alfred Knopf.

Hirst, P.
1975 *Durkheim, Bernard and epistemology.* London: Routledge.

Hitchcock, R.
1978 *Kalahari cattle posts: A regional study of hunter-gatherers, pastoralists, and agriculturalists in the western sandveld region, Botswana.* Gaborone: Government Printer.

Hobsbawm, E.
1983 Introduction: Inventing traditions. In *The invention of tradition,* ed. E. Hobsbawm and T. Ranger, pp. 1–14. Cambridge: Cambridge University Press.

Iliffe, J.
1979 *A modern history of Tankanyika.* Cambridge: Cambridge University Press.
1917 Deutsch-Herero-Wörterbuch. *Abhandlung der Hamburgischen Kolonialinstitut* 32. Hamburg: Friederichsen.

Katjavivi, P.
1988 *A history of resistance in Namibia.* London: John Currey.

Kienetz, A.
1977 The key role of the Orlam migrations in the early Europeanization of South-West Africa (Namibia). *International Journal of African Historical Studies* 10:553–72.

Köhler, O.
1975 Der Khoisan Sprachbereich. In *Die Völker Afrikas und ihre traditionellen Kulturen.* ed. H. Baumann, pp. 305–37. Wiesbaden: Fritz Steiner.

Lau, B.
1979 A critique of the historical sources and historiography relating to the "Damaras" in precolonial Namibia. B.A. thesis (honors), University of Cape Town.
1981 Thank God the Germans came: Vedder and Namibian historiography. In *Collected Seminar Papers,* ed. C. Saunders, pp. 24–53. Cape Town: University of Cape Town.
1982 The emergence of commando politics in Namaland, southern Namibia: 1800–1870. M.A. thesis (history), University of Cape Town.

1984 "Pre-colonial" Namibian historiography: "What is to be done? Conference on Research Priorities in Namibia, Institute of Commonwealth Studies, University of London.

Leacock, E.
1972 Introduction. In *The origin of the family, private property, and the state,* by F. Engels, pp. 7–67. New York: International.

Leacock, E., and R. Lee
1982 Introduction. In *Politics and history in band societies,* ed. E. Leacock and R. Lee, pp. 1–20. Cambridge: Cambridge University Press.

Lee, R.
1965 Subsistence ecology of !Kung Bushmen. Ph.D. diss. (anthropology), University of California, Berkeley.
1979 *The !Kung San: Men, women, and work in a foraging society.* Cambridge: Harvard University Press.

Lee, R. and I. DeVore, eds.
1968 *Man the hunter.* Chicago: Aldine.

Leepile, M.
1988 When manna falls from heaven. *Mmegi wa Dikang* 5 (18–24 June): 8–9.
1966 *The savage mind.* Chicago: University of Chicago Press.
1967 *The scope of anthropology.* Trans. from *Leçon inaugural* (1960) by S. Ortner Paul and R. Paul. London: Jonathan Cape.

Loomis, C., and J. McKinney
1957 Introduction. In *Gemeinschaft und Gesellschaft,* by F. Tönnies, trans. C. Loomis and J. McKinney, pp. 1–29. New York: Harper and Row.

Lubbock, J.
1913 *Prehistoric times as illustrated by ancient remains and the manners and customs of modern savages.* New York: Henry Holt. Facsimile reprint of 1865 original.

Malinowski, B.
1972 Khoisan resistance to the Dutch in the seventeenth and eighteenth centuries. *Journal of African History* 8:55–80.

Marks, S., and A. Atmore, eds.
1980 *Economy and society in pre-industrial South Africa.* London: Longman. Marks, S., and S. Trapido, eds.
1987 *The politics of race, class, and nationalism in twentieth century South Africa.* London: Longman.

Marshall, L.

1957 The kin terminology system of the !Kung Bushmen. *Africa* 27:1–25.

1976 *The !Kung of Nyae Nyae.* Cambridge: Harvard University Press.

Marx, K.

1906 *Capital.* New York: Kerr. Reprint of 1867 original.

Marx, K. and F. Engels

1977 *The German ideology.* New York: International. Unpublished original dated 1846.

Mautle, G.

1986 Bakgalagadi-Bakwena relationships: A case of slavery, c. 1840–c. 1930. *Botswana Notes and Records* 18:19–32.

Miers, S.

1983 Botlhanka/Bolata under colonial rule. Seminar paper, Department of History, University of Botswana.

Miers, S., and M. Crowder

1988 Botlhanka/Bolata under colonial rule. In *The end of slavery in Africa*, ed. S. Miers and R. Roberts, pp. 172–200. Madison: University of Wisconsin Press.

Morgan, L.

1964 *Ancient society.* New York: Kerr. Facsimile reprint of 1877 original.

Moritz, W.

1980 Erkundungsreise ins Ovamboland 1857: Tagebuch Carl Hugo Hahn. *Aus alten Tagen in Südwest*, 4, Schwäbisch Gmünd.

Murdock, G.

1959 *Africa: Its peoples and their culture history.* New York: McGraw-Hill.

Nangati, F.

1980 Constraints on precolonial economy: The Bakwaen state c. 1820–1885. *Pula: Botswana Journal of African Studies* 2:125–38.

Nienaber, G.

1952 Die woord "Boesman." *Theoria* 4:36–40.

Palmer, R., and N. Parsons, eds.

1977 *The roots of rural poverty in central and southern Africa.* Berkeley and Los Angeles: University of California Press.

Parkington, J.

1984 Soaqua and Bushman: Hunters and robbers. In *Past and present in hunter gatherer studies*, ed. C. Schrire, pp. 151–74. Orlando, Fla.: Academic Press.

Parsons, N.

1977 The economic history of Khama's country in Botswana, 1844–1930. In *The roots of rural poverty in central and southern Africa*, ed. R. Palmer and N. Parsons, pp. 113–43. Berkeley and Los Angeles: University of California Press.

1983 *A new history of southern Africa.* Marshalltown: Heinemann.

Pitt-Rivers, A.

1906 *The evolution of culture and other essays.* Oxford: Clarendon Press.

Pratt, M.

1985 Scratches on the face of the country; or, What Mr. Barrow saw in the land of the Bushmen. In *Race, writing, and difference*, ed. H. Gates, Jr., pp. 119–43. *Critical Inquiry* 12.

1986 Fieldwork in common places. In *Writing culture: The poetics and politics of ethnography*, ed. J. Clifford and G. Marcus, pp. 27–50. Berkeley and Los Angeles: University of California Press.

Radcliffe-Brown, A.

1923 The methods of ethnology and social anthropology. *South African Journal of Science* 20:142–43.

Ranger, T.

1983 The invention of tradition in colonial Africa. In *The invention of tradition*, Ed. E. Hobsbawm and T. Ranger, pp. 211–62. Cambridge: Cambridge University Press.

Schwartz, S.

1977 Introduction. In *Naming, necessity, and natural kinds*, ed. S. Schwartz, pp. 9–41. Ithaca: Cornell University Press.

Sillery, A.

1952 *The Bechuanaland Protectorate.* Oxford: Oxford University Press.

Snyman, J.

1969 *An introduction to the !Xũ language.* Cape Town: Balkema.

1975 *Žu|'hōasi phonologie en woordeboek.* Cape Town: Balkema.

Sorokin, P.

1957 *Contemporary sociological theories.* New York: Harper and Row.

Steward, J.

1938 *Basin-plateau aboriginal socio-political groups.* Bulletin 120. Washington, D.C.: Smithsonian Institution, Bureau of American Ethnology.

Stocking, G.

1987 *Victorian anthropologists.* New York: Free Press.

Tabler, E.
1973 *Pioneers of South West Africa and Ngamiland: 1738–1880*. Cape Town: Balkema.

Thomas, E.
1959 *The harmless people*. New York: Alfred Knopf.

Tlou, T.
1972 A political history of northwestern Botswana to 1906. Ph.D. diss. (history), University of Wisconsin.

Tönnies, F.
1957 *Gemeinschaft und Gesellschaft*. Trans. C. Loomis and J. McKinney. New York: Harper and Row. Originally published 1887.

Traill, A.
1974 *The compleat guide to the Koon*. Communication 1. Johannesburg: African Studies Institute.

Tylor, E.
1909 *Anthropology*. New York: Appleton. Originally published 1881.

Van Der Post, L.
1958 *The lost world of the Kalahari*. New York: William Morrow.

Vedder, H.
1938 *South West Africa in early times: Being the story of South West Africa up to the time of Maharero's death in 1890*. London: Frank Cass.

Vossen, R.
1984 Studying the linguistic and ethno-history of the Khoe-speaking (central Khoisan) peoples of Botswana: Research in progress. *Botswana Notes and Records* 16:19–36.

White, L.
1959 *The evolution of culture*. New York: McGraw-Hill.

Wiley, D.
1985 The center cannot hold. Ph.D. diss. (history), Yale University.

Wilmsen, E.
1982a Exchange, interaction, and settlement in northwestern Botswana. In *Settlement in Botswana*, ed. R. Hitchcock and M. Smith, pp. 98–109. Marshalltown: Heinemann.

1982b Migration patterns of Remote Area Dwellers. In *Migration in Botswana: Patterns, causes, and consequences*, ed. C. Kerven, pp. 337–76. Gaborone: Central Statistics Office.

1983 The ecology of illusion: Anthropological foraging in the Kalahari. *Reviews in Anthropology* 10:9–20.

1989 Those who have each other: Land tenure of San-speaking peoples. In *We are here: Politics of aboriginal land tenure*, ed. E. Wilmsen, pp. 43–67. Berkeley and Los Angeles: University of California Press.

Wily, L.
1979 Official policy toward San (Bushmen) hunter-gatherers in modern Botswana: 1966–1978. Gaborone: National Institute of Development and Cultural Research.

Worsaae, P.
1849 *The primeval antiquities of Denmark*. Copenhagen: Royal Danish National Museum.

Wright, J.
1986 Politics, ideology and the invention of 'Nguni. In *Resistance and ideology in settler societies*, ed. T. Lodge, pp. 96–118. Johannesburg: Raven Press.

15

FORAGERS, GENUINE OR SPURIOUS? SITUATING THE KALAHARI SAN IN HISTORY[1]

JACQUELINE S. SOLWAY AND RICHARD B. LEE

One of the dominant themes of critical anthropology in the 1970s and 80s has been the critique of ethnographic models that depict societies as isolated and timeless. Where an older generation of anthropologists tended to see societies as autonomous and self-regulating, the newer generation has discovered mercantilism and capitalism at work in societies hitherto portrayed as, if not pristine, then at least well beyond the reach of the "world system." Thus the Nuer (Gough 1971, Newcomer 1972, Sacks 1979, Kelly 1985), Samoans (Freeman 1983), Tallensi (Worsley 1956), Kachin (Friedman 1975, 1979; Nugent 1983), Maya (Lewis 1951, Wasserstrom 1982), and many other "classic" cases have been the subject of critical scrutiny. These studies have sought to resituate these peoples in the context of wider

regional and international economies, polities, and histories (see Wolf 1982).

Studies of hunting-and-gathering peoples have been strongly influenced by this revisionism (see, e.g., Endicott 1988; Woodburn 1988; Ingold, Riches, and Woodburn 1988; Healand and Reid 1989; Howell, cited in Lewin 1989; Bower 1989; Lewin 1989). It was in the spirit of this endeavor that we produced a critical analysis of the impact of the fur trade on the 19th-century Kalahari San (Solway and Lee 1981). A number of other scholars have focussed on the San, uncovering the early interactions between San foragers and Bantu farmers, herders, and traders within the complex historical dynamics of the Kalahari Desert (Schrire 1980, 1984a; Wilmsen 1983; Gordon 1984; Denbow 1984, 1986; Parkington 1984; Denbow and Wilmsen

[1] Solway wishes to acknowledge the generosity of the Social Sciences and Humanities Research Council of Canada for a post-doctoral fellowship for support during the writing of this article. Earlier versions of it were presented at the annual meetings of the American Anthropological Association (1981) and the Canadian Anthropology Society (1989) and at the Universities of Massachusetts and Connecticut. We thank the participants in these meetings for their useful suggestions, which we have not always followed. We particularly want to thank Alan Barnard, Alec Campbell, Peter Carstens, Norman Chance, John Cole, Moitaly Dikgogwane, Christine Gailey, Rob Gordon, Bob Hitchcock, Tim Ingold, Art Keene, Sue Kent, Michael Lambek, Michael Levin, Ben Magubane, Toby Morantz, Shuichi Nagata, Tom Patterson, Peter Rigby, Larry Robbins, Gerald Sider, Jeffery Tsheboagae, Diana Wylie, and John Yellen. Responsibility for errors and interpretations rests with us.

1986).[2] In their zeal to discover links and to dispel myths of pristinity, however, these scholars are in danger of erecting new straw men and of doing violence of a different kind to the data – imputing links where none existed and assuming that where evidence exists for trade it implies the surrender of autonomy. What is perhaps most troubling about the Kalahari revisionism is its projection of a spurious uniformity on a vast and diverse region.

In this paper we present two case studies that demonstrate the varied nature and consequences of San contact with non-San in the Kalahari. By examining the different historical experiences of two San groups, one largely dependent on its Bantu-speaking neighbours and the other (until recently) substantially autonomous, we intend to make clear that contact may take many forms, not all of which lead to dependency, abandonment of foraging, or incorporation into "more powerful" social formations.

The attribution of dependency to societies formerly considered autonomous resonates with other themes in the culture of late capitalism. Borrowing an image from the popular film *The Gods Must Be Crazy*, we call this view the "Coke Bottle in the Kalahari Syndrome," whereby modernity falls mysteriously from the sky, setting in motion an inevitable spiral of cultural disintegration that can only be checked by the removal of the foreign element. This is clearly a caricature, but it reveals the common and unstated perception of foraging societies as so delicately balanced and fragile that they cannot accommodate innovation and change. Sahlin's (1968:2) summary law "Cultural dominance goes to technological pre-dominance" could be the foragers' epitaph. The "Coke Bottle in the Kalahari" imagery also bears a subtext, the rueful recognition of the unlimited capacity of "advanced societies" to consume everything in their path.

We challenge the notion that contact automatically undermines foragers and that contemporary foragers are to be understood only as degraded cultural residuals created through their marginality to more powerful systems. We consider the possibility that foragers can be autonomous without being isolated and engaged without being incorporated. And we follow Marx (1977 [1887]:89–92) in proposing that exchange can occur in the absence of "exchange value." Further, our argument calls into question any model of social change that implies linearity; the historical record reveals protracted processes, with fits and starts, plateaus and reversals, and varied outcomes. While many historical foragers have assimilated to other societies, a number, such as the African Pygmies and the foragers of South and Southeast Asia, have developed stable forms of interaction with agricultural neighbours and persisted alongside them, sometimes for centuries (see, e.g., Leacock and Lee 1982, Endicott 1988, Peterson 1978). The fact that foragers have coexisted with farmers for so long is testimony to the resilience of their way of life. The position adopted here is that 20th-century foragers are neither pristine nor totally degraded and encapsulated. The historical status of African foraging peoples must be seen as the complex product of the dynamics of the foraging mode of production itself, of long interaction between foragers, farmers, and herders, and finally of dynamics growing out of their linkages with world capitalism.

The Problem

By the mid-20th century, San societies in Botswana exhibited a wide range of "adaptations." Along the Nata, Botletli, and Okavango Rivers there were "black" San who fished, owned cattle, and practiced agriculture

---

[2]   Lee (1965) had already noted the diversity of non-foraging adaptations among the contemporary San.

(Cashdan 1987, Tlou 1985, Hitchcock 1987); in the Ghanzi freehold zone of western Botswana many San had become farm labourers, dependent squatters on their traditional lands (Guenther 1985, Russell 1976); in the Game Reserve areas of Khutse and the Central Kalahari, the /Gwi and other San groups lived relatively independent lives, hunting and gathering, raising small stock, and gardening (Kent 1989*a*, Tanaka 1980, Silberbauer 1981); and in the central sandveld many San lived clustered around Tswana cattle posts, where the men were employed as herders (Hitchcock 1978).

The historical antecedents of this diversity have been difficult to discern. Until the 1970s the available archaeological evidence indicated that the Kalahari had been a stronghold of hunter-gatherer societies and the diversity was the product of the last few hundred years (Phillipson (1977). Recent excavations, however (Denbow 1980, 1984, 1986; Wilmsen 1983, 1989; Denbow and Wilmsen 1983, 1986), have demonstrated a much earlier Iron Age presence, in parts of the Kalahari as early as A.D. 500. Later Stone Age (LSA) sites, commonly associated with populations ancestral to San hunter-gatherers, are present as well and in some areas remain predominant, but a number of these sites have Iron Age materials indicating contact between farmers and foragers. Thus the time depth of contact with non-hunters has increased from a few centuries to a millennium or more, and the presence of "exotic" goods is evidence for regional trade between hunters and non-hunters.

A second line of evidence for the revisionists springs from rereadings of 19th-century accounts of exploration and trade in the Kalahari interior. Gordon (1984), for one, has argued that the interior San were so deeply involved in trade, warfare, and diplomacy that they bore little resemblance to the "autonomous" societies described by 20th-century ethnographers. A closely related issue is the question of San servitude for black overlords. Indeed, many 19th- and 20th-century sources describe the San as living in a condition close to serfdom, a perception that has coloured observations of them.

The revisionists have used these lines of evidence to call into question the claims to authenticity of a number of foraging peoples studied by Marshall (1976), Lee and DeVore (1976), Lee (1979), Silberbauer (1981), Tanaka (1980), and others. Schrire (1980, 1984*b*), for example, argues that the San are not hunter-gatherers at all but failed pastoralists who oscillate between herding and foraging from century to century.[3] Labelling recent ethnographies of the San "romantic accounts of Bushman isolation and independence," Denbow (1986:1) dismisses them as "an ahistorical and timeless caricature." He suggests that whatever hunters persisted through the long period of contact did so not as autonomous societies but as "part of long-standing regional systems of interaction and exchange involving neighboring peoples with quite different economic and socio-political orientations" (p. 27). Wilmsen (1983), the most outspoken critic, referencing the perspective pioneered by Wolf, challenges the idea that the flexible egalitarian sharing documented for several San groups has anything to do with the dynamics of a foraging mode of production, concluding that "it is more than merely possible that the San are classless today precisely because they are the underclass in an intrusive class structure" (p. 17). . . .

The questions raised by the revisionists are challenging ones, and the claims they make go well beyond the reinterpretation of Kalahari archaeology. Yet it is an open question how

---

[3] Schrire's model in turn is drawn from Elphick's (1977) studies of the 17th-century Cape San, who were observed to move into herding as opportunities arose and back to foraging when the livestock was lost or stolen.

much of their revision arises from the data and how much rests on unexamined inference and assumption. It will be useful to set out their claims as a series of propositions in order to clarify the boundary between fact and interpretation. They propose that (1) the Iron Age settlement of the Kalahari is earlier than previously thought, and therefore (2) hunter-gatherers were absorbed into regional economic networks and (3) ceased to exist as independent societies well before the historic period. They go on to argue that (4) if these societies continue to exhibit characteristics associated with hunting and gathering it is because of (a) their poverty (Wilmsen) or (b) their resistance to domination by stronger societies (Schrire). Of these only Point 1 can be considered well established; Points 2 and 3 draw unwarranted conclusions from scanty data while Point 4 relies heavily on discourses that are as ideological as they are analytical.

What kinds of questions need to be asked in order to evaluate the conflicting claims of the Kalahari ethnographers and their critics? It is necessary, first, for both parties to attend to issues of regional variation. Some foragers certainly were drawn into farming and herding centuries ago, and some of these became part of regional economic systems, but, as we spell out below, both archaeology and ethnohistory contradict the view of a uniform grid of economic interdependency throughout the Kalahari. Second, we need to sensitize ourselves to the assumptions we make about the nature of "contact." For some "contact" appears to be unconsciously equated with "domination." The possibility of trade or exchange *without* some form of domination is excluded from the range of outcomes. When considering the Kalahari we need to ask further whether the conditions for domination existed there before, say, 1850. Were the societies with which the foragers came in contact after A.D. 500 sufficiently powerful to compel San servitude? Again the evidence shows that outcomes were variable and that in a number of areas the foraging life persisted. Third, and related, we need to examine our assumptions about the transformative power of the commodity – the view that when a society is linked to another by trade or tribute that linkage will necessarily transform social organization and create dependency. Are there other outcomes possible in which exchange relations do not undermine existing relations of production? Finally, we need to assess the evidence for San servitude; the contradictions in the literature suggest that appearances may be deceiving and in some cases San subordination may be more apparent then real. . . .

Case Studies

The Western Kweneng San

Many San peoples today live on the fringes of Bantu communities or white-owned farms;[4] the Western Kweneng San are one example. In contrast to the Dobe San, whose contact with non-San has traditionally been intermittent, these Southern San have lived amongst Bantu-speaking peoples for at least 200 years. The peoples of the Dutlwe area, in the southern Kalahari 250km west of Gaborone (fig 15.1[1], include three intermarrying San groups

---

[4]   For some the fringes are more social than physical, and San live, as servants, in Tswana, Kgalagadi, or Herero households. At the same time, many San live literally on the outskirts of Bantu communities or, in the case of the Ghanzi district, of white-owned farms and oscillate between client-like relations with their Bantu employers, hunting and gathering, and stock raising and agriculture. Such arrangements are described for much of Botswana (see, e.g., Silberbauer and Kuper 1966, Guenther 1986, Solway 1987, Vierich 1982, Hitchcock 1987, Kent 1989, Biesele et al. 1989). In the densely settled eastern regions of Botswana, San tend to be tightly linked to Tswana communities and have little opportunity to hunt and gather or to claim a "hinterland" area to which to retreat (Motzafi 1985). In the southern and central Kalahari, where settlement is relatively sparse, San generally maintain more options and greater cultural integrity and economic diversity.

(Tshassi, Kwa, and Khute) and the Bantu-speaking Kgalagadi. The Kwena, a Tswana chiefdom, occupy the better-watered eastern edge of the desert.[5] The dominant Tswana-Kgalagadi cultural model posits a hierarchical social order in which the San and other servile peoples occupy the social and physical margins. This "Tswanacentric" model does not, however, fit everywhere with the same precision, nor has it fit equally through time. The historical record reveals a variety of linkages between San and their neighbours, with a variety of consequences. San encapsulation within the orbit of Bantu-speaking peoples and loss of autonomy have been neither automatic nor, in most instances, complete. The San of Western Kweneng have not always worked for their Bantu neighbours, nor, in spite of the pronouncements of current Kalahari residents, is there anything "natural" about the state of affairs that exists today.

The pre- and protohistoric period Oral traditions obtained from current residents indicate that relations between Kgalagadi and San were largely symbiotic in the early period.[6] All were nomadic and lived primarily by hunting and gathering, although the Kgalagadi may have practiced some horticulture. After 1820 new waves of Kgalagadi, refugees of the wars of the turbulent period known as the Difaqane, retreated into the desert with their goats, sheep, and dogs. The Kgalagadi credit the San with having taught them desert skills, and the San made use of Kgalagadi animals, especially hunting dogs. According to the Kgalagadi,

their ancestors were able to migrate to western Kweneng with their goats and sheep in the early 19th century because the animals could obtain virtually all of their moisture from melons during the trek. These new immigrants chose a more sedentary life than their predecessors, and the pans on which they settled were also San water sources. In a Mokgalagadi's words, "The Basarwa [San] were already here. They just move around a lot. . . . They were not driven away."

The fur-trade period In the period following 1840 the Kwena, who themselves had fared badly during the Difaqane (Thompson 1975:396), were attempting to reassert and consolidate their hold on the Kalahari periphery. Threatened from the east by the Boers, they were eager to accumulate Western trade goods, particularly guns (Livingstone 1857:39).[7] To do so they needed desert products such as furs, ostrich feathers, skins, and ivory, and vast quantities of these were obtained from the peoples of the area as tribute; Livingstone writes (p. 50) that while he was living among the Kwena he observed "between twenty and thirty thousand skins . . . made up into karosses; part of them were worn by the inhabitants and part sold to traders."

The San participated only indirectly in the tribute system; they and the Kgalagadi were the primary producers, hunting and preparing skins, but in most cases it was the Kgalagadi (and usually only the elite among them) who dealt with the Kwena.[8] The San hunted with dogs and occasionally with guns owned by

[5] The southern Kalahari, drier than the north, has no year-round standing water, but the pans that dot the desert have high water tables and hold water, often salty, for varying periods of time after the rains.

[6] Ethnohistorical data on the western Kweneng for the 19th century are limited. Maps in Livingstone (1857), MacKenzie (1971 [1871]), and Chapman (1971 [1868]) exclude the area, and Leistner (1967:30) notes that the mid-19th-century explorers avoided the "inhospitable southern wastes." Oral traditions collected in the field by Solway in 1977–79 and 1986 (Solway 1987) and by Okihiro (1976) contain few specific data on transactions between the ethnic groups in the 19th century. We know of no archaeological work in the region.

[7] In 1852 the Boers attacked the Kwena capital and killed 60 Africans. Livingstone (1857:121), whose home was destroyed in this raid, notes that African refugees from the Boers came to Kwena afterward, buttressing their power. In terms of trade, the Kwena capital remained the center and launch point to the north until the 1860s (Parsons 1977:119).

[8] Like the San of the Central district described by Hitchcock (1987:234), the Dutlwe-area San may well have engaged directly in trade with Europeans, but there is little evidence to support this view. Few traders ventured into western Kweneng.

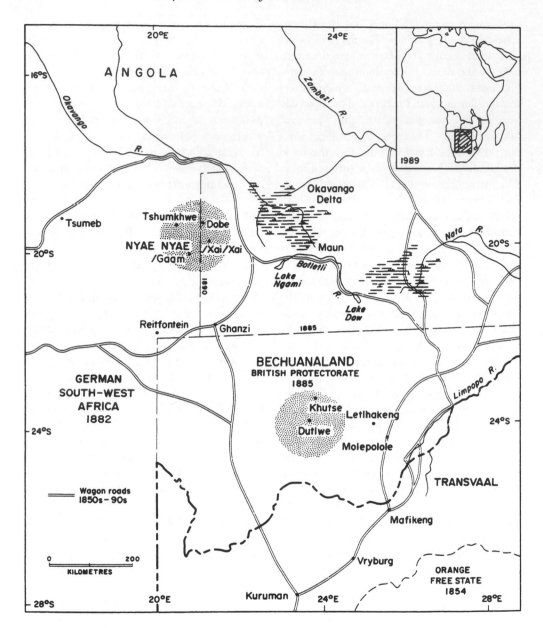

Figure 15.1 [1]   The 19th-century Kalahari, with relevant contemporary boundaries and political divisions superimposed.

others; they brought the hides and often some of the meat to the owners and kept a portion of the meat for themselves (see, e.g., Silberbauer and Kuper 1966, Hitchcock 1987, Schapera and van der Merwe 1945, Stow 1964 [1905]). Tobacco, grown and/or obtained by trade, was a central commodity in the system, exchanged for skins and labour. Contact between Kgalagadi and San was concentrated in the winter months, when the fur-bearing animals were most desirable and water most scarce. In this period there was little difference in the objective conditions of life of San and Kgalagadi. Their relations were less coercive than Kwena-Kgalagadi relations and resembled trade more than tribute.

Towards the end of the 19th century the Kwena's control over the periphery began to break down. The desert was difficult to police; Kwena rule was thin and maintained largely through periodic displays of force. The Kgalagadi as a result were able to begin to accumulate property, especially cattle (see Okihiro 1976; Schapera and van der Merwe 1945:5), thus laying the groundwork for an agro-pastoral base that did not develop among the Kweneng San. Inequalities between the San and some Kgalagadi also began to grow. The Kgalagadi attempted to replicate in their relations with the San the Tswana hierarchical model that subordinated them to the Kwena, but the material conditions for institutionalized servitude were absent.

In 1885, with the imposition of British colonial rule, the tribute system was officially disbanded; the Kgalagadi were allowed to trade their goods, and instead of tribute a tax, of which Kwena chiefs received 10%, was collected (although in practice the transition from tribute to tax was not automatic)

(Schapera and van der Merwe 1945:6). The colonial state was intrigued by the San and voiced concern over their condition, but in fact the new government had little direct impact on their life.

A colonial officer travelling through western Kweneng in 1887 considered the San the Kgalagadi's "slaves pure and simple," but at the same time he reported, "They have no fixed residence, often living miles from water and living on the melons and roots, changing their abode, as these are scarce or plentiful" (Botswana National Archives 1887a:17). (If the San had truly been slaves they would not have been following the melons but would have been working for the Kgalagadi.) This apparent contradiction emerges repeatedly; the San are described as slaves and yet as "scoundrels, snakes, and rascals" who will not stay in one place and move about as they wish (Botswana National Archives 1877b; cf. MacKenzie 1871:128–32 for the Central district). Again, an 1899 report states that the Masarwa (San) "lives a nomadic life in a wild state and hunts for the masters" (HC. 24, quoted in Schapera and van der Merwe 1945:4), thus portraying them as simultaneously enserfed and nomadic foragers.[9] . . .

Agro-pastoralism The fur trade remained for some time the primary link between San and Kgalagadi. The Kgalagadi elite who owned cattle in the early 20th century relied upon their poorer relatives rather than San for herding labour. At the same time, the development of agro-pastoral production was beginning to undermine the San's foraging base. Permanent settlement, population increase, cattle herding, and agriculture combined to reduce the environment's hunting-and-gathering potential. The desert-

[9]   Russell's (1976) analysis of Ghanzi San subordination contains similar contradictions. It is reported that "in the Bushman view [the Boers' arrival] presented an alternative to Tswana overlordship" (p. 189), yet a 1910 Boer petition is quoted as requesting that "the Bushmen be placed in a location . . . for being in such a wild state they are very little use as servants." Motzafi (1986) notes that in the Tswana world view the San's "wild" qualities emerge as much from their lack of social standing as from their association with the bush. Thus, for the Tswana, "wildness" and servility are not necessarily incompatible. It is doubtful that this cultural understanding can be attributed to the European view.

ification noted by elderly residents and by ecologists alike can be traced not simply to overhunting but to human habitation (Campbell and Child 1971, Leistner 1967). Every bush or tree cleared to make way for cultivation, especially plowing, reduces the ground cover, disrupts root systems, facilitates erosion and reduces the soil's inability to absorb and retain moisture. It was increasingly only in the bush, away from the better water sources, that the San could maintain their autonomy. The Central Kalahari has remained (by law) free of large-scale village and livestock development and served as a "hinterland" for the San, a place where their culture and mode of subsistence have persisted and where many Western Kweneng San claim roots, refuge, and restoration. . . .

The organic link By the 1940s, local agropastoralism was well established. With trading revenues and migrant labourers' wages, the Kgalagadi accumulated cattle and plows and imported new well-digging techniques that permitted expansion of the livestock sector. Cultivated water sources such as wells and boreholes came to be considered the private property of the group that dug them,[10] and eventually many of the better-watered pans (which probably had been dry-season homes of the San [Vierich 1977]) were associated with the Kgalagadi; now to obtain drinking water the San had to enter into unequal relations with the Kgalagadi. Plow agriculture and animal husbandry increased the workload at precisely the time when able-bodied young Kgalagadi men were leaving for contract work on the South African mines, and it was San labour that filled the gap (Solway 1987). By the 1950s the San had become the Kgalagadi's casual labour force. The Kgalagadi today frequently try to minimize the importance of San labour and like to think of themselves as humanitarian for "helping" them, but when pressed many will quietly admit, "We are lucky, we have Bushmen."

That the Kgalagadi's greater demand for labour occurred in concert with the growing precariousness of foraging in the area was not a result of conscious conspiracy, but neither was it a coincidence. The Kgalagadi's new productive base altered the environment; it changed their labour demands, transformed property relations over water sources, and increasingly distinguished the Kgalagadi from the San. In the 19th century differences in material conditions between the groups were small, but by the mid-20th century the hierarchical model in which the San occupy a marginal and servile position more closely matched reality than it had in the past. Hunting for the Kgalagadi had not undermined the San's foraging subsistence strategy; it is doubtful whether the Kgalagadi of the 19th century had the resources or power to compel San servitude, except in the very short term. The Kgalagadi of the 20th century, in contrast, had control of water, milk, grain, and purchased items such as tobacco, clothing, guns, and wagons, and these resources, in the face of diminishing returns from foraging, tied the San to them more thoroughly than in the past. New kinds of work that followed the rhythm of the agricultural and livestock cycle resulted in more intimate and regular association than that created by the hunting arrangements. With the expansion of Kgalagadi agriculture, San women entered the workforce in greater numbers, which meant that San social reproduction increasingly took place in the Kgalagadi's domain. Today, a few San live permanently as domestic servants with Kgalagadi; the Kgalagadi claim to "take

---

[10] Peters (1983, 1984) presents a structurally similar case in which common property (pasture) surrounding private property (borehole) becomes identified with the private and treated as such. Again, for the Ghanzi area it is reported that "Boer skill at digging wells gave them an economic advantage over Bushmen for the first time. The further decline of the water table necessitated the more complex technology and capitalization of borehole and pump, and Bushmen dependence accelerated" (Russell 1976:190).

these San as our children," but they are children who never achieve adult status. There are a number of San homesteads on the periphery of the villages, their populations waxing and waning with the seasons. The spatial marginality neatly reflects the San's social marginality and positioning somewhere between village and bush.

Although the hinterland persists and some San forage full-time in it (Kent 1989, Silberbauer 1981), most Western Kweneng San work for the Kgalagadi at least during the agricultural season, arriving "after the flowers appear on the melon plants." Sixty years ago, coming to the village and working for the Kgalagadi was seen as a "break" from foraging in an increasingly unproductive environment. Now the village end of the cycle has taken precedence, and most San are resigned to the fact that they can make a living only by working for the Kgalagadi, begging, or accepting government aid. Foraging offers only an occasional supplement. Some San still return to the bush in the wet season. According to one woman, "We are happy to be away from the Kgalagadi. There are water roots and berries. If we come upon a tortoise or a dead animal we will eat and dance all night. We only come back because of thirst."

The Dobe San

The Dobe area, 700 km north of Dutlwe, was far from the turmoil of 19th-century colonial southern Africa.[11] The Dobe people were not affected by the Difaqane, though they had heard about it, and they were not subject to tribute. More important, the wave of black settlement did not reach them until 1925. Surrounded by a waterless belt 70–200 km in depth, the Dobe area is difficult of access even today; it would have been accessible to Iron Age peoples with livestock for only a few months in years of high rainfall, and even then only after an arduous journey. It would be risky to assume that contemporary patterns of contact (or lack of contact) were characteristic of all periods of prehistory. Fortunately, the data of archaeology can be brought to bear on this kind of question.

The pre- and protohistoric period Despite the abundant evidence of Iron Age settlement elsewhere in northwestern Botswana dating from A.D. 500 or earlier and despite concerted efforts to find the same in the Dobe area, there is no archaeological evidence of Iron Age occupation of the area until the 20th century (Brooks 1989, Yellen and Brooks n.d.). What does exist in Later Stone Age archaeological

---

[11]   Although the !Kung San of the Dobe-Nyae/Nyae area are arguably the most thoroughly documented hunting-and-gathering society in this century, they are markedly underrepresented in the historical literature. Tabler's (1973) definitive compendium contains only 10 references (out of 334) to Europeans who entered the area prior to 1900. Thus the classic accounts of Baines (1973 [1864]), Chapman (1971 [1868]), Galton (1889), Anderson (1856), and Livingstone (1857) refer only elliptically to the peoples of the central !Kung interior. The earliest firsthand account, that of Passarge, dates from 1907, while Wilhelm's observations from the period 1914–19 were not published until 1954.

In his ethnohistorical examination of !Kung exchange, Gordon (1984) uncritically conflates accounts from all over northern Namibia, distorting the picture of 19th-century !Kung San by portraying a number of highly acculturated and distant San peoples as if they were San of the central !Kung interior; less than 20% of his material refers to the !Kung of the Dobe-Nyae/Nyae area. For example, he refers to a group of San controlling a rich copper mine near Tsumeb and marketing 50–60 tons of ore each year as if they were !Kung (pp. 212–13), but the San in question are the Nama-speaking Heikum and Tsumeb is located 400 km west of Dobe.

Sources of data for this case study consist of extensive interviews with San, Tswana, and Herero informants between 40 and 80 years of age, mainly during three years of fieldwork between 1963 and 1969. A number of the older informants had been alive at the turn of the century. All informants drew upon older oral histories and oral traditions. Individual accounts were checked for consistency against the growing corpus of material, and follow-up visits were made to resolve discrepancies wherever possible. These accounts were placed in the context of the growing historical literature for the region, including Tlou (1985), Tlou and Campbell (1984), Vedder (1966 [1938]), Drechsler (1980), Parsons (1982), Palmer and Parsons (1977), and Clarence-Smith (1979).

deposits, along with a classic stone tool kit, is a few fragments of pottery and a few iron implements, items best interpreted as evidence of intermittent trade with Iron Age settlements to the east and north.

!Kung oral traditions reinforce this view. Elders speak of their ancestors' maintaining long-term trade relations with "Goba" while maintaining their territorial organization and subsistence as hunter-gatherers in the Dobe area and to the west of it. Some have gone as far as to insist that the first visitors on a large scale to their area were whites rather than blacks. According to !Xamn!a, who was born at the turn of the century, "The first outsiders to come to /Xai/Xai were /Ton [European] hunters. . . . They used to shoot guns with bullets one and one-half inches thick. But this was before I was born. My wife's father, Toma!gain, worked for the /Tons." When asked which of the Tswana ruling clans had first arrived in the Dobe area in the last century, a !Goshe elder emphatically replied, "None! The !Tons [Europeans] were first." And when asked if his "fathers" knew of blacks of any origin in the area, he replied, 'No, we only knew ourselves."

The picture that emerges from the archaeological, ethnohistorical, and oral-historical evidence can be sketched as follows: The Dobe area has been occupied by hunting-and-gathering peoples for at least several thousand years. The evidence of unbroken LSA deposits 100 cm or more in depth, with ostrich eggshells and indigenous fauna from bottom to top, with a scattering of pottery and iron, and with European goods in surface levels supports a picture of relative continuity.[12] At some point between A.D. 500 and 1500, the interior !Kung established trade relations with

"Goba" to the east and northeast and carried on trade with them in which desert products – furs, honey, and ivory – were exchanged for iron, tobacco, ceramics, and possibly agricultural products. It is unclear whether the Goba made reciprocal visits to the Dobe area or even whether the ceramics that are found are of outside origin.[13] . . .

The fur-trade period Two kinds of economic networks were involved in the San articulation with the "world system": indirect involvement through black intermediaries – the Goba and later the Tswana – and direct contact with European hunters and traders. The indirect form resembled the precolonial African trade that the San had carried on for centuries and therefore involved no basic restructuring of relations of production. The direct European trade, while intense and disruptive, did not last very long. It was not until the 1920s and 30s, with the arrival of black settlers in the Dobe area, that basic production relations began to be modified and incorporative processes set in motion.

Several accounts exist of the lively trade that went on in the "Gaamveld" between the "Bushmen" and Afrikaner, German, and English hunter-traders in the period 1870–90 (Lee 1979:78; Solway and Lee 1981). The first European known to have visited the Dobe-Nyae/Nyae area was Hendrik van Zyl, whom Ramadjagote Harry, a Tswana born in 1903, describes as "the hunter who was responsible for killing all the elephants and rhinos in the west." Tabler (1973:114) confirms that in 1877 alone van Zyl's party killed 400 elephants in the Gaamveld and took out 8,000 lb. of ivory. !Kung recall the period with a great deal of affection as a time of intense social activity and economic prosperity. They were provided

---

[12] For example, at Nxai Nxai, excavated by Wilmsen (1978), Levels 6–10 (60–100 cm) produced 4 sherds, Levels 1–5 (10–50 cm) 32, and the surface levels 348. Fragments of a single bovine maxilla found in the 60cm level were identified as domesticated cow. That no further examples of domesticates have been found has led some archaeologists to suggest that this specimen was intrusive (Yellen and Brooks n.d.).

[13] Some !Kung insisted that their ancestors had made the pottery from local clays. With the advent of European iron pots, the art was lost.

with guns and ate enormous quantities of meat. One could find no trace of regret in these accounts for the carnage and diminution of wildlife; elephants, regarded as pests by the !Kung, are rarely hunted today. The legacy of this brief but intense irruption for the Dobe-area people can be briefly set out. One small family of !Kung, fully integrated into the Dobe community, is acknowledged to be descended from a member of van Zyl's party and a local !Kung woman. Few other impacts are evident. Even though firearms were widely distributed to African populations (Marks and Atmore 1971) and though many 19th-century-vintage weapons remained in African hands into the 1960s, only a single !Kung man, a tribal constable who had purchased his weapon with wages, possessed a gun in 1963.

A second instance of European presence, also short-lived, was the cattle drives sent by a group of Afrikaner trekkers from Angola to the Transvaal via Lewisfontein (!Kangwa), a large perennial spring in the centre of the Dobe area. The "Dorsland" Trekkers reached Angola only in 1880, and according to Clarence-Smith (1979:59–60) the trek route had fallen into disuse by 1900 (see also Gordon 1984:202).

Since most European goods – iron pots, beads, etc. – continued to be obtained through Bantu intermediaries, one would be hard put to argue that the sporadic European presence from 1870 to 1900 had transformed !Kung society. On the other hand, it is likely that the European penetration of the !Kung interior was the catalyst for incursions by Tswana and others.

!Kung call the period after the departure of the Europeans and before the arrival of permanent black settlers *koloi* (wagon), a reference to the ox-carts used by the Tswana from the 1880s to about 1925. A number of Tswana had been employed on the European hunting parties as hunters, trackers, and gun bearers. After 1880 Tswana hunter-traders with wagons began making their own trips to the Dobe area; this was part of the general expansion of the Tawana state after 1874 (Tlou

1985:49). In the !Kung oral traditions it is the !Kung and not the Tswana who are the initiators of this trade. As !Xamn!a tells it,

When the Europeans left, the Zhu/twasi were all alone. My ≠*tum* [father-in-law] said, "Let's go to the Tswana, bring their cattle here and drink their milk." So then my ≠*tum* organized the younger men and went east to collect the cattle. . . . Then they chopped a brush-fence kraal under the camel thorn trees and kraaled them there. The Tswana came up to visit and hunt, then they went back leaving the San drinking the milk. Then my ≠*tum* got *shoro* [tobacco] from the Tswana and smoked it. When the *shoro* was all finished the young men collected all the steenbok skins and went east to bring back more *shoro*. The boys shouldered the tobacco and brought it back. Later they drove the cattle out to Hxore Pan where they built a kraal and ate the *tsin* beans of Hxore while the cattle drank the water. So they lived, eating *tsin*, hunting steenbok and duiker, and drinking milk. When Hxore water was dry, they loaded the pack oxen with sacks of *tsin* [for the !Kung to eat] and drove them back to /Xai/Xai. At the end of the season the cattle boys loaded the pack oxen with bales and bales of eland biltong and went east with it to collect the balls of *shoro* and sometimes bags of corn. These they would deliver to my ≠*tum*.

This account provides a good description of two forms of economic linkage: the barter system, in which desert products are exchanged for agricultural and manufactured products, and the *mafisa* system, whereby well-to-do Tswana farm out cattle to others – fellow tribesmen or members of subordinate groups. The first form of linkage does not lead to incorporation and loss of autonomy, especially when the level of trade is modest and the element of coercion is absent. *Mafisa*, by contrast, does alter the character of production at the levels of both forces and relations. Animal husbandry places foragers in a different relation to land and to predators and necessitates a shift in the patterns of labour deployment. Energy is drawn away from hunting and reallocated to herding, and in return the producers are rewarded with a more secure food source, at least in the short run. At the level of production relations, *mafisa* is a form of loan-cattle – labour exchange set in the context of a patron-client relationship.

Briefly, the *mafisa* system in northwestern Ngamiland operated as follows (see also Tlou 1985:52): The San client maintained the herd on behalf of the Tswana patron, who retained ownership of the beasts. In return San could consume all the milk the herd produced and the meat of any animal that had died of natural causes, including predation. A tally was kept of beasts lost, and all animals had to be accounted for when the patron made a periodic visit. If he was satisfied with the performance of the *mafisa* holder he might pay him a calf, but this was not obligatory. If he was not satisfied he could withdraw his animals and seek another client. Similarly, the client was free to withdraw his services – with notice – and either leave *mafisa* entirely or seek another patron and a new herd of cattle.

On the face of it, *mafisa* appears to resemble a system of agrarian dependency: ownership of the means of production, in this case cattle, is in the hands of the overlord who at his whim can withdraw the herd and thus deprive the client of his livelihood. Clients therefore existed, it would seem, in a highly vulnerable state of dependency. Only a minority of Dobe-area people became involved in *mafisa*, however, and families with cattle retained links with families fully immersed in hunting and gathering, which remained viable as an alternative economic strategy throughout the *koloi* period and beyond. Had *mafisa* been the only means of subsistence for the people of the Dobe area, then the withdrawal of the

cattle would have caused a crisis in subsistence and the threat of it would have been sufficient to produce a condition of virtual serfdom. But the *mafisa* families were not peasants; they were islands of pastoralism in a sea of hunting and gathering, with benefits flowing in both directions. When cattle were withdrawn, as they often were, the bush was there to fall back on, and that same bush beckoned as an alternative if the responsibilities of keeping cattle grew too onerous.

Thus we have to consider seriously the !Kung's view of *mafisa* as something that operated in their favour. Far from having the system forced upon them or being forced into it by circumstance, !Kung who entered into it did so voluntarily, for the opportunity it provided to supplement a foraging diet with milk and occasional beef. Some of the men who went into *mafisa* did become "big men" of a sort, acting as brokers in transactions between San and black. But a large majority of !Kung remained hunter-gatherers and never relinquished their claims to foraging *n!ores*, the collectively owned hunting lands that were the foundations of their communal mode of production (see Lee 1979:333–69; 1981). In fact, many of the ranges where cattle were grazed were superimposed on these *n!ores*, and the herds were managed by members of the groups that held them. Thus the niche that had sustained the communal foraging mode of production was modified and expanded to encompass *mafisa* cattle husbandry without destroying the preexisting adaptation.[14]

Agro-pastoralism Permanent settlement by non-San came late to the Dobe area. Starting in the mid-1920s, Herero pastoralists moved into the area at cattle posts both east and west of the Namibian border.[15] The Herero began to deepen the waterholes and dig new ones to accommodate increased numbers of cattle. . . . By the late 1950s the job of herdboy had

---

[14]   The *mafisa* cattle may well have degraded the environment, but the appearance of these effects was delayed.

[15]   The Herero had been driven out of Namibia by the German colonists in 1904–5, and, cattleless, had sought refuge among the Tswana in Bechuanaland. Through *mafisa* they had quickly rebuilt their herds.

become normative for Dobe-area !Kung men between the ages of 15 and 25.[16] . . . Eventually most men returned to their camps to marry and raise families, but some married men stayed on in a semi-permanent arrangement with Herero families.

By the 1960s an alternative economy had begun to crystallize, and the Dobe !Kung were found distributed between two kinds of living groups. About 70% lived in camps – bandlike multifamily units whose members engaged in a mixed economy of foraging, *mafisa* herding, and some horticulture. The rest lived in client groups consisting of retainers and their families attached to black cattle posts. Despite the variety of economic strategies that supported them, camps continued to exhibit the characteristic patterns of collective ownership of resources and food sharing that have been documented for hunter-gatherers around the world (Lee 1979, Leacock and Lee 1982). . . .

The stage was now set for the final act in the transformation of the Dobe-area !Kung from a relatively autonomous people with longstanding but non-decisive linkages to the larger regional pastoral, tributary, and mercantile economy to a people bound to the region and the world by ties of dependency. Having survived long-distance trade, contacts with European hunters, Tswana overlordship, *mafisa* herding, direct employment on cattle posts, even forced resettlement in Namibia, the !Kung became dependent largely as a consequence of the inability of their land to support a foraging mode of production. The bush had always been the backdrop ' to economic change, giving the !Kung security and a degree of freedom not available to the great majority of the agrarian societies of southern Africa. Tlou (1985:54) speaks of the

Tswana's difficulties in exacting tribute or service from the "BaSarwa" (San) and concludes, "The sandbelt BaSarwa rarely became serfs because they could easily escape into the Kgalagadi Desert." By 1970, however, four decades of intensive and expanding pastoralism had begun to take their toll on the capacity of the environment to support hunting and gathering. Cattle grazing and the pounding of hooves had destroyed the grass cover over many square kilometres and reduced the available niches for dozens of species of edible roots and rhizomes. Goat browsing had destroyed thousands of berry bushes and other edible plants. The reduction or removal of these food sources placed added pressure on the remaining human food sources; for example, mongongo nut harvests noticeably diminished in the 1980s. The drilling of a dozen boreholes in Bushmanland, Namibia just to the west of Dobe, in the early 1980s aggravated these trends by lowering the water table. Hunting remained viable but became subject to much stricter controls by the Game Department, and many men fearing arrest, stopped hunting.[17] The effect of these changes was seriously to undermine the foraging option and to force the Dobe-area !Kung into dependency on the cattle posts and particularly the state. The latter responded with large-scale distribution of food relief between 1980 and 1987, which further deepened dependency.

Discussion

What common and contrasting patterns of change can be discerned by a comparative analysis of the two case studies?

---

[16]   The gradual shift of the Dobe-area !Kung onto the cattle posts contrasted sharply with developments in the adjacent Nyae/Nyae area. In 1960, 800–1,000 !Kung were rapidly recruited to a South African settlement scheme at Tsumkhwe (Volkman 1983, Marshall 1980). The effects of the settlement on the Dobe !Kung are discussed in Lee (1979).

[17]   In 1987 after an aerial survey indicated that game was plentiful the administration eased the game regulations, and hunting increased but still without guns.

In the earliest period for which we have information, the pre- and protohistoric (ca. 1820), the Western Kweneng San were already sharing their land with Bantu-speaking Kgalagadi, who mediated their contact with the wider world. The Dobe San, by contrast, were in unmediated though distant and intermittent contact with riverine peoples to their east and north. A second point of difference concerns the nature of social formations on the San peripheries after 1830. The Kwena in the south became more mobile and expansive, ranging widely in search of trade and tribute, while the neighbours of the northern !Kung were sedentary, river-orientated peoples who did not expand into the arid interior.

The fur-trade period (mid-19th century) was marked by social, political, and economic turbulence, yet by the time its ripple effects reached the interior of the Kalahari the impact was often attenuated.[18] If in Parsons's (1977:119) terms the 19th-century Tswana economies were becoming the "periphery of the periphery" of European capitalism, then surely the Kalahari must have been the "deep periphery." Driven by trade and external threat, strong chiefdoms arose in the south. The Kwena's need for guns to defend themselves against the Boers was a powerful impetus for the articulation of tributary and mercantile systems. Guns could only be obtained in exchange for desert products. The Kwena subjugated the Kgalagadi, who in turn enlisted the San to aid in primary production. While unequal exchange characterized British–Kwena and Kwena–Kgalagadi relationships, the Kgalagadi–San relationship was symbiotic if not entirely equal. In contrast, Dobe was part of a much more tenuous and extended trade network. The Ngwato occupied the pivotal position between mercantile and tributary networks. Their junior partners were the Tawana, nominal

overlords of Ngamiland, who, in turn relied on Yei and Mbukushu ("Goba") intermediaries to acculumate desert products from the San, including the distant !Kung. The Tawana's power was contested by other chiefs, and they were never able to consolidate their hold on the hinterland as effectively as the Kwena (Parsons 1977; Livingstone 1857; Tlou 1985: 66–67). As a consequence there was less pressure on the !Kung to enter the system, and when they did they were able to retain more control over the terms of trade. In neither instance, however, did the fur trade have much impact on the internal organization of San societies. San exchanged their products after the completion of the productive process. Linkage was predominantly through the sphere of exchange, not production, and intervention in San society remained limited (see Bonner 1983 and Harries 1982 on similar processes elsewhere).

The expansion of herding and farming to the remoter Kalahari did not signal the end of the fur trade, but the incorporation of cattle into the desert economy shifted the priorities in the deployment of land and labour. Western Kweneng San and Dobe San entered the cattle economy under different circumstances and with different statutes. In Dutlwe, Kgalagadi acquired cattle and rendered them as *mafisa* to their poorer relatives; eventually San became their herdboys. Because cattle were kept in the village, not at distant cattle posts, San herders were in regular interaction with their employers and had their subordinate status frequently reinforced. In Dobe it was the San themselves who entered into *mafisa*, a privilege they held exclusively until the 1920s. The Tawana were absentee cattle owners; the Dobe San bore responsibility for the productive enterprise, made routine decisions, and determined their daily activities. This arrangement was much more compatible with foraging than

---

[18]   Exceptions, of course, exist. Tlou and Campbell (1984:109) describe a battle between the Ngwaketse and the Amandebele in the Dutlwe area ca. 1830. The skirmish was brief, and neither group remained in the area, nor had either been resident there for any appreciable length of time.

the Western Kweneng San's situation. In neither case did even a majority of the San enter into cattle service. Many relatively independent groups remained on the peripheries of villages and cattle posts, subsisting on wild foods and continuing to provide furs for the trade. Reciprocity between foraging and non-foraging San allowed each group to enjoy the fruits of the other's labour. In lean years the foraging San would provide a safety net and alternative subsistence for their "employed" relatives, and even in good years San contact with pastoralists was largely limited to certain seasons. At all times the hinterland provided a cultural point of reference and locus of reproduction. Thus in both cases the complete incorporation, as dependents, of the San into the agro-pastoral system was delayed as long as the bush held the possibility of an alternative livelihood.[19] An important source of the continued viability of the San's foraging option was the strength of the egalitarian and reciprocal communal relations of reproduction that characterized life in the bush. As even the revisionists (e.g., Wilmsen 1989:66) acknowledge, this way of life, while far from ideal, provides an extraordinarily rich and meaningful existence for those who practice it. Communally based societies offer their members a sense of social security, entitlement, and empowerment (Lee 1988, n.d.; Rosenberg n.d.). Aspects of this quality of life persist in both Dutlwe and Dobe even today.[20]

Several factors combined to undermine the viability of the dual subsistence economy of the Dutlwe and Dobe San. Expansion of the numbers of cattle through natural increase, purchase with wages from other areas, and migration of cattle keepers (as in Dobe after 1954), along with expanding opportunities for migrant wage labour, especially in the 1960s, created a rapidly increasing need for San labour. . . .

The retreat from foraging by the San began as the agro-pastoral complex drew larger and larger numbers of labourers, male and female, into its employ. In the last analysis, however, a critical factor in moving the San into a position of dependency has been environmental degradation, which has, like an unintended scorched-earth policy, deprived them of an alternative means of livelihood. In the south, dependency increased throughout the century, and many San entered into a relationship of perpetual minor status. . . .

Foragers Genuine and Spurious: The Limitations of World Systems

What kinds of socioeconomic arrangements characterized the Kalahari San in the 19th and 20th centuries, and what kinds of explanatory frameworks best account for them? These questions must be approached at two levels: the level of fact, in which the archaeological, ethnohistoric, and ethnographic evidence is set out and interrogated, and the level of discourse, in which the explanatory frameworks themselves become the focus of interrogation.

The archaeological record shows a diversity of economic adaptations in the 19th century and earlier. The interaction of Stone Age with Iron Age cultures resulted in dramatic economic shifts in some areas, while in other areas the effects were more subtle. Kalahari trade was widespread, and in many instances

---

[19] Both the Kgalagadi and the Herero were "devolved" pastoralists with the socioeconomic infrastructure to facilitate the rapid reabsorption of livestock into the cultural system. If, as is suggested by Schrire (1980), the San were also "devolved" pastoralists, why did they not follow in their neighbours' path and become predominantly pastoralists in the 20th century?

[20] These qualities may coexist with dependency, but we see no reason to believe that they are caused by it. For a recent statement of what primitive communalism is and is not, see Lee (n.d.).

when tributary formations emerged in the 19th century ties of domination/subordination were superimposed on preexisting linkages. But not all San groups experienced this pattern of early linkage and later subordination. Interrelationships were strongest on the river systems and the margins of the desert and weaker as one moved into the interior. Thus there were large areas of semi-arid southern Africa that lay outside tributary orbits, where trade was equal, non-coercive, and intermittent and where independent – but not isolated – social formations persisted into the 20th century.

In attempting to explain this situation, it is important, first, to recognize that trade and exchange cannot simply be equated with domination and loss of autonomy. Exchange is a fundamental part of human life and appears in all cultural settings (Mauss 1925, Lévi-Strauss 1949). Hunter-gatherer peoples have participated in exchange with farming and market societies for hundreds of years (in India, South-east Asia, and East Africa) while maintaining a foraging mode of production (Leacock and Lee 1982). Even with "hunters in a world of hunters," exchange was part of social life (see, e.g., Thomson 1949, Wilmsen 1974, Earle and Ericson 1977, Ericson 1977, Torrence 1986). The evidence for long-established trade relations between foragers and others has been glossed by some as evidence for the fragility of the foraging mode of production. But if it was so fragile, why did it persist?

Throughout these debates about the status of Kalahari and other foragers there has been a lack of attention to the meanings of key terms. Just what is meant by "autonomy," "dependency," "independence," "integration," and "servitude" is rarely made clear. Without consistent, agreed-upon definitions it will be difficult or impossible to resolve the issues with which we are concerned. "Autonomy," for example, has a wide range of uses. Given its currency, it is remarkable how unreflexive its anthropological uses have been. We will confine our discussion to economic autonomy, since much of the debate in hunter-gatherer studies seems to revolve around it. One of the rhetorical devices of the revisionist view of hunter-gatherers is to equate autonomy with isolation – a definition so stringent that no society can possibly satisfy it. But autonomy is not isolation and no social formation is hermetically sealed; we take it as given that all societies are involved in economic exchanges and political relations with their neighbours.

As an economic concept, autonomy refers to economic self-sufficiency,[21] and self-sufficiency in turn hinges not on the *existence* of trade – since all societies trade – but on whether that trade is indispensable for the society's survival. To demonstrate autonomy one must demonstrate self-reproduction. Dependency therefore may be defined as the inability of a society to reproduce itself without the intervention of another.[22]

Politically, two kinds of autonomy may be provisionally defined: imposed and asserted.[23] In the former, the economic autonomy of a subject group may serve the interests of the dominant group. Subordinates are encouraged to pursue their habitual activities at their own pace while providing goods or services – often on equitable terms – to the dominant group. In the latter, the autonomous group asserts its claims through its own strengths and political

---

[21]　Political autonomy, by contrast, hinges not on a society's capacity to reproduce itself but on the willingness of other (dominating) societies to let it remain autonomous. Neither Dutlwe nor Dobe could be said to have been politically autonomous in the 1960s.

[22]　For example, Memmi's (1984:185) definition of dependence as "a relationship with a real or ideal being, object, group, or institution that involves more or less accepted compulsion and that is connected with the satisfaction of a need" is consistent with our own usage.

[23]　We are indebted to Gerald Sider for this suggestion and some of the discussion that follows.

will. In practice these two forms may be difficult to distinguish, and which form is
considered to be present will depend heavily
on subjective judgements both by the peoples
involved and by observers.[24] Thus the Mbuti
pygmies observed by Turnbull (1962) appear
to be entirely subservient to their black neighbours while they are in the villages but quite
autonomous in the forest.

Autonomy is best regarded not as a thing or
a property of social systems but as a relationship – between social groups and between a
group and its means of production. At any
given moment a society may exhibit elements
of both autonomy and dependency, and it
should be possible to assess the degree of each
through empirical investigation.

The camp-dwelling people of the Dobe area
were economically self-sufficient during the
1960s. They owned the bulk of their means of
production and paid no rent, tribute, or taxes
in money or kind. They hunted and gathered
for the large majority of their subsistence
requirements and for the rest tended *mafisa*
cattle or worked as herdboys for their Herero
neighbours. The latter tasks provided income
that was a welcome supplement but not essential to survival. How can we demonstrate its
non-essentiality? First, San *mafisa* holders and
herdboys were observed to leave "service"
without visible detriment to their well-being.
In fact, it was common for young men to work
on cattle for a few years and then return to the
bush at marriage (Lee 1979:58, 406–8). More
compelling, in the drought of 1964, Herero
crops failed and cows were dry, yet the San
persevered without evident difficulty. In fact,
the Herero women were observed gathering

wild foods alongside their San neighbours
(Lee 1979:255). Since the San carried on
through this period without visible hardship
(Lee 1979:437–41) despite the withdrawal of
Herero resources, it is clear that the latter were
not essential to their reproduction.

These lines of evidence argue for the
economic autonomy of some Dobe !Kung in
the 1960s. Obviously a great deal more could
be said on the question of autonomy, especially
from the cultural and political points of
view. Even the simplest historical judgements will involve a series of mediating
judgements concerning economy, polity,
voluntarism and coercion. Automatically classifying second-millennium San societies as
dependent, incorporated, or "peasant-like"
seems no more legitimate than classifying
them as "primitive isolates."

Turning to "servitude," we are confronted
with a literature replete with reports of San
"dependency," "serfdom," "slavery,"
"vassalage," and the like.[25] In contrast to the
early sources cited above (and see Wilson
1975:63), which tended to portray all San as
dominated, recent ones such as Silberbauer
and Kuper (1966), Tlou (1977), Russell and
Russell (1979), Hitchcock (1987), and Motzafi
(1986) employ these terms more critically, but
even here usage tends to be imprecise.
Silberbauer and Kuper (1966), for example,
use the term "serfdom" but note its inapplica-
bility – the San being bound neither to the soil
nor to a particular master. Guenther
(1985:45Q) reinforces the ambiguity when he
speaks of a "benignly paternalistic form of
serfdom" that departs from the European
pattern. Tlou (1977), Wilson (1975), and

---

[24]   The subjectivity involved in determining whether a given autonomy is asserted or imposed has been a major problem
in articulation theory (e.g., Foster-Carter 1978, Clarence-Smith 1985) regarding whether a given "tribal" communal
social formation was preserved because its maintenance was "functional" for capitalism (Wolpe 1972) or because the
local system and the local people were strong enough to resist (Beinart 1985).

[25]   The issue received international attention in the late 1920s and 1930s, when a series of reports was commissioned
by the London Missionary Society, the British, and the Ngwato chief concerning the status of the San in the Ngwato
Reserve. The question was whether the San were in a state of slavery. As might have been predicted, there was no
consensus, and while instances of hereditary servitude were noted it was clear that this condition was not general and
that many San persisted in their "miserable nomadic existence" (Tagart 1933, quoted in Miers and Crowder 1988:188).

Biesele et al. (1989) use the term "clientship" to refer to a loose association between peoples with unequal access to resources that they distinguish from the classic patron–client relationship. Russell and Russell (1979:87) further qualify the term "clientship" by contrasting the rights and obligations of "employed" San with those of "client" San. The latter are said to maintain a "foot in both worlds," one in the bush and one on the farm. Thus in their terms clientship is a partial relationship from which San can disengage.

Difficulties on several levels are encountered when we try to pin down the forms and content of San servitude and dependence. First, it is obvious that terms such as serfdom and chattel slavery, developed in a specific European context, are not easily grafted onto Kalahari social relations. More specifically, the language that is used in the Kalahari itself appears to overstate the degree of dependence. Both Vierich (1982) and Solway were struck by the exaggerated descriptions of servitude by San and black alike. The cultural vocabulary of superior/subordinate relations further illustrates the difficulty of translating words the lack cognates in the language of the observer. Silberbauer and Kuper, for example, show that the Sekgalagadi term *munyi*, used for "master" in San–black relations, is also used for the senior in asymmetrical kin relations, i.e., "elder brother." It denotes authority but falls short of our concept of mastership or ownership. Similarly, they note that the Tswana "jural model" of *bolata* (hereditary servitude) signifies something stricter than actually exists. This misunderstanding, they assert, may be the reason social commentators from 19th-century missionaries to 20th-century anthropologists have assumed that *bolata* was worse in the past and only recently has become more humane. They argue that "the practice of serfdom in Bechuanaland is much more humane than the indigenous jural model would lead one to expect: in the past some observers may have been led into assuming that the jural model represented the past, while the easy-going actuality was equated with the enlightened present" (p. 172).

At the level of concrete social relations, there is a puzzling incongruity between the exaggerated degree of inequality described by Kalahari residents and the relative ease (and frequency) with which the San "serfs" disappear into the desert for periods of time, leaving their "masters" high and dry. Vierich (1982:282) has argued that "interdependence" more accurately describes the relationship between San and non-San and that San simply "play the beggar" to get handouts. While this may be overstating the case, clearly there is a disjunction between model and practice. In no instance in which hereditary serfdom has been asserted by Kgalagadi in theory has it been observed in practice. The Dutlwe-area San may be dependent and have to work for someone at some time, but they retain some choice of when to work and for whom. An observer will find some San in relations of dependency and others not, but closer examination will reveal that the same individuals will move into clientship, out to the bush, and back again to clientship. Wealthy blacks will have full-time San labourers living in their compounds while their neighbours rarely or never retain San clients.[26] The full-time labourers living with blacks will be the most conspicuous to casual observers, and this may account for the prevalence of this kind of report in both the early and the more recent literature, but such reports fail to do justice to the complexity and fluidity of the situation. We certainly do not want to minimize the degree of San dependence and subjection to discrimination, but we

---

[26] Ethnic boundaries may also be blurred, and in many instances poorer blacks and San live similar lives, intermarry, and defy any neat ethnic categorization or hierarchy.

would suggest that this is best seen as a product of underdevelopment and not a primordial condition.

Hunter-Gatherer and Agrarian Discourse: Making the Transition

We have traced in some detail the historical pathways followed by the Dutlwe and Dobe San as they changed from autonomous foragers to clients and labourers increasingly subject to and dependent upon local, national, and world economies. In order to understand these processes it is necessary to make a second transition, from discourse about hunter-gatherers to discourse about agrarian societies and the emerging world system.

In agrarian discourse structures of domination are taken as given; it is the *forms* of domination and the modes of exploitation and surplus extraction that are problematic (Amin 1972, Hindess and Hirst 1975, Shanin 1972). In the literature on the agrarian societies of the Third World, stratification, class and class struggle, patriarchy, accumulation, and immiseration constitute the basic descriptive and analytical vocabulary. In hunter-gatherer discourse it is not the forms of domination that are at issue but *whether domination is present.* This question is often side-stepped or ignored.

We are not alone in our concern about the tendency for the discourse of domination to be imposed on precapitalist societies. Beinart (1985:97), for example, dealing with the Eastern Cape – an area under far greater pressure than the Kalahari – cautions against granting omnipotence to capitalism or the state or assuming that the migrant-labour system automatically destroys the integrity of rural societies:

> Even in so coercive an environment as South Africa, the patterns of domination were constrained – in part – by fear of the consequences of other routes and in part by the defensive responses of the dominated. Certainly, capital and the state . . . had only

limited power to shape social relationships in those areas which were left under African occupation. . . . the fact that a migrant works for a wage, even for a number of years, does not necessarily determine the totality of his, much less his family's, class position and consciousness. The importance of defensive struggles in the rural areas, amongst communities which included seasoned migrants, has generally been underestimated.

Silberbauer (1989:206–7) challenges the view that hunter-gatherer contacts with other societies necessarily preclude autonomy:

> [The] concept of coexisting states, tribes, and hunter-gatherer bands can be found accurately documented in any authoritative history of the appropriate part of Africa. It does not require that any of the coexisting societies be in a state of compulsory, day-to-day mutualism with all others. Interaction can occur at sufficiently low intensity and be of such a quality as to allow hunters and gatherers (for instance) to retain cultural, social, and political, and economic autonomy (i.e., in the philosophical sense, not in that of isolated, complete independence). At least in southern Africa and Australia that state of affairs persisted only when the hunter-gatherers were able to retain control of enough resources of sufficient variety to be largely . . . self-sustaining.

Perhaps the most serious consequence of imposing agrarian discourse on hunter-gatherers is that it robs the latter of their history. What is at issue here is an intellectual neo-colonialism that seeks to recreate their history in the image of our own. This revisionism trivializes these people by making their history entirely a reactive one. Even at its best revisionism grants historical animation and dignity to the San only by recasting their history as the history of oppression. But is their oppression by us the only thing, or even the main thing, that we want to know about foraging peoples? The majority of the world's foragers are, for whatever reason, people who have resisted the temptation (or threat) to become like us: to live settled lives at high densities and to accept the structural inequalities that characterize most of the world. Many former foragers – and that includes most of us – now live in stratified, entrepreneurial, bureaucratic society, but not all have followed this route, and the presence or absence of inequality and domination can be investigated empirically.

Ultimately, in understanding the histories of Third World societies or of our own, we will have to rely on the histories of specific instances and not allow preconceptions to sway us. This caveat applies equally to those who would place the hunter-gatherers in splendid isolation and those who would generalize the power relations of contemporary capitalism to most of the world's people through most of their historical experience.

References

AMIN, S, 1972. Underdevelopment and dependence in black Africa: Origins and contemporary forms. *Journal of Modern African Studies* 10:503–24.

ANDERSON, C. 1856. *Lake Ngami*. London: Hurst.

BAINES, T. 1973 (1864). *Explorations in South West Africa*. Salisbury: Pioneer Head.

BARNARD, ALAN. 1989. The lost world of Laurens van der Post? CURRENT ANTHROPOLOGY 30:104–15.[AB]

BEINHART, W. 1986. Chieftaincy and the concept of articulation: South Africa ca. 1900–1950. *Canadian Journal of African Studies* 19(1):91–98.

BIESELE, M., M. GUENTHER, R. HITCHCOCK, R. LEE, AND J. MACGREGOR. 1989. Hunters, clients, and squatters: The contemporary socioeconomic status of Botswana Basarwa. *African Studies Monographs* 9:109–51.

BONNER, P. 1983. *King, commoners, and concessionnaires: The evolution and dissolution of the 19th-century Swazi state.* Cambridge/New York: Cambridge University Press.

BOTSWANA NATIONAL ARCHIVES. 1887a. HC 14/2 Despatch, Administrator, British Bechuanaland to Governor, Capetown, forwarding copy of a report and a map by Captain Goold-Adams of a police patrol from Molepolole to Lehututu.

———. 1887b. HC 153/1 High Commission for South Africa. On Bakgalagadi and Bushmen slavery.

BOWER, B. 1989. A world that never existed. *Science News* 135:264–66.

BROOKS, A. 1989. Past subsistence and settlement patterns in the Dobe area: An archaeological perspective. Paper presented at the 88th annual meeting of the American Anthropological Association, Washington, D.C., November.

CAMPBELL, A., AND G. CHILD. 1971. The impact of man on the environment of Botswana. *Botswana Notes and Records* 3:91–110.

CASHDAN, ELIZABETH. 1987. Trade and its origins on the Botetli River. *Journal of Anthropological Research* 43:121–38.

CHAPMAN, J. 1971 (1868). *Travels in the interior of South Africa (1849–1863): Hunting and trading journeys from Natal to Wavis Bay and visits to Lake Ngami and Victoria Falls.* Edited by E. Tabler. Cape Town: Balkema.

CLARENCE-SMITH, W. 1979. *Slaves, peasants, and capitalists in southern Angola 1840–1926.* Cambridge and New York: Cambridge University Press.

———. 1985. "Thou shall not articulate modes of production." *Canadian Journal of African Studies* 19:19–23.

DENBOW, J. 1980. Early Iron Age remains in the Tsodilo Hills, northwestern Botswana. *South African Journal of Science* 76:474–75.

———. 1984. "Prehistoric herders and foragers of the Kalahari: The evidence for 1500 years of interaction," in *Past and present in hunter-gatherer studies*. Edited by C. Schrire, pp. 175–93. Orlando: Academic Press.

———. 1986. A new look at later prehistory of the Kalahari. *Journal of African History* 27:3–28.

———. n.d. Congo to Kalahari: Data and hypotheses about the political economy of the western stream of the Early Iron Age. *African Archaeological Review* 8. In press. [JD]

DENBOW, J., AND E. WILMSEN. 1983. Iron Age

pastoral settlements in Botswana. *South African Journal of Science* 79:405–8.

———. 1986. Advent and the course of pastoralism in the Kalahari. *Science* 234:1509–15.

DRECHSLER, H. 1980. *Let us die fighting: The Nama and Herero war against Germany*. London: Zed.

EARLE, T., AND J. E. ERICSON. Editors. 1977. *Exchange systems in prehistory*. New York: Academic Press.

ENDICOTT, K. 1988. Can hunter-gatherers survive in the rain forest without trade? Paper presented at the University of Toronto, April.

ERICSON, J. E. 1977. "Egalitarian exchange systems in California: A preliminary view," in *Exchange systems in prehistory*. Edited by T. Earle and J. E. Ericson, pp. 109–206. New York: Academic Press.

FOSTER-CARTER, A. 1978. The modes of production controversy. *New Left Review* 107:44–77.

FREEMAN, D. 1983. *Margaret Mead in Samoa*. Cambridge: Harvard University Press.

FRIEDMAN, J. 1975. "Tribes, states, and transformations," in *Marxist analyses in social anthropology*. Edited by M. Bloch, pp. 161–202. London: Tavistock.

———. 1979. *System, structure, and contradiction in the evolution of "Asiatic" social formations*. Copenhagen: National Museum of Denmark.

GALTON, F. 1889. *Narrative of an explorer in tropical Africa*. London: Ward and Lock.

GORDON, ROBERT J. 1984. "The !Kung in the Kalahari exchange: An ethnohistorical perspective," in *Past and present in hunter-gatherer studies*. Edited by C. Schrire, pp. 195–224. Orlando: Academic Press.

GOUGH, K. 1971. "Nuer kinship: A re-examination," in *The translation of culture*. Edited by T. O. Beidelmann, pp. 79–120. London: Tavistock.

GUENTHER, MATHIAS G. 1979. *The farm Bushmen of Ghanzi District, Botswana*. Stuttgart: Hoschschul Verlag. [AB]

GUENTHER, M. 1986. "Acculturation and assimilation of the Bushmen," in *Contemporary studies on Khoisan*. Edited by I. R. Vossen and K. Keuthmann, pp. 347–73. Hamburg: Helmut Buske Verlag.

HARRIES, P. 1982. "Kinship, ideology, and the nature of pre-colonial labour migration," in *Industrialism and social change in South Africa*.

Edited by S. Marks and R. Rathbone. London: Longman.

HEADLAND, T., AND L. REID. 1989. Hunter-gatherers and their neighbors from prehistory to the present. CURRENT ANTHROPOLOGY 30:43–66.

HINDESS, B., AND P. HIRST. 1976. *Pre-capitalist modes of production*. London: Routledge and Kegan Paul.

HITCHCOCK, ROBERT K. 1978, *Kalahari cattle posts: A regional study of hunter-gatherers, pastoralists, and agriculturalists in the Western Sandveld Region, Central District, Botswana*. 2 vols. Gaborone: Government Printer.

———. 1987. Socioeconomic change among the Basarwa in Botswana: An ethnohistorical analysis. *Ethnohistory* 34:219–55.

INGOLD, T., D. RICHES, AND J. WOODBURN. Editors. 1988. *Hunters and gatherers*. Vol. I. *History, evolution, and social change*. Oxford: Berg.

KELLY, R., 1986. *The Nuer conquest*. Ann Arbor: University of Michigan Press.

KENT, S. 1989a. The cycle that repeats: Shifting subsistence strategies among Kalahari Basarwa. Paper presented at the 88th annual meeting of the American Anthropological Association, Washington, D.C., November.

———. 1989b. And justice for all: The development of political centralization among newly sedentary foragers. *American Anthropologist* 91:703–11. [SK]

LEACOCK, E., AND R. LEE. Editors 1982. *Politics and history in band societies*. Cambridge and New York: Cambridge University Press.

LEE, R. 1965. Subsistence ecology of !Kung Bushmen. Ph.D. diss., University of California, Berkeley, Calif. [ENW]

———. 1979. *The !Kung San: Men, women, and work in a foraging society*. Cambridge: Cambridge University Press.

———. 1984. *The Dobe !Kung*. New York: Holt, Rinehart and Winston. [AB, ENW]

———. 1988. "Reflections on primitive communism," in *Hunters and gatherers*, vol. 1. Edited by T. Ingold, D. Riches, and J. Woodburn, pp. 252–68. Oxford: Berg.

———. n.d. "Primitive communism and the origins of social inequality," in *The evolution of political systems*. Edited by S. Upham. Cambridge and New York: Cambridge University Press. In press.

LEE, R. .B, AND I. DEVORE. Editors. 1968. *Man the hunter*. Chicago: Aldine. [BGT]

———. 1976. *Kalahari hunter-gatherers*. Cambridge: Harvard University Press.

LEISTNER, O. 1967. *The plant ecology of the southern Kalahari*. Pretoria: Government Printer.

LÉVI-STRAUSS, C. 1949. *The elementary structures of kinship*. Boston: Beacon Press.

LEWIN, R. 1989. New views emerge on hunters and gatherers. *Science* 240:1146–48.

LEWIS, O. 1951. *Life in a Mexican village: Tepoztlán restudied*. Urbana: University of Illinois Press.

LIVINGSTONE, DAVID. 1857. *Missionary travels and researches in South Africa*. London: John Murray.

MACKENZIE, J. 1971. (1871). *Ten years north of the Orange River: A story of everyday life and work among the South African tribes from 1859 to 1869*. Edinburgh: Edmonston and Douglas.

MARKS, S., AND A. ATMORE. 1917. Firearms in southern Africa: A survey. *Journal of African History* 7:517–30.

MARSHALL, L. K. 1976. *The !Kung Bushmen of Nyae/Nyae*. Cambridge: Harvard University Press.

MARX, KARL. 1965 (1857–58). *Pre-capitalist economic formations*. New York: International Publishers. [TCP]

———. 1977 (1887). *Capital*. Vol. 3. New York: International Publishers.

MAUSS, M. 1925. Essai sur le don. *Année Sociologique* 1:30–186.

MEMMI, A. 1984. *Dependence*. Boston: Beacon.

MIERS, S., AND M. CROWDER. 1988. "The politics of slavery in Bechuanaland: Power struggles and the plight of the Basarwa on the Bamangwato Reserve, 1926–1940," in *The end of slavery in Africa*. Edited by S. Miers and R. Roberts, pp. 172–202. Madison: University of Wisconsin Press.

MOTZAFI, P. 1986. Whither the "true Bushmen": The dynamics of perpetual marginality. *Sprache und Geschichte in Afrika* 7:295–328.

NEWCOMER, P. 1972. The Nuer and the Dinka: An essay on origins and environmental determinism. *Man* 7:5–11.

NUGENT, D. 1983. Closed systems and contradiction in the Kachin in and out of history. *Man* 17:508–27.

OKIHIRO, G. 1976. Hunters, herders, cultivators, and traders: Interaction and change in the Kgalagadi, nineteenth century. Ph.D. diss., University of California, Los Angeles, Calif.

PALMER, R., AND N. PARSONS. 1977. Editors. *The roots of rural poverty in central and southern Africa*. Berkeley: University of California Press.

PARKINGTON, J. 1984. "Soaqua and Bushmen: Hunters and robbers," in *Past and present in hunter-gatherer studies*. Edited by C. Schrire, pp. 151–74. Orlando: Academic Press.

PARSONS, N. 1977. "The economic history of Khama's country in Botswana, 1844–1930," in *The roots of rural poverty in central and southern Africa*. Edited by R. Palmer and N. Parsons, pp. 113–42. Berkeley: University of California Press.

———. 1982. *A new history of southern Africa*. Gaborone: Macmillan, Boleswa.

PASSARGE, S. 1907. *Die Buschmänner der Kalahari*. Berlin: Reimer and Vohsen.

PETERS, P. 1983. Cattlemen, borehole syndicates, and privatization in the Kgatleng District, Botswana: An anthropological history of the transformation of a commons. Ph.D. diss., Boston University, Boston, Mass.

———. 1984. Struggles over water, struggles over meaning: Cattle, water, and the state in Botswana. *Africa* 54(3):29–49.

PETERSON, J. .T. 1978. Hunter-gatherer/farmer exchange. *American Anthropologist* 80:335–51.

PHILLIPSON, D. 1977. *The prehistory of southern and central Africa*. London: Heinemann.

ROSENBERG, H. n.d. "Complaint discourse, aging, and caregiving among the Kung San of Botswana," in *The cultural context of aging: World-wide perspectives*. Edited by J. Sokolovsky. Boston: Bergin and Garvey. In press.

RUSSELL, M, 1976. Slaves or workers? Relations between Bushmen, Tswana, and Boers in the Kalahari. *Journal of Southern African Studies* 2:178–97.

RUSSELL, M. AND M. RUSSELL, 1979. *Afrikaners of the Kalahari: White minority in a black state*. Cambridge: Cambridge University Press.

SACKS, K. 1979. Causality and change on the Upper Nile.. *American Ethnologist* 6:437–48.

SAHLINS, M. 1968. *Tribesmen*. Englewood Cliffs: Prentice Hall.

SCHAPERA, I., AND D. F. VAN DER MERWE. 1945. *Note on tribal groupings, history, and customs of the Bakgalagadi*. Communications for the School of African Studies, n.s., 13.

SCHRIRE, CARMEL. 1980. An enquiry into the evolutionary status and apparent identity of San hunter-gatherers. *Human Ecology* 8:9–32.

——. Editor. 1984a. *Past and present in hunter-gatherer studies.* Orlando: Academic Press.

——. 1984b. "Wild surmises on savage thoughts," in *Past and present in hunter-gatherer studies.* Edited by C. Schrire, pp. 1–25. Orlando: Academic Press.

SHANIN, T. Editor. 1972. *Peasants and peasant societies.* New York: Penguin books.

SILBERBAUER, GEORGE B. 1981. *Hunter and habitat in the central Kalahari Desert.* Cambridge: Cambridge University Press.

——. 1989. On the myth of the "savage other." CURRENT ANTHROPOLOGY 30:206–7.

SILBERBAUER, G. B., AND A. KUPER. 1966. Kgalagadi masters and their Bushmen serfs. *African Studies* 25:171–79.

SOLWAY, J. 1987. Commercialization and social differentiation in a Kalahari village. Ph.D. diss., University of Toronto, Toronto, Ont.

SOLWAY, J., AND R. B. LEE. 1981. The Kalahari fur trade. Paper presented at the 80th annual meeting of the American Anthropological Association, Los Angeles, Calif.

STOW, G. W. 1964 1905) *The native races of South Africa.* Cape Town: C. Struik.

TABLER, E. 1973. *Pioneers of South West Africa and Ngamiland.* Cape Town: Balkema.

TAGART, E. S. B. 1993. *Report on the conditions existing among the Masarwa in the Banangwato Reserve of the Bechuanaland Protectorate and certain other matters appertaining to the natives living therein.* Pretoria: Government Printer.

TANAKA, J. 1980. *The San hunter-gatherers of the Kalahari: A study in ecological anthropology.* Tokyo: University of Tokyo Press.

THOMSON, D. 1949. *Economic structure and the ceremonial exchange cycle in Arnhem Land.* Melbourne: Angus and Robertson.

TLOU, T. 1977. "Servility and political control: Botlhanka among the Batawana of northwestern Botswana, ca. 1750–1906," in *Slavery in southern Africa.* Edited by S. Miers and I. Kopytoff, pp. 367–90. Madison: University of Wisconsin Press.

——. 1986. *A history of Ngamiland, 1750 to 1906: The formation of an African state.* Gaborone: Macmillan.

TLOU, T., AND A. CAMPBELL. 1984. *A history of Botswana.* Gaborone: Macmillan.

TORRENCE, R. 1986. *Production and exchange of stone tools.* Cambridge: Cambridge University Press.

TURNBULL, C. 1962. *The forest people.* New York: Simon and Schuster.

VEDDER, H. 1966 (1938). *South West Africa in early times.* London: Frank Cass.

VIERICH, H. (ESCHE). 1977. *Interim report on survey of Basarwa in Kweneng.* Gaborone: Ministry of Local Government and Lands.

——. 1982a. The Kua of the southeastern Kalahari: A study of the socio-ecology of dependency. Ph.D. diss., University of Toronto, Toronto, Ont.

——. 1982b. "Adaptive flexibility in a multi-ethnic setting: The Basarwa of the southern Kalahari," in *Politics and history in band societies.* Edited by Eleanor Leacock and Richard Lee, pp. 213–22. Cambridge: Cambridge University Press. (RKH)

VOLKMAN, T. 1983. *The San in transition.* Vol. 1. Cambridge: Cultural Survival.

WASSERSTROM, R. 1982. *Class and society in Chiapas.* New York: Columbia University Press.

WILHELM, J. 1954 (1914–19). *Die !Kung Buschleute.* Jahrbuch des Museums für Völkerkunde zu Leipzig 12.

WILMSEN, E. 1974 *Lindenmeier: A Pleistocene hunting society.* New York: Harper and Ron.

——. 1978. Prehistoric and Historic Antecedents of a Ngamiland Community. *Botswana Notes and Records,* 10:5–18.

——. 1983. The ecology of illusion: Anthropological foraging in the Kalahari. *Reviews in Anthropology* 10:9–20.

——. 1989a. "Those who have each other: San relations to land," in *We are here: Politics of aboriginal land tenure.* Edite by Edwin Wilmsen, pp. 43–67. Berkeley: University of California Press.

——. 1989b. *Land filled with flies: A political economy of the Kalahari.* Chicago: University of Chicago Press. [MG, ENW]

——. n.d. The antecedents of contemporary pastoralism in western Ngamiland. *Botswana Notes and Records.* In press. [JEY]

WILMSEN, E., AND D. DURHAM. 1988. "Food as a function of seasonal environment and social history," in *Coping with uncertainty.* Edited by G. Harrison and I. de Garine, pp. 52–87.

Cambridge: Cambridge University Press. [ENW]

WILSON, M. 1975. "The hunters and herders," in *The Oxford history of South Africa*, vol. I. Edited by M. Wilson and L. Thompson, pp. 40–75. Oxford: Oxford University Press.

WOLF, E. 1982. *Europe and the people without history*. Berkeley: University of California Press.

WOLPE, H. 1972. Capitalism and cheap labour-power in South Africa: From segregation to apartheid. *Economy and Society* 1(4).

WOODBURN, J. 1988. "African hunter-gatherer social organization: Is it best understood as a product of encapsulation?" in *Hunters and gatherers*, vol. I. Edited by T. Ingold, D. Riches, and J. Woodburn, pp. 31–64. Oxford: Berg.

WORSLEY, P. 1956. The kinship system of the Tallensi: A reevaluation. *Journal of the Royal Anthropological Institute* 86:37–77.

YELLEN, JOHN E., AND ALISON S. BROOKS. n.d. The Late Stone Age archaeology of the !Kangwa and /Xai/Xai Valleys, Ngamiland Botswana. *Botswana Notes and Records*. In press.

PART IV

WITCHCRAFT, SCIENCE, AND RATIONALITY: THE TRANSLATION OF CULTURE

San healer, Kalahari, 1965.
Photo: Irven DeVore. Anthro-Photo File, no. 3632.

WITCHCRAFT, SCIENCE, AND RATIONALITY: THE TRANSLATION OF CULTURE

16   David Livingstone. 1858. "Conversations on Rain-making" pp. 22–27. In *Missionary Travels and Researches in South Africa*. London: Murray.

17   E. E. Evans-Pritchard. 1937. "The Notion of Witchcraft Explains Unfortunate Events," pp. 18–32. In *Witchcraft, Magic, and Oracles among the Azande*. Oxford: Clarendon.

18   Peter Winch. 1964. "Understanding a Primitive Society." In Bryan R. Wilson (ed.), *Rationality*. Oxford: Basil Blackwell, pp. 78–112.

19   Robin Horton. 1970. "African Traditional Thought and Western Science." pp. 131–172. In Bryan R. Wilson (ed.), *Rationality*. Oxford: Basil Blackwell.

20   Peter Geschiere. 1992. "Kinship, Witchcraft and the Market: Hybrid Patterns in Cameroonian Societies." pp. 159–176. In Roy Dilley ed., *Contesting Markets: Analyses of Ideology, Discourse and Practice*. Edinburgh: University of Edinburgh Press.

Introduction

The readings in this section are organized around the topic of witchcraft beliefs among the Azande of southern Sudan and Northern Zaire. We chose these readings because, as a whole, they define the parameters and content of one of the most influential debates in the history of anthropology: a debate over the differences and similarities between European and African modes of thought.

The debate began after the publication of Evans-Pritchard's *Witchcraft, Oracles, and Magic among the Azande* (1937), a work that had a profound impact on both the cross-cultural study of modes of thought and the philosophy of science and rationality, and led

many scholars to reflect critically upon some of the most important issues in the history of anthropology. Stanley J. Tambiah (1990:3) poses the questions raised by the rationality debate:

1 How do we understand and represent the modes of thought and action of other societies, other cultures?

2 Since we have to undertake this task from a Western baseline so to say, how are we to achieve the "translation of cultures," i.e. understand other cultures as far as possible in their own terms but in our language, a task which also entails the mapping of the ideas and practices onto Western categories of understanding, and hopefully modifying these in turn to evolve a

language of anthropology as a comparative science?

Evans-Pritchard was forced to address these epistemological questions because he wanted to explain one mode of thought, that of the Azande, in terms of another, that of science. In other words, Evans-Pritchard understood that the translation of culture is a fundamental task of anthropology.

In Southern Africa, nearly 80 years before Evans-Pritchard published his study, the British explorer David Livingstone confronted the problem of how to understand a way of thinking radically different from his own. For the purpose of explaining the Tswana belief in rain-making, Livingstone constructed the dialogue included in this section, a dialogue between himself (a medical doctor) and a Tswana "rain doctor." As the dialogue proceeds, we come to appreciate the intelligence, logic, and coherence of rain making beliefs; we also come to question the long-standing assumption that science is "rational" and reflects truth while magical beliefs are irrational and mystify reality. In Livingstone's writings, we can also discern the roots of one of Evans-Pritchard's most important arguments: that if we understand the cultural premises and social contexts of thought and action, then beliefs in supernatural causation no longer seem bizarre, irrational or fallacious. Indeed, they may seem perfectly reasonable.

Evans-Pritchard takes the appreciation of an African mode of thought a bit further than Livingstone by analyzing in great detail the principles upon which Azande explanations are based, and by attempting to adopt for himself the Azande way of thinking. He finds that, in contrast to science, the Azande overlook certain inconsistencies in logic because they do not have an integrated theory of supernatural cause and effect. For example, the Azande believe that witchcraft substance is hereditarily transmitted down the male line. The substance predisposes people to carry out acts of witchcraft, and can be revealed through postmortem autopsy. For Evans-Pritchard, a positive finding of witchcraft substance in a person would implicate his whole clan, since the clan is a group of people biologically related through a patriline. However, despite their biological model of witchcraft inheritance, the Azande do not generalize from single cases of witchcraft to whole groups. This apparent contradiction would pose serious problems for a scientific theory, but the Azande do not formulate their beliefs as abstract and logically coherent and sustainable theories. Rather, witchcraft beliefs are produced and reproduced continuously as the Azande try to explain new misfortunes. Witchcraft is not a "thing" in and of itself, or a state of being, but rather an action (Ulin 1984:24). Beliefs are realized through practice.

In trying to adopt Zande thinking for himself, Evans-Pritchard suggests that Zande thought can be reasonable even for the scientifically trained European. While living with the Azande, he says, "I too used to react to misfortunes in the idiom of witchcraft" (1937: 45). He realized that societies can have multiple rationalities, and that, even in England, people do not always think scientifically. Evans-Pritchard thus warns us not to characterize societies in terms of single modes of thought. As Tambiah puts it, "we should avoid caricatures of both primitive and modern mentalities, and should not represent Westerners as thinking scientifically all the time when scientific activity is a special one practiced in very circumscribed circumstances. One must compare like with like, our everyday thought with their everyday thought" (1990:92).

Despite his apparent cultural relativism, Evans-Pritchard is unequivocal that scientific explanations of misfortune are superior to those of the Azande. He writes: "Witches, as the Azande conceive them, clearly cannot exist" (1937:18). In other words, though witchcraft beliefs are logical, they are wrong. Because the Azande do not form hypotheses and test them against an empirical reality, their explanations are necessarily unacceptable to the Western scientist. Peter Winch claims (in Chapter 18) that Evans-Pritchard's comparison of scientific and Azande thought is a "category mistake." Winch argues that Azande and scientific thought operate according to very different rules and premises, and so cannot be used to evaluate one another. To employ the categories of science, as Evans-Pritchard does, distorts Azande thought. Not only does the scientific explanation of witchcraft reify beliefs embedded in practice, it also makes Zande thought into a reflection of science. In a remarkable passage (p. 319, this volume), Winch quotes Evans-Pritchard at length and then repeats the quotation with the words "Azande" and "mystical" transposed to "Europeans" and "scientific." The meaning and logic of both quotations are the same. The clever parody makes the Azande into scientists, thus revealing Evans-Pritchard's category mistake. Livingstone falls into the same trap as Evans-Pritchard, for his dialogue imposes onto the rain maker the categories and logic of scientific thought. The medical doctor forces the Tswana rain maker to debate not only as a "doctor" but in the terms of positivism, rather than in terms of his own making (Comaroff and Comaroff, 1991:254). For Winch, both Livingstone and Evans-Pritchard are guilty of perpetuating the hegemony of science, of dictating the manner in which thought is represented. Cultural translation is possible, Winch suggests, but only if scientists are willing to modify and extend their own categories. "Since it is we who want to understand the Zande category, it appears that the onus is on us to extend our understanding so as to make room for the Zande category, rather than to insist on seeing it in terms of our own ready-made distinction between science and non-science." (Winch, p. 102).

Winch's argument did not go uncontested. In a provocative article (Chapter 19), Robin Horton argues that what he calls "African thought" and "Western science" *can* be fruitfully compared with one another. He proposes that African societies are "closed," meaning that people do not look critically at their ideas, or search for alternative explanations, about the world. According to Horton, scientific societies, on the other hand, are "open" to the extent that they never accept, absolutely, a given theory of the world, and always look for alternatives. The former societies take their orthodox modes of explanation to the level of sacred beliefs, while the latter minimize the role of belief, faith, and certainty.

Of importance to all of the chapters in this part is an implicit argument that there is such a thing as a "mode of thought." However, Horton goes much further in his debate with Winch and Evans-Pritchard when he assumes that there are patterns and essences to be found among the modes of thought of different populations, that a multitude of different societies can share a common way of thinking, and that groups of societies can be compared to other groups of societies. Only then is it possible for Horton to juxtapose "Africa" to "western science."

In Chapter 20, Geschiere, like other social anthropologists working on systems of belief today (Comaroff and Comaroff, 1993; Rowlands and Varnier, 1988), emphasizes the continued salience of idioms of witchcraft and sorcery in contemporary sub-saharan Africa. His piece departs somewhat from the confines of the debate begun about the Azande by exploring the ways in which the social relations of supernatural belief become implicated in local economies in southern Cameroon. Yet he continues the previous authors' interests in making comparisons between Europe and Africa, and makes several points about their juxtaposition. First, although many European and North American observers assume that markets and market behaviors constitute distinct spheres of social activity, the Cameroonian cases show us otherwise. Secondly, based on his conclusions from the Cameroonian evidence, Geschiere also urges us to rethink how, even in so-called "western" economies, religion, politics, kinship, and culturally distinctive rationalities, play vital and constitutive roles. (This is a point raised in Part Two of this volume on economics, where we discuss the issue of economic "rationality"). Third, economic organizations that have conventionally been characterized by kinship relations, such as the segmentary societies of Africa, are not necessarily incompatible with the structures and functions of the impersonal, capitalist market. Indeed, many African societies form syncretic economic organizations, combinations of many different elements and sources. Finally, this essay is about how Africans have tried to manage the recent penetration of capitalist forces into local economies of long standing. This is a crucial problem for many Africans today, especially with the wide-ranging and intensive actions of both governmental and non-governmental development agencies, including the World Bank and U.S. AID, to develop markets in Africa that more closely resemble those in the U.S. and Europe. To quote Geschiere, "It is by studying markets as outcomes of specific social struggles that one can analyse both the cultural construction of metaphors of the market and the varying strategies by which people try to get access to or protect themselves from new market conditions."

R ferences

Comaroff, Jean and John L. Comaroff, eds. 1993. *Modernity & its Malcontents: Ritual and Power in Postcolonial Africa*. Chicago: University of Chicago Press.

Rowlands, R. and J. P. Varnier. 1988. "Sorcery and the State in Cameroon." *Man* 23 (1):118–132.

Tambiah, Stanley Jeyaraja. 1990. *Magic, Science, Religion and the Scope of Rationality*. Cambridge: Cambridge University Press.

Ulin, Robert C. 1984. *Understanding Cultures: Perspectives in Anthropology and Social Theory*. Austin: University of Texas Press.

Suggested Readings

Adorno, Theodor, et al. eds. 1976. *The Positivist Dispute in German Sociolog* New York: Harper and Row.

Agassi, Joseph and Ian Charles Jarvie, eds. 1987. *Rationality: The Critical View*. Boston and Dordrecht: M. Nijhoff.

Bates, R., V. Y. Mudimbe, and J. O'Barr, eds. 1993. *Africa and the Disciplines: The Contribution of Research in Africa to the Social Sciences and Humanities*. Chicago: University of Chicago Press.

Benn, S. I. and G. W. Mortimore. 1976. *Rationality and the Social Sciences: Contributions to the Philosophy and Methodology of the Social Sciences*. London: Routledge and Kegan Paul.

Bloombill, Greta. 1962. *Witchcraft in Africa*. Capetown: H. Timmins.

Comaroff, Jean. 1984. *Body of Power, Spirit of Resistance*. Chicago: University of Chicago Press.

Comaroff, Jean and John L. Comaroff. 1991. *Of Revelation and Revolution, Vol 1: Christianity, Colonialism and Consciousness in South Africa*. Chicago: University of Chicago Press.

Devisch, Rene. 1993. *The Khita Gyn-Eco-Logical Healing Cult among the Yaka*. Chicago: University of Chicago Press.

Durkheim, Emile. 1965. *The Elementary Forms of the Religious Life*. New York: The Free Press.

Evans-Pritchard, E. E. 1956. *Nuer Religion*. London: Oxford University Press.

Frazer, Sir James G. 1994 [1900]. *The Golden Bough: A Study in Magic and Religion*. London: Oxford University Press.

Geertz, Clifford. 1973. *The Interpretation of Cultures*. New York: Basic Books.

Good, Byron. 1994. *Medicine, Rationality and Experience: An Anthropological Perspective*. Cambridge: Cambridge University Press.

Harwood, Alan. 1970. *Witchcraft, Sorcery and Social Categories of the Safwa*. London: Oxford University Press for the IAI.

Heald, Suzette. 1982. "The Making of Men." *Africa*, 52:15–35.

Horton, Robin and Ruth Ferguson, eds. 1973. *Modes of Thought: Essays on Thinking in Western and Non-Western Societies*. London: Faber.

Jarvie, Ian Charles. 1984. *Rationality and Relativism: in Search of a Philosophy and History of Anthropology*. London: Routledge and Kegan Paul.

Jules-Rosette, Benetta. 1978. "The Veil of Objectivity: Prophecy, Divination and Social Inquiry." *American Anthropologist*, 80:549–71.

Karp, Ivan and Charles Bird, eds. 1980. *Explorations in African Systems of Thought*. Bloomington: Indiana University Press.

Kekes, John. 1973. "Towards a Theory of Rationality." *Philosophy of Social Science*, 3(4):275–88.

Levi-Strauss, Claude. 1966. *The Savage Mind*. Chicago: University of Chicago Press.

Macfarlane, Alan. 1970. *Witchcraft in Tudor and Stuart England: A Regional and Comparative View*. London: Routledge and Kegan Paul.

Mair, Lucy. 1970. *Witchcraft*. New York: McGraw-Hill.

Malinowski, Bronislaw. 1948. *Magic, Science and Religion*. Boston: Beacon.

Margolis, J. M. Krausz and R. M. Burian, eds. 1986. *Rationality, Relativism and the Human Sciences*. Boston and Dordrecht: M. Nijhoff.

Marwick, Max, ed. 1970. *Witchcraft and Sorcery*: Selected Readings. Middlesex: Penguin.

Mbiti, J. S. 1969. *African Religions and Philosophy*. New York: Praeger.

Middleton, John. 1963. *Witchcraft and Sorcery in East Africa*. London: Routledge and Kegan Paul.

Nadel, S. F. 1952. "Witchcraft in Four African Societies." *American Anthropologist*. 54:18–29.

Packard, Randall M. 1980. "Social Change and the History of Misfortune among the Bashu of Eastern Zaire." In Karp, Ivan and Charles Bird, eds. 1980. *Explorations in African Systems of Thought*. Bloomington: Indiana University Press. pp. 237–266.

Parrinder, Geoffrey. 1970. *Witchcraft: European and African*. London: Faber and Faber.

Popper, Karl. 1966. *The Open Society and its Enemies*. Fifth Edition. London: Hutchison.

Ranger, T. O. 1982. "The Death of Chaminuka: Spirit Mediums, Nationalism and the Guerilla War in Zimbabwe." *African Affairs*. pp. 349–69.

Riesman, Paul. 1977. *Freedom in Fulani Social Life*. Chicago: University of Chicago Press.

Tambiah, Stanley Jeyaraja. 1985. *Culture, Thought and Social Action: An Anthropological Perspective*. Cambridge: Harvard University Press.

Turner, Victor. 1967. *The Forest of Symbols: Aspects of Ndembu Ritual*. Ithaca: Cornell University Press.

Turner, Victor. 1969. *The Ritual Process: Structure and Anti-Structure*. London: Routledge.

Wilson, Bryan. 1970. *Rationality*. Oxford: Blackwell.

Winch, Peter. 1958. *The Idea of a Social Science and its Relation to Philosophy*. London: Routledge and Kegan Paul.

Wittgenstein, Ludwig. 1953. *Philosophical Investigations*. New York: Macmillan.

16

CONVERSATIONS ON RAIN-MAKING

DAVID LIVINGSTONE

The place where we first settled with the Bakwains is called Chonuane, and it happened to be visited, during the first year of our residence there, by one of those droughts which occur from time to time in even the most favored districts of Africa.

The belief in the gift or power of *rain-making* is one of the most deeply-rooted articles of faith in this country. The chief Sechele was himself a noted rain-doctor, and believed in it implicitly. He has often assured me that he found it more difficult to give up his faith in that than in any thing else which Christianity required him to abjure. I pointed out to him that the only feasible way of watering the gardens was to select some good, never-failing river, make a canal, and irrigate the adjacent lands. This suggestion was immediately adopted, and soon the whole tribe was on the move to the Kolobeng, a stream about forty miles distant. The experiment succeeded admirably during the first year. The Bakwains made the canal and dam in exchange for my labor in assisting to build a square house for their chief. They also built their own school under my superintendence. Our house at the River Kolobeng, which gave a name to the settlement, was the third which I had reared with my own hands. A native smith taught me to weld iron; and having improved by scraps of information in that line from Mr. Moffat, and also in carpentering and gardening, I was

becoming handy at almost any trade, besides doctoring and preaching; and as my wife could make candles, soap, and clothes, we came nearly up to what may be considered as indispensable in the accomplishments of a missionary family in Central Africa, namely, the husband to be a jack-of-all-trades without doors, and the wife a maid-of-all-work within. But in our second year again no rain fell. In the third the same extraordinary drought followed. Indeed, not ten inches of water fell during these two years, and the Kolobeng ran dry; so many fish were killed that the hyenas from the whole country round collected to the feast, and were unable to finish the putrid masses. A large old alligator, which had never been known to commit any depredations, was found left high and dry in the mud among the victims. The fourth year was equally unpropitious, the fall of rain being insufficient to bring the grain to maturity. Nothing could be more trying. We dug down in the bed of the river deeper and deeper as the water receded, striving to get a little to keep the fruit-trees alive for better times, but in vain. Needles lying out of doors for months did not rust; and a mixture of sulphuric acid and water, used in a galvanic battery, parted with all its water to the air, instead of imbibing more from it, as it would have done in England. The leaves of indigenous trees were all drooping, soft, and shriveled, though not dead; and those of the mimosæ were closed at midday, the same as they are at night. In the midst of this dreary drought, it was wonderful to see those tiny creatures, the ants, running about with their accustomed vivacity. I put the bulb of a thermometer three inches under the soil, in the sun, at midday, and found the mercury to stand at 132° to 134°; and if certain kinds of beetles were placed on the surface, they ran about a few seconds and expired. But this broiling heat only augmented the activity of the long-legged black ants: they never tire; their organs of motion seem endowed with the same power as is ascribed by physiologists to the muscles of the human heart, by which that part of the frame never becomes fatigued, and which may be imparted to all our bodily organs in that higher sphere to which we fondly hope to rise. Where do these ants get their moisture? Our house was built on a hard ferruginous conglomerate, in order to be out of the way of the white ant, but they came in despite the precaution; and not only were they, in this sultry weather, able individually to moisten the soil to the consistency of mortar for the formation of galleries, which, in their way of working, is done by night (so that they are screened from the observation of birds by day in passing and repassing toward any vegetable matter they may wish to devour), but, when their inner chambers were laid open, these were also surprisingly humid. Yet there was no dew, and, the house being placed on a rock, they could have no subterranean passage to the bed of the river, which ran about three hundred yards below the hill. Can it be that they have the power of combining the oxygen and hydrogen of their vegetable food by vital force so as to form water?

Rain, however, would not fall. The Bakwains believed that I had bound Sechele with some magic spell, and I received deputations, in the evenings, of the old counselors, entreating me to allow him to make only a few showers: "The corn will die if you refuse, and we shall become scattered. Only let him make rain this once, and we shall all, men, women, and children, come to the school, and sing and pray as long as you please." It was in vain to protest that I wished Sechele to act just according to his own ideas of what was right, as he found the law laid down in the Bible, and it was distressing to appear hard-hearted to them. The clouds often collected promisingly over us, and rolling thunder seemed to portend refreshing showers, but next morning the sun would rise in a clear, cloudless sky; indeed, even these lowering appearances were less frequent by far than days of sunshine are in London.

The natives, finding it irksome to sit and wait helplessly until God gives them rain from heaven, entertain the more comfortable idea that they can help themselves by a variety of preparations, such as charcoal made of burned bats, inspissated renal deposit of the mountain cony – *Hyrax capensis* – (which, by the way, is used, in the form of pills, as a good antispasmodic, under the name of "stone-sweat"),[1] the internal parts of different animals – as jackals' livers, baboons' and lions' hearts, and hairy calculi from the bowels of old cows – serpents' skins and vertebrae, and every kind of tuber, bulb, root, and plant to be found in the country. Although you disbelieve their efficacy in charming the clouds to pour out their refreshing treasures, yet, conscious that civility is useful everywhere, you kindly state that you think they are mistaken as to their power. The rain-doctor selects a particular bulbous root, pounds it, and administers a cold infusion to a sheep, which in five minutes afterward expires in convulsions. Part of the same bulb is converted into smoke, and ascends toward the sky; rain follows in a day or two. The inference is obvious. Were we as

---

[1]   The name arises from its being always voided on one spot, in the manner practiced by others of the rhinocerontine family; and, by the action of the sun, it becomes a black, pitchy substance.

much harassed by droughts, the logic would be irresistible in England in 1857.

As the Bakwains believed that there must be some connection between the presence of "God's Word" in their town and these successive and distressing droughts, they looked with no good will at the church bell, but still they invariably treated us with kindness and respect. I am not aware of ever having had an enemy in the tribe. The only avowed cause of dislike was expressed by a very influential and sensible man, the uncle of Sechele. "We like you as well as if you had been born among us; you are the only white man we can become familiar with (thoaéla); but we wish you to give up that everlasting preaching and praying; we can not become familiar with that at all. You see we never get rain, while those tribes who never pray as we do obtain abundance." This was a fact; and we often saw it raining on the hills ten miles off, while it would not look at us "even with one eye." If the Prince of the power of the air had no hand in scorching us up, I fear I often gave him the credit of doing so.

As for the rain-makers, they carried the sympathies of the people along with them, and not without reason. With the following arguments they were all acquainted, and in order to understand their force, we must place ourselves in their position, and believe, as they do, that all medicines act by a mysterious charm. The term for cure may be translated "charm" (*alaha*).

Medical Doctor. Hail, friend! How very many medicines you have about you this morning! Why, you have every medicine in the country here.

Rain Doctor. Very true, my friend; and I ought; for the whole country needs the rain which I am making.

M.D. So you really believe that you can command the clouds? I think that can be done by God alone.

R.D. We both believe the same thing. It is God that makes the rain, but I pray to him by means of these medicines, and, the rain coming, of course it is then mine. It was *I* who made it for the Bakwains for many years, when they were at Shokuane; through my wisdom, too, their women became fat and shining. Ask them; they will tell you the same as I do.

M.D. But we are distinctly told in the parting words of our Savior that we can pray to God acceptably in his name alone, and not by means of medicines.

R.D. Truly! but God told us differently. He made black men first, and did not love us as he did the white men. He made you beautiful, and gave you clothing, and guns, and gunpowder, and horses, and wagons, and many other things about which we know nothing. But towards us he had no heart. He gave us nothing except the assegai, and cattle, and rainmaking; and he did not give us hearts like yours. We never love each other. Other tribes place medicines about our country to prevent the rain, so that we may be dispersed by hunger, and go to them, and augment their power. We must dissolve their charms by our medicines. God has given us one little thing, which you know nothing of. He has given us the knowledge of certain medicines by which we can make rain. *We* do not despise those things which you possess, though we are ignorant of them. We don't understand your book, yet we don't despise it. *You* ought not to despise our little knowledge, though you are ignorant of it.

M.D. I don't despise what I am ignorant of; I only think you are mistaken in saying that you have medicines which can influence the rain at all.

R.D. That's just the way people speak when they talk on a subject of which they have no knowledge. When we first opened our eyes, we found our forefathers making rain, and we follow in their footsteps. You, who send to Kuruman for corn, and irrigate your garden, may do without rain; *we* cannot manage in that way. If we had no rain, the cattle would have no pasture, the cows give no milk, our children become lean and die, our wives run away to other tribes who do make rain and have corn, and the whole tribe become dispersed and lost; our fire would go out.

M.D. I quite agree with you as to the value of the rain; but you can not charm the clouds by medicines. You wait till you see the clouds come, then you use your medicines, and take the credit which belongs to God only.

R.D. I use my medicines, and you employ yours; we are both doctors, and doctors are not deceivers. You give a patient medicine. Sometimes God is pleased to heal him by means of your medicine; sometimes not – he dies. When he is cured, you take the credit of what God does. I do the same. Sometimes God grants us rain, sometimes not. When he does, we take the credit of the charm. When a patient dies, you don't give up trust in your medicine, neither do I when rain fails. If you wish me to leave off my medicines, why continue your own?

M.D. I give medicine to living creatures within my reach, and can see the effects, though no cure follows; you pretend to charm the clouds, which are so far above us that your medicines never reach them. The clouds usually lie in one direction, and your smoke goes in another. God alone can command the clouds. Only try and wait patiently; God will give us rain without your medicines.

R.D. Mahala-ma-kapa-a-a!! Well, I always thought white men were wise till this morning. Who ever thought of making trial of starvation? Is death pleasant, then?

M.D. Could you make it rain on one spot and not on another?

R.D. I wouldn't think of trying. I like to see the whole country green, and all the people glad; the women clapping their hands, and giving me their ornaments for thankfulness, and lullilooing for joy.

M.D. I think you deceive both them and yourself.

R.D. Well, then, there is a pair of us (meaning both are rogues).

The above is only a specimen of their way of reasoning, in which, when the language is well understood, they are perceived to be remarkably acute. These arguments are generally known, and I never succeeded in convincing a single individual of their fallacy, though I tried to do so in every way I could think of. Their faith in medicines as charms is unbounded. The general effect of argument is to produce the impression that you are not anxious for rain at all; and it is very undesirable to allow the idea to spread that you do not take a generous interest in their welfare. An angry opponent of rain-making in a tribe would be looked upon as were some Greek merchants in England during the Russian war.

17

THE NOTION OF WITCHCRAFT EXPLAINS UNFORTUNATE EVENTS

E. E. EVANS-PRITCHARD

I

Witches, as the Azande conceive them, clearly cannot exist. None the less, the concept of witchcraft provides them with both a natural philosophy by which the relations between men and unfortunate events are explained, and, also, a ready and stereotyped means of reacting to such events. Witchcraft beliefs also embrace a system of values which regulate human conduct.

Witchcraft is ubiquitous. It plays its part in every activity of Zande life; in agricultural, fishing, and hunting pursuits; in domestic life of homesteads as well as in communal life of district and court; it is an important theme of mental life in which it forms the background of a vast panorama of oracles and magic; its influence is plainly stamped on law and morals, etiquette and religion; it is prominent in technology and language; there is no niche or corner of Zande culture into which it does not twist itself. If blight seizes the ground-nut crop it is witchcraft; if the bush is vainly scoured for game it is witchcraft; if women laboriously bale water out of a pool and are rewarded by but a few small fish it is witchcraft; if termites do not rise when their swarming is due and a cold useless night is spent in waiting for their flight it is witchcraft;

if a wife is sulky and unresponsive to her husband it is witchcraft; if a prince is cold and distant with his subject it is witchcraft; if a magical rite fails to achieve its purpose it is witchcraft; if, in fact, any failure or misfortune falls upon anyone at any time and in relation to any of the manifold activities of his life it may be due to witchcraft. The Zande attributes all these misfortunes to witchcraft unless there is strong evidence, and subsequent oracular confirmation, that sorcery or some other evil agent has been at work, or unless they are clearly to be attributed to incompetence, breach of a taboo, or failure to observe a moral rule.

To say that witchcraft has blighted the ground-nut crop, that witchcraft has scared away game, and that witchcraft has made so-and-so ill is equivalent to saying in terms of our own culture that the ground-nut crop has failed owing to blight, that game is scarce this season, and that so-and-so has caught influenza. Witchcraft participates in all misfortunes and is the idiom in which Azande speak about them and in which they explain them. To us witchcraft is something which haunted and disgusted our credulous forefathers. But the Zande expects to come across witchcraft at any time of the day or night. He would be just as surprised if he were not brought into daily contact with it as we would be if confronted by its appearance. To him there is nothing miraculous about it. It is expected that a man's hunting will be injured by witches, and he has at his disposal means of dealing with them. When misfortunes occur he does not become awestruck at the play of supernatural forces. He is not terrified at the presence of an occult enemy. He is, on the other hand, extremely annoyed. Someone, out of spite, has ruined his ground-nuts or spoilt his hunting or given his wife a chill, and surely this is cause for anger! He has done no one harm, so what right has anyone to interfere in his affairs? It is an impertinence, an insult, a dirty, offensive trick! It is the aggressiveness and not the eeriness of these actions which Azande emphasize when speaking of them, and it is anger and not awe which we observe in their response to them.

Witchcraft is not less anticipated than adultery. It is so intertwined with everyday happenings that it is part of a Zande's ordinary world. There is nothing remarkable about a witch – you may be one yourself, and certainly many of your closest neighbours are witches. Nor is there anything awe-inspiring about witchcraft. We do not become psychologically transformed when we hear that someone is ill – we expect people to be ill – and it is the same with Zande. They expect people to be ill, i.e. to be bewitched, and it is not a matter for surprise or wonderment.

I found it strange at first to live among Azande and listen to naïve explanations of misfortunes which, to our minds, have apparent causes, but after a while I learnt the idiom of their thought and applied notions of witchcraft as spontaneously as themselves in situations where the concept was relevant. A boy knocked his foot against a small stump of wood in the centre of a bush path, a frequent happening in Africa, and suffered pain and inconvenience in consequence. Owing to its position on his toe it was impossible to keep the

cut free from dirt and it began to fester. He declared that witchcraft had made him knock his foot against the stump. I always argued with Azande and criticized their statements, and I did so on this occasion. I told the boy that he had knocked his foot against the stump of wood because he had been careless, and that witchcraft had not placed it in the path, for it had grown there naturally. He agreed that witchcraft had nothing to do with the stump of wood being in his path but added that he had kept his eyes open for stumps, as indeed every Zande does most carefully, and that if he had not been bewitched he would have seen the stump. As a conclusive argument for his view he remarked that all cuts do not take days to heal but, on the contrary, close quickly, for that is the nature of cuts. Why, then, has his sore festered and remained open if there were no witchcraft behind it? This, as I discovered before long, was to be regarded as the Zande explanation of sickness.

Shortly after my arrival in Zandeland we were passing through a government settlement and noticed that a hut had been burnt to the ground on the previous night. Its owner was overcome with grief as it had contained the beer he was preparing for a mortuary feast. He told us that he had gone the previous night to examine his beer. He had lit a handful of straw and raised it above his head so that light would be cast on the pots, and in so doing he had ignited the thatch. He, and my companions also, were convinced that the disaster was caused by witchcraft.

One of my chief informants, Kisanga, was a skilled woodcarver, one of the finest carvers in the whole kingdom of Gbudwe. Occasionally the bowls and stools which he carved split during the work, as one may well imagine in such a climate. Though the hardest woods be selected they sometimes split in process of carving or on completion of the utensil even if the craftsman is careful and well acquainted with the technical rules of his craft. When this happened to the bowls and stools of this particular craftsman he attributed the misfortune to witchcraft and used to harangue me about the spite and jealousy of his neighbours. When I used to reply that I thought he was mistaken and that people were well disposed towards him he used to hold the split bowl or stool towards me as concrete evidence of his assertions. If people were not bewitching his work, how would I account for that? Likewise a potter will attribute the cracking of his pots during firing to witchcraft. An experienced potter need have no fear that his pots will crack as a result of error. He selects the proper clay, kneads it thoroughly till he has extracted all grit and pebbles, and builds it up slowly and carefully. On the night before digging out his clay he abstains from sexual intercourse. So he should have nothing to fear. Yet pots sometimes break, even when they are the handiwork of expert potters, and this can only be accounted for by witchcraft. 'It is broken – there is witchcraft,' says the potter simply. . . .

II

In speaking to Azande about witchcraft and in observing their reactions to situations of misfortune it was obvious that they did not attempt to account for the existence of phenomena, or even the action of phenomena, by mystical causation alone. What they explained by witchcraft were the particular conditions in a chain of causation which related an individual to natural happenings in such a way that he sustained injury. The boy who knocked his foot against a stump of wood did not account for the stump by reference to witchcraft, nor did he suggest that whenever anybody knocks his foot against a stump it is necessarily due to witchcraft, nor yet again did he account for the cut by saying that it was caused by witchcraft, for he knew quite well that it was caused by the stump of wood. What he attributed to witchcraft was that on this particular occasion, when exercising his usual care, he struck his foot against a stump of

wood, whereas on a hundred other occasions he did not do so, and that on this particular occasion the cut, which he expected to result from the knock, festered whereas he had had dozens of cuts which had not festered. Surely these peculiar conditions demand an explanation. Again, every year hundreds of Azande go and inspect their beer by night and they always take with them a handful of straw in order to illuminate the hut in which it is fermenting. Why then should this particular man on this single occasion have ignited the thatch of his hut? Again, my friend the wood-carver had made scores of bowls and stools without mishap and he knew all there was to know about the selection of wood, use of tools, and conditions of carving. His bowls and stools did not split like the products of craftsmen who were unskilled in their work, so why on rare occasions should his bowls and stools split when they did not split usually and when he had exercised all his usual knowledge and care? He knew the answer well enough and so, in his opinion, did his envious, back-biting neighbours. In the same way, a potter wants to know why his pots should break on an occasion when he uses the same material and technique as on other occasions; or rather he already knows, for the reason is known in advance, as it were. If the pots break it is due to witchcraft.

We shall give a false account of Zande philosophy if we say that they believe witchcraft to be the sole cause of phenomena. This proposition is not contained in Zande patterns of thought, which only assert that witchcraft brings a man into relation with events in such a way that he sustains injury.

In Zandeland sometimes an old granary collapses. There is nothing remarkable in this. Every Zande knows that termites eat the supports in course of time and that even the hardest woods decay after years of service. Now a granary is the summerhouse of a Zande homestead and people sit beneath it in the heat of the day and chat or play the African hole-game or work at some craft. Consequently it may happen that there are people sitting beneath the granary when it collapses and they are injured, for it is a heavy structure made of beams and clay and may be stored with eleusine as well. Now why should these particular people have been sitting under this particular granary at the particular moment when it collapsed? That it should collapse is easily intelligible, but why should it have collapsed at the particular moment when these particular people were sitting beneath it? Through years it might have collapsed, so why should it fall just when certain people sought its kindly shelter? We say that the granary collapsed because its supports were eaten away by termites; that is the cause that explains the collapse of the granary. We also say that people were sitting under it at the time because it was in the heat of the day and they thought that it would be a comfortable place to talk and work. This is the cause of people being under the granary at the time it collapsed. To our minds the only relationship between these two independently caused facts is their coincidence in time and space. We have no explanation of why the two chains of causation intersected at a certain time and in a certain place, for there is no interdependence between them.

Zande philosophy can supply the missing link. The Zande knows that the supports were undermined by termites and that people were sitting beneath the granary in order to escape the heat and glare of the sun. But he knows besides why these two events occurred at a precisely similar moment in time and space. It was due to the action of witchcraft. If there had been no witchcraft people would have been sitting under the granary and it would not have fallen on them, or it would have collapsed but the people would not have been sheltering under it at the time. Witchcraft explains the coincidence of these two happenings.

III

I hope I am not expected to point out that the Zande cannot analyse his doctrines as I have done for him. It is no use saying to a Zande "Now tell me what you Azande think about witchcraft" because the subject is too general and indeterminate, both too vague and too immense, to be described concisely. But it is possible to extract the principles of their thought from dozens of situations in which witchcraft is called upon to explain happenings and from dozens of other situations in which failure is attributed to some other cause. Their philosophy is explicit, but is not formally stated as a doctrine. A Zande would not say "I believe in natural causation but I do not think that that fully explains coincidences, and it seems to me that the theory of witchcraft offers a satisfactory explanation of them", but he expresses his thought in terms of actual and particular situations. He says "a buffalo charges", "a tree falls", "termites are not making their seasonal flight when they are expected to do so", and so on. Herein he is stating empirically ascertained facts. But he also says "a buffalo charged and wounded so-and-so", "a tree fell on so-and-so and killed him", "my termites refuse to make their flight in numbers worth collecting but other people are collecting theirs all right", and so on. He tells you that these things are due to witchcraft, saying in each instance, "So-and-so has been bewitched." The facts do not explain themselves or only partly explain themselves. They can only be explained fully if one takes witchcraft into consideration.

One can only obtain the full range of a Zande's ideas about causation by allowing him to fill in the gaps himself, otherwise one will be led astray by linguistic conventions. He tells you "So-and-so was bewitched and killed himself" or even simply that "So-and-so was killed by witchcraft". But he is telling you the ultimate cause of his death and not the secondary causes. You can ask him "How did he kill himself?" and he will tell you that he committed suicide by hanging himself from the branch of a tree. You can also ask "Why did he kill himself?" and he will tell you that it was because he was angry with his brothers. The cause of his death was hanging from a tree, and the cause of his hanging from a tree was his anger with his brothers. If you then ask a Zande why he should say that the man was bewitched if he committed suicide on account of his anger with his brothers, he will tell you that only crazy people commit suicide, and that if everyone who was angry with his brothers committed suicide there would soon be no people left in the world, and that if this man had not been bewitched he would not have done what he did do. If you persevere and ask why witchcraft caused the man to kill himself the Zande will reply that he supposes someone hated him, and if you ask him why someone hated him your informant will tell you that such is the nature of men.

For if Azande cannot enunciate a theory of causation in terms acceptable to us they describe happenings in an idiom that is explanatory. They are aware that it is particular circumstances of events in their relation to man, their harmfulness to a particular person, that constitutes evidence of witchcraft. Witchcraft explains *why* events are harmful to man and not *how* they happen. A Zande perceives how they happen just as we do. He does not see a witch charge a man, but an elephant. He does not see a witch push over a granary, but termites gnawing away its supports. He does not see a psychical flame igniting thatch, but an ordinary lighted bundle of straw. His perception of how events occur is as clear as our own.

IV

Zande belief in witchcraft in no way contradicts empirical knowledge of causes and effect. The world known to the senses is just as real to them as it is to us. We must not be deceived by their way of expressing causation and imagine that because they say a man was killed by witchcraft they entirely neglect the secondary causes that, as we judge them, were the true causes of his death. They are foreshortening the chain of events, and in a particular social situation are selecting the cause that is socially relevant and neglecting the rest. If a man is killed by a spear in war, or by a wild beast in hunting, or by the bite of a snake, or from sickness, witchcraft is the socially relevant cause, since it is the only one which allows intervention and determines social behaviour.

Belief in death from natural causes and belief in death from witchcraft are not mutually exclusive. On the contrary, they supplement one another, the one accounting for what the other does not account for. Besides, death is not only a natural fact but also a social fact. It is not simply that the heart ceases to beat and the lungs to pump air in an organism, but it is also the destruction of a member of a family and kin, of a community and tribe. Death leads to consultation or oracles, magic rites, and revenge. Among the causes of death witchcraft is the only one that has any significance for social behaviour. The attribution of misfortune to witchcraft does not exclude what we call its real causes but is superimposed on them and gives to social events their moral value.

Zande thought expresses the notion of natural and mystical causation quite clearly by using a hunting metaphor to define their relations. Azande always say of witchcraft that it is the *umbaga* or second spear. When Azande kill game there is a division of meat between the man who first speared the animal and the man who plunged a second spear into it. These two are considered to have killed the beast and the owner of the second spear is called the *umbaga*. Hence if a man is killed by an elephant Azande say that the elephant is the first spear and that witchcraft is the second spear and that together they killed the man. If a man spears another in war the slayer is the first spear and witchcraft is the second spear and together they killed him.

Since Azande recognize plurality of causes, and it is the social situation that indicates the relevant one, we can understand why the doctrine of witchcraft is not used to explain every failure and misfortune. It sometimes happens that the social situation demands a common-sense, and not a mystical, judgement of cause. Thus, if you tell a lie, or commit adultery, or steal, or deceive your prince, and are found out, you cannot elude punishment by saying that you were bewitched. Zande doctrine declares emphatically "Witchcraft does not make a person tell lies"; "Witchcraft does not make a person commit adultery"; "Witchcraft does not put adultery into a man. 'Witchcraft' is in yourself (you alone are responsible), that is, your penis becomes erect. It sees the hair of a man's wife and it rises and becomes erect because the only 'witchcraft' is, itself" ('witchcraft' is here used metaphorically); "Witchcraft does not make a person steal"; "Witchcraft does not make a person disloyal." Only on one occasion have I heard a Zande plead that he was bewitched when he had committed an offence and this was when he lied to me, and even on this occasion everybody present laughed at him and told him that witchcraft does not make people tell lies.

If a man murders another tribesman with knife or spear he is put to death. It is not necessary in such a case to seek a witch, for an objective towards which vengeance may be directed is already present. If, on the other hand, it is a member of another tribe who has speared a man his relatives, or his prince, will take steps to discover the witch responsible for the event.

It would be treason to say that a man put to death on the orders of his king for an offence against authority was killed by witchcraft. If a man were to consult the oracles to discover the witch responsible for the death of a relative who had been put to death at the orders of his king he would run the risk of being put to death himself. For here the social situation excludes the notion of witchcraft as on other occasions it pays no attention to natural agents and emphasizes only witchcraft. Also, if a man were killed in vengeance because the oracles said that he was a witch and had murdered another man with his witchcraft then his relatives could not say that he had been killed by witchcraft. Zande doctrine lays it down that he died at the hand of avengers because he was a homicide. If a man were to have expressed the view that his kinsman had been killed by witchcraft and to have acted upon his opinion by consulting the poison oracle, he might have been punished for ridiculing the king's poison oracle, for it was the poison oracle of the king that had given official confirmation of the man's guilt, and it was the king himself who had permitted vengeance to take its course.

In these situations witchcraft is irrelevant and, if not totally excluded, is not indicated as the principal factor in causation. As in our own society a scientific theory of causation, if not excluded, is deemed irrelevant in questions of moral and legal responsibility, so in Zande society the doctrine of witchcraft, if not excluded, is deemed irrelevant in the same situations. We accept scientific explanations of the causes of disease, and even of the causes of insanity, but we deny them in crime and sin because here they militate against law and morals which are axiomatic. The Zande accepts a mystical explanation of the causes of misfortune, sickness, and death, but he does not allow this explanation if it conflicts with social exigencies expressed in law and morals.

For witchcraft is not indicated as a cause for failure when a taboo has been broken. If a child becomes sick, and it is known that its father and mother have had sexual relations before it was weaned, the cause of death is already indicated by breach of a ritual prohibition and the question of witchcraft does not arise. If a man develops leprosy and there is a history of incest in his case then incest is the cause of leprosy and not witchcraft. In these cases, however, a curious situation arises because when the child or the leper dies it is necessary to avenge their deaths and the Zande sees no difficulty in explaining what appears to us to be most illogical behaviour. He does so on the same principles as when a man has been killed by a wild beast, and he invokes the same metaphor of "second spear". In the cases mentioned above there are really three causes of a person's death. There is the illness from which he dies, leprosy in the case of the man, perhaps some fever in the case of the child. These sicknesses are not in themselves products of witchcraft, for they exist in their own right just as a buffalo or a granary exist in their own right. Then there is the breach of a taboo, in the one case of weaning, in the other case of incest. The child, and the man, developed fever, and leprosy, because a taboo was broken. The breach of a taboo was the cause of their sickness, but the sickness would not have killed them if witchcraft had not also been operative. If witchcraft had not been present as "second spear" they would have developed fever and leprosy just the same, but they would not have died from them. In these instances there are two socially significant causes, breach of taboo and witchcraft, both of which are relative to different social processes, and each is emphasized by different people.

But where there has been a breach of taboo and death is not involved witchcraft will not be evoked as a cause of failure. If a man eats a forbidden food after he has made powerful punitive magic he may die, and in this case the cause of his death is known beforehand, since it is contained in the conditions of the situation in which he died even if witchcraft was also operative. But it does not follow that he will die. What does inevitably follow is that the medicine he has made will cease to operate against the person for whom it is intended and will have to be destroyed lest it turn against the magician who sent if forth. The failure of the medicine to achieve its purpose is due to breach of a taboo and not to witchcraft. If a man has had sexual relations with his wife and on the next day approaches the poison oracle it

will not reveal the truth and its oracular efficacy will be permanently undermined. If he had not broken a taboo it would have been said that witchcraft had caused the oracle to lie, but the condition of the person who had attended the seance provides a reason for its failure to speak the truth without having to bring in the notion of witchcraft as an agent. No one will admit that he has broken a taboo before consulting the poison oracle, but when an oracle lies everyone is prepared to admit that a taboo may have been broken by someone.

Similarly, when a potter's creations break in firing, witchcraft is not the only possible cause of the calamity. Inexperience and bad workmanship may also be reasons for failure, or the potter may himself have had sexual relations on the preceding night. The potter himself will attribute his failure to witchcraft, but others may not be of the same opinion.

Not even all deaths are invariably and unanimously attributed to witchcraft or to the breach of some taboo. The deaths of babies from certain diseases are attributed vaguely to the Supreme Being. Also, if a man falls suddenly and violently sick and dies, his relatives may be sure that a sorcerer has made magic against him and that it is not a witch who has killed him. A breach of the obligations of blood-brotherhood may sweep away whole groups of kin, and when one after another of brothers and cousins die it is the blood and not witchcraft to which their deaths are attributed by outsiders, though the relatives of the dead will seek to avenge them on witches. When a very old man dies, unrelated people say that he has died of old age, but they do not say this in the presence of kinsmen, who declare that witchcraft is responsible for his death.

It is also thought that adultery may cause misfortune, though it is only one participating factor, and witchcraft is also believed to be present. Thus is it said that a man may be killed in warfare or in a hunting accident as a result of his wife's infidelities. Therefore, before going to war or on a large-scale hunting expedition a man might ask his wife to divulge the names of her lovers.

Even where breaches of law and morals do not occur witchcraft is not the only reason given for failure. Incompetence, laziness, and ignorance may be selected as causes. When a girl smashes her water-pot or a boy forgets to close the door of the hen-house at night they will be admonished severely by their parents for stupidity. The mistakes of children are due to carelessness or ignorance and they are taught to avoid them while they are still young. People do not say that they are effects of witchcraft, or if they are prepared to concede the possibility of witchcraft they consider stupidity the main cause. Moreover, the Zande is not so naïve that he holds witchcraft responsible for the cracking of a pot during firing if subsequent examination shows that a pebble was left in the clay, or for an animal escaping his net if someone frightened it away by a move or a sound. People do not blame witchcraft if a woman burns her porridge nor if she presents it undercooked to her husband. And when an inexperienced craftsman makes a stool which lacks polish or which splits, this is put down to his inexperience.

In all these cases the man who suffers the misfortune is likely to say that it is due to witchcraft, but others will not say so. We must bear in mind nevertheless that a serious misfortune, especially if it results in death, is normally attributed by everyone to the action of witchcraft, especially by the sufferer and his kin, however much it may have been due to a man's incompetence or absence of self-control. If a man falls into a fire and is seriously burnt, or falls into a game-pit and breaks his neck or his leg, it would undoubtedly be attributed to witchcraft. Thus when six or seven of the sons of Prince Rikita were entrapped in a ring of fire and burnt to death when hunting cane-rats their death was undoubtedly due to witchcraft.

Hence we see that witchcraft has its own logic, its own rules of thought, and that these do not exclude natural causation. Belief in witchcraft is quite consistent with human responsibility and a rational appreciation of nature. First of all a man must carry out an activity according to traditional rules of technique, which consist of knowledge checked by trial and error in each generation. It is only if he fails in spite of adherence to these rules that people will impute his lack of success to witchcraft.

V

It is often asked whether primitive people distinguish between the natural and the supernatural, and the query may be here answered in a preliminary manner in respect to the Azande. The question as it stands may mean, do primitive peoples distinguish between the natural and the supernatural in the abstract? We have a notion of an ordered world conforming to what we call natural laws, but some people in our society believe that mysterious things can happen which cannot be accounted for by reference to natural laws and which therefore are held to transcend them, and we call these happenings supernatural. To us supernatural means very much the same as abnormal or extraordinary. Azande certainly have no such notions of reality. They have no conceptions of "natural" as we understand it, and therefore neither of the "supernatural" as we understand it. Witchcraft is to Azande an ordinary and not an extraordinary, even though it may in some circumstances be an infrequent, event. It is a normal, and not an abnormal, happening. But if they do not give to the natural and supernatural the meanings which educated Europeans give to them they nevertheless distinguish between them. For our question may be formulated, and should be formulated, in a different manner. We ought rather to ask whether primitive peoples perceive any difference between the happenings which we, the observers of their culture, class as natural and the happenings which we class as mystical. Azande undoubtedly perceive a difference between what we consider the workings of nature on the one hand and the workings of magic and ghosts and witchcraft on the other hand, though in the absence of a formulated doctrine of natural law they do not, and cannot, express the difference as we express it.

The Zande notion of witchcraft is incompatible with our ways of thought. But even to the Azande there is something peculiar about the action of witchcraft. Normally it can be perceived only in dreams. It is not an evident notion but transcends sensory experience. They do not profess to understand witchcraft entirely. They know that it exists and works evil, but they have to guess at the manner in which it works. Indeed, I have frequently been struck when discussing witchcraft with Azande by the doubt they express about the subject, not only in what they say, but even more in their manner of saying it, both of which contrast with their ready knowledge, fluently imparted, about social events and economic techniques. They feel out of their depth in trying to describe the way in which witchcraft accomplishes its ends. That it kills people is obvious, but how it kills them cannot

be known precisely. They tell you that perhaps if you were to ask an older man or a witch-doctor he might give you more information. But the older men and the witch-doctors can tell you little more than youth and laymen. They only know what the others know: that the soul of witchcraft goes by night and devours the soul of its victim. Only witches themselves understand these matters fully. In truth Azande experience feelings about witchcraft rather than ideas, for their intellectual concepts of it are weak and they know better what to do when attacked by it than how to explain it. Their response is action and not analysis.

There is no elaborate and consistent representation of witchcraft that will account in detail for its workings, nor of nature which expounds its conformity to sequences and functional interrelations. The Zande actualizes these beliefs rather than intellectualizes them, and their tenets are expressed in socially controlled behaviour rather than in doctrines. Hence the difficulty in discussing the subject of witchcraft with Azande, for their ideas are imprisoned in action and cannot be cited to explain and justify action.

18

UNDERSTANDING A PRIMITIVE SOCIETY*

PETER WINCH

1 The Reality of Magic

An anthropologist studying a primitive people with beliefs that we cannot possibly share and practices we cannot comprehend wishes to make those beliefs and practices intelligible to himself and his readers. This means presenting an account of them that will somehow satisfy the criteria of rationality demanded by the culture to which he and his readers belong: a culture whose conception of rationality is deeply affected by the achievements and methods of the sciences, and one which treats such things as a belief in magic or the practice of consulting oracles as almost a paradigm of the irrational. The strains inherent in this situation are very likely to lead the anthropologist to adopt the following posture: *We* know that Zande beliefs in the influence of witchcraft, the efficacy of magic medicines, the role of oracles in revealing what is going on and what is going to happen, are mistaken, illusory. Scientific methods of investigation have shown conclusively that there are no relations of cause and effect such as are implied by these beliefs and practices. All we can do then is to show how such a

system of mistaken beliefs and inefficacious practices can maintain itself in the face of objections that seem to us so obvious.[1]

Now although Evans-Pritchard goes a very great deal further than most of his predecessors in trying to present the sense of the institutions he is discussing as it presents itself to the Azande themselves, still, the last paragraph does, I believe, pretty fairly describe the attitude he himself took at the time of writing this book. There is more than one remark to the effect that "obviously there are no witches"; and he writes of the difficulty he found, during his field work with the Azande, in shaking off the "unreason" on which Zande life is based and returning to a clear view of how things really are. This attitude is not an unsophisticated one but is based on a philosophical position ably developed in a series of papers published in the 1930s in the unhappily rather inaccessible *Bulletin of the Faculty of Arts* of the University of Egypt. Arguing against Lévy-Bruhl, Evans-Pritchard here rejects the idea that the scientific understanding of causes and effects which leads us to reject magical ideas is evidence of any superior intelligence on our part. Our scien-

* This paper was first published in the *American Philosophical Quarterly* I, 1964, pp. 307–24.

[1] At this point the anthropologist is very likely to start speaking of the "social function" of the institution under examination. There are many important questions that should be raised about functional explanations and their relations to the issues discussed in this essay; but these questions cannot be pursued further here.

tific approach, he points out, is as much a function of our culture as is the magical approach of the "savage" a function of his:

> The fact that we attribute rain to meteorological causes alone while savages believe that Gods or ghosts or magic can influence the rain-fall is no evidence that our brains function differently from their brains. It does not show that we 'think more logically' than savages, at least not if this expression suggests some kind of hereditary psychic superiority. It is no sign of superior intelligence on my part that I attribute rain to physical causes. I did not come to this conclusion myself by observation and inference and have, in fact, little knowledge of the meterological process that lead to rain, I merely accept what everybody else in my society accepts, namely that rain is due to natural causes. This particular idea formed part of my culture long before I was born into it and little more was required of me than sufficient linguistic ability to learn it. Likewise a savage who believes that under suitable natural and ritual conditions the rainfall can be influenced by use of appropriate magic is not on account of this belief to be considered of inferior intelligence. He did not build up this belief from his own observations and inferences but adopted it in the same way as he adopted the rest of his cultural heritage, namely by being born into it. He and I are both thinking in patterns of thought provided for us by the societies in which we live.
>
> It would be absurd to say that the savage is thinking mystically and that we are thinking scientifically about rainfall. In either case like mental processes are involved and, moreover, the content of thought is similarly derived. But we can say that the social content of our thought about rainfall is scientific, is in accord with objective facts, whereas the social content of savage thought

about rainfall is unscientific since it is not in accord with reality and may also be mystical where it assumes the existence of suprasensible forces.[2]

In a subsequent article on Pareto, Evans-Pritchard distinguishes between "logical" and "scientific."

> Scientific notions are those which accord with objective reality both with regard to the validity of their premisses and to the inferences drawn from their propositions . . . Logical notions are those in which according to the rules of thought inferences would be true were the premisses true, the truth of the premisses being irrelevant . . .
>
> A pot has broken during firing. This is probably due to grit. Let us examine the pot and see if this is the cause. That is logical and scientific thought. Sickness is due to witchcraft. A man is sick. Let us consult the oracles to discover who is the witch responsible. That is logical and unscientific thought.[3]

I think that Evans-Pritchard is right in a great deal of what he says here, but wrong, and crucially wrong, in his attempt to characterize the scientific in terms of that which is "in accord with objective reality." Despite differences of emphasis and phraseology, Evans-Pritchard is in fact hereby put into the same metaphysical camp as Pareto: for both of them the conception of "reality" must be regarded as intelligible and applicable *outside* the context of scientific reasoning itself, since it is that to which scientific notions do, and unscientific notions do not, have a relation. Evans-Pritchard, although he emphasizes that a member of scientific culture has a different conception of reality from that of a Zande believer in magic, wants to go beyond merely

---

[2] E. E. Evans-Pritchard, "Lévy-Bruhl's Theory of Primitive Mentality," *Bulletin of the Faculty of Arts*, University of Egypt, 1934.
[3] "Science and Sentiment," *Bulletin of the Faculty of Arts*, ibid., 1935.

registering this fact and making the differences explicit, and to say, finally, that the scientific conception agrees with what reality actually is like, whereas the magical conception does not.

It would be easy, at this point, to say simply that the difficulty arises from the use of the unwieldy and misleadingly comprehensive expression "agreement with reality"; and in a sense this is true. But we should not lose sight of the fact that the idea that men's ideas and beliefs must be checkable by reference to something independent – some reality – is an important one. To abandon it is to plunge straight into an extreme Protagorean relativism, with all the paradoxes that involves. On the other hand great care is certainly necessary in fixing the precise role that this conception of the independently real does play in men's thought. There are two related points that I should like to make about it at this stage.

In the first place we should notice that the check of the independently real is not peculiar to science. The trouble is that the fascination science has for us makes it easy for us to adopt its scientific form as a paradigm against which to measure the intellectual respectability of other modes of discourse. Consider what God says to Job out of the whirlwind: "Who is this that darkeneth counsel by words without knowledge? . . . Where wast thou when I laid the foundations of the earth? declare, if thou hast understanding. Who hath laid the measures thereof, if thou knowest? or who hath stretched the line upon it . . . Shall he that contendeth with the Almighty instruct him? he that reproveth God, let him answer it." Job is taken to task for having gone astray by having lost sight of the reality of God; this does not, of course, mean that Job has made any sort of theoretical mistake, which could be put right, perhaps, by means of an experiment.[4] God's reality is certainly independent of what any man may care to think, but what that

reality amounts to can only be seen from the religious tradition in which the concept of God is used, and this use is very unlike the use of scientific concepts, say of theoretical entities. The point is that it is *within* the religious use of language that the conception of God's reality has its place, though, I repeat, this does not mean that it is at the mercy of what anyone cares to say; if this were so, God would have no reality.

My second point follows from the first. Reality is not what gives language sense. What is real and what is unreal shows itself *in* the sense that language has. Further, both the distinction between the real and the unreal and the concept of agreement with reality themselves belong to our language. I will not say that they are concepts of the language like any other, since it is clear that they occupy a commanding, and in a sense a limiting, position there. We can imagine a language with no concept, of, say, wetness, but hardly one in which there is no way of distinguishing the real from the unreal. Nevertheless we could not in fact distinguish the real from the unreal without understanding the way this distinction operates in the language. If then we wish to understand the significance of these concepts, we must examine the use they actually do have—*in* the language.

Evans-Pritchard, on the contrary, is trying to work with a conception of reality which is *not* determined by its actual use in language. He wants something against which the use can itself be appraised. But this is not possible; and no more possible in the case of scientific discourse than it is in any other. We may ask whether a particular scientific hypothesis agrees with reality and test this by observation and experiment. Given the experimental methods, and the established use of the theoretical terms entering into the hypothesis, then the question whether it holds or not is

---

[4]   Indeed, one way of expressing the point of the story of Job is to say that in it Job is shown as going astray by being induced to make the reality and goodness of God contingent on what happens.

settled by reference to something independent of what I, or anybody else, care to think. But the general nature of the data revealed by the experiment can only be specified in terms of criteria built into the methods of experiment employed and these, in turn, make sense only to someone who is conversant with the kind of scientific activity within which they are employed. A scientific illiterate, asked to describe the results of an experiment which he "observes" in an advanced physics laboratory, could not do so in terms relevant to the hypothesis being tested; and it is really only in such terms that we can sensibly speak of the "results of the experiment" at all. What Evans-Pritchard wants to be able to say is that the criteria applied in scientific experimentation constitute a true link between our ideas and an independent reality, whereas those characteristic of other systems of thought – in particular, magical methods of thought – do not. It is evident that the expressions "true link" and "independent reality" in the previous sentence cannot themselves be explained by reference to the scientific universe of discourse, as this would beg the question. We have then to ask how, by reference to what established universe of discourse, the use of those expressions *is* to be explained; and it is clear that Evans-Pritchard has not answered this question.

Two questions arise out of what I have been saying. First, is it in fact the case that a primitive system of magic, like that of the Azande, constitutes a coherent universe of discourse like science, in terms of which an intelligible conception of reality and clear ways of deciding what beliefs are and are not in agreement with this reality can be discerned! Second, what are we to make of the possibility of understanding primitive social institutions, like Zande magic, if the situation is as I have outlined? I do not claim to be able to give a satisfactory answer to the second question. It

raises some very important and fundamental issues about the nature of human social life, which require conceptions different from, and harder to elucidate than, those I have hitherto introduced. I shall offer some tentative remarks about these issues in the second part of this essay. At present I shall address myself to the first question.

It ought to be remarked here that an affirmative answer to my first question would not commit me to accepting as rational all beliefs couched in magical concepts or all procedures practiced in the name of such beliefs. This is no more necessary than is the corresponding proposition that all procedures "justified" in the name of science are immune from rational criticism. A remark of Collingwood's is apposite here:

> Savages are no more exempt from human folly than civilized men, and are no doubt equally liable to the error of thinking that they, or the persons they regard as their superiors, can do what in fact cannot be done. But this error is not the essence of magic; it is a perversion of magic. And we should be careful how we attribute it to the people we call savages, who will one day rise up and testify against us.[5]

It is important to distinguish a system of magical beliefs and practices like that of the Azande, which is one of the principal foundations of their whole social life and, on the other hand, magical beliefs that might be held, and magical rites that might be practised, by persons belonging to our own culture. These have to be understood rather differently. Evans-Pritchard is himself alluding to the difference in the following passage: "When a Zande speaks of witchcraft he does not speak of it as we speak of the weird witchcraft of our own history. Witchcraft is to him a commonplace happening and he seldom passes a day without mentioning it . . . To us

---

[5] R. G. Collingwood, *Principles of Art*, Oxford (Galaxy Books), 1958, p. 67.

witchcraft is something which haunted and disgusted our credulous forefathers. But the Zande expects to come across witchcraft at any time of the day or night. He would be just as surprised if he were not brought into daily contact with it as we would be if confronted by its appearance. To him there is nothing miraculous about it."[6]

The difference is not merely one of degree of familiarity, however, although, perhaps, even this has more importance than might at first appear. Concepts of witchcraft and magic in our culture, at least since the advent of Christianity, have been parasitic on, and a perversion of other orthodox concepts, both religious and, increasingly, scientific. To take an obvious example, you could not understand what was involved in conducting a Black Mass, unless you were familiar with the conduct of a proper Mass and, therefore, with the whole complex of religious ideas from which the mass draws its sense. Neither would you understand the relation between these without taking account of the fact that the Black practices are rejected as *irrational* (in the sense proper to religion) in the system of beliefs on which these practices are thus parasitic. Perhaps a similar relation holds between the contemporary practice of astrology and astronomy and technology. It is impossible to keep a discussion of the rationality of Black Magic or of astrology within the bounds of concepts peculiar to them; they have an essential reference to something outside themselves. The position is like that which Socrates, in Plato's *Gorgias*, showed to be true of the Sophists' conception of rhetoric: namely, that it is parasitic on rational discourse in such a way that its irrational character can be shown in terms of this dependence. Hence, when we speak of such practices as "superstitious," "illusory," "irrational," we have the weight of our culture behind us; and this is not just a matter of being on the side of the big battal-

ions, because those beliefs and practices belong to, and derive such sense as they seem to have, from the same culture. This enables us to show that the sense is only apparent, in terms which are culturally relevant.

It is evident that our relation to Zande magic is quite different. If we wish to understand it, we must seek a foothold elsewhere. And while there may well be room for the use of such critical expressions as "superstition" and "irrationality", the kind of rationality with which such terms might be used to point a contrast remains to be elucidated. . . .

Early in his book Evans-Pritchard defines certain categories in terms of which his descriptions of Zande customs are couched.

MYSTICAL NOTIONS . . . are patterns of thought that attribute to phenomena supra-sensible qualities which, or part of which, are not derived from observation or cannot be logically inferred from it, *and which they do not possess.*[7] COMMON-SENSE NOTIONS . . . attribute to phenomena only what men observe in them or what can logically be inferred from observation. So long as a notion does not assert something which has not been observed, it is not classed as mystical even though it is mistaken on account of incomplete observation . . . SCIENTIFIC NOTIONS. Science has developed out of common sense but is far more methodical and has better techniques of observation and reasoning. Common sense uses experience and rules of thumb. Science uses experiment and rules of Logic . . . *Our body of scientific knowledge and Logic are the sole arbiters of what are mystical, common sense, and scientific notions.* Their judgments are never absolute. RITUAL BEHAVIOUR. Any behaviour that is accounted for by mystical notions. *There is no objective nexus* between the behaviour and the event it is intended to cause. Such behaviour is usually intelligible to us only when we know the mystical notions associated with it. EMPIRICAL

---

[6] *Witchcraft, Oracles and Magic among the Azande*, p.64.

BEHAVIOUR. Any behaviour that is accounted for by common-sense notions.[8]

It will be seen from the phrases which I have italicized that Evans-Pritchard is doing more here than just defining certain terms for his own use. Certain metaphysical claims are embodied in the definitions: identical in substance with the claims embodied in Pareto's way of distinguishing between "logical" and "non-logical" conduct.[9] There is a very clear implication that those who use mystical notions and perform ritual behaviour are making some sort of mistake, detectable with the aid of science and logic. I shall now examine more closely some of the institutions described by Evans-Pritchard to determine how far his claims are justified.

Witchcraft is a power possessed by certain individuals to harm other individuals by "mystical" means. Its basis is an inherited organic condition, "witchcraft-substance" and it does not involve any special magical ritual or medicine. It is constantly appealed to by Azande when they are afflicted by misfortune, not so as to exclude explanation in terms of natural causes, which Azande are perfectly able to offer themselves within the limits of their not inconsiderable natural knowledge, but so as to supplement such explanations. "Witchcraft explains *why*[10] events are harmful to man and not *how*[10] they happen. A Zande perceives how they happen just as we do. He does not see a witch charge a man but an elephant. He does not see a witch push over the granary, but termites gnawing away its supports. He does not see a psychical flame igniting thatch, but an ordinary lighted bundle of straw. His perception of how events occur is as clear as our own."[11]

The most important way of detecting the influence of witchcraft and of identifying witches is by the revelations of oracles, of which in turn the most important is the "poison oracle". This name, though convenient, is significantly misleading in so far as, according to Evans-Pritchard, Azande do not have our concept of a poison and do not think of, or behave towards, *benge* – the substance administered in the consultation of the oracle – as we do of and towards poisons. The gathering, preparation, and administering of *benge* is hedged with ritual and strict taboos. At an oracular consultation *benge* is administered to a fowl, while a question is asked in a form permitting a yes or no answer. The fowl's death or survival is specified beforehand as giving the answer "yes" or "no". The answer is then checked by administering *benge* to another fowl and asking the question the other way round. "Is Prince Ndoruma responsible for placing bad medicines in the roof of my hut? The fowl DIES giving the answer 'Yes' ... Did the oracle speak truly when it said that Ndoruma was responsible? The fowl SURVIVES giving the answer 'Yes'." The poison oracle is all-pervasive in Zande life and all steps of any importance in a person's life are settled by reference to it.

A Zande would be utterly lost and bewildered without his oracle. The mainstay of his life would be lacking. It is rather as if an engineer, in our society, were to be asked to build a bridge without mathematical calculation, or a military commander to mount an extensive coordinated attack without the use of clocks. These analogies are mine, but a reader may well think that they beg the question at issue. For, he may argue, the Zande practice of consulting the oracle, unlike my technological and military examples, is completely unintelligible and rests on an obvious illusion. I shall now consider this objection.

First I must emphasize that I have so far

---

[7] The italics are mine throughout this quotation.
[8] Op. cit., p. 12.
[9] For further criticism of Pareto see Peter Winch, *The Idea of a Social Science*, pp. 95–111.
[10] Evans-Pritchard's italics.
[11] Op. cit., p. 72.

done little more than note the *fact*, conclusively established by Evans-Pritchard, that the Azande *do* in fact conduct their affairs to their own satisfaction in this way and are at a loss when forced to abandon the practice – when, for instance, they fall into the hands of European courts. It is worth remarking too that Evans-Pritchard himself ran his household in the same way during his field researches and says: "I found this as satisfactory a way of running my home and affairs as any other I know of."

Further, I would ask in my turn: *to whom* is the practice alleged to be unintelligible? Certainly it is difficult for us to understand what the Azande are about when they consult their oracles; but it might seem just as incredible to them that the engineer's motions with his slide rule could have any connection with the stability of his bridge. But this riposte of course misses the intention behind the objection, which was not directed to the question whether anyone in fact understands, or claims to understand, what is going on, but rather whether what is going on actually does make sense: i.e., in itself. And it may seem obvious that Zande beliefs in witchcraft and oracles cannot make any sense, however satisfied the Azande may be with them.

What criteria have we for saying that something does, or does not, make sense? A partial answer is that a set of beliefs and practices cannot make sense in so far as they involve contradictions. Now it appears that contradictions are bound to arise in at least two ways in the consultation of the oracle. On the one hand two oracular pronouncements may contradict each other; and on the other hand a self-consistent oracular pronouncement may be contradicted by future experience. I shall examine each of these apparent possibilities in turn.

Of course, it does happen often that the oracle first says "yes" and then "no" to the same question. This does not convince a Zande of the futility of the whole operation of consulting oracles: obviously, it cannot, since

otherwise the practice could hardly have developed and maintained itself at all. Various explanations may be offered, whose possibility, it is important to notice, is built into the whole network of Zande beliefs and may, therefore, be regarded as belonging to the concept of an oracle. It may be said, for instance, that bad *benge* is being used; that the operator of the oracle is ritually unclean; that the oracle is being itself influenced by witchcraft or sorcery; or it may be that the oracle is showing that the question cannot be answered straightforwardly in its present form, as with "Have you stopped beating your wife yet?" There are various ways in which the behaviour of the fowl under the influence of *benge* may be ingeniously interpreted by those wise in the ways of the poison oracle. We might compare this situation perhaps with the interpretation of dreams.

In the other type of case: where an internally consistent oracular revelation is apparently contradicted by subsequent experience, the situation may be dealt with in a similar way, by references to the influence of witchcraft, ritual uncleanliness, and so on. But there is another important consideration we must take into account here too. The chief function of oracles is to reveal the presence of "mystical" forces – I use Evans-Pritchard's term without committing myself to his denial that such forces really exist. Now though there are indeed ways of determining whether or not mystical forces are operating, these ways do not correspond to what we understand by "empirical" confirmation or refutation. This indeed is a tautology, since such differences in "confirmatory" procedures are the main criteria for classifying something as a mystical force in the first place. Here we have one reason why the possibilities of "refutation by experience" are very much fewer than might at first sight be supposed.

There is also another closely connected reason. The spirit in which oracles are consulted is very unlike that in which a scientist makes experiments. Oracular revelations are not treated as hypotheses and, since their sense derives from the way they are treated in their context, they therefore *are not* hypotheses. They are not a matter of intellectual interest but the main way in which Azande decide how they should act. If the oracle reveals that a proposed course of action is fraught with mystical dangers from witchcraft or sorcery, that course of action will not be carried out; and then the question of refutation or confirmation just does not arise. We might say that the revelation has the logical status of an unfulfilled hypothetical, were it not that the context in which this logical term is generally used may again suggest a misleadingly close analogy with scientific hypotheses.

I do not think that Evans-Pritchard would have disagreed with what I have said so far. Indeed, the following comment is on very similar lines:

> Azande observe the action of the poison oracle as we observe it, but their observations are always subordinated to their beliefs and are incorporated into their beliefs and made to explain them and justify them. Let the reader consider any argument that would utterly demolish all Zande claims for the power of the oracle. If it were translated into Zande modes of thought it would serve to support their entire structure of belief. For their mystical notions are eminently coherent, being interrelated by a network of logical ties, and are so ordered that they never too crudely contradict sensory experience but, instead, experience seems to justify them. The Zande is immersed in a sea of mystical notions, and if he speaks about his poison oracle he must speak in a mystical idiom.[12]

To locate the point at which the important philosophical issue does arise, I shall offer a parody, composed by changing round one or two expressions in the foregoing quotation.

> Europeans observe the action of the poison oracle just as Azande observe it, but their observations are always subordinated to their beliefs and are incorporated into their beliefs and made to explain them and justify them. Let a Zande consider any argument that would utterly refute all European scepticism about the power of the oracle. If it were translated into European modes of thought it would serve to support their entire structure of belief. For their scientific notions are eminently coherent, being interrelated by a network of logical ties, and are so ordered that they never too crudely contradict mystical experience but, instead, experience seems to justify them. The European is immersed in a sea of scientific notions, and if he speaks about the Zande poison oracle he must speak in a scientific idiom.

Perhaps this too would be acceptable to Evans-Pritchard. But it is clear from other remarks in the book to which I have alluded, that at the time of writing he would have wished to add: and the European is right and the Zande wrong. This addition I regard as illegitimate and my reasons for so thinking take us to the heart of the matter.

It may be illuminating at this point to compare the disagreement between Evans-Pritchard and me to that between the Wittgenstein of the *Philosophical Investigations* and his earlier *alter ego* of the *Tractatus Logico-Philosophicus*. In the *Tractatus* Wittgenstein sought "the general form of propositions": what made propositions possible. He said that this general form is: "This is how things are"; the proposition was an articulated model, consisting of elements standing in a definite relation to each other. The proposition was true when there existed a corresponding arrangement of elements in reality. The proposition was capable of saying something

---

[12]   Ibid., p. 319.

because of the identity of structure, of logical form, in the proposition and in reality.

By the time Wittgenstein composed the *Investigations* he had come to reject the whole idea that there must be a general form of propositions. He emphasized the indefinite number of different uses that language may have and tried to show that these different uses neither need, nor in fact do, all have something in common, in the sense intended in the *Tractatus*. He also tried to show that what counts as "agreement or disagreement with reality" takes on as many different forms as there are different use of language and cannot, therefore, be taken as given *prior* to the detailed investigation of the use that is in question.

The *Tractatus* contains a remark strikingly like something that Evans-Pritchard says.

> *The limits of my language mean the limits of my world.* Logic fills the world: the limits of the world are also its limits. We cannot therefore say in logic: This and this there is in the world, and that there is not.
>
> For that would apparently presuppose that we exclude certain possibilities, and this cannot be the case since otherwise logic must get outside the limits of the world: that is, if it could consider these limits from the other side also.[13]

Evans-Pritchard discusses the phenomena of belief and scepticism, as they appear in Zande life. There *is* certainly widespread scepticism about certain things, for instance, about some of the powers claimed by witchdoctors or about the efficacy of certain magic medicines. But, he points out, such scepticism does not begin to overturn the mystical way of thinking, since it is necessarily expressed in terms belonging to that way of thinking.

> In this web of belief every strand depends on every other strand, and a Zande cannot get outside its meshes because this is the only world he knows. The web is not an external structure in which he is enclosed. It is the texture of his thought and he cannot think that his thought is wrong.[14]

Wittgenstein and Evans-Pritchard are concerned here with much the same problem, though the difference in the directions from which they approach it is important too. Wittgenstein, at the time of the *Tractatus*, spoke of "language", as if all language is fundamentally of the same kind and must have the same kind of "relation to reality"; but Evans-Pritchard is confronted by two languages which he recognizes as fundamentally different in kind, such that much of what may be expressed in the one has no possible counterpart in the other. One might, therefore, have expected this to lead to a position closer to that of the *Philosophical Investigations* than to that of the *Tractatus*. Evans-Pritchard is not content with elucidating the differences in the two concepts of reality involved; he wants to go further and say: our concept of reality is the correct one, the Azande are mistaken. But the difficulty is to see what "correct" and "mistaken" can mean in this context.

Let me return to the subject of contradictions. I have already noted that many contradictions we might expect to appear in fact do not in the context of Zande thought, where provision is made for avoiding them. But there are some situations of which this does not seem to be true, where what appear to us as obvious contradictions are left where they are, apparently unresolved. Perhaps this may be the foothold we are looking for, from which we can appraise the "correctness" of the Zande system.

Consider Zande notions about the inheritance of witchcraft. I have spoken so far only

[13]   Wittgenstein, *Tractatus Logico-Philosophicus*, 5. 6–5. 61.
[14]   Evans-Pritchard, op. cit., p. 194.

of the role of oracles in establishing whether or not someone is a witch. But there is a further and as we might think, more "direct" method of doing this, namely by post-mortem examination of a suspect's intestines for "witchcraft-substance". This may be arranged by his family after his death in an attempt to clear the family name of the imputation of witchcraft. Evans-Pritchard remarks: "To our minds it appears evident that if a man is proven a witch the whole of his clan are *ipso facto* witches, since the Zande clan is a group of persons related biologically to one another through the male line. Azande see the sense of this argument but they do not accept its conclusions, and it would involve the whole notion of witchcraft in contradiction were they to do so."[15] Contradiction would presumably arise because a few positive results of post-mortem examinations, scattered among all the clans, would very soon prove that everbody was a witch, and a few negative results, scattered among the same clans, would prove that nobody was a witch. Though, in particular situations, individual Azande may avoid personal implications arising out of the presence of witchcraft-substance in deceased relatives, by imputations of bastardy and similar devices, this would not be enough to save the generally contradictory situation I have sketched. Evans-Pritchard comments: "Azande do not perceive the contradiction as we perceive it because they have no theoretical interest in the subject, and those situations in which they express their belief in witchcraft do not force the problem upon them."[16]

It might now appear as though we had clear grounds for speaking of the superior rationality of European over Zande thought, in so far as the latter involves a contradiction which it makes no attempt to remove and does not

even recognize: one, however, which is recognizable as such in the context of European ways of thinking. But does Zande thought on this matter really involve a contradiction? It appears from Evans-Pritchard's account that Azande do not press their ways of thinking about witches to a point at which they would be involved in contradictions.

Someone may now want to say that the irrationality of the Azande in relation to witchcraft shows itself in the fact that they do not press their thought about it "to its logical conclusion". To appraise this point we must consider whether the conclusion we are trying to force on them is indeed a logical one; or perhaps better, whether someone who does press this conclusion is being more rational than the Azande, who do not. Some light is thrown on this question by Wittgenstein's discussion of a game.

> such that whoever begins can always win by a particular simple trick. But this has not been realized – so it is a game. Now someone draws our attention to it – and it stops being a game.
>
> What turn can I give this, to make it clear to myself? – For I want to say: "and it stops being a game" – not: "and now we see that it wasn't a game."
>
> That means, I want to say, it can also be taken like this: the other man did not *draw our attention* to anything; he taught us a different game in place of our own. But how can the new game have made the old one obsolete? We now see something different, and can no longer naïvely go on playing.
>
> On the one hand the game consisted in our actions (our play) on the board; and these actions I could perform as well now as before. But on the other hand it was essential to the game that I blindly tried to win; and now I can no longer do that.[17]

[15]   Ibid., p. 24.
[16]   Ibid., p.25.
[17]   L. Wittgenstein, *Remarks on the Foundations of Mathematics*, Pt. II, Para. 77. Wittgenstein's whole discussion of "contradiction" in mathematics is directly relevant to the point I am discussing.

There are obviously considerable analogies between Wittgenstein's example and the situation we are considering. But there is an equally important difference. Both Wittgenstein's games; the old one without the trick that enables the starter to win and the new one with the trick, are in an important sense on the same level. They are both *games*, in the form of a contest where the aim of a player is to beat his opponent by the exercise of skill. The new trick makes this situation impossible and this is why it makes the old game obsolete. To be sure, the situation could be saved in a way by introducing a new rule, forbidding the use by the starter of the trick which would ensure his victory. But our intellectual habits are such as to make us unhappy about the artificiality of such a device, rather as logicians have been unhappy about the introduction of a Theory of Types as a device for avoiding Russell's paradoxes. It is noteworthy in my last quotation from Evans-Pritchard however, that the Azande, when the possibility of this contradiction about the inheritance of witchcraft is pointed out to them, do *not* then come to regard their old beliefs about witchcraft as obsolete. "They have no theoretical interest in the subject." This suggests strongly that the context from which the suggestion about the contradiction is made, the context of our scientific culture, is not on the same level as the context in which the beliefs about witchcraft operate. Zande notions of witchcraft do not constitute a theoretical system in terms of which Azande try to gain a quasi-scientific understanding of the world.[18] This in its turn suggests that it is the European, obsessed with pressing Zande thought where it would not naturally go – to a contradiction – who is guilty of misunderstanding, not the Zande. The European is in fact committing a category-mistake.

Something else is also suggested by this

discussion: the forms in which rationality expresses itself in the culture of a human society cannot be elucidated *simply* in terms of the logical coherence of the rules according to which activities are carried out in that society. For as we have seen, there comes a point where we are not even in a position to determine what is and what is not coherent in such a context of rules, without raising questions about the point which following those rules has in the society. No doubt it was a realization of this fact which led Evans-Pritchard to appeal to a residual "correspondence with reality" in distinguishing between "mystical" and "scientific" notions. The conception of reality is indeed indispensable to any understanding of the point of a way of life. But it is not a conception which can be explicated as Evans-Pritchard tries to explicate it, in terms of what science reveals to be the case; for a form of the conception of reality must already be presupposed before we can make any sense of the expression "what science reveals to be the case."

2. Our Standards and Theirs

. . . In a discussion of Wittgenstein's philosophical use of language games[19] Mr Rush Rhees points out that to try to account for the meaningfulness of language solely in terms of isolated language games is to omit the important fact that ways of speaking are not insulated from each other in mutually exclusive systems of rules. What can be said in one context by the use of a certain expression depends for its sense on the uses of that expression in other contexts (different language games). Language games are played by men who have lives to live – lives involving a wide variety of different interests, which have all kinds of different bearings on each other. Because of

---

[18]   Notice that I have *not* said that Azande conceptions of witchcraft have nothing to do with understanding the world at all. The point is that a different form of the concept of understanding is involved here.

[19]   Rush Rhees, "Wittgenstein's Builders," *Proceedings of the Aristotelian Society*, vol. 20, 1960, pp. 171–86.

this, what a man says or does may make a difference not merely to the performance of the activity upon which he is at present engaged, but to his *life* and to the lives of other people. Whether a man sees point in what he is doing will then depend on whether he is able to see any unity in his multifarious interests, activities, and relations with other men; what sort of sense he sees in his life will depend on the nature of this unity. The ability to see this sort of sense in life depends not merely on the individual concerned, though this is not to say it does not depend on him at all; it depends also on the possibilities for making such sense which the culture in which he lives does, or does not, provide.

What we may learn by studying other cultures are not merely possibilities of different ways of doing things, other techniques. More importantly we may learn different possibilities of making sense of human life, different ideas about the possible importance that the carrying out of certain activities may take on for a man, trying to contemplate the sense of his life as a whole. This dimension of the matter is precisely what MacIntyre misses in his treatment of Zande magic; he can see in it only a (misguided) technique for producing consumer goods. But a Zande's crops are not just potential objects of consumption: the life he lives, his relations with his fellows, his chances for acting decently or doing evil, may all spring from his relation to his crops. Magical rites constitute a form of expression in which these possibilities and dangers may be contemplated and reflected on – and perhaps also thereby transformed and deepened. The difficulty we find in understanding this is not merely its remoteness from science, but an aspect of the general difficulty we find, illustrated by MacIntyre's procedure, of thinking about such matters at all except in terms of "efficiency of production" – production, that is, for consumption. This again is a symptom of what Marx called the "alienation" characteristic of

man in industrial society, though Marx's own confusions about the relations between production and consumption are further symptoms of that same alienation. Our blindness to the point of primitive modes of life is a corollary of the pointlessness of much of our own life.

I have now explicitly linked my discussion of the "point" of a system of conventions with conceptions of good and evil. My aim is not to engage in moralizing, but to suggest that the concept of *learning from* which is involved in the study of other cultures is closely linked with the concept of *wisdom*. We are confronted not just with different techniques, but with new possibilities of good and evil, in relation to which men may come to terms with life. An investigation into this dimension of a society may indeed require a quite detailed inquiry into alternative techniques (e.g., of production), but an inquiry conducted for the light it throws on those possibilities of good and evil. A very good example of the kind of thing I mean is Simone Weil's analysis of the techniques of modern factory production in *Oppression and Liberty*, which is not a contribution to business management, but part of an inquiry into the peculiar form which the evil of oppression takes in our culture.

In saying this, however, I may seem merely to have lifted to a new level the difficulty raised by MacIntyre of how to relate our own conceptions of rationality to those of other societies. here the difficulty concerns the relation between our own conceptions of good and evil and those of other societies. A full investigation would thus require a discussion of ethical relativism at this point. I have tried to show some of the limitations of relativism in an earlier paper.[20] I shall close the chapter with some remarks which are supplementary to that.

I wish to point out that the very conception of human life involves certain fundamental notions – which I shall call "limiting notions"

---

[20] Peter Winch, "Nature and Convention," *Proceedings of the Aristotelian Society*, vol. 20, 1960, pp. 231–52.

– which have an obvious ethical dimension, and which indeed in a sense determine the "ethical space", within which the possibilities of good and evil in human life can be exercised. The notions which I shall discuss very briefly here correspond closely to those which Vico made the foundation of his idea of natural law, on which he thought the possibility of understanding human history rested: birth, death, sexual relations. Their significance here is that they are inescapably involved in the life of all known human societies in a way which gives us a clue where to look, if we are puzzled about the point of an alien system of institutions. The specific forms which these concepts take, the particular institutions in which they are expressed, vary very considerably from one society to another; but their central position within a society's institutions is and must be a constant factor. In trying to understand the life of an alien society, then, it will be of the utmost importance to be clear about the way in which these notions enter into it. The actual practice of social anthropologists bears this out, although I do not know how many of them would attach the same kind of importance to them as I do.

I speak of a "limit" here because these notions, along no doubt with others, give shape to what we understand by "human life," and because a concern with questions posed in terms of them seems to me constitutive of what we understand by the "morality" of a society. In saying this, I am of course, disagreeing with those moral philosophers who have made attitudes of approval and disapproval, or something similar, fundamental in ethics, and who have held that the *objects* of such attitudes were conceptually irrelevant to the conception of morality. On that view, there might be a society where the sorts of attitude taken up in *our* society to questions about relations between the sexes were reserved, say for questions about the length people wear their hair, and *vice versa*. This seems to me incoherent.

In the first place, there would be a confusion in *calling* a concern of that sort a "moral" concern, however passionately felt. The story of Samson in the Old Testament confirms rather than refutes this point, for the interdict on the cutting of Samson's hair is, of course, connected there with much else: and preeminently, it should be noted, with questions about sexual relations. But secondly, if that is thought to be merely verbal quibbling, I will say that it does not seem to me a merely conventional matter that T. S. Eliot's trinity of "birth, copulation and death" happen to be such deep objects of human concern. I do not mean that they are made such by fundamental psychological and sociological forces, though that is no doubt true. But I want to say further that the very notion of human life is limited by these conceptions.

Unlike beasts, men do not merely live but also have a conception of life. This is not something that is simply added to their life; rather, it changes the very sense which the word "life" has, when applied to men. It is no longer equivalent to "animate existence." When we are speaking of the life of man, we can ask questions about what is the right way to live, what things are most important in life, whether life has any significance, and if so what.

To have a conception of life is also to have a conception of death. But just as the "life" that is here in question is not the same as animate existence, so the "death" that is here in question is not the same as the end of animate existence. My conception of the death of an animal is of an event that will take place in the world; perhaps I shall observe it – and my life will go on. But when I speak of "my death," I am not speaking of a future event in my life;[21] I am not even speaking of an event in anyone else's life. I am speaking of the cessation of my world. That is also a cessation of my ability to do good or evil. It is not just that *as a matter of fact* I shall no longer be able to do good or evil

---

[21]   Cf. Wittgenstein, *Tractatus Logico-Philosophicus*, 6.431–6.4311.

after I am dead; the point is that my very *concept* of what it is to be able to do good or evil is deeply bound up with my concept of my life as ending in death. If ethics is a concern with the right way to live, then clearly the nature of this concern must be deeply affected by the concept of life as ending in death. One's attitude to one's life is at the same time an attitude to one's death.

This point is very well illustrated in an anthropological datum which MacIntyre confesses himself unable to make any sense of.

> According to Spencer and Gillen some aborigines carry about a stick or stone which is treated *as if* it is or embodies the soul of the individual who carries it. If the stick or stone is lost, the individual anoints himself as the dead are anointed. Does the concept of "carrying one's soul about with one" make sense? Of course we can redescribe what the aborigines are doing and transform it into sense, and perhaps Spencer and Gillen (and Durkheim who follows them) misdescribe what occurs. But if their reports are not erroneous, we confront a blank wall here, so far as meaning is concerned, although it is easy to give the rules for the use of the concept.[22]

MacIntyre does not say why he regards the concept of carrying one's soul about with one in a stick "thoroughly incoherent." He is presumably influenced by the fact that it would be hard to make sense of an action like this if performed by a twentieth-century Englishman or American; and by the fact that the soul is not a material object like a piece of paper and cannot, therefore, be carried about in a stick as a piece of paper might be. But it does not seem to me as hard to see sense in the practice, even from the little we are told about it here. Consider that a lover in our society may carry about a picture or lock of hair of the beloved; that this may symbolize for him his

relation to the beloved and may, indeed, change the relation in all sorts of ways: for example, strengthening it or perverting it. Suppose that when the lover loses the locket he feels guilty and asks his beloved for her forgiveness: there might be a parallel here to the aboriginal's practice of anointing himself when he "loses his soul." And is there necessarily anything irrational about either of these practices? Why should the lover not regard his carelessness in losing the locket as a sort of betrayal of the beloved? Remember how husbands and wives may feel about the loss of a wedding ring. The aborigine is clearly expressing a concern with his life as a whole in this practice; the anointing shows the close connection between such a concern and contemplation of death. Perhaps it is precisely this practice which makes such a concern possible for him, as religious sacraments make certain sorts of concern possible. The point is that a concern with one's life as a whole, involving as it does the limiting conception of one's death, if it is to be expressed *within* a person's life, can necessarily only be expressed quasi-sacramentally. The form of the concern shows itself in the form of the sacrament.

The sense in which I spoke also of sex as a "limiting concept" again has to do with the concept of a human life. The life of a man is a man's life and the life of a woman is a woman's life: the masculinity or the femininity are not just *components* in the life, they are its *mode*. Adapting Wittgenstein's remark about death, I might say that my masculinity is not an experience in the world, but my way of experiencing the world. Now the concepts of masculinity and femininity obviously require each other. A man is a man in relation to women; and a woman is a woman in relation to men.[23] Thus the form taken by man's relation to women is of quite fundamental importance for the significance he can attach to his own

[22] Alasdair MacIntyre *Is Understanding Religion Compatible with Believing?* read to the Segsquicentennial Seminar of the Princeton Theological Seminar (1962).

[23] These relations, however, are not simple converses. See Georg Simmel, "Das Relative und das Absolute im Geschlechter-Problem" in *Philosophische Kultur*, Leipzig, 1911.

life. The vulgar identification of morality with sexual morality certainly *is* vulgar; but it is a vulgarization of an important truth.

The limiting character of the concept of birth is obviously related to the points I have sketched regarding death and sex. On the one hand, my birth is no more an event in my life than is my death; and through my birth ethical limits are set for my life quite independently of my will: I am, from the outset, in specific relations to other people, from which obligations spring which cannot but be ethically fundamental.[24] On the other hand, the concept of birth is fundamentally linked to that of relations between the sexes. This remains true, however much or little may be known in a society about the contribution of males and females to procreation; for it remains true that man is born of woman, not of man. This, then, adds a new dimension to the ethical institutions in which relations between the sexes are expressed.

I have tried to do no more, in these last brief remarks, than to focus attention in a certain direction. I have wanted to indicate that forms of these limiting concepts will necessarily be an important feature of any human society and that conceptions of good and evil in human life will necessarily be connected with such concepts. In any attempt to understand the life of another society, therefore, an investigation of the forms taken by such concepts – their role in the life of the society – must always take a central place and provide a basis on which understanding may be built.

Now since the world of nations has been made by men, let us see in what institutions men agree and always have agreed. For these institutions will be able to give us the universal and eternal principles (such as every science must have) on which all nations were founded and still preserve themselves.

We observe that all nations, barbarous as well as civilized, though separately founded because remote from each other in time and space, keep these three human customs: all have some religion, all contract solemn marriages, all bury their dead. And in no nation, however savage and crude, are any human actions performed with more elaborate ceremonies and more sacred solemnity than the rites of religion, marriage and burial. For by the axiom that "uniform ideas, born among peoples unknown to each other, must have a common ground of truth", it must have been dictated to all nations that from these institutions humanity began among them all, and therefore they must be most devoutly guarded by them all, so that the world should not again become a bestial wilderness. For this reason we have taken these three eternal and universal customs as the first principles of this Science.[25]

---

[24] For this reason, among others, I think A. I. Melden is wrong to say that present-child obligations and rights have nothing directly to do with physical genealogy. Cf. Melden, *Rights and Right Conduct*. Oxford: Blackwell, 1959.
[25] Giambattista Vico, *The New Science*, paras. 332–333.

19

African Traditional Thought and Western Science

ROBIN HORTON

The "Closed" and "Open" Predicaments

Turning to the differences in African thought and Western science, I start by isolating one which strikes me as the key to all the others, and go on to suggest how the latter flow from it.

What I take to be the key difference is a very simple one. It is that in traditional cultures there is no developed awareness of alternatives to the established body of theoretical tenets; whereas in scientifically oriented cultures, such an awareness is highly developed. It is this difference we refer to when we say that traditional cultures are "closed" and scientifically oriented cultures "open."[1]

One important consequence of the lack of awareness of alternatives is very clearly spelled out by Evans-Pritchard in his pioneering work on Azande witchcraft beliefs. Thus he says:

> I have attempted to show how rhythm, mode of utterance, content of prophecies, and so forth, assist in creating faith in witch-doctors, but these are only some of the ways in which faith is supported, and do not entirely explain belief. Weight of tradition alone can do that . . . There is no incentive to agnosticism. All their beliefs hang together, and were a Zande to give up faith in witch-doctorhood, he would have to surrender equally his faith in witchcraft and oracles . . . In this web of belief every strand depends upon every other strand, *and a Zande cannot get out of its meshes because it is the only world he knows. The web is not an external structure in which he is enclosed. It is the texture of his thought and he cannot think that his thought is wrong.*[2]

And again:

---

[1] Philosophically minded readers will notice here some affinities with Karl Popper, who also makes the transition from a "closed" to an "open" predicament crucial for the take-off from tradition to science. For me, however, Popper obscures the issue by packing too many contracts into his definitions of "closed" and "open." Thus, for him, the transition from one predicament to the other implies not just a growth in the awareness of alternatives, but also a transition from communalism to individualism, and from ascribed status to achieved status. But as I hope to show in this essay, it is the awareness of alternatives which is crucial for the take-off into science. Not individualism or achieved status: for there are lots of societies where both of the latter are well developed, but which show no signs whatever of take-off. In the present context, therefore, my own narrower definition of "closed" and "open" seems more appropriate.

[2] E. E. Evans-Pritchard, *Witchcraft, Oracles and Magic among the Azande*, Oxford, 1936, p. 194. (See Chapter 17, this volume, for an excerpt from this book.)

And yet Azande do not see that their oracles tell them nothing! Their blindness is not due to stupidity, for they display great ingenuity in explaining away the failure and inequalities of the poison oracle and experimental keenness in testing it. It is due rather to the fact that their intellectual ingenuity and experimental keenness are conditioned by patterns of ritual behaviour and mystical belief. Within the limits set by these patterns, they show great intelligence, but it cannot operate beyond these limits. Or, to put it in another way; *they reason excellently in the idiom of their beliefs, but they cannot reason outside, or against their beliefs because they have no other idiom in which to express their thoughts.*[3]

In other words, absence of any awareness of alternatives makes for an absolute acceptance of the established theoretical tenets, and removes any possibility of questioning them. In these circumstances, the established tenets invest the believer with a compelling force. It is this force which we refer to when we talk of such tenets as sacred.

A second important consequence of lack of awareness of alternatives is that any challenge to established tenets is a threat of chaos, of the cosmic abyss, and therefore evokes intense anxiety.

With developing awareness of alternatives, the established theoretical tenets come to seem less absolute in their validity, and lose something of their sacredness. At the same time, a challenge to these tenets is no longer a horrific threat of chaos. For just as the tenets themselves have lost some of their absolute validity, a challenge to them is no longer a threat of absolute calamity. It can now be seen as nothing more threatening than an intimation that new tenets might profitably be tried. Where these conditions begin to prevail, the stage is set for change from a traditional to a scientific outlook.

Here, then, we have two basic predicaments: the "closed" – characterized by lack of awareness of alternatives, sacredness of beliefs, and anxiety about threats to them; and the "open" – characterized by awareness of alternatives, diminished sacredness of beliefs, and diminished anxiety about threats to them.

Now, as I have said, I believe all the major differences between traditional and scientific outlooks can be understood in terms of these two predicaments. In substantiating this, I should like to divide the differences into two grounds: those directly connected with the presence of absence of a vision of alternatives; and those directly connected with the presence or absence of anxiety about threats to the established beliefs.[4]

Differences Connected With the Presence or Absence of a Vision of Alternatives

(a) Magical versus non-magical attitude to words

A central characteristic of nearly all the traditional African world-views we know of is an assumption about the power of words, uttered under appropriate circumstances, to bring into being the events or states they stand for.

The most striking examples of this assumption are to be found in creation mythologies where the supreme being is said to have formed the world out of chaos by uttering the names of all things in it. Such mythologies occur most notably in Ancient Egypt and among the peoples of the Western Sudan.

In traditional African cultures, to know the name of a being or thing is to have some

---

[3]   Ibid., p. 338.
[4]   In this abridged version of the paper only the former are discussed. For a discussion of differences connected with anxiety about threats to established beliefs the reader is referred to the original version of the paper, in *Africa*, XXVII, No. 2, esp. pp. 167ff.

degree of control over it. In the invocation of spirits, it is essential to call their names correctly; and the control which such correct calling gives is one reason why the true or "deep" names of gods are often withheld from strangers, and their utterance forbidden to all but a few whose business it is to use them in ritual. Similar ideas lie behind the very widespread traditional practice of using euphemisms to refer to such things as dangerous diseases and wild animals: for it is thought that use of the real names might secure their presence. Yet again, it is widely believed that harm can be done to a man by various operations performed in his name – for instance, by writing his name on a piece of paper and burning it.

Through a very wide range of traditional African belief and activity, it is possible to see an implicit assumption as to the magical power of words.

Now if we take into account what I have called the basic predicament of the traditional thinker, we can begin to see why this assumption should be so deeply entrenched in his daily life and thought. Briefly, no man can make contact with reality save through a screen of words. Hence no man can escape the tendency to see a unique and intimate link between words and things. For the traditional thinker this tendency has an overwhelming power. Since he can imagine no alternative to his established system of concepts and words, the latter appear bound to reality in an absolute fashion. There is no way at all in which they can be seen as varying independently of the segments of reality they stand for. Hence they appear so integrally involved with their referents that any manipulation of the one self-evidently affects the other.

The scientist's attitude to words is, of course, quite opposite. He dismisses contemptuously any suggestion that words could have an immediate, magical power over the things they stand for. Indeed, he finds magical notions amongst the most absurd and alien

trappings of traditional thought. Though he grants an enormous power to words, it is the indirect power of bringing control over things through the functions of explanation and prediction.

Why does the scientist reject the magician's view of the words? One easy answer is that he has come to know better: magical behaviour has been found not to produce the results it claims to. Perhaps. But what scientist has ever bothered to put magic to the test? The answer is, none; because there are deeper grounds for rejection – grounds which made the idea of testing beside the point.

To see what these grounds are, let us return to the scientist's basic predicament – to his awareness of alternative idea-systems whose ways of classifying and interpreting the world are very different from his own. Now this changed awareness gives him two intellectual possibilities. Both are eminently thinkable; but one is intolerable, the other hopeful.

The first possibility is simply a continuance of the magical worldview. If ideas and words are inextricably bound up with reality, and if indeed they shape it and control it, then, a multiplicity of idea-systems means a multiplicity of realities, and a change of ideas means a change of things. But whereas there is nothing particularly absurd or inconsistent about this view, it is clearly intolerable in the extreme. For it means that the world is in the last analysis dependent on human whim, that the search for order is a folly, and that human beings can expect to find no sort of anchor in reality.

The second possibility takes hold as an escape from this horrific prospect. It is based on the faith that while ideas and words change, there must be some anchor, some constant reality. This faith leads to the modern view of words and reality as independent variables. With its advent, words come "unstuck from" reality and are no longer seen as acting magically upon it. Intellectually, this second possibility is neither more nor less respectable than the first. But it has the great advantage of being tolerable whilst the first is horrific.

That the outlook behind magic still remains an intellectual possibility in the scientifically oriented cultures of the modern West can be seen from its survival as a nagging undercurrent in the last 300 years of Western philosophy. This undercurrent generally goes under the labels of "Idealism" and "Solipsism"; and under these labels it is not immediately recognizable. But a deeper scrutiny reveals that the old outlook is there all right – albeit in a strange guise. True, Idealism does not say that words create, sustain, and have power over that which they represent. Rather, it says that material things are "in the mind". That is, the mind creates, sustains, and has power over matter. But the second view is little more than a post-Cartesian transposition of the first. Let me elaborate. Both in traditional African cosmologies and in European cosmologies before Descartes, the modern distinction between "mind" and "matter" does not appear. Although everything in the universe is underpinned by spiritual forces, what moderns would call "mental activities" and "material things" are both part of a single reality, neither material nor immaterial. Thinking, conceiving, saying, etc. are described in terms of organs like heart and brain and actions like the uttering of words. Now when Descartes wrote his philosophical works, he crystallized a half-way phase in the transition from a personal to an impersonal cosmological idiom. Whilst "higher" human activities still remained under the aegis of a personalized theory, physical and biological events were brought under the aegis of impersonal theory. Hence thinking, conceiving, saying, etc. became manifestations of "mind", whilst all other happenings became manifestations of "matter". Hence whereas before Descartes we have "words over things", after him we have "mind over matter" – just a new disguise for the old view.

What I have said about this view being intellectually respectable but emotionally intolerable is borne out by the attitude to it of modern Western philosophers. Since they are duty bound to explore all the alternative possibilities of thought that lie within the grasp of their imaginations, these philosophers mention, nay even expound, the doctrines of Idealism and Solipsism. Invariably, too, they follow up their expositions with attempts at refutation. But such attempts are, just as invariably, a farce. Their character is summed up in G. E. Moore's desperate gesture, when challenged to prove the existence of a world outside his mind, of banging his hand with his fist and exclaiming: "It is there!" A gesture of faith rather than of reason, if ever there was one!

With the change from the "closed" to the "open" predicament, then, the outlook behind magic becomes intolerable; and to escape from it people espouse the view that words vary independently of reality. Smug rationalists who congratulate themselves on their freedom from magical thinking would do well to reflect on the nature of this freedom!

(b) Ideas-bound-to-occasions versus ideas-bound-to-ideas

Many commentators on the idea-systems of traditional African cultures have stressed that, for members of these cultures, their thought does not appear as something distinct from and opposable to the realities that call it into action. Rather, particular passages of thought are bound to the particular occasions that evoke them.

Let us take an example. Someone becomes sick. The sickness proves intractable and the relatives call a diviner. The latter says the sickness is due to an ancestor who has been angered by the patient's bad behaviour towards his kinsmen. The diviner prescribes placatory offerings to the spirit and reconciliation with the kinsmen, and the patient is eventually cured. Now while this emergency is on, both the diviner and the patient's relatives may justify what they are doing by reference to some general statements about the kinds of circumstance which arouse ancestors to cause sickness. But theoretical statements of this kind are very much matters of occasion, not likely to be heard out of context or as part of a general discussion of "what we believe."

If ideas in traditional culture are seen as bound to occasions rather than to other ideas, the reason is one that we have already given in our discussion of magic. Since the member of such a culture can imagine no alternatives to his established system of ideas, the latter appear inexorably bound to the portions of reality they stand for. They cannot be seen as in any way opposable to reality.

In a scientifically oriented culture such as that of the Western anthropologist, things are very different. The very word "idea" has the connotation of something opposed to reality. Nor is it entirely coincidental that in such a culture the historian of ideas is considered to be the most unrealistic kind of historian. Not only are ideas dissociated in people's minds from the reality that occasions them: they are bound to other ideas, to form wholes and systems perceived as such. Belief-systems take shape not only as abstractions in the minds of anthropologists, but also as totalities in the minds of believers.

Here again, this change can be readily understood in terms of a change from the "closed" to the "open" predicament. A vision of alternative possibilities forces men to the faith that ideas somehow vary whilst reality remains constant. Ideas thus become detached from reality – nay, even in a sense opposed to it. Furthermore, such a vision, by giving the thinker an opportunity to "get outside" his own system, offers him a possibility of his coming to see it *as a system.*

(c) Unreflective versus reflective thinking

At this stage of the analysis there is no need for me to insist further on the essential rationality of traditional thought. I have already made it

far too rational for the taste of most social anthropologists. And yet, there is a sense in which this thought includes among its accomplishments neither logic or Philosophy.

Let me explain this, at first sight, rather shocking statement. It is true that most African traditional world-views are logically elaborated to a high degree. It is also true that, because of their eminently rational character, they are appropriately called "philosophies." But here I am using "Logic" and "Philosophy" in a more exact sense. By Logic, I mean thinking directed to answering the question: "What are the general rules by which we can distinguish good arguments from bad ones?" And by Philosophy, I mean thinking directed to answering the question: "On what grounds can we ever claim to know anything about the world?" Now Logic and Philosophy, in these restricted senses, are poorly developed in traditional Africa. Despite its elaborate and often penetrating cosmological, sociological, and psychological speculations, traditional thought has tended to get on with the work of explanation, without pausing for reflection upon the nature or rules of this work. Thinking once more of the "closed" predicament, we can readily see why these second-order intellectual activities should be virtually absent from traditional cultures. Briefly, the traditional thinker, because he is unable to imagine possible alternatives to his established theories and classifications, can never start to formulate generalized norms of reasoning and knowing. For only where there are alternatives can there be choice, and only where there is choice can there be norms governing it. As they are characteristically absent in traditional cultures, so Logic and Philosophy are characteristically present in all scientifically oriented cultures. Just as the "closed" predicament makes it impossible for them to appear, so the "open" predicament makes it inevitable that they must appear. For where the thinker can see the possibility of alternatives to his established idea-system, the question of choice at once arises, and the development of norms governing such choice cannot be far behind.[5]

(d) Mixed versus segregated motives

This contrast is very closely related to the preceding one. The goals of explanation and prediction are as powerfully present in traditional African cultures as they are in cultures where science has become institutionalized. In the absence of explicit norms of thought, however, we find them vigorously pursued but not explicitly reflected upon and defined. In these circumstances, there is little thought about their consistency or inconsistency with other goals and motives. Hence wherever we find a theoretical system with explanatory and predictive functions, we find other motives entering in the contributing to its development.

Despite their cognitive preoccupations, most African religious systems are powerfully influenced by what are commonly called "emotional needs" – i.e. needs for certain kinds of personal relationship. In Africa, as elsewhere, all social systems stimulate in their members a considerable diversity of such needs; but, having stimulated them, they often prove unwilling or unable to allow them full opportunities for satisfaction. In such situations the spirits function not only as theoretical entities but as surrogate people providing opportunities for the formation of ties forbidden in the purely human social field. The latter function they discharge in two ways. First, by providing non-human partners with whom people can take up relationships forbidden with other human beings. Second, though the mechanism of possession, by allowing people to "become" spirits and so to play roles *vis-à-vis* their fellow men which they are debarred from playing as ordinary human beings.

There is little doubt that because the theoretical entities of traditional thought happen to be people, they give particular scope for the working of emotional and aesthetic motives. Here, perhaps, we do have something about the personal idiom in theory that does militate indirectly against the taking up of a scientific attitude; for where there are powerful emotional and aesthetic loadings on a particular theoretical scheme, these must add to the difficulties of abandoning this scheme when cognitive goals press towards doing so. Once again, I should like to stress that the mere fact of switching from a personal to an impersonal idiom does not make anyone a scientist, and that one can be unscientific or scientific in either idiom. In this respect, nevertheless, the personal idiom does seem to present certain difficulties for the scientific attitude which the impersonal idiom does not.

Where the possibility of choice has stimulated the development of Logic, Philosophy, and norms of thought generally, the situation undergoes radical change. One theory is judged better than another with explicit reference to its efficacy in explanation and prediction. And as these ends become more clearly defined, it gets increasingly evident that no other ends are compatible with them. People come to see that if ideas are to be used as efficient tools of explanation and prediction, they must not be allowed to become tools of anything else. (This, of course, is the essence of the ideal of "objectivity.") Hence there grows up a great watchfulness against seduction by the emotional or aesthetic appeal of a theory.

---

[5] See Ernest Gellner, *Thought and Change*, London, 1964, for a similar point exemplified in the Philosophy of Descartes p. 105.

Differences Connected with the Presence or Absence of Anxiety about Threats to the Established Body of Theory

(e) Protective versus destructive attitude towards established theory

Both in traditional Africa and in the science-oriented West, theoretical thought is vitally concerned with the prediction of events. But there are marked differences in reaction to predictive failure.

In the theoretical thought of the traditional cultures, there is a notable reluctance to register repeated failures of prediction and to act by attacking the beliefs involved. Instead, other current beliefs are utilized in such a way as to "excuse" each failure as it occurs, and hence to protect the major theoretical assumptions on which prediction is based. This use of *ad hoc* excuses is a phenomenon which social anthropologists have christened "secondary elaboration".[6]

The process of secondary elaboration is most readily seen in association with the work of diviners and oracle-operators, who are concerned with discovering the identity of the spiritual forces responsible for particular happenings in the visible, tangible world, and the reasons for their activation. Typically, a sick man goes to a diviner, and is told that a certain spiritual agency is "worrying" him. The diviner points to certain of his past actions as having excited the spirit's anger, and indicates certain remedial actions which will appease this anger and restore health. Should the client take the recommended remedial action and yet see no improvement, he will be likely to conclude that the diviner was either fraudulent or just incompetent, and to seek out another expert. The new diviner will generally point to another spiritual agency and

another set of arousing circumstances as responsible for the man's condition, and will recommend fresh remedial action. In addition, he will probably provide some explanation of why the previous diviner failed to get at the truth. He may corroborate the client's suspicions of fraud, or he may say that the spirit involved maliciously "hid itself behind" another in such a way that only the most skilled of diviners would have been able to detect it. If after this the client should still see no improvement in his condition, he will move on to yet another diviner – and so on, perhaps, until his troubles culminate in death.

What is notable in all this is that the client never takes his repeated failures as evidence against the existence of the various spiritual beings named as responsible for his plight, or as evidence against the possibility of making contact with such beings as diviners claim to do. Nor do members of the wider community in which he lives ever try to keep track of the proportion of successes to failures in the remedial actions based on their beliefs, with the aim of questioning these beliefs. At most, they grumble about the dishonesty and wiles of many diviners, whilst maintaining their faith in the existence of some honest, competent practitioners.

In these traditional cultures, questioning of the beliefs on which divining is based and weighing up of successes against failures are just not among the paths that thought can take. They are blocked paths because the thinkers involved are victims of the closed predicament. For them, established beliefs have an absolute validity, and any threat to such beliefs is a horrific threat of chaos. Who is going to jump from the cosmic palm-tree when there is no hope of another perch to swing to?

Where the scientific outlook has become firmly entrenched, attitudes to established beliefs are very different. Much has been

---

[6]　The idea of secondary elaboration as a key feature of prescientific thought-systems was put forward with great brilliance and insight by Evans-Pritchard in his *Witchcraft, Oracles and Magic*. All subsequent discussions, including the present one, are heavily indebted to his lead.

made of the scientist's essential scepticism towards establishing beliefs; and one must, I think, agree that this above all is what distinguishes him from the traditional thinker. But one must be careful here. The picture of the scientist in continuous readiness to scrap or demote established theory contains a dangerous exaggeration as well as an important truth. As an outstanding modern historian of the sciences has recently observed,[7] the typical scientist spends most of his time optimistically seeing how far he can push a new theory to cover an ever-widening horizon of experience. When he has difficulty in making the theory "fit", he is more likely to develop it than to scrap it out of hand. And if it does palpably fail the occasional test, he may even put the failure down to dirty apparatus or mistaken meter-reading – rather like the oracle operator! And yet, the spirit behind the scientist's action *is* very different. His pushing of a theory and his reluctance to scrap it are not due to any chilling intuition that if his theory fails him, chaos is at hand. Rather, they are due to the very knowledge that the theory is not something timeless and absolute. Precisely because he knows that the present theory came in at a certain epoch to replace a predecessor, and that its explanatory coverage is far better than that of the predecessor, he is reluctant to throw it away before giving it the benefit of every doubt, but this same knowledge makes for an acceptance of the theory which is far more qualified and far more watchful than that of the traditional thinker. The scientist is, as it were, always keeping account, balancing the successes of a theory against its failures. And when the failures start to come thick and fast, defence of the theory switches inexorably to attack on it.

If the record of a theory that has fallen under a cloud is poor in all circumstances, it is ruthlessly scrapped. The collective memory of the European scientific community is littered with the wreckage of the various unsatisfactory theories discarded over the last 500 years – the earth-centred theory of the universe, the circular theory of planetary motion, the phlogiston theory of chemical combination, the aether theory of wave propagation, and perhaps a hundred others. Often, however, it is found that a theoretical model once assumed to have universal validity in fact has a good predictive performance over a limited range of circumstances, but a poor performance outside this range. In such a case, the beliefs in question are still ruthlessly demoted; but instead of being thrown out altogether they are given a lesser status as limiting cases of more embracing generalities – still useful as lower-level models as or guides to experience within restricted areas. This sort of demotion has been the fate of theoretical schemes like Newton's Laws of Motion (still used as a guide in many mundane affairs, including much of the business of modern rocketry) and the "Ball-and-Bond" theory of chemical combination.

This underlying readiness to scrap or demote established theories on the ground of poor predictive performance is perhaps the most important single feature of the scientific attitude. It is, I suggest, a direct outcome of the "open" predicament. For only when the thinker is able to see his established idea-system as one among many alternatives can he see his established ideas as things of less than absolute value. And only when he sees them thus can he see the scrapping of them as anything other than a horrific, irretrievable jump into chaos.

(f) Protective versus destructive attitude to the category-system

If someone is asked to list typical features of traditional thinking, he is almost certain to mention the phenomenon known as "taboo." "Taboo" is the anthropological jargon for a

---

[7] T. Kuhn, *The Structure of Scientific Revolutions*, Chicago, 1962.

reaction of horror and aversion to certain actions or happenings which are seen as monstrous and polluting. It is characteristic of the taboo reaction that people are unable to justify it in terms of ulterior reasons: tabooed events are simply bad in themselves. People take every possible step to prevent tabooed events from happening, and to isolate or expel them when they do occur.

Taboo has long been a mystery to anthropologists. Of the many explanations proposed, few have fitted more than a small selection of the instances observed. It is only recently that an anthropologist has placed the phenomenon in a more satisfactory perspective by the observation that in nearly every case of taboo reaction, the events and actions involved are ones which seriously defy the established lines of classification in the culture where they occur.[8]

Perhaps the most important occasion of taboo reaction in traditional African cultures is the commission of incest. Incest is one of the most flagrant defiances of the established category-system: for he who commits it treats a mother, daughter, or sister like a wife. Another common occasion for taboo reaction is the birth of twins. Here, the category distinction involved is that of human beings versus animals – multiple births being taken as characteristic of animals as opposed to men. Yet another very generally tabooed object is the human corpse, which occupies, as it were, a classificatory no-man's land between the living and the inanimate. Equally widely tabooed are such human bodily excreta as faeces and menstrual blood, which occupy the same no-man's land between the living and the inanimate.

Taboo reactions are often given to occur-rences that are radically strange or new; for these too (almost by definition) fail to fit in to the established category system. A good example is furnished by a Kalabari story of the coming of the Europeans. The first white man, it is said, was seen by a fisherman who had gone down to the mouth of the estuary in his canoe. Panic-stricken, he raced home and told his people what he had seen: whereupon he and the rest of the town set out to purify themselves – that is, to rid themselves of the influence of the strange and monstrous thing that had intruded into their world.

A sort of global taboo reaction is often evoked by foreign lands. As the domains of so much that is strange and unassimilable to one's own categories, such lands are the abode *par excellence* of the monstrous and the abominable. The most vivid description we have of this is that given for the Lugbara by John Middleton.[9] For this East African people, the foreigner is the inverted perpetrator of all imaginable abominations from incest downwards. The more alien he is, the more abominable. Though the Lugbara attitude is extreme, many traditional cultures would seem to echo it in some degree.[10]

Just as the central tenets of the traditional theoretical system are defended against adverse experience by an elaborate array of excuses for predictive failure, so too the main classificatory distinctions of the system are defended by taboo avoidance reactions against any event that defies them. Since every system of belief implies a system of categories, and vice versa, secondary elaboration and taboo reaction are really opposite sides of the same coin.

From all this it follows that, like secondary elaboration, taboo reaction has no place among

---

[8]   This observation may well prove to be a milestone in our understanding of traditional thought. It was first made some years ago by Mary Douglas, who has developed many of its implications in her book *Purity and Danger*. Though we clearly disagree on certain wider implications, the present discussion is deeply indebted to her insights.

[9]   Middleton, op. cit.

[10]   This association of foreign lands with chaos and pollution seems to be a universal of prescientific thought-systems. For this, see Mircea Eliade, *The Sacred and the Profane*, New York, 1961, esp. Chapter I.

the reflexes of the scientist. For him, whatever defies or fails to fit in to the established category-system is not something horrifying, to be isolated or expelled. On the contrary, it is an intriguing "phenomenon" – a starting point and a challenge for the invention of new classifications and new theories. It is something every young research worker would like to have crop up in his field of observation – perhaps the first rung on the ladder of fame. If a biologist ever came across a child born with the head of a goat, he would be hard put to it to make his compassion cover his elation. And as for social anthropologists, one may guess that their secret dreams are of finding a whole community of men who sleep for preference with their mothers!

(g) The passage of time: bad or good?

In traditional Africa, methods of time-reckoning vary greatly from culture to culture. Within each culture, again, we find a plurality of time-scales used in different contexts. Thus there may be a major scale which locates events either before, during, or after the time of founding of the major institutions of the community: another scale which locates events by correlating them with the life-time of deceased ancestors: yet another which locates events by correlating them with the phases of the seasonal cycle: and yet another which uses phases of the daily cycle.

Although these scales are seldom inter-related in any systematic way, they all serve to order events in before–after series. Further, they have the very general characteristic that vis-à-vis "after," "before" is usually valued positively, sometimes neutrally, and never negatively. Whatever the particular scale involved, then, the passage of time is seen as something deleterious or at best neutral.

Perhaps the most widespread, everyday instance of this attitude is the standard justification of so much thought and action: "That is what the old-time people told us." (It is usually this standard justification which is in the forefront of the anthropologist's mind when he applies the label "traditional culture.")

On the major time-scale of the typical traditional culture, things are thought of as having been better in the golden age of the founding heroes than they are today. On an important minor time-scale, the annual one, the end of the year is a time when everything in the cosmos is run-down and sluggish, overcome by an accumulation of defilement and pollution.

A corollary of this attitude to time is a rich development of activities designed to negate its passage by a "return to the beginning." Such activities characteristically depend on the magical premise that a symbolic statement of some archetypal event can in a sense recreate that event and temporarily obliterate the passage of time which has elapsed since its original occurrence.[11]

These rites of recreation are to be seen at their most luxuriant in the ancient cultures of the western Sudan – notably in those of the Bambara and Dogon. In such cultures, indeed, a great part of everyday activity is said to have the ulterior significance of recreating archetypal events and acts. Thus the Dogon labouring in the fields recreates in his pattern of cultivation the emergence of the world from the cosmic egg. The builder of a homestead lays it out in a pattern that symbolically recreates the body of the culture-hero Nommo. Even relations between kin symbolize and recreate relations between the primal beings.[12]

---

[11]   In these rites of recreation, traditional African thought shows its striking affinities with prescientific thought in many other parts of the world. The world-wide occurrence and meaning of such rites was first dealt with by Mircea Eliade in his *Myth of the Eternal Return*. A more recent treatment, from which the present analysis has profited greatly, is to be found in the chapter entitled "Le Temps Retrouvé" in Claude Lévi-Strauss, *La Pensée*.

[12]   See M. Griaule, and G. Dieterlen, "The Dogon", in D. Forde (ed.), *African Worlds*, London, 1954, and M. Griaule, *Conversations with Ogotemmêli*, London, 1965 (translation of *Dieu d'Eau*).

One might well describe the Western Sudanic cultures as obsessed with the annulment of time to a degree unparalleled in Africa as a whole. Yet other, less spectacular, manifestations of the attempt to "get back to the beginning" are widely distributed over the continent. In the West African forest belt, for instance, the richly developed ritual dramas enacted in honour of departed heroes and ancestors have a strong recreative aspect. For by inducing these beings to possess specially selected media and thus, during festivals, to return temporarily to the company of men, such rituals are restoring things as they were in olden times.[13]

On the minor time-scale provided by the seasonal cycle, we find a similar widespread concern for recreation and renewal. Hence the important rites which mark the end of an old year and the beginning of a new one – rites which attempt to make the year new by a thorough-going process of purification of accumulated pollutions and defilements.

This widespread attempt to annul the passage of time seems closely linked to features of traditional thought which I have already reviewed. As I pointed out earlier, the new and the strange, in so far as they fail to fit into the established system of classification and theory, are intimations of chaos to be avoided as far as possible. Advancing time, with its inevitable element of non-repetitive change, is the vehicle *par excellence* of the new and the strange. Hence its effects must be annulled at all costs. Rites of renewal and recreation, then, have much in common with the process of secondary elaboration and taboo behaviour. Indeed, their kinship with the latter can be seen in the idea that the passage of the year is essentially an accumulation of pollutions, which it is the function of the renewal rites to remove. In short, these rites are the third great defensive reflex of traditional thought.[14]

When we turn from the traditional thinker to the scientist, we find this whole valuation of temporal process turned upside down. Not for the scientist the idea of a golden age at the beginning of time – an age from which things have been steadily falling away. For him, the past is a bad old past, and the best things lie ahead. The passage of time brings inexorable progress. As C. P. Snow has put it aptly, all scientists have "the future in their bones".[15] Where the traditional thinker is busily trying to annul the passage of time, the scientist may almost be said to be trying frantically to hurry time up. For in his impassioned pursuit of the experimental method, he is striving after the creation of new situations which nature, if left to herself, would bring about slowly if ever at all.

Once again, the scientist's attitude can be understood in terms of the "open" predicament. For him, currently held ideas on a given subject are one possibility amongst many. Hence occurrences which threaten them are not the total, horrific threat that they would be for the traditional thinker. Hence time's burden of things new and strange does not hold the terrors that it holds for the traditionalist. Furthermore, the scientist's experience of the way in which successive theories, overthrown after exposure to adverse data, are replaced by ideas of ever greater predictive and explanatory power, leads almost inevitably to a very positive evaluation of time. Finally, we must remember that the "open" predicament, though it has made people able to tolerate threats to their beliefs, has not been able to supply them with anything comparable to the

---

[13]　For some interesting remarks on this aspect of West African ritual dramas, see C. Tardits, "Religion, Epic, History: Notes on the Underlying Functions of Cults in Benin Civilizations, *Diogenes*, No. 37, 1962.

[14]　Lévi-Strauss, I think, is making much the same point about rites of renewal when he talks of the continuous battle between prescientific classificatory systems and the non-repetitive changes involved in the passage of time. See Lévi-Strauss, op. cit.

[15]　C. P. Snow, *The Two Cultures and the Scientific Revolution*, Cambridge, 1959, p. 10.

cosiness of the traditional thinker ensconced amidst his established theories. As an English medical student, newly exposed to the scientific attitude, put it:

> You seem to be as if when learning to skate, trying to find a nice hard piece of ice which you can stand upright on instead of learning how to move on it. You continue trying to find something, some foundation piece which will not move, whereas everything will move and you've got to learn to skate on it.[16]

The person who enjoys the moving world of the sciences, then, enjoys the exhilaration of the skater. But for many, this is a nervous, insecure sensation, which they would fain exchange for the womb-like warmth of the traditional theories and their defences. This lingering sense of insecurity gives a powerful attraction to the idea of progress. For by enabling people to cling to some hoped-for future state of perfect knowledge, it helps them live with a realization of the imperfection and transience of present theories.

Once formed, indeed, the idea of Progress becomes in itself one of the most powerful supports of the scientific attitude generally. For the faith that, come what may, new experience must lead to better theories, and that better theories must eventually give place to still better ones, provides the strongest possible incentive for a constant readiness to expose oneself to the strange and the disturbing, to scrap current frameworks of ideas, and to cast about for replacements.

Like the quest for purity of motive, however, the faith in progress is a double-edged weapon. For the lingering insecurity which is one of the roots of this faith leads all too often to an excessive fixation of hopes and desires on an imagined Utopian future. People cling to such a future in the same way that men in pre-scientific cultures cling to the past. And

in doing so, they inevitably lose much of the traditionalist's ability to enjoy and glorify the moment he lives in. Even within the sciences, an excessive faith in progress can be dangerous. In sociology, for instance, it has led to a number of unfruitful theories of social evolution.

At this point, I should like to draw attention to a paradox inherent in the presentation of my subject. As a scientist, it is perhaps inevitable that I should at certain points give the impression that traditional African thought is a poor, shackled thing when compared with the thought of the sciences. Yet as a man, here I am living by choice in a still-heavily-traditional Africa rather than in the scientifically oriented Western subculture I was brought up in. Why? Well, there may be lots of queer, sinister, unacknowledged reasons. But one certain reason is the discovery of things lost at home. An intensely poetic quality in everyday life and thought, and a vivid enjoyment of the passing moment – both driven out of sophisticated Western life by the quest for purity of motive and the faith in progress. How necessary these are for the advance of science; but what a disaster they are when they run wild beyond their appropriate bounds! Though I largely disagree with the way in which the "Négritude" theorists have characterized the differences between traditional African and modern Western thought, when it gets to this point I see very clearly what they are after.

In modern Western Europe and America the "open" predicament seems to have escaped precariousness through public acknowledgement of the practical utility of the sciences. It has achieved a secure foothold in the culture because its results maximize values shared by "closed-" and "open-" minded alike. Even here, however, the "open" predicament has nothing like a universal sway. On the con-

---

[16] M. L. Johnson Abercrombie, *The Anatomy of Judgement*, London, 1960, quoted on p. 131.

trary, it is almost a minority phenomenon. Outside the various academic disciplines in which it has been institutionalized, its hold is pitifully less than those who describe Western culture as "science-oriented" often like to think.

It is true that in modern Western culture, the theoretical models propounded by the professional scientists do, to some extent, become the intellectual furnishings of a very large sector of the population. The moderately educated layman typically shares with the scientist a general predilection for impersonal "it-" theory and a proper contempt for "thou-" theory. Garbled and watered-down though it may be, the atomic theory of matter is one of his standard possessions. But the layman's ground for accepting the models propounded by the scientist is often no different from the young African villager's ground for accepting the models propounded by one of his elders. In both cases the propounders are deferred to as the accredited agents of tradition. As for the rules which guide scientists themselves in the acceptance or rejection of models, these seldom become part of the intellectual equipment of members of the wider population. For all the apparent up-to-dateness of the content of his world-view, the modern Western layman is rarely more "open" or scientific in his outlook than is the traditional African villager.

20

KINSHIP, WITCHCRAFT AND THE MARKET: HYBRID PATTERNS IN CAMEROONIAN SOCIETIES[1]

PETER GESCHIERE

The aim of this chapter is to study various reflections on the market in south and west Cameroon. The focus will be on kinship and witchcraft/sorcery[2] spheres of life that in the west are not primarily associated with the market. In the societies discussed here, however, it is difficult to separate these spheres from "the market". To understand how these groups are coping with the impact of the world market – to recognize their own reflections on what western people call "the forces of the market" and the peculiar expressions of these forces at the local level – it is especially the more intimate sphere of life, like kinship and sorcery, that we have to study.

The penetration of the market into these personal spheres – which still constitute the core of the local patterns of organization – is all the more surprising since several of these groups did not know the institution of a market-place until the colonial conquest (around 1900). This applies especially to the societies of the southern forests where exchanges between the groups were couched in terms of kinship and an ideology of reciprocity. Yet, it is precisely in these societies "without markets" that nowadays idioms of the market have emerged with surprising force on nodal points of the kinship organization: in funeral rites and marriage ceremonies, in sexual relations and the domestic division of labour. Apparently an ideology of reciprocity and market-like behaviour can go very well together.

The Duala on the coast and the Bamiléké and the "Grassfielders" in the western mountains had a much longer experience with the market-place as an institution. Especially in the mountains, social formations had developed which were based on a regional network

---

[1] My thanks to Roy Dilley who was untiring in giving me his stimulating comments.

[2] I use both "witchcraft" and "sorcery" for lack of better terms. In several respects, these terms distort the meaning of the African terms of which they are supposed to be the translation. The problem is especially that both "sorcery" and "witchcraft" have strong pejorative overtones, while the African terms often have a much broader meaning, covering also more positive aspects of the occult forces. A more general translation like "occult forces" would therefore be preferable. However, terms like "sorcery", "witchcraft" or "*sorcellerie*" have been appropriated by Africans. Nowadays, they return time and again in the newspapers and there are current debates about, for instance, "*Développement et Sorcellerie*". To relate to these current debates, I use, albeit with misgivings, the same terms. I shall use both terms interchangeably since in the Cameroonian societies discussed here, it is difficult to distinguish sharply between "witchcraft" and "sorcery".

of trade, linked to long-distance exchanges (Warnier 1985). During colonial and post-colonial times, these groups adapted relatively well to the new market conditions. The more successful entrepreneurs in present-day Cameroon come from these areas. However, even though the market penetrated fairly easily in these areas, developments hardly corresponded to classical economic theory. Here, specific metaphors of the market emerged, especially couched in a discourse of witchcraft, which were of direct – albeit variable – consequence to economic behaviour.

A comparison of these different examples can help in deconstructing western notions of the market.[3] During my first fieldwork one of the most shocking experiences – an unexpected kind of "culture shock" – was the confrontation with market-like behaviour in what to me were intimate spheres of life. Precisely because I was shocked, I came to realize to what extent my own western notions of the market were culturally circumscribed.[4] Such an experience makes one conscious of the fact that the western image of the market does not reflect a self-evident reality but rather a specific folk model which has become enormously influential by its scientific elaboration in economics (and in economic anthropology).

In a more specific sense these examples can serve to indicate the untenability of a standard feature of western stereotypes of the market: the notion that "traditional" forms of organization will by definition resist the impact of "modern" market forces. This vague but general notion has particularly impeded better insight into the various ways in which African societies tried to cope with the further penetration of the world market in colonial and post-colonial times. The ongoing significance of old organization patterns, although in constant transformation, has certainly influenced the impact of the market. But often these modern transformations of "traditional" idioms prove to express not a refusal of the market as such but rather a determined struggle to gain access to it on the people's own terms.

The main merit of a collection of articles edited by Parry and Bloch (1989) on a parallel topic – the penetration of money in non-western societies – is in my opinion that it effectively defuses this stereotype of a self-evident resistance of "traditional" societies to money and the market. Like the penetration of the market, monetization is not an automatic process: its variations and diverging trajectories are determined by different cultural constructs of money, which certainly do not always imply a refusal of money as something evil or threatening.[5] The classical image from Marx – and many other authors – of money "as an acid attacking the very fabric of society" (Bloch 1989:169) is often not very helpful. In the literature of Africa, examples abound of how precisely the upholders of the old order – the elders – welcomed money and used it to reinforce their position.[6]

Yet I wonder whether Bloch is not over-playing his hand when he concludes from this that the specific role of money is to be drastically relativized: in his analysis monetization seems to play only a minor role in processes of

---

[3] Compare also Gudeman 1986.

[4] Compare similar experiences described by Bloch 1989 and Harris 1989.

[5] The problem here seems to be anthropology's predilection for clear-cut binary oppositions (societies with and without markets, pre-money societies and monetarized ones and so on) all of which amount to the basic opposition "them and us". It has been clear for some time already that in practice such oppositions are untenable. Yet Harris (1989:236) warns that such oppositions are still "built into the very structure of anthropology as a discipline" as does Appadurai (1986:12): "anthropology is [still] excessively dualistic" (compare also Geschiere in press).

[6] Compare for instance, Parkin (1972) on the "cultural paradox" of Giriama elders promoting the impact of the money economy which came to undermine their own position; or Dupré (1982); compare also Appadurai (1986:26) on money as a "Trojan horse of change".

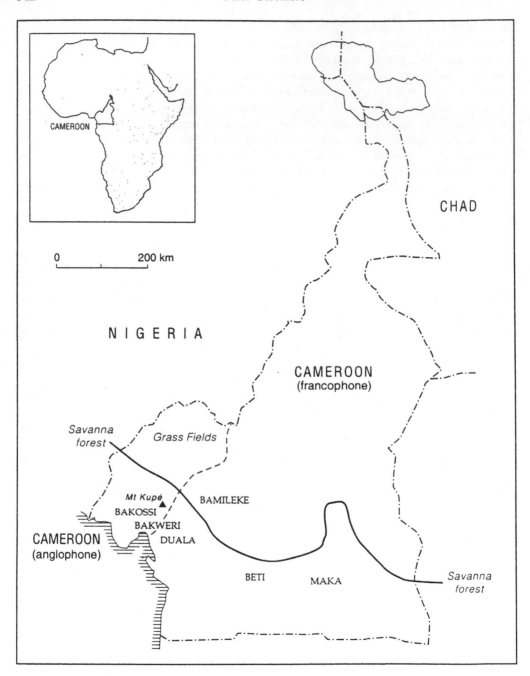

Figure 20.1 [1]   Various Groups in south and West cameroon.

change.[7] For the societies discussed here, the penetration of money as a (more) general means of payment did constitute an important turning point and the circulation of money did start processes with dynamics of their own. The unintended consequences – unintended to all parties involved and often highly variable – of the monetization of bridewealth in many parts of Africa are good examples that money can play a specific and independent role.

Similar caveats against an all too drastic deconstruction apply in my view to debates on the notion of "the market". It is doubtless highly worthwhile to bring out the folk model behind western scientific constructions of the market. Yet, such attempts at deconstruction should not hide that these western constructions have acquired considerable force on a global scale. The Cameroonian societies where I worked have had dramatic experiences of the capriciousness of market forces and the image of "the market" as an impersonal agent is to them therefore all too real. The devastating effects of the recent crisis – many peasants suddenly have no cash because they simply cannot sell their cash-crops any more – are only one example of this. All markets introduce an open-endedness in social networks which may be experienced as a threat, and the deepening penetration of the world market reinforces this vulnerablity.

Especially in view of the recent crisis in Africa, it is urgent to gain more insight into the different ways in which local societies have tried to cope with "the market". This will also influence their reactions to the renewed emphasis on "the market" by the main development agencies. To analyse such pressing issues, it seems we have to retain a notion of "the market" (which equals the world market?). Yet, at the same time we have to problematize the concept by bringing out the cultural premises behind it. In this respect, a comment by Mahmood Mamdani on IMF

policies in the Third World is important. "The IMF's point of view is ahistorical, having forgotten that the market, in Africa as in Europe, has never existed as a God-given entity; it is always created, *through social struggle*" (my emphasis, Mamdani 1990:457). It is by studying markets as outcomes of specific social struggles that one can analyse both the cultural construction of metaphors of the market and the varying strategies by which people try to get access to or protect themselves from new market conditions.

The aim of this chapter is to discuss metaphors of the markets in various Cameroonian societies as cultural constructs. Yet this emphasis on specific cultural logics should not imply that there is an absolute discontinuity with western metaphors – that these societies are locked into another kind of thinking. On the contrary, one is struck by the creative hybridization of endogenous concepts and modern (western) patterns. Moreover, we shall see that these various metaphors have highly different implications for the way people react to the further penetration of the world market: they can imply a refusal of new market conditions, but can also encourage efforts to gain access to new markets. The question is to what extent we can relate, in view of Mamdani's dictum, the various metaphors and their differing implications to specific social struggles?

1 The Segmentary Societies of Southern Cameroon and The Market

Prior to the colonial conquest (around 1900), social forms of organization in south Cameroon corresponded in many respects to the classical model of "segmentary societies". A good example are the Maka in the remote south eastern forests, where I have done

[7] Compare Bloch (1989:169–70) and Parry and Bloch (1989:16.19).

fieldwork since 1971. Before 1900, the Maka lived in small autonomous villages, formally constituted by a patrilineal segment to which in practice a varying number of matrilateral kin (*mita*, "nephews") and clients (*miloua*) were associated. A village was ruled by a council of elders who had authority over the young men and the women of their family. There was no central authority above the village level and, even between neighbouring villages, relations were marked by hostility and the constant threat of violence. But there were also regular exchanges especially between related villages. These exchanges primarily concerned women and prestige goods which were controlled by the elders: bundles of small iron bars (*mimbes*), other iron objects, bags of locally produced salt. In their stories about the past, my Maka informants always discussed these exchanges in terms of reciprocity. Two groups could thus meet to put an end to a blood feud. On such an occasion, the receiving group had to offer a girl for each man killed, in order to "restore a life" to the other group. A few weeks later, this group had in its turn to act as a host and offer a girl for each man they had killed. Similarly, regarding marriage, the elder of the groom had to offer over a period of time a series of bridal gifts to the bride's elder. But on receiving the gifts, the elder was under a strict obligation to use these goods in order to "buy" a woman on behalf of his own group (Geschiere 1982).

A network of exchanges, especially between affines, bridged the gap between patrilineal villages. When in the course of the nineteenth century the traders from the European factories on the coast penetrated even deeper into the forests of the interior, they were channelled into this network of affinity and kinship.[8]

After 1905 the Maka were subdued by the Germans. In 1914 this part of Cameroon was conquered by the French. Both Germans and French considered the Maka region to be particularly backward. The Germans, who had to make a considerable effort to subdue the Maka, called them "*die Primitivisten aller Primitiven.*" One of the reasons for this contempt was that the Maka seemed to be impervious to the forces of "the market." As one of the first French administrators expressed it: these "*primitifs imprévoyants*" did not react to "*la loi de l'offre et de la demande qui est un puissant levier pour l'action productive chez les peuples civilisés*". And he tersely formulated what was both to the French and the Germans the obvious remedy to this insensitivity: "*l'unique remède est l'obligation au travail*"[9] Up to 1940, the rather desperate efforts of the successive colonial administrators to stimulate the "*mise en valeur*" of the area were all based on coercion: forced levying of labour, "*cultures forcées*" of cash-crops and many other attempts to enforce strict administrative control in order to stimulate the productive activities of the villagers.

However, after 1945, the Maka suddenly proved to be less "resistant to the market". After forced labour and other coercive government schemes had been abolished, and when higher prices made the advantages of cash-cropping clear, the villagers rapidly began to expand their cocoa and coffee plantations on their own initiative. Since then, the penetration of the market and a money economy has proceeded in a less spasmodic manner. Since the 1950s, nearly every family head in the

---

[8]   Witz (1972:100) describes this process in detail. When a trader wanted to establish contacts in a region unknown to him, the obvious way to do so was by marrying one of his daughters to someone from this area. Then he could profit from the kinship and affinity networks of his son-in-law to expand his trade network. Thus, new trade goods mainly entered the existing circuits by means of the exchange of women and prestige goods. Near the coast, bride-prices already consisted of European goods towards the end of the nineteenth century.

[9]   Chef de la région Briaud, Abong-Mbang, to Commissaire de la République, Douala, 14.12.1920; Archives Nationales, Yaoundé, APA 111643.

village has had an annual cash income from the sale of his cocoa and coffee harvests. The woman's food plots still assure the basic subsistence of the villagers. But many women earn a little money on the side by the sale of some of their products. Moreover, many young men and women have succeeded in getting salaried jobs in town, for shorter or longer periods. Money has become an integral part of the domestic economy in nearly all households.[10]

2 Market and Kinship

When I started my fieldwork in this area, I was already familiar with the colonial history of the Maka and the many problems the French had had in mobilizing the Maka for the "*mise en valeur*" of the area. I had read some of the colonial administrators' long complaints of the insensitivity of these people to "the law of supply and demand." Therefore, I was all the more surprised, not to say shocked, by the mercenary behaviour of the villagers, especially at occasions where it was, in my view, highly inappropriate. My first experience of this came as soon as on the second day after I had settled in the village, when I was invited to a wake for someone who had died a year ago. The women's dancing group was supposed to honour the occasion by dancing, in principle from sunset to dawn. Their dance, very "traditional" and very impressive, was however interrupted rudely, only an hour after they had started. One of the women had discovered a coin of 10 francs CFA in the bowl where all the bystanders were supposed to put their offerings, and she accused me of having made this ridiculously small offering. All the

women joined in her protests. Their leader added that in any case the people were not offering enough for their dancing and five minutes later the group marched off. Nobody could make them return. I was very indignant, not only because I felt unjustly accused, I had certainly not put this coin there, but also since I felt that a dead man's wake was not the appropriate occasion for such mercenary behaviour.

I was to encounter many more examples of similar behaviour, but of a more structural kind. The second week after my arrival I assisted for the first time at a Maka funeral. To the Maka, funeral rites are one of the climaxes in the "acting out" of the kinship organization. Especially when the deceased is a prominent man or woman, people gather from all the neighbouring villages to participate in the rites. The Maka say that a deceased person is an important link in the network between the patrilineal groups. Therefore, all the groups involved have to participate in order to reaffirm these links. This leads to the theatrical "performances" in which the complex balance of solidarity and hostility between the groups involved is "acted out", especially between the patrilineal kin of the dead and the other parties involved: "mothers'-brothers," "daughters-in-law," "sons-in-law" and "sisters'-sons," all of whom are supported by their own patrilineal kin.[11]

Daughters-in-law especially play a spectacular part. Their relation to their husband's family is highly ambivalent: they have to be ostentatiously obedient, particularly to their father-in-law, but they can also indulge in small "rituals of rebellion," mocking the old man and singing lewd songs to his face. The funeral of their father-in-law, or of one of his "brothers", is a special occasion for such

---

[10] Since 1988, however, the market for cash-crops has collapsed. In 1988, the cooperative which had a monopoly over the sale of cocoa and coffee in the area, ceased paying farmers. In subsequent years, farmers were paid after much delay and at much lower prices. This has had dramatic consequences for most households.

[11] All these terms are used in a highly "classificatory" sense. "Daughters-in-law" include all the women that have married into the patrilineage of the deceased, the "sisters'-sons" are all the sons of women born to the patrilineage of the deceased but who married elsewhere, and so on.

"ritual rebellion." As soon as the *tam-tam* of mourning has sounded, the daughters-in-law start to "enliven" the scene: they dance and sing all night, mock the patrilineal kin of the deceased, and engage them in "dancing duels" to humiliate them. They are obliged to behave in this way, and the more aggressive their performance, the more satisfied the deceased's spirit is supposed to be, for their display shows that he has acquired numerous, "dynamic" women for his group.

The climax of their performance is the *kombok*. The women suddenly appear dressed up in the deceased's clothes. Aided by the sons-in-law, who are dressed as warriors, they attack the deceased's house which is shaken dangerously. The patrilineal kin offer symbolic resistance. But after a few skirmishes, the daughters-in-law suddenly rush off with the bier on their shoulders, the body bouncing up and down. They "hide" in the bushes just outside the village, singing merrily and dancing. The first time I witnessed this, I could not help feeling that all this was not the appropriate way to "honour" the deceased. But I was really shocked by what followed. The elder of the deceased's group has "to buy back" the body from the daughters-in-law, and this requires hard bargaining. The elder then claims for instance that there is no money since the cocoa harvest has not yet been sold. He counts out a few banknotes, but the women push him away, saying that they should be better remunerated for all the care they have lavished upon the deceased. The elder adds a few banknotes, but the women continue to refuse using different arguments and so on. Usually, they accept once the elder has raised his prices again. Especially in the beginning, such scenes strongly reminded me of the flea market near my house in Holland, and I realized that I found such behaviour utterly inappropriate at a funeral.

Moreover, this is certainly not the only moment for bargaining at a funeral. Just before the actual burial, the elders of the deceased's group have to "buy the body" once more, this time from the mother's-brothers. Unlike the daughters-in-law, this last group has a very strong sanction at their disposal. They have to bury the body and they may leave without doing so, if they are not satisfied with the price offered to them. On this occasion therefore, the bargaining has more serious undertones. The elders of both groups confront each other – next to the open grave – with much rhetorical prowess. The slamming of banknotes and fists, again accompanies fairly banal arguments: there is no money, because the tax has just been paid, the other party still has not paid an outstanding debt and so on. The amounts paid on these occasions are also substantially higher (in the 1970s they were usually several ten thousands of francs CFA, in other words amounts up to £100) but they can vary considerably.

These negotiations with the daughters-in-law and the mother's-brothers are the most spectacular moments of bargaining, but in the coulisses many more exchanges take place with other groups of kin. Moreover, the rites seem to be constantly enriched by new "inventions". In 1973, when I attended the funeral of a young woman I noticed that the road through the village had been blocked by a rope and some branches. Apparently, the rope had been attached by the women of the same generation as the deceased. All the men who wanted to pass had to pay a few coins to the women. This led to unexpected complications when a French priest, who regularly visited the villages and who was known for his fierce temper, approach at great speed in his car. It seemed at first that he wanted to drive right through the barrier but at the last moment desisted. One of the women explained that he had to pay some money whereupon the priest replied that he had never heard of this. When the women insisted, he became red in the face and started to shout that this was a heathen custom, that they were turning their funerals into a market with all this money business and so on, and so forth. He restarted the engine and the women just had the time to lower the rope, else he would have broken it. I was especially surprised by the comment of my assistant, himself a staunch Catholic. "Le Père is right, this is a new thing and the women are exaggerating. They borrowed this from Yaoundé (the capital). These women, they are making a market of everything."

The kinship organization of the Maka offers many more occasions for hard bargaining. Another key-moment in this respect is the conclusion of a marriage when the groom's group comes to the bride's village to offer bride-price. Again the elders of both groups have to confront each other with much rhetorical display and again the arguments used are often highly prosaic. The groom's elder has to offer a protracted series of presents: bottles of whiskey, crates of beer, demijohns of red wine, blankets, wrappers and so on, but the climax is the counting of the money and the bargaining over the bride-price. The groom's elder solemnly counts out the notes, one after another, while everybody looks on in dead silence. When he stops, the bride's family – the women foremost – utter their indignation with shrill cries of protest. The bride's elder declares in stately manner that this offer is an insult to the family and that he is not prepared to give his daughter away so cheaply. His opponents reply with the usual arguments – everybody knows that there is no money now, it is the slack season and so on. And again, a final agreement is only reached after hard bargaining.

In this context as well, it is not self-evident that an agreement will be reached. I know of cases where the bride's elder has rejected the offer and the groom has had to return without his bride. Moreover, the amounts on which both parties agreed varied considerably. There is a certain standard: in the 1970s for instance prices fluctuated between 80,000 and 100,000 francs CFA (about £160–200) but there were also cases in the village where I lived when considerably more (up to 120,000 francs CFA) or less (60,000 francs CFA) had been paid.[12] Sometimes only part of the agreed sum is paid, with the promise to settle the rest later. This invariably leads to serious complications, especially when the couple's first children are born. Then the bride's family insist on all sorts of extra payments.

All this bargaining has, of course, a ritual aspect. The negotiations between the groom's elder and the bride's representative follow fixed patterns, but despite this ritual canalization, the bargaining can lead to conflicts which are all too real. Especially in cases when part of the sum has to be paid later or when there are conflicts about subsidiary payments for the children, it is not uncommon that one of the parties takes the matter to court – to the village chief or, which is more serious, to the offical courts in town. People can be heavily fined or even imprisoned, particularly in the latter cases.

The Maka are certainly not exceptional in their strong emphasis on monetary affairs during kinship rituals. Their western neighbours for instance, the Beti, have acquired a certain reputation for the hard bargaining that takes place during their marriage ceremonies. The Beti, a prominent group in present-day Cameroon, have similar patterns of organization to the Maka. But due to their central position in Cameroon – Yaoundé, the capital, is in their territory – they became much earlier and much deeper involved in modern politico-economic developments. With them the penetration of a money economy into kinship rituals seems to have taken on even more spectacular forms. One of the newest fashions during their marriage ceremonies is, for instance, that the groom's party has to pay additional money in order to buy the "plane

---

[12] In the 1980s the price rose to 150,000 francs CFA (nearly £300), but then also considerable variations were possible. It is not yet clear how the recent collapse of the cash-crop market and the concomitant problems of raising money will affect the level of the bride-price in the villages.

ticket" for the bride. Only after enough money has been put on the table is the bride, who was hiding in one of the neighbouring houses, "flown in." Of special interest is that people from other parts of Cameroon – from the west or the north – profess to be shocked by such extremely mercenary behaviour. "With these people a marriage becomes an auction" said one of my informants.

Moreover, this monetarization of kinship, affinity and other personal relations is certainly not confined to formal occasions, like funerals or weddings. One could quote also the numerous complaints – often by men – about the monetarization of sexual relations. "*Aujourd'hui les femmes se mettent elles-mêmes sur le marché*", as one of my neighbours bitterly remarked. The young men especially complain that it becomes impossible for them to conclude a decent marriage. Again, such complaints refer particularly to women from the southern forests groups.

One can of course quote many parallel examples from other parts of Africa of how money and hard bargaining quite easily penetrate intimate spheres of life. It seems, moreover, that this trend is especially strong in societies which until fairly recently could be characterized as "societies without markets" – that is societies which prior to colonial rule had little or no direct experience of the market as a "place". Apparently, this did not impede the rapid spread of principles of the market right into the core institutions of these societies.

3 Discussion: "Reciprocity" versus "The Market"?

An obvious question is whether these practices of hard bargaining at funerals, weddings and other personal occasions are something new: are they to be seen as consequences of the penetration of the money economy in colonial times – a perversion of local rituals by the impact of "the market"? Or are they rather continuations of older patterns of behaviour?

Some authors emphasize the dramatic effects of the penetration of money and the market in these societies. As early as 1948, Furnivall insisted that the most uninhibited forms of capitalism emerged, not in the countries of its origin, but on the periphery where the market had penetrated from outside and where it was therefore much less impeded by social restraints.[13] Following this perspective, one could suppose that precisely in societies like those of the Beti and the Maka, where the market was something new, money and hard bargaining could penetrate all the more easily into personal spheres of life.

On the other hand, our examples of hard bargaining have many precedents in more "traditional" contexts. There are similar examples in classical anthropological monographs – even in their archetype, Malinowski's *Argonauts*. In this perspective, the bargaining of the Maka over bridewealth and funeral exchanges might rather be a continuation of older patterns of behaviour. Moreover, according to some, such haggling would not be related to real markets but rather to gift exchange, social prestige and reciprocity.[14]

A rapid summary of a few historical data can help to answer these questions. It is clear that in these societies money penetrated into personal spheres of life almost immediately

---

[13] Furnivall (1948) developed this view in discussing colonial developments in Burma and the all-pervasive influence of market forces in this colony.

[14] Compare Polanyi (1957:263) who speaks of "haggling with fixed prices" – apparently to make a contrast with true market situations. Compare also the critique on Malinowski for rigidly opposing gift exchange (equalled with prestige) and trade (equalled with profit) in his analysis of the *kula* (see Hart 1986 and Bloch 1989:169).

after the colonial conquest. In the Maka area, money had already emerged around 1930 in the bride-prices. At first it still constituted a complement to the *mimbesj*, the bundles of small iron bars which were traditionally the main prestige goods. But around 1935 the *mimbesj* seem to have disappeared altogether from the marriage payments. This is fairly early, because in those years money must have hardly circulated within the villages.[15]

A more spectacular example of how quickly money could spread comes from the Beti area. In 1913, Paul Rohrbach a German journalist from the *Frankfurter Zeitung*, travelled along the road from Kribi on the coast to Yaoundé in the interior. This road had only recently been constructed (after 1900) to facilitate the rapidly growing rubber trade. Already in 1903, according to some estimates, 1,000 carriers passed daily on this road (Wirz 1972:137). Rohrbach was surprised to see groups of women standing along the road and singing a cheerful song. On his request his boy, who spoke "*Neger-Englisch*" translated their song: "We are happy to sleep with the strangers who pass. But they have to pay us well. Else we run away when they want to have us." Whereupon the boy added: "Oh, these Yaoundé people, they like money too much".[16]

The boy's comment in particular is quite striking. There is a remarkable contrast here with the later complaints of the French administrators who considered these people to be insensitive to "*la loi d'offre et de demande*". Instead, it seems that the villagers were so keen on earning money that they did it by means which were fairly shocking, both to the European and his boy from the coast. This rather suggests that these societies knew remarkably few barriers to the spread of money.[17]

The introduction of money must nonetheless have constituted an important turning point. It must have greatly facilitated the development of hard bargaining during kinship rituals described above. Prior to this such ritual "payments" had to be made in prestige goods which lend themselves less easily to haggling. Moreover, it was more difficult to use these goods for individualistic pursuits. The prestige goods received as bridewealth, for instance, could in principle only be used to acquire a new woman for the group. But as soon as money penetrated bridewealth, things became different. In contrast to the old prestige goods, money could be used for any purpose. In the French archives, complaints about "*l'escroquerie de la dot*" – bridewealth swindling – had already emerged by the 1920s. Complaints by women that their elders had "eaten" their bridewealth – that is, had used it for personal consumption, often for buying western luxury goods, instead of keeping it to acquire a wife for a son – are nearly as old. The fact that money offered new possibilities for enrichment must have greatly reinforced the stimulus to bargain in the exchanges between kin groups.

But this does not mean that the developments in these forest societies did correspond to Furnivall's image of "capitalism" and the market spreading without any restriction or social channelling in peripheral areas. On the contrary, among the Cameroonian forest

---

[15] Until the end of the 1930s, French administrators really had to squeeze tax money from the villages. Nearly all of the little money the villagers earned – mostly by working on European plantations in the area – was drained from the villages by the tax collections. Only after 1945, did money begin to circulate more regularly (see Geschiere 1983).

[16] *Frankfurter Zeitung*, 25.5.1913; see also Staatsarchiv Potsdam, Reichskolonialamt, Bnd 4, file 4226, p. 57.

[17] Nowadays, money has penetrated into all sorts of relations. As an exception one could mention that there is now a strong ban on any attempt to use money in order to acquire land. At least in the Maka area, any rumour that someone is trying to sell or rent his land for money, evokes fierce reactions from his own kin who reproach him for tempering with their communal domain. However, it seems that these fierce reactions are fairly new; probably they are related to the feeling that there is a growing pressure on land. At least in the beginning of the colonial period, "chiefs" – in reality often colonial strawmen – did "sell" land to Europeans and their auxiliaries for money – mostly for derisory low sums.

groups, the spread of money and the market clearly followed the circuits in the local patterns of organization. The more spectacular manifestations of bargaining emerged in the relations between the kin groups – that is, in the local arenas regulating the exchanges of prestige goods and women. From folk tales, it is clear that these encounters between such groups had always been marked by an atmosphere of confrontation and intimidation. The Maka have a saying: "Marriage is war" which means that one can only marry one's potential enemies. Marriage is only possible outside the bounds of kinship – that is outside the sphere of peace. The fact that marriage is possible implies automatically that there is the danger of "war." No wonder that in these relations of affinity, one has to prove one's worth with much ostentation in the face of a partner who could always turn into an enemy.

In some respects, therefore, the hard bargaining at weddings and funerals does continue the old rivalry between lineages linked by ties of affinity. It fits in with the precarious balance between aggression and solidarity which some anthropologists call "a joking relationship." In this sense, one could say that the new contacts with the market economy have been integrated into a traditional idiom of exchange. But one should add that the exchanges are now carried out with a completely new means of payment: money. This innovation is of great consequence for the practical effects of the bargaining. Money has given a new dimension to the relations between elders and young men, which is of crucial importance in these societies. The young began to complain, for instance, about the elders "eating" the bridewealth. From their side the elders apparently viewed the monetization of the bridewealth as an opportunity to gain access to the money economy on their own terms: they felt free continually to raise the bride price – the amounts demanded increased steadily – and to use at least part of the money for their own consumption.

The monetization of marriage and funeral exchanges also had direct consequences for the way in which these societies became integrated into the colonial economy – or, in broader perspective, into the world market. Rey (1971) tried to show for an area in north-west Congo that the monetisation of the bridewealth played an important role in solving the labour problem of the *colons* and the colonial authorities. This interpretation applies to the Maka area as well. In my interviews with the first migrants from the village where I lived (they had left the village as young men in the 1930s) one of the standard answers to the question, why they had left, was that their parents wanted them to earn money for the bridewealth. Thus, in a very direct sense, the development of the "market of kinship" was related to more orthodox markets of labour and commodities.

Against this background it seems clear that the practices of hard bargaining discussed above cannot be explained as simply a continuation of old forms of rivalry – after all, money adds a new aspect to this rivalry which is of crucial importance to the encapsulation of these societies in the colonial economy. But neither can this hard bargaining be viewed, à la Furnivall, as simply a result of the perverting influence of money – the monetization process was channelled into the local circuits of exchange between the groups. Instead the "market of kinship" seems to be a hybridization of old forms of rivalry and new idioms of the market.

In this light it may be clear why the old conceptual opposition anthropologists tended to make between "reciprocity" and "the market" is not very useful: it is of little help in understanding the importance of such forms of hybridization for the present-day predicament of these societies. Of course elements of reciprocity in the exchange of gifts and "ostentatious consumption" to enhance one's status are to be recognized in the examples discussed above. At funerals and weddings in Maka villages, for instance, bargaining always takes place in public and is marked by much pathos and theatre. The examples above indicate, however, that such "traditional" forms of rivalry and exchange are easily linked to new market conditions. Apparently, the opposition between idioms of "reciprocity" and "the market" is not that absolute. The above also provides a clue of how to analyze such processes of hybridization. It seems characteristic that the articulation of local patterns and new market conditions took form around a crucial contradiction in these societies – around bridewealth, that is in direct relation to the struggle between young men and elders over the redistribution of women and prestige-goods. It was because they were grafted upon this old contradiction that the new market conditions could so rapidly transform these societies from the inside.

4 Sorcery and Other Metaphors of The Market

In many respects, societies in the western parts of Cameroon nowadays offer a marked contrast to the southern forest societies. The most successful entrepreneurs in present-day Cameroon come from western groups like the Bamiléké or the Grassfielders and from Duala on the coast. In these societies other metaphors of the market dominate.

Historically it is of importance that these societies knew the institution of the market-place much earlier than the southern forest groups. The Duala on the coast had intensive contacts with European traders, probably from the 1600s onwards. These trade contacts stimulated the rise of "kingues" and new forms of authority which surpassed the old kinship networks of Duala society. In the western Grassfields and the Bamiléké area, a complex regional network of market-trade had already developed centuries before, and this constituted the base for the emergence of even stronger chieftaincies in this area (Warnier 1985). The Bamiléké area was probably already in contact with the coastal trade by the

seventeenth century. Consequently, these groups had experience of different types of money over a long period; local iron hoes as means of payment had been superseded by "brass manillas" and beads (and occasionally cowries from trade to the north and the northeast with the Hausa). These moneys were used not only for bridewealth or long-distance trade but also for local exchanges (Warnier 1985:90, 149).

To these societies, the further penetration of the European market and the introduction of European money after the colonial conquest was therefore less of a rupture than in the forest areas. These groups also adapted themselves relatively well to the new market conditions. This does not mean, however, that developments in these areas followed the classical economic paradigm. Of interest in that especially in these more "entrepreneurial" societies a very powerful metaphor of "the market" emerged in terms of sorcery and occult power. According to some, this metaphor has deep historical roots: it might even refer to earlier experiences of the slave trade. But it has remained up to the present day of great importance to people's perceptions of "the market" – albeit that there are important regional variations in the ways these beliefs affect people's reactions to new economic opportunities.

The archetype of this belief is the *ekong* of the Duala, the first group to come into contact with the European trade. To the Duala, *ekong* is a special form of witchcraft which is closely related to wealth, especially to new forms of wealth. *Ekong* people do not eat their victims as witches are commonly supposed to do, but they transform them into something like "zombies" and put them to work. There is a special connection with Mount Kupe, about sixty miles to the north of Duala, in the land of the Bakossi. *Ekong* people are supposed to send their victims there and make them work on "invisible plantations." Their new wealth is explained as the fruit of their victims' labour.

Bureau illustrates how this *ekong* belief functions in modern Duala, nowadays the economic capital of Cameroon:

> A person who is interested in *ekong* goes to visit an "ekoneur" [French for "*ekong* owner" – a neologism which is commonly used], who puts him to sleep by hypnosis. In his dreams, this person will see a land where money flows and many labourers work for him. An estate owner will offer him his plantations on condition that he offers the life of, for instance, his mother in return. His first reaction will be to refuse. When he wakes up, the "ekoneur" will say to him "Now you have seen, now you know what you have to do". His client will ask for some time to think about it. Some day he will make up his mind. (Bureau 1962:141; compare also Mallart Guimera 1981:115)

De Rosny, a Catholic priest, who studied these beliefs in Duala in the 1970s, gives a vivid picture of the other side – the anxiety of the potential victims:

> when someone dreams that he is taken away as a slave, his hands tied, towards the river or the Ocean and that he cannot see the faces of his capturers, he knows that he has to see a *nganga* (witch-doctor) as soon as possible. (de Rosny 1981:93)

"Ekoneurs" are supposed to steal their victims' bodies from the grave and then "sell" them to one of their customers.

This idea of "selling someone" and de Rosny's dream picture seem indeed to refer to the old practices of the slave trade. So does the fact that the Duala and other groups in the area tend to make a close connection between *ekong* and the Europeans. This is what de Rosney found out to his distress. He had visited an old *nganga* (witch-doctor) and a chief in a village near Duala and he had offered them both a bottle of whiskey. When he wanted to leave again, he found the road was blocked by youths from the village who behaved very aggressively and refused to let him pass. Apparently, both the chief and the *nganga* were suspected of having *ekong*. The rumour that a white stranger had come to offer them a present, was apparently enough to resurrect old fears of people being "sold" to the whites.[18]

De Rosny rightly points out, however, that contemporary *ekong* beliefs also reflect more modern forms of the market. He emphasizes that *ekong* as such existed among the Duala long before the colonial conquest. In these earlier days, *ekong* was a well-respected association of chiefs, notables and traders – that is, of those groups who controlled access to the market and the trade with the Europeans. Nowadays the *ekong* have been "democratized": it seems to be in the reach of anybody who wants to have a try at it. According to de Rosny, there is a direct link here with economic changes which have occurred since the colonial conquest – such as the development of new forms of wage labour and the spread of money – by which access to the market became no longer the prerogative of family-heads or rich traders. All this has certainly not made the economy more transparent. Rising and falling prices of cash-crops and the uncertainty of the labour market have become crucial for the survival of most city people. But these "forces of the market" are absolutely unpredictable, certainly for the ordinary people, and they seem to be outside everybody's control. One of the attractions of *ekong* beliefs is – according to de Rosny – that they can "integrate" the mysteries of the market. They have persisted among the popular strata because they can still offer at least some form of explanation for the glaring differences in wealth under the new market conditions. Just as the market has been

---

[18]   Other aspects of *ekong* rumours are more reminiscent of the forced colonial labour recruitments. The Bakweri (the western neighbours of the Duala), for instance, believe that the victims are transported *in lorries* to Mount Kupé. The Bakossi, to the north of the Duala, talk about huge working camps on Mount Kupé (Ardener 1970; Balz 1984).

"democratized," so *ekong* now seems to have become much more widespread.

At first sight, this metaphor seems to characterize the market as something unequivocally weird. In this respect, *ekong* seems to correspond to the stereotype, which is still so common among western observers and development experts, of sorcery/witchcraft as a "traditional barrier" to modern changes and "development." However, on further consideration, things turn out to be more complicated. The *ekong* belief has not remained restricted to the Duala, but has also emerged throughout the western and southwestern regions of present-day Cameroon. In these areas it has been closely related to the progressive penetration of the market economy and to new opportunities for enrichment. But among the various groups this metaphor of the market has different implications. In some areas, *ekong* beliefs seem to express less a refusal than an eagerness to participate in the market. Clearly, the same metaphor allows for different reactions to the new market conditions.

Among the Bakweri, the western neighbours of the Duala, these beliefs have strong negative connotations. They use the term *nyongo* for representations that are nearly identical to the Duala *ekong*. Older Bakweri even claim that *nyongo* was introduced to their area by the Duala. This is supposed to have happened quite recently, probably at the beginning of the colonial era (Fisiy and Geschiere 1991). Prior to that time, the Bakweri, living on the steep slopes of Mount Cameroon, were largely bypassed by the trade routes from the coast into the interior. Only towards the end of the nineteenth-century were they affected by the efforts of Duala traders to create cocoa plantations and recruit labour for these plantations in the interior (Wirz 1972). The Bakweri elders, who now tell stories of how the Duala brought the *nyongo* to their land, often add fairly negative comments about the avariciousness and the venality of the Duala traders.

To the Bakweri, this *nyongo* is still unequivocally evil. In a seminal study, Ardener (1970) showed how, for a long time, this belief constituted a formidable barrier against any attempt to profit from the new opportunities for enrichment. People did not even dare to build the new type of house with a tinned roof – in this region the new status symbol – because then they would certainly be accused of *nyongo* witchcraft. In 1955, at the time when Ardener worked in this area, there was a sudden breakthrough, when people from Lysoka (a Bakweri village) brought in Obasinjom from the Banyangi (more than 160 miles to the north). This powerful *juju* was supposed to be able to flush out *nyongo* witches and take their powers from them. There followed an intensive anti-*nyongo* campaign during which village after village was cleansed. Significantly, all this coincided with the "banana-boom" in this area. Due to better transport facilities and a new co-operative organization, the bakweri peasants had for the first time a chance to profit greatly from the colonial market economy by cultivating bananas. But they could only do so after Obasinjom had liberated them from *nyongo*. People felt free to profit from the "banana-boom" only because this *juju* had put an end to *nyongo*. Now they could even build modern houses without being suspected of this dreadful form of witchcraft.

Of course, *nyongo* was not completely eradicated. There have been rumours about *nyongo* up to the present day. Recently, Obasinjom even experienced a spectacular revival in the mountain villages – apparently because there was growing unrest about *nyongo* activities. Again, there seems to be a direct link with a sudden economic change – this time the serious crisis and the austerity measures drawn up by the state since 1987. Up till today, *nyongo* remains something evil to the Bakweri which has to be combated and eradicated at all costs.

De Rosny (1981) described similar attitudes in present-day Duala. To the city people, *ekong* is an omnipresent evil lurking everywhere in their modern, urban surroundings. The *nganga* (witch-doctors) who figure in his book see themselves as protagonists in a continuous war against *ekong*. But, as remarked earlier, the image of *ekong* was not always so negative among the Duala. According to de Rosny it was formerly (probably prior to the colonial conquest when Duala society was still a slave society)[19] a respected association of notables and rich traders. De Rosny (1981:92) underlines that, in those days, the *ekong* "did not yet have the odious character it has acquired today."

In this respect, there is a striking contrast with more recent developments among the Bamiléké and the Grassfielders, in the western mountains, who now have the reputation of being the most entrepreneurial groups in Cameroon. Here similar conceptions prevail but they are called *kupe* (after the mountain) or *famla* (after a quarter of Bafoussam, the new centre of Bamilékéland). Again these beliefs refer to the "selling" of one's own relatives, to the stealing of the bodies of the victims who are transported to Mount Kupé and to new riches created by the labour of these "spirits." But in these societies the condemnation of these practices seems to be less unequivocal than among the Bakweri or the Duala. Apparently there are here special possibilities to "whitewash" the wealth thus acquired.

These areas are of special interest, since, as remarked above, entrepreneurs from this area are supposed to dominate now important sectors of the national economy. Indeed rumours of *famla* abound especially about the Bamiléké entrepreneurs, who now control important assets in Yaoundé and Duala. But in practice, this hardly seems to affect their position. Apparently, their *famla* associations are supposed to be so well organized that it would be futile to try and combat them. The

only way to escape them is by moving away. This seems to be the other side of the famous *dynamisme bamiléké*[20] – their propensity to migrate and their economic success throughout Cameroon. *Famla* and *kupe* are popularly considered to be the obvious explanation of the success of these entrepreneurs. This endogenous metaphor of the market has thus acquired considerable importance for the national economy.

The question is of course why precisely in these areas such beliefs were accepted as a more or less normal element of entrepreneurship. In another article (Fisiy and Geschiere 1991) – to which I can only briefly refer here for reasons of space – we tried to explain this by the special position of the chiefs (*fons*) in these societies and their role in processes of accumulation. It seems that *kupe* is fairly new to the Grassfields and the same might be true for *famla* among the Bamiléké.[21] But it is clear that these beliefs fitted in very well with special patterns of accumulation that had developed in these areas over the last centuries. Warnier's challenging interpretations of the relation between chieftaincy and trade in the Grassfields indicate how important the *fon's* role was to the expansion of networks of accumulation (Warnier 1985). For each chieftaincy, the *fon's* prestige determined the scope of its trade relations and inversely the success of its traders reinforced the prestige of its *fon*. The main export products were palm-oil, iron objects and slaves. According to Warnier (1990) one of the peculiarities of this area was that the export of slaves was based mainly on the sale of people by their own kin. He tries to show how enterprising individuals in this area could realize their ambitions by delivering people from their own group – often less protected youths from the larger compounds – into the hands of slave dealers. A key element

---

[19] Compare Wirz 1972 and Austen 1977; in this respect as well there seems to be a direct link between *ekong* and slavery.
[20] The title of a book by Jean-Louis Dongmo (1981) about the rise of the Bamiléké entrepreneurs.
[21] The term *famla* might not be older than the colonial period. See Miaffo and Warnier (in press), Pool 1989, Pradelles de Latour 1991, Rowlands (in press) and Warnier 1985 and 1990.

of the *famla* conception, the "selling" of one's own relatives, would therefore be derived from a historical reality.

Another characteristic of the relations in these chieftaincies is that, in the last resort, it is the *fon* who legitimizes the wealth of his subjects. The relation to his court determines whether wealth is considered to be social or asocial (Fisiy and Geschiere 1991). This principle is of direct relevance ot the integration of new forms of wealth. By dedicating one's wealth to the *fon*, modern entrepreneurs can "whitewash" their riches, despite all rumours of *famla*. Conversely, any form of accumulation which is not related to the court is bound to be considered as asocial. This may explain why modern entrepreneurs from these areas are so keen to reinforce their links with the court, for instance by buying "traditional" titles in the associations around the throne. The *fons* for their part seem to be eager to participate in the new forms of accumulation by creating all sorts of pseudo-traditional titles and selling them to the new rich (Goheen in press). Again, this is not really an innovation. After all, the position of the *fon* has always been based on their control of the networks of accumulation.

To summarize: in the societies of the west, the strong position of the *fon* – his ideologically heavily buttressed control over accumulation – offers an institutional arrangement to legitimize wealth begotten by *famla*, which is lacking in the south-western societies.[22] In the west therefore, this type of belief functions less

as a barrier to new forms of accumulation and more as a powerful incentive to try and profit from the new opportunities in the market economy.[23]

5 Conclusion

The comparison above, brief and limited by a lack of space, raises a whole array of questions which should be further elaborated. Here, I can only mention a few.

First of all, these various metaphors of the market do indeed raise questions concerning the cultural construction of our own (that is western) market notions. The very fact that westerners tend to be shocked by the uninhibited display of market-like behaviour – such as haggling over money – in kinship rituals and other intimate spheres, begs the question of how exactly we construct a conceptual distinction between kinship and economy or "the market." In an interesting argument, Bloch (1989:172) tries to show how vital such distinctions are to the reproduction of capitalist relations: in his view they serve to maintain the separation, which is basic to capitalism, between the individual as private citizen and as worker (compare also Strathern 1985). Yet, how exactly these distinctions are reproduced in western thinking is not yet very clear.

More specifically, our examples can serve to defuse the current western stereotype of "traditional" societies almost by definition resisting the market. All the examples above

---

[22] Among the strongly segmentary Bakweri, chieftaincy was only weakly developed (according to some there were no real chiefs prior to the colonial conquest). The Duala had their "kingues" whose position was highly dependent on their contracts with European traders and who lacked the elaborate ideological reinforcement of the *fons* in the west; after the colonial conquest, the Duala "kingues" lost much of their influence.

[23] The Bakossi, half-way between Duala and the Bamiléké in the interior, exhibit yet another pattern. Mount Kupé the magic mountain, is in their territory and *ekong*-like ideas – here called *ekom* – are strongly developed among them. In their conception, *ekom* is not necessarily evil. It seems rather to be considered as a piece of good luck is someone succeeds in enriching himself with the help of *ekom*. This seems related to the idea that the zombies who are slaving away on the invisible plantations on Mount Kupé are mainly people from other groups (Bakweri, Duala). Among the Bakossi, these beliefs seem to reflect a sort of ideal of absentee landlordism which corresponds to the way Bakossi tried (and try) to profit from strangers – formerly slaves, now immigrants – by making them work on their ancestral lands (compare Balz 1984 and Ejedepang-Koge 1971).

indicate that things are much more ambiguous than this. The various metaphors embody elements of fear and can be seen as attempts to control the market, for instance by personalizing it. But they can at the same time encourage determined efforts to gain access to the market and the unknown opportunities offered by new market conditions. It is rather striking, for instance, that even the elders, whose position of authority was supposedly threatened by the penetration of money into these societies, seemed to have put up little resistance. Apparently they allowed money to penetrate rapidly into the central kinship rituals. This suggests that, instead of resisting the impact of money and the market, they welcomed these specific opportunities for gaining access to new riches.

In this sense, Appadurai (1986:57) seems right to conclude that such cultural constructions – around exchange, commodities, money or the market – are "political" and should be studied as such. They cannot simply be analyzed in relation to specific cultural or symbolical logics – by which one risks overrating their stability and coherence – but they have to be related to changing political relations. Without further specification, however, the term "political" risks becoming an inane label. Some indication is required of how the different political conditions and implications of these metaphors are to be analyzed – how we are to relate them to "specific social struggles."[24] Or, to be more concrete, how are we to explain that the metaphors discussed above could have such different implications for the way these societies reacted to the penetration of the world market?

At least for the societies discussed here, a valuable lead might be found in Rey's insistence on the key role of local contradictions in the articulation of these societies with new market conditions (Rey 1971 and 1973). To Rey, these local contradictions and the alliances of local power-holders with capitalist interest groups were crucial in the subjection of African societies to capitalism.[25] However, these contradictions differed according to region, as did the ways in which they were transformed and articulated with new politico-economic inequalities. The modern transformations of these local contradictions offer, therefore, a good starting-point for analyzing different trajectories – scenarios – in the articulation of local forms of organization with new relations of control and opportunity (compare Rey 1973, Geschiere in press).

This focus on local relations of power and their different articulations with new inequalities seems helpful to clarify the different tenor of the examples discussed above. It can serve to specify how we have to study the "politics" of these metaphors. For instance, to understand the different ways in which "the market of kinship" affected the reactions of these societies to the penetration of the world market, variations in the position of the elders and their position vis-à-vis the new power relations seem to be crucial. In the same way, the different implications of sorcery metaphors of the market proved to be related to specific power relations – in this case to the strong position of the chiefs among the Bamiléké and the Grassfielders, a position which was reinforced during the colonial period. Because these chiefs still had the power to "whitewash" the new wealth, even when there were

---

[24] Compare the quotation from Mamdani in the introduction above.

[25] I realize, of course, that it takes some courage nowadays to resurrect these discussions of the 1970s on modes of production and their articulation. It seems no accident that these debates ended in a cul-de-sac due to the heavy jargon and the obsession with definition and classification of modes of production. Probably these debates focused too much on the notion of "mode of production" (which proved to be fairly cumbersome) and thereby neglected the more open and creative notion of "articulation." It seems therefore still worthwhile to pursue Rey's explorations around this latter notion (compare also Laclau and Mouffe 1985 and in general van Binsbergen and Geschiere 1985).

rumours of sorcery, these metaphors could have a special impact here – less levelling and more congenial to accumulation than in other societies.

These are, of course, only sketchy comments. A real comparison would require more space. Yet, the above discussion may indicate how local metaphors of the market express creative processes of hybridization. Such processes are better understood in terms of analyzing variations in time and space à la Rey, than by the kind of binary oppositions –

such as "reciprocity" versus "the market" – which still tend to inform much anthropological discourse. The emphasis on hybridization and variations may serve to gain deeper insight into the recent predicament of these societies: at a time when conditions on the world market are dramatically deteriorating for them, they are confronted by a renewed emphasis on "the market" by development agencies. Such paradoxes indicate the wider context in which these local metaphors of the market have to be analysed.

References

Appadurai, A. 1986. "Introduction: Commodities and the Politics of Value," in A. Appadurai (ed.), *The Social Life of Things*. Cambridge: Cambridge University Press.

Ardener, E. 1970. "Witchcraft, Economics and the Continuity of Belief," in M. Douglas (ed.), *Witchcraft Confessions and Accusations*. London: Tavistock. pp. 141–60

Austen, R. A. 1977. "Slavery among Coastal Middlemen: the Duala of Cameroon," in S. Miers and I. Kopytoff (eds.), *Slavery in Africa*. Madison: Wisconsin University Press. pp. 305–33.

Balz, H. 1984. *Where the Faith has to Live. Studies in Bakossi Society and Religion*. Basel: Basel Mission.

Binsbergen, W. M. J. van, and P. Geschiere (eds.), 1985. *Old Modes of Production and Capitalist Encroachment: Anthropological Explorations in Africa*. London: Kegan Paul; Leiden: Afrika Studiecentrum.

Bloch, M. 1989. "The Symbolism of Money in Imerina," in J. Parry & M. Bloch (eds.), *op. cit.*, pp.165–191.

Bureau, R. 1962. *Ethno-sociologie religieuse des Douala et apparentés*. Yaoundé: Recherches et Etudes Camerounaises 7/8.

Dupré, G. 1982. *Un ordre et sa destruction*, Paris: ORSTOM.

Dongmo, J. -L. 1981. *Le dynamisme bamiléké*. Yaoundé.

Ejedepang-Koge, S. N. 1971. *The Tradition of a People: Bakossi*. Yaoundé.

Ejedepang-Koge, S. N. 1975. *Tradition and Change*

in *Peasant Activities: A Study of the Indigenous People's Search for Cash in the South West Province of Cameroon*. Yaoundé.

Fisiy, C. and P. Geschiere, 1991. "Sorcelierie et accumulation. Variations Régionales." *Critique of Anthropology* 11(3): pp. 25–77.

Furnivall, J. S. 1948. *Colonial Policy and Practice*. Cambridge: Cambridge University Press.

Geschiere, P. 1982. *Village Communities and the State: Changing Relations in Maka Villages (S. E. Cameroon)*. London: Kegan Paul International; Leiden: African Studies Centre.

Geschiere, P. 1983. "European Planters, African Peasants and the Colonial State: Alternatives in the 'mise en valeur' of Makaland, Southeast Cameroun, during the Interbellum," *African Economic History*, 12: 83–108.

Geschiere, P. 1988. "Sorcery and the State", *Critique of Anthropology*, 8: 35–63.

Geschiere, P. in press, "Anthropologists and the Crisis in Africa: Beyond Conceptual Dichotomies?." The Hauge: IMWOO.

Geschiere, P. & P. Konings (eds.), in press. *Les Itinéraires d'Accumulation au Cameroun*. Leiden: African Studies Centre; Paris: Karthala.

Goheen, M. in press, "Men own the fields, Women own the Crops: Gender and Accumulation in Nso," in P. Geschiere & P. Konings (eds.) *op. cit.*.

Gudeman, S. 1986. *Economics as Culture: models and metaphors of livelihood*. London: Routledge & Kegan Paul.

Harris, O. 1989. "The Earth and the State: The Sources and Meanings of Money in Northern

Potosí, Bolivia," in J. Parry & M. Bloch (eds.), *op. cit.* pp. 232–69.

Hart, K. 1986. "Heads or Tails? Two Sides of the Coin," *Man*, 21 (4):637–56.

Laclau, E. and C. Mouffe, 1985. *Hegemony and Socialist Strategy, Towards a Radical-Democratic Politics*, London: Verso.

Mallart Guimera, L. 1981. *Ni dos, ni ventre*, Paris: Société d'ethnographie.

Mamdani, M. 1990. "Uganda: Contradictions in the IMF programme and perspective," *Development and Change*, 21: 427–67.

Miaffo, D. and J. -P. Warnier, in press. "Accumulation et ethos de la notabilité chez les Bamiléké," in P. Geschiere and P. Konings, (eds.) *op. cit.*

Parkin, D. 1972. *Palms, Wine and Witnesses*. London: Intertext Books.

Parry J. and M. Bloch, 1989. "Introduction: Money and the Morality of Exchange," in J. Parry & M. Bloch (eds.), *op. cit.* pp. 1–33.

Parry J. and M. Bloch (eds.) 1989. *Money and the Morality of Exchange*, Cambridge: Cambridge University Press.

Polanyi, K. 1957. "The Economy as Instituted Process," in K. Polanyi, C. M. Arensberg and H. W. Pearson, *Trade and Market in the Early Empires*. New York: Free Press.

Pool, R. 1989. *There Must Have Been Something – Interpretation of Illness and Misfortune in a Cameroon Village.* Amsterdam: University of Amsterdam.

Pradelles de Latour, C. -H. 1991. *Ethnopsychanalyse en pays bamiléké*. Paris: EPEL.

Rey, P. -P. 1971. *Colonialisme, néo-colonialism et transition au capitalisme*. Paris: Maspero.

Rey, P. -P. 1973. *Les Alliances de classes*. Paris: Maspero.

Rosny, E. de, 1981. *Les yeux de ma chèvre – Sur les pas des maîtres de la nuit en pays douala*. Paris: Plon.

Rowlands, in press. "Economic Dynamism and Cultural Stereotyping in the Bamenda Grassfields," in P. Geschiere and P. Konings, (eds), *op. cit.*

Rowlands, M. & J. -P. Warnier, 1988. "Sorcery, Power and the Modern State in Cameroon," *Man* (N.S.), 23: 118–132.

Strathern, M. 1985. "Kinship and Economy: Constitutive Orders of a Provisional Kind," *American Ethnologist*, 12: 191–209.

Warnier, J. -P. 1985. *Echanges, developpement et hiérarchies dans le Bamenda précolonial (Cameroun)*. Stuttgart: Steiner.

Warnier, J. -P. 1990. "Traite sans raids au Cameroun," *Cahiers d'Etudes Africaines*, 113: 5–32.

Wirz, A. 1972. *Vom Sklavenhandel zum kolonialen Handel – Wirtschaftsraume and Wirtschaftsformen in Kamerun vor 1914*. Zurich: Atlantis.

PART V

ANCESTORS, GODS, AND THE
PHILOSOPHY OF RELIGION

Dogon shrine, Mali.
Photo: V. Sills.

ANCESTORS, GODS, AND THE PHILOSOPHY OF RELIGION

21   Marcel Griaule. 1948. *Conversations with Ogotemmêli: An Introduction to Dogon Religious Ideas.* pp. 11–34. Oxford University Press.

22   Paulin J. Hountondji. 1983. *African Philosophy, Myth and Reality.* pp. 55–70. Bloomington: Indiana University Press.

23   Karin Barber. 1981. "How Man Makes God in West Africa: Yoruba Attitudes Towards the Òrìṣà," *Africa* 51(3): 724–44.

24   Igor Kopytoff. 1971. "Ancestors as Elders in Africa," *Africa* 41(2): 129–42

Introduction

In 1931 French anthropologist Marcel Griaule, together with eight colleagues affiliated with the Musée de l'Homme in Paris, set out on a twenty-one month expedition, known as the Dakar–Djibouti Mission, which crossed the continent of Africa from the Atlantic Ocean to the Red Sea along the lower perimeter of the Sahara (Clifford, 1988: 55). The aim of the mission was to collect and record, as thoroughly as possible, local knowledge and material culture in order to document fully the arts, cultures, and religious beliefs of the vast territories in sub-Saharan Africa which, at the time, were under French colonial rule.

In the course of this extensive "scientific" expedition, Griaule first came in contact with the Dogon people who inhabit the rocky cliffs of the Bandiagara escarpments in what is today the Republic of Mali. Following his initial visit, Griaule returned to the Dogon region on many occasions, writing extensively on their masking and ritual traditions, on their concept of the body and soul, and on indigenous nomenclature and systems of classification and taxonomy.

Sometime in the late 1940s, Griaule was introduced to an elderly sage named Ogotemmêli who had lost his sight many years earlier in a hunting accident. This wise, blind Dogon man from the village of lower Ogol opened Griaule's eyes for the first time to the complexity and intellectual "depth" of African religious beliefs by recounting in a long series of interviews the elaborate creation myth of the Dogon universe. Written in the form of a series of object lessons, Griaule published *Conversations with Ogotemmêli* in 1948 as an attempt to present to the outside world a unified Dogon cosmology and complete philosophical system of thought (Van Beek, 1991: 139).

Griaule's writings on the Dogon were preceded just a few years earlier by the publication of a book entitled *Bantu Philosophy* (1945) written by a Belgian missionary named Placide Tempels. In this detailed and extensive volume, Tempels presented Bantu notions of magic and witchcraft as a rational and highly structured philosophy operating within a unified system of thought. Both Tempels (writing about a Bantu-speaking people) and Griaule (writing about a non-Bantu-speaking people) were battling eurocentric stereotypes of African religious beliefs which, at the time, saw them as largely disorganized superstitions characterized by animism and ancestor-worship. Making his case for the complexity and sophistication of Dogon religion, Griaule wrote in the preface to his book that "these people live by a cosmology, a metaphysic, and a religion which put them on a par with the peoples of antiquity, and which Christian theology might indeed study with profit" (1965 ed.: 2).

Griaule's contribution to the study of Dogon cosmology came to typify French scholarship on African systems of thought. It differed from the British school – such as Evans-Pritchard's Azande ethnography for example (see Part IV in this volume) – in two fundamental ways. First, Griaule argued that Dogon religion and ontology were just as complex and rigorous as any European belief system, and that therefore it should be accorded equal weight in an anthropology of world cosmologies and indigenous intellectual beliefs. Evans-Pritchard, in contrast, argued that Azande witchcraft was rational within the logic of its own universe of meaning, but that the Azande were not "rational" when judged by European values and standards of "objective" truth. The second aspect of Griaule's work which makes it typical of French writing on African systems of thought is his emphasis on intellectual coherence and narrative symbolic meaning. Unlike Evans-Pritchard and other British anthropologists or the early to mid twentieth century, the focus of Griaule's Dogon ethnography is not on ritual *behavior* or the *practice* of belief systems in the course of daily life (cf. Richards, 1966).

In his discussion of Western writings about African systems of thought, Malian philosopher Paulin J. Hountondji criticizes both Tempels and Griaule. According to Hountondji, these authors present . African

"philosophy" as an unarticulated intellectual system about which African people themselves are uncritical and largely unaware. Hountondji argues that Western observers of African societies have often assumed that "everybody always agrees with everybody else" (1983: 60). Griaule, for example, spins the words of a single Dogon man into the cultural fabric of an entire ethnic group's philosophy and cosmology. Contrary to this, however, men and women in African societies, like individuals everywhere, have widely divergent perspectives and contentious worldviews. Meanings are arrived at through debate and dialogue – and not simply through monolithic consent and the putative unanimity of collective opinion (Gyekye, 1995: xvii).

This false, essentialist construction of African systems of thought arises, according to Hountondji, out of a certain Western perspective which assumes that critical knowledge about Africa can only come from outside – where the Western observer somehow "sees" more than indigenous Africans can possibly see themselves. While Griaule argued that Dogon cosmology was highly complex and formed a comprehensive system of belief, he suggested at the same time that this unity was apparent only to the detached, "scientific" gaze of the outside observer. While insiders were able to recite myths and dwell upon certain isolated philosophical problems, the broader structures and implications of this universal system of thought largely eluded them.

The seminal work of Tempels and Griaule set forth a framework of investigation which was followed for years to come not only by subsequent European authors but also by an emerging group of African philosophers and scholars. Thus, in his critique of the literature on African philosophy, Hountondji takes issue not only with Tempels but also with Alexis Kagame, a Rwandan (Tutsi) historian and philosopher, whose book *La philosophie bantoue-rwandaise de l'Être* (1956) is a direct follow-up study of Tempels' work on Bantu ontology. Rather than begin from his own knowledge of Bantu culture, Kagame simply clarifies points made by Tempels, and corrects errors of fact here and there. An authentic and meaningful African philosophy, according to Hountondji, must spring from African intellectual discourse and must not simply refine and build upon Western models of Africa. But where, then, is this philosophy to be found today? According to Hountondji, this kind of African philosophy is "yet to come." In a comparison of the current dialogues on African philosophy, anthropologist Andrew Apter notes that for Hountondji, "So-called traditional African thought with its oral forms of expression and transmission may constitute a wisdom, but it lacks the power of sustained *critical reflection* that real philosophy demands." (1992: 90).

An important question, however, remains as to whether or not such a philosophy is indeed possible. What is an "authentic" African knowledge or philosophy? Who has the authority to construct or discern an African philosophy? Can African scholars, trained for the most part in European academic institutions, shed Western models of representation and intellectual precedents in order to create a pure, genuine Africanist discourse? And, furthermore, did authors like Tempels and Griaule do more harm than good in our understanding of African ontology and religion? These are difficult questions which remain at the heart of any discussion of African systems of thought.

The problem with the reproduction of European-derived models of African religious beliefs is that concepts and phrases often take on assumed meanings which are quite misleading and very different from the phenomena they are intended to describe. This point is clearly addressed in Igor Kopytoff's article "Ancestors as Elders in Africa" where the author presents a critical rethinking of the category "ancestors" in the religious beliefs of the Suku people of southwestern Zaire.

Contrary to Western beliefs about life and death, Kopytoff argues that there is a continuum between the category living "elders" and that of deceased "ancestors," and that the structural relationship between elder and junior is more important to the Suku than the existential boundary which separates the living from the dead. Kopytoff argues that concepts which commonly appear in African studies literature, such as "ancestor worship" and "ancestor cults," imply a powerful spiritual and religious element which simply is not found in Suku relationships with the dead. Ancestors are considered to be the eldest members of the lineage who are appealed to in times of crisis and misfortune. The fact that they are deceased and living in the other worlds is less critical to their power of redemption than the fact that they are elders and therefore the most senior members of a particular lineage.

Kopytoff's article makes clear that African religion does not operate in a realm which is separate from society, but rather religion is modeled on society itself. This important point is picked up again in Karin Barber's article on the nature of Yoruba relations with the gods. "How Man Makes God in West Africa" builds upon a classic essay by British anthropologist Meyer Fortes entitled *Oedipus and Job in West African Religion* which was published in 1959. In this essay, Fortes examines the way in which the Tallensi people of Ghana use religious concepts to order and explain key aspects of an individual's passage through the cycle of life. He identifies two sociological concepts, abstracted from African religions in general, which help explicate different types of structural relationships between humans and gods. In the first relationship, which he calls the Oedipal principle, human actions are governed by fate and destiny. Individuals are believed to take no personal responsibility for their lives, and thus place all actions and consequences in the hands of omnipotent gods and spiritual forces which are outside the realm of human influence.

In the second type of relationship, which Fortes calls the Jobian principle, individuals assume responsibility for their lives and believe that events are shaped by human actions which are only mediated in part by supernatural forces and divine justice. Throughout the course of their life, men and women can forge "contractual relationships" with the gods and, in so doing, try to subvert and overcome the elements of fate and destiny that otherwise govern the unfolding of their existence (Fortes, 1983 ed.: 4–6). Within every world religion and system of thought there is a delicate balance between the principles of divinely imposed destiny, on the one hand, and self-determination, on the other. While Fortes concludes that Tallensi relations to the gods are largely Oedipal in nature, Barber demonstrates that Yoruba individuals forge their own destiny and thus, according to this sociological scheme, their religious convictions would be classified according to Jobian principles.

Barber concludes her essay by remarking that "It seems clear that it was this willingness to try something new that conditioned the way Islam and Christianity were received" (1981: 741). In other words, in their search for spiritual guidance and protection, the Yoruba did not limit themselves to gods in the Yoruba religious universe, but explored with confidence and ease the potential benefits of other world religions. Because Yoruba beliefs are continually produced and reproduced through individual action, Islam and Christianity were not taken as a threat to a pre-existing or established order but were viewed as complementary systems of worship and belief. Kwame Anthony Appiah has written that "Most Africans, now, whether converted to Islam or Christianity or not, still share the beliefs of their ancestors in an ontology of invisible beings" (1992: 134). Thus, because Islam and Christianity did not overthrow existing religious beliefs, any study of Muslim and Christian religions in Africa must therefore begin with the roots of African religious thought. Although the readings for this book do not cover specifically the emergence or presence of Islam and Christianity in Africa, bibliographic suggestions for reading in these areas are listed at the end of this section.

References

Appiah, Kwame Anthony. 1992. *In My Father's House: Africa in the Philosophy of Culture*. New York: Oxford University Press.

Apter, Andrew. 1992. "*Que Faire?* Reconsidering Inventions of Africa," *Critical Inquiry* 19(1): 87–104.

Clifford, James. 1988. "Power and Dialogue in Ethnography: Marcel Griaule's Initiation." In *The Predicament of Culture: Twentieth-Century Ethnography, Literature, and Art*. Cambridge, MA: Harvard University Press.

Fortes, Meyer. 1983. *Oedipus and Job in West African Religion*. Cambridge: Cambridge University Press. First published in 1959.

Griaule, Marcel. 1965. *Conversations with Ogotemmêli: An Introduction to Dogon Religious Ideas*. London: Oxford University Press for the International African Institute.

Gyekye, Kwame. 1995. *An Essay on African Philosophical Thought: The Akan Conceptual Scheme*. Philadelphia: Temple University Press. First published 1987.

Kagame, Alexis. 1956. *La philosophie bantoue-rwandaise de l'Être*. Brussels: Academie royale des sciences coloniales.

Richards, A. I. 1966. "African Systems of Thought: An Anglo-French Dialogue," *Africa* 286–98.

Tempels, Placide. 1945. *La Philosophie bantoue*. Elisabethville: Louvania. English edition 1959; *Bantu Philosophy*. Paris: Presence Africaine.

Van Beek, Walter E. A. 1991. "Dogon Restudied: A Field Evaluation of the Work of Marcel Griaule," *Current Anthropology* 32(2): 139–58.

Suggested Readings

Blakely, Thomas D., Walter E. A. van Beek, and Dennis L. Thomson, eds. 1994. *Religion in Africa*. Portsmouth, NH: Heinemann.

Forde, Daryll, ed. 1954. *African Worlds: Studies in the Cosmological Ideas and Social Values of African Peoples*. London: Published for the International African Institute by the Oxford University Press.

Fortes, Meyer. 1987. *Religion, Morality, and the Person: The Essays on Tallensi Religion*. New York: Cambridge University Press.

Fortes, Meyer, and Germaine Dieterlen, eds. 1965. *African Systems of Thought*. London: Oxford University Press for the International African Institute.

Goody, Jack. 1962. *Death, Property, and the Ancestors: A Study of the Mortuary Customs of the Lodagga of West Africa*. Standford: Standford University Press.

Jahn, Janheinz. 1961. *Muntu: An Outline of the New African Culture*. New York: Grove Press.

Karp, Ivan, and Charles S. Bird, eds. 1980. *Explorations in African Systems of Thought*. Bloomington: Indiana University Press.

Lawal, Babatunde. 1977. "The Living Dead: Art and Immortality among the Yoruba of Nigeria," *Africa* 47 (1): 50–61.

Lawson, E. Thomas. 1984. *Religions of Africa: Traditions in Transformation*. San Francisco: Harper & Row.

MacGaffey, Wyatt. 1986. *Religion and Society in Central Africa: The BaKongo of Lower Zaire*. Chicago: The University of Chicago Press.

Mbiti, John S. 1991. *Introduction to African Religion*. Portsmouth, NH: Heinemann.

Middleton, John. 1960. *Lugbara Religion*. London: Oxford University Press.

Oruka, H. Odera, ed. 1990. *Sage Philosophy: Indigenous Thinkers and Modern Debate on African Philosophy*. New York: E. J. Brill.

Ranger, Terence O., and Isaria N. Limambo, eds. 1972. *The Historical Study of African Religion*. London: Heinemann.

Ray, Benjamin C. 1976. *African Religions: Symbol, Ritual, and Community*. Englewood Cliffs, NJ: Prentice-Hall.

Twesigye, Emmanuel K. 1987. *Common Ground: Christianity, African Religion, and Philosophy*. New York: Peter Lang.

Van Binsbergen, Wim. 1981. *Religious Change in Zambia*. London: Routledge & Kegan Paul.

Zahan, Dominique. 1979. *The Religion, Spirituality, and Thought of Traditional Africa*. Chicago: University of Chicago Press.

Further readings on Islam and Christianity in Africa

Bond, George, Walton Johnson, and Sheila S. Walker, eds. 1979. *African Christianity: Patterns of Religious Continuity*. New York: Academic Press.

Bravmann, René A. 1974. *Islam and Tribal Art in West Africa*. Cambridge: Cambridge University Press.

Clarke, Peter Bernard. 1982. *West Africa and Islam: A study of Religious Development from the 8th to the 20th Century*. London: Edward Arnold.

——. 1986. *West Africa and Christianity*. London: Edward Arnold.

Cruise O'Brien, Donal B., and Christian Coulon. 1988. *Charisma and Brotherhood in African Islam*. Oxford: Clarendon Press.

Falola, Toyin, and Biodun Adediran. 1983. *Islam and Christianity in West Africa*. Ife-Ife, Nigeria: University of Ife Press.

Kritzeck, James. 1969. *Islam in Africa*. New York: Van Nostrand-Reinhold.

Lewis, I. M. 1980. *Islam in Tropical Islam*. London: International African Institute in association with Hutchinson University Library for Africa.

Nyang, Sulayman S. 1984. *Islam, Christianity, and African Industry*. Brattleboro, VT. : Amara Books.

Olupona, Jacob K. and Sulayman S. Nyang, eds. 1993. *Religious Plurality in Africa: Essays in Honour of John S. Mbiti*. Berlin; New York: Mouton de Gruyter.

Sanneh, Lamin. 1983. *West African Christianity*. London: Allen Unwin.

Sanneh, Lamin O. 1989. *The Jakhanke Muslim Clerics: A Religious and Historical Study of Islam in Senegambia*. Lanham, MD: University Press of America.

Smith, Mary F. 1981. *Baba of Karo: A Woman of the Muslim Hausa*. New Haven and London: Yale University Press. First published 1954.

Trimingham, John Spencer. 1962. *A History of Islam in West Africa*. London: Oxford University Press.

——. 1964. *Islam in East Africa*. Oxford: Clarendon.

——. 1968. *The Influence of Islam upon Africa*. New York: Praeger.

Zoghby, Samir M. 1978. *Islam in Sub-Saharan Africa: A Partially Annotated Guide*. Washington, D.C.: Library of Congress.

21

CONVERSATIONS WITH OGOTEMMÊLI

MARCEL GRIAULE

First Day: Ogotemmêli

Lower Ogol, like all Dogon Villages, was a collection of houses and granaries all crowded together, flat roofs of clay alternating with cone-shaped roofs of straw. Picking one's way along its narrow streets of light and shade, between the truncated pyramids, prisms, cubes or cylinders of the granaries and houses, the rectangular porticoes, the red or white altars shaped like umbilical hernias, one felt like a dwarf lost in a maze. Everything was mottled by the rains and the heat; the mud-walls were fissured like the skins of pachyderms. Over the walls of the tiny court-yards might be seen, under the floors of the granaries, fowls, yellow dogs, and sometimes great tortoises, symbols of the patriarchs.

At a turn of the street there was a door, shaped with an axe, but, even when new, it could never have fitted the entrance built of earthen pillars with a pediment of wooden blocks. The door was as wide as a man's two shoulders; winter rains had ploughed wave-like furrows in the wood between which the knots looked like open eyes. Drought, clutching hands, and the muzzles of goats had worn it away so that it grated on its hinges and

swung back against the wall with a bang like a gong, revealing a squalid courtyard, which belonged to the most remarkable man of the plains and rocks from Oropa to Nimbé, Asakarba and Tintam.

The white man stepped over the scanty midden of an old man with no family. A row of cabins, broken by a low door on the ground floor and a flat panel on the floor above, stood in the middle of the courtyard forming a façade which concealed the main building behind it. In the pediment were ten swallows' nests, and the edge of the roof was adorned by eight cones with flat stone tops. To right and left were six granaries in a row like big dice, two of them facing the neighbouring house, to which they belonged. Of the other four one was empty, another rickety, and the third split across like a half-bitten fruit. Only one of them was in use: it was half full of grain.

Opposite, between the main building and the granaries, a low house, in which there were faint sounds of life, completed the enclosure of the courtyard. On the right in a store-room open to the sky there was a perpetual whirl of down blown about by a light breeze.

The man accompanying the European pronounced the usual words of greeting.

Immediately a voice replied clearly and distinctly:

"God brings you! God brings you!"

"Greetings! How is your health?"

Slowly the voice drew nearer. From the shadows of the interior came the sound of hands feeling their way along walls and wood-work. A stick tapped on the floor: there was a sound of hollow earthenware: some tiny chickens made their way out one by one through the cat-hole, thrust out by the great being who was approaching.

At last there appeared a brown tunic, drawn in at the seams and frayed by long use like the standards of the warriors of old. Then a head bent beneath the lintel of the door, and the man stood up to his full height, turning towards the stranger a face that no words can describe.

"Greetings!" he said, "Greetings to those who are athirst!"

The thick lips spoke the purest Sanga language. So alive were they that one saw nothing else. All the other features seemed to be folded away, particularly as, after the first words, the head had been bent. The cheeks, the cheek-bones, the forehead and the eyelids seemed all to have suffered the same ravages; they were creased by a hundred wrinkles which had caused a painful contortion as of a face exposed to too strong a light or battered by a hail of stones. The eyes were dead.

The two visitors came from outside, and might therefore be supposed to have been working in the heat. Accordingly the old man leaning on his stick greeted them with the words:

"Welcome! Welcome after weariness! Welcome from the sun!"

The longest task of the first day was the choice of a place for the conversations. The space in front of the dwelling-house, even if the aged Ogotemmêli remained indoors, and even if the white man bent his head towards him and spoke in low tones as if in the confessional, was, according to Ogotemmêli, open to the objection that interviews there might excite the eternal curiosity of the women. The minute courtyard on the other side of the building, on the other hand, which was exposed to all the winds from the north, might be watched by children hidden in the ruined granary. There remained the courtyard itself with its wretched dung-heap, its hollow stone, its ashes and its dilapidated wall with a gap in the middle of it just high enough for curious eyes to look through.

Ogotemmêli still hesitated; he had much to say about the inconvenience of the courtyard for the purpose of conversations between men of mature years. The European for his part did not open his mouth except to agree; he even stressed the indiscreet nature of walls and the stupidity of men and, naturally, the uncon-scionable curiosity of women and their insatiable thirst for novelties. All these precau-tions interested him: they seemed so out of proportion to the simple sale of an amulet.

In the end Ogotemmêli sat down on the threshold of the lower door of the main façade; doubled up, with his face bent downwards and his hands crossed above his head, his elbows resting on his knees, he waited.

The white man was beginning to realize that the sale of the amulet was only a pretext. There was no reference to it in the subsequent conversations, and the underlying reason for the old man's action never transpired. But from various details it appeared, as time went on, that Ogotemmêli wished to pass on to the foreigner, who had first visited the country fifteen years before, and whom he trusted, the instruction which he himself had received first from his grandfather and later from his father.

But he was waiting. He was perplexed by the result of his own approaches to this man whom he could not see. Not that the man was unknown to him: for fifteen years he had been hearing about groups of Europeans, who came, under this man's guidance, to live rough and to ride about the country studying the customs of the people.

He had even followed their work since the

beginning, for he had been closely associated with Ambibê Babadyé, the great dignitary of the masks and the white man's regular informant, who had only recently died. Many times in the last fifteen years Ambibê had come to Ogotemmêli for information and advice. From what Ambitê had told him, and from the reports of a number of other persons, he had formed a correct idea of the aims and objects of his interlocutor and his unwearying passion for research.

But the situation was unique. How was one to instruct a European? How could one make him understand things and rites and beliefs? Moreover this white man had already found out about the masks, and knew their secret language. He had been all over the country in every direction, and about some of its institutions he knew as much as he knew himself. How then to set about it?

The European relieved him of his embarrassment.

"When your gun exploded in your face, what were you firing at?"

"At a porcupine."

The white man was trying by an indirect approach to lead the conversation to hunting and the attitude towards the animal world, and so to totemism.

"It was an accident," said the old man. "But it was also a last warning. I knew by divination that I was to give up hunting if I wanted to protect my children. Hunting is a work of death, and it attracts death. I have had twenty-one children, and now only five are left."

All the tragedy of African mortality was in his words, and all the deep questionings of these men about death and their defencelessness in the face of it. They clung to their beliefs, as do all men everywhere, but though beliefs may console and explain, they cannot avert the experience.

It was on this plane of suffering that Ogotemmêli's personality was revealed, in itself and in its relation with supernatural powers. From the age of fifteen he had been initiated in the mysteries of religion by his grandfather. After the latter's death his father had continued the instruction. It seemed that the "lessons" had gone on for more than twenty years, and that Ogotemmêli's family was not one that took these things lightly.

Ogotemmêli himself, no doubt, had from a very early age shown signs of an eager mind and considerable shrewdness. Until he lost his sight, he was a mighty hunter who, though one-eyed from childhood as a result of smallpox, would always come back from the chase with a full bag, while the others were still toiling in the gorges. His skill as a hunter was the fruit of his profound knowledge of nature, of animals, of men and of gods. After his accident he learnt still more. Thrown back on his own resources, on his altars and on whatever he was able to hear, he had become one of the most powerful minds on the cliffs.

Indeed his name and his character were famous throughout the plateau and the hills, known (as the saying was) to the youngest boy. People came to his door for advice every day and even by night.

Phrygian caps were even now showing above the walls, and the women were making signs from a distance. It was time to go, and make room for the clients. But contact had now been made, and the conversations thereafter came about by tacit consent, according to a sort of programme and at convenient times.

Second Day: The First Word and the Fibre Skirt

Ogotemmêli, seating himself on his threshold, scraped his stiff leather snuff-box, and put a pinch of yellow powder on his tongue.

"Tobacco," he said, "makes for right thinking."

So saying, he set to work to analyse the world system, for it was essential to begin with the dawn of all things. He rejected as a detail of no interest, the popular account of how the fourteen solar systems were formed from flat circular slabs of earth one on top of the other.

He was only prepared to speak of the service-able solar system; he agreed to consider the stars, though they only played a secondary part.

"It is quite true," he said, "that in course of time women took down the stars to give them to their children. The children put spindles through them and made them spin like fiery tops to show themselves how the world turned. But that was only a game."

The stars came from pellets of earth flung out into space by the God Amma, the one God. He had created the sun and the moon by a more complicated process, which was not the first known to man but is the first attested invention of God: the art of pottery. The sun is, in a sense, a pot raised once for all to white heat and surrounded by a spiral of red copper with eight turns. The moon is the same shape, but its copper is white. It was heated only one quarter at a time. Ogotemmêli said he would explain later the movements of these bodies. For the moment he was concerned only to indicate the main lines of the design, and from that to pass to its actors.

He was anxious, however, to give an idea of the size of the sun.

"Some," he said, "think it is as large as this encampment, which would mean thirty cubits. But it is really bigger. Its surface area is bigger than the whole of Sanga Canton."

And after some hesitation he added:

"It is perhaps even bigger than that."

He refused to linger over the dimensions of the moon, nor did he ever say anything about them. The moon's function was not impor-tant, and he would speak of it later. He said however that, while Africans were creatures of light emanating from the fullness of the sun, Europeans were creatures of the moonlight: hence their immature appearance.

He spat out his tobacco as he spoke. Ogotemmêli had nothing against Europeans. He was not even sorry for them. He left them to their destiny in the lands of the north.

The God Amma, it appeared, took a lump of clay, squeezed it in his hand and flung it from him, as he had done with the stars. The clay spread and fell on the north, which is the top, and from there stretched out to the south, which is the bottom, of the world, although the whole movement was horizontal. The earth lies flat, but the north is at the top. It extends east and west with separate members like a foetus in the womb. It is a body, that is to say, a thing with members branching out from a central mass. This body, lying flat, face upwards, in a line from north to south, is femi-nine. Its sexual organ is an anthill, and its clitoris a termite hill. Amma, being lonely and desirous of intercourse with this creature, approached it. That was the occasion of the first breach of the order of the universe.

Ogotemmêli ceased speaking. His hands crossed above his head, he sought to dis-tinguish the different sounds coming from the courtyards and roofs. He had reached the point of the origin of troubles and of the primordial blunder of God.

"If they overheard me, I should be fined an ox!"

At God's approach the termite hill rose up, barring the passage and displaying its masculinity. It was as strong as the organ of the stranger, and intercourse could not take place. But God is all-powerful. He cut down the termite hill, and had intercourse with the excised earth. But the original incident was destined to affect the course of things for ever; from this defective union there was born, instead of the intended twins, a single being, the *Thos aureus* or jackal, symbol of the diffi-culties of God. Ogotemmêli's voice sank lower and lower. It was no longer a question of women's ears listening to what he was saying; other, non-material, ear-drums might vibrate to his important discourse. The European and his African assistant, Sergeant Koguem, were leaning towards the old man as if hatching plots of the most alarming nature.

But, when he came to the beneficent acts of God, Ogotemmêli's voice again assumed its normal tone.

God had further intercourse with his

earth-wife, and this time without mishaps of any kind, the excision of the offending member having removed the cause of the former disorder. Water, which is the divine seed, was thus able to enter the womb of the earth and the normal reproductive cycle resulted in the birth of twins. Two beings were thus formed. God created them like water. They were green in colour, half human beings and half serpents. From the head to the loins they were human: below that they were serpents. Their red eyes were wide open like human eyes, and their tongues were forked like the tongues of reptiles. Their arms were flexible and without joints. Their bodies were green and sleek all over, shining like the surface of water, and covered with short green hairs, a presage of vegetation and germination.

These spirits, called Nummo, were thus two homogeneous products of God, of divine essence like himself, conceived without untoward incidents and developed normally in the womb of the earth. Their destiny took them to Heaven, where they received the instructions of their father. Not that God had to teach them speech, that indispensable necessity of all beings, as it is of the world-system; the Pair were born perfect and complete; they had eight members, and their number was eight, which is the symbol of speech.

They were also of the essence of God, since they were made of his seed, which is at once the ground, the form, and the substance of the life-force of the world, from which derives the motion and the persistence of created being. This force is water, and the Pair are present in all water: they *are* water, the water of the seas, of coasts, of torrents, of storms, and of the spoonfuls we drink.

Ogotemmêli used the terms "Water" and "Nummo" indiscriminately.

"Without Nummo," he said, "it was not even possible to create the earth, for the earth was moulded clay and it is from water (that is, from Nummo) that its life is derived."

"What life is there in the earth?" asked the European.

"The life-force of the earth is water. God moulded the earth with water. Blood too he made out of water. Even in a stone there is this force, for there is moisture in everything.

"But if Nummo is water, it also produces copper. When the sky is overcast, the sun's rays may be seen materializing on the misty horizon. These rays, excreted by the spirits, are of copper and are light. They are water too, because they uphold the earth's moisture as it rises. The Pair excrete light, because they are also light."

While he was speaking, Ogotemmêli had been searching for something in the dust. He finally collected a number of small stones. With a rapid movement he flung them into the courtyard over the heads of his two interlocutors, who had no time to bend down. The stones fell just where the Hogon's cock had been crowing a few seconds before.

"That cock is a squalling nuisance. He makes all conversation impossible."

The bird began to crow again on the other side of the wall, so Ogotemmêli sent Koguem to throw a bit of wood at him. When Koguem came back, he asked whether the cock was now outside the limits of the Tabda quarter.

"He is in the Hogon's field," said Koguem. "I have set four children to watch him."

"Good!" said Ogotemmêli with a little laugh. "Let him make the most of what remains to him of life! They tell me he is to be eaten at the next Feast of Twins."

He returned to the subject of the Nummo spirits, or (as he more usually put it, in the singular) of Nummo, for this pair of twins, he explained, represented the perfect, the ideal unit.

The Nummo, looking down from Heaven, saw their mother, the earth, naked and speechless, as a consequence no doubt of the original incident in her relations with the God Amma. It was necessary to put an end to this state of disorder. The Nummo accordingly came down to earth, bringing with them fibres pulled from plants already created in the heavenly regions. They took ten bunches of these fibres, corresponding to the number of their ten fingers, and made two strands of them, one for the front and one for behind. To this day masked men still wear these appendages hanging down to their feet in thick tendrils.

But the purpose of this garment was not merely modesty. It manifested on earth the first act in the ordering of the universe and the revelation of the helicoid sign in the form of an undulating broken line.

For the fibres fell in coils, symbol of tornadoes, of the windings of torrents, of eddies and whirlwinds, of the undulating movement of reptiles. They recall also the eight-fold spirals of the sun, which sucks up moisture. They were themselves a channel of moisture, impregnated as they were with the freshness of the celestial plants. They were full of the essence of Nummo: they *were* Nummo in motion, as shown in the undulating line, which can be prolonged to infinity.

When Nummo speaks, what comes from his mouth is a warm vapour which conveys, and itself constitutes, speech. This vapour, like all water, has sound, dies away in a helicoid line. The coiled fringes of the skirt were therefore the chosen vehicle for the words which the Spirit desired to reveal to the earth. He endued his hands with magic power by raising them to his lips while he plaited the skirt, so that the moisture of his words was imparted to the damp plaits, and the spiritual revelation was embodied in the technical instruction.

In these fibres full of water and words, placed over his mother's genitalia, Nummo is thus always present.

Thus clothed, the earth had a language, the first language of this world and the most primitive of all time. Its syntax was elementary, its verbs few, and its vocabulary without elegance. The words were breathed sounds scarcely differentiated from one another, but nevertheless vehicles. Such as it was, this ill-defined speech sufficed for the great works of the beginning of all things.

In the middle of a word Ogotemmêli gave a loud cry in answer to the hunter's halloo which the discreet Akundyo, priest of women dying in childbirth and of stillborn children, had called through the gap in the wall.

Akundyo first spat to one side, his eye riveted on the group of men. He was wearing a red Phrygian cap which covered his ears, with a raised point like a uraeus on the bridge of the nose in the fashion known as "the wind blows". His cheek-bones were prominent, and his teeth shone. He uttered a formal salutation to which the old man at once replied and the exchange of courtesies became more and more fulsome.

"God's curse," exclaimed Ogotemmêli, "on any in Lower Ogol who love you not!"

With growing emotion Akundyo made shift to out-do the vigour of the imprecation.

"May God's curse rest on me," said the blind man at last, "if I love you not!"

The four men breathed again. They exchanged humorous comments on the meagreness of the game in the I valley. Eventually Akundyo took his leave of them, asserting in the slangy French of a native soldier that he was going to "look for porcupine", an animal much esteemed by these people.

The conversation reverted to the subject of speech. Its function was organization, and therefore it was good; nevertheless from the start it let loose disorder.

This was because the jackal, the deluded and deceitful son of God, desired to possess speech, and laid hands on the fibres in which language was embodied, that is to say, on his mother's skirt. His mother, the earth, resisted this incestuous action. She buried herself in her own womb, that is to say, in the anthill, disguised as an ant. But the jackal followed her. There was, it should be explained, no other woman in the world whom he could desire. The hole which the earth made in the anthill was never deep enough, and in the end she had to admit defeat. This prefigured the even-handed struggles between men and women, which, however, always end in the victory of the male.

The incestuous act was of great consequence. In the first place it endowed the jackal with the gift of speech so that ever afterwards he was able to reveal to diviners the designs of God.

It was also the cause of the flow of menstrual blood, which stained the fibres. The resulting defilement of the earth was incompatible with the reign of God. God rejected that spouse, and decided to create living beings directly. Modelling a womb in damp clay, he placed it on the earth and covered it with a pellet flung out into space from heaven. He made a male organ in the same way and having put it on the ground, he flung out a sphere which stuck to it.

The two lumps forthwith took organic shape; their life began to develop. Members separated from the central core, bodies appeared, and a human pair arose out of the lumps of earth.

At this point the Nummo Pair appeared on the scene for the purpose of further action. The Nummo foresaw that the original rule of twin births was bound to disappear, and that errors might result comparable to those of the jackal, whose birth was single. For it was because of his solitary state that the first son of God acted as he did.

"The jackal was alone from birth," said Ogotemmêli, "and because of this he did more things than can be told."

The Spirit drew two outlines on the ground, one on top of the other, one male and the other female. The man stretched himself out on these two shadows of himself, and took both of them for his own. The same thing was done for the woman. Thus it came about that each human being from the first was endowed with two souls of different sex, or rather with two principles corresponding to two distinct persons. In the man the female soul was located in the prepuce; in the woman the male soul was in the clitoris.

But the foreknowledge of the Nummo no doubt revealed to him the disadvantages of this makeshift. Man's life was not capable of supporting both beings: each person would have to merge himself in the sex for which he appeared to be best fitted.

The Nummo accordingly circumcised the man, thus removing from him all the femininity of his prepuce. The prepuce, however, changed itself into an animal which is "neither a serpent nor an insect, but is classed with serpents". This animal is called a *nay*. It is said to be a sort of lizard, black and white like the pall which covers the dead. Its name also means "four", the female number, and "Sun", which is a female being. The *nay* symbolized the pain of circumcision and the need for the man to suffer in his sex as the woman does.

The man then had intercourse with the woman, who later bore the first two children of a series of eight, who were to become the ancestors of the Dogon people. In the moment of birth the pain of parturition was concentrated in the woman's clitoris, which was excised by an invisible hand, detached itself and left her, and was changed into the form of a scorpion. The pouch and the sting symbolized the organ: the venom was the water and the blood of the pain.

The European, returning through the millet field, found himself wondering about the significance of all these actions and counteractions, all these sudden jerks in the thought of the myth.

Here, he reflected, is a Creator God spoiling his first creation; restoration is effected by the excision of the earth, and then by the birth of a pair of spirits, inventive beings who construct the world and bring to it the first spoken words; an incestuous act destroys the created order, and jeopardizes the principle of twin-births. Order is restored by the creation of a pair of human beings, and twin-births are replaced by dual souls. (But why, he asked himself, twin-births at all?)

The dual soul is a danger; a man should be

male, and a woman female. Circumcision and excision are once again the remedy. (But why the *nay*? Why the scorpion?)

The answers to these questions were to come later, and to take their place in the massive structure of doctrine, which the blind old man was causing to emerge bit by bit from the mists of time.

Over the heads of the European and Koguem the dark millet clusters stood out against the leaden sky. They were passing through a field of heavy ears, stiffly erect and motionless in the breeze. When the crop is backward and thin, the ears are light and move with the slightest breath of wind. Thin crops are therefore full of sound. An abundant crop, on the other hand, is weighed down by the wind and bows itself in silence.

Third Day: The Second Word and Weaving

Anyone entering the courtyard upset its arrangements. It was so cramped that the kites, most cunning of all the acrobats of the air, could not get at the poultry. In a hollow stone there were the remains, or rather, the dregs of some millet-beer, which the poultry, cock, hen and chickens, were glad to drink. So was a yellow and white striped dog with tail erect like an Ethiopian sabre. When the door banged, all these creatures dispersed, leaving the court-yard to the humans.

Ogotemmêli, ensconced in his doorway, proceeded to enumerate the eight original ancestors born of the couple created by God. The four eldest were males: the four others were females. But by a special dispensation, permitted only to them, they were able to fertilize themselves, being dual and bisexual. From them are descended the eight Dogon families.

For humanity was organizing itself in this makeshift condition. The permanent calamity of single births was slightly mitigated by the grant of the dual soul, which the Nummo traced on the ground beside women in child-birth. Dual souls were implanted in the new-born child by holding it by the thighs above the place of the drawings with its hands and feet touching the ground. Later the super-fluous soul was eliminated by circumcision, and humanity limped towards its obscure destiny.

But the divine thirst for perfection was not extinguished, and the Nummo Pair, who were gradually taking the place of God their father, hand in mind projects of redemption. But, in order to improve human conditions, reforms and instruction had to be carried out on the human level. The Nummo were afraid of the terrifying effect of contact between creatures of flesh and blood on the one hand and purely spiritual beings on the other. There had to be actions that could be understood, taking place within the ambit of the beneficiaries and in their own environment. Men after regenera-tion must be drawn towards the ideal as a peasant is drawn to rich farmland.

The Nummo accordingly came down to earth, and entered the anthill, that is to say, the sexual part of which they were themselves the issue. Thus, they were able, among other tasks, to defend their mother against possible attempts by their elder, the incestuous jackal. At the same time, by their moist, luminous, and articulate presence, they were purging that body which was for ever defiled in the sight of God, but was nevertheless capable of acquiring in some degree the purity required for the activities of life.

In the anthill the male Nummo took the place of the masculine element, which had been eliminated by the excision of the termite-hill clitoris, while the female Nummo took the place of the female element, and her womb became part of the womb of the earth.

The Pair could then proceed to the work of regeneration, which they intended to carry out in agreement with God and in God's stead.

"Nummo in Amma's place," said Ogotemmêli, "was working the work of Amma."

In those obscure beginnings of the evolution of the world, men had no knowledge of death, and the eight ancestors, offspring of the first human couple, lived on indefinitely. They had eight separate lines of descendants, each of them being self-propagating since each was both male and female.

The four males and the four females were couples in consequence of their lower, i.e. of their sexual, parts. The four males were man and woman, and the four females were woman and man. In the case of the males it was the man, and in the case of the females it was the woman, who played the dominant role. They coupled and became pregnant each in him or herself, and so produced their offspring.

But in the fullness of time an obscure instinct led the eldest of them towards the anthill which had been occupied by the Nummo. He wore on his head as head-dress and to protect him from the sun, the wooden bowl he used for his food. He put his two feet into the opening of the anthill, that is of the earth's womb, and sank in slowly as if for a parturition *a tergo*.

The whole of him thus entered into the earth, and his head itself disappeared. But he left on the ground, as evidence of his passage into that world, the bowl which had caught on the edges of the opening. All that remained on the anthill was the round wooden bowl, still bearing traces of the food and the finger-prints of its vanished owner, symbol of his body and of his human nature, as, in the animal world, is the skin which a reptile has shed.

Liberated from his earthly condition, the ancestor was taken in charge by the regenerating Pair. The male Nummo led him into the depths of the earth, where, in the waters of the womb of his partner he curled himself up like a foetus and shrank to germinal form, and acquired the quality of water, the seed of God and the essence of the two Spirits.

And all this process was the work of the Word. The male with his voice accompanied the female Nummo who was speaking to herself and to her own sex. The spoken Word entered into her and wound itself round her womb in a spiral of eight turns. Just as the helical band of copper round the sun gives to it its daily movement, so the spiral of the Word gave to the womb its regenerative movement.

Thus perfected by water and words, the new Spirit was expelled and went up to Heaven.

All the eight ancestors in succession had to undergo this process of transformation; but, when the turn of the seventh ancestor came, the change was the occasion of a notable occurrence.

The seventh in a series, it must be remembered, represents perfection. Though equal in quality with the others, he is the sum of the feminine element, which is four, and the masculine element, which is three. He is thus the completion of the perfect series, symbol of the total union of male and female, that is to say of unity.

And to this homogeneous whole belongs especially the mastery of words, that is, of language; and the appearance on earth of such a one was bound to be the prelude to revolutionary developments of a beneficent character.

In the earth's womb he became, like the others, water and spirit, and his development, like theirs, followed the rhythm of the words uttered by the two transforming Nummo.

"The words which the female Nummo spoke to herself," Ogotemmêli explained, "turned into a spiral and entered into her sexual part. The male Nummo helped her. These are the words which the seventh ancestor learnt inside the womb."

The others equally possessed the knowledge of these words in virtue of their experiences in the same place; but they had not attained the mastery of them nor was it given to them to develop their use. What the seventh ancestor had received, therefore, was the perfect knowledge of a Word – the second Word to be heard on earth, clearer than the first and not, like the first, reserved for particular recipients, but destined for all mankind. Thus he was able to achieve progress for the world. In particular, he enabled mankind to take precedence over God's wicked son, the jackal. The latter, it is true, still possessed knowledge of the first Word, and could still therefore reveal to diviners certain heavenly purposes; but in the future order of things he was to be merely a laggard in the process of revelation.

The potent second Word developed the powers of its new possessor. Gradually he came to regard his regeneration in the womb of the earth as equivalent to the capture and occupation of that womb, and little by little he took possession of the whole organism, making such use of it as suited him for the purpose of his activities. His lips began to merge with the edges of the anthill, which widened and became a mouth. Pointed teeth made their appearance, seven for each lip, then ten, the number of the fingers, later forty, and finally eighty, that is to say, ten for each ancestor.

These numbers indicated the future rates of increase of the families; the appearance of the teeth was a sign that the time for new instruction was drawing near.

But here again the scruples of the Spirits made themselves felt. It was not directly to men, but to the ant, avatar of the earth and native to the locality, that the seventh ancestor imparted instruction.

At sunrise on the appointed day the seventh ancestor Spirit spat out eighty threads of cotton; these he distributed between his upper teeth which acted as the teeth of a weaver's reed. In this way he made the uneven threads of a warp. He did the same with the lower teeth to make the even threads. By opening and shutting his jaws the Spirit caused the threads of the warp to make the movements required in weaving. His whole face took part in the work, his nose studs serving as the block, while the stud in his lower lip was the shuttle.

As the threads crossed and uncrossed, the two tips of the Spirit's forked tongue pushed the thread of the weft to and fro, and the web took shape from his mouth in the breath of the second revealed Word.

For the Spirit was speaking while the work proceeded. As did the Nummo in the first revelation, he imparted his Word by means of a technical process, so that all men could understand. By so doing he showed the identity of material actions and spiritual forces, or rather the need for their co-operation.

The words that the Spirit uttered filled all the interstices of the stuff: they were woven in the threads, and formed part and parcel of the cloth. They were the cloth, and the cloth was the Word. That is why woven material is called *soy*, which means "It is the spoken word". *Soy* also means "seven", for the Spirit who spoke as he wove was seventh in the series of ancestors.

While the work was going on, the ant came and went on the edge in the opening in the breath of the Spirit, hearing and remembering his words. The new instruction, which she thus received, she passed on to the men who lived in those regions, and who had already followed the transformation of the sex of the earth.

Up to the time of the ancestors' descent into the anthill, men had lived in holes dug in the level soil like the lairs of animals. When their attention was drawn to the bowls which the ancestors had left behind them, they began to notice the shape of the anthill, which they thought much better than their holes. They copied the shape of the anthill accordingly, making passages and rooms as shelters from the rain, and began to store the produce of the crops for food.

They were thus advancing towards a less primitive way of life; and, when they noticed the growth of teeth round the opening, they imitated these too as a means of protection against wild beasts. They moulded great teeth of clay, dried them and set them up round the entrances to their dwellings.

At the moment of the second instruction, therefore, men were living in dens which were already, in some sort, a prefiguration of the place of revelation and of the womb into which each of them in due course would descend to be regenerated. And, moreover, the human anthill, with its occupants and its store-chambers for grain, was a rudimentary image of the system which, much later, was to come down to them from Heaven in the form of a marvellous granary.

These dim outlines of things to come predisposed men to take advice from the ant. The latter, after what it had seen the Spirit do, had laid in a store of cotton-fibres. These it had made into threads and, in the sight of men, drew them between the teeth of the anthill entrance as the Spirit had done. As the warp emerged, the men passed the thread of the weft, throwing it right and left in time to the opening and shutting movements of the jaws, and the resulting web was rolled round a piece of wood, fore-runner of the beam.

The ant at the same time revealed the words it had heard and the man repeated them. Thus there was recreated by human lips the concept of life in motion, of the transposition of forces, of the efficacy of the breath of the Spirit, which the seventh ancestor had created; and thus the interlacing of warp and weft enclosed the same words, the new instruction which became the heritage of mankind and was handed on from generation to generation of weavers to the accompaniment of the clapping of the shuttle and the creaking of the block, which they call the "creaking of the Word".

All these operations took place by daylight, for spinning and weaving are work for the day-time. Working at night would mean weaving webs of silence and darkness.

Fourth Day: The Third Word and the Granary of Pure Earth

Ogotemmêli had no very clear idea of what happened in Heaven after the transformation of the eight ancestors into Nummo. It is true that the eight, after leaving the earth, having completed their labours, came to the celestial region where the eldest Pair, who had trans-formed them, reigned. It is true also that these elders had precedence of the others, and did not fail to impose on them at once a form of organization and rules of life.

But it was never quite clear why this celestial world was disturbed to the point of disintegration, or why these disorders led to a reorganization of the terrestrial world, which had nothing to do with the celestial disputes. What is certain is that in the end the eight came down to earth again in a vast apparatus of symbols, in which was included a third and definitive Word necessary for the working of the modern world.

All that could be gathered from Ogotemmêli, by dint of patient attention to his words, was the evasive answer:

"Spirits do not fall from Heaven except in anger or because they are expelled."

It was obvious that he was conscious of the infinite complexity of the idea of God or the Spirits who took his place, and was reluctant to explain it. However an outline, slight but nevertheless adequate, of this obscure period was eventually obtained.

The Nummo Pair had received the trans-formed eight in Heaven. But though they were all of the same essence, the Pair had the rights of the elder generation in relation to the newcomers, on whom they imposed an organization with a network of rules, of which the most onerous was the one which separated them from one another and forbade them to visit one another.

The fact was that, like human societies in which numbers are a source of trouble, the celestial society would have been heading for disorder, if all its members had gathered together.

Though this rule was their security, the new generation of Nummo, however, proceeded to break it and thereby overthrew their destiny; and this was how it came about.

God had given the eight a collection of eight different grains intended for their food, and for these the first ancestor was responsible. Of the eight, the last was the *Digitaria*, which had been publicly rejected by the first ancestor when it was given to him, on the pretext that it was so small and so difficult to prepare. He even went so far as to swear he would never eat it.

There came, however, a critical period when all the grains were nearly exhausted except the last. The first and second ancestors, who incidentally had already broken the rule about separation, met together to eat this last food. Their action was the crowning breach of order, confirming as it did their first offence by a breach of faith. The two ancestors thereby became unclean – that is to say, of an essence incompatible with life in the celestial world. They resolved to quit that region, where they felt themselves to be strangers, and the six other ancestors threw in their lot with them and made the same decision. Moreover, they proposed to take with them when they left anything that might be of use to the men they were going to rejoin. It was then that the first ancestor, no doubt with the approval and perhaps with the help of God, began to make preparations for his own departure.

He took a woven basket with a circular opening and a square base in which to carry the earth and puddled clay required for the construction of a world-system, of which he was to be one of the counsellors. This basket served as a model for a basket-work structure of considerable size which he built upside down, as it were, with the opening, twenty cubits in diameter, on the ground, the square base, with sides eight cubits long, formed a flat roof, and the height was ten cubits. This framework he covered with puddled clay made of the earth from heaven, and in the thickness of the clay, starting from the centre of each side of the square, he made stairways of ten steps each facing towards one of the cardinal points. At the sixth step of the north staircase he put a door giving access to the interior in which were eight chambers arranged on two floors.

The symbolic significance of this structure was as follows:

The circular base represented the sun.

The square roof represented the sky.

A circle in the centre of the roof represented the moon.

The tread of each step being female and the rise of each step male, the four stairways of ten steps together prefigured the eight tens of families, offspring of the eight ancestors.

Each stairway held one kind of creature, and was associated with a constellation, as follows:

The north stairway, associated with the Pleiades, was for men and fishes;

The south stairway, associated with Orion's Belt, was for domestic animals.

The east stairway, associated with Venus, was for birds.

The west stairway, associated with the so-called "long-tailed Star", was for wild animals, vegetables, and insects.

In fact, the picture of the system was not easily or immediately grasped from Ogotemmêli's account of it.

"When the ancestor came down from Heaven," he said at first, "he was standing on a square piece of Heaven, not a very big piece, about the size of a sleeping-mat, or perhaps a bit bigger."

"How could he stand on this piece of Heaven?"

"It was a piece of celestial earth."

"A thick piece?"

"Yes! As thick as a house. It was ten cubits high with stairs on each side facing the four cardinal points."

The blind man had raised his head, which was almost always bent towards the ground. How was he to explain these geometrical forms, these steps, these exact measurements? The European had begun by thinking that what was meant was a tall prism flanked by four stairways forming a cross. He kept returning to this conception in order to get it quite clear, while the other, patiently groping in the darkness which enveloped him, sought for fresh details.

At last his ravaged face broke into a kind of smile: he had found what he wanted. Reaching into the inside of his house and lying almost flat on his back, he searched among a number of objects which grated or sounded hollow as they scraped the earth under his hand. Only his thin knees and his feet were still visible in the embrasure of the doorway; the rest disappeared in the shadows within. The front of the house looked like a great face with the mouth closed on two skinny shin-bones.

After much tugging, an object emerged from the depths and appeared framed in the doorway. It was a woven basket, black with dust and soot of the interior, with a round opening and a square base, crushed and broken, a wretched spectacle.

The thing was placed before the door, losing several strands in the process, while the whole of the blind man's body reappeared, his hand still firmly grasping the basket.

"Its only use now is to put chickens in," he said.

He passed his hands slowly over its battered remains, and proceeded to explain the world-system.

22

AFRICAN PHILOSOPHY, MYTH AND REALITY*

PAULIN J. HOUNTONDJI

I must emphasize that my theme is African philosophy, myth *and* reality, whereas one might have expected the conventional formula, myth *or* reality? I am not asking whether it exists, whether it is a myth *or* a reality. I observe that it does exist, by the same right and in the same mode as all the philosophies of the world: in the form of a *literature*. I shall try to account for this misunderstood reality, deliberately ignored or suppressed even by those who produce it and who, in producing it, believe that they are merely reproducing a pre-existing thought through it: through the insubstantiality of a transparent discourse, of a fluid, compliant ether whose only function is to transmit light. My working hypothesis is that such suppression cannot be innocent: this discursive self-deception serves to conceal something else, and this apparent self-obliteration of the subject aims at camouflaging its massive omnipresence, its convulsive effort to root in reality this fiction filled with itself. Tremendous censorship of a shameful text, which presents itself as impossibly transparent

and almost non-existent but which also claims for its object (African pseudo-philosophy) the privilege of having always existed, outside any explicit formulation.

I therefore invert the relation: that which exists, that which is incontrovertibly given is that literature. As for the object it claims to restore, it is at most a way of speaking, a verbal invention, a *muthos*. When I speak of African philosophy I mean that literature, and I try to understand why it has so far made such strenuous efforts to hide behind the screen, all the more opaque for being imaginary, of an implicit "philosophy" conceived as an unthinking, spontaneous, collective system of thought, common to all Africans or at least to all members severally, past, present and future, of such-and-such an African ethnic group. I try to understand why most African authors, when trying to engage with philosophy, have so far thought it necessary to project the misunderstood reality of their own discourse on to such palpable fiction.

Let us therefore tackle the problem at a

---

* This is a rewritten and updated version of a lecture "stammered" at the University of Nairobi on 5 November 1973, at the invitation of the Philosophical Association of Kenya, under the title "African philosophy, myth and reality" (cf. *Thought and Practice*, vol. I, no. 2, Nairobi, 1974, pp. 1–16). The same lecture was delivered at Cotonou on 20 December 1973 and at Porto-Novo on 10 January 1974, under the sponsorship of the National Commission for Philosophy of Dahomey.

higher level. What is in question here, substantially, is the idea of *philosophy*, or rather, of *African philosophy*. More accurately, the problem is whether the word "philosophy," when qualified by the word "African," must retain its habitual meaning, or whether the simple addition of an adjective necessarily changes the meaning of the substantive. What is in question, then, is the universality of the word "philosophy" throughout its possible geographical applications.

My own view is that this universality must be preserved – not because philosophy must necessarily develop the same themes or even ask the same questions from one country or continent to another, but because these differences of *content* are meaningful precisely and only as differences of *content*, which, as such, refer back to the essential unity of a single discipline, of a single style of inquiry.

The present chapter will therefore endeavour to develop the conclusions of the first two. In particular, it will attempt to show, first, that the phrase "African philosophy," in the enormous literature that has been devoted to the problem, has so far been the subject only of mythological exploitation and, second, that it is nevertheless possible to retrieve it and apply it to something else: not to the fiction of a collective system of thought, but to a set of philosophical discourses and texts.

I shall try to evince the existence of such texts and to determine both the limits and essential configurations, or general orientations, of African philosophical literature.

The Popular Concept of African Philosophy

Tempels' work will serve us as a reference.[1] More than once Tempels emphasizes that "Bantu philosophy" is experienced but not thought and that its practitioners are, at best, only dimly conscious of it:

> let us not expect the first Black-in-the-street (especially if he is young) to give us a systematic account of his ontological system. Nevertheless, this ontology exists; it penetrates and informs all the primitive's thinking and dominates all his behaviour. Using the methods of analysis and synthesis of our own intellectual disciplines, we can and therefore must do the "primitive" the service of looking for, classifying and systematizing the elements of his ontological system.(p.15)

And further on:

> We do not claim that Bantus are capable of presenting us with a philosophical treatise complete with an adequate vocabulary. It is our own intellectual training that enables us to effect its systematic development. It is up to us to provide them with an accurate account of their conception of entities, in such a way that they will recognize themselves in our words and will agree, saying: "You have understood us, you know us now completely, you 'know' in the same way we 'know'."(p.24)

It is quite clear, then: the black man is here regarded, in Eboussi-Boulaga's words, as the "Monsieur Jourdain of philosophy."[2] Unwitting philosopher, he is the rival in silliness

---

[1]   P. Tempels, *La Philosophie Bantoue* (Paris: Présence Africaine 1949) (AS 601). The letters AS, followed by a number, refer to the "bibliography of African thought" published by the Rev. Father Alphonse Smet, in *Cahiers philosophiques africains* no. 2 (July–December 1972), Lubumbashi. This "bibliography," despite the fact that it lumps together philosophical and non-philosophical (i.e. sociological, ethnological, even literary) texts, is nevertheless a useful instrument for any research on African literature or Western literature concerning Africa. The number following the letters AS indicates the number of the text in Smet's "Bibliography."

[2]   F. Eboussi-Boulaga, "Le Bantou problématique," *Présence Africaine*, no.66 (1968)

of Molière's famous character, who spoke in prose without knowing it. Ignorant of his own thoughts, he needs an interpreter to translate them for him, or rather an interpreter who, having formulated these thoughts with the white world in mind, will accidently drop a few crumbs which will inspire the Bantu, when he picks them up, with boundless gratitude.

We have already mentioned Césaire's criticism. That very necessary political critique, we said, stopped short because it failed to follow up its own theoretical implications. To aim cautious criticisms, "not at Bantu philosophy, but at the political uses to which it is being put,"[3] was to avoid questioning the genealogy of the concept itself and to treat its appearance in scientific literature as an accident, as though its only function were this very political one. It was, in fact, tantamount to shying away from an exposure of the profoundly conservative nature of the ethnophilosophical project itself.

It follows that not only *Bantu Philosophy* but the whole of ethno-philosophical literature must be subjected to an expanded and more profound version of Césaire's political criticism. For if, as a result of what might be called the ethnological division of labour (a sort of scientific equivalent of the military scramble for the Third World by the great powers), Tempels can pass for the great specialist in the Bantu area, and if, too, his reconstruction of African "philosophy" is the more sensational because of his one-to-one contrasts between this African pseudo-philosophy and an equally imaginary European philosophy,[4] similar attempts have been made by other European authors for other regions of Africa. To quote only a few, Marcel Griaule has devoted to the Dogons of the present-day Republic of Mali a book currently regarded as a classic of Dogon wisdom, *Dieu d'eau*,[5] followed by another, in collaboration with Germaine Dieterlen, entitled *Le Renard pâle*.[6] Dominique Zahan has made known to the world the religion, the spirituality and what he calls the "philosophy" of the Bambara.[7] Louis-Vincent Thomas has carried out painstaking research among the Diola of Senegal and has expatiated on their wisdom, their system of thought or, as he calls it, their "philosophy."[8]

As might have been expected, the example of these European authors has been widely followed at home. Many Africans have plunged into the same field of research, correcting on occasion – but without ever questioning its basic assumptions – the work of their Western models. Among them is the

[3]   Aimé Césaire, *Discours sur le colonialisme* (Paris: Editions Réclame 1950) (AS 95), p.45.

[4]   Comparisons between the "world-view" of Third World peoples and European philosophy involve stripping the latter also of its history, its internal diversity and its richness and reducing the multiplicity of its works and doctrines to a "lowest common denominator." This common stock-in-trade of European philosophy is represented in Tempels by a vague system of thought made up of Aristotle, Christian theology and horse sense.

[5]   AS 214.

[6]   M. Griaule and G. Dieterlen, *Le Renard pâle* (Paris: Publications of the Institute of Ethnology 1965) (AS 220).

[7]   Dominique Zahan, *Sociétés d'initiation bambara: le n'domo, le koré,* (Paris/The Hague: Mouton 1963 (AS 718); *La Dialectique du verbe chez les Bambara* (Paris–The Hague: Mouton 1963) (AS 713); *La Viande et la Graine, mythologie dogon* (Paris: Présence Africaine 1968) (AS 719); *Religion, spiritualité et pensée africaines* (Paris: Payot 1970) (AS 716). See my review of this last book in *Les Etudes philosophiques*, no.3 (1971).

[8]   Louis-Vincent Thomas, *Les Diola. Essai d'analyse fonctionnelle sur une population de Basse-Casamance*, vols. I and II (Dakar: Mémoires de l'Institut Français d'Afrique Noire 1959) (not mentioned in AS); "Brève esquisse sur la pensée cosmologique du Diola", *African Systems of Thought*, prefaced by M. Fortes and G. Dieterlen (OUP 1965) (AS 620); "Un Système philosophique sénégalais: la cosmologie des Diola," *Présence Africaine*, nos. 32–3 (1960) (AS 638); *Cinq Essais sur la mort africaine*, Publications de la Faculté des Lettres et Sciences humaines (Philosophie et Sciences sociales) Dakar no. 3 (1969) (AS 621); "La Mort et la sagesse africaine. Esquisse d'une anthropologie philosophique," *Psychopathologie Africaine*, no. 3 (1967). See also other texts by the same author, cited in AS 617–39.

abbé Alexis Kagamé of Rwanda, with his *Philosophie bantou–rwandaise de l'être*.[9] Then there is Mgr Makarakiza of Burundi, who published in 1959 a study entitled *La Dialectique des barundi*.[10] The South African priest Antoine Mabona distinguished himself in 1960 with an article entitled "African philosophy," then in 1963 with a text on "The depths of African philosophy" and finally in 1964 with a meditation on "La spiritualité africaine."[11] In this concert Father A. Rahajarizafy has sounded the note of the Great Island by trying to define Malagasy "philosophy" in an article of 1963 on "Sagesse malgache et théologie chrétienne."[12] In 1962, François-Marie Lufuluabo, a Franciscan from the former Belgian Congo, appeared in the firmament with a booklet, *Vers une théodicée bantoue*, followed in 1963 by an article entitled "La Conception bantoue face au christianisme," signing off in 1964 with another booklet on *La Notion luba-bantoue de l'être*.[13] Then, in 1965, his compatriot, the abbé Vincent Mulago, devoted a chapter to African "philosophy" in his *Visage africain du christianisme*.[14] The former Protestant clergyman Jean-Calvin Bahoken, of Cameroun, was clearing his *Clairières métaphysiques africaines*[15] in 1967, and two years later the Kenyan pastor John

Mbiti, probably fascinated by his own childhood, revealed to the world in a now classic work, *African Religions and Philosophy*, the fact that the African ignores the future, hardly knows the present and lives entirely turned towards the past.[16]

Before we go on with the catalogue, let us note that all the authors we have just quoted are churchmen, like Tempels himself. This explains their main preoccupation, which was to find a psychological and cultural basis for rooting the Christian message in the African's mind without betraying either. Of course, this is an eminently legitimate concern, up to a point. But it means that these authors are compelled to conceive of philosophy on the model of religion, as a permanent, stable system of beliefs, unaffected by evolution, impervious to time and history, ever identical to itself.

Let us now turn to the lay authors, with, here again, only a few examples. We cannot but mention Léopold Sédar Senghor, whose chatty disquisitions on "negritude" are often buttressed by an analysis of what he called, as early as 1939, the black man's "conception of the world," a phrase which he later replaced, under the influence of Tempels, with the "black metaphysic."[17] There are also the

---

[9] AS 294. See also, by the same author, "L'Ethnologie des Bantu," *Contemporary Philosophy. A Survey*, ed. Raymond Klibansky, vol. IV (Florence 1971) (AS 754).

[10] AS 347.

[11] Mongameli Antoine Mabona, "Philosophie africaine," *Présence Africaine*, no.30 (1960) (AS 342); "The Depths of African Philosophy," *Personnalité africaine et Catholicisme* (Paris: Présence Africaine 1963) (AS 343); "La Spiritualité africaine," *Présence Africaine* no. 52 (1964) (AS 344).

[12] A. Rahajarizafy, "Sagesse malgache et théologie chrétienne," *Personnalité africaine et Catholicisme* (Paris: Présence Africaine 1963) (AS 504).

[13] Respectively, AS 341; "La Conception bantoue face au christianisme," *Personnalité africaine et Catholicisme* (Paris: Présence Africaine 1963); AS 339.

[14] AS 414. The chapter in question is the eighth, entitled "Philosophical outline"; "Dialectique existentielle des Bantous et sacramentalisme," *Aspects de la culture noire* (Paris 1958) (AS 410).

[15] Jean-Calvin Bahoken, *Clairières métaphysiques africaines* (Paris: Présence Africaine 1967) (AS 46).

[16]John Mbiti, *African Religions and Philosophy* (Heinemann 1969) (AS 372); *Concepts of God in Africa* (New York: Praeger 1970) (AS 375); *New Testament Eschatology in an African Background. A Study of the encounter between New Testament theology and African traditional concepts* (OUP 1971).

[17] See in particular the texts (written between 1937 and 1963) collected in *Liberté I. Négritude et humanisme*. As a theory of "negritude," the Senghorian ethnology was always, above all, an ethnopsychology concerned essentially with defining the "Negro soul," where sociology (usually idyllic descriptions of "Negro society") and aesthetic analyses

Nigerian Adesanya, author of an article published in 1958 on "Yoruba metaphysical thinking";[18] the Ghanaian William Abraham, author of a book which is remarkable in many ways, *The Mind of Africa*[19] (I believe that a book can be instructive, interesting, useful, even if it is founded on erroneous assumptions); the late-lamented Kwame Nkrumah, whose famous *Consciencism* can hardly be regarded as his best publication;[20] the Senegalese Alassane N'Daw, who devoted several articles to the subject;[21] the Camerounian Basile-Juleat Fouda, author of a doctoral thesis defended at Lille in 1967 on "La Philosophie négro-africaine de l'existence" (unpublished);[22] the Dahomean Issiaka Prosper Laleye, also the author of a thesis, "La Conception de la personne dans la pensée traditionnelle yoruba,"[23] presented in 1970 at the Catholic University of Fribourg, in Switzerland; the Nigerian J. O. Awolalu, author of an article entitled "The Yoruba

philosophy of life."[24] And there are many others.[25]

Without being motivated quite so restrictively as the church ethnophilosophers, these authors were none the less intent on locating, beneath the various manifestations of African civilization, beneath the flood of history which has swept this civilization along willy-nilly, a solid bedrock which might provide a foundation of certitudes: in other words, a system of beliefs. In this quest, we find the same preoccupation as in the negritude movement – a passionate search for the identity that was denied by the colonizer – but now there is the underlying idea that one of the elements of the cultural identity is precisely "philosophy", the idea that every culture rests on a specific, permanent, metaphysical substratum.

Let us now ask the cruicial question: is this the usual meaning of the word "philosophy?" Is it the way it is understood, for instance, in the phrases "European philosophy,"

(commentaries, many of them excellent, on various works of art) are used mainly to reinforce this fantasy psychology. However, *ethnopsychology* always betrays the ambition to become an *ethnophilosophy* by accounting for the black "conception of the world" as well as for the psychological characteristics. The project is clearly formulated in the celebrated 1939 article "Ce que l'homme noir apporte" ("The black man's contribution") in which the black "conception of the world," however, still appears as a psychological quality: an animism, or rather, according to Senghor, an anthropopsychism. This is no longer so in the 1956 text "The Black African aesthetic" and the 1959 text on the "Constitutive elements of a civilization of Black African inspiration" *Liberté I*, pp. 202–17 and 252–86: apart from a few alterations, these are reprints of Senghor's reports to the First International Congress of Black Writers and Artists, Paris 1956, and to the Second Congress, Rome 1959. Explicitly referring to Tempels, but still wishing to *explain* the black's "metaphysics" in terms of black "psychophysiology," Senghor defines it rather as a system of ideas, an "existential ontology" (ibid., pp. 203–4, 264–8).

The reader will therefore readily understand that I should feel reluctant to situate ethnophilosophy "in the wake of negritude" or to treat it as a "(late) aspect of the negritude movement", as Marcien Towa does in *Essai sur la problématique philosophique dans l'Afrique actuelle* (Yaoundé: Editions Clé 1971), pp. 23, 25. If *African* ethnophilosophers are undoubtedly part of the negritude movement, they owe the philosophical pretensions of their nationalist discourse rather to the ethnophilosophy of *European* Africanists.

[18] A. Adesanya, "Yoruba metaphysical thinking," *Odu*, no.5 (1958) (AS 15).

[19] W. Abraham, *The Mind of Africa* (Chicago: University of Chicago Press and Weidenfeld & Nicolson 1962) (AS 5).

[20] AS 436 and 438.

[21] Alassane N'Daw, "Peut-on parler d'une pensée africaine?," *Présence Africaine* no. 58 (1966) (AS 420); "Pensée africaine et développement," *Problèmes sociaux congolais* (Kinshasa: CEP SI Publications 1966–7) (AS 419).

[22] This unpublished thesis is mentioned here mainly because it is discussed at length by Marcien Towa in his critique of ethnophilosophy (Towa, *Essai sur la problématique philosophique* pp. 23–33) (AS 646).

[23] Subtitled "A phenomenological approach" and prefaced by Philippe Laburthe-Tolra (Berne: Herbert Lang 1970) (AS 325).

[24] The article was published in *Présence Africaine*, no. 73 (1970) (AS 39).

[25] For instance, G. De Souza, *La Conception de "Vie" chez les Fon* (Cotonou: Editions du Bénin 1975): a doctoral thesis defended in 1972.

"nineteenth-century philosophy", etc.? Clearly not. It seems as though the word automatically changes its meaning as soon as it ceases to be applied to Europe or to America and is applied to Africa. This is a well-known phenomenon. As our Kenyan colleague Henry Odera humorously remarks:

> What may be a superstition is paraded as "African religion," and the white world is expected to endorse that it is indeed a religion but an African religion. What in all cases is a mythology is paraded as "African philosophy," and again the white culture is expected to endorse that it is indeed a philosophy but an African philosophy. What is in all cases a dictatorship is paraded as "African democracy," and the white culture is again expected to endorse that it is so. And what is clearly a de-development or pseudo-development is described as "development," and again the white world is expected to endorse that it is development – but of course "African development."[26]

Words do indeed change their meanings miraculously as soon as they pass from the Western to the African context, and not only in the vocabulary of European or American writers but also, through faithful imitation, in that of Africans themselves. That is what happens to the word "philosophy": applied to Africa, it is supposed to designate no longer the specific discipline it evokes in its Western context but merely a collective world-view, an implicit, spontaneous, perhaps even unconscious system of beliefs to which all Africans are supposed to adhere. This is a vulgar usage of the word, justified presumably by the supposed vulgarity of the geographical context to which it is applied.

Behind this usage, then, there is a myth at work, the myth of primitive unanimity, with its suggestion that in "primitive" societies – that is to say, non-Western societies – everybody always agrees with everybody else. It follows that in such societies there can never be individual beliefs or philosophies but only collective systems of belief. The word "philosophy" is then used to designate each belief-system of this kind, and it is tacitly agreed among well-bred people that in this context it could not mean anything else.

One can easily detect in this, one of the founding acts of the "science" (or rather the pseudo-science) called ethnology, namely, the generally tacit thesis that non-Western societies are absolutely specific, the silent postulate of a difference in *nature* (and not merely in the *evolutionary stage* attained, with regard to particular types of achievement), of a difference in *quality*, (not merely in quantity or *scale*) between so-called "primitive" societies and developed ones. Cultural anthropology (another name for ethnology) owes its supposed autonomy (notably in relation to sociology) to this arbitrary division of the human community into two types of society which are taken, arbitrarily and without proof, to be fundamentally different.[27]

But let us return to the myth of unanimity. It would seem at first sight that this theoretical consensus postulated by ethnophilosophy among all members of each "primitive" community should produce a parallel consensus, at the level of results if not of methods, among all ethnophilosophers studying the same community. But, curiously enough, instead of an ideal consensus, a fine unanimity whose transparency would have revealed the spontaneous unanimity of all those "primitive philosophers," ethnophilosophical literature offers us a rich harvest of not only diverse but also sometimes frankly contradictory works.

[26] Henry Oruka Odera, "Mythologies as African philosophy," *East Africa Journal*, vol. IX, no. 10 (October 1972) (not mentioned in AS).
[27] See, on this point, Ola Balogun, "Ethnology and its ideologies," *Consequence*, no. 1 (1974). See also my article on "Le Mythe de la philosophie spontanée," *Cahiers Philosophiques Africains*, no. 1 (1972).

We have noted above such divergences between Tempels and Kagamé. It would probably be easy to find similar differences between the many other works relating to the "traditional" thought of Bantus or Africans in general, if one could overcome one's understandable boredom, read all of them one by one, examine them patiently and juxtapose all the views they contain.

But I can see the objection being raised that such differences are normal, that the diversity of works is a source of wealth and not of weakness, that the internal contradictions of ethnophilosophy can be found in any science worthy of the name – physics, chemistry, mathematics, linguistics, psychoanalysis, sociology, etc. – that they are a sign of vitality, not inconsistency, a condition of progress rather than an obstacle in the path of discovery. It may be added that, as in all sciences, a reality may exist without being immediately understood, and that consequently it is not surprising if an implicit system of thought can be reconstructed only as a result of long, collective and contradictory research.

The only thing this objection overlooks is the "slight difference" between the sciences cited and ethnophilosophy that they do not postulate anything remotely comparable with the supposed unanimity of a human community; that in these sciences, moreover, a contradiction is never stagnant but always progressive, never final or absolute but indicative of an *error*, of the *falsity* of a hypothesis or thesis, which is bound to emerge from a rational investigation of the object itself, whereas a contradiction between two ethnophilosophical theses is necessarily circular, since it can never be resolved by experimentation or any other method of verification. The point is that an ethnophilosophical contradiction is necessarily *antinomal* in the Kantian sense; thesis and antithesis are equally demonstrable – in other words, equally gratuitous. In such a case contradiction does not generate synthesis but simply demonstrates the need to re-examine the very foundations of the discipline and to provide a critique of ethnophilosophical reason and perhaps of ethnological reason too.

Ethnophilosophy can now be seen in its true light. Because it has to account for an imaginary unanimity, to interpret a text which nowhere exists and has to be constantly reinvented, it is a science without an object, a "crazed language"[28] accountable to nothing, a discourse that has no referent, so that its falsity can never be demonstrated. Tempels can then maintain that for the Bantu being is power, and Kagamé can beg to differ: we have no means of settling the quarrel. It is clear, therefore, that the "Bantu philosophy" of the one is not the philosophy of the Bantu but that of Tempels, that the "Bantu–Rwandais philosophy" of the other is not that of the Rwandais but that of Kagamé. Both of them simply make use of African traditions and oral literature and project on to them their own philosophical beliefs, hoping to enhance their credibility thereby.

That is how the functioning of this thesis of a collective African philosophy works: it is a smokescreen behind which each author is able to manipulate his own philosophical views. It has nothing beyond this ideological function: it is an indeterminate discourse with no object.

Towards a New Concept of "African Philosophy"

Behind and beyond the ethnological pretext, philosophical views remain. The dogma of unanimism has not been completely sterile,

[28] That is, "Language gone mad." I have borrowed this phrase from the Zaïrois V. Y. Mudimbe, whose book *L'Autre Face du royaume. Une introduction à la critique des langages en folie* (Lausanne: L'Age d'homme 1973) ranks among the finest works written to this day *on* (not *of*) ethnology.

since it has at least generated a quite distinctive philosophical literature.

Here we must note a surprising fact:
while they were looking for philosophy in a
place where it could never be found – in the
collective unconscious of African peoples, in
the silent folds of their explicit discourse –
the ethnophilosophers never questioned the
nature and theoretical status of their own
analyses. Were these relevant to philosophy?
There lay the true but undetected problem.
For if we want to be scientific, we cannot apply
the same word to two things as different as a
spontaneous, implicit and collective world-
view on the one hand and, on the other, the
deliberate, explicit and individual analytic
activity which takes that world-view as its
object. Such an analysis should be called
"philosophology" rather than "philosophy"
or, to use a less barbarous term, "metaphilosophy" – but a metaphilosophy of the
worst kind, an inegalitarian metaphilosophy,
not a dialogue and confrontation with an
existing philosophy but a reduction to silence,
a denial, masquerading as the revival of an
earlier philosophy.

For we know that in its highly elaborated
forms philosophy is always, in a sense, a
metaphilosophy, that it can develop only by
reflecting on its own history, that all new
thinkers must feed on the doctrines of their
predecessors, even of their contemporaries,
extending or refuting them, so as to enrich the
philosophical heritage available in their own
time. But in this case metaphilosophy does not
rely on an exploitation of extra-philosophical
data or on the arbitrary over-interpretation of
social facts which in themselves bear no relation to philosophy. Metaphilosophy signifies,
rather, a philosophical reflection on discourses
which are themselves overtly and consciously
philosophical. Ethnophilosophy, on the other
hand, claims to be the description of an
implicit, unexpressed world-view, which
never existed anywhere but in the anthropologist's imagination. Ethnophilosophy is a
pre-philosophy mistaking itself for a meta-

philosophy, a philosophy which, instead of
presenting its own rational justification, shelters lazily behind the authority of a tradition
and projects its own theses and beliefs on to
that tradition.

If we now return to our question, namely,
whether philosophy resides in the world-view
described or in the description itself, we can
now assert that if it resides in either, it must be
the second, the description of that vision, even
if this is, in fact, a self-deluding invention that
hides behind its own products. African philosophy does exist therefore, but in a new sense,
as a literature produced by Africans and
dealing with philosophical problems.

A contradiction? Oh no! Some may be
surprised that, having patiently dismantled
the ethnophilosophical machine, we should
now be trying to restore it. They have simply
failed to understand that we are merely recognizing the existence of that literature as
philosophical literature, whatever may be its
value and *credibility*. What we are acknowledging is what it *is*, not what it *says*. Having
laid bare the mythological assumptions on
which it is founded (these having suppressed
all question of its status), we can now pay
greater attention to the fact of its existence as
a determinate form of philosophical literature
which, however mystified and mystifying it
may be (mystifying because mystified), nevertheless belongs to the history of African
literature in general.

Let us be accurate: the issue here is only
African ethnophilosophy. A work like *Bantu
Philosophy* does not belong to African philosophy, since its author is not African; but
Kagamé's work is an integral part of African
philosophical literature. In other words,
speaking of African philosophy in a new sense,
we must draw a line, within ethnophilosophical literature in general, between African and
non-African writers, not because one category
is better than the other, or because both might
not, in the last analysis, say the same thing, but
because, the subject being *African* philosophy,
we cannot exclude a geographical variable,

taken here as empirical, contingent, extrinsic to the content or significance of the discourse and as quite apart from any questions of *theoretical connections*. Thus Tempels' work, although it deals with an African subject and has played a decisive role in the development of African ethnophilosophy, belongs to *European* scientific literature, in the same way as anthropology in general, although it deals with non-Western societies, is an embodiment of Western science, no more and no less.

A happy consequence of this demarcation is that it emphasizes certain subtle nuances and occasional serious divergences which might otherwise have passed unnoticed and which differentiate African authors whom we initially grouped together as ethnophilosophers. It is thus possible to see the immense distance which separates, for instance, Bahoken's *Clairières métaphysiques africaines*,[29] justifiably assessed as a perfect example of ideological twaddle designed by an apparently nationalistic African to flatter the exotic tastes of the Western public from Kwame Nkrumah's *Consciencism*, written chiefly for the African public and aimed at making it aware of its new cultural identity, even though Nkrumah's book, unfortunately, partakes of the ethnological conception that there can be such a thing as a collective philosophy.

Another even more important consequence is that this African philosophical literature can now be seen to include philosophical works of those African authors who do not believe in the myth of a collective philosophy or who reject it explicitly. Let me cite a few of these. Fabien Eboussi-Boulaga's fine article "Le Bantou problématique"[30] has already been mentioned. Another Camerounian, Marcien Towa, has given us a brilliant critique of ethnophilosophy in general, the *Essai sur la problématique philosophique dans l'Afrique actuelle*, followed by an incisive criticism of the Senghorian doctrine of negritude, *Léopold Sédar Senghor: négritude ou servitude?*[31] Henry Oruka Odera of Kenya has published a fine article entitled "Mythologies as African philosophy".[32] The Béninois (former Dahomeyan) Stanislas Spero Adotevi earned fame in 1972 with his brilliant book *Négritude et négrologues*.[33]

But more than that: African philosophical literature includes works which make no attempt whatever to broach the problem of "African philosophy", either to assert or to deny its existence. In fact, we must extend the concept to include all the research into Western philosophy carried out by Africans. This broadening of the horizon implies no contradiction: just as the writings of Western anthropologists on African societies belong to Western scientific literature, so the philosophical writings of Africans on the history of

---

[29] How revealing that this work was published in France "with the help of the Centre National de la Recherche Scientifique."

[30] I have mentioned this article as the most vigorous and complete critique of Tempels to date for its rigorous analysis of the contradictions in his work. Eboussi-Balaga shows that these can ultimately be reduced to

> an interplay of value and counter-value . . . which characterizes the colonizer's judgements on the colonized. Bantuism is partly admirable and partly abominable. It is valuable when the colonized wish to forsake it for equality: then they are reminded that they are losing their "souls". But Bantuism becomes a vile hotchpotch of degenerate magical practices when the colonizer wishes to affirm his pre-eminence and legitimize his power. ("Le Bantou problématique," p. 32)

However, Eboussi does not totally reject the idea of an "ethnological philosophy," a philosophy which would abandon the search for an "ontological substratum for social reality," would deal with the "mythical discourse of 'native theorists'," instead of bypassing it with scorn (ibid., p.9). On this point I believe a more radical view should be taken.

[31] Towa, *Essai sur la problématique philosophique; Léopold Sédar Senghor: négritude ou servitude?* (Yaoundé: Editions Cié 1971) (AS 647).

[32] Odera, "Mythologies as African philosophy."

[33] S. A. Adotevi, *Négritude et négrologues* (Paris: Union Générale d'Editions, Coll. 10/18 1972) (not mentioned in AS).

Western thought are an integral part of African philosophical literature. So, obviously, African philosophical works concerning problems that are not specially related to African experience should also be included. In this sense, the articles by the Ghanaian J. E. Wiredu on Kant, on material implication and the concept of truth,[34] are an integral part of African philosophy, as are analyses of the concept of freedom or the notion of free will[35] by the Kenyan Henry Odera or the Nigerian D. E. Idoniboye. The same can be said of the research on French seventeenth-century philosophy by the Zaïrois Elungu Pere Elungu, *Etendue et connaissance dans la philosophie de Malebranche*,[36] of the epistemological introduction to *Théologie positive et théologie spéculative*[37] by his fellow countryman Tharcisse Tshibangu. The work of the Camerounian N'joh Mouelle, particularly *Jalons* and *De la médicocrité à l'excellence. Essai sur la signification humaine du développement*,[38] may also be placed in this category, although their subjects are not only universal but also linked with the present historical situation of Africa.

By the same token we may readily claim works like those of the Ashanti scholar Anton-Wilhelm Amo, who studied and taught in German universities during the first half of the eighteenth century, as belonging to African philosophical literature, although this may be regarded as a borderline case, since Amo was trained almost entirely in the West. But is not this the case with almost every African intellectual even today?[39]

The essential point here is that we have produced a radically new definition of African philosophy, the criterion now being the geographical origin of the authors rather than an alleged specificity of content. The effect of this is to broaden the narrow horizon which has hitherto been imposed on African philosophy and to treat it, as now conceived, as a methodical inquiry with the same universal aims as those of any other philosophy in the world. In short, it destroys the dominant mythological conception of Africanness and restores the simple, obvious truth that Africa is above all a continent and the concept of Africa an empirical, geographical concept and not a metaphysical one. The purpose of this "demythologizing" of the idea of Africa and African philosophy is simply to free our faculty for theorizing from all the intellectual impediments and prejudices which have so far prevented it from getting off the ground.

---

[34] J. E. Wiredu, "Kant's synthetic *a priori* in geometry and the rise of non-Euclidean geometries," *Kantstudien*, Heft 1, Bonn (1970) (not in AS); "Material implication and 'if . . . then'," *International Logic Review*, no. 6, Bologna (1972) (not in AS); "Truth as opinion," *Universitas*, vol. 2, no. 3 (new series), University of Ghana (1973) (not in AS); "On an African orientation in philosophy", *Second Order*, vol. 1, no. 2, University of Ife (1972) (not in AS).

[35] H. Odera, "The meaning of liberty," *Cahiers Philosophiques Africains*, no. 1, Lubumbashi (1972) (not in AS); D. E. Idoniboye, "Freewill, the linguistic philosopher's dilemma," *Cahiers Philosophiques Africains*, no. 2, Lubumbashi (1972) (not in AS).

[36] E. P. Elungu, *Etendue et connaissance dans la philosophie de Malebranche* (Paris: Vrin 1973) (not in AS). One may also mention the unpublished thesis defended in Paris in 1971 by the Senegalese A. R. N'Diaye, "L'Ordre dans la philosophie de Malebranche."

[37] T. Tshibangu. *Théologie positive et théologie spéculative* (Louvain/Paris: Béatrice-Nauwelaerts 1965) (not in AS).

[38] E. N'joh Mouellé, *Jalons: recherche d'une mentalité neuve* (Yaoundé: Editions Clé 1970) (AS 775); *De la médiocrité à l'excellence. Essai sur la signification humaine du développement* (Yaoundé: Editions Clé 1970) (AS 432).

[39] More generally, this new definition of African philosophy opens up the possibility of a history of African philosophy, whereas the very notion of such a history was unthinkable in the ideological context of ethnophilosophy. If African philosophy is seen not as an implicit world-view but as the set of philosophical writings produced by Africans, we can at last undertake to reconstruct their chequered history, including those of Afro-Arab authors like Ibn Khaldun, Al Ghazali, etc., whatever may be the historical and theoretical distance between these texts.

Final Remarks

There can no longer be any doubt about the existence of African philosophy, although its meaning is different from that to which the anthropologists have accustomed us. It exists as a particular form of scientific literature. But, of course, once this point is established, many questions remain. For instance, how shall we distinguish philosophical literature from other forms of scientific literature, such as mathematics, physics, biology, linguistics, sociology, etc., inasmuch as these disciplines also develop as specific forms of literature? In other words, what is the particular object and area of study of philosophy? In more general terms, what relation is there between scientific literature and non-scientific literature (for instance, artistic literature), and why must we include philosophical literature in the first rather than the second?

This is not the place to answer these questions. All that we have tried to do so far has been to clear the ground for questions of this kind, since they presuppose that philosophy is recognized simply as a theoretical discipline and nothing else, a discipline which, like any other, can develop only in the form of literature.

Moreover, such questions can never receive definite and immutable answers, for the definition of a science must be revised constantly in the light of its own progress, and the articulation of theoretical discourse in general – by which we mean the demarcation of the various sciences – is itself subject to historical change. At this point, it is true, a much harder question, or series of questions, arises: how is the object of a science determined? What conditions, economic, historical, ideological or other, contribute to fixing the frontiers of a discipline? How is a new science born? How does an old science die or cease to be considered a science?[40]

This is not the place to answer these questions either. But at least there is one thing we are in a position to affirm: no science, no branch of learning can appear except as an event in language or, more precisely, as the product of discussion. The first thing to do, then, is to organize such discussions in the midst of the society where the birth of these sciences is desired. In other words, whatever the specific object of philosophy may be, the first task of African philosophers today, if they wish to develop an authentic African philosophy, is to promote and sustain constant free discussion about all the problems concerning their discipline instead of being satisfied with a private and somewhat abstract dialogue between themselves and the Western world.[41] By reorienting their discourse in this way, they will easily overcome the permanent temptation of "folklorism" that limits their research to so-called African subjects – a temptation which has owed most of its strength to the fact that their writings have been intended for a foreign public.

It is indeed a strange paradox that in present conditions the dialogue with the West can only encourage "folklorism," a sort of collective cultural exhibitionism which compels the "Third World" intellectual to "defend and illustrate" the peculiarities of his tradition for the benefit of a Western public. This seemingly universal dialogue simply encourages the

---

[40]   For a consideration of these questions and some representative answers, see: L. Althusser, *For Marx* (1965), trans. B. Brewster (Allen Lane 1969); L. Althusser, *et al., Reading Capital* (New Left Books 1970); G. Bachelard, *La Formation de l'esprit scientifique* (1947) (Paris: Vrin 1969); *Le Nouvel Esprit scientifique* (1934), 9th ed. (Paris: PUF 1966); G. Canguilhem, *Etudes d'histoire et de philosophie des sciences* (Paris: Vrin 1968); M. Foucault, *The Birth of the Clinic* (1972), trans. A. M. Sheridan Smith (Tavistock 1973); *The Order of Things* (1966), (Tavistock 1970); *The Archaeology of Knowledge* (1969), trans. A. M. Sheridan Smith (Tavistock 1972).

[41]   It is worth mentioning here the part that can be played in promoting this new type of dialogue by the departments of philosophy in African universities and the philosophical associations (e.g. the Inter-African Council for Philosophy) and their respective journals.

worst kind of cultural particularism, both because its supposed peculiarities are in the main purely imaginary and because the intellectual who defends them claims to speak in the name of his whole people although they have never asked him to do so and are usually unaware that such a dialogue is taking place.

On the contrary, it is to be hoped that when Africans start discussing theoretical problems among themselves, they will feel spontaneously the need to gather the broadest possible information on the scientific achievements of other continents and societies. They will take an interest in these achievements not because they will be held to be the best that can be attained but in order to assess more objectively, and if necessary improve, their own achievements in the same areas.

The paradox is therefore easily removed: interlocutors of the same origin rarely feel the need to exalt their own cultural particularities. Such a need arises only when one faces people from other countries and is forced to assert one's uniqueness by conforming to the current stereotypes of one's own society and civilization. Universality becomes accessible only when interlocutors are set free from the need to assert themselves in the face of others; and the best way to achieve this in Africa today is to organize internal discussion and exchange among all the scientists in the continent, within each discipline and – why not? – between one discipline and another, so as to create in our societies a scientific tradition worthy of the name. The difficult questions we have been asking concerning the origins, the definition, the boundaries, the evolution and the destiny of the various sciences, and more particularly the nature of philosophy and its relation to other disciplines, will then find their answers in the concrete history of our theoretical literature.

We must therefore plunge in and not be afraid of thinking new thoughts, of simply *thinking*. For every thought is new if we take the word in its active sense, even thought about past thoughts, provided we are not

content simply to repeat hallowed themes, catechetically and parrot-fashion, with a pout or a purr, but on the contrary boldly re-articulate these themes, justify them, give them a new and sounder foundation. Conversely, every blustering declaration of loyalty to a so-called "modern" doctrine will be at best mere folklore – when it does not turn out to be an objective mystification – unless it is accompanied by some intellectual effort to *know*, *understand* and *think out* the doctrine by going beyond the more sensational formulations to the problematic on which it is founded. We cannot go on acting a part indefinitely. The time has come for theoretical responsiblity, for taking ourselves seriously.

In Africa now the individual must liberate himself from the weight of the past as well as from the allure of ideological fashions. Amid the diverse but, deep down, so strangely similar catechisms of conventional nationalism and of equally conventional pseudo-Marxism, amid so many state ideologies functioning in the Fascist mode, deceptive alibis behind which the powers that be can quietly do the opposite of what they say and say the opposite of what they do, amid this immense confusion in which the most vulgar police state pompously declares itself to be a "dictatorship of the proletariat" and neo-Fascists mouthing pseudo-revolutionary platitudes are called "Marxist-Leninists," reducing the enormous theoretical and political subversive power of Marxism to the dimensions of a truncheon, in which, in the name of revolution, they kill, massacre, torture the workers, the trade unionists, the executives, the students: in the midst of all this intellectual and political bedlam we must all open our eyes wide and clear our own path. Nothing less will make discussions between free and intellectually responsible individuals possible. Nothing less will make a philosophy possible.

As can be seen, then, the development of African philosophical literature presupposes the removal of a number of political obstacles. In particular, it requires that democratic liberties and especially the right of free criticism, the suppression of which seems to constitute the sole aim and *raison d'être* of the official ideologies, should be acknowledged and jealously guarded. It is impossible to philosophize in Africa today without being aware of this need and of the pricelessness of freedom of expression as a necessary condition for all science, for all theoretical development and, in the last resort, for all real political and economic progress, too.

Briefly, and in conclusion, African philosophy exists, but it is not what it is believed to be. It is developing objectively in the form of a literature rather than as implicit and collective thought, but as a literature of which the output remains captive to the unanimist fallacy. Yet, happily, it is possible to detect signs of a new spirit. The liberation of this new spirit is now the necessary precondition of any progress in this field. To achieve that we must begin at the beginning; we must restore the right to criticism and free expression which are so seriously threatened by our regimes of terror and ideological confusion.

In short, it is not enough to recognize the existence of an African philosophical literature. The most important task is to transform it from the simple collection of writings aimed at non-African readers and consequently upholding the peculiarities of a so-called African "world-view" that it is today into the vehicle of a free and rigorous discussion among African philosophers themselves. Only then will this literature acquire universal value and enrich the common international heritage of human thought.

23

HOW MAN MAKES GOD IN WEST AFRICA: YORUBA ATTITUDES TOWARDS THE ÒRÌṢÀ

KARIN BARBER

I

The idea that gods are made by men, not men by gods, is a sociological truism. It belongs very obviously to a detached and critical tradition of thought imcompatible with faith in those gods. But Yoruba traditional religion contains built into it a very similar notion, and here, far from indicating scepticism or decline of belief, it seems to be a central impulse to devotion. The *òrìṣà* ("gods") are, according to Yoruba traditional thought, maintained and kept in existence by the attention of humans. Without the collaboration of their devotees, the *òrìṣà* would be betrayed, exposed and reduced to nothing. This notion seems to have been intrinsic to the religion since the earliest times. How can such an awareness be part of a devotee's "belief"? Rather than speculate abstractly, as Rodney Needham does (Needham 1972), about whether people of other cultures can be said to "believe" at all, it seems more interesting to take a concrete case like the Yoruba one where there is an unexpected – even apparently paradoxical – configuration of ideas, and to ask how these ideas are constituted.[1] Only by looking at them as part of a particular kind of society, with particular kinds of social relationships, can one see why such a configuration is so persuasive. The notion that men make gods is by no means unique to Yoruba thought. It is present to some degree in a number of traditional West African religions, and in some, such as the

---

[1] What Needham is really interested in is whether or not there is a universally-experienced, discriminable inner state corresponding to the concept "belief." He concludes that there is not, and that therefore one should not presume to talk about the "beliefs" of other cultures. From this standpoint, the Yoruba example would probably be seen as further proof of his conclusion: if the Yoruba state of mind towards their gods is in some ways reminiscent of a Western man's scepticism, this indicates that their experience of belief (if there is such an experience) is not the same. The question which I think ought to be addressed, on the other hand, is what are the differences of *structure* – the structure of society and of ideas – which allows something apparently similar to scepticism to play such a different role. The particular configuration of ideas which makes up the Yoruba devotional attitude only makes sense in particular social and historical circumstances. The nature of the "experience" of belief seems to me to be less important than the nature of the social context which makes certain notions persuasive or not persuasive.

Kalabari one, it can be seen in an even more explicit form than in the Yoruba one. A comparison may help to show how it is the constitution of social relationships which makes such a notion not just acceptable but central to the religious thought of the society.

Relations between humans and *òrìṣà* are in some sense a projection of relations between people in society. I would like to suggest that if the Yoruba see the *òrìṣà's* power as being maintained and augmented by human attention, this is because they live in a kind of society where it is very clear that the *human* individual's power depends in the long run on the attention and acknowledgement of his fellow-men. It is a hierarchical society, dominated by the institution of divine kingship and articulated by a series of chiefly titles of different grades and ranks. But the dynamic impulse in political life is the rise of self-made men. Individuals compete to make a position for themselves by recruiting supporters willing to acknowledge their greatness. Titles are positions of power, but they are not hereditary; they are achieved by men who must first have established themselves. The title system itself is quite flexible, allowing a man in a small position to enlarge it by his own efforts; and it is also possible for men to by-pass the title system and become important in the town in a variety of other ways. There is, then, a lot of scope for self-aggrandisement; but the self-made man, rather like the Big Man of New Guinea, is only "big" if other people think so. He has to secure their attention by display and distribution of wealth and by using his influence as a Big Man to protect them and intervene on their behalf. If he is not able to do this, he will not attract a following.

In the same way, in Yoruba traditional thought an *òrìṣà's* power and splendour depend on its having numerous attentive (and wealthy) devotees to glorify its name. An *òrìṣà* without devotees fades into insignificance as far as the human community is concerned. The devotee can choose, within limits, which *òrìṣà* she will devote herself to.[2] If her original *òrìṣà* fails to give her what she desires – a child, success in trading, recovery from a protracted illness – she may approach other *òrìṣà* until she finds one that responds to her request.

By contrast, in a society where roles are ascribed and there is little scope for self-aggrandisement, notions of the reciprocity of the human—god relationship do not seem to arise. Among the Tallensi of Northern Ghana, for instance, humans' relations with the Ancestors are a one-way affair: the Ancestors are omnipotent and demanding, humans are passive and obedient. To put the Yoruba case in perspective, then, let us look very briefly at the contrasting case of the Tallensi.

II

According to Meyer Fortes (Fortes 1945, 1949, 1959), the Tallensi were subsistence farmers who rarely produced a surplus and who had little material wealth. There was little division of labour except according to sex. In such an economic system there was very little scope for an individual to enrich himself at the expense of his fellow-men.

Tallensi society was based on a patrilineal lineage system in which the status and role of every member was strictly determined by his position in the genealogical grid, and could not

---

[2] Devotees were, of course, both male and female. Some cults were exclusive to men – for instance Orò and Egúngún, whose secrets women were not allowed to know. In most cults however men and women played an equally prominent part. It is hard to estimate what things were like in the days when all the cults were still well-attended but it is clear that some cults – such as Ogún – attracted more men than women, while others – such as Òsun, Òtin and Òya – attracted mostly women. I give preference to the female pronoun where cults were attended by both men and women. This is partly in protest against the standard male-oriented usage and partly because in the town where I worked there were more practising women devotees than men.

be altered by his own efforts. Leadership at every level of segmentation devolved automatically upon the most senior member or that segment, and beneath him the position of every other lineage member was likewise fixed according to rules of genealogical seniority. At the lowest level of segmentation, the son was a minor, totally subordinate to the father, who acted on his behalf in matters political, economic, jural and ritual. Great stress was laid on co-operation, deference to elders, conformity to social norms.[3]

Fortes shows how Tallensi religious ideas derived from, and reinforced with moral and ritual injunctions, this ascriptive and authoritarian social structure. The most important spiritual beings in their cosmology were the Ancestors. The shrine of each ancestor was in the custody of the head of the segment that that ancestor founded. The shrines were approached only on prescribed occasions through the segment head himself and in the presence of the representatives of all the subsegments of that segment. No outsider could spontaneously come and participate. Thus there was a hierarchy of Ancestors corresponding to the hierarchy of lineage segments, and the individual's relationship with the Ancestors was regulated by his position in the lineage.

The individual's attitude to the Ancestors was one of passive acceptance. He never took the initiative, never spontaneously offered to communicate with the Ancestors through prayers and sacrifices. Even on routine occasions like harvest ceremonies, he waited for the Ancestors to demand an offering before he – often grudgingly – gave it. The Ancestors were pictured as domineering authority figures, an image of the father vastly magnified and empowered; and though they were just, they were also often capricious and unreasonable. All the human could do was to submit and accept their dominion over him.

This was true even of the "Destiny" ancestors who accounted for and represented the individuality of each person's life and character. For though each man had his own unique cluster of "Destiny" ancestors, nevertheless it was the ancestors who chose him, not he them; and once they had revealed themselves to him, he had to serve them to the end of his life. He could not approach new ones of his own accord if the original ones failed him, and indeed they could not be thought of as "failing" him, only as justly punishing him for some known or unknown transgression. Besides, all the Ancestors were similar in character so there was nothing to choose between them.

The individual then was not regarded as having any power to alter the course of his life by aligning in his support the help of spiritual beings. A large part of his religious life was performed by his segment head on behalf of the collectivity.[4] The social structure dictated which Ancestor he worshipped, with whom and on what occasions, and he took no steps on his own behalf. The notion of Destiny, though it did account for the fact that some men were more successful than others, did not represent the ideal of individual ambition or self-improvement – it rather explained why some men were better than others at conforming to the limited, ascribed roles society presented them with.

---

[3] It seems probable that Fortes, because of his own theoretical predilections, has over-emphasized the rigidly ascriptive nature of the society. There are hints of this, especially in *The Dynamics of Clanship*, where, for instance, he mentions the alacrity with which individuals took advantage of the colonial imposition of Native Authority headmen to enrich themselves far beyond what had been possible traditionally. This suggests that respect for and conformity to conventions of ascriptive seniority were not as deeply entrenched as he makes out. Nevertheless it is clear that Tale society, compared with the Yoruba, *did* offer relatively little scope or encouragement to individual ambition.

[4] It is significant that even the Earth Cult, which in some clans was an important complement to the Ancestor cult, was an affair of maximal lineages, not of individuals. As a rule, the only individuals who approached the Earth shrines of their own accord were "pilgrims" from other groups outside Taleland.

III

The following analysis of a Yoruba example is based on research done in Òkukù, a small but historically important town in the Odò-Òtìn district of the Ọsun area of Ọ̀yọ̀ State, Nigeria.[5] Yoruba political structures are well known to be of great diversity, and no attempt is being made to generalize the conclusions. However, it is evident that the fundamental political structure of Òkukù is similar to that of other Ọ̀yọ̀-area towns, though much simpler than that of the big ones. The description of traditional institutions as they have survived to the present day is filled out with oral accounts of them as they were in the nineteenth century. There is not enough evidence to show whether or not they were very different before this period: it seems likely, however, that the turmoil of the nineteenth-century wars heightened characteristics of flexibility and openness which were already present.[6]

The fundamental political unit, the town, was composed of a number of localized lineages each with a high proportion of attached (and partly attached) "guest" or stranger elements. The head of the town was the *ọba*, a sacred ruler who was chosen in rotation from each of the four sections of the very large royal lineage. He was the nominal owner of the land, and retained residual rights over it; he was set apart by his enormous household of wives, servants, office-holders and (at least till the end of the nineteenth century) slaves, a household which was maintained by the labour of the townspeople; and he was backed by a powerful and pervasive ideology of royalty.

Each lineage was represented and presided over by its *baálé* or family head, who was chosen by his fellow-elders on grounds of seniority and position and who acted as *primus inter pares* in concert with them. But he did gain additional prestige from being the head of a large number of people, and in some compounds he also had rights over a special tract of farmland on which he could require all his compound members to work from time to time. Because of this prestige, the *baálé* could usually acquire a town chieftaincy title – most *baálé* were also chiefs, though many chiefs were not *baálé*.

The chiefs shared the government of the town, and the income that derived from this, with the *ọba*. The chiefs fell into three grades, each of which was internally ranked. The most important were the senior town chiefs (*iwarefa*), the top six of whom were the kingmakers. Each of the senior titles belonged to a

---

[5]   Òkukù's population, estimated from the 1977–8 electoral register, was about 18,000 adult males and females. Of these only about ten per cent were practising traditional worshippers. More than half were Christians, the rest Muslims. Information was collected during a three-year period of field-work (1974–7). Information about lineage history and Big Men is mainly drawn from two series of interviews, one with all the Baálé of the compounds, the other with 75 representatives of three age groups (old, middle-aged and young men) in which detailed and circumstantial reminiscences of their own lives and those of prominent men they remembered were elicited. Information about cults was based mainly on prolonged participation in cult meetings, rituals and festivals, and also on interviews with leading devotees and explanations of the meaning of the *oríkì* of various *òrìṣà* from the performers. All the cults still existing in Òkukù were covered.

[6]   Òkukù was mid-way between the Ìlorin camp, Ọ̀fà, and the Ìbàdàn camp, Ìkìrun. It was overrun and evacuated several times, and on the last occasion the population stayed for 17 years in Ìkìrun before returning to resettle Òkukù in 1893. There was no military organization in Òkukù: instead the fighting men in the town arranged their own raiding expeditions, merely reporting the results to the Oba and chiefs. Even during the wars the social structure never became as flexible as that of Ìbàdàn, which during the 19th century was a society of Big Men pure and simple without the constrains of any traditionally-given hierarchy; on the other hand it never had the complex interlocking systems of hierarchy of Old Ọ̀yọ̀, where hereditary privilege apparently became established by the late 18th century. According to some informants, the title system was not so important "in the old days" as it has now become. Personal *oríkì* (praise poems) suggested that the 19th century was the hey-day of Big Men, but all the oral literature shows that elements of competition and self-aggrandisement were deeply rooted in the culture and had almost certainly been present long before the 19th century.

single lineage – by and large, the older lineages in the town.[7] Below them were the junior town chiefs, *aládàá*. There were more numerous and acted as followers to the senior chiefs, accompanying them to meetings at the palace but not actually participating. Most of these titles could be bestowed by the *ọba* on his own nominee in any compound. Then there were the palace chiefs, who were influential because they were close to the *ọba* and enjoyed his special trust.

The chiefs represented the interests of their lineage members in the councils when necessary, but they also formed an important interest-group in their own right, and spent a lot of their time pursuing alliances and rivalries amongst themselves which were of no interest to the lineage members at large. There was a constant struggle between the *ọba* (the crown) and the senior chiefs, collectively known as *àwọn ìlú* ("the town"). There was also constant rivalry over relative rank among the chiefs themselves. The system was fairly flexible, and though precedents were often appealed to, all interested parties sought to create new precedents by pushing their claims further than ever before. Between 1800 and the present day, the order of rank of the top three senior chiefs has been changed at least three times as a result of such struggles; junior titles have also been promoted to senior status and formerly open titles appropriated by a single lineage.

But more important than this is the fact that people could make a place for themselves which was out of all proportion to their formal position in the chiefly hierarchy. One

example in Òkukù in the late nineteenth century was Ẹlẹ́m ọna. He was the *baálé* of a small lineage and holder of an unimportant palace title. But because of his astuteness in building up a huge household and great wealth and farms for himself, he came to be the most famous of all Òkukù's Big Men. At the height of his power he rivalled the *ọba* himself.[8] Another example was Omíkúnlé a young and untitled warrior in the Ìlorin-Ìbàdàn wars who was given the nickname "Balógun" (after the Ìbàdàn general) and became so great as a result of his leadership of the fighting men of the town that the title was eventually adopted into the formal hierarchy and is now the most important of the four titles that the compound currently holds.

But if men could enlarge their positions within the chiefly hierarchy, they could also by-pass it on occasion and become Big Men without ever being given a title. The reign of Oyèékúnlé (1917–1932) was torn by a long feud between the *ọba* and a faction of chiefs. But in accounts of the feud that I have been given, the leaders of the two sides were Fáwándé and Tóyìnbó the first of whom had no chieftaincy title and the second of whom held only the palace title Sóbalójú. What made them great was their reputation as deadly medicine-men, for the feud was fought out in terms of incapacitating or eliminating enemies with *oògùn* (magical medicine) and *ọfọ̀* (incantations).

The ways in which men (and also women)[9] could make themselves big were diverse, and new opportunities came up with new historical situations – two of the greatest periods of

---

[7] However, on at least two occasions the *ọba* succeeded in taking away a senior title from the lineage that "owned" it and giving it to another.

[8] During the royal Olóòkù festival he is said to have set himself up on his own throne with all his attendants, facing the *ọba* across the *ọba's* market-place. When the *ọba's* drummers warned him "*Ẹlẹ́mọ̀nà rọra, ọba kó lo jẹ*" (Ẹlẹ́mọna go easy, you're not the *ọba*), his own drummers would reply *Èytí tí mo n jẹ yìi, ó ju ọba lọ*" (The position I hold here is greater than an *ọba's*).

[9] There were a number of 19th and early 20th century Big Women in Òkukù. One of them used her terrible reputation as a witch to seize other people's farmland, which she hired bondsmen to work on. Another was the first trader to sell imported alcohol in the town.

opportunity being the nineteenth-century wars and the early twentieth-century expansion of the market for cash crops. But at some stage in all routes to bigness, the person had to acquire the support of a large household and a wider group of followers and hangers-on. Usually (though not always) this was achieved through display and distribution of wealth. Even in pre-colonial days surplus was deliberately produced and sold both in the local and the long-distance markets. Trading on a large scale was characteristic of the economy. Crafts such as blacksmithing, weaving and pottery were specialist productions which enjoyed widespread markets. Before it was sacked and re-founded in the eighteenth century, Òkukù (then known as Kọọkin) was said to have had 140 blacksmiths who obtained their iron ore from the mines at Èjìgbò and supplied the whole area from Ìlá to Ọ̀yọ́ with tools and weapons. There seems always to have been scope for enterprising people to make themselves wealthy.

Some of the nineteenth- and early twentieth-century Big Men in Òkukù were said to have had an initial advantage because of a craft in which they specialised. Ẹlẹ́mọ̀nà, mentioned above, started life as a carver. Others had an edge through an inheritance, often from the mother's side; others again were credited with exceptional skill as farmers, or the good fortune of having many younger brothers to work for them and enable them to expand their farms. During the Ìlọrin-Ìbàdàn wars, young men who did well could enrich themselves by selling the slaves they captured and by marrying the female ones. When the Lagos–Kano railway reached Òkukù in 1904, entrepreneurs who were quick to see its possibilities built themselves up in commercial yam-farming and yam-trading. Others acquired capital by working as young men in

wage-labour before coming home to set up as farmers. Once an initial advantage had been established, the pattern of development was generally similar. The extra money was used to hire extra labour in the form of *ìwọ̀fa* (bondsmen whose labour constituted the interest on a loan taken out by one of their senior relatives).[10] By the 1930s, when commercial farming suddenly expanded in response to the demand for cocoa and kola, people had also begun to hire paid labourers. *Ìwọ̀fa* and labourers were used to expand the Big Man's farm, and until commercial farming really got under way, there was no shortage of land: labour was the only limitation on the expansion of farms. Wealth was used to expand the household through the marriage of more wives and the rearing of more children. A successful man could also expect relatives, matrilateral was well as patrilateral, to send some of their children to live with him to enjoy the benefits of a large and well-to-do household. "Followers" who were not actually resident in the compound would also gather; visitors would come to stay, sometimes settling permanently and becoming "*òrẹ́dẹbí*" ("friends-become-family"). Ties of kinship were manipulated to bring dependants and hangers-on flocking round a wealthy man.

Recruitment of people was crucial in a Big Man's rise in two ways. First, they were actual factors in the production of wealth, as labour on the Big Man's farm and – in the case of wives – also as the producers of the future labour of the children they bore. And second, in a fairly flexible social structure where individuals could make their own position for themselves, attendant people were the index of how much support and acknowledgement the man commanded, and thus how important he was. A man without "people" would not

---

[10]   According to Oroge (Oroge 1971) *ìwọ̀fa* only became an important source of labour after slavery had been banned in the late 19th century. It seems from oral evidence however that slaves were not much used in Òkukù in the 19th century for labour: instead almost all of them were sold. The oral literature shows that *ìwọ̀fa* as an institution had certainly existed from the earliest times.

presume to contest a chieftaincy title,[11] while one of the most important ways that acquisition of such a title strengthened a man's political power was that it brought him, or put him in charge of, more people.[12]

Reminiscences of elders suggest that a great many men, if not all, strove to become big. The picture we get is of innumerable people building themselves up and competing to acquire their own circle of hangers-on. A few seemed to have been so outstanding that they overshadowed the rest, but almost everyone was in the game. Their competitiveness comes out in the qualities admired in a Big Man. In their *oríkì* (attributive poetry) we see that they were praised not only for their generosity, magnificence, style and personal splendour, but also for toughness, unassailability, intransigence, and power – often conceived in terms of the ability to perpetrate outrages with impunity. The Big Man was pictured as rising above the malicious attacks of jealous rivals and at the same time getting away with any attacks he made on *them*. He was seen as an isolated individual pitted against enemies who strove day and night to undo him. No-one could be trusted. Whereas the Tallensi said that relations between humans were essentially amicable, and that all misfortune and death was caused by the Ancestors, the Yoruba say that humans are one another's enemies, and most misfortunes are caused by the nefarious activities of *ayé*, the "world," or more specifically the witches and wizards, and evil people employing their services.

Yoruba cosmology presents a picture of Man, a solitary individual, picking his way (aided by his Orí or Destiny, chosen by himself before coming to earth) between a variety of forces, some benign, some hostile, many ambivalent, seeking to placate them and ally himself with them in an attempt to thwart his rivals and enemies in human society. Among the hostile powers are the *eníyán* or witches, and the Ajogun which are personified evils such as Death, Loss, Sickness, etc. Among the benign ones are the ancestors who revisit their descendants in the guise of *egúngún* (masquerades), and the *òrìṣà*. Over them all is Olódùmarè, the High God who is not approached directly by humans, and his two intermediaries, Èṣù the ambivalent trickster and Òrúnmìlà the god of wisdom who reveals Olódùmarè's will to humans through divination.[13]

Unlike the Tallensi, then, the Yoruba have a great variety of spiritual forces to deal with. The pantheon as a whole and the relationships between all these forces are mainly the concern of the *babaláwo*, the highly-trained specialist Ifá priests, who master a great corpus of divination verses dealing with every aspect of the cosmology. Ordinary individuals, though they consult Ifá constantly, have a more partial view of the cosmology determined by the particular powers and cults they are involved with. These are drawn principally from among the *egúngún* and *òrìṣà*.

The *òrìṣà* are said to have been people living on earth who on their departure from it were

---

[11] In the early years of this century a junior title then held by *ilé* Olúọde fell vacant and the compound members asked a respectable elder, Ògùnlékè, to take the title. Ògùnlékè, however, refused on the grounds that his household was too small, he did not have enough children to back him up, and without these he would not be able to withstand the jealous attacks his appointment would arouse. The lineage had an attached female branch which had hitherto been debarred from taking any title: but this branch was headed by a bold and enterprising man who also had a large household. "Ọdélàdé lágidi, ó làyá, ó sì bìmọ púpọ̀" (Ọdélàdé was stubborn, he was bold, and he also had a great many children): Ọdélàdé not only got the title, he later managed to get it converted into the senior title that accompanied the role of Baálé.

[12] If the title went with the role of Baálé, the holder was actually at the head of a large body of people who would refer their political and other problems to him and whom he could, to some extent, guide and mobilise. If the title did not accompany the role of Baálé, the holder still gained followers who hoped to go through him to the *ọba*.

[13] For a full and clear exposition of Yoruba cosmology see (Abímbọ́lá 1975).

deified.[14] Each *òrìṣà* has its own town of origin, its own personality and special attributes, its own taboos and observances, and its own corpus of *oríkì*. Many *òrìṣà* are mythologically connected with rivers, hills and natural forces and seem to be nature spirits which have been combined with culture heroes and thus humanised (whereas pure nature spirits, *iwin*, remain outside in the bush and do not play an important part in human affairs).

Egúngún are of several types, some more closely associated with the ancestors than others. As well as the anonymous, plain-robed *eégún rere* (good *egúngún*) which belong to the compound as a whole and represent the collectivity of ancestors of that compound, there are the highly individual *eégún nlá* (big *egúngún*) and *eégún alágbo* (medicine-empowered *egúngún*) which, though they are revered by the whole compound as ancestral figures, also represent the particular Big Men who founded them as a monument to their own glory. The *eégún alágbo* in particular, with their flamboyant dress, ferocity and dangerous attacks on rival *egúngún*, convey the spiritual essence of human competitive struggle for dominance, as well as ancestral benignity. There are also numerous small *egúngún* which have only a residual association with the ancestors: the *pàkàá*, which are carried by young boys on certain festival days. Moreover, *egúngún* are not the only means of communication with the ancestors. The dead can appear to the living in dreams, or their wishes can be made known through Ifá, and the descendant can then approach them directly at the *ojú oórì*, the grave where the dead person is buried inside the house and which is a kind of shrine. Offerings and prayers can be made there, and the dead can be summoned back by the chanting of their *oríkì*. Questions are asked and are answered through the medium of kola in a simple form of divination.[15]

The *egúngún* cult is for everybody, though there are specialist *egúngún* priests too, and the *egúngún* festival is a long and spectacular affair in which every household in the town participates. But *òrìṣà* are worshipped only by their own cult members, and it is here that the elements of individual personality, choice and man–god reciprocality, which contrast so markedly with the Tallensi religion, are most apparent.

Just as the Big Man operates within the framework of the political title system, so the individual's relationship with his or her *òrìṣà* exists in a broader cult organisation.

The major public event for each cult is its annual festival, in which many non-members participate in a peripheral way. These festivals are co-ordinated into a yearly cycle, each festival following the last at intervals fixed by tradition. A further integrating factor is that the ultimate authority over every cult is the *oba*. It is he who ratifies the fixing of the date of every festival (*idajo*). He is represented by a member of his household or by his own Ifá priest at every festival sacrifice, and on their return from the shrine, the devotees always go to the palace to dance before the *oba* and ask his blessing.

Some festivals enact political and civic themes which are as important as the worship of the *òrìṣà* itself. The Olóókù festival – which is the biggest in the cycle, and the one for which everyone comes home from their farms – is essentially a royal and civic festival. The *òrìṣà* Olóókù is tended throughout the year

---

[14]   A few special ones who participated in the original creation of the world were said to have come down to earth from heaven and returned there: Òrúnmìlà, Obàtálá and Èṣù were among them.

[15]   Although the ancestors were addressed in a direct, personal fashion at the *ojú oórì*, it cannot be said that they are regarded simply as "elders" (see Kopytoff 1971, chapter 24, this volume). Chants addressed to them stress the idea that after human invocation and sacrifice, they *return* to the world of their descendants from another world, and the journey is pictured as an arduous one covering an immense distance. Moreover, each stage of the funeral ceremony progressively separates the soul or spirit from the body, until on the seventh day it appears as an *egúngún* and is escorted to the place of its final departure.

only by the Àwòrò Olóókù and the members of his very small compound. But Olóókù is the town's guardian spirit, and everyone participates in its festival. In it an ancient power struggle is ceremonially re-enacted in a mock wrestling-match between the ọba and the Àwòrò lóókù. Much of the festival is concerned with the glorification of royalty and the display and ritual propitiation of the ọba's ancient beaded crowns. Another festival in which political themes are prominent is that of Ọtìn, a female river deity. In this festival the opposition and interdependence of "town" and "crown" are symbolically affirmed in a confrontation between the ọba and the *arugbá Ọtìn*, who is chosen alternately from the two leading senior chiefs' compounds.[16] The importance of each cult festival's role in the affirmation of the town's political unity is seen most clearly when there is *disharmony* and the leaders of one cult or another refuse to do their part. This is considered a disgrace to the town and is used as a strong expression of disapproval of the ọba.

The public civic role of the cults is reflected in their internal organisation, for the leading members of the cult take titles which are often modelled on town chieftaincy titles. These titles are ranked and also denote specific functions within the cult. Moreover, cult titles can assume a function in the town which is actually equivalent to a chieftaincy title: this happens when a "stranger" segment, attached to a lineage but debarred from taking a title belonging to that lineage, grows big enough to feel the need for its own distinctive head. Such segments often take over a high-ranking cult title and make it their own, even calling themselves, as a group, after it.

But the core of the religion lies not in the public framework but in the personal bond between each devotee and the spiritual being she serves. In what follows I concentrate mainly of *òrìṣà*, not including Ifá.

Unlike the Tallensi devotee the Yoruba one does not have to approach spiritual beings through a hierarchy of elders. Even at the sacrifices made during the annual festival, where the role of the titled priests is most prominent, individual devotees will approach the shrine with their own offerings and have kola cast for them personally. Such occasions often take hours because of the crowds of women waiting to put in their own private plea to the *òrìṣà*. During the rest of the year, devotees attend more informally to their home shrines. Each compound in which an *òrìṣà* is worshipped usually has at least one home shrine for it: either a small room off the living corridor (*ọ̀dẹ̀dẹ̀*) or a small hut built outside in the compound courtyard. It is quite common for a compound to have several shrines to different *òrìṣà*; some will be approached by the whole household, others perhaps by only one or two women who have a special relationship with that *òrìṣà*. Many compounds have a "family" *òrìṣà* determined by their hereditary profession, their town of origin or other factors.[17] All members of the household approach its shrine but some will be more deeply involved in the cult than others, and some will have other *òrìṣà* as well.

A very deeply involved devotee approaches the shrine first thing every morning, uttering a prayer and offering some small item such as kola. Every fourth day is the *òrìṣà*'s special day, on which all the devotees in the household gather early in the morning. The most senior

---

[16] The *arugbá* Ọtìn is a young girl whose office is to carry the *igbá* (calabash) of Ọtìn on the festival days. She serves a seven year term. The calabash is said to contain sacred objects which the *oba* must not see, on pain of bringing ruin to the town.

17 William Bascom, writing about the Ifè almost forty years ago, says that most of the *òrìṣà* belonged to particular compounds or quarters: those which could be worshipped by anyone in the town were exceptions. This was not the case in present-day Òkukù. Bascom's conclusion, that *òrìṣà* belonged to families because they were thought of as ancestors, is surely a distortion. (Bascom 1944).

devotee utters prayers and incantations, an offering is made, kola cast to see if it is accepted, and then women devotees chant the òrìṣà's *oríkì*.

In some cults, devotees from other compounds join in on this occasion. Less frequently – in some cults every nine days, in others every sixteen, in others every calendar month – all the cult members assemble in the cult head's house, and after the normal devotions eat a meal together, make their contributions to their *ajo* (a rotating fund drawn on by each member in turn) and sometimes spend the whole day there gossiping and singing cult songs. But the devotee can approach the shrine whenever she wishes, on an impulse of supplication or gratitude. The communication can be as brief and apparently casual as she likes. Nor is the devotee always restricted to one place of worship. The hunter's gun, for instance, is a symbol of Ògún and wherever the hunter puts his gun down can be a temporary shrine of Ògún.

Again unlike the Tallensi devotee, the Yoruba one has a degree of choice as to which òrìṣà she pays special attention to. Attachment to a particular òrìṣà can arise in several ways. Where the cult is a family one, the older devotees will be succeeded by children of the household who have been showing special interest or who are deemed on general grounds of character to be suitable.[18] A devotee who dies always has to be replaced, but who is chosen depends on the circumstances. Some cults, including those of Ọya, Ṣàngó and Ṣọ̀pọ̀nnọ̀n, have an inner circle of devotees who alone are allowed to participate in the mysteries of the cult and to be possessed by the òrìṣà. In these cults each initiated member (*adóṣù*) will make sure she has a young person marked out to succeed her and be initiated when she dies. Such children will be selected

after consultation with Ifá, and the *babaláwo* consulted will take the prospective candidates' character and inclinations into account. But adults can also approach a new òrìṣà of their own accord. A woman who fails to conceive for several years may appeal to an òrìṣà who has given a child to a friend of hers, or to one whose style and personality appeal to her. This tends to happen most frequently at the annual festivals. If after supplication and offerings she does conceive a child, she will keep her part of the bargain by continuing to worship the òrìṣà, participating at least in its festival, at which time she will make it an offering such as a chicken, pounded yam or kola, and join the other devotees in their dances and processions. Often the child itself will be put into the cult as a full member. People can also appeal to a new òrìṣà or relief from sickness or ill-luck; they might be guided to it by Ifá. If relief is granted, they will see this as a sign that they should become devotees of the òrìṣà for life. New òrìṣà can also be brought into the family by the wives, who continue to worship their own family òrìṣà installing a personal shrine in their husband's house. When a compound wife dies, a successor will be found among the children to take over her shrine. As in the other cases, the person chosen might be someone who has of her own accord shown an interest in that òrìṣà, or it might be someone picked on general grounds of suitablity of character by the compound elders in conjunction with the Ifá priest. Or a household might decide that it would be advantageous to have a link with a certain cult, in which case, if there is not already a member of that cult in the compound, one of the children can be sent to work part-time for a priest of the cult in another compound to receive instruction and initiation in return. (This is most common in the case of the Ifá cult, because divination is a

---

[18]   I have been using the present tense because the description is based on observation of contemporary Òkukù. However, this account of how devotees are chosen is in part a reconstruction. Nowadays the cults are so short of members that it is often difficult for them to find an heir to a devotee when she dies. Sometimes they choose very young children or babies just to satisfy the requirement that the devotee be replaced; and sometimes devotees of other *òrìṣa* are pushed into taking over a cult they have no interest in.

profitable as well as prestigious occupation). Adjustments can be made in all these cases to match the devotee with an *òrìṣà* of appropriate character – for each *òrìṣà* has its own temperament and generates its own atmosphere and mood. Such adjustments are not as freely made as has elsewhere been suggested, for there are many constraints: the person selected to succeed another devotee does not actually have much say in the matter herself, except insofar as she has expressed her preferences by her past behaviour; and an *òrìṣà* cannot just be casually abandoned if it fails to respond to a devotee's needs – or it might get its revenge by inflicting further misfortunes.[19] nevertheless, adjustments *are* being made gradually and continuously. People usually have the *òrìṣà* they want and identify with.

The sense of personal involvement and identification is strengthened by a feature of the religion which has been insufficiently remarked on: the multiple manifestations of "one" *òrìṣà*. Many *òrìṣà* are worshipped quite widely. Some belong to a particular locality (those associated with certain rivers, hills, etc.) but many have devotees not only in several towns but throughout large parts of the Yoruba-speaking area. Nevertheless, each devotee can feel that she has her "own" Oya, Sango, or whatever it is. This is because each *òrìṣà* is divided into countless versions, each with its own subsidiary name, *oríkì*, personality and taboos.

In Òkukù, for instance, I was told that *"Orúkọ métadínlógún ni òrìṣà Ṣòpọ̀nnọ̀n pín si"* (the òrìṣà Ṣòpọ̀nnọ̀n divides into seventeen names). Each of the seventeen belongs to an individual or a small group of devotees. Each manifestation had an original worshipper who discovered that manifestation's own particular taboo by reacting violently to something and becoming possessed immediately after his initiation into the cult as an *adóṣù* (in this case all the initiates I heard about were men). But once the idiosyncratic taboo had been discovered, other worshippers were drawn to that manifestation and the taboo applied to them all. Waríwarùn, for instance, cannot endure to have one of his devotees beaten. If this happens, the devotee in question will be possessed instantly by Ṣòpọ̀nnọ̀n ; drummers will have to be called and sacrifices made before he is released from the possession. Àbàtà's devotees must not hear the sound of a cooking pot being scraped, Adégbọ̀nà's must not have water splashed on them, and so on. The *oríkì* show that each manifestation has a different colouring to his personality. All are tough, violent and overwhelmingly powerful: but these qualities are expressed in subtly different imagery for each. Àbàtà ("Swamp") shows his toughness by dirtying his devotees' gifts in the mud associated with his name (thus flouting with impunity all the conventions about receiving gifts):

Gùnyán lẹ́bẹ́ gbé fAyìílẹ́rẹ́ o
Olówó orí àjikí
Erè ni òó fi ṣe
Rokà lẹ́bẹ́ gbé fAyìílẹ́rẹ́ o
Erẹ̀ ni òó fi ṣe . . .[20]

Prepare fine light pounded yam for Ayílẹ́rẹ̀
My husband whom we rise to greet
And he'll dirty it in the mud
Prepare fine light yam-flour pudding for Ayílẹ́rẹ̀
And he'll dirty it in the mud . . .

The *oríkì* Ògáálá, on the other hand, are full of imagery of iron, especially the branding iron which Ṣòpọ̀nnọ́n uses to mark his smallpox victims:

---

[19]   Ulli Beier, for instance, writes perceptively about the importance of personalities in Yoruba religion but he tends to suggest that each individual will be drawn into the cult that suits his personality and will thenceforth be psychically fused with his *òrìṣà* – as if the individual was completely free to choose the cult he liked. (Beier 1959). Bascom (1944) says that people who inherited *òrìṣà* were free to abandon the lot if they so desired, and became "sceptics." Perhaps there *was* more freedom before the decline of traditional religion, but it is clear that there were also family and cult restraints.
[20]   From a Ṣòpọ̀nnọ́n chant performed by Oyádọla during the Ṣòpọ̀nnọ́n festival, Òkukù 1977.

Ó nírín ó labẹ ó ní yanyanturu
Irin'nà, okọ ọrun mi
Irin tí Agbédàjó ti ń fi ń kọmọ kò téèékanna . . .[21]

He has iron, he has knives, he has all kinds of
　　things
Hot iron, my original husband
The branding iron Agbédàjó uses to scarify
　　people is smaller than a finger-nail . . .

The many manifestations of Enlè, a hunter-
and river-god, were known as *ibú* (pools). The
oríkì of each *ibú*, bringing out different shades
of the *òrìṣà* 's personality (one dwelling on his
prowess as a hunter, another on his drinking,
another on the might of the deep river) are
chanted in turn at the Enle festival, as well as
being collectively invoked with the refrain.

Eníbúmbú, olódò-odò olómi-omi
All you pools, all you rivers, all you waters.

Each manifestation is thought of as being a
distinct personality. This can be illustrated by
an example from the Òṣun cult. In recent times
in Òkukù there have been four manifestations
of Òṣun (though there may be more elsewhere): Ijumu, Iponda (whose taboo is
guinea-corn beer), IbúŃlà and Ẹdan. Each of
them had, until recently, several devotees from
various compounds. But as the number of
traditional worshippers dwindled it became
harder to find successors to devotees who died,
and eventually a single woman ended up as the
last devotee of both Edan and Ìjùmù. She
worshipped both of them, keeping their
calabashes – their concrete symbol and location – separate, greeting each of them
separately on Òṣun's weekly day, and casting
kola separately before each.

Most *òrìṣà* seem to be fragmented in this
way. With some the number of manifestations
is determinate and there are stories explaining
how the fragmentation occurred: it is said, for

instance, that a quarrel between Ọya and
Ògún (her first husband) led to a fight in which
Ọya used her magical staff to break Ògùn into
seven pieces, while Ògún used his to break Ọya
into nine.[22] It is said that each of the 256 *odú* of
Ifá has its "own" Èṣù. But in other cults it
seems that the number of manifestations is
indefinite and that a new one may be established or discovered by an especially powerful
devotee who wants to set himself apart from
his fellow cult-members. This seemed to be
the case in Òkukù with the Sàngó cult, where
some of the versions of Sango were called after
their devotees' personal names.

The intimate personal involvement of
devotee and *òrìṣà* is mutual. The *òrìṣà*
possesses the devotee; but the devotee also, in
a different sense, "possesses" the *òrìṣà*. many
òrìṣà mount (*gùn*) certain of their devotees,
especially at the climactic moments of festivals
or on other highly-charged ritual occasions.
The devotee's face, voice and movements
change as the *òrìṣà* enters and empowers her or
him. During the Sàngó festival the *adóṣù* take
it in turns to hold a feast for their fellow cult-
members. The high point of the feast is when,
amidst frenzied drumming, chanting and
invocation of the *òrìṣà* , Sàngó enters the *adóṣù*
(usually a man) who, with a great exultant
shout, strips off his ritual costume and begins
to perform astonishing feats of magic and
physical endurance. Sòpònnón devotees are
also possessed by their *òrìṣà* when their taboo
is broken as has been mentioned. Devotees can
become possessed at the shrine of their *òrìṣà* –
for instance, at the annual festival sacrifice –
when they are chanting its *oríkì*. In possession,
the *òrìṣà*'s personality invades and colours the
devotee's, and even after it has withdrawn its
imprint is left on the devotee.

At the same time the devotee "possesses"
the *òrìṣà* in the sense that she is the special
custodian of her "own" version of it. Her own

---

[21]　From the same chant.
[22]　This story is also told in "Òòṣà Ọya ní ilú Ọyọ́", B.A. long essay, University of Ifè, June 1978 by Bridget Mojíṣola
Òkédìjí.

style and personality affect the way the manifestation is regarded. The *òrìṣà* belonging to a powerful, wealthy, charismatic devotee will be more highly regarded than one belonging to an insignificant person. Each colours the other's personality.

Devotee and *òrìṣà* are mutually defining. The devotee – especially if she is an *adóṣu* – will be addressed and referred to as Ìyá Ṣàngó, Ìyá Olótin, etc. The devotees of Enlè address each other by the names of their own *ibú* (e.g. Ojútù, Alámò, Owáálà, Abátàn, Ìyámòkín, Áánú) at cult gatherings. At the same time the *òrìṣà* is known through the devotee who "owns" it. Some versions of *òrìṣà*, as we have seen, were named after their owners. All versions could be saluted with the *oríkì orílè* (lineage attributions) of their respective owners. One devotee of Enlè told me that the principal difference between the various *ibú* was the *oríkì orílè* attributed to them by virtue of their attachment to particular devotees. *Oríkì* are the most intimate and cherished keys to a person's identity. The closeness of the personal bond between *òrìṣà* and devotee is revealed in the way that each can be saluted with the *oríkì* of the other.

It is clear that the ordinary devotee usually finds satisfaction in one cult and is more or less indifferent to the rest of the pantheon. The inner cult members in particular tend to dissociate themselves from the activities of other cults and even feel them to be rivals. Some people, of course, worship a family *òrìṣà* as well as a personal one, and many people participate in the annual worship of those *òrìṣà* like Olóókù and Òtìn which are thought of as belonging to the whole town. In recent times, with the dramatic decline of traditional worship, many old men and women find themselves in charge of several different inherited *òrìṣà*. But the living core of the religion certainly seems to have been an individual's direct, spontaneous and intimate relationship with her "own" *òrìṣà*. The importance of this relationship and the depth of involvement of course varied. For the inner circle it was

certainly a whole way of life. These cult members spend all their time together on the *òrìṣà*'s weekly day and on cult meeting days. During the festival, each member takes her turn to feast the others, and in the days when cults were well-attended this could have meant months of communal eating at four-day intervals. If she spent most of her life in the cult, on her death she cannot depart this world until she is released, by final secret rituals, from her cult membership. Cults with *adóṣu* have special rituals to remove the *oṣu* (a magical substance applied to the head on initiation). Members of the family are not allowed to approach the corpse until the cult members have arrived and performed the ritual. In one such ceremony that I witnessed, performed for a Ṣàngó *adóṣu*, there was a very strong feeling that the Ṣàngó cult owned the devotee and could claim her even against the will of the family. Some cults are very expensive to join, especially those, like Òrìṣà Oko, Ṣòpònnón and Ṣàngó, which have elaborate initiation rituals. Once having joined, the devotee is committed to it and will not want to waste more money supporting other cults. There is a sense of community and mutual obligation among the members of a cult, reinforced by the taboos which they jointly observe and by the feeling that they all share the same type of personality.

Each devotee concentrates on her own *òrìṣà* and tries to enhance its glory through her attentions. This involves not only making offerings and chanting *oríkí*, but also spending money as lavishly as possible on her day to give the feast. In return, the *òrìṣà* is asked to give blessings and protection. Paramount among the blessings people desire is children; after that come wealth, health and long life. Protection is solicited against rivals and enemies, and the *òrìṣà* is asked to bring about their downfall. A good example of the reciprocality of the relationship is seen in the assertion of the Ọya devotees that *because* the cult is so expensive, Ọya will *therefore* be obliged to make them successful in trade so that they can fulfil their obligations to her in style.

Everyone asks for the same things from her *òrìṣà*, and everyone therefore credits her own *òrìṣà* with the power to bestow them. The same qualities of generosity, life-giving power, destructive power and personal magnificence are attributed to all the *òrìṣà* by their own devotees. Beneficent power gives people children: the *òrìṣà* is often described in *oríkì* as a creator who forges children's heads or limbs, and also as a parent who cherishes the devotee as if she were herself a baby. Destructive power protects one from one's enemies: it is invoked in imagery of blood, fire and iron; the *òrìṣà* is often described as committing violent and outrageous acts with impunity, to show that he can get away with anything, withstand anyone.[23] Personal magnificence enhances reputation: it is the outward sign of greatness, and is described in images of riches, sumptuous garments, beads, beauty, elegance, graceful dancing and so on. Not all the *òrìṣà* have these qualities in the same proportions. Olooku is a "white" deity, primarily beneficent, and his nickname is "iwin èrò" (mild spirit). Ọtìn and Èsile are praised most for giving children, Ṣòpònnón, Sàngó and Ògún for their savage destructive power which their devotees beg them to turn on others and not on themselves. But all *òrìṣà* do have, in different degrees, all these qualities, because every *òrìṣà* has to be able to fulfil all the needs of the devotee. The language of all their *oríkì* is strikingly similar. In many cases the very same attributions are applied to several *òrìṣà*, one devotee borrowing from another without any feeling of incongruity to glorify her own subject.[24] Her concern is not to draw sharp distinctions between the various *òrìṣà* but to elevate and enhance her own so that it will be able to bless and protect her. One can see this in the stories devotees tell about their own *òrìṣà*. In the Ifá corpus, the two co-wives of

---

[23] Both humans and *òrìṣa* are admired for being able to do outrageous things and get away with it. There are many examples in the *oríkì* of the *òrìṣa*. Several of the *òrìṣa* are called "*Oṣìkà a-namo-àna-ŕe*" (Wicked fellow who beats his own in-laws' children). Òrìṣa Ògìyán (a "version" of Ọbàtálá) mistreats his in-laws even more savagely:

> *Jagunlabí bá jọmọ àna rè sínú ọtí*
> *Ó gbégi sónsó bojú olóore*
> *Ó fesè elése bogíyan eèrùn*
> Jagunlabí went and threw his in-laws' child into boiling guinea-corn beer
> He sharpened a stick and thrust it into his benefactor's eye
> One who shoved someone else's foot into an ant-heap

In-laws were the most respected of relatives. Enlè is credited with attacking another highly-respected category of people, widows:

> *Sá pónpó topó*
> *Fàtàrí opó nàpó*
> *Ó wáá rọtí lóọ opó*
> *Láwìn, éè san!*
> Stands over the widow with a cudgel
> Bashes the widow's skull against the house-post
> He went and bought beer from a widow
> On credit, he didn't pay!

Ṣòpònnón is said to have killed someone else's goat and then got that man to grind the pepper to cook it in. The element of humour in these examples is characteristic: the Big Men's exploits are thought to be scandalous and amusing.

[24] The similarity between the oríkì of Sàngo and Èṣù, noticed by (Westcott and Morton-Williams 1962) is actually part of a much more general phenomenon. I have found the same units of *oríkì* in chants addressed to Sàngo, Èsilè and Enlè; and some units of praise – e.g. those relating to the gift of children – can be applied to almost all *òrìṣà*.

Sàngó – Ọya and Ọ̀ṣun – are presented as contrasting types. Ọya is tough, fierce, harsh and vain, while Ọ̀ṣun the senior wife is mild, patient, long-suffering and kind. A story told to me by an Ọya devotee emphasized this contrast and gloried in Ọya's violence, which is an aspect of her power. But when an Ọ̀ṣun devotee talked about Ọ̀ṣun , he chose stories that stressed her mischievous, capricious awkwardness, her stubbornness and her primacy among all the female *òrìṣà*, concluding triumphantly *"Obìnrin bí ọkunrin ni"* (She's a woman who behaves like a man). This was the aspect of her nature that made her a valuable protector and ally in his struggle against the world.

Thus the Yoruba gods are at once fragmented and fused. They are fragmented because of the intense personal nature of the *òrìṣà*–devotee relationship, which makes each devotee desire her *own* version of the *òrìṣà* imprinted with her own personality and identity. They are fused because, underlying their differences of character and ambience, all the *òrìṣà* share the same qualities and do the same things for their devotees.[25] The Yoruba pantheon contains many figures oddly linked and merging with each other: *òrìṣà* that are said to be "the same", and yet not the same, *òrìṣà* that are partly refractions of each other and partly distinct. In Òkukù there is Otòmpòrò, a mask brought out during the Ọ̀tìn festival which has a fierce wild personality and behaves like an *egúngún*. It is said to be the "husband" of the female *òrìṣà* Òtìn (who in her own legend was married to the oba of Ọ̀tan), but it also *is* a manifestation of Òtìn along with a whole collection of other masks both male and female. There is also Arère, a female counterpart to the fearful male hunter god Òrìṣà Oko. Arère is said to be Òrìṣà Oko's wife but also a *kind* of Òrìṣà Oko, though less powerful than

the male one. There is Lóógun-Ède, who is described as the youngest son of Ọ̀ṣun, but who (according to the oldest Ọ̀ṣun devotee in the town) is also a fierce male version of Ọ̀ṣun herself: *"Lóógun- Ède? Osun ni!"* (Lóógun-Ède? He's Ọ̀ṣun!) As J. R. O. Òjò has pointed out (Òjò 1977) there is no clearly agreed-upon hierarchy or other ordering of the *òrìṣà* in the pantheon. Each one is all things to its own devotees.

If the Tallensi Ancestor is a magnified image of the father, the Yoruba *òrìṣà* seems in some ways very much like a magnified image of the Big Man. Big Men, like *òrìṣà*, exist in large numbers and achieve importance in diverse ways with diverse powers. Instead of occupying fixed positions in relation to each other, both *òrìṣà* and Big Men can be made bigger or smaller by the attention, or withdrawal of attention, of their own group of supporters. Both have a reciprocal relationship with these supporters. Both have to offer them, in return for their support, protection against enemies, guidance when problems arise, influence to make things go well. They provide not only material benefits, but their own prestige, of which the supporter partakes. In both cases, then, it is a relationship of mutual interest, for the supporter builds up the reputation of his protector and then benefits from it. The same qualities of character are admired in *òrìṣà* as in Big Men – except that the underlying ethic of decency and restraint which tempers the excesses attributed to Big Men is often absent in the *oríkì* of *òrìṣà*, who are pictured as much more extreme in their power, violence and grandeur than humans. Like the followers of a Big Man, devotees have a certain amount of choice as to who they decide to support. Though often bound by tradition, habit and family connections, there is nevertheless room for adjustment. If the Big

---

[25] Idowu (1962) tells the story of how a single, original arch-divinity called Òrìṣà was smashed into fragments when his slave rolled a massive boulder down a hillside at him. Ọ̀rúnmìlà collected the pieces, deposited some at the arch-divinity's town of Iranje and distributed the rest all over the world. Thus the differentiation of cults began. All the *òrìṣà* were originally one.

Man or *òrìṣà* disappoints him, he can take his problems elsewhere. The main difference is that the devotee plays a far more active role in building up the *òrìṣà* than the supporter does in building up the Big Man. The *òrìṣà* themselves are not particularly competitive;[26] it is their devotees who try to raise them higher than other *òrìṣà*. It is the devotees who spend conspicuously to increase the prestige of their *òrìṣà*. Indeed, the devotee seems here to be combining the roles of supporter and Big Man. He adulates his *orisa* and by doing so increases his own stature.

IV

Because of the reciprocal nature of the relationship, and because the devotee can, if the worst comes to the worst, transfer her main allegiance to another *òrìṣà*, she can afford to be forthright and demanding. The chants in which the devotees pour out praise and gratitude to the *òrìṣà* also contain strongly-worded requests for further blessings, reminders that the relationship should be reciprocal, and even semi-serious threats. Far from adopting the tone of passive acceptance that characterised the Tallensi attitude to the Ancestors, the Yorùbá devotee keeps her *òrìṣà* up to the mark. One devotee of Èsìlè took as the refrain to her chant this reminder:

> *Eni ó gabani là a gbà*
> The person who helps us is the one we help

A Ṣàngó devotee threatens to defect to another cult if blessings are not forthcoming:

Ṣàngó bọ́ ọ gbè mí, ojúti ara tìẹ ni
Ṣàngó, bí n ò sìn ó, ojúti ara tèmi ni
Ṣàngó bọ́ ọ gbè mì n ó lọ rèẹ ya Ọ̀sun
Ṣàngó bọ́ ọ gbè mì n ó lọ rèẹ ṣègbàgbọ́
Ṣàngó bọ́ ọ ba gbè mí ó, Erin-fibi-ládugbó-sojú
Erin-gbogbo-ló-káwọ́-ìjà-léri, n ò ní í kírun
Bọ́ ọ bá gbè mí nkọ́, Erin-fibi-ládugbó-sojú,
Ọ̀rẹ́ oníbàtá, mo lémi ò ní í ṣegbàgbó
Atóbájayé, bọ́ ọ gbè mí n ò ní í y Osun
Ṣíjú ègbè wò mí, Olúkòso Gbágídíyarí[27]

Ṣàngó, if you don't bless me the shame is your own
Ṣàngó, if I don't serve you, the shame is mine
Ṣàngó, if you don't bless me, I will go and make an Ọ̀sun image
Ṣàngó, if you don't bless me I'll go and turn Christian
But Ṣàngó, if you do bless me, Elephant-with-eyes-as-large-as-water-drums
All-elephants-carry-fighting-arms-on-their-heads, I won't become a Muslim
And if you bless me, Elephant-with-eyes-as-large-as-water-drums,
Friend of the *bàtá*-drummers, I say I won't turn Christian
One worthy to enjoy the world with, if you bless me I won't go and make an image o f Ọ̀sun
Open the eyes of blessing on me, lord of Kòso, Gbágídíyarí.

But the Yoruba perception of *òrìṣà*-devotee mutual dependence goes much deeper than this. What it comes down to is a conception of something very like collusion between *òrìṣà* and devotee. It was a passage from *Èṣù pípè* (the *oríkì* chant addressed to the trickster deity Èṣù) that first brought this to my attention:

---

[26] In a way, Ifá is an exception to this. The whole Ifá cult is hegemonic and countless Ifá stories present Ọ̀rúnmìlà as succeeding where all the other *òrìṣà* fail, being the only one who has solutions to problems, and so on. However, in character Ọ̀rúnmìlà is not competitive – it is just that, according to the Ifá corpus, he is by nature wiser than all the others. The continual emphasis on Ọ̀rúnmìlà's superiority seems to be evidence in support of Robin Horton's theory that the Ifá cult was the ideology of an expanding political power and was imposed on the hitherto-existing *òrìṣà* cults from above. (Horton, 1979).

[27] From a *Ṣàngó pípè* chant performed by Àjíkẹ, Ìyá Ṣàngó Ìgbàyè, on the occasion of Baálè Ṣàngó's feast during the Ṣàngó festival, 1976.

Èṣù mọ́ se mí lódè ilẹ̀ yìi láéláé
Bí ń bá ń seégún á yídó
Áá ṣiṣọ lórí
Áá ní ò sí nńkan 'bẹ
Talẹ́talẹ́ ọlọ́kọ rẹ á dìgbèsè
Èṣù mọ́ ṣe mí lóde ilẹ̀ yìi láèláé
Bí ń bá ń sòrìṣà áá fòìṣàa rẹ̀ ya pẹ̀ẹ̀rẹ̀
Olóíṣà íí, áá ní ò sí nńkan 'be
Talẹ̀talẹ́ ọlọ̀kọ rẹ̀ á dìgbèsè[28]

Èṣù don't ever attack me in this world
If he attacks a masquerade it will roll out a
    mortar
It will pull the cloth off its head
It will say there's nothing there
By evening its patron will have run into debt
Èṣù don't ever attack me in this world
If he attacks a devotee, the devotee will give
    his òrìṣà's secret away
This devotee will say there's nothing there
By evening the òrìṣà's owner will have run
    into debt.

The devotees get together to maintain the
òrìṣà's "secret," and once this secret is betrayed
by a foolish devotee, the òrìṣà is reduced to an
empty word, an object of ridicule. The devotees are in charge of the òrìṣà's reputation, and
if they do not collaborate with the òrìṣà to
preserve it, the whole impressive front
presented to the world will be ruined. What
the passage makes very clear is that this collaboration is also to the devotee's advantage. It is
the "owner" of the òrìṣà who would suffer most
if his òrìṣà were disgraced. Only a crazy person
(to be afflicted by Èṣù is to be temporarily
bereft of reason) would expose his òrìṣà, for the
disgrace would rebound on him. He would
have deprived himself of his background
support, and "by evening the òrìṣà's owner will
have run into debt."

The chanter is not saying that there is
"really" nothing to the òrìṣà or egúngún, that it
is all a hoax put over by human beings. The
suggestion is rather that every reasonable
person will do his best to make sure that his

òrìṣà is a force to be reckoned with. The òrìṣà
depends on human collaboration, but that does
not mean that the òrìṣà does not really exist. On
the contrary, it *does* exist, and the proof of this
is its inextricable, intimate bond of mutual
dependence with humans.

We have only to look at the model from
which this conception was derived for it to
become very clear. Without the co-operation
of his followers (in the form of attention,
service, respect, praise, etc.) the Big Man
would cease to be "big"; he would become
nothing. But this does not mean that the Big
Man's power is illusory. The recognition
accorded him by his followers makes it
possible for him to wield influence and get
things done. He really is "big"; but his bigness
depends on his being acknowledged as such.

It is unlikely that the passage quoted above was
inspired by scepticism arising from contact
with rival belief systems such as Islam and
Christianity. It seems, on the contrary, to
express a conception that is at the very heart of
traditional Yoruba religion. The pattern of collaboration of devotee with òrìṣà for the benefit
of both of them is embedded in the while institutional religious order. When a Ṣàngó priest is
possessed by Ṣàngó at the climax of the annual
festival, he performs all kind of feats.
Nowadays his tricks include setting fire to a
bunch of dry grass with his breath,[29] pouring
sand into an apparently empty gourd and then
producing groundnuts from it, plucking
sweets and cigarettes out of thin air to distribute to the crowd and so on. All the fraternity of
adóṣù know not only how these tricks are done,
but also how some members of the cult went to
the market-place the night before to prepare
the ground in secret. This does not mean that
they are deceiving their fellow-townsmen, so
much as that they are presenting Ṣàngó's glory
to its best advantage. Another case in point is
the *egúngún* cult. All men and boys are entitled

---

[28] Èṣù pípè contained in a chant addressed to Enlẹ̀ performed by Ẹre-Òṣun, daughter of *ilé* Ẹlẹ́mòṣó Awo, 1977.

to take part in *egúngún* celebrations and "carry" at least some types of masquerade. The masquerades are known as *ará ọrun* (denizens of heaven) and women are not supposed to know that there is a living man under the costume. To show that she knows is for a woman an extremely grave ritual transgression. Recently in Òkukù an elderly woman praise-singer walked in on a partly unmasked *egúngún* during the festival: the *egúngún* had come to one of the priests' houses to refresh itself with palm wine before continuing its progress round the town. Instead of running away, the over-excited woman boldly began to chant the *oríkì* not only of the *egúngún* but also of its human carrier, addressing the man to his face. She was thrown out and driven back to her husband's compound, and a few weeks later a retributive party of *egúngún* came out to punish her. She and her family escaped in time, but everything in the compound was destroyed – water pots were smashed and livestock hacked to pieces. It was only after many months of negotiation and the payment of a heavy fine that she was allowed to set foot in the town again. Women, of course, *do* know that *egúngún* are carried by men. In a chant performed during the *egúngún* festival vigil, a woman lamented:

Ará dá obìnrin tí ìí fi mawo
Obìnrin ò mọ̀gbàlẹ̀
Ìbá ṣe póbìnrin lè mawo
Mbá gbénú èkú wèkú[30]

Woman can do nothing about it, they are not
  allowed to know the secret cult
Women cannot know the sacred grove

If women were allowed to know the secret
  cult
I would wear one masquerader's costume on
  top of another . . .

She insists that women can know nothing about the cult and in the same breath shows indirectly that she *does* in fact know that it is living men who carry the *egúngún* costumes. The important thing is not women's actual ignorance, but the maintenance of a respectful silence about their knowledge. It is a matter of keeping up appearances for the sake of the ancestors' dignity. The woman collaborates to keep the *egúngún*'s "secret" – which is no secret – so that its splendid beneficent power will remain intact for her to profit from.

The word *awo*, so fundamental a concept in Yoruba religion, as well as meaning "secret" also means something like "sacred mystery" or "spiritual power". It is by being made into a "secret" that a spiritual being gets its authority. It has been said "If something we call '*awo*' has nothing in it to frighten the uninitiated, let's stop calling it '*awo*'; but if we put a stone in a gourd and make a couple of taboos to stop people looking into it, it's become an '*awo*'. The face of a denizen of heaven is '*awo*' for the very reason that if you removed its costume you might find nothing there."[31] Human collusion to keep the "secret" endows the object with spiritual power: perhaps what the "secret" really comes down to in the end is the open secret that gods are made by men.

---

[30]   From an *egúngún* vigil lament performed by Erẹ-Òṣun in 1976.

[31]   This formulation is translated from the Yoruba which runs as follows: "*Bí a bá pe nńkan ní "awo" tí kò sí ní ohun tí í fi í pá ọgbèrì láyà, ẹ jẹ́ á yé perú wọn láwo; ṣùgbọ́n bókùúta bá wọnú agbè tán, táa sì fèèwọ̀ méji ti yíyọjú wò rẹ̀ nídìí, ó ti dawo. Torí i wí pé tí a bá ṣìṣọ lójú ará ọrun a lè má bàá ará ọrun níbẹ̀ náà loju ará ọrun fi di awo.*" It is taken from B.A. Degree Long Essay, University of Ifẹ, 1980, '*Ọdún Ẹbẹkùn ní ilú Iresi*, by Michael Oládèjo Afolayan. Although the author is not a traditional worshipper, enquiry has shown that this formulation (which is in highly proverbial language) is acceptable to traditional worshippers. Also relevant is the story told in Bascom (1944) about a man called Amáiyégún who is *turned into* a being with spiritual authority before the eyes of a crowd by being literally invested with secrecy: as he covers his legs and arms one by one with a special costume, the crowd sings "*E wà wẹṣẹ̀ awo rèbètè-rébété*" (Come and see the foot, a fine secret) etc. and the mystery comes into being.

V

What I have tried to argue is that this notion, which at first glance looks like scepticism, is in fact at the heart of the Yoruba devotional attitude, and that this can be understood in the light of the system of social relations from which the notion is derived.

In a highly ascriptive society like that of the Tallensi, where everybody's role is defined and limited by powerful social norms, spiritual beings are conceived of as authoritarian and unaffected by what humans think of them. It is a one-way relationship in which the Ancestors are a "given" that the living can only accept and passively submit to.

In a Yoruba town like Òkukù, on the other hand, the social structure, though hierarchical, is open and relatively fluid. Instead of prescribing roles, it enjoins men (and women too) to make themselves into whatever they can, and places no limits on what they can achieve; instead it encourages the impulse of ambition to take any route it can find and go as far as it can. Men make themselves, by attracting supporters; and in such a society it is also conceived that men make their gods by being their supporters. If no-one supports a Big Man any more, he loses his power; if devotees abandon their òrìṣà it falls into oblivion. The fundamental devotional impulse is to glorify the òrìṣà and strengthen its reputation so that it in turn will bless the devotee. The glorification is spontaneous and voluntary and the relation is seen as reciprocal, for the devotee is free, within limits, to attach herself to a new òrìṣà if her first one fails her.

The argument will be strengthened if we consider an even more extreme contrast with the Tallensi case, the Kalabari. The Tallensi and Kalabari could be seen at opposite poles of a continuum, as far as this particular argument is concerned, with the Yoruba example somewhere in the middle. All the Kalabari villages appear to have been open and achievement-oriented, and the largest and

most important of them, New Calabar, developed into a trading state composed of highly active and competitive "Houses", each of which was led by an elected leader who was chosen for his ability and ambition and was often quite young. These Houses, to remain effective trading and slaving units, had to keep up their numbers, and they did this by capturing strangers and incorporating them into the House. People as supporters were here even more important to an ambitious leader's success than in the Yoruba case. The Kalabaris' three principal orders of spiritual beings (Lineage Ancestors, Village Heroes and Water Spirits) can be invoked and thus temporarily confined in a carved figure or in the person of a living carrier; then they can be made to listen to demands, rebuked and even punished for bad behaviour. Kalabari say that it was they who gave the spirits power in the first place by making offerings and uttering praises and invocations: Hence the proverb "*Tomi, ani oru beremare*" – It is men that make the gods important. (Horton 1970). Conversely, humans can strip a troublesome spirit of the powers they have given it. Horton gives an account of a water spirit one of whose manifestations was a shark; when sharks began to infest the creek, the human community destroyed the spirit's cult objects and drank a shark's blood, and by this means wiped out the spirit's power over people of New Calabar. According to Horton, the Kalabari "compare the spirits with men of influence, who are only big so long as their followers follow them, and who become nothing when their followers fade away". Here the notion that men make gods, and the social model from which the notion is derived, is completely explicit.

The Yoruba conviction that the òrìṣà need human attention in no way questions the existence of spiritual beings as a category. Olodumare, the source and background of the spiritual order, is always there even though humans do not worship him directly:

Òrìṣà ló ń pa'ni í dà
On on pa Òrìṣà á dà

It is Òrìṣà (Supreme Being) who can change
being
No-one changes Orisa[32]

It is rather that, because of the element of choice in the system, the survival in the human community of any particular *òrìṣà* depends on human collaboration. The Yoruba attitude to the *òrìṣà* could perhaps be seen as a case of what Jack Goody calls "limited scepticism" (Goody 1975) in the sense that if one *òrìṣà* fails, the devotee is free to experiment with another, and thus there is room for a gradual adjustment

and introduction of new norms. It seems clear that it was this willingness to try something new that conditioned the way Islam and Christianity were received, rather than Islam and Christianity which introduced a new attitude of scepticism.[33] However, scepticism – even the limited sort – does not seem quite the right word to apply to a religion whose central impulse is the ecstatic personal communication of devotee with *òrìṣà*. In this society power, whether human or divine, is adulated. Adulation increases the power. Once a devotee has settled for the *òrìṣà* that suits her, therefore, she throws herself heart and soul into its service, for she knows that enhancing its power is ultimately to her own benefit.

References

Abímbólá, 'Wande 1975 *Ifá: an Introduction to Ifá Literary Corpus* London: Oxford University Press.

Bascom, William 1944 "The sociological role of the Yoruba cult group." *American Anthropologist* 46 (1), part 2, 47–73

Beier, Ulli 1959 *A Year of Sacred Festivals in one Yoruba Town*. Lagos: Nigeria Magazine Special Publication, ed. D. W. MacRow.

Fortes, Meyer 1945 *The Dynamics of Clanship among the Tallensi*. London: Oxford University Press for the International African Institute

—— 1949 *The Web of Kinship among the Tallensi*, London: OUP for the IAI

—— 1959 *Oedipus and Job in West African Religion*. Cambridge University Press

Goody, Jack 1975 "Religion, social change and the sociology of conversion," in J. Goody (ed.), *Changing Social Structure in Ghana*, London: International African Institute, 91–117

Horton, Robin 1970 "A hundred years of change in Kalabari religion," in John Middleton (ed.),

Black Africa. London: Macmillan, 192–221

—— 1979 "Ancient Ife: a reassessment." *Journal of the Historical Society of Nigeria*, 9 (4)

Idowu, B. 1962 *Olódùmarè: God in Yoruba Belief*. London: Longmans

Kopytoff, Igor 1971 "Ancestors as elders in Africa." *Africa* 41 (2), 129–142

Needham, Rodney 1972 *Belief, Language and Experience* Oxford: Blackwell

Òjó, J. R. O. 1977 "The hierarchy of Yoruba cults: an aspect of Yoruba cosmology." Paper presented in the seminar series of the Department of African Languages and Literatures, University of Ife, Nigeria.

Oroge, E. A. 1971 *The Institution of Slavery in Yorubaland with particular reference to the Nineteenth Century*. University of Birmingham, Ph.D. thesis.

Westcott, J. and P. Morton-Williams 1962 "The symbolism and ritual context of the Yoruba *laba* Shango." *Journal of the Royal Anthropological Institute* 92, 23–37

---

[32] Quoted by Rowland Abiodun in his paper "Mythical allusions in Yoruba ritualistic art: *orí-inú*, visual and verbal metaphor", presented at the International Conference on the Relations Between Verbal and Visual Arts in Africa, October 10–14th, 1980, Philadelphia, Pa. The quoted lines are in Ifè dialect.

[33] The fact that Christianity and Islam were seen as additional choices in a system already full of alternatives is indicated in the passage of *Sàngó pípè* quoted above. The singer looks at the Òṣun cult, Christianity and Islam as equally plausible alternatives if she decides to defect from Ṣàngó.

24

ANCESTORS AS ELDERS IN AFRICA[1]

IGOR KOPYTOFF

Ancestor cults and ancestor worship loom large in the anthropological image of sub-Saharan Africa and few would disagree with Fortes that "comparatively viewed, African ancestor worship has a remarkably uniform structural framework" (Fortes, 1965:122). The general pattern may be quickly summarized. Ancestors are vested with mystical powers and authority. They retain a functional role in the world of the living, specifically in the life of their living kinsmen; indeed, African kin-groups are often described as communities of both the living and the dead. The relation of the ancestors to their living kinsmen has been described as ambivalent, as both punitive and benevolent and sometimes even as capricious. In general, ancestral benevolence is assured through propitiation and sacrifice; neglect is believed to bring about punishment. Ancestors are intimately involved with the welfare of their kin-group but they are not linked in the same way to every member of that group. The linkage is structured through the elders of the kin-group, and the elders' authority is related to their close link to the ancestors. In some sense the elders are the representatives of the ancestors and the mediators between them and the kin-group.

Fortes has extended our theoretical understanding of African ancestor worship more recently by further clarifying some of its structural features (1965). Amplifying Gluckman's (1937) distinction between ancestor cults and the cults of the dead, Fortes brings out the importance of the "structural matrix of [African] ancestor worship", noting *inter alia* the relative lack of elaboration and indeed interest among the Africans in the cosmography of the afterworld in which the ancestors reside. The African emphasis is clearly not on how the dead live but on the manner in which they affect the living. Different ancestors are recognized as relevant to different structural contexts (as, for example, in groups of different genealogical levels); not all but only certain dead with particular structural positions are worshipped as ancestors; and the behaviour of ancestors reflects not their individual personalities but rather a particular legal status in the political-jural domain.

In this chapter I shall describe some activities and relationships among the Suku of south-western Congo (Kinshasa). It will be apparent that the description conforms to the generalized pattern of African ancestor cults

---

[1] The first version of this paper was delivered at the 67th Annual Meeting of the American Anthropological Association, 21–4 November 1968, at Seattle, Washington, under the title: "African 'Ancestor Cults' without Ancestors?"

and is congruent with Fortes's analysis. But, I shall show that there are difficulties in characterizing the Suku complex as an "ancestor cult" and shall bring in additional data on Suku lineage structure. I shall then contend that Fortes's analysis, while pointing in the right direction, does not go far enough because it does not take the final step of shedding the ethnocentric connotations of the very term "ancestor" – connotations that have a bearing on theory. I shall also try to show that by viewing what have been called African ancestor cults as part of the eldership complex, we can account more simply for many of Fortes's generalizations and at the same time make redundant some of the problems he raises.

The fundamental social and jural group among the Suku is the corporate matrilineage, generally consisting of some thirty-five to forty persons. Married couples live virilocally, and males live patrilocally at least until their father's death and often beyond. The membership of a matrilineage is dispersed over several villages but within an area that is not too large to preclude easy communication, consultations, and joint action in important matters. The matrilineage is a corporate unit in economic, political, jural, and religious respects. Each matrilineage is centred in a particular village which bears its name and is its administrative and ritual head-quarters, containing the formal lineage head (the oldest male member) and, usually, several other older members (Kopytoff, 1964, 1965).

The dead members of the lineage, as a collectivity, are appealed to in times of crisis (such as a serious sickness or a series of misfortunes) and, more regularly, on such occasions as the marriages of women of the lineage, the breaking of sexual taboos affecting these women, the coming-out ceremony for infants, and, yearly, before the large communal hunts of the dry season. The general pattern is as follows: the head of the lineage and two or three older men of his generation go at night to the grave – any grave – of a deceased member of the lineage who was older than any of them. The Suku have no special burying places and graves are dug at random in the bush outside the lineage centre or near crossroads; the graves are not maintained and they eventually return to bush, so that the site of a particular grave is usually forgotten in time. The location of recent graves is of course remembered, and the lineage head and the older men usually go to the grave of the last deceased man who was older than they. The other appropriate place to address the dead is at the crossing of paths.

At the grave or at the cross-roads, the old men "feed" the dead certain foods considered to be their favourite: particular kinds of forest mushroom and wild roots, palm wine, and sometimes even manioc, the Suku staple. A small hole is dug in the ground and the food is put into it. Communication with the dead takes the form of a conversational monologue, patterned but not stereotyped, and devoid of repetitive formulae. One speaks the way one speaks to living people: "You, [such and such], your junior is ill. We do not know why, we do not know who is responsible. If it is you, if you are angry, we ask your forgiveness. If we have done wrong, pardon us. Do not let him die. Other lineages are prospering and our people are dying. Why are you doing this? Why do you not look after us properly?" The words typically combine complaints, scolding, sometimes even anger, and at the same time appeals for forgiveness.

At the coming-out ceremonies for infants and at marriages, the dead members of the lineage are informed of the event; pleas are made for their approval and their efforts in insuring the success of the newborn or of the marriage and the children that will be born to it. Before the large communal hunts of the dry season, the dead members are asked to extend good luck to the enterprise. They are told that the people are hungry for meat, they are reprimanded for not granting enough meat, and they are shamed that their own people should be eating less well than other lineages. Finally, dead members of the lineage are always referred to publicly by the living elders on all ceremonial occasions involving the lineage as a unit.

These activities clearly fit the general pattern of African "ancestor cults". The ancestors are seen as retaining their role in the affairs of their kin-group and only of their kin-group. They are propitiated with "sacrifices". They are seen as dispensing both favours and misfortune; they are often accused of being capricious and of failing in their responsibilities, but, at the same time, their actions are related to possible lapses on the part of the living and are seen as legitimately punitive. The features of the "cult" emphasize the nature of the social relationship while details of the life of ancestors in the other world are de-emphasized and are, indeed, of little interest to the Suku. It is primarily the jural context that dominates the relationship with the ancestors and not the personal characteristics they may have had when they were alive.

There is, however, one immediate problem that arises in calling this an "ancestor cult": the Suku have no term that can be translated as "ancestor". These dead members of the lineage are referred to as *bambuta*. Literally, *bambuta* means the "big ones", the "old ones", those who have attained maturity, those older than oneself; collectively, the term refers to the ruling elders of a lineage. A *mbuta* (singular) is literally anyone who is older than ego. The meaning is comparative. Eldership is not an absolute state of being old; being a *mbuta* is always relative to someone who is younger. Within the lineage, a *mbuta* is any older adult, older siblings as well as those of the generations above. My *bambuta* collectively are all the members of the lineage who are older than I, whether they are alive or dead. In jural contexts, where authority is vested overwhelmingly in the males, the term is effectively narrowed to all my male seniors. The lineage is thus divided into two named groups: those above me who are my *bambuta*,

and those below me – my *baleke* – to whom I am an elder. By contrast, no semantic distinction is made within the lineage between those who are alive and those who are dead.

An elder – any elder – represents to a junior the entire legal and mystical authority of the lineage. The very fact of eldership confers upon a person mystical powers over the junior. He can curse his junior in the name of the lineage, thereby removing from him the mystical protection of the lineage. The curse can be formal and public, but it can also be secret and even unconscious. To use a contemporary metaphor, a Suku is under the "umbrella" of the power of his lineage; removal of this protection exposes him to the outside world, and the world is a dangerous place to be in when one is not attached to a kin-group. As the Suku phrase it, a curse "opens the road to misfortune", though it does not actively cause misfortune. An elder's curse, always implicitly made in the name of the lineage, can only be removed by an older elder – one to whom the previous elder is a junior.

Lineage authority and the representation of the lineage to the outside world are organized on a continuum of age, that is, of relative eldership. Within this formal continuum based purely on relative age, there is also the principle of generational solidarity. Lineage members of the same generation are closer to each other and tend toward greater though never actual equality. Thus, the inequality of power and authority is most pronounced between generations. It is most presumptuous for the junior generation to question, under normal circumstances, the decisions of the senior generation and the ways in which they have been arrived at. It is the generation above me that represents to me the full authority of the lineage; generational solidarity as well as inter-generational distance means that, unless I have knowledge to the contrary, I must assume that the decision of one senior represents the decision of all seniors. This generational structure also expresses a continuum of authority. If I am middle-aged, the decision by elders of the generation above me carries for me the authority of all the senior generations above me. To a junior in the generation below me, my decision similarly carries the authority of my generation together with all the generations senior to it. To the junior, then, lineage authority is most directly embodied in the generation immediately above him, and it is presumptuous for him to go over their heads, so to speak, to yet more senior generations. Conversely, the authority of eldership is most directly exercised upon those of the generation immediately below, as they in turn properly exercise it over the generation below them. Exercising authority over the second lower generation, over the heads of the intervening one, is somewhat inappropriate. This results in muting the outward expression of authority between the alternating generations of a lineage, a pattern congruent with the relaxed etiquette between alternating generations.

In any context, the lineage is fully and legally represented by the oldest adult member of the lineage who is present. Let me give a few examples. In common with many Central African peoples, the name of the lineage is formally carried by the head of that lineage. Thus, the head of the lineage Kusu is addressed as Kusu. But this general rule expresses a more complex structure. The identification of the lineage's name with the person extends to the entire membership of the lineage; it is the lineage as a whole, *qua* corporate group, that holds the title. Cunnison (1951), writing on the Luapula peoples, has analysed this particular usage in which a person discussing his lineage and its history in the past, will refer to it by the pronoun "I." A similar usage exists among the Suku. The oldest lineage member who is present in any situation can refer to himself by the name of his lineage, and is so addressed by others. For example, an infant who is a member of the royal lineage is addressed as *Mini Kongo*, the title of the Suku king, as long as no other older member of the royal lineage is present. The

moment an older member arrives on the scene, the title is shifted to him. A young man of Kusu lineage will refer to himself as Kusu and, a moment later, after an older lineage mate has arrived, he will refer to him as Kusu and will cease applying the title to himself. Ultimately, of course, if all the members of the lineage are present, the title Kusu devolves upon the oldest male member of the lineage who is also its formal head.

The continuum of eldership in representing the lineage has a jural significance in interlineage relations. let me illustrate with an extreme example. A young man became angry with his elders and, without consulting anyone, sold to another lineage a hunting area belonging to his own. The transaction was fully legal, since he was a legitimate spokesman for his lineage in the context in which the transaction took place. His own lineage was, of course, incensed by the action; in the old days he might have been sold or even killed. But the significant point here is that the legality of the transaction was not questioned.

In short, to those on the outside, a lineage is represented by the oldest member present. Within the lineage, the lineage is represented to any one member by any older member present and, collectively, by all older members living and dead. The principle of eldership operating within the lineage corresponds, in its external relations, to its "chieftainship" (*kimfumu*). Lineage "chieftainship" is also a relative, not an absolute matter; for the outside world, it is carried by the oldest member present. Thus, the Suku say that "everyone is a chief" – just as everyone is an elder.

Let us consider now some additional features of the ritual preceding the collective hunt of the dry season. Before the hunting season begins every Suku secures hunting luck by obtaining reassurance that the lineage wishes him well, that he continues to be under its protection. This reassurance can in principle be obtained verbally from any elder; more appropriately, it is obtained from anyone in the generation above. Young men go to the middle-aged and the middle-aged go to the old. There is a pattern in asking for luck: one beseeches, one complains, one reproves, one asks forgiveness. On his part, the older man signifies his goodwill by giving the junior some *pemba* (white clay); he also uses the occasion to remind the young man of his obligations to the old, to scold him lightly for his past misde-meanours, and to ask his forgiveness for past misfortunes. The manner of addressing the living elder is the same as the one used in addressing the dead. The Suku regard the two activities as being not merely analogous but identical, and the differences between them as incidental and contextual. Everyone goes to his elder. If I am young, I go to my elders who happen to be alive. The old people go to their elders; but since these are dead, they are to be found at the grave or at the cross-roads at night. Given the continuum of eldership, the use of any grave, as long as the dead is older than the petitioner, is understandable. Also understandable in this context is the neglect of older graves. In the light of the structure of eldership, this neglect does not represent a "weak" ancestor cult nor does it indicate shallowness of lineage structure.

If there be a "cult" here, it is a cult of *bambuta*, of elders living and dead. Every junior owes *buzitu* ("honour," "respect") to his seniors, be they "elders" or "ancestors" in Western terminology. A single set of prin-ciples regulates the relationship between senior and junior; a person deals with a single category of *bambuta* and the line dividing the living from the dead does not affect the struc-ture of the relationship. Where the line is relevant is in the method of approaching the elder. The dead must of necessity be approached differently from the living; inter-action with them necessarily appears one sided and conversations with them necessarily become monologues. Also, interaction with them is necessarily less frequent and when it occurs, it is formal – but no less formal than is the interaction with living elders on cere-monial occasions. The offer of palm wine is normal at all formal occasions when a junior approaches a senior; but dead elders, in their capacity of the dead, also have their preferred foods – the special forest mushroom and roots. Thus, it is the special methods of approach, inevitably characterizing dealings with the dead as opposed to the living, that gives these dealings the special cast that makes us, as anthropologists and outsiders, call it a "cult." The dead *qua* dead also know more and see things that living elders do not; they are, therefore, more powerful and can sometimes be more helpful. Also, though the reasons for action by any elder are often obscure to the juniors, actions by dead elders are particularly obscure since no explanations from them are ever possible. In short, there is a difference in the manner in which the dead are approached, in contrast to the living. But the difference is related to their different physical states, even while they remain in the same structural position *vis-à-vis* their juniors. . . .

The Western ethnocentric conviction that "ancestors" must be separated from living "elders" conditions the cognitive set with which we approach African data and theorize about them. Not only is our term "ancestor" – meaning an ascendant who is dead – denotatively ethnocentric but it is also conno-tatively so. Western cultural tradition (which includes ghosts) accepts that the dead can be endowed with extraordinary powers. The dead belong to what we call the "supernatural world". A Western anthropologist, working in an African society, finds it easy to accept without much further questioning that the dead, including the "ancestors," should be believed capable of extraordinary doings, that they should "mystically" confer benefits, that they should visit sickness upon the living, that they should have "supernatural" powers. Such beliefs about the dead are culturally acceptable to us, and it is appropriate that such dead should have a "cult." But living people in our cultural conceptions do not have such "mystical" powers merely because they happen to be older. If they are said by Africans to have such powers, these must be "derived" from elsewhere; and the ancestors, being dead, are seen as an appropriate source.[2]

Our interpretations have had two opposing emphases. In the ethnographies, dealing descriptively with African beliefs, it has generally been held that Africans see the powers of the elders as derivative from the power of the ancestors. By contrast, on the theoretical level (where our cultural assumptions come to the fore and where ancestors cannot "exist" except as a symbol and an abstraction), the directionality of the explanation is exactly reversed; the powers with which ancestors are endowed become a "projection" of the palpable powers of living elders. This latter interpretation is the gist of Fortes's (1965) formulation. But what, then, of the mystical powers that elders hold directly and on their own, as among the Suku? Are they in turn to be seen as re-projections from the ancestors? When we see the powers over the juniors of both living elders and ancestors as derivative from eldership *per se*, both the above interpretations of the "sources" of power come to be beside the point. The problems they attempt to solve arise in the first place from an ethnocentric categorization of the ethnographic data.

The reformulation of the problem around the broader category of "eldership" carried other semantic implications for anthropological terminology (and consequently for the theory built on this terminology). We talk of ancestor "cults" and even of ancestor "worship." In their modern meanings[3] these English words are culturally appropriate in describing dealings with the dead and the supernatural. By contrast, we would hesitate to apply the terms "cult" and "worship" to relations with the living. Yet, if the Suku and others "worship" their dead elders, then they also "worship" their living elders. If they have a "cult" of dead elders, the same "cult" applies to the living. Obversely, if the living elders are only "respected," then so are the "ancestors," and no more than that.

These points are very well illustrated by Kenyatta (1938: 265–8), with his inside view of Kikuyu culture, when he discusses "ancestors." "In this account, I shall not use that term [worship], because from practical experience I do not believe that the Gikuyu worship their ancestors. . . . I shall therefore use the term 'communion with ancestors'". Kenyatta's European analogy is revealing: "There appears to be such communion with ancestors when a European family, on special occasions, has an empty chair, the seat of a dead member, at table during a meal. This custom might be closely equated with Gikuyu behaviour in this respect." "The words 'prayer' and 'worship', *gothaithaiya, goikia-mokoigoro*, are never used in dealing with the ancestors' spirits. These words are reserved for solemn rituals and sacrifices directed to the power of the unseen." As to the question of what is so often called "sacrifice": "The gifts which an elder gives to the ancestors' spirits, as when a sheep is sacrificed to them, and which perhaps seem to an outsider to be prayers directed to the ancestors, are nothing but the tributes symbolizing the gifts which the departed elders would have received had they been alive, and which the living elders now receive."

---

[2] To introduce a personal note, I had no difficulty in the field in accepting the idea that the dead "ancestors" should have "supernatural" powers. But I must have driven my informants to distraction by insisting on pursuing the question of the "why" and the "where from" of the powers of the living elders. It took a kind of methodological (and cultural) leap of faith to accept as a terminal ethnographic datum that if the dead can appropriately do supernatural things, why not also the living?

[3] The English word "worship" carried, to be sure, a less religious connotation in Old English, referring merely to "dignity," "honour," and "worthiness" – appropriate to one aspect of the African relationship with both elders and ancestors, but still missing its associated aspect of familiarity that, when necessary, allows scolding.

By using terms such as "cult," "worship," and "sacrifice," we introduce semantic paradoxes which we then feel compelled to explain. Thus, in the International African Institute's Salisbury seminar (Fortes and Dieterlen, 1965:18), "the view that ancestors are generally represented as punitive in character was discussed at length." The need to understand why an object of "worship" should be "punitive" arises from the semantics of the terms used. We are told in the report on the seminar that "Professor Mitchell concluded that ancestors seemed to be normally ambivalent, inflicting punishment to demonstrate the legitimate authority and exercising benevolence when appealed to. He linked this up with some remarks of Dr. Turner, who gave instances of ancestor worship being significant in group rituals of solidarity and expiation aimed at restoring amity within a community. Such rituals, Professor Mitchell suggested, would be directed towards the ancestors in their benevolent aspect, whereas in the case of misfortune the punitive aspect would be invoked in order to provide an interpretation." Such theoretical involution is unnecessary. The attitude to elders (dead or alive) is normally ambivalent; they both punish and exercise benevolence, and they necessarily participate in restoring amity within the lineage. Mitchell's complex theoretical interpretation ignores what almost every ethnography and every general descriptive statement on African ancestor "cults" have always stressed: that African lineages are communities of both the living and the dead. Gluckman and Fortes rightly stress that "ancestor cults" are not the same thing as the cults of the dead. But this irrelevance of the "deadness" of ancestors has implications for the very idiom in which theoretical problems are cast.

Once we recognize that African "ancestors" are above all elders and to be understood in terms of the same category as living elders, we shall stop pursuing a multitude of problems of our own creation. There is nothing startling that the attitude to elders wielding authority should be ambivalent. Fortes (1965:133) makes the important point that what matters in ancestors is their jural status, that (speaking of the Tallensi) "the personality and character, the virtues or vices, success or failures, popularity or unpopularity of a person during his lifetime make no difference to his attainment of ancestorhood". But, we should add, neither do these variations make a difference in the authority invested in eldership; what matters in *formal* relations is the formal status, in dead elders as well as those alive. "It is not the whole man, but only his jural status as the parent (or parental personage, in matrilineal systems) vested with authority and responsibility, that is transmuted into ancestorhood" (ibid.). But from the point of view proposed here, what occurs is not a "transmutation" but a *retention* of status by the now dead elder. The status, that is, remains unaffected by death, while one's purely personal and idiosyncratic relationship with the elder is necessarily changed. Similarly, when Fortes states: "Ancestor worship is a representation or extension of the authority component in the jural relations of successive generations," we can restate this more simply and, I would claim, more realistically and more in keeping with African conceptions as follows: "Elders, after they die, maintain their role in the jural relations of successive generations." In Fortes's theory, people are believed to "acquire", upon death, the power to intervene in the life of their juniors. I would claim that they "continue" to have that power.

Such rephrasing simplifies the interpretation of ethnographic data. Thus, in Fortes's formulation, the son begins "officiating" in the "cult" only upon his father's death because he now become a jural adult (Fortes, 1965: 130–2). This succession means "ousting a predecessor", and "sacrifice" to the ancestors may be a psychologically reassuring mode of ritual reparation; the ancestor cult becomes a psychological "refuge" (Fortes, 1965:140–1, 1945:9). Without questioning the psychological dynamics specific to the Tallensi, one may suggest another formulation that would seem to be more appropriate for dealing with the general phenomenon of "sacrifice" in African "ancestor cults," since these guilt feelings and their relief cannot be shown to exist in all of these societies. We see among the Tallensi a continuum of inter-generational eldership. The power of the kin-group is represented to me (a Tale) by my father, as his father represents it to him. My father "worships" (respects) and "sacrifices" (gives tribute) to his dead father, as I respect and give tribute to him. When my father dies, my relationship with him continues (Fortes, 1959:48ff.). The chain of relationships over the generations remains unaltered, though the method of interaction with my father becomes necessarily different when he is dead. If we express this difference by speaking of "worship" and "sacrifice," in contrast to "respect" and "gift or tribute," it is because we, as Westerners, find such terms more appropriate to express dealings with the dead. And, further, "sacrifice," "expiation," and "guilt" is a comfortable semantic cluster for us. But there is surely a danger here of trans-muting the semantic biases of the observer's culture into problems of the ethnology of the observed.

By treating the phrase "ancestor cults" as a rather misleading way of referring to an aspect of the relationship with elders in general, a matter that Fortes sees as a puzzle can be re-examined in a new light. The puzzle is in the fact that the Tiv and the Nuer, with genealog-ically based social systems not unlike those of the Tallensi, lack "ancestor worship" (Fortes, 1965:140). There is indeed a puzzle if one insists upon seeing the ancestor cult as a *symbolic projection* of the social system. In the view presented here, on the other hand, the ancestor cult is an integral *part* of the system of relationship with elders. The relationship with

dead elders (that is, "ancestors") is seen as being on the same symbolic plane as that with living elders and not as secondary to it or derivative from it. From this point of view the over-all structural similarities among Tallensi, Tiv, and Nuer should not be expected to result in similar ancestor cults. Other facts would seem to be more relevant to the relationship with ancestors *qua* dead elders: the meaning and structure of eldership, the nature of the authority attributed to it, and the beliefs about the effect of death upon the elder's role.

For the Tiv, the question to be asked is: what is there in the Tiv relationship with elders that makes for relative indifference to dead elders? Pervasive Tiv egalitarianism de-emphasizes the authority of eldership and indeed exacerbates the authority problems that inhere in such segmentary systems (Bohannan, 1953:31ff.). Neither genealogical position nor age confer, of themselves, special powers on the living, while the dead are believed to have no effect on the living (ibid:83). In short, Tiv elders *qua* elders have little influence on the lives of their juniors, be the elders alive or dead. Their formal authority here is minimal and genealogically shallow. Though a relationship with the dead is not entirely lacking (Bohannan, 1969:i:35ff., and 43), it is confined to one's parents. As to the Nuer, here also elders do not carry authority and power simply by virtue of their eldership (Evans-Pritchard, 1940:179–80). The elders' passage into the other world does not change their situation in this respect.

Though "ancestor cults" should not be equated with cults of the dead, beliefs about the dead are nevertheless relevant, as illus-trated by the Songye who may also be said to lack an "ancestor cult", but for rather different reasons. Here, living elders have authority; once they die, however, the relationship with them as dead elders does not last because they become reincarnated in their grandchildren.[4]

---

[4] Personal communication from Dr. Alan P. Merriam.

To conclude,[5] the selection by anthropologists of the phrases "ancestor cult" and "ancestor worship," in dealing with African cultures, is semantically inappropriate, analytically misleading, and theoretically unproductive. Fortes has rightly emphasized that the essential features of these activities are to be found not so much in the fact that the people concerned are dead as in the structural matrix in which they are placed. But he does not go far enough. By retaining the term "ancestor" (rather than use, say, "dead elders"), he continues to give undue weight in his interpretations to the fact that the persons are dead. The term "ancestor" sets up a dichotomy where there is a continuum. By conceptually separating living elders from ancestors, we unconsciously introduce Western connotations to the phenomena thus labelled and find ourselves having to deal with paradoxes of our own creation and with complex solutions to them. It is striking that African "ancestors" are more mundane and less mystical than the dead who are objects of "worship" should be in Western eyes. African elders, on the other hand, look more mystical to us than we are willing to allow the living to be. Similarly, Africans treat their living elders more "worshipfully" than the English term "respect" conveys, and they treat the ancestors with less "respect" and more contentiousness than the term "worship" should allow.

These are all paradoxes that stem from the difficulty of our vocabulary to accommodate to the fact that African living elders and dead ancestors are more similar to each other than the Western living and dead can be, that an elder's social role does not radically change when he crosses the line dividing the living from the dead, and that African "ancestorship" is but an aspect of the broader phenomenon of "eldership." The initial theoretical problem here is not so much that of uncovering deep psychological and symbolic processes as it is of probing African cultural categories and of finding adequate translations of these into the Western language used for theorizing. The terminological recasting that is proposed here (with a consequent recasting of the cognitive categories of the theorist) suggests that our understanding of variations in what we have called "ancestor cults" must begin with the analysis of eldership in particular African societies. Finally, these redefinitions also resolve the puzzle of finding "ancestor cults" to be, on the one hand, so very characteristic of Africa as a culture area and, on the other, to be inexplicably and erratically absent here and there within the area. No such problem arises when we realize that the cultural trait to be examined is not "ancestorship" but the more widely distributed African recognition of "eldership."

---

[5]   In this paper, I have discussed only the elders/ancestors of the descent group itself, and I have made no reference to the "extra-descent group ancestor cults" discussed by McKinght (1967). Briefly summarized, McKnight's point is that the "extra-descent group ancestors" (that is, paternal ancestors in the matrilineal systems, and maternal ones in the patrilineal) are not benevolent as they should be in terms of Radcliffe-Brown's theory of extension of sentiments. McKnight shows that the relations with the kin-group of the "residual parent" need not duplicate the sentiments of the relationship with that parent. Thus, in a patrilineal society, one can be on the warmest of terms with one's mother and her brother and still have strained and even hostile relations with their kin-group as a corporate entity and with other relatives in it. And it is these latter relations that condition the relations with the "extra-descent group ancestors." McKnight's mode of analysis is consistent with the one used here. I would merely use the term "relationship with the dead elders of the extra-descent group" instead of "extra-descent group ancestor cults."

References

BOHANNAN, LAURA and PAUL. 1953. *The Tiv of Central Nigeria*. London.

—— 1969. *A Source Notebook on Tiv Religion (v. I: Cosmos, Soma, Psyche and Disease)*. New Haven, Conn.

CUNNISON, IAN. 1951. *History on the Luapula*, Rhodes-Livingstone Papers, 21.

EVANS-PRITCHARD, E. 1940. *The Nuer*. Oxford.

FORTES, MEYER. 1945. *The Dynamics of Clanship among the Tallensi*. London.

—— 1959. *Oedipus and Job in West African Religion*. Cambridge.

—— 1965. "Some Reflections on Ancestor Worship", in *African Systems of Thought*, ed. M. Fortes and G. Dieterlen. London.

—— and DIETERLEN, G. (eds.). 1965. *African Systems of Thought*. London.

GLUCKMAN, M. 1937. "Mortuary Customs and the Belief in Survival after Death among the South-Eastern Bantu", *Bantu Studies*, xi.

HOMBURGER, L. 1941. *Les Langues négro-africaines et les peuples qui les parlent*. Paris.

KENYATTA, JOMO. 1938. *Facing Mount Kenya: The Tribal Life of the Gikuyu*. London.

KOPYTOFF, IGOR. 1964. "Family and Lineage among the Suku of the Congo", in *The Family Estate in Africa*, ed. Robert F. Gray and P. H. Gulliver. London.

—— 1965. "The Suku of Southwestern Congo", in *Peoples of Africa*, ed. James L. Gibbs, Jr. New York.

McKNIGHT, J. D. 1967. "Extra-Descent Group Ancestor Cults in African Societies", *Africa*, xxxvii. 1–21.

SAPIR, EDWARD. 1921. *Language*. New York (reprinted 1949).

WILSON, MONICA. 1957. *Rituals of Kinship among the Nyakyusa*. London.

For the terms for "ancestors" and "elders" in the African languages mentioned, I have used the following sources: Mary Douglas, *The Lele of the Kasai*, London, 1963; Walter Sangree, *Age, Prayer, and Politics in Tiriki, Kenya*, London, 1966; and the dictionaries of the respective languages by the following: C. W. R. Tobias and R. H. C. Turvey 1954 (Ovambo/Kwanyama), W. Holman Bentley 1887 (Kongo), R. P. A. Semain 1923 (Songye), G. Hulstaert 1952 (Nkundo/Lomongo), M. Guthrie 1935 (Ngala), M. Mamet 1955 (Ntomba), J. Whitehead 1899 (Bobangi), Edwin W. Smith 1907 and J. Torrend 1931 (Ila), C. M. Doke 1933 and 1963 (Lamba), G. M. Sanderson 1954 (Yao), C. Taylor 1959 (Ankole), Herbert W. Woodward 1882 (Bondei), C. S. Louw 1915 (Karanga), D. McJ. Malcolm 1966 and C. M. Doke and B. W. Vilakazi 1958 (Zulu), R. P. Alexandre 1953 (Mossi), B. F. and W. E. Welmers 1968 (Igbo), Charles A. Taber 1965 (Sango), A. Vekens 1928 (Mangbetu).

PART VI

ARTS AND AESTHETICS

Nighttime drumming, Kong, Côte d'Ivoire, 1982.
Photo: Christopher B. Steiner.

ARTS AND AESTHETICS

25   Simon Ottenberg. 1972. "Humorous Masks and Serious Politics among the Afikpo Ibo," pp. 99–121. In *African Art and Leadership* edited by Douglas Fraser and Herbert M. Cole. Madison: University of Wisconsin Press.

26   James W. Fernandez. 1966. "Principles of Opposition and Vitality in Fang Aesthetics," *The Journal of Aesthetics and Art Criticism* 25(1) : 53–64.

27   Uri Almagor. 1987. "The Cycle and Stagnation of Smells: Pastoralists–Fishermen Relationships in an East African Society," *Res: Anthropology and Aesthetics* 13 : 107–22.

28   David Coplan. 1985. *In Township Tonight! South Africa's Black City Music and Theatre.* London: Longman.

The presence of art on the African continent stretches back to prehistory when engravings and paintings were first made on granite rock surfaces by bands of migrating hunters and gatherers, possibly as far back as 13,000 years ago. Most of these images, at least those which have survived to the present day, represent the way of life in the Later Stone Age, depicting wild animals, human figures engaged in hunting activities, and assemblages of people gathered, perhaps, for the purpose of dance or ritual (see Lewis-Williams 1983; Garlake 1995).

Three-dimensional sculptural art first appears in the last millennium B.C., among the Nok culture, which flourished in what is today central Nigeria. The Nok produced a wide assortment of terracotta sculpture representing both animal and human figures (Fagg 1977; Jemkur 1992). Many of these objects, some of which have been recovered nearly intact, show remarkable attention to detail – elaborately styled hair, intricate necklace and bead ornaments, and a distinctive treatment of the head, nose, nostrils, and mouth that "clearly set these figurines apart from other prehistoric West African terracotta traditions" (Fagg, 1994: 82). To date, archaeology in sub-Saharan Africa has revealed the presence of a number of other major art-producing cultures, including, for example, ancient sites excavated at Igbo–Ukwu, Ife, Owo, and Jenne-Jeno (see Willett,1967; Shaw, 1977; Eyo, 1980; McIntosh, 1994). From the twelfth to fifteenth centuries, royal artisans in the Kingdom of Benin produced a large corpus of exquisite bronze figures and plaques which were used as altarpieces on commemorative shrines, as well as to decorate and enhance the palace interior (see also Part X).

While much has been learned about ancient Africa through archaeology and the analysis of early artifacts, a great deal has also been learned about Africa, both past and present, through research into the vast array of contemporary arts which are produced today for use in both secular and religious contexts. While artifacts made of bronze and terracotta have survived in the archaeological record, most objects made of wood have disintegrated due to the harsh climates of tropical Africa which quickly erode wooden materials. Thus, most wooden masks and statues which still play a vital role in African life today are, for the most part, only about a hundred years old at the most.

The study of African art in Europe and America developed largely in conjunction with the discipline of anthropology at the beginning of this century. Some of the earliest works on African art were written in order to further particular claims within a broader debate between diffusionist and evolutionist schools of thought (Haddon, 1902). African art was used, in this context, either as visual evidence for the spread of cultural traits from innovative centers to imitative peripheries, or as evidence for the social evolution of cultures – from groups which were supposedly capable of only naturalistic representation to those which had presumably graduated to the mastery of geometric stylization and abstract forms (Silver, 1979).

Following in the footsteps of late Victorian anthropology, artists in Europe began to "discover" for themselves the objects of African art that were beginning to make their way into both private art collections and museums of ethnography. Writers, artists, and intellectuals, like Maurice Vlarninck, André Derain, Guillaume Apollinaire, Georges Braque, Paul Klee, Ernst Ludwig Kirchner, Emil Nolde, and Constantin Brancusi were all impacted to some degree by the power of African aesthetics and what they perceived as the refiguring of the human form in African sculptural traditions.

Perhaps the best known example of Africa's influence on modern European art, however, is Pablo Picasso's *Les Demoiselles d'Avignon*, which was completed in 1907. Art historians have consistently noted the striking formal affinity between certain African mask styles and the "mask-like" faces of two of the five women that are the subject of this remarkable painting. Yet, only recently have scholars tried to link Picasso's interest in African art to a broader concern regarding French colonial policy in Africa. Art historian Patricia Leighten has suggested that Picasso, and many of his circle, embraced African art as a symbol of their antinationalist sentiments and, specifically, their disdain for the Colonial Party's assertion of France's national destiny and the so-called *mission civilisatrice* to the "undeveloped" peoples of Africa and Asia (Leighten 1990: 611). *Les Demoiselles d'Avignon* was completed on the heels of stunning disclosures made to the French public in 1905–6 of European military atrocities against the indigenous populations in the French and Belgian Congos. Thus, Leighten concludes, "Far from only wanting to borrow formal motifs from African forms, Picasso purposely challenged and mocked Western artistic traditions with his allusions to black Africa, with its unavoidable associations of white cruelty and exploitation" (1990: 610).

The interest that was generated in African art by European intellectuals flowed back once again into anthropology, and became absorbed into the discipline's new theories and methods of study. As the field of anthropology altered its emphasis from diffusion to context, and from evolution to function, the study of African art followed in its path. Drawing upon the new discourse of anthropology, and in particular taking a lead from the models and theories developed by Bronislaw Malinowski and A. R. Radcliffe-Brown, the focus in the study of African art beginning sometime in the 1940s and 1950s was to become the indigenous context – which would reveal the place of art within a balanced holistic system of social and cultural functions. In this sense, art was understood simply as one of many vital organs in the proper maintenance and functioning of a stable social organism.

Simon Ottenberg's essay, "Humorous Masks and Serious Politics among the Afikpo

Ibo" (Igbo) provides a classic example of how a functionalist approach may serve to locate the role of art (in this case masks and masking) in the maintenance of a balanced system of political power within an uncentralized or acephalous African society. Ottenberg argues that harmony and social equilibrium are maintained in Afikpo Ibo society through the regulated use of masks by junior males in a performative ritual known as the Okumkpa. Behind the relative anonymity of a wooden face mask, young men permit themselves to criticize their elders and to vent their dissatisfactions with village politics and social regulations. Without the masks, Ottenberg argues, the young men could never allow themselves such open and direct challenges to the established rule of the elders. The elders, for their part, permit the Okumkpa to take place because it allows youths to vent their frustrations without actually challenging or disrupting the established socio-political order. After the Okumkpa performance, which inverts hierarchy in a controlled context, power relations are reestablished and continue to function in the same way that they did before.

Given the relatively small size of Afikpo Ibo society, where each individual knows everyone else in the village, Ottenberg's analysis of the Okumkpa raises an interesting question about the role played by masks in concealing a person's identity. Are the young men really anonymous behind their wooden face mask? Or rather do the elders recognize the masker's identity, but respect the anonymity which the mask supposedly offers? In other words, is the mask's capacity to hide individual identity simply a "structural relationship" which is acknowledged by both mask-wearer and mask-viewer? Might the mask, in this regard, be compared to the powdered wig of a British judge or barrister which marks an individual's social role and sanctifies his or her authority without actually hiding the person's true identity?

Another school of thought in anthropology which, at one point, had an impact on the study and analysis of African art is structuralism – an approach that was largely developed in France by Claude Lévi-Strauss and which became very influential in the 1950s and 1960s. Structural analysis in anthropology seeks to locate the "permutable codes" by which structural relations are transposed from one plane of reality to another (Adams, 1973: 265). In other words, structuralism attempts to identify identical, or at least similar, structural formations, such as "binary oppositions" (that is, ordering the world according to symbolic principles of dualism or structured pairs), in multiple spheres of cultural expression, including the organization of social groups, class ranking, myth, ritual, art, and collective practices (Nodelman, 1970).

The impact of structuralism on the study of African art is perhaps best exemplified in James Fernandez's article "Principles of Opposition and Vitality in Fang Aesthetics." Using a structuralist approach, Fernandez demonstrates how binary oppositions are reflected in the construction of reliquary figures, the layout of the village community, in the concept of self, and throughout the entire social organization. Fernandez uses art objects as a vehicle to penetrate more deeply into an understanding of Fang culture. The formal principles of Fang sculpture (opposition and vitality) are taken by the anthropologist as clues to a more complex puzzle of aesthetic structural principles.

Recent approaches to the study of African art have challenged what has come to be perceived as an overemphasis on local context. In so doing, the unit of analysis has been expanded not only to include contacts within and among a wide range of proximate ethnic groups (Kasfir, 1984), but also to include the impact of world religions and global travel on local art use and production. Art historian René Bravmann (1974), for example, has explored the articulation of Islam with indigenous African beliefs. Far from obliterating so-called "traditional" art forms, Bravmann has shown how the production and use of art in West Africa has adapted to the religious demands of Islam and created "syncretic" art forms which blend into a single cultural expression Muslim and indigenous religious values (see Introduction for more on the notion of syncretism in African cultures). In another important instance of aesthetic assemblage and cultural syncretism, art historian Henry Drewal (1988) has explored the incorporation of European and Hindu beliefs about mermaids and snake-charmer goddesses into the worship and art associated with a pan-African religious cult known as Mami Wata. Drewal has shown in his research how the circulation of myths in the world system of the imagination produces a new religion and a new art form which combines indigenous beliefs about water spirits with foreign images of the "other."

Much of the research on African art today focuses on the hybridity of indigenous expressive cultures. Rather than look for "pure" aesthetic forms as anthropologists often did in the past – that is, art forms that were putatively "untouched" by European or other foreign contact – Africanist scholars today acknowledge outside influence and transcultural communication and, in their writings, often seek to demonstrate how Africans in fact celebrate artistic innovation and how artists and performers experiment with the foreign, the strange, and the new.

Those who collect African art in Europe and America often imagine that there is a "precolonial aesthetic" – an art style that originated in pristine conditions and remained unchanged for centuries until it was "contaminated" by European exploration and, later, colonialism. Although there were indeed precolonial art forms, it does not follow that these arts simply remained unchanged. Novelty and innovation have almost always played a key role in African visual and expressive cultures. People everywhere, however, tend to imagine the past as a time of "authenticity" and as a glorified moment which somehow was able to repro-

duce itself unchanged until outside forces caused irrevocable damage to the "ancient" practices.

This way of thinking about the relationship between the past and the present is not limited to European attitudes toward Africa, but is also manifested in African attitudes toward Europe. In a fascinating interview with West African painter Tamessir Dia, for example, art critic Thomas McEvilley captured a profound irony of postcolonial discourse about Western society. Wandering the streets of Venice in 1993, during an exhibition of contemporary art in which his work was featured, Dia contemplated the disjuncture between classical Italian art and architecture and what he perceived to be the mundane character of modern Italy:

> I keep looking at present-day Italians and try to compare them with the Italians of the past and wonder how they did such great things in the past. When I look around, not only are the architectural monuments extraordinary, but the paintings as well. I don't see any link between the relics of the past and what I see today. I keep wondering, Are these the same people? (McEvilley 1993: 10)

In his commentary on this interview, McEvilley concludes that for "an African to exert such a judgment on the West is a profound reversal of the colonial relationship" (1993: 10).

Recent studies of African art have begun not only to question the (over) emphasis placed on local context, at the expense of a more translocal or global perspective, but they have also thrown into doubt the privileged place of pre-colonial masks and statues in the definition of what constitutes "real" art in Africa. In his research on the African art market in Côte d'Ivoire, for example, Christopher Steiner (1994) has demonstrated how the category "African art" is continually reinvented and redefined by speculators and connoisseurs in the international art market. Objects that were once classified as "curios" or "artifacts" come to be reclassified as "art."

In this process, objects are given not only new monetary worth but also new cultural and political value.

Unlike art historians, who generally see the art object as their primary unit of study, anthropologists like Fernandez, for instance, use art as a means of studying society more broadly. The study of art in this case is thus not intended as an end in itself, but rather it is a methodological tool to gain access to a wider view of social organization or to penetrate a "deeper" level of cultural knowledge. Art history and anthropology are disciplines that are clearly related to one another, but each brings a different perspective to the subject of African art (Adams, 1989; Ben-Amos, 1989). In both art history and anthropology, however, the study of African art has been heavily influenced by perspectives and trends in Western scholarship. When functionalism was in vogue, for example, many anthropologists viewed African art through the lens of functionalist theory. As functionalism waned and lost favor in the field of anthropology as a whole, so too did its application to the study of African art. The question, then, is how much of our understanding of African art emerges from Western cultural assumptions about art and aesthetics, and how much is guided by the application of models and interpretations formed in other academic domains?

Philosopher V. Y. Mudimbe has reached the conclusion in his work that the term "African art" itself, in Western academic discourse, is a constructed category which fails to address indigenous African aesthetic perceptions and sensibilities. "What is called African art," writes Mudimbe, "covers a wide range of objects introduced into a historicizing perspective of European values since the eighteenth century" (1986:3). How can we understand African art without being guided by Western models of art and aesthetic theory?

One of the basic problems in the study of African art is the emphasis that has been placed on durable material objects. Most studies of African art begin with collections of art that have been assembled in museums in Europe and America starting in the sixteenth century. These collections of what is known in the parlance of anthropology as material culture are usually silent about the cultural context in which they were originally created and used. In some cases, what is important about the object is not its physical presence which endures in a museum collection, but rather its performative character which can only be exhibited in its indigenous cultural milieu. Art historian Robert Farris Thompson (1974) has pointed out that much African art was not meant to be experienced in the static environment of an exhibition gallery but was intended to be seen in motion. In its original context, for example, a viewer could not study the features of a wooden mask in detail but can only catch a fleeting glimpse of the object as a masked dancer swirled and spun before a gathered crowd in the village square. The aesthetic experience of seeing a mask in motion is very different from seeing a mask in a glass cabinet – artificially suspended in time and space.

Just as motion is an important component to the aesthetic dimension of an African mask, so too is sound. Most masks when danced in ritual performance are accompanied by distinct noises and otherworldly voices. These sounds, rather than any visual qualities of the wooden mask itself, are often what distinguish one mask type from another (Lipschitz, 1988). Seen in the silent realm of a museum cabinet these acoustic qualities of a mask's aesthetic configuration would be totally missed and overlooked.

In his essay "The Cycle and Stagnation of Smells," anthropologist Uri Almagor draws our attention to yet another domain of aesthetic and sensory experience as he explores the cultural construction of smell among pastoralists and fishermen in southwest Ethiopia. He demonstrates that judgments of smell are not based on objectively measurable values but are produced by cultural preconceptions and ideological bias. What smells "good" to the pastoralists in Almagor's study is not objectively any better smelling than the smell of fish which they classify as "bad." Smells that are perceived as pleasant and unpleasant are used by social groups to draw boundaries between themselves and others, and to establish relationships of hierarchy and metaphors of power.

Almagor's essay underscores quite brilliantly the importance of including non-material forms of cultural expression in any study of African "art" and aesthetics. An equally powerful example that serves to further illuminate this important admonition may be found in the work of anthropologist Jeremy Coote on the aesthetics of the cattle-keeping Nilotes of the Southern Sudan. Following in the footsteps of Evans-Pritchard (1934, 1940: 16–50), Coote has demonstrated that although the Nuer and Dinka, for example, make no "art objects" it would "be absurd to claim that they have no visual aesthetic" (1992: 245). Nilotic languages have an extraordinary number of terms to describe the color configurations of cattle, and both Nuer and Dinka aesthetic sensibilities are played out in the idiom of bovine beauty.

Finally, in "In Township Tonight! South Africa's Black City Music and Theatre", ethnomusicologist David Coplan reconstructs the history of urban music in a black South African township. His essay raises three points that are important to emphasize in this overview of African arts and aesthetics. First, Coplan draws attention to music as a major form of expressive culture in Africa. Although music has been studied in various parts of the African continent (Berliner, 1978; Keil, 1979; Waterman, 1990), its place in southern Africa, where emphasis on the visual arts is often not as pronounced as it is in West and Central Africa, adds an important dimension to our understanding of African arts and aesthetics.

Second, Coplan's article demonstrates the complex trans-Atlantic relationship between African–American music and the fashioning of urban cultural life in South Africa. While a significant amount of work has been done to reconstruct the African roots of African–American expressive culture (Price and Price, 1980; Thompson, 1984), few people have demonstrated with such clarity and detail the debt of African artists to black American culture. Coplan underscores that the process of transcultural blending and syncretic adaptation does not move only in one direction, from Africa to the Americas, but historically has also moved in reverse from America back to Africa. Furthermore, his analysis is of particular significance to the study of African music today, as source and influence become intertwined and mixed up in the global ethnoscape of what is called "world beat" music (Meintjes, 1990; Feld, 1995).

Third, Coplan's article raises an important point about the creation of an indigenous black African voice in South Africa. He demonstrates how music created solidarity from the period between 1940 and 1960 among the inhabitants of the townships. It is through this expression of solidarity in the arts that political battles against apartheid were later to be fought (for parallel examples of resistance in the visual arts, see Poster Book Collective 1991). Commenting on the role of the arts in confronting political oppression, the Reverend Desmond Tutu noted in 1988:

> When the San painted their exquisite rock paintings, they did so because they believed that these gave them power in the hunt. But the power they received from these paintings was the power of the knowledge that to be human is to be creative as well. . . . The art [of the South African townships] is in large measure a protest against race-obsessed bureaucrats who like to classify people into neat little packages, but who are nonetheless smart enough to ban cultural events because they know that culture can undermine racist exploitative ideology. Through art, and through creativity, blacks can transcend the claustrophobia of their physical environment. (quoted in Younge, 1988: 6)

The recent turn of events in South Africa – the dismantling of apartheid and the coming of free elections – bear out Desmond Tutu's faith not only in the capacity of culture to unite a divided nation, but more generally in the power of the arts to capture, represent, and on occasion even put into action the spirit of aesthetic expression that characterize the many diverse societies on the African continent.

References

Adams, Monni. 1973. "Structural Aspects of a Village Art," *American Anthropologist* 75(2) : 265–79.

Adams, Monni. 1989. "African Visual Arts from an Art Historical Perspective," *African Studies Review* 32(2) : 55–103.

Ben-Amos, Paula. 1989. "African Visual Arts from a Social Perspective," *African Studies Review* 32(2) : 1–54.

Berliner, Paul. 1978. *The Soul of Mbira: Music and Traditions of the Shona People of Zimbabwe.* Berkeley: University of California Press.

Bravmann, René A. 1974. *Islam and Tribal Art in West Africa.* Cambridge: Cambridge University Press.

Coote, Jeremy. 1992. " 'Marvels of Everyday Vision': The Anthropology of Aesthetics and the Cattle-Keeping Nilotes," pp. 245–73. In *Anthropology, Art, and Aesthetics,* edited by Jeremy Coote and Anthony Shelton. Oxford: Clarendon Press.

Drewal, Henry John. 1988. "Performing the Other: Mami Wata Worship in Africa," *The Drama Review* 32(2) : 160–85.

Evans-Pritchard, E. E. 1934. "Imagery in Ngok Dinka Cattle-Names," *Bulletin of the School of Oriental and African Studies* 7(3): 623–28.

—— 1940. *The Nuer: A Description of the Modes of Livelihood and Political Institutions of a Nilotic Peoples.* Oxford: Clarendon Press.

Eyo, Ekpo. 1980. *Treasures of Ancient Nigeria.* New York: Knopf.

Fagg, Angela. 1994. "Thoughts on Nok," *African Arts* 27(3) : 79–83, 103.

Fagg, Bernard. 1977. *Nok Terracottas.* London: Ethnographica for the National Museum of Lagos.

Feld, Steven. 1995. "From Schizophonia to Schismogenisis: The Discourses and Practices of World Music and World Beat," pp. 96–126. In *The Traffic in Culture: Refiguring Art and Anthropology,* edited by George E. Marcus and Fred R. Myers. Berkeley: University of California Press.

Garlake, Peter. 1995. *The Hunter's Vision: The Prehistoric Art of Zimbabwe.* Seattle: University of Washington Press.

Haddon, Alfred C. 1902. *Evolution in Art: As Illustrated by the Life-Histories of Designs.* New York: Walter Scott.

Jemkur, J. F. 1992. *Aspects of the Nok Culture.* Zaria: Ahmadu Bello University Press.

Kasfir, Sidney Littlefield. 1984. "One Tribe, One Style? Paradigms in the Historiography of African Art," *History in Africa* 11: 163–93.

Keil, Charles. 1979. *Tiv Song.* Chicago: University of Chicago Press.

Leighten, Patricia. 1990. "The White Peril and *L'art nègre*: Picasso, Primitivism, and Anticolonialism," *The Art Bulletin* 72(4): 609–30.

Lewis-Williams, J. David. 1983. *The Rock Art of Southern Africa.* Cambridge: Cambridge University Press.

Lifschitz, Edward. 1988. "Hearing is Believing: Acoustic Aspects of Masking in Africa," pp. 221–29. In *West African Masks and Cultural Systems.* Sidney L. Kasfir, ed. Tervuren, Beligium: Musée Royal de l'Afrique Centrale.

Meintjes, Louise. 1990. "Paul Simon's *Graceland,* South Africa, and the Mediation of Musical Meaning," *Ethnomusicology* 34(1): 34–73.

McEvilley, Thomas. 1993. *Fusion: West African Artists at the Venice Biennale.* New York: The Museum for African Art.

Mudimbe, V. Y. 1986. "African Art as a Question Mark," *African Studies Review* 29(1): 3–4.

Nodelman, Sheldon. 1970. "Structural Analysis in Art and Anthropology," pp. 79–93. In *Structuralism,* edited by Jacques Ehermann. Garden City, N. J.: Anchor Books.

Poster Book Collective. 1991. *Images of Defiance:*

South African Resistance Posters of the 1980s. South African History Archive. Johannesburg: Raven Press.

Price, Sally, and Richard Price. 1980. *Afro–American Arts of the Suriname Rain Forest.* Los Angeles: Museum of Cultural History, and Berkeley: University of California Press.

Shaw, Thurstan. 1977. *Unearthing Igbo–Ukwu: Archaeological Discoveries in Eastern Nigeria.* New York and Ibadan, Nigeria: Oxford University Press.

Silver, Harry R. 1979. "Ethnoart," *Annual Review of Anthropology* 8: 267–307.

Steiner, Christopher B. 1994. *African Art in Transit.* Cambridge: Cambridge University Press.

Thompson, Robert Farris. 1974. *African Art in Motion.* Los Angeles: University of California Press.

Thompson, Robert Farris. 1984. *Flash of the Spirit: African and Afro–American Art and Philosophy.* New York: Vintage Books.

Waterman, Christopher A. 1990. *Juju: A Social History and Ethnography of an African Popular Music.* Chicago: University of Chicago Press.

Willett, Frank. 1967. *Ife in the History of West African Sculpture.* New York: McGraw-Hill.

Younge, Gavin. 1988. *Art of the South African Townships.* New York: Rizzoli.

Suggested Readings

Arnoldi, Mary Jo. 1995. *Playing with Time: Art and Performance in Central Mali.* Bloomington: Indiana University Press.

Arnoldi, Mary Jo, Christraud M. Geary, Kris L. Hardin, eds. 1996. *African Material Culture.* Bloomington: Indiana University Press.

Barber, Karin. 1987. "Popular Arts in Africa," *African Studies Review* 30: 1–78, 113–32.

Barkan, Elazar, and Ronald Bush, eds. 1995. *Prehistories of the Future: The Primitivist Project and the Culture of Modernism.* Stanford: Stanford University Press.

Biebuyck, Daniel, ed. 1969. *Tradition and Creativity in Tribal Art.* Berkeley: University of California Press.

Blier, Suzanne Preston. 1987. *The Anatomy of Architecture: Ontology and Metaphor in Batammaliba Architectural Expression.* Cambridge: Cambridge University Press.

Blier, Suzanne Preston. 1995. *African Vodun: Art, Psychology, and Power.* Chicago: University of Chicago Press.

Brett-Smith, Sarah. 1994. *The Making of Bamana Sculpture: Creativity and Gender.* Cambridge: Cambridge University Press.

Chernoff, John Miller. 1981. *African Rhythm and African Sensibility: Aesthetics and Social Action in African Musical Idioms.* Chicago: University of Chicago Press.

Cole, Herbert M. 1989. *Icons: Ideals and Power in the Art of Africa.* Washington, D.C.: Smithsonian Institution Press.

Coote, Jeremy, and Anthony Shelton, eds. 1992. *Anthropology, Art, and Aesthetics.* Oxford: Oxford University Press.

Coplan, David B. 1994. *In the Time of Cannibals: The Word Music of South Africa's Basotho Migrants.* Chicago: University of Chicago Press.

d'Azevedo, Warren L., ed. 1973. *The Traditional Artist in African Societies.* Bloomington: Indiana University Press.

Fernandez, James. 1977. *Fang Architectonics.* Philadelphia: Institute for the Study of Human Issues.

Forge, Anthony, ed. 1973. *Primitive Art and Society.* London: Oxford University Press.

Goldwater, Robert, 1986. *Primitivism in Modern Art.* Cambridge, MA: The Belknap Press of Harvard University Press. First published 1938.

Jules-Rosette, Bennetta. 1984. *The Messages of Tourist Art: An African Semiotic System in Comparative Perspective.* New York: Plenum Press.

Karp, Ivan, and Stephen D. Lavine, eds. 1991. *Exhibiting Cultures: The Poetics and Politics of Museum Display.* Washington, D.C.: Smithsonian Institution Press.

Marcus, George E. and Fred R. Myers, eds. 1995. *The Traffic in Culture: Refiguring Art and Anthropology.* Berkeley: University of California Press.

National Museum of African Art. 1990. *African Art Studies: The State of the Discipline.* Washington, D.C.: Smithsonian Institution.

Ottenberg, Simon. 1975. *Masked Rituals of Afikpo: The Context of an African Art.* Seattle: University of Washington Press.

Price, Sally. 1989. *Primitive Art in Civilized Places.* Chicago: University of Chicago Press.

Rhodes, Colin. 1994. *Primitivism and Modern Art.* London: Thames and Hudson.

Robinson, Deanna C., Elizabeth Buck, and Marlene Cuthbert, eds. 1991. *Music at the Margins: Popular Music and Global Cultural Diversity.* Newbury Park, N.J.: Sage.

Rubin, Arnold, ed. 1988 *Marks of Civilization: Artistic Transformations of the Human Body.* Los Angeles: Museum of Cultural History, University of California.

Schildkrout, Enid, and Curtis A. Keim. 1990. *African Reflections: Art from Northeastern Zaire.* Seattle: University of Washington Press.

Stoller, Paul. 1989. *The Taste of Ethnographic Things: The Senses in Anthropology.* Philadelphia: University of Pennsylvania Press.

Thompson, Robert Farris. 1973. "An Aesthetic of the Cool," *African Arts* 7(1): 40–6.

Vogel, Susan. 1991. *Africa Explores: 20th Century African Art.* New York: The Center for African Art.

25

HUMOROUS MASKS AND SERIOUS POLITICS AMONG AFIKPO IBO

SIMON OTTENBERG

Compared to their actions in ordinary life how do African men behave when they don masks and special costumes? Masking is behavior of a stylized and ritualized kind, and differs, therefore, from activity of a day-to-day nature. The question is more complex, it seems to me, than simply whether the man who puts on a goat mask is supposed to look and perhaps act like a goat or not. The same man wearing the same mask may be differently interpreted at various dances. The study of masking, then, forces us to look deeply into the specific behavior of the performers and into the relationship of their actions to crucial elements of the social structure of the society. For often the masked players symbolically represent both social tensions and political matters in their performances.

Ethnographic Background

Afikpo, the subject of this study, is a village-group composed of twenty-two villages inhabited by some 30,000 persons in southeastern Nigeria.[1] It is one of several hundred village-groups of Ibo (Igbo) who live in this portion of Nigeria and whose total population probably comprises some eight million. The Afikpo, like other Ibo, are sedentary horticulturalists with clearly delineated villages composed of well-defined social groupings. Like other Ibo, they have never formed themselves into a highly centralized political system; for many years the Afikpo village-group has had considerable autonomy in matters of traditional leadership and social control. The Afikpo are unusual for Ibo, however, in having double unilineal descent, each person belonging to corporate matrilineal groupings, which are nonresidential, dispersed, landholding descent groups, as well as to patrilineal groupings, residential groupings (associated with ancestral shrines) which form the basic units of the political system.

The typical Afikpo village is composed of

Note: Field research was carried out at Afikpo in eastern Nigeria between December 1951 and March 1953, while on an Area Research Fellowship from the Social Science Research Council, with the aid of an additional grant from the Program of African Studies, Northwestern University. Further research was conducted there between September 1959 and June 1960 on a National Science Foundation grant.

[1] See Phoebe Ottenberg 1958, 1965; Simon Ottenberg 1955, 1965, 1968a, 1968b, 1968c, 1970, 1971; Simon and Phoebe Ottenberg 1962.

several hundred to several thousand persons and generally consists of a number of patrilineages, often unrelated, each agnatic group living in its own compound more or less at the edge of the village common. Each village also has a distinct system of male age-sets, there being some twenty sets in all. Each set covers about a three-year span, the men being first formed into sets in their late twenties. Sets are grouped together into grades, the oldest forming the elders' grade, which rules the village; certain younger sets perform cooperative and communal labor at the elders' discretion. These age-sets form the basis of the authority system, in which age is a primary criterion, and they also help unite men of different descent groups into a common social organization.

The male elders rule the village by common agreement amongst themselves. There are no formal village chiefs or heads; consensus is the rule. Some elders, of course, are "more equal than others," because they are outstanding speakers, have influence through their wealth and the size of their landholding, or come from influential descent groups. Fundamentally it is an egalitarian situation for persons of the same age and sex, and an authoritarian one for younger and older individuals. Too much personal power among elders, or in any Afikpo for that matter, is frowned upon.

Each village has a secret society with its own secret initiation bush, its special spirit, and a host of rituals which its members carry out in the six months following the harvest season when the society is active. All village males join the society, generally before they reach adulthood. For men it is a universal association, since without membership a man is sociologically a boy and is excluded from most adult activities. The society is thus secret only with reference to women and children.

The tripartite authority structure of the Afikpo secret society must be mentioned

briefly. The first unit includes the priest and assistant priest of the society's shrine, who are aided in carrying out sacrifices and other ritual activities by a small group of interested persons.[2] These persons are generally but not necessarily elders. The second unit comprises men who have taken senior titles within the society and who have the right to settle certain village disputes which the elders themselves cannot resolve. Again, many are elders, but there are exceptions. Third, the village elders as a group have some control over the society's activities. All three of these units – and some persons are members of two or three – act cooperatively to see that the various initiations, sacrifices, dances, plays, and the other activities of the society are effectively carried out. No highly centralized authority rules the secret society, just as there is none for the village.

Many of the society's activities are kept secret from noninitiates. These forbidden rituals include initiation ceremonies, title ceremonies of the society, the production of mysterious noises at night associated with mystical spirits, and sacrifices to the spirit of the society at its central shrine. But there is also a class of plays, dances, and musical performances carried out by society members which are open to the public; these affairs are extremely popular and well attended by men, women, and children. One of the more important types of play, consisting of a series of skits and dances, is the subject of this paper. The Okumkpa play, which lasts three to four hours or so, is performed in the village common and attended not only by local villagers but by many other Afikpo as well.

The Okumkpa Play

The Okumkpa is presented in the half of the year following the yam harvest (from about

---

[2]   In some Afikpo villages there are no formal positions of priest and assistant priest, but there is nevertheless a similar type of ritual group.

Plate 25.1 [6.1]: Ibo, Afikpo. A dancer wearing the *nne Mgbo* (mother of Mgbo) mask. The raffia backing to the mask and the method of attachment to the face are visible. Mgbom village. Ht. 9" (22.8 cm). *(Photograph: author, 1960.)*

September to February), when the secret society is active in the villages. This half of the year is one in which the highly achievement-oriented Ibo of Afikpo (Simon Ottenberg 1958, 1971; LeVine 1966) turn their attention to realigning social relationships. It is the period when men take important titles by joining special title societies, thus raising their status and sometimes their power and influence. And it is the time when the elders have the opportunity to judge cases and disputes, especially in land matters. It is thus a period of productivity in social relationships. In the other half of the year attention focuses on gaining material wealth and subsistence through farming and fishing. Social ties become less a focus of concern, the manual labor of individuals and groups more so. This work period provides wealth in foodstuffs which become resources for use in the ceremonial season; during this time new social tensions arise which are attended to in the following period. The secret-society play should be seen in this context.

As is true in virtually all of the public performances, of Afikpo village secret societies, the players in the Okumkpa wear masks. They are believed to be spirits rather than people. Though most players are individually recognizable by their manner of dancing, walking, singing, and in other ways, the fiction is maintained that they are not really humans at all, but a general form of spirit (*mma* at Afikpo, *mmo* or *mau* elsewhere in Ibo country). If a wife sees her husband dancing in costume, she is not supposed to recognize him, nor to compliment him on his dress or dancing at a later time, though men can do so among themselves, as all are members of the secret society. But the crucial act of placing a mask on the face of a secret-society member changes his status from "mortal" to "spirit," and thus allows him to behave in certain ways with respect both to other players and to unmasked members of the audience.

The masks themselves have a characteristic

Plate 25.2 [6.2]: Ibo, Afikpo. Another *nne Mgbo* mask. This is sometimes said to resemble a monkey or chimpanzee but is clearly female in character. *Nne Mgbo* is usually considered a very beautiful mask at Afikpo because of its whiteness and clearly delineated features. Mgbom village. Ht. 9" (22.8 cm) *(Photograph: author, 1960.)*

Plate 25.3 [6.3]: Ibo, Afikpo. A group of Okumkpa players sitting in the village common. Ugly masks (*okpesu umuruma*) are at the right front and left front and are about 12" (30.5 cm) in height. There is an Ibibio-style mask at front center, which is about 11" (27.9 cm) high, and a "queen" mask (*opa nwa*) toward the right, which is about 22" (55.8 cm) high. Mgbom village. *(Photograph: author, 1960).*

Plate 25.4 [6.4]: Ibo, Afikpo. The prayer beads and other aspects of the costumes of the actors are put on (and the beads played with) in ways designed to ridicule Moslems. Mgbom village. *(Photograph: author, 1960.)*

Afikpo style which differs from other Ibo mask styles.[3] Masks almost invariably have a vertical orientation and are narrower than the human head. Afikpo masks project forward from the face, the projection being markedly increased by bands of raffia which are tied to the back of the mask and hold it in front of the face as seen in Plate 25.1. The masks are faces, not half or full heads, or helmets. Some are of animals – a goat, a monkey, a bird. Plate 25.2 depicts *nne Mgbo* (mother of Mgbo), often considered a monkey or chimpanzee mask by the Afikpo. Some are stylized human faces with additional designs and projections added to them. In this second group some are male, others female, and some represent either sex or no gender at all. A variety of these masks may be seen in Plate 25.3. One mask often represents a white person. A third group of masks consists of the ugly ones; they are distortions of human faces – something like the Iroquois False Face

Society masks – with bulging cheeks, crooked noses and mouths, and ears that are out of line; these ugly masks, which often represent old men, are often dark or black in contrast to the other masks, which have brighter colors, making particular use of white. These ugly masks; which often represent old men, can be seen in Plate 25.4.

Some elements seem common to all the Okumkpa masks. Many have a human quality to them – even the animal masks – but they are almost as un-Negroid as one could make them. The noses have a high bridge. The faces lack everted lips, and in other ways do not look like actual Ibo people, as if the Afikpo wished to produce a clearly recognizable human face, yet one as distinct from their own as possible. They appear to be saying that these faces are, after all, not really theirs, but those of some other type of being. The masks are, of course, only a part of the total costume, though

[3] For other Afikpo masks and related local styles, see Bravmann 1970, pp. 65–67; Starkweather 1968, nos. 1–66; Jones 1939.

Plate 25.5 [6.5]: Ibo, Afikpo. The actors are playing out a skit. The main body of the performers is in the background. Mgbom village. *(Photograph: author, 1960.)*

Plate 25.6 [6.6]: Ibo, Afikpo. Two men dancing about between skits. They are allowed great freedom to dance in any style they wish, and sometimes, as here, do so grotesquely. Mgbom village. *(Photograph: author, 1960.)*

perhaps the most important part, for they make the man into a spirit.

The same "non-Afikpo" appearance prevails in the costumes. With the exception of khaki shorts, which have been adopted for general use, the costumes are not in any way like the usual dress of Afikpo men. This is evident from Plates 25.5 and 25.6. Animal skins worn on the back, porcupine-quill hats, and raffia shoulder-hangings and skirts indicate that this is the clothing of beings who are not Afikpo men. Red plastic waist beads, normally worn by unmarried girls, are often used as part of the costume, thereby confusing the sexual identity of the dancer.

A real social distance between the players and the audience is established through the use of mask and costume in Okumkpa performances. In our society, when we watch a performance, the players are likely to be personally less well known to us and less involved in direct social relationships with us than is the case in Africa. Masks in Afikpo help to create an illusion of distance between player and audience – people who are otherwise on close social terms.

Each Okumkpa mask has a name, and its wearer is expected to dance or play, at least at times, in character with the quality of the mask. But while masks are spirits, they are not particularly powerful; they do not give the wearer the right to try disputes, to judge cases, to wield everyday political power. There are no specific shrines associated with masks. Initiates may own, commission, or rent a mask for a play, or their part in the play may be assigned by the play leaders. Thus individuals do not have a close, personal relationship with a particular *mma* spirit.

Normally, Okumkpa consists of a series of

Plate 25.7 [6.7]: Ibo, Afikpo. The mask of the senior of the two play leaders. Known as *nnade okumkpa* (father of the Okumkpa), this mask is newly made. Often the leaders' masks are very old and are believed to have special spiritual qualities associated with them. Mgbom village. Ht. 12" (30.3 cm). *(Photograph: author, 1960.)*

skits and songs presented annually in some of the larger Afikpo villages, but the content of the plays changes every year, somewhat as variations on a recurrent theme. The play is led by two young men who volunteer for the work and who obtain the village elders' permission to prepare it. They gather their friends, peers, and relatives in the village and other volunteers in the settlement – generally it is men in their twenties and thirties that take part. The players rehearse secretly at night in the bush for several weeks. Some older men who enjoy performing may also take part and will advise the players and judge the quality of the acts before the public performance. The play is kept secret from nonsociety members until it is given. Its two organizers lead the actual performance, wearing special masks which indicate their roles. Such masks can be seen in Plate 25.7 and on the two leaders in the background in Plate 25.4. After the play is presented the songs may be sung by secret-society members of any village who choose to do so; some popular ones are heard for many years afterwards.

In general the authority relationships among the Okumpka players are voluntaristic, cooperative, and not tied directly to the authority system of the secret society. If young men do not come forward to organize a play in a given year, none will be presented; the elders do not seem to pressure strongly for it. The players are not pushed by the elders to perform in a certain way, nor is their material censored. The young men are essentially free from the usual authority of the elders. This is so even though the latter decide on what day the play is to be given and may insist that members of certain younger age-sets take part, mainly as dancers, to make the play more impressive.

An Okumkpa play may involve over a hundred actors, singers, and musicians, all masked and costumed. They sit in the center of the village common facing the section where the village elders sit; the performers move out from there to act in the skits and to dance between the scenes. Part of such a masked group may be seen in Plate 25.3 and two dancers in Plate 25.6. Only the leaders stand apart. The players wear some ten different types of masks, which constitute the whole repertory for the Afikpo, with exceptions.[4] The Okumkpa masks blend together the history of Afikpo (Simon Ottenberg 1968a, chap. 2). Some are based on styles of the nearby Edda and Okpoha village-groups of Ibo, with which Afikpo has common historical ties; some are of Ibibio origin, an area with which the Afikpo have long had trading contacts, and some appear to be indigenous to the area, though probably of non-Ibo origin, coming from the general Cross River area of which Afikpo is a part. As we have seen, some represent animals, others male and female human-like spirits, one a white person; some are of older spirit-persons, some appear as younger beings. The masked players as a group symbolize a totality of history, man, and nature at Afikpo. They are surrounded on all sides by an audience seated in the heart of the village – the group common – which also represents the totality of human life in the community.

The skits and songs are considered humorous by the Afikpo; they are intended to evoke laughter and other pleasurable responses from the audience, and they certainly do so. None of the Afikpo masks have movable parts. They very immobility requires the careful and full use of vocal contrasts to handle subtleties, and the exaggeration of bodily movements in the skits to convey impressions of persons and indicate emotional states. These features accentuate the differences between the masked skits and songs on the one hand and everyday Afikpo behavior on the other. The masks become mobile only through the skillful use of the voice and body movement.

---

[4] These exceptions include a special calabash mask worn during the initiation of a man's eldest son into the secret society, certain cloth masks, and masks that noninitiate boys make and use in play in the village.

Although Afikpo do not distinguish sharply between the types of skits, we can group them into three basic varieties:

a   The first tells of single living individuals who have acted in foolish or greedy ways. Such persons may be men or women of any age. There are tales of men who are henpecked by their wives, who ask their wives' permission before doing things which are strictly male matters, such as taking titles. Tales tell of a man who always drinks too much at ceremonies and gets sick and vomits. As in all of these skits and songs the person is named, and specific details concerning him are often sung and acted out. The skit may tell of a man who performed an important ceremony, but was too cheap to hire a palm-wine tapper, and so climbed the tree himself, fell down, and broke his leg. Or of a person who became so interested in the nearby Catholic mission that he forgot how to speak his own tongue and now can say only English prayers – "Our Father who art in heaven, Our Father who art in heaven" – over and over again. Such commentaries seem to be reminders of how individuals in a wide range of social roles should behave. They comment on the need to follow proper procedures and etiquette, to act as persons of their particular sex and age are supposed to.

b   A second category of skits and songs concerns females, often groups of women rather than individuals. The men may sing that women should remember that if they wish to have children they should not sing the secret-society songs (which they are wont to do in modified form) or the spirit of the society will render them barren. Or that in the old days when the women went naked and fired their pots in the open, none broke; but now they wear clothes and shoes and their pots are not as good as they used to be and break in firing. This is because the women do not keep to custom nowadays.

The secret society is seen strictly as a male affair. In Afikpo the sex polarity in status and role is sharp: the economic and social activities of the sexes are clearly separated, and they spend little time together (Phoebe Ottenberg 1958). Nevertheless, in a culture which emphasizes individual achievement as this one does, and which is today under considerable pressure for social change, the traditional polarity is breaking down. Men admit that it is now hard to "keep women in their place." These songs and skits are attempts to reaffirm role differentiation. Men sing that women are after all women – they should not forget their natural functions of bearing children, raising them, and cooking, or try to change their ways. Women, for example, are not supposed to know any of the secrets of the secret society. If they do, it is thought that they will fail to bear children unless cleansing rituals are performed. Nor for similar reasons are they to touch the masked dancers. Wives of men who carve masks are not to know that their husbands, who do this work in secret, so occupy themselves, even though the women may grind some of the dyes used in decorating the masks for their men. In short, Afikpo men see these plays, as well as other aspects of the secret society, as reinforcing the distinctiveness of males in contrast to females, and as helping to maintain an authority structure in which men dominate the government and the decision-making in village and family affairs while females play largely domestic roles.

c   A third category of skits and songs involves criticisms and ridicule of named leaders of the villages. These are generally elders or in some cases enterprising middle-aged men. The skits and songs generally involve a number of basic themes. One is about "palaver" men, those who engage in an argument or dispute for its own sake and so gather bribes and personal rewards at the expense of others, disrupting the normal tendencies toward cooperation and peace. Another theme criticizes the type of village leader who in a dispute sides with the group that he expects will give him the most money and food. One skit cites a man who collected money from Afikpo villages ostensibly to prosecute a court case between the Afikpo and the Nigerian government, but who actually used the money for himself. Or players may sing, again giving names, that certain elders are too shy to speak in public though they have no physical defects and can speak well, suggesting that they should come forward and give their views. In short, these brief dramas say that certain elders are foolish men who make unwise decisions for their own personal goals rather than for the whole community. They are enjoined to listen to what is being said at the plays, to help their own people, and to stop causing trouble, disruption, and dissension.

In a consensus society which also emphasizes individual achievement, there is always a tendency for some elders to try to usurp power, to go too far beyond the consensus principle. These men usually act on their own, and for personal gain, while appearing to represent their groups. Thus the consensus system of leadership at Afikpo makes for a sort of contradiction: men should be personally ambitious, but without disturbing the principle of group control. It is hard to regulate some elders and make them act as elders should. The contradiction at Afikpo is expressed both in the fear and in the admiration found there for the "big palaver man." For this reason too, elders themselves (who attend the plays in large numbers and enjoy many aspects of them) often think the dances, skits, and songs extremely funny – especially if they are about other elders, and more especially other elders whom they themselves think have acted inappropriately. The plays may also serve to articulate to some elders points that other elders find difficult to express directly themselves amongst their peers. The skits and songs therefore act as a sort of authority equalizer, just as wealth-distribution ceremonies, so characteristic of Afikpo, act to prevent any individual person from obtaining economic dominance. From the point of view of the elders, therefore, the plays have ultimately desirable goals. In another skit the leaders argue endlessly and foolishly in a divorce case. This is cleverly acted out, with side comments by the play-leaders about how some men love to talk. One skit concerns some Afikpo leaders who converted to Islam allegedly for personal gains. This can be seen in Plate 25.4 where they are sitting together hoping for funds from the Moslems as a reward for conversion. The skit goes on to say that they were foolish to change religions for personal gain, and in the

long run they lost money – that they are greedy men.

Another point brought out by Okumkpa actors and singers is that when elders engage in foolish conflicts, they are liable to be killed by poison, sorcery, or other mystical means. The plays emphasize a point strongly believed in at Afikpo, namely, that disputes and conflicts by their nature kill persons, and that attempts should therefore be made to avoid them. Such disagreements kill good leaders as well as "palaver men" who stir up a dispute for personal reasons. One song, for example, tells of an argument between villages over ownership of a palm grove. The singers call upon certain named elders to give up the dispute because the grove belongs to a certain village. They sing of other prominent elders in Afikpo who died during the dispute; their deaths must be attributed to the conflict itself. This is, in fact, an old quarrel which has been going on for many years and which has cost the Afikpo a great deal of time and money without any settlement being reached. The players voice the anxiety of the public, that the elders should make peace with one another and not divert their strength into useless conflicts.

The kinds of comments these masked figures – young and middle-aged men – make concerning their leaders would be, Afikpo admit, impossible to utter, unmasked, in public. The political structure of the village is such that no young or middle-aged man would normally dare to make such statements at village councils. If he did so he would be quickly shouted down and probably fined by the elders. In fact, deferential behavior is invariably exhibited toward persons senior in age to oneself as defined by the age-set system. Younger brothers are expected to obey their older ones and not to try to outdo them in taking titles or in other political or commercial enterprises. Sons likewise may not speak up against their fathers at public meetings, nor may they take more titles than their fathers have taken while the latter are alive.

The comments about the leaders made by

the Okumkpa masked dancers are therefore of an unusual nature and are so recognized by the Afikpo. This is proved by the wide interest taken in them on the part of the audience, an interest shared by the elders and other leaders present. Names of offenders are freely given, and specific situations which have occurred, or are believed to have taken place, are acted out and sung about. If the named persons are in the audience, they are not allowed to become angry, for to show annoyance or disgust is considered very bad form. They are, in fact, expected to give the actors or singers pennies or shillings to show their approval of an act well done. In practice, however, criticized leaders react in a variety of ways. Some are so happy to have their names mentioned, even if in a derogatory manner, that they are not actually angered. They may be pleased at this recognition that they have special power or influence. Others are very upset and may privately try to take revenge on the play-producers at some future time through land-case litigation or other devices; but this is considered very bad form. Thus the pattern is generally maintained that the Okumkpa plays are very funny affairs and not to be taken too seriously. It is appropriate that the masked and costumed characters are light-hearted, amusing, and sometimes ridiculous. To become overly serious is to spoil the game – to invite factionalism. Even a mask carver was referred to as "that funny man who makes masks," as one who does not have a serious or major occupation, compared, say, to iron-smithing or palm-wine tapping. It is obvious, on the other hand, that carvers' services are indispensable, for masks are of vital importance to any activities of the secret society. But a kind of make-believe about the plays establishes them as effective devices for airing tensions in the village and for getting comments across that are otherwise difficult to articulate. Because people do recognize that the carver plays a serious and important role with high status, the content of the plays is more than make-believe or play-acting. In fact,

I would argue that the play does have serious underlying intent.

For the young men *do* have honest grievances against the elders. Their comments are often serious, and they have no other effective ways of getting their complaints heeded short of refusing outright to cooperate with the elders, something which they rarely do. What in effect happens is that while elders normally make moral and judicial judgments on the behavior of the young men, in the plays the situation is reversed. Here the youths say to the elders: "Look, in such and such a situation you and you and you acted poorly and unethically." The characters who act out the misbehavior of the elders often use the dark ugly masks, with gestures and voices that are exaggerated and grotesque. They make fun of a leader who has a limp or speaks in a certain manner as part of their castigation of him. It is as if they are saying that the elders being portrayed are ugly, deviating, and foolish. The point is made indirectly at other times in Okumkpa, for all of the skits are about foolish people; generally, one skit is about the most foolish man in the village, and another about the most foolish woman. The latter skit usually involves a young dancer who wears the "queen" mask, *opa nwa* (carrier-child), which may be seen in Plate 25.3.

The spiritual forces of the Afikpo community are normally under the guidance of senior men who control and direct sacrifices and other religious rituals, in which young men play only supportive roles, supplying materials to be used in sacrifice and food for the feasts that accompany some religious activities. But in the Okumpka plays the younger men, as masked spirit dancers (*mma*), *are* the spirits and control and direct affairs. The elders, as ordinary members of the audience, sit passively, having only the secular role of reacting to the players. This is another aspect of the reversal of the leadership roles of elders and younger men that occurs through the masked plays.

Functional Analysis

A tentative functional analysis of these plays may be in order. Functional theory is not by any means well established to day, and between the earlier thinking of Emile Durkheim (1926), Alfred R. Radcliffe-Brown (1935), and Bronislaw Malinowski (1939, 1944) and the present day, it has been severely criticized (for example, Cancian 1960; Dore 1961; Erasmus 1967; Gregg and Williams 1948; Hempel 1959; Homans 1964; van den Berghe 1963) or developed in modified forms (Parsons 1951; Levy 1952; Merton 1949; Spiro 1952, 1961). Much anthropological writing on Africa has used functional analysis implicitly, and without making what was involved clear. I will try a somewhat more explicit formulation here.

First, the Okumkpa plays stress normal and expected behavior by ridiculing deviancy; a wide range of deviant acts may be dramatized. The emphasis is on maintaining traditional roles, traditional forms of sex polarity, and traditional leadership. When the players are asked why they perform such skits and songs, they answer in specific terms. The manifest function of them, intended and recognized, is to make fun of and to ridicule that which the Afikpo consider to be the foolish acts of specific individuals and sometimes of specific groups. It is the anthropologist who generalizes the totality of actions as functioning in a latent manner to attempt to reduce deviancy, to uphold traditional custom, and to attack abnormality. Curiously, the young men are those who in Afikpo press for change the most, yet simultaneously they also are the ones who emphasize tradition in their plays. Why is this so? The leaders and style-setters of the plays seem quite traditionalistic compared with some other young men; those who are considered most "progressive" do not seem to play leading roles, although they often take part. Again, the young men as a whole – whether conservative or innovative – do not wish the elders to make the judgments about new

conditions, for they do not feel that the elders understand them. Nor do the youths wish women to determine for themselves what changes to implement. Men today see changes in women's behavior as a threat to themselves. The Afikpo recognize that women are more independent and self-sufficient than they were formerly when they had to go to the farms under the protection of men and when they rarely traveled to distant markets or traded extensively in their own area. Afikpo women have a saying today: "When a woman has money, what is a man!" Thus, the young men see certain aspects of social change as desirable, but others as a threat to their position; in some ways they are conservative, in others they wish to play the controlling role in change.

A second major recognized and intended aim of some of the Afikpo skits and songs is to maintain sex polarity, the dominance of men over women and the restricted social and economic role of women in the face of changing conditions. Here the function of the play is seen in general terms, as many activities of the secret society are viewed, as a way of keeping women in their traditional roles. The means of coercion is the threat of barrenness in a society in which children are highly valued and where a person's status and prestige, male or female, is partly dependent on whether or not he or she has children, especially sons. The onus for failure to have children is placed on the women in Afikpo society, as can be seen in these plays and elsewhere and is associated with the angering of supernatural spirits through some form of female misbehavior.

Yet there also seems to be a latent function involved at the psychological level which the Afikpo do not verbalize. The fact is that men are extremely anxious about their failure to produce offspring even though the women are generally blamed for this, at least at first. A man must have at least a son to have status and to perform certain ceremonies and titles. Many children bring him considerable prestige and publicly symbolize his sexuality. The plays and skits, like other aspects of Afikpo life, operate to project strong, though rarely expressed, male anxieties about childlessness upon the women, particularly upon "misbehaving" females who are identified by a male definition. Women who have passed menopause sometimes flaunt the secrecy of the society. They may say: "I am an old woman now, what can the secret-society spirit do to me. I will die anyway!" The extent to which men are somewhat annoyed and bothered by such acts may be contrasted with their real displeasure if women of childbearing age do the same. This greater annoyance suggests that male anxiety over childlessness is a serious problem in Afikpo society.

A third major function of Okumkpa plays centers around the use of the theatrical situation to air anxieties and aggressive feelings that the young men hold concerning the elders. Here again the Afikpo see as a manifest function the fact that the plays and songs ridicule the elders who do not behave as elders should, who are greedy, foolish, bribe-takers, and so on. This is quite obvious, but we have to go further to see some latent functions as well. I take it that egalitarian gerontocracy in Afikpo inevitably leads to younger men developing some resentments and hostilities toward their elders. In one sense the system of political authority in these villages is a projection of the family situation. The psychological features in man which make the young rebel against their fathers in the home context also operate by extension at the village level. Criticisms of the elders' actions in the village are a very limited and ritualized working out of youths' feelings against the authority of their fathers at home. Plays provide a way of handling aggressive feelings without changing the form of village social organization. The young men apparently do not really want radically to alter this form of government, and are in fact committed to it. They see long-term rewards in the status quo, even though they are restless with it.

The question why such aggressive tenden-

cies, such criticisms, cannot be brought out openly at public meetings in the village, except in a highly circumspect manner, is crucial to the analysis here. I suggest that such tactics would be highly disruptive. The few attempted cases that I have seen were put down with short shrift by the elders, whom the youths both respect and fear, and whose place they desire some day to take themselves. I do not think we could postulate that village unity or Afikpo society would disintegrate or disappear if direct public aggression by clearly identified youths took place, although changes would occur. The theme of "social collapse unless aggressions are strongly displaced" is an old one in functional analysis, but is also moot. The fact seems to be that the young men, on the whole, are committed to the system to which they themselves sometimes object (Simon Ottenberg 1955), and they are not interested in radically altering it. Further, they are well aware that the elders hold the ultimate sources of power – the control and regulation of supernatural forces. Those "progressive" individuals who are not happy in this system of authority generally live outside the villages or elsewhere in Nigeria and take only a limited part in village matters.

The criticisms of the Afikpo elders also serve other latent functions, which are occasionally recognized in specific cases. One purpose is to reduce individualism among the elders and thus to maintain egalitarianism by criticizing those who draw too much power to themselves. Some elders support this view as well, for the ideal of consensus as a basis for decision-making and the fear of village domination by single individuals are both strong sentiments. In this sense the skits and songs concerned with the elders are a functional equivalent of the witchcraft accusations among the Tiv, which are directed toward powerful individuals (Bohannan 1958). Both are attempts to reduce and contain such power. Conflict among the elders seems to stir anxiety among many persons in the Afikpo village, and attempts through the plays to reduce faction-

alism and get the elders to pose as a cooperative group may reduce such feelings.

A further function, again one that is mainly
latent and that needs little comment, is that the
Okumkpa plays seem to help develop or maintain a sense of pride and accomplishment in the
village as a unit, to maintain a sense of the
whole, of persons acting and working together
regardless of individual kinship and residential
ties. Many other Afikpo come and see these
plays and persons remark on which villages
have produced good plays in a given year and
which have not. Intervillage rivalry, which also
finds expression in wrestling and whipping
contests and in other secret-society plays and
dances, is enhanced and maintained by this
particular form of play. The theater becomes a
symbolic and public statement of the state of
village organization.

The use of masks and costumes as "screens"
helps to facilitate the outlet of anxieties and
aggressive feelings without fear either of
counterattack or any reorganization of the
authority structure. I take it that here, as in the
case of mother-in-law jokes in our own society,
the humor expressed is related to some anxiety
and tension. I do not mean to imply, however,
that there is a natural tendency for a society to
maintain itself or for equilibrium situations
automatically to assert themselves in a society
through such plays. Following Homans
(1964), I suggest that individuals in the village
are not anxious, in terms of their goals, to
change its organization drastically at this point
in time; they are interested in it as it is, and
their orientation toward it is what maintains it,
rather than there being any natural tendency
toward equilibrium or stability.

The plays also can be looked at as dysfunctional, though I think to a relatively small
degree. They may lead to anger on the part of
elders and others who have been ridiculed and
criticized. Such anger is often directed toward
the leaders of the play, with consequent
gestures of noncooperation toward the men
involved (for example, pressuring to oust them
from land they are using on loan). Thus every

play seems to leave some residue of ill-will in
the village, though this does not seriously
affect the operation of the village organization
and usually occurs between individuals rather
than groups.

It is also worth noting that the rather free-
floating authority structure of the players'
group within the larger authority system of the
secret society and the village is no accident.
This autonomy gives players the freedom to
act as they would not be able to if they were
directly under the authority of the village
elders, the priests' group, or the titled group of
the secret society. Such functional autonomy
(Gouldner 1959) is necessary for the effective
preparation and performance of the plays. In
order to be prepared and performed a play and
its creators must be in a certain structural
arrangement vis-à-vis society at large, here one
of relative freedom to create, independent
from the elders.

Three queries concerning this sort of analysis may now be considered. The first question
is: what sort of things are *not* acted or sung
about in these plays? I see two major
omissions: matters having to do with the
secret-society's priests (and other religious
officials at Afikpo) and sexual references.
Plays may criticize the priests of Afikpo's
spirit shrines and diviners, but only indirectly
– for example, by reminding priests in general
that other priests who have failed to perform
their work effectively in the past have died
before their time. Beyond this, there seems to
be no attack on religious leaders, probably
because of their direct association with very
powerful spirits. As *mma* spirits, the masked
actors are free to criticize elders in their role as
secular leaders, but not as religious heads.
This fits well with the Afikpo view. Spirits are
guardians of morality, but as a rule they are
not believed to be critical or hostile to other
spirits.

With regard to sexual matters, it is interesting to note that apart from an occasional
reference, such matters are generally not
treated in Okumkpa plays, though there is

plenty of deviation from sexual norms at Afikpo which could be used as material. Rather, certain unmasked public song and dance festivals are held annually which do treat the actions and misbehavior of individuals, again giving names and details. The singers are young people – male and female – of certain ages. We have to ask why these performances can be given openly and not through the use of masked plays, and why women can take an active part in them. The answer is in a sense a test of the fitness of the analysis presented above. At this moment I cannot provide a fully satisfactory explanation, but I suggest that a primary factor is that sexual deviancy from the norm is not taken very seriously in Afikpo unless it involves a few special forms, such as sexual relationships between members of the same matrilineal clan. In fact, virtually everyone in Afikpo is involved in non-normative sexual acts, assuming it is even possible to determine accurately what normative sexuality is for this area. Further, many of these cases involve persons in different villages – which cases are therefore not purely internal matters – and also matrilineal groupings which do not have a residential base; thus the frictions that arise over these affairs often cut across villages, rather than merely affecting intravillage relationships. Hence the authority structure of the village is generally not involved, even if the violators of sexual norms are elders.

A second problem arises out of the fact that we are basing at least part of this analysis on hypotheses concerning individual anxieties and aggressive feelings. I have imputed these to the young men in terms of a general theory of father-son ties and some known facts about young men and elders at Afikpo and in other societies. But I really lack proof for Afikpo. We might learn more by using psychologically sensitive data, or, if a village in Afikpo could be found which did not carry out such plays, or did so very rarely, an examination of its authority structure and sex polarity and a careful search for functional equivalents of the masked plays might be made. A few small villages in Afikpo do not produce Okumkpa plays, but at the time they were investigated, I did not have this question in mind.

A third problem is that of evaluating what the plays really *do* to people, other than amusing and pleasing them. How are persons actually affected by them, what really is their impact on the audience – on a short-term or long-range basis? As we have seen, songs from the plays may be sung by many persons for months, even years, after the original performance, and both songs and skits are discussed in the village and elsewhere for a long time afterwards; their influence clearly extends beyond the day they are first presented, and beyond a second neighboring village where the play is sometimes given again a few days after its original performance. I have mentioned the attempt in Okumkpa plays to maintain sex polarity and egalitarian leadership. I would add that the plays seem to be primarily tension-reducing devices; they point up moral and ethical standards, they attempt to reduce individualism in leadership, they help to give a village a sense of identity and unity as against other villages, and so on. But it seems that in the analysis I have presented, and in others of like kind, we have yet to develop techniques for accurately gauging how effective the plays actually are in accomplishing these tasks. We do not, at present, have sensitive field tools to achieve this purpose. Furthermore, traditional field work techniques are inadequate in this context, so that new and more accurate tools of a different order will have to be devised. Functional analysis of the sort presented here is at a very simple and crude level operationally. It can indicate manifest intentions and latent functions, but it has few techniques for measuring actual consequences.

In any case, while the Afikpo plays themselves are humorous, popular, well attended, and very much enjoyed, much of the subject matter clearly is serious and directly tied to questions of authority and control in the village. The secrecy of the dancers, achieved through the use of masks and costume as concealing forms, is a method of publicly revealing what persons gossip about privately, or simply do not know. The masked players, through a ritual role reversal of leadership, become devices through which the secrets of the "other world" are revealed and explained. Thus masked secrecy is a mechanism to undo secrets.

References

BATESON, GREGORY
1936 *Naven.* Cambridge, England.

BOHANNAN, PAUL
1958 "Extra-Processual Events in Tiv Political Institutions." *American Anthropologist* 60, no. 1: 1–12.

BRAVMANN, RENÉ A.
1970 *West African Sculpture.* Index of Art in the Pacific Northwest, no. 1. Seattle.

CANCIAN, FRANCESCA
1960 "Functional Analysis of Change." *American Sociological Review* 25, no. 6: 818–827.

DORE, RONALD P.
1961 "Function and Cause." *American Sociological Review* 26, no. 6: 843–853.

DURKHEIM, EMILE
1926 *The Elementary Forms of the Religious Life.* 2d rev. ed. New York. Translation of *Les formes élémentaires de la vie religieuse.* Paris, 1912.

ERASMUS, CHARLES J.
1967 "Obviating the Functions of Functionalism." *Social Forces* 45, no. 3: 319–328.

GOULDNER, ALVIN W.
1959 "Reciprocity and Autonomy in Functional Theory." In *Symposium on Sociological Theory*, edited by L. Gross, pp. 241–270. New York.

GREGG, DOROTHY, AND WILLIAMS, ELGIN
1948 "The Dismal Science of Functionalism." *American Anthropologist* 50, no. 4: 594–611.

HEMPEL, CARL G.
1959 "The Logic of Functional Analysis." In *Symposium on Sociological Theory*, edited by L. Gross, pp. 271–307. New York.

HOMANS, GEORGE C.
1964 "Bringing Man Back In." *American Sociological Review* 29, no. 6: 809–818.

JONES, G. I.
1939 "On the Identity of Two Masks From S. E. Nigeria in the British Museum." *Man* 39, art. 35: 33–34.

LEVINE, ROBERT A.
1966 *Achievement Motivation in Nigeria.* Chicago.

LEVY, MARION J., JR.
1952 *The Structure of Society.* Princeton.

MALINOWSKI, BRONISLAW
1939 "The Group and the Individual in Functional Analysis." *American Journal of Sociology* 44, no. 6: 938–964.

1944 *A Scientific Theory of Culture and Other Essays.* Chapel Hill.

MERTON, ROBERT K.
1949 "Manifest and Latent Functions." In *Social Theory and Social Structure*, edited by R. Merton, pp. 21–81. Glencoe, Ill.

OTTENBERG, PHOEBE
1958 "The Changing Economic Position of Women Among the Afikpo Ibo." In *Continuity and Change in African Cultures*, edited by William R. Bascom and Melville J. Herskovits, pp. 205–223. Chicago.

1965 "The Afikpo Ibo of Eastern Nigeria." In *Peoples of Africa*, edited by James L. Gibbs, Jr., pp. 1–39. New York.

OTTENBERG, SIMON
1955 "Improvement Associations Among the Afikpo Ibo." *Africa* 25, no. 1: 1–28.

1958 "Ibo Receptivity to Change." In *Continuity and Change in African Cultures*, edited by William R. Bascom and Melville J. Herskovits, pp. 130–143. Chicago.

1965 "Inheritance and Succession in Afikpo." In *Studies in the Laws of Succession in Nigeria*, edited by J. Duncan M. Derrett, pp. 33–90. London.

1968a *Double Descent in an African Society: The Afikpo Village-Group.* American Ethnological Society, Monograph 47. Seattle.

1968b "Statement and Reality: The Renewal of an Igbo Protective Shrine." *International Archives of Ethnography* 51: 143–162.

1968c "The Development of Credit Associations in the Changing Economy of an African Society." *Africa* 38, no. 3: 237–252.

1970 "Personal Shrines at Afikpo." *Ethnology* 9, no. 1: 26–51.

1971 *Leadership and Authority in an African Society: The Afikpo Village-Group.* American Ethnological Society, Monograph 52. Seattle.

OTTENBERG, SIMON AND PHOEBE

1962 "Afikpo Markets: 1900–1960." In *Markets in Africa*, edited by Paul Bohannan and George Dalton, pp. 117–168. Evanston, Ill.

PARSONS, TALCOTT

1951 *The Social System.* Glencoe, Ill.

RADCLIFFE-BROWN, ALFRED R.

1935 "On the Concept of Function in Social Science." *American Anthropologist* 37, no. 3: 394–402.

1957 *The Natural Science of Society.* Glencoe, Ill.

SPIRO, MELFORD

1952 "Ghosts, Ifaluk and Teleological Functionalism." *American Anthropologist* 54, no. 4: 497–503.

1961 "Social Systems, Personality and Functional Analysis." In *Studying Personality Cross-Culturally*, edited by Bert Kaplan, pp. 93–127. Evanston, Ill.

STARKWEATHER, FRANK

1968 *Igbo Art: 1966.* Museum of Art, University of Michigan, Ann Arbor.

VAN DEN BERGHE, PIERRE L.

1963 "Dialectic and Functionalism." *American Sociological Review* 28, no. 5: 695–704.

26

Principles of Opposition and Vitality in Fang Aesthetics*

James W. Fernandez

I

As part of his introductory argument to *The Elementary Forms of the Religious Life*. Durkheim raises a seminal point that has rarely since been adequately followed up in the literature or tested in the field. It is a point that he had raised previously, with Mauss, in an article, "On Some Forms of Primitive Classification," which appeared in his *Journal de l'Annee Sociologique* in 1904.[1] If we examine some excerpts from Durkheim's argument we will see its relevance to the topic we have before us – Principles of Opposition and Vitality in Fang Aesthetics. He is speaking about the way in which Australian and North American Indian tribes lay out space.

> Among the Zuni, for example, the pueblo contains seven quarters. Each of these is a group of clans which has had a unity. Now their space also contains seven quarters and each of these seven quarters of the world is in intimate connection with a quarters of the pueblo that is to say with a group of clans. One division is thought to be in relation with the north, another represents the west, etc. [Moreover] each quarter of the pueblo has its characteristic color which symbolizes it.[2]

Since Durkheim's perspective is a sociological one, this material leads him directly to affirm that "the social organization has been the model for the spatial organization and a reproduction of it," an affirmation which he easily translates later into the book's major point – that social life has been the source of the religious life.

The relevance of these facts of social and spatial organization to aesthetic problems should be clear, for aesthetics, after all, has as one of its primary concerns the manner in which values, whether colors or tones or even words for the poet, are formally arranged in space. Presumably if one is able to tie up spatial

* Read at the Seminar in the African Humanities, Indiana University, March 20, 1963. This research, undertaken in Equatorial Africa, was supported by the Ford Foundation and the Program of African Studies, Northwestern University. For the invitation to address the seminar and for helpful comments I am grateful to Alan Merriam and Roy Sieber.

[1]   Now translated with an introduction by Rodney Needham. *Primitive Classification* (Chicago, 1963).
[2]   Emile Durkheim, *The Elementary Forms of the Religious Life*. Trans. from the French by Joseph Ward Swain (London, n.d.), p. 12.

organization with social organization he shall have said either one of two things. Either aesthetic preference responds more than we realize to social structure or social structure is itself to some extent the expression of an aesthetic preference.

More directly relevant for the body of our discussion, however, is Durkheim's further discussion in which, talking about the distinction between right and left in the primitive's organization of space, he suggests that in primitive societies the idea of contradiction is dominant. We have not clearly recognized this, he says, because in our own societies the principle of identity dominates scientific thought. But our present logical bias notwithstanding, our doctrine of the excluded middle and our inability to contemplate unresolved contradictions, the idea of contradiction has been historically of the greatest importance. In primitive thought and in the mythologies that linger on in our own day Durkheim argues:

> We are continually coming upon things which have the most contradictory attributes simultaneously, who are at the same time one and many, material and spiritual, who can divide themselves up indefinitely without losing anything of their constitution. In mythology it is an axiom that the part is worth the whole.[3]

In the contradiction between the sacred and the profane Durkheim is of course to give us full explication of not only the importance of contradiction in primitive societies but indeed the necessity of it. Unfortunately, these two categories have never been fully understood and the overtones of the terms have tended to mystify the reader.

Rather than pursuing Durkheim in the direction of the sacred and the profane I shall take up this notion of contradiction as it manifests itself in Fang culture. I shall be interested in the idea in a number of areas of Fang life, but it must be kept in mind that my basic interest in it is as it is central to their aesthetic – their notions, that is, of preferred form in object and action. For what is aesthetically pleasing to the Fang has, as I shall attempt to show, a vitality that arises out of a certain relationship of contradictory elements. The Fang not only live easily with contradictions; they cannot live without them.

It is well known to Africanists that a good many peoples of that continent possess uncentralized political systems in which order and stability, however, are achieved through lineage structure and a principle called segmentary opposition. Of these people one might truly say that they cannot live without contradictions. The Fang, though highly uncentralized, do not have fully functioning lineages and by the period of field work, 1958–1960, had only the relics of segmentary opposition. In this they are like the rest of the Bantu of north-western equatorial Africa. For these people other kinds of evidence such as that introduced here are relevant.

Fang discourse in the area of aesthetics provides a direct translation for the word *vitality* (*eniñ*, or, more exactly, the capacity to survive). It is more difficult to find a substantive to translate the word *contradiction*. They speak of things which are in the general sense contradictory, adverbially in circumlocution as not being close to one another (*ka bi* – not approximate – not congenial and by extension not possible) or as standing opposite from each other (*mam me ne mfa ayat*). It is immediately apparent that they have a spatial analogy in mind when they speak of what we would call contradictions and, therefore, I have taken as the most satisfactory translation for Durkheim's term the word *opposition*, since the spatial analogy is in this word as well. There are difficulties in this translation for

---

[3] Durkheim, p. 13.

quite obviously what is contradictory may include more than what is simply in opposition. Contradiction may imply inconsistency which is not necessarily opposition. I shall ignore this difficulty, however, and limit myself to the principle of opposition as a portion of the idea of contradiction.

II

These notions of opposition and vitality first stood out for me in my data when I was querying the Fang as regards their famed ancestor figures. I had a collection of some twelve of these figures of various qualities,

individual styles, and dates of manufacture (most of them recent unfortunately), and I simply asked each informant to select those he especially preferred and those he especially disliked, explaining why. I accepted the thesis, incidentally, that there is such a thing as art criticism in non-literate society and that art lies not so much in the act of creation but comes into being in the relationship between creation and criticism – the artist and his critics. As events turned out among the Fang, there is indeed a lively spirit of art criticism. It flows around the carver as he is in the process of turning out his statue in the men's council house, and it influences his work. If I can take one of our local concepts here in vain, it

Plate 26.1: [Male] Figure (H. 13 inches). *Mwan bian.
Demaniacion Akurnam.* Spanish Crimea. Collected 1959.
Photo by A. Bouchard.

Plate 26.2: Female Figure (H. 17 inches). *Eyima bieri.*
District d'Oyem, Gabon. Collected 1959.
Photo by A. Bouchard.

becomes possible to speak of an opposition between the carver and his village critics. Very often the villagers consider themselves the final cause of the statue and apply what social pressures they can to the efficient cause, the carver, to see that the work turns out to their expectations. The carver in his turn must reach some sort of accommodation with his critics and what this is depends upon the personalities involved. In some Fang villages the carver retreats from the council house to the solitude of the banana plantation behind the village and in these villages respect for the carver is sometimes even institutionalized though he cannot expect to escape his critics when the statue is completed. Carvers do not have much status or power in Fang society, though they are esteemed; therefore, they cannot expect to impose aesthetic acquiescence upon their clients. Nevertheless, it is a curious fact that I never found a case in which a statue was refused. The view seems to prevail that any statue can serve its function atop the reliquary whether it is aesthetically satisfying or not.

Given this custom of criticism, what, then, was the response of these eight informants, two of them carvers themselves, to the twelve figures? In explaining that response one must remember that it is the product of the evolution of Fang attitudes toward their ancestral figures as well as the evolution of the figures themselves. The Fang ancestor figure of the last thirty or forty years is a different object than the aboriginal one, and the thesis that the full figure was a stimulus response to European religious statuary is not to be rejected out of hand – probably by indirect acculturation from the coastal peoples of the southern Gabon, more particularly the Loango Vili and Balumbo who traded far up the coast and inland in the last half of the last

century. In any case, as Tessmann has affirmed,[4] the aboriginal ancestral statue was simply a head carved on a stem thrust down into the top of the round bark barrel containing the ancestral skulls. Tessmann does not point out what informants make clear – that the bark barrel (*nsuk*) was taken as the belly or torso belonging to the head. The stomach, thorax, and sometimes viscera, it might be mentioned, are the centers of power and thought while the head is simply the organ of apprehension and direction enabling what fundamentally belongs to the torso to be willfully put to use. The Fang entertain a lively sense of opposition between the head and the torso which might be summed up appropriately in our aphorism "your eyes are bigger than your stomach." The hope of the Fang is that the head and the stomach should work together in complementary fashion though they do not always succeed in doing so. In any case the original reliquary (*bieri*) was conceived as a head (the carving) and a stomach (the bark barrel). These two elements had a relationship of complementary opposition. They worked together to accomplish the vital purposes of the cult though they were really in some sense opposing entities.

As Tessmann has further shown, the Fang ancestor carving changed from simply a head to a half figure, and finally to a full figure which perched on top of the bark (*nsuk*).[5] What took place, as I intend to show from the remarks of my informants, was a shift from the opposition between bark (*nsuk*) and carving to an opposition or oppositions within the carving itself, a tension which, as in the aboriginal situation, was a source of the carving's vitality. Accompanying this change in form of Fang statuary was a change in function. This change is signaled by Tessmann's remark that in his day the *eyima bieri* statues were very easy to purchase.[6] The Fang were eager to sell them

[4]   Gunter Tessmann, *Die Pangwe*. Volkerkundliche Monographie eines Westafrikanischen Negerstammes (Berlin, 1913), II, 117.
[5]   Tessmann, p. 118.
[6]   Tessmann, p. 117.

– in strong contrast to the reliquary which was impossible to obtain. By the 1940s and '50s, however, and this was the ethnographer's personal experience, it became difficult indeed to buy or even view these statuettes which were practically all secreted away from the zealous eye of administration and missionary. It is clear that the Fang had come to attach considerable importance to the figure itself. Here again there is, conceivably, another example of stimulus diffusion, for the Fang were bound to have remarked the importance laid upon religious statuary and graphic representations of the deity in Christianity, and were bound to reflect more respectfully upon their own figurations of the supernatural. It is of equal interest that only in recent years have pieces of cranial bone been actually worked into small concavities in the statuettes themselves. This custom, as well, is probably to be traced to the long-standing custom among the Loango, but what is of greater interest is that it represents to some degree a transfer of the function to the reliquary to the statue itself. In sum, the statue, the latter-day Fang ancestor statue, is a much more awesome and much different object from its predecessors. It is a much more autonomous object. Something of this awe was reflected in the approach of those informants called upon for an aesthetic critique of those statues which had already been in use. Insofar as it is always difficult to render an adequate aesthetic judgment of that which is at the same time sacred, so the informants' response to these figures seemed truncated by comparison to their response to the others. Apparently having rested on top of the craniums, they were somehow thenceforth removed from everyday aesthetic judgment.

In setting my informants before the statues arranged in a row, I tried to limit myself to the question, Which figures do you like the most and why? (*wa dan nyugue beyime beze Amu dze.*) In some cases I had to prompt an explanation for the informants, especially the carvers who hesitated apparently to criticize the work of another and tended to limit themselves to indi-

cating their preference. But at no time was any aesthetic criteria suggested to the informant as a means of eliciting a response. I cannot enter here into a complete analysis of their responses, but I will suggest the pertinent features. Their statements were full of words, of course, suggesting the finished or unfinished quality of the particular object, was it smooth, and had it been completely cut out from the wood from which it was made or were there still traces of its rougher origins? They talked about the balance (*bibwe*) of the object and whether its various quadrants balanced with the rest. If one leg or one arm or one shoulder was proportionately differently carved than its opposite, this was practically

Plate 26.3: Male and Female Figures.
Photo by A. Bouchard

always a cause for comment and criticism. (Criticism was advanced against the two figures pictured here on this basis). There should be balance in the figure, and the proportions of opposite members whether legs or arms or eyes or breasts should display that. Without this balance of opposite members, it was said – and this is the important comment – the figure would not be a real one (*a se fwo mwan bian*), it would have no life or vitality within it (*eniñ e se ete*). I must confess that those features that seemed to have what *we* would call movement or vitality were not those selected by my informants. They generally picked those whose presentation and posture were stolid, formal, even – and perhaps this is the best word – suppressed.

This whole idea that vitality is obtained through the balance of opposite members in the statue was a clue of some importance in my understanding of Fang culture. This idea, is, of course, crucial to our discussion and it deserves further examination. The Fang generally, and not only these informants, argue, when speaking of their statuettes, that they are "our traditional photographs." "They are our way of representing living persons as the European represents them in photographs." Now it is rarely argued that these statues represent particular living persons, just living persons in general. They are not portraits. But despite their quite obvious stylization the Fang insist that they are in some sense accurate portrayals of living persons. Now I have come to believe after lengthy discussions on this matter – for example, the Fang recognize well enough that the proportions of these statues are not the proportions of living men – that what the statue represents is not necessarily the truth physically speaking, of a human body but a vital truth about human beings, that they keep opposites in balance. Both the statues and men have this in common and therefore the statues in this sense are accurate portrayals – accurate representions of living beings. They express, if they are well done, a fundamental principle of

vitality. I am obliged to say, however, that this is an inference developed from my informants' remarks.

Though I think it unnecessary here to reconcile Fang statements with what has been disclosed above, it is often said that the *eyima bieri* gathers its power from its association with the craniums in the bark barrel and is nothing without it. This is, of course, primarily true of the *eyima bieri* before pieces of bone were actually placed within it and it became a *mwan biañ* (literally, *medicine child*). It also should be noted that once a year during the initiation cycle of the ancestral cult the statues were taken off their reliquaries and danced as puppets above a palm thatch partition. Here, too, the object was to animate them, vitalize them, give them life. Whatever implications may be drawn from these further facts in respect to the vitality of the statuettes, it may, in any case, be concluded that it was important that they possessed this quality and that the aesthetic reaction to the figures was conditioned by that requirement.

Before considering the principles of opposition and vitality in other areas of Fang life. I should mention one further opposition – though not a spatial opposition – which the Fang feel add quality to these statues. If one looks closely at these statues, one finds that the great majority of them have infantile or child-like features. The obvious feature is the protruding stomach and umbilical rupture which figures so largely in many statues. The umbilical rupture is primarily characteristic of infants and children, less characteristic of the strengthened stomach wall of adults. Another infantile feature lies in the stylization of the eyes obtained by nailing round disks of tin into the orbital cavities. This feature was first called to my attention by my clerk; who remarked the wide open glare of an infant as being like that of an *eyima*. Research bore out the relevancy of that association for many Fang. Finally the proportions of the statue – the large torso, the big head, and the flexed, disproportionately small legs are definitely infantile in character. Now the opposition contained here lies in the fact that the statue presents both an infantile and an ancestral aspect. While the Fang argue that the statues represent age, the ancestors, and their august powers in their descendants' affairs, they also recognize the infantile qualities of the figures themselves.

There are, of course, cosmological and theological explanations for this juxtaposition of contradictory qualities in the statues. Among these is the fact that the newborn are felt to be especially close to the ancestors and are only gradually weaned away by ritual and time to human status. Another explanation for the infantile quality lies in the primary concern of the ancestral cult in fertility and increase. An infantile representation is an apt expression of the desire for children. More important than that, I would argue, however, is the fact that these contradictory qualities in the ancestor figure give it a vitality for the Fang that it would not possess if the *eyima* simply figures an aged person or an infant.

There is one other important and familiar opposition in African traditional sculpture, that between male and female elements as found in androgynous sculpture, particularly from the western Sudan. Unfortunately, because the presence of Fang statues embodying a male–female opposition would greatly enhance my argument as to the achievement of vitality through opposition, there are to my knowledge no clear-cut examples of such sculpture among the Fang. Where such statues are found in Africa the argument we are developing here may apply.

III

I turn now to a discussion of opposition and vitality in other areas of Fang life with the object of suggesting that these principles at work in their aesthetic reaction to their ancestor figures are found more broadly in their culture. First impressions support me here. The Fang village, when approached from the equatorial rain forest, with its two long rows of huts facing each other across a narrow barren court, provokes in the observer the immediate impression of opposition. And it would seem that the existence of oppositions in their society is recognized in the way the Fang lay out their villages. In fact, the minor segment of the clan (the *mvogabot*) is often defined as those brothers who build opposite each other because, it is said, it is better to shout insults across the court of the village to your distant brother than whisper them in his ears as your neighbor. This spatial opposition prevails even within the family (*ndebot*, house of people), and the Fang say *nda mbo, binoñ bibañ* (one house, two beds) to imply that opposition and resultant division lie even in this smallest social unit, the domestic household of the extended family. Equally it may be noted that the arrangement and mechanics of dispute in the men's council house follow this plan of opposition. In the *aba* there are two rows of benches upon which the disputants sit facing each other and between which the witnesses or judges rise, one at a time, to make their statements.

The opposition which exists within the minor segment (*mvogabot*) is that of lineage relatives whose relationship is distant enough, usually more than four generations deep, as to no longer impose strong allegiance. Their tenuous relationship is signified by spatial opposition in building arrangement. *Ndebot*, houses of people, extended families within the *mvogabot*, build side by side in the lengthening double row of houses with which we are familiar, so long as they feel strong allegiance. But they build opposite when they no longer feel the close bonds. A feeling of separation and instability within the lineage is expressed by spatial opposition. It is necessary to point out, however, that the spatial opposition of village structure is not conceived as an undesirable end in itself but is regarded as necessary. One row of houses without its opposite does not constitute a village; such a village cannot be good, pleasing, or functional. Two opposite rows of houses, it is said, stand off the forest and in the old days of internecine strife provided a closed, fortified rectangle against surprise attack. Moreover, the social antagonisms of lineage members living on opposite sides of the court are one important source, it is admitted, of the animation (*elulua*) and vitality (*eniñ* – the word is actually used) that is one of the desired features of village life. Here, then, as well, opposition is associated with vitality. What is aesthetically appropriate is socially necessary. The oppositions we have noted are part of a larger scheme guaranteeing social viability.

Now the achievement of viability in the social structure through complementary opposition of equivalent segments has been, as mentioned above, fully demonstrated by anthropologists in respect to segmentary kinship systems. Though the Fang recognize segments within their lineages and though these seem to be vestiges of corporate kinship groups, those segments do not now have full corporate character. Hence they do not provide complete data in respect to the notion of complementary opposition. It is possible, however, to examine the same principle in full blown operation among the Fang in the kinship mechanism known as complementary filiation – the tendency to trace relationship of ascending generations alternately to male and female progenitors and progenitrix. Thus the *ndebot* is traced to a woman founder, the *mvogabot* to a male, the next segment beyond that to a female, and eventually to the clan ' which is traced to a male. Now the point here is that male and female qualities are to the Fang opposing ones. The principal connotation of male origin is divisiveness and conflict: the principal connotation of female origin is unity and common purpose. Moreover, these connotations accord with the nature of the various segmentary groups as they are traced

to either male or female. The *ndebot* seen as founded by a female is cohesive and fairly stable. The *mvogabot* traced to a male founder is divisive and volatile and so on up to the clan level whose male origin accords with its characteristic potential for dispersion and division.

The Fang argue when questioned about this custom that no clan, lineage, or segment can be created by men alone; hence they must trace their kin groups to both male and female. They argue in effect, if I may be permitted to summarize the drift of a good bit of field material on this point, that the viability of the kin group lies in the fact that it is anchored in opposing qualities male and female which, however, due to their distribution at different levels of the lineage, achieve complementary opposition. The lineage structure systematically distributes maleness and femaleness so that these two opposing qualities do not clash at the same level. In the same way the village layout distributes opposition in space so that these oppositions are complementary and not conflictive.

It may be argued, I think, that this manipulation of male and female elements in the lineage genealogy gives evidence of a "kind of experimentation or play of fashion," as Kroeber called it,[7] in which the Fang are using and distributing the different valences of maleness and femaleness in the social structure in order to provide for themselves an aesthetically satisfying fiction. The distribution of these opposites, maleness and femaleness, in other words, satisfies aesthetic criteria and in doing so provides for viability. The opposition between maleness and femaleness is not only found in the social structure, incidentally, but is carried throughout Fang world view and is evident in dualistic sets such as hot (male) and cold (female), night and moon (female) and day and sun (male), earth (female) and sky (male). These sets of oppositions suggest an

---

[7] A. L. Kroeber, "Basic and Secondary Patterns of Social Structure" in *The Nature of Culture* (Chicago, 1952), p. 217.

elemental opposition – a dualism in fact – in Fang culture itself which though it has clear manifestation in social structure does not exhaust its importance there but lies behind all cultural manifestations.

I shall return to this problem of dualism in the conclusion. I want first, in a final attempt to link the principles of opposition and vitality, however, to consider what the Fang mean by maturity and what for them are the sources of maturity. For I think it may be argued that a truly mature man is an object of aesthetic appreciation.

The mature man (*nyamoro*, real man) is a man between thirty-five and fifty-five, at the height of his powers. The idea of his maturity and of his power stems, in good part, from the Fang theory of physiology. This is not an easily clarified subject. What *is* clear is that a man receives his essential forces and powers from the blood of his mother and the sperm of his father. The maternal element goes to make the flesh, blood, and bloody organs of the body cavity, particularly the heart. The paternal element goes to make up his bones, sinews, and brains. Just as the creation of the child is dependent upon the harmonious working together of these ordinarily incompatible elements, blood and sperm, so the full power of the adult is dependent upon the working together of the two sets of body members which the two essential substances of coitus have brought into being. A man with strong brain, bones, and sinew but with weak blood, organs, and heart, will confront life as inadequately as he who has strong blood but weak sinews. The brain, the bones, and the sinews are the center of the will, the driving force, the determination of a man, while the blood and the heart are the sources of reflection, deliberation, and thought (*asiman*, thought, that which gives direction to determination). Taking direction without determination is as useless to the Fang as determination expressed without direction. In a complete man, as in a vital ancestral figure, these opposing sets of attributes are held in balance so as to work together in complementary fashion. Out of the complementary relationship between opposites, life – vitality – is most fully achieved by the *nyamoro*. He, the mature man, most successfully combines the biological heritage of female blood and male seminal fluid – willful determination and thoughtful direction. Youth tends to be too active, too willful; age, too deliberative, too tranquil. Here appears again vitality arising out of the appropriate relationship between opposites.

There is not space to examine the principles of opposition and vitality in Fang aesthetic reactions to other manifestations of their culture. These principles at work might best be shown in Fang comment upon traditional dances where their gustatory appreciation in the vitality of the dance rises out of the presence of oppositions: the male drummers, the female dancers; the low sound of the drum, the high pitched and falsetto voices of the women; and, of course, the customary scheme by which the dancers face each other in two opposed lines. These principles of opposition and vitality might also be followed into the new syncretist cult of Bwiti as they express themselves in the ritual under elaboration in that cult. Even without these further examples, I hope it is sufficiently clear that when Fang assume a posture of aesthetic scrutiny the presence of skillfully related oppositions constitutes an important part of their delight and appreciation. This is so because vitality arises out of complementary opposition and for them what is aesthetically satisfying is the same as what is vitally alive.

IV

The data derived from the Fang, the extent to which the principle of opposition arises in many different areas of Fang life, indicate that there is an underlying duality in Fang culture. This duality is manifestly institutionalized in the latter-day syncretist cult of Bwiti – a religious movement designed to restore integrity, harmony, and regularity to lives greatly disturbed by acculturation. The Fang members of Bwiti oppose the left hand to the right hand in ways that Hertz[8] long ago argued, they oppose the earth to the sky, male to female, northeast to southwest, night to day, hot to cold. In fact, it is easy to construct for the Fang Bwitist a table of symbolic classification – sets of opposed values such as we have given above – in which the pairs of opposite terms are analogically related by what Needham[9] calls the "principle of complementary dualism." This principle has been explored recently by Needham for the Purum and Meru, Beidelman for the Kaguru, and Faron for the Mapuche.[10] While such systematic analysis of the coherence of symbolic values and the relation of the dualistic symbol system to the social structure are important extensions of the original Durkheimian insight, I have limited myself here, using terms from the Fang's own aesthetic vocabulary, to show how aesthetic appreciation rests upon the presence of vitality in the object or action and that this in turn rests upon the appropriate relationship – whether this be a balanced relationship or a complementary relationship – between opposites.

Two larger questions remain to be considered. Anthropologists sometimes employ the term *logico-aesthetic integration* to refer to the manner in which the disparate elements of culture were brought into some systematic relationship. The first question then is how does logico–aesthetic integration obtain in a dualistic culture where oppositions play such an important role? Second, what about this overarching question – the impact of social structure upon aesthetic principles? Is it because opposition is a fact of social life that it becomes such an important component of aesthetic appreciation?

In respect to logico-aesthetic integration – if we mean by that the extent to which patterns of behavior conform coherently to a given logic and a given set of aesthetic principles – two things are to be said. First, if one admits that analogy is a kind of logic, then there is no reason why integration should not prevail in a system of analogic oppositions; and in fact we have argued that this is the only kind of integration that makes sense to the Fang. Second, in respect to the aesthetic component of this integration, it must be pointed out that true aesthetic integration of a total culture, if not an impossibility, can only, in any case, be the consequence of "relentless concentration on the whole life process as an art." Thompson has argued that this exists among the Hopi.[11] I do not find it among the Fang. They are too materialistic and opportunistic to be constantly preoccupied with living out all of life in an aesthetically satisfying manner. For most Fang passable interrelationships – relationships which are functional, goal-reaching, and gratifying – can be established without benefit of much aesthetic elaboration. But it should also be said, and this is a measure perhaps of acculturative disintegration, that there is, except among the members of Bwiti, less concern with the aesthetic satisfactions offered by objects and actions than formerly. One can see this in an increased tendency towards shabby and unbalanced construction in village layout and upkeep. Formerly the Fang

[8]   Robert Hertz, *Death and the Right Hand* (London, 1960).
[9]   Rodney Needham, "The Left Hand of the Mugwe: An Analytical Note on the Structure of Meru Symbolism," *Africa*, XXX, 1 (Jan. 1960), 20–33.
[10]   T. O. Beidelman, "Right and Left Hand among the Kaguru; A Note on Symbolic Classification" *Africa*, XXXL, 3 (July 1961), 250–257. Louis Faron, "Symbolic Values and the Integration of Society among the Mapuche of Chile," *American Anthropologist*, LXIV, 6 (Dec. 1962), 1151–1164.
[11]   Laura Thompson, "Logico-Aesthetic Integration in Hopi Culture," *American Anthropologist*, XLVII (1945), 540–553.

proceeded on the road to gratification with more emphasis on aesthetic means and with more realization that aesthetic experience itself was an important kind of gratification.

Despite this negative data, there are still many actions and objects in Fang life that provoke a posture of aesthetic criticism. I have examined some of them, notably the ancestor figures and the behavior of a mature man. And of course aesthetic principles may be in operation in Fang culture even though no deliberate and overt attempt is made on the part of the culture carriers to apply or make out these principles. In fact, instead of asking, To what extent do aesthetic principles reflect the necessities of social structure? it might rather be stated inversely, To what extent does social structure reflect aesthetic principles? Is society aesthetic preference drawn large?

Conclusion

To such large questions only large answers can be given. The data suggests that what are given in Fang life, what are basic, are two sets of oppositions. One is spatial, right and left, northeast and southwest; the other is qualitative, male and female. Both the social structure and the aesthetic life elaborate on these basic oppositions and create vitality in so doing. This elaboration, however, in both areas is creative, a fashioning in some sense according to what is pleasing. To this extent the social structure is no different than the ancestral figure; it is the expression of aesthetic principles at work. And the fundamental principle at work among the Fang is in doubleness, duality, and opposition lie vitality, in oneness and coincidence, death.

In both aesthetics and the social structure the aim of the Fang is not to resolve opposition and create identity but to preserve a balanced opposition. This is accomplished either through alternation as in the case with complementary filiation or in the behavior of a full man; or it is done by skillful aesthetic composition in the same time and space as is the case with the ancestor statues or cult ritual. This objective is reflected in inter-clan relations. The Fang, like many non-literate people, lived in a state of constant enmity with other clans. However, their object was not that of exterminating each other or otherwise terminating the hostility in favor of one clan or another. The hostility was regarded as a natural condition of social life, and their concern was to keep this enmity in permanent and balanced opposition.[12] So in their aesthetic life, they aimed at a permanent and balanced opposition. In this permanent tension between opposites lay the source of vitality in Fang life. When this balanced arrangement is upset, as it has been by acculturation, then one can only expect that some of the vitality will go out of that life.

---

[12]   This point has been made by Joan Rayfield, "Duality Run Wild," *Explorations*, No. 5 (1955), pp. 54–67.

27

The Cycle and Stagnation of Smells: Pastoralists–Fishermen Relationships in an East African Society

URI ALMAGOR

Smells are daily matters. In some cultures – one might almost call them olfactory cultures – smells have meaning on economic, social, and cosmological levels, serving as a means of classifying the natural and social universe. One such society, in which the notions of "cycle" and "stagnation" of smells come to the fore, is the Dassanetch of Southwest Ethiopia. Among them, as in other pastoral societies of East Africa, the complex relationships between pastoralists and fishermen are characterized by the pastoralists' feelings of superiority, with smell playing an important part in this distinction. In the present paper, attitudes toward the eating of fish are used as the basis for discussing their relationships.

The fifteen thousand or so Dassanetch people inhabit the area north of Lake Turkana on both sides of the Omo River in Southwest Ethiopia. Their mixed economy is based on cattle and small stock pastoralism, flood retreat cultivation, and a little fishing.[1] Fishing is the main economic activity of several hundred people who live near the shores of Lake Turkana. They use crude hooks and spears and sometimes beat the water in the river or in inundated flats to trap fish in nets. Individuals may fish standing in shallow water (See Plate 27.1) or from dugouts (See Plate 27.2). The Dassanetch regard themselves as pastoralists, however. Their social relationships are based on transactions in livestock, and their values, identities, and main ceremonies are all related to, and centered on, cattle.

Pastoralists, Fishermen, and the Eating of Fish

In the different pastoral societies of East Africa, we find one or more of the following attitudes connected with the eating of fish. The Dassanetch, as part of the complex relationships between pastoralists and fishermen,

---

[1] Fishing as a major economic activity is practiced by two small tribal sections (Riele and Elele), and as a marginal occupation by a few individuals from the Inkabelo, Inkoria, and Oro tribal sections. For more details on the pastoral economy of the Dassanetch and the place of fishing in it, see Almagor (1978).

Plate 27.1 [1]: Fishing with a hook and line.

show a combination of all these attitudes. First, there is the taboo against eating fish, usually backed by the belief that eating (or even touching) fish pollutes or harms people, or may harm cattle or the fertility of women (see, for example, Lienhart 1961: 204–205; Huntingford 1969: 109).

A second attitude is that fish are not taboo, but pastoralists do not like fish and rarely eat it. Fish is regarded as an inferior species, and eating it is "not done," just as in many societies one does not eat snakes or certain birds (see, for example, Buxton 1972: 273; Huntingford 1953: 45; Gulliver and Gulliver 1953: 62).

A third option is for fish to be eaten occasionally. A purely pastoral way of life usually is not sufficient for survival, and pastoralists must supplement their diet with other products, including fish, if it is available. In this situation, the relationship between pastoralists and fishermen is a reciprocal one. In times of want, such as dry months or a drought, pastoralists often eat fish and even engage in fishing (see, for example, Buxton 1973: 206; Lewis 1972: 34–36, 130; Driberg 1922; Evans-Pritchard 1940: 70, 82; Spencer 1973: 216–217; Huntingford 1953: 61).[2]

Although objects of taboo are not always regarded with distaste, nor are distasteful objects always or even commonly subjected to taboo, one can see the logic in combinations of the first and second attitudes, or of the second and third, which may be found in different societies. One may reasonably assume that the

---

[2]   A. Khazanov (personal communication) tells me that the nomads of the Eurasian steppes, semideserts, and deserts never consider fish as "forbidden food"; the variations in consuming it depended on local conditions and the need to supplement the pastoralists' diet (see also Khazanov 1984: 42–43).

Plate 27.2 [2]: Fishing from a dugout in the Omo River

distaste will be set aside when dairy food is in short supply and survival is at stake. Even when all three attitudes are found in one society, they may not be contradictory, for one can envisage a near-disaster situation when eating fish becomes the norm. It is somewhat puzzling, however, to find that even when dairy food is plentiful the taboo against fish is sometimes breached, as it is among the Dassanetch, and that pastoralists eat fish and engage in reciprocal relations with fishermen. The subject is complicated, not only because contradictions among ideas permeate these relationships, but because these contradictions are connected to the theme of hierarchy and exchange, as expressed in different frames of reference (the category, the group, and social relationship) and at different levels (the cultural, the social, and the economic) that may be independent of one another.

One way of ascribing meaning to these frames of reference, the contradiction of the ideas underlying the hierarchical relationships between the two groups and their coexistence, is through the analysis of smells. In analyzing these issues through the notion of smells I take into consideration the specific qualities of odors that illuminate the complexity of the relationships. The central subject of this paper is inclusion and exclusion in the exchange relations between two groups. Inevitably, this will bring to the fore such issues as contradiction of principles, relationships of avoidance and exchange, and complementarity in economic activities. I will attempt to interweave these issues and explain them through the variable of smells, taking into consideration the specific qualities of odors that illuminate the complexity of the relationships.

Because smell has qualities of both the actual and the ideal (e.g., the many metaphors and expressions that are connected with smell), it can serve as a device for stereotyping groups of people. Thus, when odors are associated with certain people or groups of people, they become an expression par excellence of differences; the very mention of smell in relation to a particular ethnic or occupational group has clear implications of avoidance and contempt.

Second, although we cannot grade smells on a universal scale as culturally independent variables (see Osborne 1977), all cultures distinguish between "attractive" and "repellent" smells. Moreover, although cultures may differ widely as to which smells they classify as being close to one pole or the other, these smells can symbolize social extremes or groups that are considered to represent oppositions. In this polar distinction there is a general tendency to classify those smells which have to do with creation, growth, and maturation in nature, such as smells of freshness, flowers, and so on, as lying close to the "positive" pole. On the other hand, smells associated with decay in nature, such as bodily wastes and corruption, are close to the "negative" pole.

Third, the meaning attributed to a specific smell derives from the association of a smell with a specific context. Odors are thus classified within a framework of meaning in which there are dynamic relationships and associations between natural objects and or situations, and cultural contexts. This association is conventionalized to such a degree that "... just as an odor permeates a place, an occasion, a situation, so the context comes to permeate the odor-sign and becomes inseparably part of it" (Gell 1977: 30–31). Meaning is not referred to here as the way in which people understand their world and communicate about it with one another, but in the sense of reference – due to the constitution and interrelation of two phenomena – smell on the one hand and object, person, relations, group, and so forth on the other.

Fourth, smells can help in "mapping" divisions and processes in society and nature. Smells rarely are objects in themselves, but rather a medium or a device to point out the state of an object that has undergone a process of change or moved from one location to another between the poles. (I refer here to Lévi-Strauss, who mentioned smell, in passing, in the context of the "Culinary Triangle" – as a means to identify the stage of the transformation from the raw to the cooked, from nature to culture.)

Fifth, odors are regarded as mutable. They come and go, and thereby draw our attention to cyclic processes in nature. Note, however, that there is no cycle of smell as such; rather, smells are manifestations or signs of other cycles and phenomena in nature and culture. But the attribution of value to the sources of these manifestations in the form of idioms and in terms of smells has a great significance for the study of various facets of the role of smell in the relationship between various social groups.

All told, smell comes into being, serves as a vehicle for an awareness of an object or situation, and fades away. In this process, smell has an elusive quality, for smell points to accessibility to objects or of a possible change or shift of boundaries. But when a smell has evaporated, what has in fact escaped? And what is the difference between a smell that evaporates and one that lingers? Where does the smell go? To say that it comes from nature, undergoes a cultural process, and returns to nature is too general. What we can do is, tentatively, to link the above five points and see whether they carry us further. If the meaning of smells is culturally constructed but falls under diametrically different classifications of "good" and "bad" smells associated with growth and decay in nature, and is closely associated with different cultural contexts for which they become typical, then smells can help to explain intergroup relations or, in the case under discussion, the exchange relations between pastoralists and fishermen through their respective association with various phenomena in nature.

It should be noted, however, that the central subject of this paper is inclusion and exclusion in the exchange relations between two groups. Inevitably, it will bring to the fore several issues, such as contradiction of principles, relationships of avoidance and exchange, and their complementarity in economic activities. nonetheless, the direction of analysis is an attempt to interweave all of the above issues and explain them through the variable of smells.

Pastoralists, Fishermen, and their Smells

As pastoralists, the Dassanetch are well aware of the crucial importance of smell for cattle; almost every aspect of the cattle's lives is associated with smell. To give just a few examples: there is the cow-calf relationship, in which the cow starts lactating only after smelling her newborn calf, and if a calf dies, the cow must smell the stuffed carcass in order to give milk; the mutual smelling when the cow and calf

Plate 27.3 [3]: Ritual smearing of manure.

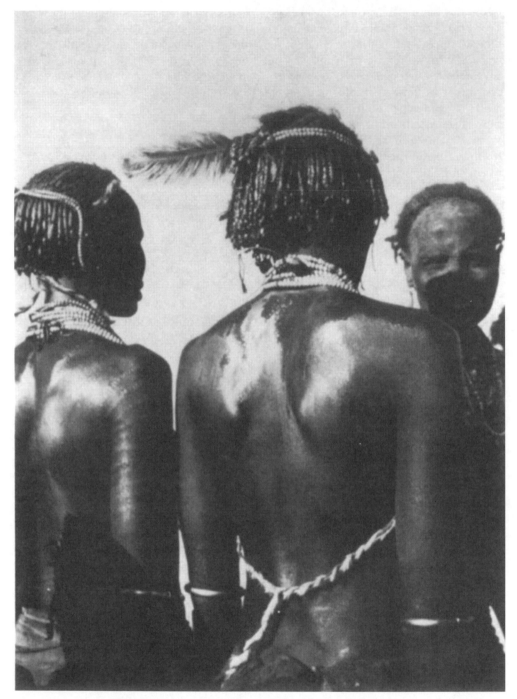

Plate 27.4 [4]: Dassanetch women with *ghee* shining on their shoulders.

Plate 27.5 [5]: Milking in a dry-season cattle camp. (Note the shining *ghee* on the shoulders of the standing girl.)

meet after being separated all day long while the cow was grazing; the bull that sniffs the cow before service; and the ability of cattle to smell and find good grazing grounds or an invisible source of water, or to alert to the presence of predators at night, all from quite a distance.

Perhaps it is the function of smell in the various activities of cattle and the identification of pastoralists with their livestock that makes the Dassanetch so aware of smells and, consequently, of the important role of odors in various domains of their lives.

Body smells and body decorations are two fundamental elements that express a man's personal identity; and it is only natural that pastoralists, whose identification with their livestock is so strong, should decorate themselves with bones and hides of cattle and smell like cattle. This is not so much because they work with cattle or spend a good deal of their time near cattle, but mainly because they anoint themselves with the body products of cattle. They often wash their hands in cattle urine; men smear manure on their bodies (See Plate 27.3) to advertise the fertility of their

Plate 27.6 [6]: A fishermen's settlement.

herds; and nubile girls and fertile women smear *ghee* on their shoulders, heads, hair, and bosoms to ensure fertility (See Plates 27.4 and 27.5). But most important, the Dassanetch explicitly say that the smell of *ghee* serves to attract men and is the "perfume," so to speak, of women.

Naturally, the smell of everything connected with cattle is considered good – "naturally" because for the Dassanetch cattle is the "perfect animal," not only because cattle is considered a divine gift, but also due to the centrality of cattle in their lives. It embodies three spheres: subsistence, social relationships through transactions, and values in rituals. But the smell of cattle differs from other good smells – such as flowers,[3] lush grazing, dew, or the land after rainfall – in that the smell of cattle is what distinguishes the Dassanetch, as pastoralists, from other people. This distinction is pointed out in comparison with other people along the Omo River who engage in agriculture (e.g., the Murle and Kere), or neighboring pastoral tribes such as the Turkana and the Gabbra, or tribal sections and groups among the Dassanetch who engage mainly in fishing. All these, the pastoral Dassanetch say, smell differently from themselves. While reference to the smells of all the above peoples is in terms of the different use of pastoral or agricultural products, both of which are considered good smells, the smell of

---

[3] Most Dassanetch plants are odorless. The few exceptions are Pluchea dioscordis, Cymbopogon schoenathus, Basilicum polystachyon, and Acacia brevispica Harms, whose flowers are odorous (see Carr 1977: 301–306). I am grateful to A. Danin for his help in this matter.

those engaged in fishing is considered bad, almost to the point of revulsion.

Furthermore, the reference to the bad smell of fish and fishermen is not merely at the level of statements or general notions of differences; it is also sometimes visibly expressed by the attitudes of the pastoralists toward fishermen. I first noticed this when I saw some pastoralists walking by the fishermen's huts on the shores of Lake Turkana (See Plate 27.6); they held their noses until they left the area. Throughout my fieldwork the pastoralists referred to fishermen as *den fedudukha* (i.e., stinking). The interesting thing here is that the attitude toward fishermen rests on the belief that their bad smell is "contagious" and can bring disaster to cattle, or, more specifically, can jeopardize the fertility of one's herd.

This belief derives from the notion that fish are antithetical to cattle. While the basis for the creation of cattle's life and continuity is dependent on the sexual act that a bull performs on cows, there is no similar concept of a visible act attributed to fish. Fish are considered to exist in a kind of inexhaustible, asexual reservoir. Furthermore, smell is specifically applied to the sexual act in cattle in the way the Dassanetch describe the way a bull approaches a cow. "No one teaches a bull how to perform the sexual act and where to insert his sexual organ," they say. "The bull is led to the right place by smelling the vagina of the cow." With fish, they add, there is no sexual act, since fish lack genitalia and also have no olfactory organ.[4]

This distinction between fertility of cattle on the one hand and lack of fertility in fish on the other is expressed in the opposition between plenty as being a divine gift attributed to cattle that smell good, vis-à-vis the notion of poor people (*gal dies*), which in Dassanetch

language is the same word for people whose life centers around fish, who stink. Furthermore, this opposition between the two is expressed in many restrictions in daily life and sayings, all of which are intended to deep the sphere of fertility symbolized by the bull and focused on its performance away from fishermen and fish. Three features concerning fertility are noticeable here.

First, although fishermen may possess cattle (a point elaborated on below), they do not keep their cattle near their homes, nor do they herd them, but keep them with pastoralist friends or their affines.[5] But most of all, fishermen are barred by custom from owning a bull, and thus must rely on the services of the bulls of their pastoralist bond partners or affines. Even so, such services should not take place when a fisherman is nearby and watching. Furthermore, Dassanetch people often chase away visiting fishermen from their livestock enclosures. Dassanetch informants explain that the bad smell of fishermen can infect the cattle – for if such a bad smell "catches" a cow, the smell of fish will deter the bull.

Second, the Dassanetch say of women who are past their reproductive period that their body is like *duna*, i.e., dry as the third growth of sorghum crops, and that their vagina smells like fish (*nyegude le at beh*). Actually, the reference is to old women, and more than referring to actual smell it expresses a link between the lack of fertility of both old women and fish and implies that such women do not attract men sexually.

Third, although fishermen may consume milk, they are prohibited by custom from making or using *ghee*. *Ghee*, I was told by my informants, is "connected to fertility, and fishermen should not touch it." My informants were referring not only to the liquid itself, but

---

[4]   As a matter of fact, fish have a well-developed olfactory organ, which is naturally adapted to an underwater environment (see Wright 1982: 182).
[5]   Cf. Evans-Pritchard (1940: 70).

Plate 27.7 [7]: A vessel made of cattle hide in which *ghee* is kept.

also to the special vessel in which *ghee* is kept, which bears the symbol of fertility (See Plate 27.7).[6]

In all these, an offensive odor is an invisible sign of fish and fishermen, which are considered antithetical to and a polluting category to cattle and pastoralists, and thus are the objects of taboo.

Besides the taboo against fish and fishermen, the Dassanetch pastoralists express revulsion at the very idea of eating fish. Yet, despite the taboo, they do eat fish, for example, when they visit their fishermen affines or part-

ners, mainly during the dry season.[7] When I asked why they eat food that might harm them and their cattle, they replied that since the food was proffered as a gift, they might insult their hosts by refusing it. Thus the answer was not in terms of need for food, but in terms of an inability to refuse a gift. Indeed, answers were not always consistent. When I asked pastoralists who were eating fish while visiting a fisherman which was polluting, the fish itself or its smell, they answered, "True, the smell is bad, but the food is good," suggesting a distinction between the smell and its source. Another time an informant told me the fish itself is taboo regardless of whether or not it has a bad smell. Other informants stated that one cannot distinguish between fish and its smell, for the nature of fish is that it has a bad smell, and that sometimes this smell becomes "very bad" (*sum den*). Another time, pastoralists who were eating fish said they could not smell anything bad.[8] I mention all these answers not to show confusion among informants, but to point out different levels of association between objects and contexts, and hence different interpretations of the fisherman–pastoralist relationship.

Eating fish occasionally is seen as totally different from a situation of prolonged drought when dairy food is not enough for subsistence. Then almost the entire population of pastoralists may resort to fishing. here the raison d'être is the shortage of food; the Dassanetch say that such a situation is of "another sort" (*hela takha*): not only is the taboo against fish lifted, but the bad smell of fish or fishermen is not an issue.

As already noted, there are no taboos on interaction with fishermen. Throughout the

---

[6] Cf. an interesting similarity among the Dinka, where the contrast between women and fishing is expressed by the notions of "women as sources of life, and the prototype of masters of the fishing-spear as a dispenser of 'life'" (Lienhardt 1961: 205).

[7] It should be noted that during the dry season most pastoralists stay near the settlements and houses of fishermen, because at that time of year the pastoralists return to the sources of water near the lake and the river.

[8] Perhaps they were referring to what is known as "olfactory fatigue," which occurs when the receptors become saturated with a certain smell; this may explain why one can tolerate an unpleasant smell after an initial aversion to it.

Plate 27.8 [8]: A dugout with fishermen guiding cattle across the Omo River.

year pastoralists may borrow fishing equipment (See Plate 27.1) from their fishermen friends. Also, pastoralists often ask fishermen to guide cattle across the Omo River with their dugouts (See Plate 27.8). But most of all the interaction between the two groups is expressed in the fact that pastoralists marry the daughters of fishermen and thus become their affines. However, in a society whose values are predominantly pastoral, and where cattle transactions serve as the main mechanism of establishing affinal ties and bond partnership, marrying a fisherman's daughter or entering into a bond with a man whose source of livelihood is considered polluting is somehow incompatible and needs an explanation.

Two points concerning pastoralist–fishermen intermarriages should be noted. First, it is a one-sided marriage. Pastoral men marry fisherwomen, but not vice versa. The Dassanetch say that no man will give his daughter to a fisherman. Indeed, throughout my field work I did not encounter even one such case. Second, the daughters of fishermen usually are married through betrothal (one form of marriage, out of four). However, unlike the betrothal procedure among pastoralists, where a girl's betrothal (at the end of the first or the beginning of the second decade of her life) is only an agreement to establish marriage in the future, the betrothal of a fisherman's daughter involves the removal of the girl to the household of the groom's father, or father's brother. Here, the Dassanetch say, she has many years to get rid of the smell of fish, and becomes an ordinary "pastoral girl," or as the Dassanetch put it (by then), "she knows cattle" (*gwo ok*).[9]

---

[9]   *Prima facie* such a marriage seems to be an advantage, for the groom is not under constant pressure to transfer

Obviously, such a marriage in due course brings cattle to a fisherman as bridewealth, when it is paid. Dassanetch men transfer bridewealth gradually – usually not more than several beasts each year. Although this process may take a long time to complete, a fisherman may nevertheless accumulate a small herd of cattle.

Two restrictions, however, significantly limit the possible benefits that a fisherman may gain from his own cattle. First, since a fisherman does not keep his cattle, he does not usually enjoy the products of his livestock. Although he goes from time to time to the cattle camps to bring milk to his family, this journey involves humiliation that always reminds a fisherman of his low and marginal status. Young herders tend to laugh at him and refer to him as being "smelly." He is given milk taken from his own cows by one of the herders (usually an affine).

Even this is done with some customary restriction. A fisherman does not enter a live-stock camp on his own initiative: he stands at a distance and waits until one of the herders brings him milk. Furthermore, when one of the fisherman's beasts suddenly dies, he is entitled to take and use the meat. Yet what happens in actuality is that the fishermen usually are told about the incident relatively late, often after chunks of the meat have already been taken away by other people. The infuriated fisherman has no choice but to take home the little meat that is left. Since fish-ermen do not participate in ritual meat eating – that is, where meat is roasted and when only men may take part – he and his household, and perhaps some neighbors, may eat the meat in the only way available to them, which is also the way women eat meat, namely, boiled.

Second, a fisherman must, like any pastoralist, undergo the main ceremony in a man's life. This is the *dimi* ceremony, which every man who has fathered a daughter some eight to ten years earlier must undergo. The purpose of this ceremony is to bring the girl to be blessed for her future marriage and fertility. A father undergoes this ceremony just once, when his eldest daughter is at the appropriate age (i.e., before her first menstruation), and the blessing conferred on her is extended to all his daughters, even those not yet born. If, as noted, such a girl may marry a pastoralist, she obviously needs the formal religious blessing; otherwise she will not be able to marry a pastoralist.

Fishermen must undergo the *dimi* cere-mony, but many pastoralists are not keen on participating, let alone undergoing it, along-side fishermen. A situation that may throw light on this attitude occurred during the cere-mony of 1969. Rain, usually welcomed by pastoralists, is feared as a bad omen during the *dimi* ceremony, which takes place at the height of the dry season. In Dassanetch concepts rain is associated with menstruation, and when heavy rain suddenly fell during the *dimi* cere-mony, people said it was because the daughter of a certain fisherman was too old, implying that she had already had her first menstruation before the ceremony and suggesting that the fisherman had disrupted the order of events in nature.

One of the salient features of the *dimi* cere-mony is the lavish slaughter of livestock and the entertainment of many guests;[10] after the ceremony, which lasts about three weeks, a man is left with virtually no livestock. A fisher-man who undergoes this ceremony may lose his entire herd in a ceremony that is intended

bridewealth, and when he does, the cattle returns to him and his family. However, bridewealth is transferred gradually and is not onerous, so that even poor people can afford it. Most people with whom I talked preferred not to have affinal relations with fishermen. This is in spite of the fact that a person's social identity is determined mainly through his or her father. Such a marriage is associated with the notion of "poor people" and carries a certain stigma. Nevertheless, such intermarriages do take place (for more details see Almagor 1978: ch. 7, 8).

[10] A fisherman can, of course, eat roasted fish, but he can participate in the *dimi* ceremony and serve meat to his guests because boiled meat is the only form of meat consumed during that ceremony.

to bring fertility to other people and to which his own daughter may contribute. Why, then – since they do not keep them, are unable to accumulate herds, and most of all are deprived of their dairy products – do fishermen need cattle at all? Subsistence is not their major gain. For the fishermen, cattle serve other purposes, mainly in social relationships with pastoralists. In other words, cattle invested in different bonds and received from and returned to affines is the fisherman's only means of establishing links with pastoral Dassanetch society, whose values and identity are theirs as well.

In this connection one wonders how fishermen perceive their own smell and what their attitude is toward the smell of cattle. The smell of the body products of cattle cannot be said "objectively" to be more or less pleasant than the smell of fish. It is rather the meaning and the social context that the Dassanetch attach to cattle and fish which cause them to perceive these smells as they do. In both cases, fish and cattle, smells are associated with separate spaces and different social groups. Further, although cattle herders are the prestigious majority of the people and are not confined to a certain location, there is another, more fundamental difference: paradoxically, to any outside observer, the personal smell of herders is much stronger and more evocative than that of fishermen. Herders, unlike fishermen, renew the smell with which they are associated by smearing manure and *ghee* on their bodies on frequent ritual occasions, at which time the idea of plenty and fertility is symbolically expressed. On the other hand, fishermen enter the river and the lake more often than any other Dassanetch, and the smell of their bodies changes. Nevertheless, the Dassanetch concept is that the fishermen permanently stink. Here the stinking smell of fish is associated with specific occupational, social, and

ecological contexts and particularly by a cultural meaning that attributes to fish the notion of nonfertility and independence of cyclical changes in nature.

Fishermen are aware that the smell of fish is unpleasant to pastoralists. Obviously, fishermen will not say that they stink, for smell, whether of a group or of a person, is a matter of one's identity.[11] But the degree to which fishermen have institutionalized pastoral values is not so much in that they themselves like the smell of cattle, but mainly in that they are aware that their bodies and clothes may smell of fish and may cause harm to the fertility of cattle, for, as Douglas and Wildavsky noted, ". . . society produces its own selected view of natural environment, a view which influences its choice of danger" (1982: 8).

Elusive and Permanent Smells

There are, apart from fish, various sources of bad smells. First are objects connected with acts, or rather outputs, of the human body – feces, urine, and intestinal gas. According to Dassanetch concepts not every substance exuded by the human body need necessarily produce a bad smell. Thus menstrual blood and semen are considered to have no smell, or a neutral one, and according to Dassanetch views, the best time for a woman to conceive is during her menstruation. (This concept is significant, for, as will be shown below, the Dassanetch do not conceive the bad smell of a person as emanating from something inherent in his body. The fact that the two substances that "create" a person, according to the Dassanetch, have no smell should be seen in connection with the concept of the lack of body smells.) Second are those things which are rotten, mainly human and animal cadavers. Third is the smell of burning. Although not

---

[11] Note a remark by Wittgenstein: "Nobody can truthfully say of himself that he is filth. Because if I do say it, though it can be true in a sense, this is not a truth by which I can be penetrated; otherwise I should either have to go mad or change myself" (1984: 32e).

considered a bad smell, it shares some of the qualities with the above two. Smoke rises from two different sources – the burning of dry fields so that they may serve as a more nutritious grazing area the following year, and the smell of burned wood either for cooking or for a ritual meal where meat is roasted. Although burning takes place throughout the year, the burning of fields and the eating of meat occur mainly during the dry season.

What is most important for our discussion is the Dassanetch view that bad smells, which ascend to the sky like smoke, are invisible; both bad smells and smoke are absorbed in the clouds, which later produce rain. Asked if the smell of fish also ascends to the clouds, they were disturbed by the very question and answered, "No, rain is for cattle; the smell of fish stays with them all the time." Bad smells accumulate mainly in the dry seasons, which are followed by two rainy seasons (March–April and October–November), but there is no direct cause-and-effect relationship between bad smells and rains. it is more a notion of natural transfiguration, similar to the way Walens describes smoke as "visible transfer of material from the world of humans to the world of the spirits and the heavens" (1981: 9).

However, the Dassanetch do not conceive of rain as depending on bad smells and smoke in the sense that little or no rain implies more bad smells and burning and hence more clouds. Rather, rain depends on the will of God. Indeed, when droughts occur they refer to God as preventing the rains, and not to the lack of smoke and bad smells.

The Dassanetch say that rain, like menstrual blood (which is called *ir ma dezit*, i.e., "the rain of a woman"), has no smell. But rains bring the revival and growth of grazing grounds on which cattle depend, and with it good smell, thereby closing a cycle.

By and large, the cycle of smells among the Dassanetch accompanies the cycle in nature where growth, decline, and death represent a process that starts with good smells that derive from nature, undergo cultural process, and in due course change into bad smells and eventually disappear in nature to reappear in the form of good smells accompanying a new growth. But the above examples point to a more complicated structure of relations among three cycles – of man, cattle, and nature – which on the one hand are formally independent of each other, but on the other hand (and in reality) are interdependent. Smell may be seen here as an element that links these three cycles, hence its importance in the pastoral cycle. Let us look at these in greater detail.

The first is the cycle of man. A man is born into a household and at a certain stage of his life, when he matures, he marries, leaves his natal household, and establishes an independent neolocal one, at which time he withdraws his herd from his father's household. Thus the developmental cycle of a man's household depends not only on the regular cycle of rains and growth in nature but also on the cycle of growth and replacement of livestock. The second cycle, that of cattle, obviously depends first on the cyclical events of rains and the growth of grass, and also on the husbandry of men, who establish households. Finally, the cycle in nature depends both on man – who in the cultural process produces burning and bad smells – and on livestock, which by grazing enable growth of new pastures, and through burning becomes edible objects.

In these interdependent cycles, cattle are the intermediary element, for they stand between nature and culture and also belong to both. Cattle products serve the three cycles – manure helps to fertilize the land and milk is consumed by calves and by people. The dual position of cattle as belonging to both nature and culture is reflected in the smells they produce. Their own smell and smells of their body excretions are considered good, similar to those that come from nature. On the other hand, cattle embody the basic cultural values and serve as metaphors for the social processes; in death, however, they leave the cultural realm and their carcasses produce a bad smell. But there is more: in the cyclical relations between man and cattle, a sequence of reversals occurs, the output of one serving as the input of the other. Thus the output of man and culture in general, which is expressed in bad smells and smoke, bring, after their transfiguration, rain and the growth of grass for cattle; the output of cattle, mainly milk, serves as the input for man, and the attractive smell of *ghee* is used to enhance fertility. Thus smells bring to the fore the notion of fertility and the cultural significance of the identity of man with cattle.

In these cycles smell not only is a powerful metaphor of transformation from cultural objects to natural ones in the forms of bad smells, smoke, and clouds; it is also a meeting point between natural instincts and cultural continuity, for the Dassanetch say that both bulls and men are attracted to their female counterparts by smell.

The association of smells with cattle and fish represent for the Dassanetch two realms, and through their contrast the pastoralist man is aware of his proper relations with nature. One realm is of good smells, which derive from nature, clearly connected with fertility and depending on the cyclical order in nature. The other realm is of bad smells, for bad smells inevitably accompany the continuity of social life. The question is, how does society handle such a phenomenon of bad and unpleasant smells that are an integral part of its existence and cannot be avoided?

The way the Dassanetch deal with this phenomenon is through the cyclical notion of smells, which conceptually and dialectically turns "bad" smells into "good" ones through the mediating link of nature. Nature for the Dassanetch is the ultimate receptacle of bad smells, and it is also the source of good smells. The cycle of smell among the Dassanetch is expressed in the transfiguration of smoke and

bad smells into clouds. In other tribal societies this transfiguration takes other forms, but basically it has the same meaning. The underlying principle is that fresh nature in the raw and the newness of growth follows the rotten, the overripe, and the burnt. The question is how the transformation from the latter to the former takes place. The cultural meaning given to the dematerialization of substances that are the sources of bad smells in the cyclical process of recreation (e.g., spreading feces and menstrual blood on the fields, or the burial of the rotten and decayed for the purpose of growth)[12] indicates a concept that the forces in nature make the transformation. Thus the evaporation of bad smell is in itself an act of transformation – for the evaporation of bad smell *severs the association* among the object, the source or the context, and the smell with which it is identified, thus enabling new growth that is accompanied by a new good smell.

Pastoralists are obsessed with periodic change. Absence of change is feared, for it may bring overgrazing, shortage of food, and hardship. The cycle of nature is never safe, however, for there is a weak link at the point where various elements in culture and in nature are ripe, used, rotten, and blighted to their change to a fresh beginning. Attributing the change to a natural transfiguration of smells reaffirms the concept of change as inherent to social life, much as different smells accompany the changing seasons and conditions of pastoral existence.

As noted, however, there is a spectrum of bad smell. For the Dassanetch, the extreme cultural form is the stench of fish.[13] Fish is part of nature but, to them, is not connected to fertility nor dependent on any cycle in nature, not even that of the ebb and flow of the river and lake. Thus, unlike other bad smells, which come and go, stimulate awareness, and

---

[12]   Cf. Panoff (1970).

[13]   It is "cultural," for the stench of hyena for the Dassanetch is even worse, but the hyena belongs to the realm of nature.

evaporate, the bad smell of fish is a kind of stagnation and is permanently connected with the *gal dies* people.

Smells and Boundaries

Smells, as noted, are part of man's experience in different contexts, and he organizes various odors by attaching them to various elements of his experience within a framework of meaning. Since smells and contexts become inseparable and one permeates the other, the implication of an enduring bad smell that is identified with a certain group is of a permanent context, which stands against cycles in nature. However, the features of smell as a temporary evocative element, elusive and evaporating, are connected with the diversity, overlapping, and changing of experiences that a person undergoes in his daily activities and in which smells play a role as one of many phenomenological components. Hence an inevitable contrast between a permanent smell associated with a certain group and other smells associated with changing contexts comes to the fore and provides the first step in explaining the meaning of these two realms.

Several points should be noted here. First, the difficulty the Dassanetch have in specifying what afflicts – the smell or the fish – can be interpreted in terms of the close association of a smell with a context, so much so that it is difficult to distinguish between them.

Second, smell attracts attention not only to the manner in which it is associated with an object. Its specific meaning, in the whole framework of meaning, is also valued when the object is placed or arranged vis-à-vis similar objects and activities. A smell that does not change, to paraphrase Eliade's term, is "eternally present" and seems to contradict the laws of nature, of rhythm or periodic changes, of growth and creation, and of smells that come, evaporate, and return. Furthermore, the cyclical recurrence of smells asserts the notion of renewal, changeability, and

new beginning, and gives the illusion of hope, accessibility, mobility, and temporal changes. But a permanent smell identified with a certain group of people maintains its original meaning even in changing circumstances. Its exposure to different social contexts does not become merged with other smells; it simply indicates that it is out of context, attracting attention to the source of the smell and, by allusion, to the object. It creates disharmony with the immediate environment when emitted and hence evokes most strongly the dividing social boundaries. Unlike fading smells, such a permanent smell underscores the absoluteness of social boundaries. If a smell represents an object that is not subject to renewal, the tendency is to spatially and socially segregate it, allowing as little contact as possible with other objects that can potentially be transformed.

Third, the avoidance of relationships with people who are said to exude a permanent bad odor is often expressed in the notion that their smell can afflict and disturb the cosmic and/or natural forces of change and transformation.

All told, there are two kinds of bad smells. First is a bad smell that is part of nature, of the order of change, and is structured in space and in time. For pastoralists, smell is connected with their cyclical conception of time that permeates their annual activities. In a cyclical concept there is no sharp polarization of "good" and "bad" – bad is relative and temporary, for there is a dialectical relation between them, and time will turn bad into good. Here there is no notion of a polluting smell. Second is the bad smell of fishermen that is totally different from the above bad smells. Fishermen are engaged in the same production and consumption without periodic changes. The pastoralists' conception of time seems to be of no relevance to them. Furthermore, it can be said that fishermen are "outside the framework of time," or – to use Geertz's (1966) term – they are in a state of "detemporalized time." But the reason why the smell of fish is considered polluting does not derive from fish being "anomalous" in Douglas's (1966) concepts, but from certain qualities that render fish a specific entity, antithetical to cattle: fish defy the basic order underlying the pastoralists' worldview.

But once the rhythm of nature is disturbed by prolonged droughts or extended periods of inundation and floods (both of which cause food shortages), the pastoralists step outside the periodicity structure of their socio-economic activities and join those who are "outside the framework of time" and engage in fishing and become (although temporarily) stinking people.

The apparent paradox here lies in the selective attitudes toward nature; the cycle of nature on which pastoralists depend is tenuous, but positively sanctioned, while a reservoir of plenty in nature is negated. These contrasting attitudes are expressed in smells that here serve as an ideology, so to speak, for the supremacy of pastoral people over the nonpastoralists in their midst. The good smell is attributed to those who are affected by the "natural rhythm," no matter how unpredictable it may be. Fish and fishermen are a constant reminder to pastoralists of the reversibility of the natural rhythm and hence a potential threat to their well-being. Fishermen threaten the cosmological cycle through their polluting smell.

Conclusion

The hierarchical relationship between the two Dassanetch groups, whose relations are based on complex contradictory principles and taboos, as well as complementarity and economic exchange, can be analyzed in Dumont's terms. His concept of hierarchy as the relation between the encompassing and the contrary is compatible with the Dassanetch pastoralists (superiors) who include in their social world the fishermen (inferiors).

Central to Dumont's argument is the thesis that in hierarchical opposition the superior

encompasses the inferior at one level, but that at another level relations may be reversed. Among the Dassanetch, we see this in the shift from a pastoral way of life to fishing during a severe drought. Then pastoralists become, in a sense, subordinated to fishermen; they must rely on the fishermen's knowledge and techniques. However, although the relationship between pastoralists and fishermen includes elements of pollution and nonpollution, the purity–impurity basis of the encompassing and the encompassed is far from an exhaustive explanation of the whole and its hierarchical levels.

The Dassanetch holistic idea of order is based on pastoral values. Although it includes both bad and good smells, this order does not include the polluting smell of fish and fishermen, who are antithetical to pastoral values and thus tantamount to disorder. The polluting smell can disrupt the cycles of nature, men, and cattle; it represents stepping outside the framework of time and space to "something different." Dumont alludes to the situation of being outside society (1980: n. 96c) when he discusses, in connection with world renunciation, "the dichotomy . . . between cultivated or inhabited space and wild space, 'forest' or jungle, the village and hermitage (*asrama*) in which dwells the man who has left society." Allen's (1985: 27) point in this matter is even more succinct: "The ambiguity as to whether . . . 'others' are inside or outside the boundaries of the cosmos . . . corresponds to the wider problem of whether or not Order embraces Chaos. . . ." Indeed, it seems that this issue can be dealt with through the concepts of inclusion and exclusion, as Apthrope (1984) did in summarizing his work on hierarchy and opposition. But in order to see the significance of the dialectics of inclusion and exclusion of fishermen in the pastoralists' world, I suggest that we incorporate the notions of category, group, and relationships as distinctly expressed in the pastoralists' attitudes toward fishermen.

The distinction among the three follows,

more or less, the one made by Witherspoon (1975: 37). A category exists at the cultural level – it is a set of conceptually defined elements that share a common theme. It is part of the taxonomies people use in classifying their world. A group exists at the social level and it refers to ". . . an aggregate of real persons which make decisions, take collective actions, and/or hold property" and often share distinct territory, way of life, and identity. Relationships also exist at the social level. They are based on individual interests and alliances and different levels of exchange. Relationships, as Witherspoon argued, may exist independently of category and group. However, unlike Witherspoon, whose categories and groups are based on descent relationship, it is often the other way around when nondescent relationships are at stake, that is, relationships derive from the notions of category and group, and thereby are characterized and limited by them. Thus, among the Dassanetch, these three notions do not merely coexist at different levels that could be juxtaposed; they assume different realities in the relations either between people or between people and cosmic powers.

As a category, fish and fishermen stand outside the compatibility of the social and the natural orders, both of which are based on a cyclical principle of fertility. The polluting stagnant smell of fish and fishermen gives ideological expression to the category of fish and fishermen as being excluded from that order, but at the same time it notes that the smell constitutes a potential threat to the process of fertility on which that cyclical order is based. It is smell that delineates the two categories by fending off and creating a conceptual separation from anything that has to do with fish. In other words, smell gives the taboo against fish a supernatural dimension and it should be seen in terms of the unambiguous, distinct relations that the two sections (pastoralists and fishermen) have with nature and cosmic powers.

While fish and fishermen as a category are excluded from the pastoralists' order, they are included as a semiautonomous group of persons at the periphery of society. The prominent feature of such inclusion is the very fact that pastoralist men marry fishermen's daughters, so that some of the girls who are the potential basis for the fishermen's demographic growth are constantly taken out to be the wives of pastoralists. Thus fishermen remain a small group, unable to grow and subordinated to pastoralists. Furthermore, as an outside group they may share some of the pastoralists' values, and indeed are permitted to possess cattle. But here again they cannot fully enjoy the benefits that other pastoralists gain from their herds. The attitude toward fishermen as a group is expressed in describing them as "stinking." Yet pastoralists cannot deny the fishermen's dignity and the usefulness of their function, thus acknowledging their autonomy.

As to relationships, one can find a range of attitudes from disgust to toleration, along with personal ties, mutual visits, and eating together, as well as avoidance. All of these coexist in a setting of contradictions, in which (a) although fish are antithetical to cattle, fishermen may own cattle as long as young pastoralists herd their livestock; (b) fish and fishermen are perceived as a potential threat to fertility, yet fishermen's daughters are taken as wives; (c) fishermen, despite their association with fish (lack of fertility), undergo a ceremony whose raison d'être is to bring fertility to pastoralists; (d) fishermen are considered to stink, but in the dry season many pastoralists visit them in their villages; (e) fish are considered to have a bad smell and are the object of taboo, and yet are eaten by many pastoralists.

These contradictions may be explained along the lines noted above – that the element of relationships derive from the former two elements of category and group. Thus what apparently seem to be opposites are in fact a reference to two different realities that are taken as not being connected, but are simultaneously employed in what Schutz (1962: vol.

1, 219) called "vivid present" – a synchroniza-
tion of interaction between two groups, which
in this case includes the activities, notions, and
attitudes associated with different realities,
although the Dassanetch are not aware of this.
Here lies the significance of the coexistence of
oppositions and contradictions in everyday
life, for taboo and pollution are associated with
a reality that is taken as standing outside the
order of things. Fishermen stand somewhere
between outside "order" in the conceptual
sense and the pastoral order of which they are
a part. Their inclusion in the pastoral order
helps pastoralists to define their own world
and particularly their relation to nature. The
conceptual exclusion of fishermen, however,
delineates the limits of that order and is a
constant reminder of the frailty of its continuation.

Hence, in spite of potential endangering
elements of disorder that exist in time of order,
order and disorder are two distinct forms of
social and cosmic realities, and the former does
not encompass the latter. The significance of
this is accentuated in times of disorder, when
there is no notion of pollution or "stinking."
One may argue here that, obviously, when
almost all the people survive on fish, there
cannot be a rejection of their only source of
food. But there is more to it than that. Fish
endanger the cosmic order, when there is
order. The polluting smell can bring the cycles
in that order to a halt. But when there is no
order, there is nothing left to endanger.
Perhaps the best example of this is when the
drought is over, and pastoralists return to
engage in their routine pastoral activities: they
do not undergo a purification ritual, because
they came from a reality where fish were not
considered taboo and their smell was not
polluting.[14]

The complementarity between that which
encompasses and that which is encompassed
can also be applied to the cycle of smells. Bad
smells encompass good smells that underwent
a *cultural* process, and equally, good smells
encompass bad smells that underwent a *natural* transfiguration. The question that comes
to the fore is, what makes smell an appropriate expression of the complex relationships
between pastoralists and fishermen?

True, to speak of the smell of fish in general
terms without specifying the different kinds of
smells associated with fish or fishermen, let
alone other "bad smells," is to refer to a loose
concept that does not contain the causal relations between smells and objects. However,
from a cultural point of view the causal relation
between smells and pollution, for example, is
not really relevant. For the Dassanetch it is not
entirely clear whether a bad smell is an expression of pollution or of something having
become polluted and inedible because it has a
bad smell. Nor does it matter. To them it is one
context. To insist on defining a particular kind
of smell and its source is to move to another
kind of argument. What is important for our
purpose is that that loose concept, by being
loose, has several qualities that make it an ideal
notion that can explain something or refer to
an object while at the same time that very
notion may be used or be referred to as its
opposite. Smells that are perceived dichoto-
mously as pleasant or unpleasant can translate
any kind of social difference into "oppositions." Furthermore, reference to different
objects or situations in terms of good or bad
smells brings them under the same heading of
logically opposing differences.

Theophrastus (ca. 320 B.C.), who was probably the first person to write an essay on odors,
realized that smells function sometimes as a

---

[14]   There is a certain similarity here with the *dimi* ceremony. *Dimi* is a reality of its own, and differs in time and space
from routine activities and time (for more details see Almagor 1983). *Dimi* stands for fertility, and no one should come
to the ceremony with a spear, let alone engage in killing animals, which act is antithetical to the raison d'être of the ceremony. But the livestock slaughtered during the ceremony to entertain guests is killed *outside* the *dimi* village. When the
men who have just slaughtered the beasts return to the *dimi* village, they do not undergo any act of purification.

distance sense and sometimes as a *contact* sense. Unlike the notion of purity, which internally distinguishes a group vis-à-vis others, the alleged smell that is attributed to a group of people is "imposed," so to speak, by others on that group. Indeed, a certain bad smell serves to draw a line and reject a group of persons to the margins of culture or even to a space that conceptually exists outside society. At the same time the smell of everything connected with cattle enables that very group of fishermen to identify themselves with something beyond their cultural mould.

Two aspects concerning the issue of smell and context stand out. First, the notion of "stinking" fishermen is not an allusion to anything inherent in their bodies or an unremovable part in their biology that causes them to stink. Nor does the reference to them as stinking have to do with the functions of the body. Rather, the idea is that the human body has no smells (the notion that semen and menstrual blood have no smells is a case in point). The smells of both pastoralists and fishermen are cultural smells that are "imposed" on the human body from outside. There is a differentiation here between the smell and its human carrier, which enables the Dassanetch to put a wedge between smell and person and to ascribe it to social circumstances and changing contexts.

Second, a smell identified with a specific context has the quality of a tautology, for there is a vicious circle here – the smell permeates the context and the context permeates the smell. This is why smell can sometimes represent the object of taboo, or be thought of as polluting, and sometimes be assigned to the fish itself without the Dassanetch being able to distinguish between them. Smell and context are assumed to inform about the same thing and can therefore substitute for each other. However, smell is often described in general terms, and as such it contains several different smells that, although closely related, are distinctly different and could be associated with different contexts. Thus with similar smells the principle of signification may refer to different contexts, some of which may be not only unrelated but even contradictory. Therefore, several *culturally* related but physiologically different smells (e.g., manure, milk, *ghee*) may allude to one context of pastoralism. Alternatively, the alleged same smell of fish may "denote," or "stand for" or "refer" to, several contradictory contexts, as the case of including and excluding fishermen indicates. To elaborate on this subject would require another paper. I should, however, note that here lies a possibility for extending the straightforward identification of smell and context to other meanings through the cultural construction of different forms of signification of smells.

I do not imply, of course, that only through the interpretations of the various meanings of smells in the relationships between individuals and groups in one society can we expect to unravel the complexity of these issues, let alone arrive at an overview of the structure of hierarchy and the processes of exchange in that society. Since smells contain elements of both classification (i.e., they are arranged along an axis of polarization) and articulation (through contexts and events), it is worth examining them empirically in other societies as well, for they may provide insights into other realms of social life.

References

Allen, N. J.
1985 "Hierarchical Opposition and Some Other Types of Relation," in R. H. Barnes, D. de Coppet, and R. J. Parkin (eds.), *Contexts and Levels.* Oxford: JASO Occasional Papers, no. 4, pp. 21–32.

Almagor, U.
1978 *Pastoral Partners.* Manchester: Manchester University Press.
1983 "Colours that Match and Clash," *Res* 5, pp. 49–73.

Apthrope, R.
1984 "Hierarchy and Other Social Relations: Some Categorical Logic," in J. –C. Galey (ed.), *Différences, valeurs, hiérarchie: Textes offerts à Louis Dumont.* Paris: Editions de l'Ecole de Hautes Etudes en Sciences Sociales.

Barnes, R. H.
1985 "Hierarchy Without Caste," in R. H. Barnes, D. de Coppet, and R. J. Parkin (eds.), *Contexts and Levels.* Oxford: JASO Occasional Papers, no. 4, pp. 8–20.

Barnes, R. H., D. de Coppet, and R. J. Parkin (eds.)
1985 *Contexts and Levels: Anthropological Essays on Hierarchy.* Oxford: JASO Occasional Papers, no. 4.

Buxton, J.
1973 *Religion and Healing in Mandari.* Oxford: At the Clarendon Press.

Carr, C. J.
1977 *Pastoralism in Crisis.* Chicago: University of Chicago, Department of Geography Research Paper no. 180.

Douglas, M.
1966 *Purity and Danger.* London: Routledge and Kegan Paul.

Douglas, M., and A. Wildavsky
1982 *Risk and Culture.* Berkeley: University of California Press.

Driberg, J. H.
1922 "A Preliminary Account of the Didinga," *Sudan Notes and Records,* vol. 5.

Dumont, L.
1980 *Homo Hierarchicus: The Caste System and Its Implications* (revised English edition). Chicago: University of Chicago Press.

Evans-Pritchard, E. E.
1940 *The Nuer.* Oxford: At the Clarendon Press.

Geertz, Clifford
1966 *Person, Time and Conduct in Bali: An Essay in Cultural Analysis.* Yale Southeast Asia Program, Cultural Report Series, no. 14.

Gell, A.
1977 "Magic, Perfume, Dream . . ." in I. M. Lewis (ed.), *Symbols and Sentiments* London: Academic Press, pp. 25–38.

Gulliver, P., and P. H. Gulliver
1953 *The Central Nilo-Hamites* London: International African Institute.

Hobart, M.
1985 "Texte est un con," in R. H. Barnes, D. de Coppet, and R. J. Parkin (eds.), *Contexts and Levels.* Oxford: JASO Occasional Papers no. 4, pp. 33–53.

Huntingford, G. W. B.
1953 *The Northern Nilo-Hamites.* London: International African Institute.
1969 *The Southern Nilo-Hamites.* London: International African Institute.

Khazanov, A.
1984 *Nomads and the Outside World.* Cambridge: Cambridge University Press.

Lewis, B. A.
1972 *The Murle.* Oxford: At the Clarendon Press.

Lienhardt, G.
1961 *Divinity and Experience.* Oxford: At the Clarendon Press.

Osborne, H.
1977 "Odours and Appreciation," *British Journal of Aesthetics,* vol. 17, pp. 37–48.

Panoff, F.
1970 "Food and Faeces: A Melanesian Rite," *Man,* vol. 5, pp. 237–252.

Schutz, A.
1962 *Collected Papers I: The Problems of Social Reality.* edited and introduced by M. Natanson. The Hague: Nijhoff.

Spencer, P.
1973 *Nomads in Alliance.* London: Oxford University Press.

Theophrastus
ca. 320BC "Concerning Odours," in his *Enquiry into Plants,* (320 B.C.) *Odours, and Weather Signs,* translated by Sir Arthur Hort 1916. London and New York, vol. 2: 327–389.

Walens, S.
1981 *Feasting with Cannibals.* Princeton: Princeton University Press.

Witherspoon, G.
1975 *Navajo Kinship and Marriage.* Chicago: University of Chicago Press.

Wittgenstein, L.
1984 *Culture and Value* translated by P. Winch. Chicago: University of Chicago Press.

Wright, R. H.
1982 *The Sense of Smell.* Boca Raton, Fla.: CRC Press, Inc.

28

IN TOWNSHIP TONIGHT!
SOUTH AFRICA'S BLACK CITY MUSIC
AND THEATRE

DAVID COPLAN

Sophiatown – culture and community, 1940–60

In 1897, an investor named H. Tobiansky bought 237 acres of land four and a half miles west of the centre of Johannesburg. After failing to sell it to the government as a "Coloured location," Tobiansky planned a private leasehold township for low-income whites and named it after his wife, Sophia. But Sophiatown's distance from the city, poor drainage, and proximity to the municipal sewage depository at Newlands made it difficult to attract tenants and buyers. By 1910, lots were being sold without discrimination, creating a racially mixed area that became increasingly black. The extension of unrestricted purchase to the adjacent areas of Martindale and Newclare in 1912 and the City Council's establishment in 1918 of Western Native Township (WNT) on the Newlands site further discouraged white residence. These Western Areas, as they were collectively called, soon constituted the largest suburban black residential area in South Africa.[1]

The government specifically exempted Sophiatown from the ownership restrictions of the Urban Areas Act but did not designate it a recognised location, so that municipal services did not keep pace with the expanding population. Despite the Act, Johannesburg's industries needed labour. The government did nothing to inhibit the flow of African families to the city, and the African population increased from 229 122 to 384 628 between 1936 and 1946.[2] As the slumyards were cleared, their residents fled to freehold areas. The population of Sophiatown, a freehold location, rose from 12 000 in 1928 to 28 500 in 1937, very near planned capacity. Though Sophiatown was also "proclaimed" (marked for removal) in 1934, the government was not prepared to absorb the cost of housing its residents or the thousands swelling the permanent urban workforce.

Furthermore, Africans preferred the free-

---

[1] Andre Proctor, "Class struggle, segregation and the city: a history of Sophiatown, 1905–1940", in B. Bozzoli, Johannesburg, 1979, p. 57.

[2] *Ibid.*, p. 62.

hold areas. As Sophiatown grew, houses stood vacant in municipal locations like Western Native Township, and workers' hostels reported many openings. Though it shared the social and economic problems of the slum-yards and municipal locations, Sophiatown offered a greater sense of permanence and self-direction. The refusal of Africans to move to the municipal locations was partly a political protest "against the authorities trying to rob them further of the alternative life and value systems they had created for themselves in the yards".[3]

Ownership of real estate gave Sophiatown a sense of community, with institutions and a social identity that served as a defence against the dehumanisation of the labour system. Sophiatown's autonomy was more self-perceived than actual, since it existed at the tolerance of the government, and whites in fact owned or controlled nearly 77 per cent of its total area.[4] Sophiatown's economy afforded few sources of capital accumulation. A few house owners established themselves in retail, service, real estate, trades, and even the professions; but many residents could profit only from crime and the liquor trade.

To some extent, middle-class and working-class Africans developed different organisational patterns and outlooks on city life. The performing arts reflected these differences and highlight for us three issues central to the relationship between performance culture and the urban African community:

1) cultural autonomy – the struggle between the black community and white commercial interests for the control of African culture;

2) disorder – the losing effort to establish social accountability, institutions, and settings for the creation of community in a segregated context;

3) the role of performers – their position in the social conflict and their relationship to their audience.

Sophiatown pinpoints these issues because of what it was and what it symbolised. It was an organic community that allowed a freedom of action, association, and expression available only in freehold areas. Located in South Africa's industrial and financial capital, Sophiatown set the pace, giving urban African culture its pulse, rhythm, and style during the 1940s and 50s. Noisy and dramatic, its untarred, potholed streets ran by the communal water taps and toilets and the rectangular jumble of yards walled in with brick, wood, and iron. A new synthesis of African culture sprang up here, shouting for recognition. Materially poor but intensely social; crime-ridden and violent but neighbourly and self-protective; proud, bursting with music and writing, swaggering with personality, simmering with intellectual and political militance, Sophiatown was a slum of dreams, a battleground of the heart.

Sophiatown, produced leaders in many fields, and Africans in other cities looked to them for inspiration. The location became a symbol as well as a partial realisation of their aspirations. The role of performance in the social world of Sophiatown was of course conditioned by the relations between the urban African community and the white power structure.

On the whole, Sophiatown was less proletarian than the slumyards. Opportunities for property ownership, family and neighbourhood life, and relative freedom from government interference attracted the growing middle-class. African professionals like Dr A. B. Xuma, MD, president of the African National Congress from 1939 to 1949, built impressive houses there and made the suburb both a symbol and a centre of efforts to

---

[3] *Ibid.*, p. 81
[4] *Ibid.*, p. 76.

gain entrance to the dominant society. Its white, Asian, and Coloured residents and shopowners were generally accepted as members of the community. Shebeen society, primarily a working-class innovation, flourished among all of Sophiatown's varied population. Some drinking houses – Aunt Babe's, The House on Telegraph Hill, The Back of the Moon – became genuine nightclubs where the elite of the African business, sporting, entertainment, and underworlds came to talk, listen, and dance to recordings of the latest American jazz.

Other gatherings included backyard parties organised around a wedding, celebration, or spontaneous get-together. These yards were similar to the old slumyards, and houseowners rented out rows of shacks built around the edges of their own backyards. Tenant families lived in one room, cooked in the open, and shared a common tap. Here neighbourhood musicians entertained, often imitating popular foreign and local performers in the hope of one day appearing on concert and dance hall stages themselves.

Community life integrated traditional African reciprocity with the cash economy. The drinking patterns of the shebeen were indispensable not only to the *stokfels* but also to middle-class voluntary associations. Attendance was obligatory at weddings, funerals, and birth receptions, where refreshments were purchased and contributions collected. Westernising Africans who sought to change the pattern were not understood, and attempts to eliminate the charge for refreshments, for example, turned the parties into gate-crashing mêlées.[5]

Frequently, middle-class sponsors hired established bands and vocal groups for their parties and fund-raisers. The musicians' professional competence, behaviour, and appearance not only reflected new urban cultural ideals but helped to define them as

well. Professional musicians preferred American "international" performance styles and strained to pull the urban African public along with them. Their success in promoting orchestral jazz gave African listeners a sense of connection with the world black community, and expressed modern African identity through technical brilliance and African roots.

Recordings became a widespread source of entertainment and status for urban African families. Imports were scarce during the early 1940s due to the war and an American musicians' strike. Local performers were encouraged to fill the gap with their own versions of American hits in the hope of capturing a greater share of the record market. American and British magazines and Wilfred Sentso's local publication *African Sunrise* kept African jazz enthusiasts informed about overseas musical trends and personalities. They could see and hear black performers like Lena Horne, Bill Robinson, Cab Calloway and Ethel Waters in films such as *Stormy Weather*, *Cabin in the Sky*, and *Black Velvet*. These productions electrified the cultural atmosphere of black Johannesburg and permanently influenced local speech, dress, and stage shows. Impressed by these films, Zuluboy Cele hired Emily Koenane as the first female vocalist to front a major African orchestra, the Jazz Maniacs. The Pitch Black Follies and Merry Blackbirds followed suit with Snowy Radebe and Marjorie Pretorius. By the end of the 1940s Sophiatown's Dolly Rathebe and Bulawayo's Dorothy Masuku were more popular than most male vocal quartets and specialised in African cover versions of American jazz favourites. African men readily adopted "zoot suits" and American slang, and English-speaking Sophiatown residents proudly referred to their community as "Little Harlem."

A contributor to *Inkundla ya Bantu* (*Bantu Forum*) criticized the adoption of European

---

[5]   Mia Brandel-Syrier, *Reeftown Elite*, London, 1971, p. 60.

culture as a movement away from an "Africa that is ours, into an 'Africa' that is of the Whiteman's making." Arguing that "we deny our music the opportunity to speak to the outside world in its own language," he praised not only indigenous music but Afro–American spirituals as well:

> They speak to the world in a language evolved by Africa in a foreign environment . . . they make the world understand the things we stand for . . . We want not to be Europeanised Africans but civilised Africans.[6] . . .

While African stage variety concerts and jazz ("jive") dances continued to attract working-class as well as middle-class patrons, the majority of urban Africans were less Westernised than their school-trained entertainers. The continuing *marabi* audience admired American jazz and clothing styles as symbols of international urban black culture. But they still demanded music that was recognisably their own and expressed the ethnic variety of location society and culture.

For working-class Africans, Sophiatown represented a struggle for things more basic than inclusion in the wider society; a fight for survival amid high rents, poverty, over-crowding, wage slavery, victimisation, and police harassment. Patterns of working-class life that had evolved in the inner city slum-yards were more fully developed and integrated into the new social environment of Sophiatown.

Living conditions were little better in Sophiatown, but there Africans had their own regular streets and neighbourhoods rather than the haphazard industrial backyards of the city fringes. The communal water taps, toilets and showerhouses of Sophiatown, though insanitary and inadequate, are remembered today as casual meeting places where the better-off and educated mixed with their humbler neighbours.[7]

Though subject to intense pressures, family life, friendship networks and neighbourhood recreation became social defences against a hostile city. In contrast to the slumyards' tran-sience and lack of social co-operation, Africans in Sophiatown developed a strong community identity. Entertainment played its part, and "more than anything else it was the backyard shebeens and dance parties that gave expres-sion to this new proletarian identity."[8] Anyone in search of a party had only to follow the sounds of musical uproar to the crowds of people dancing in the backyards or the street.

By the 1940s, the latest popular working-class dance music combined African melody and rhythm with the rhythms of American swing, jitterbug and even Latin American rumba and conga. Developed by black South African bandsmen, the new style was called *tsaba-tsaba*. It is played in duple time, and its rhythm has several distinctive African / Afro–American features, including rushed second and fourth beats, the freedom to accent any of the four beats, and a polyrhythmic sense of two beats against three. Although some Africans asserted that *tsaba-tsaba* developed from *marabi*, the rhythms of the two styles are quite distinct, and they seem to be related more through social function and category than content. . . .

Street music, a part of Johannesburg's popular culture since before the turn of the century, remained a focus of communal socia-bility in Sophiatown. Special occasions brought some of the best-trained African brass bands down from Rustenburg. No middle-class location wedding was complete without a uniformed brass band leading the procession from the church to the reception. If two bands crossed paths in the streets, competitions often

---

6   *Inkundla ya Bantu*, 17 June 1944.
7   Essop Patel (ed.), *The World of Nat Nakasa* Johannesburg, 1975, p. 21.
8   Proctor, "Class struggle, segregation and the city", p. 81.

resulted, each band listening politely to the other. Untrained Pedi groups from Sophiatown bought instruments second hand and imitated the Rustenburgers, collecting coins from onlookers or accompanying a *stokfel* parade. When two of these Pedi bands met, they tried to blow each other off the street. Captain Marcus Roe of the Native Military Corps trained and led an African brass band during the 1930s, and during the 40s and 50s the City Engineers and Non-European Affairs Departments formed their own African bands to perform at hostels, parks, beerhalls and other public places. . . .

This music came eventually to be known as *kwela*, a term given currency by mass-media distribution. The influence of the recording industry on *kwela* street performance was evident, as penny whistlers walked about the streets playing requests for "a tickey per record". They identified song tempos as "78" or "82" from the rpms of commercial discs, and ended their street "records" with a fade-out.[9] Donald Swanson's 1950 film, *The Magic Garden*, one of the first to use African actors and a location setting, featured penny whistler Willard Cele playing his own compositions in an Alexandra street. These were later released as "Penny Whistle Blues" and "Penny Whistle Boogie" (Gallotone GE1123), highly popular with African audiences. Recognition by the entertainment media greatly increased the respectability of penny whistle music among urban Africans,[10] who began to regard it as authentic expression of their urban culture rather than as an indolent pastime of juvenile delinquents. . . .

Though Africans had been listening to white municipal radio stations since the 1920s, broadcasting for Africans only began in 1941 in Durban with a five-minute report of war news in Zulu by K. E. Masinga. This service was extended to Johannesburg and the Eastern Cape, increased to 15 and then 35 minutes, and made available to migrant workers through ground-line rediffusion hook-ups to their hostels. Masinga, a talented writer, introduced African radio drama with the help of the broadcaster and ethnomusicologist Hugh Tracey. The first play was Masinga's musical script of a Zulu folktale, *Chief Above and Chief Below* (1939), with original songs by the author in traditional idiom. Tracey was a purist, dedicated to rescuing traditional forms from imported and urban musical influences. Musical dramas based on folk sources and rural settings enabled him to insert traditional music into urban radio programming. The plays proved popular, especially among the migrant hostel dwellers. For more urbanised listeners, the Gay Gaeties leader J. P. Tutu composed a number of musical plays in Zulu for the Johannesburg branch of the South African Broadcasting Corporation.

Town music forms dominated the SABC programmes while the rediffusion hook-ups emphasized neo-traditional and syncretic styles popular with non-literate workers. Tracey[11] recalled that at first Zulu hostel residents complained about items from other African ethnic groups on "their" service. By the late 1940s, however, they admitted enjoying the variety, a reflection of African workers' increasing ethnic tolerance.

The SABC had a regular programme on Tuesday, Thursday, and Saturday, from 9.45 to 10.20 am. Its wide variety of African musical styles did not entirely please any sector of the Johannesburg audience. As the only African programme, however, it was extremely popular. It also increased cultural communication, exposing urban Africans to traditional music and migrants to African "township jazz". Radio dramas of all kinds

---

[9]   Gerhard Kubik, *The Kachamba Brothers Band*, Manchester, 1974, pp. 1, 10–13.
[10] Rycroft, "The new 'town' music," p. 56.
[11] Hugh Tracey, interview, 10 June 1975.

enjoyed general popularity. Following his election to the International Mark Twain Society for his adaptations of Shakespeare in 1953, K. E. Masinga's Zulu translations of *King Lear* and *The Tempest* were serialised over SABC.[12]

By the early 1950s the SABC was presenting different African languages and musical styles on separate days. Once a week jazz pianist-composer Gideon Nxumalo entertained urban Africans with his regular feature, "This Is Bantu Jazz." He was principally responsible for the wide distribution of a new term for the *majuba* African jazz, *mbaqanga*. This term, coined by Jazz Maniacs' trumpeter Michael Xaba, originally referred in Zulu to a kind of traditional steamed maize bread. Among musicians, it meant that the music was both the Africans' own, the homely cultural sustenance of the townships, and the popular working-class source of the musicians' "daily bread."

Another name for this blend of African melody, *marabi* and jazz was *msakazo*, a derogatory term meaning "broadcast." The record companies, taking advantage of the commercial possibilities of radio, processed or "mass produced" the music in the studios, pursuing a common denominator of urban African taste. In 1952, a commercial company installed a rediffusion service in Soweto's Orlando township, even though residents objected[13] that Orlando needed lights, schools, paved streets and adequate housing more than rediffusion. The African National Congress feared that radio would become an instrument of government propaganda. Others attacked it as a "back-to-the-kraal, apartheid and never-never-land service" that used African languages (rather than English) and migrant and *msakazo* music in a "develop-along-your-own-lines pattern."[14]

The co-ordinated expansion of radio and recording studios for Africans increasingly swallowed up the performers. African journalists decried white exploitation and urged greater community support for artists.[15] In the late 1940s and 50s, however, political and social pressures pushed professional African artists into the arms of white entrepreneurs.

As early as the Second World War, a few African bands performed unofficially at white nightclubs in Johannesburg. In 1942, white musicians who feared cut-rate African competition managed to get the Jazz Maniacs expelled from the Paradise Nightclub, claiming that the band were not members of the fledgling white musicians' union. Offering to join the union and pay dues, the Maniacs found themselves barred from the union also.[16] African musicians did continue to find work at white clubs until the late 1950s, but their position remained tenuous and insecure. . . .

In 1952, white promoter Alfred Herbert organised his first *African Jazz and Variety* show at Johannesburg's Windmill Theatre, presenting some of the city's best performers before white audiences. The promise of regular pay and exposure to a wider audience attracted the professionals, particularly since Herbert allowed them to organize their own programme, based on the established African stage company format. The show was highly successful. Like Ike Brooks, Herbert himself was a product of the South African Anglo-Jewish music hall tradition. He began to take a more sophisticated directorial approach, tailoring succeeding shows to the tastes of his liberal white and largely Jewish audience. By

[12] *Cape Argus*, 12 November 1954.
[13] *Bantu World*, 9 August 1952.
[14] *Ilanga Lase Natal*, 16, 19 August 1952.
[15] *Ibid.*, 11 January, 2 April 1947.
[16] Peter Rezant tells a similar story about the Merry Blackbirds *cf.* Muff Andersson, *Music in the Mix*, Johannesburg, 1981, p. 24.

1956, *African Jazz* and *Variety* was featuring
Dolly Rathebe singing in Yiddish. The
show's programme for the late 1950s read like
a roster of the most famous names in black
Johannesburg show business, and featured
performers were paid £35 a week.

As a producer, Herbert exploited his
performers, even abandoning them to their
own devices when tours to Central and East
African or other parts of Southern Africa ran
into financial trouble. Nevertheless, his efforts
to keep their personal as well as professional
lives on an even keel and the lack of other
performance opportunities kept performers
with him up until the mid-60s. Herbert's
directional influence on the development of
urban African performing arts and on the
relation of professional performers to the
African community was more significantly
harmful than his financial misdealings. *African
Jazz and Variety* became more a burlesque
than a representation of the traditions of urban
African artistry. In 1959, the show included a
rural pastiche written by Herbert entitled
"Kraal Tone Poem", presenting "the songs,
the dances, the life and the laughter from the
home of jazz, the Kraal."[17] Though billed as an
"original vernacular ethnic" show, its central
feature was "sexy dancing [by] a crowd of
snappy-looking African lovelies clad in
leopard-skin bikinis,"[18] and Herbert described
his 1961 show, *Drums of Africa*, as showing
off "the sexulating rawness and glamour of
some of the most beautiful non-European
women."[19] None of these talents, of course,
was shown to blacks.

Clearly black performers could not serve the
cultural needs of the black community under
Herbert's direction. But professional artists
who wanted to reach out beyond their local
audience had few alternatives. Only a white

employer could easily get performance permits and the vital "musicians' pass" entitling
performers to "go to any town under the
European promoter, who is held responsible
for their activities."[20]

Performers were caught between the
recording studios and the promoters in an
apartheid society. Walter Nhlapo advised that
"unless music lovers band together and offer
employment to musicians in the form of
concerts and record clubs, commercialism will
kill music as we know it."[21]

Sophiatown's culturally self-conscious,
American-oriented elite had taken steps to
support local jazz by forming the Sophiatown
Modern Jazz Club in 1955. By that time, the
bebop styles of Charlie Parker and Dizzy
Gillespie were a powerful influence on local
musicians. A number of innovative groups
were playing the new jazz, including Mackay
Davashe's Shantytown Sextet, and trumpeter
Elijah Nkonyane's Elijah Rhythm Kings.
During the next two years, led by jazz enthu-
siast Cameron "Pinocchio" Mokaleng, the
Modern Jazz Club sponsored a series of well-
organized Sunday "jam sessions" at the Odin
Cinema Sophiatown. After the initial session,
"Jazz at the Odin" involved white as well as
black musicians. The series was a milestone for
jazz and creative interaction across racial lines
in South African music. This new music was
not well understood by the urban African
population as a whole. Yet the prestige of jazz
and of black American performance culture
drew in the most urbanised people of
Sophiatown. To appreciate jazz was a mark of
urban sophistication and social status, even
among *tsotsis* and gangsters; and by the late
1950s a genuine appreciation of the new styles
had taken hold. By then, however, the Modern
Jazz Club was dying along with Sophiatown.

[17]   Programme, *African Jazz and Variety*, 1959.
[18]   *Cape Argus*, 5 January 1965.
[19]   Johannesburg *Star*, 4 March 1961.
[20]   Alfred Herbert, *Star*, 4 March 1961.
[21]   *Bantu World*, 15 February 1956.

Forced to leave Johannesburg because of pass regulations, Pinocchio Mokaleng fled into bitter exile in Britain.

Though "Jazz at the Odin" involved individual musicians and not formal bands, the sessions did lead to the formation of the Jazz Epistles (*Verse 1*, Continental 14 ABC18341). They included bop stylist Dollar Brand (piano), Kippie Moeketsi (alto), Jonas Gwangwa (trombone), Hugh Masekela (trumpet), Johnny Gertse, (guitars) and Early Mabuza (drums). The Jazz Epistles helped to establish an influential "main stream" modern jazz movement, which claimed national attention among urban black South Africans during the 1960s.

Not all the effects of white involvement in urban black performing arts were negative. During the late 1950s, inter-racial cooperation helped to keep musical professionalism alive in South African jazz and set the stage for international recognition of black South African performers. Nor were all whites exploitative or patronising. The Anglican missionary Father Trevor Huddleston, an energetic religious leader, social worker, educator, fund-raiser, and champion of urban African rights, also took an active interest in the welfare of black performing artists in Johannesburg. His encouragement of Hugh Masekela, Jonas Gwangwa, and many others led to the formation of the Huddleston Jazz Band during the 50s. When Huddleston was recalled in 1954, a farewell concert attracted more than 200 performers and netted more than four thousand dollars for its sponsor, the Union of Southern African Artists ("Union Artists").

Union Artists began as an inter-racial effort to protect the professional rights of black performers. Under the leadership of clothing workers' trade unionist, Guy Routh, and later, the theatrical personality Ian Bernhardt, Union Artists successfully arranged royalty payments to Solomon Linda, Spokes Mashiyane, and Mackay Davashe. They also engineered the boycott by British Equity of all segregated shows in South Africa.

After Routh departed for England, Bernhardt emphasised the promotional aspects of Union Artists. The Huddleston concert provided the means to acquire permanent premises in Dorkay House. There Bernhardt initiated a programme to locate, train, and present African musical performers, before a multiracial audience. So began a series of talent contests and small "festivals" leading to the production of the famous Township Jazz and Dorkay Jazz concert series, which began at Selbourne Hall in 1957 and continued until 1966. The concerts were highly successful, and many top African performers including Dolly Rathebe, Thandi Klassens, Letta Mbulu, Sophie Mcina, Patience Gqwabe, the Jazz Epistles, and Jazz Dazzlers appeared. Among the early highlights was a benefit in 1957 for the families of the murdered journalist Henry Nxumalo and stage comedian Victor Mkhize. The city took one-third of the proceeds as entertainment tax.

These concerts allowed musicians to perform in secure, well-organised circumstances, but without artistic interference from whites. Though audiences were segregated, the series did gain African jazz musicians a wider multi-racial following and greatly revived interest in jazz within the Johannesburg black community. In addition to concerts, Union Artists organised the African Music and Drama Association (AMDA) at Dorkay House, where performers such as Wilson Silgee could instruct their younger colleagues. Some performers accused Union Artists of exploitation and its African management committee members of favouritism, but most were pleased with their artistic freedom and broadened opportunities. Artists received some cash for concert appearances, though some resented the condescending taint of amateurism implicit in the talent search. Pianist Dollar Brand (Abdullah Ibrahim) complained, "Ian Bernhardt only gives out trophies, and one is enough!".[22]

Township Jazz was at best a pale and somewhat disembodied shadow of the old concert-and-dances of the black community. Todd Matshikiza remarked in 1957 that he would gladly have given up the opportunity to play in City Hall to perform again with the Harlem Swingsters at the old Jig Club in WNT.[23]

The culmination of this phase in the history of Dorkay House as a centre of black performance activity was the birth of the musical play, *King Kong*, in 1959. *King Kong* was based on the tragic career of South African black heavyweight boxing champion Ezekial "King Kong" Dhlamini. Its creators intended it to be a model of fruitful co-operation between blacks and whites in the international entertainment field. With production, direction, script, and musical direction by whites, but using black musical actors and musicians and a score by Todd Matshikiza, the show proposed to combine the polish and style of Broadway with the cultural vitality and resources of the townships. The musical actors included the members of the Manhattan Brothers and Woody Woodpeckers vocal groups, with Nathan Mdledle as King Kong and Miriam Makeba as his lady love, Joyce. The fiery Jazz Dazzlers Orchestra, led by MacKay Davashe, included members of the Shantytown Sextet, Harlem Swingsters, and Huddleston Jazz Band. The music was big band, but ten-year-old Lemmy Mabaso was also on hand, electrifying audiences with his penny whistle *kwela* solos. The play did not make a strong political statement; but it did show something of the hardships, violence, and frustration of African township life. The show infused African musical and dramatic stage traditions into a narrative structure, and presented a mixture of African and Western song and dance. There was jazz, a *tsotsis* knife dance based on Sotho *mokorotlo* war dancing, and a dance celebrating King Kong's release from prison that echoed the traditional Zulu welcome for a returning hero.[24]

King Kong was an immediate, overwhelming success with Johannesburg people of all races. A broadly South Africa production, it challenged the best of international musical theatre. The show's producer, Leon Gluckman, naively imagined it might create a more sympathetic attitude among whites towards urban blacks:

> Any white person who has seen the show will think twice now before he pushes an African out of the way on a street corner. It's not politics, but a question of human relations.[25]

King Kong arrived in London, where its black performers believed they had left the restrictions and parochialism of the townships and entered the international performing world for good. But international attitudes towards African had left South African behind. In 1960, African nationalism, independence and cultural resurgence were already dominant movements. White as well as black critics complained about the show's lack of political force:

> Politically, *King Kong* is about as dynamic as a bag of laundry. Everything including the gangsters and the social misery, has been agreeably prettified . . . A full-blooded entertainment this may be but a whistle and a wiggle are no match for the policy of *apartheid*. One swallow of black and white collaboration doesn't make a summer of South Africa's bleak shame.[26]

---

[22]   *Drum*, December 1959.
[23]   *Drum*, August 1957.
[24]   Harry Bloom, *King Kong*, London, 1961, pp. 52, 65.
[25]   Johannesburg *Star*, 7 August 1959.
[26]   Robert Muller, quoted in Andersson, *Music in the Mix*, p. 34.

In fairness, the show would never have been granted wide public exposure in South Africa if the system had been frontally attacked. Implicit in the production was the dream, no less than the illusion, of a better, more humane South Africa. The financial rewards for performers were hardly a dream come true, however. While Todd Matshikiza got £80 per week and the leading instrumental soloist Kippie Moeketsi got £35, most actors and band members made only £15.[27]

Artistically, white playgoers expected an "African" (traditional) display, and so were disturbed by its modern, hybrid nature and considered it inauthentic. Because *King Kong* was presented in the style of European musical theatre, the actors appeared amateurish to London audiences. Nevertheless, the show ran for a year; and many of the cast, including Miriam Makeba and the four Manhattan Brothers, stayed on to pursue performing careers outside South Africa. Matshikiza's music underwent significant transformation at the hands of the music director, Stanley Glasser, who essentially removed the African township character from the London arrangements. This change was clearly perceived by urban black South Africans back home, who gave the London cast album an indifferent reception. Ethnomusicologist A.A. Mensah noted:

> The White collaborators . . . had changed to gain the upper hand and had introduced splendid arrangements but in doing so had missed some of the basic elements in the conception of modern entertainment music held by Black South Africans.[28]

In the Johannesburg of 1959, *King Kong* represented at once an ultimate achievement and final flowering of Sophiatown culture. The white suburb of Triomf rose where Sophia-town had stood. *King Kong* was both a presentation and a symbol of the character and indestructibility of Johannesburg urban African community. The show was imitated by Alfred Herbert and other producers, but the most important was the tireless Wilfred Sentso, whose productions *Washerwoman* (1959) and *Frustrated Black Boy* (1961) unflinchingly portrayed African suffering through the medium of musical theatre. During the 1960s, African director-playwrights adopted the *King Kong* model. Without white interference or assistance, they produced a self-supporting, indigenous urban musical theatre. Today, this theatre represents the most socially and politically significant art form in the black townships.

The 1950s witnessed changes in the social personality, status, and self-image of professional performers in the urban community. Opportunities in performing for white and black audiences, recording, and broadcasting continued to offer at least some African musicians the chance to earn a living from performance activity alone. The Manhattan Brothers, for example, earned five hundred dollars a week as a group during the best periods of the early 1950s, despite the violence at African shows. Still, performers' efforts to get out of the township environment and into the white and international arenas reinforced the ambivalence that many urban Africans felt towards them.

Ever since the emergence of the African dance musician around the turn of the century, urban and mission school Africans had looked upon professional popular musicians as social deviants, drinkers, gamblers, and womanizers unaccountable to either traditional or Christian social morality. In contrast, amateur choral and keyboard musicians who were active in the schools and churches and middle-class professions were highly respected. So

[27] Andersson, *Music in the Mix*, p. 34.
[28] Mensah, "Jazz – the round trip", p. 134.

were performers who appeared exclusively at middle-class minstrel concerts and European-style dances. Middle-class youngsters who showed an interest in professional perfor-mance, however, were warned against leading the dissolute life of a "ragtimer."[29] Dambuza Mdledle recalled that the Manhattan Brothers' parents "could not foresee a future for their clean-living lads 'eating music' and mixing with musicians, whose bad behaviour and drunken habits were legendary."[30]

During the 1940s, African jazz musicians benefited from their associations with black American performance culture and from their ability to express the cultural aspirations of their audiences. Nevertheless, working-class dance forms such as *tsaba-tsaba* and the occasions where they were performed per-petuated the "ragtimer" image. Like their black American counterparts,[31] professional black South African musicians began to complain that their performances were socially accepted but that they as persons were not:

> It seemed to us that musicians were only regarded as human beings while they were on stage and performing. After that nobody cared about them.[32]

H.I.E. Dhlomo defended performers, saying,

> We either do not appreciate the value of or we expect too much of our creative artists. We ignore their contributions and do not think them 'Leaders' and patriots unless they play a prominent part in our social and polit-ical life.[33]

The attempt to model themselves upon Duke Ellington or Lena Horne and to cultivate the image of the impeccably dressed, smoothly mannered, glamorous American jazzman or woman heightened both the status and popu-larity of African performers during the 1940s. Amid the bitterness and fragmentation of African society in Soweto in the late 1950s and 60s, the image of the hard-drinking, *dagga*-smoking "hep cat" reduced jazz musicians once again to the status of social marginals.

The performers' desire to escape the urban African community professionally aroused resentment among many of their fellow Africans, who saw no chance of doing them-selves. People being strangled by the wider system criticized musicians who played in white nightclubs and City Hall concerts as self-important and sometimes violently attacked them. Bloke Modisane noted bitterly:

> The African directs his aggression, perhaps more viciously, against his own group, particularly against the more successful Africans who are resented for being successful.[34]

The notion that African professional performers had sold out to the white enter-tainment industry and abandoned their people persisted alongside genuine admiration of the *African Jazz and Variety*, *Township Jazz*, and *King Kong* performers.

Internally, the jazz performance com-munity itself suffered from exploitation, professional insecurity, and modes of cultural production that discouraged integrity and stylistic development. Both black and white promoters frequently violated the terms of their agreements with musicians. Non-professional promoters could simply with-draw from the entertainment field after a more or less successful attempt to make a

---

[29]   *Bantu World*, 15 May 1954.
[30]   Quoted in Y. Huskisson, *Bantu Composers of Southern Africa*, Johannesburg, 1969, p. 98.
[31]   Hentoff and Shapiro, *Hear Me Talkin' To Ya*, p. 330.
[32]   Nathan Mdledle, *Bantu World*, 13 March 1954.
[33]   *Ilanga Lase Natal*, 16 August 1952.
[34]   Bloke Modisane, *Blame Me On History*, London, 1963, p. 59.

quick profit. They could always find new performers to replace those unhappy with past treatment.

Working conditions contributed to a rapid turnover of personnel within the bands despite the high level of demand for their services. With so few outlets for independent achievement and public recognition, band members often quarrelled over money, leadership and personal prestige. Promoters found this lack of unity easy to exploit. Performers frequently left established groups and set up new ensembles of their own, since a disproportionate amount of revenues, recognition and authority normally went to the group leader-manager.

Professionally insecure younger musicians were no longer taking the time and effort to develop reading and other technical skills common among the older generation. This trend was reinforced by the new system of Bantu Education, which in the late 1950s closed some mission schools, brought others under government control, and replaced their curriculum with one designed to educate Africans for subservience. Music education suffered along with instruction in all other fields. Even earlier, however, the *Voice of Africa* complained:

> African artists are talented but fail to reach the top because they are intoxicated by immediate success to the extent of leaving off the hard work of practising, and depend on inspiration in their performances, which invariably results in failure and the artists' disappearance and despair.[35]

The development of African broadcasting did nothing to encourage stylistic innovation or continuity. Producers like the SABC's Michael Kittermaster insisted on making their own artistic judgements over the protests of African performers. Most often, temporary ensembles were created at Broadcasting House for specific programmes. The Radio Rhythm Boys, for example, included King Force Silgee (tenor), Todd Matshikiza (piano), Thomas Khoza (drums), and Fats Dunjwa (bass), all drawn from different local bands.

New African record producers like Rupert Bopape preferred to hire musicians individually for standard *msakazo* recordings. Professional urban musicians expressed disgust with the new system[36] while the producers disliked the jazzmen's sense of artistic and professional independence and found their demands for better pay and working conditions troublesome. Bopape replaced the middle-class players with working-class and migrant performers and instituted a system of rigid studio control. Performance units were rehearsed incessantly and the musical results became his property. Bopape, though not a musician himself, has more than 1 000 compositions copyrighted in his name, including Aaron Lerole's "Tom Hark". Lerole received about £8 for "Tom Hark", and performers got about £6 for a recording.

Bopape built on the vocal *mbaqanga* of Miriam Makeba, Letta Mbulu, Susan Gabashane, Sylvia Moloi, and Thandi Mpambane's (later Klassens) Quad Sisters to create a style called *simanje-manje* (Zulu: "now-now"). Makeba and the others performed African melodies in the close harmony style of the American Andrews Sisters. The new music, pioneered by Joyce Mogatusi's Dark City Sisters, coached by Aaron Lerole, showed less American influence. It employed a simplified version of traditional part structure, set rural songs to urban rhythms derived from *marabi* and *tsaba-tsaba*, and was played at a rapid tempo by back-up groups of three reeds plus electric bass, guitar, and drumset. Musicologist

³⁵ *Voice of Africa*, May 1950.
³⁶ Oscar Mvungana, *Bantu World*, 20 August 1955.

Andrew Tracey notes that the "principle of parts cutting a cycle at different points is very noticable in black urban *mbaqanga* bands."[37]

Bopape used spoken introductions in *tsotsi-taal,* to liven up recordings by the female quartets and Lerole's Black Mambazo group. Searching the mines, hostels, and even the rural areas, Bopape discovered some outstanding talents whose neo-traditional music could be processed into the new style. These included Simon "Mahlathini" Nakbinde, who developed his remarkable sense of rhythm and phrasing as well as his talents as a composer and choreographer as the leader of a group of eighteen traditional wedding singers during the 1950s. At that time, deep-voiced Aaron Lerole led the pioneering Black Mambazo, which included Mahlathini's cousin Zeph Nkabinde. Influenced by Lerole, Mahlathini developed his rasping bass "goat voice" *(ukubodla*; Zulu "to bellow, roar")[38] and sang in praise of traditional values. The goat voice had roots in Nguni male traditional singing.

After Lerole quit Bopape at EMI in 1961, Bopape went to Gallo where he helped make Mahlathini famous. Soon every *simanje-manje* group had to have its male "groaner," as they are called, leading a female quartet with solos sung in the goat voice style. Mahlathini performed in traditional animal skins as well as in Western costume, and with the help of his female group, the Mohotella Queens, innovated new stage dance routines based on traditional steps and urban jive. This was music for people who were urbanizing but not Westernizing, as well as for migrants and even rural listeners influenced by urban culture. The new *mbaqanga* sold well in both urban and rural South Africa and in other countries of Southern and Central Africa. Performers such as Mahlathini still enjoy enormous prestige among urban workers who maintain strong links with the rural areas. Mahlathini sings nostalgically of the moral superiority and social security of traditional society, and reminds audiences of their rural roots. In the midst of urban hardship and insecurity, this musical glorification of African traditions appeals strongly to landless proletarians. For them, Nkabinde is *Indoda Mahlathini* ("Mahlathini The Man"), and his deep groaning voice embodies all the masculine power of the traditional Nguni *imbongi* (praise poet).

The commercial success of this music was based in part on the new social and demographic realities of urban African communities. As rural people continued their townward migration, the old locations of the Western Areas, Pimville, and Eastern Native Township were destroyed, and the people redistributed in the vast, anomic rental townships of Soweto. With the possible exception of Orlando, begun in 1932, there was as yet no feeling of community in Soweto, whose endless rows of identical brick "matchbox" houses reflected the authorities' view of the urban black population as mere "temporary sojourners" in the towns.

Urban Africans lost, at least temporarily, the sense of direction and identity once embodied in Sophiatown and its way of life. Africans protested against the destruction of Sophiatown far more strongly than they had objected to removal from the slumyards, because its streets, houses and institutions seemed so much more truly their own. As Father Huddleston lamented, "When Sophiatown is finally obliterated and its people scattered, I believe that South Africa will have lost not only a place but an ideal."[39]

Even as government bulldozers were levelling its houses, Sophiatown generated a

---

[37]   Andrew Tracey, quoted in Andersson, *Music in the Mix*, p. 13.

[38]   cf. J. Clegg, "The music of Zulu immigrant workers in Johannesburg – a focus on concertina and guitar," in *Papers Presented at the Symposium on Ethnomusicology*, Grahamstown, 1981, p. 6.

[39]   Huddleston, *Naught For Your Comfort*, p. 137.

cultural flowering unequalled in the urban history of South Africa. Principally in the pages of *Drum* magazine and the *Bantu World*, Henry Nxumalo, Can Themba, Stanley Motjuadi, Casey Motsisi, Arthur Maimane, Todd Matshikiza, Walter Nhlapo, Nat Nakasa and many others produced the best investigative journalism, short fiction, satirical humour, social and political commentary, and musical criticism South Africa had ever seen. Musical creativity and appreciation and intellectual discussion flourished in the backyards and shebeens. The great dance orchestras, soloists, and song and dance groups of the day packed Sophiatown's clubs, cinemas, and halls. Even as a memory, Sophiatown serves as a symbol; a legendary point of reference for an older generation of black writers and artists of every sort. Today, amid growing racial and political tension, a number of African performers and organizers are renewing the quest for artistic and professional autonomy that Sophiatown embodied. Watered by the spirit of Black Consciousness, a new creative growth has sprouted and, like the thorny aloe, flourishes in the barren landscape of apartheid.

PART VII

SEX AND GENDER STUDIES IN AFRICA

Woman spinning cotton fiber, Fakaha, Côte d'Ivoire, 1988.
Photo: Christopher B. Steiner.

Sex and Gender Studies in Africa: Economy and Society

29   Ester Boserup. 1970. "The Economics of Polygamy," pp. 37–52. In Ester Boserup, *Women's Role in Economic Development*. London: George Allen and Unwin.

30   Mona Etienne. 1980. "Women and Men, Cloth and Colonization: the Transformation of Production–Distribution Relations among the Baule (Ivory Coast)," pp. 214–238. In Mona Etienne and Eleanor Leacock, eds. *Women and Colonization*. New York: Praeger.

31   Judith Van Allen. 1982. "'Sitting on a Man.': Colonialism and the Lost Political Institutions of Igbo Women," *Canadian Journal of African Studies*, In 6 (2): 165–181.

32   Karen Tranberg Hansen. 1989. "Body Politics: Sexuality, Gender, and Domestic Service in Zambia," *Journal of Women's History*, 2 (1): 120–142.

Introduction

The subjects of sex and gender include a wide array of theoretical issues and ethnographic topics, only some of which can be covered in a single part. Topics not addressed explicitly in this part include homosexuality, conceptions of femininity and masculinity, labor migrancy, marriage systems, health care, nutrition and fertility, among others. Of course, gender studies permeate the anthology as a whole, in works by Hutchinson, Grinker, Comaroff and Comaroff, and others. Focusing primarily on relations between men and women in Nigeria, Côte d'Ivoire and Zambia, the four readings in this part address the ways in which differing ideas about men and women, and their social roles, become integral parts of African political–economic life. In order to more fully contextualize these particular readings within the larger literature, however, we shall use the next few pages to outline some of the central theoretical problems in gender studies in Africa, and elsewhere.

Some anthropologists and historians working in Africa today on sex and gender concerns refer to themselves as "feminist anthropologists" (Moore, 1988), a term that deserves some critical attention. The term "feminist," as it is used in the social sciences, often characterizes specifically those works that identify the sources of women's oppression and struggles for economic and political autonomy (Cutrufelli, 1983), and that seek changes in oppressive institutions, such as female genital mutilation (usually cliteridectomy), prostitution, and marriage customs (such as polygamy and the levirate). However, anthropologist Henrietta Moore disagrees strongly that feminist works are works "about women" or about advocacy. She writes (1988: vii),

> The identification of feminist concerns with women's concerns has been one of the strategies employed in the social sciences to marginalize the feminist critique. This marginalization is quite unjustified . . . The basis for the feminist critique is not the study of women, but the analysis of gender relations, and of gender as a structuring principle in all human societies.

Indeed, the works of authors who characterize themselves with terms such as "feminist" or the more neutral and non-ideological sounding "gender studies" emerged together in the early 1970s, as scholars and activists began to address the invisibility of women in academic literature, and to suggest that the cultural analysis of gender categories is central, rather than a marginal specialization, to both theory and method in anthropology. Of course, women were never totally absent from ethnographies of the first part of the twentieth century, especially because anthropologists focused so much on kinship and marriage. Moreover, scholars such as Audrey Richards and Hermann Baumann took special care in the 1920s to write about the sexual division of labor in Africa, and Evans-Pritchard wrote a small, but important, case report on Azande transvestites. The problem, Moore says, "was not, therefore, one of empirical study, but rather one of *representation*" (1988: 1, our emphasis). If there is an absence, we would suggest, it is an absence of studies of men and masculinity, for men have often been taken to represent the dominant cultural patterns of society, while women have been taken as the empty category to be explained (some notable exceptions include; Hewlett, 1991; Moodie, 1994).

How have women figured in anthropological accounts?

Did anthropologists elicit information from them?

Were their voices heard?

Why did it take so long for gender to become a central focus of anthropological representation?

In the last twenty years, anthropologists have increasingly focused their attention in Africa on the study of gender, sex, and women. Anthropologists and historians, such as Caroline Bledsoe, Jane Guyer, Sara Berry, Ester Boserup, Jean Comaroff, Christine Oppong, Christine Obbo, Kristin Mann, Henrietta Moore, and Anne Whitehead, to name only a few, are among those who have helped to produce a significant body of work on African gender studies. Given that anthropologists have been studying Africa since the beginnings of the European colonization of Africa, it is reasonable to ask why it took so long for work on gender to begin. The answer lies in the fact that gender studies *anywhere* are of relatively recent origin.

"Gender" can be used generally to refer to the cultural construction of maleness and femaleness, and "sex" to refer to the division of human beings into male and female. This is a distinction that might well be called into question as a cultural construction in its own right, but the distinction has some heuristic, if not analytical, value. If one accepts that the human world is divided, naturally, into two sexes – and, it must be stressed, that until the early 1700s, Western Europeans believed that there was only one sex in the world – male (Lacqueur, 1990), and there are reasonable arguments for more than two sexes (Butler, 1990) – then the anthropological question becomes:

What does the division between the sexes mean to people in different times and places?

How are biological distinctions made symbolically and socially meaningful?

How does cross-cultural analysis influence the way

we think about the limits and possibilities of sex and gender categories?

Margaret Mead's early work in the Pacific islands of Oceania was perhaps the first to explicitly address the differences in sex and gender across different cultures in detail. In New Guinea, in the late 1930s, Mead studied three societies – the Arapesh, the Mundugumor, and the Tchambuli (also called the Chambri) – whose assumptions about the differences between men and women stood in stark contrast to those of Mead's social world in the United States. Arapesh held that there are no fundamental differences between men and women, that both are naturally maternal, nurturing, and nonaggressive. Mundugumor too believed that there were no fundamental differences but that men and women are both aggressive, proud, violent, and harsh. Finally, Tchambuli believed that men were, in Mead's terms, naturally feminine whereas women were naturally masculine. What this comparative study tell us is that people tend to naturalize differences between men and women, but that the form that naturalization takes is culturally variable. We must ask: Of all the ways that human beings could organize and conceptualize their worlds, why do they do it in this or that particular way? Human beings often assert that culturally constructed phenomena are really "natural" phenomena, because then they seem more real and truthful, and not subject to change.

Following Mead's research, anthropologists, in and out of Africa, have sought to explain the extraordinary diversity of beliefs about sex and gender that are taken to be so axiomatic or natural, and to explicate the complex relations between those beliefs and other aspects of culture, including art, myth, ritual, economics, and political systems. Some, such as Sherry Ortner and Michelle Rosaldo, have addressed the problem of a universal sexism: the ways in which men are frequently construed (and extolled) as "cultural" – producing and practicing technologies, and controlling a society's economic and symbolic resources – and the ways in which women are frequently construed (and denigrated) as "natural," performing sexual, reproductive and childrearing functions. Others, such as Marilyn Strathern and Brad Shore have noted that the "the same axes that divide and distinguish male from female (and indeed rank male over female), also cross-cut the gender categories, producing internal distinctions and gradations within them" (Ortner and Whitehead, 1981: 9; Grinker, 1994: 74–75). In other words, the categories of male–female domination become categories of domination between men. Indeed, in Chapter 13 of this volume, Roy Richard Grinker's work in Zaire describes how gender categories used to distinguish men from women are used also to distinguish between whole ethnic groups. To some extent, gender becomes a free-floating set of symbols, even an artifice, applicable to myriad aspects of human existence that lie far beyond observable everyday relations between men and women.

All of these authors thus argue that the ramifications of gender concepts are complex and wide-ranging. A related argument is that we must always question the utility and validity of comparative categories, even the categories "man" and "woman." Taking aim at some recent feminist literature, Chandra Mohanty levels a harsh critique against authors who essentialize "third world women," that is, authors who create a singular, monolithic, homogeneous category of person. She contends that the process of homogenization is also, perhaps unwittingly, a process of oppression, appropriated by western feminists as a way to characterize poor, non-western women, as ahistorical, undifferentiated victims who can be used for western feminist advocacy. According to Mohanty, many authors try to achieve solidarity for "women" throughout the world, but by doing so they also tend to represent women as powerless and dependent, and to reinforce ethnocentric beliefs about sex and gender. As Mohanty puts it, they risk saying that "They cannot represent themselves; they must be represented" (1994: 216).

The first reading in this part deals with polygynous marriage, a practice that appears throughout the continent of Africa, in which a man has more than one wife. This term should be distinguished from the more general term "polygamy," which refers to someone, male or female, having more than one spouse, and thus includes the specific term "polyandry," in which a woman has more than one husband. Polyandry is uncommon in Africa, having been outlawed in Nigeria and elsewhere during colonization, and occurs most frequently in north India, Tibet, and Nepal (Sangree and Levine, 1978). Throughout Africa, many men and women consider polygyny to be an ideal form of marriage, though the expense of paying bridewealth and supporting a large family often proves prohibitive for men. There are other difficulties as well. Among the Lese and Efe of northeastern Zaire, for example, all men strive to have more than one wife, but even those who achieve their goal, and can support their families financially, find it difficult to keep peace in the family. Jealousies and competition between co-wives, and disputes over access to land and other resources, often make polygynous marriages more unstable than monogamous ones. In West Africa, some high ranking men were known to have had hundreds of wives, but the most common number of spouses in polygynous marriages is two, with one woman the principal or senior wife. In Muslim marriages in Africa, and elsewhere, Qur'anic scripture dictates no more than four wives, for beyond that, the Prophet Mohammed believed, a man would not be able to attend to his family with sufficient care. Beyond two, rivalries become especially intense as alliances and factions among co-wives may emerge. In most polygynous marriages in Africa, wives commonly occupy separate huts in the same compound, may till different plots of land, and feed their children separately.

Although there are a number of important issues that arise in the study of polygamy, Boserup writes primarily about its economic logic. Drawing on data from throughout Africa, but most specifically from the Yoruba of Nigeria, Boserup outlines the relationships between polygamy, women's status, and farming.

Why would some men want polygynous marriages?

Why would some women want polygynous marriages?

Is "women's" position debased in polygynous societies?

Is the co-wife only a "guest" in her husband's house and village, with few rights of her own?

Although Boserup does not address these questions directly, it is useful to consider how ethnocentric it would be for people who live in monogamous societies to automatically assume that African polygyny has primarily negative effects on women's lives. Polygyny offers a degree of freedom not available to women in monogamous unions, allowing women to travel more frequently, engage in entrepreneurial or trade activities, or visit friends and relatives. If a woman is ill, there are others who can care for her children; if she is absent, others can care for her garden. In northeastern Zaire, where women suffer from a high rate of infertility, infertile women can ensure their position within a village by bringing in an additional wife who can reproduce where she could not. Among the Lovedu of West Africa, woman–woman marriage served precisely this function, as a woman married another woman who would then have a sexual reproductive relationship with the first woman's husband. The Lovedu (Krige, 1943) are also notable in that they are one of the few African societies whose supreme ruler, the Rain Queen, was a woman. It is also difficult to extrapolate from a single custom a generalized status. As Robert Murphy notes, married women in France were allowed to have their own bank accounts only in 1968, but most West African women have always had the right to control their finances (1979: 67). Yet, polygamy is an issue on which there is little agreement, and local activists throughout Africa continue to press for the abolition of polygyny and other customs they deem harmful to women, such as circumcision and bridewealth. Depending upon one's perspective, bridewealth can appear as akin to purchase or prostitution, and polygamy as an excuse for male domination. In addition to the many women's organizations and legal advocacy groups in Africa speaking and writing on polygamy and human rights, the many perspectives on polygamy also appear in the writings of many African poets and novelists (see, for example, Mariama Ba, *So Long a Letter*). Of course this debate goes on.

In the next piece, Mona Etienne traces the historical impact of European colonization on male–female relations among the Baule of Côte d'Ivoire. Although this article might just as easily appear in the next part on colonization, we include it here because Etienne's concern with the interconnections between economic and gender relations complements the other readings in this part. Her focus on cloth is especially important for us as we consider the implications of part two, "Economics as a Cultural System," and part six, "Arts and Aesthetics." In precolonial days, Baule women controlled the production and distribution of cloth, one of the more valuable artistic and practical products in Baule life, while men controlled the staple food, yams. Although there were many male weavers, women controlled their end products because they owned the thread itself. Exchanges of cloth were vital to establishing all sorts of social relations, especially marriages, linkages between neighbouring villages, and long distance trade. Trading or selling cloth could make a man or woman wealthy, or at least help them to achieve a high level of prestige; but even more importantly, cloth gave women a

significant amount of power and influence in Baule society. Women and men were equally dependent upon one another, the one for food, the other for cloth.

During the French colonization of Côte d'Ivoire, however, Baule men and women were required to pay taxes, and to fulfill colonial administration quotas on agricultural production. As one result, women were sometimes forced to cultivate men's crops, such as yams, and to cultivate cotton for cash rather than for local social purposes. In addition, men, especially male weavers, could now buy thread directly from factories established by the French, thus bypassing women and alienating them from the whole production–distribution process. Consequently, women's power has decreased significantly, especially within marriages, and women today sell their labor so that they can get cash. Men remunerate them as they wish because they no longer depend upon them for any essential products.

Etienne also tells us of the important role women played in the struggle for independence, and how the state today distributes cloths, with images of national symbols, to women for political advertisement. Cloth continues to be highly valued, but it is given to women rather than given by them. Judith Van Allen also writes about women's power, and how colonialism, in this case by the British, resulted in a loss of the influence women exercised in the non-centralized political institutions of the Igbo of Nigeria. Van Allen notes that Igbo politics have always involved diffuse power relations, with status largely achieved, rather than ascribed, and the women using meetings (*mikiri*) to regulate market activity, call boycotts and strikes, and otherwise consult about women's interests that oppose men's interests. Specific actions taken against men were metaphorically referred to as "sitting on a man."

When the British colonial administration attempted to define lines of political authority among the Igbo – to produce a "native administration" consistent with the policy of "indirect rule" – they chose to ignore local political institutions of both Igbo men and women. The disastrous results of their selective blindness, and their unwillingness to include women in the new systems of local government, can be seen in Van Allen's depiction of one of the greatest demonstrations of women's power in African history: the Women's War.

Political reforms instituted by the British in 1933 did little to address women's needs, and further marginalized the women from economic and political power centers. The diffuse political system on which women's power and influence once depended was gone, as was any legitimate system of self-help, or the method of "sitting on a man." All were replaced by Native Courts, the participation in which was exclusively male, and the practice of which was geared toward men's interests. Van Allen and Etienne's articles suggest that, while colonial administrations throughout Africa consistently argued that westernization and the introduction of modern political structures and values would expand the rights and freedoms of all individuals, women's political participation withered, giving way instead to the British ideal of the politically invisible Victorian woman.

In order to highlight the differences between sex and gender, and to demonstrate how African women's gender roles were constituted by race, class, and colonization, Karen Tranberg Hansen's article addresses another aspect of the relation between colonialism and gender: domestic servants in Northern Rhodesia (current day Zambia). It should also be noted that Hansen's focus on the so-called "domestic unit" or household complements a host of previous studies that have questioned the household as a distinct and isolated "unit of analysis" and have described the complex ways in which different individuals and groups co-operate and compete with another's economic activities (Peters, 1994; Moock, 1992; Guyer, 1981). In contrast to South Africa, and Southern

Rhodesia, where domestic servants were predominantly female, Northern Rhodesian domestic servants were almost all male – despite concerted efforts of the British colonial administration to recruit men into what the British deemed to be more productive economic activities.

One of the reasons why Northern Rhodesian domestic servants were male is that the colonists were newcomers to Africa. Whereas South African white men and women had been in Africa for long periods of time (their ancestors arriving in South Africa as early as the seventeenth century), white women in Northern Rhodesia arrived in large numbers only after World War II. These newcomers brought with them ideas about Africans that were relatively absent in other parts of Africa where Europeans had long been settled. For example, British women in Northern Rhodesia believed that African women were hypersexualized and promiscuous, and so they did not want African women in their households. They might be unable to control such women, and they feared that the women might seduce their husbands. Neither white men or women believed, however, that there was a strong likelihood of interracial sex between African men and white women, and so African men were seen as the more ideal, least dangerous, servants. Hansen tells us that, even in post-colonial Zambia, wealthy Zambian women want male servants. However, instead of denigrating women in general as hypersexual, these Zambians denigrate lower class women as hypersexual. In this article on the complexities of gender and sex identities, we thus find that the colonial British and wealthy Zambians, have similar ideas about gender and sex, but that these ideas are culturally constructed from different perspectives. In Zambia, class differences are now used to characterize sexuality where previously racial differences were used.

References

Cutrufelli, Maria Rose, 1983. *Women of Africa: Roots of Oppression*. Nicolas Romano, trans. London: Zed Press.

Guyer, J. I. 1981. "Household and Community in African Studies." *African Studies Review*, vol. 24, (2/3):, pp. 87–137.

Hewlett, Barry. 1991. *Intimate Fathers: The Nature and Context of Aka Pygmy Paternal Care*. Ann Arbor: University of Michigan.

Krige, Eileen. 1943. *The Realm of the Rain Queen: A Study of the Pattern of Lovedu Society*. London: Oxford University Press.

Lacqueur, Thomas. 1990. *Making Sex: Body and Gender from the Greeks to Freud*. Cambridge, MA: Harvard University Press.

Mohanty, Chandra Talpade. 1991. Under Western Eyes: Feminist Scholarship and Colonial Discourses. In Mohantry, Chandra Talpade, Ann Russo and Lourdes Torres, eds. *Third World Women and the Politics of Feminism*. pp.51–80. Bloomington: Indiana University Press.

Moodie, T. Dunbar with Vivienne Ndatshe. 1994. *Going for Gold: Men, Mines and Migration*. Berkeley and Los Angeles: University of California Press.

Mook, Joyce Lewenger, ed. 1992. *Diversity, Farmer Knowledge and Sustainability*. Ithaca: Cornell University Press.

Moore, Henrietta. 1988 *Feminist Anthropology*. Minneapolis: University of Minnesota Press.

Moore, Henrietta and Megan Vaughan. 1994. *Cutting Down Trees: Gender, Nutrition, and Agricultural Change in the Northern Province of Zambia, 1890–1990*. Portsmouth, NH: Heinemann.

Murphy, Robert. 1979. *Overture to Social Anthropology*. Princeton: Prentice-Hall.

Ortner, Sherry B. and Harriet Whitehead, eds. 1981. "Introduction: Accounting for Sexual Meanings." In *Sexual Meanings: The Cultural Construction of Gender and Sexuality*, pp. 1–28. Cambridge: Cambridge University Press.

Peters, Pauline, 1994. *Dividing the Commons: Politics, Policy and Culture in Botswana*. Charlottesville: University of Virginia Press.

Sangree, Walter H. and Nancy E. Levine, eds. 1978. Women with Many Husbands: Polyandrous. Alliance and Marital Flexibility in Africa and Asia. Special Issue: *Journal of Comparative Family Studies*, 11(3).

Suggested Readings

Adepoju, Aderanti and Christine Oppong, eds. 1994. *Gender, Work and Population in Sub-Saharan Africa*. Portsmouth, NH: Heinemann.

Ardener, E. 1962. *Divorce and Fertility: An African Study*. London: Oxford University Press.

Ba, Mariama. 1981. *So Long a Letter*. Oxford: Heinemann.

Bay, Edna G. 1982. *Women and Work in Africa*. Boulder: Westview.

Bledsoe, Caroline H. 1980. *Women and Marriage in Kpelle Society*. Stanford: Stanford University Press.

Clark, Gracia. 1994. *Onions are my Husband: Survival and Accumulation by West African Market Women*. Chicago: University of Chicago Press.

Creevey, Lucy, ed. 1986. *Women Farmers in Africa: Rural development in Mali and the Sahel*. Syracuse, NY: Syracuse University Press.

Grinker, Roy Richard. 1994. *Houses in the Rainforest: Ethnicity and Inequality among Farmers and Foragers in Central Africa*. Berkeley: University of California Press.

Guyer, Jane I. 1984. *Family and Farm in Southern Cameroon*. Boston: Boston University African Studies Center.

Guyer, Jane I. 1988. "The Multiplication of Labor: Historical Methods in the Study of Gender and Agricultural Change in Modern Africa. *Current Anthropology* 29: 247–72.

Hay, Margaret Jean. 1995. *African Women South of the Sahara* 2nd edition. New York: Longmann.

Hay, Margaret Jean and Marcia Wright, eds. 1982. *African Women and the Law: Historical Perspectives*. Boston: Boston University African Studies Center.

Heald, Suzette. 1982. "The Making of Men." *Africa*, 52: 15–35.

Issacs, Gordon and Brian McKendrick. *Male Homosexuality in South African Identity: Formation, Culture and Crisis.*

Jacobson-Widding, Anita. 1991. *Body and Space: Symbolic Models of Unity and Division in African Cosmology and Experience.* Uppsala and Stockholm, Sweden: Upsaliensis Academie.

Kratz, Corinne A. 1994. *Affecting Performance: Meaning, Movement and Experience in Okiek Women's Initiation.* Washington, D. C.: Smithsonian Institution Press.

Llewelyn-Davies, Melissa. 1981. "Women, Warriors and Patriarchs. In Ortner, Sherry B, and Harriet Whitehead, eds. 1981. *Sexual Meanings: The cultural Construction of Gender and Sexuality*, pp. 330–358. Cambridge: Cambridge University Press.

Mafeje, A. 1991. *African Households and Prospects for Agricultural Revival in Sub-Saharan Africa.* Codresia Working Papers. Dakar: Codresia.

Obbo, Christine. 1980. *African Women.* London: Zed Press.

Oppong. C. 1974. *Marriage among a Matrilineal Elite.* Cambridge: Cambridge University Press.

Murray, Colin. 1981. *Families Divided: The Impact of Migrant Labour in Lesotho.* Johannesburg: Raven.

Parkin, David. 1975. *Town and Country in Central and Eastern Africa.* United Kingdom: IAI.

Paulme, Denise, ed. 1963, *Women of Tropical Africa.* H. M. Wright, trans. London: Routledge and Kegan Paul.

p'Bitek, Okot. 1966. *Song of Lawino.* Nairobi: East African Publishing House.

Rosaldo, Michelle Z. and Louise Lamphere. 1974. *Woman, Culture and Society.* Stanford: Stanford University Press.

Schuster, Ilsa. 1979. *New Women of Lusaka.* New York: Mayfield.

Steady, Filomina Chiona, ed. 1985. *The Black Woman Cross-Culturally.* Rochester, Vermont: Schenkman Books.

29

THE ECONOMICS OF POLYGAMY

ESTER BOSERUP

Some years ago, UNESCO held a seminar on the status of women in South Asia. The seminar made this concluding statement after a discussion of the problem of polygamy: "Polygamy might be due to economic reasons, that is to say, the nature of the principal source of livelihood of the social group concerned, e.g. agriculture, but data available to the Seminar would not permit any conclusions to be drawn on this point".[1]

It is understandable that such a cautious conclusion should be drawn in Asia where the incidence of polygamy is low and diminishing. In Africa, however, polygamy is widespread, and nobody seems to doubt that its occurrence is closely related to economic conditions. A report by the secretariat of the UN Economic Commission for Africa (ECA) affirms this point: "One of the strongest appeals of polygamy to men in Africa is precisely its economic aspect, for a man with several wives commands more land, can produce more food for his household and can achieve a high status due to the wealth which he can command".[2]

It is self explanatory, given women's input in African farming, that a man can get more food if he has more land and more wives to cultivate it. But why is it that the more wives

he has got, the more land he can command, as the ECA statement says? The explanation lies in the fact that individual property in land is far from being the only system of land tenure in Africa. Over much of the continent, tribal rules of land tenure are still in force. This implies that members of a tribe which commands a certain territory have a native right to take land under cultivation for food production and in many cases also for the cultivation of cash crops. Under this tenure system, an additional wife is an additional economic asset which helps the family to expand its production.

In regions of shifting cultivation, where women do all or most of the work of growing food crops, the task of felling the trees in preparation of new plots is usually done by older boys and very young men, as already mentioned. An elderly cultivator with several wives is likely to have a number of such boys who can be used for this purpose. By the combined efforts of young sons and young wives he may gradually expand his cultivation and become more and more prosperous, while a man with a single wife has less help in cultivation and is likely to have little or no help for felling. Hence, there is a direct relationship

---

[1] Appadorai, 19.
[2] UN. ECA., *Wom. Trad. Soc*, 5.

between the size of the area cultivated by a family and the number of wives in the family. For instance, in the Bwamba region of Uganda, in East Africa, it appeared from a sample study that men with one wife cultivated an average of 1.67 acres of land, while men with two wives cultivated 2.94 acres, or nearly twice as much. The author of the study describes women in this region as "the cornerstone and the limiting factor in the sphere of agricultural production" and notes that almost all the men desire to have additional wives. A polygamic family is "the ideal family organization from the man's point of view".[3]

In female farming communities, a man with more than one wife can cultivate more land than a man with only one wife. Hence, the institution of polygamy is a significant element in the process of economic development in regions where additional land is available for cultivation under the long fallow system. There is an inverse correlation between the use of female family labour and the use of hired labour. It seems that farmers usually either have a great deal of help from their wives, or else they hire labour. Thus farmers in polygamic communities have a wider choice in this than have farmers in monogamic communities. In the former community, the use of additional female family labour is not limited to the amount of work that one wife and her children can perform; the total input of labour can be expanded by the acquisition of one or more additional wives.

This economic significance of polygamy is not restricted to the long fallow system of cultivation. In many regions, farmers have a choice between an expansion of cultivation by the use of more labour in long fallow cultivation, with a hoe, or an expansion by the transion to shorter fallow with ploughs drawn

by animals.[4] In such cases, three possible ways of development present themselves to the farmer: expansion by technical change (the plough); expansion by hierarchization of the community (hired labour); or expansion by the traditional method of acquiring additional wives. In a study of economic development in Uganda, Audrey Richards pointed to this crucial role of polygamy as one of the possible ways to agricultural expansion: "It is rare to find Africans passing out of the subsistence farm level without either the use of additional labour (read: hired labour E.B.), the introduction of the plough, which is not a practical proposition in Buganda; or by the maintenance of a large family unit, which is not a feature of Ganda social structure at the moment.[5]

In the same vein, Little's classical study of the Mende in the West African state of Sierra Leone concluded that "a plurality of wives is an agricultural asset, since a large number of women makes it unnecessary to employ much wage labour".[6] At the time of Little's study (i.e. in the 1930s), it was accepted in the more rural areas that nobody could run a proper farm unless he had at least four wives. Little found sixty-seven wives to the twenty-three cultivators included in his sample and an average of 842 households. He describes how the work of one wife enables him to acquire an additional one: "He says to his first wife, 'I like such and such a girl. Let us make a bigger farm this year.' As soon as the harvest is over for that year, he sells the rice and so acquires the fourth wife."[7]

Little's study is thirty years old, and the incidence of polygamy has declined since then. But, although households with large numbers of wives seem to have more or less disappeared in most of Africa, polygamy is still extremely

[3] Winter, 24.
[4] Simons, 79–80.
[5] Richards 1952, 204.
[6] Little 1951, 141–2.
[7] Little 1951, 141–2, 145.

Table 29.1 [4]   Incidence of Polygamy in Africa

Country in which sample areas are located		Average number of wives per married men	Polygamic marriages as percentage of all existing marriages
Senegal	A	1.1	24
	B	1.3	23
	C	1.3	21
Sierra Leone		2.3	51
Ivory Coast		1.3	27
Nigeria	A	2.1[a]	63
	B	1.5	
Cameroon		1.0–1.3[b]	
Congo	A	1.3	11
	B	1.2	17
South Africa			14
Uganda	A	1.7	45
	B	1.2	

[a]   The figures refer to male heads of families, while married sons living with these seem to be excluded.
[b]   The lowest ratio refers to unskilled workers, the highest ratio to own-account workers.

Table 29.1 *Senegal: Sample A and B*, UN. ECA. Polygamy, 9–10, 70,000 persons in Dakar in 1955 and 1960. *Sample* C, Boutillier, 1962, 31, 33; 1,265 persons in the Valley of Senegal, 1957–8. Sierra Leone: Little 1948, 9–10n, 842 households in Mende Country, 1937. *Ivory Coast*: Boutillier 1960,45, sample of 3,764 persons, 1955–6. *Nigeria: Sample A*, Galetti, 71-2; 776 families in the Yoruba region, 1950–1. *Sample B*, Mortimore, 679, sample of 5,103 persons in Kano district, 1964. *Cameroon*: Gouellain, 260, population in New-Bell, Douala, 1956. *Congo: Sample A and B*, Balandier 1955, 136. Brazzaville and Delisie, 1952. *South Africa*: Reynders 260, sample of 1,180 households in Bantu areas, 1950–1. *Uganda: Sample A*, Winter, 23, sample of seventy-one families in Bwamba, 1951. *Sample B*, Katarikawe, 8, sample of fifty-nine families in Kiga resettlement schemes, 1956–6.

widespread and is considered an economic advantage in many rural areas. The present situation can be gleaned from Table 29.1, which brings together the results of a number of sample studies about the incidence of polygamy. It is seen that none of the more recent studies shows such a high incidence of polygamic marriages as in the period of Little's old study. Most of the studies show an average number of around 1.3 wives per married man.[*]

In most cases over one-fifth of all married men were found to have more than one wife at the time of enquiry.[†]

The acquisition of an additional wife is not always used as a means of becoming richer through the expansion of cultivation. In some cases, the economic role of the additional wife enables the husband to enjoy more leisure. A village study from Gambia showed that in the village, where rice is produced by women, men who had several wives to produce rice for them produced less millet (which is a crop produced

[*]   Some of the samples were taken in urban areas, where the incidence of polygamy is often, though not always lower than in rural areas.
[†]   To evaluate correctly this figure for the incidence of polygamy it must be taken that some of the married men, at the time of the enquiry, had one wife only because they were at an early stage of their married life, while others were older men living in monogamous marriage because they had lost other wives by death or divorce. Therefore, the figure for the incidence of polygamy would have been considerably higher if it were to show the proportion of men who have more than one wife at some stage of their married life.

Table 29.2 [5]   Rights and duties of Yoruba Women

Percentage of Women with the following rights and duties:

Wife receives from husband	Wife contributes to household:				
	as self-employed, family aid and housewife	as self-employed, and housewife	as family aid and housewife	as housewife	Total
Nothing	8	11			19
Part of food	32	16			48
All food	15	11	1	1	28
Food, clothing and cash	1		3	1	5
Total	56	38	4	2	100

Table 29.2. Galetti 77, sample of 144 women in seventy-three families in Yoruba region, 1951–2.

by men) than did men with only one wife.[8] Likewise, in the villages in the Central African Republic men with two wives worked less than men with one wife, and they found more time for hunting, the most cherished spare time occupation for the male members of the village population.[9]

Undoubtedly, future changes in marriage patterns in rural Africa will be closely linked to future changes in farming systems which may lessen (or enhance) the economic incentive for polygamic marriages. Of course, motives other than purely economic considerations are behind a man's decision to acquire an additional wife. The desire for numerous progeny is no doubt often the main incentive. Where both the desire for children and the economic considerations are at work, the incentives for polygamy are likely to be so powerful that religious or legal prohibition avails little.

A study of the Yoruba farmers of Nigeria has this to say: "There are no doubt other reasons why polygamy prevails in the Yoruba country as in other regions of the world; but the two which seem to be most prominent in

the minds of Yoruba farmers are that wives contribute much more to the family income that the value of their keep and that the dignity and standing of the family is enhanced by an increase of progeny. While these beliefs persist the institution of polygamy will be enduring, even in families which have otherwise accepted Christian doctrine. The Yoruba farmer argues that the increased output from his farms obtainable without cash expense when he has wives to help him outweighs the economic burden of providing more food, more clothing and larger houses.[10]

The Status of Younger Wives

It is easy to understand the point of view of the Yoruba farmers quoted above when one considers the contribution to family support which women make in this region. Economic relations between husband and wife among the Yoruba differ widely from the common practise of countries where wives are normally supported by their husbands. Only 5 per cent

8   Haswell, 10.
9   Georges, 18, 25, 31.
10   Galetti, 77.

of the Yoruba women in the sample reproduced in Table 29.2 received from their
husbands everything they needed – food,
clothing and some cash – and only 2 per cent
of them did no work other than domestic activities. A large majority were self-employed (in
agriculture, trade or crafts) and many helped a
husband on his farm in addition to their self-
employment and their domestic duties. Most
of these self-employed women had to provide
at least part of the food for the family as well as
clothing and cash out of their own earnings.
Nearly one-fifth of the women received
nothing from their husband and had to provide
everything out of their own earnings; nevertheless they performed domestic duties for the
husband and half of them also helped him on
his farm.

There may not be many tribes in Africa
where women contribute as much as the
Yorubas to the upkeep of the family, but it is
normal in traditional African marriages for
women to support themselves and their children and to cook for the husband, often using
food they produce themselves. A small sample
from Bamenda in the West African Cameroons showed that the women contributed 44
per cent of the gross income of the family.[11]
Many women of pastoral tribes, for instance
the Fulani tribe of Northern Nigeria and
Niger, are expected to provide a large part of
the cash expenses of the family out of their own
earnings from the sale of the milk and butter
they produce. They cover the expenditure on
clothing for their children and themselves as
well as buying food for the family.[12] In many
regions of East Africa, women are traditionally
expected to support themselves and many
women are said to prefer to marry Moslems
because a Moslem has a religious duty to
support his wife.

In a family system where wives are
supposed both to provide food for the family –
or a large part of it – and to perform the usual
domestic duties for the husband, a wife will
naturally welcome one or more co-wives to
share with them the burden of daily work.
Therefore, educated girls in Africa who
support the cause of monogamous marriage
as part of a modern outlook are unable to rally
the majority of women behind them.[13]
In the Ivory Coast, an opinion study indicated
that 85 per cent of the women preferred to
live in polygamous rather than monogamous
marriage. Most of them mentioned domestic
and economic reasons for their choice.[14]

In many cases, the first wife takes the initiative in suggesting that a second wife, who can
take over the most tiresome jobs in the household, should be procured. A woman marrying
a man who already has a number of wives often
joins the household more or less in the capacity
of a servant for the first wife, unless it happens
to be a love match.[15] It was said above that in
most parts of the world there seems to be an
inverse correlation between the use of female
labour and the use of hired labour in agriculture, i.e. that most farmers have some help
either from their wives or from hired labour.
However, in some regions with widespread
polygamy, hired labour is a *supplement* to the
labour provided by several wives, in the sense
that the tasks for which male strength is
needed are done by hired labour, while the
other tasks are done by wives. In such cases the
husband or his adult sons act only as
supervisors.

Reports from different parts of Africa,
ranging from the Sudan to Nigeria and the
Ivory Coast, have drawn attention to this
frequent combination of male labourers and
wives of polygamous cultivators working

11. Kaberry, 141.
12. Forde, 203; Dupire 1960, 79.
13. UN. ECA., *Polygamy*, 32.
14. Boutillier 1960, 120.
15. Little 1951, 133.

Table 29.3 [6]   Age Distribution of Married Moslem Population of Dakar in Senegal

| | Percentages | | |
Age Group:	First Wives	Later Wives	Husbands
Below 25 years	12	35	
25–34 years	49	44	10
35–49 years	35	19	59
50 years and over	4	2	31
All ages	100	100	100

together in the fields under the supervision of one or more male family members.[16] In such cases, the availability of male labour for hire is not a factor which lessens the incentive to polygamous marriages. On the contrary, it provides an additional incentive to polygamous marriages as a means of expanding the family business without changing the customary division of labour between the two sexes. Little reported that in Sierra Leone men with several wives sometimes used them to ensnare male agricultural labourers and get them to work for them without pay.[17]

In regions where polygamy is the rule, it is likely, for obvious demographic reasons, that many males will have to postpone marriage, or even forego it. Widespread prostitution or adultery is therefore likely to accompany widespread polygamy, marriage payments are likely to be insignificant or non-existant for the bride's family and high for the bridegroom's family, sometimes amounting to several years' earnings of a seasonal labourer.[18] This will induce parents to marry off their daughters rather young, but in a period like the present, where each generation of girls is numerically larger than the previous one, the difference in age between the spouses will be narrower than it was previously.

Figures from Dakar, the capital of Senegal, shown in Table 29.3 illustrate the importance of the age difference between the spouses. Here, the average marriage age for women is 18 years, and the average age of first marriage for men is between 27 and 28 years. The average age difference between men and their second wives is over 15 years, and nearly all wives belong to age groups which are larger than those to which their husbands belong.[19] No less than 90 per cent of married men belong to the relatively small generations over 35, as can be seen from the table, while only 39 per cent of their first wives and 21 per cent of their second wives belong to these generations.

Economic policy during the period of colonial rule in Africa contributed to the introduction or reinforcement of the customary wide difference in marriage age of young men and girls. In order to obtain labour for head transport, construction works, mines and plantations, the Europeans recruited young villagers at an age where they might have married had they stayed on in the village. Instead they married after their return several years later. The result was an age structure in the villages with very few young men in the age group between 20 and 35 and the need to marry young girls to much older men who had returned from wage labour.

The difference between the numbers of boys and girls in villages where the custom of taking away wage labourers before marriage

[16]   Baumann, 307; Forde, 45; Boutillier 1960, 97; Gosselin, 521.
[17]   Little 1951, 141; 1948, 11.
[18]   Forde, 75n.
[19]   UN. ECA., *Polygamy*, 24.

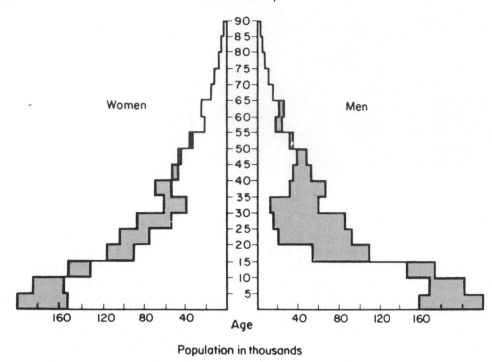

Shaded portion represents persons absent from the African areas

Figure 29.1 [3] Sex and Age Structure of Population in African Areas of South Rhodesia in 1956

persists, can be seen from Figure 29.1 which gives the age distribution in Rhodesian villages as reported in a study by J. Clyde Mitchell.[20] In the age groups 20–35 nearly all the men are away and the number of women in these age groups is several times higher than that of the men. In many other parts of Africa, recruitment for mines, plantations and urban industries results in similarly abnormal age distributions in the villages where the labourers are recruited.

Normally, the status of the younger wife is inferior as befits the assistant or even servant to the first wife. This can be explained partly as a result of the wide age difference between husband and wife and between first and younger wife, but the historical background of the institution of polygamy must also be kept in mind. Domestic slavery survived until fairly recently in many parts of Africa, and the legal ban on slavery introduced by European colonial powers provided an incentive for men to marry girls whom otherwise they might have kept as slaves.

In a paper published as recently as 1959, it is mentioned that in the Ivory Coast women were still being pawned by husbands or fathers to work in their creditor's fields, together with his own wives and daughters and without pay until the debt was paid off, when they were free to return to their own families.[21] Today, such arrangements may be rare in Africa, but it is

20. Mitchell, *Soc. Backgr.*, 80.
21. d'Aby, 49.

probable that the bride price for an additional wife is sometimes settled by the cancellation of a debt from the girl's family to the future husband, which would come to much the same thing in terms of real economic relationships.

Embodied in Moslem law is the well-known rule that all wives must be treated equally, which implies that the younger wives must not be used as servants for the senior wives. Moreover, a limit is set to the use of wives for expansion of the family business, partly by limiting the allowable number of wives to four, and partly by making the husband responsible for the support of his wives. We have already mentioned that this serves to make Moslem men desirable marriage partners for many African girls in regions where girls married to non-Moslems are expected to support themselves and their children by hard work in the fields. Because of this principle of equal treatment, first wives in orthodox Moslem marriages may desist from making the younger wives perform the most unpleasant tasks. Often in African families – Moslem and non-Moslem – each wife has her own hut or house and cooks independently, while the husband in regular succession will live and eat with each of his wives. Even so, the wife gains by not having to feed her husband all the time, and we sometimes find that women prefer polygamy even where the wives are treated equally.

In most of Africa the rule is that a wife may leave her husband provided that she pays back the bride price. In regions where wives must do hard agricultural work, many young girls wish to find money to enable them to leave a much older husband, and many husbands fear that their young wives will be able to do so.[22] This makes older men take an interest on one hand in keeping bride prices at a level which makes it difficult for women to earn enough to pay them back and on the other hand in preventing their young wives from obtaining money incomes. Later we shall see what role these conflicting interests between men and women are playing in development policy.

Work Input and Women's Status

Polygamy offers fewer incentives in those parts of the world where, because they are more densely populated than Africa, the system of shifting cultivation has been replaced by the permanent cultivation of fields ploughed before sowing. However, in some regions where the latter system prevails, polygamy may have advantages. This is true particularly where the main crop is cotton, since women and children are of great help in the plucking season.[23] But in farming systems where men do most of the agricultural work, a second wife can be an economic burden rather than an asset. In order to feed an additional wife the husband must either work harder himself or he must hire labourers to do part of the work. In such regions, polygamy is either non-existent or is a luxury in which only a small minority of rich farmers can indulge. The proportion of polygamic marriages is reported to be below 4 per cent in Egypt, 2 per cent in Algeria, 3 per cent in Pakistan and Indonesia.[24] There is a striking contrast between this low incidence of polygamy and the fact that in many parts of Africa South of the Sahara one-third to one-fourth of all married men have more than one wife.

In regions where women do most of the agricultural work it is the bridegroom who must pay bridewealth, as already mentioned, but where women are less actively engaged in agriculture, marriage payments come usually from the girl's family. In South and East Asia the connection between the work of women

---

[22]   Winter, 23.
[23]   Arnaldez, 50.
[24]   UN. ECA., *Wom. N. Afr.*, 41; Appadorai, 18.

and the direction of marriage payments is close and unmistakable. For instance, in Burma, Malaya and Laos women seem to do most of the agricultural work and bride prices are customary.[25] The same is true of Indian tribal people, and of low-caste peoples whose women work. By contrast, in the Hindu communities, women are less active in agriculture, and instead of a bride price being paid by the bridegroom, a dowry has to be paid by the bride's family.[26] A dowry paid by the girl's family is a means of securing for her a good position in her husband's family. In the middle of the nineteenth century it was legal for a husband in Thailand to sell a wife for whom he had paid a bride price, but not a wife whose parents had paid a dowry to the husband.[27]

Not only the payment of a dowry but also the use of the veil is a means of distinguishing the status of the upper class wife from that of the "servant wife." In ancient Arab society, the use of the veil and the retirement into seclusion were means of distinguishing the honoured wife from the slave girl who was exposed to the public gaze in the slave market.[28] In the Sudan even today it appears to be a mark of distinction and sophistication for an educated girl to retire into seclusion when she has finished her education.[29]

In communities where girls live in seclusion, and a large dowry must be paid when they marry, parents naturally come to dread the burden of having daughters. In some of the farming communities in Northern India, where women do little work in agriculture and the parents know that a daughter will in due course cost them the payment of a dowry, it was customary in earlier times to limit the

number of surviving daughters by infanticide. This practise has disappeared, in its outward forms, but nevertheless the ratio of female to male population in these districts continues to be abnormal compared to other regions of India and to tribes with working women living in the same region. A recent study of regional variations in the sex ratio of population in India[30] reached the conclusion that the small number of women in the Northern districts could not be explained either by undernumeration of females, or by migration, or by a low female birthrate. The only plausible hypothesis would be that mortality among girls was higher than among boys. The conclusion drawn was that "the persistence of socio-cultural factors are believed to be largely responsible for the excess of female mortality over the male."[31] One of these socio-cultural factors seem to be a widespread supposition that milk is not good for girls, but is good for boys. There is also a tendency to care more for sick boys than for sick girls.[32]

In a study from a district in Central India with a deficit of women, the author is very outspoken about the neglect of girls: "The Rajputs always preferred male children. . . . Female infanticide, therefore, was a tolerated practise. . . . Although in the past 80 years the proportion of the females to males has steadily risen yet there was always a shortage of women in the region. . . . When interrogated about the possibility of existence of female infanticide, the villagers emphatically deny its existence. . . . It was admitted on all hands that if a female child fell ill, then the care taken was very cursory and if she died there was little sorrow. In fact, in a nearby village a cultivator had

25 MiMi Khaing, 109; Swift, 271; Lévy, 264.
26. Mitham, 283–4.
27. Purcell, 295.
28 Izzedin, 299.
29 Tothill, 245.
30. Visaria, 334–71.
31 Visaria, 370.
32 Karve, 103–4.

twelve children – six sons and six daughters. All the daughters fell ill from time to time and died. The sons also fell ill but they survived. The villagers know that it was by omissions that these children had died. Perhaps there has been a transition from violence to non-violence in keeping with the spirit of the times."[33] The report adds that "no records of birth or deaths are kept. . . . it was enjoined upon the Panchayat (village council) to keep these statistics, but they were never able to fulfil the task".[34] It is explicitly said in the study that the district is one where wives and daughters of cultivators take no part in field work. In some cases, the shortage of women in rural communities in North India induce the cultivators to acquire low caste women from other districts, or from other Indian States, against the payment of a bride price.[35] This need not be an infringement on caste rules. Although it is usually forbidden for a man to marry a woman of a higher caste, men of higher caste may have the right to marry women of lower castes.[36] This may then entail the payment of a bride price instead of the receipt of a dowry as would be customary in the husband's own subcaste.

To summarize the analysis of the position of women in rural communities, two broad groups may be identified: the first type is found in regions where shifting cultivation predominates and the major part of agricultural work is done by women. In such communities, we can expect to find a high incidence of polygamy, and bride wealth being paid by the future husband or his family. The women are hard working and have only a limited right of support from their husbands, but they often enjoy considerable freedom of movement and some economic independence from the sale of their own crops.

The second group is found where plough cultivation predominates and where women do less agricultural work than men. In such communities we may expect to find that only a tiny minority of marriages, if any, are polygamous; that a dowry is usually paid by the girl's family; that a wife is entirely dependent upon her husband for economic support; and that the husband has an obligation to support his wife and children, at least as long as the marriage is in force.

We find the first type of rural community in Africa South of the Sahara, in many parts of South East Asia and in tribal regions in many parts of the world. We also find this type among descendents of negro slaves in certain parts of America.[37] The second type predominates in regions influenced by Arab, Hindu and Chinese culture.

Of course, this distinction between two major types of community is a simplification, like any other generalization about social and economic matters. This must be so because many rural communities are already in transition from one type of technical and cultural system to another, and in this process of change some elements in a culture lag behind others to a varying degree. For example, some communities may continue to have a fairly high incidence of polygamy or continue to follow the custom of paying bride price long after the economic incentive for such customs has disappeared as agricultural techniques changed.

In many rural communities hired labour is replacing the work of women belonging to the cultivator family. Where this happens, the economic incentive for polygamy may disappear, since additional wives are liable to become an economic burden. This, of course, is true only if it is assumed that the women

---

[33] Chatnager, 61–2.
[34] Bhatnagar, 65.
[35] Nath, May 1965, 816.
[36] Majumdar, 61.
[37] Bastide, 37ff.

who give up farm work retire into the purely domestic sphere. It is another matter if the women substitute farming by another economic activity such as trade.

In the type of rural community where women work hard, it is a characteristic that they are valued both as workers and as mothers of the next generation and, therefore, that the men keenly desire to have more than one wife. On the other hand, in a rural community where women take little part in field work, they are valued as mothers only and the status of the barren woman is very low in comparison with that of the mother of numerous male children. There is a danger in such a community that the propaganda for birth control, if successful, may further lower the status of women both in the eyes of men and in their own eyes. This risk is less in communities where women are valued because they contribute to the well-being of the family in other ways, as well as breeding sons.

References

Appadorai, A., *The Status of Women in South Asia*, Bombay 1954.

Arnaldez, Roger, "Le Coran et L'emancipation de la Femme", in Mury, Gilbert (ed.) *La Femme à la Recherche d'elle-même*, Paris 1966.

Bastide, Roger, Les Amériques Noires, Paris 1967.

Baumann, Hermann, "The Division of Work according to Sex in African Hoe Culture", in *Africa*, Vol. I, 1928.

Bhatnagar, K. S., *Dikpatura, Village Survey*, Monographs No. 4, Madhya Pradesh, Part VI, Census of India 1961, Delhi 1964, processed.

Boutillier, J. L., *Bongouanou Côte d'Ivoire*, Paris 1960.

Boutillier, J. L., et al., *La Moyenne Vallée de Sénégal*, Paris 1962.

d'Aby, F. J. Amon, "Report on Côte d'Ivoire", in International Institute of Differing Civilizations, *Women's Role in the Development of Tropical and Sub-Tropical Countries*, Brussels 1959.

Dupire, Marguerite, "Situation de la Femme dans une Société Pastorale (Peul Wo Da Be-Nomades du Niger)" in Paulme, Denise (ed.) *Femmes d'Afrique Noire*, Paris 1960.

Forde, Daryll, "The Rural Economies" in Perham, Margery (ed.), *The Native Economies of Nigeria*, London 1946.

Galletti, R., Baldwin, K. D .S. and Dina, I. O., *Nigerian Cocoa Farmers*, London 1956.

Georges, M. M. and Guet, Gabriel, *L'emploi du Temps du Paysan dans une Zone de L'oubangui Central 1959–60*, Bureau pour le Developpement de la Production Agricole, Paris 1961, processed.

Gouellain, R., "Parenté et affinités ethniques dans l'écologie du "Grand Quartier" de New-Bell, Douala in Southall, A. (ed.), *Social Change in Modern Africa*, London 1961.

Haswell, M. R., *The Changing Pattern of Economic Activity in a Gambia Village*, HMS London 1963, processed.

Izzeddin, Nejla, *The Arab World*, Chicago 1953.

Kaberry, Phyllis M., *Women of the Grassfields. A Study of the Economic Position of Women in Bamenda, British Cameroons.* Colonial Office, Research Publication No. 14, London 1952.

Karve, Irawati, "The Indian Woman in 1975" in *Perspectives, Supplement to the Indian Journal of Public Administration*, January–March 1966.

Katarikawe, E., "Some Preliminary Results of a Survey of Kiga Resettlement Schemes in Kigezi, Ankoll and Toro Districts, Western Uganda", *Research Paper Makerere University College*, R.D.R. 31, processed.

Lévy, Banyen Phimmasone, "Yesterday and today in Laos: a Girl's Autobiographical Notes", in Ward, Barbara E. (ed.) *Women in the New Asia, The Changing Social Roles of Men and Women in South and South-East Asia*, UNESCO 1963.

Little, K. L., "The Changing Position of Women in the Sierra Leone Protectorate", in *Africa*, Vol. XVIII, 1948.

Little, K. L., *The Mende of Sierra Leone. A West African People in Transition*, London 1951.

Majumdar, D. N., "About Women in Patrilocal Societies in South Asia", in Appadorai, A. (ed), *The Status of Women in South Asia*, Bombay 1954.

Mi Mi Khaing, "Burma, Balance and Harmony", in

Ward, Barbara E. (ed.), *Women in the New Asia, The Changing Social Roles of Men and Women in South and South-East Asia*, UNESCO 1963.

Mitchell, J. Clyde, "Wage Labour and African Population Movements in Central Africa", in Barbour, K. M. and Prothero, R. M. (ed.), *Essays on African Population*, London 1961.

Mitchell, J. Clyde, *Sociological Background to African Labour*, Salisbury 1961.

Nath, Kamla, "Women in the New Village", in *The Economic Weekly*. May 1965.

Purcell, V., "Report on Burma, Thailand and Malaya", in International Institute of Differing Civilizations, *Women's Role in the Development of Tropical and Sub-Tropical Countries*, Brussels 1959.

Reynders, H. J. J., "The Geographical Income of the Bantu Areas in South Africa", in Samuels, L. H. (ed.), *African Studies in Income and Wealth*, London 1963.

Richards, Audrey I., *Land, Labour and Diet in Northern Rhodesia. An Economic Study of the Bemba Tribe*, London 1939.

Richards, Audrey I., *Economic Development and Tribal Change*, Cambridge 1952.

Simons, H. J., *African Women. Their Legal Status in South Africa*, Evanston 1968.

Swift, Michael, "Men and Women in Malay Society", in Ward, Barbara E. (ed.) *Women in the New Asia. The Changing Social Roles of Men and Women in South and South-East Asia*, UNESCO 1963.

Tothill, J. D., *Agriculture in the Sudan*, London 1954.

United Nations Economic Commission for Africa, "Polygamie, Famille et Fait Urbain (Essai sur le Sénégal); *Workshop on Urban Problems*, Addis Ababa 1963, processed.

United Nations Economic Commission for Africa, "The Employment and Socio-Economic Situation of Women in some North African Countries" *Workshop on Urban Problems*, Addis Ababa 1963, processed.

United Nations Economic Commission for Africa, "Women in the Traditional African Societies," *Workshop on Urban Problems*, Addis Ababa 1963, processed.

Visaria, Pravin M., "The Sex Ratio of the Population of India and Pakistan and Regional Variations During 1901 – 61" in Bose, Ashish (ed.) *Pattern of Population Change in India 1951 – 61*, Bombay 1967.

Winter, E.H., "Bwamba Economy", *East African Studies"*, No. 5, Kampala 1955.

30

WOMEN AND MEN, CLOTH AND COLONIZATION: THE TRANSFORMATION OF PRODUCTION – DISTRIBUTION RELATIONS AMONG THE BAULE

MONA ETIENNE*

European interest in West Africa can be traced to antiquity, although direct contact was limited and its extent is not well known. Until the fifteenth century, West African goods reached Mediterranean Europe via the trans-Saharan trade, developed by the Carthaginians before their conquest by the Roman Empire. It is believed that Dieppois merchants established trading posts along the Upper Guinea Coast between 1364 and 1413, but early French overseas expansion focused on the Mediterranean and coastal North Africa. Maritime contact with West Africa developed only in the fifteenth century, when Portugal emerged as the foremost European colonial power, and the Atlantic seaboard became the first zone of regular contact between Europe and Africa south of the Sahara. The Portuguese traded along the coast for ivory, gold, spices, cloth, and slaves. They estab-lished coastal forts and missions, as well as sugar plantations and a cloth-dyeing center (using African dyeing methods) on offshore islands. There was some inland penetration.

Toward the mid-sixteenth century, the annexation of Portugal by Spain, growing interest in the Americas, and new sources of wealth in the Far East drew European attention away from Africa. With the expansion of the plantation economy in the Americas, however, the slave trade along the West African coast was renewed and reached unprecedented intensity in the eighteenth century. Some six million West Africans were shipped across the Atlantic. Because European traders acquired slaves almost entirely through agreements with African rulers and entrepreneurs and confined their activity to those stretches of the coast that were geographically and politically most accessible,

* This chapter is a revised version of an article originally published in *Cahiers d'Etudes africaines* XVII (1), 65, 1977:41–64. Some of the more specialized footnotes have been omitted and references have been updated. I thank Christine Gailey, Eleanor Leacock, and Susan Vogel for revision suggestions.

direct contact remained primarily coastal and ultimately was concentrated along the seaboard from the Gold Coast eastward and southward to the Cameroons. The demands of the slave trade nevertheless affected inland peoples throughout West Africa, causing raiding, wars of conquest and flight migration.

Progressive abolition of the Atlantic slave trade in the first half of the nineteenth century contributed to the renewal of "legitimate" trade and a new interest in West Africa as a source of foodstuffs and raw materials for industrial Europe, but did not immediately lead to inland penetration and conquest. For the most part, African entrepreneurs continued to satisfy the demands of European traders. Inland products reached the coast through established and adaptable trade networks, and palm oil – in high demand during the nineteenth century – was produced by coastal peoples. Again, the absence of direct colonial intervention did not preclude an indirect impact of European contact on the interior as well as the coast. It influenced productive activity and consumer needs and notably intensified the importance of domestic slavery. Most West African societies nevertheless maintained their sovereignty vis-à-vis European powers and some increased their prosperity, albeit at the expense of others. Coastal traders interacted autonomously with their European counterparts; coastal rulers commanded respect and controlled by treaties the establishment of trading counters by European firms. This situation was to change radically in the last quarter of the nineteenth century.

European industrial and economic expansion took on new momentum in the second half of the nineteenth century. The need for raw materials and foodstuffs increased, as did the need for markets for manufactured goods and opportunities for capital investment. At the same time, improved technology in naval construction rendered formerly difficult parts of the West African coast more accessible and made expanded trade more feasible by making

transportation more rapid and far less costly. (The first British steamship arrived in West Africa in 1851, but the steamship did not affirm its ascendancy over the sailing ship until the 1880s). The steamship and heightened demand for products and markets brought newcomers to West Africa and perturbed preexisting trade relations, creating rivalries among both Europeans and their African partners. The ensuing economic disorder was compounded by the "Great Depression" (1873–95) and a deterioration in the terms of trade to the detriment of primary producers, making Africans less amenable to European demands. These rivalries and this discontent sometimes materialized in violent conflict, leading trading firms, primarily British and French, to call for the intervention of their home governments.

These pressures coincided with new developments in European political rivalries. France, a major colonial power in the seventeenth century, had by the end of the Napoleonic Wars (1815) lost its most valuable overseas possessions and spheres of influence to Great Britain (although it retained Senegal, its earliest West African colony). Renewed colonial efforts had led in 1830 to the conquest and occupation by settlers of Algeria and, after 1843, to annexations in the Pacific. But France remained far behind Great Britain, both in industrial and economic development and as a world power, a situation that was not improved by the Franco–Prussian War (1870) or internal political conflict. In the early years of the Third Republic (1871–1940), colonialism was to become a weapon in the struggle within the ruling class between the republican vanguard of industrial capitalism and more conservative elements, allied with the Church and remnants of the aristocracy.

The last quarter of the nineteenth century was marked by intense rivalry among European powers – and the United States – to gain control of the rest of the world. By establishing effective occupation as a ground rule for official annexation, the Conference of

Berlin (1884–85) precipitated the "scramble" for Africa, with Great Britain and France the principal competitors. When partition was completed, France had acquired the greater part of West Africa. Inland penetration and conquest, actively pursued from the 1880s on, ended in the early years of the twentieth century.

This classical period of European imperialism stands in contrast to the dominant forms of overseas expansion in the past: on the one hand, scattered trading posts and spheres of influence and on the other (outside of West Africa), settlement colonies. Europeans no longer transported Africans elsewhere to exploit their labor, as in the slave trade, nor did they send expatriates to alienate and exploit African land, as in settlement colonization. Instead, they promoted a more systematic form of exploitation by using African labor to extract wealth from African land according to the demands of the colonial power, resorting to military force when necessary.

In France, lucid protagonists of this exploitation, who understood that short-term costs would bring long-term benefits, asserted themselves against the protests of the working class and the opposition of the old-guard bourgeoisie. In Ivory Coast, which became a colony in 1893, early administrators were representatives of the new ruling class – republican, anticlerical, and conscious of the economic goals they implemented. In the Ivory Coast hinterland, the proud and prosperous Baule, who had until then profited by coastal trade without ever encountering a European, rapidly experienced the full impact of the new colonialism, undisguised by missionizing and deterred only temporarily by their own resistance.

The Baule are a population of about one million occupying some 35,000 square kilometers in the center-east of Ivory Coast, beyond the pale of precolonial Islamic penetration from the north, well inland from the coast and marginal to West African kingdoms and major trade routes.[1] They are believed to have emerged as a cultural entity in the seventeenth and eighteenth centuries and their origin is very heterogeneous: preexisting Mande-Dyula, Voltaic and Kru elements, and groups of Akan immigrants, the first we know of from Denkyera and then, toward 1730, from Ashanti. The Akan, sometimes by conquest, sometimes peaceably, assimilated – or were assimilated by – the previous inhabitants of the region. Although many came from state societies, they failed in their attempts to constitute or reconstitute – a state. Effective centralization of authority was limited in scope and short-lived; political formations were subject to rapid change; stratification was never clearly defined or rigidly established (see P. de Salverte-Marmier 1965; P.de Salverte-Marmier, M.-A. de Salverte-Marmier, and P. Etienne 1965; Chauveau 1972a, 1972b, 1973; Weiskel 1976, 1977).

Because neither the coast nor the hinterland was easily accessible, we have no eyewitness accounts and little secondary information concerning the Baule before the end of the nineteenth century. For the same reason, they were affected only very indirectly by the Atlantic slave trade. It is probable, however, that the genesis of Baule society as we know it was strongly influenced by the violent impact of the slave trade on the Gold Coast hinterland, where slave raiding and political rivalry within and between African states sent unprecedented numbers of migrants westward

[1] Where specific references are not given, the source of my data is fieldwork in 1962 and 1963 among rural Baule of the Bouaké region, sponsored by the Ivory Coast government's Ministère du Plan, and in 1974–75 among urban Baule of Abidjan, supported by grant No. 3067 from the Wenner-Gren Foundation for Anthropological Research. I am grateful to the Ivory Coast government (Ministère de la Recherche scientifique) and to the University of Abidjan (Institut d'Ethnologie) for their authorization to pursue research in Abidjan. I thank Jean-Louis Boutillier, Ariane Deluz, Nicole-Claude Mathieu, and Claudine Vidal for contributing their suggestions to the original version of this chapter.

to a safer region. The reconstruction of Baule history also suggests that active trade relations with the Akan heartland to the east existed until the intensification of European trade along the Ivory Coast in the nineteenth century diverted Baule trade southward. The Baule are believed to have exchanged cloth and gold, and perhaps captives, for firearms and other European goods, which reached the hinterland of the Gold Coast (now Ghana) at a much earlier period. With the development of the palm-products trade in the nineteenth century, coastal populations directly to the south increased their production, and with it their purchasing power, and became desirable trading partners, offering and receiving much the same goods as those exchanged in the eastward trade.

The colonization of the Baule, documented by Weiskel (1977), began in 1893, when the French officer Marchand conquered Tiassalé, a trading post on their southern border, and then penetrated inland. Impressed by Baule prosperity, he recognized the economic potential of the region. At first amenable to new commercial relations and willingly responding to the demand for wild rubber that marked the early years of colonization, the Baule reacted violently from the very beginning to French attempts to interfere with their productive relations by mobilizing their labor or that of their captives. The French did not immediately pursue total military conquest, both because it was made difficult by Baule techniques of guerrilla warfare and because collaborative arrangements were reached whereby the colonial administration limited its demands and the Baule acceded to them. Until 1908, phases of armed conflict alternated with phases of relative peace and prosperity.

By 1909, however, the situation had changed: the economic status of the colony was unsatisfactory and, in any case, economic control was necessary if the potential of Baule land and labor was to be exploited. The new governor, Angoulvant, having provoked a revolt by tax reforms and attempts to force the Baule to produce cash crops under administrative and military control obtained support for total conquest, which he pursued by systematic search-and-destroy missions. The last Baule resistance was overcome in 1911. In 1912, the railroad reached Bouaké, an early military outpost in the heart of the Baule north, now the second largest city in Ivory Coast.

Baule Society in the Preconquest Period

In spite of their conquests and their resistance to colonization, the Baule do not appear as a people of warriors. Farming was and still is the essential productive activity; hunting and gathering, although secondary, were more important in the past. Crafts, now marginal, were essential in precolonial times and cotton-cloth production was particularly important. Uncultivated vegetable fibres were used for certain purposes (baskets, mats) and bark cloth was used for bedding. The continuing ritual importance of bark cloth as a gift from husband to mother-in-law "to replace the mat her daughter wet as a baby" may be a reminder of earlier times, but we find no clear evidence, as we do for other peoples, of a time when the Baule went unclothed or wore only bark cloth or raffia.

Marriage seems always to have been characterized by considerable freedom of choice, even in cases of childhood betrothal; there was no bridewealth, but only brideservice and symbolic gifts, primarily of consumable goods.[2] Descent, in the past as in the present,

---

[2]   Young women legitimately could – and did – reject the man they had been betrothed to in childhood. Exceptions to the general rule concerning bridewealth occurred in marriage with members of neighboring patrilineal societies and in one type of marriage practised by the wealthy and noble (see P. Etienne and M. Etienne 1971:172–73).

was cognatic, although the inheritance of wealth, including captives,[3] and of positions of authority was generally matrilineal. Because of the cognatic principle, group membership was indeterminate and depended both on the informal power relationship between maternal and paternal kin and on individual choice. It also depended very much on women, who, as mothers, tended to determine de facto group membership of children by attaching them to the domestic group with which they themselves elected residence.

These structural factors seem to have played a decisive role in determining the autonomy and mobility that are still characteristic of Baule people in general and Baule women in particular. Correlative with this autonomy and mobility we find between women and men, or between juniors and elders, no indication of clearly established relationships of subordination–domination and no mechanisms whereby husbands or elders could systematically appropriate the surplus production of wives or juniors, although in practice they might sometimes profit by it. (Even captives – at least the captive-born as opposed to those newly acquired – could control property during their lifetime.) The obligation to increase the sacred treasure of the kin group could perhaps have served such a purpose; it seems, however, to have weighed most heavily on the kin-group head and those who hoped to succeed to this position.

Land, the source of all subsistence, was available to all and all were subsistence producers, but durable wealth, especially in the form of gold and cloth, was important. Moreover, not only were there local barter of subsistence products, ritual gift-giving, and non-commodity exchange of prestige goods, both among the Baule and with neighboring societies, but there were forms of trade that can be defined as commodity exchange in the context of a noncapitalist society.[4] There was a system of gold weights and gold served as currency (see Chauveau 1972b; Meillassoux 1974: 263–75, 286). To control distribution of a product therefore could have real economic implications, not merely prestige value, as would be the case if production were only for subsistence use and ritual exchange.

Very schematically, this is the context of an analysis that will attempt to describe one limited instance of the impact of colonization on the relations between women and men.

All productive activity in Baule society was based on the sexual division of labor. In the case of some essential subsistence products, production was entirely the responsibility of one or the other sex and the producer was the "owner" of the product or, in other words, controlled its distribution. In the case of other products, both sexes contributed to production, each being in charge of specific tasks or phases of the production process; the sex that was considered to have initiated the process and taken responsibility for it "owned" the product or controlled its distribution. In both cases, the wife or husband who controlled an essential product had to provide for the subsistence needs of the other spouse and their children. When one sex controlled the product but the other had shared in its production, this latter could also receive a share of any surplus in exchange for his or her labor.

Thus, Baule marriage appears very much as an association between a woman and a man, not only for purposes of reproduction and childrearing, but also for purposes of production – the two being, of course, closely related. Although no social or supernatural sanctions

---

[3] *Captives*, a term I prefer to *slaves*, were numerous and important in Baule society. They were to all appearances assimilated through marriage and were never a separate caste or class, but their status was transmitted matrilineally and, in the matriline, was never lost.

[4]   There were, however, no large towns and no local or regional marketplaces, but only borderland markets or trading posts. (see Chauveau 1972b).

rigidly enforced the division of labor and a woman or man could, if necessary and possible, occasionally do the work of the other sex, this division of labor was clearly defined, maintained, and perpetuated by the socialization process. Possible deviation was further restricted by sex-specialized competence in tasks that required complex skills. . . .

Two products were both labor-demanding and vital to subsistence in Baule society: yams and cloth. Yams were the basic crop and, although survival was objectively conceivable without them, it would have been considered a miserable existence. To eat only cassava was "famine".

Cloth, too, was essential to everyday life. Although children were clothed only to protect them from chilly weather and men might wear only their breechcloth maintained by a waist band for farming work, the untailored cotton cloth (*tanni*) covering the breechcloth and falling below the knees was a minimum that clearly marked the transition from puberty to womanhood. Later in life, additional *tanni* – one for carrying a baby – were the mark of the married woman. The draped or wrapped cloth was worn during leisure hours and in public places by all adults. (To go naked or with only a breechcloth in public places is one symptom of madness among the Baule and even casual observers note the extreme modesty of men as well as women.)

Both yams and cloth required the labor of both sexes in the different phases of production. In the case of yams, it was the man who initiated production and took responsibility for it; he also controlled distribution. In the case of cloth, it was the woman who initiated

production, took responsibility for it, and controlled distribution.

As suggested above, although cloth is not nourishment, if we define needs by a people's own values – and so we must – it was as essential as yams in the context of subsistence. Beyond subsistence, both products played an important role in precolonial Baule society in that they were exchanged on various occasions and thus marked the establishment and perpetuation of social relationships between individuals and groups. Gifts of yams by the man marked the phases of what was a very gradual marriage process. Helping to nourish a young wife-to-be, especially during pregnancy, was an obligation in establishing rights – as husband and father – as was contributing labor to the production of in-laws yams. Cloth was equally indispensable in establishing the conjugal partnership. In defining marriage, older women today rarely fail to describe the production and distribution process, specifying the mutual obligations of wife and husband. Here, too, affines were involved: *tanni* were exchanged reciprocally between parents of the wife and husband.[5]

The Importance of Cloth

While the yam – a perishable foodstuff – remained primarily confined to the subsistence sector,[6] the woman-controlled product, cloth – no doubt because of its durability – circulated more widely and played a greater variety of roles.[7] Once the production process terminated, surplus production – what was not needed for everyday family use – became, with gold and gold ornaments, the most valuable

---

[5] Meillassoux stresses the importance of cloth as bridewealth among the Guro (1974:195, 216). It is interesting that in Baule marriage this valuable durable product is exchanged reciprocally between affines. Meillassoux also says that the Guro woman gives her skeins of thread to her husband or to others (:194). This would mean that she does not control the end-product.

[6] At trading and gold-prospecting centers in general, and, during the 1890s, in the war-ravaged regions to the north of the Baule – where captives could be bought with cassava – foodstuffs did function as commodities, but these were exceptional circumstances.

[7] Leacock suggest the importance of the study of cloth and notes the physical and functional characteristics that make it a potential commodity par excellence (1975:613–14).

type of property produced by the Baule themselves. It was given at funerals, sometimes buried with the deceased, displayed on special occasions, and conserved in the sacred treasure that was guarded by each kin-group head. Thus, within Baule society, besides its subsistence function, cloth had an essential function in what can be considered the ritual and prestige sector.

Even more important, unlike yams, cloth was not confined to intrasocietal relations, but was very important in relations with people of neighboring societies. For example, it was traded directly with the Guro for iron and cattle, and with other groups for captives. It is not always clear whether this direct trade with neighbors can necessarily be characterized as commodity exchange.[8] To the south, however, and especially at Tiassalé, cloth served to acquire salt, guns, and gunpowder from coastal peoples who traded directly with the Europeans. These commodities, although prized by the Baule themselves for their use value, were also traded, again with the Guro and other peoples, for iron, captives, and other goods. To the north, Islamic conquerors furnished captives in great numbers in exchange both for Baule gold and for guns and gunpowder acquired with gold and cloth (see Chauveau 1972a, 1972b, 1974). Therefore, besides its subsistence, ritual, and prestige functions, cloth was important in long-distance trade and seems clearly to have served as a form of currency and/or commodity.

Cloth was, of course, also art in that esthetic appreciation was decisive in determining the value of Baule cloth. But, as has been frequently noted for non-Western societies, no object was "art for art's sake" independently of its utilitarian or ritual function.

That the original distribution of such a valuable and polyvalent product was the woman's domain inevitably gave her power and autonomy both in the conjugal relationship and in Baule society in general. Further, since women participated even in long-distance trade, either directly or by delegation,[9] there is no reason to believe that the emergence of a precolonial form of commodity exchange would necessarily have resulted in their losing control of cloth when it entered that sector.

There were, however, in the production process itself, possibilities for the man to minimize the woman's control of the product. As we shall see, they opened a breach in the subsistence model that would later become a radical breakdown.

The Production and Distribution Process

In order to understand the transformations introduced by colonial conquest and penetration – as opposed to contact – it is necessary first to examine the production process and the way in which it established the woman's rights over the product, as well as the mode of distribution on the domestic level, that is, on the level of the household, which is also the production unit.

The Baule practiced rotational bush-fallow cultivation, in which settlements are fixed and land is cultivated for one to three years – with annual rotations, successions, and crop mixtures (intercropping) – and then left fallow for four to ten years to restore fertility. A plot

---

[8] According to Meillassoux, cloth was not traded directly for captives between Baule and Guro (1974:267). Further, in some instances at least, Baule–Guro trade cannot be defined as commodity exchange, but rather had sociopolitical functions (:266–67). Craft production in the two societies was similar and cloth was traded in both directions.

[9] Baule trade was of the "expedition" type, as defined by Meillassoux (Chauveau 1972b:6). Both women and men could mandate another individual, generally a dependent – son, daughter, other kinsperson, even a trusted captive – to carry out this unspecialized and often dangerous activity for them. The same was true of gold prospecting, a related activity. The grandmother of one of my informants had been sent south by her mother to trade cloth. She returned with both gold and captives.

would originally be prepared for yams. The initial and heaviest work of clearing it, breaking the ground, and preparing mounds for planting, as well as staking of the young plants, was the man's job. Although he received assistance from the woman in burning and clearing away the brush and in planting, this initial phase of labor was his responsibility and this is the reason given for his "ownership" of the yam crop.

A man, however, always prepared a plot for a given woman, generally his wife, though sometimes his sister, mother, or other kinswoman. The Baule were polygynous, but, when a man had more than one wife, each co-wife would have her separate plot. That a plot was "for" a woman meant (1) that the yam crop was to feed her and her children, as well as the man, for whom she cooked; (2) that she would do female tasks, such as weeding and helping to plant and harvest yams on this plot; and (3) that the plot was hers to exploit by inter-cropping between the yam mounds and also after the yams were harvested. She used this last right to grow cotton, always an intercrop, as well as various other intercrops and secondary crops (condiments, corn, cassava, rice).

Because she had this use right over the yam plot, and because she initiated, tended, and took responsibility for these crops, the woman had ownership of the end-product and could dispose of it unreservedly, once family subsistence needs were taken care of. All of these raw products, with the exception of cotton, were also transformed by the woman herself in cooking. In the case of cotton, the first phase of transformation was the woman's responsibility. She cleaned the cotton, carded it, and spun it into thread. Thus, she owned this thread. She also made vegetable dye (indigo) to color it. But only men did weaving and sewing. She therefore turned the skeins of cotton over to her husband, who wove them

into bands and sewed the bands together to make *tanni*. The man wove according to the woman's instructions relative to her estimation of the necessary repartition between immediate family needs and other uses, although they discussed this together. Because he was simply accomplishing one phase of the labor process *for her* and even though he well knew which cloth was for himself, he would turn over to his wife all of the final product and only then receive from her his lot.[10] This, then, was the model for the domestic or home production of cloth. It also exemplifies the model of reciprocity and interdependency in the marriage relationship, a combining of individual rights, cooperative labor, and responsibility for the other's needs.

The question we must ask at this point, before examining postconquest changes, is whether the model was always the reality. Did it always happen that way or were there other possibilities? Clearly, there could be no guarantee that a woman would produce and spin exactly the amount of cotton that her husband could or would weave. A woman who produced large quantities of cotton thread could be married to a man who was a mediocre or unenthusiastic weaver; a man who was an expert and dedicated weaver could be married to a woman whose production of thread was insufficient to satisfy his productive capacity. This imbalance could open a breach in the model of wife–husband production and could eventually create opportunities for men to control the product of their weaving, even if they did not control the raw material. They could form partnerships with other women, even strangers, or obtain thread from these women in other ways. In the case of a partnership, it is likely that a man who was an expert weaver and who approached a woman who had a large surplus of thread would sometimes be able to bargain with her to his advantage. An

[10]   See P. Etienne for a somewhat different explanation of distribution rights and for an interesting comparison between the wife-husband and the client-craftsperson relationship (1968:796; 1971:241).

old widow who spent much time spinning and had no man to weave for her would be glad to get cloth for her needs in this way, and the man would be able to appropriate more of the surplus production, as he no doubt would if he used the thread of some dependent woman, such as his own captive. If he could purchase thread – or even cotton – outright, he could control the product completely, but there is no indication that this practice, if it existed, was widespread.

Women, too, could profit by the imbalance in wife–husband productivity and the breach in the subsistence model, depending on the availability of cotton thread and the extrafamilial demands of weavers. Further, according to the same principle that governed other areas of production, the daughter, younger sister, or other dependent kinswoman of an adult woman assisted the latter, contributing her production to that of her elder. The junior partner would receive either part of what she had produced (cotton or thread) or part of the final product (cloth) for her personal use. There was in this relationship the opportunity for the older woman to take advantage of the younger woman's surplus production. Finally, an adult woman – married or unmarried – could have a yam plot prepared "for her" by a kinsman or by her male captive and, like the wife who worked her husband's plot, use it to grow cotton that she would spin into thread and have woven for her. Informants emphasize the spinning–weaving relationship as a marital obligation and it is not clear, outside of the marital relationship, to what extent a woman was obliged to give her thread to spin to the man whose yam plot she grew cotton on. If there was such an obligation, it would have been especially strong when the man was unmarried or, relative to his productive capacity, insufficiently supplied by his wife or wives. When he was the woman's dependent, particularly her own captive, she could certainly gain an advantage, whether by disposing freely of her thread or by appropriating more than the usual share of the finished product, the general rule being that the mistress – or master – controlled the surplus production of a captive.

Opportunities for women or men to appropriate each other's surplus production, therefore, depended on particular circumstances and precise relationships. It was, however, the finished product that circulated outside the domestic sphere and it was the man who finished the product. This suggests that any opportunity to break away from the wife–husband partnership could tip the balance in his favor and that any systematic deviation from the domestic production model in general could favor men's control of cloth. Such a deviation seems to have existed.

One can say that there was no specialization in Baule society in the sense that all craftspeople were also their own subsistence producers, relying on others, kin as well as captives, to tend their crops only partially or occasionally when they were not available. There was, however, semispecialization in the sense that certain crafts – for instance, goldsmithing – were not known by all.[11] This was not the case for weaving, a craft of all adult men, but, besides the general variability in expertise, certain types of cloth among the most sought after were specialties, both regionally and individually. Itinerant weavers, especially during the dry season, when agricultural work was light, would go from village to village, weaving to order, as would male dyeing specialists.[12]

---

[11] These craft specialties could be learned from a stranger or transmitted by a parent or kinsperson of the same sex.

[12] Women, however, prepared indigo and did certain types of dyeing. See Boser-Sarivaxévanis for a technical study of West African weaving and dyeing (1969, 1972a, 1972b, 1975). She documents the remarkable complexity of dyeing techniques, whether of cloth or of thread, and the unusual variability, sometimes within the same cultural group, of the gender assignment of this craft (1969:194–95).

This semispecialization and the importance of cloth in the prestige sector certainly could facilitate and encourage any tendency on the part of the weaver to gain control of the product, eventually by gaining control of the raw material. Further, although the prestige function of cloth and this kind of specialization do not in themselves imply commodity exchange,[13] commodity exchange, as I have shown, clearly existed – with cloth as an important item – and certainly served as a motivation to control it.

These factors – the durable value of cloth in the prestige sector, its function in commodity exchange, and the female–male production relations that were not strictly confined to the wife–husband relationship – created a breach in the subsistence model. This breach could not, however, in and of itself lead to a total breakdown of existing production–distribution relations, removing the control of cloth from women.

What about the fact that weaving differs from spinning in offering a wider range of expertise and variability, an infinity of esthetic possibilities? (basic designs were traditional but, inevitably, there were innovations.) In a word, as perceived by a Westerner, weaving is an art whereas spinning is a simple, monotonous, and repetitious technique. Should not the fact that he was the "artist" have favored control of cloth by the man? This, however, was not the Baule perception, in spite of their capacity for esthetic discrimination and its confirmation by the value attributed to Baule cloth throughout the region. What they perceived was that without the original cotton, without the spun thread, no weaving, no woven cloth, splendid or ordinary, was possible. That is why the woman, who grew the cotton and spun the thread, controlled the product.

The Postconquest Period

The preconquest contact period certainly accentuated the importance of Baule cloth both in the prestige sector of the economy, since there were greater opportunities to accumulate wealth, and as a commodity in long-distance trade. Although neither the Baule nor their cloth were directly involved in coastal trade with Europeans, they did, as indicated above, take part in this trade indirectly but actively, the Baule furnishing cloth to coastal peoples who were in direct contact, using it as currency to obtain European commodities both for their own use and for trade with other groups. For cloth production at least, this involvement apparently resulted in changes that were for the most part quantitative. One of the factors that were to determine radical qualitative change was the introduction of imported cloth. This was present during that period but was not widespread and, in itself, could only have a limited impact on Baule production relations.

What would ultimately be decisive was colonial conquest and penetration. Several precise changes introduced in the different economic sectors were to converge and complement each other in breaking down the precolonial production-distribution relationship, divesting women of their control over an essential and valuable product. One must see these changes as interrelated and intermeshing, mutually reinforcing each other. They will, therefore, be examined in what seems to be the logical order of their importance rather than in the strict chronological order of their occurrence.

---

[13]   It is important not to confuse "prestige sector" and commodity exchange – and also not to assume, as does Weiskel (1977), that it was necessarily the most valued cloth that circulated as a commodity. An informant showed me a very old piece of ordinary, undyed cloth, with the remark: "This (not the richly woven *tanni*) is what we used to get salt and guns at Tiassalé." It is significant that ordinary, undyed cloth, which women most clearly controlled, could circulate as a commodity or as currency.

Colonial Penetration and the Breakdown of the Precolonial Production–Distribution Relationship

Although European cloth and perhaps thread – other than what may have been obtained by unravelling cloth – were introduced by preconquest trade (Boser-Sarivaxévanis 1969, 1972a), imported thread seems to have been used only occasionally and partially in the oldest existing specimens of Baule cloth – dating back no further that the late eighteenth or early nineteenth century (Boser-Sarivaxévanis 1972a:13; 1972b:53). Museum specimens collected in 1910 and examined by R. Boser-Sarivaxévanis (1972a:179–80) are all made with native thread, except for some decorative use of factory-made thread. Many later specimens, however, are composed mainly of factory-made thread(:179 ff.)

Colonization rapidly provided new opportunities to acquire factory-made thread. In 1923 a textile factory was established by R. Gonfreville just outside of Bouaké (M.-A. de Salverte-Marmier 1965:6). Producing both cloth and thread for the local market, "Gonfreville," as it came to be called, grew into what is practically a "company town" and in 1973 was still the largest textile factory in Ivory Coast.

Weavers could purchase Gonfreville thread with cash, thus freeing themselves from dependence on their wives' home production or on the production of other Baule women, making the woman's role in cloth production appear inessential and her control of the product unjustified. The availability of Gonfreville thread, decisive in destroying precolonial production relations, also contributed to what was to become a flagrant disproportion between women's spinning and men's weaving, a disproportion confirmed by recent sales figures of the textile industry.[14]

Although factory-made thread favors the weaver's control of his product, its growing use has not been simply a question of availability and of choice on his part. There is a real scarcity of homespun thread, determined by causes other than lack of demand. If we examine the agricultural sector, the reasons for this scarcity become clear. It is not that the Baule no longer produce cotton or that Baule women no longer contribute to its production. On the contrary, as we shall see, the Baule produce more cotton than ever and the role of Baule women in the production of both cotton and thread is still essential, but, mediated by cash and the capitalist commodity economy, it has become invisible. . . .

Attempts to force the Baule to grow cotton as an unmixed crop proved that they were more knowledgeable than the colonizer; crowded cotton is destroyed by parasites. In spite of the "war effort" (World War II), postwar production figures made it clear that the choice was between intercropping, with its limited yield, and insecticide treatments, permitting the development of cotton as a high-yield unmixed crop. Furthermore (especially since forced labor had recently been abolished), higher yields were necessary to bring the higher revenues, relative to input, that would encourage farmers to grow cotton as a cash crop (Royer and Boutillier et al. n.d.:9–10). As a result, a heavy technical-assistance apparatus was instituted for research, for intervention during the different phases of production, and even for marketing (Pezet 1965; Benetière and Pezet 1965; Ripailles 1965). From sowing to selling, cotton became the focus of agricultural development experts, the principal buyer being Gonfreville (Pezet 1965:24).

There were also attempts to make cotton a first-year crop. They tended to be unsuccessful both for technical reasons and

---

[14.] Already in 1945, of 162 tons of thread produced by Gonfreville, 77 tons were sold to Baule weavers (Benetière and Pezet 1965:24). In 1963 weavers purchased 72 million francs worth of factory thread, whereas women's homespun cotton was valued at only 8 million francs (Fride 1965:204).

because the Baule preferred to save the best soil for yams (Pezet 1965:9–10; Benetière and Pezet 1965:25). Cotton was therefore developed as a second-year main crop on previously exploited yam plots. As we have seen, the second-year use of the yam plot, like intercropping, was traditionally the woman's right. Cash-crop cotton however, because it involved considerable preparatory work, could be considered a new beginning. Furthermore, this preparatory work, like the following phases of labor, was directed by agricultural experts and their extension agents. Just as the colonial administration – when it demanded that more cotton be produced – had addressed its demands to men, early and later agricultural experts and their male extension agents, when they introduced new techniques, addressed their teaching to men. It is, therefore, not surprising that cash-crop cotton, like other cash crops, became the man's domain.[15] At the same time, especially in the more densely populated areas, the takeover of second-year exploitation of the yam plot for cash cropping, by intruding on their use rights, could divest women of their means of production or, more precisely, of their object of production. . . .

As in agricultural development and forced labor, the colonizer did not generally intervene directly to collect the head tax, but specified the goals to be attained and used native agents and the native hierarchy (manipulated, of course, by the colonial administration) as intermediaries. Whether it was because of the way in which orders were given, because the "head of family" concept was convenient, or for other reasons related to precolonial

wife–husband obligations, the man became responsible for his wife's head tax. To be the primary target of taxation made the acquisition of cash a vital need for men, rather than for women, tending to justify and reinforce their control of cotton as a cash crop.[16]

While the burden of taxation made cash a necessity for men and while cotton grown by them, willingly or unwillingly, provided the necessary cash the expanding commodity economy also made cash useful to purchase the Gonfreville thread that was both advantageous and indispensable in replacing homespun thread. At the same time, cash-crop cotton made Gonfreville thread more available and contributed to making homespun thread less available. There were, however, in the agricultural sector, still other changes that reinforced men's economic position.

Besides cotton, other cash crops such as cocoa and coffee, were introduced for export purposes. They, too, became men's domain. With the growing need to feed urban populations, the yam itself sometimes became a cash crop, the entire harvest being sold wholesale after enough were set aside for subsistence needs and turned over to the adult women of the family. Here again, the right of each woman to "her" separate yam plots tended to be alienated. Cocoa and coffee – coffee is particularly important as a source of income – have not been the focus of as much technical intervention as cotton; but they are perennial, not annual plants and can therefore compound the alienation of women's use rights by giving a new meaning to permanent rights over land, whereas in the past only use rights and rights over crops existed. Eventually, this shift in

[15]   Boserup notes the generality of this phenomenon – the control of cash crops by men – in developing countries and relates it to the intervention of experts and development agents (1970:53–57). It is my experience that they are not unaware of women's rights, but simply ignore them or are sometimes consciously determined to transform women into the helpmates of men, in spite of observations that point to the low revenues of women as a source of conflict between the sexes (see M. Etienne and P. Etienne et al. 1965b:107; Fride et al. 1965:153).

[16]   Boserup notes that taxation in the colonial context was meant to serve more as a means of drawing the colonized into the cash economy than as a source of income (1970:19). She sees its relationship to cash cropping, but not to the takeover of cash crops by men.

meaning of land rights, combined with the use of wage labor, could eliminate women's use rights completely.[17]

Wage labor, however, is still the exception rather than the rule among the Baule. With the development of cash cropping, women have remained active in agricultural production. Because men's cash income is now as necessary to them as to their husbands, women continue to fulfill the conjugal obligation to assist a spouse, pursuing such tasks as weeding and harvesting for which they were traditionally responsible. The harvesting and shelling of coffee beans are particularly arduous and time-consuming tasks.[18] The principle of retributing a spouse for her or his labor remains operative and women receive some share of the profits. Because they do not control cash crops, however, they are dependent on the men for their reward. Their remuneration tends to be arbitrary, and disproportionately low when compared both to labor input and to the monetary value of the product.

Perhaps more important, the labor time devoted to men's cash crops is not available for other activities. Intercropping of cotton and other products on the yam plot continues, as does second-year production of foodstuffs necessary for subsistence. Surplus production of cassava, peanuts, and other women's crops can be retailed or even wholesaled in small quantities at the local marketplace, but women often do not have time for their own agricultural production, just as they do not have time for carding and spinning cotton. These productive activities, quantitatively, finan-

cially, and by their economic function, have become far less important than those controlled by men.

In conclusion, the scarcity of homespun thread and the widespread use of factory-made thread, resulting in women's loss of control over handwoven cloth, are two related aspects of what has been a fundamental transformation of production relations. The impact of this transformation was to be compounded by another intrusion of the expanding commodity economy: the widespread marketing of industrial commodities in general and of factory-made cloth in particular. Like other commodities, factory-made cloth will inevitably be more available to men insofar as men control more cash.

Baule Cloth and Factory Cloth

. . . As imported cloth, Gonfreville cloth, and now the cloth of other local textile factories has become widely available, it has tended to replace Baule cloth for everyday use and less important gifts. Gonfreville even makes imitations of handmade cloth and of handwoven bands that can be sewn together to make a *tanni*. This enhances the prestige value of authentic Baule cloth more appreciated than ever as a symbol of wealth and for ceremonial occasions, both among the Baule (see P. Etienne 1968:813–17) and among other Ivory Coast peoples.

Thus, in both the subsistence and prestige sectors, cloth now circulates as a commodity. Subsistence need – that is, the everyday necessity to clothe one's body – is satisfied by

---

[17]   The changed meaning of land rights can also lead to the sale of land, generally to the disadvantage of women (see Boserup 1970:57–61). The Baule, however, are buyers rather than sellers of land. Women, *provided they have the financial means to begin with*, can thus regain an advantage. Some of my urban informants owned coffee and cocoa farms in the regions south of Baule country. Wage labor, too, can sometimes work to the advantage of women. A woman can ask for land; if it is available, and control the product, if she can find a dependent man to work for her (or do all the work herself). Wage laborers, a convenient substitute for captives, can serve this purpose. Further, when men use wage labor – generally for coffee in the wealthier villages – women can sometimes devote more time to their own crops and even get husbands to help them, again *provided that land is available*. These are, however, exceptions to the general rule that cash cropping and wage labor (by promoting cash cropping) tend to alienate women's land rights.

[18]   Pounding foodstuffs is a woman's task, but men do take part in the pounding of coffee beans.

the factory-made commodity, while hand-made cloth itself has become almost entirely a commodity, with its circulation restricted to the ritual and prestige sector,[19] losing its function as a subsistence product that both served a basic need and consolidated the relationship between wife and husband. If precolonial commodity exchange of cloth opened a breach in the subsistence model, colonization and capitalist commodity exchange alone could lead to this total breakdown, transforming all cloth into a commodity and divesting Baule cloth of its primary subsistence function.

A corollary of this transformation is that "art," in the form of weaving, has become dissociated from functional or subsistence production. Baule cloth has long been appreciated for its beauty and variety, but, as long as it was also an everyday necessity, this dissociation could not occur. Because art and life were one and because woman's labor was the indispensable origin of the production process, the considerable skill or "art" required of the weaver could not radically affect her control of the product. Thus, we see that at the same time that art tends to emerge as a separate domain – distinct from everyday life and reflecting the generalized subordination of Baule society to the colonizer's commodity economy – it emerges as a male-controlled domain, reflecting the generalized subordination of women to men.

Women and Cloth Today: Alienation and the Reversal of a Relationship

A major consequence of the changes analyzed above has been the reversal of the relationship between women and cloth; once an object that

women controlled because it was their product, cloth has become, in a sense, an object that controls them. Much of what has been described here could have been systematically described in terms of alienation, the concept being applied in its different connotations to the different aspects and phases of the process analyzed.

The Gonfreville textile factory is one instance in which the concept of alienation imposes itself, so flagrant and obvious, almost ironical is the changed relationship between producer and product. In 1950 the factory started employing Baule women (M. A. de Salverte-Marmier 1965:6,9) and has continued to employ them extensively in several departments as wage laborers (:6–12). Thus, on the most manifest level, simply as factory workers they are alienated from their own product in the immediately given context of capitalist production. This alienation, however, is founded on a more complex historical process of alienation. The very production process in which Baule women sell their labor to produce thread and cloth has been a key factor in destroying a production process in which they controlled the same product.

The alienated labor of Baule women also appears in other phases of the new process, since they contribute to growing cash-crop cotton for Gonfreville cloth and thread; here the productive activity itself is much the same as in the past, but its meaning and function are entirely different. Meanwhile, traditional, woman-controlled production of cotton, by intercropping, and of thread continues but has become practically a remnant of the past, playing no essential role in the economy. Further, what primarily motivates women to sell their labor for wages is the need to acquire the cloth they once produced and in a sense, to regain control of this product by controlling

[19]   The principal economic activity of one urban woman informant was to buy Baule cloth in rural villages and sell it to well-off employees and civil servants, going from office to office to vend her wares. Some women sell factory cloth at the market place, but they by no means control this sector as do Ashanti women in Ghana.

their own cash.[20] Thus, multiple processes of alienation converge with the Baule women as their focal point or subject.

Alienated production means the producer's control of the product is replaced by the product's control of the producer. In the case of the Gonfreville factory worker, the relationship between woman and cloth has been visibly reversed in this way. If we move from the sector of production to the sector of consumption – and we must in a commodity economy that radically dissociates the two – this same reversal of the relationship between woman and cloth manifests itself. Control of the consumer by the product is, of course, a generalized characteristic of the modern capitalist commodity economy. In this case, however, we will see that it is particularly striking – a magnified and oversimplified illustration, almost a caricature, of the more general relationship.

Although handmade cloth is now confined to the prestige sector, subsistence needs being satisfied by factory-made cloth, the latter also occupies an important position in the prestige sector. All the values and functions previously attributed to the one have been extended to the other. To clothe one's body is a necessity. To have cloth in quantity and quality beyond the mere necessity of clothing one's body is a constantly pursued goal. For women in particular, the brightly colored cloth specially designed for the African market and imported from England or Holland – and the less valued local—factory cloth – is the most sought after commodity. . . .

As did handmade cloth, factory cloth also tends to materialize the relationship between woman and man, and especially between wife and husband. But now this materialization of the personal relationship takes another form. Instead of emerging from the cooperative production process with one spouse's labor being restituted by the other's gift of the final product, it is mediated by the commodity economy. The principles of wife–husband cooperation in production and of compensating the participating partner for her or his labor remain operative, but the woman is the participating partner for products that bring cash and cash has become indispensable. The equilibrium of an economy where both sexes had control over essential products – and these could be acquired in no other way than through the woman man production partnership – has disappeared, as have the rules governing distribution in a context where labor produced use values rather than commodities. At the same time, cash and cloth have become interchangeable, although it is cloth that tends to measure the value of cash, rather than the reverse. (A woman who receives a sum of money will estimate its value by the amount of cloth she can buy more naturally than she will estimate the value of cloth by its purchase price.)

Thus, the woman who contributes her labor to her husband's production of cotton or coffee will receive cash or cloth in amounts which she considers arbitrary and which, in fact, very much depend on the man's "generosity." Abusively low remuneration is facilitated by the man's knowledge that the woman cannot reciprocate, as she could when she too controlled essential products. As a result, the wife–husband production relationship is becoming a constant source of conflict. Because the production relationship has always been the foundation of marriage, and because cloth and cash now tend to be the measure of a husband's affection and respect, the whole personal relationship is also conflict-laden.

Inevitably, many women prefer to remain unmarried and all seek to acquire their own cash, whether at Gonfreville, on southern

---

[20]   Women in the sample studied by M.-A. de Salverte-Marmier are all of rural origin; almost all live in nearby villages and they are for the most part unmarried (1965:9, 16–19). They devote a considerable portion of their salary to the purchase of cloth (:15).

coffee and cocoa farms, or in town, through wage labor, petty trade, or sometimes prostitution (see P. Etienne and M. Etienne 1968). Whether in prostitution, the preconjugal relationship, or marriage itself, a woman may try to appropriate the man's advantage by constant demands for cloth and cash, but this hardly restitutes her autonomy. To pursue wealth is not entirely new. In the past women also traded and sought to acquire gold and captives, as well as prestige cloth woven by experts, and they were not always anxious to marry.[21] What is new is a transformation of the woman–man production relationship that replaces interdependency by dependency in the most essential areas of subsistence. Here, as in the Gonfreville factory, the relationship to the object cloth is reversed. Women no longer control cloth but are controlled by it. This formulation is more than an elegant abstraction. when we move from the interindividual relationship and the general production–distribution relationship to women's relationship to the political power structure in contemporary Ivory Coast, the way in which cloth has become, if not the controlling agent itself, at least the means by which control is exercised; is clearly perceptible.

Ivory Coast women – and Baule women in particular – played an important and very active role in the struggle for independence.[22] The national party (Ivory Coast is a one-party state) continues to rely heavily on women's support without always maintaining adequate communication to justify their mobilization on various occasions. When such mobilization is necessary, cloth is distributed. For example, when the party wants to organize a mass demonstration to welcome a visiting head of

state, cloth is produced in a local factory especially for the occasion – often with portraits of the Ivory Coast president and the visitor – and is distributed to the women, especially to those who are known supporters of the party and influential in the community. Here, besides motivating the women to take part in the demonstration, the cloth serves as a uniform for politico-esthetic purposes. In other circumstances, cloth is distributed as a reward for services rendered or expected. The traditional point of reference for this practice is to be found in the principle of materializing a relationship and rewarding labor. Cloth, because it has always served this purpose, and because it is highly valued and sought after, is an excellent vehicle, made even more appropriate by its display function. As in other areas, the modern power structure uses traditional models and values astutely. what colonization and the capitalist commodity economy have taken from Baule women, the state now returns in a different form and in different circumstances.

Cloth has become a prime motivation for supporting the party and the focus of attention for the recipients. The women themselves experience this relationship with ambivalence, sometimes appearing entirely absorbed in the pursuit of cloth as a party handout, sometimes expressing with bitterness the feeling of being manipulated by gifts of cloth. They do not explicitly formulate the contrast between present and past as I have done here.

They do however perceive it and reflect it in their behavior, often going through the motions of an activity that, once essential, has become anachronistic, while actively engaged in more realistic pursuits. One case illustrates this contradiction: that of a very old woman

---

[21] It is said that noble and wealthy women did not marry. This refers more to a de facto that a de jure situation and is related to the fact that viri-local marriage prevents woman from succeeding to positions of authority.

[22] In 1949 they marched on the Prison of Grand-Bassam to liberate political prisoners and many were maimed and injured in a violent encounter with colonial troops (see Diabaté 1975). The demonstration used as a model a Baule women's ritual *adjanu*, a precolonial form of symbolic warfare that can be directed against village men or against enemies. The power of *adjanu* is both verbal and visual; its visual weapon is nudity.

who, from early colonial times, had adapted to change with intelligent opportunism, becoming the "native wife" of early administrators, serving as an intermediary in their dealings with the population, acquiring wealth and prestige that were maintained in the post-independence period, when she shifted her allegiance to the new government and its party, for whom she continues to play much the same role that she had played for the colonial administration, seeing for her purposes very little difference between the two. Throughout a life that began before colonization, she has maximized every opportunity available to an illiterate woman and avidly collected factory-made cloth. Yet she continues to spin her cotton in the town compound, explaining that young kinswomen in her village grow it and that she returns each year to collect it and to give the thread to kinsmen for weaving – pointing with pride at this activity that in the past defined a woman's social reality, no doubt getting some profit from it in the present, but pretending to ignore what she obviously knows: that the spinning she carries on almost obsessively has meaning only in reference to a world that is becoming obsolete.

References

Benetière, Jean-Jacques and Pierre Pezet. 1965. "Histoire de l'agriculture en zone baoulé." In Côte d'Ivoire, Ministère du Plan, Étude régionale de Bouaké." 1962–1964, doc. 2. Abidjan.

Boser-Sarivaxévanis, Renée. 1969. Aperçus sur la teinture á l'indigo en Afrique occidentale. Basel.

—. 1972a. Les tissus de l'Afrique occidentale: méthode de classification et catalogue raisonné des étoffes tissées de l'Afrique de l'Ouest. Basel.

—. 1972b. "Les tissus de l'Afrique occidentale á dessin réservé par froissage." Ethnologische Zeitschrift Zürich 1:53–59.

—. 1975. "Recherche sur l'histoire des textiles traditionnels tissés et teints de l'Afrique occidental." Verhandlungen der Naturforschenden Gesellschaft in Basel. 86:301–41.

Boserup, Ester. 1970. Woman's Role in Economic Development. London: Allen and Unwin.

Chauveau, Jean-Pierre. 1972a. Les cadres socio-historiques de la production dans la région de Kokumbo (pays Baoulé, Côte d'Ivoire). 1: La période précoloniale. Petit-Bassam (Abidjan): ORSTOM.

—. 1972b. Note sur la place du Baoulé dans l'ensemble économique ouest-africain. Petit-Bassam (Abidjan): ORSTOM.

—. 1973. Note sur la morphologie matrimoniale de Kokumbo (pays Baoulé Côte d'Ivoire). Perspective historique. Petit-Bassam (Abidjan): ORSTOM.

Diabaté, Henriette. 1975 La Marche des femmes sur Grand-Bassam. Abidjan, Dakar: Les Nouvelles Editions africaines.

Etienne, Mona, and Pierre Etienne, et al. 1965a. "L'organisation sociale des Baoulé". In Côte d'Ivoire, Ministère du Plan. Le peuplement. Étude règionale de Bouké, 1962–1964, vol. Abidjan.

—. 1965b. "Essai de monographie d'un village de savane: Diamelassou." In Côte d'Ivoire, Ministère du Plan, Étude régionale de Bouaké, 1962–1964, doc. 4. Abidjan.

Etienne, Pierre. 1968. "Les aspects ostentatoires due système économique baoulé." Économies et Sociétés 2:793–817.

Etienne, Pierre, and Mona Etienne. 1968 "L'émigration baoulé actuelle." Cahiers d'Outre-mer 21:155–95.

Fride, B. et al. 1965. Éléments pour une monographie du village de Kouakou-Broukrou." In Côte d'Ivoire, Ministère du Plan, Étude régionale de Bouaké, 1962–1964, doc. 5. Abidjan.

Leacock, Eleanor. 1975. "Class, Commodity, and the Status of Women." In R. Rohrlich-Leavitt, ed., Women Cross-Culturally: Change and Challenge. The Hague: Mouton.

Meillassoux, Claude. 1974. Anthropologie économique des Gouro de Côte d'Ivoire (1st ed. 1964). The Hague: Mouton.

Pezet, Pierre. 1965. "Le coton dans la zone baoulé."

In Côte d'Ivoire, Ministère du Plan, *Étude régionale de Bouaké, 1962–1964*, doc. 6. Abidjan.

J. Royer, J.-L. Boutillier, et al. n.d. Enquête agricole par sondage dans le cercle de Bouaké, juillet 1954–janvier 1955. Abidjan: Côte d'Ivoire. Service de la Statistique et de la Mécanographie.

Salverte-Marmier, M.-A. de. 1965. "Les ouvriéres de l'industrie textile." In Côte d'Ivoire, Ministère du Plan, *Étude régionale de Bouaké, 1962–64*. doc. 9. Abidjan.

Salverte-Marmier, P. de. 1965. "L'organisation politique et la structure territoriale." In Côte d'Ivoire, Ministère du Plan, *Le peuplement. Étude régionale de Bouaké, 1962–64*. vol. 1. Abidjan.

Salverte-Marmier, P. de, M.-A. de Salverte-Marmier and P. Etienne. 1965. "Les étapes du peuplement." In Côte d'Ivoire, Ministère du Plan, *Le peuplement. Étude régionale de Bouaké. 1962–64*, vol. 1. Abidjan.

Weiskel, Timothy C. 1976. "L'histoire socio-économique des peuples baule: problèmes et perspectives de recherche." *Cahiers d'Études africaines* 16: 357–95.

—. 1977. "French Colonial Rule and the Baule Peoples: Resistance and Collaboration, 1889–1911." Ph.D. diss., Oxford University.

31

"SITTING ON A MAN": COLONIALISM AND THE LOST POLITICAL INSTITUTIONS OF IGBO WOMEN[1]

JUDITH VAN ALLEN

In the conventional wisdom, Western influence has "emancipated" African women – through the weakening of kinship bonds and the provision of "free choice" in Christian monogamous marriage, the suppression of "barbarous" practices, the opening of schools, the introduction of modern medicine and hygiene, and sometimes, of female suffrage.

But Westernization is not an unmixed blessing. The experience of Igbo women under British colonialism shows that Western influence can sometimes weaken or destroy women's traditional autonomy and power without providing modern forms of autonomy or power in exchange. Igbo women had a significant role in traditional political life. As individuals, they participated in village meetings with men. But their real political power was based on the solidarity of women, as expressed in their own political institutions – their "meetings" (*mikiri* or *mitiri*), their market networks, their kinship groups, and their right to use strikes, boycotts and force to effect their decisions.

British colonial officers and missionaries, both men and women, generally failed to see the political roles and the political power of Igbo women. The actions of administrators weakened and in some cases destroyed women's bases of strength. Since they did not appreciate women's political institutions, they made no efforts to ensure women's participation in the modern institutions they were trying to foster.

Igbo women haven't taken leadership roles in modern local government, nationalist movements and national government and what roles they *have* played have not been investigated by scholars. The purpose in describing their *traditional* political institutions and source of power is to raise the question of *why* these women have been "invisible" historically, even though they forced the colonial authorities to pay attention to them briefly. We suggest that the dominant view among British colonial officers and missionaries was that politics was a man's concern. Socialized in Victorian England, they had internalized a set of values and attitudes about what they considered to be the natural and proper role of

---

[1] An earlier version of this paper was presented at the Annual Meeting of The African Studies Association, Denver, Colorado, November, 1971.

women that supported this belief. We suggest further that this assumption about men and politics has had a great deal to do with the fact that no one has even asked, "Whatever happened to Igbo women's organizations?" even though all the evidence needed to justify the question has been available for 30 years.

Igbo Traditional Political Institutions[2]

Political power in Igbo society was *diffuse*. There were no specialized bodies or offices in which legitimate power was vested, and no person, regardless of his status or ritual position, had the authority to issue *commands* which others had an obligation to obey. In line with this diffusion of authority, the right to enforce decisions was also diffuse: there was no "state" that held a monopoloy of legitimate force, and the use of force to protect one's interests or to see that a group decision was carried out was considered legitimate for individuals and groups. In the simplest terms, the British tried to create specialized political institutions which commanded authority and monopolized force. In doing so they took into

account, eventually, Igbo political institutions dominated by men but ignored those of the women. Thus, women were shut out from political power.

The Igbo lived traditionally in semi-autonomous villages, which consisted of the scattered compounds of 75 or so patri-kinsmen; related villages formed "village-groups" which came together for limited ritual and jural purposes. Villages commonly contained several hundred people; but size varied, and in the more densely populated areas there were "village-groups" with more than 5,000 members.[3] Disputes at all the levels above the compound were settled by group discussion until mutual agreement was reached.[4]

The main Igbo political institution seems to have been the village assembly, a gathering of all adults in the village who chose to attend. Any adult who had something to say on the matter under discussion was entitled to speak – as long as he *or she* said something the others considered worth listening to; as the Igbo say, "a case forbids no one."[5]

Matters dealt within the village assembly were those of concern to all – either common problems for which collective action was

---

[2] The Igbo-speaking peoples are heterogeneous and can only be termed a "tribe" on the basis of a common language and a contiguous territory. They were the dominant group in southeastern Nigeria, during the colonial period numbering more than three million according to the 1931 census. The Igbo in Owerri and Calabar Provinces, the two southernmost provinces, were relatively homogeneous politically, and it is their political institutions which are discussed here. Studies in depth were done of the Igbo only in the 1930s, but traditional political institutions survived "underneath" the native administration, although weakened more in some areas than in others. There were also many informants who remembered life in the pre-colonial days. The picture of Igbo society drawn here is based on reports by two Englishwomen, Leith-Ross and Green, who had a particular interest in Igbo women; the work of a government anthropological officer, Meek; a brief report by Harris, and the work of educated Igbo describing their own society. Uchendu and Onwuteaka. See M. M. Green. *Igbo Village Affairs* (London: Frank Cass & Co., Ltd., 1947: page citations to paperback edition. New York: Frederick A. Praeger, 1964); J.S. Harris. "The Position of Women in a Nigerian Society", *Transactions of the New York Academy of Sciences*, Series II, Vol.2, No. 5, 1940; Sylvia LEITH-ROSS, *African Women* (London: Faber and Faber, 1939); C. K. MEEK. *Law and Authority in a Nigerian Tribe* (London: Oxford University Press, 1957, orig. publ. 1937); J. C. ONWUTEAKA "The Aba Riot of 1929 and its Relation to the System of Indirect Rule". *The Nigerian Journal of Economic and Social Studies*. November 1965; Victor C. UCHENDU, *The Igbo of Southeast Nigeria* (New York: Holt, Rinehart and Winston, 1965).
[3] Daryll FORDE and G. I. JONES. *The Ibo- and Ibibio-Speaking Peoples of South-Eastern Nigeria* (London: International African Institute, 1950), p. 39; J. S. HARRIS, *op. cit.*, p.141.
[4] Victor C. UCHENDU, *op. cit.*, pp. 41–44.
[5] *Ibid.*, p. 41; M. M. GREEN, *op. cit.*, pp. 76–79.

appropriate ("How can we make our market 'bigger' than the other villages' markets?") or conflicts which threatened the unity of the village.[6]

Decisions agreed on by the village assembly did not have the force of law in our terms, however. Even after decisions had been reached, social pressure based on consensus and the ability of individuals and groups to enforce decisions in their favour played a major part in giving the force of law to decisions. As Green[7] put it:

> (O)ne had the impression . . . that laws only establish themselves by degrees and then only in so far as they gain general acceptance. A law does not either exist or not exist: rather it goes through a process of establishing itself by common consent or of being shelved by a series of quiet evasions.

Persuasion about the rightness of a particular course of action in terms of tradition was of primary importance in assuring its acceptance and the leaders were people who had the ability to persuade.

The mode of political discourse was that of proverb, parable and metaphor drawn from the body of Igbo tradition.[8] The needed political knowledge was accessible to the average man or woman, since all Igbo were reared with these proverbs and parables. Influential speech was the creative and skillful use of tradition to assure others that a certain course of action was both a wise and right thing to do. The accessibility of this knowledge is indicated by an Igbo proverb: "If you tell a proverb to a fool, he will ask you its meaning."

The leaders of Igbo society were men and women who combined wealth and generosity with "mouth" – the ability to speak well. Age combined with wisdom brought respect but age alone carried little influence. The senior elders who were ritual heads of their lineages were very likely to have considerable influence, but they would not have achieved these positions in the first place if they had not been considered to have good sense and good character.[9] Wealth in itself was no guarantee of influence: a "big man" or "big woman" was not necessarily a wealthy person, but one who had shown skill and generosity in helping other individuals and, especially, the community.[10]

Men owned the most profitable crops such as palm oil, received the bulk of the money from bridewealth, and, if compound heads, presents from the members. Through the patrilineage, they controlled the land, which they could lease to non-kinsmen or to women for a good profit. Men also did most of the long-distance trading which gave higher profit than local and regional trading which was almost entirely in women's hands.[11]

Women were entitled to sell the surplus of their own crops and the palm kernels which were their share of the palm produce. They might also sell prepared foods or the products of special skills, for instance, processed salt, pots and baskets. They pocketed the entire profit, but their relatively lower profit levels kept them disadvantaged relative to the men in acquiring titles and prestige.[12]

For women as well as for men, status was largely achieved, not ascribed. A woman's

[6]   J. S. HARRIS, *op. cit.*, pp. 142–43; Victor C. UCHENDU, *op. cit.*, pp. 34, 42–43.

[7]   M. M. GREEN. *op. cit.*, p. 137.

[8]   The sources for this description are Uchendu and personal conversations with an Igbo born in Umu-Domi village of Onicha clan in Afikpo division who, however, went to mission schools from the age of seven and speaks Union Igbo rather than his village dialect.

[9]   Victor C. UCHENDU, *op. cit.*, p. 41.

[10]   *Ibid.*, p. 34; C. K. MEEK, *op. cit.*, p. 111.

[11]   M. M. GREEN, *op. cit.*, pp. 32–42.

[12]   Sylvia LEITH-ROSS, *op. cit.*, pp. 90–92, 138–39, 143.

status was determined more *by her own achievements* than by the achievements of her husband. The resources available to men were greater, however; so that while a woman might rank higher among women than her husband did among men, very few women could acquire the highest titles, a major source of prestige.[13]

At village assemblies men were more likely to speak than were women; women more often spoke only on matters of direct concern to them.[14] Title-holders took leading parts in discussion, and were more likely to take part in "consultation." After a case had been thoroughly discussed, a few men retired in order to come to a decision. A spokesman then announced the decision, which could be accepted or rejected by the assembly.[15]

Apparently no rule forbade women to participate in consultations but they were invited to do so only rarely. The invited women were older women, for while younger men might have the wealth to acquire the higher titles and thus make up in talent what they lacked in age, younger women could not acquire the needed wealth quickly enough to be eligible.[16]

Women, therefore, came second to men in power and influence. While status and the political influence it could bring were achieved and there were no formal limits to women's political power, men through their ascriptive status (members of the patrilineage) acquired wealth which gave them a head start and a life-long advantage over women. The Igbo say that "a child who washes his hands clean deserves to eat with his elders."[17] But at birth some children were given water and some were not.

Women's Political Institutions

Since political authority was diffuse, the settling of disputes, discussions about how to improve the village or its market, or any other problems of general concern were brought up at various gatherings such as funerals, meetings of kinsmen to discuss burial rituals, and the marketplace, gatherings whose ostensible purpose was not political discussion.[18]

The women's base of political power lay in their own gatherings. Since Igbo society was patrilocal and villages were exogamous, adult women resident in a village would almost all be wives, and others were divorced or widowed "daughters of the village" who had returned home to live. Women generally attended age-set gatherings (*ogbo* in their natal villages, performed various ritual functions, and helped to settle disputes among their "brothers."[19] But the gatherings which performed the major role in self-rule among women and which articulated women's interests *as opposed* to those of men were the village–wide gatherings of all adult women resident in a village which under colonialism came to be called *mikiri* or *mitiri* (from "meeting").[20]

Mikiri were held whenever there was a need.[21] In *mikiri* the same processes of discussion and consultation were used as in the village assembly. There were no official leaders; as in the village, women of wealth and generosity who could speak well took leading roles. Decisions appear often to have been announced initially by wives telling their husbands. If the need arose, spokeswomen – to contact the men, or women in other villages – were chosen through general discussion. If the

13 C. K. MEEK, *op. cit.*, p 203; Victor C. UCHENDU, *op. cit.*, p. 86.
14 M. M. Green *op. cit.*, p. 169.
15 Victor C. UCHENDU, *op. cit.*, p. 410.
16 C. K. MEEK, *op. cit.*, p. 203.
17 Victor C. UCHENDU, *op. cit.*, p. 19.
18 C. K.MEEK, *op. cit.*, p. 125; M. M.GREEN, *op. cit.*, pp. 132–38.
19 M. M. GREEN *op. cit.*, pp. 217–320.
20 Sylvia LEITH-ROSS, *op. cit.*, pp. 106–08.
21 M. M. GREEN, *op. cit.*, pp. 178–216.

announcement of decisions and persuasion were not sufficient for their implementation, women could take direct action to enforce their decisions and protect their interests.[22]

Mikiri provided women with a forum in which to develop their political talents among a more egalitarian group than the village assembly. In *mikiri*, women could discuss their particular interests as traders, farmers, wives and mothers. These interests often were opposed to those of the men, and where individually women couldn't compete with men, collectively they could often hold their own.

One of the *mikiri's* most important functions was that of a market association, to promote and regulate the major activity of women: trading. At these discussions prices were set, rules established about market attendance, and fines fixed for those who violated the rules or who didn't contribute to market rituals. Rules were also made which applied to men. For instance, rowdy behavior on the part of young men was forbidden. Husbands and elders were asked to control the young men. If their requests were ignored, the women would handle the matter by launching a boycott or a strike to force the men to police themselves or they might decide to "sit on" the individual offender.[23]

"Sitting on a man" or a woman, boycotts and strikes were the women's main weapons. To "sit on" or "make war on" a man involved gathering at his compound, sometimes late at night, dancing, singing scurrilous songs which detailed the women's grievances against him and often called his manhood into question, banging on his hut with the pestles women used for pounding yams, and perhaps demolishing his hut or plastering it with mud and roughing him up a bit. A man might be sanctioned in this way for mistreating his wife, for

violating the women's market rules, or for letting his cows eat the women's crops. The women would stay at his hut throughout the day, and late into the night, if necessary, until he repented and promised to mend his ways.[24] Although this could hardly have been a pleasant experience for the offending man, it was considered legitimate and no man would consider intervening.

In tackling men as a group, women used boycotts and strikes. Harris describes a case in which, after repeated request by the women for the paths to the market to be cleared (a male responsibility), all the women refused to cook for their husbands until the request was carried out.[25] For this boycott to be effective, *all* women had to cooperate so that men could not go and eat with their brothers. Another time the men of a village decided that the women should stop trading at the more distant markets from which they did not return until late at night because the men feared that the women were having sexual relations with men in those towns. The women, however, refused to comply since opportunity to buy in one market and sell in another was basic to profit-making. Threats of collective retaliation were enough to make the men capitulate.

As farmers, women's interest conflicted with those of the men as owners of much of the larger livestock – cows, pigs, goats and sheep. The men's crop, yams, had a short season and was then dug up and stored, after which the men tended to be careless about keeping their livestock out of the women's crops. Green reports a case in which the women of a village swore an oath that if any woman killed a cow or other domestic animal on her farm the others would stand by her.[26]

A woman could also bring complaints about her husband to the *mikiri*. If most of the

---

[22]   *Ibid.*, p. 140; Sylvia Leith-Ross, *op. cit.*, pp. 106–107.
[23]   J. S. Harris *op.cit.*, pp. 146–47.
[24]   *Ibid.*, pp. 146–48; M. M. Green, *op. cit.*, pp. 196–97; Sylvia Leith-Ross. *op. cit.*, p. 109.
[25]   J.S. Harris, *op. cit.*, pp. 146–147.
[26]   M. M. Green, *op. cit.*, pp. 210–11.

women agreed that the husband was at fault, they would collectively support her. They might send spokeswomen to tell the husband to apologize and to give her a present, and, if he was recalcitrant they might "sit on" him. They might also act to protect a right of wives. Harris describes a case of women's solidarity to maintain sexual freedom:

> The men . . . were very angry because their wives were openly having relations with their lovers. The men . . . met and passed a law to the effect that every woman . . . should renounce her lover and present a goat to her husband as a token of repentance . . . The women held . . . secret meetings and, a few mornings later, they went to a neighboring [village], leaving all but suckling children behind them . . . [The men] endured it for a day and a half and then they went to the women and begged their return . . . [T]he men gave [the women] one goat and apologized informally and formally.[27]

Thus through *mikiri* women acted to force a resolution of their individual and collective grievances.

Colonial Penetration

Into this system of diffuse authority, fluid and informal leadership, shared rights of enforcement, and a more or less stable balance of male and female power, the British tried to introduce ideas of "native administration" derived from colonial experience with chiefs and emirs in northern Nigeria. Southern Nigeria was declared a protectorate in 1900, but it was ten years before the conquest was effective. As colonial power was established in what the British perceived as a situation of "ordered anarchy," Igboland was divided into Native Court Areas which violated the autonomy of villages by lumping many unrelated villages into each court area. British District Officers were to preside over the courts, but were not always present as there were more courts than officers. The Igbo membership was formed by choosing from each village a "representative" who was given a warrant of office. These Warrant Chiefs were also constituted the Native Authority. They were required to see that the orders of the District Officers were executed in their own villages and were the only link between the colonial power and the people.[28]

It was a violation of Igbo concepts to have one man represent the village in the first place and more of a violation that he should give orders to everyone else. The people obeyed the Warrant Chief when they had to, since British power backed him up. In some places Warrant Chiefs were lineage heads or wealthy men who were already leaders in the village. But in many places they were simply ambitious, opportunistic young men who put themselves forward as friends of the conquerors. Even the relatively less corrupt Warrant Chief was still, more than anything else, an agent of the British.[29]

The people avoided using Native Courts when they could do so. But Warrant Chiefs could force cases into the Native Courts and could fine people for infractions of rules. By having the car of the British, the Warrant Chief could himself violate traditions and even British rules, and get away with it since his version would be believed.[30]

Women suffered particularly under the arbitrary rule of Warrant Chiefs, who were

---

[27] J. S. HARRIS, *op. cit.*, 146–47.
[28] Daryll FORDE. "Justice and Judgment among the Southern Ibo under Colonial Rule", unpublished paper prepared for Interdisciplinary Colloquium in African Studies, University of California, Los Angeles, pp. 9–13.
[29] *Ibid.*, pp. 9–13; J. C. ANENE, *Southern Nigeria in Transition*, 1885–1906 (New York : The Cambridge University Press, 1967), p. 259; C. K. MEEK, *op. cit.*, pp. 328–30.
[30] Daryll FORDE, *op. cit.*, p.12.

reported as having taken women to marry without conforming to the customary process, which included the woman's right to refuse a particular suitor. They also helped themselves to the women's agricultural produce, and to their domestic animals.[31]

Recommendations for reform of the system were made almost from its inception both by junior officers in the field and by senior officers sent out from headquarters to investigate. But no real improvements were made.[32]

Aba and The Women's War

The Native Administration in the years before 1929 took little account of either men's or women's political institutions. In 1929, women in southern Igboland became convinced that they were to be taxed by the British. This fear on top of their resentment of the Warrant Chiefs led to what the British called the Aba Riots, and the Igbo, the Women's War. The rebellion provides perhaps the most striking example of British blindness to the political institutions of Igbo women. The women, "invisible" to the British as they laid their plans for Native Administration, suddenly became highly visible for a few months, but as soon as they quieted down, they were once again ignored, and the reforms made in Native Administration took no account of them politically.[33]

In 1925 Igbo men paid taxes, although during the census count on which the tax was based the British had denied that there was to be any taxation. Taxes were collected without too much trouble. By 1929, the prices for palm products had fallen, however, and the taxes, set at 1925 levels, were an increasingly resented burden.[34] In the midst of this resentment, an overzealous Assistant District Officer in Owerri Province decided to update the census registers by recounting households and household property, which belonged to women. Understandably, the women did not believe his assurances that new taxes were not to be invoked. They sent messages through the market and kinship networks to other villages and called a *mikiri* to decide what to do.

In the Oloko Native Court area of Owerri Province, the women decided that as long as only men were approached in a compound and asked for information, the women would do nothing. They wanted clear evidence that they were to be taxed before they acted.[35] If any woman was approached, she was to raise the alarm and they would meet to discuss retaliation.

On November 23, the agent of the Oloko Warrant Chief, Okugo, entered a compound and told a married woman, Nwanyeruwa, to count her goats and sheep. She retorted angrily, "Was your mother counted?" Thereupon "they closed, seizing each other by the throat."[36] Nwanyeruwa's report to the

---

[31] J. C. ONWUTEAKA, *op. cit.*, p. 274.

[32] C. K. MEEK, *op. cit.*, pp. 329–30; Harry A. GAILEY, *The Road to Aba* (New York: New York University Press, 1970), pp. 66–74.

[33] Information on the Women's War is derived mainly from Gailey and Perham, who based their descriptions on the reports of the two Commissions of Enquiry, issued as Sessional Papers of the Nigerian Legislative Council, Nos. 12 and 28 of 1930, and the Minutes of Evidence issued with the latter. Gailey also used the early 1930s Intelligence Reports of political officers. Meek and Afigbo also provide quotations from the reports which were not, unfortunately, available to me in full. See Margery PERHAM, *Native Administration in Nigeria* (London: Oxford University Press, 1937); Idem, *Lugard: The Years of Adventure, 1858–1898* (London: Collins, 1956); Idem, *Lugard: The Years of Authority, 1898–1945* (London: Collins, 1960); A. E. AFIGBO, "Igbo Village Affairs", *Journal of the Historical Society of Nigeria* 4: 1, December 1967.

[34] Harry A. GAILEY, *op. cit.*, pp. 94–95; C. K. MEEK, *op. cit.*, pp. 330–31.

[35] Harry A. GAILEY, *op. cit.*, pp. 107–8.

[36] Margery PERHAM, *Native Administration in Nigeria, op. cit.*, p. 207.

Oloko women convinced them that they were to be taxed. Messengers were sent to neighboring areas. Women streamed into Oloko from all over Owerri Province. They massed in protest at the district office and after several days of protest meetings succeeded in obtaining written assurances that they were not to be taxed, and in getting Okugo arrested. Subsequently he was tried and convicted of physically assaulting women and of spreading news likely to cause alarm. He was sentenced to two years' imprisonment.[37]

News of this victory spread rapidly through the market *mikiri* network, and women in 16 Native Court areas attempted to get rid of their Warrant Chiefs as well as the Native Administration itself. Tens of thousands of women became involved, generally using the same traditional tactics, though not with the same results as in Oloko. In each Native Court area, the women marched on Native Administration centers and demanded the Warrant Chiefs' caps of office and assurances that they would not be taxed. In some areas the District Officers assured the women to their satisfaction that they were not to be taxed and the women dispersed without further incident. But the British in general stood behind the Warrant Chiefs; at that point they interpreted the women's rebellion as motivated solely by fear of taxation and Oloko was the only area in which a Warrant Chief had directly provoked the women's fears of taxation by counting their property.

Women in most areas did not get full satisfaction from the British, and, further, some British district officers simply panicked when faced by masses of angry women and acted in ways which made negotiation impossible.

In most of the Native Court areas affected, women took matters into their own hands –

they "sat on" Warrant Chiefs and burned Native Court buildings, and, in some cases, released prisoners from jail. Among the buildings burned were those at Aba, a major administrative center from which the British name for the rebellion is derived. Large numbers of police and soldiers, and on one occasion Boy Scouts, were called in to quell the "disturbances." On two occasions, clashes between the women and the troops left more than 50 women dead and 50 wounded from gunfire. The lives taken were those of women only – no men, Igbo or British, were even seriously injured. The cost of property damage – estimated at more than £60,000, was paid for by the Igbo, who were heavily taxed to pay for rebuilding the Native Administration centers.[38]

The rebellion lasted about a month. By late December, "order" was somewhat restored but sporadic disturbances and occupation by government troops continued into 1930. In all, the rebellion extended over an area of six thousand square miles, all of Owerri and Calabar Provinces, containing about two million people.[39]

The British generally saw the rebellion as "irrational" and called it a series of "riots." They discovered that the market network had been used to spread the rumor of taxation, but they did not inquire further into the concerted action of the women, the grassroots leadership, the agreement on demands, or even into the fact that thousands of women showed up at native administration centers dressed in the same unusual way: wearing short loincloths, their faces smeared with charcoal or ashes, their heads bound with young ferns, and in their hands carrying sticks wreathed with young palms.[40]

In exonerating the soldiers who fired on the

[37]   Harry A. GAILEY, *op. cit.*, pp. 108–13.
[38]   S. O. ESIRE, "The Aba Riots of 1929", *African Historian*, Vol. 1, No. 3 (1965): 13; J. S. HARRIS, *op. cit.*, p. 143; Margery PERHAM, *Native Administration in Nigeria, op. cit.*, pp. 209–12.
[39]   Harry A. GAILEY, *op. cit.*, p. 137; Margery PERHAM, *Native Administration in Nigeria, op. cit.*, pp. 209–12.
[40]   J. S. HARRIS, *op. cit.*, pp. 147–48; Margery PERHAM, *Native Administration in Nigeria, op. cit.*, pp. 207ff; C. K. MEEK, *op. cit.*, p. ix.

women, a Commission of Enquiry spoke of the "savage passions" of the "mobs," and one military officer told the Commission that "he had never seen crowds in such a state of frenzy." Yet these "frenzied mobs" injured no one seriously, which the British found "surprising."[41]

It is not surprising if the Women's War is seen as the traditional practice of "sitting on a man," only on a larger scale. Decisions were made in *mikiri* to respond to a situation in which women were acutely wronged by the Warrant Chiefs' corruption and by the taxes they believed to be forthcoming. Spokeswomen were chosen to present their demands for the removal of the Warrant Chiefs and women followed their leadership, on several occasions sitting down to wait for negotiations or agreeing to disperse or to turn in Warrant Chiefs' caps. [42] Traditional dress, rituals and "weapons" for "sitting on" were used: the head wreathed with young ferns symbolized war, and sticks, bound with ferns or young palms, were used to invoke the powers of the female ancestors.[43] The women's behavior also followed traditional patterns: much noise, stamping, preposterous threats and a general raucous atmosphere were all part of the institution of "sitting on a man". Destroying an offender's hut – in this case the Native Court buildings – was clearly within the bounds of this sanctioning process.

The Women's War was coordinated throughout the two provinces by information sent through the market *mikiri* network. Delegates travelled from one area to another and the costs were paid by donations from the women's market profits.[44] Traditional rules

were followed in that the participants were women – only a few men were involved in the demonstrations – and leadership was clearly in the hands of women.

The absence of men from the riots does not indicate lack of support. Men generally approved, and only a few older men criticized the women for not being more respectful toward the government. It is reported that both men and women shared the mistaken belief that the women, having observed certain rituals, would not be fired upon. The men had no illusions of immunity for themselves, having vivid memories of the slaughter of Igbo men during the conquest.[45] Finally, the name given the rebellion by the Igbo – the Women's War – indicates that the women saw themselves following their traditional sanctioning methods of "sitting on" or "making war on" a man.

Since the British failed to recognize the Women's War as a collective response to the abrogation of rights, they did not inquire into the kinds of structures the women had that prepared them for such action. They failed to ask, "How do the women make group decisions? How do they choose their leaders?" Since they saw only a "riot," they explained the fact that the women injured no one seriously as "luck," never even contemplating that perhaps the women's actions had traditional limits.

Because the women – and the men – regarded the inquiries as attempts to discover whom to punish, they did not volunteer any information about the women's organizations. But there is at least some question as to whether the British would have understood

---

[41] Margery PERHAM, *Native Administration in Nigeria, op. cit.*, pp. 212–19.

[42] *Ibid.*, pp. 212ff.

[43] Harris reports a curse sworn by the women on the pestles: "It is I who gave birth to you. It is I who cook for you to eat. This is the pestle I use to pound yams and coco yams for you to eat. May you soon die!" See J. S. HARRIS, *op. cit.*, pp. 143–45.

[44] Harry A. GAILEY *op. cit.*, p. 112.

[45] Margery PERHAM, *Native Administration in Nigeria, op. cit.*, pp. 212ff; J. C. ANENE, *op. cit.*, pp. 207–24; S. O. EUKE, *op. cit.*, p. 11; C. K. MEEK, *op. cit.*, p. x.

them if they had. The market network was discovered, but suggested no further lines of inquiry to the British. The majority of District Officers thought that the men organized the women's actions and were secretly directing them. The Bende District Officer and the Secretary of the southern Province believed that there was a secret "Ogbo Society" which exercised control over women and was responsible for fomenting the rebellion.[46] And the women's demands that they did not want the Native Court to hear cases any longer and that all white men should go to their own country, or, at least, that women should serve on the Native Courts and one be appointed District Officer – demands in line with the power of women in traditional society – were ignored.[47]

All these responses fall into a coherent pattern: *not* of purposeful discrimination against women with the intent of keeping them from playing their traditional political roles, but of a prevailing blindness to the possibility that women had *had* a significant role in traditional politics and should participate in the new system of local government. A few political officers were "of the opinion that, if the balance of society is to be kept, the women's organizations should be encouraged alongside those of the men."[48] Some commissioners even recognized "the remarkable character of organization and leadership which some of the women displayed" and recommended that "more attention be paid to the political influence of women."[49] But these men were the exception: their views did not prevail. Even in the late 1930s when the investigations of

Leith-Ross and Green revealed the decreasing vitality of women's organizations under colonialism, the British still did not include women in the reformed Native Administration. When political officers warned that *young men* were being excluded, however, steps were taken to return their traditional political status.[50]

"Reforms" and Women's Loss of Power

In 1933 reforms were enacted to redress many Igbo grievances against the Native Administration. The number of Native Court Areas was greatly increased and their boundaries arranged to conform roughly to traditional divisions. Warrant Chiefs were replaced by "massed benches" – allowing large numbers of judges to sit at one time. In most cases it was left up to the villages to decide whom and how many to send.[51] This benefitted the women by eliminating the corruption of the Warrant Chiefs, and it made their persons and property more secure. But it provided no outlet for collective action, their real base of power.

As in the village assembly, the women could not compete with the men for leadership in the reformed Native Administration because as individuals they lacked the resources of the men.[52] In the various studies done on the Igbo in the 1930s, there is only one report of a woman being sent to the Native Court and her patrilineage had put up the money for her to take her titles.[53]

Since the reformed Native Administration

---

[46]　Harry A. GAILEY, *op. cit.*, pp. 130ff.
[47]　Sylvia LEITH-ROSS, *op. cit.*, p. 165; Margery PERHAM, *Native Administration in Nigeria, op. cit.*, pp. 165ff.
[48]　Margery PERHAM, *Native Administration in Nigeria, op. cit.*, p. 246.
[49]　A. E. AFIGBO, *op. cit.*, p. 187.
[50.]　C. K. MEEK, *op. cit.*, p. 203.
[51]　Margery PERHAM, *Native Administration in Nigeria, op. cit.*, pp. 365ff.
[52]　C. K. MEEK, *op. cit.*, p. 203.
[53.]　*Ibid.*, pp. 158–159. She was divorced and had to remain unmarried as a condition of her family's paying for her title as they wanted to be sure to get their investment back when future initiates paid their fees to the established members. If she remarried, her husband's family, and not her own, would inherit her property.

actually took over many functions of the village assemblies, women's political participation was seriously affected. Discussions on policy no longer included any adult who wished to take part but only members of the native courts. Men who were not members were also excluded, but men's interests and point of view were represented, and, at one time or another, many men had some chance to become members; very few women ever did.[54]

The political participation and power of women had depended on the diffuseness of political power and authority within Igbo society. In attempting to create specialized political institutions on the Western model with participation on the basis of individual achievement, the British created a system in which there was no place for group solidarity, no place for what thereby became "extra-legal" or simply illegal forms of group coercion, and thus very little place for women.

The British reforms undermined and weakened the power of the women by removing many political functions from *mikiri* and from village assemblies. In 1901 the British had declared all jural institutions except the Native Courts illegitimate, but it was only in the years following the 1933 reforms that Native Administration local government became effective enough to make that declaration meaningful. When this happened, the *mikiri* lost vitality.[55] Although what has happened to them since has not been reported in detail. The reports that do exist mention the functioning of market women's organizations but only as pressure groups for narrow economic

interest[56] and women's participation in Igbo unions as very low in two towns.[57]

The British also weakened women's power by outlawing "self-help" – the use of force by individuals or groups to protect their own interests by punishing wrongdoers. This action – in accord with the idea that only the state may legitimately use force – made "sitting on" anyone illegal, thereby depriving women of one of their best weapons to protect wives from husbands, markets from rowdies, or coco yams from cows.[58]

The British didn't know, of course, that they were banning "sitting on a man"; they were simply banning the "illegitimate" use of force. In theory, this didn't hurt the women as wife-beaters, rowdies and owners of marauding cows could be taken to court. But courts were expensive, and the men who sat in them were likely to have different views from the women's on wife-beating, market "fun" and men's cows. By interfering with the traditional balance of power, the British effectively eliminated the women's ability to protect their own interests and made them dependent upon men for protection against men.

Since the British did not understand this, they did nothing to help women develop new ways of protecting their interest within the political system. (What the women *did* do to try to protect their interests in this situation should be a fruitful subject for study.) What women *did not* do was to participate to any significant extent in local government or, much later, in national government, and a large part of the responsibility must rest on the British, who removed legitimacy from women's traditional political institutions and

---

[54]   Sylvia LEITH-ROSS, *op. cit.*, pp. 171–72; Lord HAILEY, *Native Administration in the British African Territories, Part III, West Africa* (London: H. M. Stationary Office, 1951). pp. 160–65.

[55]   Sylvia LEITH-ROSS, *op. cit.*, pp. 110, 163, 214.

[56]   Henry L. BRETTON, "Political Influence in Southern Nigeria", in Herbert J. SPIRO (ed.), *Africa: The Primacy of Politics* (New York: Random House, 1966), p. 61.

[57]   Audrey C. SMOCK, *Ibo Politics: The Role of Ethnic Unions in Eastern Nigeria*, (Cambridge: The Harvard University Press, 1971), pp. 65, 137.

[58]   Sylvia LEITH-ROSS, *op. cit.*, p. 109.

did nothing to help women move into modern political institutions.

Missionary Influence

The effect of the colonial administration was reinforced by the missionaries and mission schools. Christian missions were established in Igboland in the late 19th century. They had few converts at first, but their influence by the 1930s was considered significant, generally among the young.[59] A majority of Igbo eventually "became Christians" – they had to profess Christianity in order to attend mission schools, and education was highly valued. But regardless of how nominal their membership was, they had to obey the rules to remain in good standing, and one rule was to avoid "pagan" rituals. Women were discouraged from attending *mikiri* where traditional rituals were performed or money collected for the rituals, which in effect meant all *mikiri*.[60]

Probably more significant, since *mikiri* were in the process of losing some of their political functions anyway, was mission education. English and Western education came to be seen as increasingly necessary for political leadership – needed to deal with the British and their law – and women had less access to this new knowledge than men. Boys were more often sent to school, for a variety of reasons generally related to their favored position in the patrilineage.[61] But even when girls did go, they tended not to receive the same type of education. In mission schools, and increasingly in special "training homes" which dispensed with most academic courses, the girls were taught European domestic skills and the Bible, often in the vernacular. The missionaries' avowed purpose in educating girls was to train them to be Christian wives and mothers, not for jobs or for citizenship.[62] Missionaries were not necessarily against women's participation in politics   clergy in England, as in America, could be found supporting women's suffrage. But in Africa their concern was the church, and for the church they needed Christian families. Therefore, Christian wives and mothers, not female political leaders, was the mission's aim. As Mary Slessor, the influential Calabar missionary said: "God-like motherhood is the finest sphere for women, and the way to the redemption of the world."[63]

Victorianism and Women's Invisibility

The missionaries' beliefs about woman's natural and proper role being that of a Christian helpmate and the administration's refusal to take the Igbo women seriously when

---

[59]   *Ibid.*, pp. 109–18; C. K. MEEK, *op. cit.*, p. xv. Maxwell states that by 1925 there were 26 mission stations and 63 missionaries (twelve of them missionary wives) in Igboland. The earliest station was established in 1857, but all but three were founded after 1900. Fifteen mission stations and 30 missionaries were among Igbo in Owerri and Calabar Provinces. See J. Lowry MAXWELL, *Nigeria: The Land, the People and Christian Progress* (London: World Dominion Press, 1926), pp. 150–52.

[60]   Sylvia LEITH-ROSS, *op. cit.*, p. 110; J. F. Ade AJAYI, *Christian Missions in Nigeria, 1841–1891: The Making of a New Elite* (Evanston, Ill.: The Northwestern University Press, 1965), pp. 108–9.

[61]   Sylvia LEITH-ROSS, *op. cit.*, pp. 133, 196–97, 316.

[62]   *Ibid.*, pp. 189–90. According to Leith-Ross, in the "girls' training homes . . . the scholastic education given was limited, in some of the smaller homes opened at a later date almost negligible, but the domestic training and the general civilizing effect were good." Evidence of these views among missionaries can be found in J. F. Ade AJAYI, *op. cit.*, pp. 65, 142–44; G. T. BASDEN, *Edith Warner of the Niger* (London: Seeley, Service and Co., Ltd., 1927), pp. 13, 16, 33, 55, 77, 86; Josephine C. BULIFANT, *Forty Years in the African Bush* (Grand Rapids, Mich.: Zondervan Publishing House, 1950), pp. 163 and passim; W. P. LIVINGSTONE, *Mary Slessor of Calabar* (New York: George H. Doran Co., m.d.), pp. iii–vi; J. Lowry MAXWELL, *op. cit.*, pp. 55, 118.

[63]   W. P. LIVINGSTONE, *op. cit.*, p. 328.

they demanded political participation, are understandable in light of the colonialists having been socialized in a society dominated by Victorian values. It was during Queen Victoria's reign that the woman's-place-is-in-the-home ideology hardened into its most recent highly rigid form.[64] Although attacked by feminists, it remained the dominant mode of thought through that part of the colonial period discussed here; and it is, in fact, far from dead today, when a woman's primary identity is most often seen as that of wife and mother even when she works 40 hours a week outside the home.[65]

We are concerned here primarily with the Victorian view of women and politics which produced the expectation that men would be active in politics, but women would not. The ideal of Victorian womanhood – attainable, of course, by only the middle class, but widely believed in throughout society – was of a sensitive, morally superior being who was the hearthside guardian of Christian virtues and sentiments absent in the outside world. Her mind was not strong enough for the appropriately masculine subjects: science, business, and politics.[66] A woman who showed talent in

these areas did not challenge any ideas about typical women: the exceptional woman simply "had the brain of a man," as Sir George Goldie said of Mary Kingsley.[67]

A thorough investigation of the diaries, journals, reports, and letters of colonial officers and missionaries would be needed to prove that most of them held these Victorian values. But preliminary reading of biographies, autobiographies, journals and "reminiscences," and the evidence of their own statements about Igbo women at the time of the Women's War, strongly suggest the plausibility of the hypothesis that they were deflected from any attempt to discover and protect Igbo women's political role by their assumption that politics isn't a proper, normal place for women.[68]

When Igbo women with their Women's War forced the colonial administrators to recognize their presence, their brief "visibility" was insufficient to shake these assumptions. Their behavior was simply seen as aberrant. When they returned to "normal," they were once again invisible. Although there was a feminist movement in England during that time, it had not successfully challenged

---

[64] Page SMITH, *Daughters of the Promised Land* (Boston: Little, Brown and Co., 1970), pp. 58–76; Doris STENTON, *The English Woman in History* (London: George Allen and Unwin, Ltd., 1957), pp. 312–44.

[65] Eva FIGES, *Patriarchal Attitudes* (New York: Stein and Day, 1970); Ruth E. HARTLEY, "Children's Concepts of Male and Female Roles", *Merrill-Palmer Quarterly*, January 1960.

[66] Walter E. HOUGHTON, *The Victorian Frame of Mind, 1830 – 1870* (New Haven: The Yale University Press, 1957), pp. 349–53. Numerous studies of Victorian and post-Victorian ideas about women and politics describe these patterns. In addition to Houghton, Smith and Stenton, see, for example, Kirsten AMUNDSEN, *The Silenced Majority* (Prentice-Hall, 1971): Jessie BERNARD, *Women and the Public Interest* (Aldine-Atherton, 1971): John Stuart MILL and Harriet TAYLOR MILL, *Essays on Sex Equality* (University of Chicago Press, 1970); Martha VICINUS (ed.), *Suffer and Be Still: Women in the Victorian Age* (Indiana University Press, 1972); Cecil WOODHAM-SMITH *Florence Nightingale, 1820–1910* (McGraw-Hill, 1951). It was not until 1929 that all English women could vote; women over 30 who met restrictive property qualifications got the vote in 1918.

[67] Stephen GWYNN, *The Life of Mary Kingsley* (London: Macmillan and Co., Ltd., 1932), p. 252. Mary Kingsley along with other elite female "exceptions" like Flora Shaw Lugard and Margery Perham, all of whom influenced African colonial policy, held the same values as men, at least in regard to women's roles. They did not expect ordinary women to have political power any more than the men did, and they showed no particular concern for African women.

[68] See, for non-missionary examples, J. C. ANENE, *op. cit.*, pp. 222–34; W. R. CROCKER, *Nigeria: A Critique of British Colonial Administration* (London: George Allen and Unwin, Ltd., 1936); C. K. MEEK, *op. cit*; Mary H. KINGSLEY, *Travels in West Africa* (London: Macmillan and Co., Ltd., 1897); Idem, *West African Studies* (London: Macmillan and Co., Ltd., 1899); Margery PERHAM, *op. cit.*; A.H. St. John WOOD, "Nigeria : Fifty Years of Political Development among the Ibos", in Raymond APTHORPE (ed.) *From Tribal Rule to Modern Government* (Lusaka, Northern Rhodesia: Rhodes–Livingston Institute for Social Research, 1960).

basic ideas about women nor made the absence of women from public life seem to be a problem which required remedy. The movement had not succeeded in creating a "feminist" consciousness in any but a few "deviants," and such a consciousness is far from widespread today; for to have a "feminist" consciousness means that one *notices* the "invisibility" of women. One *wonders* where the women are – in life and in print.

Understanding the assumptions about women's roles prevalent in Victorian society – and still common today – helps to explain how the introduction of supposedly modern political structures and values could reduce rather than expand the political lives of Igbo women. As long as politics is presumed to be a male realm, no one wonders where the women went. The loss of Igbo women's political institutions – in life and in print – shows the need for more Western scholars to develop enough of a feminist consciousness to start wondering.

32

BODY POLITICS: SEXUALITY, GENDER, AND DOMESTIC SERVICE IN ZAMBIA*

KAREN TRANBERG HANSEN

Many maids come in the house as innocent as a new born babe. But the attitudes of some women to treat their maids almost like slaves or rivals certainly changes their outlook and behavior towards house work. Do you blame the maids if they look at the husband as a prize catch?[1]

During the colonial period in Northern Rhodesia and today in independent Zambia, employers of domestic servants prefer to hire men. Rather than reducing domestic service in that country to an archaic remnant of a once widespread form of wage labor relationship in the west, I view it as a comparative and historical problem whose similiarities to, and differences from, domestic service in other times and places must be explained. Such an approach yields insights into those aspects of servant/employer relationships that inhere in their structure and those that are mediated by historical and cultural factors. My special concern in this paper is with the historical and cultural factors in that I seek to explore a culturally constructed gender convention invested with ambiguous sexual meanings that have not been seriously examined in the Africanist research context. For this reason, I barely treat the comparative and structural questions that I have dealt with at length elsewhere.[2] The paper, thus, is an attempt at approaching an analysis of some effects on

*   This paper draws on extensive archival research begun in 1982, and field research in Zambia, 1983–85, including the collection of life history data from retired employers of colonial servants in Great Britain (5 interviews; 19 written communications) and Zambia (a minority of the white employers of servants interviewed as part of the sample survey), elderly servants (16 men; 12 women), and a sample survey in 187 servant employing households in Lusaka involving separate interviews with the chief domestic servant and the employer. Parts of the research were funded in 1982 by the McMillan Fund and the Office of International Programs at the University of Minnesota, from 1983–85 by the U.S. National Science Foundation grant no. BNS 8303507, and by faculty grants from Northwestern University in 1985 and 1986. Versions of this paper have been presented on several occasions, among them the seminar series on Women, Colonialism and Commonwealth, at the Institute of Commonwealth Studies, University of London, June 25, 1987. Among the many who have offered critical comments and suggestions, I am grateful to Carol B. Eastman for constructive advice and to Margaret Strobel for continuous prodding and for always being a stimulating critic.

[1] Geoff Zulu, "Maids Wreaking Havoc in Homes," *Zambia Daily Mail* Weekend Entertainment Section, May 27, 1989.
[2] Karen Tranberg Hansen, *Distant Companions: Servants and Employers in Zambia*, 1900–1985 (Ithaca, N.Y.: Cornell University Press, 1989).

gender relations across race and class of culturally constructed notions of gender and
sexuality.[3] Last but not least, because of the
near total silence in the conventional source
materials about sexual interaction across race
and class lines, the paper is also a demonstration of the challenge and difficulty of
attempting to think through and write about
engendered cultural constructions whose
meanings today's readers may find troublesome.

By bringing cultural and ideological factors
to bear on my analysis of the gender question
in domestic service in Zambia, I argue that
structural and ideological factors operate in
complex and at times contradictory interaction
to shape social action and practice. I mobilize
these culturally constructed notions in the
context of a historical case study in which I
seek to illustrate the effects of such ideas on
actual social interaction across race, gender,
and class. The case under scrutiny is the failed
attempt by colonial officials in Northern
Rhodesia during the post-World War II years
to recruit African women into domestic
service. The ensuing discussion, labelled the
African womanpower debate in the colonial
correspondence, provides dramatic evidence
of the workings of colonial gender ideology
and of the social impacts of its sexual assumptions. In the paper's first section, I present the
empirical and theoretical backdrop for my
subsequent analysis. I next identify the strands
of the womanpower debate and then briefly

delineate the historical background against
which cultural notions of gender and sexuality
emerged. I go on to explore how the race,
gender, and class dynamics in white colonial
households were affected by these notions. I
finally discuss and explain why such ideas
persist in changed form, but for different
reasons, in domestic service in postcolonial
Zambia and bring out a peculiar body politic
between the madam, as female employers of
servants invariably are called in southern
Africa, her female servant, and the madam's
husband.

Background and Problem

The existing studies of domestic service in
Africa pertain almost exclusively to the
southern region.[4] The South African studies
offer a kaleidoscopic story of women of all
races and men passing through domestic
service. After the abolition of slavery in
1834, poor Afrikaner women and British
women brought over from Europe worked as
domestics in white households. As members
of household staffs consisted mainly of
African men, the presence of these white
women proved problematic, and they were
replaced by African men soon after the turn
of the century. African men persisted in
domestic service on the Witwatersrand till the
late 1930s but were replaced by "coloured"
and African women in the Cape much

---

[3] Because of the nature of my sources, most of my discussion of European or white attitudes refers to the British. The
fact that African, Asian ("Indians"), and Afrikaans-speaking households also employed servants does not mean that the
master–servant relationship in British households was atypical or out of the ordinary. On the contrary, since the British
were the dominant group in political terms, they set the norms and standards against which social interaction and practices were evaluated.

[4] Among the chief studies are Michael G. Whisson and William Weil, *Domestic Servants: A Microcosm of "The Race
Problem"* (Johannesburg: Institute of Race Relations; 1971); Eleanor Preston-Whyte, "Race Attitudes and Behavior: The
Case of Domestic Employment in White South African Homes," *African Studies* 35 (1976):71–89; special issue on
domestic labor of the *South African Labour Bulletin* 6(1980); Jacklyn Cock, *Maids and Madams: A Study in The Politics
of Exploitation* (Johannesburg: Ravan Press, 1980); and Suzanne Gordon, *A Talent for Tomorrow: Life Stories of South
African Servants* (Johannesburg: Ravan Press, 1985).

earlier.[5] With growing demand for African men's labor on the mines, women gradually became more numerous in domestic service also on the Witwatersrand. Today in South Africa, domestic service is considered an African woman's job, and it remains a life-long occupation through which married and unmarried women as well as single mothers pursue a series of dead-end jobs.[6]

In Southern Rhodesia, domestic service remained a male occupational preserve longer than in South Africa.[7] Recent research by Janet Bujra is likely to unravel the gender dynamics in domestic service in Tanzania.[8] But for much of the rest of Africa, our knowledge about gender and domestic service remains anecdotal. There is a widespread assumption that African men, rather than women, everywhere were the first to be recruited into domestic service during the colonial period and that women have been replacing them to different degrees after independence. The challenge to scholarship is not to take these assumptions for granted but to examine the changing interaction of structural, historical, and cultural factors involved in producing particular gender conventions in employment. Although the ways in which such factors have combined across space and time may result in similar employment conventions, the individual factors may carry varying weight because they are invested with different cultural meanings and thus, as in the case I am about to explore, produce conclusions that may be at variance

with those of scholars who have explored the gender dynamics in domestic service elsewhere.

Colonial officials in Northern Rhodesia often referred to experiences in South Africa and Southern Rhodesia when arguing about the direction of change in the colony. By the post–World War II years, African women had established a strong presence in domestic service in South Africa and were beginning to take on this job in larger numbers also in Southern Rhodesia. These experiences influenced the thinking of colonial officials in Northern Rhodesia when, during the post–World War II years, they became increasingly preoccupied with labor shortages. The copper mining industry was booming in the wake of the Korean war, secondary industry was developing, and labor was scarce across town and country. In their concern to alleviate the labor shortage, they suggested a solution: the recruitment of African women into domestic service in order to release men for more productive work elsewhere. The African womanpower campaign they set into motion for that purpose between the late 1940s and 1956 was a failure.

If colonial officials were to succeed in staging a gender transition from male to female in domestic service in Northern Rhodesia, they would have needed ingenuity, for domestic service in that country was defined in gender terms as an African man's job. During the early decades of white settlement, some

---

[5]   Charles van Onselen, "The Witches of Suburbia: Domestic Service on the Witwatersrand, 1890–1914," in van Onselen, ed., *Studies in the Social and Economic History of the Witwatersrand 1886–1914* (London: Longman, 1982), 2 vols., *New Nineveh*, 2: 1–73; Deborah Gaitskell, Judy Kimble, Moira Maconachie, and Elaine Unterhalter, "Race, Class and Gender: Domestic Workers in South Africa," *Review of African Political Economy* 27/28 (1984): 86–108.

[6]   Eleanor Preston-Whyte develops this point in "Families without Marriage: A Zulu Case Study," in *Social System and Transition in South Africa: Essays in Honour of Eileen Krige*, ed. John Argyle and Eleanor Preston-Whyte (Cape Town: Oxford University Press, 1978), 55–85.

[7]   Duncan G. Clarke, *Domestic Workers in Rhodesia: The Economics of Masters and Servants* (Gwelo: Mambo Press, 1974), and chapters on servants and employers in A. K. Weinrich, *Mucheke: Race, Status, and Politics in a Rhodesian Community* (New York: Holmes and Meier, 1976).

[8]   Janet Bujra, "Men at Work in the Tanzanian Home: How Did They Ever Learn?" in *Domesticity: African Constructions of Space, Work and Gender*, ed. Karen Tranberg Hansen (New Brunswick: Rutgers University Press, forthcoming).

white women had been employed as governesses and ladies' companions in colonial households. As more whites settled, a small number of African women, many of whom were "coloureds" from South Africa, were hired as "nurses" or nannies, but even in this field, juveniles (meaning "nurse boys") were taken on more frequently than African women. Although more women have entered the occupation after independence in 1964, they are greatly outnumbered by men who continue to be preferred as domestic workers.

The question of gender in domestic service has to a large extent been considered self-evident in the existing scholarship on the transformations of this occupation in the west and its ongoing changes in the Third World.[9] The historical experience of the west, of women replacing men servants towards the end of the seventeenth century, their employment peaking in the early decades of the twentieth century, and the occupation's decline as a major source of urban wage income for women as new job opportunities opened up elsewhere, has been linked in the main to economic and demographic changes.[10] Extrapolating from the twentieth-century employment pattern of women domestics in the west when making predictions about the place of gender in the process of socio-economic change in Third World countries, much existing scholarship has underestimated the singularity of this pattern.[11]

The issue of domestic service, as Belinda Bozzoli has observed, "can better be understood as the outcome of a complex series of domestic struggles, rather than institution designed to serve the interests of capital in an uncomplicated fashion."[12] The unsuccessful outcome of the African womanpower campaign was not the result only of labor market factors. Nor is today's predominance of men as paid domestic workers in Zambia to be solely attributed to the lack of postcolonial labor market developments. Scholarship on gender construction promises to flesh out the question of gender in domestic service in more detail, qualifying overly economistic accounts by actively implicating cultural and ideological factors in analysis.

Gender roles, as Michelle Rosaldo has pointed out, are not the product of the tasks women undertake or of their biology. Rather, their construction is a result of the meanings women's activities acquire through actual social interaction.[13] Cautioning against conflating gender and sexuality, Patricia Caplan has encouraged us to raise questions about whether, and if so, how, when, and why they

[9]   Recent Third World studies include Elsa M. Chaney and Mary Garcia Castro, eds., *Muchachas No More: Household Workers in Latin America and the Caribbean* (Philadelphia: Temple University Press, 1989); Jacklyn Cock, *Maids & Madams: A Study of the Politics of Exploitation* (Johannesburg: Ravan Press, 1980); and Shellee Coleen and Roger Sanjek, eds., *At Work in Homes: Household Workers in Third World Countries* (Washington, DC: American Ethnological Society, forthcoming).

[10]   On these changes in the west, see for example, Faye E. Dudden, *Serving Women: Household Service in Nineteenth-Century America* (Middletown, Conn: Wesleyan University Press, 1983); David Katzman, *Seven Days a Week: Women and Domestic Service in Industrializing America* (New York: Oxford University Press, 1978); Sarah Maza, *The Uses of Loyalty: Domestic Service in Eighteenth Century France* (Princeton, N.J.: Princeton University Press, 1983); Pamela Horn, *The Rise and Fall of the Victorian Servant* (New York: St. Martin's Press, 1975). On race and domestic service in America, see Evelyn Nakano Glenn, *Issei, Nisei, War Bride: Three Generations of Japanese American Women in Domestic Service* (Philadelphia: Temple University Press 1986); Judith Rollins, *Between Women: Domestics and Their Employers* (Philadelphia: Temple University Press, 1985).

[11]   See for example, Ester Boserup, *Woman's Role in Economic Development* (New York: St. Martin's Press, 1970), and David Chaplin, "Domestic Service and Industrialization," *Comparative Studies in Sociology* 1 (1978): 97–127.

[12]   Belinda Bozzoli, "Marxism, Feminism and South African Studies," *Journal of Southern African Studies* 9(1983): 159.

[13]   Michelle Z. Rosaldo, "The Use and Abuse of Anthropology: Reflections on Feminism and Cross-cultural Understanding," *Signs* 5(1980): 399–400.

become linked.[14] Notions of gender and sexuality were not given at the onset of the colonial encounter in Northern Rhodesia but created through it and the processes it set into motion. Although the lives of both colonizer and colonized were influenced by sexual attitudes and practices, sexuality has been placed on the scholarly agenda of colonial history only recently, and the exploration of African women's and men's experience of sexuality has barely begun.[15] Sexuality, considered as symbols pertaining to gender and to eroticism, is invested with culturally variable meanings.[16] In Northern Rhodesia, its meanings were manipulated and used by women and men of both races in ways that reflected the impact of race, class, and gender and other factors on the structure of their society. I suggest in this paper that African women's gender role hinged on constructed notions of sexuality that were the products of interactions across race and sex from the onset of colonial rule and onwards. These ideas came to the fore in the case under scrutiny, which enables me to tease out the convergence of gender and sexuality that invested the gender construction of the African female servant with ambiguous sexual meanings.

The African Womanpower Campaign

Gender and Wage Labor in Northern Rhodesia

As in much of the rest of the southern part of the African continent, the development of the migrant labor system in Northern Rhodesia from the last decades of the nineteenth century through the time of the Great Depression resulted in a geographical division of labor in which African men were recruited into wage labor on farms and in mines, while African women remained in the rural areas working the fields and taking care of children and the old. The viability of village life depended overwhelmingly on women's work, which also subsidized migrant workers substandard wages without cost to the administration.[17] Deteriorating rural conditions and lack of agricultural extension services had by the 1930s adversely affected rural livelihoods, prompting more and more women and children to migrate to towns.[18] African women were largely excluded from urban wage labor, and many secured a living by joining men as wives or consorts and/or by trading or marketing.[19] Despite the dubious nature of colonial statistics and lack of gender categorized employment data till 1951, the available statistics show that very few African women

---

[14] Pat Caplan, ed., *The Cultural Construction of Sexuality* (London: Tavistock, 1987).

[15] Ronald Hyam, "Empire and Sexual Opportunity," *Journal of Imperial and Commonwealth History* 14 (1986): 34–90. For studies concerning the former British colonies, see Kenneth Ballhatchet, *Race, Sex and Class under the Raj* (London: Weidenfeld and Nicolson, 1980), and Amirah Inglis, *The White Women's Protection Ordinance: Sexual Anxiety and Politics in Papua* (London: Sussex University Press, 1974). For American discussions of sexuality, see Ann Snitow, Christine Stansell, and Sharon Thompson, eds. *Powers of Desire: The Politics of Sexuality* (New York: Monthly Review Press, 1983).

[16] Sherry B. Ortner, and Harriet Whitehead, "Introduction: Accounting for Sexual Meanings," in *Sexual Meanings: The Cultural Construction of Gender and Sexuality*, ed. Sherry B. Ortner and Harriet Whitehead (New York: Cambridge University Press, 1981), ix.

[17] Lionel Cliffe, "Labour Migration and Peasant Differentiation: Zambian Experiences," *Journal of Peasant Studies* 5 (1978): 326–46.

[18] Andrew Roberts, *A History of Zambia* (London: Heinemann, 1976), 190–94.

[19] George Chauncey, Jr., "The Locus of Reproduction: Women's Labour in the Zambian Copperbelt, 1927–153," *Journal of Southern African Studies* 7 (1981): 135–64.

were employed in domestic service. A total of 250 African women compared to 30,000 men domestic servants were enumerated in 1951 when the occupation formed the third largest male employment category after mining and agriculture.[20] During World War II, when Northern Rhodesia experienced extreme food scarcities, the colonial government tried to stem the urban influx of women and children, devising a variety of measures to get them back to the villages as food producers.[21] These attempts were largely ineffectual. Due to growing white immigration and continued migration of rural Africans, the urban populations increased rapidly during the decade 1946–56, and the previous era's skewed adult sex ratios of both Africans and whites became more balanced.[22] To increase productivity, the colonial administration copied the practice followed since the 1930s by some of the mining companies, allowing African male workers to live with wives and dependents.[23] During the early 1940s, primary education was for the first time made compulsory for urban African children between 12 and 16 years of age. Newly established welfare departments involved themselves in shaping African urban patterns of leisure and in the teaching of western notions of domesticity to urban African women.[24] These, and other developments, contributed to the creation of a more stabilized urban African community.

The scope the colonial administration grudgingly had granted African urbanites to organize their households was not left undisturbed. When labor shortages grew during the post-World War II period, the colonial administration sought to intrude in order to tap the available labor supply. Assuming that units of labor were mutually interchangeable, they argued that African women should replace men in domestic service to release the latter for work elsewhere.[25] The ambiguous and at times contradictory attitudes of whites and Africans, males and females, to the question of employing women in domestic service was laid open in the debate that followed.

The Debate About African Womanpower

Being female or male was far from an irrelevant factor in the Northern Rhodesia labor market, and, for historical reasons, domestic service had become construed in gender terms as male. In the view of male administrators and white women, there were three chief "problems" that made the prospective employment of African female domestic servants difficult. There was no housing for them, they were not trained, and their men would object. They claimed that African women could not work as servants in white households until hostels were built for them outside of the white residential areas. Living there under the supervision of a white woman, they would be less likely to become involved with men. The reverse had never been argued, namely the need to house African men servants away from their employers' residences in order to reduce their possible sexual involvement with white madams. It seems that white women in Northern Rhodesia had been accustomed to African men servants living in their backyards for decades. Why now this fuss about African women?

It was argued over and over again that

[20]   Hansen, *Distant Companions*, 130.

[21]   Helmuth Heisler, *Urbanization and the Government of Migration* (New York: St. Martin's Press, 1974), 63–84.

[22]   George Kay, *A Social Geography of Zambia* (London: London University Press, 1967), 26–27.

[23]   Roberts, *A History of Zambia*, 190–94.

[24]   Hortense Powdermaker, *Coppertown: Changing Africa* (New York: Harper and Row, 1962), 109–12.

[25]   Unless otherwise specified, the discussion in this part is based on files deposited at the National Archives of Zambia (NAZ). Direct quotes are taken from the following files: NAZ/NR 3/143 md/14. Labour Department. Native Labour Conditions. Labour Supplies. Woman Power; NAZ/NR 2/27. African Welfare. General Correspondence; and NAZ/SEC 5/331. Native Labour. General Policy 1949–51.

African women needed education before they would be able to go into service. African women, it seems, were not considered domestic "by nature." And white women appear to have been unwilling to socialize them into domestic labor on the job as they had done with previous generations of African men servants. In the past, men's work as servants had not been deemed problematic because they had little education. On the contrary, in the early days of settlement, and according to my informants, up through the 1940s if not later, many employers avoided "mission boys" (Africans who had received some education) who were considered rogues of the first order, and several white madams had, indeed, preferred "raw natives," that is, young men fresh from the villages, whom they trained themselves. Holding African women's lack of education against them, white women chose to disregard that the curriculum in girls' schools, such as they were at this point in time, was heavy on domestic science subjects with the intention of making African women into good mothers and proud housewives. Yet these mutually contradictory attitudes did not cancel each other out. In the view of white madams, African women servants were less controllable than men; they were less tractable and caused more problems in the running of the white colonial household. Training of African women, wrote four white women in a 1950 letter to a newspaper's editor, should be undertaken by "honest-to-goodness women with a sound knowledge of Rhodesian homes . . . [because] only women who have lived among Africans have a glimmering idea of the primitive condition of the African female."[26]

These, and other comments made during the debate, indicate white women's doubt that African women would be able to take over from men in domestic service, and they themselves made little effort to see to it that they were. Nor did white male officials of the labor department who, at a 1950 conference, declared African women as "absolutely raw material." In spite of advocating the employment of African women servants, the colonial administration did little to facilitate it, resisting suggestions from churches and philanthropic groups to finance both training and hostels for women servants.[27]

As for African men, colonial authorities described them as "loath, not without some reason, to allow their wives to work away from home." The colonial assumption was that African wives would involve themselves sexually with other men. I suggest that several additional factors may have influenced African men's attitudes toward women's work as domestics. Their reluctance to send wives, sisters, and daughters into service in colonial white households may reflect their unwillingness to expose women to a demeaning work relationship for which very low wages were paid. The matter of wages was never addressed in the debate. The few African women who did participate in a short-lived African Charwoman Scheme at the copperbelt town of Ndola in 1954 preferred to change from an hourly basis to "whole time employment as being more secure." Their statement implies that part-time domestic service hardly was worthwhile economically.

Last but not least, paid household service conflicted with the demands placed on African women's own domestic labor as broadly defined in cultural terms among the region's different ethnic groups. Across much of Africa, women and men regard the home as

---

[26] "Letter to the Editor," *Central African Post*, December 14, 1950; 3.

[27] Churches and missions in Northern Rhodesia never involved themselves in housing and training women domestics to the same extent that they did in the south. On South Africa, see Deborah Gaitskell, " 'Christian Compounds for Girls': Church Hostels for African Women in Johannesburg, 1907–1970," *Journal of Southern African Studies* 6(1979): 44–69. On Southern Rhodesia, National Archives of Zimbabwe S/1561/48. Female Domestic Labour. Labour Memoranda and Minutes, 1941–1947. Report on Native Female Domestic Service, November 17, 1932.

women's place and childcare and household tasks as their most important endeavors. Married women's ability to prioritize this work was, and continues to be, influenced by cultural practices that shape gender relations within households and by the viability of their household economy. This viability is affected by the region's productive potential, by the economic needs and political capacity of the state to incorporate women as wage laborers, and by women's personal initiatives. Single women, and women who entered short-term relations with men, may have preferred their own work or self-employment to ill-paid wage labor in domestic service. African women in Northern Rhodesia were thus better able to resist the colonial government's sudden attempt to incorporate them into domestic service than their sisters in South Africa where the proletarianization process had eroded household viability much earlier.[28]

In Northern Rhodesia's urban African communities in the postwar years, the demands on women's domestic work from within their own households did not differ much by class. This is reflected in the re-actions of three African men of elite status in the colonial structure who took part in a radio debate in 1952 about women servants.[29] They objected to the idea of women going into service in white households because they had enough to attend to in their own households. When colonial authorities complained that urban African women were idle and lazy, they failed to recognize the time-consuming tasks of food processing and preparation and the

constant demands that children and their care placed on women. Despite mentioning the need for childcare facilities for urban African women, authorities never attended to it. Thus, beyond African men's sexual needs for women, authorities drew no conclusions about contending claims on women's labor from within their own households.

Perhaps most importantly, the African women themselves, crucial actors to the outcome of the campaign to hire them as domestic servants, were not called upon to express their opinion. But although the debate gave them no voice, they spoke by their action, preferring to do their own work at home or in trade. The African women of the early 1950s are likely to have shared the view on domestic service held by the women I interviewed in Lusaka in the 1980s as part of my follow-up research of low-income household develop-ments since the early 1970s: a woman with small children just doesn't leave her own household to attend to someone else's.[30] And if she does, it is as a last resort, for who wants to be ordered around by another woman all the time on a slave wage?

The debate about hiring African women for domestic service dragged on through the first half of the 1950s. The number of women domestics had increased to 855 in 1956 when a total of 33,000 men were employed in the occupation.[31] The labor commissioner was clearly fed up. His longhand remarks at the end of the official correspondence in 1956 indicate his frustrations: "It is a pity but I do not think we can force the issue any more."

---

[28] Bozzoli's account, 149–55, of the differential proletarianization of women in South Africa reckons both with the capacity of indigenous societies and of the state to subordinate women's labor. See Gaitskell et al. for an account of the different gender patterns in domestic service in South Africa. Due to a complex interplay of diverse economic and polit-ical settler motives and to the uneven displacement and increasingly impoverishment of local African groups, domestic service developed predominantly as a labor sphere for women in the Cape and the Orange Free State from the time of emancipation in 1834, and in the Natal and Transvaal the gender transition from male to female was well on its way in domestic service by the 1930s.

[29] As reported in the radio magazine, the colonial administrator made available for Africans, *The African Listener* 1, January 25, 1952, 17.

[30] Karen Tranberg Hansen, "Urban Women and Work in Africa: A Zambian Case," *TransAfrica Forum* 4 (1987): 9–24.

[31] Hansen, *Distant Companions*, 132.

There was no need to do so. The postwar boom had been succeeded by an economic downturn, beginning in 1954, when for the first time in many years labor was plentiful. The unemployment figures for all races grew when copper prices dropped sharply in 1957. The ensuing recession lasted through the first years after independence in 1964. The argument that African women should replace men in domestic service so as to release them for more productive work elsewhere was no longer heard.

Sexual Imagery and Ideology of Gender

Although economic factors had pushed toward the employment of African women in domestic service during the post-World War II economic boom, the effort between the late 1940s and 1956 to recruit them was a dismal failure. This was not only due, as the participants in the debate claimed, to lack of suitable housing for women servants, their lack of education, or the opposition of African men. Although these factors certainly influenced the outcome, they masked the more important issue of sexuality. African women's gender, I suggest, had become constructed in the white mind in a highly selective and idiosyncratic manner that accentuated their sexuality. This notion of sexuality was a by-product of pre-World War I interaction between white men and African women in the days when the white sex ratio was skewed and white settlement yet too scattered and small for social pressures for European notions of "civilized standards" to become effective. These relationships set the scene for later developments of sexual and gender relations across race. Although the way in which late-Victorian, early Edwardian

society defined the sexuality of white men and women played a likely role in the shaping of their reactions to sexual relationships in what they considered as "darkest Africa," an analysis of its role lies beyond the scope of this paper.

When white women came to the colony in larger numbers from the post-World War II years and on, they used the distorted image of African women's sexuality strategically to refrain from employing them in their own households. The image of overexaggerated sexuality colonial white women ascribed to African women was informed by normative notions of moral laxity and looseness which this generation of whites attributed to African social organization in general and to such marriage and descent practices as polyandry and matriliny in particular. Turn-of-the-century white perceptions of matriliny (the practice of tracing descent in the female line that was prevalent among many local African groups) and of polyandry (the practice of women having more than one "husband" at the same time widely reported in the literature on the region)[32] had come to constitute an ambiguous image of African women as the embodiment of sexuality associated with a "savage" eroticism in need of control. The Baila, noted a native commissioner in 1923 about one of the matrilineal, polyandrous groups in the district he administered, are "chiefly noted for their low state of morality." "These remarks," he continued, were "not much out of place if applied to the Balenje or Balovale.... Morally the sub-district ... might now be called the brothel of Northern Rhodesia."[33]

Although the pronounced invidious stance in colonial whites' interpretation of African social organization lessened as the years went on, the sedimented cultural weight of this

---

[32]   For example, V. W. Brelsford, "Lubamba: A Description of the Baila Custom," *Journal of the Royal Anthropological Society of Great Britain and Ireland* 64(1933): 433–39.
[33]   NAZ/BS 3/3003. Prostitution and Temporary Unions of Women of Mumbwa Sub-District in Settled Areas, 1923–24.

image helped to construe the gender division of labor in domestic service in terms that made African men better suited for it than women. So much taken for granted was this division of labor in the outlook of white women from the employing class that in my interviews and correspondence with postwar residents of Northern Rhodesia, who now have retired to England, I appeared to be questioning what to them were common-sense statements. Women's standard answer to my question of why so few African women worked as servants then was that it simply did not come into question or that it just was not done. Men's standard answer was that it was not looked well upon having an African woman servant for, given the legacy of pioneer days, the suspicion lingered that she was sexually available to the master of the house. Whether such statements are true or false, the ideology they express had significance by affecting social practice, in this case the convention of not employing African women as servants.

Sexual and Gender Dynamics

The impact that deep-seated European cultural assumptions about African women's sexuality had on the outcome of the campaign to hire them for domestic service must be viewed in the light of the power dynamics between colonial white women and men within the private household and in society beyond it. The campaign to hire African women workers for domestic service had been the product of male officials who, vaguely doubting it would work, could easily argue in the abstract the pros and cons of male versus female labor for domestic service. They left to their wives the practical matters involving servants and their management. I suggest that

the difficulties to which white officials had alluded when anticipating the failure of the campaign concerned the sexual ramifications of the scheme. Their gender became African women's liability and not an asset that "naturally" predisposed them for domestic work. Young African girls were considered dangerous in colonial households for they were assumed to be sexually precocious, and married African women were suspected of adulterous sexual assignations. Then there was the unspoken question of how an African woman servant and the white madam's husband would confront one another.

It is not surprising that colonial white women defended their place as mistresses of their own households when encouraged by male officials to hire African women. White women in Northern Rhodesia had little scope for autonomous activity and power acquisition in their own right in this class and race conscious society. To understand this, we must reckon with their status as incorporated wives whose ascribed social character was a function of their husbands' occupation and culture.[34] Their private lives easily merged into officialdom and made their role into that of "silent partner." Emily Bradley, the wife of a long-time colonial officer in Northern Rhodesia from 1929–42 used that term. In a mores and customs handbook Bradley wrote for a fictitious bride-to-be of a young colonial officer, she told her that it was "the rule rather than the exception out there . . . that the men can get along without us."[35]

White colonial women were well aware of their limited powers. What these women said about interracial sexuality remains unarticulated in the public discourse of the late colonial period's strained racial atmosphere, no doubt silenced by the need to keep up propriety in white "civilized society." These were events of

---

[34] Shirley Ardener, "Introduction," in *The Incorporated Wife* (London: Croom Helm, 1984), 1.
[35] Emily Bradley, *Dearest Priscilla. Letters to the Wife of a Colonial Civil Servant* (London: Max Parrish, 1950), 112, 168–69.

which it was not polite to talk in public, although there was substantial intimate knowledge about them.[36] But writers in the literary vein captured popularly shared sentiments. Women's knowledge about inter-racial sex and their reactions are illustrated dramatically in the only novel by best-selling Southern Rhodesia writer, Gertrude Page, whose plot features sex between a white male administrator and an African woman and is set in Northern Rhodesia.[37] On her outward journey to marry a white administrator, the British bride-to-be in the novel is informed about his African "harem" by a woman fellow-passenger. The bringer of unspeakable news explained to her friend that many white women overlooked their husbands' sexual habits; they had no choice, she said. Colonial white women's chief choice was to identify with their husbands, regardless of the latters' extramarital involvements.[38]

But there were other choices: departure for one thing. Employing language and sentiments that we today find objectionable, a contemporary white woman observer recalled this choice when she "thought of the game rangers and planters and men of the administration, too, who had gone to England and brought back pretty young English brides who, when they discovered that their husbands owned large families of coloured piccanins [children of mixed racial parentage] had fled as fast as their sturdy legs could carry them, back to their homes across the sea."[39] Her comments on colonial life in the 1940s at the small town of Fort Jameson (now Chipata) in the eastern part of the country showed empathy neither for such white men nor these

African women: "the native women themselves [are] a travesty of womanhood as we [women] of the West understand it."[40]

Because of their position, white men were in contact with a broader range of people and more on the move than white women. Yet white women did have other choices than condoning their men's extramarital affairs or quitting the scene. These were but two of several possible ones, involving both sexes and the two races. Liaisons between white women and African men were another choice, though one Europeans considered even more despicably than relations between white men and African women. They did occur but were not widespread.[41] Judging from contemporary writers such as those quoted above and the women I interviewed, white women were very conscious of themselves as the embodiment of white womanhood and the propriety expected of them in their roles as wives to powerful men.

The decision to play the role of incorporated wife to the hilt may have been these women's best choice. Given the dominant ideology of exclusivity in race and sex that developed over the preceding decades in response to what whites saw as "uncivilized" surroundings, it is perhaps not surprising that colonial white women drew clear distinctions by sex in their household employment practices. Since white women considered them to be potential if not actual prostitutes in any case, African women would cause too many problems for the proper running of a white "civilized" household. White women were unwilling to dispense with their men servants. They used the unexpected political platform created by the campaign for African womanpower to their own advantage:

---

[36] Such evidence can be culled from historical accounts, biography, memoirs, and travel descriptions; for example V. W. Brelsford, *Generations of Men: The European Pioneers of Northern Rhodesia* (Lusaka: Government Printer, 1965). For details, see Hansen, 87–98.

[37] Gertrude Page, *The Silent Rancher* (London: Hurst and Blackett, 1909).

[38] *Ibid*, 272, 282.

[39] Barbara Carr, *Not for Me the Wilds* (Cape Town: Howard Timmis, 1965), 174–75.

[40] *Ibid*.

[41] This information draws on my interviews with retired colonial white householders and on anecdotal evidence, since the published literature is almost totally reticent about sexual liaisons between colonial white women and African men.

keeping the men servants they had been used to for so long rather than upsetting the already delicate race, sex, and class hierarchy within the colonial household. Being aware of white men's sexual involvement with African women, white women may have seen any possibility for such liaisons as placing themselves in jeopardy. A very similar ideology affects interaction across gender and class in Zambian servant-employing households today. Although its terms rarely are charged with the colonial era's racial notions, they produce the same effects on interaction within domestic service as did the distinctions called on in the colonial discourse: they mark a class divide.

The Postcolonial Sexuality Argument

Postcolonial Changes

The recession Zambia experienced in the immediate postindependence years gave way to an economic expansion lasting into the first half of the 1970s. New economic reforms stimulated the indigenization of the economy and changed demographics brought about changes within the servant employing class after independence. The expatriate population declined and, unlike in the past, the majority of today's employers of servants are black Zambians. Servants earn low wages, which makes them affordable by a broad cross-section of society, including some segments of low-income earners. In addition to paid servants or instead of them, many Zambian householders make use of the unpaid labor of young relatives in return for upkeep. Yet in postcolonial Zambia, men still dominate in domestic service in terms of numbers of people employed. This state-

ment is based on my own conservative estimate, for domestic service has not been enumerated as a separate category of the labor force since 1968. That year, some 36,491 men and 1,758 women were employed as paid servants in private households.[42] The Zambia National Provident Fund has of late begun to provide statistics on servant employment for pension purposes. The 1983 count showed 45,760 registered servants of both sexes across the country's towns.[43] The ZNPF figures give a poor indication of the extent and nature of domestic employment. Far from all employers register their servants, and the ZNPF figures are not categorized by sex or task specialization.[44] My own sample survey of workers and employers in 187 servant-keeping households in mid- to upper-income areas in the capital city, Lusaka, showed that women comprised between one-third and one-fourth of the domestic workers, and that the majority of these women had been hired for one particular task: childcare. My findings suggest that domestic service in Zambia in the mid-1980s forms the single largest sector of the paid wage labor force, outnumbering employment in mining, which has dropped steadily. Domestic service kept on growing when overall employment shrank in the economic decline that set in during the first half of the 1970s and has persisted to this day.

Women, Men, and Domestic Service

In the mid-1980s Zambia, domestic service continues to be an important entry-level occupation for people with few marketable skills and for migrants newly arrived from the countryside. Although more women work in domestic service than during the colonial period, the occupation is not in my view at the present time undergoing a gender transition in

---

[42] Hansen, *Distant Companions*, 132. If relatives who do household work in return for their upkeep were counted as servants, the total number would be much larger.

[43] Central Statistical Office, *Monthly Digest of Statistics* 21, no. 23 (1985), supplement, 8.

[44] One third of the employers in my survey had registered their servants.

which women are replacing men. Most of the women who enter service are not taking over men's jobs but doing something different. They are, in the main, hired as nannies and to perform tasks associated with childcare. They may do other things within the house, but these are secondary to their main duty: child-care. Men, thus, remain employed as the chief domestic workers, and the expanded number of women who today work as nannies is contributing to the extension of an occupa-tional domain without transforming its long established gender division of labor.

Because of the difference in childbearing and childrearing patterns between Zambian women today and the white women of the colonial era, a special niche has opened up within domestic service for women to work as paid nannies for other wealthier Zambian women. This is not to say that African women never worked as nannies during the colonial period. Some certainly did, as I noted at the outset, and persons who employed African women went to great length to relate the trou-blesome nature of their employment to me. The point is, rather, that the African female nanny then was a "rare bird," as one of their contemporary employers expressed it. She was the exception, not the rule. Many colonial white women used paid childcare facilities for their children during the daytime. To push the pram and to wash the nappies at home, they more often employed "nurse boys" than African women. Few colonial white women worked away from home until the post-World War II years. These white women had fewer children than today's Zambian women house-holders. Because children usually were sent away to schools in what then was Southern Rhodesia, to South Africa or Great Britain, their mothers had fewer worries about their day-to-day supervision than have postcolonial Zambian women who bear children much more frequently and with shorter intervals.

Zambian women, thus, need nannies to attend to their children while they themselves go out to work. And many Zambian women who do not work away from home want relief from childcare if they can afford it. Childcare facilities and nursery schools do not have suf-ficient places for the growing number of preschool children. Even if places were avail-able, they would be too expensive for most Zambian mothers.

My study shows that women who work in domestic service fall into two broad categories of marital status: 35 percent of women servants (compared to 67 percent men) were married and lived with their spouses; 13 percent of women servants had not married (compared to 20 percent men); and 52 percent of women supported their own households after separa-tion, divorce, or widowhood (compared to 13 percent men). The married women were, in the main, nannies in Zambian and expatriate households; they earned median range wages; and they all lived out, often walking long distances to and from work. The unmarried women were young school drop-outs from rural areas who had come to town, sometimes leaving a child behind with relatives. They worked in the very low paid jobs, primarily as nannies in Zambian households, and they sometimes lived in there. The single heads of households tended to be middle aged, close to or beyond the end of their child-bearing years, often long-term urban residents who worked in better paid jobs especially in expatriate households with larger servant staffs, and they lived out.

In my interviews with them, Zambian madams described their "nanny problems" as beginning at the birth of their first child. At this point in their household's development cycle, they typically fetch, or are brought, a female relative from the countryside, often a teenage girl who has dropped out of school or whose parents are unable to pay for her edu-cation. She is fed and clothed and shares sleeping space with members of the house-hold, yet is at their beck and call. She rarely lasts from the birth of one baby to the next, which is to say that she is employed for at most two to three years before being dismissed.

Problems of discipline readily arise, for young girls develop a dislike for being ordered around, and they want to do things their own way. They want freedom to explore the city as well. If they stay for three years, they are generally returned by their urban relations or collected by their parents or guardians in order not to "detain" them for too long since this may reduce their marriage chances. The longer they stay in town, the more likely they are to become "spoiled," that is, made pregnant, which reduces the size of bridewealth their fathers or guardians may claim. After their trials with young country relatives, Zambian women turn to paid women servants and their problems with nannies grow rather than diminish. Many of the Zambian women I interviewed preferred to hire rural women new to town for they assume them to be less venturesome in matters of sex. They deliberately do not keep them too long, for with length of stay develops familiarity and a fear of likely intimate encounters with the male household head. These problems last for as long as they have preschool children, and they typically "go through" more nannies than they care to remember. Once their last-born child has entered school or the older children are considered responsible enough to watch their younger siblings, Zambian women employ men servants.

Evaluated poorly, paid miserably, and spoken of in invidious terms, paid domestic work does not in the Zambian view constitute proper women's work for it is not considered "natural" for a woman with small children to leave her household to attend to someone else's. In my interviews, Zambian madams recounted their experiences of employing women servants in a troubled voice: women servants are insolent and cheeky; they do only the work they feel like doing; in addition, they steal; they go through your panties and toiletries. But worst of all, before you know it they move into the bedroom and take over the house.[45] The sexuality issue, thus, continues to shape the gender construction of women servants in postcolonial Zambia, although those who frame it have changed in terms of race. But this shift is largely irrelevant for women whom circumstances leave no other option than paid domestic work. Their gender role continues to be constructed in sexual terms.

Body politics

The persistence, if not growth, of domestic service in postcolonial Zambia masks changes at several levels of society alluded to in the foregoing discussion at the same time as the apparent continuity of gender construction reveals a sexually charged contest that is fueled by growing economic disparity between servants and employers. Zambian women householders attribute their problems in domestic service to the loose morals of their female domestics whom they claim to be always on the lookout for a man either to marry or to "keep them nicely." Being kept nicely in Zambia means receiving shelter, food, and occasional clothing. Poor women's attempts to secure their own and their independents' livelihood through support from a spouse or consort clash with middle-to-upper income Zambian women's needs for childcare: the woman who takes a job as a nanny seeks to quit as soon as she has some economic means in her own household.

To account for this, we must grapple with the power dynamics within the household between the sexes and the way these dynamics enter into, and affect, women's and men's places in the wider social context. Most urban studies in Zambia have shown that male/female relations are difficult and very

---

[45] Stories about women servants who usurp the place of the wife abound and are featured on and off in popular magazines and newspaper columns, among them, "Georgette, My Wife," *Woman's Exclusive* 5 (1983): 7, 9, 17, and popular Zambian columnist Kapelwa Musonda, "House Servant Outwits Owner," *Times of Zambia*, January 8, 1985, 4.

unstable.[46] Regardless of the ethnic background of the towns' heterogeneous populations, the gender dynamics within private households turn on an age- and male-based hierarchy of authority. Across class, male/female relations are largely authoritarian and asymmetric, and, although there are exceptions, husbands generally assume domestic authority. Many marital relations are fraught with tensions, in part due to the persistence of customary marriage practices that permit polygyny and, perhaps influenced by this, to the existence of a double standard that condones extramarital sex for men. Zambian madams anticipate and fear their husbands' extramarital affairs, not only with women domestics but with the wife's young relatives, women at the workplace, or women they meet at bars or on the streets. To attract their man's love and assure his financial support, Zambian women will go to great expense to buy love medicines.[47] Yet they also know that they cannot rely on men. Unlike in many West African countries, cultural norms in Zambia do not oblige men to distribute part of their resources to wives for household purposes. Even if Zambian men have ample economic means, only a portion of their income reaches their own households.

While women seek to get and maintain support from men, they are also concerned to ensure the day-to-day survival of their children and to make some economic gains in their own right. As they grow older, and their children are leaving the household, Zambian women become less concerned with the pursuit of men's attentions and concentrate more of their efforts on making an income they control themselves. This shift helps account for the dual participation pattern in domestic service identified earlier: the young women

who come and go in the low paid jobs are struggling to establish their own households, whereas the middle-aged and older women in longer-term employment and at better wages often are single heads of households after the death or divorce of a husband. Men may come and go in their lives for they do not mind being kept nicely, yet they do not want them around on a permanent basis.

These tensions characterize gender relations in Zambian households across class. Because of the sexual double standard, men may feel freer than women to pursue sex and change partners. Zambian women householders seek to identify themselves sexually as their husbands' women at the same time as they are aware that husbands have other choices. They will make statements to that effect, if not about their own husbands then about a neighbor's. A sexualized gender role is attributed not only to female domestics but to any category of women a wife perceives as a threat to her marriage. To prevent compromising sexual affairs from happening within their own households, Zambian women prefer to employ men servants. Their distrust of their women domestics expresses itself in an idiom of sexuality that accentuates and dramatizes their women servants' struggle for a livelihood. It also distances them from their less fortunate sisters who may have neither husbands nor homes of their own. Underneath these expressions lies a difference of lifestyle, a class gap, which they make sure not to bridge. Yet they do have much in common: the servant wants a person to support her and her children so that she no longer needs to do someone else's domestic work, and her female employer wants a husband, certainly to support her children, and to legitimate her economic and social pursuits as a mature social person, properly married.

---

[46] Bonnie B. Keller, "Marriage and Medicine: Women's Search for Love and Luck," *African Social Research* 26 (1978): 489–505; "Marriage by Elopement," *African Social Research* 27 (1979): 565–85; and Ilsa M. G. Schuster, *New Women of Lusaka* (Palo Alto, Ca: Mayfield Publishing Corporation, 1979).

[47] Keller, "Marriage," Benetta Jules-Rosette, *Symbols of Change. Urban Transition in a Zambian Community* (Norwood, N. J.: Ablex Publishing Corporation, 1981), 129–63.

The gender role Zambian women house-holders attribute to their women servants is a product of the way they interpret sexual activities and interaction in general, and it produces a special body politic within their own households. Since they believe that their women servants may indulge in sexual affairs with their husbands, they restrict them by rules that reduce their opportunity for contact with the male head of household. The chief rules revealed in my study concerned bedrooms and the preparation of food. In colonial white households, male servants commonly entered bedrooms, bringing in the early morning tea; they made the beds and washed the underwear of white male and female employers alike; cooks were almost without exception men, for white householders claimed that Zambian women "cannot cook." In postcolonial Zambian households, these activities and domains have become reorganized spatially in sexually charged terms: the bedroom is the private space from which even children, aside from infants, are excluded; madams and their daughters wash their own underwear; and food preparation is a domain of activity in which the wife exerts individual care to please her husband.[48] In most of the Zambian households I studied, neither men nor women servants were allowed to enter bedrooms, and in several of them, the women servants were asked not to cook for the madam's husband. In these cases, the Zambian women householders feared that the female servant would mix love potions into the husband's food in order to attract his sexual attentions. Those servants who did cook were mostly men, and even in some of these cases, the wife took personal charge of preparing her husband's main meals.

Only because of their need for child care do they tolerate the presence of their Zambian nannies. As these nannies come and go, their madams' problems with them are reenacted, and the structured inequality between the two main protagonists is recreated anew. While couched in sexual idioms, the contest between women servants and employers is a battle over the status quo. Their shared interest in men creates a sexual antagonism that further distances these two categories of women who have such different marketable skills and are involved in fundamentally different relationships to the economy.

The Gender Question in Domestic Service: The Zambian Case

Few scholars today speak unequivocally about how economic change is affecting the gender division of labor; rather, they are turning toward much finer grained analyses. My account shares this concern in its attempt to free this field of studies from constraining assumptions, to anchor it in time, and to leave analytical space for the human social actor. I have suggested that interaction between whites and Africans during the early colonial period was instrumental in constructing a female gender role that in a selective and idiosyncratic manner accentuated African women's sexuality. Thus, a culturally constructed notion of gender must be reckoned with when we seek to explain the division of labor that evolved in private household employment in Northern Rhodesia's towns from the close of the depression years and

---

[48] Activities associated with sex and food preparation were in the rural societies described in the ethnographic literature from this region as surrounded by special precautions: spatial segregation by age of sleeping quarters, restrictions on women's cooking for men and handling of artifacts at the time of menstruation; and abstinence from intercourse before important celebrations and events. For examples of some of these practices, see Audrey Richards, *Chisungu. A Girl's Initiation Ceremony among the Bemba of Zambia* (London: Faber and Faber Ltd., 1951), Victor W. Turner, *The Drums of Affliction. A Study of Religious Processes among the Ndembu of Zambia* (Oxford: Clarendon; 1969), and C. M. N. White, "Elements in Luvale Beliefs and Rituals," *Rhodes–Livingstone Papers*, no. 32 (1961).

onwards. Over time, the ideology embodied in the female gender construct was articulated by the white dominant class and absorbed into social practice to the point of "naturalizing" a convention of not employing African women in wage labor and particularly not in domestic service. In the late 1940s and early 1950s, when by all accounts African women were readily available in towns, authorities argued in vain for their recruitment into domestic service. Believing that they knew what was good for them, white male colonial officials, white madams, and African men did not solicit African women's opinion when discussing the possibility of them working as servants in colonial white households. The chief performers absented themselves: white women did not want African women in their homes for fear of their sexuality, and African women, having different priorities, resisted this sudden claim on their labor power. The coming of independence has not broken this employment practice, although differences having to do with class rather than race help to account for its persistence and to explain why, in the view of some social segments in Zambia today, women's easy virtue remains a notion that exercises constraints on their employability.

My conclusions may be at variance with those of scholars who have explored the gender dynamics in domestic service in other African countries and elsewhere.[49] If so, our differences may have to do in part with the variable meanings with which notions of gender and sexuality are invested and with the ways in which they are transformed or persist as societies undergo change. While recognizing the constraining effects of economic and demographic processes on domestic service in Zambia, I have in this paper been chiefly concerned with the cultural and idiosyncratic dimension of gender construction and the resulting body politics that both influenced and were the products of domestic struggles across race and class. In my attempt to account for the influence of culturally constructed notions of gender on private household employment practices, I have purposefully sought to problematize common sense knowledge about sexuality by asking questions about, rather than contributing to, the folklore of domestic service. Gender ideology, in short, has a legitimate place on the research agenda as part of the study of socioeconomic change and its effects on women and men.

---

[49] Laurel Bossen describes a Latin American variation on this theme involving different cultural factors than those prevalent in the Zambian case: "Wives and Servants: Women of Middle-Class Households, Guatemala City," in *Urban Life. Readings in Urban Anthropology*, ed. G. Gmelch and W. Zenner (New York: St. Martin's Press, 1980), 190–200.

PART VIII

EUROPE IN AFRICA: COLONIZATION

Colonial officer in portage, Equatorial Africa, c. 1900. From *L'Homme: races et coutumes.*
Paris: Librairie Larousse, 1931.

EUROPE IN AFRICA: COLONIZATION

33   Frederick D. Lugard. 1922. "Methods of Ruling Native Races," pp. 193–213. *The Dual Mandate in British Tropical Africa*. London: Blackwood.

34   Walter Rodney. 1972. From *How Europe Underdeveloped Africa*, pp. 205–229. Washington, D.C.: Howard University Press.

35   Terence Ranger. 1983. "The Invention of Tradition in Colonial Africa," pp. 211–262. In Eric Hobsbawm and Terence Ranger (eds), *The Invention of Tradition*. Cambridge: Cambridge University Press.

36   Ngugi wa Thiong'o. 1981. From *Detained: A Writer's Prison Diary*. London: Heinemann.

By the time of colonization, in the late 1800s, Europeans had already been in close contact with Africans for hundreds of years. For example, by the eighth century, the Islamic world included parts of north and eastern Africa, leather and bead goods arrived in southern Europe from Africa as early as the thirteenth century, and Portugese traders opened up trade routes in central southern Africa, along the Zambezi river, in 1511. Dutch settlers, later called Afrikaners (or "Boers") arrived in southern Africa in 1652, when the Dutch East India Company established itself there, and throughout the seventeenth, eighteenth and nineteenth centuries, following the European conquest of the New World, Dutch, French and British traders and settlers in the Americas looked to Africa as their source of slave labor.

Why did Europeans go to Africa? And once they went, why did they decide to colonize? Clearly there were economic, political and military reasons for establishing contacts, as the European empire sought to secure more and more of the world for its economic and political gains. For example, the British heavily invested in India as part of the British empire. To get to India, where there was a rich trade in spices, and where thousands of British citizens lived and worked, one had to go around Africa past the Cape of Good Hope at the southern tip of the continent, or through the Suez Canal. Because the British wanted to protect their economic supply route, they became active in colonizing the regions that controlled the two pathways, and even intervened in military activities that affected them (for example, defending the Ottoman empire against Russia during the late 1870s since the Ottoman empire at that time bordered the route through the Red Sea).

When the Industrial Revolution began in western Europe, huge amounts of capital became available for investment in Africa, and Africa became a source of new materials for Europe. During the late 1800s, for example, King Leopold II of Belgium financed his own private corporation (the Congo Free State) by exploiting rich rubber and ivory resources in what is today Zaire. Colonization,

– permanent settlement and incorporation into the political, economic, and social system of the parent country – rather than simply exploitation, helped to secure the African lands as parts of an empire. It must be noted, however, that empire was not always profitable (Fieldhouse, 1984). Leopold, for example, lost huge sums of money when the central African rubber supply was exhausted (Grinker, 1994:31; Jewsiewicki, 1983:99). The growth of science during the enlightenment, including research on racial categories, was an additional motivator for travel to Africa, and was in many ways linked with missionary expedition and settlement. If the world was the creation of God, then science sought to reveal the complexity of God's world. That work necessitated categorizing and studying, as well as converting, human beings in all their physical and cultural forms. Finally, increased medical knowledge during the nineteenth century made it possible for Europeans to travel to Africa without large numbers of casualties due to tropical disease. Although Europeans may have wanted to go to Africa in greater numbers and for more lengthy periods of time, they could not do so safely until the cause of malaria was discovered in the 1840s, and it was discovered that quinine worked as a prophylactic against the malaria parasites. Still, for quite some time West Africa was known in Europe as "the white man's grave."

By 1885, a "scramble for Africa" began in which different European nations, namely, Portugal, Holland, Germany, Belgium, France and England, sought to carve up Africa as integral parts of its empires. Much like a jigsaw puzzle, Europeans at the Berlin Conference of 1884–1885 made decisions on paper about which piece belonged to which nation, constructing borders in what appeared at times almost arbitrary fashion, often right through the center of particular ethnic group territories. Colonization became necessary as Europeans competed for control over the territories. Article 35 of the Berlin Act, signed during the conference (Uzoigwe, 1990: 15),

stipulated that "an occupier of any such coastal possessions had also to demonstrate that it possessed sufficient 'authority' there 'to protect existing rights, and, as the case may be, freedom of trade and of transit under the conditions agreed upon'."

The social impact of the mapping on Africa and Africans was profound. The Bakongo, for example, became subjects in Portuguese, French, and Belgian colonies; and the Azande became subjects in British and Belgian colonies. Although decided by European powers more than a century ago, almost all of these borders, and the separation of ethnic groups into two or more distinct nation-states, are maintained today in independent, post-colonial, Africa. The Berlin conference thus illuminates how map-making has long been an essential part of political domination.

Although all of the colonizers participated in the Berlin conference, it would be quite misleading to think that the term "colonization" characterizes all of the activities of all Europeans in Africa during the so-called "colonial period," for there are many different kinds of colonizations, the variability determined by the culture and history of the colonizers as well as the types of societies and economies they colonized. Not only were there vast differences in how one country, such as England, colonized places as different as Nigeria and Swaziland, not to mention the differences between India and most African territories, but France, England, Portugal and Germany, among others, had distinct methods of domination. England followed Frederick Lugard's directives, some of which are included in the reading by Lugard in this part, to act paternalistically as the trustee of the colonized, and to rule *indirectly*. This meant that local African officials would mediate between the British and the people. Indirect rule was a practical alternative to direct rule, especially because in some places there were simply too few British to act as administrators, and because the British knew from previous experiences that it was impossible to abolish completely African political and social organizations, and so they needed to work with them rather than against them. With the exception of North Africa, the French and Portuguese, in contrast, sought to rule more directly over their subjects, treating local officials more as compliant subjects than as administrators.

Perhaps the most important and influential document on colonial rule, Lugard's "Dual Mandate" outlined the method of indirect rule, the legitimation of "native authority," and the system of taxation. Taxes, Lugard wrote, formed "the basis of the whole system" (1922:201), and thus constituted the development of both colonial bureaucracies and new categories of persons – colonial elites – who stood outside the pre-existing class structures of African societies. As Betts and Asiwaju (1990: 149) note:

> The tax system was the one which most obviously encouraged the bureaucratic development of colonial rule. It assigned a common function to the administrator and the African chief, who, in assessing and collecting the tax, often in conjunction with local councils of elders or notables, reminded everyone of the regulatory power of the new system. Furthermore, after tax collectors as such, there soon appeared administrative agents who became part of the new colonial elite.

In the long history of Africa, the period of colonial rule from the 1880s to the 1960s, may seem miniscule. Yet, colonialism had a profound impact on the present and future lives of all Africans – as well as on the present and future lives of the colonists. Indeed, there is a single point so obvious that it is often overlooked: colonialism not only produced the colonized, it also produced colonizers (Weiskel, 1980; Comaroff and Comaroff, 1991; Thomas, 1994). The essays included in this part highlight the complex relations between Europe and Africa during the colonial period. They also help us see that the effects of colonialism constitute a legacy that

extends far beyond the historical point at which it ended, and when African nations became officially independent (Stoller, 1995). Walter Rodney's essay, for example, boldly details the oppressive effects of capitalism on African societies, but makes clear that European imperial capital was nothing *without* Africa. In a famous quotation, Frantz Fanon says: "Europe is literally the creation of the third world." Ranger shows how Britain invented Africa, often in its own image, an argument parallelled closely in Chapter 41 by Jean and John Comaroff.

One of the common and misleading assumptions about the colonization of Africa is that it was primarily a process of conquer and rule. Certainly, that is a fair characterization as countless Africans died from European military campaigns, various other atrocities, and diseases introduced from Europe. Although these forms of domination are the easiest to see, they sometimes mask other forms of domination, exploitation, and oppression that are subtle, even elusive, and pernicious. These are the modes of power that radically change people's awareness of themselves and others, that have profound psychological implications, and forever alter the meaning of one's culture. Jean and John Comaroff (1991:15) thus write, "The point, now commonplace, is that the essence of colonization inheres less in political overrule than in seizing and transforming 'others' by the very act of conceptualizing, inscribing, and interacting with them on terms not of their own choosing."

An example of such hegemony, used by the Comaroffs and by the editors of this volume, is the discussion between Livingstone and the raindoctor (see Chapter 16), in which the raindoctor is fashioned into a scientist of sorts, who must adopt the discourse of the colonizer, and cannot be evaluated in his own terms, according to his own worldview. Other examples can be found in the Africans' denigration of their own culture and glorification of European culture, in the abandonment of local forms of religion and the embracing of Christianity and other imported belief systems, and the priority so often given to Western forms of medicine over African medicines that have been efficacious for centuries. As additional examples, the "nation" becomes the natural unit of political organization, novelists and poets write in European languages and thus not in the languages in which they may actually think and feel, and the notions of Africa and blackness become reified as things that actually exist in the world, rather than as cultural constructions that emerged out of European contact. African history is long and ancient, but Africans have frequently been made to feel that their history began when Europeans arrived at their shores.

Along with the Comaroffs, it is useful to distinguish between two forms of power relation, "ideology" and "hegemony." The former might refer to agentive power, in which there is an identifiable instrument of power that speaks, coerces, expresses itself openly and directly. Ideologies are thus contestable, because that which is said, known, and recognized, can also be argued against. Hegemony, on the other hand, can refer to relations of power that are elusive, unrecognized, taken for granted, and therefore all the more powerful and uncontestable.

> Power also presents, or rather hides, itself in the forms of everyday life. Sometimes ascribed to transcendental, suprahistorical forces (gods or ancestors, nature or physics, biological instinct or probability), these forms are not easily questioned. Being "natural" and "ineffable," they seem to be beyond human agency, notwithstanding the fact that the interests they serve may be all too human. This kind of *nonagentive* power proliferates outside the realm of institutional politics, saturating such things as aesthetics and ethics, built form and bodily representation, medical knowledge and mundane usage. What is more, it may not be experienced as power at all, since its effects are rarely wrought by overt compulsion. They are internalized, in their negative guise, as constraints; in their neutral guise, as conventions; and, in their positive guise, as values. Yet the silent power of the sign, the unspoken authority of habit, may be as effective as the most violent coercion in shaping, directing, even dominating social thought and action" (Comaroff and Comaroff, 1991: 22).

When we say that categories and identities are constructed or invented through forms of power, it is not to say that they are false or unreal, only that they are not essential, natural, or outside of culture and history. The categories are so well constructed, in fact – so hegemonic – that they appear to be natural and true. We usually don't question that people are organized into male and female, although we know that human beings could organize the world otherwise; many English speakers don't question that the neutral pronoun in English is "he"; and few people question that the nation is the natural, or normal, unit of political organization in the world.

Truth is established often through power directed upon the body, whether through medicine, capitalism's labour, religion or racism. These truth regimes, as Michel Foucault called them, destroy the possibility of even asking whether those truths are valid or not – because the method of evaluating validity is bound up with the forms and techniques of power that created the so-called truth. It is as if we determine the outcome of a medical malpractice case in court on the basis of what 6 out of ten doctors say. What is most disturbing about all of this is that, if Foucault is right, then power is capillary, everywhere moving in all directions. There is no agent to resist because we are all agents. The jailer, as he puts it, is as much a subject of surveillance, knowledge, and power as the prisoner. Ngugi wa Thiong'o leads us precisely in this direction, as he argues that many Africans – the colonial elite – unwittingly became simultaneously subjects and agents of power; that is, they became the instruments of the same hegemonic forces that constructed them. Ngugi's examples, combined with those of Ranger and Rodney, help us to see the great force of colonialism, its lasting strength and malignancy.

References

Betts, R.F. and A.I. Asiwaju. 1990. "Methods and Institutions of European Domination." In A. Adu Boahen, ed. *General History of Africa, volume VII: Africa under Colonial Domination, 1880–1935*, pp. 143–152. James Currey – California – UNESCO.

Comaroff Jean and John Comaroff. 1991. *Of Revelation and Revolution, Volume 1: Christianity, Colonialism, and Consciousness in South Africa*. Chicago: University of Chicago Press.

Grinker, Roy Richard. 1994. *Houses in the Rain Forest: Ethnicity and Inequality among Farmers and Foragers in Central Africa*. Berkeley: University of California Press.

Fieldhouse, Dennis K. 1984. *Economics and Empire, 1830–1914*. New York: Macmillan.

Lugard, Frederick. 1922. *The Dual Mandate in Tropical Africa*. London: Blackwood.

Jewsiewicki, Bogumil. 1983. "Rural Society and the Belgian Colonial Economy". In *The History of Central Africa*, vol. 2. eds David Birmingham and Phyllis Martin. pp. 95–125.

Stoller, Paul. 1995. *Embodying Colonial Memories: Spirit Possession, Power and the Hauka in West Africa*. New York and London: Routledge.

Thomas, Nicholas. 1994. *Colonialism's Culture: Anthropology, Travel, and Government*. Princeton: Princeton University Press.

Uzoigwe, G.N. 1990. "European Partition and Conquest of Africa: An Overview." In A. Adu Boahen, ed. *General History of Africa, volume VII: Africa under Colonial Domination, 1880–1935*, pp. 10–24. James Currey – California – UNESCO.

Weiskel, Timothy. 1980. *French Colonial Rule and the Baule Peoples: Resistance and Collaboration, 1889 – 1911*. Oxford: Clarendon Press.

Suggested Readings

Ajayi, J. 1968. "The Continuity of African Institutions under Colonialism." In T.O. Ranger, ed. *Emerging Themes in African History*. Proceedings of the International Congress of African Historians, Dar es Salaam, 1965. Nairobi and London: East African Publishing House. Distributed by Northwestern University Press.

Asad, Talal. 1975. *Anthropology and the Colonial Encounter*. London: Ithaca Press.

Atkins, Keletso. 1989. *The Moon is Dead! Give us Money!: The Cultural Origins of an African Work Ethic, Natal, South Africa, 1843–1900*.

Balandier, George. "The Colonial Situation." In Pierre L. Van den Berghe, ed. *Africa: Social Problems of Change and Conflict*. San Francisco, California: Chandler Publishing Company.

Blout, J.M. 1993. *The Colonizer's Model of the World: Diffusionism and Eurocentric History*. New York: Guilford.

Boahen, A. Adu. 1987. *African Perspectives on Colonialism*. Baltimore: Johns Hopkins University Press.

Callaway, Helen. 1992. "Dressing for Dinner in the Bush: Rituals of Self-definition and British Imperial Authority." In Ruth Barnes and Joanne B. Eicher, ed. *Dress and Gender: Making and Meaning*. Oxford: Berg.

Cesaire, Aime. 1972 (1955). *Discourse on Colonialism*. Trans. Joan Pinkham. New York: Monthly Review Press.

Crowder, Michael. 1968. *West Africa Under Colonial Rule*. Evanston, Il: Northwestern University Press.

Crowder, Michael. 1988. *The Flogging of Phinehas McIntosh: A Tale of Colonial Folly and Injustice, Bechuanaland, 1933*. New Haven: Yale University Press.

Dirks, Nicholas (ed.). 1992. *Colonialism and Culture*. Ann Arbor: University of Michigan Press.

Fanon, Frantz. *The Wretched of the Earth*. 1963. New York: Grove Press.

Fernandez, James W. 1979. "Africanization, Europeanization, Christianization." *History of Religions* 18: 284–292.

Fernandez, James W. 1982. *Bwiti: An Ethnography of the Religious Imagination in Africa*. Princeton: Princeton University Press.

Forde, Daryll. 1939. "Government in Umor: A Study of Social Change and Problems of Indirect rule in a Nigerian Village Community." *Africa* 12: 129–62.

Harms, Robert, ed. 1994. *Paths Toward the Past: African Historical Essays in Honor of Jan Vansina*. Atlanta: African Studies Association Press.

Kuper, Adam. 1973. "Anthropology and Colonialism." In Kuper, Adam. *Anthropology and Anthropologists: The Modern British School*. pp. 99–120. London: RKP.

Mannoni, O. 1990 (1948). *Prospero and Caliban: The Psychology of Colonization*. Ann Arbor: University of Michigan Press.

Memmi, Albert. 1974. *The Colonizer and the Colonized*. London: Souvenir Press.

Palmer, Robin and Neil Parsons, eds. 1977. *The Roots of Rural Poverty in Central and Southern Africa*. Berkeley: University of California Press.

Said, Edward. 1978. *Orientalism*. New York: Vintage Books.

Said, Edward, 1989. "Representing the Colonized: Anthropology's Interlocuters." *Critical Inquiry* 15: 205–225.

Van Onselen, Charles. 1976. *Chibaro: African Mine Labour in southern Rhodesia, 1900–1933*. London: Pluto Press.

Young, Robert J.C. 1995. *Colonial Desire: Hybridity in Theory, Culture, and Race*. London and New York: Routledge.

33

THE DUAL MANDATE IN BRITISH TROPICAL AFRICA: METHODS OF RULING NATIVE RACES

FREDERICK D. LUGARD

The principle of co-operation – Divergent methods of self-government: (*a*) Representative government: The new system in India; (*b*) Complete independence the goal; (*c*) Dependent native rule – The Fulani of Nigeria – Recognition of the principle of rule through chiefs – Advanced communities in Nigeria – Relations with British staff – Revenues of native administrations – Courts and jurisdiction – The village unit – Essential features of the system – Application to non-Moslem States – Limitations to independence: (*a*) Armed forces; (*b*) Taxation; (*c*) Legislation; (*d*) Land; (*e*) Control of aliens – Disposal of revenue – Alien races as native rulers – Education of native rulers – Misuse of the system – System must vary with local traditions – Administrative procedure – Succession – Extra-territorial allegiance.

If continuity and decentralisation are, as I have said, the first and most important conditions in maintaining an effective administration, co-operation is the key-note of success in its application – continuous co-operation between every link in the chain, from the head of the administration to its most junior member, – co-operation between the Government and the commercial community, and, above all, between the provincial staff and the native rulers. Every individual adds his share not only to the accomplishment of the ideal, but to the ideal itself. Its principles are fashioned by his quota of experience, its results are achieved by his patient and loyal application of these principles, with as little interference as possible with native customs and modes of thought.

Principles do not change, but their mode of application may and should vary with the customs, the traditions, and the prejudices of each unit. The task of the administrative officer is to clothe his principles in the garb of evolution, not of revolution; to make it apparent alike to the educated native, the conservative Moslem, and the primitive pagan, each in his own degree, that the policy of the Government is not antagonistic but progressive – sympathetic to his aspirations and the safeguard of his natural rights. The Governor looks to the administrative staff to keep in touch with native thought and feeling, and to report fully to himself, in order that he in turn may be able to support them and recognise their work.

When describing the machinery of

Government in an African dependency, I spoke of the supervision and guidance exercised by the Lieut.-Governor, the Residents, and the District Officers over the native chiefs. In this chapter I propose to discuss how those functions should be exercised.

Lord Milner's declaration that the British policy is to rule subject races through their own chiefs is generally applauded, but the manner in which the principle should be translated into practice admits of wide differences of opinion and method. Obviously the extent to which native races are capable of controlling their own affairs must vary in proportion to their degree of development and progress in social organisation, but this is a question of adaptation and not of principle. Broadly speaking, the divergent opinions in regard to the application of the principle may be found to originate in three different conceptions.

The first is that the ideal of self-government can only be realised by the methods of evolution which have produced the democracies of Europe and America – viz., by representative institutions in which a comparatively small educated class shall be recognised as the natural spokesmen for the many. This method is naturally in favour with the educated African. Whether it is adapted to peoples accustomed by their own institutions to autocracy – albeit modified by a substantial expression of the popular will and circumscribed by custom – is naturally a matter on which opinions differ. The fundamental essential, however, in such a form of Government is that the educated few shall at least be representative of the feelings and desires of the many – well known to them, speaking their language, and versed in their customs and prejudices.

In present conditions in Africa the numerous separate tribes, speaking different languages, and in different stages of evolution, cannot produce representative men of education. Even were they available, the number of communities which could claim separate representation would make any central and really representative Council very unwieldy. The authority vested in the representatives would be antagonistic (as the Indian Progressives realise[1]) to that of the native rulers and their councils, – which are the product of the natural tendencies of tribal evolution, – and would run counter to the customs and institutions of the people.[2]

An attempt to adapt these principles of Western representative Government to tropical races is now being made in India. It is at present an Eastern rather than an African problem, but as a great experiment in the method of Government in tropical countries, the outcome of which "many other native races in other parts of the world are watching with strained attention," it demands at least a passing reference here.

Though the powers entrusted to the elected representatives of the people are at first restricted under the dyarchical system (which reserves certain subjects for the Central Authority), the principle of government by an educated minority, as opposed to government by native rulers, is fully accepted. It must be admitted that there is a considerable body of well-informed opinion in India and England – voiced here by the India Association, Lord Sydenham (who speaks with the authority of an ex-Governor of Bombay), and others – which expresses much misgiving as to the wisdom of placing all political power "in the hands of a disaffected minority unrepresentative of India," and regards it as "an

---

[1] "The extremist Press," says Sir Valentine Chirol, "has already frequently denounced ruling princes and chiefs as intolerable obstacles to the democratic evolution of 'Swaraj'" (Home Rule). – "Times," 10th February 1921.

[2] Chief Ofori asserts to this effect. "We claim and we insist," say the spokesmen of the educated natives, while denouncing the present system, and advocating a new policy, "that such a policy can be adequately carried out only by giving an effective position in the legislatures to ourselves."

attempt to govern India by the narrowest of oligarchies, whose interests often conflict with those of the millions."[3]

The experiment has so far shown much promise of success, but the real test is not merely whether the native councillors show moderation and restraint as against extremists of their own class, but whether, when legislation has to be enacted which is unpopular with the illiterate masses and the martial races of India, there may be a reluctance to accept what will be called "Babu-made law," though it would have been accepted without demur as the order of "the Sirkar" – the British Raj.

It is, of course, now too late to adopt to any large extent the alternative of gradually transforming the greater part of British India into native States governed by their own hereditary dynasties, whose representatives in many cases still exist, and extending to them the principles which have so successfully guided our relations with the native States in India itself, and in Malaya in the past. It is one thing to excite an ignorant peasantry against an alien usurper, but quite another thing to challenge native ruler.

Such a system does not exclude the educated native from participation in the government of the State to which he belongs, as a councillor to the native ruler, but it substitutes for direct British rule, not an elected oligarchy but a form of government more in accord with racial instincts and inherited traditions. It may be that while dyarchy and representative government may prove suitable to Bengal, and perhaps to some other provinces, the alternative system may be found to be best adapted to Mohamedan States, and to other of the warlike races of India, where representatives of the ancient dynasties still survive. Time alone will show. I shall recur to this subject in the next chapter.

The second conception is that every advanced community should be given the widest possible powers of self-government under its own ruler, and that these powers should be rapidly increased with the object of complete independence at the earliest possible date in the not distant future. Those who hold this view generally, I think, also consider that attempts to train primitive tribes in any form of self-government are futile, and the administration must be wholly conducted by British officials. This in the past has been the principle adopted in many dependencies. It recognised no alternative between a status of independence, like the Sultans of Malaya, or the native princes of India, and the direct rule of the district commissioner.

But the attempt to create such independent States in Africa has been full of anomalies. In the case of Egbaland, where the status had been formally recognised by treaty, the extent to which the Crown had jurisdiction was uncertain, yet, as we have seen, international conventions, including even that relating to the protection of wild animals, which was wholly opposed to native customary rights, were applied without the consent of the "Independent" State, and powers quite incompatible with independence were exercised by the Suzerain.[4]

The paramount chief might receive ceremonial visits from time to time from the Governor, and even perhaps be addressed as "Your Royal Highness," and vested with titular dignity and the tinsel insignia of office. His right to impose tolls on trade, and to exact whatever oppressive taxes he chose from his peasantry, was admitted, but his authority was subject to constant interference. The last-joined District Officer, or any other official, might issue orders, if not to him, at any rate to any of his subordinate chiefs, and the native

---

[3] "Times," 22nd December 1913. See also "Spectator," 5th February 1921.

[4] That one of the stipulations of the Egba "Treaty of Commerce and Friendship" of 1893 should be the prohibition of human sacrifice, indicates that the community was hardly ripe for self-government.

ruler had no legal and recognised means of enforcing his commands. He was necessarily forbidden to raise armed forces – on which in the last resort the authority of the law must depend – and could not therefore maintain order.

The third conception is that of rule by native chiefs, unfettered in their control of their people as regards all those matters which are to them the most important attributes of rule, with scope for initiative and responsibility, but admittedly – so far as the visible horizon is concerned – subordinate to the control of the protecting Power in certain well-defined directions. It recognises, in the words of the Versailles Treaty, that the subject races of Africa are not yet able to stand alone, and that it would not conduce to the happiness of the vast bulk of the people – for whose welfare the controlling Power is trustee – that the attempt should be made.

The verdict of students of history and sociology of different nationalities, such as Dr Kidd,[5] Dr Stoddard,[6] M. Beaulieu,[7] Meredith Townsend,[8] and others is unanimous that the era of complete independence is not as yet visible on the horizon of time. Practical administrators (among whom I may include my successor, Sir P. Girouard, in Northern Nigeria) have arrived at the same conclusion.

The danger of going too fast with native races is even more likely to lead to disappointment, if not to disaster, than the danger of not going fast enough. The pace can best be gauged by those who have intimate acquaintance alike with the strong points and the limitations of the native peoples and rulers with whom they have to deal.

The Fulani of Northern Nigeria are, as I have said, more capable of rule than the indigenous races, but in proportion as we consider them an alien race, we are denying self-government to the people over whom they rule, and supporting an alien caste – albeit closer and more akin to the native races than a European can be. Yet capable as they are, it requires the ceaseless vigilance of the British staff to maintain a high standard of administrative integrity, and to prevent oppression of the peasantry. We are dealing with the same generation, and in many cases with the identical rulers, who were responsible for the misrule and tyranny which we found in 1902. The subject races near the capital were then serfs, and the victims of constant extortion. Those dwelling at a distance were raided for slaves, and could not count their women, their cattle, or their crops their own. Punishments were most barbarous, and included impalement, mutilation, and burying alive.[9] Many generations have passed since British rule was established among the more intellectual people of India – the inheritors of centuries of Eastern civilisation – yet only to-day are we tentatively

---

[5.] Dr Kidd writes: "There never has been, and never will be within any time with which we are practically concerned, such a thing as good government in the European sense of the tropics by the natives of these regions." He describes the collapse of prosperity in the West Indies and Guiana which followed the false conception that the British tropics, if given control of their own destinies, would develop into modern states – and points to the gloomy picture of Hayti, &c. – "Control of the Tropics," pp. 37, 51, 73, &c.

[6.] "Unless every lesson of history is to be disregarded, we must conclude that black Africa is unable to stand alone." – "The Rising Tide of Colour," p. 102.

[7] "Les noirs d'Afrique sont au milieu de l'humanité des mineurs qui pour parvenir à un certain état de civilisation . . . ont besoin d'être dirigés, guidés, gouvernés pendant un bon nombre de dizaines d'années par les Européans. Il convient que chaque nation qui a la résponsibilité d'une Colonie Africaine puisse sur son territoire d'une absolue souverainité." —Beaulieu, *loc. cit.*, vol. i. pp. 361, 364.

[8] "None of the black races have shown within historic times the capacity to develop civilisation." — "Asia in Europe," p.92, quoted by the American writer, Dr Stoddart. He gives his reasons at great length for his conclusions.

[9] The dungeon at Kano is thus described: "A small doorway 2 ft. 6 in. by 18 in. gives access into it; the interior is divided by a thick mud wall (with a similar hole in it) into two compartments, each 17 ft. by 7 ft. and 11 ft. high. This wall was pierced with holes at its base, through which the legs of those sentenced to death were thrust up to the thigh,

seeking to confer on them a measure of self-government. "Festina lente" is a motto which the Colonial Office will do well to remember in its dealings with Africa.

That the principle of ruling through the native chiefs is adopted by the different governments of British Tropical Africa can be seen from recent local pronouncements. The Governor of Sierra Leone, in his address to the Legislative Council last December (1920), remarks that "nine-tenths of the people enjoy autonomy under their own elected chiefs . . . European officers are the technical advisers, and helpers of the tribal authority." The Governor of the Gold Coast on a similar occasion observed: "The chiefs are keenly appreciative of our policy of indirect rule, and of the full powers they retain under their native institutions."[10] The powers retained by the Kabaka of Uganda and his Council are very wide indeed.[11]

The system adopted in Nigeria is therefore only a particular method of the application of these principles – more especially as regards "advanced communities," – and since I am familiar with it I will use it as illustrative of the methods which in my opinion should characterise the dealings of the controlling power with subject races.

The object in view is to make each "Emir" or paramount chief, assisted by his judicial Council, an effective ruler over his own people. He presides over a "Native Administration" organised throughout as a unit of local government. The area over which he exercises jurisdiction is divided into districts under the control of "Headmen," who collect the taxes in the name of the ruler, and pay them into the "Native Treasury," conducted by a native treasurer and staff under the supervision of the chief at his capital. Here, too, is the prison for native court prisoners, and probably the school. Large cities are divided into wards for purposes of control and taxation.

The district headman, usually a territorial magnate with local connections, is the chief executive officer in the area under his charge. He controls the village headmen, and is responsible for the assessment of the tax, which he collects through their agency. He must reside in his district and not at the capital. He is not allowed to pose as a chief with a

---

and they were left to be trodden on by the mass of other prisoners till they died of thirst and starvation. The place is entirely air-tight and unventilated, except for one small doorway or rather hole in the wall through which you creep. The total space inside is 2618 cub.ft., and at the time we took Kano 135 human beings were confined here each night, being let out during the day to cook their food, &c., in a small adjoining area. Recently as many as 200 have been interned at one time. As the superficial ground area was only 238 square feet, there was not, of course, even standing room. Victims were crushed to death every night – their corpses were hauled out each morning. The stench, I am told, inside the place when Col. Morland visited it was intolerable though it was empty, and when I myself went inside three weeks later the effluvium was unbearable for more than a few seconds. A putrid corpse even then lay near the doorway." – Northern Nigeria Annual Report, 1902, p. 29.

[10] Captain Armitage says of the northern territories: "The powers of the chiefs had largely lapsed, and it was the custom to put, one might almost say, the village idiot on the stool. Our policy has been to re-establish the powers of several big chiefs, and it has been a remarkable success."

[11] Before Uganda had been declared a British protectorate, and control assumed by the British Government, I wrote (in 1893): "The object to be aimed at in the administration of this country is to rule through its own executive government . . . the Resident should rule through and by the chiefs." – "The Rise of our East African Empire," vol. i. pp. 649, 651.

Uganda proper is divided into *Sazas* each of which has a *Lukiko*, which assembles weekly and deals with minor cases. They are inspected by the district officers, and report to the Central Lukiko at the capital. This consists of some forty Saza chiefs presided over by the Kabaka with his Katikiro and other ministers. The native administration has 20 per cent of the native tax – about £16,000. The system, says the Governor, "is an excellent example of the best results of indirect rule." – "United Empire," June 1920, p. 395.

Sir H. Low and Sir F. Swettenham testify from their experience in Malaya that "the only way to deal with the people is through their recognised chiefs and headmen."

retinue of his own and duplicate officials, and is summoned from time to time to report to his chief. If, as is the case with some of the ancient Emirates, the community is a small one but independent of any other native rule, the chief may be his own district headman.

A province under a Resident may contain several separate "Native Administrations," whether they be Moslem Emirates or pagan communities. A "division" under a British District Officer may include one or more headmen's districts, or more than one small Emirate or independent[12] pagan tribe, but as a rule no Emirate is partly in one division and partly in another. The Resident acts as sympathetic adviser and counsellor to the native chief, being careful not to interfere so as to lower his prestige, or cause him to lose interest in his work. His advice on matters of general policy must be followed, but the native ruler issues his own instructions to his subordinate chiefs and district heads – not as the orders of the Resident but as his own, – and he is encouraged to work through them, instead of centralising everything in himself – a system which in the past had produced such great abuses. The British District Officers supervise and assist the native district headmen, through whom they convey any instructions to village heads, and make any arrangements necessary for carrying on the work of the Government departments, but all important orders emanate from the Emir, whose messenger usually accompanies and acts as mouthpiece of a District Officer.

The tax – which supersedes all former "tribute," irregular imposts, and forced labour – is, in a sense, the basis of the whole system, since it supplies the means to pay the Emir and all his officials. The district and village heads are effectively supervised and assisted in its assessment by the British staff. The native treasury retains the proportion assigned to it (in advanced communities a half), and pays the remainder into Colonial Revenue.

There are fifty such treasuries in the northern provinces of Nigeria, and every independent chief, however small, is encouraged to have his own. The appropriation by the native administration of market dues, slaughterhouse fees, forest licences, &c., is authorised by ordinance, and the native administration receives also the fines and fees of native courts. From these funds are paid the salaries of the Emir and his council, the native court judges, the district and village heads, police, prison warders, and other employees. The surplus is devoted to the construction and maintenance of dispensaries, leper settlements, schools, roads, courthouses, and other buildings. Such works may be carried out wholly or in part by a Government department, if the native administration requires technical assistance, the cost being borne by the native treasury.

The native treasurer keeps all accounts of receipts and expenditure, and the Emir, with the assistance of the Resident, annually prepares a budget, which is formally approved by the Lieut.-Governor.

In these advanced communities the judges of the native courts – which I shall describe in a later chapter – administer native law and custom, and exercise their jurisdiction independently of the native executive, but under the supervision of the British staff, and subject to the general control of the Emir, whose "Judicial council" consists of his principal officers of State, and is vested with executive as well as judicial powers. No punishment may be inflicted by a native authority, except through a regular tribunal. The ordinances of government are operative everywhere, but the native authority may make by-laws in modification of native custom – e.g., on matters of sanitation, &c., – and these, when approved by the Governor, are enforced by the native courts.

The authority of the Emir over his own people is absolute, and the profession of an alien creed does not absolve a native from the

---

[12.] By the term "independent" in this connection is meant "independent of other native control."

obligation to obey his lawful orders; but aliens – other than natives domiciled in the Emirate and accepting the jurisdiction of the native authority and courts – are under the direct control of the British staff. Townships are excluded from the native jurisdiction.

The village is the administrative unit. It is not always easy to define, since the security to life and property which has followed the British administration has caused an exodus from the cities and large villages, and the creation of innumerable hamlets, sometimes only of one or two huts, on the agricultural lands. The peasantry of the advanced communities, though ignorant, yet differs from that of the backward tribes in that they recognise the authority of the Emir, and are more ready to listen to the village head and the Council of Elders. "The development of self-government in India," says Lord Sydenham, "should begin with the *Panchayet*" (Village Council).[13] This is the base and unit of the Nigerian system.

Subject, therefore, to the limitations which I shall presently discuss, the native authority is thus *de facto* and *de jure* ruler over his own people. He appoints and dismisses his subordinate chiefs and officials. He exercises the power of allocation of lands, and with the aid of the native courts, of adjudication in land disputes and expropriation for offences against the community, these are the essential functions upon which, in the opinion of the West African Lands Committee, the prestige of the native authority depends. The lawful orders which he may give are carefully defined by ordinance, and in the last resort are enforced by Government.

Since native authority, especially if exercised by alien conquerors, is inevitably weakened by the first impact of civilised rule,

it is made clear to the elements of disorder, who regard force as conferring the only right to demand obedience, that government, by the use of force if necessary, intends to support the native chief. To enable him to maintain order he employs a body of unarmed police, and if the occasion demands the display of superior force he looks to the Government – as, for instance, if a community combines to break the law or shield criminals from justice – a rare event in the advanced communities.

The native ruler derives his power from the Suzerain, and is responsible that it is not misused. He is equally with British officers amenable to the law, but his authority does not depend on the caprice of an executive officer. To intrigue against him is an offence punishable, if necessary, in a Provincial Court. Thus both British and native courts are invoked to uphold his authority.

The essential feature of the system (as I wrote at the time of its inauguration) is that the native chiefs are constituted "as an integral part of the machinery of the administration. There are not two sets of rulers – British and native – working either separately or in co-operation, but a single Government in which the native chiefs have well-defined duties and an acknowledged status equally with British officials. Their duties should never conflict. and should overlap as little as possible. They should be complementary to each other, and the chief himself must understand that he has no right to place and power unless he renders his proper services to the State."

The ruling classes are no longer either demi-gods, or parasites preying on the community. They must work for the stipends and position they enjoy. They are the trusted delegates of the Governor, exercising in the Moslem States the well-understood powers of

---

[13]   "Times," 10th August 1917. The Indian Commission of 1912 reported in favour of re-establishing the *Panchayet* which previous reforms had tended to destroy. They are created in response to a demand for greater participation in the control of their own affairs, and are supported by voluntary taxation alone. – ("Times," 19/12/1917.) In Egypt the "Omdehs" of the villages were Government officials whose qualification was ownership of ten acres of land. The system inevitably led to great abuse and tyranny. – (Sir V. Chirol, "Times," 1/1/20.)

"Wakils" in conformity with their own Islamic system, and recognising the King's representative as their acknowledged Suzerain. . . .

Pending the growth of a fuller sense of public responsibility and of an enlightened public opinion, some check may be afforded by the preparation of annual estimates of revenue and expenditure in a very simple form. These should require the approval of the Governor (or of the Lieut.-Governor), as the colonial estimates require that of the Secretary of State, and any subsequent alteration should require the like sanction. While refraining as far as possible from interference in detail, the Lieut.-Governor can, by suggestion and comparison, effect some co-ordination and uniformity where desirable, and can best discriminate between the scope which may be allowed to an individual, and the grant of extended powers of universal application.[14]

The habits of a people are not changed in a decade, and when powerful despots are deprived of the pastime of war and slave-raiding, and when even the weak begin to forget their former sufferings, to grow weary of a life without excitement and to resent the petty restrictions which have replaced the cruelties of the old despotism, it must be the aim of Government to provide new interests and rivalries in civilised progress, in education, in material prosperity and trade, and even in sport.[15]

There were indeed many who, with the picture of Fulani misrule fresh in their memory, regarded this system when it was first inaugurated with much misgiving, and believed that though the hostility of the rulers to the British might be concealed, and their vices disguised, neither could be eradicated, and they would always remain hostile at heart. They thought that the Fulani as an alien race of conquerors, who had in turn been conquered, had not the same claims for consideration as those whom they had displaced, even though they had become so identified with the people that they could no longer be called aliens.

But there can be no doubt that such races form an invaluable medium between the British staff and the native peasantry. Nor can the difficulty of finding any one capable of taking their place, or the danger they would constitute to the State if ousted from their positions, be ignored. Their traditions of rule, their monotheistic religion, and their intelligence enable them to appreciate more readily than the negro population the wider objects of British policy while their close touch with the masses – with whom they live in daily intercourse – mark them out as destined to play an important part in the future, as they have done in the past, in the development of the tropics.

Both the Arabs in the east and the Fulani in the west are Mohamedans, and by supporting their rule we unavoidably encourage the spread of Islam, which from the purely administrative point of view has the disadvantage of being subject to waves of fanaticism, bounded by no political frontiers. In Nigeria it has been the rule that their power should not be re-established over tribes

---

[14.] Some difference between the Colonial Office and local opinion arose in connection with these funds. The Secretary of State directed that they should only be used for works which the Government would not otherwise have undertaken, and refused contributions made to the cost of the war – limitations which seemed to hamper the utility of the projects undertaken, and to fetter the discretion and wound the susceptibilities of the chiefs and their councils. Opinions also differed as to the extent of the control over these large sums which should in the present stage of evolution be exercised by the Governor, and as to the desirability of some special accounting and audit staff, without unnecessary interference or time-wasting "red-tape." These, however, were not matters of vital importance. The principle at issue was that of dependent rule as opposed to independence, and perhaps the local opinion, in its insistence on the advisability of the former, was betrayed into too narrow a view in regard to financial control.

[15.] As Professor Elliott-Smith has justly observed, a people becomes decadent, and population decreases, not so much from war or disease as from lack of interests in life.

which had made good their independence, or imposed upon those who had successfully resisted domination.

On the other hand, the personal interests of the rulers must rapidly become identified with those of the controlling Power. The forces of disorder do not distinguish between them, and the rulers soon recognise that any upheaval against the British would equally make an end of them. Once this community of interest is established, the Central Government cannot be taken by surprise, for it is impossible that the native rulers should not be aware of any disaffection.[16]

This identification of the ruling class with the Government accentuates the corresponding obligation to check malpractices on their part. The task of educating them in the duties of a ruler becomes more than ever insistent; of inculcating a sense of responsibility; of convincing their intelligence of the advantages which accrue from the material prosperity of the peasantry, from free labour and initiative; of the necessity of delegating powers to trusted subordinates; of the evils of favouritism and bribery; of the importance of education, especially for the ruling class, and for the filling of lucrative posts under Government; of the benefits of sanitation, vaccination, and isolation of infection in checking mortality; and finally, of impressing upon them how greatly they may benefit their country by personal interest in such matters, and by the application of labour-saving devices and of scientific methods in agriculture.

Unintentional misuse of the system of native administration must also be guarded against. It is not, for instance, the duty of a native administration to purchase supplies for native troops, or to enlist and pay labour for public works, though its agency within carefully defined limits may be useful in making known Government requirements, and seeing that markets are well supplied. Nor should it be directed to collect licences, fees, and rents due to Government, nor should its funds be used for any purpose not solely connected with and prompted by its own needs.

I have throughout these pages continually emphasised the necessity of recognising, as a cardinal principle of British policy in dealing with native races, that institutions and methods, in order to command success and promote the happiness and welfare of the people, must be deep-rooted in their traditions and prejudices. Obviously in no sphere of administration is this more essential than in that under discussion, and a slavish adherence to any particular type, however successful it may have proved elsewhere, may, if unadapted to the local environment, be as ill-suited and as foreign to its conceptions as direct British rule would be.

The type suited to a community which has long grown accustomed to the social organisation of the Moslem State may or may not be suitable to advanced pagan communities, which have evolved a social system of their own, such as the Yorubas, the Benis, the Egbas, or the Ashantis in the West, or the Waganda, the Wanyoro, the Watoro, and others in the East. The history, the traditions, the idiosyncracies, and the prejudices of each must be studied by the Resident and his staff, in order that the form adopted shall accord with natural evolution, and shall ensure the ready co-operation of the chiefs and people.

Before passing to the discussion of methods applicable to primitive tribes, it may be of interest to note briefly some of the details – as apart from general principles – adopted in Nigeria among the advanced communities.

Chiefs who are executive rulers are graded – those of the first three classes are installed by

---

[16] Soon after the establishment of British rule in Northern Nigeria more than one "Mahdi" arose, and obtained a fanatical following, but in every case the Fulani Emir actively assisted in suppressing the disturbance. In the Sudan thirteen Mahdis arose between 1901 and 1916. – F.O. Handbook 98, p.43. The Germans in East Africa, in order to check the spread of Islam, encouraged pig-breeding. – Cmd. 1428/1921, p. 30.

the Governor or Lieut.-Governor, and carry a staff of office surmounted for the first class by a silver, and for the others by a brass crown. Lower grades carry a baton, and are installed by the Resident, or by the Emir, if the chief is subordinate to him. These staves of office, which are greatly prized, symbolise to the peasantry the fact that the Emir derives his power from the Government, and will be supported in its exercise. The installation of an Emir is a ceremonial witnessed by a great concourse of his people, and dignified by a parade of troops. The native insignia of office, and a parchment scroll, setting out in the vernacular the conditions of his appointment, are presented to him. The alkali (native judge) administers the following oath on the Koran: "I swear in the name of God, well and truly to serve His Majesty King George V. and his representative the Governor of Nigeria, to obey the laws of Nigeria and the lawful commands of the Governor, and of the Lieut.-Governor, provided that they are not contrary to my religion, and if they are so contrary I will at once inform the Governor through the Resident. I will cherish in my heart no treachery or disloyalty, and I will rule my people with justice and without partiality. And as I carry out this oath so may God judge me." Pagan chiefs are sworn according to their own customs on a sword.

Native etiquette and ceremonial must be carefully studied and observed in order that unintentional offence may be avoided. Great importance is attached to them, and a like observance in accordance with native custom is demanded towards British officers. Chiefs are treated with respect and courtesy. Native races alike in India and Africa are quick to discriminate between natural dignity and assumed superiority. Vulgar familiarity is no more a passport to their friendship that an assumption of self-importance is to their

respect.[17] The English gentleman needs no prompting in such a matter – his instinct is never wrong. Native titles of rank are adopted, and only native dress is worn, whether by chiefs or by schoolboys. Principal chiefs accused of serious crimes are tried by a British court, and are not imprisoned before trial, unless in very exceptional circumstances. Minor chiefs and native officials appointed by an Emir may be tried by his Judicial Council. If the offence does not involve deprivation of office, the offender may be fined without public trial, if he prefers it, in order to avoid humiliation and loss of influence.

Succession is governed by native law and custom, subject in the case of important chiefs to the approval of the Governor, in order that the most capable claimant may be chosen. It is important to ascertain the customary law and to follow it when possible, for the appointment of a chief who is not the recognised heir, or who is disliked by the people, may give rise to trouble, and in any case the new chief would have much difficulty in asserting his authority, and would fear to check abuses lest he should alienate his supporters. In Moslem countries the law is fairly clearly defined, being a useful combination of the hereditary principle, tempered by selection, and in many cases in Nigeria the ingenious device is maintained of having two rival dynasties, from each of which the successor is selected alternately.

In pagan communities the method varies; but there is no rigid rule, and a margin for selection is allowed. The formal approval of the Governor after a short period of probation is a useful precaution, so that if the designated chief proves himself unsuitable, the selection may be revised without difficulty. Minor chiefs are usually selected by popular vote, subject to the approval of the paramount chief. It is a rule in Nigeria that no slave may be

---

[17] "The Master said: the nobler sort of man is dignified but not proud; the inferior man proud but not dignified. The nobler sort of man is easy to serve yet difficult to please. In exacting service from others he takes account of aptitudes and limitations." – "The Sayings of Confucius," L. Giles, p. 65.

appointed as a chief or district headman. If one is nominated he must first be publicly freed.

Small and isolated communities, living within the jurisdiction of a chief, but owing allegiance to the chief of their place of origin – a common source of trouble in Africa – should gradually be absorbed into the territorial jurisdiction. Aliens who have settled in a district for their own purposes would be subject to the local jurisdiction.

34

How Europe Underdeveloped Africa

WALTER RODNEY

THE BLACK MAN CERTAINLY HAS TO PAY DEAR FOR CARRYING THE WHITE MAN'S
BURDEN.

—GEORGE PADMORE
(West Indian) Pan-Africanist, 1936

In the colonial society, education is such that it serves the colonialist . . . In a regime of slavery,
education was but one institution for forming slaves.

—Statement of FRELIMO (Mozambique Liberation Front)
Department of Education and Culture, 1968

The Supposed Benefits of Colonialism to Africa

Socio-Economic Services

Faced with the evidence of European exploitation of Africa, many bourgeois writers would concede at least partially that colonialism was a system which functioned well in the interests of the metropoles. However, they would then urge that another issue to be resolved is how much Europeans did for Africans, and that it is necessary to draw up a balance sheet of colonialism. On that balance sheet, they place both the credits and the debits, and quite often conclude that the good outweighed the bad. That particular conclusion can quite easily be challenged, but attention should also be drawn to the fact that the process of reasoning is itself misleading. The reasoning has some sentimental persuasiveness. It appeals to the common sentiment that "after all there must

be two sides to a thing." The argument suggests that, on the one hand, there was exploitation and oppression, but, on the other hand, colonial governments did much for the benefit of Africans and they developed Africa. It is our contention that this is completely false. Colonialism had only one hand – it was a one-armed-bandit.

What did colonial governments do in the interest of Africans? Supposedly, they built railroads, schools, hospitals, and the like. The sum total of these services was amazingly small.

For the first three decades of colonialism, hardly anything was done that could remotely be termed a service to the African people. It was in fact only after the last war that social services were built as a matter of policy. How little they amounted to does not really need illustrating. After all, the statistics which show that Africa today is underdeveloped are the statistics representing the state of affairs at the end of colonialism. For that matter, the figures at the end of the first decade of African independence in spheres such as health, housing, and education are often several times higher than the figures inherited by the newly independent governments. It would be an act of the most brazen fraud to weigh the paltry social amenities provided during the colonial epoch against the exploitation, and to arrive at the conclusion that the good outweighed the bad.

Capitalism did bring social services to European workers – firstly, as a by-product of providing such services for the bourgeoisie and the middle class, and later as a deliberate act of policy. Nothing remotely comparable occurred in Africa. In 1934, long before the coming of the welfare state to Britain, expenditure for social services in the British Isles amounted to 6 pounds 15 shillings per person. In Ghana, the figure was 7 shillings 4 pence per person, and that was high by colonial standards. In Nigeria and Nyasaland, it was less that 1 shilling 9 pence per head. None of the other colonizing powers were doing any better, and some much worse.

The Portuguese stand out because they boasted the most and did the least. Portugal boasted that Angola, Guinea, and Mozambique have been their possessions for five hundred years, during which time a "civilizing mission" has been going on. At the end of five hundred years of shouldering the white man's burden of civilizing "African natives," the Portuguese has not managed to train a single African doctor in Mozambique, and the life expectancy in eastern Angola was less than thirty years. As for Guinea-Bissau, some insight into the situation there is provided by the admission of the Portuguese themselves that Guinea-Bissau was more neglected than Angola and Mozambique!

Furthermore, the limited social services within Africa during colonial times were distributed in a manner that reflected the pattern of domination and exploitation. First of all, white settlers and expatriates wanted the standards of the bourgeoisie or professional classes of the metropoles. They were all the more determined to have luxuries in Africa, because so many of them came from poverty in Europe and could not expect good services in their own homelands. In colonies like Algeria, Kenya, and South Africa, it is well known that whites created an infrastructure to afford themselves leisured and enjoyable lives. It means, therefore, that the total amenities provided in any of those colonies is no guide to what Africans got out of colonialism.

In Algeria, the figure for infant mortality was 39 per 1,000 live births among white settlers; but it jumped to 170 per 1,000 live births in the case of Algerians living in the towns. In practical terms, that meant that the medical, maternity, and sanitation services were all geared towards the well-being of the settlers. Similarly, in South Africa, all social statistics have to be broken down into at least two groups – white and black – if they are to be interpreted correctly. In British East Africa there were three groups: firstly, the Europeans, who got the most; then, the Indians, who took most of what was left; and thirdly, the Africans, who came last in their own country.

In predominantly black countries, it was also true that the bulk of the social services went to whites. The southern part of Nigeria was one of the colonial areas that was supposed to have received the most from a benevolent mother country. Ibadan, one of the most heavily populated cities in Africa, had only about 50 Europeans before the last war. For those chosen few, the British colonial government maintained a segregated hospital service of 11 beds in well-furnished surroundings. There were 34 beds for the half-million blacks. The situation was repeated in other areas, so that altogether the 4,000 Europeans in the country in the 1930s had 12 modern hospitals, while the African population of at least 40 million had 52 hospitals.

The viciousness of the colonial system with respect to the provision of social services was most dramatically brought out in the case of economic activities which made huge profits, and notably in the mining industry. Mining takes serious toll of the health of workers, and it was only recently in the metropoles that miners have had access to the kind of medical and insurance services which could safeguard their lives and health. In colonial Africa, the exploitation of miners was entirely without responsibility. In 1930, scurvy and other epidemics broke out in the Lupa gold fields of Tanganyika. Hundreds of workers died. One should not wonder that they had no facilities which would have saved some lives, because in the first place they were not being paid enough to eat properly. . . .

Many Africans trekked to towns, because (bad as they were) they offered a little more than the countryside. Modern sanitation, electricity, piped water, paved roads, medical services, and schools were as foreign at the end of the colonial period as they were in the beginning – as far as most of rural Africa was concerned. Yet, it was the countryside that grew the cash crops and provided the labor that kept the system going. The peasants there knew very little of the supposed "credits" on the colonial balance sheet. . . .

Within individual countries, considerable regional variations existed, depending on the degree to which different parts of a country were integrated into the capitalist money economy. Thus, the northern part of Kenya or the south of Sudan had little to offer the colonialists, and such a zone was simply ignored by the colonizing power with regard to roads, schools, hospitals, and so on. Often, at the level of the district of a given colony, there would be discrimination in providing social amenities, on the basis of contribution to exportable surplus. For instance, plantations and companies might build hospitals for their workers, because some minimum maintenance of the workers' health was an economic investment. Usually, such a hospital was exclusively for workers of that particular capitalist concern, and those Africans living in the vicinity under sub-

sistence conditions outside the money economy were ignored altogether. . . .

The financial institutions of colonial Africa were even more scandalously neglectful of indigenous African interests than was the case with the European-oriented communications system. The banks did very little lending locally. In British East Africa, credit to Africans was specifically discouraged by the Credit to Natives (Restriction) Ordinance of 1931. Insurance companies catered almost exclusively to the interests of white settlers and capitalist firms. The policy of colonial reserves in metropolitan currencies can also be cited as a "service" inimical to Africans. The Currency Boards and central banks which performed such services denied Africa access to its own funds created by exports. Instead, *the colonial reserves in Britain, France, and Belgium represented African loans to and capital investment in Europe.*

It is necessary to re-evaluate the much glorified notion of "European capital" as having been invested in colonial Africa and Asia. The money available for investment in the capitalist system was itself the consequence of the previous robbery of workers and peasants in Europe and the world at large. In Africa's case, the capital that was invested in nineteenth-century commerce was part of the capital that had been derived from the trade in slaves. The Portuguese government was the first in Europe to ship captives from Africa and the last to let go of slave trading. Much of the profit slipped out of Portuguese hands, and went instead to Britain and Germany; but the Portuguese slave trade nevertheless helped the Portuguese themselves to finance later colonial ventures, such as joint capitalist participation in agricultural and mining companies in Angola and Mozambique.

As indicated earlier, many of the entrepreneurs from the big European port towns who turned to importing African agricultural produce into Europe were formerly carrying on the trade in slaves. The same can be said of many New England firms in the United

States. Some of the biggest "names" in the colonial epoch were capitalist concerns whose original capital came from the trade in slaves or from slavery itself. Lloyds, the great insurance underwriting and banking house, falls into this category, having been nourished by profits from the slave territories of the West Indies in the seventeenth and eighteenth centuries; and the ubiquitous Barclays Bank had its antecedents in slave trading. Worms et Compagnie is a French example of the same phenomenon. Back in the eighteenth century, Worms had strong links with the French slave trade, and it grew to become one of the most powerful financial houses dealing with the French empire in Africa and Asia, with particular concentration of Madagascar and the Indian Ocean.

The example of Unilever and the UAC reinforces the point that Africa was being exploited by capital produced out of African labor. When Lever Brothers took over the Niger Company in 1929, they became heirs to one of the most notorious exploiters of nineteenth-century Africa. The Niger Company was a chartered company with full governmental and police powers during the years 1885 to 1897. In that period, the company exploited Nigerians ruthlessly. Furthermore, the Niger Company was itself a monopoly that had bought up smaller firms tracing their capital directly to slave trading. Similarly, when the UAC was born out of the merger with the Eastern and African Trading Company, it was associated with some more capital that grew from a family tree rooted in the European slave trade. The capital at the disposal of the big French trading firms CFAO and SCOA can also be traced in the same way.

The process of capital accumulation and reproduction in East Africa lacks the continuity of West Africa. Firstly, Arabs as well as Europeans were participants in the slave trade from East Africa. Secondly, the Germans intervened in 1885, although they had not been previously involved; while the French (who had led the European slave trade in East Africa during the eighteenth and nineteenth centuries) concentrated on colonizing the Indian Ocean islands rather that the East African mainland. Thirdly, German colonialism did not last beyond the 1914 – 18 war. Even so, on the British side, the capital and profits of the colonizing East Africa Company reappeared in the trading firm of Smith Mackenzie.

The capital that was invested in colonial Africa in later years was a continuation of the nineteenth century, along with new influxes from the metropoles. If one inquired closely into the origins of the supposedly new sources, quite a few would have been connected very closely to previous exploitation of non-European peoples. However, it is not necessary to prove that every firm trading in Africa had a firsthand or secondhand connection with the European slave trade and with earlier exploitation of the continent. It is enough to remember that Europe's greatest source of primary capital accumulation was overseas, and that the profits from African ventures continually outran the capital invested in the colonies.

A conservative bourgeois writer on colonial Africa made the following remarks about the South African gold and diamond industries:

> Apart from the original capital subscribed [in the diamond industry], all capital expenditure was provided for out of profits. The industry also yielded large profits to the international firms which dealt in diamonds. These had a peculiar importance, because a considerable portion of the wealth accumulated by diamond firms was later used in the development of the [gold industry] of the Rand.

Similarly, in Angola the *Diamang* diamond company was an investment that quickly paid for itself, and was then producing capital. The combined profits of that company for the years 1954 and 1955 alone came to the total of invested capital plus 40 per cent. The excess over investment and maintenance costs was of course expatriated to Portugal, Belgium and the U.S.A., where the shareholders of the *Diamang* were resident; and Angola was thereby investing in those countries.

In this sense, the colonies were the generators of the capital rather than the countries into which foreign capital was plowed.

Capital was constantly in motion from metropole to some part of the dependencies, from colonies to other colonies (via the metropoles), from one metropole to another, and from colony to metropole. But because of the superprofits created by non-European peoples ever since slavery, the net flow was from colony to metropole. What was called "profits" in one year came back as "capital" the next. Even progressive writers have created a wrong impression by speaking about capital "exports" from Europe to Africa and about the role of "foreign" capital. What was foreign about the capital in colonial Africa was its ownership and not its initial source.

Apologists for colonialism are quick to say that the money for schools, hospitals, and such services in Africa was provided by the British, French, or Belgian taxpayer, as the case may have been. It defies logic to admit that profits from a given colony in a given year totaled several million dollars and to affirm nevertheless that the few thousand dollars allocated to social services in that colony was the money of European taxpayers! The true situation can accurately be presented in the following terms: African workers and peasants produced for European capitalism goods and services of a certain value. A small proportion of the fruits of their efforts was retained by them in the form of wages, cash payments, and extremely limited social services, such as were essential to the maintenance of colonialism. The rest went to the various beneficiaries of the colonial system. . . .

Capitalism as a system within the metropoles or epicenters had two dominant classes: firstly, the capitalists or bourgeoisie who owned the factories and banks (the major means for producing and distributing wealth); and secondly, the workers or proletariat who worked in the factories of the said bourgeoisie. Colonialism did not create a capital-owning and factory-owning class among Africans or even inside Africa; nor did it create an urbanized proletariat of any significance (particularly outside South Africa). In other words, capitalism in the form of colonialism failed to perform in Africa the tasks which it had performed in Europe in changing social relations and liberating the forces of production.

It is fairly obvious that capitalists do not set out to create other capitalists, who would be rivals. On the contrary, the tendency of capitalism in Europe from the very beginning was one of competition, elimination, and monopoly. Therefore, when the imperialist stage was reached, the metropolitan capitalists had no intention of allowing rivals to arise in the dependencies. However, in spite of what the metropoles wanted, some local capitalists did emerge in Asia and Latin America. Africa is a significant exception in the sense that, compared with other colonized peoples, far fewer Africans had access even to the middle rungs of the bourgeois ladder in terms of capital for investment.

Part of the explanation for the lack of African capitalists in Africa lies in the arrival of minority groups who had no local family ties which could stand in the way of the ruthless primary accumulation which capitalism requires. Lebanese, Syrian, Greek, and Indian businessmen rose from the ranks of petty traders to become minor and sometimes substantial capitalists. Names like Raccah and Leventis were well known in West Africa, just as names like Madhvani and Visram became well known as capitalists in East Africa.

There were clashes between the middlemen and the European colonialists, but the latter much preferred to encourage the minorities rather than see Africans build themselves up. For instance, in West Africa the businessmen from Sierra Leone were discouraged both in their own colony and in other British posses- sions where they chose to settle. In East Africa, there was hope among Ugandans in particular that they might acquire cotton gins and perform some capitalist functions connected with cotton growing and other activities. However, when in 1920 a Development Commission was appointed to promote commerce and industry, it favored firstly Europeans and then Indians. Africans were prohibited by legislation from owning gins.

Taking Africa as a whole, the few African businessmen who were allowed to emerge were at the bottom of the ladder and cannot be considered as "capitalists" in the true sense. They did not own sufficient capital to invest in large-scale farming, trading, mining, or industry. They were dependent both on European-owned capital and on the local capital of minority groups.

That European capitalism should have failed to create African capitalists is perhaps not so striking as its inability to create a working class and to diffuse industrial skills throughout Africa. By its very nature, colonialism was prejudiced against the estab- lishment of industries in Africa, outside of agriculture and the extractive spheres of mining and timber felling. Whenever internal forces seemed to push in the direction of African industrialization, they were deliber- ately blocked by the colonial governments acting on behalf of the metropolitan industri- alists. Groundnut-oil mills were set up in Senegal in 1927 and began exports to France. They were soon placed under restrictions because of protests of oil-millers in France. Similarly in Nigeria, the oil mills set up by Lebanese were discouraged. The oil was still sent to Europe as a raw material for industry, but European industrialists did not then welcome even the simple stage of processing groundnuts into oil on African soil.

Many irrational contradictions arose throughout colonial Africa as a result of the non-industrialization policy: Sudanese and Ugandans grew cotton but imported manufac- tured cotton goods, Ivory Coast grew cocoa and imported tinned cocoa and chocolate.

The tiny working class of colonial Africa covered jobs such as agricultural labor and domestic service. Most of it was unskilled, in contrast to the accumulating skills of capitalism proper. When it came to projects requiring technical expertise, Europeans did the supervision – standing around in their helmets and white shorts. Of course, in 1885 Africans did not have the technical know-how which had evolved in Europe during the eight- eenth and nineteenth centuries. That difference was itself partly due to the kind of relations between Africa and Europe in the pre-colonial period. What is more significant, however, is the incredibly small number of Africans who were able to acquire "modern" skills during the colonial period. In a few places, such as South Africa and the Rhodesias, this was due to specific racial discrimination in employment, so as to keep the best jobs for whites. Yet, even in the absence of whites, lack of skills among Africans was an integral part of the capitalist impact on the continent.

It has already been illustrated how the presence of industry in Europe fostered and multiplied scientific techniques. The reverse side of the coin was presented in Africa: no industry meant no generation of skills. Even in the mining industry, it was arranged that the most valuable labor should be done out- side Africa. It is sometimes forgotten that it is labor which adds value to commodities through the transformation of natural prod- ucts. For instance, although gem diamonds have a value far above their practical useful- ness, the value is not simply a question of their being rare. Work had to be done to locate the diamonds. That is the skilled task of a geologist, and the geologists were of course Europeans. Work had to be done to dig the diamonds out, which involves mainly physical labor. Only in that phase were Africans from South Africa, Namibia, Angola, Tanganyika, and Sierra Leone brought into the picture.

Subsequently, work had to be done in cutting and polishing the diamonds. A small portion of this was performed by whites in South Africa, and most of it by whites in Brussels and London. It was on the desk of the skilled cutter that the rough diamond became a gem and soared in value. No Africans were allowed to come near that kind of technique in the colonial period.

Much of the dynamism of capitalism lay in the way that growth created more opportunities for further growth. Major industries had by-products, they stimulated local raw-material usage, they expanded transport and the building industry – as was seen in the case of Unilever. In the words of the professional economists, those were the beneficial "back-word and forward linkages." Given that the industries using African raw materials were located *outside* Africa, then there could be no beneficial backward and forward linkages *inside* Africa. After the Second World War, Guinea began to export bauxite. In the hands of French and American capitalists, the bauxite became aluminum. In the metropoles, it went into the making of refactory material, electrical conductors, cigarette foil, kitchen utensils, glass, jewel bearings, abrasives, light-weight structures, and aircraft. Guinean bauxite stimulated European shipping and North American hydro–electric power. In Guinea, the colonial bauxite mining left holes in the ground.

With regard to gold, the financial implications in Europe were enormous and African gold played its part in the development of the monetary system and of industry and agriculture in the metropoles. But, like bauxite and other minerals, gold is an exhaustible resource. Once it is taken out of a country's soil, that is an absolute loss that cannot be replaced. That simple fact is often obscured so long as production continues, as in South Africa; but it is dramatically brought to attention when the minerals have actually disappeared during the colonial epoch. For instance, in the south of Tanganyika, the British mined gold as fast

as they could from 1933 onwards at a place called Chunya. By 1953, they had gobbled it all up and exported it abroad. By the end of the colonial period, Chunya was one of the most backward spots in the whole of Tanganyika, which was itself known as the poor Cinderella of East Africa. If that was modernization, and given the price paid in exploitation and oppression, then Africans would have been better off in the bush.

Industrialization does not only mean Agriculture itself has been industrialized in capitalist and socialist countries by the intensive application of scientific principles to irrigation, fertilizers, tools, crop selection, stock breeding. (The most decisive failure of colonialism in Africa was its failure to change the technology of agricultural production.) The most convincing evidence as to the superficiality of the talk about colonialism having "modernized" Africa is the fact that the vast majority of Africans went into colonialism with a hoe and came out with a hoe. Some capitalist plantations introduced agricultural machinery, and the odd tractor found its way into the hands of African farmers; but the hoe remained the overwhelmingly dominant agricultural implement. Capitalism could revolutionize agriculture in Europe, but it could not do the same for Africa.

In some districts, capitalism brought about technological backwardness in agriculture. On the reserves of southern Africa, far too many Africans were crowded onto inadequate land, and were forced to engage in intensive farming, using techniques that were suitable only to shifting cultivation. In practice, that was a form of technical retrogression, because the land yielded less and less and became destroyed in the process. Wherever Africans were hampered in their use of their ancestral lands on a wide-ranging shifting basis, the same negative effect was to be found. Besides, some of the new cash crops like groundnuts and cotton were very demanding on the soil. In countries like Senegal, Niger, and Chad, which were already on the edge of the desert, the steady cultivation led to soil impoverishment and encroachment of the desert.

White racist notions are so deep-rooted within capitalist society that the failure of African agriculture to advance was put down to the inherent inferiority of the African. It would be much truer to say that it was due to the white intruders, although the basic explanation is to be found not in the personal ill-will of the colonialists or in their racial origin, but rather in the organized viciousness of the capitalist/colonialist system.

Failure to improve agricultural tools and methods on behalf of African peasants was not a matter of a bad decision by colonial policymakers. It was an inescapable feature of colonialism as a whole, based on the understanding that the international division of labor aimed at skills in the metropoles and low-level manpower in the dependencies. It was also a result of the considerable use of force (including taxation) in African labor relations. People can be forced to perform simple manual labor, but very little else. This was proven when Africans were used as slaves in the West Indies and America. Slaves damaged tools and carried out sabotage, which could only be controlled by extra supervision and by keeping tools and productive processes very elementary. Slave labor was unsuitable for carrying out industrial activity, so that in the U.S.A. the North went to war in 1861 to end slavery in the South, so as to spread true capitalist relations throughout the land. Following the same line of argument, it becomes clear why the various forms of forced agricultural labor in Africa had to be kept quite simple, and that in turn meant small earnings.

Capitalists under colonialism did not pay enough for an African to maintain himself and family. This can readily be realized by reflecting on the amounts of money earned by African peasants from cash crops. The sale of produce by an African cash-crop farmer rarely brought in 10 pounds per year and often it was less than half that amount. Out of that, a peasant had to pay for tools, seeds, and transport and he had to repay the loan to the middleman before he could call the remainder his own. Peasants producing coffee and cocoa and collecting palm produce tended to earn more than those dealing with cotton and groundnuts, but even the ordinary Akwapim cocoa farmer of Chagga coffee farmer never handled money in quantities sufficient to feed, clothe, and shelter his family. Instead, subsistence farming of yams or bananas continued as a supplement. That was how the peasant managed to eat, and the few shillings earned went to pay taxes and to buy the increasing number of things which could not be obtained without money in the middlemen's shops – salt, cloth, paraffin. If he was extremely lucky, he would have access to zinc sheets, bicycles, radios, and sewing machines, and would be able to pay school fees. It must be made quite clear that those in the last category were extremely few.

One reason why the African peasant got so little for his agricultural crops was that his labor was unskilled. That was not the whole explanation, but it is true that a product such as cotton jumped in value during the time it went through the sophisticated processes of manufacture in Europe. Karl Marx, in clarifying how capitalists appropriated part of the surplus of each worker, used the example of cotton. He explained that the value of the manufactured cotton included the value of the labor that went into growing the raw cotton, plus part of the value of the labor that made the spindles, plus the labor that went into the actual manufacture. From an African viewpoint, the first conclusion to be drawn is that the peasant working on African soil was being exploited by the industrialist who used African raw material in Europe or America. Secondly, it is necessary to realize that the African contribution of unskilled labor was valued for less than the European contribution of skilled labor. . . .

Within any social system, the oppressed find some room to maneuver through their own initiative. For instance, under the slave regime of America and the West Indies, Africans found ways and means of gaining small advantages. They would flatter and "con" the slavemasters, who were so arrogant and bigoted that they were readily fooled. Similarly, under colonialism many Africans played the game to secure what they could. Africans in positions like interpreters, police, and court officials often had their way over the ruling Europeans. However, that should not be mistaken for power or political participation or the exercise of individual freedom. Under slavery, power lay in the hands of the slave masters: under colonialism, power lay in the hands of the colonialists. The loss of power for the various African states meant a reduction in the freedom of every individual.

Colonialism was a negation of freedom from the viewpoint of the colonized. Even in quantitative terms it could not possibly bring modern political liberation to Africans comparable to the little that had been achieved by capitalism as an improvement of feudalism. In its political aspects, capitalism in the metropoles included constitutions, parliaments, freedom of the press. All of those things were limited in their application to the European working class, but they had existed in some form or fashion in the metropoles ever since the American War of Independence and the French Revolution. But Jules Ferry, a former French colonial minister, explained that the French Revolution was not fought on behalf of the blacks of Africa. Bourgeois liberty, equality, and fraternity was not for colonial subjects. Africans had to make do with bayonets, riot acts, and gunboats.

Negative Character of the Social, Political, and Economic Consequences

. . . During the centuries of pre-colonial trade, some control over social, political, and economic life was retained in Africa, in spite of the disadvantageous commerce with Europeans. That little control over internal matters disappeared under colonialism. Colonialism went much further than trade. It meant a tendency towards direct appropriation by Europeans of the social institutions within Africa. Africans ceased to set indigenous cultural goals and standards, and lost full command of training young members of the society. Those were undoubtedly major steps backward.

The Tunisian, Albert Memmi, puts forward the following proposition:

> The most serious blow suffered by the colonized is being removed from history and from the community. Colonization usurps any free role in either war or peace, every decision contributing to his destiny and that of the world, and all cultural and social responsibility.

Sweeping as that statement may initially appear, it is entirely true. The removal from history follows logically from the loss of power which colonialism represented. The power to act independently is the guarantee to participate actively and *consciously* in history. To be colonized is to be removed from history, except in the most passive sense. A striking illustration of the fact that colonial Africa was a passive object is seen in its attraction for white anthropologists, who came to study "primitive society." Colonialism determined that Africans were no more makers of history than were beetles – objects to be looked at under a microscope and examined for unusual features.

The negative impact of colonialism in political terms was quite dramatic. Overnight, African political states lost their power, independence, and meaning – irrespective of whether they were big empires or small polities. Certain traditional rulers were kept in office, and the formal structure of some kingdoms was partially retained, but the substance of political life was quite different. Political power had passed into the hands of foreign overlords. Of course, numerous African states in previous centuries had passed through the cycle of growth and decline. But colonial rule was different. So long as it lasted, not a single African state could flourish.

To be specific, it must be noted that colonialism crushed by force the surviving feudal states of North Africa; that the French wiped out the large Moslem state of the Western Sudan, as well as Dahomey and kingdoms in Madagascar; that the British eliminated Egypt, the Mahdist Sudan, Asante, Benin, the Yoruba kingdoms, Swaziland, Matabeleland, the Lozi, and the East African lake kingdoms as great states. It should further be noted that a multiplicity of smaller and growing states were removed from the face of Africa by the Belgians, Portuguese, British, French, Germans, Spaniards, and Italians. Finally, those that appeared to survive were nothing but puppet creations. For instance, the Sultan of Morocco retained nominal existence under colonial rule which started in 1912; and the same applied to the Bey of Tunis; but Morocco and Tunisia were just as much under the power of French colonial administrators as neighboring Algeria, where the feudal rulers were removed altogether.

Sometimes, the African rulers who were chosen to serve as agents of foreign colonial rule were quite obviously nothing but puppets. The French and the Portuguese were in the habit of choosing their own African "chiefs"; the British went to Iboland and invented "warrant chiefs"; and all the colonial powers found it convenient to create "superior" or "paramount" rulers. Very often, the local population hated and despised such colonial stooges. There were traditional rulers such as the Sultan of Sokoto, the Kabaka of Buganda, and the Asantehene of Asante, who retained a great deal of prestige in the eyes of Africans, but they had no power to act outside the narrow boundaries laid down by colonialism, lest they find themselves in the Seychelles Islands as "guests of His Majesty's Government."

One can go so far as to say that colonial rule meant the effective eradication of African political power throughout the continent, since Liberia and Ethiopia could no longer function as independent states within the context of continent-wide colonialism. Liberia in particular had to bow before foreign political, economic, and military pressures in a way that no genuinely independent state could have accepted; and although Ethiopia held firm until 1936, most European capitalist nations were not inclined to treat Ethiopia as a sovereign state, primarily because it was African, and Africans were supposed to be colonial subjects.

The pattern of arrest of African political development has some features which can only be appreciated after careful scrutiny and the taking away of the blinkers which the colonizers put on the eyes of their subjects. An interesting case in point is that of women's role in society. Until today, capitalist society has failed to resolve the inequality between man and woman, wich was entrenched in all modes of production prior to socialism. The colonialists in Africa occasionally paid lip service to women's education and emancipation, but objectively there was deterioration in the status of women owing to colonial rule.

A realistic assessment of the role of women in independent pre-colonial Africa shows two contrasting but combined tendencies. In the first place, women were exploited by men through polygamous arrangements designed to capture the labor power of women. As always, exploitation was accompanied by oppression; and there is evidence to the effect that women were sometimes treated like beasts of burden, as for instance in Moslem African societies. Nevertheless, there was a counter-tendency to insure the dignity of women to greater or lesser degree in all African societies. Mother-right was a prevalent feature of African societies, and particular women held a variety of privileges based on the fact that they were the keys to inheritance.

More important still, some women had real

power in the political sense, exercised either through religion or directly within the politico-constitutional apparatus. In Mozambique, the widow of an Nguni king became the priestess in charge of the shrine set up in the burial place of her deceased husband, and the reigning king had to consult her on all important matters. In a few instances, women were actually heads of state. Among the Lovedu of Transvaal, the key figure was the Rain-Queen, combining political and religious functions. The most frequently encountered role of importance played by women was that of "Queen Mother" or "Queen Sister." In practice, that post was filled by a female of royal blood, who might be mother, sister, or aunt of the reigning king in places such as Mali, Asante, and Buganda. Her influence was considerable, and there were occasions when the "Queen Mother" was the real power and the male king a mere puppet.

What happened to African women under colonialism is that the social, religious, constitutional, and political privileges and rights disappeared, while the economic exploitation continued and was often intensified. It was intensified because the division of labor according to sex was frequently disrupted. Traditionally, African men did the heavy labor of felling trees, clearing land, building houses, apart from conducting warfare and hunting. When they were required to leave their farms to seek employment, women remained behind burdened with every task necessary for the survival of themselves, the children, and even the men as far as foodstuffs were concerned. Moreover, since men entered the money sector more easily and in greater numbers than women, women's work became greatly inferior to that of men within the new value system of colonialism: men's work was "modern" and women's was "traditional" and "backward." Therefore, the deterioration in the status of African women was bound up with the consequent loss of the right to set indigenous standards of what work had merit and what did not.

One of the most important manifestations of historical arrest and stagnation in colonial Africa is that which commonly goes under the title of "tribalism." That term, in its common journalistic setting, is understood to mean that Africans have a basic loyalty to tribe rather than nation and that each tribe still *retains* a fundamental hostility towards its neighboring tribes. The examples favored by the capitalist press and bourgeois scholarship are those of Congo and Nigeria. Their accounts suggest that Europeans tried to make a nation out of the Congolese and Nigerian peoples, but they failed, because the various tribes had their age-long hatreds; and, as soon as the colonial power went, the natives *returned* to killing each other. To this phenomenon, Europeans often attach the word "atavism," to carry the notion that Africans were returning to their primitive savagery. Even a cursory survey of the African past shows that such assertions are the exact opposite of the truth.

It is necessary to discuss briefly what comprises a tribe – a term that has been avoided in this analysis, partly because it usually carries derogatory connotations and partly because of its vagueness and the loose ways in which it is employed in the literature on Africa. Following the principle of family living, Africans were organized in groups which had common ancestors. Theoretically, the tribe was the largest group of people claiming descent from a common ancestor at some time in the remote past. Generally, such a group could therefore be said to be of the same ethnic stock, and their language would have a great deal in common. Beyond that, members of a tribe were seldom all members of the same political unit and very seldom indeed did they all share a common social purpose in terms of activities, such as trade and warfare. Instead, African states were sometimes based entirely on part of the members of a given ethnic group or (more usually) on an amalgamation of members of different ethnic communities.

All of the large states of nineteenth-century

Africa were multi-ethnic, and their expansion was continually making anything like "tribal" loyalty a thing of the past, by substituting in its place national and class ties. However, in all parts of the world, that substitution of national and class ties for purely ethnic ones is a lengthy historical process; and, invariably there remains for long periods certain regional pockets of individuals who have their own narrow, regional loyalties, springing from ties of kinship, language, and culture. In Asia, the feudal states of Vietnam and Burma both achieved a considerable degree of national homogeneity over the centuries before colonial rule. But there were pockets of "tribes" or "minorities" who remained outside the effective sphere of the nationstate and the national economy and culture.

In the first place, colonialism blocked the further evolution of national solidary, because it destroyed the particular Asian or African states which were the principal agents for achieving the liquidation of fragmented loyalties. In the second place, because ethnic and regional loyalties which go under the name of "tribalism" could not be effectively resolved by the colonial state, they tended to fester and grow in unhealthy forms. Indeed, the colonial powers sometimes saw the value of stimulating the internal tribal jealousies so as to keep the colonized from dealing with their principal contradiction with the European overlords –

i.e., the classic technique of divide and rule. Certainly, the Belgians consciously fostered that; and the racist whites in South Africa had by the 1950s worked out a careful plan to "develop" the oppressed African population as Zulu, as Xhosa, and as Sotho so that the march towards broader African national and class solidarities could be stopped and turned back.

The civil war in Nigeria is generally regarded as having been a tribal affair. To accept such a contention would mean extending the definition of tribe to cover Shell Oil and Gulf Oil! But, quite apart from that, it must be pointed out that nowhere in the history of pre-colonial independent Nigeria can anyone point to the massacre of Ibos by Hausas or any incident which suggests that people up to the nineteenth century were fighting each other because of ethnic origin. Of course there were wars, but they had a rational basis in trade rivalry, religious contentions, and the clashes of political expansion. What came to be called tribalism at the beginning of the new epoch of political independence in Nigeria was itself a product of the way that people were brought together under colonialism so as to be exploited. It was a product of administrative devices, of entrenched regional separations, of differential access by particular ethnic groups into the colonial economy and culture.

35

THE INVENTION OF TRADITION IN COLONIAL AFRICA

TERENCE RANGER

Introduction

The 1870s, 1880s and 1890s were the time of a great flowering of European invented tradition – ecclesiastical, educational, military, republican, monarchical. They were also the time of the European rush into Africa. There were many and complex connections between the two processes. The concept of Empire was central to the process of inventing tradition within Europe itself, but the African empires came so late in the day that they demonstrate the effects rather than the causes of European invented tradition. Deployed in Africa, however, the new traditions took on a peculiar character, distinguishing them from both their European and Asian Imperial forms.

By contrast to India many parts of Africa became colonies of white settlement. This meant that the settlers had to define themselves as natural and undisputed masters of vast numbers of Africans. They drew upon European invented traditions both to define and to justify their roles, and also to provide models of subservience into which it was sometimes possible to draw Africans. In Africa, therefore, the whole apparatus of invented school and professional and regimental traditions became much more starkly a matter of command and control than it was

within Europe itself. Moreover, in Europe these invented traditions of the new ruling classes were to some extent balanced by the invented traditions of industrial workers or by the invented "folk" cultures of peasants. In Africa, no white agriculturalist saw himself as a peasant. White workers in the mines of southern Africa certainly drew upon the invented rituals of European craft unionism but they did so partly because they were rituals of exclusiveness and could be used to prevent Africans being defined as workers.

By contrast to India, once again, Africa did not offer to its conquerors the framework of an indigenous imperial state nor existing centralized rituals of honour and degree. Ready connections between African and European systems of governance could only be made at the level of the monarchy; Africa possessed, so the colonisers thought, dozens of rudimentary kings. Hence in Africa the British made an even greater use of the idea of "Imperial Monarchy" than they did within Britain or India. The "theology" of an omniscient, omnipotent and omnipresent monarchy became almost the sole ingredient of imperial ideology as it was presented to Africans. For the Germans, too, the Kaiser stood as the dominant symbol of German rule. The French had the more difficult task of incorporating Africans into a republican tradition.

But serviceable as the monarchical ideology was to the British, it was not enough in itself to provide the theory or justify the structures of colonial governance on the spot. Since so few connections could be made between British and African political, social and legal systems, British administrators set about inventing African traditions for Africans. Their own respect for "tradition" disposed them to look with favour upon what they took to be traditional in Africa. They set about to codify and promulgate these traditions, thereby transforming flexible custom into hard prescription.

All this is part of the history of European ideas, but it is also very much part of the history of modern Africa. These complex processes have to be understood before a historian can arrive at any understanding of the particularity of Africa before colonialism; many African scholars as well as many European Africanists have found it difficult to free themselves from the false models of colonial codified African "tradition". However, the study of these processes is not only a part of historiography but of history. The invented traditions imported from Europe not only provided whites with models of command but also offered many Africans models of "modern" behaviour. The invented traditions of African societies – whether invented by the Europeans or by Africans themselves in response – distorted the past but became in themselves realities through which a good deal of colonial encounter was expressed. . . .

Bringing Africans into the Traditions of Governance

. . . There were two very direct ways in which Europeans sought to make use of their invented traditions to transform and modernize African thought and conduct. One was the acceptance of the idea that *some* Africans could become members of the governing class of colonial Africa, and hence the extension to such Africans of training in a neo-traditional context. The second – and more common – was an attempt to make use of what European invented traditions had to offer in terms of a redefined relationship between leader and led. The regimental tradition, after all, defined the roles of both officers and men; the great-house tradition of rural gentility defined the roles of both masters and servants; the public school tradition defined the roles of both prefects and fags. All this might be made use of to create a clearly defined hierarchical society in which Europeans commanded and Africans accepted commands, but both within a shared framework of pride and loyalty. Thus if the traditions which workers and peasants had made for themselves in Europe did not exercise much influence on Africans under colonialism, invented European traditions of subordination exercised a very considerable influence indeed.

The best illustration of the first idea – that some Africans might be turned into governors by exposure to British neo-tradition – is perhaps the famous school, King's College, Budo, in Uganda. The fullest account is by G.P. McGregor, who perceptively points out that the provision of elementary education was only just being taken seriously in Britain itself in the 1870s as part of the process of bringing the majority of the population to its place in the vocational and educational hierarchy. Hence the spread of elementary schools in Buganda at the end of the nineteenth century was a remarkably little-delayed extension of the same process to the African empire. But in Buganda, while this sort of education seemed appropriate enough to the peasant cultivator majority, the Anglican missionaries did not feel that it was suitable for the Ganda aristocracy.

So far little or nothing had been done for the children of the upper classes [wrote Bishop Tucker], who in many respects were worse off than the children of the peasants. We felt strongly that if the ruling classes of the country were to exercise in the days to come an influence for good upon their people and to have a sense of responsibility towards them, it was essential that something should be done for the education of these neglected children, on the soundest possible lines . . . by the discipline of work and games in a boarding school so as to build character as to enable the Baganda to take their proper place in the administrative, commercial and industrial life of their own country.[1]

In short, in Buganda the missionaires aimed to place on top of British-style elementary education a structure of British-style secondary education of a neo-traditional kind. They were always clear that their aim was "the adaptation of our English Public School method to the African scene." They succeeded to an extraordinary extent. King's College was built on the Coronation Hill of the Baganda kings, so that "both Coronation Services of this century have been held" in the college chapel; "though some of the traditional ceremonies were observed," the service "followed many of the features of the English coronation service."[2] The English Public School house spirit (was) quickly established," and the Gandan members of Turkey House petitioned that its name be changed to Canada House so as to go with England House, South Africa House and Australia House – Turkey seemed "distinctly unimperial." The school motto, again said to have been chosen at the request of the pupils, was a Gandan version of Cecil Rhodes's dying words, "So little done – so much to do."

McGregor quotes a letter from a Gandan pupil written in the first year of the school's existence, which enables us to see this remarkable process of socialization through Gandan eyes.

First in the mornings when we have got up we arrange properly our beds. If you do not arrange it properly there is judgement or rebuke when the Europeans make a visit . . . On the front of our cups there is a likeness of a lion. That it is by which the scholars of Budo may be known. And no-one may eat any thing in the cubicle, nor coffee which they chew, but only in the verandah where food is eaten. We sing one hymn and pray and then we learn English . . . When we come out at four, we go and play football, on one side eleven and on the other side eleven, and we arrange every man in his place, goal-keeper, and back men and ba-half-back and ba-forward.[3]

Everyone agreed that Budo had managed to create that intangible thing, "the spirit of the school." It was present at Budo

at its best, as we have breathed it in England after generations of experiment – the spirit of the team, of discipline, of local patriotism – and very remarkable has been the translation of it into the heart of Africa.

Sir Phillip Mitchell thought that Budo was "one of the few places here which has a soul." Expatriate teachers later came to criticize "the Budonian habit of defending worthless traditions merely on the grounds that they have always been there."[4]

Whatever the tensions of doing so within the imperial framework which so firmly subordinated the Gandan ruling class to British administrative officers, and the Gandan monarchy to the imperial crown, there is no

[1] G.P. McGregor, *Kings College, Budo: The First Sixty Years* (London, 1967), pp. 6, 16.
[2] *Ibid.*, pp. 35–6.
[3] *Ibid.*, pp. 17–18.
[4] *Ibid.*, pp. 54, 117, 124.

doubt that the missionaries created at Budo a successful complex of new traditions, which worked themselves out parallel to an increasing ceremonialism of the role of the Kabaka and the other Ugandan kings so as to achieve a synthesis not unlike that accomplished in nineteenth-century England. The Golden Jubilee ceremonies of the college – "We had four Kings at the high table" – were also a ritual expression of the commitment of a large section of the Gandan ruling class to these by now hallowed invented traditions.[5] But the Budo experiment was not to become a general model; the British themselves came to regret their original alliance with the Ganda chiefs, and to believe that real modernizing change could not be brought about through their agency. Real modernizing change would be the product of European commanders loyally supported by African subordinates.

Various traditions of subordination were available. One was the tradition of the hierarchy of the great house. Part of the self-image of the European in Africa was his prescriptive right to have black servants – at the height of the labour crisis in the South African mines, there were more black men employed in Johannesburg as domestic servants than as mine workers.[6] In 1914 Frank Weston, bishop of Zanzibar, contrasted Islamic community in Africa with Christian differentiation. The African Christian, he wrote, has nothing to adhere to but "a few Europeans who pass him in the street; he is beneath them; they may be kind to him; he may perhaps be a steward in their dining room, or a butler . . . but Brotherhood? Well, it is not yet."[7] There was no impulse towards "Brotherhood" in colonial Africa. For most Europeans the favoured image of their relationship with Africans was

that of paternal master and loyal servant. It was an image readily transferred to industrial employment. Throughout southern Africa, African employees were not defined as workers but instead controlled and disciplined under the terms of Masters and Servants Acts.

Few whites in Africa, however, maintained domestic establishments of a size which would have allowed the full "traditional" panoply of the British servant hierarchy. A more elaborate application of European neo-traditions of subordination came with the restructuring of African armies. In Sylvanus Cookey's fascinating account of this process, the French emerge as the first and most imaginative manipulators of the military invented tradition. Faideherbe in the 1850s disbanded his demoralized pressed levies and attracted African volunteers with "seduisant" uniforms, modern arms, Koranic oaths of allegiance and crash courses in the military glory of the French tradition.

> It was even suggested from Paris, as a means of instilling at an early age a sense of the military mode in the young Africans and preparing them for a military career, that the children of the *tirailleurs* should be provided uniforms and miniature equipment similar to those of their parents.[8]

The British were slower to follow such a policy. But in the face of the French threat they also moved to regularize their African regiments. Lugard devoted his meticulous passion for detail to the transformation of his Nigerian levies from a "rabble" to a disciplined and effective fighting force. Soon he came to esteem them highly; official praise was lavished on them for their conduct in

---

[5]   *Ibid.*, p. 136
[6]   Charles van Onselen, "The Witches of Suburbia: Domestic Service on the Witwatersrand, 1890–1914" (unpublished MS.).
[7]   Frank Weston, "Islam in Zanzibar Diocese," *Central Africa*, xxxii, no. 380 (Aug. 1914).
[8]   S.J. Cookey, "Origins and pre-1914 Character of the Colonial Armies in West Africa" (Univ. of California, Los Angeles, colloquium paper, 1972).

campaigns in the Gold Coast and northern Nigeria; a regimental tradition was being built up as rapidly as the spirit of Budo. Lugard's administration was largely staffed by army officers; in East Africa, too, "governments were largely military in character during these early years," and Professor George Shepperson has commented on

> the narrowness of the line between the civilian and the military . . . It was through its forces as much as its missions that European culture was brought to the in digenous inhabitants of British Central Africa.[9] . . .

There was a rough periodization in all this. European invented traditions were important for Africans in a series of overlapping phases. The military neo-tradition, with its clearly visible demarcations of hierarchy and its obvious centrality to the workings of early colonialism, was the first powerful influence. Its impact reached a climax – particularly in eastern Africa – with the campaigns of the first world war. Thereafter, especially in British Africa, the military presence declined.[10] The military mode became less influential that the modes of missionary employment or the bureaucratic build-up of Africans in state and business employment. But the debate over the sequence of influence or the debate over which neo-tradition was in the end most influential – a debate that sways to and fro as African kings, surrounded by neo-traditional trappings, dominate some new African states; as bureaucratic élites triumph in others; and Mazrui's "lumpen-militariat" control yet others – is less important in the end than an assessment of the overall effect of these processes of neo-traditional socialization.

This was surely very large indeed. European invented traditions offered Africans a series of clearly defined points of entry into the colonial world, though in almost all cases it was entry into the subordinate part of a man/master relationship. They began by socializing Africans into acceptance of one or other readily available European neo-traditional modes of conduct – the historical literature is full of Africans proud of having mastered the business of being a member of a regiment or having learnt how to be an effective practitioner of the ritual of nineteenth-century Anglicanism. The process often ended with serious challenges to the colonial power, often couched in terms of the socializing neo-traditions themselves. . . . This is a pattern worked out by Martin Channock for the school teacher traditionalists of Nyasaland, and in greater detail by John Iliffe for Tanganyika.[11] In its varying forms it underlay a good deal of what we call nationalism. It is distressing, but not in the least surprising, that Kenneth Kaunda in his search for a personal ideology to help him on the road to national leadership found solace and inspiration in Arthur Mee's Books for Boys.[12]

If we return for a moment to the question of "modernization" through the use of European invented traditions, both their advantages and their limitations to the colonisers become plain. They *did* serve to separate out Africans into relatively specialized categories – the askari, the teacher, the servant and so on – and to provide a rudimentary professionalization of African workers. Embedded in the neo-traditions of governance and subordination,

---

[9] George Shepperson, "The Military History of British Central Africa: A Review Article," *Rhodes–Livingstone Journal*, no. 26 (Dec. 1959), pp. 23–33.
[10] Tony Clayton, "Concepts of Power and Force in Colonial Africa, 1919–1939." Institute of Commonwealth Studies seminar (Univ. of London, Oct. 1978).
[11] Martin Channock "Ambiguities in the Malawian Political Tradition," *Afrcian Affairs*,. lxxiv, no. 296 (July 1975); John Iliffe, *A Modern History of Tanganyika* (Cambridge, 1979).
[12] Kenneth Kaunda, *Zambia Shall be Free* (London, 1962). p. 31.

there were very clear-cut requirements for the observance of industrial time and work discipline – the neatly, even fanatically, prescribed segments of the schoolboys' day at Budo; the drill square as source and symbol of discipline and punctuality. On the other hand, the invented traditions which were introduced to Africans were those of governance rather than of production. Industrial workers may have been categorized as "servants", but for a very long time the true domestic servant commanded a much greater prestige and could manipulate the reciprocities contained in the master/servant relationship from which the industrial worker was cut off. Industrial workers and peasants never had access to the clear-cut and prestigious ceremonials of the soldier, the teacher, the clerk – except insofar as they assumed them for themselves in the costumes of carnival or competitive dance.[13] And as we have seen, where craft union traditions did exist Africans were specifically excluded from them. African industrial workers were left to work out for themselves a consciousness and mode of behaviour appropriate to their condition.[14]

This was one of the many reasons for the relatively high prestige among Africans in colonial Africa of non-productive employment. And at the same time, if the new traditions of subordination had begun "usefully" to define certain sorts of specializations, they gave rise later to profoundly conservative conceptualizations of these specializations, making African teachers, ministers and soldiers notoriously resistant to subsequent attempts at modernizing change. . . .

Europeans and "Tradition" in Africa

The invented traditions of nineteenth-century Europe had been introduced into Africa to allow Europeans and certain Africans to combine for "modernizing" ends. But there was an inherent ambiguity in neo-traditional thought. Europeans belonging to one or other of the neo-traditions believed themselves to have a respect for the customary. They liked the idea of age-old prescriptive rights and they liked to compare the sort of title which an African chief possessed with the title to gentlemanliness which they laid claim to themselves. A profound misunderstanding was at work here. In comparing European neo-traditions with the customary in Africa the whites were certainly comparing unlike with unlike. European invented traditions were marked by their inflexibility. They involved sets of recorded rules and procedures – like the modern coronation rites. They gave reassurance because they represented what was unchanging in a period of flux. Now, when Europeans thought of the customary in Africa, they naturally ascribed to it these same characteristics. The assertion by whites that African society was profoundly conservative – living within age-old rules which did not change; living within an ideology based on the absence of change; living within a framework of clearly defined hierarchical status – was by no means always intended as an indictment of African backwardness or reluctance to modernize. Often it was intended as a compliment to the admirable qualities of tradition, even though it was a quite misconceived compliment. This attitude towards "traditional" Africa became more marked as whites came to realize in the 1920s and 1930s that rapid economic transformation was just not

---

[13]   Terence Ranger, *Dance and Society in Eastern Africa* (London, 1975).
[14]   For a discussion of recent literature on African worker consciousness see, Peter Gutkind, Jean Copans and Robin Cohen, *African Labour History* (London, 1978), introduction; John Higginson, "African Mine Workers at the Union Minière du Haut Katanga", American Historical Association (Dec. 1979).

going to take place in Africa and that most Africans had to remain members of rural communities, or as some whites came to dislike the consequences of the changes which *had* taken place. The African collaborators, playing their role within one or other of the introduced European traditions, then came to seem less admirable than "real" Africans, still presumed to be inhabiting their own, appropriate universe of tradition.

The trouble with this approach was that it totally misunderstood the realities of pre-colonial Africa. These societies had certainly valued custom and continuity but custom was loosely defined and infinitely flexible. Custom helped to maintain a sense of identity but it also allowed for an adaptation so spontaneous and natural that it was often unperceived. Moreover, there rarely existed in fact the closed corporate consensual system which came to be accepted as characteristic of "traditional" Africa. Almost all recent studies of nineteenth-century pre-colonial Africa have emphasized that far from there being a single "tribal" identity, most Africans moved in and out of multiple identities, defining themselves at one moment as subject to this chief, at another moment as a member of that cult, at another moment as part of this clan, and at yet another moment as an initiate in that professional guild. These overlapping networks of association and exchange extended over wide areas. Thus the boundaries of the "tribal" polity and the hierarchies of authority within them did *not* define conceptual horizons of Africans. As Wim van Binsbergen remarks, in criticizing Africanist historians for their acceptance of something called "Chewa identity" as a useful organizing concept for the past:

Modern Central Africa tribes are not so much survivals from a pre-colonial past but rather largely colonial creations by colonial

officers and African intellectuals . . . Historians fail to qualify the alleged Chewa homogeneity against the historical evidence of incessant assimilation and dissociation of peripheral groups . . . They do not differentiate between a seniority system of rulers imposed by the colonial freezing of political dynamics and the pre-colonial competitive, shifting, fluid imbalance of power and influence.[15]

Similarly, nineteenth-century Africa was *not* characterized by lack of internal social and economic competition, by the unchallenged authority of the elders, by an acceptance of custom which gave every person – young and old, male and female – a place in society which was defined and protected. Competition, movement, fluidity were as much features of small-scale communities as they were of larger groupings. Thus Marcia Wright has shown, in a stimulating account of the realities of late nineteenth-century society in the Lake Tanganyika corridor, that economic and political competition overrode the "customary securities" offered to women by marriage or extended kinship relations. Women constantly found themselves being shaken out of the niches in which they had sought security, and constantly tried to find new niches for themselves. Later on, of course, and in the twentieth century, the dogmas of customary security and immutably fixed relationships grew up in these same societies, which came to have an appearance of *ujamaa* style solidarity; the nineteenth-century time of "rapid change", in which "formal structural factors" became relatively less important than "personal resilience and powers of decision," gave way to stablization. As Marcia Wright remarks:

the terms of the reconstruction were dictated by the colonial authorities in the years after 1895, when pacification came to mean immo-

[15]   Review of S.J. Ntara, *History of the Chewa*, ed. Harry Langworthy, by W.M.J. Van Binsbergen, *African Social Research* (June 1976), pp. 73–5.

bilization of populations, re-inforcement of ethnicity and greater rigidity of social definition.[16]

Hence "custom" in the Tanganyika corridor was much more of an invention than it was a restoration. In other places, where the competitive dynamic of the nineteenth century had given many opportunities for young men to establish independent bases of economic, social and political influence, colonialism saw an establishment of control by elders of land allocation, marriage transactions and political office. Small-scale gerontocracies were a defining feature of the twentieth rather than of the nineteenth century.

Some part of these twentieth-century processes of "immobilization of populations, re-inforcement of ethnicity and greater rigidity of social definition"were the necessary and unplanned consequences of colonial economic and political change – of the break up of internal patterns of trade and communication, the defining of territorial boundaries, the alienation of land, the establishment of Reserves. But some part of them were the result of a conscious determination on the part of the colonial authorities to "re-establish" order and security and a sense of community by means of defining and enforcing "tradition". Administrators who had begun by proclaiming their support for exploited commoners against rapacious chiefs ended by backing "traditional" chiefly authority in the interests of social control.[17] Missionaires who had begun by taking converts right out of their societies so as to transform their consciousness in "Christian villages" ended by proclaiming the virtues of "traditional" small-scale community. Everyone sought to tidy up and make more comprehensible the infinitely complex situation which they held to be a result of the "untraditional" chaos of the nineteenth century. People were to be "returned" to their tribal identities; ethnicity was to be "restored" as the basis of association and organization.[18] The new rigidities, immobilizations and ethnic identifications, while serving very immediate European interests, could nevertheless be seen by the whites as fully "traditional" and hence as legitimated. The most far-reaching inventions of tradition in colonial Africa took place when the Europeans believed themselves to be respecting age-old African custom. What were called customary law, customary land-rights, customary political structure and so on, were in fact *all* invented by colonial codification.

There is a growing anthropological and historical literature on these processes which it is not possible to summarize here. But a few striking statements will give an indication of the argument. Thus John Iliffe describes the "creation of tribes" in colonial Tanganyika:

> The notion of the tribe lay at the heart of indirect rule in Tanganyika. Refining the racial thinking common in German times, administrators believed that every African belonged to a tribe, just as every European belonged to a nation. The idea doubtless owed much to the Old Testament, to Tacitus and Caesar, to academic distinctions between tribal societies based on status and modern societies based on contract, and to the post-war anthropologists who preferred "tribal" to the more pejorative word "savage." Tribes were seen as cultural units "possessing a common language, a single social system, and an established common law." Their political and social systems rested on kinship. Tribal membership was hereditary. Different tribes were related genealogically . . . As unusually well-informed officials knew, this stereotype bore little relation to Tanganyika's kaleidoscopic

16. Marcia Wright, "Women in Peril," *African Social Research* (Dec. 1975), p. 803.
17. Henry Meebelo, *Reaction to Colonialism* (Manchester, 1971).
18. Terence Ranger, "European Attitudes and African Realities: The Rise and Fall of the Matola Chiefs of South-East Tanzania," *Journal of African History*, xx, no. 1 (1979), pp. 69–82.

history, but it was the shifting sand on which Cameron and his disciples erected indirect rule by "taking the *tribal* unit." They had the power and they created the political geography.[19]

Elizabeth Colson describes the evolution of "customary land law" in much the same way:

> The newly created system was described as resting on tradition and presumably derived its legitimacy from immemorial custom. The degree to which it was a reflection of the contemporary situation and the joint creation of colonial officials and African leaders . . . was unlikely to be recognized.

The point is not merely that so-called custom in fact concealed new balances of power and wealth, since this was precisely what custom in the past had always been able to do, but that these particular constructs of customary law became codified and rigid and unable so readily to reflect change in the future. Colson remarks that

> colonial officers expected the courts to enforce long-established custom rather than current opinion. Common stereotypes about African customary law thus came to be used by colonial officials in assessing the legality of current decisions, and so came to be incorporated in "customary" systems of tenure.[20]

Similarly, Wyatt MacGaffey has shown how the Bakongo peoples moved from a pre-colonial situation of "processes of dispersal and assimilation;" of "the shunting of subordinate populations of slaves and pawns;" of "a confusion of debts, assets, scandals and grievances," into a colonial situation of much more precise and static definition of community and of land rights.

In the evolution of tradition, the touchstone of merit was very often the presiding judge's concept of customary society, derived ultimately from . . . a lingering European image of the African kingdom of Prester John . . . Court records contain evidence of the evolution for forensic purposes away from the magical in the direction of the evidential and refutable . . . Those whose traditions lost a case came back a year or two later with better traditions.

Once again, my point is not so much that "traditions" changed to accommodate new circumstances but that at a certain point they had to stop changing; once the "traditions" relating to community identity and land right were written down in court records and exposed to the criteria of the invented customary model, a new and unchanging body of tradition had been created.

> Eventually there resulted a synthesis of the new and the old, which is now called "custom". The main features of customary society, responding to the conditions that developed between 1908 and 1921, assumed their present form in the 1920s.[21]

Around the same time Europeans began to be more interested in and sympathetic towards the "irrational" and ritualistic aspects of "tradition". In 1917 an Anglican mission theologian suggested that for the first time missionaries in the field should "collect information with regard to the religious ideas of the black man", so that their relationship to traditional society could be understood. "In the twentieth century we are no longer contented to cut the knot, as the nineteenth century did, and say: Science has put an end to these superstitions."[22] After the first world war, Anglicans

---

[19]   John Iliffe, *A Modern History of Tanganyika*, pp. 323–4.

[20]   Elizabeth Colson, "The Impact of the Colonial Period on the Definition of Land Rights," in Victor Turner (ed.), *Colonialism in Africa* (Cambridge, 1971), iii. pp. 221–51.

[21]   Wyatt MacGaffey, *Custom and Government in the Lower Congo* (California, 1970), pp. 207–8.

[22]   "The Study of African Religion," *Central Africa*, xxxv, no. 419 (Nov. 1917), p. 261.

in East Africa, faced with the need to re-construct rural society after the ravages of the fighting and the subsequent impact of the depression, began to make anthropological analyses of those aspects of "traditional" ritual which had contributed towards social stability. Out of such inquiry came the well-known policy of missionary "adaptation," which produced its most developed example in the Christianized initiation ceremonies of the Masasi diocese in south-eastern Tanganyika.[23] More generally, there emerged from this kind of thought and practice – with its emphasis upon rituals of continuity and stability – a concept of immemorial "African Traditional Religion" which did less than justice to the variety and vitality of pre-colonial African religious forms.

African Manipulation of Invented Custom

All this could not have been achieved, of course, without a good deal of African partici-pation. As John Iliffe writes:

> The British wrongly believed that Tanganyikans belonged to tribes; Tanganyikans created tribes to function within the colonial framework . . . [The] new political geography . . . would have been transient had it not co-incided with similar trends among Africans. They too had to live amidst bewildering social complexity, which they ordered in kinship terms and buttressed with invented history. Moreover, Africans wanted effective units of action just as officials wanted effective units of govern-ment . . . Europeans believed Africans belonged to tribes; Africans built tribes to belong to.[24]

We have already seen in the case of the Tumbuka paramountcy how African rulers and mission-educated "modernizers" could combine in an attempt to manipulate the symbols of monarchy. Iliffe shows how similar alliances helped to build up the ideas and structures of "tribal" tradition.

> During the twenty years after 1925 Tanganyika experienced a vast social reorga-nization in which Europeans and Africans combined to create a new political order based on mythical history . . . Analysing the system [of indirect rule] one officer concluded that its main supporters were the progressive chiefs . . . It is clear that they were the key figures in indirect rule. Its chief virtue was indeed to release their energies . . . The native administrations employed many members of the local elite . . . Even educated men without native administration posts generally acknowledged hereditary authority . . . In return many chiefs welcomed educated guidance.

Iliffe describes progressive chiefs and mission-educated Africans combining in a programme of "progressive traditionalism."

> Just as later nationalists sought to create a national culture, so those who built modern tribes emphasized tribal culture. In each case educated men took the lead . . . The problem was to synthesize, to "pick out what is best from (European culture) and dilute it with what we hold". In doing so, educated men naturally reformulated the past, so that their syntheses were actually new creations.[25]

One area in which African intellectuals inter-acted with "adaptation" missionary theory was in the invention of "Traditional Religion."

[23]   Terence Ranger, "Missionary Adaptation and African Religious Institutions," in Terence Ranger and Isaria Kimambo (eds.), *The Historical Study of African Religion* (London, 1972), pp. 221–51.
[24]   Iliffe, *op. cit.*, p. 324.
[25]   *Ibid.*, pp. 327–9, 334.

It was not until missionaries studied African religions carefully during the 1920s that most Africans dared to consider their attitudes publicly. Michel Kikurwe, a Zigua teacher and cultural tribalist, envisaged a golden age of traditional African society . . . Samuel Sehoza pioneered the idea that indigenous religious beliefs had prefigured Christianity.

Like the missionaries these men emphasized the function of religion in stablilizing society.

> In each district [wrote Kikurwe] men and women were busy to help one another, they taught their children the same laws and traditions. Every Chief tried as much as he could to help and please his people, and likewise his people did the same in turn, they all knew what was lawful and unlawful, and they knew that there was a powerful God in heaven.[26]

It is easy enough to see the personal advantages which these inventors of tradition stood to gain. The successful teacher or minister who stood at the right hand of a paramount was a man of very real power. The African clergy who constructed the model of "Traditional Religion" as the inspiring ideology of stable pre-colonial communities were making a claim to do the same for modern African societies by means of "adapted" Christianity.[27] Yet Iliffe concludes that

> it would be wrong to be cynical. The effort to create a Nyakyusa tribe was as honest and constructive as the essentially similar effort forty years later to create a Tanganyikan nation. Both were attempts to build societies in which men could live well in the modern world.[28]

But there was still an ambiguity in invented African tradition. However much it may have been used by the "progressive traditionalists" to inaugurate new ideas and institutions – like compulsory education under the Tumbuka paramountcy – codified tradition inevitably hardened in a way that advantaged the vested interests in possession at the time of its codification. Codified and reified custom was manipulated by such vested interests as a means of asserting or increasing control. This happened in four particular situations; though it was not restricted to them.

Elders tended to appeal to "tradition" in order to defend their dominance of the rural means of production against challenge by the young. Men tended to appeal to "tradition" in order to ensure that the increasing role which women played in production in the rural areas did not result in any diminution of male control over women as economic assets. Paramount chiefs and ruling aristocracies in polities which included numbers of ethnic and social groupings appealed to "tradition" in order to maintain or extend their control over their subjects. Indigenous populations appealed to "tradition" in order to ensure that the migrants who settled amongst them did not achieve political or economic rights.

The Use of "Tradition" by Elders Against Youth

The colonial reification of rural custom produced a situation very much at variance with the pre-colonial situation. The pre-colonial movement of men and ideas was replaced by the colonial custom-bounded, microcosmic local society. It was important for the colonial authorities to limit regional interaction and thus to prevent a widening of focus on the part of Africans. For this reason they were prepared to back collaborators at the local level and to endorse their dominance. But at the

---

[26] *Ibid.*, pp. 335–6.
[27] Ranger, "Missionary Adaptation and African Religious Institutions."
[28] Iliffe, *op. cit.*, pp. 324–5.

same time the colonial powers wanted to extract labour from these rural societies, so that young men were being drawn to places of employment very much more distant than the range of journeying in the pre-colonial past. These young men were expected to be at one and the same time workers in a distant urban economy and acceptant citizens in the tightly defined micro-cosmic society.

This situation created many tensions. Returning migrants came back into a society tightly controlled by the elders; the elders, in turn, were alarmed at the new skills and funds possessed by the migrants. The elders stressed their customary, prescriptive rights which gave them control of land and women, and hence of patronage. MacGaffey describes the colonial Bakongo village in these terms:

> A man remains a cadet until he is about forty, perhaps longer . . . He is at the beck and call of his elders, whose tone towards him is often peremptory. Young men speak of their elders as jealous and fault-finding. The status of young men is that of the client . . . The control exercised over their dependants by the elders is a function of their managerial monopoly in routine public affairs.

This managerial monopoly is largely a function of the elders' control of "traditional" knowledge, on which claims to land and resources are based. MacGaffey records "the objection of elders" when "bright young men busily took notes" at a land hearing case, and thus threatened to break the elders monopoly.[29]

The response of young men to this manipulation of "tradition" could take one of two forms. The key object was to outflank the elders and their sphere of local, but colonially invented, tradition. This could be done by adopting one or other of the European neo-

traditions. Thus returning migrants often established themselves as catechists – whether recognized by the missions or not – and set up their own villages on new principles of organization, as it will be remembered was the case with the uniformed congregations of western Kenya. This was easier to do, however, in the earlier colonial period before both European church and European state began to insist on a proper subordination to custom. In MacGaffey's village, the young men, deprived of a real escape, took refuge in a fantasy one.

> For those who are young in years a degree of compensation is provided by the Dikembe, a social club catering to the unmarried men . . . Dikembe culture, an interesting caricature of the serious magico-religious beliefs and principles of the older generation which it defies, contains the seeds of an anti-society . . . The doors of the bachelor huts bear such inscriptions as "Palais d'Amour" in Gothic lettering . . . The culture of the Dikembe is that of *billisme,* whose heroes are the stars of romantic French and American movies [and] takes its name from Buffalo Bill, "sheriff due quartier Santa Fe, metro d'amour."[30]

These light-hearted absurdities conceal a serious attempt to discredit "custom," endorsed as it is by the whites, through the subversive effects of European fantasy.

However, another path had also been open to the young in the colonial period and before the rise of the nationalist parties. This had been to outflank the reified "custom" of the elders by appeals to more dynamic and transformative aspects of the traditional. Recent commentators have increasingly seen the very widespread witchcraft eradication movements of the colonial period, with their promise of a society freed from evil, in this sort of way. MacGaffey describes how in his Bakongo village the management of witchcraft accusation

---

[29]   MacGaffey, *op. cit.*, pp. 208, 222–3.
[30]   *Ibid.*, pp. 223–4.

by the elders caused great discontent, and led to the arrival of a "prophet" who undertook to eliminate witchcraft, an achievement which would deprive the elders of a potent form of social control. The result was "the temporary paralysis of the elders." Roy Willis has shown how in rural south-western Tanganyika in the 1950s young men tried to break the control exercised by elders over land and local "routine public affairs", by making use of a series of witchcraft eradication movements, which out-flanked invented custom by an appeal to the pre-social Golden Age.[31]

Of the many other analyses which support the argument, I will content myself with citing a particularly cogent, and as yet unpublished, account of the well-known Watch Tower sectarian movement in southern and central Africa. Sholto Cross concludes:

> The three mining belts of settler Africa . . . provide the central focus of the movement and the migrant labourer was the main bearer . . . The migrant system which existed in these territories . . . prolonged the period in which the Africans could be regarded as bound by their tribal culture . . . yet at the same time policies designed to promote labour mobility were instituted which undermined the economic basis of this tribal culture . . . The rate of change in the indus-trial areas far outstripped that in the rural hinterlands, yet the migrant labourers continued to move between the two worlds of town and country . . . The proliferation of Watch Tower villages [was caused by] the series of restraints placed upon the returning migrant. Customary authorities were jealous of the new men, whose way of life empha-sized urban values . . . The prevalence of women and youth in the rural Watch Tower suggests that economic cleavages were rein-forced by other forms of differentiation . . .

The forward looking ideas of the hoped-for liberation (promised) by millenial Watch Tower were such that customary authority itself became a major object of attack.[32]

The Use of "Tradition" by Men Against Women

Denise Paulme's *Women of Tropical Africa*, though concerned to refute a stereotyped European image of oppressed African woman-hood, nevertheless brought out very clearly two things. The first was the practical break-down under colonialism of many customary institutions regulating the relations between the sexes, a breakdown almost always dis-advantagious economically to women. The second was the constant appeal by men to "tradition." Anne Laurentin asserted in her chapter in the collection that

> remembrance of the good old days is accom-panied by nostalgic regret on the part of older men . . . Among young and old alike there is a profoundly anti-feminist spirit which springs from a feeling of impotence upon realizing that women will refuse to return to the state of dependence they knew a century ago. The old people lay the blame for the fall in the birthrate on women.[33]

To my mind Laurentin is confusing complaints about increasing female indepen-dence with its reality. Elders reasserted their control over local affairs by their complaints of the breach of tradition by the young; men reasserted their dominance over a changing economic and social system by their complaints of the breach of tradition by women.

---

[31] Roy Willis, "Kamcape: An Anti-Sorcery Movement in South-West Tanzania," *Africa*, xxxi, no. 1 (1968).

[32] Sholto Cross, "The Watch Tower Movement in South Central Africa, 1908–1945" (Univ. of Oxford doctoral thesis, 1973), pp. 431–8.

[33] Anne Laurentin, "Nzakara Women," in Denise Paulme (ed.)., *Women of Tropical Africa* (California, 1963), pp. 431–8.

A more recent collection of essays on African women makes the point clearly. As Caroline Ifeka-Moller reminds us, colonial records on African "tradition", on which the new invented custom was based, were exclusively derived from male informants, so that "indigenous female belief" remained unrecorded. Thus "men's dominance in society, that is their control over religious beliefs and political organization" was expressed even more clearly in colonial invented custom than it had ever been before. Neither in the works of indirect rule ethnographers nor of adaptation missiologists – nor of mission-educated African intellectuals – was much attention paid to the traditions of women.[34] Moreover, African men were quite prepared to appeal to the colonial authority to enforce "custom" upon women once it had been defined. In southern Rhodesia, and elsewhere in the zone of industrial labour migration, officials imposed punishments for adultery and enforced paternal control over marriage in response to constant complaints by male "traditionalists".[35] Meanwhile, in the absence of male migrants, women were playing a larger and larger part in rural production.

Once again, women had two possible means of asserting themselves against male-dominated custom. They might turn to missionary Christianity and its notions of female rights and duties, or they might seek to use the counter-propositions available within African culture. Sometimes women sought to develop rites of female initiation, which had in the past constituted a balance to male ritual influence in the microcosm. Sometimes they sought to draw on twentieth-century forms of regional cultic association and on macrocosmic prophet movements in order to challenge the constraints of the bounded society of invented custom.

One or two recent studies have sought to explore these female initiatives. Richard Stuart, in an unpublished paper, shows how Chewa women made use of a missionary import, the Mothers' Union:

> An equilibrium between the equally important sphere of women and public sphere of men had developed among the Chewa of east central Africa by the end of the nineteenth century. [This] was disrupted by the impact of African and European invasions, and the effects of Christianity, Commerce and Civilization. These undermined the historic bases of Chewa society, and provided men with access to new forms of wealth and power denied to women. During the colonial period, neo-traditionalists attempted to maintain this disequilibrium between men and women, and to restructure society on a paternalistic and individualistic basis. One attempt to counter this process, to enable women to make the transformation from small to large scale societies on their own terms, was made by the Anglican women's organization, the Mothers' Union or *Mpingo wa Amai*. This met with an immediate response when it was introduced in the early 1930s, enabling Chewa women to redefine historic roles and institutions within the changed circumstances and to respond to novel problems raised. It achieved some success in maintaining the status of women.[36]

Sherilyn Young's "Fertility and Famine" is a study of the alternative strategy. In summary version her account of her southern Mozambique case runs:

> Colonial forced labour in the twentieth century supplemented migration in draining the labour power of the Tsonga and Chopi.

---

[34] Caroline Ifeka–Moller, "Female Militancy and Colonial Revolt", in S. Ardener (ed.), *Perceiving Women* (London, 1975).
[35] Eileen Byrne, "African Marriage in Southern Rhodesia, 1890–1940" (Univ. of Manchester B.A. research thesis, 1979).
[36] Richard Stuart, "Mpingo wa Amai – the Mothers' Union in Nyasaland" (unpublished MS.).

Large settler plantations were carved out of their existing agricultural lands. A run of famines and ecological disasters between 1908 and 1922 ensured heavy dependence on the export of labour. The agricultural revival of the 1920s was predominantly that of a female peasantry, producing the bulk of Southern Mozambique's cashews and groundnuts . . . When [in] the Second World War a system of forced labour was resorted to, women had to produce cash crops, especially cotton, for four days a week, under male supervisors. Adaptation to such changes can be seen in the growth of spirit possession cults among the people, dominated by women. Southern Mozambique society survives with a striking distinction between a local female peasantry and an emigrant male semi-proletariat.[37]

Conclusion

African politicians, cultural nationalists and, indeed, historians are left with two ambiguous legacies from the colonial invention of traditions. One is the body of invented traditions imported from Europe which in some parts of Africa still exercises an influence on ruling class culture which it has largely lost in Europe itself. In his *Prison Diary* Ngugi wa Thiong'o (See Chapter 36, this volume) writes savagely of the contemporary Kenyan élite:

> The members of a comprador bourgeoisie of a former settler colony count themselves lucky. They don't have to travel and reside abroad to know and copy the culture of the imperialist bourgeoisie: have they not learnt it all from the colonial settler representatives of metropolitan culture? Nurtured in the womb of the old colonial system, they have matured to their full compradorial heights, looking to the local Europeans as the alpha

and omega of gentlemanly refinement and lady-like elegance. With racial barriers to class mobility thrown open, the deportment of a European gentleman – rosebuds and pins in coat lapels, spotless white kerchiefs in breast pockets, tail-coats, top-hats and gold-chained pocket watches – is no longer in the realm of dreams and wishes . . . The most popular columns in the old settler papers . . . were the social pages . . . Well, the columns are now back in the glossy bourgeois monthlies . . . The settler played golf and polo, went to horse-races or on the royal hunt in red-coats and riding-breeches . . . The black pupils now do the same, only with greater zeal: golf and horses have become "national" institutions.[38]

Other new states, less open to Ngugi's charges, express their national sovereignty with the national anthems, flags and rallies which Eric Hobsbawm describes for nineteenth-century Europe. Representing as they do new multi-ethnic territorial states the African nations are much less engaged in the invention of past "national cultures" than were the Scottish or Welsh Romantics.

The second ambiguous legacy is that of "traditional" African culture; the whole body of reified "tradition" invented by colonial administrators, missionaries, "progressive traditionalists," elders and anthropologists. Those like Ngugi who repudiate bourgeois élite culture face the ironic danger of embracing another set of colonial inventions instead. Ngugi himself solves the difficulty by embracing the tradition of Kenyan popular resistance to colonialism. As this chapter suggests, young men, women, immigrants – the exploited groups with whom Ngugi has sympathy – *have* sometimes been able to tap the continued vitality of the mingled continuity and innovation which resides within indigenous cultures as they have continued to

---

[37]   Sherilyn Young, "Fertility and Famine: Women's Agricultural History in Southern Mozambique," in Palmer and Parsons (eds.), *Roots of Rural Poverty*.
[38]   Ngugi wa Thiong'o, *Detained: A Writer's Prison Diary* (London, 1981), pp. 58–9.

develop underneath the rigidities of codified colonial custom.

As for historians, they have at least a double task. They have to free themselves from the illusion that the African custom recorded by officials or by many anthropologists is any sort of guide to the African past. But they also need to appreciate how much invented traditions of all kinds have to do with the history of Africa in the twentieth century and strive to produce better founded accounts of them than this preliminary sketch.

Terence Ranger has returned to the issues raised in this chapter in "The Invention of Tradition Revisited: The Case of Colonial Africa," in Terence Ranger and Olufemi Vaughan, eds., *Legitimacy and the State in Twentieth-Century Africa*, St Antony's/ Macmillan, 1993, pp. 62–111.

36

DETAINED: A WRITER'S PRISON DIARY

NGUGI WA THIONG'O

A colonial affair . . . the phrase keeps on intruding into the literary flow of my mind and pen . . . a colonial affair in an independent Kenya . . . It is as if the phrase has followed me inside Kamĩtĩ Prison to mock at me.

In 1967, just before returning home from a three-year stay in England, I had signed a contract with William Heinemann to write a book focusing on the social life of European settlers in Kenya. The literary agent who negotiated the contract – he was also the originator of the idea – put it this way: "Theirs is a world which has forever vanished, but for that very reason, many readers will find an account of it still interesting."

The title? *A Colonial Affair!*

I had agreed to do the book because I strongly held that the settlers were part of the history of Kenya: the seventy years of this destructive alien presence could not be ignored by Kenyans.

Heaven knows, as they would say, that I tried hard to come to terms with the task. I dug up old newspapers and settlers' memoirs to get an authentic feeling of the times as the settlers lived it. A writer must be honest. But in the end I was unable to write the book. I could not quite find the right tone. The difficulty lay in more than my uncertainty as to whether or not "their world" had really vanished. An account of their social life would have to include a section on culture, and I was by then

convinced that a Draculan idle class could never produce a culture.

For the settlers in Kenya were really parasites in paradise. Kenya, for them, was a huge winter home for aristocrats, which of course meant big game hunting and living it up on the backs of a million field and domestic slaves, the *Watu* as they called them. Coming ashore in Mombasa, as was clearly shown by the photographic evidence in the 1939 edition of Lord Cranworth's book, *Kenya Chronicles*, was literally on the backs of Kenyan workers. "No one coming into a new country," he writes, "could desire a more attractive welcome. We were rowed ashore in a small boat and came to land on the shoulders of sturdy Swahili natives." This was in 1906. By 1956, Sir Evelyn Baring, the governor, could still get himself photographed being carried, like a big baby, in the arms of a Kenyan worker. Thus by setting foot on Kenyan soil at Mombasa, every European was instantly transformed into a blue-blooded aristocrat. An attractive welcome: before him, stretching beyond the ken of his eyes, lay a vast valley garden of endless physical leisure and pleasure that he must have once read about in the *Arabian Nights* stories. The dream in fairy tales was now his in practice. No work, no winter, no physical or mental exertion. Here he would set up his own fiefdom. Life in these fiefdoms is well captured in Gerald Henley's novels

Consul at Sunset and *Drinkers of Darkness*. Whoring, hunting, drinking, why worry? Work on the land was carried out by gangs of African "boys." Both *Consul at Sunset* and *Drinkers of Darkness* are fiction. Observed evidence comes from the diaries of a traveller. In her 1929–30 diaries, now brought out together under the title *East African Journey*, Margery Perham described the same life in minute detail:

> We drove out past the last scattered houses of suburban Nairobi, houses very much like their opposite numbers in England. But here ordinary people can live in sunlight; get their golf and their tennis more easily and cheaply than at home; keep three or four black servants; revel in a social freedom that often turns, by all accounts, into licence, and have the intoxicating sense of belonging to a small ruling aristocracy . . . certainly, on the surface, life is very charming in Nairobi, and very sociable with unlimited entertaining; all the shooting, games and bridge anyone could want. And in many houses a table loaded with drinks, upon which you can begin at any hour from 10.00am onwards, and with real concentration from 6.00pm.

And, so, beyond drinking whisky and whoring each other's wives and natives (what Margery Perham prudishly calls social freedom turned "by all accounts, into licence") and gunning natives for pleasure in this vast happy valley – oh, yes, are you married or do you live in Kenya? – the settlers produced little. No art, no literature, no culture, just the making of a little dominion marred only by niggers too many to exterminate, the way they did in New Zealand, and threatened by upstart "Gĩkuyu agitators."

The highest they reached in creative literature was perhaps Elspeth Huxley and she is really a scribbler of tourist guides and anaemic settler polemics blown up to the size of books. The most creative things about her writing are her titles – *The Flame Trees of Thika* and *The Mottled Lizard*, for instance – because in them she lets herself be inspired by native life and landscape. Beyond the title and the glossy covers, there is only emptiness, and emptiness as a defence of oppression has never made a great subject for literature.

Their theatre, professional and amateur, never went beyond crude imitation and desperate attempts to keep up with the West End or Broadway. This theatre never inspired a single original script or actor or critic.

In science, they could of course display Leakey. But Leakey's speciality was in digging up, dating and classifying old skulls. Like George Eliot's Casaubon, he was happier living with the dead. To the Leakeys, it often seems that the archaeological ancestors of Africans were more lovable and noble than the current ones – an apparent case of regressive evolution. Colonel Leakey, and even Lewis Leakey, hated Africans and proposed ways of killing off nationalism, while praising skulls of dead Africans as precursors of humanity. The evidence is there in black and white: L.S.B. Leakey is the author of two anti-Mau Mau books – *Mau Mau and the Kikuyu* and *Defeating Mau Mau.*

In art, their highest achievement was the mural paintings on the walls of the Lord Delamere bar in the Norfolk Hotel, Nairobi.* The murals stand to this day and they still attract hordes of tourists who come to enjoy racist aesthetics in art. But the murals in their artistic mediocrity possess a revealing historical realism.

On one wall are depicted scenes drawn from the English countryside: fourteen different postures for the proper deportment of an English gentleman; fox-hunting with gentlemen and ladies on horseback surrounded on

---

* On 31 December 1980 the Norfolk Hotel was bombed, reportedly by revolutionaries. But the Lord Delamere bar remained intact.

all sides by well-fed hounds panting and wagging tails in anticipation of the kill to come; and of course the different pubs, from the White Hart to the Royal Oak, waiting to quench the thirst of the ladies and gentlemen after their blood sports. Kenya is England away from England, with this difference: Kenya is an England of endless summer tempered by an eternal spring of sprouting green life.

On another wall are two murals depicting aspects of settler life in that Kenya. One shows the Norfolk – the House of Lords as it was then known – in 1904. Here again are English ladies and gentlemen – some on horseback, others sitting or standing on the verandah – but all drinking hard liquor served them by an African waiter wearing the servant's uniform of white *kanzu*, red fez, and a red band over his shoulder and front. In the foreground is an ox-wagon with two Africans: one, the driver, lashing at the dumb oxen; and the other, the pilot, pulling them along the right paths. The ribs of the "pushing boy" and the "pulling boy" are protruding, in contrast to the fully fleshed oxen and members of "the House of Lords". But the most prominent feature in this mural is "a rickshaw boy" with grinning teeth holding up this human-powered carriage for a finely dressed English lady to enter. Oxen-powered wagons for English survival goods; African powered carriages for English lords and ladies. Eleanor Cole, in her 1975 random recollections of pioneer settler life in Kenya, writes:

> Transport in Nairobi in those days was by rickshaw, one man in front between the shafts and one behind, either pushing or acting as a brake. People had their private rickshaws and put their rickshaw men in uniform. There were also public ones for hire.

The other mural depicts the same type of royal crowd at Nairobi railway station. At the forefront, is a well-fed dog wagging its tail before its lord and master. But amidst the different groups chatting or walking, stands a lone bull-necked, bull-faced settler in riding breeches with a hat covering bushy eyebrows and a grey moustache. He could have been a Colonel Grogan or a Lord Delamere or any other settler. The most representative feature about him is the *sjambok* he is firmly holding in his hands.

The rickshaw. The dog. The *sjambok*. The ubiquitous underfed, wide-eyed, uniformed native slave.

In March 1970, Colonel Grogan and four associates flogged three "rickshaw boys" outside a Nairobi court-house. The "boys" were later taken to hospital with lacerated backs and faces. Their crime? They had had the intention of alarming two white ladies by raising the rickshaw shafts an inch too high! The rhetoric of the magistrate when later Grogan, Bowkes, Gray, Fichat, and Low were summoned before him for being members of an unlawful assembly, left not the slightest doubt about the sadistic brutality of the deeds of these sons of English nobility and graduates of Cambridge:

> From the first to the last it appears to me that out of all the people present assisting at the flogging of these men, there was no one of that number who ever took the trouble to satisfy himself as to whether these natives had ever done anything deserving of punishment at all. There was no trial of any sort nor any form or pretence of trial. These boys were neither asked whether they had any defence or explanation to give, nor does it appear that they ever had any opportunity of making one. Grogan, who ordered the flogging, has himself stated that no plea or defence which they might have made would have diverted him from his purpose. This is a very unpleasant feature in the case and I consider it about as bad as it can be. Yet, in my opinion, it is further aggravated by the fact that the place selected for this unlawful act was directly in front of a courthouse.

Sweet rhetoric versus bitter reality: the culprits, all found guilty, were given prison terms ranging from seven to thirty days. Prison? Their own houses where they were free to receive and entertain guests! Elsewhere, in the plantations and estates, the "bwana" would simply have them shot and buried them, or fed them to his dogs.

In 1960, Peter Harold Poole shot and killed Kamame Musunge for throwing stones at Poole's dogs in self-defence. To the settlers, dogs ranked infinitely higher than Kenyans; and Kenyans were either children (to be paternalisticly loved but not appreciated, like dogs) or mindless scoundrels (to be whipped or killed). In his autobiography, *Words*, Sartre has made the apt comment that "when you love children and dogs too much, you love them instead of adults." The settlers' real love was for dogs and puppies. Thus, to hit an attacking dog was a worse crime than killing a Kenyan. And when Poole was sentenced to death, the whole colonial *Herrenvolk* cried in unison against this "miscarriage of justice." Peter Harold Poole had done what had been the daily norm since 1895.

In 1918, for instance, two British peers flogged a Kenyan to death and later burnt his body. His crime? He was suspected of having an intention to steal property. The two murderers were found guilty of a "simple hurt" and were fined two-thousand shillings each. The governor later appointed one of them a member of a district committee to dispense justice among the 'natives'. The gory details are there in Macgregor Ross's book *Kenya From Within*. Justice in a *sjambok*!

I thought about this in my cell at Kamĩtĩ prison and suddenly realized I had been wrong about the British settlers. I should have written that book. For the colonial system *did* produce a culture.

But it was the culture of legalized brutality, a ruling-class culture of fear, the culture of an oppressing minority desperately trying to impose total silence on a restive oppressed majority. This culture was sanctified in the colonial administration of P.C., D.C., DO., Chiefs, right down to the askari. At Kamĩtĩ, we called it the Mbwa Kali culture.

Culture of silence and fear: the diaries and memoirs of the leading intellectual lights of the old colonial system contain full literary celebration of this settler culture. We need go no further than Colonel Meinertzhagen's *Kenya Diaries* and Baroness Blixen's *Out of Africa*.

Meinertzhagen was a commanding officer of the British forces of occupation. But he is far better known in history as the assassin of Koitalel, the otherwise unconquerable military and political leader of the Nandi people. This is what happened. Under Koitalel's inspiring leadership, the Nandi people had waged a ten-year armed struggle against the foreign army of occupation, humiliating British officers, one after the other. Enter Meinertzhagen, a gentleman. Unable to defeat the Nandi guerrilla army, the colonel invited Koitalel to a peace parley on some "neutral" ground. But only on one condition. Both men would come unarmed. Having been led to believe that the British wanted to discuss surrender terms and guarantees of safe retreat from Nandi country, Koitalel accepted. Put innocence against brutality and innocence will lose. There could be no finer illustration of this than the encounter between Koitalel and Meinertzhagen. Koitalel stretched an empty hand in greeting. Meinertzhagen stretched out a hidden gun and shot Koitalel in cold blood. The incident is recorded in *Kenya Diaries* as an act of British heroism!

Similar deeds of British colonial heroism are recorded in the same diaries.

The scene now shifts to Gĩkũyũ country, where people once again fought with tremendous courage against the better armed foreign invaders. So fierce was the struggle that in 1902 Meinertzhagen was forced to make the grudging but prophetic admission that, even if they triumphed over the people, this would only be a temporary victory: the British could never hold the country for more than fifty years. In one of several battles in Mūrang'a, a British officer was captured by the national defence army in Mūrūka and was handed to the people for justice. They killed him. Months later, Meinertzhagen stole into Mūrūka on a market day, had the whole market surrounded, and ordered a massacre of every single soul – a cold-blooded vengeance against defiant husbands and sons. Thereafter he embarked on a campaign of pillage, plunder and more murder. Meinertzhagen wrote in his diary: "Every soul was either shot or bayonetted . . . we burned all huts and razed the banana plantations to the ground . . . Then I went home and wept for brother officer killed."

Baroness Blixen was the separated wife of the big game hunter-cum-settler Baron von Blixen. From him she got no children but incurable syphilis. As if in compensation for unfulfilled desires and longings, the baroness turned Kenya into a vast erotic dreamland in which her several white lovers appeared as young gods and her Kenyan servants as usable curs and other animals. It is all there in her two books, *Shadows on the Grass* and *Out of Africa*. In the latter, her most famous, she celebrates a hideous colonial aesthetic in an account she entitles Kitosch's story:

> Kitosch was a young native in the service of a young white settler of Molo. One Wednesday in June, the settler lent his brown mare to a friend, to ride to the station on. He sent Kitosch there to bring back the mare, and told him not to ride her, but to lead her. But Kitosch jumped on the mare, and rode her back, and on Saturday the settler, his master, was told of the offence by a man who had seen it. In punishment the settler, on Sunday afternoon, had Kitosch flogged, and afterwards tied up in his store, and here late on Sunday night Kitosch died.

The outcome of the trial in the High Court at Nakuru turned to rest solely on the intentions of the victim. It transpired by a hideous logic that Kitosch had actually wanted to die and he was therefore responsible for his death. In Anglo-Saxonland, it seems colonized natives have a fiendish desire for suicide that absolves white murderers:

> Kitosch had not much opportunity for expressing his intentions. He was locked up in the store, his message, therefore comes very simply, and in a single gesture. The night watch states that he cried all night. But it was not so, for at one o'clock he talked with toto, who was in the store with him, because the flogging had made him deaf. But at one o'clock he asked the toto to loosen his feet, and explained that in any case he could not run away. When the toto had done as he asked him, Kitosch said to him that he wanted to die. A little while after, he rocked himself from side to side, cried: "I am dead!" and died.

Medical science was even brought in to support the wish-to-die theory. This was supposed to be a psychological peculiarity of the African. He wants to die, and he dies. The irony is not Blixen's. She accepts the theory. What, of course, Kitosch said was, "Nataka kufa" which means: "I am about to die, or I am dying." But that is not the issue. It is the verdict and the conclusion. The settler was found guilty of "grievous hurt." And for a "grievous hurt" to a Kenyan, the foreign settler got two years in jail, probably on his own farm! It is not recorded how much more grievous hurt he committed later.

The fault is not Blixen's manner of telling the story – all the details are there – but her total acceptance of the hideous theory and her attempts to draw from it aesthetic conclusions meant to have universal relevance and validity:

> By this strong sense in him of what is right and decorous, the figure of Kitosch, with his firm will to die, although now removed from us by many years, stands out with a beauty of its own. In it is embodied the fugitiveness of wild things who are, in the hour of need, conscious of a refuge somewhere in existence; who go when they will; of whom we can never get hold.

The African is an animal: the settler is exoner-
ated. Not a single word of condemnation for
this practice of colonial justice. No evidence of
any discomfiture. And for this, generations of
western European critics from Hemingway to
John Updike have showered her with praises.
Some neo-colonial Africans too. But I err too
in saying the African was considered an
animal. In reality they loved the wild game but
Africans were worse, more threatening,
instinctless, unlovable, unredeemable sub-
animals merely useful for brute labour. In *Out
of Africa*, Karen Blixen says that her knowledge of wild game was useful in her later
contact with Africans!

What of course is disgusting is the attempt
by writers like Blixen to turn acts of cold-
blooded murder and torture of these "black
suppliers of brute labour" into deeds of heroic
grandeur. It makes words lose their meaning
or perhaps it is proof that the meaning of a
word depends on the user. Galbraith Cole
shot dead a Masai national in cold blood.
The subsequent trial was a pre-arranged
farce, rehearsed to the letter and gesture by all
three parties, prosecutor, judge and murderer
(all European of course), in such a way that on
the records the Kenyan murdered would
emerge guilty of unbearable armed provocation. But the settler was too arrogant to hide
his murderous intentions behind a glossy
mask of lies. As later reported by Karen
Blixen, this is how the farce reached a climax
of absurdity:

> The Judge said to Galbraith, "It's not, you
> know, that we don't understand that you
> shot only to stop the thieves." "No,"
> Galbraith said, "I shot to kill. I said that I
> would do so."
>
> "Think again, Mr Cole", said the judge.
> "We are convinced that you only shot to stop
> them."
>
> "No, by God," Galbraith said, "I shot to
> kill."

He was acquitted. But Blixen reported Cole's
admission as an act of unparalleled greatness.
In a book, *Silence will Speak*, the same literary
glorification of the settler culture of murder
and torture is shamelessly repeated in 1977 by
one Errol Trzebinksi.

Robert Ruark, in *Something of Value* and
Uhuru, was to outdo the Huxleys, the Blixens,
the Trzebinskis, in raising the reactionary
settler culture of violence to the level of
universality, and anybody upsetting it was
seen as Hades' harbinger of doom and everlasting darkness.

Meinertzhagen, the soldier-assassin turned
writer; Karen Blixen, the baroness of blighted
bloom turned writer; Robert Ruark, the big-
game hunter turned writer – theirs is a literary
reflection of that colonial culture of silence and
fear best articulated in a dispatch by an early
governor, Sir A. R. Hardinge, on 5 April 1897:

> Force and the prestige which rests on a belief
> in force, are the only way you can do
> anything with those people, but once beaten
> and disarmed they will serve you. Tempor-
> izing is no good . . . These people must learn
> submission by bullets – it's the only school;
> after that you may begin more modern and
> humane methods of education, and if you
> don't do it this year you will have to next, so
> why not get it over? . . . In Africa to have
> peace you must first teach obedience, and the
> only tutor who impresses the lesson properly
> is the sword.

Thus the above acts of animal brutality were
not cases of individual aberration but an integral part of colonial politics, philosophy and
culture. Reactionary violence to instil fear and
silence was the very essence of colonial settler
culture.

Now a comprador bourgeoisie is, by its very
economic base, a dependent class, a parasitic
class in the *kupe** sense. It is, in essence, a

---

*   *Kupe*, tick; *mnyapala*, overseer.

mnyapala class, a handsomely paid supervisor for the smooth operation of foreign economic interests. Its political inspiration and guidance come from outside the country. This economic and political dependency is clearly reflected in its imitative culture – excrescences of New York, Los Angeles and London. For this class, as Frantz Fanon once put it, has an extreme, incurable wish for permanent identification with the culture of the imperialist bourgeoisie. Here this class faces insurmountable difficulties and contradictions. For to truly and really become an integral part of that culture, they would have to live and grow abroad. But to do so would remove the political base of their economic constitution as a class: their control of the state of a former colony and hence their ability to mortgage a whole country and its people for a few million dollars. So this class can only admire that culture from an undesirable distance and try to ape it the best they can within the severe limitations of territory and history, but with the hope that their children will be fully uninhibited and unlimited in their Euro–Americanism.

They will order suits straight from Harrods of London or *haute couture* from Paris; buy castles and estates abroad and even build seaside and country villas there; now and then go on holidays abroad to relax and shop and bank. At home, they will meticulously groom, with the country's precious and hard-earned foreign currency reserves, a privileged elite caste of imported foreign experts and advisors, at the same time setting up a school system reproducing what they assume obtains abroad. They will send their children to the most expensive boarding schools abroad, or else approach EEC countries to build worthwhile international-class *lycées* at home for the super-elite children of the super-wealthy.

But the members of a comprador bourgeoisie of a former settler colony count themselves lucky; they don't have to travel and reside abroad to know and copy the culture of the imperialist bourgeoisie: have they not learnt it all from the colonial settler repre-

sentatives of metropolitan culture? Nurtured in the womb of the old colonial system, they have matured to their full compradorial heights, looking up to the local Europeans as the alpha and omega of gentlemanly refinement and ladylike elegance. With racial barriers to class mobility thrown open, the deportment of a European gentleman – rosebuds and pins in coat lapels, spotless white kerchiefs in breast pockets, tail-coats, top-hats and gold-chained pocket watches – is no longer in the realm of dreams and wishes. Thus in a very recent book edited by Elspeth Huxley, *Pioneer's Scrapbook*, there is an approving comment about this cultural imitation:

> Henry Scott died . . . on 11 April 1911 and was buried at Kikuyu. He was succeeded in the following year by Dr J. W. Arthur, who had come to Kikuyu in 1907: a man of great personal charm and driving force, who exercised a tremendous influence over the younger Kikuyu. His habit of wearing a rosebud or carnation in his lapel is perpetuated by some of the leading politicians of the present day who were small children at Kikuyu in the late twenties.

Lady Eleanor Cole, wife of the infamous Galbraith Cole, in her otherwise dry, humourless, random recollections of settler life in Kenya, writes enthusiastically about the social scene in the Nairobi of 1917:

> Nairobi was very social and people gave formal dinner parties, at which the women were dressed in long skirted low-necked gowns and men in stiff shirts and white waistcoats or in uniform. Men and women were carefully paired, and you were taken to dinner on the arm of your partner. There were strict rules of precedence, and woe betide the hostess who ignored them.

She is describing the Nairobi of 1917, but she could as easily have been describing Nairobi of the 1970s; only the latter Nairobi's wastefulness behind the feudal formality surpasses the former in sheer opulence.

The most popular columns in the old settler papers, *The Sunday Post* and *The Kenya Weekly News*, were the social pages listing who was who at this or that function at this or that club or at so and so's residence. The columns used to make hearts flutter, in tears or joy, depending of course on whether or not one was included. Those who appeared more regularly, especially at functions in exclusive clubs and residences, were regarded with envious awe and admiration by the less fortunate aspirants. After independence, the columns ceased to be, as did the two newspapers.

Well, the columns are now back in the glossy bourgeois monthlies *Viva* and *Chic* and in the Aga Khan-owned tabloid, *The Daily Nation*. They are even more popular. The columns are still a cause for joy or sorrow to many an expectant lady and gentleman. Only that this time, among the main European and Asian actors are to be found upper-crust Kenyan blacks holding, on their gentlemanly arms, ladies bedecked with gold and diamonds holding a goblet of liquor.

Lessons learnt in the Hardinge school of philosophy. First through the bullet and the sword. Then through the more "humane" and "modern" methods. The character and the behaviour of the more successful pupils would have pleased Governor Hardinge and all the other tutors, from Eliot to Malcolm Macdonald, in that famous school of colonial philosophy. First the gun, cow them; then the pen, take their minds prisoner; then filter them and pick out the top loyalists and bribe them numb with some semblance of power and wealth. And see the results.

Thus, the settler played golf and polo, went to horse-races or on the royal hunt in red-coats and riding-breeches, a herd of yapping and growling hounds on the chase. The black pupils now do the same, only with greater zeal: golf and horses have become "national" institutions.

The settler prostituted women, as when Karl Peters publicly hanged his African mistress because she preferred the company of her Kenyan brothers to his own. His pupils today have gone into the whole game with greater gusto: tourism, as practised today, can only thrive on the virtual prostitution of the whole country, becoming a sacred industry with shrines, under the name of hotels and lodges in all the cities and at the seaside. The modern-day Karl Peters need not use the gun to deter rivals. The name of the game now is money.*

The settler built exclusive betting clubs, drank neat whisky on the verandah of his huge mansion, or indulged in countless sundowners and cocktail parties. Their pupils continue the process: gambling casinos and strip-tease joints get full state support and legal encouragement.

The settler despised peasant languages which he termed vernacular, meaning the language of slaves, and believed that the English language was holy. Their pupils carry this contempt a stage further: some of their early educational acts on receiving the flag were to ban African languages in schools and to elevate English as the medium of instruction from primary to secondary stages. In some schools, corporal punishment is meted out to those caught speaking their mother tongues; fines are extorted for similar offences. Men at the top will fume in fury at fellow Africans who mispronounce English but will laugh with

---

* I was too hasty when I wrote this. The *Standard* of 1 October 1980 carried this report: "American sailor Frank Joseph Sundstrom, who admitted killing a Kenyan, Monicah Njeri, in her Mombasa flat after an evening of sex, was yesterday discharged on the condition that he signed a bond of shs. 500 to be of good behaviour for the next two years." Sundstrom, who was with the U.S.S. *La Salle*, which was then paying a "good will" visit to Kenya, was tried before a white judge, L.G.E. Harris, and a white prosecutor, Nicholas Harwood. The government has granted military facilities to the U.S.A., and the *La Salle* was visiting Kenya from the U.S. Middle East fleet poised to suppress any genuine anti-imperialist nationalist uprisings in the area. The massive anger of Kenyan people at the judgement forced the retirement of Justice Harris, but a whole four months or so after the infamous judgement and even then with full benefits.

pride at their own inability to speak a single correct sentence of their own African languages. In some government departments, the ability to speak the Queen's English, exactly like an upper-class English gentleman, is the sole criterion for employment and promotion. But since few, if any, Africans can speak the language exactly like those native to it, only Englishmen get employed or promoted to critical positions of authority.

The settler loathed any intellectually challenging literature or any genuine creative expression, beyond imitations of sugary comedies from London performed by amateurs wearing robes flown from abroad to give the whole tear-jerking acrobatics a touch of the real thing. To him, African culture was a curious museum-piece or an esoteric barbaric show for the amusement of tittering ladies and gentlemen desiring glimpses of savagery. Their comprador pupils too hate books and they loathe any theatre or music that challenges their betrayal. If a certain book is in vogue, they will buy it and ask their wives or children to go through it and tell them briefly what the fuss is all about. They also loathe African culture except when it can be used to rationalize their betrayal. But they will invite a few traditional dancers to do acrobatics for visitors from abroad, later summing up the whole show with polite applause and patronizing wonder: how do these people manage such bodily contortions?

The settler built goodwill churches to thank a white God for delivering the white race from the toils of Adam and invited his African labourers to share in the joyful tidings. The settler believed in charity to passively grateful African serfs: a bit of the plunder back to the plundered? Here these dutiful pupils surpass themselves in their singular zeal to excecute the same. Charity donations and church-going become "national" imperatives and moral yardsticks for political acceptance. The cult of ostentatious godliness is raised to new ethical planes. The propertied few compete in donating money for erecting several churches in a rural village that cannot boast of a single decent primary school, much less food or water. The imperialist evangelical drive of colonial missions is now led by the state and its wealthy blacks, with the same message: trust and obey. Spiritual leaders are trotted out in a string to calm rising disgust by promising future bounty for obedient souls. There is a pathetic side to the whole exercise in apemanship exhibited by these successful pupils of Hardinge's school of philosophy.

In the 1950s a blue-blooded settler memsahib whose education never went beyond riding Arab ponies and bashing the keys of the piano, sought and found solace for her early widowhood in joining the anti-Mau Mau, anti-communist, Moral Rearmament crusade. Accompanied by a MRM team flown from its headquarters in Switzerland, paid for by the financial gnomes of Zurich, she visited schools and colleges and detention camps showing pro-imperialist religious films like *The Forgotten Factor, Freedom, The Crowning Experience* in which anti-colonial guerrillas suddenly give up their armed struggle for liberation on learning about the presumed transforming power of the four moral absolutes of honesty, unselfishness, purity and love. Her theme? Give up guns for holy kisses. Beware of godless communism.

Well? Soldierly religious words never die. In the 1970s the same words reappear in speeches by a senior cabinet minister, intellectual conqueror of universities in Africa and abroad, at fund-raising ceremonies for more and more goodwill churches. His theme? Beware of godless communism! This foreign ideology is against our African traditions. We are Christians and capitalists by birth and ancestry.

Thus far for the modern and humane features of Hardinge's school of philosophy. Playing golf and polo, gambling at modern casinos and horse-races, ogling at naked women in strip-tease clubs, creating a modern happy valley for moneyocrats from Germany and America, televising ostentatious displays of well-groomed holiness and Churchillian extravaganzas at weekends, speaking English with an upper-class English accent, all these seem harmless imitations although far reaching in their consequences. They can be fought if there's democracy. Reality is anyway more powerful than a million imitations.

Unfortunately, it is the repressive features of colonial culture – Hardinge's sword and bullet, as the only insurance of continuing their life-style – that seem to have most attracted the unqualified admiration of the compradors. The settler with the *sjambok* lording it over a mass of "pulling and pushing nigger boys", that figure so meticulously preserved on the walls of "The Lord Delamere" in the Norfolk Hotel, seems the modern ideal for the post-colonial ruling class.

How else can it be explained that the 1966 laws of detention, sedition and treason, reproduce, almost word for word, those in practice between 1951 and 1961 during the high noon of colonial culture?

Submission through the sword and the bullet! And only later is it possible to achieve the same through the modern "peaceful" methods of churches, schools, theatres, television, cinema, colonial history, junk literature – all run, supervised and approved by foreigners!

The fact is that the comprador bourgeoisie would like to resurrect the imagined grandeur and dubious dignity of colonial culture. The unilateral arbitrary arrest and detention of Kenyans opposed to imperialist culture was a major step towards reconstruction of the new colonial Jerusalem, where people would for ever sing in unison: "Trust and obey, for there is no other way, to be happy amidst us, except to trust and obey."

"Arise colonial Lazarus" is their celebratory call to divine worship at the holy shrines of imperialism:

> Our father in Europe and America
> Hallowed be thy name
> Thy kingdom come
> Thy will be done
> In our wealthy Africa
> Our willing and welcoming Africa
> As it was done in the colonial past.
> Give us this day our daily dollar
> And forgive us our failures
> Help us triumph over those that chal-
> lenge you and us
> And give us grace and aid and the power
> to be meek and grateful
> For ever and ever, Amen.

PART IX

NATIONS AND NATIONALISM

Maasai women in southern Kenya wearing government supplied Kenya African National Union (KANU)
cloth during an election.
Photo: Adrian Arbib.

NATIONS AND NATIONALISM

37   Léopold Sédar Senghor. 1970. "Negritude: A Humanism of the Twentieth Century," pp. 179–92. In Wilfred Cartey and Martin Kilson, eds *The African Reader: Independent Africa*. New York: Vintage Books.

38   Frantz Fanon. 1967. "On National Culture," pp. 206–248. In *The Wretched of the Earth*. New York: Grove Press.

39   Bruce J. Berman. 1991. "Nationalism, Ethnicity, and Modernity: The Paradox of Mau Mau," *Canadian Journal of African Studies / Revue canadienne des Études africaines* 25(2): 181–206.

40   Christopher B. Steiner. 1992. "The Invisible Face: Masks, Ethnicity, and the State in Côte d'Ivoire, West Africa," *Museum Anthropology* 16(3): 53–57.

It is fitting to begin this section on African nationalism with an essay by Léopold Sédar Senghor who, as founder of the Mali Federation in 1959, paved the way for national independence throughout much of Francophone West Africa. As a statesman, Senghor was instrumental, by way of skillful negotiations with French president Charles de Gaulle, in gaining independence for Senegal from French colonial rule. In 1960, Senghor was unanimously elected as the first president of the independent republic of Senegal – a nation which he successfully governed for two decades until he was succeeded by Abdou Diouf. As a poet and man of letters, Senghor was an eloquent spokesman for the intellectual philosophy and cultural movement known as négritude – a term which Senghor defined succinctly as "the sum total of cultural values of the Negro–African world."

The négritude movement began in Paris during the 1930s when francophone African and Caribbean intellectuals (bound by their common legacy as colonial subjects of France), including, in particular, Léopold Senghor and Martiniquan poet Aimé Césaire, fashioned a discourse of pan-African cultural identity which was intended as a non-violent revolt against colonialism and, in particular, as a statement of protest against France's policy of cultural assimilation in Africa (Crowder, 1962). Négritude used poetry and literature to restore the validity of African culture, and to establish a positive image of "black" consciousness – a metaphor of identity which would serve as a rallying force of nationalism in the African world (Steeves, 1973: 92). In his numerous writings on the subject, Senghor (1948; 1964) stresses the indigenous wisdom of African peoples, and argues that beneath the superficial cultural idiosyncrasies that distinguish one society from another Africans are united by a profound commonality which is expressed in their democratic social structures, their religions, their work practices, their arts, and in the rhythm of African life itself (see also our general Introduction on the notion of African cultural unity). While stressing that African cultures were united, Senghor also argued that Africa was distinct from Europe and that nation-building (as a form of anticolonialism) could only emerge if the "African personality" was rescued from the suffocating pressure of European colonial culture. Senghor drew upon images of gender and temperament when he described Africa as "female, emotional, and rhythmic" in contrast to Europe which he characterized as "male, technical, and cold" (Lambert, 1993: 249). In his essay *Femmes Noires*, for example, Senghor constructed a female image of Africa in which he "portrays the woman Africa as a promised land from which the black person is alienated while in Europe" (Ibid.: 249). How different is this image from earlier European accounts of exploration which depicted Africa as an erotic and dark female body waiting to be penetrated by European colonization (see Comaroff and Comaroff, Chapter 41)? Is it possible to construct a gendered image of a continent as both a positive and negative metaphor?

There is a central contradiction in Senghor's work which forms, at least in part, the basis of Fanon's critique of négritude. While Senghor argued that "there existed in blackness a special social quality . . . he expressed this outlook in French language of such skill and precision that he was admitted to the French Academy" (Manning, 1988: 165). This point raises not only the whole issue of what language should be used to establish an "authentic" voice in African national literature (see the Introduction to Part X on the debate between Chinua Achebe and Ngugi wa Thiong'o), but also throws into question the possibility of discovering "true" African identity through the framework of European scholarly discourse. How connected was Senghor to the predicament of colonial Africa when he was writing from the perspective of an elite intellectal living and studying in Paris?

Frantz Fanon was born in Martinique and became a political activist in the Algerian National Liberation Front in the 1950s. His essay, "On National Culture," was written for the Second Congress of Black Artists and Writers which was held in Rome in 1959, and was published in 1961 as a chapter in his highly acclaimed polemic *The Wretched of the Earth*. Unlike Senghor, Fanon's agenda was more political than it was academic. His essay offers a direct critique of the négritude movement, which Fanon says does not go nearly far enough in its struggle to dismantle colonialism. He argues that Senghor's vision of independent African identity is couched in European colonial racialist terms. Rather than liberate himself from the culture of the oppressor, Fanon contends that Senghor accepts the basic premise of colonial subjugation: namely, the inferiority of the colonized. Out of the indignity engendered by racist colonial rhetoric, négritude tried to rehabilitate African culture in the eyes of the West. For Fanon, however, this was neither the way to independence nor to the formation of national identity. African nationalism cannot be founded on any attempt to redress colonial discourse (a process which, through its very negation, gives credence to European stereotypes), but rather must emerge from Africa's own struggle and on its own terms (July, 1987: 215–17).

Specifically, Fanon rejects two principle tenets of the négritude movement. First, he argues that national identity cannot emerge from the (re)construction of an idealized or nostaglic past, but must be grounded on the reality of the present – a reality which, for Fanon, involves violence against the colonial authorities. "A national culture," writes Fanon, "is not a folklore, nor an abstract populism that believes it can discover the people's true nature." Second, Fanon believed that culture is national and specific to the experience of a region or local state. The emphasis in négritude on pan-African identity functioned to diffuse the struggle against colonialism. There was no "common destiny" to be shared across Africa as a whole, but there *was* a common destiny "between the Senegalese and Guinean nations which are both dominated by the same French colonialism." What Fanon largely fails to consider, however, is the question of how diverse and multiple ethnic groups can come together to form a single national culture. While the common destiny of the Senegalese may be different from that of the Guinean, what about the common destiny of the multiple ethnic groups which comprise Senegal as a nation? Are the national goals and aspirations of the Wolof, for example, the same as those of the Serer?

The problem of multi-ethnic states is the focus of the next two essays in this part. Both of the essays broach the issue of ethnicity and nationalism from a different perspective. Bruce Berman's essay "Nationalism, Ethnicity, and Modernity: The Paradox of Mau Mau" demonstrates the contested interpretation of a political/religious movement in Kenya known as Mau Mau. The Mau Mau revolt was an armed uprising by Kikuyu peasants against the colonial state in Kenya. From the early 1950s until its suppression by British authorities in 1956, a campaign of oathing (pledging alegiance to a revolutionary cause) was used to create unity among the Kikuyu people (Green, 1990). Although Mau Mau was targeted against foreign colonial rule, it was played out as a conflict between Kikuyu loyalists and Kikuyu liberationists: only a handful of the thousand deaths were "white."

During the 1950s, when Mau Mau was still active in Kenya, the colonial authorities viewed the movement as an expression of "atavistic tribalism" – a quasi-religious cult steeped in the barbarity and violence which Europeans had come to associate with Africa (see Part X). In the 1960s, following Kenya's independence from Britain, and in an era when African political science was emerging as an important field of study in the United States, writers like John Nottingham and Carl Rosberg (1966) reconsidered the colonial interpretation of Mau Mau, and concluded

that to view Mau Mau as a form of atavistic tribalism was to buy into a colonial myth which was constructed out of an ideology of racism and European paranoia and fear. Mau Mau was to be understood instead as a form of "militant nationalism" whose struggle for liberation was predicated on "modern" and "rational" political motivations. Berman concludes that both interpretations of Mau Mau are flawed, and are based on identical premises about modernity, development, and nationalism. Drawing heavily on the influential work of Benedict Anderson (1983), and his concept of the nation as "an imagined community," Berman argues that Mau Mau was both a religious movement *and* a political movement. Mau Mau grew out of internal factionalism and dissent among the Kikuyu people. There was no unified front (either "ritual" or "national") but rather "a diverse and exceedingly fragmented collection of individuals, organizations and ideas, out of which no dominant concept of a Kikuyu imagined national community had emerged." By viewing nationalism as a political ideology which has more in common with kinship and religion than it does with the secularizing demands of the modern nation-state, Berman is able to account for the "passion" of Mau Mau in a way which no prior interpretation was able to do.

Finally, the problem of the multi-ethnic state is also considered by Christopher Steiner in his essay "The Invisible Face: Masks, Ethnicity, and the State in Côte d'Ivoire, West Africa." Steiner asks the following question: How does the Ivoirian state bring together over sixty different ethnic groups into a single, unified vision of a nation? And, furthermore, how does the state then go about marketing this image of national identity to the rest of the world, and, specifically, to European and American tourists? The Festimask, a huge masked festival organized by the Ministry of Tourism in 1987, was an attempt to present a unified image of Côte d'Ivoire to both nationals and foreigners alike. The nation state was to be encapsulated in the image of the mask, an artform which was thought to capture the "mystical" past of the nation. Through an analysis of its huge commercial failure, Steiner uses the Festimask as an object lesson in multiethnic African nationalism, demonstrating the inherent tensions between "modern" national integration and the preservation of authentic "traditions." How different, in the end, is the Festimask from the folklore and nostalgia which Fanon criticized so heavily nearly three decades ago?

References

Anderson, Benedict. 1983. *Imagined Communities: Reflections on the Origin and Spread of Nationalism*. London and New York: Verso.

Crowder, Michael. 1962. *Senegal: A Study in French Assimilationist Policy*. London: Oxford University Press.

Green, Maia. 1990. "Mau Mau Oathing Rituals and Political Ideology in Kenya: A Re-Analysis," *Africa* 60(1): 69–87.

July, Robert W. 1987. *An African Voice: The Role of the Humanities in African Independence*. Durham, NC: Duke University Press.

Lambert, Michael C. 1993. "From Citizenship to Négritude: 'Making a Difference' in Elite Ideologies of Colonized Francophone West Africa," *Comparative Studies in Society and History* 35(2): 239–62.

Manning, Patrick. 1988. *Francophone Sub-Saharan Africa, 1880–1985*. Cambridge: Cambridge University Press.

Rosberg, Carl, and John Nottingham. 1966. *The Myth of Mau Mau: Nationalism in Kenya*. New York: Praeger.

Senghor, Léopold Sédar. 1948. *Anthologie de la nouvelle poésie nègre et malgache de langue française*. Paris: Presses universitaires de France. Reprinted in 1969.

———. 1964. *On African Socialism*. Translated by Mercer Cook. New York: Praeger.

Steeves, Edna L. 1973. "Négritude and the Noble Savage," *The Journal of Modern African Studies* 11(1): 91–104.

Suggested Readings

Afigbo, A. E., and S. I. O. Okita, eds. 1985. *Museums and Nation Building*. Imo State, Nigeria: New African Publishing.

Bhabha, Homi K., ed. 1990. *Nation and Narration*. London and New York: Routledge.

Césaire, Aimé. 1969. *Return to My Native Land*. Harmondsworth: Penguin Books.

———. 1990. *Lyric and Dramatic Poetry, 1946–82*. Edited by Clayton Eshleman and Annette Smith. Charlottseville: University Press of Virginia.

Chatterjee, Partha. 1993. *Nationalist Thought and the Colonial World*. Minneapolis: University of Minnesota Press.

Coombes, Annie E. 1988. "Museums and the Formation of National and Cultural Identities," *The Oxford Art Journal* 11(2): 57–68.

Dia, Mamadou. 1961. *The African Nations and World Solidarity*. Translated by Mercer Cook. New York: Praeger.

Foster, Robert J. 1991. "Making National Cultures in the Global Ecumene," *Annual Review of Anthropology* 20: 235–60.

Gellner, Ernest. 1983. *Nations and Nationalism*. Ithaca, NY: Cornell University Press

Golan, Dafnah. 1994. *Inventing Shaka: Using History in the Construction of Zulu Nationalism*. Boulder, CO: Rienner.

Hodgkin, Thomas. 1957. *Nationalism in Colonial Africa*. New York: New York University Press.

Irele, Abiola. 1965. "Négritude or Black Cultural Nationalism," *The Journal of Modern African Studies* 3(3): 321–48.

July, Robert W. 1967. *The Origins of Modern African Thought*. New York: Praeger.

Kenyatta, Jomo. 1938. *Facing Mount Kenya: The Tribal Life of the Kikuyu*. London: Secker and Warburg.

Langley, J. Ayodele. 1973. *Pan-Africanism and Nationalism in West Africa, 1900–1945*. Oxford: Clarendon Press.

Malkki, Liisa H. 1995. *Purity and Exile: Violence, Memory, and National Cosmology among Hutu Refugees in Tanzania*. Chicago: University of Chicago Press.

Mark, Peter. 1994. "Art, Ritual, and Folklore: Dance and Cultural Identity among the Peoples of the Casamance," *Cahiers d'Etudes africaines* 136, 34(4): 563–84.

Neuberger, Benyamin. 1987. "History and African Concepts of Nationhood," *Canadian Review of Studies in Nationalism* 14(1): 161–79.

Smith, Anthony D. 1983. *State and Nation in the Third World*. Brighton: Wheatsheaf.

Verdery, Katherine. 1993. "Whither 'Nation' and 'Nationalism'?," *Daedalus* 122(3): 37–46.

Welliver, Timothy K., ed. 1993. *African Nationalism and Independence*. New York: Garland.

Williams, Braquette. 1989. "A Class Act: Anthropology and the Race to Nation Across Ethnic Terrain," *Annual Review of Anthropology* 18: 401–44.

37

NEGRITUDE: A HUMANISM OF THE TWENTIETH CENTURY

LÉOPOLD SÉDAR SENGHOR

During the last thirty or so years that we have been proclaiming negritude, it has become customary, especially among English-speaking critics, to accuse us of *racialism*. This is probably because the word is not of English origin. But, in the language of Shakespeare, is it not in good company with the words humanism and socialism? Mphahleles[1] have been sent about the world saying: "Negritude is an inferiority complex"; but the same word cannot mean both "racialism" and "inferiority complex" without contradiction. The most recent attack comes from Ghana, where the government has commissioned a poem entitled "I Hate Negritude" – as if one could hate oneself, hate one's being, without ceasing to be.

No, negritude is none of these things. It is neither racialism nor self-negation. Yet it is not just affirmation; it is rooting oneself in oneself, and self-confirmation: confirmation of one's *being*. Negritude is nothing more or less than what some English-speaking Africans have called the *African personality*. It is no different from the "black personality" discovered and proclaimed by the American New Negro movement. As the American Negro poet,

Langston Hughes, wrote after the first world war: "We, the creators of the new generation, want to give expression to our *black personality* without shame or fear . . . We know we are handsome. Ugly as well. The drums weep and the drums laugh." Perhaps our only originality, since it was the West Indian poet, Aimé Césaire, who coined the word negritude, is to have attempted to define the concept a little more closely; to have developed it as a weapon, as an instrument of liberation and as a contribution to the humanism of the twentieth century.

But, once again, what is negritude? Ethnologists and sociologists today speak of "different civilizations." It is obvious that peoples differ in their ideas and their languages, in their philosophies and their religions, in their customs and their institutions, in their literature and their art. Who would deny that Africans, too, have a certain way of conceiving life and of living it? A certain way of speaking, singing, and dancing; of painting and sculpturing, and even of laughing and crying? Nobody, probably; for otherwise we would not have been talking about "Negro art" for the last sixty years and Africa would be the

---

[1] The South African writer, Ezekiel Mphahlele, author, among other books, of *The African Image*, strongly disagrees with the concept of negritude.

only continent today without its ethnologists and sociologists. What, then, is negritude? It is – as you can guess from what precedes – *the sum of the cultural values of the black world*; that is, a certain active presence in the world, or better, in the universe. It is, as John Reed and Clive Wake call it, a certain "way of relating oneself to the world and to others."[2] Yes, it is essentially relations with others, an opening out to the world, contact and participation with others. Because of what it is, negritude is necessary in the world today: it is a humanism of the twentieth century.

"The Revolution of 1889"

But let us go back to 1885 and the morrow of the Berlin Conference. The European nations had just finished, with Africa, their division of the planet. Including the United States of America, they were five or six at the height of their power who dominated the world. Without any complexes, they were proud of their material strength; prouder even of their science, and paradoxically, of their *race*. It is true that at that time this was not a paradox. Gobineau, the nineteenth-century philosopher of racial supremacy, had, by a process of osmosis, even influenced Marx, and Disraeli was the great theoretician of that "*English race*, proud, tenacious, confident in itself, that no climate, no change can undermine." (The italics are mine.) Leo Frobenius, the German ethnologist, one of the first to apprehend the rich complexity of African culture, writes in *The Destiny of Civilizations*: "Each of the great nations that considers itself personally responsible for the 'destiny of the world' believes it possesses the key to the understanding of the whole and the other nations. It is an attitude raised from the past."

In fact, this attitude "raised from the past" had begun to be discredited toward the end of the nineteenth century by books like Bergson's *Time and Free Will*, which was published in 1889. Since the Renaissance, the values of European civilization had rested essentially on discursive reason and facts, on logic and matter. Bergson, with an eminently dialectical subtlety, answered the expectation of a public weary of scientism and naturalism. He showed that facts and matter, which are the objects of discursive reason, were only the outer surface that had to be transcended by *intuition* in order to achieve a *vision in depth of reality*.

But the "Revolution of 1889" – as we shall call it – did not only affect art and literature, it completely upset the sciences. In 1880, only a year before the invention of the word electron, a distinction was still being drawn between matter and energy. The former was inert and unchangeable, the latter was not. But what characterized both of them was their permanence and their continuity. They were both subject to a strict mechanical determinism. Matter and energy had, so to speak, existed from the beginning of time; they could change their shape, but not their substance. All we lacked in order to know them objectively in space and time were sufficiently accurate instruments of investigation and measurement.

Well, in less than fifty years, all these principles were to be outmoded and even rejected. Thirty years ago already, the new discoveries of science – quanta, relativity, wave mechanics, the uncertainty principle, electron spin – had upset the nineteenth-century notion of determinism, which denied man's free will, along with the concepts of matter and energy. The French physicist, Broglie, revealed to us the duality of matter and energy, or the wave-particle principle that underlies things; the German physicist, Heisenberg, showed us that objectivity was an illusion and that we could not observe facts without

---

[2] *Léopold Sédar Senghor: Selected Poems*, introduced and translated by John Reed and Clive Wake. See also: *Léopold Sédar Senghor: Prose and Poetry*, by the same authors.

modifying them; others showed that, on the scale of the infinitely small as on that of the immensely great, particles act on one another. Since then, the physico–chemical laws, like matter itself, could no longer appear unchangeable. Even in the field, and on the scale, where they were valid, they were only rough approximations, no more than probabilities. It was enough to scrape the surface of things and of facts to realize just how much instability there is, defying our measuring instruments, probably because they are only mechanical: *material*.

It was on the basis of these discoveries, through a combination of logical coherence and amazing intuition, of scientific experiment and inner experience, that Pierre Teilhard de Chardin was able to transcend the traditional dichotomies with a new dialectic, to reveal to us the living, throbbing unity of the universe. On the basis, then, of the new scientific discoveries, Teilhard de Chardin transcends the old dualism of the philosophers and the scientists, which Marx and Engels had perpetuated by giving matter precedence over the spirit. He advanced the theory that the stuff of the universe is not composed of two realities, but of a single reality in the shape of two phenomena; that there is not matter and energy, not even matter and spirit, but spirit–matter, just as there is space–time. Matter and spirit become a "network of relations," as the French philosopher, Bachelard, called it: energy, defined as a network of forces. In matter–spirit there is, therefore, only one energy, which has two aspects. The first, *tangential energy*, which is external, is material and quantitative. It links together the corpuscles, or particles, that make up matter. The other, *radial energy*, which is internal, is psychic and qualitative. It is centripetal force. It organizes into a complex the center-to-center relations of the internal particles of a corpuscle. Since energy is force, it follows that radial energy is the creative force, the "primary stuff of things," and tangential energy is only a residual

product "caused by the interreactions of the elementary 'centers' of the consciousness, imperceptible where life has not yet occurred, but clearly apprehensible by our experience at a sufficiently advanced stage in the development of matter" (Teilhard de Chardin). It follows that where life has not yet occurred the physico–chemical laws remain valid within the limitations we have defined above, while in the living world, as we rise from plant to animal and from animal to Man, the psyche increases in consciousness until it makes and expresses itself in freedom. "Makes itself": that is, *realizes* itself, by means of – yet by transcending – material well-being through an increase of spiritual life. "Realizes itself": by that I mean it develops in harmonious fashion the two complementary elements of the soul: the heart and the mind.

The Philosophy of Being

The paradox is only apparent when I say that negritude, by its ontology (that is, its philosophy of being), its moral law and its aesthetic, is a response to the modern humanism that European philosophers and scientists have been preparing since the end of the nineteenth century, and as Teilhard de Chardin and the writers and artists of the mid-twentieth century present it.

Firstly, African ontology. Far back as one may go into his past, from the northern Sudanese to the southern Bantu, the African has always and everywhere presented a concept of the world which is diametrically opposed to the traditional philosophy of Europe. The latter is essentially *static, objective, dichotomic*; it is, in fact, dualistic, in that it makes an absolute distinction between body and soul, matter and spirit. It is founded on separation and opposition: on analysis and conflict. The African, on the other hand, conceives the world, beyond the diversity of its forms, as a fundamentally mobile, yet unique, reality that seeks synthesis. This needs development.

It is significant that in Wolof, the main language of Senegal, there are at least three words to translate the word "spirit": *xel, sago,* or *degal,* whereas images have to be used for the word "matter": *lef* (thing) or *yaram* (body). The African is, of course, sensitive to the external world, to the material aspect of beings and things. It is precisely because he is more so than the white European, because he is sensitive to the tangible qualities of things – shape, color, smell, weight, etc. – that the African considers these things merely as signs that have to be interpreted and transcended in order to reach the reality of human beings. Like others, more than others, he distinguishes the pebble from the plant, the plant from the animal, the animal from Man; but, once again, the accidents and appearances that differentiate these kingdoms only illustrate different aspects of the same reality. This reality is *being* in the ontological sense of the word, and it is life force. For the African, matter in the sense the Europeans understand it, is only a system of signs which translates the single reality of the universe: being, which is spirit, which is life force. Thus, the whole universe appears as an infinitely small, and at the same time an infinitely large, network of life forces which emanate from God and end in God, who is the source of all life forces. It is He who vitalizes and devitalizes all other beings, all the other life forces.

I have not wandered as far as might be thought from modern ontology. European ethnologists, Africanists and artists use the same words and the same expressions to designate the ultimate reality of the universe they are trying to know and to express: "spider's web," "network of forces," "communicating vessels," "system of canals," etc. This is not very different, either, from what the scientists and chemists say. As far as African ontology is concerned, too, there is no such thing as dead matter: every being, every thing – be it only a grain of sand – radiates a life force, a sort of wave-particle; and sages, priests, kings, doctors, and artists all use it to help bring the universe to its fulfilment.

For the African, contrary to popular belief, is not passive in face of the order – or disorder – of the world. His attitude is fundamentally ethical. If the moral law of the African has remained unknown for so long, it is because it derives, naturally, from his conception of the world: from his ontology – so naturally, that both have remained unknown, denied even, by Europeans, because they have not been brought to their attention by being re-examined by each new generation of Africans.

So God tired of all the possibilities that remained confined within Him, unexpressed, dormant, and as if dead. And God opened His mouth, and He spoke at length a word that was harmonious and rhythmical. All these possibilities expressed by the mouth of God *existed* and had the vocation *to live:* to express God in their turn, by establishing the link with God and all the forces deriving from Him.

In order to explain this *morality in action* of negritude, I must go back a little. Each of the identifiable life forces of the universe – from the grain of sand to the ancestor[3] – is, itself and in its turn, a network of life forces – as modern physical chemistry confirms: a network of elements that are contradictory in appearance but really *complementary.* Thus, for the African, Man is composed, of course, of matter and spirit, of body and soul; but at the same time he is also composed of a virile and a feminine element: indeed of several "souls." Man is therefore a composition of mobile life forces which interlock: a world of solidarities that seek to knit themselves together. Because he exists, he is at once end and beginning: end of

---

[3] In African religion, the ancestors are the essential link between the living and God. This is why they are surrounded by a complex ritual so as to ensure the maintenance of this link.

the three orders of the mineral, the vegetable, and the animal, but beginning of the human order.

Let us ignore for the moment the first three orders and examine the human order. Above Man and based on him, lies this fourth world of concentric circles, bigger and bigger, higher and higher, until they reach God along with the whole of the universe. Each circle – family, village, province, nation, humanity – is, in the image of Man and by vocation, a close-knit society.

So, for the African, living according to the moral law means living according to his nature, composed as it is of contradictory elements but complementary life forces. Thus he gives stuff to the stuff of the universe and tightens the threads of the tissue of life. Thus he transcends the contradictions of the elements and works toward making the life forces complementary to one another: in himself first of all, as Man, but also in the whole of human society. It is by bringing the complementary life forces together in this way that Man reinforces them in their movement towards God and, in re-inforcing them, he reinforces himself: that is, he passes from *existing* to *being*. He cannot reach the highest form of being, for in fact only God has this quality; and He has it all the more fully as creation, and all that exists, fulfil them-selves and express themselves in Him.

Dialogue

Ethnologists have often praised the unity, the balance, and the harmony of African civiliz-ation, of black society, which was based both on the *community* and on the *person*, and in which, because it was founded on dialogue and reciprocity, the group had priority over the individual without crushing him, but allowing him to blossom as a person. I would like to emphasize at this point how much these characteristics of negritude enable it to find its place in contemporary humanism, thereby permitting black Africa to make its contribu-tion to the "Civilization of the Universal" which is so necessary in our divided but inter-dependent world of the second half of the twentieth century. A contribution, first of all, to international cooperation, which must be and which shall be the cornerstone of that civilization. It is through these virtues of negritude that decolonization has been accom-plished without too much bloodshed or hatred and that a positive form of cooperation based on "dialogue and reciprocity" has been established between former colonizers and colonized. It is through these virtues that there has been a new spirit at the United Nations, where the "no" and the bang of the fist on the table are no longer signs of strength. It is through these virtues that peace through coop-eration could extend to South Africa, Rhodesia, and the Portuguese colonies, if only the dualistic spirit of the whites would open itself to dialogue.

In fact, the contribution of negritude to the "Civilization of the Universal" is not of recent origin. In the fields of literature and art, it is contemporary with the "Revolution of 1889." The French poet, Arthur Rimbaud (1854–1891), had already associated himself with negritude. But in this article I want to concen-trate on the "Negro revolution" – the expression belongs to Emmanuel Berl – which helped to stir European plastic art at the begin-ning of this century.

Art, like literature, is always the expression of a certain conception of the world and of life; the expression of a certain philosophy and, above all, of a certain ontology. Corresponding to the philosophical and scientific movement of 1889 there was not only a literary evolution – symbolism then surrealism – but another revolution, or rather revolutions, in art, which were called, taking only the plastic arts, nabism, expressionism, fauvism, and cubism. A world of life forces that have to be *tamed* is substituted for a closed world of permanent and continuous substances that have to be *reproduced*.

Since the Greek *kouroi* (the term used for

the statues of young men in classical Greek sculpture), the art of the European West had always been based on realism; the work of art had always been an imitation of the object: a *physeôs mimêsis*, to use Artistotle's expression: a corrected imitation, "improved," "idealized" by the requirements of rationality, but imitation all the same. The interlude of the Christian Middle Ages is significant insofar as Christianity is itself of Asian origin and strongly influenced by the African, St. Augustine. To what will the artist then give expression? No longer to purely objective matter, but to his spiritual self: that is, to his inner self, his spirituality, and beyond himself to the spirituality of his age and of mankind. No longer by means of perspective, relief, and chiaroscuro, but, as the French painter, Bazaine, writes, "by the most hidden workings of instinct and the sensibility." Another French painter, André Masson, makes it more explicit when he writes: "By a simple interplay of shapes and colors legibly ordered." This interplay of shapes and colors is that of the life forces and which has been illustrated in particular by a painter like Soulages.

"Interplay of life forces": and so we come back to – negritude. As the French painter, Soulages, in fact, once told me, the African aesthetic is "that of contemporary art." I find indirect proof of this in the fact that, while the consecration and spread of the new aesthetic revolution have occurred in France, the majority of its promoters were of Slav and Germanic origin; people who, like the Africans, belong to the mystical civilizations of the senses. Of course, without the discovery of African art, the revolution would still have taken place, but probably without such vigor and assurance and such a deepening of the knowledge of Man. The fact that an art of the subject and of the spirit should have germinated outside Europe, in Africa – to which

ethnologists had not yet given its true place in world culture – was proof of the human value of the message of the new European art.

Over and above its aesthetic lesson – to which we shall return later – what Picasso, Braque and the other artists and early explorers of African art were seeking was, in the first place, just this: its human value. For in black Africa art is not a separate activity, in itself or for itself: it is a social activity, a technique of living, a handicraft in fact. But it is a major activity that brings all other activities to their fulfilment, like prayer in the Christian Middle Ages: birth and education, marriage and death, sport, even war. All human activities down to the least daily act must be integrated into the subtle interplay of life forces – family, tribal, national, world, and universal forces. This harmonious interplay of life forces must be helped by *subordinating* the lower forces – mineral, vegetable, and animal – to their relations with Man, and the forces of human society to its relations with the Divine Being through the intermediary of the Ancestral Beings.

A year or two ago I attended, on the cliffs of Bandiagara in the Mali Republic, an entertainment which was microcosm of Dogon art.[4] Even though it was but a pale reflection of the splendors of the past, this "play-concert" was an extremely significant expression of the Dogon vision of the universe. It was declaimed, sung, and danced; sculptured and presented in costume. The whole of the Dogon universe was portrayed in this symbiosis of the arts, as is the custom in black Africa. The universe – heaven and earth – was therefore *represented* through the intermediary of Man, whose ideogram is the same as that of the universe. Then the world was *re-presented* by means of masks, each of which portrayed, at one and the same time, a totemic animal, an ancestor and a spirit. Others portrayed the

---

[4]   The Dogon are a West African tribe among whom wood sculpture has achieved a very remarkable degree of excellence.

foreign peoples: nomadic Fulani[5] and white Europeans. The aim of the entertainment was, by means of the symbiosis of the arts – poetry, song, dance, sculpture, and painting, used as techniques of integration – to *re-create* the universe and the contemporary world, but in a more harmonious way by making use of African humor, which corrects distortions at the expense of the foreign Fulani and the white conquerors. But this ontological vision was an entertainment – that is, an artistic demonstration – as well: a joy for the soul because a joy for the eyes and ears.

It was perhaps – indeed, it was certainly – this last aspect of the African aesthetic lesson that first attracted Picasso and Braque when, toward 1906, they discovered African art and were inspired by it. For my part, what struck me from the start of the Dogon "play-concert," even before I tried to understand its meaning, was the harmony of form and movement, of color and rhythm, that characterized it. It is this harmony by which, as a spectator, I was moved; which, in the re-creation of reality, acts on the invisible forces whose appearances are only signs, subordinates them in a complementary fashion to one another and establishes the link between them and God through the intermediary of Man. By appearances I mean the attributes of matter that strike our senses: shape and color, timbre and tone, movement and rhythm.

I have said that these appearances are signs. They are more than that: they are meaningful signs, the "lines of force" of the life forces, insofar as they are used in their pure state, with only their characteristics of shape, color, sound, movement, and rhythm. Recently M. Lods, who teaches at the National School of Art of Senegal, was showing me the pictures his students intend exhibiting at the projected Festival of African Arts. I was immediately struck by the noble and elegant interplay of shape and color. When I discovered that the

pictures were not completely abstract, that they portrayed ladies, princes, and noble animals, I was almost disappointed. There was no need for me to be: the very interplay of colored shapes perfectly expressed that elegant nobility that characterizes the art of the northern Sudan.

This, then, is Africa's lesson in aesthetics: art does not consist in photographing nature but in taming it, like the hunter when he reproduces the call of the hunted animal, like a separated couple, or two lovers, calling to each other in their desire to be reunited. The call is not the simple reproduction of the cry of the Other; it is a call of complementarity, a *song:* a call of harmony to the harmony of union that enriches by increasing *Being.* We call it pure harmony. Once more, Africa teaches that art is not photography; if there are images they are rhythmical. I can suggest or create anything – a man, a moon, a fruit, a smile, a tear – simply by assembling shapes and colors (painting sculpture), shapes and movement (dance), timbre and tones (music), provided that this assembling is not an aggregation, but that it is ordered and, in short, rhythmical. For it is rhythm – the main virtue, in fact, of negritude – that gives the work of art its beauty. Rhythm is simply the movement of attraction or repulsion that expresses the life of the cosmic forces; symmetry and asymmetry, repetition or opposition: in short, the lines of force that link the meaningful signs that shapes and colors, timbre and tones, are.

Before concluding, I should like to pause for a moment on the apparent contradiction that must have been noticed between contemporary European art (which places the emphasis on the subject) and African art (which places it on the object). This is because the "Revolution of 1889" began by reacting, of necessity, against the superstition of the *object*; and the existentialist ontology of the African, while it is based on the being-subject, has God as its

---

[5] The Fulani are a nomadic pastoral people found throughout West Africa.

pole-object; God who is the fullness of Being. What was noticed, then, was simply a nuance. For the contemporary European, and the African, the work of art, like the act of knowing, expresses the confrontation, the embrace, of subject and object: "That penetration," wrote Bazaine, "that great common structure, that deep resemblance between Man and the world, without which there is no living form."

We have seen what constitutes for the African the "deep resemblance between Man and the world." For him, then, the act of restoring the order of the world by re-creating it through art is the reinforcement of the life forces in the universe and, consequently, of God, the source of all life forces – or, in other words, the Being of the universe. In this way, we reinforce ourselves at the same time, both as interdependent forces and as beings whose being consists in revitalizing ourselves in the re-creation of art.

38

On National Culture

FRANTZ FANON

. . . In this chapter we shall analyze the problem, which is felt to be fundamental, of the legitimacy of the claims of a nation. It must be recognized that the political party which mobilizes the people hardly touches on this problem of legitimacy. The political parties start from living reality and it is in the name of this reality, in the name of the stark facts which weigh down the present and the future of men and women, that they fix their line of action. The political party may well speak in moving terms of the nation, but what it is concerned with is that the people who are listening understand the need to take part in the fight if, quite simply, they wish to continue to exist.

Today we know that in the first phase of the national struggle colonialism tries to disarm national demands by putting forward economic doctrines. As soon as the first demands arc sct out, colonialism pretends to consider them, recognizing with ostentatious humility that the territory is suffering from serious underdevelopment which necessitates a great economic and social effort. And, in fact, it so happens that certain spectacular measures (centers of work for the unemployed which are opened here and there, for example) delay the crystallization of national consciousness for a few years. But, sooner or later, colonialism sees that it is not within its powers to put into practice a project of economic and social reforms which will satisfy the aspirations of the colonized people. Even where food supplies are concerned, colonialism gives proof of its inherent incapability. The colonialist state quickly discovers that if it wishes to disarm the nationalist parties on strictly economic questions then it will have to do in the colonies exactly what it has refused to do in its own country. . . .

Inside the political parties, and most often in offshoots from these parties, cultured individuals of the colonized race make their appearance. For these individuals, the demand for a national culture and the affirmation of the existence of such a culture represent a special battlefield. While the politicians situate their action in actual present-day events, men of culture take their stand in the field of history. Confronted with the native intellectual who decides to make an aggressive response to the colonialist theory of pre-colonial barbarism, colonialism will react only slightly, and still less because the ideas developed by the young colonized intelligentsia are widely professed by specialists in the mother country. It is in fact a commonplace to state that for several decades large numbers of research workers have, in the main, rehabilitated the African, Mexican, and Peruvian civilizations. The passion with which native intellectuals defend the existence of their national culture may be a source of amazement; but those who condemn this exaggerated passion are strangely apt to forget that their own psyche and their own selves are conveniently sheltered behind a French or German culture which has given full proof of its existence and which is un-contested.

I am ready to concede that on the plane of factual being the past existence of an Aztec civilization does not change anything very much in the diet of the Mexican peasant of today. I admit that all the proofs of a wonderful Songhai civilization will not change the fact that today the Songhais are underfed and illiterate, thrown between sky and water with empty heads and empty eyes. But it has been remarked several times that this passionate search for a national culture which existed before the colonial era finds its legitimate reason in the anxiety shared by native intellec-tuals to shrink away from that Western culture in which they all risk being swamped. Because they realize they are in danger of losing their lives and thus becoming lost to their people, these men, hotheaded and with anger in their hearts, relentlessly determine to renew contact once more with the oldest and most pre-colonial springs of life of their people.

Let us go further. Perhaps this passionate research and this anger are kept up or at least directed by the secret hope of discovering beyond the misery of today, beyond self-contempt, resignation, and abjuration, some very beautiful and splendid era whose exist-ence rehabilitates us both in regard to ourselves and in regard to others. I have said that I have decided to go further. Perhaps unconsciously, the native intellectuals, since they could not stand wonderstruck before the history of today's barbarity, decided to back further and to delve deeper down; and, let us make no mistake, it was with the greatest delight that they discovered that there was nothing to be ashamed of in the past, but rather dignity, glory, and solemnity. The claim to a national culture in the past does not only re-habilitate that nation and serve as a justification for the hope of a future national culture. In the sphere of psycho-affective

equilibrium it is responsible for an important change in the native. Perhaps we have not sufficiently demonstrated that colonialism is not simply content to impose its rule upon the present and the future of a dominated country. Colonialism is not satisfied merely with holding a people in its grip and emptying the native's brain of all form and content. By a kind of perverted logic, it turns to the past of the oppressed people, and distorts, disfigures, and destroys it. This work of devaluing pre-colonial history takes on a dialectical significance today.

When we consider the efforts made to carry out the cultural estrangement so characteristic of the colonial epoch, we realize that nothing has been left to chance and that the total result looked for by colonial domination was indeed to convince the natives that colonialism came to lighten their darkness. The effect consciously sought by colonialism was to drive into the natives' heads the idea that if the settlers were to leave, they would at once fall back into barbarism, degradation, and bestiality.

On the unconscious plane, colonialism therefore did not seek to be considered by the native as a gentle, loving mother who protects her child from a hostile environment, but rather as a mother who unceasingly restrains her fundamentally perverse offspring from managing to commit suicide and from giving free rein to its evil instincts. The colonial mother protects her child from itself, from its ego, and from its physiology, its biology, and its own unhappiness which is its very essence.

In such a situation the claims of the native intellectual are not a luxury but a necessity in any coherent program. The native intellectual who takes up arms to defend his nation's legit-imacy and who wants to bring proofs to bear out that legitimacy, who is willing to strip himself naked to study the history of his body, is obliged to dissect the heart of his people.

Such an examination is not specifically national. The native intellectual who decides to give battle to colonial lies fights on the field of the whole continent. The past is given back its value. Culture, extracted from the past to be displayed in all its splendor, is not necessarily that of his own country. Colonialism, which has not bothered to put too fine a point on its efforts, has never ceased to maintain that the Negro is a savage; and for the colonist, the Negro was neither an Angolan nor a Nigerian, for he simply spoke of "the Negro." For colonialism, this vast continent was the haunt of savages, a country riddled with superstitions and fanaticism, destined for contempt, weighed down by the curse of God, a country of cannibals – in short, the Negro's country. Colonialism's condemnation is continental in its scope. The contention by colonialism that the darkest night of humanity lay over pre-colonial history concerns the whole of the African continent. The efforts of the native to rehabilitate himself and to escape from the claws of colonialism are logically inscribed from the same point of view as that of colonialism. The native intellectual who has gone far beyond the domains of Western culture and who has got it into his head to proclaim the existence of another culture never does so in the name of Angola or of Dahomey. The culture which is affirmed is African culture. The Negro, never so much a Negro as since he has been dominated by the whites, when he decides to prove that he has a culture and to behave like a cultured person, comes to realize that history points out a well-defined path to him: he must demonstrate that a Negro culture exists.

And it is only too true that those who are most responsible for this racialization of thought, or at least for the first movement toward that thought, are and remain those Europeans who have never ceased to set up white culture to fill the gap left by the absence of other cultures. Colonialism did not dream of wasting its time in denying the existence of one national culture after another. Therefore the reply of the colonized peoples will be straight away continental in its breadth. In Africa, the native literature of the last twenty years is not a national literature but a Negro literature. The concept of negritude, for example, was the emotional if not the logical antithesis of that insult which the white man flung at humanity. This rush of negritude against the white man's contempt showed itself in certain spheres to be the one idea capable of lifting interdictions and anathemas. Because the New Guinean or Kenyan intellectuals found themselves above all up against a general ostracism and delivered to the combined contempt of their overlords their reaction was to sing praises in admiration of each other. The unconditional affirmation of African culture has succeeded the unconditional affirmation of European culture. On the whole, the poets of negritude oppose the idea of an old Europe to a young Africa, tiresome reasoning to lyricism, oppressive logic to high-stepping nature, and on one side stiffness, ceremony, etiquette, and scepticism, while on the other frankness, liveliness, liberty, and – why not – luxuriance: but also irresponsibility.

The poets of negritude will not stop at the limits of the continent. From America, black voices will take up the hymn with fuller unison. The "black world" will see the light and Busia from Ghana, Birago Diop from Senegal, Hampaté Ba from the Soudan, and Saint-Clair Drake from Chicago will not hesitate to assert the existence of common ties and a motive power that is identical. . . .

This historical necessity in which the men of African culture find themselves to racialize their claims and to speak more of African culture than of national culture will tend to lead them up a blind alley. Let us take for example the case of the African Cultural Society. This society had been created by African intellectuals who wished to get to know each other and to compare their experiences and the results of their respective research work. The aim of this society was therefore to affirm the existence of an African culture, to evaluate this culture on the plane of distinct nations, and to reveal the internal motive forces of each of their national cultures.

But at the same time this society fulfilled another need: the need to exist side by side with the European Cultural Society, which threatened to transform itself into a Universal Cultural Society. There was therefore at the bottom of this decision the anxiety to be present at the universal trysting place fully armed, with a culture springing from the very heart of the African continent. Now, this Society will very quickly show its inability to shoulder these different tasks, and will limit itself to exhibitionist demonstrations, while the habitual behavior of the members of this Society will be confined to showing Europeans that such a thing as African culture exists, and opposing their ideas to those of ostentatious and narcissistic Europeans. We have shown that such an attitude is normal and draws its legitimacy from the lies propagated by men of Western culture, but the degradation of the aims of this Society will become more marked with the elaboration of the concept of negritude. The African Society will become the cultural society of the black world and will come to include the Negro dispersion, that is to say the tens of thousands of black people spread over the American continents.

The Negroes who live in the United States and in Central or Latin America in fact experience the need to attach themselves to a cultural matrix. Their problem is not fundamentally different from that of the Africans. The whites of America did not mete out to them any different treatment from that of the whites who ruled over the Africans. We have seen that the whites were used to putting all Negroes in the same bag. During the first congress of the African Cultural Society which was held in Paris in 1956, the American Negroes of their own accord considered their problems from the same standpoint as those of their African brothers. Cultured Africans, speaking of African civilizations, decreed that there should be a reasonable status within the state for those who had formerly been slaves. But little by little the American Negroes realized that the essential problems con-fronting them were not the same as those that confronted the African Negroes. The Negroes of Chicago only resemble the Nigerians or the Tanganyikans in so far as they were all defined in relation to the whites. But once the first comparisons had been made and subjective feelings were assuaged, the American Negroes realized that the objective problems were fundamentally heterogeneous. The test cases of civil liberty whereby both whites and blacks in America try to drive back racial discrimination have very little in common in their principles and objectives with the heroic fight of the Angolan people against the detestable Portuguese colonialism. Thus, during the second congress of the African Cultural Society the American Negroes decided to create an American society for people of black cultures.

Negritude therefore finds its first limitation in the phenomena which take account of the formation of the historical character of men. Negro and African–Negro culture broke up into different entities because the men who wished to incarnate these cultures realized that every culture is first and foremost national, and that the problems which kept Richard Wright or Langston Hughes on the alert were fundamentally different from those which might confront Leopold Senghor or Jomo Kenyatta. In the same way certain Arab states, though they had chanted the marvelous hymn of Arab renaissance, had nevertheless to realize that their geographical position and the economic ties of their region were stronger even than the past that they wished to revive. Thus we find today the Arab states organically linked once more with societies which are Mediterranean in their culture. The fact is that these states are submitted to modern pressure and to new channels of trade while the network of trade relations which was dominant during the great period of Arab history has disappeared. But above all there is the fact that the political regimes of certain Arab states are so different, and so far away from each other in their conceptions, that even a cultural meeting between these states is meaningless.

Thus we see that the cultural problem as it sometimes exists in colonized countries runs the risk of giving rise to serious ambiguities. The lack of culture of the Negroes, as proclaimed by colonialism, and the inherent barbarity of the Arabs ought logically to lead to the exaltation of cultural manifestations which are not simply national but continental, and extremely racial. In Africa, the movement of men of culture is a movement toward the Negro-African culture or the Arab-Moslem culture. It is not specifically toward a national culture. Culture is becoming more and more cut off from the events of today. It finds its refuge beside a hearth that glows with passionate emotion, and from there makes its way by realistic paths which are the only means by which it may be made fruitful, homogeneous, and consistent.

If the action of the native intellectual is limited historically, there remains nevertheless the fact that it contributes greatly to upholding and justifying the action of politicians. It is true that the attitude of the native intellectual sometimes takes on the aspect of a cult or of a religion. But if we really wish to analyze this attitude correctly we will come to see that it is symptomatic of the intellectual's realization of the danger that he is running in cutting his last moorings and of breaking adrift from his people. This stated belief in a national culture is in fact an ardent, despairing turning toward anything that will afford him secure anchorage. In order to ensure his salvation and to escape from the supremacy of the white man's culture the native feels the need to turn backward toward his unknown roots and to lose himself at whatever cost in his own barbarous people. Because he feels he is becoming estranged, that is to say because he feels that he is the living haunt of contradictions which run the risk of becoming insurmountable, the native tears himself away from the swamp that may suck him down and accepts everything, decides to take all for granted and confirms everything even though he may lose body and soul. The native finds that he is expected to answer for everything, and to all comers. He not only turns himself into the defender of his people's past; he is willing to be counted as one of them, and henceforward he is even capable of laughing at his past cowardice.

This tearing away, painful and difficult though it may be, is however necessary. If it is not accomplished there will be serious psycho-affective injuries and the result will be individuals without an anchor, without a horizon, colorless, stateless, rootless – a race of angels. It will be also quite normal to hear certain natives declare, "I speak as a Senegalese and as a Frenchman . . ." "I speak as an Algerian and as a Frenchman . . ." The intellectual who is Arab and French, or Nigerian and English, when he comes up against the need to take on two nationalities, chooses, if he wants to remain true to himself, the negation of one of these determinations. But most often, since they cannot or will not make a choice, such intellectuals gather together all the historical determining factors which have conditioned them and take up a fundamentally "universal standpoint."

This is because the native intellectual has thrown himself greedily upon Western culture. Like adopted children who only stop investigating the new family framework at the moment when a minimum nucleus of security crystallizes in their psyche, the native intellectual will try to make European culture his own. He will not be content to get to know Rabelais and Diderot, Shakespeare and Edgar Allen Poe; he will bind them to his intelligence as closely as possible. . . .

But at the moment when the nationalist parties are mobilizing the people in the name of national independence, the native intellectual sometimes spurns these acquisitions which he suddenly feels make him a stranger in his own land. It is always easier to proclaim rejection than actually to reject. The intellectual who through the medium of culture has filtered into Western civilization, who has managed to become part of the body of

European culture – in other words who has exchanged his own culture for another – will come to realize that the cultural matrix, which now he wishes to assume since he is anxious to appear original, can hardly supply any figureheads which will bear comparison with those, so many in number and so great in prestige, of the occupying power's civilization. History, of course, though nevertheless written by the Westerners and to serve their purposes, will be able to evaluate from time to time certain periods of the African past. But, standing face to face with his country at the present time, and observing clearly and objectively the events of today throughout the continent which he wants to make his own, the intellectual is terrified by the void, the degradation, and the savagery he sees there. Now he feels that he must get away from the white culture. He must seek his culture elsewhere, anywhere at all; and if he fails to find the substance of culture of the same grandeur and scope as displayed by the ruling power, the native intellectual will very often fall back upon emotional attitudes and will develop a psychology which is dominated by exceptional sensitivity and susceptibility. This withdrawal, which is due in the first instance to a begging of the question in his internal behavior mechanism and his own character, brings out, above all, a reflex and contradiction which is muscular.

This is sufficient explanation of the style of those native intellectuals who decide to give expression to this phase of consciousness which is in the process of being liberated. It is a harsh style, full of images, for the image is the drawbridge which allows unconscious energies to be scattered on the surrounding meadows. It is a vigorous style, alive with rhythms, struck through and through with bursting life; it is full of color, too, bronzed, sunbaked, and violent. This style, which in its time astonished the peoples of the West, has nothing racial about it, in spite of frequent statements to the contrary; it expresses above all a hand-to-hand struggle and it reveals the

need that man has to liberate himself from a part of his being which already contained the seeds of decay. Whether the fight is painful, quick, or inevitable, muscular action must substitute itself for concepts.

If in the world of poetry this movement reaches unaccustomed heights, the fact remains that in the real world the intellectual often follows up a blind alley. When at the height of his intercourse with his people, whatever they were or whatever they are, the intellectual decides to come down into the common paths of real life, he only brings back from his adventuring formulas which are sterile in the extreme. He sets a high value on the customs, traditions, and the appearances of his people; but his inevitable, painful experience only seems to be a banal search for exoticism. The sari becomes sacred, and shoes that come from Paris or Italy are left off in favor of pampooties, while suddenly the language of the ruling power is felt to burn your lips. Finding your fellow countrymen sometimes means in this phase to will to be a nigger, not a nigger like all other niggers but a real nigger, a Negro cur, just the sort of nigger that the white man wants you to be. Going back to your own people means to become a dirty wog, to go native as much as you can, to become unrecognizable, and to cut off those wings that before you had allowed to grow.

The native intellectual decides to make an inventory of the bad habits drawn from the colonial world, and hastens to remind everyone of the good old customs of the people, that people which he has decided contains all truth and goodness. The scandalized attitude with which the settlers who live in the colonial territory greet this new departure only serves to strengthen the native's decision. When the colonialists, who had tasted the sweets of their victory over these assimilated people, realize that these men whom they considered as saved souls are beginning to fall back into the ways of niggers, the whole system totters. Every native won over, every native who had taken the pledge not only marks a failure for the colonial structure when he decides to lose himself and to go back to his own side, but also stands as a symbol for the uselessness and the shallowness of all the work that has been accomplished. Each native who goes back over the line is a radical condemnation of the methods and of the regime; and the native intellectual finds in the scandal he gives rise to a justification and an encouragement to persevere in the path he has chosen.

If we wanted to trace in the works of native writers the different phases which characterize this evolution we would find spread out before us a panorama on three levels. In the first phase, the native intellectual gives proof that he has assimilated the culture of the occupying power. His writings correspond point by point with those of his opposite numbers in the mother country. His inspiration is European and we can easily link up these works with definite trends in the literature of the mother country. This is the period of unqualified assimilation. We find in this literature coming from the colonies the Parnassians, the Symbolists, and the Surrealists.

In the second phase we find the native is disturbed; he decides to remember what he is. This period of creative work approximately corresponds to that immersion which we have just described. But since the native is not a part of his people, since he only has exterior relations with his people, he is content to recall their life only. Past happenings of the byegone days of his childhood will be brought up out of the depths of his memory; old legends will be reinterpreted in the light of a borrowed estheticism and of a conception of the world which was discovered under other skies.

Sometimes this literature of just-before-the-battle is dominated by humor and by allegory; but often too it is symptomatic of a period of distress and difficulty, where death is experienced, and disgust too. We spew ourselves up; but already underneath laughter can be heard.

Finally in the third phase, which is called the fighting phase, the native, after having tried to lose himself in the people and with the people, will on the contrary shake the people. Instead of according the people's lethargy an honored place in his esteem, he turns himself into an awakener of the people; hence comes a fighting literature, a revolutionary literature, and a national literature. During this phase a great many men and women who up till then would never have thought of producing a literary work, now that they find themselves in exceptional circumstances – in prison, with the Maquis, or on the eve of their execution – feel the need to speak to their nation, to compose the sentence which expresses the heart of the people, and to become the mouthpiece of a new reality in action.

The native intellectual nevertheless sooner or later will realize that you do not show proof of your nation from its culture but that you substantiate its existence in the fight which the people wage against the forces of occupation. No colonial system draws its justification from the fact that the territories it dominates are culturally non-existent. You will never make colonialism blush for shame by spreading out little-known cultural treasures under its eyes. At the very moment when the native intellectual is anxiously trying to create a cultural work he fails to realize that he is utilizing techniques and language which are borrowed from the stranger in his country. He contents himself with stamping these instruments with a hallmark which he wishes to be national, but which is strangely reminiscent of exoticism. The native intellectual who comes back to his people by way of cultural achievements behaves in fact like a foreigner. Sometimes he has no hesitation in using a dialect in order to show his will to be as near as possible to the people; but the ideas that he expresses and the preoccupations he is taken up with have no common yardstick to measure the real situation which the men and the women of his country know. The culture that the intellectual leans toward is often no more than a stock of particularisms. He wishes to attach himself to the people; but instead he only catches hold of their outer garments. And these outer garments are merely the reflection of a hidden life, teeming and perpetually in motion. That extremely obvious objectivity which seems to characterize a people is in fact only the inert, already forsaken result of frequent, and not always very coherent, adaptations of a much more fundamental substance which itself is continually being renewed. The man of culture, instead of setting out to find this substance, will let himself be hypnotized by these mummified fragments which because they are static are in fact symbols of negation and outworn contrivances. Culture has never the translucidity of custom; it abhors all simplification. In its essence it is opposed to custom, for custom is always the deterioration of culture. The desire to attach oneself to tradition or bring abandoned traditions to life again does not only mean going against the current of history but also opposing one's own people. When a people undertakes an armed struggle or even a political struggle against a relentless colonialism, the significance of tradition changes. All that has made up the technique of passive resistance in the past may, during this phase, be radically condemned. In an underdeveloped country during the period of struggle traditions are fundamentally unstable and are shot through by centrifugal tendencies. This is why the intellectual often runs the risk of being out of date. The peoples who have carried on the struggle are more and more impervious to demagogy; and those who wish to follow them reveal themselves as nothing more than common opportunists, in other words, latecomers.

In the sphere of plastic arts, for example, the native artist who wishes at whatever cost to create a national work of art shuts himself up in a stereotyped reproduction of details. These artists who have nevertheless thoroughly studied modern techniques and who have taken part in the main trends of contemporary painting and architecture, turn their backs on foreign culture, deny it, and set out to look for a true national culture, setting great store on what they consider to be the constant principles of national art. But these people forget that the forms of thought and what it feeds on, together with modern techniques of information, language, and dress have dialectically reorganized the people's intelligences and that the constant principles which acted as safeguards during the colonial period are now undergoing extremely radical changes.

The artist who has decided to illustrate the truths of the nation turns paradoxically toward the past and away from actual events. What he ultimately intends to embrace are in fact the castoffs of thought, its shells and corpses, a knowledge which has been stabilized once and for all. But the native intellectual who wishes to create an authentic work of art must realize that the truths of a nation are in the first place its realities. He must go on until he has found the seething pot out of which the learning of the future will emerge.

Before independence, the native painter was insensible to the national scene. He set a high value on non-figurative art, or more often specialized in still lifes. After independence his anxiety to rejoin his people will confine him to the most detailed representation of reality. This is representative art which has no internal rhythms, an art which is serene and immobile, evocative not of life but of death. Enlightened circles are in ecstasies when confronted with this "inner truth" which is so well expressed; but we have the right to ask if this truth is in fact a reality, and if it is not already outworn and denied, called in question by the epoch through which the people are treading out their path toward history.

In the realm of poetry we may establish the same facts. After the period of assimilation characterized by rhyming poetry, the poetic tom-tom's rhythms break through. This is a poetry of revolt; but it is also descriptive and analytical poetry. The poet ought however to understand that nothing can replace the reasoned, irrevocable taking up of arms on the people's side. Let us quote Depestre:

The lady was not alone;
She had a husband,
A husband who knew everything,
But to tell the truth knew nothing,
For you can't have culture without making concessions.
You concede your flesh and blood to it,
You concede your own self to others,
By conceding you gain
Classicism and Romanticism,
And all that our souls are steeped in.[1]

The native poet who is preoccupied with creating a national work of art and who is determined to describe his people fails in his aim, for he is not yet ready to make that fundamental concession that Depestre speaks of. The French poet René Char shows his understanding of the difficulty when he reminds us that "the poem emerges out of a subjective imposition and an objective choice. A poem is the assembling and moving together of determining original values, in contemporary relation with someone that these circumstances bring to the front."[2]

Yes, the first duty of the native poet is to see clearly the people he has chosen as the subject of his work of art. He cannot go forward resolutely unless he first realizes the extent of his estrangement from them. We have taken everything from the other side; and the other side gives us nothing unless by a thousand detours we swing finally round in their direction, unless by ten thousand wiles and a hundred thousand tricks they manage to draw us toward them, to seduce us, and to imprison us. Taking means in nearly every case being taken: thus it is not enough to try to free oneself by repeating proclamations and denials. It is not enough to try to get back to the people in that past out of which they have already emerged; rather we must join them in that fluctuating movement which they are just giving a shape to, and which, as soon as it has started, will be the signal for everything to be

called in question. Let there be no mistake about it; it is to this zone of occult instability where the people dwell that we must come; and it is there that our souls are crystallized and that our perceptions and our lives are transfused with light. . . .

The responsibility of the native man of culture is not a responsibility vis-à-vis his national culture, but a global responsibility with regard to the totality of the nation, whose culture merely, after all, represents one aspect of that nation. The cultured native should not concern himself with choosing the level on which he wishes to fight or the sector where he decides to give battle for his nation. To fight for national culture means in the first place to fight for the liberation of the nation, that material keystone which makes the building of a culture possible. There is no other fight for culture which can develop apart from the popular struggle. To take an example: all those men and women who are fighting with their bare hands against French colonialism in Algeria are not by any means strangers to the national culture of Algeria. The national Algerian culture is taking on form and content as the battles are being fought out, in prisons, under the guillotine, and in every French outpost which is captured or destroyed.

We must not therefore be content with delving into the past of a people in order to find coherent elements which will counteract colonialism's attempts to falsify and harm. We must work and fight with the same rhythm as the people to construct the future and to prepare the ground where vigorous shoots are already springing up. A national culture is not a folklore, nor an abstract populism that believes it can discover the people's true nature. It is not made up of the inert dregs of gratuitous actions, that is to say actions which are less and less attached to the ever-present reality of the people. A national culture is the whole body of efforts made by a people in the

---

[1] René Depestre: "Face à la Nuit."
[2] René Char, *Partage Formel.*

sphere of thought to describe, justify, and praise the action through which that people has created itself and keeps itself in existence. A national culture in underdeveloped countries should therefore take its place at the very heart of the struggle for freedom which these countries are carrying on. Men of African cultures who are still fighting in the name of African-Negro culture and who have called many congresses in the name of the unity of that culture should today realize that all their efforts amount to is to make comparisons between coins and sarcophagi.

There is no common destiny to be shared between the national cultures of Senegal and Guinea; but there *is* a common destiny between the Senegalese and Guinean nations which are both dominated by the same French colonialism. If it is wished that the national culture of Senegal should come to resemble the national culture of Guinea, it is not enough for the rulers of the two peoples to decide to consider their problems – whether the problem of liberation is concerned, or the trade-union question, or economic difficulties – from similar viewpoints. And even here there does not seem to be complete identity, for the rhythm of the people and that of their rulers are not the same. There can be no two cultures which are completely identical. To believe that it is possible to create a black culture is to forget that niggers are disappearing, just as those people who brought them into being are seeing the breakup of their economic and cultural supremacy.[3] There will never be such a thing as black culture because there is not a single politician who feels he has a vocation to bring black republics into being. The problem is to get to know the place that these men mean to give their people, the kind of social relations that they decide to set up, and the conception that they have of the future

of humanity. It is this that counts; everything else is mystification, signifying nothing.

In 1959, the cultured Africans who met at Rome never stopped talking about unity. But one of the people who was loudest in the praise of this cultural unity, Jacques Rabemananjara, is today a minister in the Madagascan government, and as such has decided, with his government, to oppose the Algerian people in the General Assembly of the United Nations. Rabemananjara, if he had been true to himself, ought to have resigned from the government and denounced those men who claim to incarnate the will of the Madagascan people. The ninety thousand dead of Madagascar have not given Rabemananjara authority to oppose the aspirations of the Algerian people in the General Assembly of the United Nations.

It is around the peoples' struggles that African-Negro culture takes on substance, and not around songs, poems, or folklore. Senghor, who is also a member of the Society of African Culture and who has worked with us on the question of African culture, is not afraid for his part either to give the order to his delegation to support French proposals on Algeria. Adherence to African-Negro culture and to the cultural unity of Africa is arrived at in the first place by upholding unconditionally the peoples' struggle for freedom. No one can truly wish for the spread of African culture if he does not give practical support to the creation of the conditions necessary to the existence of that culture; in other words, to the liberation of the whole continent.

I say again that no speech-making and no proclamation concerning culture will turn us from our fundamental tasks: the liberation of the national territory; a continual struggle against colonialism in its new forms; and an obstinate refusal to enter the charmed circle of mutual admiration at the summit.

---

[3] At the last school prize giving in Dakar, the president of the Senegalese Republic, Léopold Senghor, decided to include the study of the idea of negritude in the curriculum. If this decision was due to a desire to study historical causes, no one can criticize it. But if on the other hand it was taken in order to create black self-consciousness, it is simply a turning of his back upon history which has already taken cognizance of the disappearance of the majority of Negroes.

Reciprocal Bases of National Culture and the Fight for Freedom

Colonial domination, because it is total and tends to oversimplify, very soon manages to disrupt in spectacular fashion the cultural life of a conquered people. This cultural obliteration is made possible by the negation of national reality, by new legal relations introduced by the occupying power, by the banishment of the natives and their customs to outlying districts by colonial society, by expropriation, and by the systematic enslaving of men and women.

Three years ago at our first congress I showed that, in the colonial situation, dynamism is replaced fairly quickly by a substantification of the attitudes of the colonizing power. The area of culture is then marked off by fences and signposts. These are in fact so many defense mechanisms of the most elementary type, comparable for more than one good reason to the simple instinct for preservation. The interest of this period for us is that the oppressor does not manage to convince himself of the objective non-existence of the oppressed nation and its culture. Every effort is made to bring the colonized person to admit the inferiority of his culture which has been transformed into instinctive patterns of behavior, to recognize the unreality of his "nation," and, in the last extreme, the confused and imperfect character of his own biological structure.

Vis-à-vis this state of affairs, the native's reactions are not unanimous. While the mass of the people maintain intact traditions which are completely different from those of the colonial situation, and the artisanal style solidifies into a formalism which is more and more stereotyped, the intellectual throws himself in frenzied fashion into the frantic acquisition of the culture of the occupying power and takes every opportunity of unfavorably criticizing his own national culture, or else takes refuge in setting out and substantiating the claims of that culture in a way that is passionate but rapidly becomes unproductive.

The common nature of these two reactions lies in the fact that they both lead to impossible contradictions. Whether a turncoat or a substantialist, the native is ineffectual precisely because the analysis of the colonial situation is not carried out on strict lines. The colonial situation calls a halt to national culture in almost every field. Within the framework of colonial domination there is not and there will never be such phenomena as new cultural departures or changes in the national culture. Here and there valiant attempts are sometimes made to reanimate the cultural dynamic and to give fresh impulses to its themes, its forms, and its tonalities. The immediate, palpable, and obvious interest of such leaps ahead is nil. But if we follow up the consequences to the very end we see that preparations are being thus made to brush the cobwebs off national consciousness, to question oppression, and to open up the struggle for freedom.

A national culture under colonial domination is a contested culture whose destruction is sought in systematic fashion. It very quickly becomes a culture condemned to secrecy. This idea of a clandestine culture is immediately seen in the reactions of the occupying power which interprets attachment to traditions as faithfulness to the spirit of the nation and as a refusal to submit. This persistence in following forms of cultures which are already condemned to extinction is already a demonstration of nationality; but it is a demonstration which is a throwback to the laws of inertia. There is no taking of the offensive and no redefining of relationships. There is simply a concentration on a hard core of culture which is becoming more and more shrivelled up, inert, and empty.

By the time a century or two of exploitation has passed there comes about a veritable emaciation of the stock of national culture. It becomes a set of automatic habits, some traditions of dress, and a few broken-down institutions. Little movement can be discerned in such remnants of culture; there is no real creativity and no overflowing life. The poverty of the people, national oppression, and the inhibition of culture are one and the same thing. After a century of colonial domination we find a culture which is rigid in the extreme, or rather what we find are the dregs of culture, its mineral strata. The withering away of the reality of the nation and the death pangs of the national culture are linked to each other in mutual dependence. This is why it is of capital importance to follow the evolution of these relations during the struggle for national freedom. The negation of the native's culture, the contempt for any manifestation of culture whether active or emotional, and the placing outside the pale of all specialized branches of organization contribute to breed aggressive patterns of conduct in the native. But these patterns of conduct are of the reflexive type; they are poorly differentiated, anarchic, and ineffective. Colonial exploitation, poverty, and endemic famine drive the native more and more to open, organized revolt. The necessity for an open and decisive breach is formed progressively and imperceptibly, and comes to be felt by the great majority of the people. Those tensions which hitherto were non-existent come into being. International events, the collapse of whole sections of colonial empires and the contradictions inherent in the colonial system strengthen and uphold the native's combativity while promoting and giving support to national consciousness.

These new-found tensions which are present at all stages in the real nature of colonialism have their repercussions on the cultural plane. In literature, for example, there is relative overproduction. From being a reply on a minor scale to the dominating power, the literature produced by natives becomes differentiated and makes itself into a will to particularism. The intelligentsia, which during the period of repression was essentially a consuming public, now themselves become producers. This literature at first chooses to confine itself to the tragic and poetic style; but

later on novels, short stories, and essays are attempted. It is as if a kind of internal organization or law of expression existed which wills that poetic expression become less frequent in proportion as the objectives and the methods of the struggle for liberation become more precise. Themes are completely altered; in fact, we find less and less of bitter, hopeless recrimination and less also of that violent, resounding, florid writing which on the whole serves to reassure the occupying power. The colonialists have in former times encouraged these modes of expression and made their existence possible. Stinging denunciations, the exposing of distressing conditions and passions which find their outlet in expression are in fact assimilated by the occupying power in a cathartic process. To aid such processes is in a certain sense to avoid their dramatization and to clear the atmosphere.

But such a situation can only be transitory. In fact, the progress of national consciousness among the people modifies and gives precision to the literary utterances of the native intellectual. The continued cohesion of the people constitutes for the intellectual an invitation to go further than his cry of protest. The lament first makes the indictment; and then it makes an appeal. In the period that follows, the words of command are heard. The crystallization of the national consciousness will both disrupt literary styles and themes, and also create a completely new public. While at the beginning the native intellectual used to produce his work to be read exclusively by the oppressor, whether with the intention of charming him or of denouncing him through ethnic or subjectivist means, now the native writer progressively takes on the habit of addressing his own people.

It is only from that moment that we can speak of a national literature. Here there is, at the level of literary creation, the taking up and clarification of themes which are typically nationalist. This may be properly called a literature of combat, in the sense that it calls on the whole people to fight for their existence as a nation. It is a literature of combat, because it molds the national consciousness, giving it form and contours and flinging open before it new and boundless horizons; it is a literature of combat because it assumes responsibility, and because it is the will to liberty expressed in terms of time and space.

On another level, the oral tradition – stories, epics, and songs of the people – which formerly were filed away as set pieces are now beginning to change. The storytellers who used to relate inert episodes now bring them alive and introduce into them modifications which are increasingly fundamental. There is a tendency to bring conflicts up to date and to modernize the kinds of struggle which the stories evoke, together with the names of heroes and the types of weapons. The method of allusion is more and more widely used. The formula "This all happened long ago" is substituted with that of "What we are going to speak of happened somewhere else, but it might well have happened here today, and it might happen tomorrow." The example of Algeria is significant in this context. From 1952–53 on, the storytellers, who were before that time stereotyped and tedious to listen to, completely overturned their traditional methods of storytelling and the contents of their tales. Their public, which was formerly scattered, became compact. The epic, with its typified categories, reappeared; it became an authentic form of entertainment which took on once more a cultural value. Colonialism made no mistake when from 1955 on it proceeded to arrest these storytellers systematically.

The contact of the people with the new movement gives rise to a new rhythm of life and to forgotten muscular tensions, and develops the imagination. Every time the storyteller relates a fresh episode to his public, he presides over a real invocation. The existence of a new type of man is revealed to the public. The present is no longer turned in upon itself but spread out for all to see. The storyteller once more gives free rein to his imagination; he makes innovations and he creates a work of art. It even happens that the characters, which are barely ready for such a transformation – highway robbers or more or less anti-social vagabonds – are taken up and remodeled. The emergence of the imagination and of the creative urge in the songs and epic stories of a colonized country is worth following. The storyteller replies to the expectant people by successive approximations, and makes his way, apparently alone but in fact helped on by his public, toward the seeking out of new patterns, that is to say national patterns. Comedy and farce disappear, or lose their attraction. As for dramatization, it is no longer placed on the plane of the troubled intellectual and his tormented conscience. By losing its characteristics of despair and revolt, the drama becomes part of the common lot of the people and forms part of an action in preparation or already in progress.

Where handicrafts are concerned, the forms of expression which formerly were the dregs of art, surviving as if in a daze, now begin to reach out. Woodwork, for example, which formerly turned out certain faces and attitudes by the million, begins to be differentiated. The inexpressive or overwrought mask comes to life and the arms tend to be raised from the body as if to sketch an action. Compositions containing two, three or five figures appear. The traditional schools are led on to creative efforts by the rising avalanche of amateurs or of critics. This new vigor in this sector of cultural life very often passes unseen; and yet its contribution to the national effort is of capital importance. By carving figures and faces which are full of life, and by taking as his theme a group fixed on the same pedestal, the artist invites participation in an organized movement.

If we study the repercussions of the awakening of national consciousness in the domains of ceramics and pottery-making, the same observations may be drawn. Formalism is abandoned in the craftsman's work. Jugs, jars, and trays are modified, at first imperceptibly, then almost savagely. The colors, of which formerly there were but few and which obeyed the traditional rules of harmony, increase in number and are influenced by the repercussion of the rising revolution. Certain ochres and blues, which seemed forbidden to all eternity in a given cultural area, now assert themselves without giving rise to scandal. In the same way the stylization of the human face, which according to sociologists is typical of very clearly defined regions, becomes suddenly completely relative. The specialist coming from the home country and the ethnologist are quick to note these changes. On the whole such changes are condemned in the name of a rigid code of artistic style and of a cultural life which grows up at the heart of the colonial system. The colonialist specialists do not recognize these new forms and rush to the help of the traditions of the indigenous society. It is the colonialists who become the defenders of the native style. We remember perfectly, and the example took on a certain measure of importance since the real nature of colonialism was not involved, the reactions of the white jazz specialists when after the Second World War new styles such as the be-bop took definite shape. The fact is that in their eyes jazz should only be the despairing, broken-down nostalgia of an old Negro who is trapped between five glasses of whiskey, the curse of his race, and the racial hatred of the white men. As soon as the Negro comes to an understanding of himself, and understands the rest of the world differently, when he gives birth to hope and forces back the racist universe, it is clear that his trumpet sounds more clearly and his voice less hoarsely. The new fashions in jazz are not simply born of economic competition. We must without any doubt see in them one of the consequences of the defeat, slow but sure, of the southern world of the United States. And it is not utopian to suppose that in fifty years' time the type of jazz howl hiccuped by a poor misfortunate Negro will be upheld only by the whites who believe in it as an expression of negritude, and who are faithful to this arrested image of a type of relationship.

We might in the same way seek and find in dancing, singing, and traditional rites and ceremonies the same upward-springing trend, and make out the same changes and the same impatience in this field. Well before the political or fighting phase of the national movement, an attentive spectator can thus feel and see the manifestation of new vigor and feel the approaching conflict. He will note unusual forms of expression and themes which are fresh and imbued with a power which is no longer that of invocation but rather of the assembling of the people, a summoning together for a precise purpose. Everything works together to awaken the native's sensibility and to make unreal and inacceptable the contemplative attitude, or the acceptance of defeat. The native rebuilds his perceptions because he renews the purpose and dynamism of the craftsmen, of dancing and music, and of literature and the oral tradition. His world comes to lose its accursed character. The conditions necessary for the inevitable conflict are brought together.

We have noted the appearance of the movement in cultural forms and we have seen that this movement and these new forms are linked to the state of maturity of the national consciousness. Now, this movement tends more and more to express itself objectively, in institutions. From thence comes the need for a national existence, whatever the cost.

A frequent mistake, and one which is moreover hardly justifiable, is to try to find cultural expressions for and to give new values to native culture within the framework of colonial domination. This is why we arrive at a proposition which at first sight seems paradoxical: the fact that in a colonized country the most elementary, most savage, and the most undifferentiated nationalism is the most fervent and efficient means of defending national culture. For culture is first the expression of a nation, the expression of its preferences, of its taboos and of its patterns. It is at every stage of the whole of society that other taboos, values, and patterns are formed. A national culture is the sum total of all these appraisals; it is the result of internal and external tensions exerted over society as a whole and also at every level of that society. In the colonial situation, culture, which is doubly deprived of the support of the nation and of the state, falls away and dies. The condition for its existence is therefore national liberation and the renaissance of the state.

The nation is not only the condition of culture, its fruitfulness, its continuous renewal, and its deepening. It is also a necessity. It is the fight for national existence which sets culture moving and opens to it the doors of creation. Later on it is the nation which will ensure the conditions and framework necessary to culture. The nation gathers together the various indispensable elements necessary for the creation of a culture, those elements which alone can give it credibility, validity, life, and creative power. In the same way it is its national character that will make such a culture open to other cultures and which will enable it to influence and permeate other cultures. A non-existent culture can hardly be expected to have bearing on reality, or to influence reality. The first necessity is the re-establishment of the nation in order to give life to national culture in the strictly biological sense of the phrase.

Thus we have followed the breakup of the old strata of culture, a shattering which becomes increasingly fundamental; and we have noticed, on the eve of the decisive conflict for national freedom, the renewing of forms of expression and the rebirth of the imagination. There remains one essential question: what are the relations between the struggle – whether political or military – and culture? Is there a suspension of culture during the conflict? Is the national struggle an expression of a culture? Finally, ought one to say that the battle for freedom however fertile *a posteriori* with regard to culture is in itself a negation of culture? In short, is the struggle for liberation a cultural phenomenon or not?

We believe that the conscious and organized undertaking by a colonized people to re-establish the sovereignty of that nation constitutes the most complete and obvious cultural manifestation that exists. It is not alone the success of the struggle which afterward gives validity and vigor to culture; culture is not put into cold storage during the conflict. The struggle itself in its development and in its internal progression sends culture along different paths and traces out entirely new ones for it. The struggle for freedom does not give back to the national culture its former value and shapes; this struggle which aims at a fundamentally different set of relations between men cannot leave intact either the form or the content of the people's culture. After the conflict there is not only the disappearance of colonialism but also the disappearance of the colonized man.

This new humanity cannot do otherwise than define a new humanism both for itself and for others. It is prefigured in the objectives and methods of the conflict. A struggle which mobilizes all classes of the people and which expresses their aims and their impatience, which is not afraid to count almost exclusively on the people's support, will of necessity triumph. The value of this type of conflict is that it supplies the maximum of conditions necessary for the development and aims of culture. After national freedom has been obtained in these conditions, there is no such painful cultural indecision which is found in certain countries which are newly independent, because the nation by its manner of coming into being and in the terms of its existence exerts a fundamental influence over culture. A nation which is born of the people's concerted action and which embodies the real aspirations of the people while changing the state cannot exist save in the expression of exceptionally rich forms of culture.

The natives who are anxious for the culture of their country and who wish to give to it a universal dimension ought not therefore to place their confidence in the single principle of inevitable, undifferentiated independence written into the consciousness of the people in order to achieve their task. The liberation of the nation is one thing; the methods and popular content of the fight are another. It seems to us that the future of national culture and its riches are equally also part and parcel of the values which have ordained the struggle for freedom.

And now it is time to denounce certain pharisees. National claims, it is here and there stated, are a phase that humanity has left behind. It is the day of great concerted actions, and retarded nationalists ought in consequence to set their mistakes aright. We however consider that the mistake, which may have very serious consequences, lies in wishing to skip the national period. If culture is the expression of national consciousness, I will not hesitate to affirm that in the case with which we are dealing it is the national consciousness which is the most elaborate form of culture.

The consciousness of self is not the closing of a door to communication. Philosophic thought teaches us, on the contrary, that it is its guarantee. National consciousness, which is not nationalism, is the only thing that will give us an international dimension. This problem of national consciousness and of national culture takes on in Africa a special dimension. The birth of national consciousness in Africa has a strictly contemporaneous connection with the African consciousness. The responsibility of the African as regards national culture is also a responsibility with regard to African Negro culture. This joint responsibility is not the fact of a metaphysical principle but the awareness of a simple rule which wills that every independent nation in an Africa where colonialism is still entrenched is an encircled nation, a nation which is fragile and in permanent danger.

If man is known by his acts, then we will say that the most urgent thing today for the intellectual is to build up his nation. If this building up is true, that is to say if it interprets the manifest will of the people and reveals the eager African peoples, then the building of a nation is of necessity accompanied by the discovery and encouragement of universalizing values. Far from keeping aloof from other nations, therefore, it is national liberation which leads the nation to play its part on the stage of history. It is at the heart of national consciousness that international consciousness lives and grows. And this two-fold emerging is ultimately only the source of all culture.

39

NATIONALISM, ETHNICITY, AND MODERNITY: THE PARADOX OF MAU MAU

BRUCE J. BERMAN

Introduction: The Continuing Fascination of Mau Mau

What was Mau Mau? What was its significance in the history of Kenya or, more broadly, the history of colonial Africa? What can an understanding of Mau Mau tell us about the colonial confrontation of African "tradition" and Western "modernity"? Almost forty years after the colonial authorities in Nairobi declared a state of emergency to crush what they insisted was a savage and wholly evil secret cult, conclusive answers to these questions remain elusive. "The horror story of the Empire in the 1950s," as John Lonsdale calls it, continues to be a source of political and intellectual controversy.[1] During the 1970s and again in the mid-1980s, Kenyan intellectuals and political figures clashed over conflicting interpretations of Mau Mau, with many aging ex-Mau Mau fighters also jumping into the fray (Odhiambo, 1988; Maughan-Brown, 1985, 20–22) The historical and fictional writings on Mau Mau of Kenya's

leading intellectual dissidents, Ngugi wa Thiong'o and Maina wa Kinyatti, were factors in their detention and exile (Ngugi and Micere Mugo 1976; Ngugi 1983; wa Kinyatti 1985, 1987). Academic interest in Mau Mau has surged once more, with a whole series of monographs and papers appearing since 1986 which explore yet again its nature and place in the politics of colonial and post-colonial Kenya (Kanogo 1987; Throup 1987; Edgerton 1989; Furedi 1989; Presley 1988; Gordon 1986; Berman 1990).

Central to the debates over Mau Mau is the nature of its relationship to nationalism in Kenya. Was it a parochial tribal uprising or the central episode of Kenya's national liberation struggle? Were the Mau Mau forest fighters tribal traditionalists or nationalist patriots? Despite its military defeat by Imperial forces, did Mau Mau force the British into social and political reforms which led to independence under an African government? If Mau Mau fought for national liberation, why was it unable to articulate a trans-ethnic national

---

[1] This article is derived from a joint research project entitled "Explaining Mau Mau: A Study in the Politics of Knowledge," in which John Lonsdale and I have been engaged since 1987. While many of the ideas expressed in this article are the joint product of our work, I remain responsible for the particular interpretation offered here.

ideology? This article addresses these questions through a critical examination of the
conflicting interpretations of Mau Mau's
relationship with nationalism, followed by a
plausible reconstruction of the relationship
suggested by an understanding of the internal
conflicts in Kikuyu society in the first decade
after World War II.

Mau Mau: Anti-Nationalism or Militant Nationalism?

In the late 1940s colonial officials first became
aware of what they believed was a secret
organization among African farm labourers on
the European estates of the Rift Valley which
they named "Mau Mau." Through the years
of the Emergency from 1952 to 1960, and into
the first years of Kenya's independence after
1963, the dominant interpretation of this
phenomenon focused on its essentially tribal
and religious character. This view, with
variations, comprised the conventional
wisdom about Mau Mau shared not only by
colonial officials in Nairobi and London, white
settlers, and missionaries but also by journalists and academic commentators from Britain
and several other countries.

In the most coherent official version,[2] Mau
Mau was depicted as a savage, violent, and
depraved tribal cult, an expression of unrestrained emotion rather than reason. It sought
to turn the Kikuyu people back to "the bad old
days" before enlightened British rule had
brought the blessings of modern civilization
and development. When the first reports of
something called "Mau Mau" reached the

Provincial Administration and the Kenya
Police in 1948–49, it was immediately identified as a "dini" or religious cult. As late as
February 1953, the Commissioner of Police
was passing on reports that linked Mau Mau
with the Dini ya Msambwa, which had
violently clashed with government forces a few
years before.[3] The government also claimed
that Mau Mau had emerged among a particularly unstable people who had difficulty
adjusting to the strains of rapid social change
and modernization. Playing upon their morbid
fears and superstitions, Mau Mau turned the
Kikuyu into savage and maniacal killers.
Government intelligence reports dwelt on the
"insane frenzy" and "fanatical discipline" of
Mau Mau adherents.[4] It had been deliberately
organized, according to the government, by
cynical and unprincipled leaders, seeking only
to satisfy their own lust for power.
Furthermore, officials repeatedly insisted that
Mau Mau was not a response to economic
deprivation and material grievances arising out
of colonialism, but rather was an irrational
rejection of the benefits of development. This
view led them to stress repeatedly the essentially atavistic character of Mau Mau. As the
British parliamentary delegation which visited
Kenya in 1954 put it, "Mau Mau intentionally
and deliberately seeks to lead the Africans of
Kenya back to the bush and savagery, not
forward into progress" (*Report to the Secretary
of State*, 4). Depraved, murderous, and wholly
evil, Mau Mau had to be totally destroyed.

This characterization of Mau Mau,
repeated almost daily for several years in press
conferences, news briefs, and interviews from
government information agencies in Nairobi

---

[2] It is the official version developed by the authorities of the colonial state that is of primary interest in the present context. For an analysis of other variants of the explanation of Mau Mau among both Europeans and Africans during the Emergency, see Lonsdale (1990).

[3] The first papers on Mau Mau received by the Provincial Commissioner of Central Province (the main Kikuyu area) were filed with previous correspondence on religious sects found in the colony. See Kenya National Archives (hereafter, KNA) PC/CP8/7/4 (covering the period 1934–53); and Public Record Office, London (hereafter, PRO)/PC822/447, Commissioner of Police, "Secret Situation Report for 11 February, 1953."

[4] PRO/CO822/447, Commissioner of Police, "Secret Intelligence Report for 27 November, 1952."

and London, and widely disseminated in print and broadcasts by the press throughout the world, became and remains, especially in English-speaking countries, the image of the phenomenon in popular culture. Until the mid-1960s it received powerful support in numerous studies by academic social scientists which claimed for it the status of objective scientific knowledge. The most important of these were by Louis Leakey, Kenya's leading scholar and intellectual at the time, whose interpretive authority was reinforced by his being born and raised among the Kikuyu and being one of the few whites in Kenya who spoke their language fluently. His two books (1952 and 1954) gave definitive expression to the analysis of Mau Mau as a perverted religious cult manipulated by cynical and evil leaders, and were widely disseminated by the Kenya Government, which supplied copies to all of its administrative and police officers.[5] This explanation was quickly taken up by scholars in other countries, especially amongst American anthropologists, among whom Mau Mau was readily assimilated to existing concepts of "nativistic sects," "tribal revival movements," and "crisis cults" developed in the analysis of native American responses to white colonial expansion. Its definitive expression was a 1965 article by Gilbert Kushner in the German anthropological journal *Anthropos*, which relied primarily on Leakey for empirical evidence and fixed Mau Mau firmly within the theoretical paradigm of atavistic, violent, despairing movements among peoples being overwhelmed by the advance of modern civilization (Kushner 1965; see also Rosenstiel 1953).[6] These movements were seen as nostalgic attempts to escape the rigours of modernity; not efforts to relieve the inequities of colonial development, but its utter rejection.

Thus, Mau Mau's atavistic mind and tribal scale made it the enemy, the very antithesis, of nationalism. Mau Mau could not be an expression of nationalism because it led away from everything the latter represented as an essential part of the modernization process.

> No Western observer, not even those on the anti-colonial left, saw Mau Mau as the political expression of national integration . . . The movements symbols had nothing "Kenyan" about them. Mau Mau, uniquely, seemed to be a core radicalism which rejected the nation (Lonsdale 1989, 7).

By the mid-1960s this interpretation began to be challenged by a revisionist version of Mau Mau which depicted it as an essential, if radical, component of African nationalism in Kenya. First, memoirs of the Emergency by some of those active in Mau Mau began to be published, notably by J.M. Kariuki (1963), a politician who spent years in detention, and Waruhiu Itote (1967), who as "General China" had commanded the guerrilla forces in the forests of Mount Kenya until his capture in 1954. Both insisted that Mau Mau was a modern, rational, and nationalist political movement, not tribalist reaction, and that the fighters of the Land and Freedom Army had fought a glorious struggle for national liberation. Second, and more important for shaping a significant shift in academic opinion about Mau Mau, were two substantial works which brought together participants on opposite sides of the struggle with American social scientists. The first, *Mau Mau from Within*, is the autobiography of Karari Njama, a man of some education who had served as secretary to the guerrilla forces in the Aberdares and to its leader Dedan Kimathi, edited with extensive commentary by the radical anthropologist

---

[5] Leakey's role as both an interpreter and actor is a major part of the story of Mau Mau that has yet to be fully appreciated. We have attempted to rectify this omission in Berman and Lonsdale (1991a).

[6] So characterized, Mau Mau became a useful example for use in the comparative analysis of cults and religious movements. See, for example, Fernandez (1964) and La Barre (1971).

Donald Barnett. This text is an extended elaboration of the depiction of Mau Mau as a rational struggle for national liberation, substantially downplaying the Kikuyu cultural content and symbolism it employed. This is evident right at the beginning of the book in a preface signed by several prominent political figures, including Fred Kubai, Bildad Kaggia, and Achieng Oneko, who had been charged with Jomo Kenyatta with "organizing Mau Mau." They criticized previous accounts of it:

> There is obsessive preoccupation in these works with the sinister and the awesome. The very name "Mau Mau" is an illustration of how successful propaganda can damn an entire movement to which thousands sacrificed everything, including their lives, by attaching to it an appellation that conjures up all the clichés of the "dark continent" which still crowd the European mind. (Barnett and Njama 1966, 9)

The second challenge to the interpretation of Mau Mau as atavism is a thoroughly academic monograph, based on extensive documentary analysis and numerous interviews with African political figures, composed by John Nottingham, a maverick colonial administrator who had rejected the official version of Mau Mau, and Carl Rosberg, a political scientist from the University of California at Berkeley. They state their revisionist purpose right at the outset:

> "Mau Mau" is identified with the militant nationalism and the violence which characterized the politics of central Kenya before and during the early years of the Emergency . . . This book presents an alternative interpretation of "Mau Mau," in which we will be concerned with the modern origins of African politics and their pattern of development, with particular emphasis on the politicization and mobilization of the Kikuyu people . . . In our view, the outbreak of open violence in Kenya in 1952 occurred primarily because of a European failure rather than an African one; it was not so

much a failure of the Kikuyu people to adapt to a modern institutional setting as it was a failure of the European policy-makers to recognize the need for significant social and political reform. (Rosberg and Nottingham 1966, xvi–xvii)

Not only is Mau Mau identified as modern and nationalist but also the focus of the analysis is on the development of African anti-colonial nationalist opposition in Kenya in response to the concrete inequities and material grievances of colonial domination. African politics in Kenya is shown to be essentially instrumental and rational and grounded in material causes for which the British were largely responsible. The treatment of the specifically Kikuyu cultural forms and content which characterized Mau Mau is muted, with the Mau Mau oath, the central evidence for its supposed savage obscenity, depicted as a rational "instrument for achieving unity." The earlier interpretation of Mau Mau as savage and atavistic tribalism is subject to penetrating analysis as a "myth of Mau Mau" grounded in European racism and ethnocentrism. Only on the very last page do Rosberg and Nottingham conclude:

> Although oathing strengthened the Kikuyu organizational ability to challenge the colonial state, it nonetheless had the additional effect of limiting the institutional spread of the national movement to non-Kikuyu groups. This dilemma was not unrecognized by the Kikuyu leadership, for they envisaged the creation of other tribal oaths which would serve to mobilize and commit non-Kikuyu people to their style of militant nationalism. Lack of sufficient time and the Administration's success in compartmentalizing and controlling African political activity were two important factors that prevented this from occurring in any extensive manner. Thus, the pattern of nationalism as it unfolded stemmed from a rationally conceived strategy in search of political power within a context of structural

conditions which severely inhibited the growth of a colony-wide national organizational movement (1966, 354).[7]

Nationalism and Development: The Common Foundation of Divergent Explanations

How could such divergent, indeed contradictory, characterizations of Mau Mau develop as successive influential explanations of the phenomenon, with the "militant nationalism" model largely supplanting the "atavistic tribalism" model among Africanists by the end of the 1960s? The matter becomes even more compelling when one examines the explanations more closely and finds that they are in fact based on essentially identical premises about modernity, development, and nationalism. This paradox reveals some of the crucial difficulties involved not only in understanding Mau Mau, but in understanding the phenomenon called African nationalism. . . .

It has been clear for many years that the concept of "traditional society," and its particular expression in Africa, "tribal society," represent idealized constructs which very imperfectly reflect what is now understood about the character of pre-colonial African societies. In particular, the dominant image of traditional society as highly integrated, stable, relatively unchanging, and largely free of disruptive internal conflict has been challenged by increasing evidence of the fluidity of political boundaries and ethnic identities and the significant levels of internal conflict revealed in contemporary historical research. The concept of traditional society was not in any case based on substantial and systematically collected empirical evidence. The pre-colonial history of African societies

had barely begun to be written before the late 1960s; and the knowledge available in the late 1940s and early 1950s – largely from the haphazard and unsystematic efforts of colonial administrators and missionaries, and, for a very few African peoples, more methodical ethnographic studies by a handful of professional anthropologists – referred mostly to contemporary conditions in societies already subject to colonial rule for a generation or more. "Traditional society" represented instead the coming together of a set of seemingly incongruous assumptions and interests from a number of sources.

First, colonial administrators expressed an ideology of paternalistic authoritarianism grounded in a concept of society as an organic community, each of whose constituent parts had a specific role to play in the larger whole. Harmony and order were the basic characteristics of the organic community. While African tribal society was ignorant, impoverished, and superstition-ridden, it was also an organic community. Administrators came to see the conservation of the integrity of its institutions as instrumental for the maintenance of effective control (Berman 1990, 104–115).

While administrative ideology and its construction of tradition was imbued with a substantial element of conservative romantic irrationalism and of pastoral nostalgia for the rural community of some ill-defined golden past, it nevertheless dovetailed neatly with the far more rationalist model of traditional society of British social anthropology. The latter discipline was dominated from the 1930s until the end of colonial rule by the functionalist paradigms of Bronislaw Malinowski and A.R. Radcliffe-Brown, which emphasized the analysis of traditional societies as functionally integrated homeostatic systems in which any feature of the society was to be explained by the contribution it made to the maintenance

---

[7] The relationship between African grievances and African politics is the dominant theme of chapters II to VI, especially pages 220–233; the "Mau Mau" oath is analyzed on pages 241–262; while the European "myth of Mau Mau" is treated on pages 320–334.

of the whole. Despite mutual professional jealousy and hostility, anthropological ideas became increasingly familiar to colonial officials as anthropology was incorporated into Colonial Office training programmes, and after 1945 a growing number of social anthropologists made their way to Kenya and other colonies to conduct field research under the auspices of the Colonial Social Science Research Council. Furthermore, much anthropological work contained significant elements of an "ethnographic pastoral" (see Rosaldo 1986; Clifford 1986), complementing that of colonial officials, which idealized the harmony and order of functionally integrated traditional societies (Kuper 1983, chapters 3 and 4.)

Finally, the vision of traditional society of anthropologists and colonial officials was also significantly influenced by the interests and perspectives of African chiefs and elders, recognized in British Africa as "native authorities," who were the primary source of information about indigenous institutions and culture and sought to bolster their legitimacy by accounts that stressed their authoritative role in the maintenance of the order and harmony of pre-colonial society. In Kenya, and for the Kikuyu, all three of these elements came together in the work of Leakey, himself an initiated Kikuyu elder, who shared the images of traditional society of both colonial officials and anthropologists. . . .

This construction of traditional society was also essentially the same, if expressed in a different idiom, as that developed by American social scientists from Parsonian structural-functionalism and depicted in the now familiar dichotomies of the "pattern variables": particularism *versus* universalism, ascription *versus* achievement, affectivity *versus* neutrality, and diffuseness *versus* specificity (Leys 1982, 333–334). "Modern" societies were simply constructed as the polar opposite of traditional society on these characteristics and on numerous empirical "indicators." The distance between traditional and modern society was traversed by a universal and unilinear process of development, "from tradition to modernity." All existing societies could be ranged according to their position along this metaphorical road of social progress.

Both colonial officials and social scientists shared to a striking degree a conception of the normal course and sequence of this process of modernization. The political, economic, and cultural demands of colonialism stimulated social change by driving people out of the old "tribal" ways of doing things and pulling them into wider social arenas. As the networks of African societies increased in scale, the dependence on the small tribal community would decline, local loyalties and ethnic identities would diminish, and wider ones would develop. Under the impact of a monetary economy spread by wage labour and cash crop production, traditional social relations decline and are replaced by more instrumentally efficient modern forms.[8] The ascriptive particularism of small-scale societies would be increasingly replaced by the achievement-oriented universalism of modern secular society. Not even the most conservative District commissioner, who rued the demise of the communal solidarities of organic traditional societies, denied that the process led to a society based less on emotion and superstition and more on rationality and science. . . .

Paternalistic authoritarianism shaped the process of political progress towards the nation-state into a gradual tutelary procedure under the control of the colonial administration whereby local elites through experience in local government and administration would learn to rule and gradually be given access to more inclusive national institutions. The implicit model was of a class stratified national

---

[8]   One of the earliest expressions of these ideas was found in the first chapters of Wilson and Wilson (1945).

society led by an indigenous ruling elite sharing the outlook of their colonial rulers. As Michael Lee put it,

> Good government meant that the official classes accepted full responsibility for development schemes, neither more nor less. It was expected that local politicians and local civil servants would eventually arise to take over full responsibility, and therefore reconstitute the official classes. This process was often described as creating "a political class," which meant envisaging the creation of a native elite capable of running the machinery required to join the society of states in the international order (1967, 13–14).[9]

A former Secretary of State for the Colonies put it more bluntly and colourfully in an interview when he observed that "you can't have the institutions without a political class and you can't have a political class without the institutions" (Berman 1990, 106). This logic applied with particular force in a colony such as Kenya, with its substantial European and Asian immigrant populations. Political development for Africans was conceivable in the first instance only as ultimately part of a multiracial dominant class in which Europeans would continue to play a preponderant role for an indefinite period (Berman 1990, 301–307). . . .

While nationalist organizations and leaders could be assimilated to the rationalist social engineering of nation-building, nationalist passions could not. Colonial officials and political scientists alike shared an aversion to the fervent emotions, deep personal identification, and self-sacrificial commitment also identified with nationalism. In the aftermath of World War II, these sentiments seemed not only irrational but pernicious and destructive. According to Walker Conner, scholars presumed that the war had convinced the peoples of Western Europe that nationalism was dangerous and outmoded, and the implementation of Marxism–Leninism in Eastern Europe had made it superfluous in modern socialist societies, while in studying the Third World "ethnic heterogeneity tended to be ignored or to be cavalierly dismissed as an ephemeral phenomenon," and they "offered few if any suggestions as to how a single national consciousness was to be forged among disparate ethnic elements" (1987, 196–197). Political aversion was reinforced by intellectual disdain in the face of the theoretical incoherence and historical mystification characteristic of nationalist writing and the almost total lack of nationalist thinkers who could be recognized as great by anyone outside of the particular nation they addressed. Ernest Gellner notes: "their precise doctrines are hardly worth analyzing . . . nationalist ideology suffers from pervasive false consciousness" (1983, 124); and Benedict Anderson points to a central paradox when he notes the contrast between the "political power" of nationalisms *vs* their philosophical poverty" (Anderson 1983, 14). But while nationalist ideology holds no candle to liberalism or Marxism as intellectual doctrine, it has elicited far more intense and widespread commitment. The cenotaphs and tombs of unknown soldiers, one of the most powerful and common of nationalist symbols, are not matched, as Anderson wittily reminds us, by "a Tomb of the Unknown Marxist or a cenotaph for fallen Liberals" (Anderson 1983, 17–18).

Thus, the theory and the project of national development envisioned by either British colonial officials or American social scientists had little to say about or room for nationalism as doctrine and sentiment rooted in common history, culture, and language. Indeed, in the context of Africa, it seemed improbable that any one of the numerous "tribes" contained in

---

[9]   The principal Colonial Office statement of political development policy in the immediate post-war period came in the "Despatch from the Secretary of State to the Governors of the African Territories," 25 February 1947 (Kenya Government Library, Nairobi).

each colony could provide the basis for a national consciousness in the new nation-state they were creating. The growth of such ethno-cultural identities appeared to be dis-integrative and to recall traditional tribalism in a way that threatened both modernization and nation-building. Moreover, in Kenya, the presence of Asians and Europeans as distinctive cultural communities demanding protection of their communal rights made it inconceivable that any African cultural forms or identities could be part of the process of political development. The participation of Africans in a multi-racial dominant class had to be on the basis of their being essentially European in education, culture, and lifestyle. Officials assumed that assimilation to a dominant European culture was the natural goal for Africans and the pre-condition for the emergence of a common Kenyan nationality. As Rosberg and Nottingham note: "The Leviathan of the colonial state represented the enlightened self-interests of the African in which the new educated man could remove himself completely from the darkness of his barbaric origins into the sun of the white man's culture" (1966, 322). Multi-racialism could not mean multi-culturalism.

The difficulty of dealing with the passions of nationalist ideology and identity within the rationalist structural and materialist model of national development provided the basis for interpreting Mau Mau as either atavistic tribalism or radical nationalism. As I suggested earlier, the difference between these interpretations was vividly expressed in the readings given to the emotive ideological and cultural content of Mau Mau as contained largely in the oaths given to its recruits. During the Emergency, texts of oaths were the only evidence about Mau Mau presented to sustain the official version of its character. Colonial officials, white settlers and the British and international press were obsessed with the deviant weirdness and bestiality of the oaths as proving that Mau Mau was atavistic, savage, and evil.[10] Conversely, Njama and Barnett, Rosberg and Nottingham, and the various Mau Mau memoirists were equally intent on proving that it was a modern movement for national liberation and did so by stressing the politically instrumental character of the mass oaths and setting them within the context of a long history of African anti-colonial struggle and of accumulating grievances against the inequities of the colonial order. While this does show how divergent explanations were constructed within the common premises about tradition, modernity and national development, it does not explain why they were produced. To answer the latter question one must examine them within the particular historical contexts in which they appeared.

During the Emergency, particularly in its early phases, the British authorities in Nairobi and London had a desperate need for an explanation of Mau Mau which would accomplish several objectives, effectively achieved by characterizing it, as Cohen put it, as "a reversion to tribalism in a perverted and brutal form" (1959, 55). First, by convincing the cadres of the colonial state that Mau Mau in all its mystical and murderous obscenity was wholly evil, it enabled them to fight a nasty

---

[10]   John Lonsdale has noted the manner in which Mau Mau's "rituals of recruitment" were exploited at the time: British war propaganda had no difficulty in portraying these as utterly repugnant, debased, and by intention, debasing. . . . The paraphernalia of Mau Mau recruiting officers certainly made good copy which the press did not hesitate to exploit, if with the coy reserve which titillates as much as it repels. . . . For it was reported that the oaths became ever more deviant and bestial as the war dragged on and the insurgents became more desperate or fanatic. Many accounts left the details unsaid, allowing the readers' imaginations free to wander in fascinated self-disgust. . . . A visiting parliamentary delegation thought the recruitment rituals too dreadful to lay before the British electorate. The relevant appendix to the report was never published. It was deposited in the library of the House of Commons instead, where minds were apparently thought to be already sufficiently depraved (1989, 2).

guerrilla war in good conscience. A strong predisposition to this view already existed in the racist stereotypes of African brutishness, irrationality, and bloodthirsty violence which, in their most extreme form, kept the settler population of Kenya on a constant edge of hysterical fear of the Africans they so callously exploited, and, in more moderate form, left colonial officials uneasy about unpredictable and dangerous reactions from their African wards (Berman and Lonsdale 1991b, 6–14: Kennedy 1987, chapters 8 and 9; Maughan-Brown 1985, 81–93). Second, by stigmatizing Mau Mau as the enemy of modernizing development and nationalism, the authorities were able both to insist that it had nothing to do with African grievances and, with no sense of contradiction, to continue the project of national development through a massive programme of socio-economic reforms intended to increase substantially the incomes of both African peasants and urban workers, and also to expand rapidly education and social services in the urban locations and rural reserves. This programme was combined with a series of constitutional and political reforms which rapidly expanded African access to the central institutions of the colonial state, including the civil service.[11] Third, this characterization of Mau Mau also blunted the edge of left-wing critics of colonialism in Britain who tried to depict it as an anti-colonial liberation struggle.[12] Fourth, characterizing Mau Mau as atavistic and colonialism as progressive

also helped to moderate the potential reaction by both the United States and the Soviet Union to the use of force in the colony. In the former, it blunted deep-seated American anti-colonialism and helped sustain support for the British project of national development and gradual decolonization. As far as the Soviet Union was concerned, despite the fevered claims of extreme right-wing anti-communists in Britain and among the Kenya settlers, who saw a Russian agent behind every thorn tree, the colonial authorities well knew that there was no Soviet support or encouragement for Mau Mau, but in the Cold War deep freeze of the critical 1952–56 period, they sought to deny them any possible practical or propaganda advantage by stressing the primitive and retrogressive character of the movement.[13]

By the early 1960s the political context had changed significantly. Mau Mau had been defeated, but Kenya was rapidly moving towards independence under an African majority government. While Kenyatta was lionized as still the only real national leader, new nationalist organizations in Kenya contained an uneasy blend of old leaders, mostly Kikuyu, many of whom had spent the Emergency in detention, and a new generation of largely non-Kikuyu politicians. Externally, the crucial issue was in the development of relations between the new national government and the United States and the international agencies it dominated, which collectively controlled most of the sources of

---

[11]   This programme was called "the second prong" against Mau Mau, the first being the military campaign. The various reports, memoranda, and notes relating to it are a major source of information on official thinking during the Emergency and are found in KNA/GH4/795. For fuller analysis of the reform programme in the context of the politics of the Emergency see Berman (1990, 347–371).

[12]   The activities of the British left and various anti-colonial associations in Britain drew the particular ire of the colonial authorities, who felt that they did not understand what Mau Mau was "really" like and that their ill-informed efforts threatened to undermine the metropolitan political and economic support necessary to crush it. The first draft of the official history of Mau Mau, circulated among senior officials in Nairobi, contained a particularly virulent attack on the left-wing "friends" of Mau Mau, which was excised from the published version (KNA/GO3/2/72).

[13]   The sensitivity of the Colonial Office to reactions to Mau Mau in other countries, especially the US, is indicated in the papers contained in PRO/CO822/448 *External Repercussions on the Mau Mau Situation in Kenya*; while the concern with Soviet reactions and evaluation of possible Communist involvement is discussed in PRO/CO822/461 *Communist Aspects of the Mau Mau Situation in Kenya*.

aid and investment that would sustain the project of national development. Meanwhile, research on Africa, especially in the United States, had been rapidly expanded and professionalised into "African studies" dominated largely by political scientists. While this research was instrumental in persuading policy-makers in Britain that "territorial nationalism was a force for good, or at least a force to be reckoned with" (Lee 1967, 285),[14] Kenyan nationalism and many of its most important African political figures were tainted by the image of Mau Mau constructed during the Emergency. In the changed circumstances of this period, the former detainees and forest fighters sought to claim political legitimacy by insisting on a Mau Mau connection with nationalism and the independence struggle. . . .

The Relationship Between Mau Mau and Nationalism

The question remains as to whether there is a more. effective way of understanding the passions of nationalism that will help analyze the character of Mau Mau and its relationship with nationalism in Kenya. The necessary conceptual tools can be found, I believe, in Benedict Anderson's *Imagined Communities* (1983), one of the most important theoretical essays on nationalism in recent years. In both those attributes which conform to and those which diverge from Anderson's construction of nationalism, one can understand the distinctive character of Mau Mau and its ambiguous relationship to the more typical forms of what he calls "anti-colonial nationalism."

Anderson stresses the importance of historical sequence and precedent for understanding the development of the successive forms of nationalism and the nation-state, which is its

institutional container. Rather than originating in the primordial past, both are seen as the product of little more than two hundred years of development. He identifies the origins of nationalism and the modern state in the "creole nationalisms" of the Americas, North and South, and their movements for independence from 1775 to 1830. These revolutionary new nations provided a model that was widely discussed in Europe and available for emulation:

> Out of the American welter came these imagined realities: nation-states, republican institutions, common citizenships, popular sovereignty, national flags and anthems, etc., and the liquidation of their conceptual opposites: dynastic empires, monarchical institutions, absolutisms, subjecthoods, inherited nobilities, serfdoms, ghettos, and so forth. . . . In effect, by the second decade of the nineteenth century, if not earlier, a "model" of the independent national state was available for pirating (Anderson 1983, 78).

This model was employed by the "populist nationalisms" of Europe, which transformed diverse and fragmented ethnic groups into "nations" based on the print-languages and written records of their history and culture, and established the precedent that for each nation an independent and sovereign state was the essential condition of its legitimate existence and survival (Anderson 1983, 66–73, 78–79). In central and eastern Europe, this populist nationalism challenged the older polyglot and multi-ethnic dynastic empires of Czarist Russia, Hapsburg Austria, and Ottoman Turkey, and ignited the struggles for national self-determination which marked the 1850–1920 period. These set off the defensive and reactionary "official nationalisms," such as Romanov Russification, which attempted a "willed merger of nation and dynastic empire"

---

[14]   Lee also shows that by 1956, while in all other social sciences the majority of researchers working in British Africa were either British or citizens of the "white" Commonwealth, in political science thirteen of seventeen were Americans.

through conscious policies "adapted from the model of the largely spontaneous popular nationalisms which preceded them" (Anderson 1983, 83, 102).

The most recent variant of nationalism, according to Anderson, is the anti-colonial nationalisms of the twentieth century, for which all of the previous forms have provided accessible models of nationalism, nation-ness and the state in an international environment in which the sovereign nation-state is the dominant, indeed, unchallenged norm. This nationalism is grounded in the experience of literate and bilingual indigenous intelligentsias fluent in the language of the imperial power, schooled in its "national" history, and staffing the colonial administrative cadres up to but not including its highest levels. These new nations have been essentially isomorphic with previous imperial administrative units (Anderson 1983, 104–109, 127–128; Kitching 1985, 111–113). This perspective allows us to understand how the senior imperial administrators from the metropole were able to conceive the project of modernization and nation-building to transform colonies into nation-states, even in advance of the demands of indigenous nationalist movements.

To deal with the critical problem of the passions of nationalism, Anderson stresses the importance of understanding the nation as an imagined community:

> It is imagined because the members of even the smallest nation will never know most of their fellow-members, meet them, or even hear of them, yet in the minds of each lives the image of their communion. . . . it is imagined as a community, because, regardless of the actual inequality and exploitation that may prevail in each, the nation is always conceived as a deep, horizontal comradeship. Ultimately it is this fraternity that makes it possible, over the past two centuries, for so many millions of people, not so much to kill, as to willingly die for such limited imaginings (Anderson 1983, 15–16).

Unlike the rationalism of liberalism and Marxism, nationalism is much concerned with ultimate meanings, death and immorality. Rather than a political ideology, it has more in common with kinship and religion. It replaces the religious vision of immortality with a secular one based on the nation.

> If nation-states are widely conceded to be "new" and "historical," the nations to which they give political expression always loom out of an immemorial past, and, still more important, glide into a limitless future. It is the magic of nationalism to turn chance into destiny (Anderson 1983,19).

Language plays the central role in the creation of the imagined community in so far as it is printed and related to the spread of mass literacy. "Print language is what invents nationalism, not a particular language per se" (Anderson 1983, 122). In the European experience a diversity of dialects was reduced to a much smaller number of standardized print vernaculars, while in the creole nations of the Americas and the colonial empires of the twentieth century, the print language was primarily that of the imperial metropole. In all of these instances, the growing number of readers formed the embryo of the nationally imagined community, with the production and consumption of novels and newspapers being particularly important in making possible the imagining of the nation (Anderson 1983, 30–39, 47–49, 61–63).

The role of print language in the development of nationalism is closely linked to the development of what Anderson calls "print capitalism." Printing and book production was one of the key industries of early capitalism. The principal consumers of literature were the growing middle classes, with the bourgeoisie being the first class to achieve solidarity on a largely imagined basis rooted in universal literacy. Finally, print language is also crucially connected to the development of the modern state. The schools and universities run by the state not only spread universal literacy, but also create the studies of history, literature, and folklore through which the nation takes on concrete and permanent existence, and can systematically reproduce itself from generation to generation. The use of the language as a language of administration shapes the consciousness of the imagined national community within the state cadres (Anderson 1983, 66–69, 74, 106–109, 127). The linkage of print language and the state transforms ethnicity into nationalism and makes the possession of a sovereign state the universally demanded norm for every imagined community.

To employ Anderson's approach to nationalism in analyzing Mau Mau, it is first necessary to note the shift in the understanding of the latter that occurred during the 1970s. In the context of studies of the political economy of colonial Kenya by Marxist and neo-Marxist historians and social scientists, which focused on the incorporation of Africans into capitalist production and exchange, and the consequent processes of class formation, the view of Mau Mau shifted again; and it came to be seen as a peasant war emerging out of the growing class struggles among the Kikuyu. While the British often called the Emergency a civil war between the mass of Kikuyu who had taken the Mau Mau oath of unity, on the one hand, and a small band of "Loyalists," on the other, and Rosberg and Nottingham had analyzed at some length the major internal political conflicts among the Kikuyu, more recent research has revealed with far greater subtlety and detail the complexity of internal differentiation and class formation among the Kikuyu not only during colonialism but also before the beginning of colonial rule.[15] In contrast to the constructed image of a stable and harmonious tradition, the Kikuyu in the nineteenth century were actively expanding and colonizing new territory and already internally divided between wealthy land-owning families and landless families attached to them in a variety of forms of dependence. The highest status and civic virtue

> . . . lay in the labour of agrarian civilization directed by household heads. Honour lay in wealth, the proud fruit of burning back the forest and taming the wild, clearing a culti-vated space in which industrious dependents might establish themselves in self-respecting independence; the possibility of working one's own salvation was the subject of more Kikuyu proverbs than any other (Lonsdale 1990, 417).

The impact of colonial capitalism and the colonial state hit the Kikuyu with greater force and effect than any other of Kenya's peoples, setting off new processes of differentiation and class formation. Anderson stresses that in the development of colonial nationalism "to an unprecedented extent the key early spokesman . . . were lonely, bilingual intelligentsias unattached to sturdy local bourgeoisies," whose pilgrimage among administrative posts ending in the colonial capital was critical to their imagining of a nation (1983, 127–128). This was not true, however, for the Kikuyu or for Kenya as a whole through most of the colonial period. The intelligentsia and administrative cadres among the Kikuyu were intimately connected with the development of a petty bourgeoisie. In the particular circumstances of Kenya as a colony of white settlement, the Kikuyu servants of the colonial state consisted of local chiefs and headmen, who never served outside of their original areas, and literate clerks and artisans, who encountered their counterparts from other peoples in Kenya only when they worked in the urban crucible of Nairobi and a few of the other major towns. The pilgrimage for both the Kikuyu new wealthy and new poor was a more restricted

---

[15]   See, in particular, the careful synthesis and analysis of the evidence in Kitching (1980).

circuit between the reserves established by the colonial state, the white settler estates and towns of the Rift Valley, and the capital. From the 1920s, however, the developing elite of accumulators was internally split by a cleavage between the collaborationist chiefs and their families and supporters and a younger and more populist element organized in the Kikuyu Central Association and willing to confront colonial authority over the issue of the "stolen" lands alienated to white settlers and the missionary attack on the Kikuyu custom of female circumcision. At the other pole of the class structure, growing numbers of impoverished Kikuyu were leaving the home territories, now increasingly crowded within their fixed boundaries, to seek land and work as squatters or wage labourers on settler estates or as largely unskilled workers in the towns.

The increasing disparities of wealth and property and developing conflicts within and between the developing social classes in Kikuyu society were expressed in a vigorous internal debate, largely invisible to the British in Kenya and only now being reconstructed, over the meaning of Kikuyu-ness, the nature of the community, the value of tradition, the involvement in new forms of production and exchange, and the degree of acceptance of and assimilation to European culture.[16] Thus, the chiefs and their supporters opposed the more militant Kikuyu Central Association through the pointedly named "Kikuyu Loyal Patriots." Meanwhile, in the aftermath of the breach with the mission societies over the custom of female circumcision, two independent school associations were formed calling themselves the Kikuyu Independent Schools Association and the Kikuyu Karing'a (pure or authentic) Schools.

From the beginning, print-language and literacy in both English and Kikuyu played a crucial role in defining the terms and content of the debate. The developing petty bourgeoisie was commonly referred to as the *athomi* (literally, "the readers"). In 1928 the KCA began publishing a Kikuyu-language journal called *Muigwithania* ("The Reconciler"), with Kenyatta as its first editor. An article in an early issue on the word "association" told the readers not to say "that you do not belong to that Association. You are members of the Association since you are all Kikuyu Karing'a (real Kikuyu)" (Rosberg and Nottingham 1966, 100). In 1938 Kenyatta published in English his ethnography of the Kikuyu, written during his studies at the London School of Economics with Bronislaw Malinowski, which provided a vigorous defence of Kikuyu custom against European criticism and provided in permanent printed form his version of a pre-colonial pastoral. In this key text of an emerging Kikuyu imagined community, as well as in other writings of the period, there is a strong element of "redemptive criticism," a "present employment of the past in the hopes of reshaping the future" (Kenyatta 1938; Clark 1989, 396).[17]

By the late 1940s the Kikuyu were a deeply divided people, increasingly in conflict among themselves as well as with the colonial political and economic order. In three centres of growing unrest, a growing mass of the dispossessed and impoverished confronted the leadership of the chiefs and the athomi. In the Rift Valley, an increasing number of squatters were expelled from settler estates for refusing to accept ever-tighter restrictions on their herds and use of settler land. In the overcrowded reserves, small peasants desperately

---

[16] These themes are explored more fully in Lonsdale, "Wealth, Poverty and Civic Virtue in Kikuyu Political Thought" in Berman and Lonsdale (1992).

[17] Clark's remarks concern Leakey's ethnography, but they apply equally well to Kenyatta's. The rivalry between Kenyatta and Leakey for the intellectual leadership of the Kikuyu and its expression in the ethnographic politics of establishing the "right" version of Kikuyu society and culture is analyzed in "Louis Leakey's Mau Mau" (Berman and Lonsdale 1991a).

clung to fragmented and eroded holdings no longer capable of supporting a family, while wealthy landowners sought to expel tenants and dependents to regain land for more profitable uses. In Nairobi, a largely Kikuyu labour force struggled with growing impoverishment, inflation, and unemployment. The struggle over authentic Kikuyu-ness, over the character of the imagined community, continued unabated. At this point, however, the conceptions of propertied civic virtue

> . . . began to mock the majority rather than to inspire . . . those who had the most cause to fight colonial rule had the least chance to merit responsibility. Those whose deeds might deliver power would have no chance to enjoy it. That was the Kikuyu tragedy, a struggle over the moralities of class formation, not mental derangement" (Lonsdale 1990, 417).

The situation was complicated by the emergence of the Kenya African Union, the first attempt at a pan-ethnic "national" political organization. In this organization we do find an expression of a more typical anti-colonial nationalism. KAU had a multi-ethnic, although largely Kikuyu, leadership of bilingual literates of the type upon which Anderson focuses. It was committed to a very different vision of the imagined community, a multi-ethnic Kenya, and to moderate constitutional politics which accepted the premises of the colonial state's version of modernization and nation-building. . . .

Kikuyu struggle continued to take place in print. The dominant journal was the weekly *Mumenyereri*, edited by Henry Muoria.

> Considered the paper of Kikuyu patriotism, it published a mixture of real and imagined grievances. As tension grew in 1951 and 1952, it became uncompromising in its nationalism. Invitations to political meetings, called under the guise of "tea parties" (which usually included oathing ceremonies) at the Kikuyu Club in Nairobi's Pumwani

Location, became a regular feature of the paper (Rosberg and Nottingham 1966, 212).

There was also a considerable vernacular pamphlet literature, the most remarkable available example of which is Gakaara wa Wanjau's *Mageria no mo Mahota (The Spirit of Manhood and Perseverance for Africans)*, published in April 1952, which appeals for unity across the cleavages of "the regime of division that the white man has established over us and the bitter and destructive conflicts between ourselves this regime creates," lists all of the classes and segments of the Kikuyu and their just grievances, proclaims universal acceptance of the goals of modernization and development, enjoins the rich to "get actively involved in the people's movement," and includes this extraordinary evocation of the imagined community and the passions of nationalism:

> . . . it is vital that every African plays his own role in the struggle for African freedom. To fight for freedom does not only mean making political speeches and writing political tracts. More than that, to struggle for freedom is to be imbued with a patriotic love for your country and its people, so that you become part and parcel of its suffering and its triumphs, so that, in your spiritual unity with your people, you weep with them when they weep, and you share with them their moments of joy. It is a deep and all consuming involvement with your people. It motivates you to seek to know what is happening all the time to your people; it motivates you to always seek to further the cause of freedom and independence (Wanjau 1988, 227–243).

Wanjau speaks here of Africans and African freedom, but the language and cultural symbolism he employs are Kikuyu, and this suggests the contradictory notions of the imagined community of the nation existing during this period. For the colonial authorities, however, it was sufficiently clear to merit

Wanjau's arrest at the beginning of the Emergency and his subsequent detention for ten years.

While Mau Mau was clearly not a tribal atavism seeking a return to the past, the answer to the question of "was it nationalism?" must be yes and no. What the British called Mau Mau, and by constant repetition imposed on the consciousness of both Kenya and the outside world, was no single thing, but rather a diverse and exceedingly fragmented collection of individuals, organizations and ideas, out of which no dominant concept of a Kikuyu imagined national community had emerged. At the same time, if Mau Mau was not a nativistic revival or atavistic revitalization movement, it did emerge out of a bitterly contested process of reinterpreting and reconstructing tradition that embraced the colonial authorities as well as Kikuyu factions, Leakey as well as Kenyatta; and in which cultural beliefs and symbols were profoundly important. Mau Mau was part of a struggle over the dimensions and meaning of Kikuyu ethnicity and its problematic relationship with both the internal cleavages of class and the wider solidarities of a Kenyan nation.[18]

The colonial authorities' version of Mau Mau as a conspiratorial secret cult attached to it an illusory unity of organization and ideology. The official version also played loosely with the historical sequence of events, focusing on the limited degree of organization and unity achieved by the forest fighters under Dedan Kimathi and General China, adding the connections to the Nairobi "Central Committee," combining both with the "evidence" of oaths often extracted from detainees under torture, and then projecting all of this backward to characterize "Mau Mau" before the Emergency. What the accumulated evidence records, instead, are largely failed efforts to define a Kikuyu nationality linked to

a militant populist politics of the poor. How this was to relate to the other imagined communities in Kenya in an independent nation state was not clearly thought through. What is interesting is that the ideological cleavages of contrasting visions of the Kikuyu and Kenyan nations were reproduced within the structure of the Land and Freedom Army itself in conflicts between the literate leaders like Kimathi and Karari Njama and many of the primarily illiterate rank and file of peasants and dispossessed squatters led by men like Stanley Mathenge. "This boiled down, in essence, to the rejection by the non-literate leaders of the state-building, parliamentarist 'Freedom' component, in favour of the peasant/land component, in the forest fighters'"national-ism'" (Maughan-Brown 1985, 47). The forest fighters' own name for their movement, *ithaka na wiathi*, is perhaps better translated, according to Lonsdale, as "freedom through land" or "land and moral responsibility," which invokes "the highest civic virtue of Kikuyu elderhood, rather than the more common 'land and freedom' which invites the retrospective connotation of 'land and national independence'" (Lonsdale 1990, 416 note 118), and thus expresses the distinctive cultural content of Kikuyu internal conflicts as much as an anti-colonial liberation struggle.

The paradoxes of Mau Mau are also revealed tellingly in the career and words of Kenyatta. He both outraged and terrified British officialdom because, in their eyes, he was the obvious charismatic nationalist leader of Kenya's Africans, but used the force of his personality and his elite education to deliberately lead the Kikuyu back to the mystical witchcraft of tribal reaction rather than unite the Africans with whites in the project of national development. They convicted him of organizing Mau Mau in a flagrantly rigged trial which threw him together with men like

---

[18] Mau Mau can thus be usefully examined in the comparative context of the processes of constructing ethnicity and tradition discussed in Hobsbawn and Ranger (1983) (See Ranger, Chapter 35, this volume) and Vail (1989).

Kubai and Kaggia who actually had organized the mass oathings. But Kenyatta, and his colleagues in the KCA, spoke for the new generation of athomi who, even in opposing the chiefs and elders, always laid claim to the leadership of the Kikuyu in traditional terms as men of property and virtue. In the internal struggles among the Kikuyu before the Emergency, he stood on the opposite side from the leaders of the Kikuyu dispossessed, the squatters, urban workers and landless peasants; while as the leader of the KAU he struggled to hold together its multi-ethnic coalition. His denunciations of Mau Mau in 1952, when he equated it with poverty, irresponsibility and criminality, led its leaders to consider his assassination.[19]

Ironically, it was the Emergency which secured the victory of the very different nationalism of the multi-ethnic dominant class that came to power with independence, while Kenyatta's conviction and imprisonment for organizing Mau Mau probably saved his position as the national leader. The elite nationalism of this class was definitively formed during the Emergency itself among the Kikuyu loyalists and the educated elites from other ethnic communities, who shared literacy in English and who travelled their national pilgrimage in less than a decade through increasing access to the bureaucracy of the colonial state and to the expanding "national" political institutions at the centre, created by repeated rounds of constitutional reform. Simultaneously, with the detention or confinement in the reserves of the bulk of the Kikuyu labour force in the colony, replacements were found among other ethnic groups,

while economic reforms both raised wages and increased peasant access to cash crop markets – all of which provided a substantially widened base of support for "nationalist" goals when African political organizations were again permitted after 1957. The pressure of this multi-ethnic elite forced the pace of British withdrawal, undermined the political position of white settlers and ultimately made independence under a "multi-racial" regime impossible (Berman 1990, chapter 9). In them, the British found, rather unexpectedly, the "political class" to whom they could safely turn over power, and belatedly discovered in Kenyatta the moderate modernizing national leader.

It is hardly surprising that the attitude of the government of independent Kenya has been ambivalent about the recognition of the contributions of Mau Mau "freedom fighters," or that the divergent post-independence interpretations of Mau Mau, as the central element in the epic of national liberation or as an isolated tribal uprising, reflect a continuing cleavage between radical populist elements among the Kikuyu and the "national" dominant class (Maughan-Brown, 1985, 57–58, 258–261).[20] Kenyatta himself, after his release from prison and political rehabilitation in the early 1960s and later as President of Kenya, continued to denounce Mau Mau and equate it with criminality and disease, repeating the very type of metaphor which the British had used to describe it. Meanwhile, his government proclaimed: "we all fought for Uhuru" and refused any special recognition of the achievements of Mau Mau or the claims of the ex-forest fighters and detainees, although

---

[19] As revealed by Fred Kubai in an interview with Alan Segal broadcast in part in Granada Television's program on Kenya in its series "The End of Empire" in July 1985.

[20] Ngugi wa Thiong'o has recently analyzed the split in Kenyan intellectual life between the English-speaking, neo-colonial petty-bourgeoisie which, he claims, hi-jacked independence and the "true" nationalism represented by Mau Mau. He explicitly denounces the dominant class both for its exploitation of ethnic chauvinism and its reliance on the old imperial language while praising Mau Mau, and the work of Gakaara wa Wanjau in particular, for encouraging the emergence of a genuine indigenous African-language literature, as well as expressing "the mass political movements of an awakened peasantry and working class" (1986, 23–24, 44–45, 102–104.)

it permitted some local memorials in Kikuyuland to them and to Kimathi.[21] In 1988 the monument to the "freedom fighters," which contains no explicit reference to *ithaka na wiathi* sat forlorn and graffiti-defaced at an intersection in Nyeri town, a material expression of the continuing paradoxes of Mau Mau.

References

Anderson, Benedict. 1983. *Imagined Communities: Reflections on the Origin and Spread of Nationalism*. London: Verso.

Barnett, Donald and Karari Njama. 1966. *Mau Mau from Within: Autobiography and Analysis of Kenya's Peasant Revolt*. London: Macgibbon and Kee.

Berman, Bruce. 1990. *Control and Crisis in Colonial Kenya: The Dialectic of Domination*. London: James Currey and Athen, Ohio: Ohio University Press.

Berman, Bruce and John Lonsdale. 1991a. "Louis Leakey's Mau Mau: A Study in the Politics of Knowledge." *History and Anthropology*, forthcoming.

Berman, Bruce and John Lonsdale. 1991b. "The Shadow of Mau Mau: the Politics of Terror in Kenya." Conference on Colonialism and the Construction of Terror. Trinity College, Cambridge. March.

Berman, Bruce and John Lonsdale. 1992. *Unhappy Valley: Clan, Class and State in Colonial Kenya*. London: James Currey.

Buijtenhuijs, Robert 1973. *Mau Mau Twenty Years After: The Myth and the Survivors*. The Hague: Mouton.

Clark, Carolyn, 1989. "Louis Leakey as Ethnographer: On *The Southern Kikuyu Before 1900*. *Canadian Journal of African Studies* 23, no. 3:380–398.

Clifford, James. 1986. "On Ethnographic Allegory." In Clifford and Marcus, 98–121.

Cohen, Sir Andrew. 1959. *British Policy in Changing Africa*. London: Routledge and Kegan Paul.

Edgerton, Robert. 1989. *Mau Mau: An African Crucible*. New York: Free Press.

Fernandez, James. 1964. "African Religious Movements: Types and Dynamics." *Journal of Modern African Studies* 2, no. 4:531–549.

Furedi, Frank. 1989. *The Mau Mau War in Perspective*. London: James Currey.

Gordon, David. 1986. *Decolonization and the State in Kenya*. Boulder: Westview.

Hobsbawm, Eric and Terence Ranger. 1983. *The Invention of Tradition*. Cambridge: Cambridge University Press.

Itote, Waruhiu. 1967 *"Mau Mau" General*. Nairobi: East African Publishing House.

Kanogo, Tabitha. 1987. *Squatters and the Roots of Mau Mau*. London: James Currey.

Kariuki, J.M. 1963. *Mau Mau Detainee*. London: Penguin.

Kennedy, Dane. 1987. *Islands of White: Settler Society and Culture in Kenya and Southern Rhodesia 1890–1939*. Durham: Duke University Press.

Kenyatta, Jomo. 1938. *Facing Mount Kenya: The Tribal Life of the Kikuyu*. London: Secker and Warburg.

———. 1968. *Suffering without Bitterness: The Founding of the Kenya Nation*. Nairobi: East African Publishing House.

Kinyatti, Maina wa. 1987. *Kenya's Freedom Struggle: The Dedan Kimathi Papers*. London: Zed Press.

———. 1985. *Thunder From the Mountains: Mau Mau Patriotic Songs*. London: Zed Press.

Kitching, Gavin, 1980. *Class and Economic Change in Kenya*. New Haven: Yale University Press.

———. 1985 "Nationalism: The Instrumental Passion." *Capital and Class* 25: 98–116.

Kuper, Adam. 1983. *Anthropology and Anthropologists: the Modern British School*. London: Routledge and Kegan Paul.

Kushner, Gilbert, 1965. "An African Revitalization Movement: Mau Mau." *Anthropos* 60, nos. 1–6:763–802.

La Barre, Weston. 1971. "Materials for the Study

---

[21] Some of Kenyatta's statements denouncing "hooliganism" and oath-taking can be found in Kenyatta (1968, 147, 154, 167, 183, 189, and 204). See also Buijtenhuijs (1973, 49–53, 61–72) and Lonsdale (1990, 418–420).

of Crisis Cults: A Bibliographic Essay." *Current Anthropology* 12, no.1:3–64.

Leakey, Louis S.B. 1952. *Mau Mau and the Kikuyu.* London: Methuen.

——. 1954 *Defeating Mau Mau.* London: Methuen.

Lee, Michael. 1967. *Colonial Development and Good Government.* London: Oxford University Press.

Leys, Colin. 1982. "Samuel Huntington and the End of Classical Modernization Theory." In *Introduction to the Sociology of "Developing Societies,"* edited by Hamza Alavi and Teodor Shanin. 332–349. New York and London: Monthly Review Press.

Lonsdale, John. 1989. "The Constructions of Mau Mau." Royal Historical Society, London. December.

——. 1990. "Mau Maus of the Mind: Making Mau Mau and Remaking Kenya."*Journal of African History* 31, no.4:393–421.

Maughan-Brown, David. 1985. *Land, Freedom and Fiction.* London: Zed Press.

Odhiambo, E.S. Atieno. 1988. "The Construction of History in Kenya." Canadian Association of African Studies, Kingston Ontario, May.

Rosaldo, Renato. 1986. "From the Door of His Tent: The Fieldworker and the Inquisitor." In Clifford and Marcus.

Rosberg, Karl and John Nottingham. 1966. *The Myth of Mau Mau: Nationalism in Kenya.* New York: Frederick Praeger.

Rosenstiel, Annette. 1953. "An Anthropological Approach to the Mau Mau Problem." *Political Science Quarterly* 68: 419–432.

Thiong'o, Ngugi wa. 1983 *Barrel of a Pen: Resistance to Repression in Neo-Colonial Kenya.* Trenton, New Jersey: Africa World Press.

——. 1986. *Decolonizing the Mind: The Politics of Language in African Literature.* Nairobi: Heinemann Kenya.

Thiong'o, Ngugi wa and Micere Mugo. 1976. *The Trial of Dedan Kimathi.* London.

Throup, David. 1987. *The Economic and Social Origins of Mau Mau.* London: James Currey.

Vail, Leroy, ed. 1989. *The Creation of Tribalism in Southern Africa.* London: James Currey.

Wanjau, Gakaara wa. 1988. *Mau Mau Author in Detention: An Author's Detention Diary.* Nairobi: Heinemann Kenya.

Wilson, Godfrey and Monica Wilson. 1945. *The Analysis of Social Change, Based on Observations in Central Africa.* Cambridge: Cambridge University Press.

40

THE INVISIBLE FACE:
MASKS, ETHNICITY, AND THE STATE
IN CÔTE D'IVOIRE

CHRISTOPHER B. STEINER

This chapter examines the critical role of masks and masked performances in the Côte d'Ivoire[1] government's dual projects of (1) promoting international tourism in light of the country's most severe economic recession, and (2) fostering national unity in the face of growing ethnic factionalism and tension. Although, as I will argue, the ideological frameworks underlying these two goals are in many ways diametrically opposed to one another, I will demonstrate that the use of masks and masked dancing is an attempt on the part of the Ivoirian state to bridge the differences between these two nation-stabilizing strategies and mute their potential contradictions.

Masks and masking in Côte d'Ivoire are found in different forms in a variety of coastal and inland communities. Many of the estimated sixty ethnic groups in the country have their own style of mask carving and their own repertoire of masked dancing and performances. Although some aspects of masking are shrouded under a veil of secrecy and used only in the context of secret society activities, many forms consist largely of public displays intended purely for general entertainment. While these secular forms of masking are often carried out at the local village level, they are sometimes incorporated into public events organized by members of both regional and national government. A meeting of town mayors, a visit to a village by a district (*préfecture*) administrator, or a national tour by a high-ranking minister or diplomat are all events that would call for the performance of a masked festival. Although certain forms of secular masking probably found expression at the village level in pre-colonial times, I would argue that most public displays of masking became associated with political and bureaucratic events during colonial rule. Huge masked festivals, for example, were organized each summer by the French to celebrate Bastille Day; while smaller masked festivals were often held at the ground-breaking reception for the construction of administrative buildings, at official ceremonies for the naming of city streets, or at the unveiling of colonial monuments (see Gorer 1935:322–28).

Together with their function in national

---

[1] In order to respect the decree of 14 October 1985 by President Félix Houphouët-Boigny, the country name "Côte d'Ivoire" will not be translated into English.

Plate 40.1   Masked dancer with musicians performing at the festival of masks in Man, ca. 1979.
Photographer unknown

politics, masks and masking in post-colonial Côte d'Ivoire have, in recent years at least, played a critical role in the promotion of international tourism and the marketing of African art (Steiner forthcoming). In any one of the major marketplaces in Côte d'Ivoire, art traders line their stalls with row upon row of carved wooden masks. The major styles are attributed to the Baule, Guro, Senufo, and Dan ethnic groups. Miniature masks, called "passports," are available to tourists who do not have the room in their luggage to carry home a full-size mask.

Within the last decade, the mask has been appropriated by the Ivoirian state as a symbol of national identity or character.[2] As Duon Sadia, the Ivoirian Minister of Tourism, noted

in a 1987 interview: "Because Côte d'Ivoire does not possess pyramids or grand ancient monuments like Egypt or Mexico, and because it does not have an abundance of wildlife like some of the countries in East Africa, Côte d'Ivoire has chosen to promote itself through its only indigenous product, Ivoirian man himself – with his culture and his traditions, of which masks and masking are an integral part" (Bouabré 1987:8).[3] In another interview, the Minister of Tourism further clarified the specific function of masks in the development of the modern Ivoirian polity by noting that, "We now declare that the trademark [of Côte d'Ivoire] will be the mask, for it is representative [of this country], rather pleasing to observe, and enshrouded in an air of mystery.

[2]   The process is also reflected in the use of "traditional" symbols on West African bank notes (Francs CFA) used jointly by nations of former Afrique Occidentale Française (cf. Vogel 1991:233).
[3]   All translations from the French are by the author.

The mask could arouse the curiosity of foreign tourists and lead them to visit our country. We have [therefore] chosen the mask for we believe that it integrates several aspects of our culture and our civilization. The mask encapsulates the traditional arts of Côte d'Ivoire, and represents the strength and history of our nation" (Philmon 1982:13).

The promotion of tourism through the marketing of the image of the mask represents, in point of fact, a radical departure in the rhetoric of the Ivoirian state. Less than a decade before this recent campaign, for example, Félix Houphouët-Boigny, President of the Republic and founder of independent Côte d'Ivoire, declared to a congress of the National Democratic Party: "We are fed up with having Africa relegated, through the futile gaze of the observer, to a land of sunshine, rhythms, and innocuous folklore" (quoted in Boutillier, Fiéloux and Ormiéres 1978:5). For Houphouët-Boigny, in his first years of power after independence, both national integration and international economic success were to be found in the promotion of modern industrial technolgies rather than in a return to traditionalism or the re-creation of a "primitivist" aesthetic.

Hence, in light of this philosophy, how can one explain the state's recent shift toward traditional cultural resources and, in particular, its appropriation of the wooden mask as a symbol of national, multi-ethnic pride? I would argue that this return to traditionalism is a direct result of the nation's financial collapse following the failure of its cash-crop export economy – beginning sometime in 1980 (Brooke 1988). That is to say, as long as Côte d'Ivoire enjoyed economic prosperity through its production and export of cacao and coffee, the state used its success in the international economy as a device for rallying nationalist sentiment. It needed nothing else. Following the dramatic collapse of the price of cacao and coffee in the world market, however, politicians scrambled to find not only a new source of foreign income but also a new gathering point for nationalist sentiment. The mask was thought to be capable of achieving both. On the one hand, it fueled the Western imagination through its mystery and exotic appeal. On the other hand, it reconciled growing ethnic divisions by elevating the symbolism of the mask – with its plethora of ethnic styles and interpretations – to a single, national icon.

The first attempt by the government of Côte d'Ivoire to promote tourism and national solidarity through the use of wooden masks was the festival of masks held on April 14–15, 1979 in the town of Man, near the Liberian border in the western part of the country. The festival was organized by Bernard Dadié, the Minister of Cultural Affairs. On the whole, the festival was poorly attended, and it received very little coverage from the Ivoirian press (only three short articles in the semi-official daily newspaper *Fraternité Matin*).

The second masked festival was organized by the Minister of Tourism, Duon Sadia. It too was held in the town of Man from February 11–15, 1983. In the second festival at Man, there was a more overt effort on behalf of the government organizers to use the mask as a symbol of Côte d'Ivoire and as a mechanism for attracting the financial benefits of tourism. The masked festival at Man, Duon Sadia noted at a press conference held at the luxurious Hotel Ivoire in Abidjan, "will be the equivalent of Carnival in Rio, with an added element of the profound soul and mystery of 'non-commercialised' Africa" (Anonymous 1983:10).[4] The 1983 festival of the masks at Man was again reported by the press to be an overall failure. Very few tourists went to the festival, and the mask-bearers, who felt they were being treated without sufficient

[4] The link between an African festival and the Carnival in Rio was first made by the government of Senegal in 1974 when they tried (without success) to launch a series of "ethnic" dances which "would become as famous as the Carnival of Rio or of Nice" (Copans 1978:119).

respect, boycotted their appearance. A delegation, consisting of three ministers and a representative of the national government, had to plead in public with the masked dancers to come out and perform on the stage (Djidji 1983:11).

The Ivoirian state's appropriation of the mask reached its epitome in the summer of 1988, when the Ministries of Tourism and Culture jointly organized a national masked festival. Promoted under the name "Festimask," the festival was funded by the state at an estimated cost of $500,000. Unlike previous state-sponsored masked festivals which were organized by district administrations with the exclusive participation of local ethnic groups, the Festimask attempted to bring all the ethnic groups of Côte d'Ivoire into a single event which, not surprisingly, was held in the President's home town of Yamoussoukro, in the center of the country. The official reason reported in the national newspaper for holding the festival in Yamoussoukro, rather than Man, was because of its proximity to the economic capital and port city of Abidjan – thereby, the argument went, encouraging more expatriates and more tourists to attend the festival of masks. However, the unstated reason for the site of the event, I would argue, was to link the festival of masks and, more generally, the symbolism of masks and masking to the national government through its association with Houphouët-Boigny's natal village and place of retreat.

When the masked festival was moved to Yamoussoukro in 1988, it became not only a vehicle for promoting international tourism, it was also used as a means of stressing national unity. Since the end of the colonial period, many burgeoning African nations have had to push for national unity in the face of internal ethnic factionalism. Although cultural pluralism may be profitable within the realm of the international art market, it is often perceived as a major obstacle in the domain of centralized state politics. As Wallerstein noted

in 1960, "The dysfunctional aspects of ethnicity for national integration are obvious. The first is that ethnic groups are still particularistic in their orientation and diffuse in their obligations.... The second problem, and one which worries African political leaders more, is separatism, which in various guises is a pervasive tendency in West Africa today" (1960:137–38). Until recently, post-colonial Côte d'Ivoire had a history of successful national integration. In a country made up of approximately sixty different ethnic groups, this record of success is an impressive triumph. One of the reasons which accounts for successful integration of ethnic groups in Côte d'Ivoire is the rapid growth and expansion of the Ivoirian economy – the so-called Ivoirian "miracle" which took place from 1960 to 1980. Since a majority of Ivoirian nationals were reaping the benefits of favorable transnational trade, it was to their (economic) advantage to remain united under a national economic cause (Dozon 1985:53–54). Since the economy has weakened, however, in the past several years, it could be argued that ethnic factionalism has become an increasing concern to the representatives of the centralized Ivoirian state. Viewed in this context, then, the masked festival at Yamoussoukro was yet another way of promoting nationalist sentiment in the face of growing ethnic factionalism. The Festimask respected ethnic heterogeneity – i.e., each masked performance was associated with a different and unique ethnic style – while, at the same time, it brought disparate ethnic groups together into a single, united cause.

The Festimask stresses national unity in at least two ways. First, it aims to bring the ethnic distinctions embedded in styles of art into a single "folkloric" category. There are no longer individual ethnic masks. All masks, said the organizers of the festival, are to be thought of as members of the PDCI (Partie Democratique de Côte d'Ivoire). All masks are to be considered Ivoirian patriots struggling for the good of the modern nation–state

Plate 40.2   Masked dancer with musicians performing at the festival of masks in
Man, ca. 1979.
Photographer unknown.

(Gnangnan 1987). Secondly, the festival of masks strives to bring the concerns of the older generation (the so-called "*mentalitées traditionelles*" of the rural population) into step with national concerns, such as the promotion of international tourism and the President's long-standing campaign for West African regional peace. In the context of Festimask, the mask is a tool of the modern nation-state that serves "rational" political goals while being presented to both nationals and foreigners as a kind of "traditionalizing instrument" (Moore and Myerhoff 1977:8). At a press conference held to clarify the role of the mask in the nationalist party, the Ivoirian Minister of Tourism, Duon Sadia, said:

When we say that the mask must become militant, we mean to signal that the mask must no longer transmit the knowledge of the ancestors in a mechanical way without any explanations. The mask must become a spokesman – communicating in the common language of our culture – for the message of peace. The performance [of Festimask] is not intended to caricature our traditional values, but rather it is aimed to preserve these traditions by adapting them to the exigencies of the modern world. (Bouabré 1987:8)

The Festimask was thus intended to collapse divisions in *both* space (i.e., ethnic geography) and time (i.e., generational differences).

According to Ernest Gellner, there are at least three pre-conditions for the flourishment of state nationalism: (1) that a population be culturally homogenous without internal ethnic sub-groupings, (2) that a population be literate and capable of authoring and propagating its own history, and (3) that a population be anonymous, fluid, mobile, and unmediated in its loyalty to the state (1983:138). International tourism in most of the developing world hinges on the exact opposite criteria from those which underlie the foundation of state nationalism. First, international tourism demands that a population be as culturally and ethnically diverse as possible. In Côte d'Ivoire, for example, the tourist art market is driven by the production of a large variety of supposedly autochthonous and stereotyped ethnic arts (cf. Graburn 1984:413). Second, international tourism seeks to discover a population that is *il*literate, and without a sense of historical knowledge or a proper understanding of its geographic place within the world system. And third, international tourism calls for the existence of small-scale populations in which there is no anonymity, in which whole societies recognize each and every one of its members, and in which long-distance communication is not possible among putatively isolated groups. In essence, therefore, the demands of state nationalism and the demands of international

tourism are situated at opposite poles in the realm of possibilities concerning the individual's relationship to society.

The organization of Festimask was an attempt by the Ivoirian government to satisfy *simultaneously* both the monolithic requirements of effective state nationalism and the polymorphic demands of successful international tourism. By elevating the mask to a national icon, the state was attempting (1) to subvert ethnic differences, (2) to emphasize an indigenous form of national literacy and ethnohistorical consciousness, and (3) to create a national category of aesthetic identity through the hidden and anonymous face of the mask. At the same time, however, the state was also trying to encourage international tourism by stressing both the visual diversity in ethnic material productions and the exoticism of the masked dance itself.

Although the aims of the Festimask were both complex and diverse, its results were unambiguous. Both tourists *and* nationals judged the event as a complete failure. Tourists, on the one hand, stayed away from the Festimask because, I was told by one, they anticipated a large, staged, "tourist" event. Nationals, on the other hand, were disgusted with the Festimask because they felt they had been treated without respect – like pawns in a commercial venture. As one of the elders who attended the Festimask put it to a reporter for the national press, "My son, we went to Yamoussoukro, and we were happy for we had been invited to the village of our President. . . . But you should know that nobody took care of us; nobody even provided us with food, and that just isn't normal. Not only were we not greeted by the organizers of the festival, as is the custom, but when we [finally did get some food] it was their leftovers that we were sent to eat" (Anonymous 1987).

In conclusion, I would argue, the masked festival failed in the eyes of both Ivoirian nationals and foreign tourists for the same reason. In both instances, the Festimask was viewed as an inauthentic event because it had been, as it were, too "modern" in its tactics and too insensitive to the demands of "custom." The appropriation of the hidden face by the hidden hand resulted in a particular form of the commodification of ethnicity, in which neither the producers nor the consumers were willing to strike a bargain.

References

Anonymous
   1983   Festivale de masques à Man. *Fraternité Matin*, 7 February, p.11.
   1987   Communiqué from the Ministry of Information to the Ministry of Tourism. Archives of the Ministry of Tourism, Abidjan.
Bouabré, Paul
   1987   Festimask 1987: Le masque doit servir à la paix. *Fraternité Matin*, 16 July, p.8.
Boutillier, J-L, Michèle Fiéloux, and J-L Ormières
   1978   Le tourisme en Afrique de l'ouest. In *Le tourisme en Afrique de l'ouest*, edited by Jean-Louis Boutillier, Jean Copans, Michèle Fiéloux, Suzanne Lallemeand, and Jean-Louis Ormières. Pp.5–83. Paris: François Maspero.
Brooke, James
   1988   Ivory Coast Gambles to Prop up Cacao Prices. *The New York Times*, 21 November, section D, p.10.
Copans, Jean
   1978   Idéologies et idéologues du tourisme au Sénégal: Fabrications et contenus d'une image de marque. In *Le tourisme en Afrique de l'ouest*, edited by Jean-Louis Boutillier, Jean Copans, Michèle Fiéloux, Suzanne Lallemand, and Jean-Louis Ormières. Pp.108–40. Paris: François Maspero.
Djidji, Ambroise
   1983   Réflexion sur le festival des masques. *Fraternité Matin*, 22 February, p.10.
Dozon, Jean-Pierre
   1985   Les Bété: Une création coloniale. In *Au coeur de l'ethnie*, edited by Jean-Louis Amselle and Elikia M'Bokolo. Pp.49–85. Paris: Editions la Decouverte.
Gellner, Ernest,
   1983   *Nations and Nationalism*. Ithaca: Cornell University Press.
Gnangan, Desiré
   1987   Festivale de masque 1987. *Fraternité Matin*, 4 May, p.10.
Gorer, Geoffrey
   1935   *Africa Dances*. New York: Alfred A. Knopf.
Graburn, Nelson H.H.
   1984   The Evolution of Tourist Arts. *Annals of Tourism Research* 11:393–419.
Moore, Sally Falk, and Barbara Myerhoff (eds.)
   1977   *Secular Ritual*. Assen, The Netherlands: Van Gorcum.
Philmon, Thierry O.
   1982   Conference du Ministre Duon Sadia. *Fraternité Matin*, 2 December, pp.13–16.
Steiner, Christopher B.
   1994 *African Art in Transit*. Cambridge: Cambridge University Press.
Vogel, Susan (ed.)
   1991   *Africa Explores: 20th Century African Art*. New York: The Center for African Art.
Wallerstein, Immanuel
   1960   Ethnicity and National Integration in West Africa. *Cahiers d'Etudes Africaines* 3:129–39.

PART X

REPRESENTATION AND DISCOURSE

Europe Supported by Africa and America, engraving by William Blake. In John Gabriel Stedman, *Narrative, of a Five Years' Expedition, Against the revolted Negroes of Surinam*, vol. 2. London, 1796. Reproduced by permission of the J. Paul Getty Trust.

REPRESENTATION AND DISCOURSE

41   Jean and John Comaroff. 1991. "Africa Observed: Discourses of the Imperial Imagination," In *Of Revelation and Revolution: Christianity, Colonialism, and Consciousness in South Africa*. Vol. 1. Chicago: The University of Chicago Press.

42   Maxwell Owusu. 1978. "Ethnography of Africa: The Usefulness of the Useless," *American Anthropologist* 80(1): 310–34.

43   Cheikh Anta Diop. 1974. "The Meaning of Our Work," pp. xii–xvii. In *The African Origins of Civilization: Myth or Reality?* New York: L. Hill.

44   Kwame Anthony Appiah. 1993. "Europe Upside Down: Fallacies of the New Afrocentrism," *The Times Literary Supplement*, February 12, no. 4689, pp. 24–25.

The essays in this part address the issue of representation, and explore how "Africa" has been imagined and constructed in both Western and African discourses (see also our general Introduction). Since earliest contact between Europe and Africa, individuals on both sides of the encounter have classified and represented the other from the perspective of their own cultural assumptions and values. Although the readings here deal largely with European images of Africa and Africans, it is important to keep in mind that from the very earliest moments of encounter Africans have also generated images of Europeans.

When European seafaring travelers first set foot on the coast of Central Africa in the late fifteenth century, for example, it is reported that the local inhabitants saw them as spirits who had returned to the living from their ancestral world somewhere far off at sea. There was no category of person in Central African thought which could account for a European, so rather than invent one they were classified according to pre-existing criteria – as dead ancestors. Describing the nature of this transcultural encounter, anthropologist Wyatt MacGaffey has written that

> When the first Portuguese arrived in Kongo in 1485 they exhibited the principal characteristics of the dead: they were white in color, spoke an unintelligible language, and possessed technology superior even to that of the local priestly guild of smiths.... The first Portuguese, like their successors to the present day, were regarded as visitors from the land of the dead. (1986: 199)

Representations of Europeans in African visual art first appear in the fifteenth century in ivory carvings (saltcellars, spoons, and Catholic ritual objects) which were commissioned by Portuguese merchants from artists in coastal Sierra Leone to take back as tribute to the Portuguese crown (Curnow 1990; Blier 1993). In the sixteenth and seventeenth centuries, Europeans were extensively depicted in bronze plaques which adorned the king's palace at the royal court of Benin. In these naturalistic representations created by highly accomplished court artists, Europeans may be identified by their military dress and accoutrements, and by their beards, moustaches, and hairstyles which were characteristic of Portuguese fashion during this period (Ezra 1992: 128–29). The plaques, which hung throughout the palace in Benin City, alluded to the power of the king, whose network of influence stretched as far as Europe – a remote land from where wealthy visitors came to pay their respect to the court.

As in the earlier example from the Kongo encounter with Europeans, the Portuguese were folded almost seamlessly into prior categories of Benin social structure and religious beliefs. "Because they came from across the sea, bringing with them wealth and luxury items," writes anthropologist Paula Ben-Amos, "the Portuguese travelers were readily incorporated into (or perhaps generated) the complex of ideas associated with the god Olokun, ruler of the seas and provider of earthly wealth" (1980: 28). Sadly, yet ironically, these very plaques were among the thousands of royal artifacts which were seized by the British military in 1897, during their so-called Punitive Expedition against the oba of Benin, whose agents were charged with killing six British officers in the course of a trade negotiation putatively gone awry. Many of these objects were sold shortly thereafter at auction in London, and are now held in museums and private collections throughout Europe and North America.

The British Punitive Expedition against the court of Benin took place at the height of Europe's military aggression toward Africa – an intense period of time when all European efforts were being made to secure their colonial territories and establish resolute imperial authority abroad. African resistance to European political rule was, in some areas of the continent, defiant, powerful, and often bitter (Weiskel, 1980; Ranger, 1986). Also, during the same period, African rejection of certain export commodities undermined European mercantile aspirations of economic

growth and prosperity in what European entrepreneurs had hoped was a promising new consumer marketplace in the African colonies. Textile manufacturers in France, for example, could not understand why Africans would reject their latest industrial, factory-made cloth in favor of, what the French perceived to be, the more crude and rudimentary African handwoven fabrics (Steiner, 1985).

Not surprisingly, then, this was a period in European history which generated a vast amount of negative propaganda and denigratory stereotypes about Africa and Africans. It was also a time when technological developments in mass communications, especially newspapers and illustrated magazines, enabled large amounts of information to be disseminated quickly to a wide and eager audience (Schneider, 1982; Blanchard and Chatelier, 1993). Africans were depicted in the European press in a manner which was calculated to entitle and authorize colonial expansionist goals. During the late nineteenth century, for example, on the eve of France's military aggression against Dahomean resistance to colonial rule, the French press seized upon both textual and visual representations of human sacrifice in Dahomey. Most of these images had been constructed and disseminated over a century earlier by Archibald Dalzel, a British mercantile explorer who had published horrific images of human sacrifice in his *History of Dahomy* (1793) in order to rationalize European violence against Africans in the Atlantic slave trade (see general Introduction). The "recycling" of this negative imagery by the French press was now intended to legitimate colonial rule and, once again, rationalize European actions in Africa. As historian William Schneider notes "The mass illustrated [press] played a key role in preparing the French public for the conquest of Dahomey, which was the first episode in the French government's new policy of open colonial aggrandizement in the 1890s" (1982: 103; Campion-Vincent, 1967).

Although the colonial period produced an

abundance of racist and paternalistic images of Africa in European art, literature, mass media, and scholarship, this was not always the case. European images of Africa from about the twelfth to seventeenth centuries were predominantly "positive" ones which depicted Africans as either "noble" beings living in harmony with nature, or as political allies whose vast kingdoms and empires were believed to be commensurate with the most powerful of royal monarchies which reigned in Europe. A glorified image of Africa emerged in the twelfth and thirteenth centuries when Europeans began to view Africans as potential military partners against the spread of Islam. When the Crusaders lost Jerusalem in 1244 and their strongholds in Palestine and Syria in 1291, Ethiopia became important as a possible ally against the Muslims (Debrunner, 1979: 24). A relationship of cooperation and mutual respect between Europe and Ethiopia developed throughout the ensuing four centuries. In 1634, for example, when a school for Ethiopian linguistics was established in Rome, European Christians believed that the Ethiopian language was the "original language of paradise" (Nederveen Pieterse, 1992: 28)

Although these images do not represent the "beastliness" and "barbarism" which were to be evoked later in the colonialist representation of "darkest" Africa, they are, of course, as philosopher V. Y. Mudimbe (1988: 1994) reminds us, but one of two extremes in Europe's polarized evaluation of Africa – both of which are equally based on European fantasies rather than on African realities. Mudimbe writes:

> From Herodotus onward, the West's self-representations have always included images of people situated outside of its cultural and imaginary frontiers. The paradox is that if, indeed, these outsiders were understood as localized and far away geographically, they were nonetheless imagined and rejected as the intimate and other side of the European-thinking subject. (1994: xi).

The problem of representation has been taken up by literary critic Christopher Miller in his book, _Blank Darkness: Africanist Discourse in French_ (1985). In a chapter entitled "Deriving a Discourse," Miller explores the semantic and historical roots of the terms Africa and Africanist. Like Mudimbe, he argues that from the time of earliest contact, Africa has been imprinted with European constructs, such that at some moments Africans were represented as "noble," while at others they were judged "monstrous." Africa, according to Miller, was a "blank" space in Europe's collective imagination which could be populated with all sorts of invented creatures and entangled in the various products of European fears and desires.

As a professor of literature, and one who focuses on texts and their representations, Miller deals primarily with the question of _language_. No matter where European explorers went in Africa – whether to the most accessible regions of the continent or the most remote – they always brought back their knowledge and "discoveries" in the form of language. This language, which eventually comes to be known as Africanist discourse, is structured by its own predetermined form. That is to say, the unknown cannot be represented in language without reference to something already known. The language which was used to describe Africa was made to fit the narrative conventions of European languages and rhetoric – its models, idioms, metaphors, systems of classification, and cultural assumptions.

How different is this from the early Kongo encounter with Europeans, in which Europeans were evaluated according to pre-existing categories of thought? Does every process of transcultural representation involve locating points of intersection between the known and the unknown, the familiar and the unfamiliar, the self and the other? How would you go about describing something, say an object, to someone who had never seen anything like it before? Would you try to describe it with images or with words? Would you begin by noting what it looks like (its appearance) or what it was used for (its function)? Would you draw contrasts and comparisons between that unfamiliar object and something more commonly found in your own cultural environment?

While Miller has looked broadly at the question of representation and its discourses, Jean and John Comaroff's essay in this volume, "Africa Observed," explores the "imagined landscape" of Africa within the context of a very specific historical moment. Beginning in the late eighteenth century, they demonstrate the pervasive and profound influence of slavery in shaping European discourses about Africa. On the one hand, abolitionists argued that slavery had corrupted Africa – "deforming the normal progress of civilization" – and that Africans required emancipation and conversion to Christianity in order to be saved. On the other hand, those who opposed abolition argued that Africans were naturally incited to "savagery" and war, and that the slave trade rescued them from the fate of their own barbarism. Either way, the Comaroffs conclude, "Africa was degraded and debased."

In their attention to the European image of South Africa, in particular, the Comaroffs demonstrate how texts could be used to make specific territorial claims. Analyzing John Barrow's *Account of Travels into the Interior of Southern Africa in the Years 1797 and 1798*, for example, they argue that the author intentionally created the image of an empty landscape just waiting to be seized by British colonial rule – an "unpopulated" place inhabited only by "unregenerate natives" and "degenerate Dutchmen," both of whom fell outside British definitions of civilization and, therefore, perceived as populations without legitimate claims to the land they happened to occupy.

The Comaroffs bring into sharp focus the relationship between gender and representation in their discussion of the portrayal of Africa as woman. Sexual metaphors of pene-tration abound in the literature of African exploration, where Africa was reduced "to the body of a black female yielding herself to white male discovery" (see also McClintock, 1995). During the late eighteenth century, a new political discourse surfaced in Europe which drew explicit physically-derived contrasts between men and women. Rooted in the pseudo-objectivity of a newly emerging biological epistemology, (male) scientists claimed that men were the bearers of reason and rationality, while women's temperament was adversely affected by their dominant reproductive organs which were linked directly to the central nervous system. The denigration of Africa as female body was linked to this new gender ideology, such that women and Africans were equally devalued and made peripheral in contrast to the European ideal of "rational man."

The Comaroffs examine the issue of representation from the perspective of how European images of Africa are constructed and circulated. That is to say, their aim is to analyze and deconstruct the languages – textual strategies and visual grammars – that have been used to portray Africa in European narratives about other cultures. Maxwell Owusu's article, "Ethnography of Africa: The Usefulness of the Useless," offers a different perspective on the issue of representation by addressing an even more fundamental question: namely, how can one hope to represent the realities and complexities of a foreign culture without possessing the full extent of language skills of an indigenous speaker? Thus, rather than look strictly at the dissemination of knowledge about Africa in European texts, Owusu questions the authenticity and validity of the production of that very knowledge at the moment of transcultural encounter and interlocution.

Although there are some noteworthy exceptions, anthropologists in the early decades of this century rarely bothered to learn the indigenous language. Working through "native" interpreters versed to a greater or lesser degree in the language of the colonizer (such as French, English, or Portuguese), anthropologists collected data which was inevitably being filtered and corrupted through its various stages of translation. Beginning in the 1940s and 1950s, with the development of more intensive and long-term field research, anthropologists began to study the language of the people with whom they worked. Much of their knowledge was gained through dictionaries and grammars written by European and American missionaries who had become proficient in most African languages as a means to proselytize. But no matter how well versed one might become in a foreign tongue, it is arguable that unless one is raised and nurtured in the cultural environment of a linguistic group it may be hard, if not impossible, to capture all of a culture's subtleties and complexities. In building his argument, Owusu makes reference to a debate in anthropology which took place in the early 1940s between Margaret Mead and Robert Lowie on the necessity of "native languages as fieldwork tools." While Lowie believed that language competence was essential to understanding other cultures, Mead viewed language as a mere instrument of research which could be hired out through local interpreters. Although neither of these anthropologists worked in Africa, their debate raises interesting problems regarding language skills, the translation of culture, and the production of knowledge.

Owusu's argument is so compelling that one may wonder why anthropologists have not questioned language competence more seriously before. His answer to this problem forms part of his argument: throwing into doubt the issue of language proficiency in field research would undermine all anthropology except the study of one's own culture. Since historically the unit of study in anthropology has been non-Western societies (although this is now quickly changing), and since anthropology was a discipline dominated largely by Western scholars (although today this has significantly changed), the only people qualified to conduct field research in non-Western contexts would be those who had been identified as the observed – and not the observers. This dilemma explains why, according to Owusu, anthropologists have argued that what the stranger "discovers" in field research is an abstraction of "reality" which is unknowable to indigenous peoples themselves. The epistemological distance between anthropologists and the cultural data before them, the argument goes, allows them to somehow "see" things that would otherwise remain unnoticed by indigenous people who are too steeped in their own cultural traditions. Owusu turns this methodological canon of anthropology on its head, and argues instead that the interpretation of culture can only come from "native" anthropologists who speak the language with sufficient competence to understand the subtleties and nuances of cultural expression.

A related debate on African languages exists, within the context of African literature, between Nigerian writer and critic Chinua Achebe and exiled Kenyan author Ngugi wa Thiong'o. Writing in the early 1960s, just a few years after Nigerian independence, Achebe argued that English ought to become the adopted language of African writers. He believed that Nigerian literature should serve to promote feelings of national solidarity, and that it could only do so by assuming the form of a "national" literature written in the national language, rather than merely an "ethnic" literature written in one of the numerous indigenous languages of Nigeria – such as Hausa, Ibo, Yoruba, and so on (Achebe, 1975 ed.: 92).

Ngugi wa Thiong'o, conversely, has argued more recently that African literature should be written in the author's mother tongue. As a child listening to stories told to him in his natal Gĩkũyũ language, he learned "to value words for their meanings and nuances. Language was not a mere string of words. It had a suggestive power well beyond the immediate and lexical meaning" (1986: 9). European languages, for Ngugi, were weapons of the colonizers –

vehicles through which the African soul was held prisoner. The liberation of that expressive spirit for African authors, according to Ngugi, could only come from writing in the indigenous language of their own culture. It would seem, then, that Owusu and Ngugi are arguing from the same perspective. Both view language not simply as a tool of communication, but rather as a rich purveyor of cultural knowledge which loses its depth and meaning in the process of translation. Representation and language are thus linked in this complex matrix of culture, where they inform and predetermine one another.

The final two readings in this section offer an intertextual dialogue between two African scholars regarding African cultural unity and the relationship between Europe, ancient Egypt, and sub-Saharan Africa. Beginning with Herodotus in the fifth century B.C., scholars in Europe believed that the rise of civilization in ancient Greece could be attributed to the fact that it had been colonized by the peoples of ancient Egypt, and was shaped largely through its cultural borrowings from African cultures. This model, which historian Martin Bernal calls the Ancient Model, was accepted until the 1700s, when racism and "continental chauvism" overtook European historiography (1987: 1–2). To the European historians of the eighteenth and nineteenth centuries, Bernal writes, "it was simply intolerable for Greece, which was seen not merely as the epitome of Europe but also its pure childhood, to have been the result of the mixture of native Europeans and colonizing Africans" (1987: 2). In their efforts to redefine the cultural genesis of European civilization, these historians set forth an alternative model in which it was argued that the origin of ancient Greece was the product of European or Aryan influence. This model, which Bernal calls the Aryan Model, denies any cultural borrowings in ancient Greece from Africa. The shift between these two radically different theories of history can be attributed not to the discovery of new evidence or facts, but rather

to changing racial attitudes in Europe during the period of the Atlantic slave trade. "After the rise of black slavery and racism," Bernal concludes on this point, "European thinkers were concerned to keep black Africans as far as possible from European civilization" (1987: 30). Thus, we see once again, that the construction of history is a matter of representation, and not the cumulative growth of knowledge which leads to a higher and more objective truth. Until fairly recently, the Aryan Model was the "accepted" version of history which accounted for the rise of ancient Greek civilization.

Beginning in the mid 1940s, however, Cheikh Anta Diop, a Senegalese scholar and a strong advocate of Pan-African political unity, reversed the Aryan Model and placed conventional wisdom on its head when he argued that it was Europe that depended on Africa and not the other way around (July, 1987: 137). In scores of painstakingly researched volumes on African history and prehistory, Diop sought to demonstrate – through linguistics, archaeology, anthropology, paleontology, history, art history, chemistry, and physics – that African culture had been transmitted to Greece in ancient times across the Mediterranean, and that its influence accounted for the rise of European civilization. Europe, in other words, once again owed its existence to Africa, and in particular to the immense artistic, cultural, and technological accomplishments of ancient Egypt. At the core of Diop's argument – a point which was left somewhat ambiguous in the earlier Ancient Model – is the notion that ancient Egypt was a *black* nation, classified as a distinct African population, which had migrated north from southern Africa, rather than one associated with the ancient Near East.

Diop's work has become an important resource in the rise of the Afrocentric movement both in Europe and North America. The arguments of Afrocentrism are twofold. First it holds that most Western scholarship views the world through Eurocentric eyes (see Lambropoulos, 1993). The achievements of other cultures (especially African cultures) are subordinated to those of Europe, while racial assumptions about ancient civilizations deny that the cultural triumphs of ancient Egypt can be attributed to the accomplishments of black people. Second, Afrocentrism holds that Africa should become the center of world history. That Europe should be judged by African standards and values, and not the other way round.

In his article, "Europe Upside Down," Kwame Anthony Appiah speaks out against a rising tide of publications which embrace this new Afrocentric perspective. He argues that Afrocentrism is seriously flawed on, at least, two counts. First, he notes, that by reclassifying Egypt as a black culture, Afrocentrists have accomplished nothing but simply to reverse a Eurocentric model of world history. Impressed by the presence of many of the cultural qualities with which Europeans defined civilization – a well developed writing system, a complex political, religious, and social hierarchy, a specialized class of professional artists and artisans, and the evidence of monumental architecture – Europeans recognized ancient Egypt as the most highly (and sometimes the only) developed culture on the African continent. But, Appiah asks, what about the immense accomplishments of non-literate societies in Africa? Why should all the attention of Afrocentric discourse be focused on Egypt, when there are so many other cultures in Africa whose histories are chronicled in oral (rather than written) traditions?

The attention lavished on ancient Egypt by the Afrocentric movement implies that the rest of the continent was somehow more "primitive" or "undeveloped," and thus underscores (rather than undermines) Europe's negative evaluation of Africa.

Second, Appiah remarks that Afrocentrism mistakenly tries to locate a cultural unity on the African continent (see general Introduction). This again, he says, is a bias which grows directly out of a Eurocentric preoccupation with identifying a common core of Western culture. Appiah believes that Africa's strength derives not from its putative homogeneity but rather from its rich complexity and diversity. Elsewhere he has written that "We cannot accept . . . the presupposition that there is, even at quite a high level of abstraction, *an* African world view" (1992: 82; original emphasis). The Afrocentrist search for African cultural solidarity in a "fancied past of shared glories" should be replaced, he argues, by a less racially motivated quest for black unity – one that looks for universal struggles and shared experiences among a vast array of individuals, around Africa and the African diaspora, who each belong to their own distinctive communities (1992: 173–80). African culture is something which needs to be constructed in the present and future, and not something which can be retrieved from an invented past. As it now stands, however, Appiah concludes, Afrocentrism is simply Eurocentrism turned upside down.

References

Achebe, Chinua. 1975. *Morning Yet on Creation Day*. New York: Anchor Press and Doubleday. First published in 1964.

Appiah, Kwame Anthony. 1992. *In My Father's House: Africa in the Philosophy Culture*. New York and Oxford: Oxford University Press.

Ben-Amos, Paula. 1980. *The Art of Benin*. London: Thames and Hudson.

Bernal, Martin. 1987. *Black Athena: The Afroasiatic Roots of Classical Civilization*. Volume 1, *The Fabrication of Ancient Greece, 1785–1985*. New Brunswick, NJ: Rutgers University Press.

Blanchard, Pascal, and Armelle Chatelier, eds. 1993. *Images et Colonies*. Paris: ACHAC and SYROS.

Blier, Suzanne Preston. 1993. "Imaging Otherness

in Ivory: African Portrayals of the Portuguese ca. 1492," *The Art Bulletin* 75(3): 375–96.

Campion-Vincent, Veronique. 1967. "L'image du Dahomey dans la presse française (1890–1895): les sacrifices humaines," *Cahiers d'études africaines* 7: 27–58.

Curnow, Kathy. 1990. "Alien or Accepted: African Perspectives on the Western 'Other' in 15th- and 16th-Century Art," *Visual Anthropology Review* 6(1) : 38–44.

Dalzel, Archibald. 1793. *The History of Dahomy, an Inland Kingdom of Africa, compiled from authentic memoirs; with an introduction and notes.* London: Spilsbury & Sons.

Debrunner, Hans. W. 1979. *Presence and Prestige: Africans in Europe Before 1918.* Basel: Basler Afrika Bibliographien.

Ezra, Kate. 1992. *Royal Art of Benin: The Perls Collection in The Metropolitan Museum of Art.* New York: The Metropolitan Museum of Art and Harry N. Abrams.

July, Robert W. 1987. *An African Voice: The Role of the Humanities in African Independence.* Durham, NC: Duke University Press.

Lambropoulos, Vassilis. 1993. *The Rise of Eurocentrism: Anatomy of Interpretation.* Princeton, NJ: Princeton University Press.

McClintock, Anne. 1995. *Imperial Leather: Race, Gender and Sexuality in the Colonial Conquest.* New York and London: Routledge.

MacGaffey, Wyatt. 1986. *Religion and Society in Central Africa: The BaKongo of Lower Zaire.* Chicago: The University of Chicago Press.

Mudimbe, V. Y. 1988. *The Invention of Africa: Gnosis, Philosophy, and the Order of Knowledge.* Bloomington: Indiana University Press.

Nederveen Pieterse, Jan. 1992. *White on Black: Images of Africa and Blacks in Western Popular Culture.* New Haven and London: Yale University Press.

Ngũgĩ wa Thiong'o. 1986. *Decolonising the Mind: The Politics of Language in African Literature.* London: James Currey.

Ranger, Terence. 1986. "Resistance in Africa: From Nationalist Revolt to Agrarian Protest," pp. 32–52. In *Resistance: Studies in African, Caribbean, and Afro-American History,* edited by Gary Y. Okihiro. Amherst: University of Massachusetts Press.

Schneider, William H. 1982. *An Empire for the Masses: The French Popular Image of Africa, 1870–1900.* Westport, CT: Greenwood Press.

Steiner, Christopher B. 1985. "Another Image of Africa: Toward an Ethnohistory of European Cloth Marketed in West Africa, 1873–1960," *Ethnohistory* 32(2) : 91–110.

Weiskel, Timothy. 1980. *French Colonial Rule and the Baule Peoples: Resistance and Collaboration, 1889–1911.* Oxford: Clarendon Press.

Suggested Readings

Appiah, Kwame Anthony. 1991. "Is the Post in Postmodernism the Post in Postcolonial?," *Critical Inquiry* 17(2) : 3–36.

Apter, Andrew. 1992. "*Que Faire?* Reconsidering Inventions of Africa," *Critical Inquiry* 19(1): 87–104.

Bachollet, Raymond, Jean-Barthélemi Debost, Anne-Claude Lelieur, and Marie-Christine Peyrière. 1992. *Négripub: L'image des Noirs dans la publicité.* Paris: SOMOGY.

Barkan, Elazar. 1992. *The Retreat of Scientific Racism: Changing Concepts of Race in Britain and the United States Between the World Wars.* Cambridge: Cambridge University Press.

Campbell, Mary B. 1988. *The Witness and the Other World: Exotic European Travel Writing, 400–1600.* Ithaca: Cornell University Press.

Clinton, Jean M. 1991. *Behind the Eurocentric Veils: The Search for African Realities.* Amherst: University of Massachusetts Press.

Cohen, William B. 1980. *The French Encounter with Africans: White Response to Blacks, 1530–1880.* Bloomington: Indiana University Press.

Coombes, Annie E. 1994. *Reinventing Africa: museums, Material Culture, and Popular Imagination.* New Haven and London: Yale University Press.

Curtin, Philip D. 1964. *The Image of Africa: British Ideas and Action, 1780–1850.* 2 vols. Madison: University of Wisconsin Press.

Diop, Cheikh Anta. 1987. *Precolonial Black Africa.* Westport, Conn.: L. Hill.

Diop, Cheikh Anta. 1991. *Civilization or Barbarism:*

An Authentic Anthropology. New York: Lawrence Hills Books.

Edwards, Elizabeth, ed. 1992. *Anthropology and Photography, 1860–1920*. New Haven and London: Yale University Press.

Fabian, Johannes. 1983. *Time and the Other: How Anthropology Makes its Object*. New York: Columbia University Press.

Gould, Stephen Jay. 1981. *The Mismeasure of Man*. New York: Norton.

Hawk, Beverly G., ed. 1992. *Africa's Media Image*. New York: Praeger.

Jahn, Janheinz. 1961. *Muntu: An Outline of the New African Culture*. New York: Grove Press.

Kuper, Adam. 1988. *The Invention of Primitive Society: Transformations of an Illusion*. London and New York: Routledge.

Lips, Julius E. 1937. *The Savage Hits Back*. New Haven: Yale University Press.

Lutz, Catherine A., and Jane L. Collins. 1993. *Reading National Geographic*. Chicago: The University of Chicago Press.

Mackey, Eva. 1995. "Postmodernism and Cultural Politics in a Multicultural Nation: Contests over Truth in the *Into the Heart of Africa* Controversy," *Public Culture* 7: 403–31.

Miller, Christopher L. 1985. *Blank Darkness: Africanist Discourse in French*. Chicago: University of Chicago Press.

———. 1990. *Theories of Africans: Francophone Literature and Anthropology in Africa*. Chicago and London: The University of Chicago Press.

Mudimbe, V. Y. 1994. *The Idea of Africa*. Bloomington: Indiana University Press.

Okoye, Felix N. 1971. *The American Image of Africa: Myth and Reality*. Buffalo, NY: Black Academy Press.

Onyewuenyi, Innocent C. 1993. *The African Origin of Greek Philosophy: An Exercise in Afrocentrism*. Nsukka: University of Nigeria Press.

Price, Sally. 1989. *Primitive Art in Civilized Places*. Chicago and London: The University of Chicago Press.

Steiner, Christopher B. 1995. "Travel Engravings and the Construction of the Primitive," pp. 202–25, 416–18. In *Prehistories of the Future: The Primitivist Project and the Culture of Modernism*, edited by Elazar Barkan and Ronald Bush. Stanford: Stanford University Press.

Thornton, Robert. 1983. "Narrative Ethnography in Africa, 1850–1920: The Creation and Capture of an Appropriate Domain for Anthropology," *Man* 18(3): 502–20.

41

AFRICA OBSERVED: DISCOURSES OF THE IMPERIAL IMAGINATION

JEAN AND JOHN COMAROFF

Let us . . . contrast piety with atheism, the philosopher with the rude savage, the monarch with the Chief, luxury with want, philanthropy with lawless rapine: let us set before us in one view, the lofty cathedral and the straw-hut, the flowery garden and the stony waste, the verdant meadow and the arid sands. And when our imagination shall have completed the picture, and placed it in a light which may invite contemplation, it will, I think, be impossible not to derive from it instruction of the highest class.

William Burchell (1824:2,444)

The imagined landscape of Africa was greatly elaborated in late eighteenth-century Britain, albeit less as an end in itself than as a byproduct of the making of modern European self-consciousness (cf. Said 1978; Asad 1973; Gates 1986). Its features were formed in the context of vigorous arguments about humanity, reason, and civilization – debates that were driven by the social and cultural upheavals that accompanied the rise of capitalism and that forced the nations of Europe to refashion their sense of themselves as polities on a world map. Africa became an indispensable term, a negative trope, in the language of modernity; it provided a rhetorical ground on which a new sense of heroic history could be acted out (cf. Godzich 1987).

More than anything else, perhaps, abolitionism subsumed the great debates and discourses of the age. For it raised all the crucial issues involved in the contested relationship between European and Other, savagery and civilization, free labor and servitude, man and commodity; the ideological stuff, that is, from which a liberal hegemony was being made. As Davis (1975:350) has noted, the antislavery movement replayed Adam Smith's message in another key, making of it a program for global social transformation: that all classes of society should be recognized as sharing a natural identity of interest; that the common wealth depended on the liberty of everyone to pursue their own ends in an unfettered material and moral economy.

Abolitionism, as some have claimed, might have been a pragmatic attempt to resolve contradictions in the culture of postenlightenment Britain. And it clearly was a dispute about the merits and morals of different modes of colonial production. But it was also an exercise in mobilizing new forms of representation and communication (see Anderson 1983) to arouse the middle and laboring classes to a passion for epic reform; the controversy was widely aired in mass-circulating pamphlets, newspapers, and religious tracts, as well as in the discriminating columns of the literary reviews. And it drew upon a number of related discourses which alike had become sites for the formulation of a coherent bourgeois awareness. These discourses arose out of a number of distinct but related fields of exploration. Each aimed to construct what Heidegger (1977:115f.; see Godzich 1987:xiv) has identified as a mechanism of mastery, an explanatory scheme capable of objectifying nature and representing it to the knowing, synthesizing human subject. Most significant among them – at least in shaping the consciousness of our evangelists – were the discoveries of the geographical mission to Africa; the investigations into human essence and difference within the emerging life sciences; and the mythology of the noble savage celebrated by the romantic movement (Curtin 1964:34), which explored otherness in a variety of aesthetic genres. Each of these discourses had its own institutional context and expressive forms. But each played off the others – often in productive discord – and conduced to an increasingly rationalized debate about the nature of civilization, the civilization of nature. And together, by virtue of *both* their form and their content, they established the dark continent as a metaphysical stage on which various white crusaders struck moral postures (Achebe 1978:9).[1]

The symbolic terrain of a rarely-seen Africa, then, was being shaped by a cascade of narratives that strung together motley "scientific facts" and poetic images – facts and images

surveyed by an ever more roving European eye. As this suggests, the rhetoric of light and dark, of color and culture, was already palpable in contemporary Europe, though it had not yet taken on the full fan of connotations it was to bear in Victorian thought. Hume (1854:3,228n), after all, had argued that "there scarcely ever was a civilized nation of [Negro] complexion," and Rousseau had echoed his sentiment that blacks were mentally inferior by nature.[2] Those who opposed abolition argued that slavery was the "natural law" of Africa, as much part of the condition of savagery as the cannibalism and wanton bloodshed so luridly described by some observers (Dalzel [1793] 1799; Norris [1789] 1968). Abolitionists tended to respond by blaming the slave trade itself for deforming the normal progress of civilization (Austen and Smith 1969:79). Either way, Africa was degraded and debased.

It was also inextricably entangled in a western embrace. Romantic poets might have envisaged Africans living lives free of Europe (Brantlinger 1985:170), but the weight of public opinion at the turn of the nineteenth century suggested the opposite. So, too, did the sheer weight of evidence. Whether as purveyors or reformers of the "evil traffic," white men had written themselves into the present and future of the continent. Whatever else it might have entailed, abolitionism did not argue for European withdrawal from Africa. It made the case for the replacement of one mode of colonial extraction with another. Once emancipated, his humanity established, the savage would become a fit subject of Empire and Christendom.

In this chapter we examine each of the discourses through which Africa came to be imagined, tracing their confluence to the argument over slavery itself. In so doing, we

---

[1]   Notwithstanding our particular concerns here, it goes without saying that stereotypic images of "others," in Africa and elsewhere, predate the age of revolution. So does their metaphysical significance in European thought and representation. For a valuable history of medieval conceptions of the "monstrous races," see Friedman (1981).

[2]   On Rousseau's views in this respect, see Cook (1936); also Curtin (1964:42).

witness the rise of a more and more elaborate model of the relationship of Europe to the "dark continent": a relationship of both complementary opposition and inequality, in which the former stood to the latter as civilization to nature, savior to victim, actor to subject. It was a relationship whose very creation implied a historical imperative, a process of intervention through which the wild would be cultivated, the suffering saved. Life would imitate the masterful gestures of art and science. The "native" would be brought into the European world, but as the recipient of a gift he could never return – except by acknowledging, gratefully, his own subordination. And in this colonizing project the Christian missionary would play a special role as agent, scribe, and moral alibi. . . .

Into South Africa: Of Maps and Morals

In Britain ca. 1800, West Africa served as stereotype for the continent as a whole. The Cape of Good Hope was a secondary focus of European concern. A small colony administered since 1652 by the Dutch East India Company, it had generated little travel literature, especially in English.[3] In 1795, however, the Cape was taken over by Britain as a consequence of her war with the French, who had invaded Holland and were thought likely to seize the Dutch outpost on the sea route to the East (Harlow 1936:171f.). John Barrow, founder of the Royal Geographical Society (which was to absorb the African Association), was appointed personal secretary to Macartney, the new governor of the

Colony.[4] As Macartney's protege he had accompanied the latter to China in 1792, serving officially as comptroller to the embassy but acting also as observer of Chinese civilization (Lloyd 1970:24). Now he was sent on a tour of the South African interior to represent His Majesty and to investigate the discontents of frontier farmers, whose long-standing resistance to the Dutch Company had been transferred to the new administration.[5]

Barrow's *Account of Travels into the Interior of Southern Africa in the Years 1797 and 1798* (1801–4) was self-evidently a colonial document. A legitimation of the British annexation of the Cape, it also gave eyewitness account of the degradation of the Dutch frontiersmen, who, lacking a European "spirit of improvement and experiment," had regressed to take on the qualities of their rugged and soporific surrounds (1801–4:1,67; see also Streak 1974:5f.; Coetzee 1988:29f.). The very landscape conveyed this unrefined state to Barrow's eye, schooled as he was on nicely-demarcated European vistas of private ownership (1801–4:1,57):

> As none of the [extensive lands] are enclosed there is a general appearance of nakedness in the country . . . which . . . if divided by fences, would become sufficiently beautiful, as nature in drawing the outline has performed her part.

The Dutch had not investigated the interior systematically and, perhaps most diagnostic for Barrow, had "no kind of chart or survey, save of such districts as were contiguous to the Cape" (1801–4:1,8). This was taken to indicate lax colonial control, something that the British

---

[3] Three seventeenth-century accounts were published in Dutch and Latin (see Schapera 1933); two in German followed during the eighteenth century (Kolben 1731; Mentzel 1785–87).

[4] Barrow's biography was notably similar to that of Park. Both were self-made sons of northern British smallholders (Lloyd 1970).

[5] It will be recalled (see chapter 1) that the Cape was restored to the new Batavian Republic in 1803 under the Treaty of Amiens but was seized again by the British in 1806, after the resumption of the Napoleonic Wars (see e.g. Davenport 1969:273f.).

"spirit of commerce and adventurous industry" would remedy. The frontispiece of Barrow's book has a comprehensive map of the Cape Colony, constructed from bearings, distances, and latitudes observed during his travels. The map presents this land to Britain for the taking, its virgin scapes laid tantalizingly bare, its routes of access picked out in red.

Barrow's *Account* was also a moral geography of the interior of the Cape, one which not so much emptied the landscape of its human inhabitants (Pratt 1985) as denied them any legitimate claim to it. The text cleared the ethical ground for British colonialism by depicting the territory as a polarized human universe of unregenerate natives and degenerate Dutchmen. The dualistic vision of nature in postenlightenment imagery, to which we alluded above and shall return, speaks out here. The Dutch had negated their own humanity by treating the blacks as objects, prey to be "hunted" (1801–4:1,273); they sought to validate a "monstrous" manhood (1801–4:1,145) by exterminating nature's innocents – rather than by elevating them, and all African humanity, through forceful cultivation. Their brutal bravado was founded on a myth of savagery that Barrow feels called upon to dispel (1801–4:1,196):

> It is a common idea, industriously kept up in the colony, that the Kaffers[6] are a savage, treacherous, and cruel people, a character as false as it is unmerited . . .

Likewise, speaking of the Khoisan, he adds that the "Hottentots" (Khoi) were "mild, quiet, and timid people, perfectly harmless, honest, faithful," their timeless customary existence destroyed by Dutch abuse (1801–04: 1,151); and the "Bushmen" (San) were "like frightened children" mowed down by Boer bullets as they played with bows and arrows (1801–4: 1,273).

These observations were grounded in the very real fact of genocide; there is plenty of collateral evidence to prove that a war of extermination had been waged along the frontier against the Khoisan (see e.g., Marais 1944; Marks 1972; Elphick and Malherbe 1989). Nor is there any doubt that Barrow believed himself to be writing a *historical* account of both Boer and Bushman, explaining how each had been affected by the violent encounter with the other. Nonetheless, there is in this historiography another process at work. In building his stereotypic contrasts, Barrow, intentionally or not, was also fleshing out an imaginative structure, a set of oppositions which came to be shared by many of his contemporaries (see Coetzee 1988:29f.). The Dutch farmer was European civilization grown rotten in the African sun – his "nature" made yet more degenerate, his "indolence of body and low groveling mind" corrupted yet further by being an owner and master of slaves (Barrow 1801–4 quoted by Coetzee 1988:29; see also Philip 1828,1:367f.; Moodie 1835:1,176). He was the very antithesis of Protestant enlightenment, having wilfully permitted his own debasement. The "savage tribes," made so brutish by seventeenth-century Dutch reports (see Willem ten Rhyne in Schapera 1933), were really innocent and ignorant. They might dance and sing when moved by their childish passions, and slept in beds "like the nest of an ostrich" (1801–4:1,148,275). While "low on the scale of humanity," they were raw material for the civilizing project. For, notwithstanding their common predicament as "miserable savages" (1801–4:1,287) in opposition to the British, peoples such as the "Hottentots" had their own nobility. This *Account*, in short, validated the moral scheme of the first LMS and WMMS

---

[6] It is clear that Barrow meant "kaffir" here to include all "aborigines." In the nineteenth century the term (also "Caffre") was often used more specifically to describe the Nguni-speaking peoples of South Africa – although it was later to become a general term of abuse for blacks, much like "nigger" in the United States of America.

missionaries to South Africa, coloring their view of the white perverts and would-be black converts who peopled the interior.

Barrow's social position guaranteed him a wide readership among scholars, politicians, and the literate public. The natural historian Lichtenstein ([1815] 1930,2:12) noted at the time that in his native Germany the "journals and almanacks" vied to publish the British author's accounts of the "ignorance, the brutality, the filthiness" of the Dutch colonists. Lichtenstein himself had traveled in the interior of South Africa between 1803 and 1806 in the employ of the Dutch government. His own two volume narrative appeared in German in 1810 and 1812 and in English in 1812 [repr. 1928] and 1815 [repr. 1930]. It was highly critical of Barrow's portrayal of the Dutch farmers and their brutal domination of the "Caffres" (1928:1,59):

> I was led almost daily to ask myself whether these were really the same African colonists which the celebrated Mr Barrow represented as such barbarians, as such more than half-savages – so much did I find the reality in contradiction to his description.

Again we are reminded that images of Africa are born of European arguments about their own essential nature.[7] Barrow was accused of betraying his own kind; of failing, as an educated European, to credit the effects of the African climate and hence to understand the "rough Cape peasantry" and their relation to the blacks (1930:2,6–13). Yet, lying beneath the surfaces of the debate, is a set of shared constructs that makes the dispute possible in the first place. Lichtenstein does not really take issue with Barrow's portrayal of Africans,

although his own descriptions lack the Englishman's stress on their innocence and vulnerability. For him, "Bushmen" are miserable and voracious: "no class of savages . . . lead lives so near those of brutes" or are so low on the "scale of existence" (1930:2,244). But, he adds (1930:2,65):[8]

> The rude rough man left entirely in a state of nature, is not in himself evil and wicked. . . . [He] follows blindly the impulse of his passions, which lead him to acts, that to us, in the high point of civilization we have attained, appear as crimes . . .

Africa might have become a moral battlefield, but its representation in late eighteenth-century Europe also reflected a conceptual order fast spreading among persons "of reason," an essential humanism in terms of which man became his own measure (Foucault 1975). No longer satisfied with a notion of himself as God's passive creature, he sought to define his "place in nature" (Thomas 1984:243 et passim); that is, to assess his position on a scale of humanity rather than on a ladder to heaven. A new narrative of human types was being written, and the African was to have a definite niche in it. As a foil to the enlightened European, he was doubly devalued: human yet ignorant of salvation to begin with, he had now lost his innocence at the hands of civilization's most depraved elements, slavers and the degenerate white men of the tropics.[9] Here, as we have said, the texts of travelers and explorers became entangled in the debate over abolition (see Barrow 1801–04:1,46). But the discourse also informed, and was informed by, arguments within the related field of natural history and the emerging science of biology.

---

[7] For an account of British images of and attitudes toward the Dutch settlers, see Streak (1974), who also discusses the writings of Barrow and Lichtenstein. We are grateful to Robert Gordon for drawing our attention to this reference.

[8] Lichtenstein seems to have been the first writer in this genre to make use of missionary observations of black South Africans (see the Prefatory Note to volume 1 of his *Travels* [p.vi], republished by the Van Riebeeck Society in 1928). His work in turn became an important source of European constructions of Africa.

[9] See Curtin (1964:58f.) on the role of the "tropics" in this discourse.

The New Biology and the Great Chain of Being

In the early nineteenth century the life sciences were preoccupied with the "great chain of being" – and especially with its lower half. As Figlio (1976:25) observes, contemporary debates about man's place in nature hinged upon the relationship of the human species to the rest of the living world:

> There was a focusing upon the multi-faceted idea of animality, as opposed to an insistence upon a scalar, uni-dimensional hierarchy, with man at the top of the visible, and God at the top of the invisible, realm.

Rooted in the contrast between the animate and the inanimate, this focus on animality implied a concern with the properties of "life" common to all beings. And it fixed on man as the embodiment of perfection, since he alone had distinguished himself by using reason to discover his own essence. This in turn led inexorably to the concept of "generic human nature" (Stocking 1987:17), a notion that separated man from beast, people from objects, and rendered anomalous anything – like the slave trade – that confused them. But "human nature" was a highly abstract category. Once put to work in the world it was immediately subject to internal differentiation. This is where the chain of being served as a powerful metaphor, for it conjured up a hierarchy of distinct varieties within (a single) humankind.

In the epistemology of the time, then, the key to knowledge seemed to lie increasingly within man himself. The essence of life was in the unplumbed depths of organic being, to be grasped through the invasive thrust, the looking and naming, of the new biology (Foucault 1975). Its interior truth, merely signified in outer bodily form, gave rise to meaningful differences in the faculties and function of living beings.

African Bodies, African Nature

We have already encountered traces of this epistemology in the geographical mission, where the thrust into the African interior likened the continent to a female body. Bernhard Fabian (quoted in Nerlich 1987:179) reminds us that, in the late eighteenth century, the qualities of the scientific "spirit" were identified with the heroic "spirit" of the adventurer: the natural scientist's penetration into hitherto unknown realms had become one with the advance into regions unknown. The newly charted surfaces of the African landscape were to have a direct connection with the universe opening up within the person, for the geographical mission expanded European knowledge of the global biology of mankind. In investigating the savage, the West set up a mirror in which it might find a tangible, if inverted, self-image. Non-Europeans filled out the nether reaches of the scale of being, providing the contrast against which cultivated man might distinguish himself. On this scale, moreover, the African was assigned a particularly base position: he marked the point at which humanity gave way to animality. In treating him as the very embodiment of savagery, of deviance from a racially-defined ideal (Gould 1981:38), the travel and adventure literature gave ostensibly objective, precise descriptions of both his bodily form and his "manners and customs." In such popular accounts, in other words, African "nature" was grounded in the color, shape, and substance of the black physique.

With the rise of comparative anatomy and biology as formal sciences, the organic reduction of African society and culture took on ever greater authority. For much of the eighteenth century it had been civilization that separated savage man from his white counterpart – moral and politico-economic circumstance rather than physical endowment (Stocking 1987: 18). But the vocabulary of natural science was to strengthen and legitimize the association of dark continents with black bodies and dim minds. Comparative anatomical schemes, typically presented Africans as the most extreme contrast with Europeans – in the new technical argot, the "link" between man and beast (Curtin 1964:42). Linnaeus' *Systema Naturae*, first published in 1735, laid out in initial form what would soon become a convention of biological classification: a chromatic scale of white, yellow, red, and black races, each native to one of the four major continents (Gould 1981:35; Curtin 1964:37). As in the popular literature of travel and adventure, Africans were invariably placed at the bottom of the ladder of enlightenment, below such paler peoples as Asians or American Indians (Buffon 1791; Blumenbach 1775, 1795; White 1799). By 1778 Buffon, who had added such features as hair, stature, and physiognomy to his scheme, declared that white was the "real and natural colour of man" (quoted in West 1982:56).[10] Blumenbach took this yet further, to the shape of the skull, thereby introducing one of the more pervasive and enduring elements in the annals of racial taxonomy. He went on to claim, on this basis, that the Ethiopian was the lowliest deviation from the "most beautiful" Caucasian type (Street 1975:52ff.). The great chain of being, a vertical scale, had been set on its side, becoming also a linear history of human progress from the peripheral regions of the earth to its north European core. The hard facts of organic form, it seemed, could now explain and determine the place of men in the world.

Science, Aesthetics, and Selfhood

The life sciences, then, were part of a broader discourse about the human condition – a discourse closely tied to Europe's encounter with the non-European world. Raised to a new level of self-consciousness and authority, their "value free" knowledge found a natural vali-

dation for cultural imperialism in the inner secrets of existence. "Natural" scientists read off the degree of animality and the perfection of life from the external features of different "organisms"; for these were taken to be a function of the relative complexity, symmetry, and refinement of the faculties within. Take, for example, the influential Dutch scholar Camper, who, in a manner similar to Blumenbach, devised a scale that correlated the shape of the skull with aesthetic appearance and mental capacity: his "facial angle" measured the projection of the jaw, a protruding profile being linked with the long snouts, low brows, and sensory-bound state of animals. Applied to an eclectic array of "evidence" – including African traveler's accounts – this measurement defined and ranked national character, giving physical shape to the current philosophical concern with the relationship of race, nationality, and civilization (cf. Hume 1854).

Camper's scale extended from dog through ape to Negro, then through the European peoples to the ideal beauty of form epitomized in Greek sculpture (1821:x; see Figlio 1976:28f.). And it was rapidly publicized well beyond the scientific community, as were his more general pronouncements. Thus the preface to an English translation of his popular lectures addressed an artistic audience on the moral and aesthetic implications of the science of comparative anatomy (1821:x):

> [The] grand object was to shew, that national differences may be reduced to rules; of which the different directions of the facial line form a fundamental norma or canon . . . the knowledge of which will prevent the artist from blending the features of different nations in the same individual . . .

Nationality, physical type, and aesthetic value are condensed here into an iconography that

[10] We are indebted to Nahum Chandler for this reference, included in his unpublished paper, "Writing Absence: On Some Assumptions of Africanist Discourse in the West."

would in due course become part of the language of scientific racism. With his apartheid of the sketchpad, Camper imprinted the bodily contours of stereotypic others on the European imagination – and with them, a host of qualitative associations. His sample African profile, for instance, a distinctly bestial representation, was to become standard in nineteenth-century texts on racial difference; significantly, these texts gave prominence to images of black South Africans.

Georges Cuvier, the prestigious Swiss comparative anatomist of the early nineteenth century, took the facial angle and the biological reduction of culture to new levels of sophistication. He developed a scale to evaluate the perfection not only of the intellect but also of the introspective self, the moral core of the person. By gauging the proportion of the mid-cranial area to that of the face, he sought to reveal the degree of dependence of an organism upon external sensations; the size of the cranium itself was taken to reflect the development of reason and self-control. On this count, the "negro" stood between the "most ferocious apes" and the Europeans, who were themselves superseded by the men and deities of ancient Greek sculpture (Figlio 1976:28). But it was the neurological dimension of Cuvier's scheme (1827:1,49f.) that raised most explicitly the spiritual and moral capacity of man. For the nervous system was the site of internal animation, and its complexity determined the higher faculties of life – intelligence and volition. The latter were expressions of a "soul or sentient principle," whose source of vitality remained, at the time, a matter of serious debate. Scientists, however, were more concerned with the physical organization of this system, which was centered on a compact inner core that reached its most perfect form in the complicated brain of man. As Figlio (1976:24) explains:

> . . . this compactness [was associated] quite explicitly with the higher faculties, indeed with the sense of the 'self'. Just as the nervous system coalesced into a centre from which dependent nerves arose, so too was the sense of self increasingly solidified and distinct. Thus, a grading of this . . . concentrating of the nervous system was simultaneously a grading of animal sentience and selfhood.

And so the bourgeois subject of the new Age of Capitalism, already secure in the Protestant ethic and rational philosophy, was given incontestable grounding in biological nature. Needless to say, the inner density and refinement associated by Cuvier with self-awareness and control were held to be underdeveloped among non-Europeans. This was especially true of blacks, who were bound by the animal reflexes of survival (1827:1,97; see Curtin 1964:231):

> The negro race is confined to the south of Mount Atlas. Its characters are, black complexion, woolly hair, compressed cranium, and flattish nose. In the prominence of the lower part of the face, and the thickness of the lips, it manifestly approaches to the monkey tribe. The hordes of which this variety is composed have always remained in a state of complete barbarism.

Cuvier's writings were summarized in the British biomedical press within months of their publication and were assiduously discussed by scientists, theologians, and men of letters (Figlio 1976:35). In an age when specialist knowledge was not yet set apart by technical language, work such as this – and that of Camper – was rapidly directed to a receptive, almost insatiable public. Often, as in one widely read translation of Cuvier's *Animal Kingdom*, some "popular and entertaining matter" was added on the instincts and habits of animals and primitive man (1827:1,i–ii). The editors in this particular instance included a description of the "unhappy races" of South Africa, a telling bricolage of current European curiosity, with substantiating material drawn from the accounts of travelers like Barrow and Lichtenstein. Thus were the discoveries of geographical adventure converted into a scientific currency in which the universal value of man might be reckoned.

As these travel tales and salon exotica gained scientific credentials, they hardened into stereotypic representations of Africa. Their influence on the eye of subsequent European observations in South Africa was to be tangible. Cuvier's editors (1827:1,197), for example, provided an account of the "Bushmen" as pygmy "plunderers" who "lurk[ed]" in the complicit woods and bushes. This description seems to have been drawn directly from Lichtenstein (1928:1,68n), yet we encounter it, metaphor intact, in the "eyewitness" report given many years afterwards by the Rev. Edwards (1886:66). The interplay of other epithets in the *Animal Kingdom* – "Hottentots" as degraded and disgusting, or as swarthy, filthy, and greasy – may also be traced to Lichtenstein (1928:1,69).[11] They too were to flow from the pens of later writers who claimed the authority of firsthand experience.

One item among the potpourri of curiosities in the *Animal Kingdom* (1827:1,196) was a description of the "Hottentot Venus," an "essential black" from the Cape Colony. This unfortunate "wild" woman of Khoi ancestry had been taken to Europe and made into a traveling exhibit, shown first in England and then, by an animal trainer, in France. She died in Paris in 1815 after European audiences had gazed in fascination at her for some five years – and promptly ended up on Cuvier's dissecting table (Gould 1985:294). His famous account of her autopsy was to be reprinted twice within a decade of its publication; it centered on the anomalies of her "organ of generation," which, in its excessive development of the *labia minora*, was held to set her

kind apart from other human beings (Gilman 1985:212). Barrow, too, had written of genital aberrations of Khoisan women, and a host of anatomical reports were to follow Cuvier in focusing on the exotic, simian qualities of black female reproductive organs. A barely suppressed infatuation with the torrid eroticism of Africa made itself respectable as biological inquiry.

The story of the Hottentot Venus reminds us that Mungo Park, albeit in somewhat different idiom, had also reduced Africa to the body of a black female yielding herself to white male discovery. This mytheme, as we shall see, was repeated in both the poetry of romantic naturalists and the sober prose of our missionary crusaders. But Cuvier's writings show particularly plainly how early nineteenth-century science actually articulated and authorized such constructions – how the various products of current European fancy sailed under the colors of biological knowledge about man, woman, and nature. Nor did the ideological message of this material remain implicit. Supplementary details on African peoples in the *Animal Kingdom* (1827:1, 196) were summarized with the confident statement that "a physical obstacle to their progress seemed to be a more natural solution to [the] problem [of their lack of development] than any political or local circumstances."

The Nature of Gender

As all this suggests, the "signifying economy" (Godzich 1987:xi) of otherness took in gender as well as race. That "economy" has a long history, of course. But we need only break into it at the dawn of modernism. "Sometime in the late eighteenth century," Lacquer (1986:1) observes, "human sexual nature changed." It certainly did. With the reorganization of production and perception in the age of

---

[11] Although, as Keith Thomas (1984:42) points out, talk of Hottentots as "beasts in the skin of man" also had earlier precursors.

revolution, novel distinctions arose in the construction of gender. And they raised the problematic "nature of woman" to consciousness in Europe as never before.

Given the epistemology of the time, it was inevitable that this new consciousness should find the source of gender relations in the bodies of men and women – and that biology should be invoked to explain a division of labor already established in economy and society. The ideology of the enlightened free market might celebrate equality and a generic humanity. But its material practices sanctioned the exploitation of whole categories of people, usually on the basis of "natural" distinctions like race and sex. Such stigmatizing signs often come to imply each other: in late eighteenth-century images of Africa, the feminization of the black "other" was a potent trope of devaluation. The non-European was to be made as peripheral to the global axes of reason and production as women had become at home. Both were vital to the material and imaginative order to modern Europe. Yet both were deprived of access to its highest values. Biology again provided the authoritative terms for this simultaneous process of inclusion and disqualification.

In sum, the manner in which Africa was portrayed as woman – with reference in particular to the organs of procreation – was an extension of a gender ideology fast taking root in late eighteenth-century Europe. Here "the female body in its reproductive capacity and in its distinction from that of the male, [had come] to occupy a critical place in a whole range of political discourses" (Lacquer 1986:1). As the biology of childbearing became the essence of womanhood, it also seemed to prescribe an increasingly radical, physically-derived contrast between male and female. For centuries prior to this time, both medical and commonsense knowledge appear to have assumed that women had the same reproductive organs as men; that they were "men turned outside in" (Lacquer 1986:1). Moreover, gender identity had not been vested

in the anatomy of procreation alone but in more general features of moral and social disposition. In this respect too there was a continuity between male and female: far from "a total division of mental properties between the sexes," as Jordanova (1980:63) puts it, there had been "a continuum according to which reason dominated . . ."

Reason and intelligence were male properties, of course; men and women had thus been arrayed along a single axis whose telos was masculine (Lacquer 1986:3). But the struggle between the two qualities had occurred within rather than between individuals, each person's temperament being the product of both. Here Foucault's insight into changing perceptions of hermaphrodites throws light on the emergence of modern gender identity. In his introduction to the memoirs of Herculine Barbin (1980b:viif.), he notes that medieval canon and civil law defined them as people in whom the two sexes were juxtaposed in variable proportions. By the nineteenth century, however, it had become the task of the medical expert to "find the one true sex of the so-called hermaphrodite" (Davidson 1987), to reveal the unambiguous biological reality that underlay uncertain appearances.

The premodern language of gender had also integrated physical, mental, and social qualities, making the body an icon of moral as much as of procreative status. Jordanova (1980:49) notes that medical and philosophical writings in the eighteenth century focused on the breast as a symbol of the valued role of women in domestic nurture. The shift of attention to the uterus in nineteenth-century biology marked a retreat into the hidden recesses of gynaecological anatomy, whence female nature now seemed to emanate.

The new biology of difference and incommensurability, then, shackled women to their sexual nature as resolutely as it freed men – or at least European men – from the constraints of instinct and bodily function. "It was," one physician explained, "as if the Almighty, in creating the female sex, had taken the uterus and built up a woman around it" (Holbrook 1882; quoted in Smith-Rosenberg and Rosenberg 1973:335). Here the ideology of gender cut across contemporary models of the nervous system and became implicated in the more general definition of modern selfhood. For, by implication, women's reproductive physiology rerouted their neurological pathways, diffusing the compact density of the rational, male self. As opponents of female education were to argue, the brain and the reproductive organs simply could not develop at the same time. The uterus was assumed to be connected directly to the central nervous system, shaping its constitution and in return being affected by it (Smith-Rosenberg and Rosenberg 1973:335).

Women's sensibility was both greater and more labile than that of men, and their nervous systems lacked focus; their "fibres" were "mobile," especially "those in the uterus" (Macquart 1799; quoted in Jordanova 1980:48). Like the "low brow" non-European, the European female was played upon by strong and frequent sensations from the external environment. Her constitution was passionate and intuitive, susceptible to nervous disorders, and responsive to control by males – particularly men of science (Stocking 1987:199). A privileged relationship of sex and selfhood had been born: with the emergence of the "psyche" in later nineteenth-century thought, sexuality would become the "externalization of the hidden, inner essence of personality" (Davidson 1987:47). This development was prefigured in the vision of missionaries earlier in the century, which placed great diagnostic weight upon sexual propriety as a symptom of "moral fiber." After all, as Davidson reminds us, moral theology had once used "pervert" – a person wilfully turning to evil from good – as an antonym of "convert." There is evidence of this connotation, and of the more modern sense of "sexual deviance," in the evangelists' use of the term.

It has been pointed out (Smith-Rosenberg and Rosenberg 1973:338; Stocking 1987:199;

Jordanova 1980:49) that contemporary discourses on female nature were neither unanimous nor free of contradiction. Women were held at once to be sensitive and delicate, yet hardy and longer-lived; passionate and quintessentially sexual, yet innocent and intuitively moral. Given the political load that the anatomy of woman had come to bear, such ambiguities were bound to fuel angry dispute; it is not surprising that her body soon became an ideological battleground (Lacquer 1986:24). Feminists and antifeminists both exploited these contradictions, albeit in contrasting ways – the former being no less quick than the latter to appeal to natural differences in making their case. Anna Wheeler and William Thompson (1825; quoted in Lacquer 1986:23), for example, argued that women deserved greater political participation on grounds of their innate moral aptitude and their undesiring, even passionless dispositions. And Fuller (1855), in her manifesto, *Woman in the Nineteenth Century*, described male and female as "two sides of the great radical dualism," the female system being "electrical in movement" and "intuitive in function" (quoted in Ayala 1977:263). Thus, while the debate raged over social values, its terms reinforced the hegemony of biological determinism and ineluctable gender distinction.

The new biology, in short, gave legitimacy to an idealized image of rational man. Unlike women and non-Europeans, he was a self-contained individual and was driven by inner reason, not by sensory stimuli from the social and material environment. This image of selfhood appeared simultaneously in a wide range of late eighteenth-century moral and technical discourses; biomedical science was just one voice in a richly redundant chorus, its concern with the inner body drawing attention away from man's dialectical relation with his context. But the reduction did not go unchecked. It was countered by the social reformism of mainstream enlightenment religion and philosophy, which stressed the reconstruction of persons and, through them, the world. Humanitarian and evangelical rhetoric alike had it that the possession of a soul and the capacity to reason made every human being capable of improvement. The self could be "cultured,"[12] the will strengthened by implanting spiritual truth and by "uplifting" physical and social conditions.

Thus the biological determinism of the age was usually qualified by some attention to the effects of environment; conversely, the optimism of philanthropists and evangelists was often tempered by a suspicion that nature placed limits on the ability of some human beings to develop. Nor were scientists undivided on the issues: Gould (1981:31ff.) has distinguished "hard-" from "softliners" among significant eighteenth and nineteenth-century thinkers on the question of the African's potential for civilization.[13] While this distinction may be too rigidly drawn, there certainly were loud and lengthy arguments about the origin and implications of racial difference. Witness the debate over the role of climate in the origin of human diversity, in which some early naturalists (e.g., Buffon 1791) and biologists (e.g., Blumenbach [1775, 1795] 1969) claimed that negro physical characteristics grew out of life in the tropics (Curtin 1964:40). Here again scientific thought evoked European notions of ecology that went back at least a hundred years – in

particular, the humoral theory that "as the air is, so are the inhabitants" (cf. Hodgen 1964:283). In this legacy "southern climes" were repeatedly associated with heat and fecundity, sensuality and decay. For instance, in his defense of Cape Dutchmen against Barrow's attacks, Lichtenstein (1928:1,58) attributed their "phlegm" to the African environment. And for comparative support he quoted Goethe's similar observations of the indolent Neapolitans.

The writings of the South African missionaries suggest that they too perceived a complex connection between African bodies and landscapes. Moreover, their efforts to reform the benighted blacks were to express an unresolved conflict between the incorrigibility of natural endowment and the possibility of human improvement. Visible in the conflict, and in the entire European discourse about savagery, was an increasingly sharp – and gendered – contrast between "nature" (all that exists prior to civil society) and "civilization" or "culture" (collectively wrought existence, though not yet the modern anthropological idea of a distinct, meaningful lifeworld; see Stocking 1987:19; also note 12 above). This dichotomy was elaborated most extensively, perhaps, in the debate over the "noble savage," a chimera which relied heavily on images of Africa already in popular European circulation.

[12]   As Williams (1976:77) has noted, "culture as an independent noun, an abstract process or the product of such a process, is not important before 1C18 [the late eighteenth century] not common before mC19 [the mid-nineteenth century]." Prior to this, "culture" was a noun of process, implying the "tending *of* something," usually crops or animals. From the early sixteenth century, the tending of natural growth was gradually extended by metaphor to the process of human development.

[13]   We are indebted to Nahum Chandler for this reference also; see n. 11 above.

References

Achebe, Chinua
1959   *Things Fall Apart*. New York: Astor-Honor Inc.
1978   An Image of Africa. *Research in African Literatures* 9:1–15.

Anderson, Benedict
1983   *Imagined Communities: Reflections on the Origin and Spread of Nationalism*. London: Verso.

Asad, Talal
1973   Two European Images of Non-European Rule. In *Anthropology and the Colonial Encounter*, ed. T. Asad. London: Ithaca Press.

Austen, Ralph A., and Woodruff D. Smith
1969   Images of Africa and British Slave-Trade Abolition: The Transition to an Imperialist Ideology, 1787–1807. *African Historical Studies* 2:69–83.

Ayala, Flavia
1977   Victorian Science and the "Genius" of Woman. *Journal of the History of Ideas* 38:261–80.

Barrow, John
1801–4 *An Account of Travels into the Interior of Southern Africa in the Years 1797 and 1798*. 2 vols. London: Cadell & Davies.
1806   *A Voyage to Cochinchina*. London: Cadell & Davies.

Blumenbach, Johann F.
1969   *On the Natural Varieties of Mankind*. Translated by T. Bendyshe from the 1775/1795 editions. New York: Bergman Publishers.

Brantlinger, Patrick
1985   Victorians and Africans: The Genealogy of the Myth of the Dark Continent. *Critical Inquiry* 12:166–203.

Buffon, George L.L.
1791   *Natural History, General and Particular*. Translated by W. Smellie. London: A. Strahan.

Camper, Petrus
1821   *The Works of the Late Professor Camper, on the Connexion between the Science of Anatomy and the Arts of Drawing, Painting, Statuary*. . . . New ed., edited by T. Cogan. London: sold by J. Hearne.

Coetzee, John M.
1988   *White Writing: On the Culture of Letters in South Africa*. New Haven: Yale University Press.

Curtin, Philip D.
1964   *The Image of Africa: British Ideas and Action, 1780–1850*. Madison: University of Wisconsin Press.

Cuvier, Georges
1827–35 *The Animal Kingdom*. . . . 16 vols. London: Geo. B. Whittaker.

Dalzel, Archibald
1799   *Geschichte von Dahomy, einem Inländischen Königreich in Afrika*. Translated from *The History of Dahomey*, 1793. Leipzig: Schwickert.

Davidson, Arnold I.
1987   Sex and the Emergence of Sexuality. *Critical Inquiry*. 14:16–48.

Davis, Peter B.
1966   *The Problem of Slavery in Western Culture*. Ithaca: Cornell University Press.
1975   *The Problem of Slavery in the Age of Revolution 1770–1823*. Ithaca: Cornell University Press.

Edwards, John
1886   *Reminiscences of the Early Life and Missionary Labours of the Rev. John Edwards*. Edited by W.C. Holden. Grahamstown, South Africa: T.H. Grocott.

Elphick, Robert, and V.C. Malherbe
1989   The Khoisan to 1828. In *The Shaping of South African Society, 1652–1840*, ed. R. Elphick and H.B. Giliomee. Middletown, Conn.: Wesleyan University Press.

Figlio, Karl
1976   The Metaphor of Organization: An Historiographical Perspective on the Bio-Medical Sciences of the Early Nineteenth Century. *History of Science* 14:17–53.

Foucault, Michel
1973   *Madness and Civilization: A History of Insanity in the Age of Reason*. Translated by R. Howard. New York: Vintage Books.
1975   *The Birth of the Clinic: An Archeology of Medical Perception*. Translated by A.M. Sheridan Smith. New York: Vintage Books.

Fuller Ossoli, Sarah M.
1855   *Woman in the Nineteenth Century*. New York: Sheldon, Lamport. Original edition, 1845.

Gates, Henry L., Jr., ed.
    1986   "Race," Writing, and Difference. Chicago:
    University of Chicago Press.
Gilman, Sander L.
    1985   Black Bodies, White Bodies: Toward an
    Iconography of Female Sexuality in Late
    Nineteenth Century Art, Medicine and
    Literature. Critical Inquiry 12:204–242.
Godzich, Wlad
    1987   Foreword: In Quest of Modernity. In
    Ideology of Adventure: Studies in Modern
    Consciousness, 1100–1750, vol. 1, by Michael
    Nerlich. Translated by R. Crowley.
    Minneapolis: University of Minnesota Press.
Gould, Stephen J.
    1981   The Mismeasure of Man. New York:
    W.W. Norton & Co.
    1985   The Flamingo's Smile: Reflections in
    Natural History. New York: W.W. Norton & Co.
Harlow, Vincent T.
    1936   The British Occupations, 1795–1806. In
    The Cambridge History of the British Empire, vol.
    8, South Africa, Rhodesia and the Protectorates,
    ed. A.P. Newton and E.A. Benians. Cambridge:
    Cambridge University Press.
Heidegger, Martin
    1977   The Question Concerning Technology, and
    Other Essays. Translated by W. Lovitt. New
    York: Harper & Row.
Hodgen, Margaret T.
    1964   Early Anthropology in the Sixteenth and
    Seventeenth Centuries. Philadelphia: University
    of Pennsylvania Press.
Holbrook, Martin L.
    1882   Parturition without Pain: A Code of
    Directions for Escaping from the Primal Curse.
    New York: Fowler & Wells.
Hume, David
    1854   The Philosophical Works. 4 vols.
    Edinburgh: Adam & Charles Black; Boston:
    Little, Brown.
Jordanova, Ludmilla J.
    1980   Natural Facts: A Historical Perspective
    on Science and Sexuality. In Nature, Culture,
    and Gender, ed. C.P. MacCormack and M.
    Strathern. Cambridge: Cambridge University
    Press.
    1981   The History of the Family. In Women in
    Society: Interdisciplinary Essays, The
    Cambridge Women's Studies Group. London:
    Virago Press.

Lacquer, Thomas
    1986   Orgasm, Generation, and the Politics of
    Reproductive Biology. Representations 14:1–41.
Lichtenstein, Henry [W.H.C.]
    1928–30   Travels in Southern Africa in the
    Years 1803, 1804, 1805 and 1806. 2 vols.
    Translated from the 1812–15 edition by A.
    Plumptre. Cape Town: The Van Riebeeck
    Society.
    1973   Foundation of the Cape (1811) and About
    the Bechuanas (1807). Translated and edited by
    O.H. Spohr. Cape Town: A.A. Balkema.
Lloyd, Christopher
    1970   Mr Barrow of the Admiralty: A Life of Sir
    John Barrow, 1764–1848. London: Collins.
Marais, Johannes S.
    1944   Maynier and the First Boer Republic. Cape
    Town: Maskew Miller.
Marks, Shula
    1972   Khoisan Resistance to the Dutch in the
    Seventeenth and Eighteenth Centuries. Journal
    of African History 13:55–80.
Moodie, John W.D.
    1835   Ten Years in South Africa. 2 vols.
    London: R. Bentley.
Nerlich, Michael
    1987   Ideology of Adventure: Studies in Modern
    Consciousness, 1100–1750. 2 vols. Translated by
    R. Crowley. Minneapolis: University of
    Minnesota Press.
Norris, Robert
    1968   Memoirs of the Reign of Bossa Ahadee,
    King of Dahomey. . . . Facsimile of the 1789
    edition. London: Frank Cass.
Philip, John
    1828   Researches in South Africa; Illustrating the
    Civil, Moral, and Religious Condition of the
    Native Tribes. 2 vols. London: James Duncan.
    Reprinted, 1969; New York: Negro Universities
    Press.
Said, Edward W.
    1978   Orientalism. New York: Pantheon Books.
Schapera, Isaac
    1933   The Early Cape Hottentots, Described in
    the Writings of Olfert Dapper (1668), Willem ten
    Rhyne (1686), and Johannes Gulielmus de
    Grevenbroek (1695). Original texts and transla-
    tions by I. Schapera and B. Farrington. Cape
    Town: The Van Riebeeck Society.
Smith-Rosenberg, Carroll, and Charles Rosenberg
    1973   The Female Animal: Medical and

Biological Views of Woman and her Role in Nineteenth-century America. *Journal of American History* 40:323–56.

Stocking, George W.
1987   *Victorian Anthropology*. New York: The Free Press; London: Collier Macmillan.

Streak, Michael
1974   *The Afrikaner as Viewed by the English, 1795–1854*. Cape Town: Struik.

Street, Brian V.
1975   *The Savage in Literature: Representations of 'Primitive' Society in English Fiction, 1858–1920*. London and Boston: Routledge & Kegan Paul.

Thomas, Keith V.
1984   *Man and the Natural World: Changing Attitudes in England, 1500–1800*. Harmondsworth: Penguin.

West, Cornel
1982   *Prophesy Deliverance!: An Afro-American Revolutionary Christianity*. Philadelphia: Westminster Press.

White, Charles
1799   *An Account of the Regular Gradation in Man, and in Different Animals and Vegetables; and From the Former to the Latter*. . . . London: Printed for C. Dilly.

42

ETHNOGRAPHY OF AFRICA: THE USEFULNESS OF THE USELESS

MAXWELL OWUSU*

Toward an African Critique of African Ethnography

Hui Tzu said to Chuang Tzu, "Your teachings are of no practical use." Chuang Tzu said, "Only those who already know the value of the useless can be talked to about the useful. This earth we walk upon is of vast extent, yet in order to walk a man uses no more of it than the soles of his two feet will cover. But suppose one cut away the ground round his feet till one reached the Yellow Springs, could his patches of ground still be of any use to him for walking?" Hui Tzu said, "They would be of no use." Chuang Tzu said, "So then the usefulness of the useless is evident." [Fortes 1945:vi.]

Ethnographic fieldwork, perhaps the most interesting and certainly the most challenging and fundamental, has two principal aspects: the survey and intensive participant observation. Ethnographic research conventionally has had as its main objective the descriptive account of native cultures. That is, the provision for primarily a Western European audience of new and basic or additional and *reliable* information about non-Western – the so-called "primitive," "barbarous," "savage,"

or "backward" peoples – "the millions whose welfare" according to Fortes "is in the trust of Western civilization" (1953:46) and of whose cultures nothing or little was (is) known to *Europeans*.

Over the years, white anthropologists have effectively and successfully persuaded (seduced? convinced? reassured?) scholars the world over and intelligent laymen alike to believe, at times against their better judgment, that their ethnographies of "primitive" people

* This is a revised version of a paper prepared for delivery at the special symposium, New Directions for the Anthropological Study of African Societies, at the 74th annual meeting of the American Anthropological Association, San Francisco, 2–6 December 1975, and read in a modified form at the University of Michigan Department of Anthropology Symposium on Implications of Western Perspectives in Anthropology, winter 1976. I thank William Shack, Aidan Southall, Victor Uchendu, and Niara Sudarkasa for their useful and informed comments. The suggestions for improvement of the paper by the three anonymous referees for the *American Anthropologist* are also very well appreciated. The responsibility for the arguments presented here, however, is all mine.

are trustworthy because they are the result of painstaking, and *intensive* fieldwork, which implies *fluency* in the languages of the peoples studied (see, for instance, Staniland's recent [1975:x] well-meaning but misplaced apologetic in his work on the Dagomba).

Yet a careful reading of the typical "tribal" monograph ingeniously protected by an "ethnographic present" and written in obscure "scientific" and esoteric language demonstrates one thing: it is virtually impossible, particularly for the native anthropologist to falsify, replicate, or evaluate it *objectively*. For, frequently, it is not clear whether the accounts so brilliantly presented are about native realities at all, or whether they are about informants, about "scientific" models and imaginative speculations, or about the anthropologists themselves and their fantasies.

Whatever the message and intellectual contribution of these ethnographies, they represent a clear measure of the general distorting intellectual impact of the extension of Western politicoeconomic frontiers, of Western "discovery" of the non-Western world, which has since led, unabated, to the systematic and often forcible restructuring and transformation by Europeans of the "new" and "primitive" world in the image of Europe.

The main purpose of this article, then, is to reexamine, with particular reference to selected, highly representative ethnographic (and historical) accounts of Africa, the implications for past, current, and future research of the perennial problem of the use (lack of use, misuse, or abuse) of native languages in fieldwork. The issue of native languages as fieldwork tools was raised in the now almost forgotten or ignored 1939–40 debate, summarized and commented upon below, between Margaret Mead and Robert H. Lowie. There is ample epistemological, substantive, and methodological evidence of the urgent need to

reopen this debate. I show, for instance, on the basis of the analysis of representative selected textual references in two classic, very popular, and influential ethnographies – Evans-Pritchard's *The Nuer* (1940: See extract, Chapter 2, this volume), already in its eighth reprinting, and Meyer Fortes' *The Dynamics of Clanship among the Tallensi* (1945) usually cited with *The Nuer* – that a great majority of the very authoritative and over-quoted ethnographies of Africa by distinguished Western scholars produced particularly during the colonial period have been successfully put together without the serious and systematic benefit of the relevant local vernaculars.[1] Most of the ethnographers did not and could not have had an adequate command of the relevant indigenous languages and a ready comprehension of the natives' speech among themselves. The resulting inevitable reliance of ethnographers on semiliterate and literate native interpreter-informants who communicated in various lingua francas or the so-called contact languages, e.g., Pidgin English, Swahili, etc., did not, as we shall soon see, provide sufficient or reliable insurance against working misunderstanding between ethnographers and the people they studied and, inevitably, data quality contamination. I further demonstrate with reference to a recent fairly representative case study of local politics in Ghana (Dunn and Robertson 1974) that the use of literate native interpreter-informants may very well compound the problem of ethnographer bias in field reports and, hence, of intercultural translation. I present also some evidence from cross-cultural survey methodology to show that one critical factor that greatly contributes to systematic errors in ethnographic accounts is the lack of language familiarity or fluency.

Today, when "heavy acculturation" is the rule rather than the exception in African societies, a *prior* ability to speak and under-

---

[1] Despite conventional claims to the contrary, as George M. Foster reminds us, "anthropologists take it for granted that they must speak and understand the language of the people they study if their research results are to meet the exacting canons of excellence of contemporary fieldwork" (1969:66).

stand *several* relevant local vernaculars is essential if the ethnographer is to avoid serious factual errors and misleading theoretical conclusions. Command of several local vernaculars is necessary because of the increasing tendency of Africans to shift from language to language within a single interaction context or social field as a result of the mixing of different speech communities. Unfortunately there is a growing tendency among Africanists (and anthropologists working in other geographic areas as well) to assume rather naïvely, even as they pay lip service to the importance of the use of native languages, that since European languages are now widely used throughout Africa, satisfactory scholarly ethnographies based on fieldwork can be written without mastery of the relevant vernaculars.[2]

According to the School of Oriental and African Studies' linguistic map of Africa there are, and we need to be constantly reminded, some 1,500 living indigenous languages in very active daily use among Africa's 300 million or so inhabitants, in addition, of course, to the major European languages in use, especially by the new elites, throughout the continent. Africa's self-identity is to a significant extent defined in terms of this linguistic reality. It is this cultural reality, which has over the years successfully defied the otherwise aggressive European culture penetration, which makes ethnographic research in Africa a formidable task, even for native scholars. I then put

---

[2] One anonymous referee of this paper remarked that since, as I have argued, anthropology is a Western science, "control of a native language, however good, is not likely to produce native intuition." This may be so, but certainly language familiarity serves or should serve as a useful, indeed invaluable, check on both informants and interpreters and help improve the general quality or reliability of ethnographic data collection and description. I must strongly emphasize that my basic contention concerning the control and use of native languages in ethnographic research is *not*, as another anonymous referee suggested, a polemic about the "let-us-study-us" approach. Nor am I arguing in support of an extreme relativist position that asserts that since peoples in different cultures have often radically different ways of thinking and looking at life – philosophies of life which are expressed or embodied in their various languages – cultures (and languages) are untranslatable. This would render anthropology as the study of *other* cultures impossible.

Rather, I am arguing as many others have done before me – though their advice is yet to be seriously heeded – that *in practice*, translation of cultures is extremely difficult, and that even the *possibility* of a tolerably satisfactory translation requires that we have better than a tolerably satisfactory control of the relevant local vernaculars. This is the *sine qua non* of every good (meaningful) ethnography, which is above all a *semantic* enterprise.

Thus I totally agree with John U. Ogbu's cogent point (personal communication) that except where one studies one's own language, dialect, or subcultural group, an African ethnographer will face problems similar to those faced by foreign ethnographers in Africa and elsewhere.

Professor Ogbu's account of his personal experience based on a brief study of the Pika of Northern Malawi some years ago is worth recounting. "I had no knowledge of CiTumbuka before arriving in the field. I hired a native interpreter-informant who had some formal education and had lived in South Africa as labor migrant for a couple of years. But my interpreter-informant proved to be a handicap in some respects. As I became 'proficient' in CiTumbuka I realized that he did not always translate my questions to local people accurately; nor did he always give me in English their responses to my questions fully or accurately. I had a crash language course in the field as a way to solve the problem. This consisted of not only being taught CiTumbuka by the interpreter-informant, but also using published materials. . . . Among these materials was a bible in CiTumbuka which proved to be very useful in self-teaching, given my background in mission schools in Nigeria. Unfortunately, the fieldwork ended just at the point where I was beginning to be quite conversant with the use of the local language; that is, at the point when I could confidently tell when my interpreter-informant was making a mistake in either translating my questions or translating other informants' responses" (personal communication).

All of this underscores my main point about the crucial role of language acquisition and understanding in ethnographic research anywhere. Of course, the control of the relevant vernaculars cannot be a panacea for the total range of our epistemological problems in all aspects of our research, e.g., those associated with the dynamics of class, ethnic, racial, caste, age, sex, and individual differences. However, it cannot be disputed that the control of, for instance, lower class or upper caste dialectical differences is an indispensable first step toward meaningful ethnographies of lower class or upper caste subcultures.

forward what may be a radical solution to the epistemological and methodological dilemmas of the foreign anthropologist who still dominates the study of African societies and cultures. It is my firm belief that the continued *professionalism* in the field of African studies, the field's contribution to the science of society, and the extent to which ethnographic knowledge could be of real service to the host community and government all depend critically on the seriousness and determination with which the problem of data quality control as it relates particularly to linguistic competence is successfully tackled.

Functions of Language in Ethnography: Mead vs. Lowie

In a classic assessment of "native languages as fieldwork tools," Mead (1939) observes that "there is much misunderstanding of what is meant by *using the native language*, a phrasing which I prefer to *speaking the native language*. The latter . . . arouses the suspicion of linguistic purists, terrifies students who have not yet tried fieldwork, and puts an *undue* premium on virtuosity at the expense of emphasizing that a language is a tool, not a feather in one's cap" (1939:196; emphasis added).

She goes on to note characteristically that "we may consider the use of the native language in relation to the problems that confront the fieldworker and divide them into the need to *speak* and the need to *understand*, always bearing in mind that the fieldworker is not in the field to *talk* but to *listen*, not there to express complicated ideas of his own that will muddle and distort the natives' accounts. The demands upon him for active linguistic participation are lower than they are in any *normal* period of his life" (1939:196; emphasis added). Mead proceeds to identify the *three* functions

of language in the field as (1) the need to ask questions correctly, (2) the need to establish rapport, and (3) the need to give accurate instructions. For Mead, 20 to 30 locutions at most, with allowance for inflection (1939:197) and "one piece of scrupulously accurate habitual formal comment," (1939:199) are usually adequate for the linguistic needs.

The stress is on the command of a modicum amount of *strategic* native utterances. For if the "ethnologist [ethnographer] cannot give quick and accurate instructions to his native servants, informants and assistants . . . he will waste an enormous amount of time and energy doing mechanical tasks which he could have delegated if his tongue had been just a little better schooled" (1939:199). According to Mead, "it is also essential to know whether the natives can digest *complex* instructions or whether the instruction must be given them piecemeal sometimes permitting them to answer and repeat between each item in a series" (1939:199; emphasis added). If the fieldworker can learn to handle these three situations, Mead concludes, "he will be able to *use* the native language . . . insofar as speaking is concerned," since he naturally wishes to limit himself to the minimum in conversation, for "he is there to observe and listen" (1939:200). For Mead then "using the native language" for active participation and for obtaining "ethnological information" does not mean, as Lowie indicates in his effective and noteworthy rebuttal of Mead's *mutatis mutandis*, "what it means for a would-be authority on any *advanced contemporary civilization* viz., a *fluent* command of the vernacular, coupled with ready comprehension of the natives' speech among themselves. Such control . . . Dr Mead vehemently deprecates – almost contemptuously – as 'linguistic virtuosity'" (Lowie 1940:81; emphasis added).[3] Mead concludes on the basis of the

---

[3]   The obvious sophistry and Eurocentrism implied by Mead's foregoing remarks notwithstanding, her distinction between two broad types of study, one requiring *minimal* use of the native language and the other requiring *maximal* use of it (see particularly Mead 1939:194–196), whatever its analytic value, leads to further practical obfuscation. Under the

above considerations that since the publication of Malinowski's *Argonauts of the Western Pacific* in 1922, which marks a significant revolution in ethnographic fieldwork methods, more than 25 investigators of both sexes from England and the U.S. "have done *authentic* fieldwork *using* native tongues" (1939: 191–192; emphasis added). . . .

The *indispensable* role of the proper *contextual* use of the native language in fieldwork is justified on *scientific*, practical, and humanistic grounds.

Data Quality Control and Native Language Familiarity

. . . Since ethnographic accounts of African societies (and of other non-Western societies) have traditionally relied, admittedly, so heavily on native informants, control of informant bias is obviously a most urgent task. Three main sources of informant error are described by Naroll. These are (1) the distorting effects of indigenous cultural theory or stereotype, (2) the distorting effect of poor choice of informant by the ethnographer, and (3) the distorting influence of faulty memory of the details of a particular unique event (see 1962:80–82 for details).

Of course, informants may deliberately or unintentionally mislead, lie, or refuse to answer questions or provide needed information. That is, informants may indulge in various kinds of systematic deception. To find out whether or not any of the above-mentioned and other forms of informant or ethnographer bias (in contradistinction to random error) exist in field reports, Naroll proposes six bias-sensitive control factors or tests for the purpose and applies them to a

cross-cultural study of culture stress. The relevant control factors are (1) case reports, (2) participant observation, (3) length of stay in the field, (4) native language familiarity, (5) ethnographer's role (e.g., as scientist, government official, or missionary), and (6) explicitness and generality of report. The "provenience of the ethnographer" may also be a possible control test (see Naroll 1962:85–99 for a detailed discussion).

In this study, based on a final worldwide sample of 37 societies, including seven in Africa (1962:46), Naroll constructs an "index of culture stress" involving four adequately operationalized and transculturally equivalent substantive variables or traits, which are (1) drunken brawling, (2) defiant homicide, (3) protest suicide, and (4) witchcraft attribution. That is, the quality control factors are measured in each sample ethnography and they are then correlated with the substantive variables. If a data quality control factor – we need to stress that each separate quality control test "stands on its own feet" in regard to the observation conditions in the field (1962:22) – is significantly related in a statistical sense to a pair of substantive variables, then the effects of that control factor must be considered in the interpretation of the relationship between the bias-sensitive substantive variables or traits.

Naroll is able to show in his study of culture stress, for example that ethnographers who live in the research community for a year or more ("length of stay in the field") tend significantly more often than "short stayers" to report the presence of witchcraft. If reports on warfare are biased in the same way, with "long stayers" being more likely to report the presence of warfare than "short stayers," then cross-cultural survey researchers may discover

---

former category are studies (a) to rescue the remains of "dying cultures" and (b) of survivals of primitive culture in a hybridized cultural situation in which everyone speaks a contact language. Under the latter category of studies are (a) those of social functioning, except where a lingua franca is sufficiently widespread to enable a *male* investigator to follow social trends in specific situations without a knowledge of the vernacular, (b) those that deal with the relationship between culture and personality, and (c) those that are concerned with symbolism.

a statistically significant but spurious cross-cultural relationship between the incidence of witchcraft and that of warfare. The true relationship between witchcraft and warfare would thus be obscured because of systematic ethnographer bias in the ethnographic reporting process (1962:88–89; see also Rohner 1975 and Rohner et al. 1973 for a recent application of the data quality control technique to a cross-cultural study of the effects of parental acceptance and rejection).

Most pertinent to my argument is Naroll's observation that the quality control tests of witchcraft attribution and of protest suicide reports have produced statistically significant or near significant evidence of bias. According to him, the evidence that turned up suggests, among other things, that reports by ethnographers unfamiliar with the native language may tend consistently to underestimate suicide and witchcraft attribution rates. Naroll's language familiarity test, for instance, shows a high association between native language familiarity and high witchcraft attribution reports (1962:89–90). Naroll (1962), Rohner (1975),

and others do recognize that the effects of ethnographer bias shown by the statistical analysis of the ethnographic data could be due to a number of factors, including sampling error and coder bias.[4]

Nonetheless, the commonsense remark by Naroll (1962:90) that ethnographers who stay longer in the field and who master the native language have better – superior – rapport with informants and hence are less likely to be imposed upon or more likely to detect deception when it is tried can hardly be refuted and needs to be restated again and again.

Unfortunately, as I have implied, few ethnographers, if any, working in African societies in the 1920s, 1930s, 1940s, and 1950s – the senior anthropologists whose work laid the foundation for African studies – had any appreciable control of the native languages.[5] The ability to use effectively native African language(s) by the ethnographer would require, under normal conditions, several years of sojourn among the target and *related* peoples before one could be ready for the serious task of studying the culture.

---

[4] The subject of *probability sampling* in ethnography is a thorny one and merits a separate detailed treatment. It may suffice to note here that one of the most serious weaknesses of the ethnography of Africa, especially of colonial anthropology (and other "anthropological societies as well), has been the ethnographers' total reliance on opportunistic sampling. That is, from a few, occasional, even casual and sometimes "trained" informants or informers, they derived sweeping, if highly imaginative, generalizations about the whole society and culture. After all, anthropology must be holistic. The Nuer, for example, numbered, according to Evans-Pritchard, about 200,000 at the time of study. Evans-Pritchard tells us that he never succeeded in training informants capable of dictating texts and giving detailed description and commentaries. Information was thus collected in particles, each Nuer he met being used as a source of knowledge. We are not told how many of the 200,000 or so Nuer he met. Godfrey and Monica Wilson, in the words of the latter in her *Good Company* (1951), gathered data on the Nyakusa of Central Africa who totalled about 234,000 from only four or so key informants. Fortes' Tallensi numbered about 35,000 according to the 1931 Gold Coast census. The data on the Tallensi come from two principal informants and perhaps "the many others, too numerous to mention" who "were our faithful friends and zealous helpers" (1945:xii). Some anthropologists working in Africa, such as Günter Wagner (1949) who studied the Abaluhyia of North Nyanza, Kenya, in the 1930s, did not even consider it necessary to discuss their research methods at all. We need only stress here that we cannot without serious distortion of reality derive valid macrosociological theories or cross-cultural generalizations from our crude microsociological techniques (see Naroll 1970a, 1970b; Rohner 1975; Chilungu 1976).

[5] In a recent study, Rohner (1975:252–253) provides a reasonable, if perhaps charitable, measure of the ethnographer's proficiency in the languages of the people he is studying. Three categories or ratings of proficiency are proposed: (1) little or no knowledge of the native language, (2) some knowledge and understanding of the native language, and (3) fluency in the native language.

An ethnographer may be considered fluent in the language only when he makes an explicit statement to that effect. The ethnographer may be thought to have some knowledge and understanding of the language when he says so or when he is able to follow at least the gist of most casual conversations without being able to speak the language well enough to

But in a *colonial situation*, characterized as it was by a diffused sense of the White Man's Burden, serious misconceptions about the nature of traditional African societies and cultures, and Eurocentric intellectual orthodoxies and preconceptions, conditions could hardly have been normal, let alone ideal, as Fortes' and Evans-Pritchard's remarks, to be discussed later, attest. The ethnographer was, therefore, forced almost invariably to rely heavily on the overburdened native-servant-interpreter-informant. As Lowie concludes with characteristic candor, "We use interpreters, not because we like to, but because we have no other choice" (1940:89).

The basic epistemological issue is whether a true dialogue can be obtained between the foreign ethnographer and his native interpreter-informant, which will provide a basis for real understanding of the native's culture and society and for removing any serious mutual historical misconceptions that may hinder genuine communication where one or both parties have little or no effective control of the other's vernacular (in the phonetic, lexical, and idiomatic senses).

A related question is what constitutes *acceptable* anthropological paradigms and ethnographic findings, given the fact that the anthropology of Africa is still largely a European enterprise, dominated by European scholars who define what anthropology is? Further, given that Europeans provide the rules for "scientific" or legitimate anthropological work and also provide the criteria by which academic recognition and rewards are allocated among deserving anthropologists, both African and European, what real contribution can a native literate or semiliterate interpreter-informant make toward genuine

understanding of his society and culture? Answers to these questions may be found in part by a careful analysis of aspects of the conventional role of the literate native interpreter-informant in ethnographic fieldwork and the procedural rules by which anthropologists arrive at their data and the nature of the conclusions based on them.

The Ethnographer's Magic: The Discovery of "Structures"

There are basically three interrelated stages and processes by which data on African cultural realities have been and continue to be systematically gathered and their substance transformed and often mistranslated by Western ethnographers into the so-called valid cross-cultural, universally applicable institutional types. These stages are as follows: (1) initial, and often persistent, linguistic and pyschological (cultural and racially defined) gaps between the foreign ethnographers and the peoples they study; (2) the urgent demand for "theories" to assist the ethnographer in organizing his field data and in presenting the conclusions derived from the data; and (3) the uncritical treatment of "authoritative" ethnographic or ethnological hypotheses and hunches as accepted or established facts of native life.

First, faced with the cognitive and linguistic gap between himself and the subjects, or natives, the ethnographer is forced to apply rigidly the rather convenient rule of "scientific detachment" in fieldwork and to aim primarily, even solely, at providing sociologically intelligible accounts of the beliefs and practices of native populations. As

converse in it, except for phrases of etiquette. The ethnographer is said to have little or no knowledge of the language when he states that this is the case, speaks only English (or whatever his own native language may be) while doing fieldwork, or relies almost exlusively on interpreters.

Fourteen sub-Saharan African societies are represented in Rohner's study sample. It is significant to note that of the ten ethnographers whose language familiarity is rated, only one, Ashton (Sotho), had fluency in the language. Herskovits (Fon) had little or no knowledge of the language, and neither had Evans-Pritchard (Nuer) nor LeVine (Gusii). Fallers (Soga) was rated as having some understanding of the language, and Fortes (Tallensi) received a zero score.

Evans-Pritchard clearly indicates, sociological intelligibility means that

the social anthropologist *discovers* in a native society what no native can explain to him and what no layman, however conversant with the culture, can perceive – its basic structure. This structure cannot be seen. It is a set of abstractions, each of which, though derived, it is true, from analysis of observed behavior, is fundamentally an *imaginative construct of the anthropologist himself*. By relating these abstractions to one another logically so that they present a pattern he can see the society in its essentials and as a single whole. . . . Having isolated these patterns in one society he compares them with patterns in other societies [1968:51; emphasis added].

There are thorny problems concerning how "structures" as abstractions from reality are generated; the extent of the logical validity of the abstractions; and, more critically, the degree of their correspondence with native realities. The major "discoveries" of the Western ethnographer (and historian) can and have been made with little concern for the integrity of the cultural realities of the individuals and groups of the societies in question. For example, Chukwuemeka Onwubu, in a review essay, has recently demonstrated, through semantic analysis of Igbo terms, the error committed by Simon Ottenberg in his *Leadership and Authority in an African Society: The Afikpo Village Group* when he presents as the structural attributes of Igbo society such

taxonomic categories as subsets, grades, wards, village segments, subsegments, and clans, thus creating the impression of a formally organized village bureaucracy (Onwubu 1975:71–77).[6]

The ethnographer's magic wand, his most *personal* and prized property, seems then capable of conjuring up a fantastic array of truly head-spinning hierarchies of "structures" and reticulated "structures" of "structures," according, no doubt, to a preconceived, well rehearsed and orchestrated, little understood philosophical plan. In the main, these hierarchies have little correspondence with local realities. This ethnographic shadowboxing continues to make open transcultural scientific, even humanistic, discourse difficult and truly cumulative progress impossible. . . .

The second stage in the process by which African cultural realities are often mistransformed through mistranslation by ethnographers is associated with the urgent demand for "theories" to assist the ethnographer in organizing his field data and in presenting the conclusions derived from the data. As Fortes indicates with regard to his African data:

It is not merely a question of putting his [the ethnographer's] observations on record. Writing an anthropological monograph is itself an instrument of research and perhaps the most significant instrument of research in the anthropologist's armory. It involves breaking up the vivid kaleidoscopic reality of

---

[6] In a recent monumental work on the 18th and 19th-century Asante political system, Wilks (1975) chooses to describe and interpret the Asante historical experience in terms of culturally alien European terminology and modern concepts, such as the overall continuity of the "bureaucratic process," the "executive arm" of the "central administration" in Kumasi, and the "middle class" engaged in ideological debate over the relative merits of "free trade" vs. "state capitalism." Wilks presents the Asante political system of the period as if it were almost the exact copy of the latter-day British colonial administrative structure with its district and provincial commissioners.

The most disturbing thing about all this is that Wilks defends the application of "concepts developed in geographically and temporally different contexts" by insisting that "only thus can the Asante past be viewed within the wider perspectives of human endeavour and its place within comparative history ultimately be assured" (1975:xiv). Thus, in the interest of cross-cultural comparison, Western scholars adopt readily an approach to African societies and cultures that inevitably produces hasty and superficial cross-cultural generalizations. This type of cognitive and linguistic imperialism is very common indeed in Western "scientific" studies of non-Western peoples.

human action, thought, and emotion which lives in the anthropologist's notebooks and memory, and creating out of the pieces a coherent representation of a society, in terms of the general principles of organization and motivation that regulate it. It is a task that cannot be done without the help of theory [1945:vii].

Alas, the "theory" or "theories" generally turn out, on closer inspection, naturally to be well established, fairly orthodox Western views of society and culture, their origins and development, based on European academic and popular philosophical thought and experience, which are then applied to the whole of humanity. The power of Western science and technology and the related ability of the West to establish and maintain its political and economic domination and intellectual leadership particularly of the non-Western world have successfully turned dominant Eurocentric theories of history, culture, and society into "cosmos-centric" systems, i.e., universal systems of thought and belief (despite the popularity of the current distinctions between the so-called emic-etic approaches to ethnographic fieldwork).

The negative intellectual effects of various aspects of this type of deep-rooted Western "prejudice" or "psychocultural bondage" on anthropological studies, for example of witchcraft and caste, have been effectively argued by Hsu (1973:6–9). As Hsu points out, the major weakness in American anthropology "is found in its general theories on the determinants of human social and cultural behavior. This major weakness is in my [his] view directly attributable to the failure of white American anthropologists to consider views other than those to which their cultural conditioning has led them" (1973:9). Hsu concludes rightly that truly universally applicable theories of man can hardly emerge unless Western anthropologists break out of their near obscurantist "mental bondage" (1973:16) and recognize and accept the significance and validity of competing non-Western assumptions and theories and contrary viewpoints about man and culture not in conformity with conventional Western orthodoxy.[7]

The rather distressing difficulty for the native ethnographer brought up in the European intellectual traditions is clearly how to overcome his own Eurocentric biases; penetrate the granitic Eurocentric structural crust; and get to the deeper, graphitic, turbulent substantive layers of African cultures and societies.[8]

Third, the process of cultural mistranslation in African ethnography reaches its apogee when "authoritative" ethnographic or ethno-

[7]   Rohner has also recently pointed to one source of serious error in Western ethnographic research namely, "the bias of romanticism" (1975:203–204), expressive of a kind of "moral commitment" of anthropologists to see "their people" in a positive light, to patronize the people they study. Rohner explains the problem in terms of ethnographers' uncompromising belief in cultural relativity and the functionalist interpretation of ethnographic data. Gellner (1971:18–19) in evaluating primarily Evans-Pritchard's interpretation of Nuer religion, has equally criticized British anthropologists for being "charitable," that is for employing in the interpretation of non-Western belief systems a "hermeneutic principle" that ensures "*in advance* of inquiry that nothing may count as pre-logical, inconsistent, or categorically absurd though it may be" (1971:36; emphasis added). Gellner locates the source of this peculiar ethnographer bias both in extreme functionalism and in the problems of translation – the striving to find equivalents in English or other European languages for native statements or concepts ill-understood by the anthropologist who is not fluent in the native language, but making it a "condition of good translation that it conveys the coherence which he assumes is there" to be found in the thoughts of non-Western peoples (1971:26). My point here is not to argue whether or not non-Western thought is pre-logical, logical, or postlogical, an issue which is itself a reflection of Western philosophical prejudices, but to stress the distortions in ethnography caused by the lack of language familiarity.

[8]   Those of us natives who saw, even as undergraduate students in British universities, the dangerous limitations of tradition-bound *tribal* research in Africa and its distorting epistemological presuppositions and sterile, self-opinionated theories, and who later as *anthropologists* have attempted to transcend these limitations by venturing into the broader,

logical hypotheses and hunches are treated uncritically as accepted or established facts of native life, i.e., when, as Wagley puts it, "classificatory types, formulated in the first place for their heuristic value . . . [are] translated into developmental stages, conceived as having real existence and arranged in a hierarchy which is both chronological and qualitative" (1971:121).

Thus Sahlins, ignoring Evans-Pritchard's own caution regarding the tentative nature of the Nuer data, attempts a reanalysis of the Nuer material from an evolutionary perspective. On the basis of precategory assumptions and taking the historical validity of the Tiv–Nuer data for granted, Sahlins argues rather speciously that the Tiv–Nuer segmentary lineage organization "is a specific adaptive variety within the tribal [pre*chiefdom*, post-*band*] level of society and culture" (1967:89). He believes, in a historicist vein, that without Anglo-Egyptian intervention, the Nuer would have in time overthrown the segmentary lineage system and "catapulted themselves to the chiefdom level of evolutionary progress" (1967:119). Sahlins further contends without any precise specification that his reformulation of the Nuer social structure "leads to certain empirically testable conclusions about its genesis and incidence" (1967:90). . . .

The Problem of "Paraliterate Feedback"

In a brief, critical, and provocative survey of social anthropology in Nigeria during the colonial period, Jones (1974:280–289), colonial administrator turned professional anthropologist, comes to some hard, unflattering conclusions that may be of general application. Singling out for rare praise S. F. Nadel's work

on the Nupe, Rupert East's translation of *Akiga's Story* on the Tiv, and the essays by Forde on the Yako – one might perhaps add a few others of comparable value and usefulness to his list, e.g., Bradbury's work on the Benin – Jones is nevertheless convinced that by and large the contributions to the general field of anthropological studies, made in the course of rather hectic anthropological activity in Nigeria from the 1850s to the 1950s, have been disappointing.

> Many monographs, reports, and papers have been published by anthropologists, some of them professional, most of them amateur, most of the earlier ones self-taught, most of the later having taken some university courses on the subject. Much of their descriptive ethnography is pretty poor, and their monographs on particular people vary; those written under the influence of anthropological hypotheses in vogue at the time they were written are worse than the others (1974:286).

One may disagree with Jones on points of detail, but his basic conclusions are, I believe, valid. The generally poor quality of early African ethnography was partially due to dominant Eurocentric prejudices, distortions, and errors of fact associated with the exciting but hopeless search for the *real,* raw, exotic native based on a highly discredited conjectural history and the application of current anthropological theories. It is clear from Jones' discussion that the quality of descriptive ethnographies was adversely affected as much by the serious linguistic problems of the anthropologists as by the uncritical use of primary ethnographic data collected by the colonial governments for their own purposes. Jones notes that "the Nigerian Colonial records provide a mass of material not only for

---

historically more relevant, context of colonialism and political economy of development in Africa, are labeled, at best, *sociologists* and *political scientists*, branches of social science not much disconcerted by real issues. At worst, we are polemists, propagandists, and anything but anthropologists and scholars. (See Robertson 1975 for a frank assessment of an aspect of this problem.)

historians but also for social anthropologists as soon as they become interested in diachronic studies and social change" (1974:287). But unfortunately, Jones points out that "official government report seems to exercise a mesmerizing effect, not only on many colonial historians, but also on some anthropologists who lose sight of the point that, although its manifest function is to present the facts, its latent function is usually to cover up" (1974:287). Robertson (1975) makes a similar point with regard to colonial archives in Ghana.

However, in connection with the role of the native interpreter-informant in ethnographic fieldwork, we may observe with Jones that undoubtedly the most *alarming* consequences of colonialism and the initiation and continued control of anthropological activity in Africa by Europeans has been the effect that anthropology (and European writings on Africa generally) has had upon the *Africans* themselves.[9] It is crucial to remember in this connection that one of the subtler and more effective weapons of imperial supremacy was the European language. Subject peoples were obliged to adopt and use it if they wished to succeed in the colonial world. In time, the colonized African was made to believe that anything written in a European language was sacrosanct, infallible, and beyond question. Few natives, however, mastered the foreign language perfectly. As a result, the European (and any native who could master the European language) enjoyed unparalleled psychological (and social) advantages. There are numerous humorous examples throughout Africa of natives painfully and tragically pretending to speak and/or understand English or French in a rather hopeless effort to improve their standing in the eyes of the European. But indigenous African languages

survived and even flourished. Jones correctly identifies one of the primary sources of the confusion in the translation of cultures when he notes that

> To the average Ibo villager an anthropologist is someone who knows more about Ibo traditional culture than he does himself. Any monograph written by an anthropologist on a particular tribe and accessible to its *literate* members becomes the tribal Bible, the charter of its traditional history and culture . . .
>
> The oral tradition of many of these . . . communities has completely absorbed, and been corrupted by, the myths of the anthropologist. The Wheel has come full circle and, to paraphrase C. L. Temple's remark, "a knowledge of the beliefs and practices of the European anthropologist is now of first importance to the native" [1974:287].

Similarly, on the "authoritative" writings on the Tiv by the Bohannans, Dorward (1974) makes the following assessment.

> They too were armed with conceptual models, the most influential being that of the *segmentary lineage system* which they refined and gave substance. Like their predecessors, they too were to *create an image* of the Tiv, far more influential for being scientific. Theirs was the *"reality"* through which academics and outsiders have since come to perceive the Tiv; one might say the Nuer and the Tiv have segmentary lineage systems, thus segmentary lineage systems *exist because* we have the Tiv and the Nuer (1974:474–475; emphasis added).

Dorward also notes that "with the spread of literacy among the Tiv, the influence of the written work, and the availability of latter-day publications on the Tiv (by Europeans), the

[9]   Commenting recently on local T.V. on the Second World Black and African Festival of Arts and Culture (FESTAC) in Nigeria, Dr. Mahdi Adamu, Director of the Centre for Nigerian Culture Studies of Ahmadu Bello University, went as far as saying that the festival could not help project the true concept of African culture, for FESTAC was "an elitist phenomenon based on Western cultural values . . ." (see *FESTAC Notebook.* In *West Africa.* 13 December 1976:1,923).

extent of 'feedback' has been considerable" (1974:475; see also the warnings of Owusu [1975] and Vansina [1974] against "paraliterate feedback").

Native Scholars and Ethnography

In his *American Kinship: A Cultural Account* (1968), David Schneider presents clearly and cogently the scientific and practical arguments in favor of the central role of the native scholar in ethnographic fieldwork. His remarks merit full quotation:

> There is another reason why the study of kinship in America is especially important to Americans and that is that as Americans, this is a society and a culture which we know well. We *speak* the language *fluently*, we know the customs, and we have observed the natives in their daily lives. Indeed, we *are* [emphasis in original] the natives. Hence we are in an especially good position to keep the facts and the theory in their most *productive* relationships. *We can monitor the interplay between fact and theory where American kinship is concerned in ways that are simply impossible in the ordinary course of anthropological work.* When we read about kinship in some society *foreign* to our own we have only the facts which the author chooses to present to us, and we usually have no independent source of knowledge against which we can check his facts. It is thus very hard to evaluate his theory for ordering those facts.
>
> By the same token of course *we are able to achieve a degree of control over a large body of data which many anthropological fieldworkers hardly approach, even after one or two years in the field. Hence the quality of the data we control is considerably greater, and the grounds for evaluating the fit between fact and theory is correspondingly greater* [vi; emphasis added].

The point that needs special emphasis is that African scholars who have given serious thought to the quality of the huge masses of data on African societies and cultures written mainly by foreign anthropologists and other experts have independently long come to similar conclusions, though not all have always succeeded in articulating the theoretical and substantive issues involved as clearly and effectively as has Schneider (see for instance, Owusu 1970, 1975; Kenyatta 1962).

Fortes, Evans-Pritchard and Company and Data Quality Control

In the light of the foregoing epistemological and methodological problems raised by the comments of Schneider and others concerning ethnographer bias, let us return to the epistemological basis of the theoretical and empirical contributions to African ethnography of two most distinguished and influential founding fathers, Evans-Pritchard and Fortes.

The particular focus on the two classic ethnographies perhaps requires some further explanation: both works clearly exemplify the built-in epistemological dilemmas generally characteristic of structural-functional anthropology; they illustrate graphically the serious confusion of time levels, time scale, and perspectives associated with the ethnographer's standard use of the "ethnographic present" and the resultant structural and empirical distortions and oversimplifications of the cultural-historical processes usually found in ethnographic accounts of African societies. Thus, it is difficult, for example, to reconcile Evans-Pritchard's description of the Nuer as "an acephalous kinship state" lacking generally organized political life and legal institutions, and as a society that had, until 1928, generally remained intact (1940:271), with his very brief discussion that from about 1821, the Nuer continued to resist the Arab, British, and Egyptian intervention and invasions; that in 1920, despite large-scale military operations, including bombing and machine gunning of Nuer camps causing much loss of life and destruction of property, the Nuer remained unsubdued (1940: 132–135); and that the 1928–30 prolonged military operations conducted against Nuerland truly marked the end of serious fighting between the Nuer and the Anglo-Egyptian government. A more systematic and empirically valid description of Nuer society and polity (a) before 1821, (b) after 1821 and before 1930, and (c) after 1930 under the new administration of Anglo-Egyptian Sudan is urgently needed. John Tosh, writing recently about the Nilotic Langi of Uganda described by anthropologists along with the Nuer, etc., as "segmentary," "stateless," "amorphous," or "acephalous" societies, notes after analysis of oral traditions and documentary evidence that Lango society was far from static during the precolonial period. A comparison between 1870 and 1900, for example, "would reveal that significant structural change had occurred in that time" (1973:475). In fact, Evans-Pritchard (1949), working under more favorable research conditions, describes a similar process of structural transformation for the Bedouin society of Cyrenaica, between 1837 and 1902.

Again, *The Nuer* and Fortes' *Dynamics of Clanship among the Tallensi* (1945) show clearly the inherent essential anachronism of the ethnographic enterprise – ethnographic techniques, research orientations, "theories," terms of reference, and descriptions in the colonial age. As Margery Perham candidly notes, "while with one hand [colonial] government was trying to *preserve and control* tribal society with the other it was opening Africa to economic and other forces which were bound to undermine it" (1962:68–69). In some instances African societies had long been undermined by these forces. It was the rather thankless job of Malinowski and his students to recover rapidly the real nature and characteristics of precolonial "traditional" African societies, a task that forced structural-functional anthropologists to break their own self-imposed taboo against speculative history.

In fact, by the end of colonial rule, all indigenous African polities, including the Nuer and the Tallensi, had become for a considerable period of time constituent units of European centralized administrative bureaucracies. The inevitable result of this ethnographic anachronism is that ethnographies ended up being, by and large, neither reliable, thoroughgoing cultural histories or ethnohistories, nor valid, critical, empirical sociology.

Ethnographies neither made serious, systematic, and critical use of the available relevant documents or of oral traditions – in the latter case, no doubt, mainly because of language problems – nor did they consider sociological "theories" of modern imperialism and capitalism applicable, despite a Eurocentric approach, to the conditions of colonized natives.

Both monographs also reveal the urgent necessity for reanalyzing the data, especially on the much misunderstood, so-called "acephalous" societies within a comprehensive historical and sociological framework. For some of these societies may have been, as the Tallensi and Kokomba cases show, constituent units of precolonial chiefdoms or kingdoms, and a critical reexamination of the factors or circumstances that may have led to their subsequent structural dispersal, dissolution, and decay, or to structural destabilization and decentralization, would be interesting and informative. After all, centralized kingdoms in Africa could often tolerate varying degrees of subordinate structural autonomy and wide latitudes of policymaking independence on the part of component units without losing their identity as "states." In the final analysis, however, one could of course, speculate on what might have been the course of social and political development in Africa if there had never been a colonial era.

Finally, since the so-called acephalous, segmentary, or band societies are frequently cited by Western ethnographers as archetypical examples of "simple," "archaic," neolithic, or "savage" forms of societies, a focus on the Nuer and the Tallensi is meant to force us to reevaluate our simple-minded, ahistorical, if social Darwinist, approach to African societies and cultures.

In a revealing, perhaps forgotten, foreword to his *Dynamics of Clanship among the Tallensi*, Fortes reiterates the nature of the basic difficulties of *European* anthropologists studying African cultures, particularly in the colonial era. But instead of discussing systematically the implications for cross-cultural research of the complex intellectual and substantive issues raised by the usual fieldwork problems of the typical "outsider" ethnographers, e.g., lack of language familiarity, Fortes sidesteps the issues involved by cleverly elevating the difficulties into cardinal and universal principles of value-free scientific anthropology. He accordingly states:

> It is true that he [the anthropologist] can never feel himself completely at one with the people he is studying, however gifted he may be, *linguistically* or *psychologically*. He may make some real friends among his hosts; but he can never adopt their cultural values. If he did, he would lose that *detachment without which anything he wrote would be of no scientific value*[!][10] [1945:vii; emphasis added].

It is worth noting that the thoroughly Akanized *Okomfo* Rattray, whose rich and detailed ethnographic accounts of the Asante (Ashanti) people provided a solid empirical foundation for Fortes' own much later stimulating writings on the Asante, had better thoughts. He notes concerning ethnographic data collection.

> If these "ancients" [the older Asante men and women who can provide valuable ethnographic information] are asked to converse

through the medium of an interpreter, who often does not know English at all well and is generally quite incapable of rendering into English many of the words used in the vernacular, they usually become reticent and suspicious, or at any rate uninterested, and likely to withhold their stores of knowledge. If, however, they are able to talk freely and without the aid of an interpreter to one who has their confidence, *who they know can sympathize with them and understand not only their language, but their modes of thought and pride of race, then and then only are they likely to pour out their store of ancient lore and to lay bare their thoughts* [1969:7; emphasis added].

Yet Fortes seems to accept Rattray's position, shared by most ethnographers, that the good ethnographer thoroughly masters the native language so that he or she does not need to use an interpreter or a contact language, when he points out that in the course of two and one half years (1934–37) of fieldwork

> as there is no linguistic literature for the Tallensi, we had to learn the dialect from scratch, with the assistance of a semi-literate interpreter and the scanty literature on Mole and Dagbane. . . . By the end of our first *tour* we became proficient enough to dispense with an interpreter. Nevertheless, I know only too well that we reached but a *moderate standard in our vocabulary and in our appreciation of the finer shades of thought and feeling that can be expressed in Talni* [1945:xli; emphasis added].

Apart from linguistic problems, Fortes mentions other "extraneous difficulties," namely economic and political, which affected the quality of his data, for example "the war, bringing with it issues of far greater moment than the study of the social structure of *a remote and unimportant African people*[!]" (1945:viii; emphasis added).

---

[10] If one were to take Fortes' comments seriously, one would have to reject as scientifically useless what Western social scientists write about their own societies. Schneider's *American Kinship* for example, would have to be scientifically worthless!

Concerning the central analytical concepts of "segmentation" and "social equilibrium" as applied to the Tallensi (which go back to Durkheim and Evans-Pritchard), Fortes cautions that "their virtue lies not in their *explanatory* but in their *exploratory* value" (1945:xi; emphasis added).[11]

Evans-Pritchard and The Nuer

Similar self-critical observations and caveats, often not heeded by others, are found in the introductory remarks of Evans-Pritchard's classic, *The Nuer* (1940). We cannot afford to pooh-pooh authors' cautions. For, as Evans-Pritchard himself attests and anyone who has carefully read him knows, his account of the political development of the Islamic Order of the Sanusiya among the Bedouin tribes of Cyrenaica is definitely far superior to his discussion of the political and social institutions of the Nuer. The existence of extensive literature in Arabic on Cyrenaica, three years' residence in Egypt, travels in other Arab lands, some knowledge of Arab history and culture, experience of Bedouin, and, most crucial of all, proficiency in spoken Arabic, clearly account in large part for the relatively high substantive and analytic quality of the book (1949), which is explicitly cast in a genuine historical mold. Evans-Pritchard began his research among the Nuer of the Sudan in 1930 under very difficult circumstances, since the Nuer had only recently been subjected to harsh military suppression of a series of revolts against British colonial authority and since the area was physically difficult to reach. As Evans-Pritchard notes, "my total residence among the Nuer was . . . about a year. I do not consider a year adequate time in which to make a sociological study of a people in adverse circumstances, but serious sickness on both the 1935 and 1936 expeditions closed

investigations prematurely" (1940:14). He goes on, "Besides physical discomfort at all times, suspicion and obstinate resistance encountered in the early stages of research, *absence of interpreter, lack of adequate grammar and dictionary, and failure to procure the usual informants*, there developed a further difficulty as the inquiry proceeded" (1940:14; emphasis added). All the same, Evans-Pritchard could conclude on an intriguing note that ultimately he knew more about the Nuer than about the Azande, "about whom I am able to write a much more detailed account" (1940:15). To add to our epistemological confusion, Evans-Pritchard presents the Nuer monograph as "a contribution to the *ethnology* of a particular area rather than as a detailed *sociological* study" (1940:15; emphasis added), remembering that ethnology in Britain, as Malinowski indicates, refers to speculative and comparative theories, as opposed to the "empirical and descriptive results of the science of man" (1961:9fn).

The practical and linguistic problems did not, however, prevent Evans-Pritchard from making a two-and-a-half-month survey of the political institutions of the Anuak of the Southern Sudan in 1935 and a six-week research survey of the Nilotic Luo of Kenya in 1936, in addition to brief tours of other African peoples of the area. It is interesting that in 1936 he had hoped to study the Masai but was discouraged by the Kenya Government on the grounds that the Masai had recently tried to kill their District Commissioner (see Beidelman 1974:2–3).

The point of all these textual excursions is to demonstrate the crucial epistemological role of language understanding and the political environment – e.g., the colonial situation – in determining ethnographic research priorities and in shaping the qualitative content of research results. It is also meant to show the all-too-obvious fact that it takes a great deal of

---

[11]   These are the people who were described by British colonial administrators as the "martial races" and since 1900 had been some of the empire's dutiful forced laborers and colonial soldiers in both World War I and World War II.

time, energy, and scholarship to penetrate the hermeneutic meaning of African cosmogony and cosmology as well as years of continued interest in a single culture. Discussing the critical problems of anthropological research in Kenya Colony, I. Schapera (who has himself successfully demonstrated in his own studies of South African populations the crucial significance of many years of continuous fieldwork through native languages and has made noteworthy contributions to South African ethnography) observes that "ideally a thorough study of each of those peoples should extend over a period of roughly five to seven years" (1949:18). The fact of the matter is that time has never been on the side of most foreign anthropologists. . . .

The New Ethnography of Africa

If the vaunted aim of the ethnography of Africa is to provide, on the basis of systematic fieldwork done through native languages or native interpreter-informants, careful descriptions and explanations that can be substantiated, interpretations that have insight, generalizations that can be factually supported, and findings that can provide a clear basis for governmental policy in Africa, the record of the results of conscientious European ethnographic explorations and discoveries has been, by and large, truly disappointing. The evidence for their claims is in most cases often unclear, imprecise, or simply lacking.

Throughout this discussion I have pinpointed some of the principal sources of the ethnographic confusion and errors: Eurocentric and social Darwinist conceptions of African societies; colonial policy constraints on ethnographic research; the inherent anachronism of ethnographic data collection; the reliance on a few key, often misguided, native interpreter-informants (see for example, Chilungu's timely discussion [1976]); the "paraliterate" feedback problem; and, above

all, the ignorance of European ethnographers of native languages, even as they shouldered the heavy burden of revealing and translating African realities to the Western and Westernized world.

By this observation, we are hardly saying that there can be no validity whatsoever to the Africa of ethnographers, who by their elaborate pioneering intellectual efforts put "traditional" Africa on the map, gave Africa a new "tribal" identity, and African studies enduring, if dubious, European and, hence, world recognition.

Of course, to a growing number of well-informed African writers and critics, anthropology as a study of "primitive" peoples by "civilized" Westerners is or ought to be dead. The reasoning is quite simple: African societies and cultures on balance are no less or more "primitive" than any others. In any case, the "primitive world" as a subject of serious scholarship is spent in two related senses: (1) classical ethnographic techniques and methodology have in their Eurocentric way said all they could possibly say and (2) colonialism or modernization has transformed "the primitive world" itself out of existence. The "tribal" microcosm, if it ever existed, has vanished.

Nevertheless, the monographs and essays on Africa by such eminent and distinguished scholars as Malinowski, Evans-Pritchard, Fortes, Mair, Gluckman, Forde, Kabbery, Turner, Schapera, and the Wilsons among others, some of whom I am proud to say have been my close and respected teachers and good friends, will in the manner of our capricious ancestral spirits, for many, many years to come, continue to daunt and overwhelm us and to provide a tremendous and intriguing fascination and challenge for indigenous African scholars (a number of whom may, from a respectable distance, still take for granted the "factual" correctness of the ethnographic data). Indeed, some African historians and sociologists of precolonial Africa who have yet to find themselves, faced with overwhelming problems of research using oral traditions, are often compelled to take the line of least resistance by falling back, often too uncritically, on the only published data available – the ethnographic data, which, with all their notorious factual errors and other imperfections, are considered useful, if shaky, props in a *terra incognita*.

Yet these African scholars are sharply aware of the unavoidable historical fact that we could not and *should not* expect European and other foreign scholars, given their very different backgrounds, language problems, cognitive orientations, and intellectual and other interests, to continue to be, as was inevitably the case in the colonial era, our trusted or unquestioned guardians of Africa's collective memory.

Ethnographers have bequeathed to Africa a formidable literary colonial legacy. For all such apparently beneficial European legacies, Africa has had to pay a high cultural and cognitive price. Through their inherent distortions, the classic ethnographies will continue to provide an unfailing, sometimes the only, stimulus for African scholars to newer, bolder, better, more realistic, and more reliable ethnographic and historical research in Africa. Herein lies their lasting usefulness.

While paying lip service to the ideal of objectivity and the pursuit of truth, Western ethnographers have often demanded, unbelievably, in the past that critics must judge their famous classics not by their self-imposed and proclaimed canons of science and scholarship but by appeals to *argumentum ad hominen*. Thus Evans-Pritchard is able to say with reference to his Nuer research and data, that "A man must judge his labours by the obstacles he has overcome and the hardships he has endured and by these standards I am not ashamed of the results" (1940:9). We can indeed appreciate the practical difficulties of Western ethnographers in foreign lands and still hold them responsible for the erroneous or misleading results of their intellectual efforts.

The principal lesson to be learned from all this is that the validity and intrinsic merit of Western ethnographic "theories," research data, accounts, and interpretations of African societies and cultures, however brilliant, prolific, imaginative, and suggestive, cannot be taken for granted and incorporated uncritically into the comparative generalizations on other cultures in the future if social science is to progress. The persuasive character of ethnographic findings, which still dominate the non-Western field of scholarship – itself a function of the world power structure – is based less on their factual correctness than on the well known fact that they are mostly consistent with or have successfully molded or manipulated over the years – because of their "scientific" claims and the prestige of their authors – Western (or even thoroughly Westernized African) public opinion. They cannot, therefore, be substitutes for the well informed, critical, and original insights and real understanding based on native research and scholarship.

The simple commonsense truth is that no person, not even a de Toqueville studying African cultures, can understand another whose language he does not speak, read, and understand, and, hence, whose world view he cannot truly share. The position is already very well understood by some Western scholars. As Kenneth Hale, writing recently on the role of native knowledge in anthropological linguistics (Hymes 1972:382–297) observes, "the linguist depends upon native speakers of the language he studies. It is a prevailing fact about anthropological linguistics . . . that the linguist and the native speaker are not the same individual" (1972:384). He continues, "I question whether significant advances beyond the present state of knowledge of the world's languages can be made if important sectors of linguistics continue to be *dominated* by scholars who are not native speakers of the languages they study" (1972:385–386; emphasis added). Of course, Hale is aware that "it would be incorrect to assert that a linguist is absolutely incapable of making important observations about . . . language not his own or that such observations are of limited scientific interest. . . . Nevertheless . . . even where insights of great importance have been contributed by non-native speakers to the study of English, for example, it is possible to argue that the insights are based on intuitions which, in all essential respects closely approximate those of a native speaker" (1972–386). Hale's arguments apply with equal force to foreign ethnographic research in Africa.

To drive home the obvious point, one may very well ask how many Euro-Americans know our language beyond the usual literal dictionary translations that inevitably make a caricature of native terms and idioms and confuse local meanings and expressions? I have not met one yet, certainly not among our esteemed ethnographic "experts" and critics. And what is even more disturbing about their general attitude is that they continue to produce "authoritative" monographs and essays on African cultures without seriously worrying about the degrading effects of their language deficiencies on the quality of the data. Publishing editors often cannot ensure or do not care whether the native terms are even spelled correctly.

This type of unethical intellectual arrogance, cocksureness, or nonchalance characteristic of Western social scientists studying African societies and cultures – their insulting insistence that one could still be an African "expert" without the need to master any indigenous language – has recently led one anthropologist reveiwing Godfrey Muriuki's history of the Kikuyu, 1500–1900, to remark rather frivolously that the book, otherwise an excellent one, is "*marred* by an extraordinary profusion of place names . . . countless native terms which are not always explained. This makes the early chapters particularly hard going" (Dahlberg 1975:84; emphasis added). Although June Nash does not mention the problem of language, I would suggest that this

is at the root of the so-called crisis in contemporary fieldwork so well adumbrated and sensitively discussed by her (1975). This crisis will be perpetuated as long as we keep sending into the field graduate students with little or no linguistic training.

What emerges logically out of all this is simply that an authentic, reliable ethnography of Africa (the new sociology of Africa), which will provide material for the comparative study of other cultures, will have to satisfy at least three specific requirements. The first requirement is the mastery of the relevant African languages by Western ethnographers and other foreign social scientists doing research in Africa. Because of the relatively large size of research funding available to them and the Western world's powers of mass persuasion, these scholars and their views dominate African studies. It seems very unlikely that this particular condition will be met in the foreseeable future. Yet the very quality of ethnographic data from informants is greatly improved when the researcher speaks the relevant native language.

The second requirement is the readiness and commitment of native scholars – the Chilungus, the Uchendus, the Onoges, the Otites, the Magubanes, etc. – already aware of the dangers of uncritical adoption and application of Western social and culture theory to African conditions to do the necessary and basic research, which requires hard work and systematic effort, to take control of our literary and intellectual criticism. This condition is most likely to be satisfied but not in the short run.

The third requirement is a new frank and informed critical intellectual dialogue between the foreign Africanists and native Africanists, the former realizing that they can no longer hope for the role of unchallenged interpreters and translators of African cultures that they not too long ago took so much for granted.

African scholars today are seriously committed to emulate, as Chinua Achebe puts it, "those men of Benin, ready to guide the curious visitor to the gallery of their art, willing to listen with politeness even to his hasty opinions, but careful, most careful, to concede nothing to him that might appear to undermine their own position within their heritage or compromise the integrity of their indigenous perception" (1975:28).

References

Achebe, Chinua
  1975   *Morning Yet on Creation Day: Essays.* Garden City: Anchor Press, Doubleday.
Beidelman, Thomas O.
  1974   *A Bibliography of the Writings of E. E. Evans-Pritchard.* London: Tavistock.
Chilungu, Simeon W.
  1976   Issues in the Ethics of Research Method: An Interpretation of the Anglo-American Perspective. *Current Anthropology* 17(3): 457–481.
Dahlberg, Frances
  1975   Kiyuku [sic] History. Review of A History of the Kikuyu 1500–1900. By G. Muriuku. *Africa Today* 22(3):83–84.
Dorward, D. C.
  1974   Ethnography and Administration: A Study of Anglo-Tiv "Working Misunderstanding." *The Journal of African History* 15(3):457–477.
Dunn, John, and A. F. Robertson
  1974   *Dependence and Opportunity: Political Change in Ahafo.* African Studies Series, 9. Cambridge: Cambridge University Press.
Evans-Pritchard, Edward E.
  1940   *The Nuer. A Description of the Modes of Livelihood and Political Institutions of a Nilotic People.* Oxford: Clarendon Press.
  1949   *The Sanusi of Cyrenaica.* Oxford: Clarendon Press.
Fortes, Meyer
  1945   *The Dynamics of Clanship among the Tallensi.* London: Oxford University Press.
Foster, George M.
  1969   *Applied Anthropology.* Boston: Little, Brown.
Hsu, Francis L. K.
  1973   Prejudice and Its Intellectual Effect in American Anthropology: An Ethnographic Report. *American Anthropologist* 75(1):1–19

Jones, G. I.
  1974   Social Anthropology in Nigeria during the Colonial Period. *Africa* 44(3):280–289.
Kenyatta, Jomo
  1962   *Facing Mount Kenya.* New York: Vintage.
Lowie, Robert E.
  1940   Native Languages as Ethnographic Tools. *American Anthropologist* 42:81–89.
Mair, Lucy
  1975   Anthropology and Colonial Policy. *African Affairs* 74(295):191–195.
Malinowski, Bronislaw
  1961   *Argonauts of the Western Pacific.* New York: Dutton. (First ed., Routledge and Kegan Paul, 1922).
Mead, Margaret
  1939   Native Languages as Fieldwork Tools. *American Anthropologist* 42:(2)189–205.
Naroll, Raoul
  1962   *Data Quality Control – A New Research Technique. Prolegomena to a Cross-Cultural Study of Culture Stress.* New York: Free Press.
  1970a Data Quality Control in Cross-Cultural Surveys. In *A Handbook of Method in Cultural Anthropology.* Raoul Naroll and Ronald Cohen, eds. Pp. 927–945. New York: Natural History Press.
  1970b What Have We Learned from Cross-Cultural Surveys? *American Anthropologist* 72(6):1227–1288.
Nash, June C.
  1975   Nationalism and Fieldwork. In *Annual Review of Anthropology*, Vol. 4. Bernard J. Siegel, ed. Pp. 225–245.
Onwubu, Chukwuemeka
  1975   Igbo Society: Three Views Analyzed. *Africa Today* 22(3):71–77.
Owusu, Maxwell
  1970   *Uses and Abuses and Political Power. A*

Case Study of Continuity and Change in the Politics of Ghana. Chicago: University of Chicago Press.

1975 Anthropology and Afro-American Studies: Scholarship or Ideology? *Michigan Discussions in Anthropology* 1(1):71–95.

Perham, Margery
1962 *The Colonial Reckoning.* New York: Knopf.

Rattray, Robert S.
1969 *Ashanti.* New York: Negro Universities Press. (First ed., Oxford University Press, 1923.)

Robertson, A.F.
1975 Anthropology and Government in Ghana. *African Affairs* 74(294):51–59.

Rohner, Ronald P.
1975 *They Love Me, They Love Me Not. A Worldwide Study of the Effects of Parental Acceptance and Rejection.* New Haven: HRAF Press.

Rohner, Ronald P., Billie R. DeWalt, and Robert C. Ness
1973 Ethnographer Bias in Cross-Cultural Research: An Empirical Study. *Behaviour Science Notes* 8:275–317.

Sahlins, Marshall D.
1967 The Segmentary Lineage: An Organization of Predatory Expansion. In *Comparative Political Systems.* Ronald Cohen and John Middleton, eds. Pp. 89–119. Garden City: Natural History Press.

Schapera, Isaac
1949 Some Problems of Anthropological Research in Kenya Colony. *International African Institute Memorandum* XXIII. London: Oxford University Press.

Schneider, David M.
1968 *American Kinship: A Cultural Account.* Englewood Cliffs: Prentice-Hall.

Tosh, John
1973 *Colonial Chiefs in a Stateless Society: A Case Study from Northern Uganda.* The Journal of African History 14(3):473–490.

Vansina, Jan
1974 Traditions of Genesis. Comment. *The Journal of African History* 15(2):317–322.

Wagley, Christopher
1971 Historicism in Africa. *African Affairs* 70(279):113–124.

Wilks, Ivor
1975 *Asante in the Nineteenth Century: The Structure and Evolution of a Political Order.* Cambridge: Cambridge University Press.

Wilson, Monica
1951 *Good Company: A Study of Nyakyusa Age Villages.* International African Institute. London: Oxford University Press.

43

The Meaning of Our Work

Cheikh Anta Diop

I began my research in September 1946; because of our colonial situation at that time, the political problem dominated all others. In 1949 the RDA[1] was undergoing a crisis. I felt that Africa should mobilize all its energy to help the movement turn the tide of repression: thus I was elected Secretary General of the RDA students in Paris and served from 1950 to 1953. On July 4–8, 1951 we held in Paris the first postwar Pan African Student Union (from London) well represented by more than 30 delegates, including the daughter of the Oni of Ife, the late Miss Aderemi Tedju. In February 1953 the first issue of the *Voie de l'Afrique Noire* appeared; this was the organ of the RDA students. In it I published an article entitled "Towards a Political Ideology in Black Africa."

That article contained a résumé of *Nations nègres*, the manuscript of which was already completed. All our ideas on African history, the past and future of our languages, their utilization in the most advanced scientific fields as in education generally, our concepts on the creation of a future federal state, continental or subcontinental, our thoughts on African social structures, on strategy and tactics in the struggle for national independence, and so forth, all those ideas were clearly expressed in that article. As would subsequently be seen, with respect to the problem of the continent's political independence, the French-speaking African politicians took their own good time before admitting that this was the right political road to follow. Nevertheless, the RDA students organized themselves into a federation within France and politicized African student circles by popularizing the slogan of national independence for Africa from the Sahara to the Cape and from the Indian Ocean to the Atlantic, as our periodical attests. The archives of the FEANF (Federation of African Students in France) indicate that it did not begin to adopt anticolonialist positions until it was directed by RDA students.[2] We stressed the cultural and polit-

[1] Rassemblement Démocratique Africain (Democratic African Rally), The RDA founded in 1946, "was the first interterritorial movement in French West Africa, created before parties in territories other than Senegal or Ivory Coast had taken root." Ruth S. Morgenthau, *Political Parties on French-speaking West Africa*. Oxford: Clarendon Press, 1964, p. 302.
[2] Starting especially with the administration of Franklin, secretary general of the RDA students at Montpellier. Cf. the article by Penda Marcelle Ouegnin: "Un compte-rendu du Congrès de la FEANF organisé par les ERDA aux Sociétés savantes le 8 avril 1953," in the same bulletin cited above, May–June 1953.

Similarly, with a few exceptions, the PAI (African Independence Party) was organized by former RDA students who had returned to Africa. Various branches in France rallied to the new party which thus carried forward the RDA line and popularized the slogan of national independance that we had launched.

ical content that we included in the concept of independence in order to get the latter adopted in French-speaking Africa: already forgotten is the bitter struggle that had to be waged to impose it on student circles in Paris, throughout France, and even within the ranks of RDA students.

The cultural concept especially will claim our attention here; the problem was posed in terms of restoring the collective national African personality. It was particularly necessary to avoid the pitfall of facility. It could seem too tempting to delude the masses engaged in a struggle for national independence by taking liberties with scientific truth, by unveiling a mythical, embellished past. Those who have followed us in our efforts for more than 20 years know now that this was not the case and that this fear remained groundless.

Admittedly three factors compete to form the collective personality of a people: a psychic factor, susceptible of a literary approach; this is the factor that would elsewhere be called national temperament, and that the Negritude poets have overstressed. In addition, there are the historical factor and the linguistic factor, both susceptible of being approached scientifically. These last two factors have been the subject of our studies; we have endeavored to remain strictly on scientific grounds. Have foreign intellectuals, who challenge our intentions and accuse us of all kinds of hidden motives or ridiculous ideas, proceeded any differently? When they explain their own historical past or study their languages, that seems normal. Yet, when an African does likewise to help reconstruct the national personality of his people, distorted by colonialism, that is considered backward or alarming. We contend that such a study is the point of departure for the cultural revolution properly understood. All the headlong flights of certain infantile leftists who try to bypass this effort can be explained by intellectual inertia, inhibition, or incompetence. The most brilliant pseudo-revolutionary eloquence

ignores that need which must be met if our peoples are to be reborn culturally and politically. In truth, many Africans find this vision too beautiful to be true; not so long ago some of them could not break with the idea that Blacks are non-existent culturally and historically. It was necessary to put up with the cliché that Africans had no history and try to start from there to build something modestly!

Our investigations have convinced us that the West has not been calm enough and objective enough to teach us our history correctly, without crude falsifications. Today, what interests me most is to see the formation of teams, not of passive readers, but of honest, bold research workers, allergic to complacency and busy substantiating and exploring ideas expressed in our work, such as:

1. Ancient Egypt was a Negro civilization. The history of Black Africa will remain suspended in air and cannot be written correctly until African historians dare to connect it with the history of Egypt. In particular, the study of languages, institution, and so forth, cannot be treated properly; in a word, it will be impossible to build African humanities, a body of African human sciences, so long as that relationship does not appear legitimate. The African historian who evades the problem of Egypt is neither modest nor objective, nor unruffled; he is ignorant, cowardly, and neurotic. Imagine, if you can, the uncomfortable position of a western historian who was to write the history of Europe without referring to Greco-Latin Antiquity and try to pass that off as a scientific approach.

The ancient Egyptians were Negroes. The moral fruit of their civilization is to be counted among the assets of the Black world. Instead of presenting itself to history as an insolvent debtor, that Black world is the very initiator of the "western" civilization flaunted before our eyes today. Pythagorean mathematics, the theory of the four elements of Thales of Miletus, Epicurean materialism, Platonic idealism, Judaism, Islam, and modern science are rooted in Egyptian cosmogony and science.

One needs only to meditate on Osiris, the redeemer-god, who sacrifices himself, dies, and is resurrected to save mankind, a figure essentially identifiable with Christ.

A visitor to Thebes in the Valley of the Kings can view the Moslem inferno in detail (in the tomb of Seti I, of the Nineteenth Dynasty), 1700 years before the Koran. Osiris at the tribunal of the dead is indeed the "lord" of revealed religions, sitting enthroned on Judgement Day, and we know that certain Biblical passages are practically copies of Egyptian moral texts. Far be it from me to confuse this brief reminder with a demonstration. It is simply a matter of providing a few landmarks to persuade the incredulous Black African reader to bring himself to verify this. To his great surprise and satisfaction, he will discover that most of the ideas used today to domesticate, atrophy, dissolve, or steal his "soul," were conceived by his own ancestors. To become conscious of that fact is perhaps the first step toward a genuine retrieval of himself; without it, intellectual sterility is the general rule, or else the creations bear I know not what imprint of the subhuman.

In a word, we must restore the historical consciousness of the African peoples and reconquer a Promethean consciousness.

2. Anthropologically and culturally speaking, the Semitic world was born during protohistoric times from the mixture of white-skinned and black-skinned people in western Asia. This is why an understanding of the Mesopotamian Semitic world, Judaic or Arabic, requires constant reference to the underlying Black reality. If certain Biblical passages, especially in the Old Testament, seem absurd, this is because specialists, puffed up with prejudices, are unable to accept documentary evidence.

3. The triumph of the monogenetic thesis of humanity (Leakey), even at the stage of "Homo sapiens-sapiens," compels one to admit that all races descended from the Black race, according to a filiation process that science will one day explain. [3]

4. In *L'Afrique Noire précoloniale* (1960), I had two objectives: (1) to demonstrate the possibility of writing a history of Black Africa free of mere chronology of events, as the preface to that volume clearly indicates; (2) to define the laws governing the evolution of African sociopolitical structures, in order to explain the direction that historical evolution has taken in Black Africa; therefore, to try henceforth to dominate and master that historical process by knowledge, rather than simply to submit to it.

These last questions, like those about origins (Egypt), are among the key problems; once they are solved, a scholar can proceed to write the history of Africa. Consequently, it is evident why we are paying particular attention to the solution of such problems and of so many others which transcend the field of history.

The research pattern inaugurated by *L'Afrique Noire précoloniale* on the sociohistorical, not on the ethnographic, plane has since been utilized by many researchers. That, I suppose, is what has led them to describing the daily life of the Congolese or enlarging upon the various forms of political, economic, social, military, and judicial organization in Africa.

5. To define the image of a modern Africa reconciled with its past and preparing for its future. [4]

6. Once the perspectives accepted until now by official science have been reversed, the history of humanity will become clear and the history of Africa can be written. But any undertaking in this field that adopts compromise as its point of departure as if it were possible to split the difference, or the truth, in half, would run the risk of producing nothing

[3] Cf. Cheikh Anta Diop, "L'Apparition de l'homo-sapiens," *Bulletin de l'IFAN*, XXXII, Series II, number 3, 1970.
———, "La Pigmentation des anciens Egyptiens. Test par la mélanine," *Bulletin de l'IFAN*, 1973 (in press).
[4] Cf. Cheikh Anta Diop, *Les Fondements culturels et industriels d'un futur Etat fédéral d'Afrique Noire*.

but alienation. Only a loyal, determined struggle to destroy cultural aggression and bring out the truth, whatever it may be, is revolutionary and consonant with real progress; it is the only approach which opens on to the universal. Humanitarian declarations are not called for and add nothing to real progress.

Similarly, it is not a matter of looking for the Negro under a magnifying glass as one scans the past; a great people has nothing to do with petty history, nor with ethnographic reflections sorely in need of renovation. It matters little that some brilliant Black individuals may have existed elsewhere. The essential factor is to retrace the history of the entire nation. The contrary is tantamount to thinking that to be or not to be depends on whether or not one is known in Europe. The effort is corrupted at the base by the presence of the very complex one hopes to eradicate. Why not study the acculturation of the white man in a Black milieu, in ancient Egypt, for example?

7. How does it happen that all modern Black literature has remained minor, in the sense that no Negro African author or artist, to my knowledge, has yet posed the problem of man's fate, the major theme of human letters?

8. In *L'Unité culturelle de l'Afrique Noire*, we tried to pinpoint the features common to Negro African civilization.

9. In the second part of *Nations nègres*, we demonstrated that African languages could express philosophic and scientific thought (mathematics, physics, and so forth) [5] and that African culture will not be taken seriously until their utilization in education becomes a reality. The events of the past few years prove that UNESCO has accepted those ideas. [6]

10. I am delighted to learn that one idea proposed in *L'Afrique Noire précoloniale* – the possibilities of pre-Columbian relations between Africa and America – has been taken up by an American scholar. Professor Harold G. Lawrence, of Oakland University, is in fact demonstrating with an abundance of proof the reality of those relationships which were merely hypothetical in my work. If the sum total of his impressive arguments stands up to the test of chronology, if it can be proved in the final analyis that all the facts noted existed prior to the period of slavery, his research will have surely contributed solid material to the edifice of historical knowledge.

I should like to conclude by urging young American scholars of good will, both Blacks and Whites, to form university teams and to become involved, like Professor Lawrence, in the effort to confirm various ideas that I have advanced, instead of limiting themselves to a negative, sterile skepticism. They would soon be dazzled, if not blinded, by the bright light of their future discoveries. In fact, our conception of African history, as exposed here, has practically triumphed, and those who write on African history now, whether willingly or not, base themselves upon it. But the American contribution to this final phase could be decisive.

---

[5] In *Nations nègres*, Dr. Diop translates a page of Einstein's Theory of Relativity into Wolof, the principal language of Senegal.

[6] Bamako 1964 colloquium on the transcription of African languages, various measures taken to promote African languages, and so forth.

44

EUROPE UPSIDE DOWN: FALLACIES OF THE NEW AFROCENTRISM

KWAME ANTHONY APPIAH

In the last few years, there has been a stream of publications, especially in the United States, aimed at establishing a new basis for the study and teaching of African and African–American culture. Whether or not they actually use the word "Afrocentric" on their packaging, these books – which differ enormously in the quality of their thought and writing, as well as in their factual reliability – have a certain common set of pre-occupations, whose persistence entitles one now to speak of an Afrocentric paradigm.

This has two basic elements, one critical, the other positive, which are either argued or taken for granted. The negative thesis is that modern Western scholarship on cultural matters, high and low, is hopelessly Eurocentric. This means, to begin with, that Western scholarship understands European history, intellectual life and social institutions as an ideal type, both normatively and descriptively. But Eurocentric work also displays an inability, rooted in prejudice, to enter sympathetically into the forms of life of non-Europeans, and, especially, of black people of African descent. As a consequence, Western scholarship presupposes, so the story goes, that Africans have produced little of much cultural worth, and that cultural works of sophistication or value (like the architecture of

Great Zimbabwe or the Pyramids), even when they are in Africa, are unlikely to have been produced by black people. In support of this Eurocentric thesis, some (and occasionally a great deal of) work goes into showing that European scholars, at least since the Enlightenment, have concealed facts about the African origins of certain central elements of Western civilization; notably the Egyptian origins of the Greek "miracle" and the black African origins of the Egyptian "miracle."

This negative thesis is argued as the prolegomenon to an alternative, positive, "Afrocentric" view, in which African cultural creativity is discovered to have been at the origin of Western civilization, while Western civilization, especially modern Western civilization, is either asserted or implied to be morally depraved; incapable, in particular, of living peacefully with others. We (sometimes all of us, sometimes just those of us who are black) are urged, then, to centre on African history (and particularly the history of the Egypt of the Pharaohs) and return to African values.

The Afrocentric paradigm is not just the source of a lively body of writing; it is the basis of a movement in the United States to revise the teaching of African–American children, to provide them with an Afrocentric education.

Here the argument is that the Eurocentricity of what is taught in American schools, at best, fails to nurture, and at worst, actively damages the self-esteem of black children, and that what these children need instead is a diet of celebratory African history (held to begin in Egypt, and in an Egyptian civilization held to be black) and the transmission of African values.

These values are often now taught in the version developed by Maulana Karenga and associated with the invention of a feast called "Kwanzaa," designed to provide an African celebration to go with Christmas and Hanukkah. (American children are taught Swahili words, naming various allegedly African virtues, as their proper inheritance. There is something of an irony in the use of Swahili as an Afrocentric language, since hardly any of the slaves brought to the New World can have known it, and it was in fact being used in a culture in which slave–trading to the Arabian peninsula was a major element of the economy.) This particular brand of Afrocentrism goes under the label of "Kemetism" ("Kemet" being a name for ancient Egypt); and the whole package can be found in a recent book by Molefi Kete Asante, one of the intellectual leaders of the movement *Kemet: Afrocentricity and Knowledge*.

At least as important as any published work is a body of Afrocentric lore transmitted in public lectures and in discussion groups by figures who have tended in recent years to combine Afrocentrism with a peculiar anti-Semitism, which is preoccupied with attributing special responsibility for the ills of the black world to a Jewish conspiracy. Many of the leading rap stars seem to subscribe to such views, combining them with their well-known misogyny and homophobia, to produce a cultural brew as noxious as any currently available in popular culture. The diagnosis of this particular pathology is the subject of much current speculation among observers of African–American culture.

The scholarly end of the Afrocentric move-ment has one major hero: Cheikh Anta Diop, the Senegalese man of letters, after whom the university in Dakar is now named. Diop argued, over many years (beginning in the 1950s), for the thesis of the African origins of Greek civilization. In such works as *L'Unité culturelle de l'Afrique noire, Antériorité des civilisations nègres, Nations nègres et culture, Fondements économiques et culturels d'un état fédéral d'Afrique noir*, and *Parenté génétique de l'égyptien pharaonique et des langues négro-africaines*, he pursued a complex agenda, in which the splendours of Egypt were seen as a reason for contemporary African pride and the cultural unity derived from a common African source as the basis for modern African political unity. (For a sample of Diop's writing see Chapter 43, this volume.)

Like most cultural movements at full flood, this Afrocentrism is a composite of truth and error, insight and illusion, moral generosity and meanness. But the most striking thing about it is how thoroughly at home it is in the frameworks of nineteenth-century European thought. (One of the symptomatic features of much Afrocentric writing is that the antagonists it identifies are largely dead.) Afrocentrism, in short, seems very much to share the presuppositions of the Victorian ideologies against which it is reacting. Take, for example, the preoccupation with the ancient world. The academic curriculum of the nineteenth century traced Western civilization to roots in ancient Greece. Afrocentrists have simply challenged the old priority of the (white) Greeks, by replacing them with (black) Egyptians. There are, of course, genuine issues for discussion here about the relations between different parts of the ancient Mediterranean and the Greek "miracle." Martin Bernal (not, by my account, an Afrocentrist, because he doesn't support the positive agenda of the movement) is a hero for Afrocentrists because, in *Black Athena* (Volume One, 1987), he has taken up the challenge of refuting the modern view that the Greeks owed nothing of importance to Egypt.

So far as I can see, there is now a consensus that Bernal has convincingly demonstrated the role of prejudice against blacks and Jews in classical scholarship from the Enlightenment onwards, but has not established decisively his own positive account of ancient history.

But it is not this quite genteel academic debate that has drawn Bernal to the Afrocentrists' attention. For it is essential not only to agree with Bernal's account of ancient intellectual history but also to insist, in Diop's words, that "Ancient Egypt was a Negro civilization [and] . . . the moral fruit of their civilization is to be counted among the assets of the Black world . . . ." And on this matter Bernal has little to say. Fortunately he did not have to argue for this secondary thesis, since it is taken to be implicit in his title. *African Athena* (the title Bernal preferred) or *Egyptian Athena* would have left the racial issue open: *Black Athena* (his publisher's choice) does not.

This preoccupation with racial matters is very much a response to the ninteenth-century formulation of the issues, when to the classicism of the Enlightenment there was added the thought that the Western heritage was a racial possession. Which is to neglect not only Egyptian influences on the Greeks, but such minor embarrassments as the centrality of Jewish contributions to Western high culture, and the key role of the Arabs in maintaining the intellectual tradition that linked Plato to the Renaissance. It depends on a way of thinking about culture and biology which is bound to be discomfited by those scholars, black, brown and yellow, who have taken possession of Western culture in the twentieth century and mastered it, at the same time as many of the supposed racial heirs of the West have been immersed in popular culture "contaminated" by African rhythms.

But in our day racialism surely doesn't need arguing against in serious company. Do we not all know that the interconnections and interdependences of biology and culture are complex and multiple, that the old simplicities of racialism have not stood the test of exposure to the evidence? Perhaps, or, then again, perhaps not. After all, Afrocentrist interest in the colour of the ancient Egyptians presumably derives from the thought that if they were black then they were of the same race as contemporary black Africans and their New World cousins. And unless you conflate biology and culture, why should that matter?

It is hard to find in the Afrocentrist literature a clearer answer to this question than the passage from Diop I quoted earlier. Racial identity with the Egyptians makes their achievements a moral asset for contemporary blacks. (Of course, if Greece grew out of Egypt and "the West" grew out of Greece, then the West too is a moral asset of contemporary blacks, and its legacy of ethnocentrism presumably one of our moral liabilities. . . .But I digress.) Perhaps this is why *Black Athena* and *The African Origin of Civilization* sell so well on the streets of Harlem. And if so, this is a reason that would have been entirely congenial to the nineteenth-century Eurocentrists whom Afrocentrism aims to refute.

Once we see the essentially reactive structure of Afrocentrism – that it is simply Eurocentrism turned upside-down – we can understand where its intellectual weaknesses lie. It is not surpising, for example, that in choosing to talk about Egypt and to ignore the rest of Africa and African history, Afrocentrism shares the European prejudice against cultures without writing. Eurocentrism, finding there a literate culture and a significant architecture, set about claiming that Egypt could not be black. Afrocentrism chooses Egypt because Eurocentrism had already made a claim on it.

Similarly, we should not be suprised at one of the most tiresome features of Afrocentrism, namely its persistence in what the Beninois philosopher (and current Minister of Culture) Paulin Hountondji has called "unanimism": the view that there is *an* African culture to which to appeal. (See Hountondji, Chapter 22, this volume). It is surely preposterous to suppose that there is a single African culture, shared by everyone from the civilizations of the Upper Nile thousands of years ago to the thousand or so language-zones of contemporary Africa.

In aiming to identify some common core of African civilization, the Afrocentrists seem once again to be responding to earlier attempts to identify a common core of Western culture. One can be forgiven for wondering how unitary the West really is today. But it was always a strange idea that Alexander, Alfred and Frederick the Great had something in common with each other and with the least of their subjects, which could be called Western culture. And in Africa, where whatever continuity there has been through all this time has not been mediated by even the broken textual tradition that in some sense unites "Western culture," it is not only a strange idea but a silly one.

A final irony is that Afrocentrism, which is offered in the name of black solidarity, has, by and large, entirely ignored the work of African scholars other than Diop. (This fact tends to be concealed because African–American scholars like Asante and Karenga have adopted African names.) Thus, much play has been given to another major source-book for the Afrocentrists, Janheinz Jahn's *Muntu: African cultures and the Western world*, a work that appeared in English translation in the United States with great *éclat* in the early 1960s. The book revolves around the concept of *ntu*, the stem of the Kinyaruanda-Bantu words *muntu* (person), *kintu* (thing), *hantu* (place and time) and *kuntu* (modality); "*ntu*," Jahn wrote with the *gravitas* of revelation, "is the universal force as such."

Reading this, I found myself drawn into a fantasy in which an African scholar returns to her home in Lagos or Nairobi, with the important news that she has uncovered the key to Western culture. Soon to be published: *THING: Western culture and the African world*, a work that exposes the philosophy of *ing*, written so clearly on the face of the English language. For *ing*, in the Euro–American view, is manifestly the inner dynamic essence of the world. In the structure of the terms do*ing* and mak*ing* and mean*ing*, the English (and thus, by extension all Westerners) express their deep commitment to this conception. But the secret heart of the matter is captured in their primary ontological category of th-*ing*: every th-*ing* (or be-*ing* as their sages express the matter in the more specialized vocabulary of one of their secret societies) is not stable but ceaselessly changing. Here we see the fundamental explanation for the extraordinary neophilia of Western culture, its sense that reality is change.

The notion that there is something unitary called African culture that could thus be summarized has been subjected to devastating critique by a generation of African intellectuals. But little sign of these African accounts of African culture appears in the writings of Afrocentrism. Molefi Asante has written whole books about Akan culture without referring to the major works of such Akan philosophers as J.B. Danquah, William Abrahams, Kwasi Wiredu and Kwame Gyekye. And I am reliably informed that, on one occasion not so long ago, a distinguished Zairian intellectual was told by an African–American interlocutor that "We do not need you educated Africans coming here to tell us about African culture." . . .

RESOURCE GUIDE

I. Journals which specialize in African studies, and journals which frequently publish essays on Africa:

Advance: The Journal of the African Development Foundation. Washington, D.C.: The Foundation, Superintendent of Documents, United States G. P. O. 1986–

Africa. London: International African Institute. 1928–

Africa Today. London: Africa Journal Ltd. 1981–

African Abstracts. London: International African Institute. 1950–

African Affairs. London: Royal African Society and Oxford University Press. 1901–

African Arts. Los Angeles: University of California Press.

African Historical Studies. Brookline, Mass: African Studies Center, Boston University. 1968–1971

African Insight. Pretoria: African Institute. 1980–

African Law Studies. New York: African Law Association of America. 1969–1980

African Social Research. Manchester: Manchester University Press 1966–

African Study Monographs (also called "Kyoto University African Study Mongraphs") Kyoto, Japan: Kyoto University African Studies Center. 1981–

African Studies Review. Atlanta: African Studies Association. 1970–

American Anthropologist. Washington, D.C.: American Anthropological Assocation.1889–

American Ethnologist. Washington, D.C.: American Anthropological Association.

Anthropological Quarterly. Washington, D.C.: Catholic University of America Press. 1953–

Botswana Notes and Records. Gabarone: Botswana Society. 1969–

Canadian Journal of African Studies. Ottawa: Canadian Association of African Studies. 1967–

Comparative Studies in Society And History. Cambridge: Cambridge University Press. 1958–

Cultural Survival Quarterly. Cambridge, Mass: Cultural Survival.

Current Anthropology. Chicago: University of Chicago Press. 1960–

Cultural Anthropology: Journal for the Society of Cultural Anthropology. Washington, D.C.: American Anthropological Associaton. 1986–

Diaspora: A Journal of Transnational Studies. New York: Oxford University Press 1991–

East Africa Journal. Nairobi: East Africa Publishing House. 1964–

Ethos. Berkeley: University of California Press. 1973–

Harvard African Studies. Cambridge, Mass: Peabody Museum of Harvard University. 1917–

Horn of Africa. Summit, New Jersey: Horn of Africa Journal. 1978–

Human Relations Area Files (HRAF). HRAF Press.

International Journal of African Historical Studies. London: Oxford University Press. 1974–

Journal des Africanistes. Paris: Société des Africanistes. 1976–

Journal of African History. Cambridge: Cambridge University Press. 1960–

Journal of African Law. London: School of Oriental and African Studies, University of London. 1957–

Journal of African Studies. Washington, D.C.: Heldref. (1974–1988); Volumes 1–5, Berkeley: University of California Press; Volumes 6–15, Los Angeles: UCLA African Studies Center.

Journal of Asian and African Studies. Leiden: Brill. 1966–

Journal of Modern African Studies. Cambridge: Cambridge University Press. 1964–

Journal of Religion in Africa. Leiden: Brill. 1967–

Journal of the Royal African Society. London and New York: MacMillan. 1901–

Journal of the Royal Anthropological Institute (see also *Man*). London: Royal Anthropological Society of Great Britain and Ireland. 1907–1995 (published as *Man*) 1995–

Journal of Southern African Studies. London: Oxford University Press. 1974–

Journal of West African Language. Cambridge: Cambridge University Press in association with the Institute of African Studies, University of Ibadan, Nigeria. 1964

Man. London: Royal Anthropological Institute of Great Britain and Ireland. 1966–1995.

Mawazo. Uganda: Makerere University College. Volumes 1–4, 1967–1976.

Museum Anthropology. Washington, D.C.: American Anthropological Association. 1991–

Pan-African Journal. New York: Pan-African Student's Organization. 1968–1970; Westport, Connecticut: Greenwood Periodicals. 1971–

Présence Africaine. Paris: Présence Africaine. 1947–

Public Culture: Bulletin of the Project for Transnational Cultural Studies. Chicago: University of Chicago Press. 1988–

Rhodes-Livingstone Journal (also called "Human Problems in British Central Africa"). 1944–

Social Anthropology: The Journal of the European Association of Social Anthropologists. Cambridge: Cambridge University Press. 1993–

Transition. Oxford: Oxford University Press. 19**–

West African Journal of Education. Ibadan, Nigeria: Nigerian Institute of Education, University of Ibadan.

II. Bibliographies of African research materials:

Africa South of the Sahara. London: Europa. 1971–

Africana Journal. New York: Africana Publishing Company. 1974–

Aguolu, Christian Chukwunedu. 1973. *Ghana in the Humanities and Social Sciences, 1900–1971: A Bibliography*. Metuchen, N.J.: Scarecrow Press.

Ajayi, J. F. Ade, and Michael Crowder. 1985. *Historical Atlas of Africa*. Cambridge: Cambridge University Press.

Anafalu, Joseph C. 1981. *The Ibo-Speaking Peoples of Southern Nigeria: A Selected Annotated List of Writings, 1627–1970*. Munich: Kraus.

Anthropological Literature. Cambridge, Massachusetts: Tozzer Library, Harvard University. 1982–

Baumann, Hermann, ed. 1975–1979. *Volker afrikas und ihre traditionallen kultern*. Wiesbaden: Franz Steiner.

Bennett, Norman Robert. 1984. *The Arab state of Zanzibar: A Bibliography*. Boston: G. K. Hall.

Bhatt, Purnima Mehta. 1980. *Scholar's Guide to Washington, D. C. African Studies* Washington, D.c.: Smithsonian Institution Press.

Bibliographies in African Studies. Madison: African Studies Program, University of Wisconsin, Madison. 1987–

Bibliography of African Art. 1965. London: International African Institute.

Bibliography on Africa. 1989. Dehli, India: Department of African Studies, University of Dehli.

Bibliography on Africa. 1975. Warsaw: University of Warsaw, Centre of African Studies.

Blackhurst, Hector. 1996. *East and Northeast Africa Bibliography*. Lanham, MD: Scarecrow Press.

Bliss, Anne M. and J.A. Rigg. 1984. *Zambia*. Oxford and Santa Barbara: Clio Press.

Boeder, Robert B. 1979. *Malawi*, Oxford and Santa Barbara: Clio Press.

Boston University Libraries: Catalog of African Government Documents. 1976. Boston: G. K. Hall.

Brown, Clifton F. 1978. *Ethiopian Perspectives: A Bibliographic Guide to the History of Ethiopia*. Westport, Conn: Greenwood Press.

Bruel, Georges. 1914. *Bibliographie de l'afrique equatoriale francaise*. Paris: E. Larose.

Bullwinkle, Davis. 1989. *African Women: A General Bibliography, 1976–1985*. New York: Greenwood.

Cambridge Encyclopedia of Africa. 1981. Roland Oliver and Michael Crowder, eds. Cambridge: Cambridge University Press.

Collison, Robert L. 1981. *Uganda*. Oxford and Santa Barbara: Clio Press.

Collison, Robert L. 1982. *Kenya*. Oxford and Santa Barbara: Clio Press.

Cook, Gillian P. 1984. *Development in Africa South of the Sahara, 1970–1980: a Select annotated Bibliography*. Cape Town: University of Cape Town Libraries.

A Current Bibliography of African Affairs. Farmingdale, N.Y.: Baywood Publishing Company.

Dalby, David. 1977. *Language Map of Africa and the Adjacent Islands*. London: International African Institute.

Daly, M. W. 1983. *Sudan*. Oxford and Santa Barbara: Clio Press.

Darch, Colin. 1985. *Tanzania*. Oxford and Santa Barbara: Clio Press.

Darkowska-Nidzgorska, Olenka. 1978. *Connaissance du Gabo: Guide bibliographique*. Libreville: Universite Nationale el Hadj Omar Bongo.

DeLancy, Mark W and Virginia H. DeLancey. 1975. *A Bibliography of Cameroon*. New York: Africana Publishing Company.

Der-Houssikian, Haig. 1972. *A bibliography of African Linguistics*. Edmonton, Alberta; Champaign, Il.: Linguistic Research.

Doro, Marion E. 1984. *Rhodesia/Zimbabwe: A Bibliographic Guide to the Nationalist Period*. Boston: G. K. Hall.

Duigan, Peter. ed. 1972. *Guide to Research and Reference Works un Sub-Saharan Africa*. Stanford: Hoover Institution.

Ethnographic Survey of Africa. 1950–1977. London: International African Institute and Oxford University Press.

Fage, J. D. 1987. *A Guide to Original Sources for Precolonial Western Africa Published in European Languages*. Madison: African Studies Program, University of Wisconsin, Madison.

Gamble, David P. 1979. A General Bibliography of the Gambia. Boston: G. K. Hall.

Gibson, Gordon D. 1969. "A Bibliography of Anthropological Bibliographies: Africa." *Current Anthropology* 10: 527–66.

Gosebrink, Jean E. Meeh. "Bibliography and Sources for African Studies." In Phyllis M. Martin and Patrick O'Meara, eds. *Africa*. pp. 381–439. Second Edition. New York: MacMillan.

Grandidier, Guillaume. 1905/ 06–57. *Bibliographie de Madagascar*. Paris: Comite de Madagascar.

Gary, John. 1989. *'Ashe, Traditional Religion and Healing in Sub-Saharan Africa and the Diaspora: A Classified International Bibliography*. New York: Greenwood.

Hambly, Wilfird D. 1937. Source Book for African Anthropology. Anthropological studies, Volume 26. Chicago: Field Museum of Natural History.

Henderson, Francine I and Modisakeng, Tiny. 1982. *A Guide to Periodical Articles about Botswana, 1965–1980*. Gabarone: National Institute of Development and Cultural Research.

Hartwig, Gerald W. and William M. O'Barr. 1974. *The Student Africanist's Handbook: A Guide to Resources*. Cambridge, Massachusetts: Schenkman.

International African Institute of London: Cumulative Bibliography of African Studies. 1983. Boston: G. K. Hall.

Ita, Nduntuei O. 1971. *Bibliography of Nigeria: A Survey of Anthropological and Linguistic Writings from the Earliest Times to 1966*. London: Cass.

Izard, Françoise. 1967. *Bibliographie generale de la Haute-Volta, 1956–1965*. Paris: CNRS–CVRS.

Janvier, Genevieve. 1972–1978. *Bibliographie de la Côte d'Ivoire*. Abidjan: Université d'Abidjan.

Library of Congress: Africa South of the Sahara. An Index to Periodical Literature, 1900–1970. 1981. Boston: G.K. Hall.

Liniger-Goumaz, Max. 1974 – *Guinea Equatorial, bibliografia general*. Berne: Commission Nationale Suisse pour l'Unesco.

Luijik, J. N. van. 1969. *Selected Bibliography of Sociological and Anthropological Literature Relating to Modern and Traditional Medicine in Africa South of the Sahara*. Leiden: Afrika-Studiecentrum.

Mann, Michael et al. 1987. *A Thesaurus of African Languages: A Classified and Annotated Inventory of the Spoken Languages of Africa with an Appendix on their Written Representation*. London: Hans Zell for the International African Institute.

McIlwaine, John. 1993. *Africa: A Guide to Reference Material*. London and New York: Hans Zell.

Mitchell, Robert C. 1966. *A Comprehensive Bibliography of Modern African Religious*

Movements. Evanston: Northwestern University Press.

Murdock, George Peter. 1959. *Africa: Its People and their Culture History*. New York: McGraw Hill.

Murphy, John D. and Harry Goff. 1969. *A Bibliography of African Languages and Linguistics*. Washington, D. C.: Catholic University of America Press.

Musée de l'Homme. Bibliothèque. Paris. *Catalogue systematique de la Section Afrique* [Classified Catalog of the Africa Section]. 1970. Boston: G. K. Hall.

Musée Royale du Congo Belge. 1925/1930–1950. *Bibliographie ethnographique du Congo Belge et des regions avoisinantes*. 14 volumes. Tervuren, Belgium: Musée Royale du Congo Belge.

Musée Royale du Congo Belge. 1952–1959. *Bibliographie ethnographique du Congo Belge et des regions avoisinantes*. 10 volumes. Tervuren, Belgium: Musée Royale du Congo Belge.

Musée Royale du Congo Belge. 1962–1981. *Bibliographie enthnographique de l'Afrique sud-saharienne, sciences humaines et sociales*. 18 volumes. Tervuren, Belgium: Musée Royale du Congo Belge.

Northwestern University Catalog of the Melville Herskovits Library of African Studies, Northwestern University Library and Africana in Selected Libraries. 1978. Boston: G. K. Hall.

Nyeko, Balam. 1982. *Swaziland*. Oxford and Santa Barbara: Clio Press.

O'Connor, A.M. *Urbanization in Tropical Africa: An Annotated Bibliography*. Boston: G. K. Hall.

Ofcansky, Thomas P. 1985. *British East Africa, 1856–1963: An Annotated Bibliography*. Garland Reference Library of Social Science, Volume 158. New York Garland.

Otchere, Freda E. 1992. *African Studies Thesaurus: Subject Headings for Library Users*. Westport, Connecticut: Greenwood Press.

Paden, John N. and Edward W. Soja. 1970. *The African Experience*. Evanston: Northwestern University Press.

Panofsky, Hans. 1975. *A Bibliography of Africana*. Westport, CT: Greenwood Press.

Pearson, J. D. 1982. *International African Bibliography, 1973–1978*. New York: Wilson.

Porges, Laurence. 1967. *Bibliographie des regions du Senegal*. Dakar, Ministere du Plan et du Developpement. .

Portugal in Africa: A Bibliography of the UCLA Collection. 1972. Los Angeles: UCLA African Studies Center.

Scheub, Harold. 1977. *African Oral Narratives, Proverbs, Riddles, Poetry, and Song*. Boston: G. K. Hall.

Scheven, Yvette, ed. 1977; 1984; 1988; 1994. *Bibliographies for African Studies*. 1994, 1988, and 1984 published by Hans Zell (London and Munich); 1977 published by Crossroads Press (Los Angeles and Waltham).

Schmidt, Nancy J. 1994. *African Studies Periodicals and Other Serials Currently on Subscription, Indiana University Libraries, Bloomington*. Bloomington: African Studies Program, Indiana University Libraries.

Schmidt, Nancy J. 1994. *Sub-Saharan African Film and Filmmakers, 1987–1992: An Annotated Bibliography*. London: Hans Zell Publishers.

Schoeman, Stanley and Elna Schoeman. 1984. *Namibia*. Oxford and Santa Barbara: Clio Press.

Stanley, Janet. 1989. *The Arts of Africa: An Annotated Bibliography*. Atlanta: African Studies Association.

Stanley, Janet. 1995. *Modern African Art: A Basic Reading List*. Washington, D.C.: National Museum of African Art Library, Smithsonian Institution Libraries.

Thieme, Darius L. 1964. *African Music: A Briefly Annotated Bibliography*. Washington, D. C. Library of Congress.

Travis, Crole and Miriam Alam, eds. 1977. *Periodicals from Africa: A Bibliography and Union List of Periodicals Published in Africa*. Boston G. K. Hall.

University of London. School of Oriental and African Studies. 1963; 1968–1979. *Library Catalogue*. Boston: G. K. Hall.

Van Warmelo, Nicholas J. ed. 1977. *Anthropology of Southern Africa in Periodicals to 1950: An Analysis and Index*. Johannesburg: Witwatersrand University Press.

Varley, Douglas H. *African Native Music: An Annotated Bibliography*. London: Royal Empire Society.

Webster, John B. et al. 1967. *A Bibliography on Kenya*. Syracuse: Syracuse University Program of Eastern African Studies.

Westerman, R. C. 1994. *Fieldwork in the Library: A Guide to Research in Anthropology and Related Area Studies*. Chicago: American Library Association.

Wilding, Richard. 1976. *A Bibliography of the History and Peoples of the Swahili-Speaking World: From Earliest Times to the Beginning of the Twentieth Century*. Nairobi: Lamu Society.

Wiley, David S. et al. 1982. *Africa on Film and Videotape, 1960–1981* [a guide to 7.500 films]. East Lansing: African Studies Center, Michigan State University.

Willet, Shelagh M. and David P. Ambrose. 1980. *Lesotho: A Comprehensive Bibliography*. Oxford and Santa Barbara: Clio Press.

Williams, Geoffrey J. 1967. *A Bibliography of Sierra Leone, 1925–1967*. New York: Africana Publishing Company.

Williams, Geoffrey J. 1984. *Independent Zambia: A Bibliography of the Social Sciences, 1964–1979*. Boston: G. K. Hall.

Witherall, Julian W. 1989. *Africana Resources and Collections: Three Decades of Development and Achievement*. Metuchen, N. J.: Scarecrow Press.